Authentic Chinese Horoscopes

THE YEAR OF THE RAT

Kwok Man-ho

with Martin Palmer and Joanne O'Brien

ARROW BOOKS

Arrow Books Limited
62–65 Chandos Place, London WC2N 4NW

An imprint of Century Hutchinson Limited

London Melbourne Sydney Auckland
Johannesburg and agencies throughout
the world

First published 1987

© International Consultancy on Religion, Education and Culture 1987

Typeset by Avocet Marketing Services, Bicester, Oxon
Printed and bound in Great Britain by
Anchor Brendon Limited, Tiptree, Essex

ISBN 0 09 952840 1

CONTENTS

ACKNOWLEDGEMENTS

The authors wish to express their deep gratitude to the many people, both in the United Kingdom, Hong Kong and other parts of Asia, who gave their time, expertise and encouragement to this work. In particular, we wish to thank our colleagues at the International Consultancy on Religion, Education and Culture (ICOREC) who worked long and hard to prepare the material. To Liz Breuilly, our thanks for devising a computer programme which made it possible to construct the calendar of dates for both Chinese and English days; to Pallavi Mavani and Barbara Cousins who put the material in order and to Kerry Brown who helped make sense of it. To our friends in the Chinese communities around the world who ensured that we remained faithful to the tradition, we owe a debt of gratitude which we can never repay. Finally, to Sue Hogg and Francesca Liversidge, our editors – what can we say that can adequately express our appreciation.

Kwok Man-ho, Joanne O'Brien, Martin Palmer

INTRODUCTION

As you opened this book, you should have bowed slightly, for you are in effect coming into the presence of a traditional Chinese fortune-teller, an astrologer who will share with you secrets and traditions which stretch back thousands of years. Normally you would have to travel to one of the great temples of the Chinese world to find the astrologers in their stalls in order to discover a picture of your life which a full reading can give. Instead, through the use of this book and the assistance of the fortune-tellers and astrologers who have helped to prepare it, we invite you to explore with us the insights and messages of Chinese astrology, its myths and legends, its tales and stories, its revelations and insights.

In this book you will find two very different levels of astrology and fortune-telling. Most people will be familiar with the animal sign of their year of birth. However, the animal sign is only a small part of astrology. At a simple level it can give a brief sketch of your basic personality according to Chinese beliefs. It is in the second level, the Tzu Wei system, that the heart of this book lies. Here, with the help of the charts and calendar, you can act as your own fortune-teller. Through the Tzu Wei system you can explore the world of traditional Chinese astrology as you would do if you had walked through the side streets around a great temple and sat at the feet of a master astrologer. It takes a little time and some patience, but at the end you will be able to discover what one of the most revered systems of astrology the Chinese have ever devised has to say to you – and you alone.

There are three things we would like to stress before you begin. First, do not approach Chinese astrology as you would Western astrology. They are so different that we found any comparison of the two was impossible. There is no correlation between the twelve animals of Chinese astrology and the twelve signs of the Western zodiac, for example. This is quite simply because Western astrology is based upon a system which uses the path of the sun through the heavens, and thus looks to the constellations which lie along this path. The Chinese system focuses upon the Tzu Wei star (the Pole Star of our system – see below) and the constellations which relate to that. Nor is there a correlation between the Chinese interpretations and the assumptions that present-day Westerners bring to astrology. Neither Chinese astrology nor Chinese fortune-telling in general is concerned with psychological insights or nuances. If a Chinese fortune-teller says that you will lose your house by fire or a disaster, that is what he means. You are welcome to read into what he says more than that if you so wish, but you will be doing a disservice to the authentic nature of the reading. Obviously there is much in what a fortune-teller says that is meant to be pondered upon. But there is also much that is meant to be taken at face value because the very sharpness of the fortune-teller's language is intended to make you sit up and take stock.

Secondly, many people think that the animal signs are the most important aspect of Chinese astrology – but this is not so. You will find as you explore this book that the animal signs are only the tip of the Chinese astrological iceberg. Most Western books about Chinese astrology have failed to delve further than the animal signs, usually because they have been written by Westerners, not by practising Chinese astrologers trained in the traditional methods. Through the learning of Kwok Man-ho, we are able to offer you more than just the tip of the iceberg, though it would take us scores if not hundred of volumes to reveal to you the full depths of all the aspects of Chinese astrology.

Finally, it is important to understand that Chinese astrology is not going to give you an absolute, fixed reading. It will tell you what is likely to happen, given your eight characters – your Heavenly Stems and Earthly Branches (see below) – the gods on duty at a particular time, and so on. But your future is to a great extent in your hands. Chinese astrology warns you what may happen. But, within certain parameters, you can alter your fortune. There are many stories of people changing their fortune through acts of kindness and compassion. By understanding the influence of the past in terms of your previous lives on this life, a Chinese fortune-teller can say where this is likely to lead you in the future. A pattern can be, literally, divined. The future can be seen as mapped out if you continue along your present path. What the fortune-teller is not saying is that this is inevitable, even though the stars are involved.

So bow slightly. Be prepared to spend some time working out what Chinese astrology has to say to you through the Tzu Wei system. Then sit and reflect.

The Background to Chinese Astrology

Astrology is one of the most ancient arts of the Chinese; it is supernatural in origin and the most important of the Five Arts of divination. For thousands of years the twin arts of astrology and astronomy were the same. No distinction was made between them. Astronomers observed the stars in order to be able to see what Heaven was planning for earth – and, of course, for humanity. From the earliest days right up to the present century the astronomer-astrologers were officials of the Imperial Court. Their records, stretching back in an unbroken written line for over three thousand years, are some of the most important astronomical documents in the world. To this day, Chinese astrology continues to play a major part in the day-to-day lives of millions of Chinese around the world. Every day they use the Chinese Almanac, the T'ung Shu. The T'ung Shu lists astrological and astronomical data for each day of the Chinese year. On the basis of this certain days will be auspicious and others unlucky. Very few Chinese would dream of starting a new business or setting out on a journey on a day which the T'ung Shu declared to be a bad one.

It is in association with the Almanac, or rather, the calendrical part of the Almanac, that we first come across Chinese astronomy and astrology. If you delve into one of the oldest books of the Chinese, the *Shu Ching* or *Book of Historical Documents*, you will find the story of the Emperor Yao and the brothers Hsis and Ho. The story is traditionally set in the year 2256 BCE. The Emperor Yao wanted to produce a yearly calendar so that the people would know when the seasons began and when to plant and when to reap. So he commanded the brothers Hsis and Ho to observe 'the wide heavens, to calculate and delineate the sun, the moon and the stars' and to produce a calendar based upon their observations (*Shu Ching*, 'The

Canon of Yao', Part 1, Book 2). So legend gives astronomy and astrology a history stretching back over four thousand years, and there seems to be every likelihood that astronomical observations were being undertaken that long ago.

However, there is one very important difference between our present-day expectations of astrology and the expectations of the ancient Chinese. To the ancient Chinese astronomy-astrology revealed what was likely to happen to a state, or to the ruler of that state. It was not a system for personal fortune-telling. This example of a reading can be found in the ancient annals of China for the year 532 BCE: 'In Spring, in the king's first month, a strange star appeared in the constellation of Wu Nu. Pei Tsao of Cheng said to Tzu Ch'an: "In the seventh month, on the cyclical day Wu Tzu, the ruler of Chin, will die."' In Chinese thought the ruler was the state and vice versa.

It is not until the beginning of the Christian era that we find astrology being applied to individuals. The first example occurs c. 100 CE. From then on the number of individual astrological readings grew until an entire encyclopedia was constructed around the art (T'ang dynasty, 618–907 CE). Since that time, astrology has been part of everyday life for many Chinese. Echoes of its older role as diviner or forewarner of the fate of nations is still to be found in the modern-day Almanac. For example, in 1986 the Almanac warned that evil forces and armies would be likely to attack from the north. However, it is the personal aspect which now commands the field of Chinese astrology.

So let us now turn to the basic building blocks of Chinese astrology – the animal signs, the Heavenly Stems and the Earthly Branches, the sixty-year cycle and the Pole Star.

The Sixty-Year Cycle

Nowadays everyone seems to know their Chinese animal sign. As Chinese New Year is celebrated ever more widely in the Western world, the newspapers declare this year to be the year of the Tiger or Rabbit and so on. But why are these twelve animals important and what do they mean?

Legend ascribes the creation of the cycle of twelve creatures to the semi-mythological, semi-historical Yellow Emperor, who is supposed to have invented it in 2637 BCE. Certainly the system was in use by the time of Confucius, who lived in the fifth century BCE. It had probably been in use long before his time. Yet, strange to say, that is really all that can be said about the twelve animals. Traditional stories reveal why these particular twelve animals have been chosen; why some are wild and some are domesticated; why the cat does not feature and why the Rat is always put at the top of the list. You can read how the animals were chosen on p. 21 and one version of why the Rat comes first is given in the following legend.

One day the twelve animals of the calendar were arguing as to who should be first in the calendar. The gods, fed up with this bickering, stepped in to settle the argument. They suggested a contest. The first animal to reach the far bank of the river would be the first animal sign. All the creatures assembled on the river bank. The Rat looked up and down the line. He could see that he stood the least chance of swimming swiftly across the river, so he decided to hitch a lift. Looking at his friends, he thought that the Ox, with his great strength and tenacity, was most likely to reach the far bank first. So, as the animals plunged into the river, the Rat jumped nimbly onto the Ox's broad back. Just before the Ox climbed out onto the river bank ahead of all the others, the Rat leaped from his back and landed first. Although the other animals protested strongly that the Rat had cheated, the gods declared him the winner because he had used his head rather than just his strength to win the race. This is why the cycle of twelve yearly animal signs starts with the Rat and is followed by the Ox.

Although the twelve animals are interesting, they are only one part of the Chinese system for counting the years. The ten Heavenly Stems and the twelve Earthly Branches are far more important for time-keeping and astrology.

Chinese time is measured by a cycle of sixty years. Traditionally the Chinese do not celebrate birthdays, but when someone reaches his or her sixtieth birthday, a great feast is held in his or her honour. The sixty-year cycle is used as the main system for giving dates. What we regard as the year of Queen Victoria's death, 1901, is known to the Chinese as the 27th year of the reign of the Emperor Kuang Hsu. Confusion sets in when monarchs reign for more than sixty years – but this has not happened very often.

Sixty is a significant calendrical number because of the combination of Heavenly Stems and Earthly Branches. There are ten Heavenly Stems and twelve Earthly Branches. If you combine these two sets together, then the ten Heavenly Stems have to be repeated six times in order to match the twelve Earthly Branches, which are repeated five times, to bring you back to the start of both the Heavenly Stems and the Earthly Branches, giving you sixty pairs in all. The cycle always begins with the Heavenly Stem Chia and the Earthly Branch Tzu and looks like this:

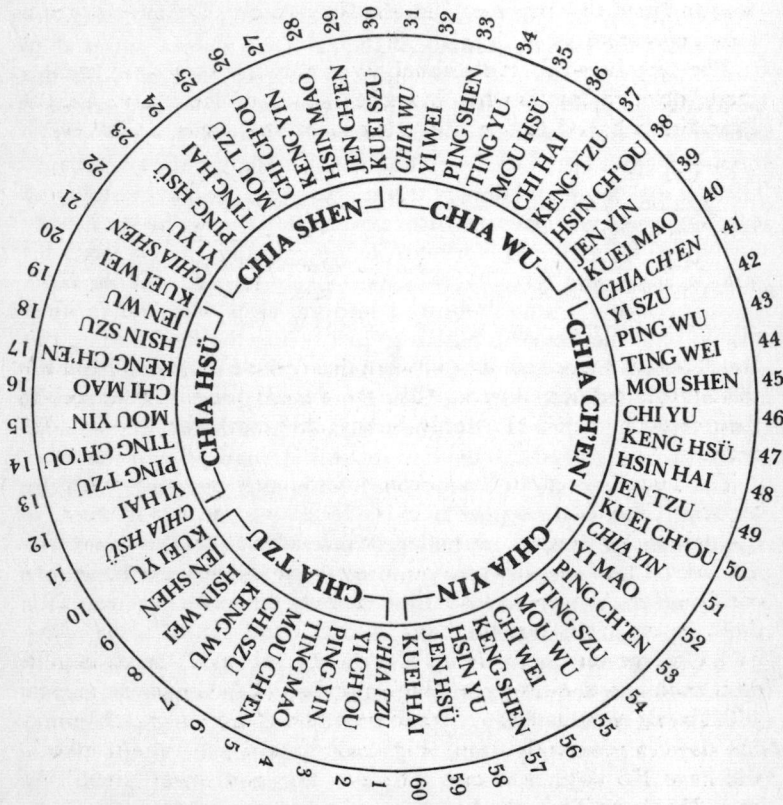

The names for the years are taken from the pairs of Heavenly Stems and Earthly Branches in the sixty-year cycle. Thus, 1988 is Mou Ch'en year, a combination of Heavenly Stem and Earthly Branch which has not occurred since 1928 and will not occur again until 2048. The characters change at the start of each Chinese New Year, which falls somewhere between 21 January and 20 February of the Western calendar.

Where or why the system of Heavenly Stems and Earthly Branches began is unknown. Suffice to say that by the time the *Shu Ching*, the *Book of Historical Documents*, was written the sixty-year cycle of the Heavenly Stems and Earthly Branches was in use. It is difficult to date accurately much of the *Shu Ching*, but by about 1000 BCE, and probably much earlier, the sixty-year cycle was accepted as a dating system.

The link between the animal signs and the sixty-year cycle is made through the Earthly Branches. Each of the twelve Earthly Branches is linked to one of the twelve animal signs, as follows:

Tzu – Rat	Wu – Horse
Ch'ou – Ox	Wei – Ram
Yin – Tiger	Shen – Monkey
Mao – Hare	Yu – Cock
Ch'en – Dragon	Hsü – Dog
Szu – Snake	Hai – Pig

It will become apparent as you work through the horoscope that it is the Earthly Branches rather than the animal signs, and especially their relation to the Heavenly Stems, that carry the key to a full reading.

The sixty-year cycle has been traditionally used to mark the months. The Chinese calendar is based on the lunar year, in contrast to the Western calendar, which is based on the solar year. The lunar and solar years do not correspond exactly: the lunar year consists of twelve moons (months), each of which lasts just over 29½ days. In order to keep the days in each lunar month as full days, each Chinese year is made up of a number of 'small' months of 29 days each and a number of 'big' months of 30 days each. A year with six big months and six small months will have a grand total of 354 days; a year with seven 'big' months and five 'small' months will have 355 days; and one with five 'big' and seven 'small' will have 353 days. Thus the lunar year falls short of the solar year by 10, 11 or 12 days. To bring the Chinese calendar into line with the seasons, and thus with the Western calendar, it is necessary to include an extra month every second or third year. This is called an intercalary month, and it comes immediately after the month it is linked with. In 1982 the extra month was month 4, and it came after the normal month 4. The next extra month came in 1984 and was number 10, following the normal month 10. The next occurrence was in 1987, the extra month being number 6. (The intercalary months are printed in italic in the Calendar Tables at the back of this book.)

Although the lunar months are numbered from 1 to 12 each year, they are also counted according to the sexagenary cycle of Heavenly Stems and Earthly Branches. The sequence is shown in the table opposite. The characters for each lunar month are determined by the Heavenly Stem for the year (column headings) and the number of the month in question (side headings). So in a year whose Heavenly Stem is Ping – 1986, for example – the 6th lunar month had the characters Yi Wei. This cycle repeats every five years, so in 1991, whose Heavenly Stem is Hsin, the 6th lunar month will also have the characters Yi Wei.

As there are twelve lunar months and twelve Earthly Branches, their relationship in the cycle always stays the same, so the 1st lunar month always has Yin as one of its characters, the 2nd Mao, the 3rd Ch'en, and so on, while the Heavenly Stems change according to the cycle.

The same cycle is used for the days as well. The old Chinese week was ten days long, so the first day of every sixth week could return to the beginning of the cycle of sixty, the Heavenly Stem Chia and the Earthly Branch Tzu.

As you can see, each year, each month and each day has its own distinctive combination of Heavenly Stem and Earthly Branch, and we will shortly explain how the system is also used for the hours. By discovering what Heavenly and Earthly characters (that means the Chinese characters) you have for the year, the month, the day and the hour of your birth, you can form an eight-character horoscope and enter properly the world of Chinese astrology. With your eight-character horoscope, the path lies open for you to explore what this ancient art has to tell you.

To find the first six characters of your horoscope – those for the year, the month and the day – you simply need to turn to the Calendar Tables at the back of this book and look up your Western date of birth. There, you will find the Heavenly Stem and Earthly Branch for your Chinese year of birth, and, in the adjacent columns, the numbers and the characters for the lunar month and

16/5

The Cycle of Heavenly Stems and Earthly Branches for the Months
(The cycle is shown in relation to the Western years 1984–93)

Heavenly Stem for the Year

Lunar Month	Chia (1984) Chi (1989)	Yi (1985) Keng (1990)	Ping (1986) Hsin (1991)	Ting (1987) Jen (1992)	Mou (1988) Kuei (1993)	The cycle repeats
1st	Ping Yin	Mou Yin	Keng Yin	Jen Yin	Chia Yin	
2nd	Ting Mao	Chi Mao	Hsin Mao	Kuei Mao	Yi Mao	
3rd	Mou Ch'en	Keng Ch'en	Jen Ch'en	Chia Ch'en	Ping Ch'en §	
4th	Chi Szu	Hsin Szu	Kuei Szu	Yi Szu	Ting Szu	
5th	Keng Wu	Jen Wu	Chia Wu‡	Ping Wu	Mou Wu	
6th	Hsin Wei	Kuei Wei	Yi Wei	Ting Wei†	Chi Wei	
7th	Jen Shen	Chia Shen	Ping Shen	Mou Shen	Keng Shen	
8th	Kuei Yu	Yi Yu	Ting Yu	Chi Yu	Hsin Yu	
9th	Chia Hsü	Ping Hsü	Mou Hsü	Keng Hsü	Jen Hsü	
10th	Yi Hai*	Ting Hai	Chi Hai	Hsin Hai	Kuei Hai	
11th	Ping Tzu	Mou Tzu	Keng Tzu	Jen Tzu	Chia Tzu	
12th	Ting Ch'ou	Chi Ch'ou	Hsin Ch'ou	Kuei Ch'ou	Yi Ch'ou	

* Extra month in 1984.   ‡Extra month in 1990.
†Extra month in 1987.   §Extra month in 1993.

for the day you were born. To simplify the tables we have used a system of codes for the Heavenly Stems and the Earthly Branches, the former being coded from A to K and the latter from 1 to 12. The codes are listed at the front of the Calendar Tables.

Your day of birth also corresponds to one of twenty-eight constellations, each of which is associated with a particular animal and these are also listed in the Calendar Tables. This group is quite separate from the animal signs for the years. The constellations change on a daily basis over twenty-eight days. In four groups of seven they are also linked to and change with the seasons. The spring, summer, autumn and winter groups correspond respectively to the four elements Wood, Fire, Metal and Water. The constellation on duty on the day of your birth will stand with you for your entire life. The characteristics of the constellational animals are as follows:

Crocodile   Unstable and slow-witted.

Dragon   Clever and quick to understand.

Badger   Slow-witted and irreligious.

Hare   Literary and impatient.

Fox   Loves dressing up; lewd, but not bad at heart.

Tiger   Quick to anger, quick to laugh, gluttonous, good-hearted.

Leopard   Brave but cruel; disliked.

Griffon   Refined and long-lived.

Ox   Unstable, with a harsh life.

Bat   Cunning; disliked.

Rat   Assenting with the lips, dissenting with the heart; spiteful.

Swallow   Loves dressing up, straightforward, quick of speech.

Pig   A difficult time in spring and summer, a better time in autumn and winter.

Porcupine   Trustworthy, kind, easily frightened.

Wolf   Knowledgeable; a good planner.

Dog   A troublemaker, loquacious, quick to laugh and quick to anger; disliked.

Pheasant   Generous.

Cock   Trustworthy.

Crow   Enjoys leisure and fortune-telling.

Monkey   Easily frightened, fond of fruit, long-lived.

Gibbon   Clever, quick-thinking, cute in appearance, cowardly.

Tapir   Powerful and kind.

Sheep   Miserly; a show-off.

Deer   Good-natured.

Horse   Outstanding; destined to meet the right people at the right time.

Stag   Kind; enjoys eating.

Serpent   Unskilful.

Earthworm   Impatient; enjoys the arts.

The last two characters of your eight-character horoscope – those for the hour of your birth – remain to be discovered. They too are based on the sexagenary cycle, but the Chinese use a different system of calculating the hours to that used in the West. The Chinese 'hour' is equivalent to two Western hours, so there are only twelve 'hours' in the Chinese day. Each one corresponds to an Earthly Branch as follows:

Tzu	11 p.m.–1 a.m.	Wu	11 a.m.–1 p.m.
Ch'ou	1 a.m.–3 a.m.	Wei	1 p.m.–3 p.m.
Yin	3 a.m.–5 a.m.	Shen	3 p.m.–5 p.m.
Mao	5 a.m.–7 a.m.	Yu	5 p.m.–7 p.m.
Ch'en	7 a.m.–9 a.m.	Hsü	7 p.m.–9 p.m.
Szu	9 a.m.–11 a.m.	Hai	9 p.m.–11 p.m.

To find the characters for your 'hour' of birth a special table is used (see p. 18), similar to the one for the months (see above). It works in much the same way, although in this case the coordinates are the Heavenly Stem for the day you were born (column headings) and the 'hour' of your birth (side headings).

Having discovered your own eight-character horoscope, and knowing your animal sign for the year, you can now turn to the fortune-teller captured in this book and begin to discover what secrets Chinese astrology holds for you.

As we mentioned earlier, there are two different systems here for you to use. The first is a quick simple guide to your basic personality according to your animal sign. As you will by now have gathered, although you are a Rat, the Rat appears five times in the sixty-year cycle, each time with a different Heavenly Stem. Thus, you are indeed a Rat, a Tzu, but are you a Chia Tzu (a Rat on the Roof), a Ping Tzu (a Rat in the Field), a Mou Tzu (a Rat in the Warehouse), a Keng Tzu (a Rat on the Beam) or a Jen Tzu (Rat on the Mountain)? Each of these different types will give a slightly different reading in the first part of the book and will be of added significance in the second.

Heavenly Stem for Day of Birth

'Hour' of Birth	Chia Chi	Yi Keng	Ping Hsin	Ting Jen	Mou Kuei
11 p.m. –1 a.m. (Tzu)	Chia Tzu	Ping Tzu	Mou Tzu	Keng Tzu	Jen Tzu
1 a.m. –3 a.m. (Ch'ou)	Yi Ch'ou	Ting Ch'ou	Chi Ch'ou	Hsin Ch'ou	Kuei Ch'ou
3 a.m. –5 a.m. (Yin)	Ping Yin	Mou Yin	Keng Yin	Jen Yin	Chia Yin
5 a.m. –7 a.m. (Mao)	Ting Mao	Chi Mao	Hsin Mao	Kuei Mao	Yi Mao
7 a.m. –9 a.m. (Ch'en)	Mou Ch'en	Keng Ch'en	Jen Ch'en	Chia Ch'en	Ping Ch'en
9 a.m. –11 a.m. (Szu)	Chi Szu	Hsin Szu	Kuei Szu	Yi Szu	Ting Szu
11 a.m. –1 p.m. (Wu)	Keng Wu	Jen Wu	Chia Wu	Ping Wu	Mou Wu
1 p.m. –3 p.m. (Wei)	Hsin Wei	Kuei Wei	Yi Wei	Ting Wei	Chi Wei
3 p.m. –5 p.m. (Shen)	Jen Shen	Chia Shen	Ping Shen	Mou Shen	Keng Shen
5 p.m. –7 p.m. (Yu)	Kuei Yu	Yi Yu	Ting Yu	Chi Yu	Hsin Yu
7 p.m. –9 p.m. (Hsü)	Chia Hsü	Ping Hsü	Mou Hsü	Keng Hsü	Jen Hsü
9 p.m. –11 p.m. (Hai)	Yi Hai	Ting Hai	Chi Hai	Hsin Hai	Kuei Hai

In the busy world of modern Chinese communities, the first system has been developed over the last hundred years or so to give a simple personality reading. Behind it lie the vast resources of the ancient art of astrology and divination. In the second part of the book we give one of the most popular systems, the Tzu Wei (Purple Star). Dating from the T'ang dynasty (618–907 CE), it was first written down by the astrologer Ch'en T'u Nan during the Sung dynasty (960–1280 CE).

The title Tzu Wei is very significant. Tzu Wei is the name of the

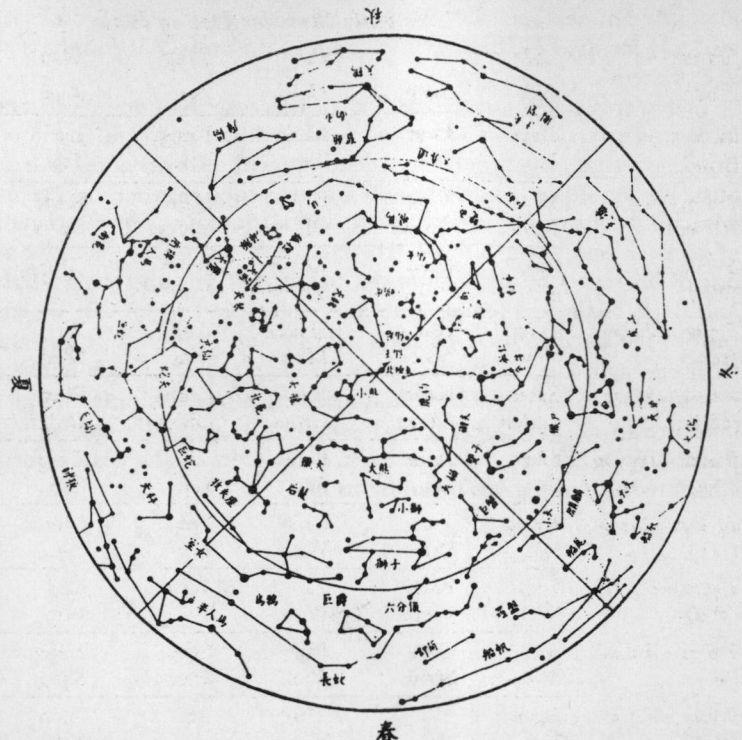

god in charge of what is variously called the Purple Planet, the Purple Star or the Pole Star. Chinese astrology is based upon the Pole Star, and to name a system after the god of that star indicates how important this system is. In Chinese astrology and astronomy the Pole Star stands as the symbol of imperial stability, for, like the Pole Star, life centred upon and circled around the figure of the Emperor. In Chinese astrology the Pole Star is the centre of the astronomical system and the astrological calendar. Its two closest constellations, Ursa Major and Ursa Minor, are seen as the North and South Measures – the measures of each person's lifespan. The god of birth dwells in the Southern Measure and the god of death in the Northern Measure. At the centre of all life, of the entire universe, stands the Pole Star – the Purple Planet or Purple Star. All other stars used in the Tzu Wei system are there because of their relation to the Pole Star. The Heavenly Stems and Earthly Branches of your eight-character horoscope are used to give a detailed reading not only for the Pole Star, but for each of the stars listed in the Tzu Wei system.

Tzu Wei is a very auspicious title for this system of divination and makes us aware that we are entering sacred and powerful territory. But as we study the animal signs and enter the world of the Purple Star, we should remember that in Chinese thought there is a triad. This triad consists of Heaven, Earth and Humanity. The interaction of Heaven and earth is made through us. We can put the universe out of harmony by disturbing the balance of yin and yang – light and dark, male and female, fire and water, and so on – or we can restore the balance through right actions and thoughts. In the end Chinese astrology presents us with a picture of our current relationship to the great cosmic forces which shape all life and give measure to all lives. But it also presents us with the challenging possibility of change, because we are also part of the cosmic force which moulds and gives meaning to life.

THE JADE KING AND THE TWELVE EARTHLY BRANCHES

The Jade King was extremely bored since he had little to do: he was waited on by his aides and servants, and because he lived in Heaven he had no idea what happened on earth. In an effort to amuse himself he summoned his chief adviser.

'I have ruled for many years,' said the King, 'but I have never seen the animals on earth. What do they look like?'

The adviser told him that there were many animals on earth. Did the Jade King wish to see them all?

'Oh no!' replied the King. 'I shall waste too much time if I do that. Instead I want you to select the twelve most interesting animals, and I will grade them according to their peculiarity.'

The adviser thought long and hard as to which animals would please the King. First of all he decided to send an invitation to the rat; he also asked the rat to pass on an invitation to his friend the cat. Further invitations were also sent to the ox, the tiger, the rabbit, the dragon, the snake, the horse, the ram, the monkey, the cock and the dog, telling them to be at the palace at six o'clock the next morning.

The rat was extremely proud to be summoned before the Jade King and set off to tell the cat their good news. The cat was delighted to hear the news, but was afraid that he might oversleep. He therefore made the rat promise to wake him early the next morning. That night the rat pondered on how handsome the cat was and how ugly he would appear in comparison. The only way to prevent the cat taking the limelight was to let him oversleep the next morning.

Early the next day eleven animals were lined up before the Jade King. When the King reached the end of the line he turned to his adviser.

'They are all very interesting, but why are there only eleven?'

The adviser had no answer and, for fear that the King would think he had not performed his task properly, he sent a servant down to earth and ordered him to catch the first animal he found and to bring it up to Heaven. The servant arrived on a road and saw a man carrying a pig, so he took the pig to the parade.

Meanwhile the rat was afraid that the King might not see him because he was so small. The only thing to do was to sit on the ox's back and play a flute. That way the King would be sure to notice him.

The King did indeed notice him, and was so delighted with this unusual animal that he gave him first place. The Jade King gave the ox second place, since he had been so kind as to let the rat sit on his back. Because the tiger looked so courageous he was given third place, and the rabbit, because of his fine white fur, was given fourth place. The King thought the dragon looked like a strong snake on legs, so he gave him fifth place. The snake was given sixth place, the horse seventh, the ram eighth, the monkey ninth, the cock tenth (he was the only bird that the adviser knew his servant could catch), and the dog was given eleventh place. The pig was ugly, but the King had no choice but to give him twelfth place.

After the ceremony had been performed the cat came dashing into the palace and begged the King to give him a chance.

'I'm sorry,' said the King. 'You are too late. I have arranged the twelve Earthly Branches and I cannot go back on my choice.'

When the cat spotted the rat, he chased him with the intention of killing him. That is why, even today, a cat cannot be friends with a rat.

Your Animal Sign Horoscope

THE SIGN OF THE RAT

The Main Attributes of Rat People

Character
You have a good heart but you are occasionally inconsiderate and selfish.

Luck
You will be lucky if you are generous and use your intelligence to the best of your ability.

Wealth
Your energetic and versatile nature will help you achieve financial success. A subsidiary business will prove to be more lucrative than your main business. Do not spend your money as soon as you have earned it.

Occupation
You will be fortunate whatever your job or profession as long as you use your intelligence wisely. You are suited to a managerial job or a career involving buying and selling.

Social life
You are open and generous at the beginning of your friendships, but the critical and petty side of your nature soon surfaces. You will have a successful social life but your friendships will be short-lived.

Business
Nobody will support your large-scale business ventures because you have a petty attitude towards your colleagues. Any small enterprises which you undertake will be successful.

Romance
You are attentive, caring and usually take the initiative. Your love life will be successful because you are not easily upset.

Marriage
You will give your full commitment to your marriage even if your parents and relatives disapprove of the match.

Parents
You are an obedient and cheerful son/daughter. One of your parents will be more sympathetic to you than the other.

Brothers and sisters
Rat people do not forgive easily so it is difficult to heal the frequent rifts between you and your brothers and sisters.

Children
You love your children dearly and encourage their studies at school and at home.

Assets
You will never own many assets because you spend your money so quickly.

Travel
You enjoy travelling more than people born in the other animal years do. You appreciate areas of outstanding natural beauty as opposed to architecture or foreign culture. The Chinese say that you roam the mountains and enjoy the waters.

Health
You will only suffer from minor illnesses during your long life.

Investment
You usually invest sensibly but do not expect large returns.

Skills
Your artistic skills are better than your intellectual skills.

Speculation
You are clever and discriminating, but you will never make great profits because others sometimes distrust you.

Hopes
You have great ambitions, but they are rarely realized because you treat others carelessly and unsympathetically.

Litigation
Your cunning nature helps you win law suits. If there is a possibility of losing a law suit you will try to settle out of court.

Lost property
Do not expect to find lost friends or property immediately; they will appear eventually.

The Character of the Rat

The Rat is first in the cycle of the twelve animals and corresponds to the Earthly Branch Tzu. Tzu is associated with the 11th month and matched to the hours of the day between 11 p.m. and 1 a.m. Wherever humans are found the Rat is also found; rats find their way into every corner of the world and can survive in any conditions.

You are gregarious, sociable, intelligent and polite. You are also strong-willed and humorous. You make friends easily but do not form any deep friendships. When you first meet someone you are open and sincere and expect to be treated in the same way. If you are cheated or deceived you quickly take revenge. You have a vivid imagination, discriminating judgement and the ability to translate your ideas into reality.

Underneath an eloquent, carefree and happy exterior you are calculating and miserly. You refuse to pay more than your fair share of expenses although you are happy to accept others' generosity. The good impression which you initially create is soon destroyed by your criticisms and pettiness. At a superficial level you know how to put others in a good mood and how to maintain a good social atmosphere.

You are impulsive and persistent in business and friendships.

You use your sharp intelligence to assess situations and then take advantage of any available opportunities. You appear to be a patient and forgiving business partner, but you secretly distrust your associates. Try to be more patient and understanding.

You will be a cooperative and loving marriage partner. A man born in this year is passionate from the beginning of a relationship, whereas a woman born in this year is usually passionate and committed after marriage. Someone born in the year of the Dragon will make a good marriage partner because both of you belong to the element Water. Your marriage will be long-lasting in spite of many arguments. You will feel confident and safe if you marry someone born in the year of the Ox. Partnerships between people born in the years of the Rat, the Dragon and the Ox are called a Three Harmony.

You will be happy if you marry someone born in the year of the Monkey provided the Monkey is not too dominant. A marriage with someone born in the year of the Snake, the Dog, the Pig or the Tiger will be happy but not perfect. Avoid marrying someone born in the year of the Horse because the Horse is too independent and honest for the Rat. A woman born in the year of the Horse on the Way (1906, 1966) should be wary of marrying a man born in the year of the Rat: she would be cheated throughout her marriage. You are suited to a marriage with someone born in the year of the Rabbit as long as your relationship is founded on a firm friendship; if your friendship is superficial your marriage will end in disaster.

You are suited to a career as a publisher, writer, commercial trader, critic, accountant, shopkeeper or musician.

Your Luck According to Your Year of Birth

1924, 1984
Born in the year of Chia Tzu, you belong to the Rat on the Roof.

You are impatient and rarely finish a job. You will be plagued by accidents and illnesses when you are young, and throughout life your brothers will be unwilling or unable to support you. If you are an eldest son you will have an unhappy marriage. If you are an eldest daughter you will be clever, active and a capable housewife.

1936, 1996
Born in the year of Ping Tzu, you belong to the Rat in the Field.

You are brave and powerful but you are also impatient. You lack a good education but you are an accomplished planner. You are not very lucky in your youth but by middle age you will be prosperous and well respected. A woman born in either of these years will be garrulous and annoying.

1948, 2008
Born in the year of Mou Tzu, you belong to the Rat in the Warehouse.

You are clever and skilled. You will have problems with your children when they are young but you have a trusting relationship with your husband/wife. A woman born in either of these years will be lucky and amenable.

1900, 1960
Born in the year of Keng Tzu, you belong to the Rat on the Beam.

You will be powerful and well respected. You are a popular and steady friend and your career will be prosperous and successful. A woman born in either of these years will be an efficient housekeeper who keeps a firm control over domestic affairs.

1912, 1972
Born in the year of Jen Tzu, you belong to the Rat on the Mountain.

You will have a difficult youth but a happy middle age. A man

born in these years seems to enjoy life but is secretly preoccupied and worried. His family relationships are unsteady and troubled but he will have the opportunity to marry a good wife. A woman born in either of these years will have an accommodating nature.

Your Luck According to Your Month of Birth

1st month
You have part of the Pig nature because you were born so close to the year of the Pig. You are independent and calm, even in times of crisis. You are popular because you are earnest and straightforward.

2nd month
You are clever, sensitive and intuitive. If you use your talents wisely everything you touch will turn to gold but do not overestimate your own abilities and avoid complacency. You have a busy social life but you upset others easily. A man born in this month likes cleanliness and a woman born in this month takes great care of her appearance. She is straightforward and gentle and enchants unknowingly.

3rd month
You are accessible and popular. Although you appear to run your business affairs with determination and confidence, you are privately concerned and worried. Your friends will recommend you to someone in a position of authority and you can expect to be offered promotion. Your romances may end painfully because you are so shy and emotional.

4th month
You are prosperous and extravagant. You never act without careful forethought but once you have accepted new responsibilities you fulfil your obligations. You never make empty promises and rarely abandon a project in the face of obstacles. A woman born in this month falls in love easily, even if her love is unrequited. She is a good communicator and will prove to be a good friend.

✓ **5th month**
You are cheerful, approachable and just. You have a natural charm and people of the opposite sex are attracted to you. Your marriage will be successful because you are honest, faithful, loving and level-headed. A man born in this month should not allow himself to be besotted by romance. He should approach work and romance sensibly and positively.

6th month
You are optimistic, open, sympathetic and can adapt to any environment. You are extrovert and extravagant, spending money on yourself and others with little thought for the future. You have many original ideas which will make your fortune. Be satisfied with your earnings; do not be too greedy. You are sensitive and responsive to romance. You will have a happy marriage once you learn to forgive your partner's faults.

7th month
You are gentle and polite in your speech and in your behaviour. You make others happy because you consider each point attentively but you rarely make close friends. You do not use other people but likewise you do not let others use you. You will change your job frequently when you are young because you want to assert your independence. Once you have found a suitable career you will dedicate yourself to it. Approach your work gradually and sensibly. You will never suffer any losses but neither will you be very successful. You are emotionally direct and once you have found the right partner you will be very happy.

8th month
Heaven has given you good fortune. You are attentive and alert and

can solve financial difficulties easily. You understand human nature and enjoy cultivating friendships. You quickly adapt to new situations or new jobs. You will enjoy any career that involves an element of risk.

9th month
You are intelligent, sensitive and disciplined. You enjoy working in a stable environment and will work hard to achieve promotion. Others often mistake your forgiving and understanding nature for flattery. You have many friends but none of them are close. You will have an unlucky love life.

10th month
You are quick-witted and perceptive. You are a good planner and never daunted by difficulties or challenges. You may have to work diligently for a long time before the value of your work is finally recognized. The Chinese say, 'One cry will startle people.' Others distrust you because you reveal your emotions easily. A man born in this month has difficulty controlling his physical desires.

11th month
You have an unsociable, moody and inflexible nature. You are quick-tempered and independent. Make an effort to listen to the opinions of others and try to be more open and tolerant. If you can improve these weak points you will be successful in politics or public relations. You have the spirit and drive of a leader, and others will respect you and learn from you. They will recognize your strength – you do not need to push yourself to the forefront. The Chinese say that 'You do not need to reveal your bones'.

12th month
You have a strong will and are adept at putting your ideas into practice but you also change your mind easily. You put all your energy into your work and have the strength to overcome problems. You are more concerned with running an efficient business than with the profits it may yield. Your creativity and intelligence will ensure a prosperous future. The extravagance and independence of women born in this month will cause many marital problems.

Your Luck According to Your Day of Birth

Born on the 1st, 10th, 19th or 28th

You are of noble bearing, independent and trustworthy. Your standards are high and you are always ready to fight for your career. You have a determined character but are overly concerned with yourself and with achieving fame and fortune. You feel the need to complete everything quickly but you frequently fail. Be careful and cautious. You are suited to a career as a civil servant or to a job in the arts. Your fortune fluctuates, and although at times you may receive unexpected money, at others you must control your spending.

Born on the 2nd, 11th, 20th or 29th

You are quiet but honest, open-hearted and extremely popular. Sometimes you like to be alone and at other times you want to be surrounded by friends. Unless you control your temper you will fall into trouble. You are suited to a career as an artistic designer, planner or literary editor. You enjoy life, even if you are in the poorest circumstances. Your fortune does not vary greatly, but your luck will improve after middle age.

Born on the 3rd, 12th, 21st or 30th

You are talented, sensitive and react quickly. You are always ready to fight for what you know is true and just. Others will avoid forming friendships with you if you are too obstinate; they wrongly assume you are too stern and difficult. You have business acumen and are suited to a disciplined job, such as the army, or to any job which has a competitive element, such as politics or the stock exchange. You must learn how to control your spending and think seriously of ways to earn more income.

Born on the 4th, 13th, 22nd or 31st

You are calm, patient and reserved. Your appearance and attitude lead others to think you are unapproachable, although in fact you are warm-hearted. If you change your approach you will be more popular. You are suited to a career as an academic, particularly in the field of theology or philosophy. Because you cannot control your spending you will lose money as easily and as quickly as you make it.

Born on the 5th, 14th or 23rd

Your fiery, obstinate nature makes it difficult for you to accept suggestions or opinions. At times your stubbornness leads to quarrels and problems. You are suited to a career in the arts, as an academic, an administrator or an advertising designer. Your intelligence enables you to work in a highly paid job. You will be lucky with money, often using it to set up new projects.

Born on the 6th, 15th or 24th

Your open, stable and cheerful character provides you with an active social life. You are affectionate and emotional and daydream so often that your mind becomes confused. Your eagerness to help others is often stifled by your indecisiveness. A career in the arts or work as a designer or social worker would be appropriate for you. You will not be very rich but will always have enough to live on.

Born on the 7th, 16th or 25th

You are an exhibitionist but when you show off nobody wants to listen to you or watch you. You enjoy an exciting life, but your head is in the clouds; you must learn to discipline yourself. You are suited to a job which allows you mobility, for example, a reporter, a traveller or an explorer. You do not want to earn a fortune and are quite content with your standard of living.

Born on the 8th, 17th or 26th

You are calm, quiet and a good judge. You have a determined and logical mind but lack social skills. You have a free spirit and are suited to self-employment. Do not buy stocks and shares or put your money in short-term investments. Your fortune is varied – it depends on your approach. There are times of wealth and times of abject poverty.

Born on the 9th, 18th or 27th

You are happy, optimistic and warm-hearted. You have an active life and are not easily troubled by minor matters. On the whole you are magnanimous but occasionally you quarrel unnecessarily with friends. It is important that you learn to control your moods. You should work as sole director or proprietor to avoid disagreements with partners. A job involving buying and selling would be suitable. You have a good income but you are extravagant.

Your Luck According to Your 'Hour' of Birth

Tzu hours: 11 p.m.–1 a.m.

You are hot-tempered, obstinate, thrifty and shy away from challenges. You are an easy target for gossip. At times you act without sufficient planning but later you regret your actions. You will be able to build a successful business, buy a home and care for your family without a family inheritance. You will achieve fame and success independently of others but if you find yourself in trouble your parents or your marriage partner will always be there to help you out.

Unlucky ages   10, 17, 35, 48, 57.

Age at death   87.

Suitable occupations   Artist, politician, architect, electrician or jobs connected with metal or water.

Unsuitable occupations   Work connected with earth.

Ch'ou hours: 1–3 a.m.

If you want a good career, leave your home town while you are young. Life will be difficult up to the age of twenty but then your fortune will change for the better. You will be wealthy in old age.

Unlucky ages   17, 22, 30, 45.

Age at death   71.

Suitable occupations Commercial trader, teacher, government official, restaurateur, academic, skilled manual worker or jobs connected with the final stages of production.

Unsuitable occupations   Work connected with wood.

Yin hours: 3–5 a.m.

You are on bad terms with your relatives and your early years will be difficult. You will not be left an inheritance and will leave your home town. After the age of forty everything will work out well. Old age will bring you power and wealth.

Unlucky ages   25, 28, 32, 38, 48.

Age at death   65.

Suitable occupations   Doctor, musician, artist, actor, travelling agent/representative.

Unsuitable occupations   Work connected with metal.

Mao hours: 5-7 a.m.

You will be very fortunate, with occasional help from your parents but none from your brothers and sisters. You will have a comfortable life and be wealthy if you work away from your home town. Marriage will be unsteady and difficult in the early years, but after middle age you will develop more satisfactory relationships and will have the chance to be wealthy.

Unlucky ages   15, 19, 54.

Age at death   71.

Suitable occupations   Mechanical engineer, actor, writer, artist, theologian or work connected with religion.

Unsuitable occupations   Work connected with fire.

Ch'en hours: 7-9 a.m.

You are clever, quick-witted and determined. Your warm-hearted nature enables you to form close friendships. Life is busy and varied, but a woman born in the Ch'en hours will be lonely. However, you will have many material possessions and a good salary. Your excessive self-confidence makes working relationships difficult.

Unlucky ages   18, 26, 35, 38.

Age at death   65.

Suitable occupations   Entrepreneur, politician, public relations officer, teacher, miner.

Unsuitable occupations   Work connected with wood.

Szu hours: 9–11 a.m.

You have outstanding talent and are able to build up your business and care for your family successfully. Family relations are troubled and you would prosper financially if you were to leave your home town. You are kind to your friends and like to help them when they are in trouble. A woman born in the Szu hours is extravagant and may have an unhappy marriage. Men and women born in these hours drink too much.

Unlucky ages   30, 35, 46, 48.

Age at death   88.

Suitable occupations   Civil or electrical engineer, architect, wood or wine merchant.

Unsuitable occupations   Work connected with water.

Wu hours: 11 a.m.–1 p.m.

You are active, clever, obstinate and extravagant. You prefer travelling to settling down to a job in your local area. A woman born in these hours is likely to have an unusual and fascinating character.

Unlucky ages   5, 11, 23, 32, 44, 53.

Age at death   84.

Suitable occupations   Doctor, nurse, politician, film actor, skilled worker, jobs in the service industries or any work connected with oil.

Unsuitable occupations   Work connected with gold.

Wei hours: 1–3 p.m.

You have a troubled relationship with your parents, brothers and sisters and marriage partner. You will have serious difficulties in middle age. A woman born in these hours is clever but will always have difficulties with her marriage because she is too active to settle down.

Unlucky ages   18, 25, 55.

Age at death   69.

Suitable occupations   Civil engineer, electrical engineer, architect, wood merchant, wine merchant.

Unsuitable occupations   Work connected with water.

Shen hours: 3–5 p.m.
You will earn money easily and spend it freely. You will be luckier if you work outside your home town. Your marriage will be harmonious although your parents will not offer you moral support. A woman born in the Shen hours will be married twice. Because you are too active ever to settle down completely it is important that you are seen to behave honourably. Too much time worrying over relationships will cause your business to fail.

Unlucky ages   18, 21, 27, 29, 41, 53.

Age at death   71.

Suitable occupations   Finance-related work – e.g. broker, public relations officer, watchmaker, manager – or work connected with metal.

Unsuitable occupations   Work connected with wood.

Yu hours: 5–7 p.m.
Your youth is difficult because of troubled family relationships. You will be separated from your brothers and sisters and will leave home when young. You may not be able to have a child but it will be possible to adopt one. A woman born in the Yu hours is warm-hearted, fond of food and can be trusted to keep a secret.

Unlucky ages   18, 24, 31, 48.

Age at death   77.

Suitable occupations   Chemist, researcher/writer, teacher, artist, technologist or work connected with the final stages of production.

Unsuitable occupations   Work connected with earth.

Hsü hours: 7–9 p.m.
You are brave, capable, hardworking and run your business alone.
You are optimistic and will have a successful life and a flourishing
career. A woman born in the Hsü hours can be vain and impatient.
You are magnanimous but on the other hand money is not
important to you. You care little for others but will have a
magnificent life.

Unlucky ages   15, 25, 34, 43, 48, 56.

Age at death   77.

Suitable occupations   Poet, writer, investor, engineer, rice or cereal
merchant, or work connected with metal and agriculture.

Unsuitable occupations   Work connected with fire.

Hai hours: 9–11 p.m.
You are manually dextrous and set yourself high standards.
Although you are warm-hearted you do not like to make too many
friends. A woman born in the Hai hours can be obstinate. Others
may be easily upset but you have the ability to forgive and forget.
You are hardworking and will be fortunate.

Unlucky ages   10, 25, 35, 38, 48, 55.

Age at death   77.

Suitable occupations   Surgeon, monk/nun, hotelier, artist, antiques
dealer or work connected with metal.

Unsuitable occupations   Work connected with fire.

Practical Advice

Remember to thank anyone who helps you.
Try to establish better relationships with your family.
Be sincere and cheerful, it will help your business prosper.
Help others even if they are not connected with your own affairs.
Do not stay silent if you feel the need to talk.
Be courageous. Accept difficult challenges.
Be careful and calm, particularly when you are driving.
If you fail, do not be afraid to try again.
Be humble. Do not try to attract attention.
Be careful where you go at night-time.
You will be fortunate if you help your friends.
Do not put off till tomorrow what you can do today.

Your Luck Year by Year

Year of the Rat
Three lucky stars, two unlucky stars.
   This is a prosperous and successful year for your business, but your unlucky stars will bring sickness or shock.

Year of the Ox
Three lucky stars, two unlucky stars.
   Do not initiate any new ventures in your private or public life. Although your three lucky stars are shining, this is not a fortunate year. Do not take any risks.

Year of the Tiger
One travelling star, one lucky star, two unlucky spirits.
   This is a good year for travel and emigration. It is also a lonely year and there may be a death in the family.

Year of the Rabbit
One lucky star, one baleful spirit.
   Someone in your family may marry during the year. There will be quarrels in your marriage and possibly problems at work. You will be the target of gossip this year.

Year of the Dragon
Three lucky stars, four unlucky stars.

During the year your business will prosper, your income will increase and you will be successful in examinations. Your unlucky stars forecast the death of an older relative or parent and a dangerous threat from one of your friends.

Year of the Snake
One lucky star, two unlucky stars.

You will suffer a serious illness or accident which may leave you scarred. Your lucky star will help you to recover.

Year of the Horse
Two baleful spirits.

This is a year of financial loss, possible imprisonment and general misfortune.

Year of the Ram
Two lucky stars, two unlucky stars.

Your business will prosper, but you will suffer an injustice during the year. You may be burgled or lose something important.

Year of the Monkey
One baleful spirit.

Choose your friends carefully this year. Keep in contact with them; you may need their support.

Year of the Cock
Four lucky stars, one unlucky star.

This is a very fortunate year for you and your family. Your business will prosper and you could marry a wealthy partner. Your bad star is not influential this year. Take care of your hands; you may damage them.

Year of the Dog
One lucky star, four unlucky stars.

This is a year of disaster, loneliness and loss. Do not climb to high places and beware of being bitten by a dog.

Year of the Pig
Four unlucky stars.

This is a fruitless and unfortunate year. You will feel weak and sick during the year, so you must be careful what you eat and drink.

Tzu Wei (Purple Star) Astrological System

INTRODUCTION

Tzu Wei (Purple Star) astrology was written down in the Sung dynasty (960–1280 AD). It was drawn together and elaborated on by the master astrologer Ch'en T'u Nan, who is also known as Ch'en Hsi I (this was an additional name taken at the age of twenty in ancient China). However, elements of the Tzu Wei system were already being practised during the T'ang dynasty (618–907 AD). It is an accurate method of fortune-telling yet has the advantage of being simple to use.

The Tzu Wei method centres on the Chinese concept of *ming* (life or fate). It attempts to explain why one person's *ming* is so different from another's. Why do some people have good fortune, social position, riches or long life, when others are unlucky, suffer tragedies, are poor or die young? How is it that some never have to work but are well off, while others have to work as labourers for a pittance?

In Tzu Wei astrology your *ming* is believed to be controlled by your horoscope. Your horoscope comes with you at birth, and is based on your year of birth, your month of birth, your day of birth and your hour of birth. This means that to understand your *ming* – to discover if your fate is good or bad – you need to examine your horoscope. The Tzu Wei method provides a means of doing this in detail.

In China the Tzu Wei method is very well known. It remains pure and distinct from the other main ancient Chinese astrological system, the Szu Chu (Four-Pole astrology). In Japan the two have been fused. If you want to study Chinese astrology, you should start with the Tzu Wei method.

In Chinese, Tzu Wei is the name of the god of the Pole Star and

Tzu Wei astrology is called *Tzu Wei Tou Shu*, which literally means 'Purple Star Calculation'. This reflects the many stages of calculation required to arrive at your horoscope.

Many stars are used to calculate your horoscope. These include the Tzu Wei stars, real and imaginary, and other real or imaginary stars. These stars are plotted on the Tzu Wei chart, which is a visual representation of your horoscope.

Drawing up the Tzu Wei chart may be time-consuming, but once complete it is easy to use. It has two particular advantages. The first is that you can read it yourself, without the help of a professional astrologer. The second is that the chart can be used to obtain readings for any time in your life. This means that you can keep it to hand and consult it to find out when, for example, it would be a good time for you to embark on a particular venture.

In the following chapters you will come across many different star names. Opposite is a list of all the stars used in the Tzu Wei system with a literal English translation of their names. The English names do not reflect to any great extent the complex nature of the stars.

The Stars in the Tzu Wei System

1 Tzu Wei *TỬ VI* Purple Star
2 Lien Chen *LIÊM TRINH* Pure Virtue Star
3 T'ien K'uei Heavenly Leader Star
4 Tso Fu and Yu Pi Left and Right Assistant Stars
5 Hua Ch'üan Transforming Authority Star
6 T'ien Chi *THIÊN CƠ* Heavenly Secret Star
7 T'ien T'ung *THIÊN ĐỒNG* Heavenly Unity Star
8 T'ai-yang *THÁI DƯƠNG* The Sun
9 T'ai-yin *THÁI ÂM* The Moon
10 T'ien Hsiang *THIÊN TƯỚNG* Heavenly Minister Star
11 T'ien Ts'un Heavenly Store Star
12 T'ien Yüeh Heavenly Halberd Star
13 Chü Men *CỰ MÔN* Great Door Star
14 Ch'i Sha *THẤT SÁT* Seven Killings Star
15 Hua Lu Transforming Salary Star
16 Wu Ch'ü *VŨ KHÚC* Military Music Star
17 T'ien Fu *THIÊN PHỦ* Southern Star
18 T'an Lang *THAM LANG* Greedy Wolf Star
19 T'ien Liang *THIÊN LƯƠNG* Heavenly Roof-Beam Star
20 P'o Chün *PHÁ QUÂN* Broken Army Star
21 Hua K'o Transforming Examination Class Star
22 Fire Star *HOA TINH*
23 Ringing Star
24 Yang Jen Sheep-Blade Star
25 T'o Lo Hump-Back Star
26 Hua Chi Transforming Jealousy Star
27 T'ien K'ung Heavenly Void Star
28 Ti Chieh Earthly Robbery Star
29 Wen Ch'ü *VĂN KHÚC* Literary Music Star   ⎫
30 Wen Ch'ang *VĂN XƯƠNG* Literary Prosperity Star ⎬ Literary Stars
31 I-ma Travelling Star
32 T'ien Yao Heavenly Beauty Star
33 T'ien Hao Heavenly Destroyer Star
34 Hung Luan Red Phoenix Star
35 T'ien Hsi Heavenly Happiness Star
36 T'ien Hsing Heavenly Punishment Star

HOW TO COMPILE
YOUR TZU WEI CHART

You will find that this first section requires a lot of looking up of tables and filling in of squares. Don't give up! Once you have followed through the twenty-one stages described below you will have unlocked the door to one of the most detailed horoscopes you will ever receive.

The Tzu Wei Chart

The Tzu Wei chart is a visual representation of your horoscope. On A4 paper first draw up the grid or *ching* (well) on which the chart is based. This consists of twelve boxes around a central square (see Figure 1). Then label each box with one of the twelve Earthly Branches as follows: the first of the Earthly Branches, Tzu, appears in the box second from the right on the bottom row. The following eleven, Ch'ou, Yin, Mao, Ch'en, Szu, Wu, Wei, Shen, Yu, Hsü and Hai appear in consecutive boxes running clockwise from the box containing Tzu (see Figure 2).

Your Lunar Birthday and Your Pa Tzu
(Eight Characters)

The Pa Tzu are the eight characters on which your horoscope is based. They are arranged in four pairs. The first pair corresponds to the year of birth, the second pair to the month, the third pair to the day and the fourth to the time. Each pair consists of a Heavenly Stem and an Earthly Branch.

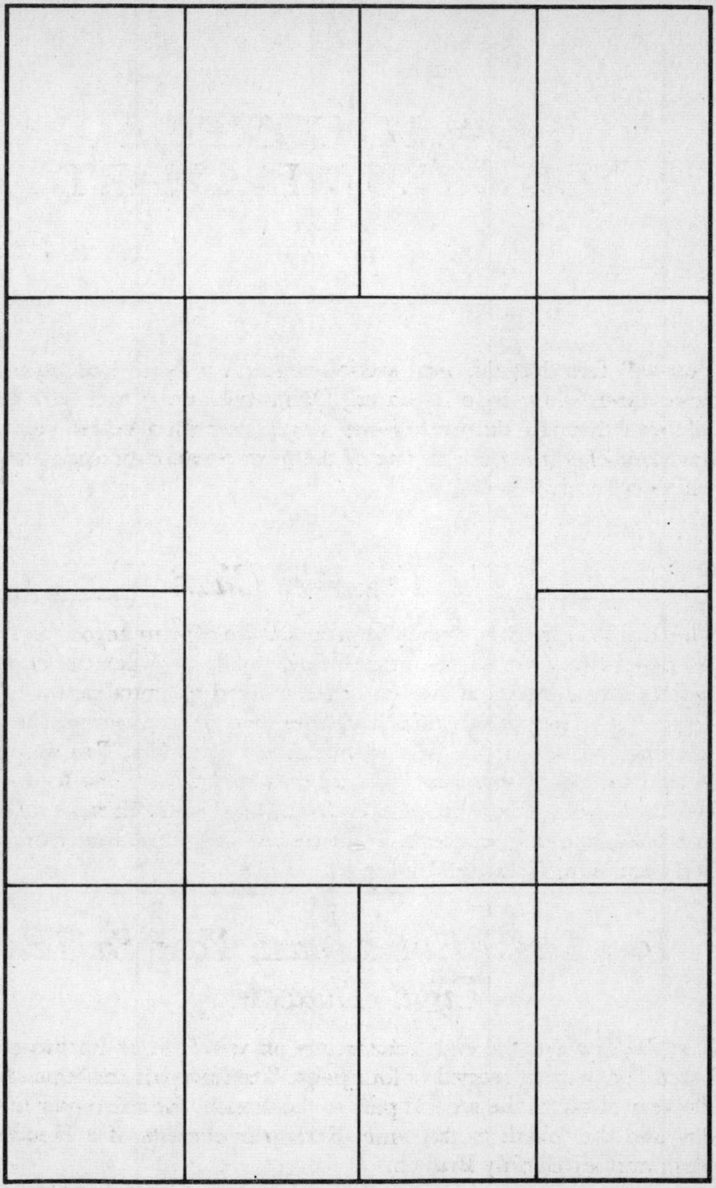

Figure 1   *The grid or ching (well)*

Figure 2   The boxes labelled with the twelve Earthly Branches —TAM?

TIEN LIANG+ TIEN KUEI HAO TIEN HSI 45-54 **WEALTH** **Szu** 6	CHI SHA ☆ 35-44 **MAN/WOMAN** YR MO JEN CHEN MOU SHEN **Wu** 5	TIEN YAO TAI YANG FIRE STR TAI YIN 25-34 **MARITAL** DAY HR CHIA TZU YI HAI **Wei** 4	LIEN CHEN ☆ 15-34 **BRO/SIS** RINGING STAR + **Shen** 3
TZU WGI ☆ TIEN HSIANG ☆ 55-64 **SICKNESS** **Ch'en** 7	EARTH		5-14 MING **Yu** 2
TIEN CHI ☆ TIEN YUEH WEN CHU ☆ TIEN HSING ☆ CHU MEN HUA CHI 65-74 **MOVING** **Mao** 9			PO CHUN ☆ TSO FU TI CHIEH + 115-124 **PARENTS** **Hsü** 1
TAN LANG+ I-MA HUA LU TAI YANG ☆ FIRE STAR ☆ TAI YIN ☆ 85-94 **OFFICIALS** 75-84 **SERVANTS** **Yin** 9	WO CHU ☆ HUA KO TIEN FU HUA CHUAN ☆ YANG JEN- 95-104 **PROSPERTY** **Ch'ou** 10	TIEN KUNG 95-104 **PROSPERTY** **Tzu** 11	TIEN TUNG ☆ TIEN TSIN WEN CHANG ☆ HUNG LUAN TO LO- 105-114 **FORTUNE** **Hai** 12

To find your eight characters you first need to convert your date and time of birth to the lunar (Chinese) calendar. The three steps of the conversion (your solar birthday, your lunar birthday and your eight characters) appear in the central square of the Tzu Wei chart.

First, at the top of the central square enter your year, month, date and hour of birth according to the solar (Western) calendar. Next, convert this to the lunar (Chinese) calendar. Look up your date of birth (solar) in the Calendar Tables which appear at the back of this book.

The Heavenly Stem and Earthly Branch for the year are shown at the start of the lunar (Chinese) year in which your birthday falls. In the case of 1 September 1986 the Chinese name for the year is Ping Yin. Thus the first pair of characters in our example of the eight-character horoscope are the Heavenly Stem Ping and the Earthly Branch Yin.

The lunar month and date are shown in the second column of the Calendar Tables. Using the same example, in 1986, 1 September is equivalent to the 27th day of the 7th lunar month.

The Chinese system of hours is shown in the table on p. 17 of the Introduction. In our example someone born at 8 p.m. would have the Earthly Branch Hsü as the character for his or her 'hour' of birth.

You are now in a position to enter the details of the year, month, date and 'hour' of birth according to the lunar calendar on the Tzu Wei chart. They go in the central square, immediately below the solar entry.

Next you need to find the characters for your eight-character horoscope. You already have the pair for the year – in our example these are Ping Yin. The characters for the month are shown in code in the third column of the Calendar Tables. Staying with our example, in 1986 the 7th month has the code C9. At the start of the Calendar Tables you will find the list of codes for the Heavenly Stems and the Earthly Branches. The Heavenly Stems are coded from A to K and the Earthly Branches from 1 to 12. The code C9 is equivalent to the Heavenly Stem Ping and the Earthly Branch Shen and these thus form the second pair of characters of the eight-character horoscope in our example and are entered in the central square of the Tzu Wei chart.

The code corresponding to the day is given in the fourth column of the Calendar Tables. Still using the same example, the 27th day

of the 7th month in Ping Yin year (1 September 1986) has the code
E9. Looking up the codes at the start of the tables, we find that this
corresponds to the Heavenly Stem Mou and the Earthly Branch
Shen, and these too are entered in the central square of the Tzu Wei
chart.

By now you should have found the first six characters for your
eight-character horoscope. The last two characters are those for
your 'hour' of birth. We have already found the Earthly Branch for
the 'hour' in our example – it is Hsü. So all that remains is to find
the Heavenly Stem for the 'hour' and this can be done using Table
1. This table is based on the Earthly Branch for your 'hour' of birth
and the Heavenly Stem for your day of birth. So if the Earthly
Branch for the 'hour' is Hsü and the Heavenly Stem for the day is
Mou, then the Heavenly Stem for the 'hour' is Jen. You can now
enter the last pair of characters of your Pa Tzu – your eight
characters – in the central square of the Tzu Wei chart, which
should look like Figure 3.

Table 1   *The Heavenly Stem for the 'Hour' of Birth*

Earthly Branch for 'Hour' of Birth	Heavenly Stem for Day of Birth				
	Chia Chi	Yi Keng	Ping Hsin	Ting Jen	Mou Kuei
Tzu	Chia	Ping	Mou	Keng	Jen
Ch'ou	Yi	Ting	Chi	Hsin	Kuei
Yin	Ping	Mou	Keng	Jen	Chia
Mao	Ting	Chi	Hsin	Kuei	Yi
Ch'en	Mou	Keng	Jen	Chia	Ping
Szu	Chi	Hsin	Kuei	Yi	Ting
Wu	Keng	Jen	Chia	Ping	Mou
Wei	Hsin	Kuei	Yi	Ting	Chi
Shen	Jen	Chia	Ping	Mou	Keng
Yu	Kuei	Yi	Ting	Chi	Hsin
Hsü	Chia	Ping	Mou	Keng	Jen
Hai	Yi	Ting	Chi	Hsin	Kuei

Finally, immediately below the eight-character entry, write the
word 'Element'. This will be filled in later. Then write your name
and today's date at the bottom of the central square.

Figure 3   *Information entered in the central square: example for 1 September 1986, 8 p.m.*

Szu	Wu	Wei	Shen
Ch'en			Yu
Mao			Hsü
Yin	Ch'ou	Tzu	Hai

Date and time of birth (solar):
1986   September   1st   8 p.m.

Date and time of birth (lunar):
Ping Yin   7th   27th   Hsü

Eight characters:
Ping Yin   Ping Shen   Mou Shen   Jen Hsü

Element:

Name:

Today's date:

The Ming Palace

Locating your Ming (Life/Fate) Palace on the Tzu Wei chart is the first step in the calculation of your horoscope.

The Ming Palace may appear in any one of the twelve boxes labelled with the Twelve Earthly Branches. To locate your Ming Palace use Table 2. Find the Earthly Branch for the month you were born in the column headings and the Earthly Branch for your 'hour' of birth in the side headings. The entry in the main body of the table is the Earthly Branch of the box in which your Ming Palace is located. For example, if you were born on 1 September 1986 at 8 p.m., the branch for the month is Shen and the branch for the 'hour' is Hsü. The Ming Palace is located in the box labelled with the Earthly Branch Hsü. The box in which the Ming Palace appears becomes the key box on the chart.

The Twelve Palaces

The Ming Palace is one of twelve palaces concerned with different aspects of your life. The other eleven palaces are the Brothers' and Sisters' Palace, the Marital Palace, the Man and Woman Palace, the Wealth Palace, the Sickness Palace, the Moving Palace, the Servants' Palace, the Officials' Palace, the Property Palace, the Fortune and Virtue Palace and the Parents' Palace. The aspects of your life with which each palace is associated are as follows:

Ming Palace
Your physical appearance, natural abilities and business success or failure are included under this palace. In short, it is concerned with good and bad luck as it affects your whole life.

Brothers' and Sisters' Palace
Your relationships with your brothers, sisters, friends and colleagues are all dealt with under this palace.

Marital Palace
This palace is concerned with your *yuanten* – the appointed fate by which you and your partner are brought together, your affinity. Is this strong or weak? After marriage will you be happy or not?

Table 2   Locating the Ming (Life/Fate) Palace

Earthly Branch for 'Hour' of Birth	Earthly Branch for Month of Birth											
	Tzu	Ch'ou	Yin	Mao	Ch'en	Szu	Wu	Wei	Shen	Yu	Hsü	Hai
Tzu	Tzu	Ch'ou	Yin	Mao	Ch'en	Szu	Wu	Wei	Shen	Yu	Hsü	Hai
Ch'ou	Hai	Tzu	Ch'ou	Yin	Mao	Ch'en	Szu	Wu	Wei	Shen	Yu	Hsü
Yin	Hsü	Hai	Tzu	Ch'ou	Yin	Mao	Ch'en	Szu	Wu	Wei	Shen	Yu
Mao	Yu	Hsü	Hai	Tzu	Ch'ou	Yin	Mao	Ch'en	Szu	Wu	Wei	Shen
Ch'en	Shen	Yu	Hsü	Hai	Tzu	Ch'ou	Yin	Mao	Ch'en	Szu	Wu	Wei
Szu	Wei	Shen	Yu	Hsü	Hai	Tzu	Ch'ou	Yin	Mao	Ch'en	Szu	Wu
Wu	Wu	Wei	Shen	Yu	Hsü	Hai	Tzu	Ch'ou	Yin	Mao	Ch'en	Szu
Wei	Szu	Wu	Wei	Shen	Yu	Hsü	Hai	Tzu	Ch'ou	Yin	Mao	Ch'en
Shen	Ch'en	Szu	Wu	Wei	Shen	Yu	Hsü	Hai	Tzu	Ch'ou	Yin	Mao
Yu	Mao	Ch'en	Szu	Wu	Wei	Shen	Yu	Hsü	Hai	Tzu	Ch'ou	Yin
Hsü	Yin	Mao	Ch'en	Szu	Wu	Wei	Shen	Yu	Hsü	Hai	Tzu	Ch'ou
Hai	Ch'ou	Yin	Mao	Ch'en	Szu	Wu	Wei	Shen	Yu	Hsü	Hai	Tzu

Man and Woman Palace

This palace covers two aspects. The first is sexual happiness and fertility. The second is your relationship with your children: are they well behaved and obedient?

Wealth Palace

This palace is concerned with your level of income and overall wealth.

Sickness Palace

This palace deals with physical health including illness and accident.

Moving Palace

There are two aspects included under this palace. The first is your success at work: do you develop and expand into new areas? The second is travel: is it auspicious or not for you to travel?

Servants' Palace

Your relationships with your inferiors, for example, staff working under you, are covered by this palace. Are they honest or do they harm you?

Officials' Palace

This palace is concerned with your relationship with your superiors: is this harmonious? A second aspect covered by this palace is whether you are suited to your job.

Property Palace

Is your family life favoured by good luck? Are you likely to own much property? This palace deals with both questions.

Fortune and Virtue Palace

This palace deals with your longevity and your physical and psychological condition. It also includes leisure activities.

Parents' Palace

This palace concerns your parents' good and bad luck, their longevity and mutual harmony. Your relationship with your parents, whether they love you and support you, is also included.

Once the Ming Palace has been located in a box, then the other eleven palaces can be assigned to the remaining eleven boxes. In Table 3 the Earthly Branch on which the Ming Palace appears is given on the side headings and the other eleven palaces in the column headings. The entry in the main body of the table is the Earthly Branch of the box in which the palace is located. For example if the Ming Palace appears in the box labelled Hsü, then the Brothers' and Sisters' Palace appears in the box labelled Yu, the Marital Palace in the box labelled Shen, the Man and Woman Palace in the box labelled Wei, and so on. Figure 4 shows how the palaces are entered on the Tzu Wei chart for our example of 1 September 1986, 8 p.m., in which the Ming Palace appears in the box labelled Hsü.

The palaces become new labels for the boxes they appear in. A palace is a place or a space. Stars which appear in a particular box affect that aspect of your life governed by the palace associated with that box.

The Five Elements

Each individual's horoscope is associated with one of the five elements: Water, Fire, Earth, Wood or Metal.

This element can be calculated from the Earthly Branch of the box in which the Ming Palace is located and the Heavenly Stem for the year of your birth. In Table 4 these Earthly Branches appear in the side headings and the Heavenly Stems in the column headings; the elements are shown in the main body of the table. For the example of 1 September 1986, 8 p.m., the Ming Palace is located in the box labelled with the Earthly Branch Hsü and the Heavenly Stem for the year of birth is Ping. This gives the element Wood.

You can now enter your element in the central square of the Tzu Wei chart under the eight-character entry.

The Tzu Wei Star

Tzu Wei (Purple Star) is the leading star of the Tzu Wei star group. It is equated with the Pole Star and is a symbol of the Pei Tou stars (the Great Bear constellation, Ursa Major).

Figure 4   *Locating the Twelve Palaces: example for 1 September 1986, 8 p.m.*

Sickness — Szu	Wealth — Wu	Man and Woman — Wei	Marital — Shen
Moving — Ch'en	Date and time of birth (solar): 1986 September 1st 8 p.m. Date and time of birth (lunar): Ping Yin 7th 27th Hsü	Eight characters: Ping Yin Ping Shen Mou Shen Jen Hsü Element: Name:	Brothers' and Sisters' — Yu
Servants' — Mao	Today's date:		Ming — Hsü
Officials' — Yin	Property — Ch'ou	Fortune and Virtue — Tzu	Parents' — Hai

Table 3   *Locating the Twelve Palaces*

Location of the Ming Palace	Brothers' and Sisters' Palace	Marital Palace	Man and Woman Palace	Wealth Palace	Sickness Palace	Moving Palace	Servants' Palace	Officials' Palace	Property Palace	Fortune and Virtue Palace	Parents' Palace
Tzu	Hai	Hsü	Yu	Shen	Wei	Wu	Szu	Ch'en	Mao	Yin	Ch'ou
Ch'ou	Tzu	Hai	Hsü	Yu	Shen	Wei	Wu	Szu	Ch'en	Mao	Yin
Yin	Ch'ou	Tzu	Hai	Hsü	Yu	Shen	Wei	Wu	Szu	Ch'en	Mao
Mao	Yin	Ch'ou	Tzu	Hai	Hsü	Yu	Shen	Wei	Wu	Szu	Ch'en
Ch'en	Mao	Yin	Ch'ou	Tzu	Hai	Hsü	Yu	Shen	Wei	Wu	Szu
Szu	Ch'en	Mao	Yin	Ch'ou	Tzu	Hai	Hsü	Yu	Shen	Wei	Wu
Wu	Szu	Ch'en	Mao	Yin	Ch'ou	Tzu	Hai	Hsü	Yu	Shen	Wei
Wei	Wu	Szu	Ch'en	Mao	Yin	Ch'ou	Tzu	Hai	Hsü	Yu	Shen
Shen	Wei	Wu	Szu	Ch'en	Mao	Yin	Ch'ou	Tzu	Hai	Hsü	Yu
Yu	Shen	Wei	Wu	Szu	Ch'en	Mao	Yin	Ch'ou	Tzu	Hai	Hsü
Hsü	Yu	Shen	Wei	Wu	Szu	Ch'en	Mao	Yin	Ch'ou	Tzu	Hai
Hai	Hsü	Yu	Shen	Wei	Wu	Szu	Ch'en	Mao	Yin	Ch'ou	Tzu

Table 4 *The Five Elements*

Location of the Ming Palace	Heavenly Stem for the Year of Birth									
	Chia	*Yi*	*Ping*	*Ting*	*Mou*	*Chi*	*Keng*	*Hsin*	*Jen*	*Kuei*
Tzu / *Ch'ou*	Water	Fire	Earth	Wood	Metal	Water	Fire	Earth	Wood	Metal
Yin / *Mao*	Fire	Earth	Wood	Metal	Water	Fire	Earth	Wood	Metal	Water
Ch'en / *Szu*	Wood	Metal	Water	Fire	Earth	Wood	Metal	Water	Fire	Earth
Wu / *Wei*	Earth	Wood	Metal	Water	Fire	Earth	Wood	Metal	Water	Fire
Shen / *Yu*	Metal	Water	Fire	Earth	Wood	Metal	Water	Fire	Earth	Wood
Hsü / *Hai*	Fire	Earth	Water	Earth	Water	Fire	Earth	Wood	Metal	Water

The location of the Tzu Wei star on the Tzu Wei chart is calculated from the number of the day on which you were born and the element of your horoscope. In Table 5 the day appears in the side headings and element in the column headings. The main body of the table gives the Earthly Branch of the box in which the Tzu Wei star should be located. In our example, 1 September 1986, 8 p.m., is equivalent to the 27th day of the 7th lunar month and the element is Wood. This means that the Tzu Wei star is located in the box labelled Hsü. In the case of this horoscope this is a particularly lucky location as both the Ming Palace and the Tzu Wei star appear in the same box.

The Tzu Wei Star Group

The Tzu Wei star group consists of five stars which form a group around the Tzu Wei star. Although the Tzu Wei star itself can be equated with the Pole Star, the other stars in the group do not correspond to other stars in the Great Bear constellation. T'ai-yang (literally, 'extreme yang') is in fact the Sun. The other stars – T'ien Chi (Heavenly Secret), Wu Ch'ü (Military Music), T'ien T'ung (Heavenly Unity) and Lien Chen (Pure Virtue) – are all imaginary.

On the Tzu Wei chart each of these stars is located in a different box, and this depends on the location of the Tzu Wei star. Table 6 gives the Earthly Branch of the box containing the Tzu Wei star in the side headings and the names of the other stars in the Tzu Wei group in the column headings. The Earthly Branch for the box in which each star is located is given in the main body of the table. For the example 1 September 1986, 8 p.m., we have already established that the Tzu Wei star appears in the box labelled Hsü. Using Table 6 we find that T'ien Chi appears in the box labelled Yu, Tai-yang is in the box labelled Wei, Wu Ch'ü in the box labelled Wu, T'ien T'ung in the box labelled Szu and Lien Chen in the box labelled Yin (see Figure 5).

T'ien Fu (Southern Star)

In Tzu Wei astrology T'ien Fu is the Southern Star. In the sky it appears opposite the Tzu Wei star. Its position on the chart depends

Figure 5   *Locating the Tzu Wei star group*

T'ien T'ung Sickness — Szu	Wu Ch'ü Wealth — Wu	T'ai-yang Man and Woman — Wei	T'ien Chi Marital — Shen
Moving — Ch'en	Date and time of birth (solar): 1986 September 1st 8 p.m. Date and time of birth (lunar): Ping Yin 7th 27th Hsü		Brothers' and Sisters' — Yu
Servants' — Mao	Eight characters: Ping Yin Ping Shen Mou Shen Jen Hsü Element: **Wood** Name: Today's date:		Tzu Wei Ming — Hsü
Lien Chen Officials' — Yin	Property — Ch'ou	Fortune and Virtue — Tzu	Parents' — Hai

Table 5   *Locating the Tzu Wei Star*

Day of Birth	Wood	Fire	Element Earth	Metal	Water
1st	Ch'en	Yu	Wu	Hai	Ch'ou
2nd	Ch'ou	Wu	Hai	Ch'en	Yin
3rd	Yin	Hai	Ch'en	Ch'ou	Yin
4th	Szu	Ch'en	Ch'ou	Yin	Mao
5th	Yin	Ch'ou	Yin	Tzu	Mao
6th	Mao	Yin	Wei	Szu	Ch'en
7th	Wu	Hsü	Tzu	Yin	Ch'en
8th	Mao	Wei	Szu	Mao	Szu
9th	Ch'en	Tzu	Yin	Ch'ou	Szu
10th	Wei	Szu	Mao	Wu	Wu
11th	Ch'en	Yin	Shen	Mao	Wu
12th	Szu	Mao	Ch'ou	Ch'en	Wei
13th	Shen	Hai	Wu	Yin	Wei
14th	Szu	Shen	Mao	Wei	Shen
15th	Wu	Ch'ou	Ch'en	Ch'en	Shen
16th	Yu	Wu	Yu	Szu	Yu
17th	Wu	Mao	Yin	Mao	Yu
18th	Wei	Ch'en	Wei	Shen	Hsü
19th	Hsü	Tzu	Ch'en	Szu	Hsü
20th	Wei	Yu	Szu	Wu	Hai
21st	Shen	Yin	Hsü	Ch'en	Hai
22nd	Hai	Wei	Mao	Yu	Tzu
23rd	Shen	Ch'en	Shen	Wu	Tzu
24th	Yu	Szu	Szu	Wei	Ch'ou
25th	Tzu	Ch'ou	Wu	Szu	Ch'ou
26th	Yu	Hsü	Hai	Hsü	Yin
27th	Hsü	Mao	Ch'en	Wei	Yin
28th	Ch'ou	Shen	Yu	Shen	Mao
29th	Hsü	Szu	Wu	Wu	Mao
30th	Hai	Wu	Wei	Hai	Ch'en

on the position of the Tzu Wei star. Table 7 gives the location of the Tzu Wei star in the left-hand column and the location of T'ien Fu in the right-hand column. For the example 1 September 1986, 8 p.m., the Tzu Wei star is in the box labelled Hsü. This means that T'ien Fu appears in the box labelled Wu.

Figure 6   *Locating the T'ien Fu star group*

T'ien T'ung Sickness — Szu	Wu Ch'ü **T'ien Fu** Wealth — Wu	T'ai-yang **T'ai-yin** Man and Woman — Wei	**T'an Lang** Marital — Shen
P'o Chün Moving — Ch'en	Date and time of birth (solar): 1986 September 1st 8 p.m. Date and time of birth (lunar): Ping Yin 7th 27th Hsü		T'ien Chi **Chü Men** Brothers' and Sisters' — Yu
Servants' — Mao	Eight characters: Ping Yin Ping Shen Mou Shen Jen Hsü Element: Wood Name: Today's date:		Tzu Wei **T'ien Hsiang** Ming — Hsü
Lien Chen Officials' — Yin	**Ch'i Sha** Property — Ch'ou	Fortune and Virtue — Tzu	**T'ien Liang** Parents' — Hai

Table 6   *Locating the Tzu Wei Star Group*

Location of Tzu Wei Star	T'ien Chi	T'ai-yang	Wu Ch'ü	T'ien T'ung	Lien Chen
Tzu	Hai	Yu	Shen	Wei	Ch'en
Ch'ou	Tzu	Hsü	Yu	Shen	Szu
Yin	Ch'ou	Hai	Hsü	Yu	Wu
Mao	Yin	Tzu	Hai	Hsü	Wei
Ch'en	Mao	Ch'ou	Tzu	Hai	Shen
Szu	Ch'en	Yin	Ch'ou	Tzu	Yu
Wu	Szu	Mao	Yin	Ch'ou	Hsü
Wei	Wu	Ch'en	Mao	Yin	Hai
Shen	Wei	Szu	Ch'en	Mao	Tzu
Yu	Shen	Wu	Szu	Ch'en	Ch'ou
Hsü	Yu	Wei	Wu	Szu	Yin
Hai	Hsü	Shen	Wei	Wu	Mao

Table 7   *Locating T'ien Fu (Southern Star)*

Location of Tzu Wei Star	T'ien Fu
Tzu	Ch'en
Ch'ou	Mao
Yin	Yin
Mao	Ch'ou
Ch'en	Tzu
Szu	Hai
Wu	Hsü
Wei	Yu
Shen	Shen
Yu	Wei
Hsü	Wu
Hai	Szu

The T'ien Fu Star Group

Like the Tzu Wei star, T'ien Fu is accompanied by a group of seven stars. Of these, T'ai-yin (the Moon) is real and the others – T'an Lang (Greedy Wolf), Chü Men (Great Door), T'ien Hsiang (Heavenly Minister), T'ien Liang (Heavenly Roof-beam), Ch'i Sha (Seven Killings) and P'o Chün (Broken Army) – are imaginary. The location of these stars depends on the location of T''ien Fu itself. Table 8 gives the Earthly Branch of the box containing T'ien Fu in the side headings and the names of the other stars in the group in the column headings. The Earthly Branches of the boxes in which these stars are to be located are given in the main body of the table. For the example 1 September 1986, 8 p.m., we already know that T'ien Fu appears in the box labelled Wu. This means that T'ai-yin appears in the box labelled Wei, T'an Lang in the box labelled Shen, Chü Men in the box labelled Yu, T'ien Hsiang in the box labelled Hsü, T'ien Liang in the box labelled Hai, Ch'i Sha in the box labelled Tzu and P'o Chün in the box labelled Ch'en.

Table 8   *Locating the T''ien Fu Star Group*

Location of T''ien Fu	T'ai-yin	T'an Lang	Chü Men	T'ien Hsiang	T'ien Liang	Ch'i Sha	P'o Chün
Tzu	Ch'ou	Yin	Mao	Ch'en	Szu	Wu	Hsü
Ch'ou	Yin	Mao	Ch'en	Szu	Wu	Wei	Hai
Yin	Mao	Ch'en	Szu	Wu	Wei	Shen	Tzu
Mao	Ch'en	Szu	Wu	Wei	Shen	Yu	Ch'ou
Ch'en	Szu	Wu	Wei	Shen	Yu	Hsü	Yin
Szu	Wu	Wei	Shen	Yu	Hsü	Hai	Mao
Wu	Wei	Shen	Yu	Hsü	Hai	Tzu	Ch'en
Wei	Shen	Yu	Hsü	Hai	Tzu	Ch'ou	Szu
Shen	Yu	Hsü	Hai	Tzu	Ch'ou	Yin	Wu
Yu	Hsü	Hai	Tzu	Ch'ou	Yin	Mao	Wei
Hsü	Hai	Tzu	Ch'ou	Yin	Mao	Ch'en	Shen
Hai	Tzu	Ch'ou	Yin	Mao	Ch'en	Szu	Yu

The Fire Star and the Ringing Star

The Fire Star is the Chinese name for Mars. The location of the Fire Star on the Tzu Wei chart is dependent on your 'hour' and year of birth. Table 9 gives the Earthly Branch for the 'hour' of birth in the side headings and the Earthly Branch for the year of birth in the column headings. The location of the Fire Star is given in the body of the table. For 1 September 1986, 8 p.m., the Earthly Branch for the 'hour' is Hsü and the Earthly Branch for the year is Yin. This means that the Fire Star is located in the box labelled Hai.

Table 9   Locating the Fire Star

Earthly Branch for 'Hour' of Birth	Earthly Branch for Year of Birth											
	Tzu	Ch'ou	Yin	Mao	Ch'en	Szu	Wu	Wei	Shen	Yu	Hsü	Hai
Tzu	Yin	Mao	Ch'ou	Yu	Yin	Mao	Ch'ou	Yu	Yin	Mao	Ch'ou	Yu
Ch'ou	Mao	Ch'en	Yin	Hsü	Mao	Ch'en	Yin	Hsü	Mao	Ch'en	Yin	Hsü
Yin	Ch'en	Szu	Mao	Hai	Ch'en	Szu	Mao	Hai	Ch'en	Szu	Mao	Hai
Mao	Szu	Wu	Ch'en	Tzu	Szu	Wu	Ch'en	Tzu	Szu	Wu	Ch'en	Tzu
Ch'en	Wu	Wei	Szu	Ch'ou	Wu	Wei	Szu	Ch'ou	Wu	Wei	Szu	Ch'ou
Szu	Wei	Shen	Wu	Yin	Wei	Shen	Wu	Yin	Wei	Shen	Wu	Yin
Wu	Shen	Yu	Wei	Mao	Shen	Yu	Wei	Mao	Shen	Yu	Wei	Mao
Wei	Yu	Hsü	Shen	Ch'en	Yu	Hsü	Shen	Ch'en	Yu	Hsü	Shen	Ch'en
Shen	Hsü	Hai	Yu	Szu	Hsü	Hai	Yu	Szu	Hsü	Hai	Yu	Szu
Yu	Hai	Tzu	Hsü	Wu	Hai	Tzu	Hsü	Wu	Hai	Tzu	Hsü	Wu
Hsü	Tzu	Ch'ou	Hai	Wei	Tzu	Ch'ou	Hai	Wei	Tzu	Ch'ou	Hai	Wei
Hai	Ch'ou	Yin	Tzu	Shen	Ch'ou	Yin	Tzu	Shen	Ch'ou	Yin	Tzu	Shen

Table 10   *Locating the Ringing Star*

Earthly Branch for 'Hour' of Birth	Earthly Branch for Year of Birth											
	Tzu	*Ch'ou*	*Yin*	*Mao*	*Ch'en*	*Szu*	*Wu*	*Wei*	*Shen*	*Yu*	*Hsü*	*Hai*
Tzu	Hsü	Hsü	Mao	Hsü	Hsü	Hsü	Mao	Hsü	Hsü	Hsü	Mao	Hsü
Ch'ou	Hai	Hai	Ch'en	Hai	Hai	Hai	Ch'en	Hai	Hai	Hai	Ch'en	Hai
Yin	Tzu	Tzu	Szu	Tzu	Tzu	Tzu	Szu	Tzu	Tzu	Tzu	Szu	Tzu
Mao	Ch'ou	Ch'ou	Wu	Ch'ou	Ch'ou	Ch'ou	Wu	Ch'ou	Ch'ou	Ch'ou	Wu	Ch'ou
Ch'en	Yin	Yin	Wei	Yin	Yin	Yin	Wei	Yin	Yin	Yin	Wei	Yin
Szu	Mao	Mao	Shen	Mao	Mao	Mao	Shen	Mao	Mao	Mao	Shen	Mao
Wu	Ch'en	Ch'en	Yu	Ch'en	Ch'en	Ch'en	Yu	Ch'en	Ch'en	Ch'en	Yu	Ch'en
Wei	Szu	Szu	Hsü	Szu	Szu	Szu	Hsü	Szu	Szu	Szu	Hsü	Szu
Shen	Wu	Wu	Hai	Wu	Wu	Wu	Hai	Wu	Wu	Wu	Hai	Wu
Yu	Wei	Wei	Tzu	Wei	Wei	Wei	Tzu	Wei	Wei	Wei	Tzu	Wei
Hsü	Shen	Shen	Ch'ou	Shen	Shen	Shen	Ch'ou	Shen	Shen	Shen	Ch'ou	Shen
Hai	Yu	Yu	Yin	Yu	Yu	Yu	Yin	Yu	Yu	Yu	Yin	Yu

The Ringing Star is an imaginary star. Its location on the Tzu Wei chart is also dependent on your 'hour' and year of birth. Use Table 10 in the same way as Table 9 to locate your Ringing Star. For the example 1 September 1986, 8 p.m., the Ringing Star is located in the box labelled Ch'ou.

The Literary Stars

There are two imaginary Literary stars – Wen Ch'ü (Literary Music) and Wen Ch'ang (Literary Prosperity). Wen Ch'u guards literature and painting and Wen Ch'ang blesses examinations. The position of these two stars on the Tzu Wei chart is dependent on your 'hour' of birth. Table 11 gives the Earthly Branch for the 'hour' in the side headings. The Earthly Branch for the location of Wen Ch'ü is given in the left-hand column and the Earthly Branch for the location of Wen Ch'ang in the right-hand column. For the example 1 September 1986, 8 p.m., the Earthly Branch for the 'hour' is Hsü. This means that Wen Ch'ü is located in the box labelled Yin and Wen Ch'ang in the box labelled Tzu.

Table 11   *Locating the Literary Stars: Wen Chü and Wen Ch'ang*

Earthly Branch for 'Hour' of Birth	Wen Ch'ü	Wen Ch'ang
Tzu	Ch'en	Hsü
Ch'ou	Szu	Yu
Yin	Wu	Shen
Mao	Wei	Wei
Ch'en	Shen	Wu
Szu	Yu	Szu
Wu	Hsü	Ch'en
Wei	Hai	Mao
Shen	Tzu	Yin
Yu	Ch'ou	Ch'ou
Hsü	Yin	Tzu
Hai	Mao	Hai

Yang Jen (Sheep-Blade Star)
and T'o Lo (Hump-Back Star)

Yang Jen (Sheep-Blade Star) and T'o Lo (Hump-Back Star) are usually inauspicious. Their location on the Tzu Wei chart depends on your year of birth. In Table 12 the Heavenly Stem for the year is given in the side headings. The Earthly Branch of the box in which Yang Jen is to be located appears in the left-hand column, and the Earthly Branch of the box in which T'o Lo is to be located appears in the right-hand column.

For the example 1 September 1986, 8 p.m., the Heavenly Stem for the year is Ping. This means that Yang Jen is located in the box labelled Wu and T'o Lo in the box labelled Ch'en (see Figure 7).

Table 12 *Locating Yang Jen and T'o Lo*

Heavenly Stem for Year of Birth	Yang Jen	T'o Lo
Chia	Mao	Ch'ou
Yi	Ch'en	Yin
Ping	Wu	Ch'en
Ting	Wei	Szu
Mou	Wu	Ch'en
Chi	Wei	Szu
Keng	Yu	Wei
Hsin	Hsü	Shen
Jen	Tzu	Hsü
Kuei	Ch'ou	Hai

By now you should have twenty different stars on your Tzu Wei chart. These are the main stars of your horoscope. The following are minor stars.

The Yearly Stars

There are three Yearly stars – T'ien Ts'un (Heavenly Store), T'ien K'uei (Heavenly Leader) and T'ien Yüeh (Heavenly Halberd).

Their position on the Tzu Wei chart depends on the Heavenly Stem for the year you were born. Table 13 shows how to locate them. For the example 1 September 1986, 8 p.m. the Heavenly

Figure 7   *Locating the Fire Star, Ringing Star, Literary Stars and Yang Jen (Sheep-Blade) and T'o Lo (Hump-Back)*

T'ien T'ung	Wu Ch'ü T'ien Fu **Yang Jen**	T'ai-yang T'ai-yin	T'an Lang
Sickness Szu	Wealth Wu	Man and Woman Wei	Marital Shen
P'o Chün **T'o Lo** Moving Ch'en	Date and time of birth (solar): 1986 September 1st 8 p.m. Date and time of birth (lunar): Ping Yin 7th 27th Hsü		T'ien Chi Chü Men Brothers' and Sisters' Yu
 Servants' Mao	Eight characters: Ping Yin Ping Shen Mou Shen Jen Hsü Element: Wood Name: Today's date:		Tzu Wei T'ien Hsiang Ming Hsü
Lien Chen **Wen Ch'ü** **Ringing Star** Officials' Yin	Ch'i Sha **Wen Ch'ang** Property Ch'ou	Fortune and Virtue Tzu	T'ien Liang **Fire Star** Parents' Hai

Table 13 *Locating the Yearly Stars*

Heavenly Stem for Year of Birth	T'ien Ts'un	T'ien K'uei	T'ien Yüeh
Chia	Yin	Ch'ou	Wei
Yi	Mao	Tzu	Shen
Ping	Szu	Hai	Yu
Ting	Wu	Yu	Hai
Mou	Szu	Wei	Ch'ou
Chi	Wu	Shen	Tzu
Keng	Shen	Wei	Ch'ou
Hsin	Yu	Wu	Yin
Jen	Hai	Szu	Mao
Kuei	Tzu	Mao	Szu

Stem for the year is Ping. This means that T'ien Ts'un is located in the box labelled with the Earthly Branch Szu, T'ien K'uei in the box labelled Hai and T'ien Yüeh in the box labelled Yu.

The Monthly Stars

There are three Monthly stars – Tso Fu (Right Assistant), Yu Pi (Left Assistant) and I-ma (Travelling Star). The position of these stars on the Tzu Wei chart depends on the Earthly Branch of the month in which you were born. Table 14 shows how to locate the monthly stars. For the example 1 September 1986, 8 p.m., the Earthly Branch for the month is Shen. This means that Tso Fu is located in the box labelled with the Earthly Branch Hsü, Yu Pi is located in the box labelled Ch'en and I-ma is located in the box labelled Yin.

The Hourly Stars

There are two Hourly stars – T'ien K'ung (Heavenly Void) and Ti Chieh (Earthly Robbery). Their positions on the Tzu Wei chart depend on the Earthly Branch for the 'hour' you were born. Table 15 shows how to locate them. For the example 1 September 1986, 8 p.m., the Earthly Branch for the 'hour' is Hsü. This means that T'ien K'ung is located in the box labelled Ch'ou and Ti Chieh in the box labelled Yu (see Figure 8).

Table 14 *Locating the Monthly Stars*

Earthly Branch for Month of Birth	Tso Fu	Yu Pi	I-ma
Tzu	Yin	Tzu	Yin
Ch'ou	Mao	Hai	Hai
Yin	Ch'en	Hsü	Shen
Mao	Szu	Yu	Szu
Ch'en	Wu	Shen	Yin
Szu	Wei	Wei	Hai
Wu	Shen	Wu	Shen
Wei	Yu	Szu	Szu
Shen	Hsü	Ch'en	Yin
Yu	Hai	Mao	Hai
Hsü	Tzu	Yin	Shen
Hai	Ch'ou	Ch'ou	Szu

Table 15 *Locating the Hourly Stars*

Earthly Branch for 'Hour' of Birth	T'ien K'ung	Ti Chieh
Tzu	Hai	Hai
Ch'ou	Hsü	Tzu
Yin	Yu	Ch'ou
Mao	Shen	Yin
Ch'en	Wei	Mao
Szu	Wu	Ch'en
Wu	Szu	Szu
Wei	Ch'en	Wu
Shen	Mao	Wei
Yu	Yin	Shen
Hsü	Ch'ou	Yu
Hai	Tzu	Hsü

The Miscellaneous Yearly Stars

There are three Miscellaneous stars whose position on the Tzu Wei chart depends on your year of birth. These are T'ien Hao (Heavenly Destroyer), Hung Luan (Red Phoenix) and T'ien Hsi

Figure 8   *Locating the Yearly, Monthly and Hourly stars*

T'ien T'ung **T'ien Ts'un** Sickness Szu	Wu Ch'ü T'ien Fu Yang Jen Wealth Wu	T'ai-yang T'ai-yin Man and Woman Wei	T'an Lang Marital Shen
P'o Chün T'o Lo **Yu Pi** Moving Ch'en	Date and time of birth (solar): 1986 September 1st 8 p.m. Date and time of birth (lunar): Ping Yin 7th 27th Hsü Eight characters: Ping Yin Ping Shen Mou Shen Jen Hsü Element: Wood		**T'ien Yüeh** **Ti Chieh** T'ien Chi Chü Men Brothers' and Sisters' Yu
 Servants' Mao	Name: Today's date:		Tzu Wei T'ien Hsiang **Tso Fu** Ming Hsü
Lien Chen Wen Ch'ü **I-ma** Officials' Yin	Ringing **T'ien K'ung** Star Property Ch'ou	Ch'i Sha Wen Ch'ang Fortune and Virtue Tzu	T'ien Liang **T'ien K'uei** Fire Star Parents' Hai

Table 16 *Locating the Miscellaneous Yearly Stars*

Earthly Branch for Year of Birth	T'ien Hao	Hung Luan	T'ien Hsi
Tzu	Ch'ou	Mao	Yu
Ch'ou	Yin	Yin	Shen
Yin	Mao	Ch'ou	Wei
Mao	Ch'en	Tzu	Wu
Ch'en	Szu	Hai	Szu
Szu	Wu	Hsü	Ch'en
Wu	Wei	Yu	Mao
Wei	Shen	Shen	Yin
Shen	Yu	Wei	Ch'ou
Yu	Hsü	Wu	Tzu
Hsü	Hai	Szu	Hai
Hai	Tzu	Ch'en	Hsü

(Heavenly Happiness). Table 16 shows how to locate these. For the example 1 September 1986, 8 p.m., the Earthly Branch for the year is Yin. This means that T'ien Hao is located in the box labelled Mao, Hung Luan in the box labelled Ch'ou and T'ien Hsi in the box labelled Wei.

The Miscellaneous Monthly Stars

There are two Miscellaneous stars whose position on the Tzu Wei chart depends on your month of birth. These are T'ien Yao (Heavenly Beauty) and T'ien Hsing (Heavenly Punishment). Table 17 shows how to locate these. For the example 1 September 1986, 8 p.m., the Earthly Branch for the month is Shen. This means that in this case T'ien Yao is located in the box labelled Wei and T'ien Hsing in the box labelled Mao.

The Transforming Stars

There are four Transforming stars – Hua Lu (Transforming Salary), Hua Ch'üan (Transforming Authority), Hua K'o (Transforming Examination Class) and Hua Chi (Transforming Jealousy).

Table 17 *Locating the Miscellaneous Monthly Stars*

Earthly Branch for Month of Birth	T'ien Yao	T'ien Hsing
Tzu	Hai	Wei
Ch'ou	Tzu	Shen
Yin	Ch'ou	Yu
Mao	Yin	Hsü
Ch'en	Mao	Hai
Szu	Ch'en	Tzu
Wu	Szu	Ch'ou
Wei	Wu	Yin
Shen	Wei	Mao
Yu	Shen	Ch'en
Hsü	Yu	Szu
Hai	Hsü	Wu

Table 18 shows how to locate them on the Tzu Wei chart. For the example 1 September 1986, 8 p.m., the Heavenly Stem for the month is Ping. This means that Hua Lu appears in the same box as T'ien T'ung (Heavenly Unity), Hua Ch'üan appears in the same box as T'ien Chi (Heavenly Secret), Hua K'o appears in the same box as Wen Ch'ang (Literary Prosperity) and Hua Chi in the same box as Lien Chen (Pure Virtue) (see Figure 9).

You should now have thirty-seven stars on your Tzu Wei chart: twenty major stars and seventeen minor stars. The major stars are strong and stable, and their degree of influence is rarely affected by the minor stars. The minor stars are unstable, and whether they are good or bad depends on the Earthly Branch of the box in which they appear. The individual readings will tell you whether a minor star is good or bad in a particular box.

The Degrees of Influence

Each of the twenty main stars has a degree of influence attached to it, depending on where it is located in the Tzu Wei chart. There are four different symbols used in this chart: * corresponds to excellent,

Table 18 *Locating the Transforming Stars*

Heavenly Stem for Month of Birth	Hua Lu	Hua Ch'üan	Hua K'o	Hua Chi
Chia	Lien Chen	P'o Chün	Wu Ch'ü	T'ai- yang
Yi	T'ien Chi	T'ien Liang	Tzu Wei	T'ai- yin
Ping	T'ien T'ung	T'ien Chi	Wen Ch'ang	Lien Chen
Ting	T'ai- yin	T'ien T'ung	T'ien Chi	Chü Men
Mou	T'an Lang	T'ai- yin	T'ai- yang	T'ien Chi
Chi	Wu Ch'ü	T'an Lang	T'ien Liang	Wen Ch'ü
Keng	T'ai- yang	Wu Ch'ü	T'ien Fu	T'ien T'ung
Hsin	Chü Men	T'ai- yang	Wen Ch'ü	Wen Ch'ang
Jen	T'ien Liang	Tzu Wei	Tien Fu	Wu Ch'ü
Kuei	P'o Chün	Chü Men	T'ai- yin	T'an Lang

☆ to good, + to poor and – to bad. The degree depends on the Earthly Branch of the box in which the star appears and can be found in Table 19. Figure 10 shows the degree of influence for each star marked on the Tzu Wei chart for the example 1 September 1986, 8 p.m.

Figure 9   *Locating the Miscellaneous and Transforming stars*

Sickness — Szu T'ien T'ung T'ien Ts'un **Hua Lu**	**Wealth — Wu** Wu Ch'ü T'ien Fu Yang Jen	**Man and Woman — Wei** T'ai-yang T'ai-yin **T'ien Hsi** **T'ien Yao**	**Marital — Shen** T'an Lang
Moving — Ch'en P'o Chün T'o Lo Yu Pi	Date and time of birth (solar): September 1st 1986 8 p.m. Date and time of birth (lunar): Ping Yin 7th 27th Hsü	Eight characters: Ping Yin Ping Shen Mou Shen Jen Hsü Element: Wood Name:	**Brothers' and Sisters' — Yu** T'ien Chi Chü Men T'ien Yüeh Ti Chieh **Hua Ch'üan**
Servants' — Mao **T'ien Hao** **T'ien Hsing**	Today's date:		**Ming — Hsü** Tzu Wei T'ien Hsiang Tso Fu
Officials' — Yin Lien Chen Wen Ch'ü I-ma **Hua Chi**	**Property — Ch'ou** Ringing Star T'ien K'ung **Hung Luan**	**Fortune and Virtue — Tzu** Ch'i Sha Wen Ch'ang **Hua K'o**	**Parents' — Hai** T'ien Liang Fire Star T'ien K'uei

Figure 10   *The degrees of influence of the main and secondary stars*

T'ien T'ung* T'ien Ts'un Hua Lu **Sickness** — Szu	Wu Ch'ü* T'ien Fu* Yang Jen— **Wealth** — Wu	T'ien Hsi T'ien Yao T'ai-yang* T'ai-yin* **Man and Woman** — Wei	T'an Lang+ **Marital** — Shen
P'o Chün* T'o Lo* Yu Pi **Moving** — Ch'en	Date and time of birth (solar): 1986 September 1st 8 p.m. Date and time of birth (lunar): Ping Yin 7th 27th Hsü	Eight characters: Ping Yin Ping Shen Mou Shen Jen Hsü	T'ien Chi* Chü Men* T'ien Yüeh Ti Chieh Hua Ch'üan **Brothers' and Sisters'** — Yu
T'ien Hao T'ien Hsing **Servants'** — Mao	Element: Wood Name:	Today's date:	Tzu Wei* T'ien Hsiang* Tso Fu **Ming** — Hsü
Lien Chen* Wen Ch'ü+ I-ma Hua Chi **Officials'** — Yin	T'ien K'ung Hung Luan Ringing Star+ **Property** — Ch'ou	Ch'i Sha* Wen Ch'ang☆ Hua K'o **Fortune and Virtue** — Tzu	T'ien Liang+ T'ien K'uei Fire Star+ **Parents'** — Hai

Table 19 The Degrees of Influence for the Main Stars

Location	Tzu Wei	T'ien Chi	T'ai-yang	Wu Ch'ü	T'ien T'ung	Lien Chen	T'ien Fu	T'ai-yin	T'an Lang	Chü Men	T'ien Hsiang	T'ien Liang	Ch'i Sha	P'o Chün	Fire and Ringing Stars	WEN CHANG/CHU Literary Stars	Yang Jen and T'o Lo
Tzu	☆	★	+	☆	★	+	☆	★	☆	☆	+	★	☆	☆	—	☆	—
Ch'ou	+	+	☆	☆	+	☆	★	☆	☆	+	★	☆	☆	+	+	☆	☆
Yin	+	+	☆	☆	☆	☆	☆	+	+	☆	☆	☆	☆	—	☆	+	—
Mao	+	☆	★	☆	☆	—	☆	+	+	☆	+	★	☆	—	+	☆	—
Ch'en	☆	☆	★	☆	☆	☆	☆	+	☆	+	☆	☆	☆	☆	—	★	★
Szu	☆	+	★	+	☆	—	☆	+	—	+	☆	+	☆	+	+	☆	—
Wu	★	★	★	☆	+	+	☆	+	☆	☆	+	★	☆	☆	☆	+	—
Wei	+	+	+	☆	+	☆	★	☆	☆	+	☆	☆	☆	—	+	☆	★
Shen	☆	☆	+	☆	+	☆	☆	☆	+	+	+	+	☆	—	—	★	—
Yu	+	☆	+	☆	☆	—	☆	★	+	+	☆	+	☆	☆	+	☆	—
Hsü	☆	☆	+	☆	☆	☆	☆	★	☆	+	☆	☆	☆	+	☆	+	☆
Hai	☆	+	+	+	☆	—	☆	★	—	+	+	+	☆	+	+	☆	—

The Great and Small Limits

The Great Limits are periods of ten years and the Small Limits periods of one year in your life. On the Tzu Wei chart each box is also labelled with Great and Small Limits. This means each box on the chart will have three different main labels, the Earthly Branch, the Palace and now the Great and Small Limits. The stars in a given box affect the period of your life shown by the limits labelling that box.

The Great Limits
To fill in the Great Limits on the Tzu Wei chart, follow these instructions.

To find out what your Great Limits (ten-year periods) are:

(a) Write down your element.

(b) Find the number corresponding to this element.

> Wood = 3
> Fire   = 6
> Metal = 4
> Water = 2
> Earth = 5

(c) Write down your first Great Limit. This ten-year period runs from the age corresponding to the number of your element:

> for Wood: 3–12 years of age
> for Fire: 6–15 years of age
> for Metal: 4–13 years of age
> for Water: 2–11 years of age
> for Earth: 5–14 years of age

(d) Calculate the series based on your first Great Limit:

> for Wood: 3–12, 13–22, 23–32, 33–42, 43–52, etc.
> for Fire: 6–15, 16–25, 26–35, 36–45, 46–55, etc.
> for Metal: 4–13, 14–23, 24–33, 34–43, 44–53, etc.
> for Water: 2–11, 12–21, 22–31, 32–41, 42–51, etc.
> for Earth: 5–14, 15–24, 25–34, 35–44, 45–54, etc.

The first Great Limit is entered in the box in which your Ming Palace appears. The others are entered in order running round the boxes on the edge of the chart.

To find out whether your Great Limits run clockwise or anticlockwise around the Tzu Wei chart:

(e) Write down whether you are a yin person (woman) or a yang person (man).

(f) Write down whether the Heavenly Stem for the year you were born is yin or yang.

Yang Heavenly Stems: Chia, Ping, Mou, Keng, Jen
Yin Heavenly Stems: Yi, Ting, Chi, Hsin, Kuei

(g) You work out whether your Great Limits run clockwise or anticlockwise around the chart as follows:

A yin person born in a year with a yin Heavenly Stem runs clockwise (yin + yin→CW).

A yang person born in a year with a yang Heavenly Stem runs clockwise (yang + yang→CW).

A yin person born in a year with a yang Heavenly Stem runs anticlockwise (yin + yang→ACW).

A yang person born in a year with a yin Heavenly Stem runs anticlockwise (yang + yin→ACW).

For the example 1 September 1986, 8 p.m., the element is Wood and the number corresponding to this element is 3. This means that the Great Limits series is 3-12, 13-22, 23-32, 33-42, 43-52, etc.

The Ming Palace is located in the box Hsü. This means that the first Great Limit labels this box. Let us suppose that the person born on this date is female (a yin person). The Heavenly Stem for the year is Ping. This is a yang Heavenly Stem.

A yin person born in a year with a yang Heavenly Stem runs anticlockwise (yin + yang→ACW).

This means that the second Great Limit appears in the box labelled Yu, the third in the box labelled Shen, and so on (Figure 11).

The Small Limits
The Small Limits are simpler to fill in on the chart. If you were born in a year with Earthly Branch:

Yin, Wu or Hsü – start from the box labelled Ch'en
Shen, Tzu or Ch'en – start from the box labelled Hsü
Szu, Yu or Ch'ou – start from the box labelled Wei

Hai, Mao or Wei – start from the box labelled Ch'ou

The first Small Limit is year 1, the second year 2, the third year 3, and so on up to year 12. Then the cycle repeats itself, so that year 13 falls in the same box as year 1, year 14 in the same box as year 2, year 15 in the same box as year 3, and so on.

The sequence is as follows:

Year	Year	Year	Year	Year	Year	Year	Year
1	13	25	37	49	61	73	85
2	14	26	38	50	62	74	86
3	15	27	39	51	63	75	87
4	16	28	40	52	64	76	88
5	17	29	41	53	65	77	89
6	18	30	42	54	66	78	90
7	19	31	43	55	67	79	91
8	20	32	44	56	68	80	92
9	21	33	45	57	69	81	93
10	22	34	46	58	70	82	94
11	23	35	47	59	71	83	95
12	24	36	48	60	72	84	96

Thus, if the Small Limit for year 1 falls in the box labelled Ch'en, so will the Small Limits for the years 13, 25, 37, 49, 61, 73 and 85.

If you are a yin person (woman) the Small Limits run anticlockwise around the chart and if you are a yang person (man) they run clockwise.

For the example 1 September 1986, 8 p.m., the Earthly Branch for the year is Yin. This means that the first Small Limit goes in the box labelled Ch'en. As the person born on this date is female, the Small Limits run anticlockwise. This means the second Small Limit goes in the box labelled Mao, the third in the box labelled Yin, and so on (see Figure 11).

The ten-year period covered by a Great Limit will also be affected by the Small Limits for each of those years. This means that although a particular ten-year period has a poor prospect, this can be modified from year to year according to the Small Limits readings.

Figure 11   *Filling in the Great and Small Limits, and borrowed stars*

T'ien T'ung* T'ien Ts'un Hua Lu **53-62 Sickness** 12 Szu	Wu Ch'ü* T'ien Fu* Yang Jen– **43-52 Wealth**	T'ai-yang* T'ai-yin* **33-42 Man and Woman** 11 Wu	T'ien Hsi T'ien Yao T'an Lang+ **23-32 Marital**	T'ien Yüeh Ti Chieh Hua Ch'üan T'ien Chi* Chü Men* **13-22** "Brothers' and Sisters'" Yu
		10 Wei		9 Shen
P'o Chün* T'o Lo* Yu Pi **63-72 Moving** 1 Ch'en	Date and time of birth (solar): 1986 September 1st 8 p.m. Date and time of birth (lunar): Ping Yin 7th 27th Hsü Eight characters: Ping Yin Ping Shen Mou Shen Jen Hsü Element: Wood Name: Today's date:			T'ien Chi* Chü Men*
T'ien Chi T'ien Hao T'ien Hsing Chü Men **73-82 Servants'** 2 Mao				8 Yu
			Tzu Wei* T'ien Hsiang* Tso Fu **3-12 Ming**	7 Hsü
Lien Chen* Wen Ch'ü+ I-ma Hua Chi **83-92 Officials'** 3 Yin	T'ien K'ung Hung Luan Ringing Star+ **93-102 Property** 4 Ch'ou	Ch'i Sha* Wen Ch'ang☆ Hua K'o **103-112 Fortune and Virtue** 5 Tzu	T'ien Liang+ T'ien K'uei Fire Star+ **113-122 Parents'**	6 Hai

Borrowing

On the Tzu Wei chart there is likely to be a concentration of stars in some palaces and very few or even no stars in others. If there are no stars in a palace this does not spell bad luck. It simply means that you have no particular fate, lucky or unlucky, for that palace.

If there are no main stars in a palace, then you can borrow the main stars from another palace according to the following rules:

The Ming Palace borrows from the Moving Palace (and vice versa)

The Brothers' and Sisters' Palace borrows from the Servants' Palace (and vice versa)

The Marital Palace borrows from the Officials' Palace (and vice versa)

The Man and Woman Palace borrows from the Property Palace (and vice versa)

The Wealth Palace borrows from the Fortune and Virtue Palace (and vice versa)

The Sickness Palace borrows from the Parents' Palace (and vice versa)

In the example 1 September 1986, 8 p.m., the Servants' Palace (in the box labelled Mao) has no main stars (see Figure 10). Using the rules outlined above, the main stars from Brothers' and Sisters' Palace can be borrowed for the Servants' Palace. These are T'ien Chi and Chü Men.

Borrowed stars influence the palace they have moved to. They also influence the ten-year period of your life covered by the Great Limit for that box and the one-year periods covered by the Small Limits.

HOW TO READ YOUR
TZU WEI CHART

The first way of reading the Tzu Wei chart is based on the palaces and these give you readings for different aspects of your life, for example, your relationship with your parents, wealth, illness. The second way of reading the Tzu Wei chart is based on the Great and Small Limits, and this can predict whether a certain ten-year period or a one-year period is auspicious or not. The following are descriptions of how to make both types of reading.

The Palaces Reading

In the following chapters the tables used to read the Tzu Wei chart are arranged by palace. At the start of each chapter is a description of the aspects of your life covered by that particular palace. There is also a list of the stars divided into four groups, according to whether a star brings good or bad luck when it appears in that particular palace. The groups are: stars which bring extremely good luck, stars which bring moderately good luck, stars which bring bad luck and stars which bring extremely bad luck.

The table for each palace gives a detailed description of the significance a star exerts in that particular palace. It also shows how its significance alters if other stars also appear in the same palace, and what degree of influence the major stars have.

The tables are arranged as follows: the star of primary concern appears in the first column. If it is a major star, its degree of influence (see p. 70/83) is specified in the second column. Other stars which may also appear in that particular palace are listed in the third column. These stars may be referred to by name – e.g. 'Either of the Literary stars', 'Yang Jen *or* T'o Lu' – or the entry may simply say 'Any' (meaning 'Any star'), 'Any lucky star' or 'No unlucky stars'. In the latter two cases you should turn to the groups of lucky and unlucky stars listed at the front of the table to identify which stars are lucky and which unlucky. Very rarely the degree of influence of these other stars may be specified in the fourth column. The reading appears in the fifth column.

Not all stars appear in all palaces. If a certain star appears in a particular palace and is not listed in the table for that palace, this means that it is an 'interrupting star' and exerts only a minor influence. You can find out whether it brings good or bad luck by looking at the list of good-luck and bad-luck stars at the start of each table. However, not all interrupting stars are important enough to be listed.

You must distinguish between 'or' and 'and' in the table. 'T'ien K'uei *or* T'o Lo appears in the Ming Palace' is a different statement to 'T'ien K'uei *and* T'o Lo appear in the Ming Palace'.

In using the chart make sure you look at the readings for all possible combinations of stars in your horoscope. In the example for 1 September 1986, 8 p.m., there are six different readings for the three stars which appear in the Ming Palace, as follows:

Example of a reading for the Ming Palace for someone born on 1 September 1986, 8 p.m. (see Figure 11)

Tzu Wei*	You are reflective and refined. Your living conditions will improve in later life. You may be wealthy and famous.
Tzu Wei* with T'ien Hsiang*	You will have good clothes and enjoy dressing well.
Tzu Wei* with Tso Fu	Your social position will be elevated.
T'ien Hsiang*	You will have a successful social life and will enjoy helping people. You will enjoy involvement on a committee or an association. People respect and support you and this will bring you promotion and a good income.

| T'ien Hsiang* with Tso Fu | You will have a position of authority and be wealthy. If you work in politics you will gain a high position. |
| Tso Fu | You are sedate and gentle. |

The Great and Small Limits Readings

The Great and Small Limits readings predict whether a particular ten-year or a one-year period in your life is lucky or unlucky. This depends on whether the stars which appear in the box are lucky or unlucky.

Let us look at the example of someone born on 1 September 1986, 8 p.m., and obtain a reading for the ten-year period of this person's life between the ages of three and twelve. There are three stars which appear in the box labelled by this Great Limit: Tzu Wei (Purple Star), T'ien Hsiang (Heavenly Minister) and Tso Fu (Left Assistant). To find out if these stars, when they appear in this particular box, are lucky or unlucky we need to look at its palace labelling. In this case the box is labelled Ming Palace. Then turn to the start of the tables for the Ming Palace and find the list of stars divided into four groups depending on whether they bring good or bad luck in the Ming Palace. Tzu Wei, T'ien Hsiang and Tso Fu all bring extremely good luck in the Ming Palace. This means that this ten-year period from ages three to twelve is extremely auspicious.

If we wish to narrow down further and obtain a reading for the year in which this person is three, we look at the Small Limits. In this case the stars which appear in the box labelled with the Small Limit 3 are Lien Chen (Pure Virtue), Wen Ch'ü (Literary Music), I-ma (Travelling Star) and Hua Chi (Heavenly Secret). This box is labelled Officials' Palace. In the Officials' Palace Lien Chen and Wen Ch'ü bring extremely good luck. I-ma brings moderately good luck. Hua Chi brings bad luck. This means that on average this third year will be fairly lucky. This will also apply to the ages of 15, 27, 39, 51, 63, 75 and 87.

The following tables, therefore, give detailed readings for each palace of each of the stars in all possible combinations. By drawing up your own individual grid of stars, palaces, and so on, you can obtain a full Tzu Wei reading for yourself.

THE MING (LIFE/FATE) PALACE

The Ming Palace is concerned with your physical appearance, your character, abilities and the likelihood of you making progress, and developments at work.

The stars which bring great good luck in the Ming Palace are:

Tzu Wei (Purple Star)
T'ien Chi (Heavenly Secret)
T'ai-yang (Sun)
T'ien Fu (Southern Star)
T'ai-yin (Moon)
T'ien T'ung (Heavenly Unity)
T'ien Hsiang (Heavenly Minister)
T'ien Liang (Heavenly Roof-Beam)

Wen Ch'ü (Literary Music)
Wen Ch'ang (Literary Prosperity)
T'ien Ts'un (Heavenly Store)
T'ien K'uei (Heavenly Leader)
T'ien Yüeh (Heavenly Halberd)
Tso Fu (Left Assistant)
Yu Pi (Right Assistant)
Hua Lu (Transforming Salary)
Hua Ch'üan (Transforming Authority)

The stars which bring moderately good luck in this palace are:

Wu Ch'ü (Military Music)
Ch'i Sha (Seven Killings)
I-ma (Travelling Star)

Hung Luan (Red Phoenix)
T'ien Hsi (Heavenly Happiness)

The stars which bring bad luck in this palace are:

Lien Chen (Pure Virtue)   T'an Lang (Greedy Wolf)

Chü Men (Great Door)
P'o Chün (Broken Army)
Fire Star
Ringing Star
Yang Jen (Sheep-Blade)
T'o Lo (Hump-Back)

T'ien Yao (Heavenly
Beauty)
T'ien Hsing (Heavenly
Punishment)
T'ien Hao (Heavenly
Destroyer

The stars which bring extremely bad luck in this palace are:

T'ien K'ung (Heavenly
Void)
Ti Chieh (Earthly Robbery)

Hua Chi (Transforming
Jealousy

Star	Degree of influence	Other stars which appear in the Ming Palace	Degree of influence	Reading
Tzu Wei	Any	Any		You are reflective and refined. Your living conditions will improve in later life. You may be wealthy and famous.
	Any	T'ien Fu		You will enjoy material well-being and good fortune.
	Any	T'an Lang		The opposite sex will bring you financial ruin or personal disaster.
	Any	T'ien Hsiang		You will have good clothes and enjoy dressing well.
	Any	Ch'i Sha		Whatever your line of work you will be in a position of authority.
	Any	Fire Star Ringing Star Yang Jen T'o Lo T'ien K'ung Ti Chieh		There will be a rift between you and your relatives. You will bring each other harm. You will live alone.
	Any	Either of the Literary stars T'ien Ts'un T'ien K'uei T'ien Yüeh Tso Fo or Yu Pi		Your social position will be elevated.

Star	Degree of influence	Other stars	Degree of influence	Reading
T'ien Chi	Any	Any		Your eyebrows are thick, your eyes alert, your forehead wide but your chin narrow. Although you have a hot temper, your heart is kind and charitable. You are intelligent, but you are always imagining things. The Chinese say: 'Clever but hindered by that cleverness.'
	* ☆	Any		You are wise and you will be successful and make great progress.
	+ −	Any		You are impatient and have a hot temper. Your imagination is too wild and you are unlikely to realize your aims.
	Any	T'ia-yin		You will be favoured by fortune in respect of social position and money.
	Any	Chü Men		You will either have a long life and little money, or you

Star	Degree of influence	Other stars	Degree of influence	Reading
				will have a lot of money and die young.
	Any	T'ien Liang		You have an aptitude for organization at work.
	Any	Fire Star, Ringing Star or either of the Literary stars		Your life will be like a wave fluctating between fortune and bad luck.
	Any	Yang Jen T'o Lo T'ien K'ung or Ti Chieh		You will be lonely and poor throughout your life.
		T'ien Ts'un T'ien K'uei T'ien Yüeh Tso Fu or Yu Pi		Your social position will be good and you will be rich.
T'ai-yang	Any	Any		Your physical appearance is round and full. You are stern and clever. You will treat people kindly and are full of energy. You have a tendency to show off. You are extravagant and will be a spendthrift.
	* ☆	Any		You will be successful in politics or finance.

Star	Degree of influence	Other stars	Degree of influence	Reading
	+ −	Any		You will become lazy even if you work hard when young.
	Any	T'ai-yin		You will be promoted to a high position. You will enjoy the authority and the renown it brings you. However, this promotion will bring you no concrete benefits. There will be no respite in the work required to build up your reputation.
	* ☆	Chü Men		You will be well known and hold a responsible position.
	+ −	Chü Men		When young, you will work hard and have success, but after middle age you will grow inattentive and lazy and start to make losses.
	* ☆	T'ien Liang		You will live in splendour and hold a high rank.
	+ −	T'ien Liang		You will be poor and unemployed, like a beggar.

Star	Degree of influence	Other stars	Degree of influence	Reading
	* ☆	Fire Star, Ringing Star *or* either of the Literary stars		Your work will run smoothly and you will be prosperous.
	+ –	Fire Star, Ringing Star *or* either of the Literary stars		Your luck will fluctuate.
	Any	Yang Jen T'o Lo T'ien K'ung *or* Ti Chieh		You are too extravagant. This will be your downfall.
	* ☆	T'ien Ts'un T'ien K'uei T'ien Yüeh Tso Fu *or* Yu Pi		You will be promoted to a high position and become rich.
	+ –	T'ien Ts'un T'ien K'uei T'ien Yüeh Tso Fu *or* Yu Pi		You will neither be wealthy nor poor.
Wu Ch'ü	Any	Any		You are physically short and slim and your voice is high and piercing. You have a strong will and are good at making decisions. You are quick-witted but sometimes impatient and hot-tempered. You rush at things and lack foresight.

Star	Degree of influence	Other stars	Degree of influence	Reading
	Any	No other unlucky stars		You will have financial success.
	Any	T'ien Fu		You will be successful in business and politics.
	Any	T'an Lang		You will be rich but miserly.
	Any	T'ien Hsiang		You will have broad knowledge. If you study subjects in more detail you will be successful.
	Any	Ch'i Sha		You are honest and discriminating. You are not prejudiced towards your friends.
	Any	P'o Chün		You will lose money and property and have a harsh life.
	Any	T'ien Ts'un		You will expand your business and make your family prosperous. You will become rich.
	Any	I-ma		You will leave your home town to expand your business. If you do not, it will go into decline and your future will be gloomy.

Star	Degree of influence	Other stars	Degree of influence	Reading
	Any	Fire Star or Ringing Star	☆	Your life will be average.
	Any	Fire Star or Ringing Star	+ −	You may have the opportunity to become wealthy and well known.
	Any	Tso Fu Yu Pi T'ien K'uei or T'ien Yüeh		You will leave your home town and your family to expand your business.
	Any	T'ien K'ung or Ti Chieh		If you try to make a lot of money, legally or illegally, you will not succeed or may die. You will have disagreements with your colleagues.
T'ien T'ung	Any	Any		Your manner is gentle, modest and warm.
	Any	No unlucky stars		You will be well known and wealthy.
	*	T'ai-yin		You will be a well-known doctor or will be given a special scholarship. You will be successful.
	+ −	T'ai-yin		Your whole life will be harsh. You will have no success.

Star	Degree of influence	Other stars	Degree of influence	Reading
	*	T'ien Liang		You will be promoted to a high position and make great profits.
	+ −	T'ien Liang		Your life will be harsh.
	Any	Chü Men		You will be plagued with troubles and arguments. The opposite sex will bring harm to your name.
	Any	T'ien Ts'un		You will be rich and noble all your life. You will be materially well off.
	Any	Fire Star Ringing Star Yang Jen T'o Lo		You will be pursued to repay your debts. If you cannot repay them you may be forced to do something illegal which will bring you trouble.
	Any	Literary stars T'ien K'uei T'ien Yüeh Tso Fu or Yu Pi		You will have a title and be well known. You will enjoy a good reputation and a peaceful and prosperous life.
Lien Chen	Any	Any		You have thick eyebrows and large eyes. You are clever and like to display your authority.

Star	Degree of influence	Other stars	Degree of influence	Reading
	Any	No unlucky stars		You will be rich and powerful.
	Any	T'ien Fu		You are likely to have a high position and be well known. You will live in splendour.
	Any	T'an Lang		You will have little money and a harsh life.
	Any	T'ien Hsiang		You are suited to business enterprise. You are not suited to work in politics or studying. Select your job carefully.
	Any	Ch'i Sha		Unless you leave your home town you will be unable to make progress at work.
	Any	P'o Chün		You will either be disabled or die young.
	Any	T'ien Ts'un		You will have social standing and be wealthy.
	Any	Fire Star Ringing Star Yang Jen T'o Lo		You are likely to break the law.
	Any	Literary stars T'ien K'uei or T'ien Yüeh		You will be rich and noble all your life.

Star	Degree of influence	Other stars	Degree of influence	Reading
	Any	Tso Fu *or* Yu Pi		Your social life will be excellent and your business prosperous.
	Any	T'ien K'ung *or* Ti Chieh		You will have accidents and unexpected expenses. This means you will be unable to save and will not be rich.
T'ien Fu	Any	Any		You treat people gently and politely. You know how to work hard and how to make progress. You are clever and if you use your abilities you will have a peaceful life.
	Any	Literary stars T'ien K'uei T'ien Yüeh		You are intelligent and will pass many examinations.
	Any	Fire Star Ringing Star Yang Jen T'o Lo		You start a project with enthusiasm but this peters out. The Chinese say you have a lion's head but a snake's tail. When you reach old age you will have an increasingly harsh life.

Star	Degree of influence	Other stars	Degree of influence	Reading
	Any	Tso Fu *or* Yu Pi		You will have a successful social life. This will provide you with opportunities to expand your business.
	Any	T'ien Ts'un		You will be able to save money and will be offered promotion.
	Any	T'ien K'ung *or* Ti Chieh		You will have a harsh life and lack material things.
T'ai-yin	Any	Any		You are good-looking.
	* ☆	Any		You will have a good education. You will be well known and have a good social position.
	+ −	Any		You will separate from your marriage partner and will die young.
	* ☆	Fire Star Ringing Star Yang Jen T'o Lo T'ien K'ung *or* Ti Chieh		You have abilities but you do not work hard. You do not make as much progress at work as you might.
	* ☆	T'ien Ts'un Literary stars T'ien K'uei T'ien Yüeh		Your polite and gentle character is well respected. You approach your work

Star	Degree of influence	Other stars	Degree of influence	Reading
		I-ma Tso Fu *or* Yu Pi		sensibly and gradually and will be promoted to a high position. You will have a prosperous life.
	+ −	Fire Star Ringing Star Yang Jen T'o Lo T'ien K'ung *and* Ti Chieh		You will succumb to overindulgence in drink and sex.
	+ −	Either of the Literary stars		You will work in the area of religion or astrology or as a medium in contact with the supernatural.
T'an Lang	Any	Any		You have protruding bones over your eyes. You are realistic and firm when making plans.
	* ☆	Any		You are not only fortunate but will also have a long life.
	+ −	Any		You like to show off your authority and intelligence. In the end you will be lost.
	Any	Fire Star Ringing Star T'ien K'uei *or* T'ien Yüeh		You will have more than enough money and material possessions.

Star	Degree of influence	Other stars	Degree of influence	Reading
	Any	Either of the Literary stars* Yang Jen *or* T'o Lo		You have just enough material possessions. You are greedy for sex. If more than one of these subordinate stars appear, you should take special care.
	Any	Tso Fu *or* Yu Pi		You will make a profit.
	Any	T'ien K'ung *or* Ti Chieh		You are over-indulgent in your desire for fame and money. This will bring disaster.
	* ☆	T'ien Ts'un		You will have great wealth.
Chü Men	Any	Any		You appear to be unfriendly but in fact you make a good friend. You are obstinate but give up easily when you have to do anything. This means that you are unlikely to succeed.
	* ☆	Any		You are a careful manager and have an aptitude for business.

*This is an exception to the general rule that the Literary stars bring good luck in the Ming Palace.

Star	Degree of influence	Other stars	Degree of influence	Reading
	+ –	Any		You are over-attentive and this means that you will suffer from nervous complaints. You have no patience to finish your work.
	Any	Fire Star Ringing Star Literary stars Yang Jen T'o Lo T'ien K'ung Ti Chieh		You are clever but you may have a short life. Sometimes your intelligence will be a drawback. You may commit suicide.
	* ☆	T'ien K'uei T'ien Yüeh Tso Fu or Yu Pi T'ien Ts'un		You will be promoted to a high position and be successful.
	+ –	T'ien K'uei T'ien Yüeh Tso Fu or Yu Pi T'ien Ts'un		You will have an average life.
T'ien Hsiang	Any	Any		You will have a successful social life and will always help others. You will enjoy working on a committee or with an association. People respect and support you and this will bring you promotion and a good income.

Star	Degree of influence	Other stars	Degree of influence	Reading
	+ –	Any		You will have a small business, e.g. street vendor.
	Any	Fire Star Ringing Star Yang Jen T'o Lo T'ien K'ung Ti Chieh		You should not expect to be rich or noble. You will have an average life.
	* ☆	Literary stars T'ien K'uei T'ien Yüeh Tso Fu *or* Yu Pi T'ien Ts'un		You will attain a position of authority and be wealthy. If you work in politics you will gain a high position.
	+ –	Literary stars T'ien K'uei T'ien Yüeh Tso Fu *or* Yu Pi T'ien Ts'un		(The same reading as above.)
T'ien Liang	Any	Any		You enjoy peaceful surroundings and you have leadership qualities. You are clever but your nature is gentle and sincere. You never display your talents.
	+ –	Any		You will have trouble in relation to the opposite sex. This will bring you into disrepute.

Star	Degree of influence	Other stars	Degree of influence	Reading
	Any	Fire Star Ringing Star Yang Jen To Lo T'ien K'ung Ti Chieh		You are likely to separate from or divorce your marriage partner. You may have other lovers.
	Any	Literary stars T'ien K'uei T'ien Yüeh Tso Fu *or* Yu Pi		You will have good luck.
	Any	T'ien Ts'un		You will have the opportunity to save vast amounts of money.
Ch'i Sha	Any	Any		Your eyes have a distinctive characteristic (perhaps a mark). Your appearance is stern and serious. You dislike compromise. You have a hot temper and never hide your feelings. You are quick to express happiness or anger.
	Any	No unlucky stars		You will be successful.
	Any	Fire Star *or* Ringing Star	☆	You may be promoted to a higher position.
	Any	Fire Star *or* Ringing Star	+ −	Your position will be average.

Star	Degree of influence	Other stars	Degree of influence	Reading
	Any	T'ien Ts'un I-ma		You will not only be rich but also noble.
	Any	T'ien K'uei T'ien Yüeh		You will be famous throughout the country or you will be a very important official.
	Any	Yang Jen T'o Lo T'ien K'ung Ti Chieh		Even if you are healthy, you may die young. You are likely to die from an accident or sudden illness.
P'o Chün	* ☆	Any		You will build up great wealth.
	+ −	Any		You will create a large business but it will destroy you.
	Any	Literary stars T'ien Ts'un T'ien K'uei T'ien Yüeh Tso Fu or Yu Pi		You will have authority and wealth.
	Any	Fire Star Ringing Star Yang Jen T'o Lo T'ien K'ung Ti Chieh		You will have a harsh and difficult life.

Star	Degree of influence	Other stars	Degree of influence	Reading
Fire Star and **Ringing Star**	Any	Any		You are taciturn. Your work is rushed and careless and you never make detailed or considered plans. You would like to run a large business but are unlikely to succeed; you have no interest in a small business.
	* ☆	Any		You will have authority and the chance of a high position.
	+ −	Any		Your life will fluctuate between good and bad luck. You are likely to die young.
Fire Star or **Ringing Star**	Any	Either of the Literary stars		You are suited to work as a labourer. You are not suited to politics or business.
	Any	Yang Jen T'o Lo		You may be deformed, disabled or have the scars of a major operation.
	* ☆	T'ien K'uei T'ien Yüeh		You will have authority and wealth.
	+ −	T'ien K'uei T'ien Yüeh		You will suffer from a long illness.

Star	Degree of influence	Other stars	Degree of influence	Reading
	* ☆	Tso Fu or Yu Pi		Your social life will be successful.
	+ −	Tso Fu or Yu Pi		You will have lasting authority and financial power.
	* ☆	T'ien K'ung Ti Chieh		You give the impression of having great authority when you really have none.
	+ −	T'ien K'ung Ti Chich		You will not have lasting authority or financial power.
	* ☆	T'ien Ts'un I-ma		You will not be short of material goods.
	+ −	T'ien Ts'un I-ma		Travel to distant places will result in an accident or a disaster. You may lose money or your life.
Wen Ch'ü or **Wen Ch'ang**	Any	Any		You have fine facial features and are intelligent. You like study. Your conduct is refined and you take care of your appearance.
	* ☆	Any		You will be successful in your occupation.
	+ −	Any		You will never have any money.

Star	Degree of influence	Other stars	Degree of influence	Reading
	Any	Yang Jen *or* T'o Lo		You are likely to be disabled and may die young. If you have a high position or are well known this will bring you no genuine benefit.
	Any	T'ien Ts'un T'ien K'uei T'ien Yüeh Tso Fu *or* Yu Pi		You will be an important person in your country.
T'ien Ts'un		Any		You will have a long life and be wealthy.
		Tso Fu *or* Yu Pi		You will be well known in business or in politics.
		T'ien K'ung Ti Chieh		You will work hard but with little success.
Yang Jen *or* **T'o Lo**	Any	Any		You are courageous and good at decision making.
	* ☆	Any		Your decision-making ability is excellent and you will make great progress in your work.
	+ −	Any		Your life will be full of disasters and you may be disabled.
	+ −	T'ien K'uei *or* T'ien Yüeh		Your life will be fortunate and long.

Star	Degree of influence	Other stars	Degree of influence	Reading
	Any	Tso Fu or Yu Pi		You will suffer from robbery. Your property may be harmed or you will lose your life.
	☆	Tso Fu or Yu Pi		You will have great wealth and long life.
	Any	T'ien K'ung Ti Chieh		You will either have financial difficulties or a short life.
T'ien K'uei or T'ien Yüeh	Any			Your character and exterior are stern. Your conduct is refined.
		Tso Fu or Yu Pi		You will have extremely good fortune. You will stay healthy and live long.
		T'ien K'ung Ti Chieh		You will suffer from recurrent illness.
Tso Fu or Yu Pi	Any			You are sedate and gentle.
		T'ien K'ung or Ti Chieh		You will make no progress in your work. Your standard of living will be below average.
T'ien K'ung or Ti Chieh	Any			You will waste time and money. You will fluctuate between success and loss.

Star	Degree of influence	Other stars	Degree of influence	Reading
		I-ma		You will die far away from home, perhaps in a foreign country.
I-ma		Any		You like travelling or your work will involve travelling.
T'ien Hao		Any		You spend money like water and fluctuate between success and loss.
Hung Luan		Any		The opposite sex likes you. You may take advantage of this.
T'ien Hsi		Any		You take nothing seriously and are always happy.
T'ien Yao		Any		You will drown in drink and sex.
T'ien Hsing		Any		You will be lonely and will easily fall into legal difficulties.
Hua Lu		Any		You will have many chances of promotion.
Hua Ch'üan		Any		You will obtain power and authority.
Hua K'o		Any		You will be lucky in examinations.

Star	Degree of influence	Other stars	Degree of influence	Reading
Hua Chi		Any		You will easily miss opportunities and are unlikely to have success.

THE BROTHERS' AND SISTERS' PALACE

The Brothers' and Sisters' Palace is concerned with the relationship between you and your brothers and sisters. This relationship is controlled by the *yuanten* (predestined attachment) between you. *Yuanten* covers a broad range of meanings. If the *yuanten* between you is strong, you love one another and will stay together. If weak, you have little feeling for one another and may separate.

The Brothers' and Sisters' Palace is also concerned with how much help, material or otherwise, you and your brothers and sisters can give each other.

The following stars bring extremely good luck in the Brothers' and Sisters' Palace:

T'ien Chi (Heavenly Secret)
T'ien T'ung (Heavenly Unity)
T'ien Fu (Southern Star)
T'ien Hsiang (Heavenly Minister)
T'ien Liang (Heavenly Roof-Beam)

T'ien K'uei (Heavenly Leader)
T'ien Yüeh (Heavenly Halberd)
Tso Fu (Left Assistant)
Yu Pi (Right Assistant)

These stars bring moderately good luck:

Tzu Wei (Purple Star)
T'ai-yang (Sun)
T'ai-yin (Moon)
Wen Ch'ü (Literary Music)

Wen Ch'ang (Literary Prosperity)
T'ien Ts'un (Heavenly Store)

These stars bring bad luck:

Wu Ch'ü (Military Music)
Fire Star
Ringing Star

These stars bring extremely bad luck:

Lien Chen (Pure Virtue)
T'an Lang (Greedy Wolf)
Chü Men (Great Door)
Ch'i Sha (Seven Killings)
P'o Chün (Broken Army)
Yang Jen (Sheep-Blade)

T'o Lo (Hump-Back)
T'ien K'ung (Heavenly
   Void)
Ti Chieh (Earthly
   Robbery)
Hua Chi (Transforming
   Jealousy)

Star	Degree of influence	Other stars which appear in the Brothers' and Sisters' Palace	Degree of influence	Reading
Tzu Wei	Any	Any		You and your brothers and sisters will support one another.
	Any	T'ien Fu T'ien Hsiang		You will receive help from your brothers and sisters.
	Any	T'an Lang		One brother or sister will marry late or not at all.
	Any	Ch'i Sha		There will be a rift between you and one of your brothers and sisters. You may harm them.
	Any	P'o Chün		There will be a rift between you and your brothers and sisters, but this will not be as serious as the situation above.
	Any	T'ien Ts'un		You will receive material support from your brothers and sisters.
	Any	Fire Star Ringing Star Yang Jen T'o Lo T'ien K'ung Ti Chieh		You will not be in harmony with your brothers and sisters.

Star	Degree of influence	Other stars	Degree of influence	Reading
	Any	Literary stars T'ien K'uei T'ien Yüeh Tso Fu *or* Yu Pi		You are in harmony with your brothers and sisters. You will stay together.
T'ien Chi	Any	Any		You will not have many brothers and sisters, but they will be a great support to you.
	+ −	Any		You will not be in harmony with your brothers and sisters.
	Any	T'ai-yin T'ien Liang		Your brothers and sisters will give you moral support.
	Any	T'ien Ts'un *or* Chü Men		You will receive material support from your brothers and sisters.
	Any	Fire Star Ringing Star Yang Jen T'o Lo T'ien K'ung *or* Ti Chieh		There will not be any harmony between you and your brothers and sisters. You will not help one another.
	Any	Literary stars T'ien K'uei T'ien Yüeh Tso Fu *or* Yu Pi		There will be great harmony between you and your brothers and sisters. Your eldest brother or sister will care for you as a parent.

Star	Degree of influence	Other stars	Degree of influence	Reading
T'ai-yang	* ☆	Any		Your brothers and sisters will help one another.
	–	Any		Not only will there be lack of harmony between your brothers and sisters, but they will actively quarrel with one another.
	Any	T'ai-yin T'ien Liang T'ien Ts'un		Your *yuanten* (predestined attachment) with your brothers and sisters will be strong. You will have a deep love for one another, will help one another and are likely to stay together.
	Any	Chü Men		Your *yuanten* (predestined attachment) with your brothers and sisters is fairly weak.
	Any	Fire Star Ringing Star Yang Jen T'o Lo T'ien K'ung Ti Chieh		You and your brothers and sisters all have differing opinions. There will be no feeling between you.
Wu Ch'ü	Any	Any		You come from a small family.

Star	Degree of influence	Other stars	Degree of influence	Reading
	Any	T'ien Fu T'ien Hsiang T'ien Ts'un		You will receive substantial material help from your brothers and sisters.
	Any	T'an Lang Ch'i Sha P'o Chün		There will be no harmony between you and your brothers and sisters and you will quarrel easily.
	Any	Fire Star Ringing Star Yang Jen T'o Lo T'ien K'ung Ti Chieh		Your *yuanten* (predestined attachment) with your brothers and sisters is weak. There will be no harmony between you, and you will be lonely.
	Any	Literary stars T'ien K'uei T'ien Yüeh Tso Fu *or* Yu Pi	Any	Although you will receive material support from your brothers and sisters you are likely to separate.
T'ien T'ung	Any	Any	Any	You will have many brothers and sisters and will be in harmony with all of them.
	Any	Chü Men		(The above reading does not hold.)

Star	Degree of influence	Other stars	Degree of influence	Reading
	Any	Fire Star Ringing Star Yang Jen T'o Lo T'ien T'ung Ti Chieh		Your brothers and sisters will be scattered in different places. You will lack harmony.
	Any	Literary stars T'ien K'uei T'ien Yüeh Tso Fu *or* Yu Pi		You will be in harmony with your brothers and sisters and help one another.
Lien Chen	Any	Any		You will have few brothers and sisters and lack harmony.
	Any	T'ien Fu T'ien Hsiang T'ien Ts'un Literary stars T'ien K'uei T'ien Yüeh Tso Fu *or* Yu Pi		You and your brothers and sisters do not help one another but you are in harmony.
	Any	T'an Lang Ch'i Sha P'o Chün Ringing Star Fire Star Yang Jen T'o Lo T'ien K'ung Ti Chieh		You will not be in harmony with your brothers and sisters and you will quarrel frequently.
T'ien Fu	Any	Any		You will have many brothers and sisters and you all will live in harmony.

Star	Degree of influence	Other stars	Degree of influence	Reading
		T'ien Ts'un		You will receive material support from your brothers and sisters.
	Any	Fire Star Ringing Star Yang Jen T'o Lo		You will have few brothers and sisters. You will be unable to help each other.
	Any	Literary stars T'ien K'uei T'ien Yüeh		You will live in harmony and help each other.
	Any	Tso Fu *or* Yu Pi		You and your brothers and sisters will help one another greatly and this will bring you business success.
	Any	T'ien K'ung Ti Chieh		You will be out of harmony with your brothers and sisters. You may fight and harm one another.
T'ai-yin	* ☆	Any		You will have many brothers and sisters and will help each other.
	–	Any		You will have few brothers and sisters and will not help one another.

Star	Degree of influence	Other stars	Degree of influence	Reading
	Any	Fire Star Ringing Star Yang Jen T'o Lo T'ien K'ung Ti Chieh		You will be in harmony even though your brothers and sisters will be scattered in many different places.
	Any	Literary stars T'ien K'uei T'ien Yüeh Tso Fu *or* Yu Pi		You and your brothers and sisters will be in harmony and will help each other.
	Any	T'ien Ts'un		You will receive material help from your brothers and sisters.
T'an Lang	☆	Any		You will have few brothers or sisters and they will not help each other.
	–	Any		Your brothers and sisters will cause you harm. You may suffer financial loss.
	Any	Any		You will be cold towards your brothers and sisters, even those born of the same parents. However, the devious nature of your brothers and sisters appeals to you.

Star	Degree of influence	Other stars	Degree of influence	Reading
	Any	Fire Star Ringing Star Yang Jen T'o Lo T'ien K'ung Ti Chieh		You will suffer a disaster caused by your brothers and sisters. In the course of doing something for them you may have an accident.
	Any	Either of the Literary stars T'ien K'uei T'ien Yüeh Tso Fu *or* Yu Pi		You and your brothers and sisters will not help one another, but you will live in harmony.
	Any	T'ien Ts'un		You will live happily with your brothers and sisters.
Chü Men	Any	Any		You will have few brothers and sisters.
	Any	T'ien Ts'un		(As above.)
	Any	Fire Star Ringing Star Yang Jen T'o Lo T'ien K'ung Ti Chieh		You and your brothers and sisters will distrust and loathe one another. You will speak ill of one another.
	Any	Either of the Literary stars Tso Fu *or* Yu Pi		Although you and your brothers and sisters will not help one another you all get on well.
T'ien Hsiang	Any	Any		You will have two or three brothers or sisters and will help one another.

Star	Degree of influence	Other stars	Degree of influence	Reading
	Any	T'ien Ts'un		You will receive material support from your brothers and sisters.
	Any	Fire Star Ringing Star Yang Jen T'o Lo T'ien K'ung Ti Chieh		Your *yuanten* (predestined attachment) for your brothers and sisters is weak so you will either be separated by circumstances or will stay together but not live in harmony.
	Any	Either of the Literary stars T'ien K'uei T'ien Yüeh Tso Fu *and* Yu Pi		You and your brothers and sisters will live in harmony and help one another. You will be close and supportive.
T'ien Liang	Any	Any		Although you will have few brothers and sisters you will all assist one another.
	Any	T'ien Ts'un		You will receive material support from your brothers and sisters.

Star	Degree of influence	Other stars	Degree of influence	Reading
	Any	Fire Star Ringing Star Yang Jen T'o Lo T'ien Kung Ti Chieh		Your *yuanten* (predestined attachment) is weak and you will not be in harmony. It is unlikely and inadvisable for you to stay together.
	Any	Literary Stars T'ien K'uei T'ien Yüeh Tso Fu *and* Yu Pi		Your feelings for your brothers and sisters will be harmonious and you will help one another.
Ch'i Sha	Any	Any		You will have three brothers or sisters.
	Any	T'ien Ts'un		You will receive material help from your brothers and sisters.
	Any	Fire Star Ringing Star Yang Jen T'o Lo T'ien K'ung Ti Chieh		You and your brothers and sisters will bring harm to one another and will quarrel constantly.
	Any	Literary stars T'ien K'uei T'ien Yüeh Tso Fu *or* Yu Pi		You will be in harmony with your brothers and sisters and you will all help each other.
P'o Chün	Any	Any		You will have many brothers and sisters but they will not help you.

Star	Degree of influence	Other stars	Degree of influence	Reading
	Any	T'ien Ts'un		You will receive material help from your brothers and sisters.
		Fire Star Ringing Star Yang Jen T'o Lo T'ien K'ung Ti Chieh		You will either have no brothers or sisters or you will live separately and not see one another.
	Any	Either of the Literary stars T'ien K'uei T'ien Yüeh Tso Fu *or* Yu Pi		You will live in harmony with your brothers and sisters and will help one another.
Fire Star *or* **Ringing Star**	Any	Any		You and your brothers and sisters will not be in harmony and your feelings for one another will be cold.
	Any	Either of the Literary stars *or* T'ien Ts'un		(These stars make the above reading weaker.)
	Any	T'ien K'uei T'ien Yüeh Tso Fu *or* Yu Pi		You will receive help from your brothers and sisters.
	Any	Yang Jen T'o Lo T'ien K'ung Ti Chieh		Your brothers and sisters will cause you worry and you will suffer a loss.

Star	Degree of influence	Other stars	Degree of influence	Reading
Wen Chü or **Wen Ch'ang**	Any	Any		You will be in harmony and receive moral support from your brothers and sisters. Your business will prosper.
	Any	T'ien Ts'un		As well as moral support, you will also receive material support from your brothers and sisters.
	Any	T'ien K'uei T'ien Yüeh Tso Fu or Yu Pi		Your brothers and sisters will help you to achieve a comfortable life.
	Any	Yang Jen T'o Lo		Your *yuanten* (predestined attachment) with your brothers and sisters is weak. You may live apart or a brother or sister may die unexpectedly.
T'ien Ts'un	Any	Any		Your brothers and sisters will receive material support from one another.
	Any	Tso Fu or Yu Pi		Your brothers and sisters will live in harmony and will help one another.

Star	Degree of influence	Other stars	Degree of influence	Reading
	Any	T'ien K'ung Ti Chieh		Your brothers and sisters will be cold towards one another. They may cause you loss.
Yang Jen *or* **T'o Lo**	Any	Any		Your brothers and sisters will be few in number.
	Any	T'ien K'uei *or* T'ien Yüeh Tso Fu *or* Yu Pi		You will have even fewer brothers and sisters than in the above case.
	Any	T'ien K'ung Ti Chieh		There will be enmity and suspicion between you and your brothers and sisters.
T'ien K'uei *or* **T'ien Yüeh**		Any		You will receive great benefit from your brothers and sisters.
		Tso Fu *or* Yu Pi		Your brothers and sisters will live in harmony and help one another.
		T'ien K'ung Ti Chieh		You will be in reasonable harmony with your brothers and sisters.
Tso Fu *or* **Yu Pi**		Any		Your brothers and sisters will live in harmony and help one another.

Star	Degree of influence	Other stars	Degree of influence	Reading
		T'ien K'ung Ti Chieh		There will be a lack of harmony between you and your brothers and sisters and you will not help one another.
T'ien K'ung *or* Ti Chieh		Any		You will care deeply for your brothers and sisters and work hard for them. They will cause you worry.
Hua Chi		Any		You will make sacrifices for your brothers and sisters.

THE MARITAL PALACE

The Marital Palace concerns the appearance, nature and character of your marriage partner and describes your relationship and love life.

These stars bring extremely good luck in the Marital Palace:

T'ai-yang (Sun)
T'ien T'ung (Heavenly Unity)
T'ien Fu (Southern Star)
T'ien Liang (Heavenly Roof-Beam)

T'ien Ts'un (Heavenly Store)
T'ien K'uei (Heavenly Leader)
T'ien Yüeh (Heavenly Halberd)

These stars bring moderately good luck:

Tzu Wei (Purple Star)
T'ien Chi (Heavenly Secret)
T'ai-yin (Moon)
T'ien Hsiang (Heavenly Minister)

Wen Ch'ü (Literary Music)
Wen Ch'ang (Literary Prosperity)

These stars bring bad luck in the Marital Palace:

Wu Ch'ü (Military Music)
Chü Men (Great Door)
Fire Star
Ringing Star

Tso Fu (Left Assistant)*
Yu Pi (Right Assistant)*
T'ien Yao (Heavenly Beauty)

*These are generally good-luck stars.

These stars bring extremely bad luck in the Marital Palace:

Lien Chen (Pure Virtue)

T'an Lang (Greedy Wolf)

Ch'i Sha (Seven Killings)

P'o Chün (Broken Army)

Yang Jen (Sheep-Blade)

T'o Lo (Hump-Back)

T'ien K'ung (Heavenly Void)

Ti Chieh (Earthly Robbery)

Hua Chi (Transforming Jealousy)

Star	Degree of influence	Other stars which appear in the Marital Palace	Degree of influence	Reading
Tzu Wei	Any	Any		Your partner's well-bred background causes marital problems. However, if you marry late (over the age of twenty-eight), even if your partner is well-bred, he/she will be attractive to you and you will live in harmony.
	Any	T'ien Fu		Your feelings for each other will be strong and you will love one another until the end.
	Any	T'an Lang		You will either separate or one of you will die before old age.
	Any	T'an Lang *and* any other lucky star		Your marriage will be long and fortunate.
		T'ien Hsiang		There will be a big discrepancy in your ages.
	Any	Ch'i Sha		You will quarrel easily and may separate or one of you may die.

Star	Degree of influence	Other stars	Degree of influence	Reading
	Any	P'o Chün		There will be a rift between you which sours your feelings for each other. You will cause each other harm. However, if the woman is older than the man, this trouble can be avoided.
	Any	T'ien Ts'un		You will receive substantial material support from your partner.
	Any	Fire Star Ringing Star Yang Jen T'o Lo T'ien K'ung Ti Chieh		There will be a rift between you and you are likely to harm your partner.
	Any	Either of Literary stars T'ien K'uei T'ien Yüeh Tso Fu or Yu Pi		Your partner will bring you great happiness in your love life.
T'ien Chi	Any	Any		If you are a man your wife will be young but impatient. If you are a woman there will be a great discrepancy between your ages.

Star	Degree of influence	Other stars	Degree of influence	Reading
	Any	T'ai-yin		If you are a man your wife will be pretty. If you are a woman your husband will be handsome.
	Any	Chü Men		Your partner will be good-looking.
	Any	T'ien Liang		Your partner will be good-looking but the difference in your ages will be great.
	Any	T'ien Ts'un		Your partner will be virtuous.
T'ai-yang	Any	Any		Your partner will help you gain promotion, but if you marry too early (e.g. at sixteen years of age) there will be a rift between you and your partner.
	Any	T'ai-yin		You will benefit greatly from your partner.
	Any	Chü Men		Your life will be average unless other unlucky stars also appear under this palace.
	Any	T'ien Liang		Your partner will be extremely virtuous and clever.

Star	Degree of influence	Other stars	Degree of influence	Reading
	Any	T'ien Ts'un		Your partner will offer you material support.
	Any	Fire Star Ringing Star Yang Jen T'o Lo T'ien K'ung Ti Chieh		There will be a rift between you and your partner and you may harm each other. If you marry late you will avoid this problem.
Wu Chü	Any	Any		You may separate from your partner or your partner may die. If you marry late you will avoid this trouble.
	Any	T'ien Ts'un		Your partner will bring you great wealth.
	Any	T'an Lang		Unless you marry late there will be a rift between you, and you will harm your partner.
	Any	T'ien Hsiang		You will not be in harmony with your partner.
	Any	Ch'i Sha		You will separate or your partner may die.

Star	Degree of influence	Other stars	Degree of influence	Reading
	Any	Fire Star Ringing Star Yang Jen T'o Lo T'ien K'ung Ti Chieh		You will quarrel and may separate or one of you may die.
	Any	Either of the Literary stars T'ien K'uei T'ien Yüeh Tso Fu *or* Yu Pi		Your partner will bring you great wealth.
T'ien T'ung	Any	Any		Your partner will be yielding and kind.
	Any	T'ai-yin		Your partner will be good-looking.
	Any	Chü Men		Your partner will be clever but is likely to die young.
	Any	T'ien Liang		You will love each other dearly and will live in harmony. Your family will have good fortune.
	Any	T'ien Ts'un		You will be united in your love for each other, and your partner will ensure that you are financially secure.

THE MARITAL PALACE 135

Star	Degree of influence	Other stars	Degree of influence	Reading
	Any	Fire Star Ringing Star Yang Jen T'o Lo T'ien K'ung Ti Chieh		You will not be in harmony. You may separate or one of you may die.
	Any	Literary stars T'ien K'uei T'ien Yüeh Tso Fu *or* Yu Pi		You will be in harmony. Your love life will be excellent.
Lien Chen	Any	Any		You will either separate or one partner may die.
	Any	T'ien Fu T'ien Hsiang T'ien Ts'un Literary stars T'ien K'uei T'ien Yüeh Tso Fu *or* Yu Pi		You will marry someone with a hot temper. You must be patient to avoid quarrels.
	Any	T'an Lang Ch'i Sha P'o Chün Fire Star Ringing Star Yang Jen T'o Lo T'ien K'ung Ti Chieh		There will be a rift between you which will not be easily reconciled. At times in your marriage you will separate.

Star	Degree of influence	Other stars	Degree of influence	Reading
T'ien Fu	Any	Any		Your partner will be very capable and will show great ability. You will receive substantial material support from him/her.
	Any	Fire Star Ringing Star Yang Jen T'o Lo T'ien K'ung Ti Chieh		Your partner will be too intelligent for you and your ideas will differ greatly. You are likely to suffer.
	Any	Either of the Literary stars T'ien K'uei T'ien Yüeh Tso Fu *or* Yu Pi		Your partner will be brilliantly capable. You will have enough material possessions and your love life will be happy.
T'ai-yin	Any	Any		Your partner will be good-looking and will have a high-class air.
	Any	Fire Star Ringing Star Yang Jen T'o Lo T'ien K'ung Ti Chieh		You will separate because your partner will be too good-looking and will attract others.
	Any	Literary stars T'ien K'uei T'ien Yüeh Tso Fu *or* Yu Pi		You will be a happy couple.

Star	Degree of influence	Other stars	Degree of influence	Reading
T'an Lang	Any	Any		You will change partner many times.
		T'ien Ts'un Fire Star Ringing Star Yang Jen T'o Lo T'ien K'ung Ti Chieh		You will divorce.
	Any	Either of the Literary stars T'ien K'uei T'ien Yüeh Tso Fu *or* Yu Pi		If you marry late you will avoid separation or the untimely death of one partner.
Chü Men	Any	Any		You will have no feeling for each other and will quarrel constantly.
	Any	T'ien Ts'un		There will be discord and you will argue constantly.
	Any	Fire Star Ringing Star Yang Jen T'o Lo T'ien K'ung Ti Chieh		You will either separate or one partner will die early.
	Any	Literary stars T'ien K'uei T'ien Yüeh Tso Fu *or* Yu Pi		You will appear to be in love and live in harmony, but this will not be the case.

Star	Degree of influence	Other stars	Degree of influence	Reading
T'ien Hsiang	Any	Any		The husband will be younger than the wife. You will be distant relatives.
	Any	T'ien Ts'un		You will both have the same aspirations and will help each other to build a strong foundation for achieving them.
	Any	Fire Star Ringing Star Yang Jen T'o Lo T'ien K'ung Ti Chieh		Your feelings for each other will not be good.
	Any	Literary stars T'ien K'uei T'ien Yüeh Tso Fu *or* Yu Pi		You will be cooperative and will forgive each other's faults.
T'ien Liang	Any	Any		Your partner will be good-looking. If you are a woman your husband will be younger than you.
	Any	T'ien Ts'un		You will respect each other. Your love life will be good.
	Any	Fire Star Ringing Star Yang Jen T'o Lo T'ien K'ung Ti Chieh		There will be discord in your marriage; you will quarrel constantly.

Star	Degree of influence	Other stars	Degree of influence	Reading
	Any	Literary stars T'ien K'uei T'ien Yüeh Tso Fu *and* Yu Pi		You will respect and love each other dearly.
Ch'i Sha	Any	Any		Early on in your marriage you will cause your partner harm.
	Any	Any lucky star		(The above reading is still true but may be delayed.)
	Any	Fire Star Ringing Star Yang Jen T'o Lo T'ien K'ung Ti Chieh		You will change your marriage partner many times.
P'o Chün	Any	Any		There will be a rift between you and your partner early on. You will cause your partner harm.
	Any	Any lucky star		(The above reading is delayed, not avoided.)
	Any	Fire Star Ringing Star Yang Jen T'o Lo T'ien K'ung Ti Chieh		You will change your partner many times. You are likely to live with your boyfriend or girlfriend rather than marry.

Star	Degree of influence	Other stars	Degree of influence	Reading
Fire Star or **Ringing Star**	* ☆	Any lucky star		You can avoid misfortune.
	+ –	Any unlucky star		You will lack harmony. You will separate or one of you may die.
Wen Ch'ü or **Wen Ch'ang**	Any	Any		Your partner will be virtuous.
Wen Ch'ü and **Wen Ch'ang**	Any	Any		You will commit adultery.
Yang Jen or **T'o Lo**	Any	Any		There will be a rift between you and your partner and you will harm each other.
Tso Fu or **Yu Pi**		Any		You will be co-operative and will progress well at work.
T'ien K'ung or **Ti Chieh**		Any		Your partner will cause you distress.
T'ien Ts'un		Any		You will receive material support from your partner. This will help you to make progress at work.

Star	Degree of influence	Other stars	Degree of influence	Reading
T'ien Yao		Any		Your partner succumbs to drink and sex.
Hua Chi		Any		There will be a rift between you and your partner.

THE MAN AND WOMAN PALACE

The Man and Woman Palace is concerned with your children. How many children will you have? What will your relationship with them be like?

The stars which bring extremely good luck in the Man and Woman Palace are:

T'ai-yang (Sun)
T'ien T'ung (Heavenly Unity)
T'ien Fu (Southern Star)

T'ai-yin (Moon)
T'ien K'uei (Heavenly Leader)
T'ien Yüeh (Heavenly Halberd)

The stars which bring moderately good luck are:

Tzu Wei (Purple Star)
T'ien Chi (Heavenly Secret)
T'ien Hsiang (Heavenly Minister)
T'ien Liang (Heavenly Roof-Beam)

Wen Ch'ü (Literary Music)
Wen Ch'ang (Literary Prosperity)
T'ien Ts'un (Heavenly Store)
Tso Fu (Left Assistant)
Yu Pi (Right Assistant)

The stars which bring bad luck are:

Wu Ch'ü (Military Music)   P'o Chün (Broken Army)

The stars which bring extremely bad luck are:

Lien Chen (Pure Virtue)
T'an Lang (Greedy Wolf)
Chü Men (Great Door)

T'o Lo (Hump-Back)
T'ien T'ung (Heavenly Unity)

Ch'i Sha (Seven Killings)

Fire Star

Ringing Star

Yang Jen (Sheep-Blade)

Ti Chieh (Earthly Robbery)

Hua Chi (Transforming Jealousy)

Star	Degree of influence	Other stars appearing in in the Man and Woman Palace	Degree of influence	Reading
Tzu Wei	Any	Any		Your children will have a successful business.
	Any	T'ien Fu		Your children will be prosperous in their work.
	Any	T'an Lang		Your children will be successful but their relationships with the opposite sex will not be good.
	Any	T'ien Hsiang		Your children will be successful in politics.
	Any	Ch'i Sha		Your children will be few. You may have only one or two boys.
	Any	P'o Chün		There will be a rift between you and your children. You will live apart.
	Any	T'ien Ts'un		Your children will save money and be rich. They will have a comfortable old age.
	Any	T'ien Ts'un and T'ien K'ung or Ti Chieh		Your children will not always be able to offer you financial support.

Star	Degree of influence	Other stars	Degree of influence	Reading
	Any	Fire Star Ringing Star Yang Jen T'o Lo T'ien K'ung T'i Chieh		There will be a rift and discord between you and your children.
	Any	Literary stars T'ien K'uei T'ien Yüeh Tso Fu *or* Yu Pi		Your children will be successful in business. They will be clever and obedient.
T'ien Chi	Any	Any		Your children will be particularly clever or even outstanding.
	Any	T'ai-yin T'ien Liang		You will have pleasant, attractive children.
	Any	Chü Men T'ien Ts'un		You will have creative children. They will be adept socially in later life.
	Any	Fire Star Ringing Star Yang Jen T'o Lo T'ien K'ung Ti Chieh		When your children are young, a parent or child may die.
	Any	Literary stars T'ien K'uei T'ien Yüeh Tso Fu *or* Yu Pi		Your children will already be outstanding in some way when they are young.

Star	Degree of influence	Other stars	Degree of influence	Reading
T'ai-yang	Any	Any		Your son will bring you renown and a high social position.
	Any	T'ai-yin Chü Men		Your *yuanten* (predestined attachment) with your children will be weak. You are likely to live apart.
	Any	T'ien Liang T'ien Fu		Your *yuanten* (predestined attachment) is strong. In old age your children will care for you. You need not worry about money or material things.
	Any	Fire Star Ringing Star Yang Jen T'o Lo T'ien K'ung Ti Chieh		You will argue with your children and will suffer as a result.
	Any	Literary Stars T'ien K'uei T'ien Yüeh Tso Fu *or* Yu Pi		Your children will have good brains and bring you renown.
Wu Ch'ü	Any	Any		There will be a rift between you and your children.

Star	Degree of influence	Other stars	Degree of influence	Reading
	Any	T'ien Fu T'ien Hsiang Either of the Literary stars T'ien Ts'un T'ien K'uei T'ien Yüeh Tso Fu *or* Yu Pi		Your children will make great progress in their work.
	Any	T'an Lang Ch'i Sha P'o Chün Fire Star Ringing Star Yang Jen T'o Lo T'ien K'ung Ti Chieh		When your children are very young there will be a lack of harmony or a parent or child may die.
T'ien T'ung	Any	Any		You will have more daughters than sons. They will all be good-looking.
	Any	T'ai-yin		You will have more daughters than sons. Their good looks will cause you many problems.
	Any	Chü Men		You will not be in harmony with your children. You will be suspicious of one another.

Star	Degree of influence	Other stars	Degree of influence	Reading
	Any	T'ien Liang		Your *yuanten* (predestined attachment) with your daughters is stronger than that with your sons. As a result you and your daughters love each other and are likely to stay together.
	Any	T'ien Ts'un		You will have substantial material help from your children.
	Any	Fire Star Ringing Star Yang Jen T'o Lo T'ien K'ung Ti Chieh		There will be no harmony between you and your children.
	Any	Either of the Literary stars T'ien K'uei Tien Yüeh Tso Fu *or* Yu Pi		Your *yuanten* (predestined attachment) is strong. You will be in harmony with your children.
Lien Chen	Any	Any		There will be a great rift between you and your children. A child or parent may die.

Star	Degree of influence	Other stars	Degree of influence	Reading
	Any	T'ien Fu T'ien Hsiang T'ien Ts'un Either of the Literary stars T'ien K'uei T'ien Yüeh Tso Fu *or* Yu Pi		Your children will be few in number. There will be no great rift between you but neither will you be in harmony.
	Any	T'an Lang Ch'i Sha P'o Chün Fire Star Ringing Star Yang Jen T'o Lo T'ien K'ung Ti Chieh		Your *yuanten* (predestined attachment) with your sons will be weak. You may separate, or a parent or son may die when the son is young.
T'ien Fu	Any	Any		You will have many children. One of them will be very wealthy.
	Any	T'ien Ts'un		(The above reading is almost certain to be true.)
	Any	Either of the Literary stars T'ien K'uei T'ien Yüeh		Your children will be intelligent. In old age you will be comfortable.
	Any	Tso Fu *or* Yu Pi		Your children will be helpful assistants to you. They will develop your family business.

Star	Degree of influence	Other stars	Degree of influence	Reading
	Any	Fire Star Ringing Star Yang Jen T'o Lo		You will have more daughters than sons.
	Any	T'ien K'ung Ti Chieh		Your children will suffer loss or a son may die.
T'ai-yin	Any	Any		You are more likely to have daughters than sons. Only a daughter will develop your business; if you have a son he will be unable to help you.
	* ☆	Any		Your children will give you happiness and moral support.
	Any	Any lucky star		(The above reading applies.)
	+ −	Any		Your children will cause you suffering.
	Any	Any unlucky star		(The above reading applies.)
T'an Lang	Any	Any		You will be full of energy and physically strong. However, it will be difficult for you to offer your children material support.

Star	Degree of influence	Other stars	Degree of influence	Reading
	Any	T'ien Ts'un		It will be easier for you to support your children than in the above case.
	Any	Fire Star Ringing Star Yang Jen T'o Lo T'ien K'ung Ti Chieh		You will lose contact with your children.
	Any	Either of the Literary stars T'ien K'uei T'ien Yüeh Tso Fu or Yu Pi		You and your children's fate is average.
Chü Men	Any	Any		Your sons will not be in harmony with you. You will all have different ideas, aspirations and interests.
	Any	T'ien Ts'un		You will quarrel constantly about money and hide your money from each other.
	Any	Fire Star Ringing Star Yang Jen T'o Lo T'ien K'ung Ti Chieh		Your relationship with your sons will deteriorate and you will quarrel constantly.

Star	Degree of influence	Other stars	Degree of influence	Reading
	Any	Either of the Literary stars T'ien K'uei T'ien Yüeh Tso Fu *or* Yu Pi		Although you will not be in harmony with your sons this will not present any great problem.
T'ien Hsiang	Any	Any		Your children will work in literary, cultural or political areas. Their careers will prosper.
	Any	T'ien Ts'un		Your children will not only flourish in the above areas, but also in finance. They will be materially well off.
	Any	Fire Star Ringing Star Yang Jen T'o Lo T'ien K'ung Ti Chieh		When your children are young they will cause many problems.
	Any	Either of the Literary stars T'ien K'uei Tien Yüeh Tso Fu *or* Yu Pi		Your children will be obedient.
T'ien Liang	Any	Any		A daughter may be outstanding.

Star	Degree of Influence	Other stars	Degree of Influence	Reading
	Any	T'ien Ts'un		Your children will make great developments in financial affairs: e.g. investment, buying and selling, lending money.
	Any	Fire Star Ringing Star Yang Jen T'o Lo T'ien K'ung Ti Chieh		Your sons will not share your ideas and you will quarrel constantly.
	Any	Either of the Literary stars T'ien K'uei T'ien Yüeh Tso Fu or Yu Pi		You will be in harmony and will give each other moral support.
Ch'i Sha	Any	Any		You will have few children (especially sons). If you do have a son it will be difficult for you to live happily together.
	Any	T'ien Ts'un		(The above unlucky reading is improved.)
	Any	Fire Star Ringing Star Yang Jen T'o Lo T'ien Kung Ti Chieh		There will be a rift between you which will never be resolved – you will argue until death.

Star	Degree of Influence	Other stars	Degree of Influence	Reading
		Literary stars T'ien K'uei T'ien Yüeh Tso Fu *or* Yu Pi		Your ideas will differ and there will be a lack of harmony. Your children will not follow your advice.
P'o Chün	Any	Any		Your sons will not be in harmony with you and you will live apart.
	Any	Any lucky star		(The above unlucky reading is improved.)
	Any	Any unlucky star		(The above unlucky reading is made worse.)
	Any	T'ien Ts'un		You will have many children. They will use their wealth to develop their businesses and will have success.
	Any	T'ien Ts'un *and* no unlucky stars		Your children will care for you in your old age.
Fire Star *or* **Ringing Star**	Any	Any		You will not be in harmony with your sons.
	☆	Any		Your children will be bad-tempered, but they will be successful.

Star	Degree of influence	Other stars	Degree of influence	Reading
	Any	Any lucky star		(As above.)
	+ –	Any		Your children will always be quarrelling with you or one child may die.
	Any	Any unlucky star		(As above.)
Wen Ch'ü or **Wen Ch'ang**	Any	Any		Your children will be clever and will do well at school. They will also be physically healthy.
	* ☆	Any		Your children will make successful progress at work.
Yang Jen or **T'o Lo**	Any	Any		Your children will frequently be ill and prone to accidents, or they may die.
T'ien K'uei or **T'ien Yüeh**		Any		Your children will be gentle, clever and quick.
Tso Fu or **Yu Pi**		Any		Your children will be very obedient.
T'ien K'ung or **Ti Chieh**		Any		Your children could cause you heartache. One of your children may disappear.

Star	Degree of Influence	Other stars	Degree of Influence	Reading
T'ien Ts'un		Any		You will have very few children – possibly just one child.
Hua Chi		Any		There will be a rift between you and you may bring harm to your children.

THE WEALTH PALACE

The Wealth Palace is concerned with your personal wealth and also your capacity for earning money.

The stars which bring extremely good luck in the Wealth Palace are:

Tzu Wei (Purple Star)
T'ai-yang (Sun)
Wu Ch'ü (Military Music)
T'ien Fu (Southern Star)

T'ai-yin (Moon)
T'ien Ts'un (Heavenly Store)
Hua Lu (Transforming Salary)

The stars which bring moderately good luck in this palace are:

T'ien Chi (Heavenly Secret)
T'ien T'ung (Heavenly Unity)
Lien Chen (Pure Virtue)
Chü Men (Great Door)
T'ien Hsiang (Heavenly Minister)
T'ien Liang (Heavenly Roof-Beam)
Ch'i Sha (Seven Killings)
P'o Chün (Broken Army)
Wen Chü (Literary Music)

Wen Ch'ang (Literary Prosperity)
T'ien K'uei (Heavenly Leader)
T'ien Yüeh (Heavenly Halberd)
Tso Fu (Left Assistant)
Yu Pi (Right Assistant)
Hua Ch'üan (Transforming Authority)
Hua K'o (Transforming Examination Class)

The stars which bring bad luck in this palace are:

T'an Lang (Greedy Wolf)	Fire Star
Yang Jen (Sheep-Blade)	Ringing Star
T'o Lo (Hump-Back)	Hua Chi (Transforming Jealousy)

The stars which bring extremely bad luck in this palace are:

T'ien K'ung (Heavenly Void)	Ti Chieh (Earthly Robbery)

Star	Degree of Influence	Other stars appearing in the Wealth Palace	Degree of Influence	Reading
Tzu Wei	Any	Any		You will work either with gold or on commission. You will gain a steady income and have many business interests. You have influential connections which will also bring you wealth.
	Any	T'ien Fu T'ien Hsiang T'ien Ts'un		You will use your renown, your position in society or your title to create a business and earn a lot of money.
	Any	T'an Lang Ch'i Sha P'o Chün		Although you know how to organize financial accounts, your income will not be quite satisfactory.
	Any	Fire Star Ringing Star Yang Jen T'o Lo T'ien K'ung Ti Chieh		You will spend a lot of money to live up to your position. You will spend too much and suffer the consequences.
	Any	Either of the Literary stars T'ien K'uei T'ien Yüeh Tso Fu or Yu Pi		You will be successful in three different areas: you will be well known, have a high social position and wealth.

Star	Degree of influence	Other stars	Degree of influence	Reading
T'ien Chi	Any	Any		You will make much money in religious matters or in the art of fortune-telling.
	–	Any		Your income will be small.
	Any	T'ai-yang Chü Men		You will earn a good income from a sideline. This will be related to your own interests.
	Any	T'ien Liang T'ien Ts'un		Your fame in religious affairs will bring you wealth.
	Any	Fire Star Ringing Star Yang Jen T'o Lo T'ien K'ung Ti Chieh		You will work hard but earn little income from it.
	Any	Either of the Literary stars T'ien K'uei T'ien Yüeh Tso Fu or Yu Pi		You will work hard, which will bring you a good position and increase your income.
T'ai-yang	* ☆	Any		You will gain a large income from a business enterprise or writing.
	–	Any		You will overspend and have very few savings.

Star	Degree of influence	Other stars	Degree of influence	Reading
	Any	T'ai-yin Chü Men		You will miss opportunities to earn money.
	Any	T'ien Liang T'ien Ts'un		You will be lucky in acquiring money; you will have an endless supply of it.
	Any	Fire Star Ringing Star Yang Jen T'o Lo T'ien K'ung Ti Chieh		You will spend too much and waste lots of money.
	Any	Either of the Literary stars T'ien K'uei T'ien Yüeh Tso Fu *or* Yu Pi		Your income and expenditure will be balanced. You will not waste money and will therefore save a reasonable amount.
Wu Chü	Any	Any		You will earn a lot of money quite unexpectedly.
	Any	Any unlucky star		You will have a large income but will be in danger of losing it.
	Any	T'ien Fu T'ien Ts'un		You will be involved in speculation. You will earn money steadily.

Star	Degree of influence	Other stars	Degree of influence	Reading
	Any	T'an Lang Ch'i Sha		Your business is likely to be in speculation.
	Any	T'an Lang Ch'i Sha *and* no other unlucky stars		You will make much money.
	Any	T'an Lang Ch'i Sha *and* any unlucky star.		You will suffer disaster.
	Any	T'ien Hsiang	Any	You will work in politics. You will work steadily and your income will increase – you will step on solid ground.
	Any	P'o Chün	Any	You will participate in speculation and are likely to lose money.
	Any	Fire Star Ringing Star Yang Jen T'o Lo	*	You will make a lot of money.
	Any	Fire Star Ringing Star Yang Jen T'o Lo	+ –	You will lose money.
	Any	T'ien K'ung Ti Chieh		Your speculation will fail due to your bad judgement. This will cause you suffering.

Star	Degree of influence	Other stars	Degree of influence	Reading
	Any	T'ien K'uei T'ien Yüeh Tso Fu *or* Yu Pi		You will receive help from your relatives and friends.
	Any	Either of the Literary stars		You will use your intelligence in business and earn a large income.
T'ien T'ung	Any	Any		You will work in a service industry. You will move from poverty to wealth. After middle age your income will be steady.
	Any	T'ai-yin T'ien Liang T'ien Ts'un T'ien K'uei T'ien Yüeh Tso Fu *or* Yu Pi		You will earn a lot of money.
	Any	Chü Men Fire Star Ringing Star Yang Jen T'o Lo T'ien K'ung Ti Chieh		You will spend money as soon as you receive it; you will never be wealthy.

Star	Degree of influence	Other stars	Degree of influence	Reading
	Any	Either of the Literary stars		You will use your creativity and intelligence to bring you success. You will save money and your wealth will grow.
Lien Chen	Any	Any		You will earn money unexpectedly.
	Any	T'ien Fu T'ien Ts'un T'ien Hsiang		You will gain great wealth from an industrial, commercial or electrical business. You will enjoy this wealth to the end of your life.
	Any	T'an Lang Ch'i Sha P'o Chün		You will earn large amounts of money unexpectedly but will spend them quickly. You will be unable to save.
	Any	Fire Star Ringing Star Yang Jen T'o Lo T'ien K'ung Ti Chieh		You are likely to earn money by illegal means.
	Any	Either of the Literary stars T'ien K'uei T'ien Yüeh Tso Fu or Yu Pi		You will have a good salary and a comfortable life.

Star	Degree of influence	Other stars	Degree of influence	Reading
T'ien Fu	Any	Any		You will be extremely rich.
	Any	Fire Star Ringing Star Yang Jen T'o Lo		Your luck in wealth will be unsteady. At times you will be rich and at times poor.
	Any .	T'ien K'ung Ti Chieh		Even if you become a billionaire you will spend all your money. In old age you will be poor.
	Any	Either of the Literary stars T'ien K'uei T'ien Yüeh		Your luck in wealth will be steady. By old age you will have many savings.
	Any	Tso Fu *or* Yu Pi		You will earn a lot of money and will use this to raise yourself in politics.
T'ai-yin	* ☆	Any		You will have a steady occupation and earn a lot of money.
	Any	Any lucky star		(As above.)
	–	Any		Your occupation will be unsteady. You will have to work hard to make money.
	Any	Any unlucky star		(As above.)

Star	Degree of influence	Other stars	Degree of influence	Reading
T'an Lang	☆	Any		Although you will not be rich in your youth, in middle age your income will increase.
	Any	Fire Star Ringing Star *or* any lucky star	Any	(As above.)
	Any	Fire Star Ringing Star	+ −	You will have a harsh life.
	Any	Any unlucky star		You will have a harsh life.
Chü Men	Any	Any		Your income will not come through trade or exchange, it will come through advising others, e.g. as a solicitor or fortune-teller.
	☆	Any		You will save money and make it grow.
	Any	Any lucky star		(As above.)
	+ −	Any		The Chinese say: 'Your hand holds water', i.e. you will spend money like water.
	Any	Any unlucky star		(As above.)

Star	Degree of influence	Other stars	Degree of influence	Reading
T'ien Liang	Any	Any		You will earn a good income from religious work, medical work and research into unusual topics.
	* ☆	Any		Money will pour in. You will be prosperous and there is no need to worry.
	–	Any		You will have a harsh life. You will work hard for nothing.
	Any	Fire Star Ringing Star Yang Jen T'o Lo T'ien K'ung Ti Chieh		When young you will suffer from poverty. In middle age you will earn more, but you will never be rich.
	Any	Literary stars T'ien K'uei T'ien Yüeh Tso Fu *or* Yu Pi		You have no need to work hard for you will always have money. Your style of living will be comfortable.
T'ien Hsiang	Any	Any		You will have a wealthy style of living.

Star	Degree of influence	Other stars	Degree of influence	Reading
	Any	Fire Star Ringing Star Yang Jen T'o Lo T'ien K'ung Ti Chieh		You need not worry about having enough to live on, but you will not be able to save money.
	Any	Either of the Literary stars T'ien K'uei T'ien Yüeh Tso Fu or Yu Pi		You will earn a good income by working in the service industry.
Ch'i Sha	Any	Any		You will gain money unexpectedly.
	Any	T'ien K'ung Ti Chieh		You will always be poor.
P'o Chün	Any	Any		You will be very rich as a result of financial speculation.
	+	Any		You will go bankrupt.
	Any	Fire Star Ringing Star Yang Jen T'o Lo T'ien K'ung or Ti Chieh		Your financial success will be insecure. You will sometimes keep your head above water and sometimes go under. You will be on the edge of bankruptcy.

Star	Degree of influence	Other stars	Degree of influence	Reading
	Any	Literary stars T'ien K'uei T'ien Yüeh Tso Fu *or* Yu Pi		Your finances will fluctuate substantially throughout your life.
	*	Literary stars T'ien K'uei T'ien Yüeh Tso Fu *or* Yu Pi		Despite the above reading, eventually you will be successful.
	+ –	Literary stars T'ien K'uei T'ien Yüeh Tso Fu *or* Yu Pi		After all the fluctuations mentioned above, you will go bankrupt.
T'ien Ts'un	Any	Any		You will be very rich, but your wealth will not come of its own accord. You must save it little by little.
	Any	T'ien K'ung Ti Chieh		You will earn money quickly but eventually lose it.
Fire Star *or* **Ringing Star**	Any	Any		Your fortunes will be unstable, both in property and money. Today you are rich and tomorrow you will be poor.

Star	Degree of influence	Other stars	Degree of influence	Reading
	Any	Either of the Literary stars		You will have good qualifications but will be unable to get a suitable job. This will bring you worry and poverty.
	Any	Yang Jen T'o Lo		You will suffer from a lack of money throughout your life.
	Any	T'ien K'uei T'ien Yüeh		Your income will be irregular – sometimes great, sometimes small.
	Any	Tso Fu *or* Yu Pi		You will earn a good income with the help of friends.
	Any	T'ien K'ung Ti Chieh		Because of rushing to produce results, you will suffer great loss.
Wen Ch'ü *or* **Wen Ch'ang**	Any	Any		Your finances and property will be stable and your income regular.
	Any	Yang Jen T'o Lo		Your income will be low and you will have to budget carefully.
	Any	T'ien K'uei T'ien Yüeh		You will have a good income without having to work very hard.

Star	Degree of influence	Other stars	Degree of influence	Reading
	Any	Tso Fu or Yu Pi		You will need assistance to find out how to earn a good income.
	Any	T'ien K'ung Ti Chieh		You will be cheated and will lose money. You will not have material wealth although you have the capacity for work. You will have a poor and harsh life.
Yang Jen or **T'o Lo**	Any	Any		You will have no reward for your hard work throughout your life. You will have a poor and harsh life.
	*	Any		You may have a regular income plus income from a sideline.
	Any	T'ien K'uei or T'ien Yüeh		Although you work hard your standard of living will only be moderately comfortable.
	Any	Tso Fu or Yu Pi		Your entire life will be harsh but there will be someone to advise you. This will help to improve your standard of living.

Star	Degree of influence	Other stars	Degree of influence	Reading
	Any	T'ien K'ung Ti Chieh		You will have a poor and harsh life.
T'ien K'uei or T'ien Yüeh		Any		Money will flow in regularly and you will have a comfortable life.
		Tso Fu or Yu Pi		You will be rich and comfortable throughout your life.
		T'ien K'ung Ti Chieh		Although you will not have great wealth you will never need to worry about your livelihood.
Tso Fu or Yu Pi		Any		With your friends' or elders' help you will be prosperous in middle age. In old age you will be comfortable, happy and rich.
		T'ien K'ung Ti Chieh		You will have just enough to live on. You will be unable to make any more money.
T'ien K'ung or Ti Chieh		Any		Out of every ten attempts nine will fail. In old age you will not have enough money.

Star	Degree of influence	Other stars	Degree of influence	Reading
Hua Lu		Any		You will have two or three opportunities to make money. Your life style will be wealthy.
Hua Chi		Any		You have no *yuanten* (predestined) attachment) with money.
Hua Ch'üan		Any		You will have a great amount of money.
Hua K'o		Any		You will have no need to worry about your livelihood. You will always be prosperous.

THE SICKNESS PALACE

The Sickness Palace is concerned with your physical health – your condition and your strength. It is also concerned with illness.

The stars which bring extremely good luck in the Sickness Palace are:

T'ien T'ung (Heavenly Unity)
T'ien Liang (Heavenly Roof-Beam)
T'ien Yüeh (Heavenly Halberd)
T'ien Fu (Southern Star)
T'ien Hsiang (Heavenly Minister)
T'ien K'uei (Heavenly Leader)

The stars which bring fairly good luck are:

Tzu Wei (Purple Star)
T'ai-yang (Sun)
T'ai-yin (Moon)
Fire Star
Ringing Star
T'ien Ts'un (Heavenly Store)
Tso Fu (Left Assistant)
Yu Pi (Right Assistant)

The stars which bring bad luck are:

T'ien Chi (Heavenly Secret)
Wen Ch'ü (Literary Music)
Wen Ch'ang (Literary Prosperity)
Wu Ch'ü (Military Music)

The stars which bring extremely bad luck are:

Lien Chen (Pure Virtue)
Chü Men (Great Door)
P'o Chün (Broken Army)
T'o Lo (Hump-Back)
Ti Chieh (Earthly Robbery)
T'an Lang (Greedy Wolf)
Ch'i Sha (Seven Killings)
Yang Jen (Sheep-Blade)
T'ien K'ung (Heavenly Void)
Hua Chi (Transforming Jealousy)

Star	Degree of influence	Other stars which appear in the Sickness Palace	Degree of influence	Reading
Tzu Wei	Any	Any		You will never suffer serious illness.
	Any	Any unlucky star		You may have nervous complaints.
T'ien Chi	Any	Any		As a child you tended to be sickly, but you will have very few serious illnesses.
	Any	T'ai-yin		You are prone to purulent boils. Your skin bruises easily.
	Any	Chü Men		You are likely to be anaemic.
	Any	T'ien Liang		You are likely to have bladder and lower abdominal problems.
	Any	Fire Star Ringing Star Yang Jen T'o Lo T'ien K'ung Ti Chieh		You will suffer from eye problems.
	Any	Either of the Literary stars T'ien K'uei T'ien Yüeh Tso Fu or Yu Pi		Your legs, arms and trunk are weak.
T'ai-yang	Any	Any		You are likely to have eye problems.
	* ☆ Any	Any Any lucky star }		The above illness will not afflict you.

Star	Degree of influence	Other stars	Degree of influence	Reading
Wu Ch'ü	Any	Any		You are likely to have nasal problems. When young you are easily hurt. You may have a scar on your hand, leg or head.
T'ien T'ung	Any	Any		You are likely to have ear problems.
	Any	T'ai-yin Chü Men		You have a weak heart.
	Any	T'ien Liang T'ien Ts'un		You have bad circulation.
		Fire Star Ringing Star Yang Jen T'o Lo T'ien K'ung Ti Chieh		You are physically weak and will suffer from minor illnesses.
	Any	Either of the Literary stars T'ien K'uei T'ien Yüeh Tso Fu or Yu Pi		You are physically strong and unlikely to become ill.

Star	Degree of influence	Other stars	Degree of influence	Reading
Lien Chen	Any	Any		You will suffer from ill health all your life.
	Any	T'ien Fu T'ien Hsiang T'ien Ts'un Either of the Literary stars T'ien K'uei T'ien Yüeh Tso Fu *or* Yu Pi		You are strong and seldom ill.
	Any	T'an Lang Ch'i Sha P'o Chün Fire Star Ringing Star Yang Jen T'o Lo T'ien K'ung Ti Chieh		You are weak and often ill.
T'ien Fu	Any	Any		You are seldom ill; even if you are unwell you recover easily.
	Any	Any unlucky star		You are likely to have gall-bladder problems or mental problems.

Star	Degree of influence	Other stars	Degree of influence	Reading
T'ai-yin	* ☆	Any		You are unlikely to suffer from illness.
	Any	Any unlucky star		
	–	Any		You will suffer from eye and liver problems and other illness. If you are a woman you are likely to suffer from gynaecological problems.
	Any	Any unlucky star		
T'an Lang	Any	Any		You are likely to suffer from venereal disease or other sexual illnesses.
Chü Men	Any	Any		When young you will have skin problems. When an adult you will have stomach problems.
T'ien Hsiang	Any	Any		You are physically strong and unlikely to be ill.
T'ien Liang	* ☆	Any		You are seldom ill and will have a long life.
	Any	Any lucky star		
	–	Any		You are likely to have a heart attack.
	Any	Any unlucky star		

Star	Degree of influence	Other stars	Degree of influence	Reading
Ch'i Sha	Any	Any		When young you are susceptible to illness, particularly intestinal problems. In middle age you are likely to suffer from piles.
P'o Chün	Any	Any		When young you are likely to get boils. Your lungs are weak.
T'ien Ts'un	Any	Any		You are physically strong and unlikely to become ill.
Fire Star *or* **Ringing Star**	Any	Any		Your bodily functions will deteriorate. You also suffer from allergies and if you have a transplant your body may reject the organ.
	Any	Either of the Literary stars		Your bodily functions are disturbed: e.g. when it is cold you sweat.
	Any	Yang Jen T'o Lo		You are unlikely to live long.
	Any	T'ien K'uei T'ien Yüeh		You will never suffer from illness.
	Any	T'ien K'ung Ti Chieh		You will suffer from many illnesses, disasters and injuries.

Star	Degree of influence	Other stars	Degree of influence	Reading
Wen Ch'ü *or* **Wen Ch'ang**	Any	Any		Your natural bodily functions will deteriorate.
Yang Jen *or* **T'o Lo**	Any	Any		You are likely to suffer injuries, such as broken bones.
T'ien K'uei *or* **T'ien Yüeh**		Any		You will be physically strong all your life and will seldom be ill.
Tso Fu *or* **Yu Pi**		Any		You will be physically strong and seldom ill.
T'ien K'ung *or* **Ti Chieh**		Any		You will have many illnesses which will make you unhappy and miserable.
Hua Chi		Any		You are physically weak and easily fall ill. You are likely to die young.

THE MOVING PALACE

The Moving Palace is concerned with your social life – how you relate to people and how best to develop your business.

The stars which bring extremely good luck in the Moving Palace are:

Tzu Wei (Purple Star)
Wu Ch'ü (Military Music)
T'ien Fu (Southern Star)
T'ien Hsiang (Heavenly Minister)
Wen Ch'ü (Literary Music)
Wen Ch'ang (Literary Prosperity)
T'ien K'uei (Heavenly Leader)
T'ien Yüeh (Heavenly Halberd)

T'ai-yang (Sun)
Lien Chen (Pure Virtue)
T'ai-yin (Moon)
T'ien Liang (Heavenly Roof-Beam)
T'ien Ts'un (Heavenly Store)
Tso Fu (Left Assistant)
Yu Pi (Right Assistant)
Hau K'o (Transforming Examination Class)

The stars which bring moderately good luck are:

T'ien Chi (Heavenly Secret)
I-ma (Travelling Star)
Hua Ch'üan (Transforming Authority)

T'ien T'ung (Heavenly Unity)
Hua Lu (Transforming Salary)

The stars which bring bad luck are:

T'an Lang (Greedy Wolf)
Ch'i Sha (Seven Killings)

Chü Men (Great Door)
T'o Lo (Hump-Back)

Fire Star   Yang Jen (Sheep-Blade)
Ringing Star

The stars which bring extremely bad luck are:

T'ien K'ung (Heavenly   Ti Chieh (Earthly Robbery)
   Void)
Hua Chi (Transforming
   Jealousy)

Star	Degree of influence	Other stars which appear in the Moving Palace	Degree of influence	Reading
Tzu Wei	Any	Any		You will have friends to help you in a foreign place.
	Any	T'ien Fu T'ien Hsiang T'ien Ts'un		You will have great success abroad. The Chinese say: 'Wear brocade and return home with honour.'
	Any	T'an Lang Ch'i Sha P'o Chün		You will have support from older people. Take care that the opposite sex does not ruin your name.
	Any	Fire Star Ringing Star T'ien K'ung Ti Chieh		When you put a plan into practice, you will often achieve the reverse of what you intended.
	Any	Either of the Literary stars T'ien K'uei T'ien Yüeh Tso Fu *or* Yu Pi		You have position, renown and money.

Star	Degree of influence	Other stars	Degree of influence	Reading
T'ien Chi	Any	Any		You should leave your home and work in a foreign country. If you stay at home you will work extremely hard for little reward. Your social connections will bring you great fortune.
	Any	T'ai-yin T'ien Ts'un Literary stars T'ien K'uei T'ien Yüeh Tso Fu *or* Yu Pi		You will always be busy and will have good fortune. You treat people well when you are abroad.
	Any	Chü Men T'ien Liang Fire Star Ringing Star Yang Jen T'o Lo T'ien K'ung Ti Chieh		Because you will not work hard it is difficult for you to save money. If you work as an artist you will be successful.
T'ai-yang	Any	Any		You are suited to living and working abroad. You should have a job in which you are physically active.

Star	Degree of influence	Other stars	Degree of influence	Reading
	Any	T'ai-yin T'ien Ts'un Literary stars T'ien Fu T'ien Yüeh Tso Fu *or* Yu Pi		You will work hard for many years and be prosperous.
	Any	Chü Men T'ien K'ung Fire Star Ringing Star Yang Jen T'o Lo Ti Chieh		You will work for a pittance.
Wu Ch'ü	Any	Any		You will always be busy but will make no money.
	Any	T'ien Fu T'an Lang T'ien Hsiang Ch'i Sha T'ien Ts'un		You will earn great sums of money unexpectedly.
	Any	P'o Chün Yang Jen T'o Lo Fire Star Ringing Star		If you leave home you will suffer or meet disasters unless you work as an artist.
	Any	Either of the Literary stars T'ien K'uei T'ien Yüeh Hua K'o		You will make progress in a foreign country. Your name will be known in distant places.

Star	Degree of influence	Other stars	Degree of influence	Reading
	Any	Tso Fu *or* Yu Pi		You will be supported by strong and powerful people and will become rich.
	Any	T'ien K'ung Ti Chieh		You will be cheated in a foreign country. You may lose money or your life may be in danger.
T'ien T'ung	Any	Any		The help that you receive from older people in foreign countries will bring business success and an introduction to a marriage partner.
	Any	T'ai-yin Chü Men		You will work extremely hard but will suffer and be miserable.
	Any	T'ien Liang T'ien Ts'un		Older people will recommend you and help you. This means you will be able to make progress.
	Any	Fire Star Ringing Star Yang Jen T'o Lo T'ien K'ung Ti Chieh		You will have many difficult times. Your plans will not work out and you will make no progress.

Star	Degree of influence	Other stars	Degree of influence	Reading
	Any	Either of the Literary stars T'ien K'uei T'ien Yüeh Tso Fu or Yu Pi		Your life will be prosperous. Your relations with people will be good and your work will go well.
Lien Chen	Any	Any		You are likely to leave home as you dislike living there.
	Any	T'ien Fu T'ien Ts'un		You will work in an unusual job. You will gain a great fortune in a foreign country.
	Any	T'an Lang Ch'i Sha		Although you will gain money unexpectedly, you will not be able to keep it for long.
	Any	T'ien Hsiang Either of the Literary stars T'ien K'uei T'ien Yüeh Tso Fu or Yu Pi		You should live away from home if you want your business to prosper. If you remain in your home town you will not succeed.
	Any	P'o Chün Fire Star Ringing Star Yang Jen T'o Lo T'ien K'ung or Ti Chieh		You are not suited to living in distant places. If you do your life or your money will be in danger.

Star	Degree of influence	Other stars	Degree of influence	Reading
T'ien Fu	Any	Any		You will get support and help from someone to increase your income.
	Any	Any unlucky star		(The unlucky star has no effect on the above reading.)
	Any	T'ien K'ung Ti Chieh		Your life and property are safe.
T'ai-yin	Any	Any		You will have a high position, renown and wealth.
	–	Any		You will suffer a disaster in a foreign country.
T'an Lang	Any	Any		You will work hard but you will lose your determination in later life.
	Any	Any lucky star		You have unusual features to your character which, when they express themselves, will bring you great wealth.
	Any	Any unlucky star		You will suffer from a robbery or a disaster which will leave you penniless.
Chü Men	Any	Any		You will have a difficult, unstable life.

Star	Degree of influence	Other stars	Degree of influence	Reading
	Any	Any lucky star		(The above reading applies.)
	Any	Any unlucky star		(The unlucky star increases your suffering.)
T'ien Hsiang	Any	Any		You will develop a successful business in a foreign country.
	Any	T'ien Ts'un		You will enjoy material stability.
	Any	Fire Star Ringing Star Yang Jen T'o Lo T'ien K'ung Ti Chieh		Your livelihood is unstable. You will easily cause others to dislike you. Your inferiors will bring you trouble.
	Any	Literary stars T'ien K'uei T'ien Yüeh Tso Fu or Yu Pi		You will have a high position, a good name and make great progress in business.
T'ien Liang	Any	Any		Someone will support you and bring you success.
Ch'i Sha	Any	Any		You will not work in one place but will have to travel a great deal.
	Any	T'ien Ts'un		You will have the opportunity to make progress in business and attain success.

Star	Degree of influence	Other stars	Degree of influence	Reading
	Any	Fire Star Ringing Star Yang Jen T'o Lo T'ien K'ung Ti Chieh		You will be forced to travel to make a living.
	Any	Either of the Literary stars T'ien Ts'un T'ien K'uei T'ien Yüeh Tso Fo *or* Yu Pi		You will be promoted to a high position, and be well known and successful in business.
P'o Chün	Any	Any		You will have a harsh life in a foreign country. Your life will be unstable.
	Any	T'ien Ts'un		You will be successful in earning money but you will have to work hard.
	Any	Fire Star Ringing Star Yang Jen T'o Lo T'ien K'ung Ti Chieh		Work where your interest lies – as an artist – then you will be prosperous. Otherwise you will not be successful.
	Any	Either of the Literary stars T'ien K'uei T'ien Yüeh Tso Fu *or* Yu Pi		You will live abroad and have a stable life.

Star	Degree of influence	Other stars	Degree of influence	Reading
Fire Star *or* **Ringing Star**	Any	Any		You will have an unstable and harsh life.
	Any	Literary stars Yang Jen T'o Lo T'ien K'ung Ti Chieh		You will have a difficult life. You will work for a pittance.
	*	T'ien Ts'un T'ien K'uei T'ien Yüeh Tso Fu *or* Yu Pi		You may make successful progress in business. If not your life will be harsh.
Wen Ch'ü *or* **Wen Ch'ang**	Any	Any		You will gain renown in a foreign country.
	Any	Any unlucky star		You will be notorious and no one will trust you.
Yang Jen *or* **T'o Lo**	*	Any		You will be successful in your work.
	–	Any		You are easily cheated – you will have a harsh and unrewarding life. Everything will be lost.
Hua Lu *or* **T'ien Ts'un**		Any		You will be successful one day.

Star	Degree of influence	Other stars	Degree of influence	Reading
T'ien K'uei or T'ien Yüeh		Any		You will have a comfortable and stable life.
Tso Fu or Yu Pi		Any		You have a competitive spirit. In business you will be successful and hold a high position.
T'ien K'ung or Ti Chieh		Any		You will suffer a great loss in a foreign country. You will be unable to recover from this.
Hua K'o		Any		Other people will admire your skills and your work. This will bring you success.
Hua Chi		Any		You work for a pittance. Your standard of living will be average.
I-ma		Any		You have to travel widely in a foreign country.
Hua Ch'üan		Any		You will be offered promotion and make good progress in your work.

THE SERVANTS' PALACE

The Servants' Palace is concerned with how your inferiors and colleagues relate to you.

The stars which bring extremely good luck in the Servants' Palace are:

T'ai-yang (Sun)	T'ien Fu (Southern Star)
T'ai-yin (Moon)	T'ien Hsiang (Heavenly
T'ien Liang (Heavenly	Minister)
Roof-Beam)	Wen Ch'ü (Literary Music)
T'ien Yüeh (Heavenly	Wen Ch'ang (Literary
Halberd)	Prosperity)
Tso Fu (Left Assistant)	T'ien Ts'un (Heavenly Store)
Yu Pi (Right Assistant)	T'ien K'uei (Heavenly
	Leader)

The stars which bring moderately good luck are:

Tzu Wei (Purple Star)	Wu Ch'ü (Military Music)
T'ien T'ung (Heavenly	Lien Chen (Pure Virtue)
Unity)	

The stars which bring bad luck are:

T'ien Chi (Heavenly Secret)	T'an Lang (Greedy Wolf)
P'o Chün (Broken Army)	Hua Chi (Transforming
Fire Star	Jealousy)
Ringing Star	

The stars which bring extremely bad luck are:

Chü Men (Great Door)	Ch'i Sha (Seven Killings)
Yang Jen (Sheep Blade)	T'o Lo (Hump-Back)
T'ien K'ung (Heavenly	Ti Chieh (Earthly Robbery)
Void)	

Star	Degree of influence	Other stars which appear in the Servants' Palace	Degree of influence	Reading
Tzu Wei	Any	Any		Your inferiors will be helpful or you will have many good friends who will assist you in business and help you to make money.
	Any	T'ien Fu T'ien Hsiang T'ien Ts'un Either of the Literary stars T'ien K'uei T'ien Yüeh Tso Fu *or* Yu Pi		You will be given a lot of help by your inferiors or servants.
	Any	T'an Lang Ch'i Sha P'o Chün Fire Star Ringing Star Yang Jen T'o Lo T'ien K'ung *or* Ti Chieh		Your inferiors will not help you, however many people there are under you.
T'ien Chi	Any	Any		Your inferiors will be cooperative.
	–	Any		You will not be liked by your inferiors or by older people.

Star	Degree of influence	Other stars	Degree of influence	Reading
	Any	T'ien Liang T'ien Ts'un Either of the Literary stars T'ien K'uei T'ien Yüeh Tso Fu *or* Yu Pi		During the first half of your life you will not be helped by your inferiors. In the second half you will always be helped by them.
	Any	T'ai-yin Chü Men Fire Star Ringing Star Yang Jen T'o Lo T'ien K'ung Ti Chieh		Not only will your inferiors not help you but they will also be jealous and suspicious.
T'ai-yang	* ☆	Any		Your inferiors and friends will be good to you. They will help you develop your work.
	+ −	Any		Your inferiors will be unable to help you. They will also be jealous and suspicious of you and of one another. They may betray you and cause you loss.
	Any	T'ai-yin T'ien Liang T'ien Ts'un		Your colleagues will help you to achieve success in your career.

Star	Degree of influence	Other stars	Degree of influence	Reading
	Any	Chü Men		You will always be on bad terms with your inferiors.
	Any	Fire Star Ringing Star Yang Jen T'o Lo T'ien K'ung Ti Chieh		Your inferiors will refuse to obey you.
	Any	Either of the Literary stars T'ien K'uei T'ien Yüeh Tso Fu or Yu Pi		You will be supported by inferiors and elders. This will bring you promotion to a high position.
Wu Ch'ü or **Wen Ch'ang**	Any	Any		Your inferiors will be supportive and help your career.
	Any	T'ien Fu T'ien Hsiang T'ien Ts'un T'ien K'uei T'ien Yüeh Tso Fu or Yu Pi		Your inferiors will be helpful, especially those of the opposite sex.
	Any	T'an Lang Ch'i Sha P'o Chün Fire Star Ringing Star Yang Jen T'o Lo T'ien K'ung Ti Chieh		You will not be helped by the opposite sex. This will make you suspicious and jealous.

Star	Degree of influence	Other stars	Degree of influence	Reading
T'ien T'ung	Any	Any		The help of your friends and inferiors will bring you great success.
	Any	T'ai-yin T'ien Liang		You will be in harmony with your inferiors. You will be respected.
	Any	Chü Men T'ien Ts'un		You will be an incompetent leader because you fail to see others' aims and ideas. Your relationship with others improves after middle age.
	Any	Fire Star Ringing Star Yang Jen T'o Lo T'ien K'ung Ti Chieh		You will be too considerate towards your inferiors. You will be cheated and suffer loss.
	Any	Either of the Literary stars T'ien K'uei T'ien Yüeh Tso Fu or Yu Pi		You will be very kind to your inferiors and they will respect you, cooperate with you and help you. You will be successful at work.

Star	Degree of influence	Other stars	Degree of influence	Reading
Lien Chen	Any	Any		You will be too stern with your inferiors. They will be unhappy and may take revenge.
	Any	T'ien Fu T'ien Hsiang T'ien Ts'un		(The unlucky reading above will be improved.)
	Any	T'an Lang Ch'i Sha P'o Chün		(The unlucky reading above will deteriorate.)
	Any	Fire Star Ringing Star Yang Jen T'o Lo T'ien K'ung Ti Chieh		Your inferiors will be rebellious.
		Either of the Literary stars T'ien K'uei T'ien Yüeh Tso Fu or Yu Pi		You will treat your inferiors too sternly. This will make them unhappy but they will not cause you harm.
T'ien Fu	Any	Any		Your inferiors and elders will respect you. Your work will be successful and you will be happy in your job. You will get on well with people.

Star	Degree of influence	Other stars	Degree of influence	Reading
	Any	T'ien Ts'un		Your inferiors will be able to help and support you. They will bring you success.
	Any	Fire Star Ringing Star Yang Jen T'o Lo		Your inferiors will disobey you. As a result your business will never make much money.
	Any	Either of the Literary stars T'ien K'uei *or* T'ien Yüeh		Your inferiors will bring you success at work.
	Any	Tso Fu *or* Yu Pi		Your inferiors will be intelligent and capable. This will bring you promotion and renown.
	Any	T'ien K'ung Ti Chieh		You will be unable to recover from the loss caused by arguments with your inferiors.
T'ai-yin	Any	Any		The reliability of your inferiors will help you achieve a successful career.
	Any	T'ien Ts'un		You will receive material help from your inferiors.

Star	Degree of influence	Other stars	Degree of influence	Reading
	Any	Fire Star Ringing Star Yang Jen T'o Lo T'ien K'ung Ti Chieh		You will not be welcomed by inferiors or elders. Your relationship with them will limit your career.
	Any	T'ien K'uei T'ien Yüeh Tso Fu *or* Yu Pi		Your inferiors and elders will respect you.
T'an Lang	Any	Any		You will have a great disaster as a result of your inferiors. Their dependence on you will be a burden.
	Any	Any lucky star		(The above reading remains the same.)
	Any	Any unlucky star		(The above reading will deteriorate.)
Chü Men	Any	Any		Your inferiors will cause you disaster and loss.
	Any	Any unlucky star		(The above reading deteriorates even further.)
T'ien Hsiang	Any	Any		You will have helpful and reliable inferiors. This means that your work will be successful.

Star	Degree of influence	Other stars	Degree of influence	Reading
	Any	T'ien Ts'un		Your inferiors will be reliable and will give you material help.
	Any	Fire Star Ringing Star Yang Jen T'o Lo T'ien K'ung Ti Chieh		Your inferiors will cause you loss.
	Any	Either of the Literary stars T'ien K'uei T'ien Yüeh Tso Fu *or* Yu Pi		Your inferiors will be strong. They will help you to achieve promotion.
T'ien Liang	Any	Any		Your inferiors will be reliable and helpful.
	Any	Any unlucky star		(The above reading turns bad.)
Ch'i Sha	Any	Any		Your inferiors will be unreliable. They will be arrogant and rebel against your instructions.
	Any	Any lucky star		(The above reading is still unavoidable.)

Star	Degree of influence	Other stars	Degree of influence	Reading
	Any	Fire Star Ringing Star Yang Jen T'o Lo T'ien K'ung Ti Chieh		Your inferiors will cause you disaster and loss.
P'o Chün	Any	Any		Your inferiors will rebel against you. You will easily make enemies.
	*	Any		You will be supported by your colleagues.
Fire Star *or* **Ringing Star**	Any	Any		You will be very kind to your inferiors but they will treat you as an enemy. This will bring you misfortune.
	Any	Either of the Literary stars		You will lose a lot of money.
	Any	Yang Jen T'o Lo		You are likely to quarrel with your inferiors, which will cause you loss.
	Any	T'ien K'uei T'ien Yüeh		Your relationship with your inferiors is quarrelsome and suspicious.
	Any	Tso Fu *or* Yu Pi		You will have no good inferiors to help you.

Star	Degree of influence	Other stars	Degree of influence	Reading
	Any	T'ien K'ung Ti Chieh		Your inferiors will cause you trouble.
Wen Ch'ü *or* **Wen Ch'ang**	Any	Any		Your inferiors and elders will be reliable and helpful.
	–	Any		(The lucky reading above deteriorates.)
Yang Jen *or* **T'o Lo**	Any	Any		Lack of support from inferiors leads to tension and failure.
T'ien K'uei *or* **T'ien Yüeh**		Any		Your inferiors will support you and help you to gain promotion.
Tso Fu *or* **Yu Pi**		Any		Your inferiors and elders will have the same aims – to maintain your good position and renown.
		T'ien K'ung Ti Chieh		Although your elders and inferiors will support you they will bring you no real benefit.
T'ien K'ung *or* **Ti Chieh**		Any		Your inferiors will rebel against you. They will bring you disaster and harm you.

Star	Degree of influence	Other stars	Degree of influence	Reading
T'ien Ts'un		Any		Your inferiors will give you financial support.
		T'ien K'ung Ti Chieh		Your inferiors will not give you financial support.
Hua Chi		Any		Because your inferiors rebel, you will suffer great loss.

THE OFFICIALS' PALACE

The Officials' Palace is concerned with how you relate to older people. It is also concerned with your career – is it fortunate or not?

The stars which bring extremely good luck in the Officials' Palace are:

Tzu Wei (Purple Star)
Lien Chen (Pure Virtue)
T'ien Ts'un (Heavenly Store)
T'ien K'uei (Heavenly Leader)
Tso Fu (Left Assistant)
Yu Pi (Right Assistant)
T'ai-yang (Sun)
T'ien Hsiang (Heavenly Minister)
Wen Ch'ü (Literary Music)
Wen Ch'ang (Literary Prosperity)
T'ien Yüeh (Heavenly Halberd)
Hua Ch'üan (Transforming Authority)

The stars which bring moderately good luck are:

T'ien Chi (Heavenly Secret)
T'ien T'ung (Heavenly Unity)
T'ai-yin (Moon)
Chü Men (Great Door)
Ch'i Sha (Seven Killings)
Hua K'o (Transforming Examination Class)
P'o Chün (Broken Army)
Wu Ch'ü (Military Music)
T'ien Fu (Southern Star)
T'an Lang (Greedy Wolf)
T'ien Liang (Heavenly Roof-Beam)
Hua Lu (Transforming Salary)

The stars which bring bad luck are:

Fire Star
Ringing Star
Yang Jen (Sheep-Blade)
T'o Lo (Hump-Back)

The stars which bring extremely bad luck are:

T'ien K'ung (Heavenly Void)   Ti Chieh (Earthly Robbery)

Star	Degree of influence	Other stars which appear in the Officials' Palace	Degree of influence	Reading
Tzu Wei	Any	Any		You will be a skilled and expert chairman, director, government official or administrator. Your work will be successful.
	Any	T'ien Fu T'ien Hsiang		Your authority will be great and your position high. You will work in financial affairs or politics. You will become well known and receive a good income.
	Any	Ch'i Sha P'o Chün		You will have unexpected success.
	Any	T'an Lang		You may use the opposite sex to gain promotion.
	Any	T'ien Ts'un		You will be promoted to a high position and acquire great wealth.
	Any	Fire Star Ringing Star Yang Jen T'o Lo T'ien K'ung Ti Chieh		Your standard of living will be average.

Star	Degree of influence	Other stars	Degree of influence	Reading
	Any	Literary stars T'ien K'uei T'ien Yüeh Tso Fu *or* Yu Pi		Your business will be favoured with good luck. You will progress smoothly to success.
T'ien Chi	Any	Any		You will have success in religious, educational, academic or cultural work.
	Any	T'ai-yin *or* Chü Men	☆	You will be well known in a distant place.
	Any	T'ai-yin *or* Chü Men	+	Although you will be well known in a distant place, your renown will not last long.
	Any	T'ien Liang T'ien Ts'un		You will have a good position and authority. You will make progress in politics or financial affairs.
	Any	Fire Star Ringing Star Yang Jen T'o Lo T'ien K'ung Ti Chieh		You will work extremely hard but will have difficult times. You will not be able to develop your work.

Star	Degree of influence	Other stars	Degree of influence	Reading
	Any	Literary stars T'ien Kuei T'ien Yüeh Tso Fu *or* Yu Pi		Although your business appears to be successful you will have no real authority and you will not reap any benefit.
T'ai-yang	Any	Any		You will have a high position and will have success in business or politics.
	Any	T'ai-yin T'ien Ts'un		You will have both a high position in life and a good income.
	*	Chü Men T'ien Liang		You will maintain a good position in life.
	–	Chü Men T'ien Liang		You will lose your position of authority.
	Any	Fire Star Ringing Star Yang Jen T'o Lo T'ien K'ung Ti Chieh		You will have an unstable and changeable life – like a boat bobbing up and down in the water without an anchor.
	Any	Literary stars T'ien K'uei T'ien Yüeh Tso Fu *or* Yu Pi		You will have a stable livelihood, not floating about without an anchor. You will work methodically and will be successful.

Star	Degree of influence	Other stars	Degree of influence	Reading
Wu Ch'ü	Any	Any		You will be successful in finance, industry and the transport business.
	Any	T'ien Fu T'ien Ts'un		You will be promoted and your life will be prosperous.
	Any	Ch'i Sha T'ien Hsiang		If you want to maintain your authority and be successful, you should leave your home town.
	Any	T'an Lang P'o Chün		Because you become involved in corruption you will lose your job if it is connected with politics. However, if you work in finance in a foreign country, you will be successful.
	Any	Fire Star Ringing Star Yang Jen T'o Lo		You will not have an outstanding life or be able to develop your business interests very far.

Star	Degree of influence	Other stars	Degree of influence	Reading
	Any	Either of the Literary stars T'o Fu *or* Yu Pi		You will be very lucky. You will be particularly successful if you work in an occupation related to finance.
		T'ien K'uei T'ien Yüeh		All aspects of your life will be stable and without any untoward events.
		T'ien K'ung Ti Chieh		You will work very hard but without reward and will have a harsh life.
T'ien T'ung	Any	Any		You will be successful in your career if you choose to work in a service industry or a career involving handicrafts.
	*	T'ai-yin Ch'u Men		As you grow older your business will improve by leaps and bounds.
	–	T'ai-yin Chü Men		You will have an uneventful life with no particular successes or failures.
	Any	T'ien Liang T'ien Ts'un		You will have authority and wealth.

Star	Degree of influence	Other stars	Degree of influence	Reading
	Any	Fire Star Ringing Star Yang Jen T'o Lo T'ien K'ung Ti Chieh		There will be many unexpected events in your life and a lot of bad luck.
	Any	Either of the Literary stars T'ien K'uei T'ien Yüeh Tso Fu *or* Yu Pi		You will achieve fame and have a good position.
Lien Chen	Any	Any		If you work in a large corporation you will have a senior position but, like the flower that opens only for the shortest time at night and then dies, so your position will be short-lived.
	Any	T'ien Ts'un		You will be rich and have good health, but you will not be well known.
	Any	P'o Chün		In your livelihood you will experience ups and downs and be generally unstable.

Star	Degree of influence	Other stars	Degree of influence	Reading
	Any	T'ien Fu T'ien Hsiang		You will have a good position in your job and eventually you will achieve fame and wealth.
	Any	T'an Lang Ch'i Sha		You will be very successful in an unusual form of business or trade and receive a large income from it. However, you will be unsuccessful if you go into politics.
	Any	Fire Star Ringing Star Yang Jen T'o Lo T'ien K'ung Ti Chieh		You will have an unsteady career and experience fluctuating luck.
		Literary stars T'ien K'uei T'ien Yüeh Tso Fu *or* Yu Pi		You will be promoted to a senior position in your job.
T'ien Fu	Any	Any		You will be successful in politics and business.
	Any	Any lucky star		Your success will be greater than the above case and will come to you earlier in life.
	Any	Any unlucky star		Your success will be late in coming.

Star	Degree of influence	Other stars	Degree of influence	Reading
	Any	T'ien K'ung Ti Chieh		You will have an uneventful life.
T'ai-yin	Any	Any		You will be successful in the building industry or government service.
	Any	Any lucky star		You will have the chance of promotion.
	* ☆	Any		
	Any	Any unlucky star		You will swing between success and failure.
	+ –	Any		
T'an Lang	Any	Any		You will have success in entertainment or cultural work.
	Any	T'ien Ts'un		You will become wealthy from entertainment or cultural work.
	Any	Fire Star Ringing Star Tso Fu *or* Yu Pi		You will have a managerial role in a financial business.
	Any	Either of the Literary stars T'ien K'uei T'ien Yüeh		You will have an influential role in politics.
	Any	Yang Jen T'o Lo T'ien K'ung Ti Chieh		Your life will be average.

Star	Degree of influence	Other stars	Degree of influence	Reading
Chü Men	Any	Any		If you use your intellience, and work either as a judge, in specialized study or in a business enterprise, you will have great success.
	Any	T'ien Ts'un		You will be successful in business and earn a lot of money.
	Any	Fire Star Ringing Star Yang Jen T'o Lo T'ien K'ung Ti Chieh		You will change jobs many times.
	Any	Either of the Literary stars T'ien K'uei T'ien Yüeh Tso Fu or Yu Pi		Whatever your job, you will be successful.
T'ien Hsiang	Any	Any		You will be successful in medicine, finance, or politics.
		Fire Star Ringing Star Yang Jen T'o Lo T'ien K'ung Ti Chieh		Whatever your job, there will be no harmony between you and your workmates. You may be cheated or lose money.

Star	Degree of influence	Other stars	Degree of influence	Reading
	Any	Literary stars T'ien K'uei T'ien Yüeh Tso Fu *or* Yu Pi		You will make great strides in politics.
T'ien Liang	Any	Any		You will go far in religion, academia, public sanitation, business, the civil service or the military.
	Any	T'ien Ts'un		You will earn a lot of money.
	Any	Fire Star Ringing Star Yang Jen T'o Lo T'ien K'ung Ti Chieh		Your life and fortune will be average.
	Any	Either of the Literary stars T'ien K'uei T'ien Yüeh Tso Fu *or* Yu Pi		You will have success in politics.
Ch'i Sha	Any	Any		You will have great success in heavy industry, the police force or the army. This star remains unaffected by other lucky or unlucky stars.

Star	Degree of influence	Other stars	Degree of influence	Reading
P'o Chün	Any	Any		You will be successful in transport, the army or the police force.
	Any	Fire Star Ringing Star Yang Jen T'o Lo T'ien K'ung Ti Chieh		You will make little progress at work.
	Any	Literary stars T'ien K'uei T'ien Yüeh		You will be promoted to a high position at work.
Fire Star *or* **Ringing Star**	Any	Any		When young your job will be unstable. In middle age it will become stable.
	+ −	Any		Your fortune fluctuates between success and failure.
	Any	Either of the Literary stars T'ien K'ung Ti Chieh		Your life will be average.
	Any	T'ien K'uei T'ien Yüeh Tso Fu *or* Yu Pi		You will have success in commerce or finance.

Star	Degree of influence	Other stars	Degree of influence	Reading
Wen Ch'ü *or* **Wen Ch'ang**	Any	Any		You will have great success in skilled academic or cultural work.
	–	Any		You have no success in the above types of work.
Yang Jen *or* **T'o Lo**	Any	Any		You will have success in the army or police force.
	–	Any		You will have no success in these types of work.
	Any	T'ien K'ung Ti Chieh		You will die while at work.
T'ien Ts'un		Any		You will have success in finance.
		T'ien K'ung Ti Chieh		You will have no success in finance.
T'ien K'uei *or* **T'ien Yüeh**		Any		Your superiors will be happy with your work. This will lead to promotion earlier than usual. You will be successful in politics.
Tso Fu *or* **Yu Pi**		Any		You will have success in politics. Your inferiors will respect you. Your colleagues will give you good recommendations.

Star	Degree of influence	Other stars	Degree of influence	Reading
T'ien K'ung or **Ti Chieh**		Any		Whatever your career, you will have a managerial role.
Hua Ch'üan		Any		Whatever your career, you will have a managerial role.
Hua Chi		Any		Your fortunes will fluctuate. At times you will keep your head above water and at times go under.

THE PROPERTY PALACE

The Property Palace is concerned with your surroundings and situation at home and how much property you own.

The stars which bring extremely good luck in the Property Palace are:

Wu Ch'ü (Military Music)
T'ai-yin (Moon)

T'ien Fu (Southern Star)
T'ien Ts'un (Heavenly Store)

The stars which bring moderately good luck are:

Tzu Wei (Purple Star)
T'ien T'ung (Heavenly Unity)
T'ien Hsiang (Heavenly Minister)
Tso Fu (Left Assistant)
Yu Pi (Right Assistant)
T'ien Liang (Heavenly Roof-Beam)

T'ai-yang (Sun)
Ch'i Sha (Seven Killings)
Wen Ch'ü (Literary Music)
Wen Ch'ang (Literary Prosperity)
T'ien K'uei (Heavenly Leader)
T'ien Yüeh (Heavenly Halberd)

The stars which bring bad luck are:

T'ien Chi (Heavenly Secret)
Chü Men (Great Door)
Fire Star
Ringing Star

Lien Chen (Pure Virtue)
P'o Chün (Broken Army)
Yang Jen (Sheep-Blade)
T'o Lo (Hump-Back)

The stars which bring extremely bad luck are:

T'an Lang (Greedy Wolf)
Ti Chieh (Earthly Robbery)

T'ien K'ung (Heavenly Void)
Hua Chi (Transforming Jealousy)

Star	Degree of influence	Other stars which appear in the Property Palace	Degree of influence	Reading
Tzu Wei	Any	Any		You will own a lot of property.
	Any	T'ien Fu T'ien Ts'un		You will own many properties. The number will increase every year.
	Any	T'an Lang P'o Chün		You will have few properties; even if you do have several properties you will eventually lose some.
	Any	T'ien Hsiang Ch'i Sha		You will own a moderate amount of property.
	Any	Literary stars T'ien K'uei T'ien Yüeh Tso Fu *or* Yu Pi		You will gain more property and its value will increase greatly.
T'ien Chi	Any	Any		Although at first you sell all your property, as time goes on you will acquire more.
	*	Chü Men T'ai-yin		You will be able to keep the property that you inherit in the family.
	–	Chü Men T'ai-yin		You will need to sell the property that you inherit.

Star	Degree of influence	Other stars	Degree of influence	Reading
	Any	T'ien Liang T'ien Ts'un		You will start buying property when you are young and will increase your holding annually.
	Any	Fire Star Ringing Star Yang Jen T'o Lo T'ien K'ung Ti Chieh		You will not own any property.
	Any	T'ien K'uei T'ien Yüeh Tso Fu or Yu Pi		You will possess a lot of property.
T'ai-yang	Any	Any		You will inherit some property and will increase the amount during your lifetime.
	–	Any		In middle age your property holdings will decrease.
	*	T'ien Liang Chü Men		You will be able to keep the property that you inherit and increase its value.
	–	T'ien Liang Chü Men		You will need to sell all your inherited property.

Star	Degree of influence	Other stars	Degree of influence	Reading
	Any	T'ai-yin T'ien Ts'un		From your early years you will buy houses and land, so that by your middle years you will have amassed a large amount of property.
	Any	Fire Star Ringing Star Yang Jen T'o Lo T'ien K'ung Ti Chieh		You will never have property.
	Any	Either of the Literary stars Tso Fu *or* Yu Pi		You will own a lot of property.
Wu Ch'ü	Any	Any		You will own a lot of property.
	Any	T'ien Fu T'ien Ts'un Fire Star Ringing Star Either of the Literary stars		You will buy a lot of property.
	Any	T'an Lang T'ien Hsiang T'ien K'uei T'ien Yüeh Tso Fu *or* Yu Pi		By the time you reach old age you will possess a lot of property.
	Any	Ch'i Sha Yang Jen T'o Lo		Because you have no interest in acquiring property, you will own none.

Star	Degree of influence	Other stars	Degree of influence	Reading
	Any	P'o Chün T'ien K'ung Ti Chieh		You will sell all the property that you inherit.
T'ien T'ung	* ☆	Any		You will not own any property until you are middle-aged.
	* ☆	Any lucky star		You will own property when you are young.
	–	Any		You will not own any property.
Lien Chen	Any	Any		You will probably not inherit any property. If you do inherit property, you will have to sell it quickly.
	Any	T'ien Fu Ch'i Sha Either of the Literary stars T'ien K'uei T'ien Yüeh Tso Fu or Yu Pi T'ien Ts'un		You will not only inherit property, but will be able to buy more throughout your life.
	Any	T'an Lang T'ien Hsiang P'o Chün Fire Star Ringing Star Yang Jen T'o Lo T'ien K'ung Ti Chieh		You will not be able to keep the property that you inherit. You will have to sell it.

Star	Degree of influence	Other stars	Degree of influence	Reading
T'ien Fu	Any	Any		You will become wealthy through buying property and increasing your stock each year.
	Any	T'ien Ts'un		You will start to buy property at an early age. By the time you reach middle age you will have a large holding.
	Any	Fire Star Ringing Star Yang Jen T'o Lo		You will buy and sell property frequently.
		Either of the Literary stars T'ien K'uei T'ien Yüeh		By old age you will have acquired a lot of property.
		Tso Fu *or* Yu Pi		You will own a lot of property and will live in a particularly splendid house.
		T'ien K'ung Ti Chieh		You will not have any property. Should you inherit any, you will have to sell it.
T'ai-yin	* ☆	Any lucky star		You will not only own a house but land too.

Star	Degree of influence	Other stars	Degree of influence	Reading
	–	Any unlucky star		You will not own any property, or you will have to sell what property you do own.
T'an Lang	Any	Any		You will not own any property.
	Any	T'ien Ts'un		By the time you reach old age you will own some property.
	Any	Fire Star Ringing Star		You will own a lot of property but will need to take care of it because there is a danger of fire.
	Any	Either of the Literary stars Tso Fu or Yu Pi		By the time you reach old age you will have acquired some property.
	Any	Yang Jen T'o Lo T'ien K'ung Ti Chieh		You will never own property.
Chü Men	*	Any lucky star		You will be able to earn money easily and buy property.
	–	Any unlucky star		You will never own property.
T'ien Hsiang	Any	Any lucky star		You will own property throughout your life and will greatly benefit from it.

Star	Degree of influence	Other stars	Degree of influence	Reading
	Any	Any unlucky star		You will own nothing.
T'ien Liang	Any	Any		You will own some property.
	Any	Any lucky star		(The above reading is improved.)
	Any	Any unlucky star		You will own very little property.
Ch'i Sha or P'o Chün	Any	Any		You will be able to keep the property that you have inherited, but will not inherit any more.
	+ –	Any unlucky star		You will have to sell the property that you have.
Fire Star or Ringing Star	Any	Any		You will either give away most of your inherited property or have to sell much of it.
	Any	Either of the Literary stars Yang Jen T'o Lo T'ien K'ung Ti Chieh		You will not be able to buy any property.
	Any	T'ien Ts'un T'ien K'uei T'ien Yüeh Tso Fu or Yu Pi		You will increase your stock of property.

Star	Degree of influence	Other stars	Degree of influence	Reading
Wen Ch'ü *or* **Wen Ch'ang**	Any	Any		You will be able to maintain your inherited property and will acquire a little more.
	–	Yang Jen T'o Lo T'ien K'ung Ti Chieh		Your stock of property will decrease.
Yang Jen *or* **T'o Lo**	Any	Any		You will lose your property.
	☆	Any		You will gain more property.
T'ien Ts'un		Any		You will not only possess a lot of property but will benefit financially from it.
T'ien K'uei *or* **T'ien Yüeh**		Any		You will be able to maintain your inherited property: a farm and farmhouse.
Tso Fu *or* **Yu Pi**		Any		You will be able to keep your inherited property.
T'ien K'ung *or* **Ti Chieh**		Any		You will lose your inherited property.
Hua Chi		Any		You will not be able to buy any property.

THE FORTUNE AND VIRTUE PALACE

The Fortune and Virtue Palace is concerned with what generally interest you – your hobbies and how you enjoy yourself.

The stars which bring extremely good luck in the Fortune and Virtue Palace are:

T'ien T'ung (Heavenly Unity)
T'ai-yin (Moon)
T'ien Liang (Heavenly Roof-Beam)
Wen Ch'ü (Literary Music)
Wen Ch'ang (Literary Prosperity)
T'ien Fu (Southern Star)
T'ien Hsiang (Heavenly Minister)
T'ien K'uei (Heavenly Leader)
T'ien Yüeh (Heavenly Halberd)
Tso Fu (Left Assistant)
Yu Pi (Right Assistant)

The stars which bring moderately good luck are:

Tzu Wei (Purple Star)
T'ien Ts'un (Heavenly Store)
T'ai-yang (Sun)
I-ma (Travelling Star)

The stars which bring bad luck are:

T'ien Chi (Heavenly Secret)
Lien Chen (Pure Virtue)
Fire Star
Ringing Star
T'ien Yao (Heavenly Beauty)
Wu Ch'ü (Military Music)
Ch'i Sha (Seven Killings)
Yang Jen (Sheep-Blade)
T'o Lo (Hump-Back)

The stars which bring extremely bad luck are:

T'an Lang (Greedy Wolf)   Chü Men (Great Door)
P'o Chün (Brokent Army)   T'ien K'ung (Heavenly Void)
Ti Chieh (Earthly Robbery)   Hua Chi (Transforming
                                 Jealousy)

Star	Degree of influence	Other stars which appear in the Fortune and Virtue Palace	Degree of influence	Reading
Tzu Wei	Any	Any		You want to work on projects connected with charity or community work without regard to personal financial rewards. You like to make friends with famous people and those in important positions.
	Any	T'ien Fu T'ien Hsiang T'ien Ts'un Either of the Literary stars T'ien K'uei T'ien Yüeh Tso Fu *or* Yu Pi		You will be comfortably off and will have no need to worry about your living expenses.
	Any	T'an Lang Ch'i Sha P'o Chün Fire Star Ringing Star Yang Jen T'o Lo T'ien K'ung Ti Chieh		You will have a hard life with little enjoyment.

Star	Degree of influence	Other stars	Degree of influence	Reading
T'ien Chi	Any	Any		You are very interested in religious, literary and cultural studies. When you are young you will have to work very hard but you will be comfortably off from your middle years onwards.
	Any	Any lucky star		It will not be material pleasures that interest you but those of the spirit. Relationships with people and ideas will form the main source of your enjoyment. You will be happy throughout your life.
	Any	Any unlucky star		Your spirit will suffer and you will have a hard life. You will not be interested in enjoying yourself.
T'ai-yang	Any	Any		You are very fond of politics and like to make friends with people in high positions.

Star	Degree of influence	Other stars	Degree of influence	Reading
Wu Ch'ü	Any	Any		You will have such a busy life that you will not have any time to enjoy yourself.
T'ien T'ung	Any	Any		You enjoy making lots of friends, especially members of the opposite sex.
Lien Chen	Any	Any	.	You are particularly fond of running and enjoy training hard. You will work in an active job.
T'ien Fu	Any	Any		You prefer to live in the countryside rather than the town. You enjoy eating and drinking.
	Any	T'ien K'ung Ti Chieh		You will not have much money and will suffer from stomach or digestive troubles. This means that you will not be interested in enjoying yourself.
T'ai-yin	Any	Any		You enjoy living in the countryside and will be involved in religious affairs.
T'an Lang	Any	Any		You will have a hard life with little enjoyment.

Star	Degree of influence	Other stars	Degree of influence	Reading
Chü Men	Any	Any		You will be so busy that you will not have time to enjoy yourself.
T'ien Liang	Any	Any		You will be interested in education and cultural affairs. You enjoy writing and will want to publish your work.
Ch'i Sha	Any	Any		You will have a hard life without enjoyment.
P'o Chün	Any	Any		You will work very hard and be very busy all your life. You will experience little enjoyment.
Fire Star or **Ringing Star Yang Jen** or **T'o Lo T'ien K'ung Ti Chieh** or **Hua Chi**	Any	Any		You will always be hardworking, so much so that you will not know how to enjoy yourself.
Wen Ch'ü or **Wen Ch'ang**	* ☆	Any		You will be very interested in cultural and artistic affairs. You will enjoy yourself very much.

Star	Degree of influence	Other stars	Degree of influence	Reading
	–	Any unlucky star		Although you have the above interests, you will be unable to follow them up.
T'ien Ts'un		Any		You will have a long and happy life and be very interested in material pleasures, such as clothes, food and drink.
T'ien K'uei or T'ien Yüeh		Any		You like working on community or charity projects.
Tso Fu or Yu Pi		Any		You greatly enjoy your social life, especially meeting the opposite sex.
I-ma		Any		You enjoy travelling and admiring beautiful views.
T'ien Yao		Any		You enjoy making friends with members of the opposite sex.

THE PARENTS' PALACE

The Parents' Palace is concerned with the relationship between you and your parents. This relationship is controlled by your *yuanten* (the predestined attachment between your parents and yourself). If your *yuanten* is strong, you will love one another and stay together. If weak, you will have little feeling for each other and may move away.

This palace is also concerned with how much material benefit and moral support your parents can give you.

The stars which bring extremely good luck in the Parents' Palace are:

T'ai-yang (Sun)
T'ai-yin (Moon)
T'ien Liang (Heavenly Roof-Beam)
T'ien Yüeh (Heavenly Halberd)

T'ien Fu (Southern Star)
T'ien Hsiang (Heavenly Minister)
T'ien K'uei (Heavenly Leader)

The stars which bring moderately good luck are:

Tzu Wei (Purple Star)
T'ien T'ung (Heavenly Unity)
T'ien Ts'un (Heavenly Store)

T'ien Chi (Heavenly Secret)
Wen Ch'ü (Literary Music)
Wen Ch'ang (Literary Prosperity)
Tso Fu (Left Assistant)
Yu Pi (Right Assistant)

The star which brings bad luck is:

Wu Ch'ü (Military Music)*

* This is generally a lucky star.

The stars which bring extremely bad luck are:

Lien Chen (Pure Virtue)	T'an Lang (Greedy Wolf)
Chü Men (Great Door)	Ch'i Sha (Seven Killings)
P'o Chün (Broken Army)	Yang Jen (Sheep-Blade)
Fire Star	T'o Lo (Hump-Back)
Ringing Star	T'ien K'ung (Heavenly Void)
Ti Chieh (Earthly Robbery)	Hua Chi (Transforming Jealousy)

Star	Degree of influence	Other stars which appear in the Parents' Palace	Degree of influence	Reading
Tzu Wei	Any	Any		You will receive many benefits from your parents.
	Any	T'ien Fu T'ien Hsiang Either of the Literary stars T'ien Ts'un T'ien K'uei T'ien Yüeh Tso Fu or Yu Pi		You will receive great moral and material support from your parents.
	Any	T'an Lang		Although you live with your parents, in spirit and feeling you are not in harmony with them.
	Any	Ch'i Sha P'o Chün		There will be a rift between you and one of your parents.
	Any	Fire Star Ringing Star Yang Jen T'o Lo T'ien K'ung Ti Chieh		Your *yuanten* (predestined attachment) with your parents is weak. You may live apart from your parents or one of them may die.
T'ien Chi	Any	Any		Your parents will give you a good education but they will not spoil you.

Star	Degree of influence	Other stars	Degree of influence	Reading
	Any	T'ai-yin T'ien Liang T'ien Ts'un		You will receive long-term benefits from your parents. This will last until your middle years.
	Any	Chü Men		You will only receive short-term benefits from your parents, or when you are young you may lose your father . or mother.
	Any	Fire Star Ringing Star Yang Jen T'o Lo T'ien K'ung Ti Chieh		You may lose one of your parents while you are young.
		Either of the Literary stars T'ien K'uei T'ien Yüeh Tso Fu or Yu Pi		Your parents are well educated. They have taught you well and this means that your business will expand and be successful.
T'ai-yang	Any	Any		You will receive many benefits from your father.
	–	Any		Your father will die or you will live apart from him when you are young.

Star	Degree of influence	Other stars	Degree of influence	Reading
	Any	T'ai-yin T'ien Liang T'ien Ts'un		Your parents will help and support you.
	Any	Chü Men		Your relationship with your father is tense and argumentative.
	Any	Fire Star Ringing Star Yang Jen T'o Lo T'ien K'ung Ti Chieh		When young you will have no *yuanten* (predestined attachment) with your father. You may live apart from him or he may not take care of you.
	Any	Either of the Literary stars T'ien K'uei T'ien Yüeh Tso Fu *or* Yu Pi		Your father will be a great help to you and will bring you social advantages.
Wu Ch'ü	Any	Any		Your *yuanten* (predestined attachment) is weak and your relationship with your parents is troubled.
	Any	T'ien Fu T'ien Hsiang T'ien Ts'un		Your *yuanten* is very strong and you are in harmony with your parents.

Star	Degree of influence	Other stars	Degree of influence	Reading
	Any	T'an Lang Ch'i Sha P'o Chün		You are not close to your parents and and will either live apart from them or one of them may die.
	Any	Fire Star Ringing Star Yang Jen T'o Lo T'ien K'ung Ti Chieh		When you are young there will be a rift between you and your parents.
	Any	Either of the Literary stars T'ien K'uei T'ien Yüeh Tso Fu *and* Yu Pi		Your parents will not only support you materially but will give you a good education and moral support.
T'ien T'ung	Any	Any		Your mother loves you dearly.
	Any	T'ai-yin T'ien Liang		Both your parents love you dearly.
	Any	Chü Men Fire Star Ringing Star Yang Jen T'o Lo T'ien K'ung Ti Chieh		Your parents do not love you. You are forever arguing. Sometimes you are very rude or cruel to one of your parents.
	Any	Literary stars T'ien Ts'un T'ien K'uei T'ien Yüeh Tso Fu *or* Yu Pi		You will be supported by your parents. They love you and give you material things.

Star	Degree of influence	Other stars	Degree of influence	Reading
Lien Chen	Any	Any		There will be a rift between you and one of your parents.
	Any	T'ien Fu T'ien Hsiang Wen Ch'ü T'ien Ts'un T'ien K'uei T'ien Yüeh Tso Fu *or* Yu Pi		When you are young you will cause your parents to worry. However, there will be no serious rift between you.
	Any	T'an Lang Ch'i Sha P'o Chün Fire Star Ringing Star Yang Jen T'o Lo T'ien K'ung Ti Chieh		When you are young there will be a rift between you and one parent. In middle age you will move away from your parents or one of them will die.
T'ien Fu	Any	Any		You will have great material support from your parents.
	Any	T'ien Ts'un		(As above.)
	Any	Fire Star Ringing Star Yang Jen T'o Lo T'ien K'ung Ti Chieh		You are likely to move away from one or other of your parents or one of them may die.

Star	Degree of influence	Other stars	Degree of influence	Reading
	Any	Either of the Literary stars T'ien K'uei T'ien Yüeh Tso Fu *or* Yu Pi		Your parents will give you many benefits which will enable you to have a comfortable and wealthy life.
T'ai-yin	Any	Any		Your *yuanten* (predestined attachment) with your mother is greater than that with your father.
	+ −	Any		Your *yuanten* with your mother is weak.
	Any	T'ien Ts'un		You will receive substantial material support from your mother.
	Any	Fire Star Ringing Star Yang Jen T'o Lo T'ien K'ung Ti Chieh		When you are young there will be a rift between you and your mother.
	Any	Literary stars T'ien K'uei T'ien Yüeh Tso Fu *or* Yu Pi		Your mother will give you great support. Your business will be prosperous.
T'an Lang	Any	Any		There will be a rift between you and both or one of your parents.

Star	Degree of influence	Other stars	Degree of influence	Reading
	+ −	Any		You have no *yuanten* (predestined attachment) with your parents.
	Any	Literary stars T'ien Ts'un Tso Fu *or* Yu Pi		In later life there will be a rift between you and your parents.
	Any	T'ien K'uei *or* T'ien Yüeh		Your *yuanten* with your parents is strong.
	Any	Fire Star Ringing Star Yang Jen T'o Lo T'ien K'ung *or* Ti Chieh		When young you will be in conflict with your parents.
Chü Men	Any	Any		Your relationship with your parents is unstable and unhappy.
	+ −	Any		There will be a rift between you and your parents and you may harm one of them.
	Any	T'ien Ts'un		(The above reading is improved.)

Star	Degree of influence	Other stars	Degree of influence	Reading
	Any	Fire Star Ringing Star Yang Jen T'o Lo T'ien K'ung *or* Ti Chieh		Your brothers' and sisters' relationship with your parents and yourself will be unstable and argumentative.
	Any	Either of the Literary stars T'ien K'uei T'ien Yüeh Tso Fu *or* Yu Pi		In later life your brothers' and sisters' relationship with you and your parents will be troubled and unhappy.
T'ien Hsiang	Any	Any		Your parents will give you material and moral support. Your *yuanten* (predestined attachment) with your parents is deep.
	Any	T'ien Ts'un		You will receive great benefits from your parents.
	Any	Fire Star Ringing Star Yang Jen T'o Lo T'ien K'ung Ti Chieh		There will be a rift between you and your parents. You may live apart or you may cause your parents to die.

Star	Degree of influence	Other stars	Degree of influence	Reading
		Either of the Literary stars T'ien K'uei T'ien Yüeh Tso Fu *or* Yu Pi		Your parents' support and encouragement helps you to achieve social success.
T'ien Liang	Any	Any		Your parents will be long-lived.
	+ −	Any		In later life there will be a rift between you and your parents.
	Any	T'ien Ts'un		Your parents will offer you substantial material support.
	Any	Fire Star Ringing Star Yang Jen T'o Lo T'ien K'ung *or* Ti Chieh		There will be a rift between you and one parent.
	Any	Literary stars T'ien K'uei T'ien Yüeh Tso Fu *or* Yu Pi		Your parents will be long-lived.
Ch'i Sha	Any	Any		Your parents will be short-lived. There will be a rift between you and one parent.

Star	Degree of influence	Other stars	Degree of influence	Reading
	Any	Any lucky star		(The above reading is unchanged, but may be delayed until later life.)
	Any	Any unlucky star		(The above unlucky reading deteriorates.)
P'o Chün	Any	Any		When young there will be a rift between you and one parent. You may harm them.
	Any	Any unlucky star		(The above reading deteriorates).
Fire Star *or* **Ringing Star**	Any	Any		You have *yuanten* (predestined attachment) with only one parent.
	Any	T'ien K'uei T'ien Yüeh		(The above reading is improved.)
	Any	Any stars other than T'ien K'uei *and* T'ien Yüeh		(The above reading deteriorates.)
Wen Ch'ü *or* **Wen Ch'ang**	Any	Any		You have *yuanten* (predestined attachment) with both parents.
	Any	T'ien K'uei T'ien Yüeh T'ien Ts'un		You will receive many benefits from your parents.

Star	Degree of influence	Other stars	Degree of influence	Reading
	Any	Yang Jen T'o Lo		There will be a rift between you and one parent.
Yang Jen or **T'o Lo**	Any	Any		There will be a rift between you and one parent. You may harm them.
	Any	T'ien K'ung Ti Chieh		There will be a rift between you and your parents.
	Any	T'ien K'ung Ti Chieh and any other lucky star		(The above reading may be delayed.)
T'ien Ts'un		Any		You will receive many benefits from your parents.
		Tso Fu or Yu Pi		Your parents will give you moral rather than material support.
		T'ien K'ung Ti Chieh		When you are young there will be a rift between you and your parents.
T'ien K'uei or **T'ien Yüeh**		Any		Your *yuanten* (predestined attachment) with your parents is strong. You will stay together.
		Tso Fu or Yu Pi		You will receive many benefits from your parents.

Star	Degree of influence	Other stars	Degree of influence	Reading
		T'ien K'ung Ti Chieh		Although T'ien K'ung and Ti Chieh are generally unlucky, they will not harm your parents because T'ien K'uei and T'ien Yüeh are strong lucky stars in this palace.
Tso Fu *or* **Yu Pi**		Any		You have *yuanten* (predestined attachment) with your parents.
T'ien K'ung *or* **Ti Chieh**		Any		Your *yuanten* (predestined attachment) with one parent is weak.
Hua Chi		Any		There will be a rift between you and one of your parents.

The Calendar Tables

Much of the material covered below has appeared earlier in the book; it is repeated here in this form to assist the reader to use the Calendar Tables as easily as possible.

The Chinese calendar uses the sexagenary cycle of Heavenly Stems and Earthly Branches for numbering the years, the months and the days (see pp. 10–17). In the pages that follow we have listed the Chinese equivalents for the Western calendar dates from 5 February 1924 to 23 January 2001. To simplify matters, in the main body of the tables we have used codes for the Heavenly Stems and Earthly Branches, and these are shown below.

The tables are divided into years according to the Chinese calendar, and each year is named by a Heavenly Stem and an Earthly Branch from the sexagenary cycle. Thus the first year, which runs from the Western date of 5 February 1924 to 23 January 1925, is Chia Tzu; the next year, from 24 January 1925 to 12 February 1926, is Yi Ch'ou; the next, from 13 February 1926 to 1 February 1927, is Ping Yin; and so on. To find the characters for your year of birth, simply turn to your Western birthday in the tables and look for the heading to the Chinese year in which it appears. For example, someone born on 10 January 1925 comes under the year Chia Tzu.

In the left-hand column of the tables are listed the days and months according to the Western calendar, 10.1 meaning 10 January. The next column gives the corresponding days and months for the Chinese calendar. Thus, in 1925, 10 January becomes 16.12 in the Chinese calendar, that is, the 16th day of the 12th month. Therefore someone born on 10 January 1925 was born on the 16th day of the 12th month in Chia Tzu year.

Note that the relationship between the Western and the Chinese calendars varies from year to year. The 10th of January will not invariably be the 16th day of the 12th month. This is because in the Chinese system the number of days in a year fluctuates between 353 and 355, with an additional intercalary month every two to three

the calendars in line (see p. 13). Thus in the tables you
so often a year with two months which have the same
.econd of which is set in italic – this is the extra month.
variable number of days in the year is also the reason why the
Chinese New Year changes from year to year in relation to the
Western calendar, falling anywhere between 21 January and 20
February.

The third column of the tables lists the codes (see below) for the
Heavenly Stems and Earthly Branches for the months. In the
example already given, 10 January 1925 has the code D2, which
gives the Heavenly Stem Ting and the Earthly Branch Ch'ou.
These are the characters for the 12th month in Chia Tzu year.

In the fourth column are the codes for the Heavenly Stems and
Earthly Branches for the days. For 10 January 1925 the code is A7,
which gives the Heavenly Stem Chia and the Earthly Branch Wu.
These are the characters for the 16th day of the 12th month in Chia
Tzu year.

The characters for the 'hours' are not listed in the Calendar – to
do so would have meant including twelve separate entries for each
day. The characters for the 'hours' can be found on p. 18.

Finally, in the right-hand column are listed the constellations.
There are twenty-eight in all and they change from day to day. For
10 January 1925 the constellation is Pheasant.

Codes for the Heavenly Stems and Earthly Branches

Heavenly Stems		Earthly Branches	
Code	Character	Code	Character
A	Chia	1	Tzu
B	Yi	2	Ch'ou
C	Ping	3	Yin
D	Ting	4	Mao
E	Mou	5	Ch'en
F	Chi	6	Szu
G	Keng	7	Wu
H	Hsin	8	Wei
J*	Jen	9	Shen
K	Kuei	10	Yu
		11	Hsü
		12	Hai

*To avoid possible confusion with the number 1, we have not used the letter I.

CHIA TZU YEAR

Solar date	Lunar date	Month HS/EB	Day HS/EB	Constellation
1924				
5. 2	1. 1	C3	A3	Pig
6. 2	2. 1	C3	B4	Porcupine
7. 2	3. 1	C3	C5	Wolf
8. 2	4. 1	C3	D6	Dog
9. 2	5. 1	C3	E7	Pheasant
10. 2	6. 1	C3	F8	Cock
11. 2	7. 1	C3	G9	Crow
12. 2	8. 1	C3	H10	Monkey
13. 2	9. 1	C3	J11	Gibbon
14. 2	10. 1	C3	K12	Tapir
15. 2	11. 1	C3	A1	Sheep
16. 2	12. 1	C3	B2	Deer
17. 2	13. 1	C3	C3	Horse
18. 2	14. 1	C3	D4	Stag
19. 2	15. 1	C3	E5	Serpent
20. 2	16. 1	C3	F6	Earthworm
21. 2	17. 1	C3	G7	Crocodile
22. 2	18. 1	C3	H8	Dragon
23. 2	19. 1	C3	J9	Badger
24. 2	20. 1	C3	K10	Hare
25. 2	21. 1	C3	A11	Fox
26. 2	22. 1	C3	B12	Tiger
27. 2	23. 1	C3	C1	Leopard
28. 2	24. 1	C3	D2	Griffon
29. 2	25. 1	C3	E3	Ox
1. 3	26. 1	C3	F4	Bat
2. 3	27. 1	C3	G5	Rat
3. 3	28. 1	C3	H6	Swallow
4. 3	29. 1	C3	J7	Pig
5. 3	1. 2	D4	K8	Porcupine
6. 3	2. 2	D4	A9	Wolf
7. 3	3. 2	D4	B10	Dog
8. 3	4. 2	D4	C11	Pheasant
9. 3	5. 2	D4	D12	Cock
10. 3	6. 2	D4	E1	Crow
11. 3	7. 2	D4	F2	Monkey
12. 3	8. 2	D4	G3	Gibbon
13. 3	9. 2	D4	H4	Tapir
14. 3	10. 2	D4	J5	Sheep
15. 3	11. 2	D4	K6	Deer
16. 3	12. 2	D4	A7	Horse
17. 3	13. 2	D4	B8	Stag
18. 3	14. 2	D4	C9	Serpent
19. 3	15. 2	D4	D10	Earthworm
20. 3	16. 2	D4	E11	Crocodile
21. 3	17. 2	D4	F12	Dragon
22. 3	18. 2	D4	G1	Badger
23. 3	19. 2	D4	H2	Hare
24. 3	20. 2	D4	J3	Fox
25. 3	21. 2	D4	K4	Tiger
26. 3	22. 2	D4	A5	Leopard
27. 3	23. 2	D4	B6	Griffon
28. 3	24. 2	D4	C7	Ox
29. 3	25. 2	D4	D8	Bat
30. 3	26. 2	D4	E9	Rat
31. 3	27. 2	D4	F10	Swallow
1. 4	28. 2	D4	G11	Pig
2. 4	29. 2	D4	H12	Porcupine
3. 4	30. 2	D4	J1	Wolf
4. 4	1. 3	E5	K2	Dog
5. 4	2. 3	E5	A3	Pheasant
6. 4	3. 3	E5	B4	Cock
7. 4	4. 3	E5	C5	Crow
8. 4	5. 3	E5	D6	Monkey
9. 4	6. 3	E5	E7	Gibbon
10. 4	7. 3	E5	F8	Tapir
11. 4	8. 3	E5	G9	Sheep
12. 4	9. 3	E5	H10	Deer
13. 4	10. 3	E5	J11	Horse
14. 4	11. 3	E5	K12	Stag
15. 4	12. 3	E5	A1	Serpent
16. 4	13. 3	E5	B2	Earthworm
17. 4	14. 3	E5	C3	Crocodile
18. 4	15. 3	E5	D4	Dragon
19. 4	16. 3	E5	E5	Badger
20. 4	17. 3	E5	F6	Hare
21. 4	18. 3	E5	G7	Fox
22. 4	19. 3	E5	H8	Tiger
23. 4	20. 3	E5	J9	Leopard
24. 4	21. 3	E5	K10	Griffon
25. 4	22. 3	E5	A11	Ox
26. 4	23. 3	E5	B12	Bat
27. 4	24. 3	E5	C1	Rat
28. 4	25. 3	E5	D2	Swallow
29. 4	26. 3	E5	E3	Pig
30. 4	27. 3	E5	F4	Porcupine
1. 5	28. 3	E5	G5	Wolf
2. 5	29. 3	E5	H6	Dog
3. 5	30. 3	E5	J7	Pheasant
4. 5	1. 4	F6	K8	Cock
5. 5	2. 4	F6	A9	Crow
6. 5	3. 4	F6	B10	Monkey
7. 5	4. 4	F6	C11	Gibbon
8. 5	5. 4	F6	D12	Tapir
9. 5	6. 4	F6	E1	Sheep
10. 5	7. 4	F6	F2	Deer
11. 5	8. 4	F6	G3	Horse
12. 5	9. 4	F6	H4	Stag
13. 5	10. 4	F6	J5	Serpent
14. 5	11. 4	F6	K6	Earthworm
15. 5	12. 4	F6	A7	Crocodile
16. 5	13. 4	F6	B8	Dragon
17. 5	14. 4	F6	C9	Badger
18. 5	15. 4	F6	D10	Hare
19. 5	16. 4	F6	E11	Fox
20. 5	17. 4	F6	F12	Tiger
21. 5	18. 4	F6	G1	Leopard
22. 5	19. 4	F6	H2	Griffon
23. 5	20. 4	F6	J3	Ox
24. 5	21. 4	F6	K4	Bat
25. 5	22. 4	F6	A5	Rat
26. 5	23. 4	F6	B6	Swallow
27. 5	24. 4	F6	C7	Pig
28. 5	25. 4	F6	D8	Porcupine
29. 5	26. 4	F6	E9	Wolf
30. 5	27. 4	F6	F10	Dog
31. 5	28. 4	F6	G11	Pheasant
1. 6	29. 4	F6	H12	Cock
2. 6	1. 5	G7	J1	Crow
3. 6	2. 5	G7	K2	Monkey
4. 6	3. 5	G7	A3	Gibbon
5. 6	4. 5	G7	B4	Tapir
6. 6	5. 5	G7	C5	Sheep
7. 6	6. 5	G7	D6	Deer
8. 6	7. 5	G7	E7	Horse
9. 6	8. 5	G7	F8	Stag
10. 6	9. 5	G7	G9	Serpent
11. 6	10. 5	G7	H10	Earthworm
12. 6	11. 5	G7	J11	Crocodile
13. 6	12. 5	G7	K12	Dragon
14. 6	13. 5	G7	A1	Badger
15. 6	14. 5	G7	B2	Hare
16. 6	15. 5	G7	C3	Fox
17. 6	16. 5	G7	D4	Tiger
18. 6	17. 5	G7	E5	Leopard
19. 6	18. 5	G7	F6	Griffon
20. 6	19. 5	G7	G7	Ox
21. 6	20. 5	G7	H8	Bat
22. 6	21. 5	G7	J9	Rat
23. 6	22. 5	G7	K10	Swallow
24. 6	23. 5	G7	A11	Pig

Solar date	Lunar date	Month HS/EB	Day HS/EB	Constellation	Solar date	Lunar date	Month HS/EB	Day HS/EB	Constellation
25. 6	24. 5	G7	B12	Porcupine	6. 9	8. 8	K10	E1	Badger
26. 6	25. 5	G7	C1	Wolf	7. 9	9. 8	K10	F2	Hare
27. 6	26. 5	G7	D2	Dog	8. 9	10. 8	K10	G3	Fox
28. 6	27. 5	G7	E3	Pheasant	9. 9	11. 8	K10	H4	Tiger
29. 6	28. 5	G7	F4	Cock	10. 9	12. 8	K10	J5	Leopard
30. 6	29. 5	G7	G5	Crow	11. 9	13. 8	K10	K6	Griffon
1. 7	30. 5	G7	H6	Monkey	12. 9	14. 8	K10	A7	Ox
2. 7	1. 6	H8	J7	Gibbon	13. 9	15. 8	K10	B8	Bat
3. 7	2. 6	H8	K8	Tapir	14. 9	16. 8	K10	C9	Rat
4. 7	3. 6	H8	A9	Sheep	15. 9	17. 8	K10	D10	Swallow
5. 7	4. 6	H8	B10	Deer	16. 9	18. 8	K10	E11	Pig
6. 7	5. 6	H8	C11	Horse	17. 9	19. 8	K10	F12	Porcupine
7. 7	6. 6	H8	D12	Stag	18. 9	20. 8	K10	G1	Wolf
8. 7	7. 6	H8	E1	Serpent	19. 9	21. 8	K10	H2	Dog
9. 7	8. 6	H8	F2	Earthworm	20. 9	22. 8	K10	J3	Pheasant
10. 7	9. 6	H8	G3	Crocodile	21. 9	23. 8	K10	K4	Cock
11. 7	10. 6	H8	H4	Dragon	22. 9	24. 8	K10	A5	Crow
12. 7	11. 6	H8	J5	Badger	23. 9	25. 8	K10	B6	Monkey
13. 7	12. 6	H8	K6	Hare	24. 9	26. 8	K10	C7	Gibbon
14. 7	13. 6	H8	A7	Fox	25. 9	27. 8	K10	D8	Tapir
15. 7	14. 6	H8	B8	Tiger	26. 9	28. 8	K10	E9	Sheep
16. 7	15. 6	H8	C9	Leopard	27. 9	29. 8	K10	F10	Deer
17. 7	16. 6	H8	D10	Griffon	28. 9	30. 8	K10	G11	Horse
18. 7	17. 6	H8	E11	Ox	29. 9	1. 9	A11	H12	Stag
19. 7	18. 6	H8	F12	Bat	30. 9	2. 9	A11	J1	Serpent
20. 7	19. 6	H8	G1	Rat	1.10	3. 9	A11	K2	Earthworm
21. 7	20. 6	H8	H2	Swallow	2.10	4. 9	A11	A3	Crocodile
22. 7	21. 6	H8	J3	Pig	3.10	5. 9	A11	B4	Dragon
23. 7	22. 6	H8	K4	Porcupine	4.10	6. 9	A11	C5	Badger
24. 7	23. 6	H8	A5	Wolf	5.10	7. 9	A11	D6	Hare
25. 7	24. 6	H8	B6	Dog	6.10	8. 9	A11	E7	Fox
26. 7	25. 6	H8	C7	Pheasant	7.10	9. 9	A11	F8	Tiger
27. 7	26. 6	H8	D8	Cock	8.10	10. 9	A11	G9	Leopard
28. 7	27. 6	H8	E9	Crow	9.10	11. 9	A11	H10	Griffon
29. 7	28. 6	H8	F10	Monkey	10.10	12. 9	A11	J11	Ox
30. 7	29. 6	H8	G11	Gibbon	11.10	13. 9	A11	K12	Bat
31. 7	30. 6	H8	H12	Tapir	12.10	14. 9	A11	A1	Rat
1. 8	1. 7	J9	J1	Sheep	13.10	15. 9	A11	B2	Swallow
2. 8	2. 7	J9	K2	Deer	14.10	16. 9	A11	C3	Pig
3. 8	3. 7	J9	A3	Horse	15.10	17. 9	A11	D4	Porcupine
4. 8	4. 7	J9	B4	Stag	16.10	18. 9	A11	E5	Wolf
5. 8	5. 7	J9	C5	Serpent	17.10	19. 9	A11	F6	Dog
6. 8	6. 7	J9	D6	Earthworm	18.10	20. 9	A11	G7	Pheasant
7. 8	7. 7	J9	E7	Crocodile	19.10	21. 9	A11	H8	Cock
8. 8	8. 7	J9	F8	Dragon	20.10	22. 9	A11	J9	Crow
9. 8	9. 7	J9	G9	Badger	21.10	23. 9	A11	K10	Monkey
10. 8	10. 7	J9	H10	Hare	22.10	24. 9	A11	A11	Gibbon
11. 8	11. 7	J9	J11	Fox	23.10	25. 9	A11	B12	Tapir
12. 8	12. 7	J9	K12	Tiger	24.10	26. 9	A11	C1	Sheep
13. 8	13. 7	J9	A1	Leopard	25.10	27. 9	A11	D2	Deer
14. 8	14. 7	J9	B2	Griffon	26.10	28. 9	A11	E3	Horse
15. 8	15. 7	J9	C3	Ox	27.10	29. 9	A11	F4	Stag
16. 8	16. 7	J9	D4	Bat	28.10	1.10	B12	G5	Serpent
17. 8	17. 7	J9	E5	Rat	29.10	2.10	B12	H6	Earthworm
18. 8	18. 7	J9	F6	Swallow	30.10	3.10	B12	J7	Crocodile
19. 8	19. 7	J9	G7	Pig	31.10	4.10	B12	K8	Dragon
20. 8	20. 7	J9	H8	Porcupine	1.11	5.10	B12	A9	Badger
21. 8	21. 7	J9	J9	Wolf	2.11	6.10	B12	B10	Hare
22. 8	22. 7	J9	K10	Dog	3.11	7.10	B12	C11	Fox
23. 8	23. 7	J9	A11	Pheasant	4.11	8.10	B12	D12	Tiger
24. 8	24. 7	J9	B12	Cock	5.11	9.10	B12	E1	Leopard
25. 8	25. 7	J9	C1	Crow	6.11	10.10	B12	F2	Griffon
26. 8	26. 7	J9	D2	Monkey	7.11	11.10	B12	G3	Ox
27. 8	27. 7	J9	E3	Gibbon	8.11	12.10	B12	H4	Bat
28. 8	28. 7	J9	F4	Tapir	9.11	13.10	B12	J5	Rat
29. 8	29. 7	J9	G5	Sheep	10.11	14.10	B12	K6	Swallow
30. 8	1. 8	K10	H6	Deer	11.11	15.10	B12	A7	Pig
31. 8	2. 8	K10	J7	Horse	12.11	16.10	B12	B8	Porcupine
1. 9	3. 8	K10	K8	Stag	13.11	17.10	B12	C9	Wolf
2. 9	4. 8	K10	A9	Serpent	14.11	18.10	B12	D10	Dog
3. 9	5. 8	K10	B10	Earthworm	15.11	19.10	B12	E11	Pheasant
4. 9	6. 8	K10	C11	Crocodile	16.11	20.10	B12	F12	Cock
5. 9	7. 8	K10	D12	Dragon	17.11	21.10	B12	G1	Crow

Solar date	Lunar date	Month HS/EB	Day HS/EB	Constellation
18.11	22.10	B12	H2	Monkey
19.11	23.10	B12	J3	Gibbon
20.11	24.10	B12	K4	Tapir
21.11	25.10	B12	A5	Sheep
22.11	26.10	B12	B6	Deer
23.11	27.10	B12	C7	Horse
24.11	28.10	B12	D8	Stag
25.11	29.10	B12	E9	Serpent
26.11	30.10	B12	F10	Earthworm
27.11	1.11	C1	G11	Crocodile
28.11	2.11	C1	H12	Dragon
29.11	3.11	C1	J1	Badger
30.11	4.11	C1	K2	Hare
1.12	5.11	C1	A3	Fox
2.12	6.11	C1	B4	Tiger
3.12	7.11	C1	C5	Leopard
4.12	8.11	C1	D6	Griffon
5.12	9.11	C1	E7	Ox
6.12	10.11	C1	F8	Bat
7.12	11.11	C1	G9	Rat
8.12	12.11	C1	H10	Swallow
9.12	13.11	C1	J11	Pig
10.12	14.11	C1	K12	Porcupine
11.12	15.11	C1	A1	Wolf
12.12	16.11	C1	B2	Dog
13.12	17.11	C1	C3	Pheasant
14.12	18.11	C1	D4	Cock
15.12	19.11	C1	E5	Crow
16.12	20.11	C1	F6	Monkey
17.12	21.11	C1	G7	Gibbon
18.12	22.11	C1	H8	Tapir
19.12	23.11	C1	J9	Sheep
20.12	24.11	C1	K10	Deer
21.12	25.11	C1	A11	Horse
22.12	26.11	C1	B12	Stag
23.12	27.11	C1	C1	Serpent
24.12	28.11	C1	D2	Earthworm
25.12	29.11	C1	E3	Crocodile
26.12	1.12	D2	F4	Dragon
27.12	2.12	D2	G5	Badger
28.12	3.12	D2	H6	Hare
29.12	4.12	D2	J7	Fox
30.12	5.12	D2	K8	Tiger
31.12	6.12	D2	A9	Leopard

1925

Solar date	Lunar date	Month HS/EB	Day HS/EB	Constellation
1. 1	7.12	D2	B10	Griffon
2. 1	8.12	D2	C11	Ox
3. 1	9.12	D2	D12	Bat
4. 1	10.12	D2	E1	Rat
5. 1	11.12	D2	F2	Swallow
6. 1	12.12	D2	G3	Pig
7. 1	13.12	D2	H4	Porcupine
8. 1	14.12	D2	J5	Wolf
9. 1	15.12	D2	K6	Dog
10. 1	16.12	D2	A7	Pheasant
11. 1	17.12	D2	B8	Cock
12. 1	18.12	D2	C9	Crow
13. 1	19.12	D2	D10	Monkey
14. 1	20.12	D2	E11	Gibbon
15. 1	21.12	D2	F12	Tapir
16. 1	22.12	D2	G1	Sheep
17. 1	23.12	D2	H2	Deer
18. 1	24.12	D2	J3	Horse
19. 1	25.12	D2	K4	Stag
20. 1	26.12	D2	A5	Serpent
21. 1	27.12	D2	B6	Earthworm
22. 1	28.12	D2	C7	Crocodile
23. 1	29.12	D2	D8	Dragon

YI CH'OU YEAR

Solar date	Lunar date	Month HS/EB	Day HS/EB	Constellation
24. 1	1. 1	E3	E9	Badger
25. 1	2. 1	E3	F10	Hare
26. 1	3. 1	E3	G11	Fox
27. 1	4. 1	E3	H12	Tiger
28. 1	5. 1	E3	J1	Leopard
29. 1	6. 1	E3	K2	Griffon
30. 1	7. 1	E3	A3	Ox
31. 1	8. 1	E3	B4	Bat
1. 2	9. 1	E3	C5	Rat
2. 2	10. 1	E3	D6	Swallow
3. 2	11. 1	E3	E7	Pig
4. 2	12. 1	E3	F8	Porcupine
5. 2	13. 1	E3	G9	Wolf
6. 2	14. 1	E3	H10	Dog
7. 2	15. 1	E3	J11	Pheasant
8. 2	16. 1	E3	K12	Cock
9. 2	17. 1	E3	A1	Crow
10. 2	18. 1	E3	B2	Monkey
11. 2	19. 1	E3	C3	Gibbon
12. 2	20. 1	E3	D4	Tapir
13. 2	21. 1	E3	E5	Sheep
14. 2	22. 1	E3	F6	Deer
15. 2	23. 1	E3	G7	Horse
16. 2	24. 1	E3	H8	Stag
17. 2	25. 1	E3	J9	Serpent
18. 2	26. 1	E3	K10	Earthworm
19. 2	27. 1	E3	A11	Crocodile
20. 2	28. 1	E3	B12	Dragon
21. 2	29. 1	E3	C1	Badger
22. 2	30. 1	E3	D2	Hare
23. 2	1. 2	F4	E3	Fox
24. 2	2. 2	F4	F4	Tiger
25. 2	3. 2	F4	G5	Leopard
26. 2	4. 2	F4	H6	Griffon
27. 2	5. 2	F4	J7	Ox
28. 2	6. 2	F4	K8	Bat
1. 3	7. 2	F4	A9	Rat
2. 3	8. 2	F4	B10	Swallow
3. 3	9. 2	F4	C11	Pig
4. 3	10. 2	F4	D12	Porcupine
5. 3	11. 2	F4	E1	Wolf
6. 3	12. 2	F4	F2	Dog
7. 3	13. 2	F4	G3	Pheasant
8. 3	14. 2	F4	H4	Cock
9. 3	15. 2	F4	J5	Crow
10. 3	16. 2	F4	K6	Monkey
11. 3	17. 2	F4	A7	Gibbon
12. 3	18. 2	F4	B8	Tapir
13. 3	19. 2	F4	C9	Sheep
14. 3	20. 2	F4	D10	Deer
15. 3	21. 2	F4	E11	Horse
16. 3	22. 2	F4	F12	Stag
17. 3	23. 2	F4	G1	Serpent
18. 3	24. 2	F4	H2	Earthworm
19. 3	25. 2	F4	J3	Crocodile
20. 3	26. 2	F4	K4	Dragon
21. 3	27. 2	F4	A5	Badger
22. 3	28. 2	F4	B6	Hare
23. 3	29. 2	F4	C7	Fox
24. 3	1. 3	G5	D8	Tiger
25. 3	2. 3	G5	E9	Leopard
26. 3	3. 3	G5	F10	Griffon
27. 3	4. 3	G5	G11	Ox
28. 3	5. 3	G5	H12	Bat
29. 3	6. 3	G5	J1	Rat
30. 3	7. 3	G5	K2	Swallow

Solar date	Lunar date	Month HS/EB	Day HS/EB	Constellation
31. 3	8. 3	G5	A3	Pig
1. 4	9. 3	G5	B4	Porcupine
2. 4	10. 3	G5	C5	Wolf
3. 4	11. 3	G5	D6	Dog
4. 4	12. 3	G5	E7	Pheasant
5. 4	13. 3	G5	F8	Cock
6. 4	14. 3	G5	G9	Crow
7. 4	15. 3	G5	H10	Monkey
8. 4	16. 3	G5	J11	Gibbon
9. 4	17. 3	G5	K12	Tapir
10. 4	18. 3	G5	A1	Sheep
11. 4	19. 3	G5	B2	Deer
12. 4	20. 3	G5	C3	Horse
13. 4	21. 3	G5	D4	Stag
14. 4	22. 3	G5	E5	Serpent
15. 4	23. 3	G5	F6	Earthworm
16. 4	24. 3	G5	G7	Crocodile
17. 4	25. 3	G5	H8	Dragon
18. 4	26. 3	G5	J9	Badger
19. 4	27. 3	G5	K10	Hare
20. 4	28. 3	G5	A11	Fox
21. 4	29. 3	G5	B12	Tiger
22. 4	30. 3	G5	C1	Leopard
23. 4	1. 4	H6	D2	Griffon
24. 4	2. 4	H6	E3	Ox
25. 4	3. 4	H6	F4	Bat
26. 4	4. 4	H6	G5	Rat
27. 4	5. 4	H6	H6	Swallow
28. 4	6. 4	H6	J7	Pig
29. 4	7. 4	H6	K8	Porcupine
30. 4	8. 4	H6	A9	Wolf
1. 5	9. 4	H6	B10	Dog
2. 5	10. 4	H6	C11	Pheasant
3. 5	11. 4	H6	D12	Cock
4. 5	12. 4	H6	E1	Crow
5. 5	13. 4	H6	F2	Monkey
6. 5	14. 4	H6	G3	Gibbon
7. 5	15. 4	H6	H4	Tapir
8. 5	16. 4	H6	J5	Sheep
9. 5	17. 4	H6	K6	Deer
10. 5	18. 4	H6	A7	Horse
11. 5	19. 4	H6	B8	Stag
12. 5	20. 4	H6	C9	Serpent
13. 5	21. 4	H6	D10	Earthworm
14. 5	22. 4	H6	E11	Crocodile
15. 5	23. 4	H6	F12	Dragon
16. 5	24. 4	H6	G1	Badger
17. 5	25. 4	H6	H2	Hare
18. 5	26. 4	H6	J3	Fox
19. 5	27. 4	H6	K4	Tiger
20. 5	28. 4	H6	A5	Leopard
21. 5	29. 4	H6	B6	Griffon
22. 5	*1. 4*	*H6*	C7	Ox
23. 5	*2. 4*	*H6*	D8	Bat
24. 5	*3. 4*	*H6*	E9	Rat
25. 5	*4. 4*	*H6*	F10	Swallow
26. 5	*5. 4*	*H6*	G11	Pig
27. 5	*6. 4*	*H6*	H12	Porcupine
28. 5	*7. 4*	*H6*	J1	Wolf
29. 5	*8. 4*	*H6*	K2	Dog
30. 5	*9. 4*	*H6*	A3	Pheasant
31. 5	*10. 4*	*H6*	B4	Cock
1. 6	*11. 4*	*H6*	C5	Crow
2. 6	*12. 4*	*H6*	D6	Monkey
3. 6	*13. 4*	*H6*	E7	Gibbon
4. 6	*14. 4*	*H6*	F8	Tapir
5. 6	*15. 4*	*H6*	G9	Sheep
6. 6	*16. 4*	*H6*	H10	Deer
7. 6	*17. 4*	*H6*	J11	Horse
8. 6	*18. 4*	*H6*	K12	Stag
9. 6	*19. 4*	*H6*	A1	Serpent
10. 6	*20. 4*	*H6*	B2	Earthworm
11. 6	*21. 4*	*H6*	C3	Crocodile
12. 6	*22. 4*	*H6*	D4	Dragon
13. 6	*23. 4*	*H6*	E5	Badger
14. 6	*24. 4*	*H6*	F6	Hare
15. 6	*25. 4*	*H6*	G7	Fox
16. 6	*26. 4*	*H6*	H8	Tiger
17. 6	*27. 4*	*H6*	J9	Leopard
18. 6	*28. 4*	*H6*	K10	Griffon
19. 6	*29. 4*	*H6*	A11	Ox
20. 6	*30. 4*	*H6*	B12	Bat
21. 6	1. 5	J7	C1	Rat
22. 6	2. 5	J7	D2	Swallow
23. 6	3. 5	J7	E3	Pig
24. 6	4. 5	J7	F4	Porcupine
25. 6	5. 5	J7	G5	Wolf
26. 6	6. 5	J7	H6	Dog
27. 6	7. 5	J7	J7	Pheasant
28. 6	8. 5	J7	K8	Cock
29. 6	9. 5	J7	A9	Crow
30. 6	10. 5	J7	B10	Monkey
1. 7	11. 5	J7	C11	Gibbon
2. 7	12. 5	J7	D12	Tapir
3. 7	13. 5	J7	E1	Sheep
4. 7	14. 5	J7	F2	Deer
5. 7	15. 5	J7	G3	Horse
6. 7	16. 5	J7	H4	Stag
7. 7	17. 5	J7	J5	Serpent
8. 7	18. 5	J7	K6	Earthworm
9. 7	19. 5	J7	A7	Crocodile
10. 7	20. 5	J7	B8	Dragon
11. 7	21. 5	J7	C9	Badger
12. 7	22. 5	J7	D10	Hare
13. 7	23. 5	J7	E11	Fox
14. 7	24. 5	J7	F12	Tiger
15. 7	25. 5	J7	G1	Leopard
16. 7	26. 5	J7	H2	Griffon
17. 7	27. 5	J7	J3	Ox
18. 7	28. 5	J7	K4	Bat
19. 7	29. 5	J7	A5	Rat
20. 7	30. 5	J7	B6	Swallow
21. 7	1. 6	K8	C7	Pig
22. 7	2. 6	K8	D8	Porcupine
23. 7	3. 6	K8	E9	Wolf
24. 7	4. 6	K8	F10	Dog
25. 7	5. 6	K8	G11	Pheasant
26. 7	6. 6	K8	H12	Cock
27. 7	7. 6	K8	J1	Crow
28. 7	8. 6	K8	K2	Monkey
29. 7	9. 6	K8	A3	Gibbon
30. 7	10. 6	K8	B4	Tapir
31. 7	11. 6	K8	C5	Sheep
1. 8	12. 6	K8	D6	Deer
2. 8	13. 6	K8	E7	Horse
3. 8	14. 6	K8	F8	Stag
4. 8	15. 6	K8	G9	Serpent
5. 8	16. 6	K8	H10	Earthworm
6. 8	17. 6	K8	J11	Crocodile
7. 8	18. 6	K8	K12	Dragon
8. 8	19. 6	K8	A1	Badger
9. 8	20. 6	K8	B2	Hare
10. 8	21. 6	K8	C3	Fox
11. 8	22. 6	K8	D4	Tiger
12. 8	23. 6	K8	E5	Leopard
13. 8	24. 6	K8	F6	Griffon
14. 8	25. 6	K8	G7	Ox
15. 8	26. 6	K8	H8	Bat
16. 8	27. 6	K8	J9	Rat
17. 8	28. 7	K8	K10	Swallow
18. 8	29. 7	K8	A11	Pig
19. 8	1. 7	A9	B12	Porcupine
20. 8	2. 7	A9	C1	Wolf
21. 8	3. 7	A9	D2	Dog
22. 8	4. 7	A9	E3	Pheasant
23. 8	5. 7	A9	F4	Cock

Solar date	Lunar date	Month HS/EB	Day HS/EB	Constellation
24. 8	6. 7	A9	G5	Crow
25. 8	7. 7	A9	H6	Monkey
26. 8	8. 7	A9	J7	Gibbon
27. 8	9. 7	A9	K8	Tapir
28. 8	10. 7	A9	A9	Sheep
29. 8	11. 7	A9	B10	Deer
30. 8	12. 7	A9	C11	Horse
31. 8	13. 7	A9	D12	Stag
1. 9	14. 7	A9	E1	Serpent
2. 9	15. 7	A9	F2	Earthworm
3. 9	16. 7	A9	G3	Crocodile
4. 9	17. 7	A9	H4	Dragon
5. 9	18. 7	A9	J5	Badger
6. 9	19. 7	A9	K6	Hare
7. 9	20. 7	A9	A7	Fox
8. 9	21. 7	A9	B8	Tiger
9. 9	22. 7	A9	C9	Leopard
10. 9	23. 7	A9	D10	Griffon
11. 9	24. 7	A9	E11	Ox
12. 9	25. 7	A9	F12	Bat
13. 9	26. 7	A9	G1	Rat
14. 9	27. 7	A9	H2	Swallow
15. 9	28. 7	A9	J3	Pig
16. 9	29. 7	A9	K4	Porcupine
17. 9	30. 7	A9	A5	Wolf
18. 9	1. 8	B10	B6	Dog
19. 9	2. 8	B10	C7	Pheasant
20. 9	3. 8	B10	D8	Cock
21. 9	4. 8	B10	E9	Crow
22. 9	5. 8	B10	F10	Monkey
23. 9	6. 8	B10	G11	Gibbon
24. 9	7. 8	B10	H12	Tapir
25. 9	8. 8	B10	J1	Sheep
26. 9	9. 8	B10	K2	Deer
27. 9	10. 8	B10	A3	Horse
28. 9	11. 8	B10	B4	Stag
29. 9	12. 8	B10	C5	Serpent
30. 9	13. 8	B10	D6	Earthworm
1.10	14. 8	B10	E7	Crocodile
2.10	15. 8	B10	F8	Dragon
3.10	16. 8	B10	G9	Badger
4.10	17. 8	B10	H10	Hare
5.10	18. 8	B10	J11	Fox
6.10	19. 8	B10	K12	Tiger
7.10	20. 8	B10	A1	Leopard
8.10	21. 8	B10	B2	Griffon
9.10	22. 8	B10	C3	Ox
10.10	23. 8	B10	D4	Bat
11.10	24. 8	B10	E5	Rat
12.10	25. 8	B10	F6	Swallow
13.10	26. 8	B10	G7	Pig
14.10	27. 8	B10	H8	Porcupine
15.10	28. 8	B10	J9	Wolf
16.10	29. 8	B10	K10	Dog
17.10	30. 8	B10	A11	Pheasant
18.10	1. 9	C11	B12	Cock
19.10	2. 9	C11	C1	Crow
20.10	3. 9	C11	D2	Monkey
21.10	4. 9	C11	E3	Gibbon
22.10	5. 9	C11	F4	Tapir
23.10	6. 9	C11	G5	Sheep
24.10	7. 9	C11	H6	Deer
25.10	8. 9	C11	J7	Horse
26.10	9. 9	C11	K8	Stag
27.10	10. 9	C11	A9	Serpent
28.10	11. 9	C11	B10	Earthworm
29.10	12. 9	C11	C11	Crocodile
30.10	13. 9	C11	D12	Dragon
31.10	14. 9	C11	E1	Badger
1.11	15. 9	C11	F2	Hare
2.11	16. 9	C11	G3	Fox
3.11	17. 9	C11	H4	Tiger
4.11	18. 9	C11	J5	Leopard
5.11	19. 9	C11	K6	Griffon
6.11	20. 9	C11	A7	Ox
7.11	21. 9	C11	B8	Bat
8.11	22. 9	C11	C9	Rat
9.11	23. 9	C11	D10	Swallow
10.11	24. 9	C11	E11	Pig
11.11	25. 9	C11	F12	Porcupine
12.11	26. 9	C11	G1	Wolf
13.11	27. 9	C11	H2	Dog
14.11	28. 9	C11	J3	Pheasant
15.11	29. 9	C11	K4	Cock
16.11	1.10	D12	A5	Crow
17.11	2.10	D12	B6	Monkey
18.11	3.10	D12	C7	Gibbon
19.11	4.10	D12	D8	Tapir
20.11	5.10	D12	E9	Sheep
21.11	6.10	D12	F10	Deer
22.11	7.10	D12	G11	Horse
23.11	8.10	D12	H12	Stag
24.11	9.10	D12	J1	Serpent
25.11	10.10	D12	K2	Earthworm
26.11	11.10	D12	A3	Crocodile
27.11	12.10	D12	B4	Dragon
28.11	13.10	D12	C5	Badger
29.11	14.10	D12	D6	Hare
30.11	15.10	D12	E7	Fox
1.12	16.10	D12	F8	Tiger
2.12	17.10	D12	G9	Leopard
3.12	18.10	D12	H10	Griffon
4.12	19.10	D12	J11	Ox
5.12	20.10	D12	K12	Bat
6.12	21.10	D12	A1	Rat
7.12	22.10	D12	B2	Swallow
8.12	23.10	D12	C3	Pig
9.12	24.10	D12	D4	Porcupine
10.12	25.10	D12	E5	Wolf
11.12	26.10	D12	F6	Dog
12.12	27.10	D12	G7	Pheasant
13.12	28.10	D12	H8	Cock
14.12	29.10	D12	J9	Crow
15.12	30.10	D12	K10	Monkey
16.12	1.11	E1	A11	Gibbon
17.12	2.11	E1	B12	Tapir
18.12	3.11	E1	C1	Sheep
19.12	4.11	E1	D2	Deer
20.12	5.11	E1	E3	Horse
21.12	6.11	E1	F4	Stag
22.12	7.11	E1	G5	Serpent
23.12	8.11	E1	H6	Earthworm
24.12	9.11	E1	J7	Crocodile
25.12	10.11	E1	K8	Dragon
26.12	11.11	E1	A9	Badger
27.12	12.11	E1	B10	Hare
28.12	13.11	E1	C11	Fox
29.12	14.11	E1	D12	Tiger
30.12	15.11	E1	E1	Leopard
31.12	16.11	E1	F2	Griffon

1926

Solar date	Lunar date	Month HS/EB	Day HS/EB	Constellation
1. 1	17.11	E1	G3	Ox
2. 1	18.11	E1	H4	Bat
3. 1	19.11	E1	J5	Rat
4. 1	20.11	E1	K6	Swallow
5. 1	21.11	E1	A7	Pig
6. 1	22.11	E1	B8	Porcupine
7. 1	23.11	E1	C9	Wolf
8. 1	24.11	E1	D10	Dog
9. 1	25.11	E1	E11	Pheasant
10. 1	26.11	E1	F12	Cock
11. 1	27.11	E1	G1	Crow
12. 1	28.11	E1	H2	Monkey
13. 1	29.11	E1	J3	Gibbon
14. 1	1.12	F2	K4	Tapir

Solar date	Lunar date	Month HS/EB	Day HS/EB	Constellation	Solar date	Lunar date	Month HS/EB	Day HS/EB	Constellation
15. 1	2.12	F2	A5	Sheep	30. 1	17.12	F2	F8	Bat
16. 1	3.12	F2	B6	Deer	31. 1	18.12	F2	G9	Rat
17. 1	4.12	F2	C7	Horse	1. 2	19.12	F2	H10	Swallow
18. 1	5.12	F2	D8	Stag	2. 2	20.12	F2	J11	Pig
19. 1	6.12	F2	E9	Serpent	3. 2	21.12	F2	K12	Porcupine
20. 1	7.12	F2	F10	Earthworm	4. 2	22.12	F2	A1	Wolf
21. 1	8.12	F2	G11	Crocodile	5. 2	23.12	F2	B2	Dog
22. 1	9.12	F2	H12	Dragon	6. 2	24.12	F2	C3	Pheasant
23. 1	10.12	F2	J1	Badger	7. 2	25.12	F2	D4	Cock
24. 1	11.12	F2	K2	Hare	8. 2	26.12	F2	E5	Crow
25. 1	12.12	F2	A3	Fox	9. 2	27.12 *	F2	F6	Monkey
26. 1	13.12	F2	B4	Tiger	10. 2	28.12	F2	G7	Gibbon
27. 1	14.12	F2	C5	Leopard	11. 2	29.12	F2	H8	Tapir
28. 1	15.12	F2	D6	Griffon	12. 2	30.12	F2	J9	Sheep
29. 1	16.12	F2	E7	Ox					

PING YIN YEAR

Solar date	Lunar date	Month HS/EB	Day HS/EB	Constellation	Solar date	Lunar date	Month HS/EB	Day HS/EB	Constellation
13. 2	1. 1	G3	K10	Deer	7. 4	25. 2	H4	C3	Gibbon
14. 2	2. 1	G3	A11	Horse	8. 4	26. 2	H4	D4	Tapir
15. 2	3. 1	G3	B12	Stag	9. 4	27. 2	H4	E5	Sheep
16. 2	4. 1	G3	C1	Serpent	10. 4	28. 2	H4	F6	Deer
17. 2	5. 1	G3	D2	Earthworm	11. 4	29. 2	H4	G7	Horse
18. 2	6. 1	G3	E3	Crocodile	12. 4	1. 3	J5	H8	Stag
19. 2	7. 1	G3	F4	Dragon	13. 4	2. 3	J5	J9	Serpent
20. 2	8. 1	G3	G5	Badger	14. 4	3. 3	J5	K10	Earthworm
21. 2	9. 1	G3	H6	Hare	15. 4	4. 3	J5	A11	Crocodile
22. 2	10. 1	G3	J7	Fox	16. 4	5. 3	J5	B12	Dragon
23. 2	11. 1	G3	K8	Tiger	17. 4	6. 3	J5	C1	Badger
24. 2	12. 1	G3	A9	Leopard	18. 4	7. 3	J5	D2	Hare
25. 2	13. 1	G3	B10	Griffon	19. 4	8. 3	J5	E3	Fox
26. 2	14. 1	G3	C11	Ox	20. 4	9. 3	J5	F4	Tiger
27. 2	15. 1	G3	D12	Bat	21. 4	10. 3	J5	G5	Leopard
28. 2	16. 1	G3	E1	Rat	22. 4	11. 3	J5	H6	Griffon
1. 3	17. 1	G3	F2	Swallow	23. 4	12. 3	J5	J7	Ox
2. 3	18. 1	G3	G3	Pig	24. 4	13. 3	J5	K8	Bat
3. 3	19. 1	G3	H4	Porcupine	25. 4	14. 3	J5	A9	Rat
4. 3	20. 1	G3	J5	Wolf	26. 4	15. 3	J5	B10	Swallow
5. 3	21. 1	G3	K6	Dog	27. 4	16. 3	J5	C11	Pig
6. 3	22. 1	G3	A7	Pheasant	28. 4	17. 3	J5	D12	Porcupine
7. 3	23. 1	G3	B8	Cock	29. 4	18. 3	J5	E1	Wolf
8. 3	24. 1	G3	C9	Crow	30. 4	19. 3	J5	F2	Dog
9. 3	25. 1	G3	D10	Monkey	1. 5	20. 3	J5	G3	Pheasant
10. 3	26. 1	G3	E11	Gibbon	2. 5	21. 3	J5	H4	Cock
11. 3	27. 1	G3	F12	Tapir	3. 5	22. 3	J5	J5	Crow
12. 3	28. 1	G3	G1	Sheep	4. 5	23. 3	J5	K6	Monkey
13. 3	29. 1	G3	H2	Deer	5. 5	24. 3	J5	A7	Gibbon
14. 3	1. 2	H4	J3	Horse	6. 5	25. 3	J5	B8	Tapir
15. 3	2. 2	H4	K4	Stag	7. 5	26. 3	J5	C9	Sheep
16. 3	3. 2	H4	A5	Serpent	8. 5	27. 3	J5	D10	Deer
17. 3	4. 2	H4	B6	Earthworm	9. 5	28. 3	J5	E11	Horse
18. 3	5. 2	H4	C7	Crocodile	10. 5	29. 3	J5	F12	Stag
19. 3	6. 2	H4	D8	Dragon	11. 5	30. 3	J5	G1	Serpent
20. 3	7. 2	H4	E9	Badger	12. 5	1. 4	K6	H2	Earthworm
21. 3	8. 2	H4	F10	Hare	13. 5	2. 4	K6	J3	Crocodile
22. 3	9. 2	H4	G11	Fox	14. 5	3. 4	K6	K4	Dragon
23. 3	10. 2	H4	H12	Tiger	15. 5	4. 4	K6	A5	Badger
24. 3	11. 2	H4	J1	Leopard	16. 5	5. 4	K6	B6	Hare
25. 3	12. 2	H4	K2	Griffon	17. 5	6. 4	K6	C7	Fox
26. 3	13. 2	H4	A3	Ox	18. 5	7. 4	K6	D8	Tiger
27. 3	14. 2	H4	B4	Bat	19. 5	8. 4	K6	E9	Leopard
28. 3	15. 2	H4	C5	Rat	20. 5	9. 4	K6	F10	Griffon
29. 3	16. 2	H4	D6	Swallow	21. 5	10. 4	K6	G11	Ox
30. 3	17. 2	H4	E7	Pig	22. 5	11. 4	K6	H12	Bat
31. 3	18. 2	H4	F8	Porcupine	23. 5	12. 4	K6	J1	Rat
1. 4	19. 2	H4	G9	Wolf	24. 5	13. 4	K6	K2	Swallow
2. 4	20. 2	H4	H10	Dog	25. 5	14. 4	K6	A3	Pig
3. 4	21. 2	H4	J11	Pheasant	26. 5	15. 4	K6	B4	Porcupine
4. 4	22. 2	H4	K12	Cock	27. 5	16. 4	K6	C5	Wolf
5. 4	23. 2	H4	A1	Crow	28. 5	17. 4	K6	D6	Dog
6. 4	24. 2	H4	B2	Monkey	29. 5	18. 4	K6	E7	Pheasant

Solar date	Lunar date	Month HS/EB	Day HS/EB	Constellation
30. 5	19. 4	K6	F8	Cock
31. 5	20. 4	K6	G9	Crow
1. 6	21. 4	K6	H10	Monkey
2. 6	22. 4	K6	J11	Gibbon
3. 6	23. 4	K6	K12	Tapir
4. 6	24. 4	K6	A1	Sheep
5. 6	25. 4	K6	B2	Deer
6. 6	26. 4	K6	C3	Horse
7. 6	27. 4	K6	D4	Stag
8. 6	28. 4	K6	E5	Serpent
9. 6	29. 4	K6	F6	Earthworm
10. 6	1. 5	A7	G7	Crocodile
11. 6	2. 5	A7	H8	Dragon
12. 6	3. 5	A7	J9	Badger
13. 6	4. 5	A7	K10	Hare
14. 6	5. 5	A7	A11	Fox
15. 6	6. 5	A7	B12	Tiger
16. 6	7. 5	A7	C1	Leopard
17. 6	8. 5	A7	D2	Griffon
18. 6	9. 5	A7	E3	Ox
19. 6	10. 5	A7	F4	Bat
20. 6	11. 5	A7	G5	Rat
21. 6	12. 5	A7	H6	Swallow
22. 6	13. 5	A7	J7	Pig
23. 6	14. 5	A7	K8	Porcupine
24. 6	15. 5	A7	A9	Wolf
25. 6	16. 5	A7	B10	Dog
26. 6	17. 5	A7	C11	Pheasant
27. 6	18. 5	A7	D12	Cock
28. 6	19. 5	A7	E1	Crow
29. 6	20. 5	A7	F2	Monkey
30. 6	21. 5	A7	G3	Gibbon
1. 7	22. 5	A7	H4	Tapir
2. 7	23. 5	A7	J5	Sheep
3. 7	24. 5	A7	K6	Deer
4. 7	25. 5	A7	A7	Horse
5. 7	26. 5	A7	B8	Stag
6. 7	27. 5	A7	C9	Serpent
7. 7	28. 5	A7	D10	Earthworm
8. 7	29. 5	A7	E11	Crocodile
9. 7	30. 5	A7	F12	Dragon
10. 7	1. 6	B8	G1	Badger
11. 7	2. 6	B8	H2	Hare
12. 7	3. 6	B8	J3	Fox
13. 7	4. 6	B8	K4	Tiger
14. 7	5. 6	B8	A5	Leopard
15. 7	6. 6	B8	B6	Griffon
16. 7	7. 6	B8	C7	Ox
17. 7	8. 6	B8	D8	Bat
18. 7	9. 6	B8	E9	Rat
19. 7	10. 6	B8	F10	Swallow
20. 7	11. 6	B8	G11	Pig
21. 7	12. 6	B8	H12	Porcupine
22. 7	13. 6	B8	J1	Wolf
23. 7	14. 6	B8	K2	Dog
24. 7	15. 6	B8	A3	Pheasant
25. 7	16. 6	B8	B4	Cock
26. 7	17. 6	B8	C5	Crow
27. 7	18. 6	B8	D6	Monkey
28. 7	19. 6	B8	E7	Gibbon
29. 7	20. 6	B8	F8	Tapir
30. 7	21. 6	B8	G9	Sheep
31. 7	22. 6	B8	H10	Deer
1. 8	23. 6	B8	J11	Horse
2. 8	24. 6	B8	K12	Stag
3. 8	25. 6	B8	A1	Serpent
4. 8	26. 6	B8	B2	Earthworm
5. 8	27. 6	B8	C3	Crocodile
6. 8	28. 6	B8	D4	Dragon
7. 8	29. 6	B8	E5	Badger
8. 8	1. 7	C9	F6	Hare
9. 8	2. 7	C9	G7	Fox
10. 8	3. 7	C9	H8	Tiger
11. 8	4. 7	C9	J9	Leopard
12. 8	5. 7	C9	K10	Griffon
13. 8	6. 7	C9	A11	Ox
14. 8	7. 7	C9	B12	Bat
15. 8	8. 7	C9	C1	Rat
16. 8	9. 7	C9	D2	Swallow
17. 8	10. 7	C9	E3	Pig
18. 8	11. 7	C9	F4	Porcupine
19. 8	12. 7	C9	G5	Wolf
20. 8	13. 7	C9	H6	Dog
21. 8	14. 7	C9	J7	Pheasant
22. 8	15. 7	C9	K8	Cock
23. 8	16. 7	C9	A9	Crow
24. 8	17. 7	C9	B10	Monkey
25. 8	18. 7	C9	C11	Gibbon
26. 8	19. 7	C9	D12	Tapir
27. 8	20. 7	C9	E1	Sheep
28. 8	21. 7	C9	F2	Deer
29. 8	22. 7	C9	G3	Horse
30. 8	23. 7	C9	H4	Stag
31. 8	24. 7	C9	J5	Serpent
1. 9	25. 7	C9	K6	Earthworm
2. 9	26. 7	C9	A7	Crocodile
3. 9	27. 7	C9	B8	Dragon
4. 9	28. 7	C9	C9	Badger
5. 9	29. 7	C9	D10	Hare
6. 9	30. 7	C9	E11	Fox
7. 9	1. 8	D10	F12	Tiger
8. 9	2. 8	D10	G1	Leopard
9. 9	3. 8	D10	H2	Griffon
10. 9	4. 8	D10	J3	Ox
11. 9	5. 8	D10	K4	Bat
12. 9	6. 8	D10	A5	Rat
13. 9	7. 8	D10	B6	Swallow
14. 9	8. 8	D10	C7	Pig
15. 9	9. 8	D10	D8	Porcupine
16. 9	10. 8	D10	E9	Wolf
17. 9	11. 8	D10	F10	Dog
18. 9	12. 8	D10	G11	Pheasant
19. 9	13. 8	D10	H12	Cock
20. 9	14. 8	D10	J1	Crow
21. 9	15. 8	D10	K2	Monkey
22. 9	16. 8	D10	A3	Gibbon
23. 9	17. 8	D10	B4	Tapir
24. 9	18. 8	D10	C5	Sheep
25. 9	19. 8	D10	D6	Deer
26. 9	20. 8	D10	E7	Horse
27. 9	21. 8	D10	F8	Stag
28. 9	22. 8	D10	G9	Serpent
29. 9	23. 8	D10	H10	Earthworm
30. 9	24. 8	D10	J11	Crocodile
1. 10	25. 8	D10	K12	Dragon
2. 10	26. 8	D10	A1	Badger
3. 10	27. 8	D10	B2	Hare
4. 10	28. 8	D10	C3	Fox
5. 10	29. 8	D10	D4	Tiger
6. 10	30. 8	D10	E5	Leopard
7. 10	1. 9	E11	F6	Griffon
8. 10	2. 9	E11	G7	Ox
9. 10	3. 9	E11	H8	Bat
10. 10	4. 9	E11	J9	Rat
11. 10	5. 9	E11	K10	Swallow
12. 10	6. 9	E11	A11	Pig
13. 10	7. 9	E11	B12	Porcupine
14. 10	8. 9	E11	C1	Wolf
15. 10	9. 9	E11	D2	Dog
16. 10	10. 9	E11	E3	Pheasant
17. 10	11. 9	E11	F4	Cock
18. 10	12. 9	E11	G5	Crow
19. 10	13. 9	E11	H6	Monkey
20. 10	14. 9	E11	J7	Gibbon
21. 10	15. 9	E11	K8	Tapir
22. 10	16. 9	E11	A9	Sheep

Solar date	Lunar date	Month HS/EB	Day HS/EB	Constellation	Solar date	Lunar date	Month HS/EB	Day HS/EB	Constellation
23.10	17. 9	E11	B10	Deer	14.12	10.11	G1	D2	Monkey
24.10	18. 9	E11	C11	Horse	15.12	11.11	G1	E3	Gibbon
25.10	19. 9	E11	D12	Stag	16.12	12.11	G1	F4	Tapir
26.10	20. 9	E11	E1	Serpent	17.12	13.11	G1	G5	Sheep
27.10	21. 9	E11	F2	Earthworm	18.12	14.11	G1	H6	Deer
28.10	22. 9	E11	G3	Crocodile	19.12	15.11	G1	J7	Horse
29.10	23. 9	E11	H4	Dragon	20.12	16.11	G1	K8	Stag
30.10	24. 9	E11	J5	Badger	21.12	17.11	G1	A9	Serpent
31.10	25. 9	E11	K6	Hare	22.12	18.11	G1	B10	Earthworm
1.11	26. 9	E11	A7	Fox	23.12	19.11	G1	C11	Crocodile
2.11	27. 9	E11	B8	Tiger	24.12	20.11	G1	D12	Dragon
3.11	28. 9	E11	C9	Leopard	25.12	21.11	G1	E1	Badger
4.11	29. 9	E11	D10	Griffon	26.12	22.11	G1	F2	Hare
5.11	1.10	F12	E11	Ox	27.12	23.11	G1	G3	Fox
6.11	2.10	F12	F12	Bat	28.12	24.11	G1	H4	Tiger
7.11	3.10	F12	G1	Rat	29.12	25.11	G1	J5	Leopard
8.11	4.10	F12	H2	Swallow	30.12	26.11	G1	K6	Griffon
9.11	5.10	F12	J3	Pig	31.12	27.11	G1	A7	Ox
10.11	6.10	F12	K4	Porcupine					
11.11	7.10	F12	A5	Wolf	1927				
12.11	8.10	F12	B6	Dog	1. 1	28.11	G1	B8	Bat
13.11	9.10	F12	C7	Pheasant	2. 1	29.11	G1	C9	Rat
14.11	10.10	F12	D8	Cock	3. 1	30.11	G1	D10	Swallow
15.11	11.10	F12	E9	Crow	4. 1	1.12	H2	E11	Pig
16.11	12.10	F12	F10	Monkey	5. 1	2.12	H2	F12	Porcupine
17.11	13.10	F12	G11	Gibbon	6. 1	3.12	H2	G1	Wolf
18.11	14.10	F12	H12	Tapir	7. 1	4.12	H2	H2	Dog
19.11	15.10	F12	J1	Sheep	8. 1	5.12	H2	J3	Pheasant
20.11	16.10	F12	K2	Deer	9. 1	6.12	H2	K4	Cock
21.11	17.10	F12	A3	Horse	10. 1	7.12	H2	A5	Crow
22.11	18.10	F12	B4	Stag	11. 1	8.12	H2	B6	Monkey
23.11	19.10	F12	C5	Serpent	12. 1	9.12	H2	C7	Gibbon
24.11	20.10	F12	D6	Earthworm	13. 1	10.12	H2	D8	Tapir
25.11	21.10	F12	E7	Crocodile	14. 1	11.12	H2	E9	Sheep
26.11	22.10	F12	F8	Dragon	15. 1	12.12	H2	F10	Deer
27.11	23.10	F12	G9	Badger	16. 1	13.12	H2	G11	Horse
28.11	24.10	F12	H10	Hare	17. 1	14.12	H2	H12	Stag
29.11	25.10	F12	J11	Fox	18. 1	15.12	H2	J1	Serpent
30.11	26.10	F12	K12	Tiger	19. 1	16.12	H2	K2	Earthworm
1.12	27.10	F12	A1	Leopard	20. 1	17.12	H2	A3	Crocodile
2.12	28.10	F12	B2	Griffon	21. 1	18.12	H2	B4	Dragon
3.12	29.10	F12	C3	Ox	22. 1	19.12	H2	C5	Badger
4.12	30.10	F12	D4	Bat	23. 1	20.12	H2	D6	Hare
5.12	1.11	G1	E5	Rat	24. 1	21.12	H2	E7	Fox
6.12	2.11	G1	F6	Swallow	25. 1	22.12	H2	F8	Tiger
7.12	3.11	G1	G7	Pig	26. 1	23.12	H2	G9	Leopard
8.12	4.11	G1	H8	Porcupine	27. 1	24.12	H2	H10	Griffon
9.12	5.11	G1	J9	Wolf	28. 1	25.12	H2	J11	Ox
10.12	6.11	G1	K10	Dog	29. 1	26.12	H2	K12	Bat
11.12	7.11	G1	A11	Pheasant	30. 1	27.12	H2	A1	Rat
12.12	8.11	G1	B12	Cock	31. 1	28.12	H2	B2	Swallow
13.12	9.11	G1	C1	Crow	1. 2	29.12	H2	C3	Pig

TING MAO YEAR

Solar date	Lunar date	Month HS/EB	Day HS/EB	Constellation	Solar date	Lunar date	Month HS/EB	Day HS/EB	Constellation
2. 2	1. 1	J3	D4	Porcupine	18. 2	17. 1	J3	K8	Dragon
3. 2	2. 1	J3	E5	Wolf	19. 2	18. 1	J3	A9	Badger
4. 2	3. 1	J3	F6	Dog	20. 2	19. 1	J3	B10	Hare
5. 2	4. 1	J3	G7	Pheasant	21. 2	20. 1	J3	C11	Fox
6. 2	5. 1	J3	H8	Cock	22. 2	21. 1	J3	D12	Tiger
7. 2	6. 1	J3	J9	Crow	23. 2	22. 1	J3	E1	Leopard
8. 2	7. 1	J3	K10	Monkey	24. 2	23. 1	J3	F2	Griffon
9. 2	8. 1	J3	A11	Gibbon	25. 2	24. 1	J3	G3	Ox
10. 2	9. 1	J3	B12	Tapir	26. 2	25. 1	J3	H4	Bat
11. 2	10. 1	J3	C1	Sheep	27. 2	26. 1	J3	J5	Rat
12. 2	11. 1	J3	D2	Deer	28. 2	27. 1	J3	K6	Swallow
13. 2	12. 1	J3	E3	Horse	1. 3	28. 1	J3	A7	Pig
14. 2	13. 1	J3	F4	Stag	2. 3	29. 1	J3	B8	Porcupine
15. 2	14. 1	J3	G5	Serpent	3. 3	30. 1	J3	C9	Wolf
16. 2	15. 1	J3	H6	Earthworm	4. 3	1. 2	K4	D10	Dog
17. 2	16. 1	J3	J7	Crocodile	5. 3	2. 2	K4	E11	Pheasant

Solar date	Lunar date	Month HS/EB	Day HS/EB	Constellation	Solar date	Lunar date	Month HS/EB	Day HS/EB	Constellation
6. 3	3. 2	K4	F12	Cock	18. 5	18. 4	B6	J1	Leopard
7. 3	4. 2	K4	G1	Crow	19. 5	19. 4	B6	K2	Griffon
8. 3	5. 2	K4	H2	Monkey	20. 5	20. 4	B6	A3	Ox
9. 3	6. 2	K4	J3	Gibbon	21. 5	21. 4	B6	B4	Bat
10. 3	7. 2	K4	K4	Tapir	22. 5	22. 4	B6	C5	Rat
11. 3	8. 2	K4	A5	Sheep	23. 5	23. 4	B6	D6	Swallow
12. 3	9. 2	K4	B6	Deer	24. 5	24. 4	B6	E7	Pig
13. 3	10. 2	K4	C7	Horse	25. 5	25. 4	B6	F8	Porcupine
14. 3	11. 2	K4	D8	Stag	26. 5	26. 4	B6	G9	Wolf
15. 3	12. 2	K4	E9	Serpent	27. 5	27. 4	B6	H10	Dog
16. 3	13. 2	K4	F10	Earthworm	28. 5	28. 4	B6	J11	Pheasant
17. 3	14. 2	K4	G11	Crocodile	29. 5	29. 4	B6	K12	Cock
18. 3	15. 2	K4	H12	Dragon	30. 5	30. 4	B6	A1	Crow
19. 3	16. 2	K4	J1	Badger	31. 5	1. 5	C7	B2	Monkey
20. 3	17. 2	K4	K2	Hare	1. 6	2. 5	C7	C3	Gibbon
21. 3	18. 2	K4	A3	Fox	2. 6	3. 5	C7	D4	Tapir
22. 3	19. 2	K4	B4	Tiger	3. 6	4. 5	C7	E5	Sheep
23. 3	20. 2	K4	C5	Leopard	4. 6	5. 5	C7	F6	Deer
24. 3	21. 2	K4	D6	Griffon	5. 6	6. 5	C7	G7	Horse
25. 3	22. 2	K4	E7	Ox	6. 6	7. 5	C7	H8	Stag
26. 3	23. 2	K4	F8	Bat	7. 6	8. 5	C7	J9	Serpent
27. 3	24. 2	K4	G9	Rat	8. 6	9. 5	C7	K10	Earthworm
28. 3	25. 2	K4	H10	Swallow	9. 6	10. 5	C7	A11	Crocodile
29. 3	26. 2	K4	J11	Pig	10. 6	11. 5	C7	B12	Dragon
30. 3	27. 2	K4	K12	Porcupine	11. 6	12. 5	C7	C1	Badger
31. 3	28. 2	K4	A1	Wolf	12. 6	13. 5	C7	D2	Hare
1. 4	29. 2	K4	B2	Dog	13. 6	14. 5	C7	E3	Fox
2. 4	1. 3	A5	C3	Pheasant	14. 6	15. 5	C7	F4	Tiger
3. 4	2. 3	A5	D4	Cock	15. 6	16. 5	C7	G5	Leopard
4. 4	3. 3	A5	E5	Crow	16. 6	17. 5	C7	H6	Griffon
5. 4	4. 3	A5	F6	Monkey	17. 6	18. 5	C7	J7	Ox
6. 4	5. 3	A5	G7	Gibbon	18. 6	19. 5	C7	K8	Bat
7. 4	6. 3	A5	H8	Tapir	19. 6	20. 5	C7	A9	Rat
8. 4	7. 3	A5	J9	Sheep	20. 6	21. 5	C7	B10	Swallow
9. 4	8. 3	A5	K10	Deer	21. 6	22. 5	C7	C11	Pig
10. 4	9. 3	A5	A11	Horse	22. 6	23. 5	C7	D12	Porcupine
11. 4	10. 3	A5	B12	Stag	23. 6	24. 5	C7	E1	Wolf
12. 4	11. 3	A5	C1	Serpent	24. 6	25. 5	C7	F2	Dog
13. 4	12. 3	A5	D2	Earthworm	25. 6	26. 5	C7	G3	Pheasant
14. 4	13. 3	A5	E3	Crocodile	26. 6	27. 5	C7	H4	Cock
15. 4	14. 3	A5	F4	Dragon	27. 6	28. 5	C7	J5	Crow
16. 4	15. 3	A5	G5	Badger	28. 6	29. 5	C7	K6	Monkey
17. 4	16. 3	A5	H6	Hare	29. 6	1. 6	D8	A7	Gibbon
18. 4	17. 3	A5	J7	Fox	30. 6	2. 6	D8	B8	Tapir
19. 4	18. 3	A5	K8	Tiger	1. 7	3. 6	D8	C9	Sheep
20. 4	19. 3	A5	A9	Leopard	2. 7	4. 6	D8	D10	Deer
21. 4	20. 3	A5	B10	Griffon	3. 7	5. 6	D8	E11	Horse
22. 4	21. 3	A5	C11	Ox	4. 7	6. 6	D8	F12	Stag
23. 4	22. 3	A5	D12	Bat	5. 7	7. 6	D8	G1	Serpent
24. 4	23. 3	A5	E1	Rat	6. 7	8. 6	D8	H2	Earthworm
25. 4	24. 3	A5	F2	Swallow	7. 7	9. 6	D8	J3	Crocodile
26. 4	25. 3	A5	G3	Pig	8. 7	10. 6	D8	K4	Dragon
27. 4	26. 3	A5	H4	Porcupine	9. 7	11. 6	D8	A5	Badger
28. 4	27. 3	A5	J5	Wolf	10. 7	12. 6	D8	B6	Hare
29. 4	28. 3	A5	K6	Dog	11. 7	13. 6	D8	C7	Fox
30. 4	29. 3	A5	A7	Pheasant	12. 7	14. 6	D8	D8	Tiger
1. 5	1. 4	B6	B8	Cock	13. 7	15. 6	D8	E9	Leopard
2. 5	2. 4	B6	C9	Crow	14. 7	16. 6	D8	F10	Griffon
3. 5	3. 4	B6	D10	Monkey	15. 7	17. 6	D8	G11	Ox
4. 5	4. 4	B6	E11	Gibbon	16. 7	18. 6	D8	H12	Bat
5. 5	5. 4	B6	F12	Tapir	17. 7	19. 6	D8	J1	Rat
6. 5	6. 4	B6	G1	Sheep	18. 7	20. 6	D8	K2	Swallow
7. 5	7. 4	B6	H2	Deer	19. 7	21. 6	D8	A3	Pig
8. 5	8. 4	B6	J3	Horse	20. 7	22. 6	D8	B4	Porcupine
9. 5	9. 4	B6	K4	Stag	21. 7	23. 6	D8	C5	Wolf
10. 5	10. 4	B6	A5	Serpent	22. 7	24. 6	D8	D6	Dog
11. 5	11. 4	B6	B6	Earthworm	23. 7	25. 6	D8	E7	Pheasant
12. 5	12. 4	B6	C7	Crocodile	24. 7	26. 6	D8	F8	Cock
13. 5	13. 4	B6	D8	Dragon	25. 7	27. 6	D8	G9	Crow
14. 5	14. 4	B6	E9	Badger	26. 7	28. 6	D8	H10	Monkey
15. 5	15. 4	B6	F10	Hare	27. 7	29. 6	D8	J11	Gibbon
16. 5	16. 4	B6	G11	Fox	28. 7	30. 6	D8	K12	Tapir
17. 5	17. 4	B6	H12	Tiger	29. 7	1. 7	E9	A1	Sheep

Solar date	Lunar date	Month HS/EB	Day HS/EB	Constellation	Solar date	Lunar date	Month HS/EB	Day HS/EB	Constellation
30. 7	2. 7	E9	B2	Deer	11.10	16. 9	G11	E3	Pig
31. 7	3. 7	E9	C3	Horse	12.10	17. 9	G11	F4	Porcupine
1. 8	4. 7	E9	D4	Stag	13.10	18. 9	G11	G5	Wolf
2. 8	5. 7	E9	E5	Serpent	14.10	19. 9	G11	H6	Dog
3. 8	6. 7	E9	F6	Earthworm	15.10	20. 9	G11	J7	Pheasant
4. 8	7. 7	E9	G7	Crocodile	16.10	21. 9	G11	K8	Cock
5. 8	8. 7	E9	H8	Dragon	17.10	22. 9	G11	A9	Crow
6. 8	9. 7	E9	J9	Badger	18.10	23. 9	G11	B10	Monkey
7. 8	10. 7	E9	K10	Hare	19.10	24. 9	G11	C11	Gibbon
8. 8	11. 7	E9	A11	Fox	20.10	25. 9	G11	D12	Tapir
9. 8	12. 7	E9	B12	Tiger	21.10	26. 9	G11	E1	Sheep
10. 8	13. 7	E9	C1	Leopard	22.10	27. 9	G11	F2	Deer
11. 8	14. 7	E9	D2	Griffon	23.10	28. 9	G11	G3	Horse
12. 8	15. 7	E9	E3	Ox	24.10	29. 9	G11	H4	Stag
13. 8	16. 7	E9	F4	Bat	25.10	1.10	H12	J5	Serpent
14. 8	17. 7	E9	G5	Rat	26.10	2.10	H12	K6	Earthworm
15. 8	18. 7	E9	H6	Swallow	27.10	3.10	H12	A7	Crocodile
16. 8	19. 7	E9	J7	Pig	28.10	4.10	H12	B8	Dragon
17. 8	20. 7	E9	K8	Porcupine	29.10	5.10	H12	C9	Badger
18. 8	21. 7	E9	A9	Wolf	30.10	6.10	H12	D10	Hare
19. 8	22. 7	E9	B10	Dog	31.10	7.10	H12	E11	Fox
20. 8	23. 7	E9	C11	Pheasant	1.11	8.10	H12	F12	Tiger
21. 8	24. 7	E9	D12	Cock	2.11	9.10	H12	G1	Leopard
22. 8	25. 7	E9	E1	Crow	3.11	10.10	H12	H2	Griffon
23. 8	26. 7	E9	F2	Monkey	4.11	11.10	H12	J3	Ox
24. 8	27. 7	E9	G3	Gibbon	5.11	12.10	H12	K4	Bat
25. 8	28. 7	E9	H4	Tapir	6.11	13.10	H12	A5	Rat
26. 8	29. 7	E9	J5	Sheep	7.11	14.10	H12	B6	Swallow
27. 8	1. 8	F10	K6	Deer	8.11	15.10	H12	C7	Pig
28. 8	2. 8	F10	A7	Horse	9.11	16.10	H12	D8	Porcupine
29. 8	3. 8	F10	B8	Stag	10.11	17.10	H12	E9	Wolf
30. 8	4. 8	F10	C9	Serpent	11.11	18.10	H12	F10	Dog
31. 8	5. 8	F10	D10	Earthworm	12.11	19.10	H12	G11	Pheasant
1. 9	6. 8	F10	E11	Crocodile	13.11	20.10	H12	H12	Cock
2. 9	7. 8	F10	F12	Dragon	14.11	21.10	H12	J1	Crow
3. 9	8. 8	F10	G1	Badger	15.11	22.10	H12	K2	Monkey
4. 9	9. 8	F10	H2	Hare	16.11	23.10	H12	A3	Gibbon
5. 9	10. 8	F10	J3	Fox	17.11	24.10	H12	B4	Tapir
6. 9	11. 8	F10	K4	Tiger	18.11	25.10	H12	C5	Sheep
7. 9	12. 8	F10	A5	Leopard	19.11	26.10	H12	D6	Deer
8. 9	13. 8	F10	B6	Griffon	20.11	27.10	H12	E7	Horse
9. 9	14. 8	F10	C7	Ox	21.11	28.10	H12	F8	Stag
10. 9	15. 8	F10	D8	Bat	22.11	29.10	H12	G9	Serpent
11. 9	16. 8	F10	E9	Rat	23.11	30.10	H12	H10	Earthworm
12. 9	17. 8	F10	F10	Swallow	24.11	1.11	J1	J11	Crocodile
13. 9	18. 8	F10	G11	Pig	25.11	2.11	J1	K12	Dragon
14. 9	19. 8	F10	H12	Porcupine	26.11	3.11	J1	A1	Badger
15. 9	20. 8	F10	J1	Wolf	27.11	4.11	J1	B2	Hare
16. 9	21. 8	F10	K2	Dog	28.11	5.11	J1	C3	Fox
17. 9	22. 8	F10	A3	Pheasant	29.11	6.11	J1	D4	Tiger
18. 9	23. 8	F10	B4	Cock	30.11	7.11	J1	E5	Leopard
19. 9	24. 8	F10	C5	Crow	1.12	8.11	J1	F6	Griffon
20. 9	25. 8	F10	D6	Monkey	2.12	9.11	J1	G7	Ox
21. 9	26. 8	F10	E7	Gibbon	3.12	10.11	J1	H8	Bat
22. 9	27. 8	F10	F8	Tapir	4.12	11.11	J1	J9	Rat
23. 9	28. 8	F10	G9	Sheep	5.12	12.11	J1	K10	Swallow
24. 9	29. 8	F10	H10	Deer	6.12	13.11	J1	A11	Pig
25. 9	30. 8	F10	J11	Horse	7.12	14.11	J1	B12	Porcupine
26. 9	1. 9	G11	K12	Stag	8.12	15.11	J1	C1	Wolf
27. 9	2. 9	G11	A1	Serpent	9.12	16.11	J1	D2	Dog
28. 9	3. 9	G11	B2	Earthworm	10.12	17.11	J1	E3	Pheasant
29. 9	4. 9	G11	C3	Crocodile	11.12	18.11	J1	F4	Cock
30. 9	5. 9	G11	D4	Dragon	12.12	19.11	J1	G5	Crow
1.10	6. 9	G11	E5	Badger	13.12	20.11	J1	H6	Monkey
2.10	7. 9	G11	F6	Hare	14.12	21.11	J1	J7	Gibbon
3.10	8. 9	G11	G7	Fox	15.12	22.11	J1	K8	Tapir
4.10	9. 9	G11	H8	Tiger	16.12	23.11	J1	A9	Sheep
5.10	10. 9	G11	J9	Leopard	17.12	24.11	J1	B10	Deer
6.10	11. 9	G11	K10	Griffon	18.12	25.11	J1	C11	Horse
7.10	12. 9	G11	A11	Ox	19.12	26.11	J1	D12	Stag
8.10	13. 9	G11	B12	Bat	20.12	27.11	J1	E1	Serpent
9.10	14. 9	G11	C1	Rat	21.12	28.11	J1	F2	Earthworm
10.10	15. 9	G11	D2	Swallow	22.12	29.11	J1	G3	Crocodile

Solar date	Lunar date	Month HS/EB	Day HS/EB	Constellation	Solar date	Lunar date	Month HS/EB	Day HS/EB	Constellation
23.12	30.11	J1	H4	Dragon	6. 1	14.12	K2	B6	Dog
24.12	1.12	K2	J5	Badger	7. 1	15.12	K2	C7	Pheasant
25.12	2.12	K2	K6	Hare	8. 1	16.12	K2	D8	Cock
26.12	3.12	K2	A7	Fox	9. 1	17.12	K2	E9	Crow
27.12	4.12	K2	B8	Tiger	10. 1	18.12	K2	F10	Monkey
28.12	5.12	K2	C9	Leopard	11. 1	19.12	K2	G11	Gibbon
29.12	6.12	K2	D10	Griffon	12. 1	20.12	K2	H12	Tapir
30.12	7.12	K2	E11	Ox	13. 1	21.12	K2	J1	Sheep
31.12	8.12	K2	F12	Bat	14. 1	22.12	K2	K2	Deer
					15. 1	23.12	K2	A3	Horse
1928					16. 1	24.12	K2	B4	Stag
1. 1	9.12	K2	G1	Rat	17. 1	25.12	K2	C5	Serpent
2. 1	10.12	K2	H2	Swallow	18. 1	26.12	K2	D6	Earthworm
3. 1	11.12	K2	J3	Pig	19. 1	27.12	K2	E7	Crocodile
4. 1	12.12	K2	K4	Porcupine	20. 1	28.12	K2	F8	Dragon
5. 1	13.12	K2	A5	Wolf	21. 1	29.12	K2	G9	Badger
					22. 1	30.12	K2	H10	Hare

MOU CH'EN YEAR

Solar date	Lunar date	Month HS/EB	Day HS/EB	Constellation	Solar date	Lunar date	Month HS/EB	Day HS/EB	Constellation
23. 1	1. 1	A3	J11	Fox	14. 3	23. 2	B4	K2	Earthworm
24. 1	2. 1	A3	K12	Tiger	15. 3	24. 2	B4	A3	Crocodile
25. 1	3. 1	A3	A1	Leopard	16. 3	25. 2	B4	B4	Dragon
26. 1	4. 1	A3	B2	Griffon	17. 3	26. 2	B4	C5	Badger
27. 1	5. 1	A3	C3	Ox	18. 3	27. 2	B4	D6	Hare
28. 1	6. 1	A3	D4	Bat	19. 3	28. 2	B4	E7	Fox
29. 1	7. 1	A3	E5	Rat	20. 3	29. 2	B4	F8	Tiger
30. 1	8. 1	A3	F6	Swallow	21. 3	30. 2	B4	G9	Leopard
31. 1	9. 1	A3	G7	Pig	22. 3	*1. 2*	*B4*	H10	Griffon
1. 2	10. 1	A3	H8	Porcupine	23. 3	*2. 2*	*B4*	J11	Ox
2. 2	11. 1	A3	J9	Wolf	24. 3	*3. 2*	*B4*	K12	Bat
3. 2	12. 1	A3	K10	Dog	25. 3	*4. 2*	*B4*	A1	Rat
4. 2	13. 1	A3	A11	Pheasant	26. 3	*5. 2*	*B4*	B2	Swallow
5. 2	14. 1	A3	B12	Cock	27. 3	*6. 2*	*B4*	C3	Pig
6. 2	15. 1	A3	C1	Crow	28. 3	*7. 2*	*B4*	D4	Porcupine
7. 2	16. 1	A3	D2	Monkey	29. 3	*8. 2*	*B4*	E5	Wolf
8. 2	17. 1	A3	E3	Gibbon	30. 3	*9. 2*	*B4*	F6	Dog
9. 2	18. 1	A3	F4	Tapir	31. 3	*10. 2*	*B4*	G7	Pheasant
10. 2	19. 1	A3	G5	Sheep	1. 4	*11. 2*	*B4*	H8	Cock
11. 2	20. 1	A3	H6	Deer	2. 4	*12. 2*	*B4*	J9	Crow
12. 2	21. 1	A3	J7	Horse	3. 4	*13. 2*	*B4*	K10	Monkey
13. 2	22. 1	A3	K8	Stag	4. 4	*14. 2*	*B4*	A11	Gibbon
14. 2	23. 1	A3	A9	Serpent	5. 4	*15. 2*	*B4*	B12	Tapir
15. 2	24. 1	A3	B10	Earthworm	6. 4	*16. 2*	*B4*	C1	Sheep
16. 2	25. 1	A3	C11	Crocodile	7. 4	*17. 2*	*B4*	D2	Deer
17. 2	26. 1	A3	D12	Dragon	8. 4	*18. 2*	*B4*	E3	Horse
18. 2	27. 1	A3	E1	Badger	9. 4	*19. 2*	*B4*	F4	Stag
19. 2	28. 1	A3	F2	Hare	10. 4	*20. 2*	*B4*	G5	Serpent
20. 2	29. 1	A3	G3	Fox	11. 4	*21. 2*	*B4*	H6	Earthworm
21. 2	1. 2	B4	H4	Tiger	12. 4	*22. 2*	*B4*	J7	Crocodile
22. 2	2. 2	B4	J5	Leopard	13. 4	*23. 2*	*B4*	K8	Dragon
23. 2	3. 2	B4	K6	Griffon	14. 4	*24. 2*	*B4*	A9	Badger
24. 2	4. 2	B4	A7	Ox	15. 4	*25. 2*	*B4*	B10	Hare
25. 2	5. 2	B4	B8	Bat	16. 4	*26. 2*	*B4*	C11	Fox
26. 2	6. 2	B4	C9	Rat	17. 4	*27. 2*	*B4*	D12	Tiger
27. 2	7. 2	B4	D10	Swallow	18. 4	*28. 2*	*B4*	E1	Leopard
28. 2	8. 2	B4	E11	Pig	19. 4	*29. 2*	*B4*	F2	Griffon
29. 2	9. 2	B4	F12	Porcupine	20. 4	1. 3	C5	G3	Ox
1. 3	10. 2	B4	G1	Wolf	21. 4	2. 3	C5	H4	Bat
2. 3	11. 2	B4	H2	Dog	22. 4	3. 3	C5	J5	Rat
3. 3	12. 2	B4	J3	Pheasant	23. 4	4. 3	C5	K6	Swallow
4. 3	13. 2	B4	K4	Cock	24. 4	5. 3	C5	A7	Pig
5. 3	14. 2	B4	A5	Crow	25. 4	6. 3	C5	B8	Porcupine
6. 3	15. 2	B4	B6	Monkey	26. 4	7. 3	C5	C9	Wolf
7. 3	16. 2	B4	C7	Gibbon	27. 4	8. 3	C5	D10	Dog
8. 3	17. 2	B4	D8	Tapir	28. 4	9. 3	C5	E11	Pheasant
9. 3	18. 2	B4	E9	Sheep	29. 4	10. 3	C5	F12	Cock
10. 3	19. 2	B4	F10	Deer	30. 4	11. 3	C5	G1	Crow
11. 3	20. 2	B4	G11	Horse	1. 5	12. 3	C5	H2	Monkey
12. 3	21. 2	B4	H12	Stag	2. 5	13. 3	C5	J3	Gibbon
13. 3	22. 2	B4	J1	Serpent	3. 5	14. 3	C5	K4	Tapir

Solar date	Lunar date	Month HS/EB	Day HS/EB	Constellation	Solar date	Lunar date	Month HS/EB	Day HS/EB	Constellation
4. 5	15. 3	C5	A5	Sheep	16. 7	29. 5	E7	D6	Swallow
5. 5	16. 3	C5	B6	Deer	17. 7	1. 6	F8	E7	Pig
6. 5	17. 3	C5	C7	Horse	18. 7	2. 6	F8	F8	Porcupine
7. 5	18. 3	C5	D8	Stag	19. 7	3. 6	F8	G9	Wolf
8. 5	19. 3	C5	E9	Serpent	20. 7	4. 6	F8	H10	Dog
9. 5	20. 3	C5	F10	Earthworm	21. 7	5. 6	F8	J11	Pheasant
10. 5	21. 3	C5	G11	Crocodile	22. 7	6. 6	F8	K12	Cock
11. 5	22. 3	C5	H12	Dragon	23. 7	7. 6	F8	A1	Crow
12. 5	23. 3	C5	J1	Badger	24. 7	8. 6	F8	B2	Monkey
13. 5	24. 3	C5	K2	Hare	25. 7	9. 6	F8	C3	Gibbon
14. 5	25. 3	C5	A3	Fox	26. 7	10. 6	F8	D4	Tapir
15. 5	26. 3	C5	B4	Tiger	27. 7	11. 6	F8	E5	Sheep
16. 5	27. 3	C5	C5	Leopard	28. 7	12. 6	F8	F6	Deer
17. 5	28. 3	C5	D6	Griffon	29. 7	13. 6	F8	G7	Horse
18. 5	29. 3	C5	E7	Ox	30. 7	14. 6	F8	H8	Stag
19. 5	1. 4	D6	F8	Bat	31. 7	15. 6	F8	J9	Serpent
20. 5	2. 4	D6	G9	Rat	1. 8	16. 6	F8	K10	Earthworm
21. 5	3. 4	D6	H10	Swallow	2. 8	17. 6	F8	A11	Crocodile
22. 5	4. 4	D6	J11	Pig	3. 8	18. 6	F8	B12	Dragon
23. 5	5. 4	D6	K12	Porcupine	4. 8	19. 6	F8	C1	Badger
24. 5	6. 4	D6	A1	Wolf	5. 8	20. 6	F8	D2	Hare
25. 5	7. 4	D6	B2	Dog	6. 8	21. 6	F8	E3	Fox
26. 5	8. 4	D6	C3	Pheasant	7. 8	22. 6	F8	F4	Tiger
27. 5	9. 4	D6	D4	Cock	8. 8	23. 6	F8	G5	Leopard
28. 5	10. 4	D6	E5	Crow	9. 8	24. 6	F8	H6	Griffon
29. 5	11. 4	D6	F6	Monkey	10. 8	25. 6	F8	J7	Ox
30. 5	12. 4	D6	G7	Gibbon	11. 8	26. 6	F8	K8	Bat
31. 5	13. 4	D6	H8	Tapir	12. 8	27. 6	F8	A9	Rat
1. 6	14. 4	D6	J9	Sheep	13. 8	28. 6	F8	B10	Swallow
2. 6	15. 4	D6	K10	Deer	14. 8	29. 6	F8	C11	Pig
3. 6	16. 4	D6	A11	Horse	15. 8	1. 7	G9	D12	Porcupine
4. 6	17. 4	D6	B12	Stag	16. 8	2. 7	G9	E1	Wolf
5. 6	18. 4	D6	C1	Serpent	17. 8	3. 7	G9	F2	Dog
6. 6	19. 4	D6	D2	Earthworm	18. 8	4. 7	G9	G3	Pheasant
7. 6	20. 4	D6	E3	Crocodile	19. 8	5. 7	G9	H4	Cock
8. 6	21. 4	D6	F4	Dragon	20. 8	6. 7	G9	J5	Crow
9. 6	22. 4	D6	G5	Badger	21. 8	7. 7	G9	K6	Monkey
10. 6	23. 4	D6	H6	Hare	22. 8	8. 7	G9	A7	Gibbon
11. 6	24. 4	D6	J7	Fox	23. 8	9. 7	G9	B8	Tapir
12. 6	25. 4	D6	K8	Tiger	24. 8	10. 7	G9	C9	Sheep
13. 6	26. 4	D6	A9	Leopard	25. 8	11. 7	G9	D10	Deer
14. 6	27. 4	D6	B10	Griffon	26. 8	12. 7	G9	E11	Horse
15. 6	28. 4	D6	C11	Ox	27. 8	13. 7	G9	F12	Stag
16. 6	29. 4	D6	D12	Bat	28. 8	14. 7	G9	G1	Serpent
17. 6	30. 4	D6	E1	Rat	29. 8	15. 7	G9	H2	Earthworm
18. 6	1. 5	E7	F2	Swallow	30. 8	16. 7	G9	J3	Crocodile
19. 6	2. 5	E7	G3	Pig	31. 8	17. 7	G9	K4	Dragon
20. 6	3. 5	E7	H4	Porcupine	1. 9	18. 7	G9	A5	Badger
21. 6	4. 5	E7	J5	Wolf	2. 9	19. 7	G9	B6	Hare
22. 6	5. 5	E7	K6	Dog	3. 9	20. 7	G9	C7	Fox
23. 6	6. 5	E7	A7	Pheasant	4. 9	21. 7	G9	D8	Tiger
24. 6	7. 5	E7	B8	Cock	5. 9	22. 7	G9	E9	Leopard
25. 6	8. 5	E7	C9	Crow	6. 9	23. 7	G9	F10	Griffon
26. 6	9. 5	E7	D10	Monkey	7. 9	24. 7	G9	G11	Ox
27. 6	10. 5	E7	E11	Gibbon	8. 9	25. 7	G9	H12	Bat
28. 6	11. 5	E7	F12	Tapir	9. 9	26. 7	G9	J1	Rat
29. 6	12. 5	E7	G1	Sheep	10. 9	27. 7	G9	K2	Swallow
30. 6	13. 5	E7	H2	Deer	11. 9	28. 7	G9	A3	Pig
1. 7	14. 5	E7	J3	Horse	12. 9	29. 7	G9	B4	Porcupine
2. 7	15. 5	E7	K4	Stag	13. 9	30. 7	G9	C5	Wolf
3. 7	16. 5	E7	A5	Serpent	14. 9	1. 8	H10	D6	Dog
4. 7	17. 5	E7	B6	Earthworm	15. 9	2. 8	H10	E7	Pheasant
5. 7	18. 5	E7	C7	Crocodile	16. 9	3. 8	H10	F8	Cock
6. 7	19. 5	E7	D8	Dragon	17. 9	4. 8	H10	G9	Crow
7. 7	20. 5	E7	E9	Badger	18. 9	5. 8	H10	H10	Monkey
8. 7	21. 5	E7	F10	Hare	19. 9	6. 8	H10	J11	Gibbon
9. 7	22. 5	E7	G11	Fox	20. 9	7. 8	H10	K12	Tapir
10. 7	23. 5	E7	H12	Tiger	21. 9	8. 8	H10	A1	Sheep
11. 7	24. 5	E7	J1	Leopard	22. 9	9. 8	H10	B2	Deer
12. 7	25. 5	E7	K2	Griffon	23. 9	10. 8	H10	C3	Horse
13. 7	26. 5	E7	A3	Ox	24. 9	11. 8	H10	D4	Stag
14. 7	27. 5	E7	B4	Bat	25. 9	12. 8	H10	E5	Serpent
15. 7	28. 5	E7	C5	Rat	26. 9	13. 8	H10	F6	Earthworm

Solar date	Lunar date	Month HS/EB	Day HS/EB	Constellation	Solar date	Lunar date	Month HS/EB	Day HS/EB	Constellation
27. 9	14. 8	H10	G7	Crocodile	5.12	24.10	K12	F4	Porcupine
28. 9	15. 8	H10	H8	Dragon	6.12	25.10	K12	G5	Wolf
29. 9	16. 8	H10	J9	Badger	7.12	26.10	K12	H6	Dog
30. 9	17. 8	H10	K10	Hare	8.12	27.10	K12	J7	Pheasant
1.10	18. 8	G10	A11	Fox	9.12	28.10	K12	K8	Cock
2.10	19. 8	G10	B12	Tiger	10.12	29.10	K12	A9	Crow
3.10	20. 8	G10	C1	Leopard	11.12	30.10	K12	B10	Monkey
4.10	21. 8	G10	D2	Griffon	12.12	1.11	A1	C11	Gibbon
5.10	22. 8	G10	E3	Ox	13.12	2.11	A1	D12	Tapir
6.10	23. 8	G10	F4	Bat	14.12	3.11	A1	E1	Sheep
7.10	24. 8	G10	G5	Rat	15.12	4.11	A1	F2	Deer
8.10	25. 8	G10	H6	Swallow	16.12	5.11	A1	G3	Horse
9.10	26. 8	G10	J7	Pig	17.12	6.11	A1	H4	Stag
10.10	27. 8	G10	K8	Porcupine	18.12	7.11	A1	J5	Serpent
11.10	28. 8	G10	A9	Wolf	19.12	8.11	A1	K6	Earthworm
12.10	29. 8	G10	B10	Dog	20.12	9.11	A1	A7	Crocodile
13.10	1. 9	J11	C11	Pheasant	21.12	10.11	A1	B8	Dragon
14.10	2. 9	J11	D12	Cock	22.12	11.11	A1	C9	Badger
15.10	3. 9	J11	E1	Crow	23.12	12.11	A1	D10	Hare
16.10	4. 9	J11	F2	Monkey	24.12	13.11	A1	E11	Fox
17.10	5. 9	J11	G3	Gibbon	25.12	14.11	A1	F12	Tiger
18.10	6. 9	J11	H4	Tapir	26.12	15.11	A1	G1	Leopard
19.10	7. 9	J11	J5	Sheep	27.12	16.11	A1	H2	Griffon
20.10	8. 9	J11	K6	Deer	28.12	17.11	A1	J3	Ox
21.10	9. 9	J11	A7	Horse	29.12	18.11	A1	K4	Bat
22.10	10. 9	J11	B8	Stag	30.12	19.11	A1	A5	Rat
23.10	11. 9	J11	C9	Serpent	31.12	20.11	A1	B6	Swallow
24.10	12. 9	J11	D10	Earthworm					
25.10	13. 9	J11	E11	Crocodile	**1929**				
26.10	14. 9	J11	F12	Dragon	1. 1	21.11	A1	C7	Pig
27.10	15. 9	J11	G1	Badger	2. 1	22.11	A1	D8	Porcupine
28.10	16. 9	J11	H2	Hare	3. 1	23.11	A1	E9	Wolf
29.10	17. 9	J11	J3	Fox	4. 1	24.11	A1	F10	Dog
30.10	18. 9	J11	K4	Tiger	5. 1	25.11	A1	G11	Pheasant
31.10	19. 9	J11	A5	Leopard	6. 1	26.11	A1	H12	Cock
1.11	20. 9	J11	B6	Griffon	7. 1	27.11	A1	J1	Crow
2.11	21. 9	J11	C7	Ox	8. 1	28.11	A1	K2	Monkey
3.11	22. 9	J11	D8	Bat	9. 1	29.11	A1	A3	Gibbon
4.11	23. 9	J11	E9	Rat	10. 1	30.11	A1	B4	Tapir
5.11	24. 9	J11	F10	Swallow	11. 1	1.12	B2	C5	Sheep
6.11	25. 9	J11	G11	Pig	12. 1	2.12	B2	D6	Deer
7.11	26. 9	J11	H12	Porcupine	13. 1	3.12	B2	E7	Horse
8.11	27. 9	J11	J1	Wolf	14. 1	4.12	B2	F8	Stag
9.11	28. 9	J11	K2	Dog	15. 1	5.12	B2	G9	Serpent
10.11	29. 9	J11	A3	Pheasant	16. 1	6.12	B2	H10	Earthworm
11.11	30. 9	J11	B4	Cock	17. 1	7.12	B2	J11	Crocodile
12.11	1.10	K12	C5	Crow	18. 1	8.12	B2	K12	Dragon
13.11	2.10	K12	D6	Monkey	19. 1	9.12	B2	A1	Badger
14.11	3.10	K12	E7	Gibbon	20. 1	10.12	B2	B2	Hare
15.11	4.10	K12	F8	Tapir	21. 1	11.12	B2	C3	Fox
16.11	5.10	K12	G9	Sheep	22. 1	12.12	B2	D4	Tiger
17.11	6.10	K12	H10	Deer	23. 1	13.12	B2	E5	Leopard
18.11	7.10	K12	J11	Horse	24. 1	14.12	B2	F6	Griffon
19.11	8.10	K12	K12	Stag	25. 1	15.12	B2	G7	Ox
20.11	9.10	K12	A1	Serpent	26. 1	16.12	B2	H8	Bat
21.11	10.10	K12	B2	Earthworm	27. 1	17.12	B2	J9	Rat
22.11	11.10	K12	C3	Crocodile	28. 1	18.12	B2	K10	Swallow
23.11	12.10	K12	D4	Dragon	29. 1	19.12	B2	A11	Pig
24.11	13.10	K12	E5	Badger	30. 1	20.12	B2	B12	Porcupine
25.11	14.10	K12	F6	Hare	31. 1	21.12	B2	C1	Wolf
26.11	15.10	K12	G7	Fox	1. 2	22.12	B2	D2	Dog
27.11	16.10	K12	H8	Tiger	2. 2	23.12	B2	E3	Pheasant
28.11	17.10	K12	J9	Leopard	3. 2	24.12	B2	F4	Cock
29.11	18.10	K12	K10	Griffon	4. 2	25.12	B2	G5	Crow
30.11	19.10	K12	A11	Ox	5. 2	26.12	B2	H6	Monkey
1.12	20.10	K12	B12	Bat	6. 2	27.12	B2	J7	Gibbon
2.12	21.10	K12	C1	Rat	7. 2	28.12	B2	K8	Tapir
3.12	22.10	K12	D2	Swallow	8. 2	29.12	B2	A9	Sheep
4.12	23.10	K12	E3	Pig	9. 2	30.12	B2	B10	Deer

CHI SZU YEAR

Solar date	Lunar date	Month HS/EB	Day HS/EB	Constellation
10. 2	1. 1	C3	C11	Horse
11. 2	2. 1	C3	D12	Stag
12. 2	3. 1	C3	E1	Serpent
13. 2	4. 1	C3	F2	Earthworm
14. 2	5. 1	C3	G3	Crocodile
15. 2	6. 1	C3	H4	Dragon
16. 2	7. 1	C3	J5	Badger
17. 2	8. 1	C3	K6	Hare
18. 2	9. 1	C3	A7	Fox
19. 2	10. 1	C3	B8	Tiger
20. 2	11. 1	C3	C9	Leopard
21. 2	12. 1	C3	D10	Griffon
22. 2	13. 1	C3	E11	Ox
23. 2	14. 1	C3	F12	Bat
24. 2	15. 1	C3	G1	Rat
25. 2	16. 1	C3	H2	Swallow
26. 2	17. 1	C3	J3	Pig
27. 2	18. 1	C3	K4	Porcupine
28. 2	19. 1	C3	A5	Wolf
1. 3	20. 1	C3	B6	Dog
2. 3	21. 1	C3	C7	Pheasant
3. 3	22. 1	C3	D8	Cock
4. 3	23. 1	C3	E9	Crow
5. 3	24. 1	C3	F10	Monkey
6. 3	25. 1	C3	G11	Gibbon
7. 3	26. 1	C3	H12	Tapir
8. 3	27. 1	C3	J1	Sheep
9. 3	28. 1	C3	K2	Deer
10. 3	29. 1	C3	A3	Horse
11. 3	1. 2	D4	B4	Stag
12. 3	2. 2	D4	C5	Serpent
13. 3	3. 2	D4	D6	Earthworm
14. 3	4. 2	D4	E7	Crocodile
15. 3	5. 2	D4	F8	Dragon
16. 3	6. 2	D4	G9	Badger
17. 3	7. 2	D4	H10	Hare
18. 3	8. 2	D4	J11	Fox
19. 3	9. 2	D4	K12	Tiger
20. 3	10. 2	D4	A1	Leopard
21. 3	11. 2	D4	B2	Griffon
22. 3	12. 2	D4	C3	Ox
23. 3	13. 2	D4	D4	Bat
24. 3	14. 2	D4	E5	Rat
25. 3	15. 2	D4	F6	Swallow
26. 3	16. 2	D4	G7	Pig
27. 3	17. 2	D4	H8	Porcupine
28. 3	18. 2	D4	J9	Wolf
29. 3	19. 2	D4	K10	Dog
30. 3	20. 2	D4	A11	Pheasant
31. 3	21. 2	D4	B12	Cock
1. 4	22. 2	D4	C1	Crow
2. 4	23. 2	D4	D2	Monkey
3. 4	24. 2	D4	E3	Gibbon
4. 4	25. 2	D4	F4	Tapi
5. 4	26. 2	D4	G5	Sheep
6. 4	27. 2	D4	H6	Deer
7. 4	28. 2	D4	J7	Horse
8. 4	29. 2	D4	K8	Stag
9. 4	30. 2	D4	A9	Serpent
10. 4	1. 3	E5	B10	Earthworm
11. 4	2. 3	E5	C11	Crocodile
12. 4	3. 3	E5	D12	Dragon
13. 4	4. 3	E5	E1	Badger
14. 4	5. 3	E5	F2	Hare
15. 4	6. 3	E5	G3	Fox
16. 4	7. 3	E5	H4	Tiger
17. 4	8. 3	E5	J5	Leopard
18. 4	9. 3	E5	K6	Griffon
19. 4	10. 3	E5	A7	Ox
20. 4	11. 3	E5	B8	Bat
21. 4	12. 3	E5	C9	Rat
22. 4	13. 3	E5	D10	Swallow
23. 4	14. 3	E5	E11	Pig
24. 4	15. 3	E5	F12	Porcupine
25. 4	16. 3	E5	G1	Wolf
26. 4	17. 3	E5	H2	Dog
27. 4	18. 3	E5	J3	Pheasant
28. 4	19. 3	E5	K4	Cock
29. 4	20. 3	E5	A5	Crow
30. 4	21. 3	E5	B6	Monkey
1. 5	22. 3	E5	C7	Gibbon
2. 5	23. 3	E5	D8	Tapir
3. 5	24. 3	E5	E9	Sheep
4. 5	25. 3	E5	F10	Deer
5. 5	26. 3	E5	G11	Horse
6. 5	27. 3	E5	H12	Stag
7. 5	28. 3	E5	J1	Serpent
8. 5	29. 3	E5	K2	Crocodile
9. 5	1. 4	F6	A3	Crocodile
10. 5	2. 4	F6	B4	Dragon
11. 5	3. 4	F6	C5	Badger
12. 5	4. 4	F6	D6	Hare
13. 5	5. 4	F6	E7	Fox
14. 5	6. 4	F6	F8	Tiger
15. 5	7. 4	F6	G9	Leopard
16. 5	8. 4	F6	H10	Griffon
17. 5	9. 4	F6	J11	Ox
18. 5	10. 4	F6	K12	Bat
19. 5	11. 4	F6	A1	Rat
20. 5	12. 4	F6	B2	Swallow
21. 5	13. 4	F6	C3	Pig
22. 5	14. 4	F6	D4	Porcupine
23. 5	15. 4	F6	E5	Wolf
24. 5	16. 4	F6	F6	Dog
25. 5	17. 4	F6	G7	Pheasant
26. 5	18. 4	F6	H8	Cock
27. 5	19. 4	F6	J9	Crow
28. 5	20. 4	F6	K10	Monkey
29. 5	21. 4	F6	A11	Gibbon
30. 5	22. 4	F6	B12	Tapir
31. 5	23. 4	F6	C1	Sheep
1. 6	24. 4	F6	D2	Deer
2. 6	25. 4	F6	E3	Horse
3. 6	26. 4	F6	F4	Stag
4. 6	27. 4	F6	G5	Serpent
5. 6	28. 4	F6	H6	Earthworm
6. 6	29. 4	F6	J7	Crocodile
7. 6	1. 5	G7	K8	Dragon
8. 6	2. 5	G7	A9	Badger
9. 6	3. 5	G7	B10	Hare
10. 6	4. 5	G7	C11	Fox
11. 6	5. 5	G7	D12	Tiger
12. 6	6. 5	G7	E1	Leopard
13. 6	7. 5	G7	F2	Griffon
14. 6	8. 5	G7	G3	Ox
15. 6	9. 5	G7	H4	Bat
16. 6	10. 5	G7	J5	Rat
17. 6	11. 5	G7	K6	Swallow
18. 6	12. 5	G7	A7	Pig
19. 6	13. 5	G7	B8	Porcupine
20. 6	14. 5	G7	C9	Wolf
21. 6	15. 5	G7	D10	Dog
22. 6	16. 5	G7	E11	Pheasant
23. 6	17. 5	G7	F12	Cock
24. 6	18. 5	G7	G1	Crow
25. 6	19. 5	G7	H2	Monkey
26. 6	20. 5	G7	J3	Gibbon
27. 6	21. 5	G7	K4	Tapir
28. 6	22. 5	G7	A5	Sheep
29. 6	23. 5	G7	B6	Deer
30. 6	24. 5	G7	C7	Horse
1. 7	25. 5	G7	D8	Stag

Solar date	Lunar date	Month HS/EB	Day HS/EB	Constellation	Solar date	Lunar date	Month HS/EB	Day HS/EB	Constellation
2. 7	26. 5	G7	E9	Serpent	13. 9	11. 8	K10	H10	Dog
3. 7	27. 5	G7	F10	Earthworm	14. 9	12. 8	K10	J11	Pheasant
4. 7	28. 5	G7	G11	Crocodile	15. 9	13. 8	K10	K12	Cock
5. 7	29. 5	G7	H12	Dragon	16. 9	14. 8	K10	A1	Crow
6. 7	30. 5	G7	J1	Badger	17. 9	15. 8	K10	B2	Monkey
7. 7	1. 6	H8	K2	Hare	18. 9	16. 8	K10	C3	Gibbon
8. 7	2. 6	H8	A3	Fox	19. 9	17. 8	K10	D4	Tapir
9. 7	3. 6	H8	B4	Tiger	20. 9	18. 8	K10	E5	Sheep
10. 7	4. 6	H8	C5	Leopard	21. 9	19. 8	K10	F6	Deer
11. 7	5. 6	H8	D6	Griffon	22. 9	20. 8	K10	G7	Horse
12. 7	6. 6	H8	E7	Ox	23. 9	21. 8	K10	H8	Stag
13. 7	7. 6	H8	F8	Bat	24. 9	22. 8	K10	J9	Serpent
14. 7	8. 6	H8	G9	Rat	25. 9	23. 8	K10	K10	Earthworm
15. 7	9. 6	H8	H10	Swallow	26. 9	24. 8	K10	A11	Crocodile
16. 7	10. 6	H8	J11	Pig	27. 9	25. 8	K10	B12	Dragon
17. 7	11. 6	H8	K12	Porcupine	28. 9	26. 8	K10	C1	Badger
18. 7	12. 6	H8	A1	Wolf	29. 9	27. 8	K10	D2	Hare
19. 7	13. 6	H8	B2	Dog	30. 9	28. 8	K10	E3	Fox
20. 7	14. 6	H8	C3	Pheasant	1.10	29. 8	K10	F4	Tiger
21. 7	15. 6	H8	D4	Cock	2.10	30. 8	K10	G5	Leopard
22. 7	16. 6	H8	E5	Crow	3.10	1. 9	A11	H6	Griffon
23. 7	17. 6	H8	F6	Monkey	4.10	2. 9	A11	J7	Ox
24. 7	18. 6	H8	G7	Gibbon	5.10	3. 9	A11	K8	Bat
25. 7	19. 6	H8	H8	Tapir	6.10	4. 9	A11	A9	Rat
26. 7	20. 6	H8	J9	Sheep	7.10	5. 9	A11	B10	Swallow
27. 7	21. 6	H8	K10	Deer	8.10	6. 9	A11	C11	Pig
28. 7	22. 6	H8	A11	Horse	9.10	7. 9	A11	D12	Porcupine
29. 7	23. 6	H8	B12	Stag	10.10	8. 9	A11	E1	Wolf
30. 7	24. 6	H8	C1	Serpent	11.10	9. 9	A11	F2	Dog
31. 7	25. 6	H8	D2	Earthworm	12.10	10. 9	A11	G3	Pheasant
1. 8	26. 6	H8	E3	Crocodile	13.10	11. 9	A11	H4	Cock
2. 8	27. 6	H8	F4	Dragon	14.10	12. 9	A11	J5	Crow
3. 8	28. 6	H8	G5	Badger	15.10	13. 9	A11	K6	Monkey
4. 8	29. 6	H8	H6	Hare	16.10	14. 9	A11	A7	Gibbon
5. 8	1. 7	J9	J7	Fox	17.10	15. 9	A11	B8	Tapir
6. 8	2. 7	J9	K8	Tiger	18.10	16. 9	A11	C9	Sheep
7. 8	3. 7	J9	A9	Leopard	19.10	17. 9	A11	D10	Deer
8. 8	4. 7	J9	B10	Griffon	20.10	18. 9	A11	E11	Horse
9. 8	5. 7	J9	C11	Ox	21.10	19. 9	A11	F12	Stag
10. 8	6. 7	J9	D12	Bat	22.10	20. 9	A11	G1	Serpent
11. 8	7. 7	J9	E1	Rat	23.10	21. 9	A11	H2	Earthworm
12. 8	8. 7	J9	F2	Swallow	24.10	22. 9	A11	J3	Crocodile
13. 8	9. 7	J9	G3	Pig	25.10	23. 9	A11	K4	Dragon
14. 8	10. 7	J9	H4	Porcupine	26.10	24. 9	A11	A5	Badger
15. 8	11. 7	J9	J5	Wolf	27.10	25. 9	A11	B6	Hare
16. 8	12. 7	J9	K6	Dog	28.10	26. 9	A11	C7	Fox
17. 8	13. 7	J9	A7	Pheasant	29.10	27. 9	A11	D8	Tiger
18. 8	14. 7	J9	B8	Cock	30.10	28. 9	A11	E9	Leopard
19. 8	15. 7	J9	C9	Crow	31.10	29. 9	A11	F10	Griffon
20. 8	16. 7	J9	D10	Monkey	1.11	1.10	B12	G11	Ox
21. 8	17. 7	J9	E11	Gibbon	2.11	2.10	B12	H12	Bat
22. 8	18. 7	J9	F12	Tapir	3.11	3.10	B12	J1	Rat
23. 8	19. 7	J9	G1	Sheep	4.11	4.10	B12	K2	Swallow
24. 8	20. 7	J9	H2	Deer	5.11	5.10	B12	A3	Pig
25. 8	21. 7	J9	J3	Horse	6.11	6.10	B12	B4	Porcupine
26. 8	22. 7	J9	K4	Stag	7.11	7.10	B12	C5	Wolf
27. 8	23. 7	J9	A5	Serpent	8.11	8.10	B12	D6	Dog
28. 8	24. 7	J9	B6	Earthworm	9.11	9.10	B12	E7	Pheasant
29. 8	25. 7	J9	C7	Crocodile	10.11	10.10	B12	F8	Cock
30. 8	26. 7	J9	D8	Dragon	11.11	11.10	B12	G9	Crow
31. 8	27. 7	J9	E9	Badger	12.11	12.10	B12	H10	Monkey
1. 9	28. 7	J9	F10	Hare	13.11	13.10	B12	J11	Gibbon
2. 9	29. 7	J9	G11	Fox	14.11	14.10	B12	K12	Tapir
3. 9	1. 8	K10	H12	Tiger	15.11	15.10	B12	A1	Sheep
4. 9	2. 8	K10	J1	Leopard	16.11	16.10	B12	B2	Deer
5. 9	3. 8	K10	K2	Griffon	17.11	17.10	B12	C3	Horse
6. 9	4. 8	K10	A3	Ox	18.11	18.10	B12	D4	Stag
7. 9	5. 8	K10	B4	Bat	19.11	19.10	B12	E5	Serpent
8. 9	6. 8	K10	C5	Rat	20.11	20.10	B12	F6	Earthworm
9. 9	7. 8	K10	D6	Swallow	21.11	21.10	B12	G7	Crocodile
10. 9	8. 8	K10	E7	Pig	22.11	22.10	B12	H8	Dragon
11. 9	9. 8	K10	F8	Porcupine	23.11	23.10	B12	J9	Badger
12. 9	10. 8	K10	G9	Wolf	24.11	24.10	B12	K10	Hare

Solar date	Lunar date	Month HS/EB	Day HS/EB	Constellation	Solar date	Lunar date	Month HS/EB	Day HS/EB	Constellation
25.11	25.10	B12	A11	Fox	29.12	29.11	C1	E9	Rat
26.11	26.10	B12	B12	Tiger	30.12	30.11	C1	F10	Swallow
27.11	27.10	B12	C1	Leopard	31.12	1.12	D2	G11	Pig
28.11	28.10	B12	D2	Griffon	**1930**				
29.11	29.10	B12	E3	Ox	1. 1	2.12	D2	H12	Porcupine
30.11	30.10	B12	F4	Bat	2. 1	3.12	D2	J1	Wolf
1.12	1.11	C1	G5	Rat	3. 1	4.12	D2	K2	Dog
2.12	2.11	C1	H6	Swallow	4. 1	5.12	D2	A3	Pheasant
3.12	3.11	C1	J7	Pig	5. 1	6.12	D2	B4	Cock
4.12	4.11	C1	K8	Porcupine	6. 1	7.12	D2	C5	Crow
5.12	5.11	C1	A9	Wolf	7. 1	8.12	D2	D6	Monkey
6.12	6.11	C1	B10	Dog	8. 1	9.12	D2	E7	Gibbon
7.12	7.11	C1	C11	Pheasant	9. 1	10.12	D2	F8	Tapir
8.12	8.11	C1	D12	Cock	10. 1	11.12	D2	G9	Sheep
9.12	9.11	C1	E1	Crow	11. 1	12.12	D2	H10	Deer
10.12	10.11	C1	F2	Monkey	12. 1	13.12	D2	J11	Horse
11.12	11.11	C1	G3	Gibbon	13. 1	14.12	D2	K12	Stag
12.12	12.11	C1	H4	Tapir	14. 1	15.12	D2	A1	Serpent
13.12	13.11	C1	J5	Sheep	15. 1	16.12	D2	B2	Earthworm
14.12	14.11	C1	K6	Deer	16. 1	17.12	D2	C3	Crocodile
15.12	15.11	C1	A7	Horse	17. 1	18.12	D2	D4	Dragon
16.12	16.11	C1	B8	Stag	18. 1	19.12	D2	E5	Badger
17.12	17.11	C1	C9	Serpent	19. 1	20.12	D2	F6	Hare
18.12	18.11	C1	D10	Earthworm	20. 1	21.12	D2	G7	Fox
19.12	19.11	C1	E11	Crocodile	21. 1	22.12	D2	H8	Tiger
20.12	20.11	C1	F12	Dragon	22. 1	23.12	D2	J9	Leopard
21.12	21.11	C1	G1	Badger	23. 1	24.12	D2	K10	Griffon
22.12	22.11	C1	H2	Hare	24. 1	25.12	D2	A11	Ox
23.12	23.11	C1	J3	Fox	25. 1	26.12	D2	B12	Bat
24.12	24.11	C1	K4	Tiger	26. 1	27.12	D2	C1	Rat
25.12	25.11	C1	A5	Leopard	27. 1	28.12	D2	D2	Swallow
26.12	26.11	C1	B6	Griffon	28. 1	29.12	D2	E3	Pig
27.12	27.11	C1	C7	Ox	29. 1	30.12	D2	F4	Porcupine
28.12	28.11	C1	D8	Bat					

KENG WU YEAR

Solar date	Lunar date	Month HS/EB	Day HS/EB	Constellation	Solar date	Lunar date	Month HS/EB	Day HS/EB	Constellation
30. 1	1. 1	E3	G5	Wolf	5. 3	6. 2	F4	A3	Gibbon
31. 1	2. 1	E3	H6	Dog	6. 3	7. 2	F4	B4	Tapir
1. 2	3. 1	E3	J7	Pheasant	7. 3	8. 2	F4	C5	Sheep
2. 2	4. 1	E3	K8	Cock	8. 3	9. 2	F4	D6	Deer
3. 2	5. 1	E3	A9	Crow	9. 3	10. 2	F4	E7	Horse
4. 2	6. 1	E3	B10	Monkey	10. 3	11. 2	F4	F8	Stag
5. 2	7. 1	E3	C11	Gibbon	11. 3	12. 2	F4	G9	Serpent
6. 2	8. 1	E3	D12	Tapir	12. 3	13. 2	F4	H10	Earthworm
7. 2	9. 1	E3	E1	Sheep	13. 3	14. 2	F4	J11	Crocodile
8. 2	10. 1	E3	F2	Deer	14. 3	15. 2	F4	K12	Dragon
9. 2	11. 1	E3	G3	Horse	15. 3	16. 2	F4	A1	Badger
10. 2	12. 1	E3	H4	Stag	16. 3	17. 2	F4	B2	Hare
11. 2	13. 1	E3	J5	Serpent	17. 3	18. 2	F4	C3	Fox
12. 2	14. 1	E3	K6	Earthworm	18. 3	19. 2	F4	D4	Tiger
13. 2	15. 1	E3	A7	Crocodile	19. 3	20. 2	F4	E5	Leopard
14. 2	16. 1	E3	B8	Dragon	20. 3	21. 2	F4	F6	Griffon
15. 2	17. 1	E3	C9	Badger	21. 3	22. 2	F4	G7	Ox
16. 2	18. 1	E3	D10	Hare	22. 3	23. 2	F4	H8	Bat
17. 2	19. 1	E3	E11	Fox	23. 3	24. 2	F4	J9	Rat
18. 2	20. 1	E3	F12	Tiger	24. 3	25. 2	F4	K10	Swallow
19. 2	21. 1	E3	G1	Leopard	25. 3	26. 2	F4	A11	Pig
20. 2	22. 1	E3	H2	Griffon	26. 3	27. 2	F4	B12	Porcupine
21. 2	23. 1	E3	J3	Ox	27. 3	28. 2	F4	C1	Wolf
22. 2	24. 1	E3	K4	Bat	28. 3	29. 2	F4	D2	Dog
23. 2	25. 1	E3	A5	Rat	29. 3	30. 2	F4	E3	Pheasant
24. 2	26. 1	E3	B6	Swallow	30. 3	1. 3	G5	F4	Cock
25. 2	27. 1	E3	C7	Pig	31. 3	2. 3	G5	G5	Crow
26. 2	28. 1	E3	D8	Porcupine	1. 4	3. 3	G5	H6	Monkey
27. 2	29. 1	E3	E9	Wolf	2. 4	4. 3	G5	J7	Gibbon
28. 2	1. 2	F4	F10	Dog	3. 4	5. 3	G5	K8	Tapir
1. 3	2. 2	F4	G11	Pheasant	4. 4	6. 3	G5	A9	Sheep
2. 3	3. 2	F4	H12	Cock	5. 4	7. 3	G5	B10	Deer
3. 3	4. 2	F4	J1	Crow	6. 4	8. 3	G5	C11	Horse
4. 3	5. 2	F4	K2	Monkey	7. 4	9. 3	G5	D12	Stag

Solar date	Lunar date	Month HS/EB	Day HS/EB	Constellation
8. 4	10. 3	G5	E1	Serpent
9. 4	11. 3	G5	F2	Earthworm
10. 4	12. 3	G5	G3	Crocodile
11. 4	13. 3	G5	H4	Dragon
12. 4	14. 3	G5	J5	Badger
13. 4	15. 3	G5	K6	Hare
14. 4	16. 3	G5	A7	Fox
15. 4	17. 3	G5	B8	Tiger
16. 4	18. 3	G5	C9	Leopard
17. 4	19. 3	G5	D10	Griffon
18. 4	20. 3	G5	E11	Ox
19. 4	21. 3	G5	F12	Bat
20. 4	22. 3	G5	G1	Rat
21. 4	23. 3	G5	H2	Swallow
22. 4	24. 3	G5	J3	Pig
23. 4	25. 3	G5	K4	Porcupine
24. 4	26. 3	G5	A5	Wolf
25. 4	27. 3	G5	B6	Dog
26. 4	28. 3	G5	C7	Pheasant
27. 4	29. 3	G5	D8	Cock
28. 4	30. 3	G5	E9	Crow
29. 4	1. 4	H6	F10	Monkey
30. 4	2. 4	H6	G11	Gibbon
1. 5	3. 4	H6	H12	Tapir
2. 5	4. 4	H6	J1	Sheep
3. 5	5. 4	H6	K2	Deer
4. 5	6. 4	H6	A3	Horse
5. 5	7. 4	H6	B4	Stag
6. 5	8. 4	H6	C5	Serpent
7. 5	9. 4	H6	D6	Earthworm
8. 5	10. 4	H6	E7	Crocodile
9. 5	11. 4	H6	F8	Dragon
10. 5	12. 4	H6	G9	Badger
11. 5	13. 4	H6	H10	Hare
12. 5	14. 4	H6	J11	Fox
13. 5	15. 4	H6	K12	Tiger
14. 5	16. 4	H6	A1	Leopard
15. 5	17. 4	H6	B2	Griffon
16. 5	18. 4	H6	C3	Ox
17. 5	19. 4	H6	D4	Bat
18. 5	20. 4	H6	E5	Rat
19. 5	21. 4	H6	F6	Swallow
20. 5	22. 4	H6	G7	Pig
21. 5	23. 4	H6	H8	Porcupine
22. 5	24. 4	H6	J9	Wolf
23. 5	25. 4	H6	K10	Dog
24. 5	26. 4	H6	A11	Pheasant
25. 5	27. 4	H6	B12	Cock
26. 5	28. 4	H6	C1	Crow
27. 5	29. 4	H6	D2	Monkey
28. 5	1. 5	J7	E3	Gibbon
29. 5	2. 5	J7	F4	Tapir
30. 5	3. 5	J7	G5	Sheep
31. 5	4. 5	J7	H6	Deer
1. 6	5. 5	J7	J7	Horse
2. 6	6. 5	J7	K8	Stag
3. 6	7. 5	J7	A9	Serpent
4. 6	8. 5	J7	B10	Earthworm
5. 6	9. 5	J7	C11	Crocodile
6. 6	10. 5	J7	D12	Dragon
7. 6	11. 5	J7	E1	Badger
8. 6	12. 5	J7	F2	Hare
9. 6	13. 5	J7	G3	Fox
10. 6	14. 5	J7	H4	Tiger
11. 6	15. 5	J7	J5	Leopard
12. 6	16. 5	J7	K6	Griffon
13. 6	17. 5	J7	A7	Ox
14. 6	18. 5	J7	B8	Bat
15. 6	19. 5	J7	C9	Rat
16. 6	20. 5	J7	D10	Swallow
17. 6	21. 5	J7	E11	Pig
18. 6	22. 5	J7	F12	Porcupine
19. 6	23. 5	J7	G1	Wolf

Solar date	Lunar date	Month HS/EB	Day HS/EB	Constellation
20. 6	24. 5	J7	H2	Dog
21. 6	25. 5	J7	J3	Pheasant
22. 6	26. 5	J7	K4	Cock
23. 6	27. 5	J7	A5	Crow
24. 6	28. 5	J7	B6	Monkey
25. 6	29. 5	J7	C7	Gibbon
26. 6	1. 6	K8	D8	Tapir
27. 6	2. 6	K8	E9	Sheep
28. 6	3. 6	K8	F10	Deer
29. 6	4. 6	K8	G11	Horse
30. 6	5. 6	K8	H12	Stag
1. 7	6. 6	K8	J1	Serpent
2. 7	7. 6	K8	K2	Earthworm
3. 7	8. 6	K8	A3	Crocodile
4. 7	9. 6	K8	B4	Dragon
5. 7	10. 6	K8	C5	Badger
6. 7	11. 6	K8	D6	Hare
7. 7	12. 6	K8	E7	Fox
8. 7	13. 6	K8	F8	Tiger
9. 7	14. 6	K8	G9	Leopard
10. 7	15. 6	K8	H10	Griffon
11. 7	16. 6	K8	J11	Ox
12. 7	17. 6	K8	K12	Bat
13. 7	18. 6	K8	A1	Rat
14. 7	19. 6	K8	B2	Swallow
15. 7	20. 6	K8	C3	Pig
16. 7	21. 6	K8	D4	Porcupine
17. 7	22. 6	K8	E5	Wolf
18. 7	23. 6	K8	F6	Dog
19. 7	24. 6	K8	G7	Pheasant
20. 7	25. 6	K8	H8	Cock
21. 7	26. 6	K8	J9	Crow
22. 7	27. 6	K8	K10	Monkey
23. 7	28. 6	K8	A11	Gibbon
24. 7	29. 6	K8	B12	Tapir
25. 7	30. 6	K8	C1	Sheep
26. 7	1. 6	K8	D2	Deer
27. 7	2. 6	K8	E3	Horse
28. 7	3. 6	K8	F4	Stag
29. 7	4. 6	K8	G5	Serpent
30. 7	5. 6	K8	H6	Earthworm
31. 7	6. 6	K8	J7	Crocodile
1. 8	7. 6	K8	K8	Dragon
2. 8	8. 6	K8	A9	Badger
3. 8	9. 6	K8	B10	Hare
4. 8	10. 6	K8	C11	Fox
5. 8	11. 6	K8	D12	Tiger
6. 8	12. 6	K8	E1	Leopard
7. 8	13. 6	K8	F2	Griffon
8. 8	14. 6	K8	G3	Ox
9. 8	15. 6	K8	H4	Bat
10. 8	16. 6	K8	J5	Rat
11. 8	17. 6	K8	K6	Swallow
12. 8	18. 6	K8	A7	Pig
13. 8	19. 6	K8	B8	Porcupine
14. 8	20. 6	K8	C9	Wolf
15. 8	21. 6	K8	D10	Dog
16. 8	22. 6	K8	E11	Pheasant
17. 8	23. 6	K8	F12	Cock
18. 8	24. 6	K8	G1	Crow
19. 8	25. 6	K8	H2	Monkey
20. 8	26. 6	K8	J3	Gibbon
21. 8	27. 6	K8	K4	Tapir
22. 8	28. 6	K8	A5	Sheep
23. 8	29. 6	K8	B6	Deer
24. 8	1. 7	A9	C7	Horse
25. 8	2. 7	A9	D8	Stag
26. 8	3. 7	A9	E9	Serpent
27. 8	4. 7	A9	F10	Earthworm
28. 8	5. 7	A9	G11	Crocodile
29. 8	6. 7	A9	H12	Dragon
30. 8	7. 7	A9	J1	Badger
31. 8	8. 7	A9	K2	Hare

Solar date	Lunar date	Month HS/EB	Day HS/EB	Constellation	Solar date	Lunar date	Month HS/EB	Day HS/EB	Constellation
1. 9	9. 7	A9	A3	Fox	13.11	23. 9	C11	D4	Tapir
2. 9	10. 7	A9	B4	Tiger	14.11	24. 9	C11	E5	Sheep
3. 9	11. 7	A9	C5	Leopard	15.11	25. 9	C11	F6	Deer
4. 9	12. 7	A9	D6	Griffon	16.11	26. 9	C11	G7	Horse
5. 9	13. 7	A9	E7	Ox	17.11	27. 9	C11	H8	Stag
6. 9	14. 7	A9	F8	Bat	18.11	28. 9	C11	J9	Serpent
7. 9	15. 7	A9	G9	Rat	19.11	29. 9	C11	K10	Earthworm
8. 9	16. 7	A9	H10	Swallow	20.11	1.10	D12	A11	Crocodile
9. 9	17. 7	A9	J11	Pig	21.11	2.10	D12	B12	Dragon
10. 9	18. 7	A9	K12	Porcupine	22.11	3.10	D12	C1	Badger
11. 9	19. 7	A9	A1	Wolf	23.11	4.10	D12	D2	Hare
12. 9	20. 7	A9	B2	Dog	24.11	5.10	D12	E3	Fox
13. 9	21. 7	A9	C3	Pheasant	25.11	6.10	D12	F4	Tiger
14. 9	22. 7	A9	D4	Cock	26.11	7.10	D12	G5	Leopard
15. 9	23. 7	A9	E5	Crow	27.11	8.10	D12	H6	Griffon
16. 9	24. 7	A9	F6	Monkey	28.11	9.10	D12	J7	Ox
17. 9	25. 7	A9	G7	Gibbon	29.11	10.10	D12	K8	Bat
18. 9	26. 7	A9	H8	Tapir	30.11	11.10	D12	A9	Rat
19. 9	27. 7	A9	J9	Sheep	1.12	12.10	D12	B10	Swallow
20. 9	28. 7	A9	K10	Deer	2.12	13.10	D12	C11	Pig
21. 9	29. 7	A9	A11	Horse	3.12	14.10	D12	D12	Porcupine
22. 9	1. 8	B10	B12	Stag	4.12	15.10	D12	E1	Wolf
23. 9	2. 8	B10	C1	Serpent	5.12	16.10	D12	F2	Dog
24. 9	3. 8	B10	D2	Earthworm	6.12	17.10	D12	G3	Pheasant
25. 9	4. 8	B10	E3	Crocodile	7.12	18.10	D12	H4	Cock
26. 9	5. 8	B10	F4	Dragon	8.12	19.10	D12	J5	Crow
27. 9	6. 8	B10	G5	Badger	9.12	20.10	D12	K6	Monkey
28. 9	7. 8	B10	H6	Hare	10.12	21.10	D12	A7	Gibbon
29. 9	8. 8	B10	J7	Fox	11.12	22.10	D12	B8	Tapir
30. 9	9. 8	B10	K8	Tiger	12.12	23.10	D12	C9	Sheep
1.10	10. 8	B10	A9	Leopard	13.12	24.10	D12	D10	Deer
2.10	11. 8	B10	B10	Griffon	14.12	25.10	D12	E11	Horse
3.10	12. 8	B10	C11	Ox	15.12	26.10	D12	F12	Stag
4.10	13. 8	B10	D12	Bat	16.12	27.10	D12	G1	Serpent
5.10	14. 8	B10	E1	Rat	17.12	28.10	D12	H2	Earthworm
6.10	15. 8	B10	F2	Swallow	18.12	29.10	D12	J3	Crocodile
7.10	16. 8	B10	G3	Pig	19.12	30.10	D12	K4	Dragon
8.10	17. 8	B10	H4	Porcupine	20.12	1.11	E1	A5	Badger
9.10	18. 8	B10	J5	Wolf	21.12	2.11	E1	B6	Hare
10.10	19. 8	B10	K6	Dog	22.12	3.11	E1	C7	Fox
11.10	20. 8	B10	A7	Pheasant	23.12	4.11	E1	D8	Tiger
12.10	21. 8	B10	B8	Cock	24.12	5.11	E1	E9	Leopard
13.10	22. 8	B10	C9	Crow	25.12	6.11	E1	F10	Griffon
14.10	23. 8	B10	D10	Monkey	26.12	7.11	E1	G11	Ox
15.10	24. 8	B10	E11	Gibbon	27.12	8.11	E1	H12	Bat
16.10	25. 8	B10	F12	Tapir	28.12	9.11	E1	J1	Rat
17.10	26. 8	B10	G1	Sheep	29.12	10.11	E1	K2	Swallow
18.10	27. 8	B10	H2	Deer	30.12	11.11	E1	A3	Pig
19.10	28. 8	B10	J3	Horse	31.12	12.11	E1	B4	Porcupine
20.10	29. 8	B10	K4	Stag	**1931**				
21.10	30. 8	B10	A5	Serpent	1. 1	13.11	E1	C5	Wolf
22.10	1. 9	C11	B6	Earthworm	2. 1	14.11	E1	D6	Dog
23.10	2. 9	C11	C7	Crocodile	3. 1	15.11	E1	E7	Pheasant
24.10	3. 9	C11	D8	Dragon	4. 1	16.11	E1	F8	Cock
25.10	4. 9	C11	E9	Badger	5. 1	17.11	E1	G9	Crow
26.10	5. 9	C11	F10	Hare	6. 1	18.11	E1	H10	Monkey
27.10	6. 9	C11	G11	Fox	7. 1	19.11	E1	J11	Gibbon
28.10	7. 9	C11	H12	Tiger	8. 1	20.11	E1	K12	Tapir
29.10	8. 9	C11	J1	Leopard	9. 1	21.11	E1	A1	Sheep
30.10	9. 9	C11	K2	Griffon	10. 1	22.11	E1	B2	Deer
31.10	10. 9	C11	A3	Ox	11. 1	23.11	E1	C3	Horse
1.11	11. 9	C11	B4	Bat	12. 1	24.11	E1	D4	Stag
2.11	12. 9	C11	C5	Rat	13. 1	25.11	E1	E5	Serpent
3.11	13. 9	C11	D6	Swallow	14. 1	26.11	E1	F6	Earthworm
4.11	14. 9	C11	E7	Pig	15. 1	27.11	E1	G7	Crocodile
5.11	15. 9	C11	F8	Porcupine	16. 1	28.11	E1	H8	Dragon
6.11	16. 9	C11	G9	Wolf	17. 1	29.11	E1	J9	Badger
7.11	17. 9	C11	H10	Dog	18. 1	30.11	E1	K10	Hare
8.11	18. 9	C11	J11	Pheasant	19. 1	1.12	F2	A11	Fox
9.11	19. 9	C11	K12	Cock	20. 1	2.12	F2	B12	Tiger
10.11	20. 9	C11	A1	Crow	21. 1	3.12	F2	C1	Leopard
11.11	21. 9	C11	B2	Monkey	22. 1	4.12	F2	D2	Griffon
12.11	22. 9	C11	C3	Gibbon					

Solar date	Lunar date	Month HS/EB	Day HS/EB	Constellation	Solar date	Lunar date	Month HS/EB	Day HS/EB	Constellation
23. 1	5.12	F2	E3	Ox	5. 2	18.12	F2	H4	Tapir
24. 1	6.12	F2	F4	Bat	6. 2	19.12	F2	J5	Sheep
25. 1	7.12	F2	G5	Rat	7. 2	20.12	F2	K6	Deer
26. 1	8.12	F2	H6	Swallow	8. 2	21.12	F2	A7	Horse
27. 1	9.12	F2	J7	Pig	9. 2	22.12	F2	B8	Stag
28. 1	10.12	F2	K8	Porcupine	10. 2	23.12	F2	C9	Serpent
29. 1	11.12	F2	A9	Wolf	11. 2	24.12	F2	D10	Earthworm
30. 1	12.12	F2	B10	Dog	12. 2	25.12	F2	E11	Crocodile
31. 1	13.12	F2	C11	Pheasant	13. 2	26.12	F2	F12	Dragon
1. 2	14.12	F2	D12	Cock	14. 2	27.12	F2	G1	Badger
2. 2	15.12	F2	E1	Crow	15. 2	28.12	F2	H2	Hare
3. 2	16.12	F2	F2	Monkey	16. 2	29.12	F2	J3	Fox
4. 2	17.12	F2	G3	Gibbon					

HSIN WEI YEAR

Solar date	Lunar date	Month HS/EB	Day HS/EB	Constellation	Solar date	Lunar date	Month HS/EB	Day HS/EB	Constellation
17. 2	1. 1	G3	K4	Tiger	13. 4	26. 2	H4	E11	Fox
18. 2	2. 1	G3	A5	Leopard	14. 4	27. 2	H4	F12	Tiger
19. 2	3. 1	G3	B6	Griffon	15. 4	28. 2	H4	G1	Leopard
20. 2	4. 1	G3	C7	Ox	16. 4	29. 2	H4	H2	Griffon
21. 2	5. 1	G3	D8	Bat	17. 4	30. 2	H4	J3	Ox
22. 2	6. 1	G3	E9	Rat	18. 4	1. 3	J5	K4	Bat
23. 2	7. 1	G3	F10	Swallow	19. 4	2. 3	J5	A5	Rat
24. 2	8. 1	G3	G11	Pig	20. 4	3. 3	J5	B6	Swallow
25. 2	9. 1	G3	H12	Porcupine	21. 4	4. 3	J5	C7	Pig
26. 2	10. 1	G3	J1	Wolf	22. 4	5. 3	J5	D8	Porcupine
27. 2	11. 1	G3	K2	Dog	23. 4	6. 3	J5	E9	Wolf
28. 2	12. 1	G3	A3	Pheasant	24. 4	7. 3	J5	F10	Dog
1. 3	13. 1	G3	B4	Cock	25. 4	8. 3	J5	G11	Pheasant
2. 3	14. 1	G3	C5	Crow	26. 4	9. 3	J5	H12	Cock
3. 3	15. 1	G3	D6	Monkey	27. 4	10. 3	J5	J1	Crow
4. 3	16. 1	G3	E7	Gibbon	28. 4	11. 3	J5	K2	Monkey
5. 3	17. 1	G3	F8	Tapir	29. 4	12. 3	J5	A3	Gibbon
6. 3	18. 1	G3	G9	Sheep	30. 4	13. 3	J5	B4	Tapir
7. 3	19. 1	G3	H10	Deer	1. 5	14. 3	J5	C5	Sheep
8. 3	20. 1	G3	J11	Horse	2. 5	15. 3	J5	D6	Deer
9. 3	21. 1	G3	K12	Stag	3. 5	16. 3	J5	E7	Horse
10. 3	22. 1	G3	A1	Serpent	4. 5	17. 3	J5	F8	Stag
11. 3	23. 1	G3	B2	Earthworm	5. 5	18. 3	J5	G9	Serpent
12. 3	24. 1	G3	C3	Crocodile	6. 5	19. 3	J5	H10	Earthworm
13. 3	25. 1	G3	D4	Dragon	7. 5	20. 3	J5	J11	Crocodile
14. 3	26. 1	G3	E5	Badger	8. 5	21. 3	J5	K12	Dragon
15. 3	27. 1	G3	F6	Hare	9. 5	22. 3	J5	A1	Badger
16. 3	28. 1	G3	G7	Fox	10. 5	23. 3	J5	B2	Hare
17. 3	29. 1	G3	H8	Tiger	11. 5	24. 3	J5	C3	Fox
18. 3	30. 1	G3	J9	Leopard	12. 5	25. 3	J5	D4	Tiger
19. 3	1. 2	H4	K10	Griffon	13. 5	26. 3	J5	E5	Leopard
20. 3	2. 2	H4	A11	Ox	14. 5	27. 3	J5	F6	Griffon
21. 3	3. 2	H4	B12	Bat	15. 5	28. 3	J5	G7	Ox
22. 3	4. 2	H4	C1	Rat	16. 5	29. 3	J5	H8	Bat
23. 3	5. 2	H4	D2	Swallow	17. 5	1. 4	K6	J9	Rat
24. 3	6. 2	H4	E3	Pig	18. 5	2. 4	K6	K10	Swallow
25. 3	7. 2	H4	F4	Porcupine	19. 5	3. 4	K6	A11	Pig
26. 3	8. 2	H4	G5	Wolf	20. 5	4. 4	K6	B12	Porcupine
27. 3	9. 2	H4	H6	Dog	21. 5	5. 4	K6	C1	Wolf
28. 3	10. 2	H4	J7	Pheasant	22. 5	6. 4	K6	D2	Dog
29. 3	11. 2	H4	K8	Cock	23. 5	7. 4	K6	E3	Pheasant
30. 3	12. 2	H4	A9	Crow	24. 5	8. 4	K6	F4	Cock
31. 3	13. 2	H4	B10	Monkey	25. 5	9. 4	K6	G5	Crow
1. 4	14. 2	H4	C11	Gibbon	26. 5	10. 4	K6	H6	Monkey
2. 4	15. 2	H4	D12	Tapir	27. 5	11. 4	K6	J7	Gibbon
3. 4	16. 2	H4	E1	Sheep	28. 5	12. 4	K6	K8	Tapir
4. 4	17. 2	H4	F2	Deer	29. 5	13. 4	K6	A9	Sheep
5. 4	18. 2	H4	G3	Horse	30. 5	14. 4	K6	B10	Deer
6. 4	19. 2	H4	H4	Stag	31. 5	15. 4	K6	C11	Horse
7. 4	20. 2	H4	J5	Serpent	1. 6	16. 4	K6	D12	Stag
8. 4	21. 2	H4	K6	Earthworm	2. 6	17. 4	K6	E1	Serpent
9. 4	22. 2	H4	A7	Crocodile	3. 6	18. 4	K6	F2	Earthworm
10. 4	23. 2	H4	B8	Dragon	4. 6	19. 4	K6	G3	Crocodile
11. 4	24. 2	H4	C9	Badger	5. 6	20. 4	K6	H4	Dragon
12. 4	25. 2	H4	D10	Hare	6. 6	21. 4	K6	J5	Badger

Solar date	Lunar date	Month HS/EB	Day HS/EB	Constellation	Solar date	Lunar date	Month HS/EB	Day HS/EB	Constellation
7. 6	22. 4	K6	K6	Hare	19. 8	6. 7	C9	C7	Gibbon
8. 6	23. 4	K6	A7	Fox	20. 8	7. 7	C9	D8	Tapir
9. 6	24. 4	K6	B8	Tiger	21. 8	8. 7	C9	E9	Sheep
10. 6	25. 4	K6	C9	Leopard	22. 8	9. 7	C9	F10	Deer
11. 6	26. 4	K6	D10	Griffon	23. 8	10. 7	C9	G11	Horse
12. 6	27. 4	K6	E11	Ox	24. 8	11. 7	C9	H12	Stag
13. 6	28. 4	K6	F12	Bat	25. 8	12. 7	C9	J1	Serpent
14. 6	29. 4	K6	G1	Rat	26. 8	13. 7	C9	K2	Earthworm
15. 6	30. 4	K6	H2	Swallow	27. 8	14. 7	C9	A3	Crocodile
16. 6	1. 5	A7	J3	Pig	28. 8	15. 7	C9	B4	Dragon
17. 6	2. 5	A7	K4	Porcupine	29. 8	16. 7	C9	C5	Badger
18. 6	3. 5	A7	A5	Wolf	30. 8	17. 7	C9	D6	Hare
19. 6	4. 5	A7	B6	Dog	31. 8	18. 7	C9	E7	Fox
20. 6	5. 5	A7	C7	Pheasant	1. 9	19. 7	C9	F8	Tiger
21. 6	6. 5	A7	D8	Cock	2. 9	20. 7	C9	G9	Leopard
22. 6	7. 5	A7	E9	Crow	3. 9	21. 7	C9	H10	Griffon
23. 6	8. 5	A7	F10	Monkey	4. 9	22. 7	C9	J11	Ox
24. 6	9. 5	A7	G11	Gibbon	5. 9	23. 7	C9	K12	Bat
25. 6	10. 5	A7	H12	Tapir	6. 9	24. 7	C9	A1	Rat
26. 6	11. 5	A7	J1	Sheep	7. 9	25. 7	C9	B2	Swallow
27. 6	12. 5	A7	K2	Deer	8. 9	26. 7	C9	C3	Pig
28. 6	13. 5	A7	A3	Horse	9. 9	27. 7	C9	D4	Porcupine
29. 6	14. 5	A7	B4	Stag	10. 9	28. 7	C9	E5	Wolf
30. 6	15. 5	A7	C5	Serpent	11. 9	29. 7	C9	F6	Dog
1. 7	16. 5	A7	D6	Earthworm	12. 9	1. 8	D10	G7	Pheasant
2. 7	17. 5	A7	E7	Crocodile	13. 9	2. 8	D10	H8	Cock
3. 7	18. 5	A7	F8	Dragon	14. 9	3. 8	D10	J9	Crow
4. 7	19. 5	A7	G9	Badger	15. 9	4. 8	D10	K10	Monkey
5. 7	20. 5	A7	H10	Hare	16. 9	5. 8	D10	A11	Gibbon
6. 7	21. 5	A7	J11	Fox	17. 9	6. 8	D10	B12	Tapir
7. 7	22. 5	A7	K12	Tiger	18. 9	7. 8	D10	C1	Sheep
8. 7	23. 5	A7	A1	Leopard	19. 9	8. 8	D10	D2	Deer
9. 7	24. 5	A7	B2	Griffon	20. 9	9. 8	D10	E3	Horse
10. 7	25. 5	A7	C3	Ox	21. 9	10. 8	D10	F4	Stag
11. 7	26. 5	A7	D4	Bat	22. 9	11. 8	D10	G5	Serpent
12. 7	27. 5	A7	E5	Rat	23. 9	12. 8	D10	H6	Earthworm
13. 7	28. 5	A7	F6	Swallow	24. 9	13. 8	D10	J7	Crocodile
14. 7	29. 5	A7	G7	Pig	25. 9	14. 8	D10	K8	Dragon
15. 7	1. 6	B8	H8	Porcupine	26. 9	15. 8	D10	A9	Badger
16. 7	2. 6	B8	J9	Wolf	27. 9	16. 8	D10	B10	Hare
17. 7	3. 6	B8	K10	Dog	28. 9	17. 8	D10	C11	Fox
18. 7	4. 6	B8	A11	Pheasant	29. 9	18. 8	D10	D12	Tiger
19. 7	5. 6	B8	B12	Cock	30. 9	19. 8	D10	E1	Leopard
20. 7	6. 6	B8	C1	Crow	1.10	20. 8	D10	F2	Griffon
21. 7	7. 6	B8	D2	Monkey	2.10	21. 8	D10	G3	Ox
22. 7	8. 6	B8	E3	Gibbon	3.10	22. 8	D10	H4	Bat
23. 7	9. 6	B8	F4	Tapir	4.10	23. 8	D10	J5	Rat
24. 7	10. 6	B8	G5	Sheep	5.10	24. 8	D10	K6	Swallow
25. 7	11. 6	B8	H6	Deer	6.10	25. 8	D10	A7	Pig
26. 7	12. 6	B8	J7	Horse	7.10	26. 8	D10	B8	Porcupine
27. 7	13. 6	B8	K8	Stag	8.10	27. 8	D10	C9	Wolf
28. 7	14. 6	B8	A9	Serpent	9.10	28. 8	D10	D10	Dog
29. 7	15. 6	B8	B10	Earthworm	10.10	29. 8	D10	E11	Pheasant
30. 7	16. 6	B8	C11	Crocodile	11.10	1. 9	E11	F12	Cock
31. 7	17. 6	B8	D12	Dragon	12.10	2. 9	E11	G1	Crow
1. 8	18. 6	B8	E1	Badger	13.10	3. 9	E11	H2	Monkey
2. 8	19. 6	B8	F2	Hare	14.10	4. 9	E11	J3	Gibbon
3. 8	20. 6	B8	G3	Fox	15.10	5. 9	E11	K4	Tapir
4. 8	21. 6	B8	H4	Tiger	16.10	6. 9	E11	A5	Sheep
5. 8	22. 6	B8	J5	Leopard	17.10	7. 9	E11	B6	Deer
6. 8	23. 6	B8	K6	Griffon	18.10	8. 9	E11	C7	Horse
7. 8	24. 6	B8	A7	Ox	19.10	9. 9	E11	D8	Stag
8. 8	25. 6	B8	B8	Bat	20.10	10. 9	E11	E9	Serpent
9. 8	26. 6	B8	C9	Rat	21.10	11. 9	E11	F10	Earthworm
10. 8	27. 6	B8	D10	Swallow	22.10	12. 9	E11	G11	Crocodile
11. 8	28. 6	B8	E11	Pig	23.10	13. 9	E11	H12	Dragon
12. 8	29. 6	B8	F12	Porcupine	24.10	14. 9	E11	J1	Badger
13. 8	30. 6	B8	G1	Wolf	25.10	15. 9	E11	K2	Hare
14. 8	1. 7	C9	H2	Dog	26.10	16. 9	E11	A3	Fox
15. 8	2. 7	C9	J3	Pheasant	27.10	17. 9	E11	B4	Tiger
16. 8	3. 7	C9	K4	Cock	28.10	18. 9	E11	C5	Leopard
17. 8	4. 7	C9	A5	Crow	29.10	19. 9	E11	D6	Griffon
18. 8	5. 7	C9	B6	Monkey	30.10	20. 9	E11	E7	Ox

Solar date	Lunar date	Month HS/EB	Day HS/EB	Constellation	Solar date	Lunar date	Month HS/EB	Day HS/EB	Constellation
31.10	21. 9	E11	F8	Bat	20.12	12.11	G1	F10	Hare
1.11	22. 9	E11	G9	Rat	21.12	13.11	G1	G11	Fox
2.11	23. 9	E11	H10	Swallow	22.12	14.11	G1	H12	Tiger
3.11	24. 9	E11	J11	Pig	23.12	15.11	G1	J1	Leopard
4.11	25. 9	E11	K12	Porcupine	24.12	16.11	G1	K2	Griffon
5.11	26. 9	E11	A1	Wolf	25.12	17.11	G1	A3	Ox
6.11	27. 9	E11	B2	Dog	26.12	18.11	G1	B4	Bat
7.11	28. 9	E11	C3	Pheasant	27.12	19.11	G1	C5	Rat
8.11	29. 9	E11	D4	Cock	28.12	20.11	G1	D6	Swallow
9.11	30. 9	E11	E5	Crow	29.12	21.11	G1	E7	Pig
10.11	1.10	F12	F6	Monkey	30.12	22.11	G1	F8	Porcupine
11.11	2.10	F12	G7	Gibbon	31.12	23.11	G1	G9	Wolf
12.11	3.10	F12	H8	Tapir					
13.11	4.10	F12	J9	Sheep	**1932**				
14.11	5.10	F12	K10	Deer	1. 1	24.11	G1	H10	Dog
15.11	6.10	F12	A11	Horse	2. 1	25.11	G1	J11	Pheasant
16.11	7.10	F12	B12	Stag	3. 1	26.11	G1	K12	Cock
17.11	8.10	F12	C1	Serpent	4. 1	27.11	G1	A1	Crow
18.11	9.10	F12	D2	Earthworm	5. 1	28.11	G1	B2	Monkey
19.11	10.10	F12	E3	Crocodile	6. 1	29.11	G1	C3	Gibbon
20.11	11.10	F12	F4	Dragon	7. 1	30.11	G1	D4	Tapir
21.11	12.10	F12	G5	Badger	8. 1	1.12	H2	E5	Sheep
22.11	13.10	F12	H6	Hare	9. 1	2.12	H2	F6	Deer
23.11	14.10	F12	J7	Fox	10. 1	3.12	H2	G7	Horse
24.11	15.10	F12	K8	Tiger	11. 1	4.12	H2	H8	Stag
25.11	16.10	F12	A9	Leopard	12. 1	5.12	H2	J9	Serpent
26.11	17.10	F12	B10	Griffon	13. 1	6.12	H2	K10	Earthworm
27.11	18.10	F12	C11	Ox	14. 1	7.12	H2	A11	Crocodile
28.11	19.10	F12	D12	Bat	15. 1	8.12	H2	B12	Dragon
29.11	20.10	F12	E1	Rat	16. 1	9.12	H2	C1	Badger
30.11	21.10	F12	F2	Swallow	17. 1	10.12	H2	D2	Hare
1.12	22.10	F12	G3	Pig	18. 1	11.12	H2	E3	Fox
2.12	23.10	F12	H4	Porcupine	19. 1	12.12	H2	F4	Tiger
3.12	24.10	F12	J5	Wolf	20. 1	13.12	H2	G5	Leopard
4.12	25.10	F12	K6	Dog	21. 1	14.12	H2	H6	Griffon
5.12	26.10	F12	A7	Pheasant	22. 1	15.12	H2	J7	Ox
6.12	27.10	F12	B8	Cock	23. 1	16.12	H2	K8	Bat
7.12	28.10	F12	C9	Crow	24. 1	17.12	H2	A9	Rat
8.12	29.10	F12	D10	Monkey	25. 1	18.12	H2	B10	Swallow
9.12	1.11	G1	E11	Gibbon	26. 1	19.12	H2	C11	Pig
10.12	2.11	G1	F12	Tapir	27. 1	20.12	H2	D12	Porcupine
11.12	3.11	G1	G1	Sheep	28. 1	21.12	H2	E1	Wolf
12.12	4.11	G1	H2	Deer	29. 1	22.12	H2	F2	Dog
13.12	5.11	G1	J3	Horse	30. 1	23.12	H2	G3	Pheasant
14.12	6.11	G1	K4	Stag	31. 1	24.12	H2	H4	Cock
15.12	7.11	G1	A5	Serpent	1. 2	25.12	H2	J5	Crow
16.12	8.11	G1	B6	Earthworm	2. 2	26.12	H2	K6	Monkey
17.12	9.11	G1	C7	Crocodile	3. 2	27.12	H2	A7	Gibbon
18.12	10.11	G1	D8	Dragon	4. 2	28.12	H2	B8	Tapir
19.12	11.11	G1	E9	Badger	5. 2	29.12	H2	C9	Sheep

JEN SHEN YEAR

Solar date	Lunar date	Month HS/EB	Day HS/EB	Constellation	Solar date	Lunar date	Month HS/EB	Day HS/EB	Constellation
6. 2	1. 1	J3	D10	Deer	24. 2	19. 1	J3	B4	Porcupine
7. 2	2. 1	J3	E11	Horse	25. 2	20. 1	J3	C5	Wolf
8. 2	3. 1	J3	F12	Stag	26. 2	21. 1	J3	D6	Dog
9. 2	4. 1	J3	G1	Serpent	27. 2	22. 1	J3	E7	Pheasant
10. 2	5. 1	J3	H2	Earthworm	28. 2	23. 1	J3	F8	Cock
11. 2	6. 1	J3	J3	Crocodile	29. 2	24. 1	J3	G9	Crow
12. 2	7. 1	J3	K4	Dragon	1. 3	25. 1	J3	H10	Monkey
13. 2	8. 1	J3	A5	Badger	2. 3	26. 1	J3	J11	Gibbon
14. 2	9. 1	J3	B6	Hare	3. 3	27. 1	J3	K12	Tapir
15. 2	10. 1	J3	C7	Fox	4. 3	28. 1	J3	A1	Sheep
16. 2	11. 1	J3	D8	Tiger	5. 3	29. 1	J3	B2	Deer
17. 2	12. 1	J3	E9	Leopard	6. 3	30. 1	J3	C3	Horse
18. 2	13. 1	J3	F10	Griffon	7. 3	1. 2	K4	D4	Stag
19. 2	14. 1	J3	G11	Ox	8. 3	2. 2	K4	E5	Serpent
20. 2	15. 1	J3	H12	Bat	9. 3	3. 2	K4	F6	Earthworm
21. 2	16. 1	J3	J1	Rat	10. 3	4. 2	K4	G7	Crocodile
22. 2	17. 1	J3	K2	Swallow	11. 3	5. 2	K4	H8	Dragon
23. 2	18. 1	J3	A3	Pig	12. 3	6. 2	K4	J9	Badger

Solar date	Lunar date	Month HS/EB	Day HS/EB	Constellation
13. 3	7. 2	K4	K10	Hare
14. 3	8. 2	K4	A11	Fox
15. 3	9. 2	K4	B12	Tiger
16. 3	10. 2	K4	C1	Leopard
17. 3	11. 2	K4	D2	Griffon
18. 3	12. 2	K4	E3	Ox
19. 3	13. 2	K4	F4	Bat
20. 3	14. 2	K4	G5	Rat
21. 3	15. 2	K4	H6	Swallow
22. 3	16. 2	K4	J7	Pig
23. 3	17. 2	K4	K8	Porcupine
24. 3	18. 2	K4	A9	Wolf
25. 3	19. 2	K4	B10	Dog
26. 3	20. 2	K4	C11	Pheasant
27. 3	21. 2	K4	D12	Cock
28. 3	22. 2	K4	E1	Crow
29. 3	23. 2	K4	F2	Monkey
30. 3	24. 2	K4	G3	Gibbon
31. 3	25. 2	K4	H4	Tapir
1. 4	26. 2	K4	J5	Sheep
2. 4	27. 2	K4	K6	Deer
3. 4	28. 2	K4	A7	Horse
4. 4	29. 2	K4	B8	Stag
5. 4	30. 2	K4	C9	Serpent
6. 4	1. 3	A5	D10	Earthworm
7. 4	2. 3	A5	E11	Crocodile
8. 4	3. 3	A5	F12	Dragon
9. 4	4. 3	A5	G1	Badger
10. 4	5. 3	A5	H2	Hare
11. 4	6. 3	A5	J3	Fox
12. 4	7. 3	A5	K4	Tiger
13. 4	8. 3	A5	A5	Leopard
14. 4	9. 3	A5	B6	Griffon
15. 4	10. 3	A5	C7	Ox
16. 4	11. 3	A5	D8	Bat
17. 4	12. 3	A5	E9	Rat
18. 4	13. 3	A5	F10	Swallow
19. 4	14. 3	A5	G11	Pig
20. 4	15. 3	A5	H12	Porcupine
21. 4	16. 3	A5	J1	Wolf
22. 4	17. 3	A5	K2	Dog
23. 4	18. 3	A5	A3	Pheasant
24. 4	19. 3	A5	B4	Cock
25. 4	20. 3	A5	C5	Crow
26. 4	21. 3	A5	D6	Monkey
27. 4	22. 3	A5	E7	Gibbon
28. 4	23. 3	A5	F8	Tapir
29. 4	24. 3	A5	G9	Sheep
30. 4	25. 3	A5	H10	Deer
1. 5	26. 3	A5	J11	Horse
2. 5	27. 3	A5	K12	Stag
3. 5	28. 3	A5	A1	Serpent
4. 5	29. 3	A5	B2	Earthworm
5. 5	30. 3	A5	C3	Crocodile
6. 5	1. 4	B6	D4	Dragon
7. 5	2. 4	B6	E5	Badger
8. 5	3. 4	B6	F6	Hare
9. 5	4. 4	B6	G7	Fox
10. 5	5. 4	B6	H8	Tiger
11. 5	6. 4	B6	J9	Leopard
12. 5	7. 4	B6	K10	Griffon
13. 5	8. 4	B6	A11	Ox
14. 5	9. 4	B6	B12	Bat
15. 5	10. 4	B6	C1	Rat
16. 5	11. 4	B6	D2	Swallow
17. 5	12. 4	B6	E3	Pig
18. 5	13. 4	B6	F4	Porcupine
19. 5	14. 4	B6	G5	Wolf
20. 5	15. 4	B6	H6	Dog
21. 5	16. 4	B6	J7	Pheasant
22. 5	17. 4	B6	K8	Cock
23. 5	18. 4	B6	A9	Crow
24. 5	19. 4	B6	B10	Monkey
25. 5	20. 4	B6	C11	Gibbon
26. 5	21. 4	B6	D12	Tapir
27. 5	22. 4	B6	E1	Sheep
28. 5	23. 4	B6	F2	Deer
29. 5	24. 4	B6	G3	Horse
30. 5	25. 4	B6	H4	Stag
31. 5	26. 4	B6	J5	Serpent
1. 6	27. 4	B6	K6	Earthworm
2. 6	28. 4	B6	A7	Crocodile
3. 6	29. 4	B6	B8	Dragon
4. 6	1. 5	C7	C9	Badger
5. 6	2. 5	C7	D10	Hare
6. 6	3. 5	C7	E11	Fox
7. 6	4. 5	C7	F12	Tiger
8. 6	5. 5	C7	G1	Leopard
9. 6	6. 5	C7	H2	Griffon
10. 6	7. 5	C7	J3	Ox
11. 6	8. 5	C7	K4	Bat
12. 6	9. 5	C7	A5	Rat
13. 6	10. 5	C7	B6	Swallow
14. 6	11. 5	C7	C7	Pig
15. 6	12. 5	C7	D8	Porcupine
16. 6	13. 5	C7	E9	Wolf
17. 6	14. 5	C7	F10	Dog
18. 6	15. 5	C7	G11	Pheasant
19. 6	16. 5	C7	H12	Cock
20. 6	17. 5	C7	J1	Crow
21. 6	18. 5	C7	K2	Monkey
22. 6	19. 5	C7	A3	Gibbon
23. 6	20. 5	C7	B4	Tapir
24. 6	21. 5	C7	C5	Sheep
25. 6	22. 5	C7	D6	Deer
26. 6	23. 5	C7	E7	Horse
27. 6	24. 5	C7	F8	Stag
28. 6	25. 5	C7	G9	Serpent
29. 6	26. 5	C7	H10	Earthworm
30. 6	27. 5	C7	J11	Crocodile
1. 7	28. 5	C7	K12	Dragon
2. 7	29. 5	C7	A1	Badger
3. 7	30. 5	C7	B2	Hare
4. 7	1. 6	D8	C3	Fox
5. 7	2. 6	D8	D4	Tiger
6. 7	3. 6	D8	E5	Leopard
7. 7	4. 6	D8	F6	Griffon
8. 7	5. 6	D8	G7	Ox
9. 7	6. 6	D8	H8	Bat
10. 7	7. 6	D8	J9	Rat
11. 7	8. 6	D8	K10	Swallow
12. 7	9. 6	D8	A11	Pig
13. 7	10. 6	D8	B12	Porcupine
14. 7	11. 6	D8	C1	Wolf
15. 7	12. 6	D8	D2	Dog
16. 7	13. 6	D8	E3	Pheasant
17. 7	14. 6	D8	F4	Cock
18. 7	15. 6	D8	G5	Crow
19. 7	16. 6	D8	H6	Monkey
20. 7	17. 6	D8	J7	Gibbon
21. 7	18. 6	D8	K8	Tapir
22. 7	19. 6	D8	A9	Sheep
23. 7	20. 6	D8	B10	Deer
24. 7	21. 6	D8	C11	Horse
25. 7	22. 6	D8	D12	Stag
26. 7	23. 6	D8	E1	Serpent
27. 7	24. 6	D8	F2	Earthworm
28. 7	25. 6	D8	G3	Crocodile
29. 7	26. 6	D8	H4	Dragon
30. 7	27. 6	D8	J5	Badger
31. 7	28. 6	D8	K6	Hare
1. 8	29. 6	D8	A7	Fox
2. 8	1. 7	E9	B8	Tiger
3. 8	2. 7	E9	C9	Leopard
4. 8	3. 7	E9	D10	Griffon
5. 8	4. 7	E9	E11	Ox

Solar date	Lunar date	Month HS/EB	Day HS/EB	Constellation	Solar date	Lunar date	Month HS/EB	Day HS/EB	Constellation
6. 8	5. 7	E9	F12	Bat	18.10	19. 9	G11	J1	Serpent
7. 8	6. 7	E9	G1	Rat	19.10	20. 9	G11	K2	Earthworm
8. 8	7. 7	E9	H2	Swallow	20.10	21. 9	G11	A3	Crocodile
9. 8	8. 7	E9	J3	Pig	21.10	22. 9	G11	B4	Dragon
10. 8	9. 7	E9	K4	Porcupine	22.10	23. 9	G11	C5	Badger
11. 8	10. 7	E9	A5	Wolf	23.10	24. 9	G11	D6	Hare
12. 8	11. 7	E9	B6	Dog	24.10	25. 9	G11	E7	Fox
13. 8	12. 7	E9	C7	Pheasant	25.10	26. 9	G11	F8	Tiger
14. 8	13. 7	E9	D8	Cock	26.10	27. 9	G11	G9	Leopard
15. 8	14. 7	E9	E9	Crow	27.10	28. 9	G11	H10	Griffon
16. 8	15. 7	E9	F10	Monkey	28.10	29. 9	G11	J11	Ox
17. 8	16. 7	E9	G11	Gibbon	29.10	1.10	H12	K12	Bat
18. 8	17. 7	E9	H12	Tapir	30.10	2.10	H12	A1	Rat
19. 8	18. 7	E9	J1	Sheep	31.10	3.10	H12	B2	Swallow
20. 8	19. 7	E9	K2	Deer	1.11	4.10	H12	C3	Pig
21. 8	20. 7	E9	A3	Horse	2.11	5.10	H12	D4	Porcupine
22. 8	21. 7	E9	B4	Stag	3.11	6.10	H12	E5	Wolf
23. 8	22. 7	E9	C5	Serpent	4.11	7.10	H12	F6	Dog
24. 8	23. 7	E9	D6	Earthworm	5.11	8.10	H12	G7	Pheasant
25. 8	24. 7	E9	E7	Crocodile	6.11	9.10	H12	H8	Cock
26. 8	25. 7	E9	F8	Dragon	7.11	10.10	H12	J9	Crow
27. 8	26. 7	E9	G9	Badger	8.11	11.10	H12	K10	Monkey
28. 8	27. 7	E9	H10	Hare	9.11	12.10	H12	A11	Gibbon
29. 8	28. 7	E9	J11	Fox	10.11	13.10	H12	B12	Tapir
30. 8	29. 7	E9	K12	Tiger	11.11	14.10	H12	C1	Sheep
31. 8	30. 7	E9	A1	Leopard	12.11	15.10	H12	D2	Deer
1. 9	1. 8	F10	B2	Griffon	13.11	16.10	H12	E3	Horse
2. 9	2. 8	F10	C3	Ox	14.11	17.10	H12	F4	Stag
3. 9	3. 8	F10	D4	Bat	15.11	18.10	H12	G5	Serpent
4. 9	4. 8	F10	E5	Rat	16.11	19.10	H12	H6	Earthworm
5. 9	5. 8	F10	F6	Swallow	17.11	20.10	H12	J7	Crocodile
6. 9	6. 8	F10	G7	Pig	18.11	21.10	H12	K8	Dragon
7. 9	7. 8	F10	H8	Porcupine	19.11	22.10	H12	A9	Badger
8. 9	8. 8	F10	J9	Wolf	20.11	23.10	H12	B10	Hare
9. 9	9. 8	F10	K10	Dog	21.11	24.10	H12	C11	Fox
10. 9	10. 8	F10	A11	Pheasant	22.11	25.10	H12	D12	Tiger
11. 9	11. 8	F10	B12	Cock	23.11	26.10	H12	E1	Leopard
12. 9	12. 8	F10	C1	Crow	24.11	27.10	H12	F2	Griffon
13. 9	13. 8	F10	D2	Monkey	25.11	28.10	H12	G3	Ox
14. 9	14. 8	F10	E3	Gibbon	26.11	29.10	H12	H4	Bat
15. 9	15. 8	F10	F4	Tapir	27.11	30.10	H12	J5	Rat
16. 9	16. 8	F10	G5	Sheep	28.11	1.11	J1	K6	Swallow
17. 9	17. 8	F10	H6	Deer	29.11	2.11	J1	A7	Pig
18. 9	18. 8	F10	J7	Horse	30.11	3.11	J1	B8	Porcupine
19. 9	19. 8	F10	K8	Stag	1.12	4.11	J1	C9	Wolf
20. 9	20. 8	F10	A9	Serpent	2.12	5.11	J1	D10	Dog
21. 9	21. 8	F10	B10	Earthworm	3.12	6.11	J1	E11	Pheasant
22. 9	22. 8	F10	C11	Crocodile	4.12	7.11	J1	F12	Cock
23. 9	23. 8	F10	D12	Dragon	5.12	8.11	J1	G1	Crow
24. 9	24. 8	F10	E1	Badger	6.12	9.11	J1	H2	Monkey
25. 9	25. 8	F10	F2	Hare	7.12	10.11	J1	J3	Gibbon
26. 9	26. 8	F10	G3	Fox	8.12	11.11	J1	K4	Tapir
27. 9	27. 8	F10	H4	Tiger	9.12	12.11	J1	A5	Sheep
28. 9	28. 8	F10	J5	Leopard	10.12	13.11	J1	B6	Deer
29. 9	29. 8	F10	K6	Griffon	11.12	14.11	J1	C7	Horse
30. 9	1. 9	G11	A7	Ox	12.12	15.11	J1	D8	Stag
1.10	2. 9	G11	B8	Bat	13.12	16.11	J1	E9	Serpent
2.10	3. 9	G11	C9	Rat	14.12	17.11	J1	F10	Earthworm
3.10	4. 9	G11	D10	Swallow	15.12	18.11	J1	G11	Crocodile
4.10	5. 9	G11	E11	Pig	16.12	19.11	J1	H12	Dragon
5.10	6. 9	G11	F12	Porcupine	17.12	20.11	J1	J1	Badger
6.10	7. 9	G11	G1	Wolf	18.12	21.11	J1	K2	Hare
7.10	8. 9	G11	H2	Dog	19.12	22.11	J1	A3	Fox
8.10	9. 9	G11	J3	Pheasant	20.12	23.11	J1	B4	Tiger
9.10	10. 9	G11	K4	Cock	21.12	24.11	J1	C5	Leopard
10.10	11. 9	G11	A5	Crow	22.12	25.11	J1	D6	Griffon
11.10	12. 9	G11	B6	Monkey	23.12	26.11	J1	E7	Ox
12.10	13. 9	G11	C7	Gibbon	24.12	27.11	J1	F8	Bat
13.10	14. 9	G11	D8	Tapir	25.12	28.11	J1	G9	Rat
14.10	15. 9	G11	E9	Sheep	26.12	29.11	J1	H10	Swallow
15.10	16. 9	G11	F10	Deer	27.12	1.12	K2	J11	Pig
16.10	17. 9	G11	G11	Horse	28.12	2.12	K2	K12	Porcupine
17.10	18. 9	G11	H12	Stag	29.12	3.12	K2	A1	Wolf

Solar date	Lunar date	Month HS/EB	Day HS/EB	Constellation	Solar date	Lunar date	Month HS/EB	Day HS/EB	Constellation
30.12	4.12	K2	B2	Dog	12. 1	17.12	K2	E3	Crocodile
31.12	5.12	K2	C3	Pheasant	13. 1	18.12	K2	F4	Dragon
1933					14. 1	19.12	K2	G5	Badger
					15. 1	20.12	K2	H6	Hare
1. 1	6.12	K2	D4	Cock	16. 1	21.12	K2	J7	Fox
2. 1	7.12	K2	E5	Crow	17. 1	22.12	K2	K8	Tiger
3. 1	8.12	K2	F6	Monkey	18. 1	23.12	K2	A9	Leopard
4. 1	9.12	K2	G7	Gibbon	19. 1	24.12	K2	B10	Griffon
5. 1	10.12	K2	H8	Tapir	20. 1	25.12	K2	C11	Ox
6. 1	11.12	K2	J9	Sheep	21. 1	26.12	K2	D12	Bat
7. 1	12.12	K2	K10	Deer	22. 1	27.12	K2	E1	Rat
8. 1	13.12	K2	A11	Horse	23. 1	28.12	K2	F2	Swallow
9. 1	14.12	K2	B12	Stag	24. 1	29.12	K2	G3	Pig
10. 1	15.12	K2	C1	Serpent	25. 1	30.12	K2	H4	Porcupine
11. 1	16.12	K2	D2	Earthworm					

KUEI YU YEAR

Solar date	Lunar date	Month HS/EB	Day HS/EB	Constellation	Solar date	Lunar date	Month HS/EB	Day HS/EB	Constellation
26. 1	1. 1	A3	J5	Wolf	20. 3	25. 2	B4	B10	Swallow
27. 1	2. 1	A3	K6	Dog	21. 3	26. 2	B4	C11	Pig
28. 1	3. 1	A3	A7	Pheasant	22. 3	27. 2	B4	D12	Porcupine
29. 1	4. 1	A3	B8	Cock	23. 3	28. 2	B4	E1	Wolf
30. 1	5. 1	A3	C9	Crow	24. 3	29. 2	B4	F2	Dog
31. 1	6. 1	A3	D10	Monkey	25. 3	30. 2	B4	G3	Pheasant
1. 2	7. 1	A3	E11	Gibbon	26. 3	1. 3	C5	H4	Cock
2. 2	8. 1	A3	F12	Tapir	27. 3	2. 3	C5	J5	Crow
3. 2	9. 1	A3	G1	Sheep	28. 3	3. 3	C5	K6	Monkey
4. 2	10. 1	A3	H2	Deer	29. 3	4. 3	C5	A7	Gibbon
5. 2	11. 1	A3	J3	Horse	30. 3	5. 3	C5	B8	Tapir
6. 2	12. 1	A3	K4	Stag	31. 3	6. 3	C5	C9	Sheep
7. 2	13. 1	A3	A5	Serpent	1. 4	7. 3	C5	D10	Deer
8. 2	14. 1	A3	B6	Earthworm	2. 4	8. 3	C5	E11	Horse
9. 2	15. 1	A3	C7	Crocodile	3. 4	9. 3	C5	F12	Stag
10. 2	16. 1	A3	D8	Dragon	4. 4	10. 3	C5	G1	Serpent
11. 2	17. 1	A3	E9	Badger	5. 4	11. 3	C5	H2	Earthworm
12. 2	18. 1	A3	F10	Hare	6. 4	12. 3	C5	J3	Crocodile
13. 2	19. 1	A3	G11	Fox	7. 4	13. 3	C5	K4	Dragon
14. 2	20. 1	A3	H12	Tiger	8. 4	14. 3	C5	A5	Badger
15. 2	21. 1	A3	J1	Leopard	9. 4	15. 3	C5	B6	Hare
16. 2	22. 1	A3	K2	Griffon	10. 4	16. 3	C5	C7	Fox
17. 2	23. 1	A3	A3	Ox	11. 4	17. 3	C5	D8	Tiger
18. 2	24. 1	A3	B4	Bat	12. 4	18. 3	C5	E9	Leopard
19. 2	25. 1	A3	C5	Rat	13. 4	19. 3	C5	F10	Griffon
20. 2	26. 1	A3	D6	Swallow	14. 4	20. 3	C5	G11	Ox
21. 2	27. 1	A3	E7	Pig	15. 4	21. 3	C5	H12	Bat
22. 2	28. 1	A3	F8	Porcupine	16. 4	22. 3	C5	J1	Rat
23. 2	29. 1	A3	G9	Wolf	17. 4	23. 3	C5	K2	Swallow
24. 2	1. 2	B4	H10	Dog	18. 4	24. 3	C5	A3	Pig
25. 2	2. 2	B4	J11	Pheasant	19. 4	25. 3	C5	B4	Porcupine
26. 2	3. 2	B4	K12	Cock	20. 4	26. 3	C5	C5	Wolf
27. 2	4. 2	B4	A1	Crow	21. 4	27. 3	C5	D6	Dog
28. 2	5. 2	B4	B2	Monkey	22. 4	28. 3	C5	E7	Pheasant
1. 3	6. 2	B4	C3	Gibbon	23. 4	29. 3	C5	F8	Cock
2. 3	7. 2	B4	D4	Tapir	24. 4	30. 3	C5	G9	Crow
3. 3	8. 2	B4	E5	Sheep	25. 4	1. 4	D6	H10	Monkey
4. 3	9. 2	B4	F6	Deer	26. 4	2. 4	D6	J11	Gibbon
5. 3	10. 2	B4	G7	Horse	27. 4	3. 4	D6	K12	Tapir
6. 3	11. 2	B4	H8	Stag	28. 4	4. 4	D6	A1	Sheep
7. 3	12. 2	B4	J9	Serpent	29. 4	5. 4	D6	B2	Deer
8. 3	13. 2	B4	K10	Earthworm	30. 4	6. 4	D6	C3	Horse
9. 3	14. 2	B4	A11	Crocodile	1. 5	7. 4	D6	D4	Stag
10. 3	15. 2	B4	B12	Dragon	2. 5	8. 4	D6	E5	Serpent
11. 3	16. 2	B4	C1	Badger	3. 5	9. 4	D6	F6	Earthworm
12. 3	17. 2	B4	D2	Hare	4. 5	10. 4	D6	G7	Crocodile
13. 3	18. 2	B4	E3	Fox	5. 5	11. 4	D6	H8	Dragon
14. 3	19. 2	B4	F4	Tiger	6. 5	12. 4	D6	J9	Badger
15. 3	20. 2	B4	G5	Leopard	7. 5	13. 4	D6	K10	Hare
16. 3	21. 2	B4	H6	Griffon	8. 5	14. 4	D6	A11	Fox
17. 3	22. 2	B4	J7	Ox	9. 5	15. 4	D6	B12	Tiger
18. 3	23. 2	B4	K8	Bat	10. 5	16. 4	D6	C1	Leopard
19. 3	24. 2	B4	A9	Rat	11. 5	17. 4	D6	D2	Griffon

Solar date	Lunar date	Month HS/EB	Day HS/EB	Constellation
12. 5	18. 4	D6	E3	Ox
13. 5	19. 4	D6	F4	Bat
14. 5	20. 4	D6	G5	Rat
15. 5	21. 4	D6	H6	Swallow
16. 5	22. 4	D6	J7	Pig
17. 5	23. 4	D6	K8	Porcupine
18. 5	24. 4	D6	A9	Wolf
19. 5	25. 4	D6	B10	Dog
20. 5	26. 4	D6	C11	Pheasant
21. 5	27. 4	D6	D12	Cock
22. 5	28. 4	D6	E1	Crow
23. 5	29. 4	D6	F2	Monkey
24. 5	1. 5	E7	G3	Gibbon
25. 5	2. 5	E7	H4	Tapir
26. 5	3. 5	E7	J5	Sheep
27. 5	4. 5	E7	K6	Deer
28. 5	5. 5	E7	A7	Horse
29. 5	6. 5	E7	B8	Stag
30. 5	7. 5	E7	C9	Serpent
31. 5	8. 5	E7	D10	Earthworm
1. 6	9. 5	E7	E11	Crocodile
2. 6	10. 5	E7	F12	Dragon
3. 5	11. 5	E7	G1	Badger
4. 5	12. 5	E7	H2	Hare
5. 6	13. 5	E7	J3	Fox
6. 6	14. 5	E7	K4	Tiger
7. 6	15. 5	E7	A5	Leopard
8. 6	16. 5	E7	B6	Griffon
9. 6	17. 5	E7	C7	Ox
10. 6	18. 5	E7	D8	Bat
11. 6	19. 5	E7	E9	Rat
12. 6	20. 5	E7	F10	Swallow
13. 6	21. 5	E7	G11	Pig
14. 6	22. 5	E7	H12	Porcupine
15. 6	23. 5	E7	J1	Wolf
16. 6	24. 5	E7	K2	Dog
17. 6	25. 5	E7	A3	Pheasant
18. 6	26. 5	E7	B4	Cock
19. 6	27. 5	E7	C5	Crow
20. 6	28. 5	E7	D6	Monkey
21. 6	29. 5	E7	E7	Gibbon
22. 6	30. 5	E7	F8	Tapir
23. 6	1. 5	E7	G9	Sheep
24. 6	2. 5	E7	H10	Deer
25. 6	3. 5	E7	J11	Horse
26. 6	4. 5	E7	K12	Stag
27. 6	5. 5	E7	A1	Serpent
28. 6	6. 5	E7	B2	Earthworm
29. 6	7. 5	E7	C3	Crocodile
30. 6	8. 5	E7	D4	Dragon
1. 7	9. 5	E7	E5	Badger
2. 7	10. 5	E7	F6	Hare
3. 7	11. 5	E7	G7	Fox
4. 7	12. 5	E7	H8	Tiger
5. 7	13. 5	E7	J9	Leopard
6. 7	14. 5	E7	K10	Griffon
7. 7	15. 5	E7	A11	Ox
8. 7	16. 5	E7	B12	Bat
9. 7	17. 5	E7	C1	Rat
10. 7	18. 5	E7	D2	Swallow
11. 7	19. 5	E7	E3	Pig
12. 7	20. 5	E7	F4	Porcupine
13. 7	21. 5	E7	G5	Wolf
14. 7	22. 5	E7	H6	Dog
15. 7	23. 5	E7	J7	Pheasant
16. 7	24. 5	E7	K8	Cock
17. 7	25. 5	E7	A9	Crow
18. 7	26. 5	E7	B10	Monkey
19. 7	27. 5	E7	C11	Gibbon
20. 7	28. 5	E7	D12	Tapir
21. 7	29. 5	E7	E1	Sheep
22. 7	30. 5	E7	F2	Deer
23. 7	1. 6	F8	G3	Horse
24. 7	2. 6	F8	H4	Stag
25. 7	3. 6	F8	J5	Serpent
26. 7	4. 6	F8	K6	Earthworm
27. 7	5. 6	F8	A7	Crocodile
28. 7	6. 6	F8	B8	Dragon
29. 7	7. 6	F8	C9	Badger
30. 7	8. 6	F8	D10	Hare
31. 7	9. 6	F8	E11	Fox
1. 8	10. 6	F8	F12	Tiger
2. 8	11. 6	F8	G1	Leopard
3. 8	12. 6	F8	H2	Griffon
4. 8	13. 6	F8	J3	Ox
5. 8	14. 6	F8	K4	Bat
6. 8	15. 6	F8	A5	Rat
7. 8	16. 6	F8	B6	Swallow
8. 8	17. 6	F8	C7	Pig
9. 8	18. 6	F8	D8	Porcupine
10. 8	19. 6	F8	E9	Wolf
11. 8	20. 6	F8	F10	Dog
12. 8	21. 6	F8	G11	Pheasant
13. 8	22. 6	F8	H12	Cock
14. 8	23. 6	F8	J1	Crow
15. 8	24. 6	F8	K2	Monkey
16. 8	25. 6	F8	A3	Gibbon
17. 8	26. 6	F8	B4	Tapir
18. 8	27. 6	F8	C5	Sheep
19. 8	28. 6	F8	D6	Deer
20. 8	29. 6	F8	E7	Horse
21. 8	1. 7	G9	F8	Stag
22. 8	2. 7	G9	G9	Serpent
23. 8	3. 7	G9	H10	Earthworm
24. 8	4. 7	G9	J11	Crocodile
25. 8	5. 7	G9	K12	Dragon
26. 8	6. 7	G9	A1	Badger
27. 8	7. 7	G9	B2	Hare
28. 8	8. 7	G9	C3	Fox
29. 8	9. 7	G9	D4	Tiger
30. 8	10. 7	G9	E5	Leopard
31. 8	11. 7	G9	F6	Griffon
1. 9	12. 7	G9	G7	Ox
2. 9	13. 7	G9	H8	Bat
3. 9	14. 7	G9	J9	Rat
4. 9	15. 7	G9	K10	Swallow
5. 9	16. 7	G9	A11	Pig
6. 9	17. 7	G9	B12	Porcupine
7. 9	18. 7	G9	C1	Wolf
8. 9	19. 7	G9	D2	Dog
9. 9	20. 7	G9	E3	Pheasant
10. 9	21. 7	G9	F4	Cock
11. 9	22. 7	G9	G5	Crow
12. 9	23. 7	G9	H6	Monkey
13. 9	24. 7	G9	J7	Gibbon
14. 9	25. 7	G9	K8	Tapir
15. 9	26. 7	G9	A9	Sheep
16. 9	27. 7	G9	B10	Deer
17. 9	28. 7	G9	C11	Horse
18. 9	29. 7	G9	D12	Stag
19. 9	30. 7	G9	E1	Serpent
20. 9	1. 8	H10	F2	Earthworm
21. 9	2. 8	H10	G3	Crocodile
22. 9	3. 8	H10	H4	Dragon
23. 9	4. 8	H10	J5	Badger
24. 9	5. 8	H10	K6	Hare
25. 9	6. 8	H10	A7	Fox
26. 9	7. 8	H10	B8	Tiger
27. 9	8. 8	H10	C9	Leopard
28. 9	9. 8	H10	D10	Griffon
29. 9	10. 8	H10	E11	Ox
30. 9	11. 8	H10	F12	Bat
1.10	12. 8	H10	G1	Rat
2.10	13. 8	H10	H2	Swallow
3.10	14. 8	H10	J3	Pig
4.10	15. 8	H10	K4	Porcupine

Solar date	Lunar date	Month HS/EB	Day HS/EB	Constellation	Solar date	Lunar date	Month HS/EB	Day HS/EB	Constellation
5.10	16. 8	H10	A5	Wolf	11.12	24.10	K12	H12	Stag
6.10	17. 8	H10	B6	Dog	12.12	25.10	K12	J1	Serpent
7.10	18. 8	H10	C7	Pheasant	13.12	26.10	K12	K2	Earthworm
8.10	19. 8	H10	D8	Cock	14.12	27.10	K12	A3	Crocodile
9.10	20. 8	H10	E9	Crow	15.12	28.10	K12	B4	Dragon
10.10	21. 8	H10	F10	Monkey	16.12	29.10	K12	C5	Badger
11.10	22. 8	H10	G11	Gibbon	17.12	1.11	A1	D6	Hare
12.10	23. 8	H10	H12	Tapir	18.12	2.11	A1	E7	Fox
13.10	24. 8	H10	J1	Sheep	19.12	3.11	A1	F8	Tiger
14.10	25. 8	H10	K2	Deer	20.12	4.11	A1	G9	Leopard
15.10	26. 8	H10	A3	Horse	21.12	5.11	A1	H10	Griffon
16.10	27. 8	H10	B4	Stag	22.12	6.11	A1	J11	Ox
17.10	28. 8	H10	C5	Serpent	23.12	7.11	A1	K12	Bat
18.10	29. 8	H10	D6	Earthworm	24.12	8.11	A1	A1	Rat
19.10	1. 9	J11	E7	Crocodile	25.12	9.11	A1	B2	Swallow
20.10	2. 9	J11	F8	Dragon	26.12	10.11	A1	C3	Pig
21.10	3. 9	J11	G9	Badger	27.12	11.11	A1	D4	Porcupine
22.10	4. 9	J11	H10	Hare	28.12	12.11	A1	E5	Wolf
23.10	5. 9	J11	J11	Fox	29.12	13.11	A1	F6	Dog
24.10	6. 9	J11	K12	Tiger	30.12	14.11	A1	G7	Pheasant
25.10	7. 9	J11	A1	Leopard	31.12	15.11	A1	H8	Cock
26.10	8. 9	J11	B2	Griffon					
27.10	9. 9	J11	C3	Ox	**1934**				
28.10	10. 9	J11	D4	Bat	1. 1	16.11	A1	J9	Crow
29.10	11. 9	J11	E5	Rat	2. 1	17.11	A1	K10	Monkey
30.10	12. 9	J11	F6	Swallow	3. 1	18.11	A1	A11	Gibbon
31.10	13. 9	J11	G7	Pig	4. 1	19.11	A1	B12	Tapir
1.11	14. 9	J11	H8	Porcupine	5. 1	20.11	A1	C1	Sheep
2.11	15. 9	J11	J9	Wolf	6. 1	21.11	A1	D2	Deer
3.11	16. 9	J11	K10	Dog	7. 1	22.11	A1	E3	Horse
4.11	17. 9	J11	A11	Pheasant	8. 1	23.11	A1	F4	Stag
5.11	18. 9	J11	B12	Cock	9. 1	24.11	A1	G5	Serpent
6.11	19. 9	J11	C1	Crow	10. 1	25.11	A1	H6	Earthworm
7.11	20. 9	J11	D2	Monkey	11. 1	26.11	A1	J7	Crocodile
8.11	21. 9	J11	E3	Gibbon	12. 1	27.11	A1	K8	Dragon
9.11	22. 9	J11	F4	Tapir	13. 1	28.11	A1	A9	Badger
10.11	23. 9	J11	G5	Sheep	14. 1	29.11	A1	B10	Hare
11.11	24. 9	J11	H6	Deer	15. 1	1.12	B2	C11	Fox
12.11	25. 9	J11	J7	Horse	16. 1	2.12	B2	D12	Tiger
13.11	26. 9	J11	K8	Stag	17. 1	3.12	B2	E1	Leopard
14.11	27. 9	J11	A9	Serpent	18. 1	4.12	B2	F2	Griffon
15.11	28. 9	J11	B10	Earthworm	19. 1	5.12	B2	G3	Ox
16.11	29. 9	J11	C11	Crocodile	20. 1	6.12	B2	H4	Bat
17.11	30. 9	J11	D12	Dragon	21. 1	7.12	B2	J5	Rat
18.11	1.10	K12	E1	Badger	22. 1	8.12	B2	K6	Swallow
19.11	2.10	K12	F2	Hare	23. 1	9.12	B2	A7	Pig
20.11	3.10	K12	G3	Fox	24. 1	10.12	B2	B8	Porcupine
21.11	4.10	K12	H4	Tiger	25. 1	11.12	B2	C9	Wolf
22.11	5.10	K12	J5	Leopard	26. 1	12.12	B2	D10	Dog
23.11	6.10	K12	K6	Griffon	27. 1	13.12	B2	E11	Pheasant
24.11	7.10	K12	A7	Ox	28. 1	14.12	B2	F12	Cock
25.11	8.10	K12	B8	Bat	29. 1	15.12	B2	G1	Crow
26.11	9.10	K12	C9	Rat	30. 1	16.12	B2	H2	Monkey
27.11	10.10	K12	D10	Swallow	31. 1	17.12	B2	J3	Gibbon
28.11	11.10	K12	E11	Pig	1. 2	18.12	B2	K4	Tapir
29.11	12.10	K12	F12	Porcupine	2. 2	19.12	B2	A5	Sheep
30.11	13.10	K12	G1	Wolf	3. 2	20.12	B2	B6	Deer
1.12	14.10	K12	H2	Dog	4. 2	21.12	B2	C7	Horse
2.12	15.10	K12	J3	Pheasant	5. 2	22.12	B2	D8	Stag
3.12	16.10	K12	K4	Cock	6. 2	23.12	B2	E9	Serpent
4.12	17.10	K12	A5	Crow	7. 2	24.12	B2	F10	Earthworm
5.12	18.10	K12	B6	Monkey	8. 2	25.12	B2	G11	Crocodile
6.12	19.10	K12	C7	Gibbon	9. 2	26.12	B2	H12	Dragon
7.12	20.10	K12	D8	Tapir	10. 2	27.12	B2	J1	Badger
8.12	21.10	K12	E9	Sheep	11. 2	28.12	B2	K2	Hare
9.12	22.10	K12	F10	Deer	12. 2	29.12	B2	A3	Fox
10.12	23.10	K12	G11	Horse	13. 2	30.12	B2	B4	Tiger

CHIA HSÜ YEAR

Solar date	Lunar date	Month HS/EB	Day HS/EB	Constellation	Solar date	Lunar date	Month HS/EB	Day HS/EB	Constellation
14. 2	1. 1	C3	C5	Leopard	26. 4	13. 3	E5	D4	Tapir
15. 2	2. 1	C3	D6	Griffon	27. 4	14. 3	E5	E5	Sheep
16. 2	3. 1	C3	E7	Ox	28. 4	15. 3	E5	F6	Deer
17. 2	4. 1	C3	F8	Bat	29. 4	16. 3	E5	G7	Horse
18. 2	5. 1	C3	G9	Rat	30. 4	17. 3	E5	H8	Stag
19. 2	6. 1	C3	H10	Swallow	1. 5	18. 3	E5	J9	Serpent
20. 2	7. 1	C3	J11	Pig	2. 5	19. 3	E5	K10	Earthworm
21. 2	8. 1	C3	K12	Porcupine	3. 5	20. 3	E5	A11	Crocodile
22. 2	9. 1	C3	A1	Wolf	4. 5	21. 3	E5	B12	Dragon
23. 2	10. 1	C3	B2	Dog	5. 5	22. 3	E5	C1	Badger
24. 2	11. 1	C3	C3	Pheasant	6. 5	23. 3	E5	D2	Hare
25. 2	12. 1	C3	D4	Cock	7. 5	24. 3	E5	E3	Fox
26. 2	13. 1	C3	E5	Crow	8. 5	25. 3	E5	F4	Tiger
27. 2	14. 1	C3	F6	Monkey	9. 5	26. 3	E5	G5	Leopard
28. 2	15. 1	C3	G7	Gibbon	10. 5	27. 3	E5	H6	Griffon
1. 3	16. 1	C3	H8	Tapir	11. 5	28. 3	E5	J7	Ox
2. 3	17. 1	C3	J9	Sheep	12. 5	29. 3	E5	K8	Bat
3. 3	18. 1	C3	K10	Deer	13. 5	1. 4	F6	A9	Rat
4. 3	19. 1	C3	A11	Horse	14. 5	2. 4	F6	B10	Swallow
5. 3	20. 1	C3	B12	Stag	15. 5	3. 4	F6	C11	Pig
6. 3	21. 1	C3	C1	Serpent	16. 5	4. 4	F6	D12	Porcupine
7. 3	22. 1	C3	D2	Earthworm	17. 5	5. 4	F6	E1	Wolf
8. 3	23. 1	C3	E3	Crocodile	18. 5	6. 4	F6	F2	Dog
9. 3	24. 1	C3	F4	Dragon	19. 5	7. 4	F6	G3	Pheasant
10. 3	25. 1	C3	G5	Badger	20. 5	8. 4	F6	H4	Cock
11. 3	26. 1	C3	H6	Hare	21. 5	9. 4	F6	J5	Crow
12. 3	27. 1	C3	J7	Fox	22. 5	10. 4	F6	K6	Monkey
13. 3	28. 1	C3	K8	Tiger	23. 5	11. 4	F6	A7	Gibbon
14. 3	29. 1	C3	A9	Leopard	24. 5	12. 4	F6	B8	Tapir
15. 3	1. 2	D4	B10	Griffon	25. 5	13. 4	F6	C9	Sheep
16. 3	2. 2	D4	C11	Ox	26. 5	14. 4	F6	D10	Deer
17. 3	3. 2	D4	D12	Bat	27. 5	15. 4	F6	E11	Horse
18. 3	4. 2	D4	E1	Rat	28. 5	16. 4	F6	F12	Stag
19. 3	5. 2	D4	F2	Swallow	29. 5	17. 4	F6	G1	Serpent
20. 3	6. 2	D4	G3	Pig	30. 5	18. 4	F6	H2	Earthworm
21. 3	7. 2	D4	H4	Porcupine	31. 5	19. 4	F6	J3	Crocodile
22. 3	8. 2	D4	J5	Wolf	1. 6	20. 4	F6	K4	Dragon
23. 3	9. 2	D4	K6	Dog	2. 6	21. 4	F6	A5	Badger
24. 3	10. 2	D4	A7	Pheasant	3. 6	22. 4	F6	B6	Hare
25. 3	11. 2	D4	B8	Cock	4. 6	23. 4	F6	C7	Fox
26. 3	12. 2	D4	C9	Crow	5. 6	24. 4	F6	D8	Tiger
27. 3	13. 2	D4	D10	Monkey	6. 6	25. 4	F6	E9	Leopard
28. 3	14. 2	D4	E11	Gibbon	7. 6	26. 4	F6	F10	Griffon
29. 3	15. 2	D4	F12	Tapir	8. 6	27. 4	F6	G11	Ox
30. 3	16. 2	D4	G1	Sheep	9. 6	28. 4	F6	H12	Bat
31. 3	17. 2	D4	H2	Deer	10. 6	29. 4	F6	J1	Rat
1. 4	18. 2	D4	J3	Horse	11. 6	30. 4	F6	K2	Swallow
2. 4	19. 2	D4	K4	Stag	12. 6	1. 5	G7	A3	Pig
3. 4	20. 2	D4	A5	Serpent	13. 6	2. 5	G7	B4	Porcupine
4. 4	21. 2	D4	B6	Earthworm	14. 6	3. 5	G7	C5	Wolf
5. 4	22. 2	D4	C7	Crocodile	15. 6	4. 5	G7	D6	Dog
6. 4	23. 2	D4	D8	Dragon	16. 6	5. 5	G7	E7	Pheasant
7. 4	24. 2	D4	E9	Badger	17. 6	6. 5	G7	F8	Cock
8. 4	25. 2	D4	F10	Hare	18. 6	7. 5	G7	G9	Crow
9. 4	26. 2	D4	G11	Fox	19. 6	8. 5	G7	H10	Monkey
10. 4	27. 2	D4	H12	Tiger	20. 6	9. 5	G7	J11	Gibbon
11. 4	28. 2	D4	J1	Leopard	21. 6	10. 5	G7	K12	Tapir
12. 4	29. 2	D4	K2	Griffon	22. 6	11. 5	G7	A1	Sheep
13. 4	30. 2	D4	A3	Ox	23. 6	12. 5	G7	B2	Deer
14. 4	1. 3	E5	B4	Bat	24. 6	13. 5	G7	C3	Horse
15. 4	2. 3	E5	C5	Rat	25. 6	14. 5	G7	D4	Stag
16. 4	3. 3	E5	D6	Swallow	26. 6	15. 5	G7	E5	Serpent
17. 4	4. 3	E5	E7	Pig	27. 6	16. 5	G7	F6	Earthworm
18. 4	5. 3	E5	F8	Porcupine	28. 6	17. 5	G7	G7	Crocodile
19. 4	6. 3	E5	G9	Wolf	29. 6	18. 5	G7	H8	Dragon
20. 4	7. 3	E5	H10	Dog	30. 6	19. 5	G7	J9	Badger
21. 4	8. 3	E5	J11	Pheasant	1. 7	20. 5	G7	K10	Hare
22. 4	9. 3	E5	K12	Cock	2. 7	21. 5	G7	A11	Fox
23. 4	10. 3	E5	A1	Crow	3. 7	22. 5	G7	B12	Tiger
24. 4	11. 3	E5	B2	Monkey	4. 7	23. 5	G7	C1	Leopard
25. 4	12. 3	E5	C3	Gibbon	5. 7	24. 5	G7	D2	Griffon

Solar date	Lunar date	Month HS/EB	Day HS/EB	Constellation
6. 7	25. 5	G7	E3	Ox
7. 7	26. 5	G7	F4	Bat
8. 7	27. 5	G7	G5	Rat
9. 7	28. 5	G7	H6	Swallow
10. 7	29. 5	G7	J7	Pig
11. 7	30. 5	G7	K8	Porcupine
12. 7	1. 6	H8	A9	Wolf
13. 7	2. 6	H8	B10	Dog
14. 7	3. 6	H8	C11	Pheasant
15. 7	4. 6	H8	D12	Cock
16. 7	5. 6	H8	E1	Crow
17. 7	6. 6	H8	F2	Monkey
18. 7	7. 6	H8	G3	Gibbon
19. 7	8. 6	H8	H4	Tapir
20. 7	9. 6	H8	J5	Sheep
21. 7	10. 6	H8	K6	Deer
22. 7	11. 6	H8	A7	Horse
23. 7	12. 6	H8	B8	Stag
24. 7	13. 6	H8	C9	Serpent
25. 7	14. 6	H8	D10	Earthworm
26. 7	15. 6	H8	E11	Crocodile
27. 7	16. 6	H8	F12	Dragon
28. 7	17. 6	H8	G1	Badger
29. 7	18. 6	H8	H2	Hare
30. 7	19. 6	H8	J3	Fox
31. 7	20. 6	H8	K4	Tiger
1. 8	21. 6	H8	A5	Leopard
2. 8	22. 6	H8	B6	Griffon
3. 8	23. 6	H8	C7	Ox
4. 8	24. 6	H8	D8	Bat
5. 8	25. 6	H8	E9	Rat
6. 8	26. 6	H8	F10	Swallow
7. 8	27. 6	H8	G11	Pig
8. 8	28. 6	H8	H12	Porcupine
9. 8	29. 6	H8	J1	Wolf
10. 8	1. 7	J9	K2	Dog
11. 8	2. 7	J9	A3	Pheasant
12. 8	3. 7	J9	B4	Cock
13. 8	4. 7	J9	C5	Crow
14. 8	5. 7	J9	D6	Monkey
15. 8	6. 7	J9	E7	Gibbon
16. 8	7. 7	J9	F8	Tapir
17. 8	8. 7	J9	G9	Sheep
18. 8	9. 7	J9	H10	Deer
19. 8	10. 7	J9	J11	Horse
20. 8	11. 7	J9	K12	Stag
21. 8	12. 7	J9	A1	Serpent
22. 8	13. 7	J9	B2	Earthworm
23. 8	14. 7	J9	C3	Crocodile
24. 8	15. 7	J9	D4	Dragon
25. 8	16. 7	J9	E5	Badger
26. 8	17. 7	J9	F6	Hare
27. 8	18. 7	J9	G7	Fox
28. 8	19. 7	J9	H8	Tiger
29. 8	20. 7	J9	J9	Leopard
30. 8	21. 7	J9	K10	Griffon
31. 8	22. 7	J9	A11	Ox
1. 9	23. 7	J9	B12	Bat
2. 9	24. 7	J9	C1	Rat
3. 9	25. 7	J9	D2	Swallow
4. 9	26. 7	J9	E3	Pig
5. 9	27. 7	J9	F4	Porcupine
6. 9	28. 7	J9	G5	Wolf
7. 9	29. 7	J9	H6	Dog
8. 9	30. 7	J9	J7	Pheasant
9. 9	1. 8	K10	K8	Cock
10. 9	2. 8	K10	A9	Crow
11. 9	3. 8	K10	B10	Monkey
12. 9	4. 8	K10	C11	Gibbon
13. 9	5. 8	K10	D12	Tapir
14. 9	6. 8	K10	E1	Sheep
15. 9	7. 8	K10	F2	Deer
16. 9	8. 8	K10	G3	Horse
17. 9	9. 8	K10	H4	Stag
18. 9	10. 8	K10	J5	Serpent
19. 9	11. 8	K10	K6	Earthworm
20. 9	12. 8	K10	A7	Crocodile
21. 9	13. 8	K10	B8	Dragon
22. 9	14. 8	K10	C9	Badger
23. 9	15. 8	K10	D10	Hare
24. 9	16. 8	K10	E11	Fox
25. 9	17. 8	K10	F12	Tiger
26. 9	18. 8	K10	G1	Leopard
27. 9	19. 8	K10	H2	Griffon
28. 9	20. 8	K10	J3	Ox
29. 9	21. 8	K10	K4	Bat
30. 9	22. 8	K10	A5	Rat
1.10	23. 8	K10	B6	Swallow
2.10	24. 8	K10	C7	Pig
3.10	25. 8	K10	D8	Porcupine
4.10	26. 8	K10	E9	Wolf
5.10	27. 8	K10	F10	Dog
6.10	28. 8	K10	G11	Pheasant
7.10	29. 8	K10	H12	Cock
8.10	1. 9	A11	J1	Crow
9.10	2. 9	A11	K2	Monkey
10.10	3. 9	A11	A3	Gibbon
11.10	4. 9	A11	B4	Tapir
12.10	5. 9	A11	C5	Sheep
13.10	6. 9	A11	D6	Deer
14.10	7. 9	A11	E7	Horse
15.10	8. 9	A11	F8	Stag
16.10	9. 9	A11	G9	Serpent
17.10	10. 9	A11	H10	Earthworm
18.10	11. 9	A11	J11	Crocodile
19.10	12. 9	A11	K12	Dragon
20.10	13. 9	A11	A1	Badger
21.10	14. 9	A11	B2	Hare
22.10	15. 9	A11	C3	Fox
23.10	16. 9	A11	D4	Tiger
24.10	17. 9	A11	E5	Leopard
25.10	18. 9	A11	F6	Griffon
26.10	19. 9	A11	G7	Ox
27.10	20. 9	A11	H8	Bat
28.10	21. 9	A11	J9	Rat
29.10	22. 9	A11	K10	Swallow
30.10	23. 9	A11	A11	Pig
31.10	24. 9	A11	B12	Porcupine
1.11	25. 9	A11	C1	Wolf
2.11	26. 9	A11	D2	Dog
3.11	27. 9	A11	E3	Pheasant
4.11	28. 9	A11	F4	Cock
5.11	29. 9	A11	G5	Crow
6.11	30. 9	A11	H6	Monkey
7.11	1.10	B12	J7	Gibbon
8.11	2.10	B12	K8	Tapir
9.11	3.10	B12	A9	Sheep
10.11	4.10	B12	B10	Deer
11.11	5.10	B12	C11	Horse
12.11	6.10	B12	D12	Stag
13.11	7.10	B12	E1	Serpent
14.11	8.10	B12	F2	Earthworm
15.11	9.10	B12	G3	Crocodile
16.11	10.10	B12	H4	Dragon
17.11	11.10	B12	J5	Badger
18.11	12.10	B12	K6	Hare
19.11	13.10	B12	A7	Fox
20.11	14.10	B12	B8	Tiger
21.11	15.10	B12	C9	Leopard
22.11	16.10	B12	D10	Griffon
23.11	17.10	B12	E11	Ox
24.11	18.10	B12	F12	Bat
25.11	19.10	B12	G1	Rat
26.11	20.10	B12	H2	Swallow
27.11	21.10	B12	J3	Pig
28.11	22.10	B12	K4	Porcupine

Solar date	Lunar date	Month HS/EB	Day HS/EB	Constellation	Solar date	Lunar date	Month HS/EB	Day HS/EB	Constellation
29.11	23.10	B12	A5	Wolf	2. 1	27.11	C1	E3	Gibbon
30.11	24.10	B12	B6	Dog	3. 1	28.11	C1	F4	Tapir
1.12	25.10	B12	C7	Pheasant	4. 1	29.11	C1	G5	Sheep
2.12	26.10	B12	D8	Cock	5. 1	1.12	D2	H6	Deer
3.12	27.10	B12	E9	Crow	6. 1	2.12	D2	J7	Horse
4.12	28.10	B12	F10	Monkey	7. 1	3.12	D2	K8	Stag
5.12	29.10	B12	G11	Gibbon	8. 1	4.12	D2	A9	Serpent
6.12	30.10	B12	H12	Tapir	9. 1	5.12	D2	B10	Earthworm
7.12	1.11	C1	J1	Sheep	10. 1	6.12	D2	C11	Crocodile
8.12	2.11	C1	K2	Deer	11. 1	7.12	D2	D12	Dragon
9.12	3.11	C1	A3	Horse	12. 1	8.12	D2	E1	Badger
10.12	4.11	C1	B4	Stag	13. 1	9.12	D2	F2	Hare
11.12	5.11	C1	C5	Serpent	14. 1	10.12	D2	G3	Fox
12.12	6.11	C1	D6	Earthworm	15. 1	11.12	D2	H4	Tiger
13.12	7.11	C1	E7	Crocodile	16. 1	12.12	D2	J5	Leopard
14.12	8.11	C1	F8	Dragon	17. 1	13.12	D2	K6	Griffon
15.12	9.11	C1	G9	Badger	18. 1	14.12	D2	A7	Ox
16.12	10.11	C1	H10	Hare	19. 1	15.12	D2	B8	Bat
17.12	11.11	C1	J11	Fox	20. 1	16.12	D2	C9	Rat
18.12	12.11	C1	K12	Tiger	21. 1	17.12	D2	D10	Swallow
19.12	13.11	C1	A1	Leopard	22. 1	18.12	D2	E11	Pig
20.12	14.11	C1	B2	Griffon	23. 1	19.12	D2	F12	Porcupine
21.12	15.11	C1	C3	Ox	24. 1	20.12	D2	G1	Wolf
22.12	16.11	C1	D4	Bat	25. 1	21.12	D2	H2	Dog
23.12	17.11	C1	E5	Rat	26. 1	22.12	D2	J3	Pheasant
24.12	18.11	C1	F6	Swallow	27. 1	23.12	D2	K4	Cock
25.12	19.11	C1	G7	Pig	28. 1	24.12	D2	A5	Crow
26.12	20.11	C1	H8	Porcupine	29. 1	25.12	D2	B6	Monkey
27.12	21.11	C1	J9	Wolf	30. 1	26.12	D2	C7	Gibbon
28.12	22.11	C1	K10	Dog	31. 1	27.12	D2	D8	Tapir
29.12	23.11	C1	A11	Pheasant	1. 2	28.12	D2	E9	Sheep
30.12	24.11	C1	B12	Cock	2. 2	29.12	D2	F10	Deer
31.12	25.11	C1	C1	Crow	3. 2	30.12	D2	G11	Horse

1935

Solar date	Lunar date	Month HS/EB	Day HS/EB	Constellation
1. 1	26.11	C1	D2	Monkey

YI HAI YEAR

Solar date	Lunar date	Month HS/EB	Day HS/EB	Constellation	Solar date	Lunar date	Month HS/EB	Day HS/EB	Constellation
4. 2	1. 1	E3	H12	Stag	8. 3	4. 2	F4	K8	Dragon
5. 2	2. 1	E3	J1	Serpent	9. 3	5. 2	F4	A9	Badger
6. 2	3. 1	E3	K2	Earthworm	10. 3	6. 2	F4	B10	Hare
7. 2	4. 1	E3	A3	Crocodile	11. 3	7. 2	F4	C11	Fox
8. 2	5. 1	E3	B4	Dragon	12. 3	8. 2	F4	D12	Tiger
9. 2	6. 1	E3	C5	Badger	13. 3	9. 2	F4	E1	Leopard
10. 2	7. 1	E3	D6	Hare	14. 3	10. 2	F4	F2	Griffon
11. 2	8. 1	E3	E7	Fox	15. 3	11. 2	F4	G3	Ox
12. 2	9. 1	E3	F8	Tiger	16. 3	12. 2	F4	H4	Bat
13. 2	10. 1	E3	G9	Leopard	17. 3	13. 2	F4	J5	Rat
14. 2	11. 1	E3	H10	Griffon	18. 3	14. 2	F4	K6	Swallow
15. 2	12. 1	E3	J11	Ox	19. 3	15. 2	F4	A7	Pig
16. 2	13. 1	E3	K12	Bat	20. 3	16. 2	F4	B8	Porcupine
17. 2	14. 1	E3	A1	Rat	21. 3	17. 2	F4	C9	Wolf
18. 2	15. 1	E3	B2	Swallow	22. 3	18. 2	F4	D10	Dog
19. 2	16. 1	E3	C3	Pig	23. 3	19. 2	F4	E11	Pheasant
20. 2	17. 1	E3	D4	Porcupine	24. 3	20. 2	F4	F12	Cock
21. 2	18. 1	E3	E5	Wolf	25. 3	21. 2	F4	G1	Crow
22. 2	19. 1	E3	F6	Dog	26. 3	22. 2	F4	H2	Monkey
23. 2	20. 1	E3	G7	Pheasant	27. 3	23. 2	F4	J3	Gibbon
24. 2	21. 1	E3	H8	Cock	28. 3	24. 2	F4	K4	Tapir
25. 2	22. 1	E3	J9	Crow	29. 3	25. 2	F4	A5	Sheep
26. 2	23. 1	E3	K10	Monkey	30. 3	26. 2	F4	B6	Deer
27. 2	24. 1	E3	A11	Gibbon	31. 3	27. 2	F4	C7	Horse
28. 2	25. 1	E3	B12	Tapir	1. 4	28. 2	F4	D8	Stag
1. 3	26. 1	E3	C1	Sheep	2. 4	29. 2	F4	E9	Serpent
2. 3	27. 1	E3	D2	Deer	3. 4	1. 3	G5	F10	Earthworm
3. 3	28. 1	E3	E3	Horse	4. 4	2. 3	G5	G11	Crocodile
4. 3	29. 1	E3	F4	Stag	5. 4	3. 3	G5	H12	Dragon
5. 3	1. 2	F4	G5	Serpent	6. 4	4. 3	G5	J1	Badger
6. 3	2. 2	F4	H6	Earthworm	7. 4	5. 3	G5	K2	Hare
7. 3	3. 2	F4	J7	Crocodile	8. 4	6. 3	G5	A3	Fox

Solar date	Lunar date	Month HS/EB	Day HS/EB	Constellation
9. 4	7. 3	G5	B4	Tiger
10. 4	8. 3	G5	C5	Leopard
11. 4	9. 3	G5	D6	Griffon
12. 4	10. 3	G5	E7	Ox
13. 4	11. 3	G5	F8	Bat
14. 4	12. 3	G5	G9	Rat
15. 4	13. 3	G5	H10	Swallow
16. 4	14. 3	G5	J11	Pig
17. 4	15. 3	G5	K12	Porcupine
18. 4	16. 3	G5	A1	Wolf
19. 4	17. 3	G5	B2	Dog
20. 4	18. 3	G5	C3	Pheasant
21. 4	19. 3	G5	D4	Cock
22. 4	20. 3	G5	E5	Crow
23. 4	21. 3	G5	F6	Monkey
24. 4	22. 3	G5	G7	Gibbon
25. 4	23. 3	G5	H8	Tapir
26. 4	24. 3	G5	J9	Sheep
27. 4	25. 3	G5	K10	Deer
28. 4	26. 3	G5	A11	Horse
29. 4	27. 3	G5	B12	Stag
30. 4	28. 3	G5	C1	Serpent
1. 5	29. 3	G5	D2	Earthworm
2. 5	30. 3	G5	E3	Crocodile
3. 5	1. 4	H6	F4	Dragon
4. 5	2. 4	H6	G5	Badger
5. 5	3. 4	H6	H6	Hare
6. 5	4. 4	H6	J7	Fox
7. 5	5. 4	H6	K8	Tiger
8. 5	6. 4	H6	A9	Leopard
9. 5	7. 4	H6	B10	Griffon
10. 5	8. 4	H6	C11	Ox
11. 5	9. 4	H6	D12	Bat
12. 5	10. 4	H6	E1	Rat
13. 5	11. 4	H6	F2	Swallow
14. 5	12. 4	H6	G3	Pig
15. 5	13. 4	H6	H4	Porcupine
16. 5	14. 4	H6	J5	Wolf
17. 5	15. 4	H6	K6	Dog
18. 5	16. 4	H6	A7	Pheasant
19. 5	17. 4	H6	B8	Cock
20. 5	18. 4	H6	C9	Crow
21. 5	19. 4	H6	D10	Monkey
22. 5	20. 4	H6	E11	Gibbon
23. 5	21. 4	H6	F12	Tapir
24. 5	22. 4	H6	G1	Sheep
25. 5	23. 4	H6	H2	Deer
26. 5	24. 4	H6	J3	Horse
27. 5	25. 4	H6	K4	Stag
28. 5	26. 4	H6	A5	Serpent
29. 5	27. 4	H6	B6	Earthworm
30. 5	28. 4	H6	C7	Crocodile
31. 5	29. 4	H6	D8	Dragon
1. 6	1. 5	J7	E9	Badger
2. 6	2. 5	J7	F10	Hare
3. 6	3. 5	J7	G11	Fox
4. 6	4. 5	J7	H12	Tiger
5. 6	5. 5	J7	J1	Leopard
6. 6	6. 5	J7	K2	Griffon
7. 6	7. 5	J7	A3	Ox
8. 6	8. 5	J7	B4	Bat
9. 6	9. 5	J7	C5	Rat
10. 6	10. 5	J7	D6	Swallow
11. 6	11. 5	J7	E7	Pig
12. 6	12. 5	J7	F8	Porcupine
13. 6	13. 5	J7	G9	Wolf
14. 6	14. 5	J7	H10	Dog
15. 6	15. 5	J7	J11	Pheasant
16. 6	16. 5	J7	K12	Cock
17. 6	17. 5	J7	A1	Crow
18. 6	18. 5	J7	B2	Monkey
19. 6	19. 5	J7	C3	Gibbon
20. 6	20. 5	J7	D4	Tapir

Solar date	Lunar date	Month HS/EB	Day HS/EB	Constellation
21. 6	21. 5	J7	E5	Sheep
22. 6	22. 5	J7	F6	Deer
23. 6	23. 5	J7	G7	Horse
24. 6	24. 5	J7	H8	Stag
25. 6	25. 5	J7	J9	Serpent
26. 6	26. 5	J7	K10	Earthworm
27. 6	27. 5	J7	A11	Crocodile
28. 6	28. 5	J7	B12	Dragon
29. 6	29. 5	J7	C1	Badger
30. 6	30. 5	J7	D2	Hare
1. 7	1. 6	K8	E3	Fox
2. 7	2. 6	K8	F4	Tiger
3. 7	3. 6	K8	G5	Leopard
4. 7	4. 6	K8	H6	Griffon
5. 7	5. 6	K8	J7	Ox
6. 7	6. 6	K8	K8	Bat
7. 7	7. 6	K8	A9	Rat
8. 7	8. 6	K8	B10	Swallow
9. 7	9. 6	K8	C11	Pig
10. 7	10. 6	K8	D12	Porcupine
11. 7	11. 6	K8	E1	Wolf
12. 7	12. 6	K8	F2	Dog
13. 7	13. 6	K8	G3	Pheasant
14. 7	14. 6	K8	H4	Cock
15. 7	15. 6	K8	J5	Crow
16. 7	16. 6	K8	K6	Monkey
17. 7	17. 6	K8	A7	Gibbon
18. 7	18. 6	K8	B8	Tapir
19. 7	19. 6	K8	C9	Sheep
20. 7	20. 6	K8	D10	Deer
21. 7	21. 6	K8	E11	Horse
22. 7	22. 6	K8	F12	Stag
23. 7	23. 6	K8	G1	Serpent
24. 7	24. 6	K8	H2	Earthworm
25. 7	25. 6	K8	J3	Crocodile
26. 7	26. 6	K8	K4	Dragon
27. 7	27. 6	K8	A5	Badger
28. 7	28. 6	K8	B6	Hare
29. 7	29. 6	K8	C7	Fox
30. 7	1. 7	A9	D8	Tiger
31. 7	2. 7	A9	E9	Leopard
1. 8	3. 7	A9	F10	Griffon
2. 8	4. 7	A9	G11	Ox
3. 8	5. 7	A9	H12	Bat
4. 8	6. 7	A9	J1	Rat
5. 8	7. 7	A9	K2	Swallow
6. 8	8. 7	A9	A3	Pig
7. 8	9. 7	A9	B4	Porcupine
8. 8	10. 7	A9	C5	Wolf
9. 8	11. 7	A9	D6	Dog
10. 8	12. 7	A9	E7	Pheasant
11. 8	13. 7	A9	F8	Cock
12. 8	14. 7	A9	G9	Crow
13. 8	15. 7	A9	H10	Monkey
14. 8	16. 7	A9	J11	Gibbon
15. 8	17. 7	A9	K12	Tapir
16. 8	18. 7	A9	A1	Sheep
17. 8	19. 7	A9	B2	Deer
18. 8	20. 7	A9	C3	Horse
19. 8	21. 7	A9	D4	Stag
20. 8	22. 7	A9	E5	Serpent
21. 8	23. 7	A9	F6	Earthworm
22. 8	24. 7	A9	G7	Crocodile
23. 8	25. 7	A9	H8	Dragon
24. 8	26. 7	A9	J9	Badger
25. 8	27. 7	A9	K10	Hare
26. 8	28. 7	A9	A11	Fox
27. 8	29. 7	A9	B12	Tiger
28. 8	30. 7	A9	C1	Leopard
29. 8	1. 8	B10	D2	Griffon
30. 8	2. 8	B10	E3	Ox
31. 8	3. 8	B10	F4	Bat
1. 9	4. 8	B10	G5	Rat

Solar date	Lunar date	Month HS/EB	Day HS/EB	Constellation	Solar date	Lunar date	Month HS/EB	Day HS/EB	Constellation
2. 9	5. 8	B10	H6	Swallow	14.11	19.10	D12	A7	Crocodile
3. 9	6. 8	B10	J7	Pig	15.11	20.10	D12	B8	Dragon
4. 9	7. 8	B10	K8	Porcupine	16.11	21.10	D12	C9	Badger
5. 9	8. 8	B10	A9	Wolf	17.11	22.10	D12	D10	Hare
6. 9	9. 8	B10	B10	Dog	18.11	23.10	D12	E11	Fox
7. 9	10. 8	B10	C11	Pheasant	19.11	24.10	D12	F12	Tiger
8. 9	11. 8	B10	D12	Cock	20.11	25.10	D12	G1	Leopard
9. 9	12. 8	B10	E1	Crow	21.11	26.10	D12	H2	Griffon
10. 9	13. 8	B10	F2	Monkey	22.11	27.10	D12	J3	Ox
11. 9	14. 8	B10	G3	Gibbon	23.11	28.10	D12	K4	Bat
12. 9	15. 8	B10	H4	Tapir	24.11	29.10	D12	A5	Rat
13. 9	16. 8	B10	J5	Sheep	25.11	30.10	D12	B6	Swallow
14. 9	17. 8	B10	K6	Deer	26.11	1.11	E1	C7	Pig
15. 9	18. 8	B10	A7	Horse	27.11	2.11	E1	D8	Porcupine
16. 9	19. 8	B10	B8	Stag	28.11	3.11	E1	E9	Wolf
17. 9	20. 8	B10	C9	Serpent	29.11	4.11	E1	F10	Dog
18. 9	21. 8	B10	D10	Earthworm	30.11	5.11	E1	G11	Pheasant
19. 9	22. 8	B10	E11	Crocodile	1.12	6.11	E1	H12	Cock
20. 9	23. 8	B10	F12	Dragon	2.12	7.11	E1	J1	Crow
21. 9	24. 8	B10	G1	Badger	3.12	8.11	E1	K2	Monkey
22. 9	25. 8	B10	H2	Hare	4.12	9.11	E1	A3	Gibbon
23. 9	26. 8	B10	J3	Fox	5.12	10.11	E1	B4	Tapir
24. 9	27. 8	B10	K4	Tiger	6.12	11.11	E1	C5	Sheep
25. 9	28. 8	B10	A5	Leopard	7.12	12.11	E1	D6	Deer
26. 9	29. 8	B10	B6	Griffon	8.12	13.11	E1	E7	Horse
27. 9	30. 8	B10	C7	Ox	9.12	14.11	E1	F8	Stag
28. 9	1. 9	C11	D8	Bat	10.12	15.11	E1	G9	Serpent
29. 9	2. 9	C11	E9	Rat	11.12	16.11	E1	H10	Earthworm
30. 9	3. 9	C11	F10	Swallow	12.12	17.11	E1	J11	Crocodile
1.10	4. 9	C11	G11	Pig	13.12	18.11	E1	K12	Dragon
2.10	5. 9	C11	H12	Porcupine	14.12	19.11	E1	A1	Badger
3.10	6. 9	C11	J1	Wolf	15.12	20.11	E1	B2	Hare
4.10	7. 9	C11	K2	Dog	16.12	21.11	E1	C3	Fox
5.10	8. 9	C11	A3	Pheasant	17.12	22.11	E1	D4	Tiger
6.10	9. 9	C11	B4	Cock	18.12	23.11	E1	E5	Leopard
7.10	10. 9	C11	C5	Crow	19.12	24.11	E1	F6	Griffon
8.10	11. 9	C11	D6	Monkey	20.12	25.11	E1	G7	Ox
9.10	12. 9	C11	E7	Gibbon	21.12	26.11	E1	H8	Bat
10.10	13. 9	C11	F8	Tapir	22.12	27.11	E1	J9	Rat
11.10	14. 9	C11	G9	Sheep	23.12	28.11	E1	K10	Swallow
12.10	15. 9	C11	H10	Deer	24.12	29.11	E1	A11	Pig
13.10	16. 9	C11	J11	Horse	25.12	30.11	E1	B12	Porcupine
14.10	17. 9	C11	K12	Stag	26.12	1.12	F2	C1	Wolf
15.10	18. 9	C11	A1	Serpent	27.12	2.12	F2	D2	Dog
16.10	19. 9	C11	B2	Earthworm	28.12	3.12	F2	E3	Pheasant
17.10	20. 9	C11	C3	Crocodile	29.12	4.12	F2	F4	Cock
18.10	21. 9	C11	D4	Dragon	30.12	5.12	F2	G5	Crow
19.10	22. 9	C11	E5	Badger	31.12	6.12	F2	H6	Monkey
20.10	23. 9	C11	F6	Hare					
21.10	24. 9	C11	G7	Fox	**1936**				
22.10	25. 9	C11	H8	Tiger	1. 1	7.12	F2	J7	Gibbon
23.10	26. 9	C11	J9	Leopard	2. 1	8.12	F2	K8	Tapir
24.10	27. 9	C11	K10	Griffon	3. 1	9.12	F2	A9	Sheep
25.10	28. 9	C11	A11	Ox	4. 1	10.12	F2	B10	Deer
26.10	29. 9	C11	B12	Bat	5. 1	11.12	F2	C11	Horse
27.10	1.10	D12	C1	Rat	6. 1	12.12	F2	D12	Stag
28.10	2.10	D12	D2	Swallow	7. 1	13.12	F2	E1	Serpent
29.10	3.10	D12	E3	Pig	8. 1	14.12	F2	F2	Earthworm
30.10	4.10	D12	F4	Porcupine	9. 1	15.12	F2	G3	Crocodile
31.10	5.10	D12	G5	Wolf	10. 1	16.12	F2	H4	Dragon
1.11	6.10	D12	H6	Dog	11. 1	17.12	F2	J5	Badger
2.11	7.10	D12	J7	Pheasant	12. 1	18.12	F2	K6	Hare
3.11	8.10	D12	K8	Cock	13. 1	19.12	F2	A7	Fox
4.11	9.10	D12	A9	Crow	14. 1	20.12	F2	B8	Tiger
5.11	10.10	D12	B10	Monkey	15. 1	21.12	F2	C9	Leopard
6.11	11.10	D12	C11	Gibbon	16. 1	22.12	F2	D10	Griffon
7.11	12.10	D12	D12	Tapir	17. 1	23.12	F2	E11	Ox
8.11	13.10	D12	E1	Sheep	18. 1	24.12	F2	F12	Bat
9.11	14.10	D12	F2	Deer	19. 1	25.12	F2	G1	Rat
10.11	15.10	D12	G3	Horse	20. 1	26.12	F2	H2	Swallow
11.11	16.10	D12	H4	Stag	21. 1	27.12	F2	J3	Pig
12.11	17.10	D12	J5	Serpent	22. 1	28.12	F2	K4	Porcupine
13.11	18.10	D12	K6	Earthworm	23. 1	29.12	F2	A5	Wolf

PING TZU YEAR

Solar date	Lunar date	Month HS/EB	Day HS/EB	Constellation
24. 1	1. 1	G3	B6	Dog
25. 1	2. 1	G3	C7	Pheasant
26. 1	3. 1	G3	D8	Cock
27. 1	4. 1	G3	E9	Crow
28. 1	5. 1	G3	F10	Monkey
29. 1	6. 1	G3	G11	Gibbon
30. 1	7. 1	G3	H12	Tapir
31. 1	8. 1	G3	J1	Sheep
1. 2	9. 1	G3	K2	Deer
2. 2	10. 1	G3	A3	Horse
3. 2	11. 1	G3	B4	Stag
4. 2	12. 1	G3	C5	Serpent
5. 2	13. 1	G3	D6	Earthworm
6. 2	14. 1	G3	E7	Crocodile
7. 2	15. 1	G3	F8	Dragon
8. 2	16. 1	G3	G9	Badger
9. 2	17. 1	G3	H10	Hare
10. 2	18. 1	G3	J11	Fox
11. 2	19. 1	G3	K12	Tiger
12. 2	20. 1	G3	A1	Leopard
13. 2	21. 1	G3	B2	Griffon
14. 2	22. 1	G3	C3	Ox
15. 2	23. 1	G3	D4	Bat
16. 2	24. 1	G3	E5	Rat
17. 2	25. 1	G3	F6	Swallow
18. 2	26. 1	G3	G7	Pig
19. 2	27. 1	G3	H8	Porcupine
20. 2	28. 1	G3	J9	Wolf
21. 2	29. 1	G3	K10	Dog
22. 2	30. 1	G3	A11	Pheasant
23. 2	1. 2	H4	B12	Cock
24. 2	2. 2	H4	C1	Crow
25. 2	3. 2	H4	D2	Monkey
26. 2	3. 2	H4	E3	Griffon
27. 2	4. 2	H4	F4	Tapir
28. 2	6. 2	H4	G5	Sheep
29. 2	7. 2	H4	H6	Deer
1. 3	8. 2	H4	J7	Horse
2. 3	9. 2	H4	K8	Stag
3. 3	10. 2	H4	A9	Serpent
4. 3	11. 2	H4	B10	Earthworm
5. 3	12. 2	H4	C11	Crocodile
6. 3	13. 2	H4	D12	Dragon
7. 3	14. 2	H4	E1	Badger
8. 3	15. 2	H4	F2	Hare
9. 3	16. 2	H4	G3	Fox
10. 3	17. 2	H4	H4	Tiger
11. 3	18. 2	H4	J5	Leopard
12. 3	19. 2	H4	K6	Griffon
13. 3	20. 2	H4	A7	Ox
14. 3	21. 2	H4	B8	Bat
15. 3	22. 2	H4	C9	Rat
16. 3	23. 2	H4	D10	Swallow
17. 3	24. 2	H4	E11	Pig
18. 3	25. 2	H4	F12	Porcupine
19. 3	26. 2	H4	G1	Wolf
20. 3	27. 2	H4	H2	Dog
21. 3	28. 2	H4	J3	Pheasant
22. 3	29. 2	H4	K4	Cock
23. 3	1. 3	J5	A5	Crow
24. 3	2. 3	J5	B6	Monkey
25. 3	3. 3	J5	C7	Gibbon
26. 3	4. 3	J5	D8	Tapir
27. 3	5. 3	J5	E9	Sheep
28. 3	6. 3	J5	F10	Deer
29. 3	7. 3	J5	G11	Horse
30. 3	8. 3	J5	H12	Stag
31. 3	9. 3	J5	J1	Serpent
1. 4	10. 3	J5	K2	Earthworm
2. 4	11. 3	J5	A3	Crocodile
3. 4	12. 3	J5	B4	Dragon
4. 4	13. 3	J5	C5	Badger
5. 4	14. 3	J5	D6	Hare
6. 4	15. 3	J5	E7	Fox
7. 4	16. 3	J5	F8	Tiger
8. 4	17. 3	J5	G9	Leopard
9. 4	18. 3	J5	H10	Griffon
10. 4	19. 3	J5	J11	Ox
11. 4	20. 3	J5	K12	Bat
12. 4	21. 3	J5	A1	Rat
13. 4	22. 3	J5	B2	Swallow
14. 4	23. 3	J5	C3	Pig
15. 4	24. 3	J5	D4	Porcupine
16. 4	25. 3	J5	E5	Wolf
17. 4	26. 3	J5	F6	Dog
18. 4	27. 3	J5	G7	Pheasant
19. 4	28. 3	J5	H8	Cock
20. 4	29. 3	J5	J9	Crow
21. 4	1. 3	J5	K10	Monkey
22. 4	2. 3	J5	A11	Gibbon
23. 4	3. 3	J5	B12	Tapir
24. 4	4. 3	J5	C1	Sheep
25. 4	5. 3	J5	D2	Deer
26. 4	6. 3	J5	E3	Horse
27. 4	7. 3	J5	F4	Stag
28. 4	8. 3	J5	G5	Serpent
29. 4	9. 3	J5	H6	Earthworm
30. 4	10. 3	J5	J7	Crocodile
1. 5	11. 3	J5	K8	Dragon
2. 5	12. 3	J5	A9	Badger
3. 5	13. 3	J5	B10	Hare
4. 5	14. 3	J5	C11	Fox
5. 5	15. 3	J5	D12	Tiger
6. 5	16. 3	J5	E1	Leopard
7. 5	17. 3	J5	F2	Griffon
8. 5	18. 3	J5	G3	Ox
9. 5	19. 3	J5	H4	Bat
10. 5	20. 3	J5	J5	Rat
11. 5	21. 3	J5	K6	Swallow
12. 5	22. 3	J5	A7	Pig
13. 5	23. 3	J5	B8	Porcupine
14. 5	24. 3	J5	C9	Wolf
15. 5	25. 3	J5	D10	Dog
16. 5	26. 3	J5	E11	Pheasant
17. 5	27. 3	J5	F12	Cock
18. 5	28. 3	J5	G1	Crow
19. 5	29. 3	J5	H2	Monkey
20. 5	30. 3	J5	J3	Gibbon
21. 5	1. 4	K6	K4	Tapir
22. 5	2. 4	K6	A5	Sheep
23. 5	3. 4	K6	B6	Deer
24. 5	4. 4	K6	C7	Horse
25. 5	5. 4	K6	D8	Stag
26. 5	6. 4	K6	E9	Serpent
27. 5	7. 4	K6	F10	Earthworm
28. 5	8. 4	K6	G11	Crocodile
29. 5	9. 4	K6	H12	Dragon
30. 5	10. 4	K6	J1	Badger
31. 5	11. 4	K6	K2	Hare
1. 6	12. 4	K6	A3	Fox
2. 6	13. 4	K6	B4	Tiger
3. 6	14. 4	K6	C5	Leopard
4. 6	15. 4	K6	D6	Griffon
5. 6	16. 4	K6	E7	Ox
6. 6	17. 4	K6	F8	Bat
7. 6	18. 4	K6	G9	Rat
8. 6	19. 4	K6	H10	Swallow
9. 6	20. 4	K6	J11	Pig
10. 6	21. 4	K6	K12	Porcupine
11. 6	22. 4	K6	A1	Wolf
12. 6	23. 4	K6	B2	Dog
13. 6	24. 4	K6	C3	Pheasant

Solar date	Lunar date	Month HS/EB	Day HS/EB	Constellation	Solar date	Lunar date	Month HS/EB	Day HS/EB	Constellation
14. 6	25. 4	K6	D4	Cock	26. 8	10. 7	C9	G5	Leopard
15. 6	26. 4	K6	E5	Crow	27. 8	11. 7	C9	H6	Griffon
16. 6	27. 4	K6	F6	Monkey	28. 8	12. 7	C9	J7	Ox
17. 6	28. 4	K6	G7	Gibbon	29. 8	13. 7	C9	K8	Bat
18. 6	29. 4	K6	H8	Tapir	30. 8	14. 7	C9	A9	Rat
19. 6	1. 5	A7	J9	Sheep	31. 8	15. 7	C9	B10	Swallow
20. 6	2. 5	A7	K10	Deer	1. 9	16. 7	C9	C11	Pig
21. 6	3. 5	A7	A11	Horse	2. 9	17. 7	C9	D12	Porcupine
22. 6	4. 5	A7	B12	Stag	3. 9	18. 7	C9	E1	Wolf
23. 6	5. 5	A7	C1	Serpent	4. 9	19. 7	C9	F2	Dog
24. 6	6. 5	A7	D2	Earthworm	5. 9	20. 7	C9	G3	Pheasant
25. 6	7. 5	A7	E3	Crocodile	6. 9	21. 7	C9	H4	Cock
26. 6	8. 5	A7	F4	Dragon	7. 9	22. 7	C9	J5	Crow
27. 6	9. 5	A7	G5	Badger	8. 9	23. 7	C9	K6	Monkey
28. 6	10. 5	A7	H6	Hare	9. 9	24. 7	C9	A7	Gibbon
29. 6	11. 5	A7	J7	Fox	10. 9	25. 7	C9	B8	Tapir
30. 6	12. 5	A7	K8	Tiger	11. 9	26. 7	C9	C9	Sheep
1. 7	13. 5	A7	A9	Leopard	12. 9	27. 7	C9	D10	Deer
2. 7	14. 5	A7	B10	Griffon	13. 9	28. 7	C9	E11	Horse
3. 7	15. 5	A7	C11	Ox	14. 9	29. 7	C9	F12	Stag
4. 7	16. 5	A7	D12	Bat	15. 9	30. 7	C9	G1	Serpent
5. 7	17. 5	A7	E1	Rat	16. 9	1. 8	D10	H2	Earthworm
6. 7	18. 5	A7	F2	Swallow	17. 9	2. 8	D10	J3	Crocodile
7. 7	19. 5	A7	G3	Pig	18. 9	3. 8	D10	K4	Dragon
8. 7	20. 5	A7	H4	Porcupine	19. 9	4. 8	D10	A5	Badger
9. 7	21. 5	A7	J5	Wolf	20. 9	5. 8	D10	B6	Hare
10. 7	22. 5	A7	K6	Dog	21. 9	6. 8	D10	C7	Fox
11. 7	23. 5	A7	A7	Pheasant	22. 9	7. 8	D10	D8	Tiger
12. 7	24. 5	A7	B8	Cock	23. 9	8. 8	D10	E9	Leopard
13. 7	25. 5	A7	C9	Crow	24. 9	9. 8	D10	F10	Griffon
14. 7	26. 5	A7	D10	Monkey	25. 9	10. 8	D10	G11	Ox
15. 7	27. 5	A7	E11	Gibbon	26. 9	11. 8	D10	H12	Bat
16. 7	28. 5	A7	F12	Tapir	27. 9	12. 8	D10	J1	Rat
17. 7	29. 5	A7	G1	Sheep	28. 9	13. 8	D10	K2	Swallow
18. 7	1. 6	B8	H2	Deer	29. 9	14. 8	D10	A3	Pig
19. 7	2. 6	B8	J3	Horse	30. 9	15. 8	D10	B4	Porcupine
20. 7	3. 6	B8	K4	Stag	1.10	16. 8	D10	C5	Wolf
21. 7	4. 6	B8	A5	Serpent	2.10	17. 8	D10	D6	Dog
22. 7	5. 6	B8	B6	Earthworm	3.10	18. 8	D10	E7	Pheasant
23. 7	6. 6	B8	C7	Crocodile	4.10	19. 8	D10	F8	Cock
24. 7	7. 6	B8	D8	Dragon	5.10	20. 8	D10	G9	Crow
25. 7	8. 6	B8	E9	Badger	6.10	21. 8	D10	H10	Monkey
26. 7	9. 6	B8	F10	Hare	7.10	22. 8	D10	J11	Gibbon
27. 7	10. 6	B8	G11	Fox	8.10	23. 8	D10	K12	Tapir
28. 7	11. 6	B8	H12	Tiger	9.10	24. 8	D10	A1	Sheep
29. 7	12. 6	B8	J1	Leopard	10.10	25. 8	D10	B2	Deer
30. 7	13. 6	B8	K2	Griffon	11.10	26. 8	D10	C3	Horse
31. 7	14. 6	B8	A3	Ox	12.10	27. 8	D10	D4	Stag
1. 8	15. 6	B8	B4	Bat	13.10	28. 8	D10	E5	Serpent
2. 8	16. 6	B8	C5	Rat	14.10	29. 8	D10	F6	Earthworm
3. 8	17. 6	B8	D6	Swallow	15.10	1. 9	E11	G7	Crocodile
4. 8	18. 6	B8	E7	Pig	16.10	2. 9	E11	H8	Dragon
5. 8	19. 6	B8	F8	Porcupine	17.10	3. 9	E11	J9	Badger
6. 8	20. 6	B8	G9	Wolf	18.10	4. 9	E11	K10	Hare
7. 8	21. 6	B8	H10	Dog	19.10	5. 9	E11	A11	Fox
8. 8	22. 6	B8	J11	Pheasant	20.10	6. 9	E11	B12	Tiger
9. 8	23. 6	B8	K12	Cock	21.10	7. 9	E11	C1	Leopard
10. 8	24. 6	B8	A1	Crow	22.10	8. 9	E11	D2	Griffon
11. 8	25. 6	B8	B2	Monkey	23.10	9. 9	E11	E3	Ox
12. 8	26. 6	B8	C3	Gibbon	24.10	10. 9	E11	F4	Bat
13. 8	27. 6	B8	D4	Tapir	25.10	11. 9	E11	G5	Rat
14. 8	28. 6	B8	E5	Sheep	26.10	12. 9	E11	H6	Swallow
15. 8	29. 6	B8	F6	Deer	27.10	13. 9	E11	J7	Pig
16. 8	30. 6	B8	G7	Horse	28.10	14. 9	E11	K8	Porcupine
17. 8	1. 7	C9	H8	Stag	29.10	15. 9	E11	A9	Wolf
18. 8	2. 7	C9	J9	Serpent	30.10	16. 9	E11	B10	Dog
19. 8	3. 7	C9	K10	Earthworm	31.10	17. 9	E11	C11	Pheasant
20. 8	4. 7	C9	A11	Crocodile	1.11	18. 9	E11	D12	Cock
21. 8	5. 7	C9	B12	Dragon	2.11	19. 9	E11	E1	Crow
22. 8	6. 7	C9	C1	Badger	3.11	20. 9	E11	F2	Monkey
23. 8	7. 7	C9	D2	Hare	4.11	21. 9	E11	G3	Gibbon
24. 8	8. 7	C9	E3	Fox	5.11	22. 9	E11	H4	Tapir
25. 8	9. 7	C9	F4	Tiger	6.11	23. 9	E11	J5	Sheep

Solar date	Lunar date	Month HS/EB	Day HS/EB	Constellation
7.11	24. 9	E11	K6	Deer
8.11	25. 9	E11	A7	Horse
9.11	26. 9	E11	B8	Stag
10.11	27. 9	E11	C9	Serpent
11.11	28. 9	E11	D10	Earthworm
12.11	29. 9	E11	E11	Crocodile
13.11	30. 9	E11	F12	Dragon
14.11	1.10	F12	G1	Badger
15.11	2.10	F12	H2	Hare
16.11	3.10	F12	J3	Fox
17.11	4.10	F12	K4	Tiger
18.11	5.10	F12	A5	Leopard
19.11	6.10	F12	B6	Griffon
20.11	7.10	F12	C7	Ox
21.11	8.10	F12	D8	Bat
22.11	9.10	F12	E9	Rat
23.11	10.10	F12	F10	Swallow
24.11	11.10	F12	G11	Pig
25.11	12.10	F12	H12	Porcupine
26.11	13.10	F12	J1	Wolf
27.11	14.10	F12	K2	Dog
28.11	15.10	F12	A3	Pheasant
29.11	16.10	F12	B4	Cock
30.11	17.10	F12	C5	Crow
1.12	18.10	F12	D6	Monkey
2.12	19.10	F12	E7	Gibbon
3.12	20.10	F12	F8	Tapir
4.12	21.10	F12	G9	Sheep
5.12	22.10	F12	H10	Deer
6.12	23.10	F12	J11	Horse
7.12	24.10	F12	K12	Stag
8.12	25.10	F12	A1	Serpent
9.12	26.10	F12	B2	Earthworm
10.12	27.10	F12	C3	Crocodile
11.12	28.10	F12	D4	Dragon
12.12	29.10	F12	E5	Badger
13.12	30.10	F12	F6	Hare
14.12	1.11	G1	G7	Fox
15.12	2.11	G1	H8	Tiger
16.12	3.11	G1	J9	Leopard
17.12	4.11	G1	K10	Griffon
18.12	5.11	G1	A11	Ox
19.12	6.11	G1	B12	Bat
20.12	7.11	G1	C1	Rat
21.12	8.11	G1	D2	Swallow
22.12	9.11	G1	E3	Pig
23.12	10.11	G1	F4	Porcupine
24.12	11.11	G1	G5	Wolf
25.12	12.11	G1	H6	Dog
26.12	13.11	G1	J7	Pheasant
27.12	14.11	G1	K8	Cock
28.12	15.11	G1	A9	Crow
29.12	16.11	G1	B10	Monkey
30.12	17.11	G1	C11	Gibbon
31.12	18.11	G1	D12	Tapir

1937

Solar date	Lunar date	Month HS/EB	Day HS/EB	Constellation
1. 1	19.11	G1	E1	Sheep
2. 1	20.11	G1	F2	Deer
3. 1	21.11	G1	G3	Horse
4. 1	22.11	G1	H4	Stag
5. 1	23.11	G1	J5	Serpent
6. 1	24.11	G1	K6	Earthworm
7. 1	25.11	G1	A7	Crocodile
8. 1	26.11	G1	B8	Dragon
9. 1	27.11	G1	C9	Badger
10. 1	28.11	G1	D10	Hare
11. 1	29.11	G1	E11	Fox
12. 1	30.11	G1	F12	Tiger
13. 1	1.12	H2	G1	Leopard
14. 1	2.12	H2	H2	Griffon
15. 1	3.12	H2	J3	Ox
16. 1	4.12	H2	K4	Bat
17. 1	5.12	H2	A5	Rat
18. 1	6.12	H2	B6	Swallow
19. 1	7.12	H2	C7	Pig
20. 1	8.12	H2	D8	Porcupine
21. 1	9.12	H2	E9	Wolf
22. 1	10.12	H2	F10	Dog
23. 1	11.12	H2	G11	Pheasant
24. 1	12.12	H2	H12	Cock
25. 1	13.12	H2	J1	Crow
26. 1	14.12	H2	K2	Monkey
27. 1	15.12	H2	A3	Gibbon
28. 1	16.12	H2	B4	Tapir
29. 1	17.12	H2	C5	Sheep
30. 1	18.12	H2	D6	Deer
31. 1	19.12	H2	E7	Horse
1. 2	20.12	H2	F8	Stag
2. 2	21.12	H2	G9	Serpent
3. 2	22.12	H2	H10	Earthworm
4. 2	23.12	H2	J11	Crocodile
5. 2	24.12	H2	K12	Dragon
6. 2	25.12	H2	A1	Badger
7. 2	26.12	H2	B2	Hare
8. 2	27.12	H2	C3	Fox
9. 2	28.12	H2	D4	Tiger
10. 2	29.12	H2	E5	Leopard

TING CH'OU YEAR

Solar date	Lunar date	Month HS/EB	Day HS/EB	Constellation
11. 2	1. 1	J3	F6	Griffon
12. 2	2. 1	J3	G7	Ox
13. 2	3. 1	J3	H8	Bat
14. 2	4. 1	J3	J9	Rat
15. 2	5. 1	J3	K10	Swallow
16. 2	6. 1	J3	A11	Pig
17. 2	7. 1	J3	B12	Porcupine
18. 2	8. 1	J3	C1	Wolf
19. 2	9. 1	J3	D2	Dog
20. 2	10. 1	J3	E3	Pheasant
21. 2	11. 1	J3	F4	Cock
22. 2	12. 1	J3	G5	Crow
23. 2	13. 1	J3	H6	Monkey
24. 2	14. 1	J3	J7	Gibbon
25. 2	15. 1	J3	K8	Tapir
26. 2	16. 1	J3	A9	Sheep
27. 2	17. 1	J3	B10	Deer
28. 2	18. 1	J3	C11	Horse
1. 3	19. 1	J3	D12	Stag
2. 3	20. 1	J3	E1	Serpent
3. 3	21. 1	J3	F2	Earthworm
4. 3	22. 1	J3	G3	Crocodile
5. 3	23. 1	J3	H4	Dragon
6. 3	24. 1	J3	J5	Badger
7. 3	25. 1	J3	K6	Hare
8. 3	26. 1	J3	A7	Fox
9. 3	27. 1	J3	B8	Tiger
10. 3	28. 1	J3	C9	Leopard
11. 3	29. 1	J3	D10	Griffon
12. 3	30. 1	J3	E11	Ox
13. 3	1. 2	K4	F12	Bat
14. 3	2. 2	K4	G1	Rat
15. 3	3. 2	K4	H2	Swallow
16. 3	4. 2	K4	J3	Pig
17. 3	5. 2	K4	K4	Porcupine
18. 3	6. 2	K4	A5	Wolf
19. 3	7. 2	K4	B6	Dog
20. 3	8. 2	K4	C7	Pheasant

Solar date	Lunar date	Month HS/EB	Day HS/EB	Constellation	Solar date	Lunar date	Month HS/EB	Day HS/EB	Constellation
21. 3	9. 2	K4	D8	Cock	2. 6	24. 4	B6	G9	Leopard
22. 3	10. 2	K4	E9	Crow	3. 6	25. 4	B6	H10	Griffon
23. 3	11. 2	K4	F10	Monkey	4. 6	26. 4	B6	J11	Ox
24. 3	12. 2	K4	G11	Gibbon	5. 6	27. 4	B6	K12	Bat
25. 3	13. 2	K4	H12	Tapir	6. 6	28. 4	B6	A1	Rat
26. 3	14. 2	K4	J1	Sheep	7. 6	29. 4	B6	B2	Swallow
27. 3	15. 2	K4	K2	Deer	8. 6	30. 4	B6	C3	Pig
28. 3	16. 2	K4	A3	Horse	9. 6	1. 5	C7	D4	Porcupine
29. 3	17. 2	K4	B4	Stag	10. 6	2. 5	C7	E5	Wolf
30. 3	18. 2	K4	C5	Serpent	11. 6	3. 5	C7	F6	Dog
31. 3	19. 2	K4	D6	Earthworm	12. 6	4. 5	C7	G7	Pheasant
1. 4	20. 2	K4	E7	Crocodile	13. 6	5. 5	C7	H8	Cock
2. 4	21. 2	K4	F8	Dragon	14. 6	6. 5	C7	J9	Crow
3. 4	22. 2	K4	G9	Badger	15. 6	7. 5	C7	K10	Monkey
4. 4	23. 2	K4	H10	Hare	16. 6	8. 5	C7	A11	Gibbon
5. 4	24. 2	K4	J11	Fox	17. 6	9. 5	C7	B12	Tapir
6. 4	25. 2	K4	K12	Tiger	18. 6	10. 5	C7	C1	Sheep
7. 4	26. 2	K4	A1	Leopard	19. 6	11. 5	C7	D2	Deer
8. 4	27. 2	K4	B2	Griffon	20. 6	12. 5	C7	E3	Horse
9. 4	28. 2	K4	C3	Ox	21. 6	13. 5	C7	F4	Stag
10. 4	29. 2	K4	D4	Bat	22. 6	14. 5	C7	G5	Serpent
11. 4	1. 3	A5	E5	Rat	23. 6	15. 5	C7	H6	Earthworm
12. 4	2. 3	A5	F6	Swallow	24. 6	16. 5	C7	J7	Crocodile
13. 4	3. 3	A5	G7	Pig	25. 6	17. 5	C7	K8	Dragon
14. 4	4. 3	A5	H8	Porcupine	26. 6	18. 5	C7	A9	Badger
15. 4	5. 3	A5	J9	Wolf	27. 6	19. 5	C7	B10	Hare
16. 4	6. 3	A5	K10	Dog	28. 6	20. 5	C7	C11	Fox
17. 4	7. 3	A5	A11	Pheasant	29. 6	21. 5	C7	D12	Tiger
18. 4	8. 3	A5	B12	Cock	30. 6	22. 5	C7	E1	Leopard
19. 4	9. 3	A5	C1	Crow	1. 7	23. 5	C7	F2	Griffon
20. 4	10. 3	A5	D2	Monkey	2. 7	24. 5	C7	G3	Ox
21. 4	11. 3	A5	E3	Gibbon	3. 7	25. 5	C7	H4	Bat
22. 4	12. 3	A5	F4	Tapir	4. 7	26. 5	C7	J5	Rat
23. 4	13. 3	A5	G5	Sheep	5. 7	27. 5	C7	K6	Swallow
24. 4	14. 3	A5	H6	Deer	6. 7	28. 5	C7	A7	Pig
25. 4	15. 3	A5	J7	Horse	7. 7	29. 5	C7	B8	Porcupine
26. 4	16. 3	A5	K8	Stag	8. 7	1. 6	D8	C9	Wolf
27. 4	17. 3	A5	A9	Serpent	9. 7	2. 6	D8	D10	Dog
28. 4	18. 3	A5	B10	Earthworm	10. 7	3. 6	D8	E11	Pheasant
29. 4	19. 3	A5	C11	Crocodile	11. 7	4. 6	D8	F12	Cock
30. 4	20. 3	A5	D12	Dragon	12. 7	5. 6	D8	G1	Crow
1. 5	21. 3	A5	E1	Badger	13. 7	6. 6	D8	H2	Monkey
2. 5	22. 3	A5	F2	Hare	14. 7	7. 6	D8	J3	Gibbon
3. 5	23. 3	A5	G3	Fox	15. 7	8. 6	D8	K4	Tapir
4. 5	24. 3	A5	H4	Tiger	16. 7	9. 6	D8	A5	Sheep
5. 5	25. 3	A5	J5	Leopard	17. 7	10. 6	D8	B6	Deer
6. 5	26. 3	A5	K6	Griffon	18. 7	11. 6	D8	C7	Horse
7. 5	27. 3	A5	A7	Ox	19. 7	12. 6	D8	D8	Stag
8. 5	28. 3	A5	B8	Bat	20. 7	13. 6	D8	E9	Serpent
9. 5	29. 3	A5	C9	Rat	21. 7	14. 6	D8	F10	Earthworm
10. 5	1. 4	B6	D10	Swallow	22. 7	15. 6	D8	G11	Crocodile
11. 5	2. 4	B6	E11	Pig	23. 7	16. 6	D8	H12	Dragon
12. 5	3. 4	B6	F12	Porcupine	24. 7	17. 6	D8	J1	Badger
13. 5	4. 4	B6	G1	Wolf	25. 7	18. 6	D8	K2	Hare
14. 5	5. 4	B6	H2	Dog	26. 7	19. 6	D8	A3	Fox
15. 5	6. 4	B6	J3	Pheasant	27. 7	20. 6	D8	B4	Tiger
16. 5	7. 4	B6	K4	Cock	28. 7	21. 6	D8	C5	Leopard
17. 5	8. 4	B6	A5	Crow	29. 7	22. 6	D8	D6	Griffon
18. 5	9. 4	B6	B6	Monkey	30. 7	23. 6	D8	E7	Ox
19. 5	10. 4	B6	C7	Gibbon	31. 7	24. 6	D8	F8	Bat
20. 5	11. 4	B6	D8	Tapir	1. 8	25. 6	D8	G9	Rat
21. 5	12. 4	B6	E9	Sheep	2. 8	26. 6	D8	H10	Swallow
22. 5	13. 4	B6	F10	Deer	3. 8	27. 6	D8	J11	Pig
23. 5	14. 4	B6	G11	Horse	4. 8	28. 6	D8	K12	Porcupine
24. 5	15. 4	B6	H12	Stag	5. 8	29. 6	D8	A1	Wolf
25. 5	16. 4	B6	J1	Serpent	6. 8	1. 7	E9	B2	Dog
26. 5	17. 4	B6	K2	Earthworm	7. 8	2. 7	E9	C3	Pheasant
27. 5	18. 4	B6	A3	Crocodile	8. 8	3. 7	E9	D4	Cock
28. 5	19. 4	B6	B4	Dragon	9. 8	4. 7	E9	E5	Crow
29. 5	20. 4	B6	C5	Badger	10. 8	5. 7	E9	F6	Monkey
30. 5	21. 4	B6	D6	Hare	11. 8	6. 7	E9	G7	Gibbon
31. 5	22. 4	B6	E7	Fox	12. 8	7. 7	E9	H8	Tapir
1. 6	23. 4	B6	F8	Tiger	13. 8	8. 7	E9	J9	Sheep

Solar date	Lunar date	Month HS/EB	Day HS/EB	Constellation	Solar date	Lunar date	Month HS/EB	Day HS/EB	Constellation
14. 8	9. 7	E9	K10	Deer	26.10	23. 9	G11	C11	Pig
15. 8	10. 7	E9	A11	Horse	27.10	24. 9	G11	D12	Porcupine
16. 8	11. 7	E9	B12	Stag	28.10	25. 9	G11	E1	Wolf
17. 8	12. 7	E9	C1	Serpent	29.10	26. 9	G11	F2	Dog
18. 8	13. 7	E9	D2	Earthworm	30.10	27. 9	G11	G3	Pheasant
19. 8	14. 7	E9	E3	Crocodile	31.10	28. 9	G11	H4	Cock
20. 8	15. 7	E9	F4	Dragon	1.11	29. 9	G11	J5	Crow
21. 8	16. 7	E9	G5	Badger	2.11	30. 9	G11	K6	Monkey
22. 8	17. 7	E9	H6	Hare	3.11	1.10	H12	A7	Gibbon
23. 8	18. 7	E9	J7	Fox	4.11	2.10	H12	B8	Tapir
24. 8	19. 7	E9	K8	Tiger	5.11	3.10	H12	C9	Sheep
25. 8	20. 7	E9	A9	Leopard	6.11	4.10	H12	D10	Deer
26. 8	21. 7	E9	B10	Griffon	7.11	5.10	H12	E11	Horse
27. 8	22. 7	E9	C11	Ox	8.11	6.10	H12	F12	Stag
28. 8	23. 7	E9	D12	Bat	9.11	7.10	H12	G1	Serpent
29. 8	24. 7	E9	E1	Rat	10.11	8.10	H12	H2	Earthworm
30. 8	25. 7	E9	F2	Swallow	11.11	9.10	H12	J3	Crocodile
31. 8	26. 7	E9	G3	Pig	12.11	10.10	H12	K4	Dragon
1. 9	27. 7	E9	H4	Porcupine	13.11	11.10	H12	A5	Badger
2. 9	28. 7	E9	J5	Wolf	14.11	12.10	H12	B6	Hare
3. 9	29. 7	E9	K6	Dog	15.11	13.10	H12	C7	Fox
4. 9	30. 7	E9	A7	Pheasant	16.11	14.10	H12	D8	Tiger
5. 9	1. 8	F10	B8	Cock	17.11	15.10	H12	E9	Leopard
6. 9	2. 8	F10	C9	Crow	18.11	16.10	H12	F10	Griffon
7. 9	3. 8	F10	D10	Monkey	19.11	17.10	H12	G11	Ox
8. 9	4. 8	F10	E11	Gibbon	20.11	18.10	H12	H12	Bat
9. 9	5. 8	F10	F12	Tapir	21.11	19.10	H12	J1	Rat
10. 9	6. 8	F10	G1	Sheep	22.11	20.10	H12	K2	Swallow
11. 9	7. 8	F10	H2	Deer	23.11	21.10	H12	A3	Pig
12. 9	8. 8	F10	J3	Horse	24.11	22.10	H12	B4	Porcupine
13. 9	9. 8	F10	K4	Stag	25.11	23.10	H12	C5	Wolf
14. 9	10. 8	F10	A5	Serpent	26.11	24.10	H12	D6	Dog
15. 9	11. 8	F10	B6	Earthworm	27.11	25.10	H12	E7	Pheasant
16. 9	12. 8	F10	C7	Crocodile	28.11	26.10	H12	F8	Cock
17. 9	13. 8	F10	D8	Dragon	29.11	27.10	H12	G9	Crow
18. 9	14. 8	F10	E9	Badger	30.11	28.10	H12	H10	Monkey
19. 9	15. 8	F10	F10	Hare	1.12	29.10	H12	J11	Gibbon
20. 9	16. 8	F10	G11	Fox	2.12	30.10	H12	K12	Tapir
21. 9	17. 8	F10	H12	Tiger	3.12	1.11	J1	A1	Sheep
22. 9	18. 8	F10	J1	Leopard	4.12	2.11	J1	B2	Deer
23. 9	19. 8	F10	K2	Griffon	5.12	3.11	J1	C3	Horse
24. 9	20. 8	F10	A3	Ox	6.12	4.11	J1	D4	Stag
25. 9	21. 8	F10	B4	Bat	7.12	5.11	J1	E5	Serpent
26. 9	22. 8	F10	C5	Rat	8.12	6.11	J1	F6	Earthworm
27. 9	23. 8	F10	D6	Swallow	9.12	7.11	J1	G7	Crocodile
28. 9	24. 8	F10	E7	Pig	10.12	8.11	J1	H8	Dragon
29. 9	25. 8	F10	F8	Porcupine	11.12	9.11	J1	J9	Badger
30. 9	26. 8	F10	G9	Wolf	12.12	10.11	J1	K10	Hare
1.10	27. 8	F10	H10	Dog	13.12	11.11	J1	A11	Fox
2.10	28. 8	F10	J11	Pheasant	14.12	12.11	J1	B12	Tiger
3.10	29. 8	F10	K12	Cock	15.12	13.11	J1	C1	Leopard
4.10	1. 9	G11	A1	Crow	16.12	14.11	J1	D2	Griffon
5.10	2. 9	G11	B2	Monkey	17.12	15.11	J1	E3	Ox
6.10	3. 9	G11	C3	Gibbon	18.12	16.11	J1	F4	Bat
7.10	4. 9	G11	D4	Tapir	19.12	17.11	J1	G5	Rat
8.10	5. 9	G11	E5	Sheep	20.12	18.11	J1	H6	Swallow
9.10	6. 9	G11	F6	Deer	21.12	19.11	J1	J7	Pig
10.10	7. 9	G11	G7	Horse	22.12	20.11	J1	K8	Porcupine
11.10	8. 9	G11	H8	Stag	23.12	21.11	J1	A9	Wolf
12.10	9. 9	G11	J9	Serpent	24.12	22.11	J1	B10	Dog
13.10	10. 9	G11	K10	Earthworm	25.12	23.11	J1	C11	Pheasant
14.10	11. 9	G11	A11	Crocodile	26.12	24.11	J1	D12	Cock
15.10	12. 9	G11	B12	Dragon	27.12	25.11	J1	E1	Crow
16.10	13. 9	G11	C1	Badger	28.12	26.11	J1	F2	Monkey
17.10	14. 9	G11	D2	Hare	29.12	27.11	J1	G3	Gibbon
18.10	15. 9	G11	E3	Fox	30.12	28.11	J1	H4	Tapir
19.10	16. 9	G11	F4	Tiger	31.12	29.11	J1	J5	Sheep
20.10	17. 9	G11	G5	Leopard					
21.10	18. 9	G11	H6	Griffon	**1938**				
22.10	19. 9	G11	J7	Ox	1. 1	30.11	J1	K6	Deer
23.10	20. 9	G11	K8	Bat	2. 1	1.12	K2	A7	Horse
24.10	21. 9	G11	A9	Rat	3. 1	2.12	K2	B8	Stag
25.10	22. 9	G11	B10	Swallow	4. 1	3.12	K2	C9	Serpent

Solar date	Lunar date	Month HS/EB	Day HS/EB	Constellation	Solar date	Lunar date	Month HS/EB	Day HS/EB	Constellation
5. 1	4.12	K2	D10	Earthworm	18. 1	17.12	K2	G11	Pig
6. 1	5.12	K2	E11	Crocodile	19. 1	18.12	K2	H12	Porcupine
7. 1	6.12	K2	F12	Dragon	20. 1	19.12	K2	J1	Wolf
8. 1	7.12	K2	G1	Badger	21. 1	20.12	K2	K2	Dog
9. 1	8.12	K2	H2	Hare	22. 1	21.12	K2	A3	Pheasant
10. 1	9.12	K2	J3	Fox	23. 1	22.12	K2	B4	Cock
11. 1	10.12	K2	K4	Tiger	24. 1	23.12	K2	C5	Crow
12. 1	11.12	K2	A5	Leopard	25. 1	24.12	K2	D6	Monkey
13. 1	12.12	K2	B6	Griffon	26. 1	25.12	K2	E7	Gibbon
14. 1	13.12	K2	C7	Ox	27. 1	26.12	K2	F8	Tapir
15. 1	14.12	K2	D8	Bat	28. 1	27.12	K2	G9	Sheep
16. 1	15.12	K2	E9	Rat	29. 1	28.12	K2	H10	Deer
17. 1	16.12	K2	F10	Swallow	30. 1	29.12	K2	J11	Horse

MOU YIN YEAR

Solar date	Lunar date	Month HS/EB	Day HS/EB	Constellation	Solar date	Lunar date	Month HS/EB	Day HS/EB	Constellation
31. 1	1. 1	A3	K12	Stag	26. 3	25. 2	B4	D6	Deer
1. 2	2. 1	A3	A1	Serpent	27. 3	26. 2	B4	E7	Horse
2. 2	3. 1	A3	B2	Earthworm	28. 3	27. 2	B4	F8	Stag
3. 2	4. 1	A3	C3	Crocodile	29. 3	28. 2	B4	G9	Serpent
4. 2	5. 1	A3	D4	Dragon	30. 3	29. 2	B4	H10	Earthworm
5. 2	6. 1	A3	E5	Badger	31. 3	30. 2	B4	J11	Crocodile
6. 2	7. 1	A3	F6	Hare	1. 4	1. 3	C5	K12	Dragon
7. 2	8. 1	A3	G7	Fox	2. 4	2. 3	C5	A1	Badger
8. 2	9. 1	A3	H8	Tiger	3. 4	3. 3	C5	B2	Hare
9. 2	10. 1	A3	J9	Leopard	4. 4	4. 3	C5	C3	Fox
10. 2	11. 1	A3	K10	Griffon	5. 4	5. 3	C5	D4	Tiger
11. 2	12. 1	A3	A11	Ox	6. 4	6. 3	C5	E5	Leopard
12. 2	13. 1	A3	B12	Bat	7. 4	7. 3	C5	F6	Griffon
13. 2	14. 1	A3	C1	Rat	8. 4	8. 3	C5	G7	Ox
14. 2	15. 1	A3	D2	Swallow	9. 4	9. 3	C5	H8	Bat
15. 2	16. 1	A3	E3	Pig	10. 4	10. 3	C5	J9	Rat
16. 2	17. 1	A3	F4	Porcupine	11. 4	11. 3	C5	K10	Swallow
17. 2	18. 1	A3	G5	Wolf	12. 4	12. 3	C5	A11	Pig
18. 2	19. 1	A3	H6	Dog	13. 4	13. 3	C5	B12	Porcupine
19. 2	20. 1	A3	J7	Pheasant	14. 4	14. 3	C5	C1	Wolf
20. 2	21. 1	A3	K8	Cock	15. 4	15. 3	C5	D2	Dog
21. 2	22. 1	A3	A9	Crow	16. 4	16. 3	C5	E3	Pheasant
22. 2	23. 1	A3	B10	Monkey	17. 4	17. 3	C5	F4	Cock
23. 2	24. 1	A3	C11	Gibbon	18. 4	18. 3	C5	G5	Crow
24. 2	25. 1	A3	D12	Tapir	19. 4	19. 3	C5	H6	Monkey
25. 2	26. 1	A3	E1	Sheep	20. 4	20. 3	C5	J7	Gibbon
26. 2	27. 1	A3	F2	Deer	21. 4	21. 3	C5	K8	Tapir
27. 2	28. 1	A3	G3	Horse	22. 4	22. 3	C5	A9	Sheep
28. 2	29. 1	A3	H4	Stag	23. 4	23. 3	C5	B10	Deer
1. 3	30. 1	A3	J5	Serpent	24. 4	24. 3	C5	C11	Horse
2. 3	1. 2	B4	K6	Earthworm	25. 4	25. 3	C5	D12	Stag
3. 3	2. 2	B4	A7	Crocodile	26. 4	26. 3	C5	E1	Serpent
4. 3	3. 2	B4	B8	Dragon	27. 4	27. 3	C5	F2	Earthworm
5. 3	4. 2	B4	C9	Badger	28. 4	28. 3	C5	G3	Crocodile
6. 3	5. 2	B4	D10	Hare	29. 4	29. 3	C5	H4	Dragon
7. 3	6. 2	B4	E11	Fox	30. 4	1. 4	D6	J5	Badger
8. 3	7. 2	B4	F12	Tiger	1. 5	2. 4	D6	K6	Hare
9. 3	8. 2	B4	G1	Leopard	2. 5	3. 4	D6	A7	Fox
10. 3	9. 2	B4	H2	Griffon	3. 5	4. 4	D6	B8	Tiger
11. 3	10. 2	B4	J3	Ox	4. 5	5. 4	D6	C9	Leopard
12. 3	11. 2	B4	K4	Bat	5. 5	6. 4	D6	D10	Griffon
13. 3	12. 2	B4	A5	Rat	6. 5	7. 4	D6	E11	Ox
14. 3	13. 2	B4	B6	Swallow	7. 5	8. 4	D6	F12	Bat
15. 3	14. 2	B4	C7	Pig	8. 5	9. 4	D6	G1	Rat
16. 3	15. 2	B4	D8	Porcupine	9. 5	10. 4	D6	H2	Swallow
17. 3	16. 2	B4	E9	Wolf	10. 5	11. 4	D6	J3	Pig
18. 3	17. 2	B4	F10	Dog	11. 5	12. 4	D6	K4	Porcupine
19. 3	18. 2	B4	G11	Pheasant	12. 5	13. 4	D6	A5	Wolf
20. 3	19. 2	B4	H12	Cock	13. 5	14. 4	D6	B6	Dog
21. 3	20. 2	B4	J1	Crow	14. 5	15. 4	D6	C7	Pheasant
22. 3	21. 2	B4	K2	Monkey	15. 5	16. 4	D6	D8	Cock
23. 3	22. 2	B4	A3	Gibbon	16. 5	17. 4	D6	E9	Crow
24. 3	23. 2	B4	B4	Tapir	17. 5	18. 4	D6	F10	Monkey
25. 3	24. 2	B4	C5	Sheep	18. 5	19. 4	D6	G11	Gibbon

Solar date	Lunar date	Month HS/EB	Day HS/EB	Constellation	Solar date	Lunar date	Month HS/EB	Day HS/EB	Constellation
19. 5	20. 4	D6	H12	Tapir	31. 7	5. 7	G9	A1	Rat
20. 5	21. 4	D6	J1	Sheep	1. 8	6. 7	G9	B2	Swallow
21. 5	22. 4	D6	K2	Deer	2. 8	7. 7	G9	C3	Pig
22. 5	23. 4	D6	A3	Horse	3. 8	8. 7	G9	D4	Porcupine
23. 5	24. 4	D6	B4	Stag	4. 8	9. 7	G9	E5	Wolf
24. 5	25. 4	D6	C5	Serpent	5. 8	10. 7	G9	F6	Dog
25. 5	26. 4	D6	D6	Earthworm	6. 8	11. 7	G9	G7	Pheasant
26. 5	27. 4	D6	E7	Crocodile	7. 8	12. 7	G9	H8	Cock
27. 5	28. 4	D6	F8	Dragon	8. 8	13. 7	G9	J9	Crow
28. 5	29. 4	D6	G9	Badger	9. 8	14. 7	G9	K10	Monkey
29. 5	1. 5	E7	H10	Hare	10. 8	15. 7	G9	A11	Gibbon
30. 5	2. 5	E7	J11	Fox	11. 8	16. 7	G9	B12	Tapir
31. 5	3. 5	E7	K12	Tiger	12. 8	17. 7	G9	C1	Sheep
1. 6	4. 5	E7	A1	Leopard	13. 8	18. 7	G9	D2	Deer
2. 6	5. 5	E7	B2	Griffon	14. 8	19. 7	G9	E3	Horse
3. 6	6. 5	E7	C3	Ox	15. 8	20. 7	G9	F4	Stag
4. 6	7. 5	E7	D4	Bat	16. 8	21. 7	G9	G5	Serpent
5. 6	8. 5	E7	E5	Rat	17. 8	22. 7	G9	H6	Earthworm
6. 6	9. 5	E7	F6	Swallow	18. 8	23. 7	G9	J7	Crocodile
7. 6	10. 5	E7	G7	Pig	19. 8	24. 7	G9	K8	Dragon
8. 6	11. 5	E7	H8	Porcupine	20. 8	25. 7	G9	A9	Badger
9. 6	12. 5	E7	J9	Wolf	21. 8	26. 7	G9	B10	Hare
10. 6	13. 5	E7	K10	Dog	22. 8	27. 7	G9	C11	Fox
11. 6	14. 5	E7	A11	Pheasant	23. 8	28. 7	G9	D12	Tiger
12. 6	15. 5	E7	B12	Cock	24. 8	29. 7	G9	E1	Leopard
13. 6	16. 5	E7	C1	Crow	25. 8	*1. 7*	*G9*	F2	Griffon
14. 6	17. 5	E7	D2	Monkey	26. 8	*2. 7*	*G9*	G3	Ox
15. 6	18. 5	E7	E3	Gibbon	27. 8	*3. 7*	*G9*	H4	Bat
16. 6	19. 5	E7	F4	Tapir	28. 8	*4. 7*	*G9*	J5	Rat
17. 6	20. 5	E7	G5	Sheep	29. 8	*5. 7*	*G9*	K6	Swallow
18. 6	21. 5	E7	H6	Deer	30. 8	*6. 7*	*G9*	A7	Pig
19. 6	22. 5	E7	J7	Horse	31. 8	*7. 7*	*G9*	B8	Porcupine
20. 6	23. 5	E7	K8	Stag	1. 9	*8. 7*	*G9*	C9	Wolf
21. 6	24. 5	E7	A9	Serpent	2. 9	*9. 7*	*G9*	D10	Dog
22. 6	25. 5	E7	B10	Earthworm	3. 9	*10. 7*	*G9*	E11	Pheasant
23. 6	26. 5	E7	C11	Crocodile	4. 9	*11. 7*	*G9*	F12	Cock
24. 6	27. 5	E7	D12	Dragon	5. 9	*12. 7*	*G9*	G1	Crow
25. 6	28. 5	E7	E1	Badger	6. 9	*13. 7*	*G9*	H2	Monkey
26. 6	29. 5	E7	F2	Hare	7. 9	*14. 7*	*G9*	J3	Gibbon
27. 6	30. 5	E7	G3	Fox	8. 9	*15. 7*	*G9*	K4	Tapir
28. 6	1. 6	F8	H4	Tiger	9. 9	*16. 7*	*G9*	A5	Sheep
29. 6	2. 6	F8	J5	Leopard	10. 9	*17. 7*	*G9*	B6	Deer
30. 6	3. 6	F8	K6	Griffon	11. 9	*18. 7*	*G9*	C7	Horse
1. 7	4. 6	F8	A7	Ox	12. 9	*19. 7*	*G9*	D8	Stag
2. 7	5. 6	F8	B8	Bat	13. 9	*20. 7*	*G9*	E9	Serpent
3. 7	6. 6	F8	C9	Rat	14. 9	*21. 7*	*G9*	F10	Earthworm
4. 7	7. 6	F8	D10	Swallow	15. 9	*22. 7*	*G9*	G11	Crocodile
5. 7	8. 6	F8	E11	Pig	16. 9	*23. 7*	*G9*	H12	Dragon
6. 7	9. 6	F8	F12	Porcupine	17. 9	*24. 7*	*G9*	J1	Badger
7. 7	10. 6	F8	G1	Wolf	18. 9	*25. 7*	*G9*	K2	Hare
8. 7	11. 6	F8	H2	Dog	19. 9	*26. 7*	*G9*	A3	Fox
9. 7	12. 6	F8	J3	Pheasant	20. 9	*27. 7*	*G9*	B4	Tiger
10. 7	13. 6	F8	K4	Cock	21. 9	*28. 7*	*G9*	C5	Leopard
11. 7	14. 6	F8	A5	Crow	22. 9	*29. 7*	*G9*	D6	Griffon
12. 7	15. 6	F8	B6	Monkey	23. 9	*30. 7*	*G9*	E7	Ox
13. 7	16. 6	F8	C7	Gibbon	24. 9	1. 8	H10	F8	Bat
14. 7	17. 6	F8	D8	Tapir	25. 9	2. 8	H10	G9	Rat
15. 7	18. 6	F8	E9	Sheep	26. 9	3. 8	H10	H10	Swallow
16. 7	19. 6	F8	F10	Deer	27. 9	4. 8	H10	J11	Pig
17. 7	20. 6	F8	G11	Horse	28. 9	5. 8	H10	K12	Porcupine
18. 7	21. 6	F8	H12	Stag	29. 9	6. 8	H10	A1	Wolf
19. 7	22. 6	F8	J1	Serpent	30. 9	7. 8	H10	B2	Dog
20. 7	23. 6	F8	K2	Earthworm	1.10	8. 8	H10	C3	Pheasant
21. 7	24. 6	F8	A3	Crocodile	2.10	9. 8	H10	D4	Cock
22. 7	25. 6	F8	B4	Dragon	3.10	10. 8	H10	E5	Crow
23. 7	26. 6	F8	C5	Badger	4.10	11. 8	H10	F6	Monkey
24. 7	27. 6	F8	D6	Hare	5.10	12. 8	H10	G7	Gibbon
25. 7	28. 6	F8	E7	Fox	6.10	13. 8	H10	H8	Tapir
26. 7	29. 6	F8	F8	Tiger	7.10	14. 8	H10	J9	Sheep
27. 7	1. 7	G9	G9	Leopard	8.10	15. 8	H10	K10	Deer
28. 7	2. 7	G9	H10	Griffon	9.10	16. 8	H10	A11	Horse
29. 7	3. 7	G9	J11	Ox	10.10	17. 8	H10	B12	Stag
30. 7	4. 7	G9	K12	Bat	11.10	18. 8	H10	C1	Serpent

Solar date	Lunar date	Month HS/EB	Day HS/EB	Constellation	Solar date	Lunar date	Month HS/EB	Day HS/EB	Constellation
12.10	19. 8	H10	D2	Earthworm	17.12	26.10	K12	K8	Bat
13.10	20. 8	H10	E3	Crocodile	18.12	27.10	K12	A9	Rat
14.10	21. 8	H10	F4	Dragon	19.12	28.10	K12	B10	Swallow
15.10	22. 8	H10	G5	Badger	20.12	29.10	K12	C11	Pig
16.10	23. 8	H10	H6	Hare	21.12	30.10	K12	D12	Porcupine
17.10	24. 8	H10	J7	Fox	22.12	1.11	A1	E1	Wolf
18.10	25. 8	H10	K8	Tiger	23.12	2.11	A1	F2	Dog
19.10	26. 8	H10	A9	Leopard	24.12	3.11	A1	G3	Pheasant
20.10	27. 8	H10	B10	Griffon	25.12	4.11	A1	H4	Cock
21.10	28. 8	H10	C11	Ox	26.12	5.11	A1	J5	Crow
22.10	29. 8	H10	D12	Bat	27.12	6.11	A1	K6	Monkey
23.10	1. 9	J11	E1	Rat	28.12	7.11	A1	A7	Gibbon
24.10	2. 9	J11	F2	Swallow	29.12	8.11	A1	B8	Tapir
25.10	3. 9	J11	G3	Pig	30.12	9.11	A1	C9	Sheep
26.10	4. 9	J11	H4	Porcupine	31.12	10.11	A1	D10	Deer
27.10	5. 9	J11	J5	Wolf	**1939**				
28.10	6. 9	J11	K6	Dog	1. 1	11.11	A1	E11	Horse
29.10	7. 9	J11	A7	Pheasant	2. 1	12.11	A1	F12	Stag
30.10	8. 9	J11	B8	Cock	3. 1	13.11	A1	G1	Serpent
31.10	9. 9	J11	C9	Crow	4. 1	14.11	A1	H2	Earthworm
1.11	10. 9	J11	D10	Monkey	5. 1	15.11	A1	J3	Crocodile
2.11	11. 9	J11	E11	Gibbon	6. 1	16.11	A1	K4	Dragon
3.11	12. 9	J11	F12	Tapir	7. 1	17.11	A1	A5	Badger
4.11	13. 9	J11	G1	Sheep	8. 1	18.11	A1	B6	Hare
5.11	14. 9	J11	H2	Deer	9. 1	19.11	A1	C7	Fox
6.11	15. 9	J11	J3	Horse	10. 1	20.11	A1	D8	Tiger
7.11	16. 9	J11	K4	Stag	11. 1	21.11	A1	E9	Leopard
8.11	17. 9	J11	A5	Serpent	12. 1	22.11	A1	F10	Griffon
9.11	18. 9	J11	B6	Earthworm	13. 1	23.11	A1	G11	Ox
10.11	19. 9	J11	C7	Crocodile	14. 1	24.11	A1	H12	Bat
11.11	20. 9	J11	D8	Dragon	15. 1	25.11	A1	J1	Rat
12.11	21. 9	J11	E9	Badger	16. 1	26.11	A1	K2	Swallow
13.11	22. 9	J11	F10	Hare	17. 1	27.11	A1	A3	Pig
14.11	23. 9	J11	G11	Fox	18. 1	28.11	A1	B4	Porcupine
15.11	24. 9	J11	H12	Tiger	19. 1	29.11	A1	C5	Wolf
16.11	25. 9	J11	J1	Leopard	20. 1	1.12	B2	D6	Dog
17.11	26. 9	J11	K2	Griffon	21. 1	2.12	B2	E7	Pheasant
18.11	27. 9	J11	A3	Ox	22. 1	3.12	B2	F8	Cock
19.11	28. 9	J11	B4	Bat	23. 1	4.12	B2	G9	Crow
20.11	29. 9	J11	C5	Rat	24. 1	5.12	B2	H10	Monkey
21.11	30. 9	J11	D6	Swallow	25. 1	6.12	B2	J11	Gibbon
22.11	1.10	K12	E7	Pig	26. 1	7.12	B2	K12	Tapir
23.11	2.10	K12	F8	Porcupine	27. 1	8.12	B2	A1	Sheep
24.11	3.10	K12	G9	Wolf	28. 1	9.12	B2	B2	Deer
25.11	4.10	K12	H10	Dog	29. 1	10.12	B2	C3	Horse
26.11	5.10	K12	J11	Pheasant	30. 1	11.12	B2	D4	Stag
27.11	6.10	K12	K12	Cock	31. 1	12.12	B2	E5	Serpent
28.11	7.10	K12	A1	Crow	1. 2	13.12	B2	F6	Earthworm
29.11	8.10	K12	B2	Monkey	2. 2	14.12	B2	G7	Crocodile
30.11	9.10	K12	C3	Gibbon	3. 2	15.12	B2	H8	Dragon
1.12	10.10	K12	D4	Tapir	4. 2	16.12	B2	J9	Badger
2.12	11.10	K12	E5	Sheep	5. 2	17.12	B2	K10	Hare
3.12	12.10	K12	F6	Deer	6. 2	18.12	B2	A11	Fox
4.12	13.10	K12	G7	Horse	7. 2	19.12	B2	B12	Tiger
5.12	14.10	K12	H8	Stag	8. 2	20.12	B2	C1	Leopard
6.12	15.10	K12	J9	Serpent	9. 2	21.12	B2	D2	Griffon
7.12	16.10	K12	K10	Earthworm	10. 2	22.12	B2	E3	Ox
8.12	17.10	K12	A11	Crocodile	11. 2	23.12	B2	F4	Bat
9.12	18.10	K12	B12	Dragon	12. 2	24.12	B2	G5	Rat
10.12	19.10	K12	C1	Badger	13. 2	25.12	B2	H6	Swallow
11.12	20.10	K12	D2	Hare	14. 2	26.12	B2	J7	Pig
12.12	21.10	K12	E3	Fox	15. 2	27.12	B2	K8	Porcupine
13.12	22.10	K12	F4	Tiger	16. 2	28.12	B2	A9	Wolf
14.12	23.10	K12	G5	Leopard	17. 2	29.12	B2	B10	Dog
15.12	24.10	K12	H6	Griffon	18. 2	30.12	B2	C11	Pheasant
16.12	25.10	K12	J7	Ox					

CHI MAO YEAR

Solar date	Lunar date	Month HS/EB	Day HS/EB	Constellation	Solar date	Lunar date	Month HS/EB	Day HS/EB	Constellation
19. 2	1. 1	C3	D12	Cock	1. 5	12. 3	E5	E11	Fox
20. 2	2. 1	C3	E1	Crow	2. 5	13. 3	E5	F12	Tiger
21. 2	3. 1	C3	F2	Monkey	3. 5	14. 3	E5	G1	Leopard
22. 2	4. 1	C3	G3	Gibbon	4. 5	15. 3	E5	H2	Griffon
23. 2	5. 1	C3	H4	Tapir	5. 5	16. 3	E5	J3	Ox
24. 2	6. 1	C3	J5	Sheep	6. 5	17. 3	E5	K4	Bat
25. 2	7. 1	C3	K6	Deer	7. 5	18. 3	E5	A5	Rat
26. 2	8. 1	C3	A7	Horse	8. 5	19. 3	E5	B6	Swallow
27. 2	9. 1	C3	B8	Stag	9. 5	20. 3	E5	C7	Pig
28. 2	10. 1	C3	C9	Serpent	10. 5	21. 3	E5	D8	Porcupine
1. 3	11. 1	C3	D10	Earthworm	11. 5	22. 3	E5	E9	Wolf
2. 3	12. 1	C3	E11	Crocodile	12. 5	23. 3	E5	F10	Dog
3. 3	13. 1	C3	F12	Dragon	13. 5	24. 3	E5	G11	Pheasant
4. 3	14. 1	C3	G1	Badger	14. 5	25. 3	E5	H12	Cock
5. 3	15. 1	C3	H2	Hare	15. 5	26. 3	E5	J1	Crow
6. 3	16. 1	C3	J3	Fox	16. 5	27. 3	E5	K2	Monkey
7. 3	17. 1	C3	K4	Tiger	17. 5	28. 3	E5	A3	Gibbon
8. 3	18. 1	C3	A5	Leopard	18. 5	29. 3	E5	B4	Tapir
9. 3	19. 1	C3	B6	Griffon	19. 5	1. 4	F6	C5	Sheep
10. 3	20. 1	C3	C7	Ox	20. 5	2. 4	F6	D6	Deer
11. 3	21. 1	C3	D8	Bat	21. 5	3. 4	F6	E7	Horse
12. 3	22. 1	C3	E9	Rat	22. 5	4. 4	F6	F8	Stag
13. 3	23. 1	C3	F10	Swallow	23. 5	5. 4	F6	G9	Serpent
14. 3	24. 1	C3	G11	Pig	24. 5	6. 4	F6	H10	Earthworm
15. 3	25. 1	C3	H12	Porcupine	25. 5	7. 4	F6	J11	Crocodile
16. 3	26. 1	C3	J1	Wolf	26. 5	8. 4	F6	K12	Dragon
17. 3	27. 1	C3	K2	Dog	27. 5	9. 4	F6	A1	Badger
18. 3	28. 1	C3	A3	Pheasant	28. 5	10. 4	F6	B2	Hare
19. 3	29. 1	C3	B4	Cock	29. 5	11. 4	F6	C3	Fox
20. 3	30. 1	C3	C5	Crow	30. 5	12. 4	F6	D4	Tiger
21. 3	1. 2	D4	D6	Monkey	31. 5	13. 4	F6	E5	Leopard
22. 3	2. 2	D4	E7	Gibbon	1. 6	14. 4	F6	F6	Griffon
23. 3	3. 2	D4	F8	Tapir	2. 6	15. 4	F6	G7	Ox
24. 3	4. 2	D4	G9	Sheep	3. 6	16. 4	F6	H8	Bat
25. 3	5. 2	D4	H10	Deer	4. 6	17. 4	F6	J9	Rat
26. 3	6. 2	D4	J11	Horse	5. 6	18. 4	F6	K10	Swallow
27. 3	7. 2	D4	K12	Stag	6. 6	19. 4	F6	A11	Pig
28. 3	8. 2	D4	A1	Serpent	7. 6	20. 4	F6	B12	Porcupine
29. 3	9. 2	D4	B2	Earthworm	8. 6	21. 4	F6	C1	Wolf
30. 3	10. 2	D4	C3	Crocodile	9. 6	22. 4	F6	D2	Dog
31. 3	11. 2	D4	D4	Dragon	10. 6	23. 4	F6	E3	Pheasant
1. 4	12. 2	D4	E5	Badger	11. 6	24. 4	F6	F4	Cock
2. 4	13. 2	D4	F6	Hare	12. 6	25. 4	F6	G5	Crow
3. 4	14. 2	D4	G7	Fox	13. 6	26. 4	F6	H6	Monkey
4. 4	15. 2	D4	H8	Tiger	14. 6	27. 4	F6	J7	Gibbon
5. 4	16. 2	D4	J9	Leopard	15. 6	28. 4	F6	K8	Tapir
6. 4	17. 2	D4	K10	Griffon	16. 6	29. 4	F6	A9	Sheep
7. 4	18. 2	D4	A11	Ox	17. 6	1. 5	G7	B10	Deer
8. 4	19. 2	D4	B12	Bat	18. 6	2. 5	G7	C11	Horse
9. 4	20. 2	D4	C1	Rat	19. 6	3. 5	G7	D12	Stag
10. 4	21. 2	D4	D2	Swallow	20. 6	4. 5	G7	E1	Serpent
11. 4	22. 2	D4	E3	Pig	21. 6	5. 5	G7	F2	Earthworm
12. 4	23. 2	D4	F4	Porcupine	22. 6	6. 5	G7	G3	Crocodile
13. 4	24. 2	D4	G5	Wolf	23. 6	7. 5	G7	H4	Dragon
14. 4	25. 2	D4	H6	Dog	24. 6	8. 5	G7	J5	Badger
15. 4	26. 2	D4	J7	Pheasant	25. 6	9. 5	G7	K6	Hare
16. 4	27. 2	D4	K8	Cock	26. 6	10. 5	G7	A7	Fox
17. 4	28. 2	D4	A9	Crow	27. 6	11. 5	G7	B8	Tiger
18. 4	29. 2	D4	B10	Monkey	28. 6	12. 5	G7	C9	Leopard
19. 4	30. 2	D4	C11	Gibbon	29. 6	13. 5	G7	D10	Griffon
20. 4	1. 3	E5	D12	Tapir	30. 6	14. 5	G7	E11	Ox
21. 4	2. 3	E5	E1	Sheep	1. 7	15. 5	G7	F12	Bat
22. 4	3. 3	E5	F2	Deer	2. 7	16. 5	G7	G1	Rat
23. 4	4. 3	E5	G3	Horse	3. 7	17. 5	G7	H2	Swallow
24. 4	5. 3	E5	H4	Stag	4. 7	18. 5	G7	J3	Pig
25. 4	6. 3	E5	J5	Serpent	5. 7	19. 5	G7	K4	Porcupine
26. 4	7. 3	E5	K6	Earthworm	6. 7	20. 5	G7	A5	Wolf
27. 4	8. 3	E5	A7	Crocodile	7. 7	21. 5	G7	B6	Dog
28. 4	9. 3	E5	B8	Dragon	8. 7	22. 5	G7	C7	Pheasant
29. 4	10. 3	E5	C9	Badger	9. 7	23. 5	G7	D8	Cock
30. 4	11. 3	E5	D10	Hare	10. 7	24. 5	G7	E9	Crow

Solar date	Lunar date	Month HS/EB	Day HS/EB	Constellation	Solar date	Lunar date	Month HS/EB	Day HS/EB	Constellation
11. 7	25. 5	G7	F10	Monkey	22. 9	10. 8	K10	J11	Ox
12. 7	26. 5	G7	G11	Gibbon	23. 9	11. 8	K10	K12	Bat
13. 7	27. 5	G7	H12	Tapir	24. 9	12. 8	K10	A1	Rat
14. 7	28. 5	G7	J1	Sheep	25. 9	13. 8	K10	B2	Swallow
15. 7	29. 5	G7	K2	Deer	26. 9	14. 8	K10	C3	Pig
16. 7	30. 5	G7	A3	Horse	27. 9	15. 8	K10	D4	Porcupine
17. 7	1. 6	H8	B4	Stag	28. 9	16. 8	K10	E5	Wolf
18. 7	2. 6	H8	C5	Serpent	29. 9	17. 8	K10	F6	Dog
19. 7	3. 6	H8	D6	Earthworm	30. 9	18. 8	K10	G7	Pheasant
20. 7	4. 6	H8	E7	Crocodile	1.10	19. 8	K10	H8	Cock
21. 7	5. 6	H8	F8	Dragon	2.10	20. 8	K10	J9	Crow
22. 7	6. 6	H8	G9	Badger	3.10	21. 8	K10	K10	Monkey
23. 7	7. 6	H8	H10	Hare	4.10	22. 8	K10	A11	Gibbon
24. 7	8. 6	H8	J11	Fox	5.10	23. 8	K10	B12	Tapir
25. 7	9. 6	H8	K12	Tiger	6.10	24. 8	K10	C1	Sheep
26. 7	10. 6	H8	A1	Leopard	7.10	25. 8	K10	D2	Deer
27. 7	11. 6	H8	B2	Griffon	8.10	26. 8	K10	E3	Horse
28. 7	12. 6	H8	C3	Ox	9.10	27. 8	K10	F4	Stag
29. 7	13. 6	H8	D4	Bat	10.10	28. 8	K10	G5	Serpent
30. 7	14. 6	H8	E5	Rat	11.10	29. 8	K10	H6	Earthworm
31. 7	15. 6	H8	F6	Swallow	12.10	30. 8	K10	J7	Crocodile
1. 8	16. 6	H8	G7	Pig	13.10	1. 9	A11	K8	Dragon
2. 8	17. 6	H8	H8	Porcupine	14.10	2. 9	A11	A9	Badger
3. 8	18. 6	H8	J9	Wolf	15.10	3. 9	A11	B10	Hare
4. 8	19. 6	H8	K10	Dog	16.10	4. 9	A11	C11	Fox
5. 8	20. 6	H8	A11	Pheasant	17.10	5. 9	A11	D12	Tiger
6. 8	21. 6	H8	B12	Cock	18.10	6. 9	A11	E1	Leopard
7. 8	22. 6	H8	C1	Crow	19.10	7. 9	A11	F2	Griffon
8. 8	23. 6	H8	D2	Monkey	20.10	8. 9	A11	G3	Ox
9. 8	24. 6	H8	E3	Gibbon	21.10	9. 9	A11	H4	Bat
10. 8	25. 6	H8	F4	Tapir	22.10	10. 9	A11	J5	Rat
11. 8	26. 6	H8	G5	Sheep	23.10	11. 9	A11	K6	Swallow
12. 8	27. 6	H8	H6	Deer	24.10	12. 9	A11	A7	Pig
13. 8	28. 6	H8	J7	Horse	25.10	13. 9	A11	B8	Porcupine
14. 8	29. 6	H8	K8	Stag	26.10	14. 9	A11	C9	Wolf
15. 8	1. 7	J9	A9	Serpent	27.10	15. 9	A11	D10	Dog
16. 8	2. 7	J9	B10	Earthworm	28.10	16. 9	A11	E11	Pheasant
17. 8	3. 7	J9	C11	Crocodile	29.10	17. 9	A11	F12	Cock
18. 8	4. 7	J9	D12	Dragon	30.10	18. 9	A11	G1	Crow
19. 8	5. 7	J9	E1	Badger	31.10	19. 9	A11	H2	Monkey
20. 8	6. 7	J9	F2	Hare	1.11	20. 9	A11	J3	Gibbon
21. 8	7. 7	J9	G3	Fox	2.11	21. 9	A11	K4	Tapir
22. 8	8. 7	J9	H4	Tiger	3.11	22. 9	A11	A5	Sheep
23. 8	9. 7	J9	J5	Leopard	4.11	23. 9	A11	B6	Deer
24. 8	10. 7	J9	K6	Griffon	5.11	24. 9	A11	C7	Horse
25. 8	11. 7	J9	A7	Ox	6.11	25. 9	A11	D8	Stag
26. 8	12. 7	J9	B8	Bat	7.11	26. 9	A11	E9	Serpent
27. 8	13. 7	J9	C9	Rat	8.11	27. 9	A11	F10	Earthworm
28. 8	14. 7	J9	D10	Swallow	9.11	28. 9	A11	G11	Crocodile
29. 8	15. 7	J9	E11	Pig	10.11	29. 9	A11	H12	Dragon
30. 8	16. 7	J9	F12	Porcupine	11.11	1.10	B12	J1	Badger
31. 8	17. 7	J9	G1	Wolf	12.11	2.10	B12	K2	Hare
1. 9	18. 7	J9	H2	Dog	13.11	3.10	B12	A3	Fox
2. 9	19. 7	J9	J3	Pheasant	14.11	4.10	B12	B4	Tiger
3. 9	20. 7	J9	K4	Cock	15.11	5.10	B12	C5	Leopard
4. 9	21. 7	J9	A5	Crow	16.11	6.10	B12	D6	Griffon
5. 9	22. 7	J9	B6	Monkey	17.11	7.10	B12	E7	Ox
6. 9	23. 7	J9	C7	Gibbon	18.11	8.10	B12	F8	Bat
7. 9	24. 7	J9	D8	Tapir	19.11	9.10	B12	G9	Rat
8. 9	25. 7	J9	E9	Sheep	20.11	10.10	B12	H10	Swallow
9. 9	26. 7	J9	F10	Deer	21.11	11.10	B12	J11	Pig
10. 9	27. 7	J9	G11	Horse	22.11	12.10	B12	K12	Porcupine
11. 9	28. 7	J9	H12	Stag	23.11	13.10	B12	A1	Wolf
12. 9	29. 7	J9	J1	Serpent	24.11	14.10	B12	B2	Dog
13. 9	1. 8	K10	K2	Earthworm	25.11	15.10	B12	C3	Pheasant
14. 9	2. 8	K10	A3	Crocodile	26.11	16.10	B12	D4	Cock
15. 9	3. 8	K10	B4	Dragon	27.11	17.10	B12	E5	Crow
16. 9	4. 8	K10	C5	Badger	28.11	18.10	B12	F6	Monkey
17. 9	5. 8	K10	D6	Hare	29.11	19.10	B12	G7	Gibbon
18. 9	6. 8	K10	E7	Fox	30.11	20.10	B12	H8	Tapir
19. 9	7. 8	K10	F8	Tiger	1.12	21.10	B12	J9	Sheep
20. 9	8. 8	K10	G9	Leopard	2.12	22.10	B12	K10	Deer
21. 9	9. 8	K10	H10	Griffon	3.12	23.10	B12	A11	Horse

Solar date	Lunar date	Month HS/EB	Day HS/EB	Constellation
4.12	24.10	B12	B12	Stag
5.12	25.10	B12	C1	Serpent
6.12	26.10	B12	D2	Earthworm
7.12	27.10	B12	E3	Crocodile
8.12	28.10	B12	F4	Dragon
9.12	29.10	B12	G5	Badger
10.12	30.10	B12	H6	Hare
11.12	1.11	C1	J7	Fox
12.12	2.11	C1	K8	Tiger
13.12	3.11	C1	A9	Leopard
14.12	4.11	C1	B10	Griffon
15.12	5.11	C1	C11	Ox
16.12	6.11	C1	D12	Bat
17.12	7.11	C1	E1	Rat
18.12	8.11	C1	F2	Swallow
19.12	9.11	C1	G3	Pig
20.12	10.11	C1	H4	Porcupine
21.12	11.11	C1	J5	Wolf
22.12	12.11	C1	K6	Dog
23.12	13.11	C1	A7	Pheasant
24.12	14.11	C1	B8	Cock
25.12	15.11	C1	C9	Crow
26.12	16.11	C1	D10	Monkey
27.12	17.11	C1	E11	Gibbon
28.12	18.11	C1	F12	Tapir
29.12	19.11	C1	G1	Sheep
30.12	20.11	C1	H2	Deer
31.12	21.11	C1	J3	Horse
1940				
1. 1	22.11	C1	K4	Stag
2. 1	23.11	C1	A5	Serpent
3. 1	24.11	C1	B6	Earthworm
4. 1	25.11	C1	C7	Crocodile
5. 1	26.11	C1	D8	Dragon
6. 1	27.11	C1	E9	Badger
7. 1	28.11	C1	F10	Hare
8. 1	29.11	C1	G11	Fox
9. 1	1.12	D2	H12	Tiger
10. 1	2.12	D2	J1	Leopard
11. 1	3.12	D2	K2	Griffon
12. 1	4.12	D2	A3	Ox
13. 1	5.12	D2	B4	Bat
14. 1	6.12	D2	C5	Rat
15. 1	7.12	D2	D6	Swallow
16. 1	8.12	D2	E7	Pig
17. 1	9.12	D2	F8	Porcupine
18. 1	10.12	D2	G9	Wolf
19. 1	11.12	D2	H10	Dog
20. 1	12.12	D2	J11	Pheasant
21. 1	13.12	D2	K12	Cock
22. 1	14.12	D2	A1	Crow
23. 1	15.12	D2	B2	Monkey
24. 1	16.12	D2	C3	Gibbon
25. 1	17.12	D2	D4	Tapir
26. 1	18.12	D2	E5	Sheep
27. 1	19.12	D2	F6	Deer
28. 1	20.12	D2	G7	Horse
29. 1	21.12	D2	H8	Stag
30. 1	22.12	D2	J9	Serpent
31. 1	23.12	D2	K10	Earthworm
1. 2	24.12	D2	A11	Crocodile
2. 2	25.12	D2	B12	Dragon
3. 2	26.12	D2	C1	Badger
4. 2	27.12	D2	D2	Hare
5. 2	28.12	D2	E3	Fox
6. 2	29.12	D2	F4	Tiger
7. 2	30.12	D2	G5	Leopard

KENG CH'EN YEAR

Solar date	Lunar date	Month HS/EB	Day HS/EB	Constellation
8. 2	1. 1	E3	H6	Griffon
9. 2	2. 1	E3	J7	Ox
10. 2	3. 1	E3	K8	Bat
11. 2	4. 1	E3	A9	Rat
12. 2	5. 1	E3	B10	Swallow
13. 2	6. 1	E3	C11	Pig
14. 2	7. 1	E3	D12	Porcupine
15. 2	8. 1	E3	E1	Wolf
16. 2	9. 1	E3	F2	Dog
17. 2	10. 1	E3	G3	Pheasant
18. 2	11. 1	E3	H4	Cock
19. 2	12. 1	E3	J5	Crow
20. 2	13. 1	E3	K6	Monkey
21. 2	14. 1	E3	A7	Gibbon
22. 2	15. 1	E3	B8	Tapir
23. 2	16. 1	E3	C9	Sheep
24. 2	17. 1	E3	D10	Deer
25. 2	18. 1	E3	E11	Horse
26. 2	19. 1	E3	F12	Stag
27. 2	20. 1	E3	G1	Serpent
28. 2	21. 1	E3	H2	Earthworm
29. 2	22. 1	E3	J3	Crocodile
1. 3	23. 1	E3	K4	Dragon
2. 3	24. 1	E3	A5	Badger
3. 3	25. 1	E3	B6	Hare
4. 3	26. 1	E3	C7	Fox
5. 3	27. 1	E3	D8	Tiger
6. 3	28. 1	E3	E9	Leopard
7. 3	29. 1	E3	F10	Griffon
8. 3	30. 1	E3	G11	Ox
9. 3	1. 2	F4	H12	Bat
10. 3	2. 2	F4	J1	Rat
11. 3	3. 2	F4	K2	Swallow
12. 3	4. 2	F4	A3	Pig
13. 3	5. 2	F4	B4	Porcupine
14. 3	6. 2	F4	C5	Wolf
15. 3	7. 2	F4	D6	Dog
16. 3	8. 2	F4	E7	Pheasant
17. 3	9. 2	F4	F8	Cock
18. 3	10. 2	F4	G9	Crow
19. 3	11. 2	F4	H10	Monkey
20. 3	12. 2	F4	J11	Gibbon
21. 3	13. 2	F4	K12	Tapir
22. 3	14. 2	F4	A1	Sheep
23. 3	15. 2	F4	B2	Deer
24. 3	16. 2	F4	C3	Horse
25. 3	17. 2	F4	D4	Stag
26. 3	18. 2	F4	E5	Serpent
27. 3	19. 2	F4	F6	Earthworm
28. 3	20. 2	F4	G7	Crocodile
29. 3	21. 2	F4	H8	Dragon
30. 3	22. 2	F4	J9	Badger
31. 3	23. 2	F4	K10	Hare
1. 4	24. 2	F4	A11	Fox
2. 4	25. 2	F4	B12	Tiger
3. 4	26. 2	F4	C1	Leopard
4. 4	27. 2	F4	D2	Griffon
5. 4	28. 2	F4	E3	Ox
6. 4	29. 2	F4	F4	Bat
7. 4	30. 2	F4	G5	Rat
8. 4	1. 3	G5	H6	Swallow
9. 4	2. 3	G5	J7	Pig
10. 4	3. 3	G5	K8	Porcupine
11. 4	4. 3	G5	A9	Wolf
12. 4	5. 3	G5	B10	Dog
13. 4	6. 3	G5	C11	Pheasant
14. 4	7. 3	G5	D12	Cock
15. 4	8. 3	G5	E1	Crow

Solar date	Lunar date	Month HS/EB	Day HS/EB	Constellation	Solar date	Lunar date	Month HS/EB	Day HS/EB	Constellation
16. 4	9. 3	G5	F2	Monkey	28. 6	23. 5	J7	J3	Ox
17. 4	10. 3	G5	G3	Gibbon	29. 6	24. 5	J7	K4	Bat
18. 4	11. 3	G5	H4	Tapir	30. 6	25. 5	J7	A5	Rat
19. 4	12. 3	G5	J5	Sheep	1. 7	26. 5	J7	B6	Swallow
20. 4	13. 3	G5	K6	Deer	2. 7	27. 5	J7	C7	Pig
21. 4	14. 3	G5	A7	Horse	3. 7	28. 5	J7	D8	Porcupine
22. 4	15. 3	G5	B8	Stag	4. 7	29. 5	J7	E9	Wolf
23. 4	16. 3	G5	C9	Serpent	5. 7	1. 6	K8	F10	Dog
24. 4	17. 3	G5	D10	Earthworm	6. 7	2. 6	K8	G11	Pheasant
25. 4	18. 3	G5	E11	Crocodile	7. 7	3. 6	K8	H12	Cock
26. 4	19. 3	G5	F12	Dragon	8. 7	4. 6	K8	J1	Crow
27. 4	20. 3	G5	G1	Badger	9. 7	5. 6	K8	K2	Monkey
28. 4	21. 3	G5	H2	Hare	10. 7	6. 6	K8	A3	Gibbon
29. 4	22. 3	G5	J3	Fox	11. 7	7. 6	K8	B4	Tapir
30. 4	23. 3	G5	K4	Tiger	12. 7	8. 6	K8	C5	Sheep
1. 5	24. 3	G5	A5	Leopard	13. 7	9. 6	K8	D6	Deer
2. 5	25. 3	G5	B6	Griffon	14. 7	10. 6	K8	E7	Horse
3. 5	26. 3	G5	C7	Ox	15. 7	11. 6	K8	F8	Stag
4. 5	27. 3	G5	D8	Bat	16. 7	12. 6	K8	G9	Serpent
5. 5	28. 3	G5	E9	Rat	17. 7	13. 6	K8	H10	Earthworm
6. 5	29. 3	G5	F10	Swallow	18. 7	14. 6	K8	J11	Crocodile
7. 5	1. 4	H6	G11	Pig	19. 7	15. 6	K8	K12	Dragon
8. 5	2. 4	H6	H12	Porcupine	20. 7	16. 6	K8	A1	Badger
9. 5	3. 4	H6	J1	Wolf	21. 7	17. 6	K8	B2	Hare
10. 5	4. 4	H6	K2	Dog	22. 7	18. 6	K8	C3	Fox
11. 5	5. 4	H6	A3	Pheasant	23. 7	19. 6	K8	D4	Tiger
12. 5	6. 4	H6	B4	Cock	24. 7	20. 6	K8	E5	Leopard
13. 5	7. 4	H6	C5	Crow	25. 7	21. 6	K8	F6	Griffon
14. 5	8. 4	H6	D6	Monkey	26. 7	22. 6	K8	G7	Ox
15. 5	9. 4	H6	E7	Gibbon	27. 7	23. 6	K8	H8	Bat
16. 5	10. 4	H6	F8	Tapir	28. 7	24. 6	K8	J9	Rat
17. 5	11. 4	H6	G9	Sheep	29. 7	25. 6	K8	K10	Swallow
18. 5	12. 4	H6	H10	Deer	30. 7	26. 6	K8	A11	Pig
19. 5	13. 4	H6	J11	Horse	31. 7	27. 6	K8	B12	Porcupine
20. 5	14. 4	H6	K12	Stag	1. 8	28. 6	K8	C1	Wolf
21. 5	15. 4	H6	A1	Serpent	2. 8	29. 6	K8	D2	Dog
22. 5	16. 4	H6	B2	Earthworm	3. 8	30. 6	K8	E3	Pheasant
23. 5	17. 4	H6	C3	Crocodile	4. 8	1. 7	A9	F4	Cock
24. 5	18. 4	H6	D4	Dragon	5. 8	2. 7	A9	G5	Crow
25. 5	19. 4	H6	E5	Badger	6. 8	3. 7	A9	H6	Monkey
26. 5	20. 4	H6	F6	Hare	7. 8	4. 7	A9	J7	Gibbon
27. 5	21. 4	H6	G7	Fox	8. 8	5. 7	A9	K8	Tapir
28. 5	22. 4	H6	H8	Tiger	9. 8	6. 7	A9	A9	Sheep
29. 5	23. 4	H6	J9	Leopard	10. 8	7. 7	A9	B10	Deer
30. 5	24. 4	H6	K10	Griffon	11. 8	8. 7	A9	C11	Horse
31. 5	25. 4	H6	A11	Ox	12. 8	9. 7	A9	D12	Stag
1. 6	26. 4	H6	B12	Bat	13. 8	10. 7	A9	E1	Serpent
2. 6	27. 4	H6	C1	Rat	14. 8	11. 7	A9	F2	Earthworm
3. 6	28. 4	H6	D2	Swallow	15. 8	12. 7	A9	G3	Crocodile
4. 6	29. 4	H6	E3	Pig	16. 8	13. 7	A9	H4	Dragon
5. 6	30. 4	H6	F4	Porcupine	17. 8	14. 7	A9	J5	Badger
6. 6	1. 5	J7	G5	Wolf	18. 8	15. 7	A9	K6	Hare
7. 6	2. 5	J7	H6	Dog	19. 8	16. 7	A9	A7	Fox
8. 6	3. 5	J7	J7	Pheasant	20. 8	17. 7	A9	B8	Tiger
9. 6	4. 5	J7	K8	Cock	21. 8	18. 7	A9	C9	Leopard
10. 6	5. 5	J7	A9	Crow	22. 8	19. 7	A9	D10	Griffon
11. 6	6. 5	J7	B10	Monkey	23. 8	20. 7	A9	E11	Ox
12. 6	7. 5	J7	C11	Gibbon	24. 8	21. 7	A9	F12	Bat
13. 6	8. 5	J7	D12	Tapir	25. 8	22. 7	A9	G1	Rat
14. 6	9. 5	J7	E1	Sheep	26. 8	23. 7	A9	H2	Swallow
15. 6	10. 5	J7	F2	Deer	27. 8	24. 7	A9	J3	Pig
16. 6	11. 5	J7	G3	Horse	28. 8	25. 7	A9	K4	Porcupine
17. 6	12. 5	J7	H4	Stag	29. 8	26. 7	A9	A5	Wolf
18. 6	13. 5	J7	J5	Serpent	30. 8	27. 7	A9	B6	Dog
19. 6	14. 5	J7	K6	Earthworm	31. 8	28. 7	A9	C7	Pheasant
20. 6	15. 5	J7	A7	Crocodile	1. 9	29. 7	A9	D8	Cock
21. 6	16. 5	J7	B8	Dragon	2. 9	1. 8	B10	E9	Crow
22. 6	17. 5	J7	C9	Badger	3. 9	2. 8	B10	F10	Monkey
23. 6	18. 5	J7	D10	Hare	4. 9	3. 8	B10	G11	Gibbon
24. 6	19. 5	J7	E11	Fox	5. 9	4. 8	B10	H12	Tapir
25. 6	20. 5	J7	F12	Tiger	6. 9	5. 8	B10	J1	Sheep
26. 6	21. 5	J7	G1	Leopard	7. 9	6. 8	B10	K2	Deer
27. 6	22. 5	J7	H2	Griffon	8. 9	7. 8	B10	A3	Horse

Solar date	Lunar date	Month HS/EB	Day HS/EB	Constellation	Solar date	Lunar date	Month HS/EB	Day HS/EB	Constellation
9. 9	8. 8	B10	B4	Stag	19.11	20.10	D12	C3	Pig
10. 9	9. 8	B10	C5	Serpent	20.11	21.10	D12	D4	Porcupine
11. 9	10. 8	B10	D6	Earthworm	21.11	22.10	D12	E5	Wolf
12. 9	11. 8	B10	E7	Crocodile	22.11	23.10	D12	F6	Dog
13. 9	12. 8	B10	F8	Dragon	23.11	24.10	D12	G7	Pheasant
14. 9	13. 8	B10	G9	Badger	24.11	25.10	D12	H8	Cock
15. 9	14. 8	B10	H10	Hare	25.11	26.10	D12	J9	Crow
16. 9	15. 8	B10	J11	Fox	26.11	27.10	D12	K10	Monkey
17. 9	16. 8	B10	K12	Tiger	27.11	28.10	D12	A11	Gibbon
18. 9	17. 8	B10	A1	Leopard	28.11	29.10	D12	B12	Tapir
19. 9	18. 8	B10	B2	Griffon	29.11	1.11	E1	C1	Sheep
20. 9	19. 8	B10	C3	Ox	30.11	2.11	E1	D2	Deer
21. 9	20. 8	B10	D4	Bat	1.12	3.11	E1	E3	Horse
22. 9	21. 8	B10	E5	Rat	2.12	4.11	E1	F4	Stag
23. 9	22. 8	B10	F6	Swallow	3.12	5.11	E1	G5	Serpent
24. 9	23. 8	B10	G7	Pig	4.12	6.11	E1	H6	Earthworm
25. 9	24. 8	B10	H8	Porcupine	5.12	7.11	E1	J7	Crocodile
26. 9	25. 8	B10	J9	Wolf	6.12	8.11	E1	K8	Dragon
27. 9	26. 8	B10	K10	Dog	7.12	9.11	E1	A9	Badger
28. 9	27. 8	B10	A11	Pheasant	8.12	10.11	E1	B10	Hare
29. 9	28. 8	B10	B12	Cock	9.12	11.11	E1	C11	Fox
30. 9	29. 8	B10	C1	Crow	10.12	12.11	E1	D12	Tiger
1.10	1. 9	C11	D2	Monkey	11.12	13.11	E1	E1	Leopard
2.10	2. 9	C11	E3	Gibbon	12.12	14.11	E1	F2	Griffon
3.10	3. 9	C11	F4	Tapir	13.12	15.11	E1	G3	Ox
4.10	4. 9	C11	G5	Sheep	14.12	16.11	E1	H4	Bat
5.10	5. 9	C11	H6	Deer	15.12	17.11	E1	J5	Rat
6.10	6. 9	C11	J7	Horse	16.12	18.11	E1	K6	Swallow
7.10	7. 9	C11	K8	Stag	17.12	19.11	E1	A7	Pig
8.10	8. 9	C11	A9	Serpent	18.12	20.11	E1	B8	Porcupine
9.10	9. 9	C11	B10	Earthworm	19.12	21.11	E1	C9	Wolf
10.10	10. 9	C11	C11	Crocodile	20.12	22.11	E1	D10	Dog
11.10	11. 9	C11	D12	Dragon	21.12	23.11	E1	E11	Pheasant
12.10	12. 9	C11	E1	Badger	22.12	24.11	E1	F12	Cock
13.10	13. 9	C11	F2	Hare	23.12	25.11	E1	G1	Crow
14.10	14. 9	C11	G3	Fox	24.12	26.11	E1	H2	Monkey
15.10	15. 9	C11	H4	Tiger	25.12	27.11	E1	J3	Gibbon
16.10	16. 9	C11	J5	Leopard	26.12	28.11	E1	K4	Tapir
17.10	17. 9	C11	K6	Griffon	27.12	29.11	E1	A5	Sheep
18.10	18. 9	C11	A7	Ox	28.12	30.11	E1	B6	Deer
19.10	19. 9	C11	B8	Bat	29.12	1.12	F2	C7	Horse
20.10	20. 9	C11	C9	Rat	30.12	2.12	F2	D8	Stag
21.10	21. 9	C11	D10	Swallow	31.12	3.12	F2	E9	Serpent
22.10	22. 9	C11	E11	Pig					
23.10	23. 9	C11	F12	Porcupine	**1941**				
24.10	24. 9	C11	G1	Wolf	1. 1	4.12	F2	F10	Earthworm
25.10	25. 9	C11	H2	Dog	2. 1	5.12	F2	G11	Crocodile
26.10	26. 9	C11	J3	Pheasant	3. 1	6.12	F2	H12	Dragon
27.10	27. 9	C11	K4	Cock	4. 1	7.12	F2	J1	Badger
28.10	28. 9	C11	A5	Crow	5. 1	8.12	F2	K2	Hare
29.10	29. 9	C11	B6	Monkey	6. 1	9.12	F2	A3	Fox
30.10	30. 9	C11	C7	Gibbon	7. 1	10.12	F2	B4	Tiger
31.10	1.10	D12	D8	Tapir	8. 1	11.12	F2	C5	Leopard
1.11	2.10	D12	E9	Sheep	9. 1	12.12	F2	D6	Griffon
2.11	3.10	D12	F10	Deer	10. 1	13.12	F2	E7	Ox
3.11	4.10	D12	G11	Horse	11. 1	14.12	F2	F8	Bat
4.11	5.10	D12	H12	Stag	12. 1	15.12	F2	G9	Rat
5.11	6.10	D12	J1	Serpent	13. 1	16.12	F2	H10	Swallow
6.11	7.10	D12	K2	Earthworm	14. 1	17.12	F2	J11	Pig
7.11	8.10	D12	A3	Crocodile	15. 1	18.12	F2	K12	Porcupine
8.11	9.10	D12	B4	Dragon	16. 1	19.12	F2	A1	Wolf
9.11	10.10	D12	C5	Badger	17. 1	20.12	F2	B2	Dog
10.11	11.10	D12	D6	Hare	18. 1	21.12	F2	C3	Pheasant
11.11	12.10	D12	E7	Fox	19. 1	22.12	F2	D4	Cock
12.11	13.10	D12	F8	Tiger	20. 1	23.12	F2	E5	Crow
13.11	14.10	D12	G9	Leopard	21. 1	24.12	F2	F6	Monkey
14.11	15.10	D12	H10	Griffon	22. 1	25.12	F2	G7	Gibbon
15.11	16.10	D12	J11	Ox	23. 1	26.12	F2	H8	Tapir
16.11	17.10	D12	K12	Bat	24. 1	27.12	F2	J9	Sheep
17.11	18.10	D12	A1	Rat	25. 1	28.12	F2	K10	Deer
18.11	19.10	D12	B2	Swallow	26. 1	29.12	F2	A11	Horse

HSIN SZU YEAR

Solar date	Lunar date	Month HS/EB	Day HS/EB	Constellation	Solar date	Lunar date	Month HS/EB	Day HS/EB	Constellation
27. 1	1. 1	G3	B12	Stag	8. 4	12. 3	J5	C11	Pig
28. 1	2. 1	G3	C1	Serpent	9. 4	13. 3	J5	D12	Porcupine
29. 1	3. 1	G3	D2	Earthworm	10. 4	14. 3	J5	E1	Wolf
30. 1	4. 1	G3	E3	Crocodile	11. 4	15. 3	J5	F2	Dog
31. 1	5. 1	G3	F4	Dragon	12. 4	16. 3	J5	G3	Pheasant
1. 2	6. 1	G3	G5	Badger	13. 4	17. 3	J5	H4	Cock
2. 2	7. 1	G3	H6	Hare	14. 4	18. 3	J5	J5	Crow
3. 2	8. 1	G3	J7	Fox	15. 4	19. 3	J5	K6	Monkey
4. 2	9. 1	G3	K8	Tiger	16. 4	20. 3	J5	A7	Gibbon
5. 2	10. 1	G3	A9	Leopard	17. 4	21. 3	J5	B8	Tapir
6. 2	11. 1	G3	B10	Griffon	18. 4	22. 3	J5	C9	Sheep
7. 2	12. 1	G3	C11	Ox	19. 4	23. 3	J5	D10	Deer
8. 2	13. 1	G3	D12	Bat	20. 4	24. 3	J5	E11	Horse
9. 2	14. 1	G3	E1	Rat	21. 4	25. 3	J5	F12	Stag
10. 2	15. 1	G3	F2	Swallow	22. 4	26. 3	J5	G1	Serpent
11. 2	16. 1	G3	G3	Pig	23. 4	27. 3	J5	H2	Earthworm
12. 2	17. 1	G3	H4	Porcupine	24. 4	28. 3	J5	J3	Crocodile
13. 2	18. 1	G3	J5	Wolf	25. 4	29. 3	J5	K4	Dragon
14. 2	19. 1	G3	K6	Dog	26. 4	1. 4	K6	A5	Badger
15. 2	20. 1	G3	A7	Pheasant	27. 4	2. 4	K6	B6	Hare
16. 2	21. 1	G3	B8	Cock	28. 4	3. 4	K6	C7	Fox
17. 2	22. 1	G3	C9	Crow	29. 4	4. 4	K6	D8	Tiger
18. 2	23. 1	G3	D10	Monkey	30. 4	5. 4	K6	E9	Leopard
19. 2	24. 1	G3	E11	Gibbon	1. 5	6. 4	K6	F10	Griffon
20. 2	25. 1	G3	F12	Tapir	2. 5	7. 4	K6	G11	Ox
21. 2	26. 1	G3	G1	Sheep	3. 5	8. 4	K6	H12	Bat
22. 2	27. 1	G3	H2	Deer	4. 5	9. 4	K6	J1	Rat
23. 2	28. 1	G3	J3	Horse	5. 5	10. 4	K6	K2	Swallow
24. 2	29. 1	G3	K4	Stag	6. 5	11. 4	K6	A3	Pig
25. 2	30. 1	G3	A5	Serpent	7. 5	12. 4	K6	B4	Porcupine
26. 2	1. 2	H4	B6	Earthworm	8. 5	13. 4	K6	C5	Wolf
27. 2	2. 2	H4	C7	Crocodile	9. 5	14. 4	K6	D6	Dog
28. 2	3. 2	H4	D8	Dragon	10. 5	15. 4	K6	E7	Pheasant
1. 3	4. 2	H4	E9	Badger	11. 5	16. 4	K6	F8	Cock
2. 3	5. 2	H4	F10	Hare	12. 5	17. 4	K6	G9	Crow
3. 3	6. 2	H4	G11	Fox	13. 5	18. 4	K6	H10	Monkey
4. 3	7. 2	H4	H12	Tiger	14. 5	19. 4	K6	J11	Gibbon
5. 3	8. 2	H4	J1	Leopard	15. 5	20. 4	K6	K12	Tapir
6. 3	9. 2	H4	K2	Griffon	16. 5	21. 4	K6	A1	Sheep
7. 3	10. 2	H4	A3	Ox	17. 5	22. 4	K6	B2	Deer
8. 3	11. 2	H4	B4	Bat	18. 5	23. 4	K6	C3	Horse
9. 3	12. 2	H4	C5	Rat	19. 5	24. 4	K6	D4	Stag
10. 3	13. 2	H4	D6	Swallow	20. 5	25. 4	K6	E5	Serpent
11. 3	14. 2	H4	E7	Pig	21. 5	26. 4	K6	F6	Earthworm
12. 3	15. 2	H4	F8	Porcupine	22. 5	27. 4	K6	G7	Crocodile
13. 3	16. 2	H4	G9	Wolf	23. 5	28. 4	K6	H8	Dragon
14. 3	17. 2	H4	H10	Dog	24. 5	29. 4	K6	J9	Badger
15. 3	18. 2	H4	J11	Pheasant	25. 5	30. 4	K6	K10	Hare
16. 3	19. 2	H4	K12	Cock	26. 5	1. 5	A7	A11	Fox
17. 3	20. 2	H4	A1	Crow	27. 5	2. 5	A7	B12	Tiger
18. 3	21. 2	H4	B2	Monkey	28. 5	3. 5	A7	C1	Leopard
19. 3	22. 2	H4	C3	Gibbon	29. 5	4. 5	A7	D2	Griffon
20. 3	23. 2	H4	D4	Tapir	30. 5	5. 5	A7	E3	Ox
21. 3	24. 2	H4	E5	Sheep	31. 5	6. 5	A7	F4	Bat
22. 3	25. 2	H4	F6	Deer	1. 6	7. 5	A7	G5	Rat
23. 3	26. 2	H4	G7	Horse	2. 6	8. 5	A7	H6	Swallow
24. 3	27. 2	H4	H8	Stag	3. 6	9. 5	A7	J7	Pig
25. 3	28. 2	H4	J9	Serpent	4. 6	10. 5	A7	K8	Porcupine
26. 3	29. 2	H4	K10	Earthworm	5. 6	11. 5	A7	A9	Wolf
27. 3	30. 2	H4	A11	Crocodile	6. 6	12. 5	A7	B10	Dog
28. 3	1. 3	J5	B12	Dragon	7. 6	13. 5	A7	C11	Pheasant
29. 3	2. 3	J5	C1	Badger	8. 6	14. 5	A7	D12	Cock
30. 3	3. 3	J5	D2	Hare	9. 6	15. 5	A7	E1	Crow
31. 3	4. 3	J5	E3	Fox	10. 6	16. 5	A7	F2	Monkey
1. 4	5. 3	J5	F4	Tiger	11. 6	17. 5	A7	G3	Gibbon
2. 4	6. 3	J5	G5	Leopard	12. 6	18. 5	A7	H4	Tapir
3. 4	7. 3	J5	H6	Griffon	13. 6	19. 5	A7	J5	Sheep
4. 4	8. 3	J5	J7	Ox	14. 6	20. 5	A7	K6	Deer
5. 4	9. 3	J5	K8	Bat	15. 6	21. 5	A7	A7	Horse
6. 4	10. 3	J5	A9	Rat	16. 6	22. 5	A7	B8	Stag
7. 4	11. 3	J5	B10	Swallow	17. 6	23. 5	A7	C9	Serpent

Solar date	Lunar date	Month HS/EB	Day HS/EB	Constellation	Solar date	Lunar date	Month HS/EB	Day HS/EB	Constellation
18. 6	24. 5	A7	D10	Earthworm	30. 8	8. 7	C9	G11	Pheasant
19. 6	25. 5	A7	E11	Crocodile	31. 8	9. 7	C9	H12	Cock
20. 6	26. 5	A7	F12	Dragon	1. 9	10. 7	C9	J1	Crow
21. 6	27. 5	A7	G1	Badger	2. 9	11. 7	C9	K2	Monkey
22. 6	28. 5	A7	H2	Hare	3. 9	12. 7	C9	A3	Gibbon
23. 6	29. 5	A7	J3	Fox	4. 9	13. 7	C9	B4	Tapir
24. 6	30. 5	A7	K4	Tiger	5. 9	14. 7	C9	C5	Sheep
25. 6	1. 6	B8	A5	Leopard	6. 9	15. 7	C9	D6	Deer
26. 6	2. 6	B8	B6	Griffon	7. 9	16. 7	C9	E7	Horse
27. 6	3. 6	B8	C7	Ox	8. 9	17. 7	C9	F8	Stag
28. 6	4. 6	B8	D8	Bat	9. 9	18. 7	C9	G9	Serpent
29. 6	5. 6	B8	E9	Rat	10. 9	19. 7	C9	H10	Earthworm
30. 6	6. 6	B8	F10	Swallow	11. 9	20. 7	C9	J11	Crocodile
1. 7	7. 6	B8	G11	Pig	12. 9	21. 7	C9	K12	Dragon
2. 7	8. 6	B8	H12	Porcupine	13. 9	22. 7	C9	A1	Badger
3. 7	9. 6	B8	J1	Wolf	14. 9	23. 7	C9	B2	Hare
4. 7	10. 6	B8	K2	Dog	15. 9	24. 7	C9	C3	Fox
5. 7	11. 6	B8	A3	Pheasant	16. 9	25. 7	C9	D4	Tiger
6. 7	12. 6	B8	B4	Cock	17. 9	26. 7	C9	E5	Leopard
7. 7	13. 6	B8	C5	Crow	18. 9	27. 7	C9	F6	Griffon
8. 7	14. 6	B8	D6	Monkey	19. 9	28. 7	C9	G7	Ox
9. 7	15. 6	B8	E7	Gibbon	20. 9	29. 7	C9	H8	Bat
10. 7	16. 6	B8	F8	Tapir	21. 9	1. 8	D10	J9	Rat
11. 7	17. 6	B8	G9	Sheep	22. 9	2. 8	D10	K10	Swallow
12. 7	18. 6	B8	H10	Deer	23. 9	3. 8	D10	A11	Pig
13. 7	19. 6	B8	J11	Horse	24. 9	4. 8	D10	B12	Porcupine
14. 7	20. 6	B8	K12	Stag	25. 9	5. 8	D10	C1	Wolf
15. 7	21. 6	B8	A1	Serpent	26. 9	6. 8	D10	D2	Dog
16. 7	22. 6	B8	B2	Earthworm	27. 9	7. 8	D10	E3	Pheasant
17. 7	23. 6	B8	C3	Crocodile	28. 9	8. 8	D10	F4	Cock
18. 7	24. 6	B8	D4	Dragon	29. 9	9. 8	D10	G5	Crow
19. 7	25. 6	B8	E5	Badger	30. 9	10. 8	D10	H6	Monkey
20. 7	26. 6	B8	F6	Hare	1.10	11. 8	D10	J7	Gibbon
21. 7	27. 6	B8	G7	Fox	2.10	12. 8	D10	K8	Tapir
22. 7	28. 6	B8	H8	Tiger	3.10	13. 8	D10	A9	Sheep
23. 7	29. 6	B8	J9	Leopard	4.10	14. 8	D10	B10	Deer
24. 7	1. 6	B8	K10	Griffon	5.10	15. 8	D10	C11	Horse
25. 7	2. 6	B8	A11	Ox	6.10	16. 8	D10	D12	Stag
26. 7	3. 6	B8	B12	Bat	7.10	17. 8	D10	E1	Serpent
27. 7	4. 6	B8	C1	Rat	8.10	18. 8	D10	F2	Earthworm
28. 7	5. 6	B8	D2	Swallow	9.10	19. 8	D10	G3	Crocodile
29. 7	6. 6	B8	E3	Pig	10.10	20. 8	D10	H4	Dragon
30. 7	7. 6	B8	F4	Porcupine	11.10	21. 8	D10	J5	Badger
31. 7	8. 6	B8	G5	Wolf	12.10	22. 8	D10	K6	Hare
1. 8	9. 6	B8	H6	Dog	13.10	23. 8	D10	A7	Fox
2. 8	10. 6	B8	J7	Pheasant	14.10	24. 8	D10	B8	Tiger
3. 8	11. 6	B8	K8	Cock	15.10	25. 8	D10	C9	Leopard
4. 8	12. 6	B8	A9	Crow	16.10	26. 8	D10	D10	Griffon
5. 8	13. 6	B8	B10	Monkey	17.10	27. 8	D10	E11	Ox
6. 8	14. 6	B8	C11	Gibbon	18.10	28. 8	D10	F12	Bat
7. 8	15. 6	B8	D12	Tapir	19.10	29. 8	D10	G1	Rat
8. 8	16. 6	B8	E1	Sheep	20.10	1. 9	E11	H2	Swallow
9. 8	17. 6	B8	F2	Deer	21.10	2. 9	E11	J3	Pig
10. 8	18. 6	B8	G3	Horse	22.10	3. 9	E11	K4	Porcupine
11. 8	19. 6	B8	H4	Stag	23.10	4. 9	E11	A5	Wolf
12. 8	20. 6	B8	J5	Serpent	24.10	5. 9	E11	B6	Dog
13. 8	21. 6	B8	K6	Earthworm	25.10	6. 9	E11	C7	Pheasant
14. 8	22. 6	B8	A7	Crocodile	26.10	7. 9	E11	D8	Cock
15. 8	23. 6	B8	B8	Dragon	27.10	8. 9	E11	E9	Crow
16. 8	24. 6	B8	C9	Badger	28.10	9. 9	E11	F10	Monkey
17. 8	25. 6	B8	D10	Hare	29.10	10. 9	E11	G11	Gibbon
18. 8	26. 6	B8	E11	Fox	30.10	11. 9	E11	H12	Tapir
19. 8	27. 6	B8	F12	Tiger	31.10	12. 9	E11	J1	Sheep
20. 8	28. 6	B8	G1	Leopard	1.11	13. 9	E11	K2	Deer
21. 8	29. 6	B8	H2	Griffon	2.11	14. 9	E11	A3	Horse
22. 8	30. 6	B8	J3	Ox	3.11	15. 9	E11	B4	Stag
23. 8	1. 7	C9	K4	Bat	4.11	16. 9	E11	C5	Serpent
24. 8	2. 7	C9	A5	Rat	5.11	17. 9	E11	D6	Earthworm
25. 8	3. 7	C9	B6	Swallow	6.11	18. 9	E11	E7	Crocodile
26. 8	4. 7	C9	C7	Pig	7.11	19. 9	E11	F8	Dragon
27. 8	5. 7	C9	D8	Porcupine	8.11	20. 9	E11	G9	Badger
28. 8	6. 7	C9	E9	Wolf	9.11	21. 9	E11	H10	Hare
29. 8	7. 7	C9	F10	Dog	10.11	22. 9	E11	J11	Fox

Solar date	Lunar date	Month HS/EB	Day HS/EB	Constellation	Solar date	Lunar date	Month HS/EB	Day HS/EB	Constellation
11.11	23. 9	E11	K12	Tiger	30.12	13.11	G1	J1	Serpent
12.11	24. 9	E11	A1	Leopard	31.12	14.11	G1	K2	Earthworm
13.11	25. 9	E11	B2	Griffon	**1942**				
14.11	26. 9	E11	C3	Ox	1. 1	15.11	G1	A3	Crocodile
15.11	27. 9	E11	D4	Bat	2. 1	16.11	G1	B4	Dragon
16.11	28. 9	E11	E5	Rat	3. 1	17.11	G1	C5	Badger
17.11	29. 9	E11	F6	Swallow	4. 1	18.11	G1	D6	Hare
18.11	30. 9	E11	G7	Pig	5. 1	19.11	G1	E7	Fox
19.11	1.10	F12	H8	Porcupine	6. 1	20.11	G1	F8	Tiger
20.11	2.10	F12	J9	Wolf	7. 1	21.11	G1	G9	Leopard
21.11	3.10	F12	K10	Dog	8. 1	22.11	G1	H10	Griffon
22.11	4.10	F12	A11	Pheasant	9. 1	23.11	G1	J11	Ox
23.11	5.10	F12	B12	Cock	10. 1	24.11	G1	K12	Bat
24.11	6.10	F12	C1	Crow	11. 1	25.11	G1	A1	Rat
25.11	7.10	F12	D2	Monkey	12. 1	26.11	G1	B2	Swallow
26.11	8.10	F12	E3	Gibbon	13. 1	27.11	G1	C3	Pig
27.11	9.10	F12	F4	Tapir	14. 1	28.11	G1	D4	Porcupine
28.11	10.10	F12	G5	Sheep	15. 1	29.11	G1	E5	Wolf
29.11	11.10	F12	H6	Deer	16. 1	30.11	G1	F6	Dog
30.11	12.10	F12	J7	Horse	17. 1	1.12	H2	G7	Pheasant
1.12	13.10	F12	K8	Stag	18. 1	2.12	H2	H8	Cock
2.12	14.10	F12	A9	Serpent	19. 1	3.12	H2	J9	Crow
3.12	15.10	F12	B10	Earthworm	20. 1	4.12	H2	K10	Monkey
4.12	16.10	F12	C11	Crocodile	21. 1	5.12	H2	A11	Gibbon
5.12	17.10	F12	D12	Dragon	22. 1	6.12	H2	B12	Tapir
6.12	18.10	F12	E1	Badger	23. 1	7.12	H2	C1	Sheep
7.12	19.10	F12	F2	Hare	24. 1	8.12	H2	D2	Deer
8.12	20.10	F12	G3	Fox	25. 1	9.12	H2	E3	Horse
9.12	21.10	F12	H4	Tiger	26. 1	10.12	H2	F4	Stag
10.12	22.10	F12	J5	Leopard	27. 1	11.12	H2	G5	Serpent
11.12	23.10	F12	K6	Griffon	28. 1	12.12	H2	H6	Earthworm
12.12	24.10	F12	A7	Ox	29. 1	13.12	H2	J7	Crocodile
13.12	25.10	F12	B8	Bat	30. 1	14.12	H2	K8	Dragon
14.12	26.10	F12	C9	Rat	31. 1	15.12	H2	A9	Badger
15.12	27.10	F12	D10	Swallow	1. 2	16.12	H2	B10	Hare
16.12	28.10	F12	E11	Pig	2. 2	17.12	H2	C11	Fox
17.12	29.10	F12	F12	Porcupine	3. 2	18.12	H2	D12	Tiger
18.12	1.11	G1	G1	Wolf	4. 2	19.12	H2	E1	Leopard
19.12	2.11	G1	H2	Dog	5. 2	20.12	H2	F2	Griffon
20.12	3.11	G1	J3	Pheasant	6. 2	21.12	H2	G3	Ox
21.12	4.11	G1	K4	Cock	7. 2	22.12	H2	H4	Bat
22.12	5.11	G1	A5	Crow	8. 2	23.12	H2	J5	Rat
23.12	6.11	G1	B6	Monkey	9. 2	24.12	H2	K6	Swallow
24.12	7.11	G1	C7	Gibbon	10. 2	25.12	H2	A7	Pig
25.12	8.11	G1	D8	Tapir	11. 2	26.12	H2	B8	Porcupine
26.12	9.11	G1	E9	Sheep	12. 2	27.12	H2	C9	Wolf
27.12	10.11	G1	F10	Deer	13. 2	28.12	H2	D10	Dog
28.12	11.11	G1	G11	Horse	14. 2	29.12	H2	E11	Pheasant
29.12	12.11	G1	H12	Stag					

JEN WU YEAR

Solar date	Lunar date	Month HS/EB	Day HS/EB	Constellation	Solar date	Lunar date	Month HS/EB	Day HS/EB	Constellation
15. 2	1. 1	J3	F12	Cock	6. 3	20. 1	J3	E7	Ox
16. 2	2. 1	J3	G1	Crow	7. 3	21. 1	J3	F8	Bat
17. 2	3. 1	J3	H2	Monkey	8. 3	22. 1	J3	G9	Rat
18. 2	4. 1	J3	J3	Gibbon	9. 3	23. 1	J3	H10	Swallow
19. 2	5. 1	J3	K4	Tapir	10. 3	24. 1	J3	J11	Pig
20. 2	6. 1	J3	A5	Sheep	11. 3	25. 1	J3	K12	Porcupine
21. 2	7. 1	J3	B6	Deer	12. 3	26. 1	J3	A1	Wolf
22. 2	8. 1	J3	C7	Horse	13. 3	27. 1	J3	B2	Dog
23. 2	9. 1	J3	D8	Stag	14. 3	28. 1	J3	C3	Pheasant
24. 2	10. 1	J3	E9	Serpent	15. 3	29. 1	J3	D4	Cock
25. 2	11. 1	J3	F10	Earthworm	16. 3	30. 1	J3	E5	Crow
26. 2	12. 1	J3	G11	Crocodile	17. 3	1. 2	K4	F6	Monkey
27. 2	13. 1	J3	H12	Dragon	18. 3	2. 2	K4	G7	Gibbon
28. 2	14. 1	J3	J1	Badger	19. 3	3. 2	K4	H8	Tapir
1. 3	15. 1	J3	K2	Hare	20. 3	4. 2	K4	J9	Sheep
2. 3	16. 1	J3	A3	Fox	21. 3	5. 2	K4	K10	Deer
3. 3	17. 1	J3	B4	Tiger	22. 3	6. 2	K4	A11	Horse
4. 3	18. 1	J3	C5	Leopard	23. 3	7. 2	K4	B12	Stag
5. 3	19. 1	J3	D6	Griffon	24. 3	8. 2	K4	C1	Serpent

Solar date	Lunar date	Month HS/EB	Day HS/EB	Constellation
25. 3	9. 2	K4	D2	Earthworm
26. 3	10. 2	K4	E3	Crocodile
27. 3	11. 2	K4	F4	Dragon
28. 3	12. 2	K4	G5	Badger
29. 3	13. 2	K4	H6	Hare
30. 3	14. 2	K4	J7	Fox
31. 3	15. 2	K4	K8	Tiger
1. 4	16. 2	K4	A9	Leopard
2. 4	17. 2	K4	B10	Griffon
3. 4	18. 2	K4	C11	Ox
4. 4	19. 2	K4	D12	Bat
5. 4	20. 2	K4	E1	Rat
6. 4	21. 2	K4	F2	Swallow
7. 4	22. 2	K4	G3	Pig
8. 4	23. 2	K4	H4	Porcupine
9. 4	24. 2	K4	J5	Wolf
10. 4	25. 2	K4	K6	Dog
11. 4	26. 2	K4	A7	Pheasant
12. 4	27. 2	K4	B8	Cock
13. 4	28. 2	K4	C9	Crow
14. 4	29. 2	K4	D10	Monkey
15. 4	1. 3	A5	E11	Gibbon
16. 4	2. 3	A5	F12	Tapir
17. 4	3. 3	A5	G1	Sheep
18. 4	4. 3	A5	H2	Deer
19. 4	5. 3	A5	J3	Horse
20. 4	6. 3	A5	K4	Stag
21. 4	7. 3	A5	A5	Serpent
22. 4	8. 3	A5	B6	Earthworm
23. 4	9. 3	A5	C7	Crocodile
24. 4	10. 3	A5	D8	Dragon
25. 4	11. 3	A5	E9	Badger
26. 4	12. 3	A5	F10	Hare
27. 4	13. 3	A5	G11	Fox
28. 4	14. 3	A5	H12	Tiger
29. 4	15. 3	A5	J1	Leopard
30. 4	16. 3	A5	K2	Griffon
1. 5	17. 3	A5	A3	Ox
2. 5	18. 3	A5	B4	Bat
3. 5	19. 3	A5	C5	Rat
4. 5	20. 3	A5	D6	Swallow
5. 5	21. 3	A5	E7	Pig
6. 5	22. 3	A5	F8	Porcupine
7. 5	23. 3	A5	G9	Wolf
8. 5	24. 3	A5	H10	Dog
9. 5	25. 3	A5	J11	Pheasant
10. 5	26. 3	A5	K12	Cock
11. 5	27. 3	A5	A1	Crow
12. 5	28. 3	A5	B2	Monkey
13. 5	29. 3	A5	C3	Gibbon
14. 5	30. 3	A5	D4	Tapir
15. 5	1. 4	B6	E5	Sheep
16. 5	2. 4	B6	F6	Deer
17. 5	3. 4	B6	G7	Horse
18. 5	4. 4	B6	H8	Stag
19. 5	5. 4	B6	J9	Serpent
20. 5	6. 4	B6	K10	Earthworm
21. 5	7. 4	B6	A11	Crocodile
22. 5	8. 4	B6	B12	Dragon
23. 5	9. 4	B6	C1	Badger
24. 5	10. 4	B6	D2	Hare
25. 5	11. 4	B6	E3	Fox
26. 5	12. 4	B6	F4	Tiger
27. 5	13. 4	B6	G5	Leopard
28. 5	14. 4	B6	H6	Griffon
29. 5	15. 4	B6	J7	Ox
30. 5	16. 4	B6	K8	Bat
31. 5	17. 4	B6	A9	Rat
1. 6	18. 4	B6	B10	Swallow
2. 6	19. 4	B6	C11	Pig
3. 6	20. 4	B6	D12	Porcupine
4. 6	21. 4	B6	E1	Wolf
5. 6	22. 4	B6	F2	Dog
6. 6	23. 4	B6	G3	Pheasant
7. 6	24. 4	B6	H4	Cock
8. 6	25. 4	B6	J5	Crow
9. 6	26. 4	B6	K6	Monkey
10. 6	27. 4	B6	A7	Gibbon
11. 6	28. 4	B6	B8	Tapir
12. 6	29. 4	B6	C9	Sheep
13. 6	30. 4	B6	D10	Deer
14. 6	1. 5	C7	E11	Horse
15. 6	2. 5	C7	F12	Stag
16. 6	3. 5	C7	G1	Serpent
17. 6	4. 5	C7	H2	Earthworm
18. 6	5. 5	C7	J3	Crocodile
19. 6	6. 5	C7	K4	Dragon
20. 6	7. 5	C7	A5	Badger
21. 6	8. 5	C7	B6	Hare
22. 6	9. 5	C7	C7	Fox
23. 6	10. 5	C7	D8	Tiger
24. 6	11. 5	C7	E9	Leopard
25. 6	12. 5	C7	F10	Griffon
26. 6	13. 5	C7	G11	Ox
27. 6	14. 5	C7	H12	Bat
28. 6	15. 5	C7	J1	Rat
29. 6	16. 5	C7	K2	Swallow
30. 6	17. 5	C7	A3	Pig
1. 7	18. 5	C7	B4	Porcupine
2. 7	19. 5	C7	C5	Wolf
3. 7	20. 5	C7	D6	Dog
4. 7	21. 5	C7	E7	Pheasant
5. 7	22. 5	C7	F8	Cock
6. 7	23. 5	C7	G9	Crow
7. 7	24. 5	C7	H10	Monkey
8. 7	25. 5	C7	J11	Gibbon
9. 7	26. 5	C7	K12	Tapir
10. 7	27. 5	C7	A1	Sheep
11. 7	28. 5	C7	B2	Deer
12. 7	29. 5	C7	C3	Horse
13. 7	1. 6	D8	D4	Stag
14. 7	2. 6	D8	E5	Serpent
15. 7	3. 6	D8	F6	Earthworm
16. 7	4. 6	D8	G7	Crocodile
17. 7	5. 6	D8	H8	Dragon
18. 7	6. 6	D8	J9	Badger
19. 7	7. 6	D8	K10	Hare
20. 7	8. 6	D8	A11	Fox
21. 7	9. 6	D8	B12	Tiger
22. 7	10. 6	D8	C1	Leopard
23. 7	11. 6	D8	D2	Griffon
24. 7	12. 6	D8	E3	Ox
25. 7	13. 6	D8	F4	Bat
26. 7	14. 6	D8	G5	Rat
27. 7	15. 6	D8	H6	Swallow
28. 7	16. 6	D8	J7	Pig
29. 7	17. 6	D8	K8	Porcupine
30. 7	18. 6	D8	A9	Wolf
31. 7	19. 6	D8	B10	Dog
1. 8	20. 6	D8	C11	Pheasant
2. 8	21. 6	D8	D12	Cock
3. 8	22. 6	D8	E1	Crow
4. 8	23. 6	D8	F2	Monkey
5. 8	24. 6	D8	G3	Gibbon
6. 8	25. 6	D8	H4	Tapir
7. 8	26. 6	D8	J5	Sheep
8. 8	27. 6	D8	K6	Deer
9. 8	28. 6	D8	A7	Horse
10. 8	29. 6	D8	B8	Stag
11. 8	30. 6	D8	C9	Serpent
12. 8	1. 7	E9	D10	Earthworm
13. 8	2. 7	E9	E11	Crocodile
14. 8	3. 7	E9	F12	Dragon
15. 8	4. 7	E9	G1	Badger
16. 8	5. 7	E9	H2	Hare
17. 8	6. 7	E9	J3	Fox

Solar date	Lunar date	Month HS/EB	Day HS/EB	Constellation
18. 8	7. 7	E9	K4	Tiger
19. 8	8. 7	E9	A5	Leopard
20. 8	9. 7	E9	B6	Griffon
21. 8	10. 7	E9	C7	Ox
22. 8	11. 7	E9	D8	Bat
23. 8	12. 7	E9	E9	Rat
24. 8	13. 7	E9	F10	Swallow
25. 8	14. 7	E9	G11	Pig
26. 8	15. 7	E9	H12	Porcupine
27. 8	16. 7	E9	J1	Wolf
28. 8	17. 7	E9	K2	Dog
29. 8	18. 7	E9	A3	Pheasant
30. 8	19. 7	E9	B4	Cock
31. 8	20. 7	E9	C5	Crow
1. 9	21. 7	E9	D6	Monkey
2. 9	22. 7	E9	E7	Gibbon
3. 9	23. 7	E9	F8	Tapir
4. 9	24. 7	E9	G9	Sheep
5. 9	25. 7	E9	H10	Deer
6. 9	26. 7	E9	J11	Horse
7. 9	27. 7	E9	K12	Stag
8. 9	28. 7	E9	A1	Serpent
9. 9	29. 7	E9	B2	Earthworm
10. 9	1. 8	F10	C3	Crocodile
11. 9	2. 8	F10	D4	Dragon
12. 9	3. 8	F10	E5	Badger
13. 9	4. 8	F10	F6	Hare
14. 9	5. 8	F10	G7	Fox
15. 9	6. 8	F10	H8	Tiger
16. 9	7. 8	F10	J9	Leopard
17. 9	8. 8	F10	K10	Griffon
18. 9	9. 8	F10	A11	Ox
19. 9	10. 8	F10	B12	Bat
20. 9	11. 8	F10	C1	Rat
21. 9	12. 8	F10	D2	Swallow
22. 9	13. 8	F10	E3	Pig
23. 9	14. 8	F10	F4	Porcupine
24. 9	15. 8	F10	G5	Wolf
25. 9	16. 8	F10	H6	Dog
26. 9	17. 8	F10	J7	Pheasant
27. 9	18. 8	F10	K8	Cock
28. 9	19. 8	F10	A9	Crow
29. 9	20. 8	F10	B10	Monkey
30. 9	21. 8	F10	C11	Gibbon
1.10	22. 8	F10	D12	Tapir
2.10	23. 8	F10	E1	Sheep
3.10	24. 8	F10	F2	Deer
4.10	25. 8	F10	G3	Horse
5.10	26. 8	F10	H4	Stag
6.10	27. 8	F10	J5	Serpent
7.10	28. 8	F10	K6	Earthworm
8.10	29. 8	F10	A7	Crocodile
9.10	30. 8	F10	B8	Dragon
10.10	1. 9	G11	C9	Badger
11.10	2. 9	G11	D10	Hare
12.10	3. 9	G11	E11	Fox
13.10	4. 9	G11	F12	Tiger
14.10	5. 9	G11	G1	Leopard
15.10	6. 9	G11	H2	Griffon
16.10	7. 9	G11	J3	Ox
17.10	8. 9	G11	K4	Bat
18.10	9. 9	G11	A5	Rat
19.10	10. 9	G11	B6	Swallow
20.10	11. 9	G11	C7	Pig
21.10	12. 9	G11	D8	Porcupine
22.10	13. 9	G11	E9	Wolf
23.10	14. 9	G11	F10	Dog
24.10	15. 9	G11	G11	Pheasant
25.10	16. 9	G11	H12	Cock
26.10	17. 9	G11	J1	Crow
27.10	18. 9	G11	K2	Monkey
28.10	19. 9	G11	A3	Gibbon
29.10	20. 9	G11	B4	Tapir
30.10	21. 9	G11	C5	Sheep
31.10	22. 9	G11	D6	Deer
1.11	23. 9	G11	E7	Horse
2.11	24. 9	G11	F8	Stag
3.11	25. 9	G11	G9	Serpent
4.11	26. 9	G11	H10	Earthworm
5.11	27. 9	G11	J11	Crocodile
6.11	28. 9	G11	K12	Dragon
7.11	29. 9	G11	A1	Badger
8.11	1.10	H12	B2	Hare
9.11	2.10	H12	C3	Fox
10.11	3.10	H12	D4	Tiger
11.11	4.10	H12	E5	Leopard
12.11	5.10	H12	F6	Griffon
13.11	6.10	H12	G7	Ox
14.11	7.10	H12	H8	Bat
15.11	8.10	H12	J9	Rat
16.11	9.10	H12	K10	Swallow
17.11	10.10	H12	A11	Pig
18.11	11.10	H12	B12	Porcupine
19.11	12.10	H12	C1	Wolf
20.11	13.10	H12	D2	Dog
21.11	14.10	H12	E3	Pheasant
22.11	15.10	H12	F4	Cock
23.11	16.10	H12	G5	Crow
24.11	17.10	H12	H6	Monkey
25.11	18.10	H12	J7	Gibbon
26.11	19.10	H12	K8	Tapir
27.11	20.10	H12	A9	Sheep
28.11	21.10	H12	B10	Deer
29.11	22.10	H12	C11	Horse
30.11	23.10	H12	D12	Stag
1.12	24.10	H12	E1	Serpent
2.12	25.10	H12	F2	Earthworm
3.12	26.10	H12	G3	Crocodile
4.12	27.10	H12	H4	Dragon
5.12	28.10	H12	J5	Badger
6.12	29.10	H12	K6	Hare
7.12	30.10	H12	A7	Fox
8.12	1.11	J1	B8	Tiger
9.12	2.11	J1	C9	Leopard
10.12	3.11	J1	D10	Griffon
11.12	4.11	J1	E11	Ox
12.12	5.11	J1	F12	Bat
13.12	6.11	J1	G1	Rat
14.12	7.11	J1	H2	Swallow
15.12	8.11	J1	J3	Pig
16.12	9.11	J1	K4	Porcupine
17.12	10.11	J1	A5	Wolf
18.12	11.11	J1	B6	Dog
19.12	12.11	J1	C7	Pheasant
20.12	13.11	J1	D8	Cock
21.12	14.11	J1	E9	Crow
22.12	15.11	J1	F10	Monkey
23.12	16.11	J1	G11	Gibbon
24.12	17.11	J1	H12	Tapir
25.12	18.11	J1	J1	Sheep
26.12	19.11	J1	K2	Deer
27.12	20.11	J1	A3	Horse
28.12	21.11	J1	B4	Stag
29.12	22.11	J1	C5	Serpent
30.12	23.11	J1	D6	Earthworm
31.12	24.11	J1	E7	Crocodile

1943

Solar date	Lunar date	Month HS/EB	Day HS/EB	Constellation
1. 1	25.11	J1	F8	Dragon
2. 1	26.11	J1	G9	Badger
3. 1	27.11	J1	H10	Hare
4. 1	28.11	J1	J11	Fox
5. 1	29.11	J1	K12	Tiger
6. 1	1.12	K2	A1	Leopard
7. 1	2.12	K2	B2	Griffon
8. 1	3.12	K2	C3	Ox

Solar date	Lunar date	Month HS/EB	Day HS/EB	Constellation	Solar date	Lunar date	Month HS/EB	Day HS/EB	Constellation
9. 1	4.12	K2	D4	Bat	23. 1	18.12	K2	H6	Deer
10. 1	5.12	K2	E5	Rat	24. 1	19.12	K2	J7	Horse
11. 1	6.12	K2	F6	Swallow	25. 1	20.12	K2	K8	Stag
12. 1	7.12	K2	G7	Pig	26. 1	21.12	K2	A9	Serpent
13. 1	8.12	K2	H8	Porcupine	27. 1	22.12	K2	B10	Earthworm
14. 1	9.12	K2	J9	Wolf	28. 1	23.12	K2	C11	Crocodile
15. 1	10.12	K2	K10	Dog	29. 1	24.12	K2	D12	Dragon
16. 1	11.12	K2	A11	Pheasant	30. 1	25.12	K2	E1	Badger
17. 1	12.12	K2	B12	Cock	31. 1	26.12	K2	F2	Hare
18. 1	13.12	K2	C1	Crow	1. 2	27.12	K2	G3	Fox
19. 1	14.12	K2	D2	Monkey	2. 2	28.12	K2	H4	Tiger
20. 1	15.12	K2	E3	Gibbon	3. 2	29.12	K2	J5	Leopard
21. 1	16.12	K2	F4	Tapir	4. 2	30.12	K2	K6	Griffon
22. 1	17.12	K2	G5	Sheep					

KUEI WEI YEAR

Solar date	Lunar date	Month HS/EB	Day HS/EB	Constellation	Solar date	Lunar date	Month HS/EB	Day HS/EB	Constellation
5. 2	1. 1	A3	A7	Ox	31. 3	26. 2	B4	E1	Leopard
6. 2	2. 1	A3	B8	Bat	1. 4	27. 2	B4	F2	Griffon
7. 2	3. 1	A3	C9	Rat	2. 4	28. 2	B4	G3	Ox
8. 2	4. 1	A3	D10	Swallow	3. 4	29. 2	B4	H4	Bat
9. 2	5. 1	A3	E11	Pig	4. 4	30. 2	B4	J5	Rat
10. 2	6. 1	A3	F12	Porcupine	5. 4	1. 3	C5	K6	Swallow
11. 2	7. 1	A3	G1	Wolf	6. 4	2. 3	C5	A7	Pig
12. 2	8. 1	A3	H2	Dog	7. 4	3. 3	C5	B8	Porcupine
13. 2	9. 1	A3	J3	Pheasant	8. 4	4. 3	C5	C9	Wolf
14. 2	10. 1	A3	K4	Cock	9. 4	5. 3	C5	D10	Dog
15. 2	11. 1	A3	A5	Crow	10. 4	6. 3	C5	E11	Pheasant
16. 2	12. 1	A3	B6	Monkey	11. 4	7. 3	C5	F12	Cock
17. 2	13. 1	A3	C7	Gibbon	12. 4	8. 3	C5	G1	Crow
18. 2	14. 1	A3	D8	Tapir	13. 4	9. 3	C5	H2	Monkey
19. 2	15. 1	A3	E9	Sheep	14. 4	10. 3	C5	J3	Gibbon
20. 2	16. 1	A3	F10	Deer	15. 4	11. 3	C5	K4	Tapir
21. 2	17. 1	A3	G11	Horse	16. 4	12. 3	C5	A5	Sheep
22. 2	18. 1	A3	H12	Stag	17. 4	13. 3	C5	B6	Deer
23. 2	19. 1	A3	J1	Serpent	18. 4	14. 3	C5	C7	Horse
24. 2	20. 1	A3	K2	Earthworm	19. 4	15. 3	C5	D8	Stag
25. 2	21. 1	A3	A3	Crocodile	20. 4	16. 3	C5	E9	Serpent
26. 2	22. 1	A3	B4	Dragon	21. 4	17. 3	C5	F10	Earthworm
27. 2	23. 1	A3	C5	Badger	22. 4	18. 3	C5	G11	Crocodile
28. 2	24. 1	A3	D6	Hare	23. 4	19. 3	C5	H12	Dragon
1. 3	25. 1	A3	E7	Fox	24. 4	20. 3	C5	J1	Badger
2. 3	26. 1	A3	F8	Tiger	25. 4	21. 3	C5	K2	Hare
3. 3	27. 1	A3	G9	Leopard	26. 4	22. 3	C5	A3	Fox
4. 3	28. 1	A3	H10	Griffon	27. 4	23. 3	C5	B4	Tiger
5. 3	29. 1	A3	J11	Ox	28. 4	24. 3	C5	C5	Leopard
6. 3	1. 2	B4	K12	Bat	29. 4	25. 3	C5	D6	Griffon
7. 3	2. 2	B4	A1	Rat	30. 4	26. 3	C5	E7	Ox
8. 3	3. 2	B4	B2	Swallow	1. 5	27. 3	C5	F8	Bat
9. 3	4. 2	B4	C3	Pig	2. 5	28. 3	C5	G9	Rat
10. 3	5. 2	B4	D4	Porcupine	3. 5	29. 3	C5	H10	Swallow
11. 3	6. 2	B4	E5	Wolf	4. 5	1. 4	D6	J11	Pig
12. 3	7. 2	B4	F6	Dog	5. 5	2. 4	D6	K12	Porcupine
13. 3	8. 2	B4	G7	Pheasant	6. 5	3. 4	D6	A1	Wolf
14. 3	9. 2	B4	H8	Cock	7. 5	4. 4	D6	B2	Dog
15. 3	10. 2	B4	J9	Crow	8. 5	5. 4	D6	C3	Pheasant
16. 3	11. 2	B4	K10	Monkey	9. 5	6. 4	D6	D4	Cock
17. 3	12. 2	B4	A11	Gibbon	10. 5	7. 4	D6	E5	Crow
18. 3	13. 2	B4	B12	Tapir	11. 5	8. 4	D6	F6	Monkey
19. 3	14. 2	B4	C1	Sheep	12. 5	9. 4	D6	G7	Gibbon
20. 3	15. 2	B4	D2	Deer	13. 5	10. 4	D6	H8	Tapir
21. 3	16. 2	B4	E3	Horse	14. 5	11. 4	D6	J9	Sheep
22. 3	17. 2	B4	F4	Stag	15. 5	12. 4	D6	K10	Deer
23. 3	18. 2	B4	G5	Serpent	16. 5	13. 4	D6	A11	Horse
24. 3	19. 2	B4	H6	Earthworm	17. 5	14. 4	D6	B12	Stag
25. 3	20. 2	B4	J7	Crocodile	18. 5	15. 4	D6	C1	Serpent
26. 3	21. 2	B4	K8	Dragon	19. 5	16. 4	D6	D2	Earthworm
27. 3	22. 2	B4	A9	Badger	20. 5	17. 4	D6	E3	Crocodile
28. 3	23. 2	B4	B10	Hare	21. 5	18. 4	D6	F4	Dragon
29. 3	24. 2	B4	C11	Fox	22. 5	19. 4	D6	G5	Badger
30. 3	25. 2	B4	D12	Tiger	23. 5	20. 4	D6	H6	Hare

Solar date	Lunar date	Month HS/EB	Day HS/EB	Constellation	Solar date	Lunar date	Month HS/EB	Day HS/EB	Constellation
24. 5	21. 4	D6	J7	Fox	5. 8	5. 7	G9	B8	Tapir
25. 5	22. 4	D6	K8	Tiger	6. 8	6. 7	G9	C9	Sheep
26. 5	23. 4	D6	A9	Leopard	7. 8	7. 7	G9	D10	Deer
27. 5	24. 4	D6	B10	Griffon	8. 8	8. 7	G9	E11	Horse
28. 5	25. 4	D6	C11	Ox	9. 8	9. 7	G9	F12	Stag
29. 5	26. 4	D6	D12	Bat	10. 8	10. 7	G9	G1	Serpent
30. 5	27. 4	D6	E1	Rat	11. 8	11. 7	G9	H2	Earthworm
31. 5	28. 4	D6	F2	Swallow	12. 8	12. 7	G9	J3	Crocodile
1. 6	29. 4	D6	G3	Pig	13. 8	13. 7	G9	K4	Dragon
2. 6	30. 4	D6	H4	Porcupine	14. 8	14. 7	G9	A5	Badger
3. 6	1. 5	E7	J5	Wolf	15. 8	15. 7	G9	B6	Hare
4. 6	2. 5	E7	K6	Dog	16. 8	16. 7	G9	C7	Fox
5. 6	3. 5	E7	A7	Pheasant	17. 8	17. 7	G9	D8	Tiger
6. 6	4. 5	E7	B8	Cock	18. 8	18. 7	G9	E9	Leopard
7. 6	5. 5	E7	C9	Crow	19. 8	19. 7	G9	F10	Griffon
8. 6	6. 5	E7	D10	Monkey	20. 8	20. 7	G9	G11	Ox
9. 6	7. 5	E7	E11	Gibbon	21. 8	21. 7	G9	H12	Bat
10. 6	8. 5	E7	F12	Tapir	22. 8	22. 7	G9	J1	Rat
11. 6	9. 5	E7	G1	Sheep	23. 8	23. 7	G9	K2	Swallow
12. 6	10. 5	E7	H2	Deer	24. 8	24. 7	G9	A3	Pig
13. 6	11. 5	E7	J3	Horse	25. 8	25. 7	G9	B4	Porcupine
14. 6	12. 5	E7	K4	Stag	26. 8	26. 7	G9	C5	Wolf
15. 6	13. 5	E7	A5	Serpent	27. 8	27. 7	G9	D6	Dog
16. 6	14. 5	E7	B6	Earthworm	28. 8	28. 7	G9	E7	Pheasant
17. 6	15. 5	E7	C7	Crocodile	29. 8	29. 7	G9	F8	Cock
18. 6	16. 5	E7	D8	Dragon	30. 8	30. 7	G9	G9	Crow
19. 6	17. 5	E7	E9	Badger	31. 8	1. 8	H10	H10	Monkey
20. 6	18. 5	E7	F10	Hare	1. 9	2. 8	H10	J11	Gibbon
21. 6	19. 5	E7	G11	Fox	2. 9	3. 8	H10	K12	Tapir
22. 6	20. 5	E7	H12	Tiger	3. 9	4. 8	H10	A1	Sheep
23. 6	21. 5	E7	J1	Leopard	4. 9	5. 8	H10	B2	Deer
24. 6	22. 5	E7	K2	Griffon	5. 9	6. 8	H10	C3	Horse
25. 6	23. 5	E7	A3	Ox	6. 9	7. 8	H10	D4	Stag
26. 6	24. 5	E7	B4	Bat	7. 9	8. 8	H10	E5	Serpent
27. 6	25. 5	E7	C5	Rat	8. 9	9. 8	H10	F6	Earthworm
28. 6	26. 5	E7	D6	Swallow	9. 9	10. 8	H10	G7	Crocodile
29. 6	27. 5	E7	E7	Pig	10. 9	11. 8	H10	H8	Dragon
30. 6	28. 5	E7	F8	Porcupine	11. 9	12. 8	H10	J9	Badger
1. 7	29. 5	E7	G9	Wolf	12. 9	13. 8	H10	K10	Hare
2. 7	1. 6	F8	H10	Dog	13. 9	14. 8	H10	A11	Fox
3. 7	2. 6	F8	J11	Pheasant	14. 9	15. 8	H10	B12	Tiger
4. 7	3. 6	F8	K12	Cock	15. 9	16. 8	H10	C1	Leopard
5. 7	4. 6	F8	A1	Crow	16. 9	17. 8	H10	D2	Griffon
6. 7	5. 6	F8	B2	Monkey	17. 9	18. 8	H10	E3	Ox
7. 7	6. 6	F8	C3	Gibbon	18. 9	19. 8	H10	F4	Bat
8. 7	7. 6	F8	D4	Tapir	19. 9	20. 8	H10	G5	Rat
9. 7	8. 6	F8	E5	Sheep	20. 9	21. 8	H10	H6	Swallow
10. 7	9. 6	F8	F6	Deer	21. 9	22. 8	H10	J7	Pig
11. 7	10. 6	F8	G7	Horse	22. 9	23. 8	H10	K8	Porcupine
12. 7	11. 6	F8	H8	Stag	23. 9	24. 8	H10	A9	Wolf
13. 7	12. 6	F8	J9	Serpent	24. 9	25. 8	H10	B10	Dog
14. 7	13. 6	F8	K10	Earthworm	25. 9	26. 8	H10	C11	Pheasant
15. 7	14. 6	F8	A11	Crocodile	26. 9	27. 8	H10	D12	Cock
16. 7	15. 6	F8	B12	Dragon	27. 9	28. 8	H10	E1	Crow
17. 7	16. 6	F8	C1	Badger	28. 9	29. 8	H10	F2	Monkey
18. 7	17. 6	F8	D2	Hare	29. 9	1. 9	J11	G3	Gibbon
19. 7	18. 6	F8	E3	Fox	30. 9	2. 9	J11	H4	Tapir
20. 7	19. 6	F8	F4	Tiger	1.10	3. 9	J11	J5	Sheep
21. 7	20. 6	F8	G5	Leopard	2.10	4. 9	J11	K6	Deer
22. 7	21. 6	F8	H6	Griffon	3.10	5. 9	J11	A7	Horse
23. 7	22. 6	F8	J7	Ox	4.10	6. 9	J11	B8	Stag
24. 7	23. 6	F8	K8	Bat	5.10	7. 9	J11	C9	Serpent
25. 7	24. 6	F8	A9	Rat	6.10	8. 9	J11	D10	Earthworm
26. 7	25. 6	F8	B10	Swallow	7.10	9. 9	J11	E11	Crocodile
27. 7	26. 6	F8	C11	Pig	8.10	10. 9	J11	F12	Dragon
28. 7	27. 6	F8	D12	Porcupine	9.10	11. 9	J11	G1	Badger
29. 7	28. 6	F8	E1	Wolf	10.10	12. 9	J11	H2	Hare
30. 7	29. 6	F8	F2	Dog	11.10	13. 9	J11	J3	Fox
31. 7	30. 6	F8	G3	Pheasant	12.10	14. 9	J11	K4	Tiger
1. 8	1. 7	G9	H4	Cock	13.10	15. 9	J11	A5	Leopard
2. 8	2. 7	G9	J5	Crow	14.10	16. 9	J11	B6	Griffon
3. 8	3. 7	G9	K6	Monkey	15.10	17. 9	J11	C7	Ox
4. 8	4. 7	G9	A7	Gibbon	16.10	18. 9	J11	D8	Bat

Solar date	Lunar date	Month HS/EB	Day HS/EB	Constellation	Solar date	Lunar date	Month HS/EB	Day HS/EB	Constellation
17.10	19. 9	J11	E9	Rat	7.12	11.11	A1	F12	Tiger
18.10	20. 9	J11	F10	Swallow	8.12	12.11	A1	G1	Leopard
19.10	21. 9	J11	G11	Pig	9.12	13.11	A1	H2	Griffon
20.10	22. 9	J11	H12	Porcupine	10.12	14.11	A1	J3	Ox
21.10	23. 9	J11	J1	Wolf	11.12	15.11	A1	K4	Bat
22.10	24. 9	J11	K2	Dog	12.12	16.11	A1	A5	Rat
23.10	25. 9	J11	A3	Pheasant	13.12	17.11	A1	B6	Swallow
24.10	26. 9	J11	B4	Cock	14.12	18.11	A1	C7	Pig
25.10	27. 9	J11	C5	Crow	15.12	19.11	A1	D8	Porcupine
26.10	28. 9	J11	D6	Monkey	16.12	20.11	A1	E9	Wolf
27.10	29. 9	J11	E7	Gibbon	17.12	21.11	A1	F10	Dog
28.10	30. 9	J11	F8	Tapir	18.12	22.11	A1	G11	Pheasant
29.10	1.10	K12	G9	Sheep	19.12	23.11	A1	H12	Cock
30.10	2.10	K12	H10	Deer	20.12	24.11	A1	J1	Crow
31.10	3.10	K12	J11	Horse	21.12	25.11	A1	K2	Monkey
1.11	4.10	K12	K12	Stag	22.12	26.11	A1	A3	Gibbon
2.11	5.10	K12	A1	Serpent	23.12	27.11	A1	B4	Tapir
3.11	6.10	K12	B2	Earthworm	24.12	28.11	A1	C5	Sheep
4.11	7.10	K12	C3	Crocodile	25.12	29.11	A1	D6	Deer
5.11	8.10	K12	D4	Dragon	26.12	30.11	A1	E7	Horse
6.11	9.10	K12	E5	Badger	27.12	1.12	B2	F8	Stag
7.11	10.10	K12	F6	Hare	28.12	2.12	B2	G9	Serpent
8.11	11.10	K12	G7	Fox	29.12	3.12	B2	H10	Earthworm
9.11	12.10	K12	H8	Tiger	30.12	4.12	B2	J11	Crocodile
10.11	13.10	K12	J9	Leopard	31.12	5.12	B2	K12	Dragon
11.11	14.10	K12	K10	Griffon	**1944**				
12.11	15.10	K12	A11	Ox					
13.11	16.10	K12	B12	Bat	1. 1	6.12	B2	A1	Badger
14.11	17.10	K12	C1	Rat	2. 1	7.12	B2	B2	Hare
15.11	18.10	K12	D2	Swallow	3. 1	8.12	B2	C3	Fox
16.11	19.10	K12	E3	Pig	4. 1	9.12	B2	D4	Tiger
17.11	20.10	K12	F4	Porcupine	5. 1	10.12	B2	E5	Leopard
18.11	21.10	K12	G5	Wolf	6. 1	11.12	B2	F6	Griffon
19.11	22.10	K12	H6	Dog	7. 1	12.12	B2	G7	Ox
20.11	23.10	K12	J7	Pheasant	8. 1	13.12	B2	H8	Bat
21.11	24.10	K12	K8	Cock	9. 1	14.12	B2	J9	Rat
22.11	25.10	K12	A9	Crow	10. 1	15.12	B2	K10	Swallow
23.11	26.10	K12	B10	Monkey	11. 1	16.12	B2	A11	Pig
24.11	27.10	K12	C11	Gibbon	12. 1	17.12	B2	B12	Porcupine
25.11	28.10	K12	D12	Tapir	13. 1	18.12	B2	C1	Wolf
26.11	29.10	K12	E1	Sheep	14. 1	19.12	B2	D2	Dog
27.11	1.11	A1	F2	Deer	15. 1	20.12	B2	E3	Pheasant
28.11	2.11	A1	G3	Horse	16. 1	21.12	B2	F4	Cock
29.11	3.11	A1	H4	Stag	17. 1	22.12	B2	G5	Crow
30.11	4.11	A1	J5	Serpent	18. 1	23.12	B2	H6	Monkey
1.12	5.11	A1	K6	Earthworm	19. 1	24.12	B2	J7	Gibbon
2.12	6.11	A1	A7	Crocodile	20. 1	25.12	B2	K8	Tapir
3.12	7.11	A1	B8	Dragon	21. 1	26.12	B2	A9	Sheep
4.12	8.11	A1	C9	Badger	22. 1	27.12	B2	B10	Deer
5.12	9.11	A1	D10	Hare	23. 1	28.12	B2	C11	Horse
6.12	10.11	A1	E11	Fox	24. 1	29.12	B2	D12	Stag

CHIA SHEN YEAR

Solar date	Lunar date	Month HS/EB	Day HS/EB	Constellation	Solar date	Lunar date	Month HS/EB	Day HS/EB	Constellation
25. 1	1. 1	C3	E1	Serpent	11. 2	18. 1	C3	B6	Dog
26. 1	2. 1	C3	F2	Earthworm	12. 2	19. 1	C3	C7	Pheasant
27. 1	3. 1	C3	G3	Crocodile	13. 2	20. 1	C3	D8	Cock
28. 1	4. 1	C3	H4	Dragon	14. 2	21. 1	C3	E9	Crow
29. 1	5. 1	C3	J5	Badger	15. 2	22. 1	C3	F10	Monkey
30. 1	6. 1	C3	K6	Hare	16. 2	23. 1	C3	G11	Gibbon
31. 1	7. 1	C3	A7	Fox	17. 2	24. 1	C3	H12	Tapir
1. 2	8. 1	C3	B8	Tiger	18. 2	25. 1	C3	J1	Sheep
2. 2	9. 1	C3	C9	Leopard	19. 2	26. 1	C3	K2	Deer
3. 2	10. 1	C3	D10	Griffon	20. 2	27. 1	C3	A3	Horse
4. 2	11. 1	C3	E11	Ox	21. 2	28. 1	C3	B4	Stag
5. 2	12. 1	C3	F12	Bat	22. 2	29. 1	C3	C5	Serpent
6. 2	13. 1	C3	G1	Rat	23. 2	30. 1	C3	D6	Earthworm
7. 2	14. 1	C3	H2	Swallow	24. 2	1. 2	D4	E7	Crocodile
8. 2	15. 1	C3	J3	Pig	25. 2	2. 2	D4	F8	Dragon
9. 2	16. 1	C3	K4	Porcupine	26. 2	3. 2	D4	G9	Badger
10. 2	17. 1	C3	A5	Wolf	27. 2	4. 2	D4	H10	Hare

Solar date	Lunar date	Month HS/EB	Day HS/EB	Constellation	Solar date	Lunar date	Month HS/EB	Day HS/EB	Constellation
28. 2	5. 2	D4	J11	Fox	11. 5	19. 4	F6	B12	Tapir
29. 2	6. 2	D4	K12	Tiger	12. 5	20. 4	F6	C1	Sheep
1. 3	7. 2	D4	A1	Leopard	13. 5	21. 4	F6	D2	Deer
2. 3	8. 2	D4	B2	Griffon	14. 5	22. 4	F6	E3	Horse
3. 3	9. 2	D4	C3	Ox	15. 5	23. 4	F6	F4	Stag
4. 3	10. 2	D4	D4	Bat	16. 5	24. 4	F6	G5	Serpent
5. 3	11. 2	D4	E5	Rat	17. 5	25. 4	F6	H6	Earthworm
6. 3	12. 2	D4	F6	Swallow	18. 5	26. 4	F6	J7	Crocodile
7. 3	13. 2	D4	G7	Pig	19. 5	27. 4	F6	K8	Dragon
8. 3	14. 2	D4	H8	Porcupine	20. 5	28. 4	F6	A9	Badger
9. 3	15. 2	D4	J9	Wolf	21. 5	29. 4	F6	B10	Hare
10. 3	16. 2	D4	K10	Dog	22. 5	*1. 4*	*F6*	C11	Fox
11. 3	17. 2	D4	A11	Pheasant	23. 5	*2. 4*	*F6*	D12	Tiger
12. 3	18. 2	D4	B12	Cock	24. 5	*3. 4*	*F6*	E1	Leopard
13. 3	19. 2	D4	C1	Crow	25. 5	*4. 4*	*F6*	F2	Griffon
14. 3	20. 2	D4	D2	Monkey	26. 5	*5. 4*	*F6*	G3	Ox
15. 3	21. 2	D4	E3	Gibbon	27. 5	*6. 4*	*F6*	H4	Bat
16. 3	22. 2	D4	F4	Tapir	28. 5	*7. 4*	*F6*	J5	Rat
17. 3	23. 2	D4	G5	Sheep	29. 5	*8. 4*	*F6*	K6	Swallow
18. 3	24. 2	D4	H6	Deer	30. 5	*9. 4*	*F6*	A7	Pig
19. 3	25. 2	D4	J7	Horse	31. 5	*10. 4*	*F6*	B8	Porcupine
20. 3	26. 2	D4	K8	Stag	1. 6	*11. 4*	*F6*	C9	Wolf
21. 3	27. 2	D4	A9	Serpent	2. 6	*12. 4*	*F6*	D10	Dog
22. 3	28. 2	D4	B10	Earthworm	3. 6	*13. 4*	*F6*	E11	Pheasant
23. 3	29. 2	D4	C11	Crocodile	4. 6	*14. 4*	*F6*	F12	Cock
24. 3	1. 3	E5	D12	Dragon	5. 6	*15. 4*	*F6*	G1	Crow
25. 3	2. 3	E5	E1	Badger	6. 6	*16. 4*	*F6*	H2	Monkey
26. 3	3. 3	E5	F2	Hare	7. 6	*17. 4*	*F6*	J3	Gibbon
27. 3	4. 3	E5	G3	Fox	8. 6	*18. 4*	*F6*	K4	Tapir
28. 3	5. 3	E5	H4	Tiger	9. 6	*19. 4*	*F6*	A5	Sheep
29. 3	6. 3	E5	J5	Leopard	10. 6	*20. 4*	*F6*	B6	Deer
30. 3	7. 3	E5	K6	Griffon	11. 6	*21. 4*	*F6*	C7	Horse
31. 3	8. 3	E5	A7	Ox	12. 6	*22. 4*	*F6*	D8	Stag
1. 4	9. 3	E5	B8	Bat	13. 6	*23. 4*	*F6*	E9	Serpent
2. 4	10. 3	E5	C9	Rat	14. 6	*24. 4*	*F6*	F10	Earthworm
3. 4	11. 3	E5	D10	Swallow	15. 6	*25. 4*	*F6*	G11	Crocodile
4. 4	12. 3	E5	E11	Pig	16. 6	*26. 4*	*F6*	H12	Dragon
5. 4	13. 3	E5	F12	Porcupine	17. 6	*27. 4*	*F6*	J1	Badger
6. 4	14. 3	E5	G1	Wolf	18. 6	*28. 4*	*F6*	K2	Hare
7. 4	15. 3	E5	H2	Dog	19. 6	*29. 4*	*F6*	A3	Fox
8. 4	16. 3	E5	J3	Pheasant	20. 6	*30. 4*	*F6*	B4	Tiger
9. 4	17. 3	E5	K4	Cock	21. 6	1. 5	G7	C5	Leopard
10. 4	18. 3	E5	A5	Crow	22. 6	2. 5	G7	D6	Griffon
11. 4	19. 3	E5	B6	Monkey	23. 6	3. 5	G7	E7	Ox
12. 4	20. 3	E5	C7	Gibbon	24. 6	4. 5	G7	F8	Bat
13. 4	21. 3	E5	D8	Tapir	25. 6	5. 5	G7	G9	Rat
14. 4	22. 3	E5	E9	Sheep	26. 6	6. 5	G7	H10	Swallow
15. 4	23. 3	E5	F10	Deer	27. 6	7. 5	G7	J11	Pig
16. 4	24. 3	E5	G11	Horse	28. 6	8. 5	G7	K12	Porcupine
17. 4	25. 3	E5	H12	Stag	29. 6	9. 5	G7	A1	Wolf
18. 4	26. 3	E5	J1	Serpent	30. 6	10. 5	G7	B2	Dog
19. 4	27. 3	E5	K2	Earthworm	1. 7	11. 5	G7	C3	Pheasant
20. 4	28. 3	E5	A3	Crocodile	2. 7	12. 5	G7	D4	Cock
21. 4	29. 3	E5	B4	Dragon	3. 7	13. 5	G7	E5	Crow
22. 4	30. 3	E5	C5	Badger	4. 7	14. 5	G7	F6	Monkey
23. 4	1. 4	F6	D6	Hare	5. 7	15. 5	G7	G7	Gibbon
24. 4	2. 4	F6	E7	Fox	6. 7	16. 5	G7	H8	Tapir
25. 4	3. 4	F6	F8	Tiger	7. 7	17. 5	G7	J9	Sheep
26. 4	4. 4	F6	G9	Leopard	8. 7	18. 5	G7	K10	Deer
27. 4	5. 4	F6	H10	Griffon	9. 7	19. 5	G7	A11	Horse
28. 4	6. 4	F6	J11	Ox	10. 7	20. 5	G7	B12	Stag
29. 4	7. 4	F6	K12	Bat	11. 7	21. 5	G7	C1	Serpent
30. 4	8. 4	F6	A1	Rat	12. 7	22. 5	G7	D2	Earthworm
1. 5	9. 4	F6	B2	Swallow	13. 7	23. 5	G7	E3	Crocodile
2. 5	10. 4	F6	C3	Pig	14. 7	24. 5	G7	F4	Dragon
3. 5	11. 4	F6	D4	Porcupine	15. 7	25. 5	G7	G5	Badger
4. 5	12. 4	F6	E5	Wolf	16. 7	26. 5	G7	H6	Hare
5. 5	13. 4	F6	F6	Dog	17. 7	27. 5	G7	J7	Fox
6. 5	14. 4	F6	G7	Pheasant	18. 7	28. 5	G7	K8	Tiger
7. 5	15. 4	F6	H8	Cock	19. 7	29. 5	G7	A9	Leopard
8. 5	16. 4	F6	J9	Crow	20. 7	1. 6	H8	B10	Griffon
9. 5	17. 4	F6	K10	Monkey	21. 7	2. 6	H8	C11	Ox
10. 5	18. 4	F6	A11	Gibbon	22. 7	3. 6	H8	D12	Bat

Solar date	Lunar date	Month HS/EB	Day HS/EB	Constellation	Solar date	Lunar date	Month HS/EB	Day HS/EB	Constellation
23. 7	4. 6	H8	E1	Rat	4.10	18. 8	K10	H2	Earthworm
24. 7	5. 6	H8	F2	Swallow	5.10	19. 8	K10	J3	Crocodile
25. 7	6. 6	H8	G3	Pig	6.10	20. 8	K10	K4	Dragon
26. 7	7. 6	H8	H4	Porcupine	7.10	21. 8	K10	A5	Badger
27. 7	8. 6	H8	J5	Wolf	8.10	22. 8	K10	B6	Hare
28. 7	9. 6	H8	K6	Dog	9.10	23. 8	K10	C7	Fox
29. 7	10. 6	H8	A7	Pheasant	10.10	24. 8	K10	D8	Tiger
30. 7	11. 6	H8	B8	Cock	11.10	25. 8	K10	E9	Leopard
31. 7	12. 6	H8	C9	Crow	12.10	26. 8	K10	F10	Griffon
1. 8	13. 6	H8	D10	Monkey	13.10	27. 8	K10	G11	Ox
2. 8	14. 6	H8	E11	Gibbon	14.10	28. 8	K10	H12	Bat
3. 8	15. 6	H8	F12	Tapir	15.10	29. 8	K10	J1	Rat
4. 8	16. 6	H8	G1	Sheep	16.10	30. 8	K10	K2	Swallow
5. 8	17. 6	H8	H2	Deer	17.10	1. 9	A11	A3	Pig
6. 8	18. 6	H8	J3	Horse	18.10	2. 9	A11	B4	Porcupine
7. 8	19. 6	H8	K4	Stag	19.10	3. 9	A11	C5	Wolf
8. 8	20. 6	H8	A5	Serpent	20.10	4. 9	A11	D6	Dog
9. 8	21. 6	H8	B6	Earthworm	21.10	5. 9	A11	E7	Pheasant
10. 8	22. 6	H8	C7	Crocodile	22.10	6. 9	A11	F8	Cock
11. 8	23. 6	H8	D8	Dragon	23.10	7. 9	A11	G9	Crow
12. 8	24. 6	H8	E9	Badger	24.10	8. 9	A11	H10	Monkey
13. 8	25. 6	H8	F10	Hare	25.10	9. 9	A11	J11	Gibbon
14. 8	26. 6	H8	G11	Fox	26.10	10. 9	A11	K12	Tapir
15. 8	27. 6	H8	H12	Tiger	27.10	11. 9	A11	A1	Sheep
16. 8	28. 6	H8	J1	Leopard	28.10	12. 9	A11	B2	Deer
17. 8	29. 6	H8	K2	Griffon	29.10	13. 9	A11	C3	Horse
18. 8	30. 6	H8	A3	Ox	30.10	14. 9	A11	D4	Stag
19. 8	1. 7	J9	B4	Bat	31.10	15. 9	A11	E5	Serpent
20. 8	2. 7	J9	C5	Rat	1.11	16. 9	A11	F6	Earthworm
21. 8	3. 7	J9	D6	Swallow	2.11	17. 9	A11	G7	Crocodile
22. 8	4. 7	J9	E7	Pig	3.11	18. 9	A11	H8	Dragon
23. 8	5. 7	J9	F8	Porcupine	4.11	19. 9	A11	J9	Badger
24. 8	6. 7	J9	G9	Wolf	5.11	20. 9	A11	K10	Hare
25. 8	7. 7	J9	H10	Dog	6.11	21. 9	A11	A11	Fox
26. 8	8. 7	J9	J11	Pheasant	7.11	22. 9	A11	B12	Tiger
27. 8	9. 7	J9	K12	Cock	8.11	23. 9	A11	C1	Leopard
28. 8	10. 7	J9	A1	Crow	9.11	24. 9	A11	D2	Griffon
29. 8	11. 7	J9	B2	Monkey	10.11	25. 9	A11	E3	Ox
30. 8	12. 7	J9	C3	Gibbon	11.11	26. 9	A11	F4	Bat
31. 8	13. 7	J9	D4	Tapir	12.11	27. 9	A11	G5	Rat
1. 9	14. 7	J9	E5	Sheep	13.11	28. 9	A11	H6	Swallow
2. 9	15. 7	J9	F6	Deer	14.11	29. 9	A11	J7	Pig
3. 9	16. 7	J9	G7	Horse	15.11	30. 9	A11	K8	Porcupine
4. 9	17. 7	J9	H8	Stag	16.11	1.10	B12	A9	Wolf
5. 9	18. 7	J9	J9	Serpent	17.11	2.10	B12	B10	Dog
6. 9	19. 7	J9	K10	Earthworm	18.11	3.10	B12	C11	Pheasant
7. 9	20. 7	J9	A11	Crocodile	19.11	4.10	B12	D12	Cock
8. 9	21. 7	J9	B12	Dragon	20.11	5.10	B12	E1	Crow
9. 9	22. 7	J9	C1	Badger	21.11	6.10	B12	F2	Monkey
10. 9	23. 7	J9	D2	Hare	22.11	7.10	B12	G3	Gibbon
11. 9	24. 7	J9	E3	Fox	23.11	8.10	B12	H4	Tapir
12. 9	25. 7	J9	F4	Tiger	24.11	9.10	B12	J5	Sheep
13. 9	26. 7	J9	G5	Leopard	25.11	10.10	B12	K6	Deer
14. 9	27. 7	J9	H6	Griffon	26.11	11.10	B12	A7	Horse
15. 9	28. 7	J9	J7	Ox	27.11	12.10	B12	B8	Stag
16. 9	29. 7	J9	K8	Bat	28.11	13.10	B12	C9	Serpent
17. 9	1. 8	K10	A9	Rat	29.11	14.10	B12	D10	Earthworm
18. 9	2. 8	K10	B10	Swallow	30.11	15.10	B12	E11	Crocodile
19. 9	3. 8	K10	C11	Pig	1.12	16.10	B12	F12	Dragon
20. 9	4. 8	K10	D12	Porcupine	2.12	17.10	B12	G1	Badger
21. 9	5. 8	K10	E1	Wolf	3.12	18.10	B12	H2	Hare
22. 9	6. 8	K10	F2	Dog	4.12	19.10	B12	J3	Fox
23. 9	7. 8	K10	G3	Pheasant	5.12	20.10	B12	K4	Tiger
24. 9	8. 8	K10	H4	Cock	6.12	21.10	B12	A5	Leopard
25. 9	9. 8	K10	J5	Crow	7.12	22.10	B12	B6	Griffon
26. 9	10. 8	K10	K6	Monkey	8.12	23.10	B12	C7	Ox
27. 9	11. 8	K10	A7	Gibbon	9.12	24.10	B12	D8	Bat
28. 9	12. 8	K10	B8	Tapir	10.12	25.10	B12	E9	Rat
29. 9	13. 8	K10	C9	Sheep	11.12	26.10	B12	F10	Swallow
30. 9	14. 8	K10	D10	Deer	12.12	27.10	B12	G11	Pig
1.10	15. 8	K10	E11	Horse	13.12	28.10	B12	H12	Porcupine
2.10	16. 8	K10	F12	Stag	14.12	29.10	B12	J1	Wolf
3.10	17. 8	K10	G1	Serpent	15.12	1.11	C1	K2	Dog

Solar date	Lunar date	Month HS/EB	Day HS/EB	Constellation	Solar date	Lunar date	Month HS/EB	Day HS/EB	Constellation
16.12	2.11	C1	A3	Pheasant	14. 1	1.12	D2	K8	Cock
17.12	3.11	C1	B4	Cock	15. 1	2.12	D2	A9	Crow
18.12	4.11	C1	C5	Crow	16. 1	3.12	D2	B10	Monkey
19.12	5.11	C1	D6	Monkey	17. 1	4.12	D2	C11	Gibbon
20.12	6.11	C1	E7	Gibbon	18. 1	5.12	D2	D12	Tapir
21.12	7.11	C1	F8	Tapir	19. 1	6.12	D2	E1	Sheep
22.12	8.11	C1	G9	Sheep	20. 1	7.12	D2	F2	Deer
23.12	9.11	C1	H10	Deer	21. 1	8.12	D2	G3	Horse
24.12	10.11	C1	J11	Horse	22. 1	9.12	D2	H4	Stag
25.12	11.11	C1	K12	Stag	23. 1	10.12	D2	J5	Serpent
26.12	12.11	C1	A1	Serpent	24. 1	11.12	D2	K6	Earthworm
27.12	13.11	C1	B2	Earthworm	25. 1	12.12	D2	A7	Crocodile
28.12	14.11	C1	C3	Crocodile	26. 1	13.12	D2	B8	Dragon
29.12	15.11	C1	D4	Dragon	27. 1	14.12	D2	C9	Badger
30.12	16.11	C1	E5	Badger	28. 1	15.12	D2	D10	Hare
31.12	17.11	C1	F6	Hare	29. 1	16.12	D2	E11	Fox
1945					30. 1	17.12	D2	F12	Tiger
1. 1	18.11	C1	G7	Fox	31. 1	18.12	D2	G1	Leopard
2. 1	19.11	C1	H8	Tiger	1. 2	19.12	D2	H2	Griffon
3. 1	20.11	C1	J9	Leopard	2. 2	20.12	D2	J3	Ox
4. 1	21.11	C1	K10	Griffon	3. 2	21.12	D2	K4	Bat
5. 1	22.11	C1	A11	Ox	4. 2	22.12	D2	A5	Rat
6. 1	23.11	C1	B12	Bat	5. 2	23.12	D2	B6	Swallow
7. 1	24.11	C1	C1	Rat	6. 2	24.12	D2	C7	Pig
8. 1	25.11	C1	D2	Swallow	7. 2	25.12	D2	D8	Porcupine
9. 1	26.11	C1	E3	Pig	8. 2	26.12	D2	E9	Wolf
10. 1	27.11	C1	F4	Porcupine	9. 2	27.12	D2	F10	Dog
11. 1	28.11	C1	G5	Wolf	10. 2	28.12	D2	G11	Pheasant
12. 1	29.11	C1	H6	Dog	11. 2	29.12	D2	H12	Cock
13. 1	30.11	C1	J7	Pheasant	12. 2	30.12	D2	J1	Crow

YI YU YEAR

Solar date	Lunar date	Month HS/EB	Day HS/EB	Constellation	Solar date	Lunar date	Month HS/EB	Day HS/EB	Constellation
13. 2	1. 1	E3	K2	Monkey	22. 3	9. 2	F4	G3	Crocodile
14. 2	2. 1	E3	A3	Gibbon	23. 3	10. 2	F4	H4	Dragon
15. 2	3. 1	E3	B4	Tapir	24. 3	11. 2	F4	J5	Badger
16. 2	4. 1	E3	C5	Sheep	25. 3	12. 2	F4	K6	Hare
17. 2	5. 1	E3	D6	Deer	26. 3	13. 2	F4	A7	Fox
18. 2	6. 1	E3	E7	Horse	27. 3	14. 2	F4	B8	Tiger
19. 2	7. 1	E3	F8	Stag	28. 3	15. 2	F4	C9	Leopard
20. 2	8. 1	E3	G9	Serpent	29. 3	16. 2	F4	D10	Griffon
21. 2	9. 1	E3	H10	Earthworm	30. 3	17. 2	F4	E11	Ox
22. 2	10. 1	E3	J11	Crocodile	31. 3	18. 2	F4	F12	Bat
23. 2	11. 1	E3	K12	Dragon	1. 4	19. 2	F4	G1	Rat
24. 2	12. 1	E3	A1	Badger	2. 4	20. 2	F4	H2	Swallow
25. 2	13. 1	E3	B2	Hare	3. 4	21. 2	F4	J3	Pig
26. 2	14. 1	E3	C3	Fox	4. 4	22. 2	F4	K4	Porcupine
27. 2	15. 1	E3	D4	Tiger	5. 4	23. 2	F4	A5	Wolf
28. 2	16. 1	E3	E5	Leopard	6. 4	24. 2	F4	B6	Dog
1. 3	17. 1	E3	F6	Griffon	7. 4	25. 2	F4	C7	Pheasant
2. 3	18. 1	E3	G7	Ox	8. 4	26. 2	F4	D8	Cock
3. 3	19. 1	E3	H8	Bat	9. 4	27. 2	F4	E9	Crow
4. 3	20. 1	E3	J9	Rat	10. 4	28. 2	F4	F10	Monkey
5. 3	21. 1	E3	K10	Swallow	11. 4	29. 2	F4	G11	Gibbon
6. 3	22. 1	E3	A11	Pig	12. 4	1. 3	G5	H12	Tapir
7. 3	23. 1	E3	B12	Porcupine	13. 4	2. 3	G5	J1	Sheep
8. 3	24. 1	E3	C1	Wolf	14. 4	3. 3	G5	K2	Deer
9. 3	25. 1	E3	D2	Dog	15. 4	4. 3	G5	A3	Horse
10. 3	26. 1	E3	E3	Pheasant	16. 4	5. 3	G5	B4	Stag
11. 3	27. 1	E3	F4	Cock	17. 4	6. 3	G5	C5	Serpent
12. 3	28. 1	E3	G5	Crow	18. 4	7. 3	G5	D6	Earthworm
13. 3	29. 1	E3	H6	Monkey	19. 4	8. 3	G5	E7	Crocodile
14. 3	1. 2	F4	J7	Gibbon	20. 4	9. 3	G5	F8	Dragon
15. 3	2. 2	F4	K8	Tapir	21. 4	10. 3	G5	G9	Badger
16. 3	3. 2	F4	A9	Sheep	22. 4	11. 3	G5	H10	Hare
17. 3	4. 2	F4	B10	Deer	23. 4	12. 3	G5	J11	Fox
18. 3	5. 2	F4	C11	Horse	24. 4	13. 3	G5	K12	Tiger
19. 3	6. 2	F4	D12	Stag	25. 4	14. 3	G5	A1	Leopard
20. 3	7. 2	F4	E1	Serpent	26. 4	15. 3	G5	B2	Griffon
21. 3	8. 2	F4	F2	Earthworm	27. 4	16. 3	G5	C3	Ox

Solar date	Lunar date	Month HS/EB	Day HS/EB	Constellation	Solar date	Lunar date	Month HS/EB	Day HS/EB	Constellation
28. 4	17. 3	G5	D4	Bat	10. 7	2. 6	K8	G5	Serpent
29. 4	18. 3	G5	E5	Rat	11. 7	3. 6	K8	H6	Earthworm
30. 4	19. 3	G5	F6	Swallow	12. 7	4. 6	K8	J7	Crocodile
1. 5	20. 3	G5	G7	Pig	13. 7	5. 6	K8	K8	Dragon
2. 5	21. 3	G5	H8	Porcupine	14. 7	6. 6	K8	A9	Badger
3. 5	22. 3	G5	J9	Wolf	15. 7	7. 6	K8	B10	Hare
4. 5	23. 3	G5	K10	Dog	16. 7	8. 6	K8	C11	Fox
5. 5	24. 3	G5	A11	Pheasant	17. 7	9. 6	K8	D12	Tiger
6. 5	25. 3	G5	B12	Cock	18. 7	10. 6	K8	E1	Leopard
7. 5	26. 3	G5	C1	Crow	19. 7	11. 6	K8	F2	Griffon
8. 5	27. 3	G5	D2	Monkey	20. 7	12. 6	K8	G3	Ox
9. 5	28. 3	G5	E3	Gibbon	21. 7	13. 6	K8	H4	Bat
10. 5	29. 3	G5	F4	Tapir	22. 7	14. 6	K8	J5	Rat
11. 5	30. 3	G5	G5	Sheep	23. 7	15. 6	K8	K6	Swallow
12. 5	1. 4	H6	H6	Deer	24. 7	16. 6	K8	A7	Pig
13. 5	2. 4	H6	J7	Horse	25. 7	17. 6	K8	B8	Porcupine
14. 5	3. 4	H6	K8	Stag	26. 7	18. 6	K8	C9	Wolf
15. 5	4. 4	H6	A9	Serpent	27. 7	19. 6	K8	D10	Dog
16. 5	5. 4	H6	B10	Earthworm	28. 7	20. 6	K8	E11	Pheasant
17. 5	6. 4	H6	C11	Crocodile	29. 7	21. 6	K8	F12	Cock
18. 5	7. 4	H6	D12	Dragon	30. 7	22. 6	K8	G1	Crow
19. 5	8. 4	H6	E1	Badger	31. 7	23. 6	K8	H2	Monkey
20. 5	9. 4	H6	F2	Hare	1. 8	24. 6	K8	J3	Gibbon
21. 5	10. 4	H6	G3	Fox	2. 8	25. 6	K8	K4	Tapir
22. 5	11. 4	H6	H4	Tiger	3. 8	26. 6	K8	A5	Sheep
23. 5	12. 4	H6	J5	Leopard	4. 8	27. 6	K8	B6	Deer
24. 5	13. 4	H6	K6	Griffon	5. 8	28. 6	K8	C7	Horse
25. 5	14. 4	H6	A7	Ox	6. 8	29. 6	K8	D8	Stag
26. 5	15. 4	H6	B8	Bat	7. 8	30. 6	K8	E9	Serpent
27. 5	16. 4	H6	C9	Rat	8. 8	1. 7	A9	F10	Earthworm
28. 5	17. 4	H6	D10	Swallow	9. 8	2. 7	A9	G11	Crocodile
29. 5	18. 4	H6	E11	Pig	10. 8	3. 7	A9	H12	Dragon
30. 5	19. 4	H6	F12	Porcupine	11. 8	4. 7	A9	J1	Badger
31. 5	20. 4	H6	G1	Wolf	12. 8	5. 7	A9	K2	Hare
1. 6	21. 4	H6	H2	Dog	13. 8	6. 7	A9	A3	Fox
2. 6	22. 4	H6	J3	Pheasant	14. 8	7. 7	A9	B4	Tiger
3. 6	23. 4	H6	K4	Cock	15. 8	8. 7	A9	C5	Leopard
4. 6	24. 4	H6	A5	Crow	16. 8	9. 7	A9	D6	Griffon
5. 6	25. 4	H6	B6	Monkey	17. 8	10. 7	A9	E7	Ox
6. 6	26. 4	H6	C7	Gibbon	18. 8	11. 7	A9	F8	Bat
7. 6	27. 4	H6	D8	Tapir	19. 8	12. 7	A9	G9	Rat
8. 6	28. 4	H6	E9	Sheep	20. 8	13. 7	A9	H10	Swallow
9. 6	29. 4	H6	F10	Deer	21. 8	14. 7	A9	J11	Pig
10. 6	1. 5	J7	G11	Horse	22. 8	15. 7	A9	K12	Porcupine
11. 6	2. 5	J7	H12	Stag	23. 8	16. 7	A9	A1	Wolf
12. 6	3. 5	J7	J1	Serpent	24. 8	17. 7	A9	B2	Dog
13. 6	4. 5	J7	K2	Earthworm	25. 8	18. 7	A9	C3	Pheasant
14. 6	5. 5	J7	A3	Crocodile	26. 8	19. 7	A9	D4	Cock
15. 6	6. 5	J7	B4	Dragon	27. 8	20. 7	A9	E5	Crow
16. 6	7. 5	J7	C5	Badger	28. 8	21. 7	A9	F6	Monkey
17. 6	8. 5	J7	D6	Hare	29. 8	22. 7	A9	G7	Gibbon
18. 6	9. 5	J7	E7	Fox	30. 8	23. 7	A9	H8	Tapir
19. 6	10. 5	J7	F8	Tiger	31. 8	24. 7	A9	J9	Sheep
20. 6	11. 5	J7	G9	Leopard	1. 9	25. 7	A9	K10	Deer
21. 6	12. 5	J7	H10	Griffon	2. 9	26. 7	A9	A11	Horse
22. 6	13. 5	J7	J11	Ox	3. 9	27. 7	A9	B12	Stag
23. 6	14. 5	J7	K12	Bat	4. 9	28. 7	A9	C1	Serpent
24. 6	15. 5	J7	A1	Rat	5. 9	29. 7	A9	D2	Earthworm
25. 6	16. 5	J7	B2	Swallow	6. 9	1. 8	B10	E3	Crocodile
26. 6	17. 5	J7	C3	Pig	7. 9	2. 8	B10	F4	Dragon
27. 6	18. 5	J7	D4	Porcupine	8. 9	3. 8	B10	G5	Badger
28. 6	19. 5	J7	E5	Wolf	9. 9	4. 8	B10	H6	Hare
29. 6	20. 5	J7	F6	Dog	10. 9	5. 8	B10	J7	Fox
30. 6	21. 5	J7	G7	Pheasant	11. 9	6. 8	B10	K8	Tiger
1. 7	22. 5	J7	H8	Cock	12. 9	7. 8	B10	A9	Leopard
2. 7	23. 5	J7	J9	Crow	13. 9	8. 8	B10	B10	Griffon
3. 7	24. 5	J7	K10	Monkey	14. 9	9. 8	B10	C11	Ox
4. 7	25. 5	J7	A11	Gibbon	15. 9	10. 8	B10	D12	Bat
5. 7	26. 5	J7	B12	Tapir	16. 9	11. 8	B10	E1	Rat
6. 7	27. 5	J7	C1	Sheep	17. 9	12. 8	B10	F2	Swallow
7. 7	28. 5	J7	D2	Deer	18. 9	13. 8	B10	G3	Pig
8. 7	29. 5	J7	E3	Horse	19. 9	14. 8	B10	H4	Porcupine
9. 7	1. 6	K8	F4	Stag	20. 9	15. 8	B10	J5	Wolf

Solar date	Lunar date	Month HS/EB	Day HS/EB	Constellation	Solar date	Lunar date	Month HS/EB	Day HS/EB	Constellation
21. 9	16. 8	B10	K6	Dog	28.11	24.10	D12	H2	Earthworm
22. 9	17. 8	B10	A7	Pheasant	29.11	25.10	D12	J3	Crocodile
23. 9	18. 8	B10	B8	Cock	30.11	26.10	D12	K4	Dragon
24. 9	19. 8	B10	C9	Crow	1.12	27.10	D12	A5	Badger
25. 9	20. 8	B10	D10	Monkey	2.12	28.10	D12	B6	Hare
26. 9	21. 8	B10	E11	Gibbon	3.12	29.10	D12	C7	Fox
27. 9	22. 8	B10	F12	Tapir	4.12	30.10	D12	D8	Tiger
28. 9	23. 8	B10	G1	Sheep	5.12	1.11	E1	E9	Leopard
29. 9	24. 8	B10	H2	Deer	6.12	2.11	E1	F10	Griffon
30. 9	25. 8	B10	J3	Horse	7.12	3.11	E1	G11	Ox
1.10	26. 8	B10	K4	Stag	8.12	4.11	E1	H12	Bat
2.10	27. 8	B10	A5	Serpent	9.12	5.11	E1	J1	Rat
3.10	28. 8	B10	B6	Earthworm	10.12	6.11	E1	K2	Swallow
4.10	29. 8	B10	C7	Crocodile	11.12	7.11	E1	A3	Pig
5.10	30. 8	B10	D8	Dragon	12.12	8.11	E1	B4	Porcupine
6.10	1. 9	C11	E9	Badger	13.12	9.11	E1	C5	Wolf
7.10	2. 9	C11	F10	Hare	14.12	10.11	E1	D6	Dog
8.10	3. 9	C11	G11	Fox	15.12	11.11	E1	E7	Pheasant
9.10	4. 9	C11	H12	Tiger	16.12	12.11	E1	F8	Cock
10.10	5. 9	C11	J1	Leopard	17.12	13.11	E1	G9	Crow
11.10	6. 9	C11	K2	Griffon	18.12	14.11	E1	H10	Monkey
12.10	7. 9	C11	A3	Ox	19.12	15.11	E1	J11	Gibbon
13.10	8. 9	C11	B4	Bat	20.12	16.11	E1	K12	Tapir
14.10	9. 9	C11	C5	Rat	21.12	17.11	E1	A1	Sheep
15.10	10. 9	C11	D6	Swallow	22.12	18.11	E1	B2	Deer
16.10	11. 9	C11	E7	Pig	23.12	19.11	E1	C3	Horse
17.10	12. 9	C11	F8	Porcupine	24.12	20.11	E1	D4	Stag
18.10	13. 9	C11	G9	Wolf	25.12	21.11	E1	E5	Serpent
19.10	14. 9	C11	H10	Dog	26.12	22.11	E1	F6	Earthworm
20.10	15. 9	C11	J11	Pheasant	27.12	23.11	E1	G7	Crocodile
21.10	16. 9	C11	K12	Cock	28.12	24.11	E1	H8	Dragon
22.10	17. 9	C11	A1	Crow	29.12	25.11	E1	J9	Badger
23.10	18. 9	C11	B2	Monkey	30.12	26.11	E1	K10	Hare
24.10	19. 9	C11	C3	Gibbon	31.12	27.11	E1	A11	Fox
25.10	20. 9	C11	D4	Tapir					
26.10	21. 9	C11	E5	Sheep	**1946**				
27.10	22. 9	C11	F6	Deer	1. 1	28.11	E1	B12	Tiger
28.10	23. 9	C11	G7	Horse	2. 1	29.11	E1	C1	Leopard
29.10	24. 9	C11	H8	Stag	3. 1	1.12	F2	D2	Griffon
30.10	25. 9	C11	J9	Serpent	4. 1	2.12	F2	E3	Ox
31.10	26. 9	C11	K10	Earthworm	5. 1	3.12	F2	F4	Bat
1.11	27. 9	C11	A11	Crocodile	6. 1	4.12	F2	G5	Rat
2.11	28. 9	C11	B12	Dragon	7. 1	5.12	F2	H6	Swallow
3.11	29. 9	C11	C1	Badger	8. 1	6.12	F2	J7	Pig
4.11	30. 9	C11	D2	Hare	9. 1	7.12	F2	K8	Porcupine
5.11	1.10	D12	E3	Fox	10. 1	8.12	F2	A9	Wolf
6.11	2.10	D12	F4	Tiger	11. 1	9.12	F2	B10	Dog
7.11	3.10	D12	G5	Leopard	12. 1	10.12	F2	C11	Pheasant
8.11	4.10	D12	H6	Griffon	13. 1	11.12	F2	D12	Cock
9.11	5.10	D12	J7	Ox	14. 1	12.12	F2	E1	Crow
10.11	6.10	D12	K8	Bat	15. 1	13.12	F2	F2	Monkey
11.11	7.10	D12	A9	Rat	16. 1	14.12	F2	G3	Gibbon
12.11	8.10	D12	B10	Swallow	17. 1	15.12	F2	H4	Tapir
13.11	9.10	D12	C11	Pig	18. 1	16.12	F2	J5	Sheep
14.11	10.10	D12	D12	Porcupine	19. 1	17.12	F2	K6	Deer
15.11	11.10	D12	E1	Wolf	20. 1	18.12	F2	A7	Horse
16.11	12.10	D12	F2	Dog	21. 1	19.12	F2	B8	Stag
17.11	13.10	D12	G3	Pheasant	22. 1	20.12	F2	C9	Serpent
18.11	14.10	D12	H4	Cock	23. 1	21.12	F2	D10	Earthworm
19.11	15.10	D12	J5	Crow	24. 1	22.12	F2	E11	Crocodile
20.11	16.10	D12	K6	Monkey	25. 1	23.12	F2	F12	Dragon
21.11	17.10	D12	A7	Gibbon	26. 1	24.12	F2	G1	Badger
22.11	18.10	D12	B8	Tapir	27. 1	25.12	F2	H2	Hare
23.11	19.10	D12	C9	Sheep	28. 1	26.12	F2	J3	Fox
24.11	20.10	D12	D10	Deer	29. 1	27.12	F2	K4	Tiger
25.11	21.10	D12	E11	Horse	30. 1	28.12	F2	A5	Leopard
26.11	22.10	D12	F12	Stag	31. 1	29.12	F2	B6	Griffon
27.11	23.10	D12	G1	Serpent	1. 2	30.12	F2	C7	Ox

PING HSÜ YEAR

Solar date	Lunar date	Month HS/EB	Day HS/EB	Constellation	Solar date	Lunar date	Month HS/EB	Day HS/EB	Constellation
2.2	1.1	G3	D8	Bat	14.4	13.3	J5	E7	Horse
3.2	2.1	G3	E9	Rat	15.4	14.3	J5	F8	Stag
4.2	3.1	G3	F10	Swallow	16.4	15.3	J5	G9	Serpent
5.2	4.1	G3	G11	Pig	17.4	16.3	J5	H10	Earthworm
6.2	5.1	G3	H12	Porcupine	18.4	17.3	J5	J11	Crocodile
7.2	6.1	G3	J1	Wolf	19.4	18.3	J5	K12	Dragon
8.2	7.1	G3	K2	Dog	20.4	19.3	J5	A1	Badger
9.2	8.1	G3	A3	Pheasant	21.4	20.3	J5	B2	Hare
10.2	9.1	G3	B4	Cock	22.4	21.3	J5	C3	Fox
11.2	10.1	G3	C5	Crow	23.4	22.3	J5	D4	Tiger
12.2	11.1	G3	D6	Monkey	24.4	23.3	J5	E5	Leopard
13.2	12.1	G3	E7	Gibbon	25.4	24.3	J5	F6	Griffon
14.2	13.1	G3	F8	Tapir	26.4	25.3	J5	G7	Ox
15.2	14.1	G3	G9	Sheep	27.4	26.3	J5	H8	Bat
16.2	15.1	G3	H10	Deer	28.4	27.3	J5	J9	Rat
17.2	16.1	G3	J11	Horse	29.4	28.3	J5	K10	Swallow
18.2	17.1	G3	K12	Stag	30.4	29.3	J5	A11	Pig
19.2	18.1	G3	A1	Serpent	1.5	1.4	K6	B12	Porcupine
20.2	19.1	G3	B2	Earthworm	2.5	2.4	K6	C1	Wolf
21.2	20.1	G3	C3	Crocodile	3.5	3.4	K6	D2	Dog
22.2	21.1	G3	D4	Dragon	4.5	4.4	K6	E3	Pheasant
23.2	22.1	G3	E5	Badger	5.5	5.4	K6	F4	Cock
24.2	23.1	G3	F6	Hare	6.5	6.4	K6	G5	Crow
25.2	24.1	G3	G7	Fox	7.5	7.4	K6	H6	Monkey
26.2	25.1	G3	H8	Tiger	8.5	8.4	K6	J7	Gibbon
27.2	26.1	G3	J9	Leopard	9.5	9.4	K6	K8	Tapir
28.2	27.1	G3	K10	Griffon	10.5	10.4	K6	A9	Sheep
1.3	28.1	G3	A11	Ox	11.5	11.4	K6	B10	Deer
2.3	29.1	G3	B12	Bat	12.5	12.4	K6	C11	Horse
3.3	30.1	G3	C1	Rat	13.5	13.4	K6	D12	Stag
4.3	1.2	H4	D2	Swallow	14.5	14.4	K6	E1	Serpent
5.3	2.2	H4	E3	Pig	15.5	15.4	K6	F2	Earthworm
6.3	3.2	H4	F4	Porcupine	16.5	16.4	K6	G3	Crocodile
7.3	4.2	H4	G5	Wolf	17.5	17.4	K6	H4	Dragon
8.3	5.2	H4	H6	Dog	18.5	18.4	K6	J5	Badger
9.3	6.2	H4	J7	Pheasant	19.5	19.4	K6	K6	Hare
10.3	7.2	H4	K8	Cock	20.5	20.4	K6	A7	Fox
11.3	8.2	H4	A9	Crow	21.5	21.4	K6	B8	Tiger
12.3	9.2	H4	B10	Monkey	22.5	22.4	K6	C9	Leopard
13.3	10.2	H4	C11	Gibbon	23.5	23.4	K6	D10	Griffon
14.3	11.2	H4	D12	Tapir	24.5	24.4	K6	E11	Ox
15.3	12.2	H4	E1	Sheep	25.5	25.4	K6	F12	Bat
16.3	13.2	H4	F2	Deer	26.5	26.4	K6	G1	Rat
17.3	14.2	H4	G3	Horse	27.5	27.4	K6	H2	Swallow
18.3	15.2	H4	H4	Stag	28.5	28.4	K6	J3	Pig
19.3	16.2	H4	J5	Serpent	29.5	29.4	K6	K4	Porcupine
20.3	17.2	H4	K6	Earthworm	30.5	30.4	K6	A5	Wolf
21.3	18.2	H4	A7	Crocodile	31.5	1.5	A7	B6	Dog
22.3	19.2	H4	B8	Dragon	1.6	2.5	A7	C7	Pheasant
23.3	20.2	H4	C9	Badger	2.6	3.5	A7	D8	Cock
24.3	21.2	H4	D10	Hare	3.6	4.5	A7	E9	Crow
25.3	22.2	H4	E11	Fox	4.6	5.5	A7	F10	Monkey
26.3	23.2	H4	F12	Tiger	5.6	6.5	A7	G11	Gibbon
27.3	24.2	H4	G1	Leopard	6.6	7.5	A7	H12	Tapir
28.3	25.2	H4	H2	Griffon	7.6	8.5	A7	J1	Sheep
29.3	26.2	H4	J3	Ox	8.6	9.5	A7	K2	Deer
30.3	27.2	H4	K4	Bat	9.6	10.5	A7	A3	Horse
31.3	28.2	H4	A5	Rat	10.6	11.5	A7	B4	Stag
1.4	29.2	H4	B6	Swallow	11.6	12.5	A7	C5	Serpent
2.4	1.3	J5	C7	Pig	12.6	13.5	A7	D6	Earthworm
3.4	2.3	J5	D8	Porcupine	13.6	14.5	A7	E7	Crocodile
4.4	3.3	J5	E9	Wolf	14.6	15.5	A7	F8	Dragon
5.4	4.3	J5	F10	Dog	15.6	16.5	A7	G9	Badger
6.4	5.3	J5	G11	Pheasant	16.6	17.5	A7	H10	Hare
7.4	6.3	J5	H12	Cock	17.6	18.5	A7	J11	Fox
8.4	7.3	J5	J1	Crow	18.6	19.5	A7	K12	Tiger
9.4	8.3	J5	K2	Monkey	19.6	20.5	A7	A1	Leopard
10.4	9.3	J5	A3	Gibbon	20.6	21.5	A7	B2	Griffon
11.4	10.3	J5	B4	Tapir	21.6	22.5	A7	C3	Ox
12.4	11.3	J5	C5	Sheep	22.6	23.5	A7	D4	Bat
13.4	12.3	J5	D6	Deer	23.6	24.5	A7	E5	Rat

Solar date	Lunar date	Month HS/EB	Day HS/EB	Constellation	Solar date	Lunar date	Month HS/EB	Day HS/EB	Constellation
24. 6	25. 5	A7	F6	Swallow	5. 9	10. 8	D10	J7	Crocodile
25. 6	26. 5	A7	G7	Pig	6. 9	11. 8	D10	K8	Dragon
26. 6	27. 5	A7	H8	Porcupine	7. 9	12. 8	D10	A9	Badger
27. 6	28. 5	A7	J9	Wolf	8. 9	13. 8	D10	B10	Hare
28. 6	29. 5	A7	K10	Dog	9. 9	14. 8	D10	C11	Fox
29. 6	1. 6	B8	A11	Pheasant	10. 9	15. 8	D10	D12	Tiger
30. 6	2. 6	B8	B12	Cock	11. 9	16. 8	D10	E1	Leopard
1. 7	3. 6	B8	C1	Crow	12. 9	17. 8	D10	F2	Griffon
2. 7	4. 6	B8	D2	Monkey	13. 9	18. 8	D10	G3	Ox
3. 7	5. 6	B8	E3	Gibbon	14. 9	19. 8	D10	H4	Bat
4. 7	6. 6	B8	F4	Tapir	15. 9	20. 8	D10	J5	Rat
5. 7	7. 6	B8	G5	Sheep	16. 9	21. 8	D10	K6	Swallow
6. 7	8. 6	B8	H6	Deer	17. 9	22. 8	D10	A7	Pig
7. 7	9. 6	B8	J7	Horse	18. 9	23. 8	D10	B8	Porcupine
8. 7	10. 6	B8	K8	Stag	19. 9	24. 8	D10	C9	Wolf
9. 7	11. 6	B8	A9	Serpent	20. 9	25. 8	D10	D10	Dog
10. 7	12. 6	B8	B10	Earthworm	21. 9	26. 8	D10	E11	Pheasant
11. 7	13. 6	B8	C11	Crocodile	22. 9	27. 8	D10	F12	Cock
12. 7	14. 6	B8	D12	Dragon	23. 9	28. 8	D10	G1	Crow
13. 7	15. 6	B8	E1	Badger	24. 9	29. 8	D10	H2	Monkey
14. 7	16. 6	B8	F2	Hare	25. 9	1. 9	E11	J3	Gibbon
15. 7	17. 6	B8	G3	Fox	26. 9	2. 9	E11	K4	Tapir
16. 7	18. 6	B8	H4	Tiger	27. 9	3. 9	E11	A5	Sheep
17. 7	19. 6	B8	J5	Leopard	28. 9	4. 9	E11	B6	Deer
18. 7	20. 6	B8	K6	Griffon	29. 9	5. 9	E11	C7	Horse
19. 7	21. 6	B8	A7	Ox	30. 9	6. 9	E11	D8	Stag
20. 7	22. 6	B8	B8	Bat	1.10	7. 9	E11	E9	Serpent
21. 7	23. 6	B8	C9	Rat	2.10	8. 9	E11	F10	Earthworm
22. 7	24. 6	B8	D10	Swallow	3.10	9. 9	E11	G11	Crocodile
23. 7	25. 6	B8	E11	Pig	4.10	10. 9	E11	H12	Dragon
24. 7	26. 6	B8	F12	Porcupine	5.10	11. 9	E11	J1	Badger
25. 7	27. 6	B8	G1	Wolf	6.10	12. 9	E11	K2	Hare
26. 7	28. 6	B8	H2	Dog	7.10	13. 9	E11	A3	Fox
27. 7	29. 6	B8	J3	Pheasant	8.10	14. 9	E11	B4	Tiger
28. 7	1. 7	C9	K4	Cock	9.10	15. 9	E11	C5	Leopard
29. 7	2. 7	C9	A5	Crow	10.10	16. 9	E11	D6	Griffon
30. 7	3. 7	C9	B6	Monkey	11.10	17. 9	E11	E7	Ox
31. 7	4. 7	C9	C7	Gibbon	12.10	18. 9	E11	F8	Bat
1. 8	5. 7	C9	D8	Tapir	13.10	19. 9	E11	G9	Rat
2. 8	6. 7	C9	E9	Sheep	14.10	20. 9	E11	H10	Swallow
3. 8	7. 7	C9	F10	Deer	15.10	21. 9	E11	J11	Pig
4. 8	8. 7	C9	G11	Horse	16.10	22. 9	E11	K12	Porcupine
5. 8	9. 7	C9	H12	Stag	17.10	23. 9	E11	A1	Wolf
6. 8	10. 7	C9	J1	Serpent	18.10	24. 9	E11	B2	Dog
7. 8	11. 7	C9	K2	Earthworm	19.10	25. 9	E11	C3	Pheasant
8. 8	12. 7	C9	A3	Crocodile	20.10	26. 9	E11	D4	Cock
9. 8	13. 7	C9	B4	Dragon	21.10	27. 9	E11	E5	Crow
10. 8	14. 7	C9	C5	Badger	22.10	28. 9	E11	F6	Monkey
11. 8	15. 7	C9	D6	Hare	23.10	29. 9	E11	G7	Gibbon
12. 8	16. 7	C9	E7	Fox	24.10	30. 9	E11	H8	Tapir
13. 8	17. 7	C9	F8	Tiger	25.10	1.10	F12	J9	Sheep
14. 8	18. 7	C9	G9	Leopard	26.10	2.10	F12	K10	Deer
15. 8	19. 7	C9	H10	Griffon	27.10	3.10	F12	A11	Horse
16. 8	20. 7	C9	J11	Ox	28.10	4.10	F12	B12	Stag
17. 8	21. 7	C9	K12	Bat	29.10	5.10	F12	C1	Serpent
18. 8	22. 7	C9	A1	Rat	30.10	6.10	F12	D2	Earthworm
19. 8	23. 7	C9	B2	Swallow	31.10	7.10	F12	E3	Crocodile
20. 8	24. 7	C9	C3	Pig	1.11	8.10	F12	F4	Dragon
21. 8	25. 7	C9	D4	Porcupine	2.11	9.10	F12	G5	Badger
22. 8	26. 7	C9	E5	Wolf	3.11	10.10	F12	H6	Hare
23. 8	27. 7	C9	F6	Dog	4.11	11.10	F12	J7	Fox
24. 8	28. 7	C9	G7	Pheasant	5.11	12.10	F12	K8	Tiger
25. 8	29. 7	C9	H8	Cock	6.11	13.10	F12	A9	Leopard
26. 8	30. 7	C9	J9	Crow	7.11	14.10	F12	B10	Griffon
27. 8	1. 8	D10	K10	Monkey	8.11	15.10	F12	C11	Ox
28. 8	2. 8	D10	A11	Gibbon	9.11	16.10	F12	D12	Bat
29. 8	3. 8	D10	B12	Tapir	10.11	17.10	F12	E1	Rat
30. 8	4. 8	D10	C1	Sheep	11.11	18.10	F12	F2	Swallow
31. 8	5. 8	D10	D2	Deer	12.11	19.10	F12	G3	Pig
1. 9	6. 8	D10	E3	Horse	13.11	20.10	F12	H4	Porcupine
2. 9	7. 8	D10	F4	Stag	14.11	21.10	F12	J5	Wolf
3. 9	8. 8	D10	G5	Serpent	15.11	22.10	F12	K6	Dog
4. 9	9. 8	D10	H6	Earthworm	16.11	23.10	F12	A7	Pheasant

Solar date	Lunar date	Month HS/EB	Day HS/EB	Constellation	Solar date	Lunar date	Month HS/EB	Day HS/EB	Constellation
17.11	24.10	F12	B8	Cock	21.12	28.11	G1	F6	Deer
18.11	25.10	F12	C9	Crow	22.12	29.11	G1	G7	Horse
19.11	26.10	F12	D10	Monkey	23.12	1.12	H2	H8	Stag
20.11	27.10	F12	E11	Gibbon	24.12	2.12	H2	J9	Serpent
21.11	28.10	F12	F12	Tapir	25.12	3.12	H2	K10	Earthworm
22.11	29.10	F12	G1	Sheep	26.12	4.12	H2	A11	Crocodile
23.11	30.10	F12	H2	Deer	27.12	5.12	H2	B12	Dragon
24.11	1.11	G1	J3	Horse	28.12	6.12	H2	C1	Badger
25.11	2.11	G1	K4	Stag	29.12	7.12	H2	D2	Hare
26.11	3.11	G1	A5	Serpent	30.12	8.12	H2	E3	Fox
27.11	4.11	G1	B6	Earthworm	31.12	9.12	H2	F4	Tiger
28.11	5.11	G1	C7	Crocodile	**1947**				
29.11	6.11	G1	D8	Dragon	1. 1	10.12	H2	G5	Leopard
30.11	7.11	G1	E9	Badger	2. 1	11.12	H2	H6	Griffon
1.12	8.11	G1	F10	Hare	3. 1	12.12	H2	J7	Ox
2.12	9.11	G1	G11	Fox	4. 1	13.12	H2	K8	Bat
3.12	10.11	G1	H12	Tiger	5. 1	14.12	H2	A9	Rat
4.12	11.11	G1	J1	Leopard	6. 1	15.12	H2	B10	Swallow
5.12	12.11	G1	K2	Griffon	7. 1	16.12	H2	C11	Pig
6.12	13.11	G1	A3	Ox	8. 1	17.12	H2	D12	Porcupine
7.12	14.11	G1	B4	Bat	9. 1	18.12	H2	E1	Wolf
8.12	15.11	G1	C5	Rat	10. 1	19.12	H2	F2	Dog
9.12	16.11	G1	D6	Swallow	11. 1	20.12	H2	G3	Pheasant
10.12	17.11	G1	E7	Pig	12. 1	21.12	H2	H4	Cock
11.12	18.11	G1	F8	Porcupine	13. 1	22.12	H2	J5	Crow
12.12	19.11	G1	G9	Wolf	14. 1	23.12	H2	K6	Monkey
13.12	20.11	G1	H10	Dog	15. 1	24.12	H2	A7	Gibbon
14.12	21.11	G1	J11	Pheasant	16. 1	25.12	H2	B8	Tapir
15.12	22.11	G1	K12	Cock	17. 1	26.12	H2	C9	Sheep
16.12	23.11	G1	A1	Crow	18. 1	27.12	H2	D10	Deer
17.12	24.11	G1	B2	Monkey	19. 1	28.12	H2	E11	Horse
18.12	25.11	G1	C3	Gibbon	20. 1	29.12	H2	F12	Stag
19.12	26.11	G1	D4	Tapir	21. 1	30.12	H2	G1	Serpent
20.12	27.11	G1	E5	Sheep					

TING HAI YEAR

Solar date	Lunar date	Month HS/EB	Day HS/EB	Constellation	Solar date	Lunar date	Month HS/EB	Day HS/EB	Constellation
22. 1	1. 1	J3	H2	Earthworm	25. 2	5. 2	K4	B12	Tiger
23. 1	2. 1	J3	J3	Crocodile	26. 2	6. 2	K4	C1	Leopard
24. 1	3. 1	J3	K4	Dragon	27. 2	7. 2	K4	D2	Griffon
25. 1	4. 1	J3	A5	Badger	28. 2	8. 2	K4	E3	Ox
26. 1	5. 1	J3	B6	Hare	1. 3	9. 2	K4	F4	Bat
27. 1	6. 1	J3	C7	Fox	2. 3	10. 2	K4	G5	Rat
28. 1	7. 1	J3	D8	Tiger	3. 3	11. 2	K4	H6	Swallow
29. 1	8. 1	J3	E9	Leopard	4. 3	12. 2	K4	J7	Pig
30. 1	9. 1	J3	F10	Griffon	5. 3	13. 2	K4	K8	Porcupine
31. 1	10. 1	J3	G11	Ox	6. 3	14. 2	K4	A9	Wolf
1. 2	11. 1	J3	H12	Bat	7. 3	15. 2	K4	B10	Dog
2. 2	12. 1	J3	J1	Rat	8. 3	16. 2	K4	C11	Pheasant
3. 2	13. 1	J3	K2	Swallow	9. 3	17. 2	K4	D12	Cock
4. 2	14. 1	J3	A3	Pig	10. 3	18. 2	K4	E1	Crow
5. 2	15. 1	J3	B4	Porcupine	11. 3	19. 2	K4	F2	Monkey
6. 2	16. 1	J3	C5	Wolf	12. 3	20. 2	K4	G3	Gibbon
7. 2	17. 1	J3	D6	Dog	13. 3	21. 2	K4	H4	Tapir
8. 2	18. 1	J3	E7	Pheasant	14. 3	22. 2	K4	J5	Sheep
9. 2	19. 1	J3	F8	Cock	15. 3	23. 2	K4	K6	Deer
10. 2	20. 1	J3	G9	Crow	16. 3	24. 2	K4	A7	Horse
11. 2	21. 1	J3	H10	Monkey	17. 3	25. 2	K4	B8	Stag
12. 2	22. 1	J3	J11	Gibbon	18. 3	26. 2	K4	C9	Serpent
13. 2	23. 1	J3	K12	Tapir	19. 3	27. 2	K4	D10	Earthworm
14. 2	24. 1	J3	A1	Sheep	20. 3	28. 2	K4	E11	Crocodile
15. 2	25. 1	J3	B2	Deer	21. 3	29. 2	K4	F12	Dragon
16. 2	26. 1	J3	C3	Horse	22. 3	30. 2	K4	G1	Badger
17. 2	27. 1	J3	D4	Stag	23. 3	*1. 2*	*K4*	H2	Hare
18. 2	28. 1	J3	E5	Serpent	24. 3	*2. 2*	*K4*	J3	Fox
19. 2	29. 1	J3	F6	Earthworm	25. 3	*3. 2*	*K4*	K4	Tiger
20. 2	30. 1	J3	G7	Crocodile	26. 3	*4. 2*	*K4*	A5	Leopard
21. 2	1. 2	K4	H8	Dragon	27. 3	*5. 2*	*K4*	B6	Griffon
22. 2	2. 2	K4	J9	Badger	28. 3	*6. 2*	*K4*	C7	Ox
23. 2	3. 2	K4	K10	Hare	29. 3	*7. 2*	*K4*	D8	Bat
24. 2	4. 2	K4	A11	Fox	30. 3	*8. 2*	*K4*	E9	Rat

Solar date	Lunar date	Month HS/EB	Day HS/EB	Constellation	Solar date	Lunar date	Month HS/EB	Day HS/EB	Constellation
31. 3	9. 2	K4	F10	Swallow	12. 6	24. 4	B6	J11	Crocodile
1. 4	10. 2	K4	G11	Pig	13. 6	25. 4	B6	K12	Dragon
2. 4	11. 2	K4	H12	Porcupine	14. 6	26. 4	B6	A1	Badger
3. 4	12. 2	K4	J1	Wolf	15. 6	27. 4	B6	B2	Hare
4. 4	13. 2	K4	K2	Dog	16. 6	28. 4	B6	C3	Fox
5. 4	14. 2	K4	A3	Pheasant	17. 6	29. 4	B6	D4	Tiger
6. 4	15. 2	K4	B4	Cock	18. 6	30. 4	B6	E5	Leopard
7. 4	16. 2	K4	C5	Crow	19. 6	1. 5	C7	F6	Griffon
8. 4	17. 2	K4	D6	Monkey	20. 6	2. 5	C7	G7	Ox
9. 4	18. 2	K4	E7	Gibbon	21. 6	3. 5	C7	H8	Bat
10. 4	19. 2	K4	F8	Tapir	22. 6	4. 5	C7	J9	Rat
11. 4	20. 2	K4	G9	Sheep	23. 6	5. 5	C7	K10	Swallow
12. 4	21. 2	K4	H10	Deer	24. 6	6. 5	C7	A11	Pig
13. 4	22. 2	K4	J11	Horse	25. 6	7. 5	C7	B12	Porcupine
14. 4	23. 2	K4	K12	Stag	26. 6	8. 5	C7	C1	Wolf
15. 4	24. 2	K4	A1	Serpent	27. 6	9. 5	C7	D2	Dog
16. 4	25. 2	K4	B2	Earthworm	28. 6	10. 5	C7	E3	Pheasant
17. 4	26. 2	K4	C3	Crocodile	29. 6	11. 5	C7	F4	Cock
18. 4	27. 2	K4	D4	Dragon	30. 6	12. 5	C7	G5	Crow
19. 4	28. 2	K4	E5	Badger	1. 7	13. 5	C7	H6	Monkey
20. 4	29. 2	K4	F6	Hare	2. 7	14. 5	C7	J7	Gibbon
21. 4	1. 3	A5	G7	Fox	3. 7	15. 5	C7	K8	Tapir
22. 4	2. 3	A5	H8	Tiger	4. 7	16. 5	C7	A9	Sheep
23. 4	3. 3	A5	J9	Leopard	5. 7	17. 5	C7	B10	Deer
24. 4	4. 3	A5	K10	Griffon	6. 7	18. 5	C7	C11	Horse
25. 4	5. 3	A5	A11	Ox	7. 7	19. 5	C7	D12	Stag
26. 4	6. 3	A5	B12	Bat	8. 7	20. 5	C7	E1	Serpent
27. 4	7. 3	A5	C1	Rat	9. 7	21. 5	C7	F2	Earthworm
28. 4	8. 3	A5	D2	Swallow	10. 7	22. 5	C7	G3	Crocodile
29. 4	9. 3	A5	E3	Pig	11. 7	23. 5	C7	H4	Dragon
30. 4	10. 3	A5	F4	Porcupine	12. 7	24. 5	C7	J5	Badger
1. 5	11. 3	A5	G5	Wolf	13. 7	25. 5	C7	K6	Hare
2. 5	12. 3	A5	H6	Dog	14. 7	26. 5	C7	A7	Fox
3. 5	13. 3	A5	J7	Pheasant	15. 7	27. 5	C7	B8	Tiger
4. 5	14. 3	A5	K8	Cock	16. 7	28. 5	C7	C9	Leopard
5. 5	15. 3	A5	A9	Crow	17. 7	29. 5	C7	D10	Griffon
6. 5	16. 3	A5	B10	Monkey	18. 7	1. 6	D8	E11	Ox
7. 5	17. 3	A5	C11	Gibbon	19. 7	2. 6	D8	F12	Bat
8. 5	18. 3	A5	D12	Tapir	20. 7	3. 6	D8	G1	Rat
9. 5	19. 3	A5	E1	Sheep	21. 7	4. 6	D8	H2	Swallow
10. 5	20. 3	A5	F2	Deer	22. 7	5. 6	D8	J3	Pig
11. 5	21. 3	A5	G3	Horse	23. 7	6. 6	D8	K4	Porcupine
12. 5	22. 3	A5	H4	Stag	24. 7	7. 6	D8	A5	Wolf
13. 5	23. 3	A5	J5	Serpent	25. 7	8. 6	D8	B6	Dog
14. 5	24. 3	A5	K6	Earthworm	26. 7	9. 6	D8	C7	Pheasant
15. 5	25. 3	A5	A7	Crocodile	27. 7	10. 6	D8	D8	Cock
16. 5	26. 3	A5	B8	Dragon	28. 7	11. 6	D8	E9	Crow
17. 5	27. 3	A5	C9	Badger	29. 7	12. 6	D8	F10	Monkey
18. 5	28. 3	A5	D10	Hare	30. 7	13. 6	D8	G11	Gibbon
19. 5	29. 3	A5	E11	Fox	31. 7	14. 6	D8	H12	Tapir
20. 5	1. 4	B6	F12	Tiger	1. 8	15. 6	D8	J1	Sheep
21. 5	2. 4	B6	G1	Leopard	2. 8	16. 6	D8	K2	Deer
22. 5	3. 4	B6	H2	Griffon	3. 8	17. 6	D8	A3	Horse
23. 5	4. 4	B6	J3	Ox	4. 8	18. 6	D8	B4	Stag
24. 5	5. 4	B6	K4	Bat	5. 8	19. 6	D8	C5	Serpent
25. 5	6. 4	B6	A5	Rat	6. 8	20. 6	D8	D6	Earthworm
26. 5	7. 4	B6	B6	Swallow	7. 8	21. 6	D8	E7	Crocodile
27. 5	8. 4	B6	C7	Pig	8. 8	22. 6	D8	F8	Dragon
28. 5	9. 4	B6	D8	Porcupine	9. 8	23. 6	D8	G9	Badger
29. 5	10. 4	B6	E9	Wolf	10. 8	24. 6	D8	H10	Hare
30. 5	11. 4	B6	F10	Dog	11. 8	25. 6	D8	J11	Fox
31. 5	12. 4	B6	G11	Pheasant	12. 8	26. 6	D8	K12	Tiger
1. 6	13. 4	B6	H12	Cock	13. 8	27. 6	D8	A1	Leopard
2. 6	14. 4	B6	J1	Crow	14. 8	28. 6	D8	B2	Griffon
3. 6	15. 4	B6	K2	Monkey	15. 8	29. 6	D8	C3	Ox
4. 6	16. 4	B6	A3	Gibbon	16. 8	1. 7	E9	D4	Bat
5. 6	17. 4	B6	B4	Tapir	17. 8	2. 7	E9	E5	Rat
6. 6	18. 4	B6	C5	Sheep	18. 8	3. 7	E9	F6	Swallow
7. 6	19. 4	B6	D6	Deer	19. 8	4. 7	E9	G7	Pig
8. 6	20. 4	B6	E7	Horse	20. 8	5. 7	E9	H8	Porcupine
9. 6	21. 4	B6	F8	Stag	21. 8	6. 7	E9	J9	Wolf
10. 6	22. 4	B6	G9	Serpent	22. 8	7. 7	E9	K10	Dog
11. 6	23. 4	B6	H10	Earthworm	23. 8	8. 7	E9	A11	Pheasant

Solar date	Lunar date	Month HS/EB	Day HS/EB	Constellation	Solar date	Lunar date	Month HS/EB	Day HS/EB	Constellation
24. 8	9. 7	E9	B12	Cock	5.11	23. 9	G11	E1	Leopard
25. 8	10. 7	E9	C1	Crow	6.11	24. 9	G11	F2	Griffon
26. 8	11. 7	E9	D2	Monkey	7.11	25. 9	G11	G3	Ox
27. 8	12. 7	E9	E3	Gibbon	8.11	26. 9	G11	H4	Bat
28. 8	13. 7	E9	F4	Tapir	9.11	27. 9	G11	J5	Rat
29. 8	14. 7	E9	G5	Sheep	10.11	28. 9	G11	K6	Swallow
30. 8	15. 7	E9	H6	Deer	11.11	29. 9	G11	A7	Pig
31. 8	16. 7	E9	J7	Horse	12.11	30. 9	G11	B8	Porcupine
1. 9	17. 7	E9	K8	Stag	13.11	1.10	H12	C9	Wolf
2. 9	18. 7	E9	A9	Serpent	14.11	2.10	H12	D10	Dog
3. 9	19. 7	E9	B10	Earthworm	15.11	3.10	H12	E11	Pheasant
4. 9	20. 7	E9	C11	Crocodile	16.11	4.10	H12	F12	Cock
5. 9	21. 7	F9	D12	Dragon	17.11	5.10	H12	G1	Crow
6. 9	22. 7	E9	E1	Badger	18.11	6.10	H12	H2	Monkey
7. 9	23. 7	E9	F2	Hare	19.11	7.10	H12	J3	Gibbon
8. 9	24. 7	E9	G3	Fox	20.11	8.10	H12	K4	Tapir
9. 9	25. 7	E9	H4	Tiger	21.11	9.10	H12	A5	Sheep
10. 9	26. 7	E9	J5	Leopard	22.11	10.10	H12	B6	Deer
11. 9	27. 7	E9	K6	Griffon	23.11	11.10	H12	C7	Horse
12. 9	28. 7	E9	A7	Ox	24.11	12.10	H12	D8	Stag
13. 9	29. 7	E9	B8	Bat	25.11	13.10	H12	E9	Serpent
14. 9	30. 7	E9	C9	Rat	26.11	14.10	H12	F10	Earthworm
15. 9	1. 8	F10	D10	Swallow	27.11	15.10	H12	G11	Crocodile
16. 9	2. 8	F10	E11	Pig	28.11	16.10	H12	H12	Dragon
17. 9	3. 8	F10	F12	Porcupine	29.11	17.10	H12	J1	Badger
18. 9	4. 8	F10	G1	Wolf	30.11	18.10	H12	K2	Hare
19. 9	5. 8	F10	H2	Dog	1.12	19.10	H12	A3	Fox
20. 9	6. 8	F10	J3	Pheasant	2.12	20.10	H12	B4	Tiger
21. 9	7. 8	F10	K4	Cock	3.12	21.10	H12	C5	Leopard
22. 9	8. 8	F10	A5	Crow	4.12	22.10	H12	D6	Griffon
23. 9	9. 8	F10	B6	Monkey	5.12	23.10	H12	E7	Ox
24. 9	10. 8	F10	C7	Gibbon	6.12	24.10	H12	F8	Bat
25. 9	11. 8	F10	D8	Tapir	7.12	25.10	H12	G9	Rat
26. 9	12. 8	F10	E9	Sheep	8.12	26.10	H12	H10	Swallow
27. 9	13. 8	F10	F10	Deer	9.12	27.10	H12	J11	Pig
28. 9	14. 8	F10	G11	Horse	10.12	28.10	H12	K12	Porcupine
29. 9	15. 8	F10	H12	Stag	11.12	29.10	H12	A1	Wolf
30. 9	16. 8	F10	J1	Serpent	12.12	1.11	J1	B2	Dog
1.10	17. 8	F10	K2	Earthworm	13.12	2.11	J1	C3	Pheasant
2.10	18. 8	F10	A3	Crocodile	14.12	3.11	J1	D4	Cock
3.10	19. 8	F10	B4	Dragon	15.12	4.11	J1	E5	Crow
4.10	20. 8	F10	C5	Badger	16.12	5.11	J1	F6	Monkey
5.10	21. 8	F10	D6	Hare	17.12	6.11	J1	G7	Gibbon
6.10	22. 8	F10	E7	Fox	18.12	7.11	J1	H8	Tapir
7.10	23. 8	F10	F8	Tiger	19.12	8.11	J1	J9	Sheep
8.10	24. 8	F10	G9	Leopard	20.12	9.11	J1	K10	Deer
9.10	25. 8	F10	H10	Griffon	21.12	10.11	J1	A11	Horse
10.10	26. 8	F10	J11	Ox	22.12	11.11	J1	B12	Stag
11.10	27. 8	F10	K12	Bat	23.12	12.11	J1	C1	Serpent
12.10	28. 8	F10	A1	Rat	24.12	13.11	J1	D2	Earthworm
13.10	29. 8	F10	B2	Swallow	25.12	14.11	J1	E3	Crocodile
14.10	1. 9	G11	C3	Pig	26.12	15.11	J1	F4	Dragon
15.10	2. 9	G11	D4	Porcupine	27.12	16.11	J1	G5	Badger
16.10	3. 9	G11	E5	Wolf	28.12	17.11	J1	H6	Hare
17.10	4. 9	G11	F6	Dog	29.12	18.11	J1	J7	Fox
18.10	5. 9	G11	G7	Pheasant	30.12	19.11	J1	K8	Tiger
19.10	6. 9	G11	H8	Cock	31.12	20.11	J1	A9	Leopard
20.10	7. 9	G11	J9	Crow					
21.10	8. 9	G11	K10	Monkey	**1948**				
22.10	9. 9	G11	A11	Gibbon	1. 1	21.11	J1	B10	Griffon
23.10	10. 9	G11	B12	Tapir	2. 1	22.11	J1	C11	Ox
24.10	11. 9	G11	C1	Sheep	3. 1	23.11	J1	D12	Bat
25.10	12. 9	G11	D2	Deer	4. 1	24.11	J1	E1	Rat
26.10	13. 9	G11	E3	Horse	5. 1	25.11	J1	F2	Swallow
27.10	14. 9	G11	F4	Stag	6. 1	26.11	J1	G3	Pig
28.10	15. 9	G11	G5	Serpent	7. 1	27.11	J1	H4	Porcupine
29.10	16. 9	G11	H6	Earthworm	8. 1	28.11	J1	J5	Wolf
30.10	17. 9	G11	J7	Crocodile	9. 1	29.11	J1	K6	Dog
31.10	18. 9	G11	K8	Dragon	10. 1	30.11	J1	A7	Pheasant
1.11	19. 9	G11	A9	Badger	11. 1	1.12	K2	B8	Cock
2.11	20. 9	G11	B10	Hare	12. 1	2.12	K2	C9	Crow
3.11	21. 9	G11	C11	Fox	13. 1	3.12	K2	D10	Monkey
4.11	22. 9	G11	D12	Tiger	14. 1	4.12	K2	E11	Gibbon

Solar date	Lunar date	Month HS/EB	Day HS/EB	Constellation	Solar date	Lunar date	Month HS/EB	Day HS/EB	Constellation
15. 1	5.12	K2	F12	Tapir	28. 1	18.12	K2	J1	Leopard
16. 1	6.12	K2	G1	Sheep	29. 1	19.12	K2	K2	Griffon
17. 1	7.12	K2	H2	Deer	30. 1	20.12	K2	A3	Ox
18. 1	8.12	K2	J3	Horse	31. 1	21.12	K2	B4	Bat
19. 1	9.12	K2	K4	Stag	1. 2	22.12	K2	C5	Rat
20. 1	10.12	K2	A5	Serpent	2. 2	23.12	K2	D6	Swallow
21. 1	11.12	K2	B6	Earthworm	3. 2	24.12	K2	E7	Pig
22. 1	12.12	K2	C7	Crocodile	4. 2	25.12	K2	F8	Porcupine
23. 1	13.12	K2	D8	Dragon	5. 2	26.12	K2	G9	Wolf
24. 1	14.12	K2	E9	Badger	6. 2	27.12	K2	H10	Dog
25. 1	15.12	K2	F10	Hare	7. 2	28.12	K2	J11	Pheasant
26. 1	16.12	K2	G11	Fox	8. 2	29.12	K2	K12	Cock
27. 1	17.12	K2	H12	Tiger	9. 2	30.12	K2	A1	Crow

MOU TZU YEAR

Solar date	Lunar date	Month HS/EB	Day HS/EB	Constellation	Solar date	Lunar date	Month HS/EB	Day HS/EB	Constellation
10. 2	1. 1	A3	B2	Monkey	5. 4	26. 2	B4	G9	Crow
11. 2	2. 1	A3	C3	Gibbon	6. 4	27. 2	B4	H10	Monkey
12. 2	3. 1	A3	D4	Tapir	7. 4	28. 2	B4	J11	Gibbon
13. 2	4. 1	A3	E5	Sheep	8. 4	29. 2	B4	K12	Tapir
14. 2	5. 1	A3	F6	Deer	9. 4	1. 3	C5	A1	Sheep
15. 2	6. 1	A3	G7	Horse	10. 4	2. 3	C5	B2	Deer
16. 2	7. 1	A3	H8	Stag	11. 4	3. 3	C5	C3	Horse
17. 2	8. 1	A3	J9	Serpent	12. 4	4. 3	C5	D4	Stag
18. 2	9. 1	A3	K10	Earthworm	13. 4	5. 3	C5	E5	Serpent
19. 2	10. 1	A3	A11	Crocodile	14. 4	6. 3	C5	F6	Earthworm
20. 2	11. 1	A3	B12	Dragon	15. 4	7. 3	C5	G7	Crocodile
21. 2	12. 1	A3	C1	Badger	16. 4	8. 3	C5	H8	Dragon
22. 2	13. 1	A3	D2	Hare	17. 4	9. 3	C5	J9	Badger
23. 2	14. 1	A3	E3	Fox	18. 4	10. 3	C5	K10	Hare
24. 2	15. 1	A3	F4	Tiger	19. 4	11. 3	C5	A11	Fox
25. 2	16. 1	A3	G5	Leopard	20. 4	12. 3	C5	B12	Tiger
26. 2	17. 1	A3	H6	Griffon	21. 4	13. 3	C5	C1	Leopard
27. 2	18. 1	A3	J7	Ox	22. 4	14. 3	C5	D2	Griffon
28. 2	19. 1	A3	K8	Bat	23. 4	15. 3	C5	E3	Ox
29. 2	20. 1	A3	A9	Rat	24. 4	16. 3	C5	F4	Bat
1. 3	21. 1	A3	B10	Swallow	25. 4	17. 3	C5	G5	Rat
2. 3	22. 1	A3	C11	Pig	26. 4	18. 3	C5	H6	Swallow
3. 3	23. 1	A3	D12	Porcupine	27. 4	19. 3	C5	J7	Pig
4. 3	24. 1	A3	E1	Wolf	28. 4	20. 3	C5	K8	Porcupine
5. 3	25. 1	A3	F2	Dog	29. 4	21. 3	C5	A9	Wolf
6. 3	26. 1	A3	G3	Pheasant	30. 4	22. 3	C5	B10	Dog
7. 3	27. 1	A3	H4	Cock	1. 5	23. 3	C5	C11	Pheasant
8. 3	28. 1	A3	J5	Crow	2. 5	24. 3	C5	D12	Cock
9. 3	29. 1	A3	K6	Monkey	3. 5	25. 3	C5	E1	Crow
10. 3	30. 1	A3	A7	Gibbon	4. 5	26. 3	C5	F2	Monkey
11. 3	1. 2	B4	B8	Tapir	5. 5	27. 3	C5	G3	Gibbon
12. 3	2. 2	B4	C9	Sheep	6. 5	28. 3	C5	H4	Tapir
13. 3	3. 2	B4	D10	Deer	7. 5	29. 3	C5	J5	Sheep
14. 3	4. 2	B4	E11	Horse	8. 5	30. 3	C5	K6	Deer
15. 3	5. 2	B4	F12	Stag	9. 5	1. 4	D6	A7	Horse
16. 3	6. 2	B4	G1	Serpent	10. 5	2. 4	D6	B8	Stag
17. 3	7. 2	B4	H2	Earthworm	11. 5	3. 4	D6	C9	Serpent
18. 3	8. 2	B4	J3	Crocodile	12. 5	4. 4	D6	D10	Earthworm
19. 3	9. 2	B4	K4	Dragon	13. 5	5. 4	D6	E11	Crocodile
20. 3	10. 2	B4	A5	Badger	14. 5	6. 4	D6	F12	Dragon
21. 3	11. 2	B4	B6	Hare	15. 5	7. 4	D6	G1	Badger
22. 3	12. 2	B4	C7	Fox	16. 5	8. 4	D6	H2	Hare
23. 3	13. 2	B4	D8	Tiger	17. 5	9. 4	D6	J3	Fox
24. 3	14. 2	B4	E9	Leopard	18. 5	10. 4	D6	K4	Tiger
25. 3	15. 2	B4	F10	Griffon	19. 5	11. 4	D6	A5	Leopard
26. 3	16. 2	B4	G11	Ox	20. 5	12. 4	D6	B6	Griffon
27. 3	17. 2	B4	H12	Bat	21. 5	13. 4	D6	C7	Ox
28. 3	18. 2	B4	J1	Rat	22. 5	14. 4	D6	D8	Bat
29. 3	19. 2	B4	K2	Swallow	23. 5	15. 4	D6	E9	Rat
30. 3	20. 2	B4	A3	Pig	24. 5	16. 4	D6	F10	Swallow
31. 3	21. 2	B4	B4	Porcupine	25. 5	17. 4	D6	G11	Pig
1. 4	22. 2	B4	C5	Wolf	26. 5	18. 4	D6	H12	Porcupine
2. 4	23. 2	B4	D6	Dog	27. 5	19. 4	D5	J1	Wolf
3. 4	24. 2	B4	E7	Pheasant	28. 5	20. 4	D6	K2	Dog
4. 4	25. 2	B4	F8	Cock	29. 5	21. 4	D6	A3	Pheasant

Solar date	Lunar date	Month HS/EB	Day HS/EB	Constellation	Solar date	Lunar date	Month HS/EB	Day HS/EB	Constellation
30. 5	22. 4	D6	B4	Cock	11. 8	7. 7	G9	E5	Leopard
31. 5	23. 4	D6	C5	Crow	12. 8	8. 7	G9	F6	Griffon
1. 6	24. 4	D6	D6	Monkey	13. 8	9. 7	G9	G7	Ox
2. 6	25. 4	D6	E7	Gibbon	14. 8	10. 7	G9	H8	Bat
3. 6	26. 4	D6	F8	Tapir	15. 8	11. 7	G9	J9	Rat
4. 6	27. 4	D6	G9	Sheep	16. 8	12. 7	G9	K10	Swallow
5. 6	28. 4	D6	H10	Deer	17. 8	13. 7	G9	A11	Pig
6. 6	29. 4	D6	J11	Horse	18. 8	14. 7	G9	B12	Porcupine
7. 6	1. 5	E7	K12	Stag	19. 8	15. 7	G9	C1	Wolf
8. 6	2. 5	E7	A1	Serpent	20. 8	16. 7	G9	D2	Dog
9. 6	3. 5	E7	B2	Earthworm	21. 8	17. 7	G9	E3	Pheasant
10. 6	4. 5	E7	C3	Crocodile	22. 8	18. 7	G9	F4	Cock
11. 6	5. 5	E7	D4	Dragon	23. 8	19. 7	G9	G5	Crow
12. 6	6. 5	E7	E5	Badger	24. 8	20. 7	G9	H6	Monkey
13. 6	7. 5	E7	F6	Hare	25. 8	21. 7	G9	J7	Gibbon
14. 6	8. 5	E7	G7	Fox	26. 8	22. 7	G9	K8	Tapir
15. 6	9. 5	E7	H8	Tiger	27. 8	23. 7	G9	A9	Sheep
16. 6	10. 5	E7	J9	Leopard	28. 8	24. 7	G9	B10	Deer
17. 6	11. 5	E7	K10	Griffon	29. 8	25. 7	G9	C11	Horse
18. 6	12. 5	E7	A11	Ox	30. 8	26. 7	G9	D12	Stag
19. 6	13. 5	E7	B12	Bat	31. 8	27. 7	G9	E1	Serpent
20. 6	14. 5	E7	C1	Rat	1. 9	28. 7	G9	F2	Earthworm
21. 6	15. 5	E7	D2	Swallow	2. 9	29. 7	G9	G3	Crocodile
22. 6	16. 5	E7	E3	Pig	3. 9	1. 8	H10	H4	Dragon
23. 6	17. 5	E7	F4	Porcupine	4. 9	2. 8	H10	J5	Badger
24. 6	18. 5	E7	G5	Wolf	5. 9	3. 8	H10	K6	Hare
25. 6	19. 5	E7	H6	Dog	6. 9	4. 8	H10	A7	Fox
26. 6	20. 5	E7	J7	Pheasant	7. 9	5. 8	H10	B8	Tiger
27. 6	21. 5	E7	K8	Cock	8. 9	6. 8	H10	C9	Leopard
28. 6	22. 5	E7	A9	Crow	9. 9	7. 8	H10	D10	Griffon
29. 6	23. 5	E7	B10	Monkey	10. 9	8. 8	H10	E11	Ox
30. 6	24. 5	E7	C11	Gibbon	11. 9	9. 8	H10	F12	Bat
1. 7	25. 5	E7	D12	Tapir	12. 9	10. 8	H10	G1	Rat
2. 7	26. 5	E7	E1	Sheep	13. 9	11. 8	H10	H2	Swallow
3. 7	27. 5	E7	F2	Deer	14. 9	12. 8	H10	J3	Pig
4. 7	28. 5	E7	G3	Horse	15. 9	13. 8	H10	K4	Porcupine
5. 7	29. 5	E7	H4	Stag	16. 9	14. 8	H10	A5	Wolf
6. 7	30. 5	E7	J5	Serpent	17. 9	15. 8	H10	B6	Dog
7. 7	1. 6	F8	K6	Earthworm	18. 9	16. 8	H10	C7	Pheasant
8. 7	2. 6	F8	A7	Crocodile	19. 9	17. 8	H10	D8	Cock
9. 7	3. 6	F8	B8	Dragon	20. 9	18. 8	H10	E9	Crow
10. 7	4. 6	F8	C9	Badger	21. 9	19. 8	H10	F10	Monkey
11. 7	5. 6	F8	D10	Hare	22. 9	20. 8	H10	G11	Gibbon
12. 7	6. 6	F8	E11	Fox	23. 9	21. 8	H10	H12	Tapir
13. 7	7. 6	F8	F12	Tiger	24. 9	22. 8	H10	J1	Sheep
14. 7	8. 6	F8	G1	Leopard	25. 9	23. 8	H10	K2	Deer
15. 7	9. 6	F8	H2	Griffon	26. 9	24. 8	H10	A3	Horse
16. 7	10. 6	F8	J3	Ox	27. 9	25. 8	H10	B4	Stag
17. 7	11. 6	F8	K4	Bat	28. 9	26. 8	H10	C5	Serpent
18. 7	12. 6	F8	A5	Rat	29. 9	27. 8	H10	D6	Earthworm
19. 7	13. 6	F8	B6	Swallow	30. 9	28. 8	H10	E7	Crocodile
20. 7	14. 6	F8	C7	Pig	1.10	29. 8	H10	F8	Dragon
21. 7	15. 6	F8	D8	Porcupine	2.10	30. 8	H10	G9	Badger
22. 7	16. 6	F8	E9	Wolf	3.10	1. 9	J11	H10	Hare
23. 7	17. 6	F8	F10	Dog	4.10	2. 9	J11	J11	Fox
24. 7	18. 6	F8	G11	Pheasant	5.10	3. 9	J11	K12	Tiger
25. 7	19. 6	F8	H12	Cock	6.10	4. 9	J11	A1	Leopard
26. 7	20. 6	F8	J1	Crow	7.10	5. 9	J11	B2	Griffon
27. 7	21. 6	F8	K2	Monkey	8.10	6. 9	J11	C3	Ox
28. 7	22. 6	F8	A3	Gibbon	9.10	7. 9	J11	D4	Bat
29. 7	23. 6	F8	B4	Tapir	10.10	8. 9	J11	E5	Rat
30. 7	24. 6	F8	C5	Sheep	11.10	9. 9	J11	F6	Swallow
31. 7	25. 6	F8	D6	Deer	12.10	10. 9	J11	G7	Pig
1. 8	26. 6	F8	E7	Horse	13.10	11. 9	J11	H8	Porcupine
2. 8	27. 6	F8	F8	Stag	14.10	12. 9	J11	J9	Wolf
3. 8	28. 6	F8	G9	Serpent	15.10	13. 9	J11	K10	Dog
4. 8	29. 6	F8	H10	Earthworm	16.10	14. 9	J11	A11	Pheasant
5. 8	1. 7	G9	J11	Crocodile	17.10	15. 9	J11	B12	Cock
6. 8	2. 7	G9	K12	Dragon	18.10	16. 9	J11	C1	Crow
7. 8	3. 7	G9	A1	Badger	19.10	17. 9	J11	D2	Monkey
8. 8	4. 7	G9	B2	Hare	20.10	18. 9	J11	E3	Gibbon
9. 8	5. 7	G9	C3	Fox	21.10	19. 9	J11	F4	Tapir
10. 8	6. 7	G9	D4	Tiger	22.10	20. 9	J11	G5	Sheep

Solar date	Lunar date	Month HS/EB	Day HS/EB	Constellation	Solar date	Lunar date	Month HS/EB	Day HS/EB	Constellation
23.10	21. 9	J11	H6	Deer	12.12	12.11	A1	H8	Cock
24.10	22. 9	J11	J7	Horse	13.12	13.11	A1	J9	Crow
25.10	23. 9	J11	K8	Stag	14.12	14.11	A1	K10	Monkey
26.10	24. 9	J11	A9	Serpent	15.12	15.11	A1	A11	Gibbon
27.10	25. 9	J11	B10	Earthworm	16.12	16.11	A1	B12	Tapir
28.10	26. 9	J11	C11	Crocodile	17.12	17.11	A1	C1	Sheep
29.10	27. 9	J11	D12	Dragon	18.12	18.11	A1	D2	Deer
30.10	28. 9	J11	E1	Badger	19.12	19.11	A1	E3	Horse
31.10	29. 9	J11	F2	Hare	20.12	20.11	A1	F4	Stag
1.11	1.10	K12	G3	Fox	21.12	21.11	A1	G5	Serpent
2.11	2.10	K12	H4	Tiger	22.12	22.11	A1	H6	Earthworm
3.11	3.10	K12	J5	Leopard	23.12	23.11	A1	J7	Crocodile
4.11	4.10	K12	K6	Griffon	24.12	24.11	A1	K8	Dragon
5.11	5.10	K12	A7	Ox	25.12	25.11	A1	A9	Badger
6.11	6.10	K12	B8	Bat	26.12	26.11	A1	B10	Hare
7.11	7.10	K12	C9	Rat	27.12	27.11	A1	C11	Fox
8.11	8.10	K12	D10	Swallow	28.12	28.11	A1	D12	Tiger
9.11	9.10	K12	E11	Pig	29.12	29.11	A1	E1	Leopard
10.11	10.10	K12	F12	Porcupine	30.12	1.12	B2	F2	Griffon
11.11	11.10	K12	G1	Wolf	31.12	2.12	B2	G3	Ox
12.11	12.10	K12	H2	Dog					
13.11	13.10	K12	J3	Pheasant	**1949**				
14.11	14.10	K12	K4	Cock	1. 1	3.12	B2	H4	Bat
15.11	15.10	K12	A5	Crow	2. 1	4.12	B2	J5	Rat
16.11	16.10	K12	B6	Monkey	3. 1	5.12	B2	K6	Swallow
17.11	17.10	K12	C7	Gibbon	4. 1	6.12	B2	A7	Pig
18.11	18.10	K12	D8	Tapir	5. 1	7.12	B2	B8	Porcupine
19.11	19.10	K12	E9	Sheep	6. 1	8.12	B2	C9	Wolf
20.11	20.10	K12	F10	Deer	7. 1	9.12	B2	D10	Dog
21.11	21.10	K12	G11	Horse	8. 1	10.12	B2	E11	Pheasant
22.11	22.10	K12	H12	Stag	9. 1	11.12	B2	F12	Cock
23.11	23.10	K12	J1	Serpent	10. 1	12.12	B2	G1	Crow
24.11	24.10	K12	K2	Earthworm	11. 1	13.12	B2	H2	Monkey
25.11	25.10	K12	A3	Crocodile	12. 1	14.12	B2	J3	Gibbon
26.11	26.10	K12	B4	Dragon	13. 1	15.12	B2	K4	Tapir
27.11	27.10	K12	C5	Badger	14. 1	16.12	B2	A5	Sheep
28.11	28.10	K12	D6	Hare	15. 1	17.12	B2	B6	Deer
29.11	29.10	K12	E7	Fox	16. 1	18.12	B2	C7	Horse
30.11	30.10	K12	F8	Tiger	17. 1	19.12	B2	D8	Stag
1.12	1.11	A1	G9	Leopard	18. 1	20.12	B2	E9	Serpent
2.12	2.11	A1	H10	Griffon	19. 1	21.12	B2	F10	Earthworm
3.12	3.11	A1	J11	Ox	20. 1	22.12	B2	G11	Crocodile
4.12	4.11	A1	K12	Bat	21. 1	23.12	B2	H12	Dragon
5.12	5.11	A1	A1	Rat	22. 1	24.12	B2	J1	Badger
6.12	6.11	A1	B2	Swallow	23. 1	25.12	B2	K2	Hare
7.12	7.11	A1	C3	Pig	24. 1	26.12	B2	A3	Fox
8.12	8.11	A1	D4	Porcupine	25. 1	27.12	B2	B4	Tiger
9.12	9.11	A1	E5	Wolf	26. 1	28.12	B2	C5	Leopard
10.12	10.11	A1	F6	Dog	27. 1	29.12	B2	D6	Griffon
11.12	11.11	A1	G7	Pheasant	28. 1	30.12	B2	E7	Ox

CHI CH'OU YEAR

Solar date	Lunar date	Month HS/EB	Day HS/EB	Constellation	Solar date	Lunar date	Month HS/EB	Day HS/EB	Constellation
29. 1	1. 1	C3	F8	Bat	16. 2	19. 1	C3	D2	Earthworm
30. 1	2. 1	C3	G9	Rat	17. 2	20. 1	C3	E3	Crocodile
31. 1	3. 1	C3	H10	Swallow	18. 2	21. 1	C3	F4	Dragon
1. 2	4. 1	C3	J11	Pig	19. 2	22. 1	C3	G5	Badger
2. 2	5. 1	C3	K12	Porcupine	20. 2	23. 1	C3	H6	Hare
3. 2	6. 1	C3	A1	Wolf	21. 2	24. 1	C3	J7	Fox
4. 2	7. 1	C3	B2	Dog	22. 2	25. 1	C3	K8	Tiger
5. 2	8. 1	C3	C3	Pheasant	23. 2	26. 1	C3	A9	Leopard
6. 2	9. 1	C3	D4	Cock	24. 2	27. 1	C3	B10	Griffon
7. 2	10. 1	C3	E5	Crow	25. 2	28. 1	C3	C11	Ox
8. 2	11. 1	C3	F6	Monkey	26. 2	29. 1	C3	D12	Bat
9. 2	12. 1	C3	G7	Gibbon	27. 2	30. 1	C3	E1	Rat
10. 2	13. 1	C3	H8	Tapir	28. 2	1. 2	D4	F2	Swallow
11. 2	14. 1	C3	J9	Sheep	1. 3	2. 2	D4	G3	Pig
12. 2	15. 1	C3	K10	Deer	2. 3	3. 2	D4	H4	Porcupine
13. 2	16. 1	C3	A11	Horse	3. 3	4. 2	D4	J5	Wolf
14. 2	17. 1	C3	B12	Stag	4. 3	5. 2	D4	K6	Dog
15. 2	18. 1	C3	C1	Serpent	5. 3	6. 2	D4	A7	Pheasant

Solar date	Lunar date	Month HS/EB	Day HS/EB	Constellation	Solar date	Lunar date	Month HS/EB	Day HS/EB	Constellation
6. 3	7. 2	D4	B8	Cock	18. 5	21. 4	F6	E9	Leopard
7. 3	8. 2	D4	C9	Crow	19. 5	22. 4	F6	F10	Griffon
8. 3	9. 2	D4	D10	Monkey	20. 5	23. 4	F6	G11	Ox
9. 3	10. 2	D4	E11	Gibbon	21. 5	24. 4	F6	H12	Bat
10. 3	11. 2	D4	F12	Tapir	22. 5	25. 4	F6	J1	Rat
11. 3	12. 2	D4	G1	Sheep	23. 5	26. 4	F6	K2	Swallow
12. 3	13. 2	D4	H2	Deer	24. 5	27. 4	F6	A3	Pig
13. 3	14. 2	D4	J3	Horse	25. 5	28. 4	F6	B4	Porcupine
14. 3	15. 2	D4	K4	Stag	26. 5	29. 4	F6	C5	Wolf
15. 3	16. 2	D4	A5	Serpent	27. 5	30. 4	F6	D6	Dog
16. 3	17. 2	D4	B6	Earthworm	28. 5	1. 5	G7	E7	Pheasant
17. 3	18. 2	D4	C7	Crocodile	29. 5	2. 5	G7	F8	Cock
18. 3	19. 2	D4	D8	Dragon	30. 5	3. 5	G7	G9	Crow
19. 3	20. 2	D4	E9	Badger	31. 5	4. 5	G7	H10	Monkey
20. 3	21. 2	D4	F10	Hare	1. 6	5. 5	G7	J11	Gibbon
21. 3	22. 2	D4	G11	Fox	2. 6	6. 5	G7	K12	Tapir
22. 3	23. 2	D4	H12	Tiger	3. 6	7. 5	G7	A1	Sheep
23. 3	24. 2	D4	J1	Leopard	4. 6	8. 5	G7	B2	Deer
24. 3	25. 2	D4	K2	Griffon	5. 6	9. 5	G7	C3	Horse
25. 3	26. 2	D4	A3	Ox	6. 6	10. 5	G7	D4	Stag
26. 3	27. 2	D4	B4	Bat	7. 6	11. 5	G7	E5	Serpent
27. 3	28. 2	D4	C5	Rat	8. 6	12. 5	G7	F6	Earthworm
28. 3	29. 2	D4	D6	Swallow	9. 6	13. 5	G7	G7	Crocodile
29. 3	1. 3	E5	E7	Pig	10. 6	14. 5	G7	H8	Dragon
30. 3	2. 3	E5	F8	Porcupine	11. 6	15. 5	G7	J9	Badger
31. 3	3. 3	E5	G9	Wolf	12. 6	16. 5	G7	K10	Hare
1. 4	4. 3	E5	H10	Dog	13. 6	17. 5	G7	A11	Fox
2. 4	5. 3	E5	J11	Pheasant	14. 6	18. 5	G7	B12	Tiger
3. 4	6. 3	E5	K12	Cock	15. 6	19. 5	G7	C1	Leopard
4. 4	7. 3	E5	A1	Crow	16. 6	20. 5	G7	D2	Griffon
5. 4	8. 3	E5	B2	Monkey	17. 6	21. 5	G7	E3	Ox
6. 4	9. 3	E5	C3	Gibbon	18. 6	22. 5	G7	F4	Bat
7. 4	10. 3	E5	D4	Tapir	19. 6	23. 5	G7	G5	Rat
8. 4	11. 3	E5	E5	Sheep	20. 6	24. 5	G7	H6	Swallow
9. 4	12. 3	E5	F6	Deer	21. 6	25. 5	G7	J7	Pig
10. 4	13. 3	E5	G7	Horse	22. 6	26. 5	G7	K8	Porcupine
11. 4	14. 3	E5	H8	Stag	23. 6	27. 5	G7	A9	Wolf
12. 4	15. 3	E5	J9	Serpent	24. 6	28. 5	G7	B10	Dog
13. 4	16. 3	E5	K10	Earthworm	25. 6	29. 5	G7	C11	Pheasant
14. 4	17. 3	E5	A11	Crocodile	26. 6	1. 6	H8	D12	Cock
15. 4	18. 3	E5	B12	Dragon	27. 6	2. 6	H8	E1	Crow
16. 4	19. 3	E5	C1	Badger	28. 6	3. 6	H8	F2	Monkey
17. 4	20. 3	E5	D2	Hare	29. 6	4. 6	H8	G3	Gibbon
18. 4	21. 3	E5	E3	Fox	30. 6	5. 6	H8	H4	Tapir
19. 4	22. 3	E5	F4	Tiger	1. 7	6. 6	H8	J5	Sheep
20. 4	23. 3	E5	G5	Leopard	2. 7	7. 6	H8	K6	Deer
21. 4	24. 3	E5	H6	Griffon	3. 7	8. 6	H8	A7	Horse
22. 4	25. 3	E5	J7	Ox	4. 7	9. 6	H8	B8	Stag
23. 4	26. 3	E5	K8	Bat	5. 7	10. 6	H8	C9	Serpent
24. 4	27. 3	E5	A9	Rat	6. 7	11. 6	H8	D10	Earthworm
25. 4	28. 3	E5	B10	Swallow	7. 7	12. 6	H8	E11	Crocodile
26. 4	29. 3	E5	C11	Pig	8. 7	13. 6	H8	F12	Dragon
27. 4	30. 3	E5	D12	Porcupine	9. 7	14. 6	H8	G1	Badger
28. 4	1. 4	F6	E1	Wolf	10. 7	15. 6	H8	H2	Hare
29. 4	2. 4	F6	F2	Dog	11. 7	16. 6	H8	J3	Fox
30. 4	3. 4	F6	G3	Pheasant	12. 7	17. 6	H8	K4	Tiger
1. 5	4. 4	F6	H4	Cock	13. 7	18. 6	H8	A5	Leopard
2. 5	5. 4	F6	J5	Crow	14. 7	19. 6	H8	B6	Griffon
3. 5	6. 4	F6	K6	Monkey	15. 7	20. 6	H8	C7	Ox
4. 5	7. 4	F6	A7	Gibbon	16. 7	21. 6	H8	D8	Bat
5. 5	8. 4	F6	B8	Tapir	17. 7	22. 6	H8	E9	Rat
6. 5	9. 4	F6	C9	Sheep	18. 7	23. 6	H8	F10	Swallow
7. 5	10. 4	F6	D10	Deer	19. 7	24. 6	H8	G11	Pig
8. 5	11. 4	F6	E11	Horse	20. 7	25. 6	H8	H12	Porcupine
9. 5	12. 4	F6	F12	Stag	21. 7	26. 6	H8	J1	Wolf
10. 5	13. 4	F6	G1	Serpent	22. 7	27. 6	H8	K2	Dog
11. 5	14. 4	F6	H2	Earthworm	23. 7	28. 6	H8	A3	Pheasant
12. 5	15. 4	F6	J3	Crocodile	24. 7	29. 6	H8	B4	Cock
13. 5	16. 4	F6	K4	Dragon	25. 7	30. 6	H8	C5	Crow
14. 5	17. 4	F6	A5	Badger	26. 7	1. 7	J9	D6	Monkey
15. 5	18. 4	F6	B6	Hare	27. 7	2. 7	J9	E7	Gibbon
16. 5	19. 4	F6	C7	Fox	28. 7	3. 7	J9	F8	Tapir
17. 5	20. 4	F6	D8	Tiger	29. 7	4. 7	J9	G9	Sheep

Solar date	Lunar date	Month HS/EB	Day HS/EB	Constellation
30. 7	5. 7	J9	H10	Deer
31. 7	6. 7	J9	J11	Horse
1. 8	7. 7	J9	K12	Stag
2. 8	8. 7	J9	A1	Serpent
3. 8	9. 7	J9	B2	Earthworm
4. 8	10. 7	J9	C3	Crocodile
5. 8	11. 7	J9	D4	Dragon
6. 8	12. 7	J9	E5	Badger
7. 8	13. 7	J9	F6	Hare
8. 8	14. 7	J9	G7	Fox
9. 8	15. 7	J9	H8	Tiger
10. 8	16. 7	J9	J9	Leopard
11. 8	17. 7	J9	K10	Griffon
12. 8	18. 7	J9	A11	Ox
13. 8	19. 7	J9	B12	Bat
14. 8	20. 7	J9	C1	Rat
15. 8	21. 7	J9	D2	Swallow
16. 8	22. 7	J9	E3	Pig
17. 8	23. 7	J9	F4	Porcupine
18. 8	24. 7	J9	G5	Wolf
19. 8	25. 7	J9	H6	Dog
20. 8	26. 7	J9	J7	Pheasant
21. 8	27. 7	J9	K8	Cock
22. 8	28. 7	J9	A9	Crow
23. 8	29. 7	J9	B10	Monkey
24. 8	*1. 7*	*J9*	C11	Gibbon
25. 8	*2. 7*	*J9*	D12	Tapir
26. 8	*3. 7*	*J9*	E1	Sheep
27. 8	*4. 7*	*J9*	F2	Deer
28. 8	*5. 7*	*J9*	G3	Horse
29. 8	*6. 7*	*J9*	H4	Stag
30. 8	*7. 7*	*J9*	J5	Serpent
31. 8	*8. 7*	*J9*	K6	Earthworm
1. 9	*9. 7*	*J9*	A7	Crocodile
2. 9	*10. 7*	*J9*	B8	Dragon
3. 9	*11. 7*	*J9*	C9	Badger
4. 9	*12. 7*	*J9*	D10	Hare
5. 9	*13. 7*	*J9*	E11	Fox
6. 9	*14. 7*	*J9*	F12	Tiger
7. 9	*15. 7*	*J9*	G1	Leopard
8. 9	*16. 7*	*J9*	H2	Griffon
9. 9	*17. 7*	*J9*	J3	Ox
10. 9	*18. 7*	*J9*	K4	Bat
11. 9	*19. 7*	*J9*	A5	Rat
12. 9	*20. 7*	*J9*	B6	Swallow
13. 9	*21. 7*	*J9*	C7	Pig
14. 9	*22. 7*	*J9*	D8	Porcupine
15. 9	*23. 7*	*J9*	E9	Wolf
16. 9	*24. 7*	*J9*	F10	Dog
17. 9	*25. 7*	*J9*	G11	Pheasant
18. 9	*26. 7*	*J9*	H12	Cock
19. 9	*27. 7*	*J9*	J1	Crow
20. 9	*28. 7*	*J9*	K2	Monkey
21. 9	*29. 7*	*J9*	A3	Gibbon
22. 9	1. 8	K10	B4	Tapir
23. 9	2. 8	K10	C5	Sheep
24. 9	3. 8	K10	D6	Deer
25. 9	4. 8	K10	E7	Horse
26. 9	5. 8	K10	F8	Stag
27. 9	6. 8	K10	G9	Serpent
28. 9	7. 8	K10	H10	Earthworm
29. 9	8. 8	K10	J11	Crocodile
30. 9	9. 8	K10	K12	Dragon
1.10	10. 8	K10	A1	Badger
2.10	11. 8	K10	B2	Hare
3.10	12. 8	K10	C3	Fox
4.10	13. 8	K10	D4	Tiger
5.10	14. 8	K10	E5	Leopard
6.10	15. 8	K10	F6	Griffon
7.10	16. 8	K10	G7	Ox
8.10	17. 8	K10	H8	Bat
9.10	18. 8	K10	J9	Rat
10.10	19. 8	K10	K10	Swallow

Solar date	Lunar date	Month HS/EB	Day HS/EB	Constellation
11.10	20. 8	K10	A11	Pig
12.10	21. 8	K10	B12	Porcupine
13.10	22. 8	K10	C1	Wolf
14.10	23. 8	K10	D2	Dog
15.10	24. 8	K10	E3	Pheasant
16.10	25. 8	K10	F4	Cock
17.10	26. 8	K10	G5	Crow
18.10	27. 8	K10	H6	Monkey
19.10	28. 8	K10	J7	Gibbon
20.10	29. 8	K10	K8	Tapir
21.10	30. 8	K10	A9	Sheep
22.10	1. 9	A11	B10	Deer
23.10	2. 9	A11	C11	Horse
24.10	3. 9	A11	D12	Stag
25.10	4. 9	A11	E1	Serpent
26.10	5. 9	A11	F2	Earthworm
27.10	6. 9	A11	G3	Crocodile
28.10	7. 9	A11	H4	Dragon
29.10	8. 9	A11	J5	Badger
30.10	9. 9	A11	K6	Hare
31.10	10. 9	A11	A7	Fox
1.11	11. 9	A11	B8	Tiger
2.11	12. 9	A11	C9	Leopard
3.11	13. 9	A11	D10	Griffon
4.11	14. 9	A11	E11	Ox
5.11	15. 9	A11	F12	Bat
6.11	16. 9	A11	G1	Rat
7.11	17. 9	A11	H2	Swallow
8.11	18. 9	A11	J3	Pig
9.11	19. 9	A11	K4	Porcupine
10.11	20. 9	A11	A5	Wolf
11.11	21. 9	A11	B6	Dog
12.11	22. 9	A11	C7	Pheasant
13.11	23. 9	A11	D8	Cock
14.11	24. 9	A11	E9	Crow
15.11	25. 9	A11	F10	Monkey
16.11	26. 9	A11	G11	Gibbon
17.11	27. 9	A11	H12	Tapir
18.11	28. 9	A11	J1	Sheep
19.11	29. 9	A11	K2	Deer
20.11	1.10	B12	A3	Horse
21.11	2.10	B12	B4	Stag
22.11	3.10	B12	C5	Serpent
23.11	4.10	B12	D6	Earthworm
24.11	5.10	B12	E7	Crocodile
25.11	6.10	B12	F8	Dragon
26.11	7.10	B12	G9	Badger
27.11	8.10	B12	H10	Hare
28.11	9.10	B12	J11	Fox
29.11	10.10	B12	K12	Tiger
30.11	11.10	B12	A1	Leopard
1.12	12.10	B12	B2	Griffon
2.12	13.10	B12	C3	Ox
3.12	14.10	B12	D4	Bat
4.12	15.10	B12	E5	Rat
5.12	16.10	B12	F6	Swallow
6.12	17.10	B12	G7	Pig
7.12	18.10	B12	H8	Porcupine
8.12	19.10	B12	J9	Wolf
9.12	20.10	B12	K10	Dog
10.12	21.10	B12	A11	Pheasant
11.12	22.10	B12	B12	Cock
12.12	23.10	B12	C1	Crow
13.12	24.10	B12	D2	Monkey
14.12	25.10	B12	E3	Gibbon
15.12	26.10	B12	F4	Tapir
16.12	27.10	B12	G5	Sheep
17.12	28.10	B12	H6	Deer
18.12	29.10	B12	J7	Horse
19.12	30.10	B12	K8	Stag
20.12	1.11	C1	A9	Serpent
21.12	2.11	C1	B12	Earthworm
22.12	3.11	C1	C11	Crocodile

Solar date	Lunar date	Month HS/EB	Day HS/EB	Constellation	Solar date	Lunar date	Month HS/EB	Day HS/EB	Constellation
23.12	4.11	C1	D12	Dragon	19. 1	2.12	D2	A3	Crocodile
24.12	5.11	C1	E1	Badger	20. 1	3.12	D2	B4	Dragon
25.12	6.11	C1	F2	Hare	21. 1	4.12	D2	C5	Badger
26.12	7.11	C1	G3	Fox	22. 1	5.12	D2	D6	Hare
27.12	8.11	C1	H4	Tiger	23. 1	6.12	D2	E7	Fox
28.12	9.11	C1	J5	Leopard	24. 1	7.12	D2	F8	Tiger
29.12	10.11	C1	K6	Griffon	25. 1	8.12	D2	G9	Leopard
30.12	11.11	C1	A7	Ox	26. 1	9.12	D2	H10	Griffon
31.12	12.11	C1	B8	Bat	27. 1	10.12	D2	J11	Ox
1950					28. 1	11.12	D2	K12	Bat
1. 1	13.11	C1	C9	Rat	29. 1	12.12	D2	A1	Rat
2. 1	14.11	C1	D10	Swallow	30. 1	13.12	D2	B2	Swallow
3. 1	15.11	C1	E11	Pig	31. 1	14.12	D2	C3	Pig
4. 1	16.11	C1	F12	Porcupine	1. 2	15.12	D2	D4	Porcupine
5. 1	17.11	C1	G1	Wolf	2. 2	16.12	D2	E5	Wolf
6. 1	18.11	C1	H2	Dog	3. 2	17.12	D2	F6	Dog
7. 1	19.11	C1	J3	Pheasant	4. 2	18.12	D2	G7	Pheasant
8. 1	20.11	C1	K4	Cock	5. 2	19.12	D2	H8	Cock
9. 1	21.11	C1	A5	Crow	6. 2	20.12	D2	J9	Crow
10. 1	22.11	C1	B6	Monkey	7. 2	21.12	D2	K10	Monkey
11. 1	23.11	C1	C7	Gibbon	8. 2	22.12	D2	A11	Gibbon
12. 1	24.11	C1	D8	Tapir	9. 2	23.12	D2	B12	Tapir
13. 1	25.11	C1	E9	Sheep	10. 2	24.12	D2	C1	Sheep
14. 1	26.11	C1	F10	Deer	11. 2	25.12	D2	D2	Deer
15. 1	27.11	C1	G11	Horse	12. 2	26.12	D2	E3	Horse
16. 1	28.11	C1	H12	Stag	13. 2	27.12	D2	F4	Stag
17. 1	29.11	C1	J1	Serpent	14. 2	28.12	D2	G5	Serpent
18. 1	1.12	D2	K2	Earthworm	15. 2	29.12	D2	H6	Earthworm
					16. 2	30.12	D2	J7	Crocodile

KENG YIN YEAR

Solar date	Lunar date	Month HS/EB	Day HS/EB	Constellation	Solar date	Lunar date	Month HS/EB	Day HS/EB	Constellation
17. 2	1. 1	E3	K8	Dragon	28. 3	11. 2	F4	J11	Pig
18. 2	2. 1	E3	A9	Badger	29. 3	12. 2	F4	K12	Porcupine
19. 2	3. 1	E3	B10	Hare	30. 3	13. 2	F4	A1	Wolf
20. 2	4. 1	E3	C11	Fox	31. 3	14. 2	F4	B2	Dog
21. 2	5. 1	E3	D12	Tiger	1. 4	15. 2	F4	C3	Pheasant
22. 2	6. 1	E3	E1	Leopard	2. 4	16. 2	F4	D4	Cock
23. 2	7. 1	E3	F2	Griffon	3. 4	17. 2	F4	E5	Crow
24. 2	8. 1	E3	G3	Ox	4. 4	18. 2	F4	F6	Monkey
25. 2	9. 1	E3	H4	Bat	5. 4	19. 2	F4	G7	Gibbon
26. 2	10. 1	E3	J5	Rat	6. 4	20. 2	F4	H8	Tapir
27. 2	11. 1	E3	K6	Swallow	7. 4	21. 2	F4	J9	Sheep
28. 2	12. 1	E3	A7	Pig	8. 4	22. 2	F4	K10	Deer
1. 3	13. 1	E3	B8	Porcupine	9. 4	23. 2	F4	A11	Horse
2. 3	14. 1	E3	C9	Wolf	10. 4	24. 2	F4	B12	Stag
3. 3	15. 1	E3	D10	Dog	11. 4	25. 2	F4	C1	Serpent
4. 3	16. 1	E3	E11	Pheasant	12. 4	26. 2	F4	D2	Earthworm
5. 3	17. 1	E3	F12	Cock	13. 4	27. 2	F4	E3	Crocodile
6. 3	18. 1	E3	G1	Crow	14. 4	28. 2	F4	F4	Dragon
7. 3	19. 1	E3	H2	Monkey	15. 4	29. 2	F4	G5	Badger
8. 3	20. 1	E3	J3	Gibbon	16. 4	30. 2	F4	H6	Hare
9. 3	21. 1	E3	K4	Tapir	17. 4	1. 3	G5	J7	Fox
10. 3	22. 1	E3	A5	Sheep	18. 4	2. 3	G5	K8	Tiger
11. 3	23. 1	E3	B6	Deer	19. 4	3. 3	G5	A9	Leopard
12. 3	24. 1	E3	C7	Horse	20. 4	4. 3	G5	B10	Griffon
13. 3	25. 1	E3	D8	Stag	21. 4	5. 3	G5	C11	Ox
14. 3	26. 1	E3	E9	Serpent	22. 4	6. 3	G5	D12	Bat
15. 3	27. 1	E3	F10	Earthworm	23. 4	7. 3	G5	E1	Rat
16. 3	28. 1	E3	G11	Crocodile	24. 4	8. 3	G5	F2	Swallow
17. 3	29. 1	E3	H12	Dragon	25. 4	9. 3	G5	G3	Pig
18. 3	1. 2	F4	J1	Badger	26. 4	10. 3	G5	H4	Porcupine
19. 3	2. 2	F4	K2	Hare	27. 4	11. 3	G5	J5	Wolf
20. 3	3. 2	F4	A3	Fox	28. 4	12. 3	G5	K6	Dog
21. 3	4. 2	F4	B4	Tiger	29. 4	13. 3	G5	A7	Pheasant
22. 3	5. 2	F4	C5	Leopard	30. 4	14. 3	G5	B8	Cock
23. 3	6. 2	F4	D6	Griffon	1. 5	15. 3	G5	C9	Crow
24. 3	7. 2	F4	E7	Ox	2. 5	16. 3	G5	D10	Monkey
25. 3	8. 2	F4	F8	Bat	3. 5	17. 3	G5	E11	Gibbon
26. 3	9. 2	F4	G9	Rat	4. 5	18. 3	G5	F12	Tapir
27. 3	10. 2	F4	H10	Swallow	5. 5	19. 3	G5	G1	Sheep

Solar date	Lunar date	Month HS/EB	Day HS/EB	Constellation	Solar date	Lunar date	Month HS/EB	Day HS/EB	Constellation
6. 5	20. 3	G5	H2	Deer	18. 7	4. 6	K8	A3	Pig
7. 5	21. 3	G5	J3	Horse	19. 7	5. 6	K8	B4	Porcupine
8. 5	22. 3	G5	K4	Stag	20. 7	6. 6	K8	C5	Wolf
9. 5	23. 3	G5	A5	Serpent	21. 7	7. 6	K8	D6	Dog
10. 5	24. 3	G5	B6	Earthworm	22. 7	8. 6	K8	E7	Pheasant
11. 5	25. 3	G5	C7	Crocodile	23. 7	9. 6	K8	F8	Cock
12. 5	26. 3	G5	D8	Dragon	24. 7	10. 6	K8	G9	Crow
13. 5	27. 3	G5	E9	Badger	25. 7	11. 6	K8	H10	Monkey
14. 5	28. 3	G5	F10	Hare	26. 7	12. 6	K8	J11	Gibbon
15. 5	29. 3	G5	G11	Fox	27. 7	13. 6	K8	K12	Tapir
16. 5	30. 3	G5	H12	Tiger	28. 7	14. 6	K8	A1	Sheep
17. 5	1. 4	H6	J1	Leopard	29. 7	15. 6	K8	B2	Deer
18. 5	2. 4	H6	K2	Griffon	30. 7	16. 6	K8	C3	Horse
19. 5	3. 4	H6	A3	Ox	31. 7	17. 6	K8	D4	Stag
20. 5	4. 4	H6	B4	Bat	1. 8	18. 6	K8	E5	Serpent
21. 5	5. 4	H6	C5	Rat	2. 8	19. 6	K8	F6	Earthworm
22. 5	6. 4	H6	D6	Swallow	3. 8	20. 6	K8	G7	Crocodile
23. 5	7. 4	H6	E7	Pig	4. 8	21. 6	K8	H8	Dragon
24. 5	8. 4	H6	F8	Porcupine	5. 8	22. 6	K8	J9	Badger
25. 5	9. 4	H6	G9	Wolf	6. 8	23. 6	K8	K10	Hare
26. 5	10. 4	H6	H10	Dog	7. 8	24. 6	K8	A11	Fox
27. 5	11. 4	H6	J11	Pheasant	8. 8	25. 6	K8	B12	Tiger
28. 5	12. 4	H6	K12	Cock	9. 8	26. 6	K8	C1	Leopard
29. 5	13. 4	H6	A1	Crow	10. 8	27. 6	K8	D2	Griffon
30. 5	14. 4	H6	B2	Monkey	11. 8	28. 6	K8	E3	Ox
31. 5	15. 4	H6	C3	Gibbon	12. 8	29. 6	K8	F4	Bat
1. 6	16. 4	H6	D4	Tapir	13. 8	30. 6	K8	G5	Rat
2. 6	17. 4	H6	E5	Sheep	14. 8	1. 7	A9	H6	Swallow
3. 6	18. 4	H6	F6	Deer	15. 8	2. 7	A9	J7	Pig
4. 6	19. 4	H6	G7	Horse	16. 8	3. 7	A9	K8	Porcupine
5. 6	20. 4	H6	H8	Stag	17. 8	4. 7	A9	A9	Wolf
6. 6	21. 4	H6	J9	Serpent	18. 8	5. 7	A9	B10	Dog
7. 6	22. 4	H6	K10	Earthworm	19. 8	6. 7	A9	C11	Pheasant
8. 6	23. 4	H6	A11	Crocodile	20. 8	7. 7	A9	D12	Cock
9. 6	24. 4	H6	B12	Dragon	21. 8	8. 7	A9	E1	Crow
10. 6	25. 4	H6	C1	Badger	22. 8	9. 7	A9	F2	Monkey
11. 6	26. 4	H6	D2	Hare	23. 8	10. 7	A9	G3	Gibbon
12. 6	27. 4	H6	E3	Fox	24. 8	11. 7	A9	H4	Tapir
13. 6	28. 4	H6	F4	Tiger	25. 8	12. 7	A9	J5	Sheep
14. 6	29. 4	H6	G5	Leopard	26. 8	13. 7	A9	K6	Deer
15. 6	1. 5	J7	H6	Griffon	27. 8	14. 7	A9	A7	Horse
16. 6	2. 5	J7	J7	Ox	28. 8	15. 7	A9	B8	Stag
17. 6	3. 5	J7	K8	Bat	29. 8	16. 7	A9	C9	Serpent
18. 6	4. 5	J7	A9	Rat	30. 8	17. 7	A9	D10	Earthworm
19. 6	5. 5	J7	B10	Swallow	31. 8	18. 7	A9	E11	Crocodile
20. 6	6. 5	J7	C11	Pig	1. 9	19. 7	A9	F12	Dragon
21. 6	7. 5	J7	D12	Porcupine	2. 9	20. 7	A9	G1	Badger
22. 6	8. 5	J7	E1	Wolf	3. 9	21. 7	A9	H2	Hare
23. 6	9. 5	J7	F2	Dog	4. 9	22. 7	A9	J3	Fox
24. 6	10. 5	J7	G3	Pheasant	5. 9	23. 7	A9	K4	Tiger
25. 6	11. 5	J7	H4	Cock	6. 9	24. 7	A9	A5	Leopard
26. 6	12. 5	J7	J5	Crow	7. 9	25. 7	A9	B6	Griffon
27. 6	13. 5	J7	K6	Monkey	8. 9	26. 7	A9	C7	Ox
28. 6	14. 5	J7	A7	Gibbon	9. 9	27. 7	A9	D8	Bat
29. 6	15. 5	J7	B8	Tapir	10. 9	28. 7	A9	E9	Rat
30. 6	16. 5	J7	C9	Sheep	11. 9	29. 7	A9	F10	Swallow
1. 7	17. 5	J7	D10	Deer	12. 9	1. 8	B10	G11	Pig
2. 7	18. 5	J7	E11	Horse	13. 9	2. 8	B10	H12	Porcupine
3. 7	19. 5	J7	F12	Stag	14. 9	3. 8	B10	J1	Wolf
4. 7	20. 5	J7	G1	Serpent	15. 9	4. 8	B10	K2	Dog
5. 7	21. 5	J7	H2	Earthworm	16. 9	5. 8	B10	A3	Pheasant
6. 7	22. 5	J7	J3	Crocodile	17. 9	6. 8	B10	B4	Cock
7. 7	23. 5	J7	K4	Dragon	18. 9	7. 8	B10	C5	Crow
8. 7	24. 5	J7	A5	Badger	19. 9	8. 8	B10	D6	Monkey
9. 7	25. 5	J7	B6	Hare	20. 9	9. 8	B10	E7	Gibbon
10. 7	26. 5	J7	C7	Fox	21. 9	10. 8	B10	F8	Tapir
11. 7	27. 5	J7	D8	Tiger	22. 9	11. 8	B10	G9	Sheep
12. 7	28. 5	J7	E9	Leopard	23. 9	12. 8	B10	H10	Deer
13. 7	29. 5	J7	F10	Griffon	24. 9	13. 8	B10	J11	Horse
14. 7	30. 5	J7	G11	Ox	25. 9	14. 8	B10	K12	Stag
15. 7	1. 6	K8	H12	Bat	26. 9	15. 8	B10	A1	Serpent
16. 7	2. 6	K8	J1	Rat	27. 9	16. 8	B10	B2	Earthworm
17. 7	3. 6	K8	K2	Swallow	28. 9	17. 8	B10	C3	Crocodile

Solar date	Lunar date	Month HS/EB	Day HS/EB	Constellation	Solar date	Lunar date	Month HS/EB	Day. HS/EB	Constellation
29. 9	18. 8	B10	D4	Dragon	4.12	25.10	D12	K10	Swallow
30. 9	19. 8	B10	E5	Badger	5.12	26.10	D12	A11	Pig
1.10	20. 8	B10	F6	Hare	6.12	27.10	D12	B12	Porcupine
2.10	21. 8	B10	G7	Fox	7.12	28.10	D12	C1	Wolf
3.10	22. 8	B10	H8	Tiger	8.12	29.10	D12	D2	Dog
4.10	23. 8	B10	J9	Leopard	9.12	1.11	E1	E3	Pheasant
5.10	24. 8	B10	K10	Griffon	10.12	2.11	E1	F4	Cock
6.10	25. 8	B10	A11	Ox	11.12	3.11	E1	G5	Crow
7.10	26. 8	B10	B12	Batr	12.12	4.11	E1	H6	Monkey
8.10	27. 8	B10	C1	Rat	13.12	5.11	E1	J7	Gibbon
9.10	28. 8	B10	D2	Swallow	14.12	6.11	E1	K8	Tapir
10.10	29. 8	B10	E3	Pig	15.12	7.11	E1	A9	Sheep
11.10	1. 9	C11	F4	Porcupine	16.12	8.11	E1	B10	Deer
12.10	2. 9	C11	G5	Wolf	17.12	9.11	E1	C11	Horse
13.10	3. 9	C11	H6	Dog	18.12	10.11	E1	D12	Stag
14.10	4. 9	C11	J7	Pheasant	19.12	11.11	E1	E1	Serpent
15.10	5. 9	C11	K8	Cock	20.12	12.11	E1	F2	Earthworm
16.10	6. 9	C11	A9	Crow	21.12	13.11	E1	G3	Crocodile
17.10	7. 9	C11	B10	Monkey	22.12	14.11	E1	H4	Dragon
18.10	8. 9	C11	C11	Gibbon	23.12	15.11	E1	J5	Badger
19.10	9. 9	C11	D12	Tapir	24.12	16.11	E1	K6	Hare
20.10	10. 9	C11	E1	Sheep	25.12	17.11	E1	A7	Fox
21.10	11. 9	C11	F2	Deer	26.12	18.11	E1	B8	Tiger
22.10	12. 9	C11	G3	Horse	27.12	19.11	E1	C9	Leopard
23.10	13. 9	C11	H4	Stag	28.12	20.11	E1	D10	Griffon
24.10	14. 9	C11	J5	Serpent	29.12	21.11	E1	E11	Ox
25.10	15. 9	C11	K6	Earthworm	30.12	22.11	E1	F12	Bat
26.10	16. 9	C11	A7	Crocodile	31.12	23.11	E1	G1	Rat
27.10	17. 9	C11	B8	Dragon					
28.10	18. 9	C11	C9	Badger	**1951**				
29.10	19. 9	C11	D10	Hare	1. 1	23.11	E1	H2	Swallow
30.10	20. 9	C11	E11	Fox	2. 1	25.11	E1	J3	Pig
31.10	21. 9	C11	F12	Tiger	3. 1	26.11	E1	K4	Porcupine
1.11	22. 9	C11	G1	Leopard	4. 1	27.11	E1	A5	Wolf
2.11	23. 9	C11	H2	Griffon	5. 1	28.11	E1	B6	Dog
3.11	24. 9	C11	J3	Ox	6. 1	29.11	E1	C7	Pheasant
4.11	25. 9	C11	K4	Bat	7. 1	30.11	E1	D8	Cock
5.11	26. 9	C11	A5	Rat	8. 1	1.12	F2	E9	Crow
6.11	27. 9	C11	B6	Swallow	9. 1	2.12	F2	F10	Monkey
7.11	28. 9	C11	C7	Pig	10. 1	3.12	F2	G11	Gibbon
8.11	29. 9	C11	D8	Porcupine	11. 1	4.12	F2	H12	Tapir
9.11	30. 9	C11	E9	Wolf	12. 1	5.12	F2	J1	Sheep
10.11	1.10	D12	F10	Dog	13. 1	6.12	F2	K2	Deer
11.11	2.10	D12	G11	Pheasant	14. 1	7.12	F2	A3	Horse
12.11	3.10	D12	H12	Cock	15. 1	8.12	F2	B4	Stag
13.11	4.10	D12	J1	Crow	16. 1	9.12	F2	C5	Serpent
14.11	5.10	D12	K2	Monkey	17. 1	10.12	F2	D6	Earthworm
15.11	6.10	D12	A3	Gibbon	18. 1	11.12	F2	E7	Crocodile
16.11	7.10	D12	B4	Tapir	19. 1	12.12	F2	F8	Dragon
17.11	8.10	D12	C5	Sheep	20. 1	13.12	F2	G9	Badger
18.11	9.10	D12	D6	Deer	21. 1	14.12	F2	H10	Hare
19.11	10.10	D12	E7	Horse	22. 1	15.12	F2	J11	Fox
20.11	11.10	D12	F8	Stag	23. 1	16.12	F2	K12	Tiger
21.11	12.10	D12	G9	Serpent	24. 1	17.12	F2	A1	Leopard
22.11	13.10	D12	H10	Earthworm	25. 1	18.12	F2	B2	Griffon
23.11	14.10	D12	J11	Crocodile	26. 1	19.12	F2	C3	Ox
24.11	15.10	D12	K12	Dragon	27. 1	20.12	F2	D4	Bat
25.11	16.10	D12	A1	Badger	28. 1	21.12	F2	E5	Rat
26.11	17.10	D12	B2	Hare	29. 1	22.12	F2	F6	Swallow
27.11	18.10	D12	C3	Fox	30. 1	23.12	F2	G7	Pig
28.11	19.10	D12	D4	Tiger	31. 1	24.12	F2	H8	Porcupine
29.11	20.10	D12	E5	Leopard	1. 2	25.12	F2	J9	Wolf
30.11	21.10	D12	F6	Griffon	2. 2	26.12	F2	K10	Dog
1.12	22.10	D12	G7	Ox	3. 2	27.12	F2	A11	Pheasant
2.12	23.10	D12	H8	Bat	4. 2	28.12	F2	B12	Cock
3.12	24.10	D12	J9	Rat	5. 2	29.12	F2	C1	Crow

HSIN MAO YEAR

Solar date	Lunar date	Month HS/EB	Day HS/EB	Constellation	Solar date	Lunar date	Month HS/EB	Day HS/EB	Constellation
6. 2	1. 1	G3	D2	Monkey	18. 4	13. 3	J5	E1	Leopard
7. 2	2. 1	G3	E3	Gibbon	19. 4	14. 3	J5	F2	Griffon
8. 2	3. 1	G3	F4	Tapir	20. 4	15. 3	J5	G3	Ox
9. 2	4. 1	G3	G5	Sheep	21. 4	16. 3	J5	H4	Bat
10. 2	5. 1	G3	H6	Deer	22. 4	17. 3	J5	J5	Rat
11. 2	6. 1	G3	J7	Horse	23. 4	18. 3	J5	K6	Swallow
12. 2	7. 1	G3	K8	Stag	24. 4	19. 3	J5	A7	Pig
13. 2	8. 1	G3	A9	Serpent	25. 4	20. 3	J5	B8	Porcupine
14. 2	9. 1	G3	B10	Earthworm	26. 4	21. 3	J5	C9	Wolf
15. 2	10. 1	G3	C11	Crocodile	27. 4	22. 3	J5	D10	Dog
16. 2	11. 1	G3	D12	Dragon	28. 4	23. 3	J5	E11	Pheasant
17. 2	12. 1	G3	E1	Badger	29. 4	24. 3	J5	F12	Cock
18. 2	13. 1	G3	F2	Hare	30. 4	25. 3	J5	G1	Crow
19. 2	14. 1	G3	G3	Fox	1. 5	26. 3	J5	H2	Monkey
20. 2	15. 1	G3	H4	Tiger	2. 5	27. 3	J5	J3	Gibbon
21. 2	16. 1	G3	J5	Leopard	3. 5	28. 3	J5	K4	Tapir
22. 2	17. 1	G3	K6	Griffon	4. 5	29. 3	J5	A5	Sheep
23. 2	18. 1	G3	A7	Ox	5. 5	30. 3	J5	B6	Deer
24. 2	19. 1	G3	B8	Bat	6. 5	1. 4	K6	C7	Horse
25. 2	20. 1	G3	C9	Rat	7. 5	2. 4	K6	D8	Stag
26. 2	21. 1	G3	D10	Swallow	8. 5	3. 4	K6	E9	Serpent
27. 2	22. 1	G3	E11	Pig	9. 5	4. 4	K6	F10	Earthworm
28. 2	23. 1	G3	F12	Porcupine	10. 5	5. 4	K6	G11	Crocodile
1. 3	24. 1	G3	G1	Wolf	11. 5	6. 4	K6	H12	Dragon
2. 3	25. 1	G3	H2	Dog	12. 5	7. 4	K6	J1	Badger
3. 3	26. 1	G3	J3	Pheasant	13. 5	8. 4	K6	K2	Hare
4. 3	27. 1	G3	K4	Cock	14. 5	9. 4	K6	A3	Fox
5. 3	28. 1	G3	A5	Crow	15. 5	10. 4	K6	B4	Tiger
6. 3	29. 1	G3	B6	Monkey	16. 5	11. 4	K6	C5	Leopard
7. 3	30. 1	G3	C7	Gibbon	17. 5	12. 4	K6	D6	Griffon
8. 3	1. 2	H4	D8	Tapir	18. 5	13. 4	K6	E7	Ox
9. 3	2. 2	H4	E9	Sheep	19. 5	14. 4	K6	F8	Bat
10. 3	3. 2	H4	F10	Deer	20. 5	15. 4	K6	G9	Rat
11. 3	4. 2	H4	G11	Horse	21. 5	16. 4	K6	H10	Swallow
12. 3	5. 2	H4	H12	Stag	22. 5	17. 4	K6	J11	Pig
13. 3	6. 2	H4	J1	Serpent	23. 5	18. 4	K6	K12	Porcupine
14. 3	7. 2	H4	K2	Earthworm	24. 5	19. 4	K6	A1	Wolf
15. 3	8. 2	H4	A3	Crocodile	25. 5	20. 4	K6	B2	Dog
16. 3	9. 2	H4	B4	Dragon	26. 5	21. 4	K6	C3	Pheasant
17. 3	10. 2	H4	C5	Badger	27. 5	22. 4	K6	D4	Cock
18. 3	11. 2	H4	D6	Hare	28. 5	23. 4	K6	E5	Crow
19. 3	12. 2	H4	E7	Fox	29. 5	24. 4	K6	F6	Monkey
20. 3	13. 2	H4	F8	Tiger	30. 5	25. 4	K6	G7	Gibbon
21. 3	14. 2	H4	G9	Leopard	31. 5	26. 4	K6	H8	Tapir
22. 3	15. 2	H4	H10	Griffon	1. 6	27. 4	K6	J9	Sheep
23. 3	16. 2	H4	J11	Ox	2. 6	28. 4	K6	K10	Deer
24. 3	17. 2	H4	K12	Bat	3. 6	29. 4	K6	A11	Horse
25. 3	18. 2	H4	A1	Rat	4. 6	30. 4	K6	B12	Stag
26. 3	19. 2	H4	B2	Swallow	5. 6	1. 5	A2	C1	Serpent
27. 3	20. 2	H4	C3	Pig	6. 6	2. 5	A7	D2	Earthworm
28. 3	21. 2	H4	D4	Porcupine	7. 6	3. 5	A7	E3	Crocodile
29. 3	22. 2	H4	E5	Wolf	8. 6	4. 5	A7	F4	Dragon
30. 3	23. 2	H4	F6	Dog	9. 6	5. 5	A7	G5	Badger
31. 3	24. 2	H4	G7	Pheasant	10. 6	6. 5	A7	H6	Hare
1. 4	25. 2	H4	H8	Cock	11. 6	7. 5	A7	J7	Fox
2. 4	26. 2	H4	J9	Crow	12. 6	8. 5	A7	K8	Tiger
3. 4	27. 2	H4	K10	Monkey	13. 6	9. 5	A7	A9	Leopard
4. 4	28. 2	H4	A11	Gibbon	14. 6	10. 5	A7	B10	Griffon
5. 4	29. 2	H4	B12	Tapir	15. 6	11. 5	A7	C11	Ox
6. 4	1. 3	J5	C1	Sheep	16. 6	12. 5	A7	D12	Bat
7. 4	2. 3	J5	D2	Deer	17. 6	13. 5	A7	E1	Rat
8. 4	3. 3	J5	E3	Horse	18. 6	14. 5	A7	F2	Swallow
9. 4	4. 3	J5	F4	Stag	19. 6	15. 5	A7	G3	Pig
10. 4	5. 3	J5	G5	Serpent	20. 6	16. 5	A7	H4	Porcupine
11. 4	6. 3	J5	H6	Earthworm	21. 6	17. 5	A7	J5	Wolf
12. 4	7. 3	J5	J7	Crocodile	22. 6	18. 5	A7	K6	Dog
13. 4	8. 3	J5	K8	Dragon	23. 6	19. 5	A7	A7	Pheasant
14. 4	9. 3	J5	A9	Badger	24. 6	20. 5	A7	B8	Cock
15. 4	10. 3	J5	B10	Hare	25. 6	21. 5	A7	C9	Crow
16. 4	11. 3	J5	C11	Fox	26. 6	22. 5	A7	D10	Monkey
17. 4	12. 3	J5	D12	Tiger	27. 6	23. 5	A7	E11	Gibbon

Solar date	Lunar date	Month HS/EB	Day HS/EB	Constellation	Solar date	Lunar date	Month HS/EB	Day HS/EB	Constellation
28. 6	24. 5	A7	F12	Tapir	9. 9	9. 8	D10	J1	Rat
29. 6	25. 5	A7	G1	Sheep	10. 9	10. 8	D10	K2	Swallow
30. 6	26. 5	A7	H2	Deer	11. 9	11. 8	D10	A3	Pig
1. 7	27. 5	A7	J3	Horse	12. 9	12. 8	D10	B4	Porcupine
2. 7	28. 5	A7	K4	Stag	13. 9	13. 8	D10	C5	Wolf
3. 7	29. 5	A7	A5	Serpent	14. 9	14. 8	D10	D6	Dog
4. 7	1. 6	B8	B6	Earthworm	15. 9	15. 8	D10	E7	Pheasant
5. 7	2. 6	B8	C7	Crocodile	16. 9	16. 8	D10	F8	Cock
6. 7	3. 6	B8	D8	Dragon	17. 9	17. 8	D10	G9	Crow
7. 7	4. 6	B8	E9	Badger	18. 9	18. 8	D10	H10	Monkey
8. 7	5. 6	B8	F10	Hare	19. 9	19. 8	D10	J11	Gibbon
9. 7	6. 6	B8	G11	Fox	20. 9	20. 8	D10	K12	Tapir
10. 7	7. 6	B8	H12	Tiger	21. 9	21. 8	D10	A1	Sheep
11. 7	8. 6	B8	J1	Leopard	22. 9	22. 8	D10	B2	Deer
12. 7	9. 6	B8	K2	Griffon	23. 9	23. 8	D10	C3	Horse
13. 7	10. 6	B8	A3	Ox	24. 9	24. 8	D10	D4	Stag
14. 7	11. 6	B8	B4	Bat	25. 9	25. 8	D10	E5	Serpent
15. 7	12. 6	B8	C5	Rat	26. 9	26. 8	D10	F6	Earthworm
16. 7	13. 6	B8	D6	Swallow	27. 9	27. 8	D10	G7	Crocodile
17. 7	14. 6	B8	E7	Pig	28. 9	28. 8	D10	H8	Dragon
18. 7	15. 6	B8	F8	Porcupine	29. 9	29. 8	D10	J9	Badger
19. 7	16. 6	B8	G9	Wolf	30. 9	30. 8	D10	K10	Hare
20. 7	17. 6	B8	H10	Dog	1.10	1. 9	E11	A11	Fox
21. 7	18. 6	B8	J11	Pheasant	2.10	2. 9	E11	B12	Tiger
22. 7	19. 6	B8	K12	Cock	3.10	3. 9	E11	C1	Leopard
23. 7	20. 6	B8	A1	Crow	4.10	4. 9	E11	D2	Griffon
24. 7	21. 6	B8	B2	Monkey	5.10	5. 9	E11	E3	Ox
25. 7	22. 6	B8	C3	Gibbon	6.10	6. 9	E11	F4	Bat
26. 7	23. 6	B8	D4	Tapir	7.10	7. 9	E11	G5	Rat
27. 7	24. 6	B8	E5	Sheep	8.10	8. 9	E11	H6	Swallow
28. 7	25. 6	B8	F6	Deer	9.10	9. 9	E11	J7	Pig
29. 7	26. 6	B8	G7	Horse	10.10	10. 9	E11	K8	Porcupine
30. 7	27. 6	B8	H8	Stag	11.10	11. 9	E11	A9	Wolf
31. 7	28. 6	B8	J9	Serpent	12.10	12. 9	E11	B10	Dog
1. 8	29. 6	B8	K10	Earthworm	13.10	13. 9	E11	C11	Pheasant
2. 8	30. 6	B8	A11	Crocodile	14.10	14. 9	E11	D12	Cock
3. 8	1. 7	C9	B12	Dragon	15.10	15. 9	E11	E1	Crow
4. 8	2. 7	C9	C1	Badger	16.10	16. 9	E11	F2	Monkey
5. 8	3. 7	C9	D2	Hare	17.10	17. 9	E11	G3	Gibbon
6. 8	4. 7	C9	E3	Fox	18.10	18. 9	E11	H4	Tapir
7. 8	5. 7	C9	F4	Tiger	19.10	19. 9	E11	J5	Sheep
8. 8	6. 7	C9	G5	Leopard	20.10	20. 9	E11	K6	Deer
9. 8	7. 7	C9	H6	Griffon	21.10	21. 9	E11	A7	Horse
10. 8	8. 7	C9	J7	Ox	22.10	22. 9	E11	B8	Stag
11. 8	9. 7	C9	K8	Bat	23.10	23. 9	E11	C9	Serpent
12. 8	10. 7	C9	A9	Rat	24.10	24. 9	E11	D10	Earthworm
13. 8	11. 7	C9	B10	Swallow	25.10	25. 9	E11	E11	Crocodile
14. 8	12. 7	C9	C11	Pig	26.10	26. 9	E11	F12	Dragon
15. 8	13. 7	C9	D12	Porcupine	27.10	27. 9	E11	G1	Badger
16. 8	14. 7	C9	E1	Wolf	28.10	28. 9	E11	H2	Hare
17. 8	15. 7	C9	F2	Dog	29.10	29. 9	E11	J3	Fox
18. 8	16. 7	C9	G3	Pheasant	30.10	1.10	F12	K4	Tiger
19. 8	17. 7	C9	H4	Cock	31.10	2.10	F12	A5	Leopard
20. 8	18. 7	C9	J5	Crow	1.11	3.10	F12	B6	Griffon
21. 8	19. 7	C9	K6	Monkey	2.11	4.10	F12	C7	Ox
22. 8	20. 7	C9	A7	Gibbon	3.11	5.10	F12	D8	Bat
23. 8	21. 7	C9	B8	Tapir	4.11	6.10	F12	E9	Rat
24. 8	22. 7	C9	C9	Sheep	5.11	7.10	F12	F10	Swallow
25. 8	23. 7	C9	D10	Deer	6.11	8.10	F12	G11	Pig
26. 8	24. 7	C9	E11	Horse	7.11	9.10	F12	H12	Porcupine
27. 8	25. 7	C9	F12	Stag	8.11	10.10	F12	J1	Wolf
28. 8	26. 7	C9	G1	Serpent	9.11	11.10	F12	K2	Dog
29. 8	27. 7	C9	H2	Earthworm	10.11	12.10	F12	A3	Pheasant
30. 8	28. 7	C9	J3	Crocodile	11.11	13.10	F12	B4	Cock
31. 8	29. 7	C9	K4	Dragon	12.11	14.10	F12	C5	Crow
1. 9	1. 8	D10	A5	Badger	13.11	15.10	F12	D6	Monkey
2. 9	2. 8	D10	B6	Hare	14.11	16.10	F12	E7	Gibbon
3. 9	3. 8	D10	C7	Fox	15.11	17.10	F12	F8	Tapir
4. 9	4. 8	D10	D8	Tiger	16.11	18.10	F12	G9	Sheep
5. 9	5. 8	D10	E9	Leopard	17.11	19.10	F12	H10	Deer
6. 9	6. 8	D10	F10	Griffon	18.11	20.10	F12	J11	Horse
7. 9	7. 8	D10	G11	Ox	19.11	21.10	F12	K12	Stag
8. 9	8. 8	D10	H12	Bat	20.11	22.10	F12	A1	Serpent

Solar date	Lunar date	Month HS/EB	Day HS/EB	Constellation	Solar date	Lunar date	Month HS/EB	Day HS/EB	Constellation
21.11	23.10	F12	B2	Earthworm	26.12	28.11	G1	G1	Leopard
22.11	24.10	F12	C3	Crocodile	27.12	29.11	G1	H2	Griffon
23.11	25.10	F12	D4	Dragon	28.12	1.12	H2	J3	Ox
24.11	26.10	F12	E5	Badger	29.12	2.12	H2	K4	Bat
25.11	27.10	F12	F6	Hare	30.12	3.12	H2	A5	Rat
26.11	28.10	F12	G7	Fox	31.12	4.12	H2	B6	Swallow
27.11	29.10	F12	H8	Tiger					
28.11	30.10	F12	J9	Leopard	**1952**				
29.11	1.11	G1	K10	Griffon					
30.11	2.11	G1	A11	Ox	1. 1	5.12	H2	C7	Pig
1.12	3.11	G1	B12	Bat	2. 1	6.12	H2	D8	Porcupine
2.12	4.11	G1	C1	Rat	3. 1	7.12	H2	E9	Wolf
3.12	5.11	G1	D2	Swallow	4. 1	8.12	H2	F10	Dog
4.12	6.11	G1	E3	Pig	5. 1	9.12	H2	G11	Pheasant
5.12	7.11	G1	F4	Porcupine	6. 1	10.12	H2	H12	Cock
6.12	8.11	G1	G5	Wolf	7. 1	11.12	H2	J1	Crow
7.12	9.11	G1	H6	Dog	8. 1	12.12	H2	K2	Monkey
8.12	10.11	G1	J7	Pheasant	9. 1	13.12	H2	A3	Gibbon
9.12	11.11	G1	K8	Cock	10. 1	14.12	H2	B4	Tapir
10.12	12.11	G1	A9	Crow	11. 1	15.12	H2	C5	Sheep
11.12	13.11	G1	B10	Monkey	12. 1	16.12	H2	D6	Deer
12.12	14.11	G1	C11	Gibbon	13. 1	17.12	H2	E7	Horse
13.12	15.11	G1	D12	Tapir	14. 1	18.12	H2	F8	Stag
14.12	16.11	G1	E1	Sheep	15. 1	19.12	H2	G9	Serpent
15.12	17.11	G1	F2	Deer	16. 1	20.12	H2	H10	Earthworm
16.12	18.11	G1	G3	Horse	17. 1	21.12	H2	J11	Crocodile
17.12	19.11	G1	H4	Stag	18. 1	22.12	H2	K12	Dragon
18.12	20.11	G1	J5	Serpent	19. 1	23.12	H2	A1	Badger
19.12	21.11	G1	K6	Earthworm	20. 1	24.12	H2	B2	Hare
20.12	22.11	G1	A7	Crocodile	21. 1	25.12	H2	C3	Fox
21.12	23.11	G1	B8	Dragon	22. 1	26.12	H2	D4	Tiger
22.12	24.11	G1	C9	Badger	23. 1	27.12	H2	E5	Leopard
23.12	25.11	G1	D10	Hare	24. 1	28.12	H2	F6	Griffon
24.12	26.11	G1	E11	Fox	25. 2	29.12	H2	G7	Ox
25.12	27.11	G1	F12	Tiger	26. 1	30.12	H2	H8	Bat

JEN CH'EN YEAR

Solar date	Lunar date	Month HS/EB	Day HS/EB	Constellation	Solar date	Lunar date	Month HS/EB	Day HS/EB	Constellation
27. 1	1. 1	J3	J9	Rat	29. 2	5. 2	K4	B6	Dog
28. 1	2. 1	J3	K10	Swallow	1. 3	6. 2	K4	C7	Pheasant
29. 1	3. 1	J3	A11	Pig	2. 3	7. 2	K4	D8	Cock
30. 1	4. 1	J3	B12	Porcupine	3. 3	8. 2	K4	E9	Crow
31. 1	5. 1	J3	C1	Wolf	4. 3	9. 2	K4	F10	Monkey
1. 2	6. 1	J3	D2	Dog	5. 3	10. 2	K4	G11	Gibbon
2. 2	7. 1	J3	E3	Pheasant	6. 3	11. 2	K4	H12	Tapir
3. 2	8. 1	J3	F4	Cock	7. 3	12. 2	K4	J1	Sheep
4. 2	9. 1	J3	G5	Crow	8. 3	13. 2	K4	K2	Deer
5. 2	10. 1	J3	H6	Monkey	9. 3	14. 2	K4	A3	Horse
6. 2	11. 1	J3	J7	Gibbon	10. 3	15. 2	K4	B4	Stag
7. 2	12. 1	J3	K8	Tapir	11. 3	16. 2	K4	C5	Serpent
8. 2	13. 1	J3	A9	Sheep	12. 3	17. 2	K4	D6	Earthworm
9. 2	14. 1	J3	B10	Deer	13. 3	18. 2	K4	E7	Crocodile
10. 2	15. 1	J3	C11	Horse	14. 3	19. 2	K4	F8	Dragon
11. 2	16. 1	J3	D12	Stag	15. 3	20. 2	K4	G9	Badger
12. 2	17. 1	J3	E1	Serpent	16. 3	21. 2	K4	H10	Hare
13. 2	18. 1	J3	F2	Earthworm	17. 3	22. 2	K4	J11	Fox
14. 2	19. 1	J3	G3	Crocodile	18. 3	23. 2	K4	K12	Tiger
15. 2	20. 1	J3	H4	Dragon	19. 3	24. 2	K4	A1	Leopard
16. 2	21. 1	J3	J5	Badger	20. 3	25. 2	K4	B2	Griffon
17. 2	22. 1	J3	K6	Hare	21. 3	26. 2	K4	C3	Ox
18. 2	23. 1	J3	A7	Fox	22. 3	27. 2	K4	D4	Bat
19. 2	24. 1	J3	B8	Tiger	23. 3	28. 2	K4	E5	Rat
20. 2	25. 1	J3	C9	Leopard	24. 3	29. 2	K4	F6	Swallow
21. 2	26. 1	J3	D10	Griffon	25. 3	30. 2	K4	G7	Pig
22. 2	27. 1	J3	E11	Ox	26. 3	1. 3	A5	H8	Porcupine
23. 2	28. 1	J3	F12	Bat	27. 3	2. 3	A5	J9	Wolf
24. 2	29. 1	J3	G1	Rat	28. 3	3. 3	A5	K10	Dog
25. 2	1. 2	K4	H2	Swallow	29. 3	4. 3	A5	A11	Pheasant
26. 2	2. 2	K4	J3	Pig	30. 3	5. 3	A5	B12	Cock
27. 2	3. 2	K4	K4	Porcupine	31. 3	6. 3	A5	C1	Crow
28. 2	4. 2	K4	A5	Wolf	1. 4	7. 3	A5	D2	Monkey

Solar date	Lunar date	Month HS/EB	Day HS/EB	Constellation	Solar date	Lunar date	Month HS/EB	Day HS/EB	Constellation
2. 4	8. 3	A5	E3	Gibbon	14. 6	22. 5	C7	H4	Bat
3. 4	9. 3	A5	F4	Tapir	15. 6	23. 5	C7	J5	Rat
4. 4	10. 3	A5	G5	Sheep	16. 6	24. 5	C7	K6	Swallow
5. 4	11. 3	A5	H6	Deer	17. 6	25. 5	C7	A7	Pig
6. 4	12. 3	A5	J7	Horse	18. 6	26. 5	C7	B8	Porcupine
7. 4	13. 3	A5	K8	Stag	19. 6	27. 5	C7	C9	Wolf
8. 4	14. 3	A5	A9	Serpent	20. 6	28. 5	C7	D10	Dog
9. 4	15. 3	A5	B10	Earthworm	21. 6	29. 5	C7	E11	Pheasant
10. 4	16. 3	A5	C11	Crocodile	22. 6	1. 5	C7	F12	Cock
11. 4	17. 3	A5	D12	Dragon	23. 6	2. 5	C7	G1	Crow.
12. 4	18. 3	A5	E1	Badger	24. 6	3. 5	C7	H2	Monkey
13. 4	19. 3	A5	F2	Hare	25. 6	4. 5	C7	J3	Gibbon
14. 4	20. 3	A5	G3	Fox	26. 6	5. 5	C7	K4	Tapir
15. 4	21. 3	A5	H4	Tiger	27. 6	6. 5	C7	A5	Sheep
16. 4	22. 3	A5	J5	Leopard	28. 6	7. 5	C7	B6	Deer
17. 4	23. 3	A5	K6	Griffon	29. 6	8. 5	C7	C7	Horse
18. 4	24. 3	A5	A7	Ox	30. 6	9. 5	C7	D8	Stag
19. 4	25. 3	A5	B8	Bat	1. 7	10. 5	C7	E9	Serpent
20. 4	26. 3	A5	C9	Rat	2. 7	11. 5	C7	F10	Earthworm
21. 4	27. 3	A5	D10	Swallow	3. 7	12. 5	C7	G11	Crocodile
22. 4	28. 3	A5	E11	Pig	4. 7	13. 5	C7	H12	Dragon
23. 4	29. 3	A5	F12	Porcupine	5. 7	14. 5	C7	J1	Badger
24. 4	1. 4	B6	G1	Wolf	6. 7	15. 5	C7	K2	Hare
25. 4	2. 4	B6	H2	Dog	7. 7	16. 5	C7	A3	Fox
26. 4	3. 4	B6	J3	Pheasant	8. 7	17. 5	C7	B4	Tiger
27. 4	4. 4	B6	K4	Cock	9. 7	18. 5	C7	C5	Leopard
28. 4	5. 4	B6	A5	Crow	10. 7	19. 5	C7	D6	Griffon
29. 4	6. 4	B6	B6	Monkey	11. 7	20. 5	C7	E7	Ox
30. 4	7. 4	B6	C7	Gibbon	12. 7	21. 5	C7	F8	Bat
1. 5	8. 4	B6	D8	Tapir	13. 7	22. 5	C7	G9	Rat
2. 5	9. 4	B6	E9	Sheep	14. 7	23. 5	C7	H10	Swallow
3. 5	10. 4	B6	F10	Deer	15. 7	24. 5	C7	J11	Pig
4. 5	11. 4	B6	G11	Horse	16. 7	25. 5	C7	K12	Porcupine
5. 5	12. 4	B6	H12	Stag	17. 7	26. 5	C7	A1	Wolf
6. 5	13. 4	B6	J1	Serpent	18. 7	27. 5	C7	B2	Dog
7. 5	14. 4	B6	K2	Earthworm	19. 7	28. 5	C7	C3	Pheasant
8. 5	15. 4	B6	A3	Crocodile	20. 7	29. 5	C7	D4	Cock
9. 5	16. 4	B6	B4	Dragon	21. 7	30. 5	C7	E5	Crow
10. 5	17. 4	B6	C5	Badger	22. 7	1. 6	D8	F6	Monkey
11. 5	18. 4	B6	D6	Hare	23. 7	2. 6	D8	G7	Gibbon
12. 5	19. 4	B6	E7	Fox	24. 7	3. 6	D8	H8	Tapir
13. 5	20. 4	B6	F8	Tiger	25. 7	4. 6	D8	J9	Sheep
14. 5	21. 4	B6	G9	Leopard	26. 7	5. 6	D8	K10	Deer
15. 5	22. 4	B6	H10	Griffon	27. 7	6. 6	D8	A11	Horse
16. 5	23. 4	B6	J11	Ox	28. 7	7. 6	D8	B12	Stag
17. 5	24. 4	B6	K12	Bat	29. 7	8. 6	D8	C1	Serpent
18. 5	25. 4	B6	A1	Rat	30. 7	9. 6	D8	D2	Earthworm
19. 5	26. 4	B6	B2	Swallow	31. 7	10. 6	D8	E3	Crocodile
20. 5	27. 4	B6	C3	Pig	1. 8	11. 6	D8	F4	Dragon
21. 5	28. 4	B6	D4	Porcupine	2. 8	12. 6	D8	G5	Badger
22. 5	29. 4	B6	E5	Wolf	3. 8	13. 6	D8	H6	Hare
23. 5	30. 4	B6	F6	Dog	4. 8	14. 6	D8	J7	Fox
24. 5	1. 5	C7	G7	Pheasant	5. 8	15. 6	D8	K8	Tiger
25. 5	2. 5	C7	H8	Cock	6. 8	16. 6	D8	A9	Leopard
26. 5	3. 5	C7	J9	Crow	7. 8	17. 6	D8	B10	Griffon
27. 5	4. 5	C7	K10	Monkey	8. 8	18. 6	D8	C11	Ox
28. 5	5. 5	C7	A11	Gibbon	9. 8	19. 6	D8	D12	Bat
29. 5	6. 5	C7	B12	Tapir	10. 8	20. 6	D8	E1	Rat
30. 5	7. 5	C7	C1	Sheep	11. 8	21. 6	D8	F2	Swallow
31. 5	8. 5	C7	D2	Deer	12. 8	22. 6	D8	G3	Pig
1. 6	9. 5	C7	E3	Horse	13. 8	23. 6	D8	H4	Porcupine
2. 6	10. 5	C7	F4	Stag	14. 8	24. 6	D8	J5	Wolf
3. 6	11. 5	C7	G5	Serpent	15. 8	25. 6	D8	K6	Dog
4. 6	12. 5	C7	H6	Earthworm	16. 8	26. 6	D8	A7	Pheasant
5. 6	13. 5	C7	J7	Crocodile	17. 8	27. 6	D8	B8	Cock
6. 6	14. 5	C7	K8	Dragon	18. 8	28. 6	D8	C9	Crow
7. 6	15. 5	C7	A9	Badger	19. 8	29. 6	D8	D10	Monkey
8. 6	16. 5	C7	B10	Hare	20. 8	1. 7	E9	E11	Gibbon
9. 6	17. 5	C7	C11	Fox	21. 8	2. 7	E9	F12	Tapir
10. 6	18. 5	C7	D12	Tiger	22. 8	3. 7	E9	G1	Sheep
11. 6	19. 5	C7	E1	Leopard	23. 8	4. 7	E9	H2	Deer
12. 6	20. 5	C7	F2	Griffon	24. 8	5. 7	E9	J3	Horse
13. 6	21. 5	C7	G3	Ox	25. 8	6. 7	E9	K4	Stag

Solar date	Lunar date	Month HS/EB	Day HS/EB	Constellation	Solar date	Lunar date	Month HS/EB	Day HS/EB	Constellation
26. 8	7. 7	E9	A5	Serpent	7.11	20. 9	G11	D6	Dog
27. 8	8. 7	E9	B6	Earthworm	8.11	21. 9	G11	E7	Pheasant
28. 8	9. 7	E9	C7	Crocodile	9.11	22. 9	G11	F8	Cock
29. 8	10. 7	E9	D8	Dragon	10.11	23. 9	G11	G9	Crow
30. 8	11. 7	E9	E9	Badger	11.11	24. 9	G11	H10	Monkey
31. 8	12. 7	E9	F10	Hare	12.11	25. 9	G11	J11	Gibbon
1. 9	13. 7	E9	G11	Fox	13.11	26. 9	G11	K12	Tapir
2. 9	14. 7	E9	H12	Tiger	14.11	27. 9	G11	A1	Sheep
3. 9	15. 7	E9	J1	Leopard	15.11	28. 9	G11	B2	Deer
4. 9	16. 7	E9	K2	Griffon	16.11	29. 9	G11	C3	Horse
5. 9	17. 7	E9	A3	Ox	17.11	1.10	H12	D4	Stag
6. 9	18. 7	E9	B4	Bat	18.11	2.10	H12	E5	Serpent
7. 9	19. 7	E9	C5	Rat	19.11	3.10	H12	F6	Earthworm
8. 9	20. 7	E9	D6	Swallow	20.11	4.10	H12	G7	Crocodile
9. 9	21. 7	E9	E7	Pig	21.11	5.10	H12	H8	Dragon
10. 9	22. 7	E9	F8	Porcupine	22.11	6.10	H12	J9	Badger
11. 9	23. 7	E9	G9	Wolf	23.11	7.10	H12	K10	Hare
12. 9	24. 7	E9	H10	Dog	24.11	8.10	H12	A11	Fox
13. 9	25. 7	E9	J11	Pheasant	25.11	9.10	H12	B12	Tiger
14. 9	26. 7	E9	K12	Cock	26.11	10.10	H12	C1	Leopard
15. 9	27. 7	E9	A1	Crow	27.11	11.10	H12	D2	Griffon
16. 9	28. 7	E9	B2	Monkey	28.11	12.10	H12	E3	Ox
17. 9	29. 7	E9	C3	Gibbon	29.11	13.10	H12	F4	Bat
18. 9	30. 7	E9	D4	Tapir	30.11	14.10	H12	G5	Rat
19. 9	1. 8	F10	E5	Sheep	1.12	15.10	H12	H6	Swallow
20. 9	2. 8	F10	F6	Deer	2.12	16.10	H12	J7	Pig
21. 9	3. 8	F10	G7	Horse	3.12	17.10	H12	K8	Porcupine
22. 9	4. 8	F10	H8	Stag	4.12	18.10	H12	A9	Wolf
23. 9	5. 8	F10	J9	Serpent	5.12	19.10	H12	B10	Dog
24. 9	6. 8	F10	K10	Earthworm	6.12	20.10	H12	C11	Pheasant
25. 9	7. 8	F10	A11	Crocodile	7.12	21.10	H12	D12	Cock
26. 9	8. 8	F10	B12	Dragon	8.12	22.10	H12	E1	Crow
27. 9	9. 8	F10	C1	Badger	9.12	23.10	H12	F2	Monkey
28. 9	10. 8	F10	D2	Hare	10.12	24.10	H12	G3	Gibbon
29. 9	11. 8	F10	E3	Fox	11.12	25.10	H12	H4	Tapir
30. 9	12. 8	F10	F4	Tiger	12.12	26.10	H12	J5	Sheep
1.10	13. 8	F10	G5	Leopard	13.12	27.10	H12	K6	Deer
2.10	14. 8	F10	H6	Griffon	14.12	28.10	H12	A7	Horse
3.10	15. 8	F10	J7	Ox	15.12	29.10	H12	B8	Stag
4.10	16. 8	F10	K8	Bat	16.12	30.10	H12	C9	Serpent
5.10	17. 8	F10	A9	Rat	17.12	1.11	J1	D10	Earthworm
6.10	18. 8	F10	B10	Swallow	18.12	2.11	J1	E11	Crocodile
7.10	19. 8	F10	C11	Pig	19.12	3.11	J1	F12	Dragon
8.10	20. 8	F10	D12	Porcupine	20.12	4.11	J1	G1	Badger
9.10	21. 8	F10	E1	Wolf	21.12	5.11	J1	H2	Hare
10.10	22. 8	F10	F2	Dog	22.12	6.11	J1	J3	Fox
11.10	23. 8	F10	G3	Pheasant	23.12	7.11	J1	K4	Tiger
12.10	24. 8	F10	H4	Cock	24.12	8.11	J1	A5	Leopard
13.10	25. 8	F10	J5	Crow	25.12	9.11	J1	B6	Griffon
14.10	26. 8	F10	K6	Monkey	26.12	10.11	J1	C7	Ox
15.10	27. 8	F10	A7	Gibbon	27.12	11.11	J1	D8	Bat
16.10	28. 8	F10	B8	Tapir	28.12	12.11	J1	E9	Rat
17.10	29. 8	F10	C9	Sheep	29.12	13.11	J1	F10	Swallow
18.10	30. 8	F10	D10	Deer	30.12	14.11	J1	G11	Pig
19.10	1. 9	G11	E11	Horse	31.12	15.11	J1	H12	Porcupine
20.10	2. 9	G11	F12	Stag					
21.10	3. 9	G11	G1	Serpent	**1953**				
22.10	4. 9	G11	H2	Earthworm	1. 1	16.11	J1	J1	Wolf
23.10	5. 9	G11	J3	Crocodile	2. 1	17.11	J1	K2	Dog
24.10	6. 9	G11	K4	Dragon	3. 1	18.11	J1	A3	Pheasant
25.10	7. 9	G11	A5	Badger	4. 1	19.11	J1	B4	Cock
26.10	8. 9	G11	B6	Hare	5. 1	20.11	J1	C5	Crow
27.10	9. 9	G11	C7	Fox	6. 1	21.11	J1	D6	Monkey
28.10	10. 9	G11	D8	Tiger	7. 1	22.11	J1	E7	Gibbon
29.10	11. 9	G11	E9	Leopard	8. 1	23.11	J1	F8	Tapir
30.10	12. 9	G11	F10	Griffon	9. 1	24.11	J1	G9	Sheep
31.10	13. 9	G11	G11	Ox	10. 1	25.11	J1	H10	Deer
1.11	14. 9	G11	H12	Bat	11. 1	26.11	J1	J11	Horse
2.11	15. 9	G11	J1	Rat	12. 1	27.11	J1	K12	Stag
3.11	16. 9	G11	K2	Swallow	13. 1	28.11	J1	A1	Serpent
4.11	17.19	G11	A3	Pig	14. 1	29.11	J1	B2	Earthworm
5.11	18. 9	G11	B4	Porcupine	15. 1	1.12	K2	C3	Crocodile
6.11	19. 9	G11	C5	Wolf	16. 1	2.12	K2	D4	Dragon

Solar date	Lunar date	Month HS/EB	Day HS/EB	Constellation	Solar date	Lunar date	Month HS/EB	Day HS/EB	Constellation
17. 1	3.12	K2	E5	Badger	31. 1	17.12	K2	J7	Pheasant
18. 1	4.12	K2	F6	Hare	1. 2	18.12	K2	K8	Cock
19. 1	5.12	K2	G7	Fox	2. 2	19.12	K2	A9	Crow
20. 1	6.12	K2	H8	Tiger	3. 2	20.12	K2	B10	Monkey
21. 1	7.12	K2	J9	Leopard	4. 2	21.12	K2	C11	Gibbon
22. 1	8.12	K2	K10	Griffon	5. 2	22.12	K2	D12	Tapir
23. 1	9.12	K2	A11	Ox	6. 2	23.12	K2	E1	Sheep
24. 1	10.12	K2	B12	Batr	7. 2	24.12	K2	F2	Deer
25. 1	11.12	K2	C1	Rat	8. 2	25.12	K2	G3	Horse
26. 1	12.12	K2	D2	Swallow	9. 2	26.12	K2	H4	Stag
27. 1	13.12	K2	E3	Pig	10. 2	27.12	K2	J5	Serpent
28. 1	14.12	K2	F4	Porcupine	11. 2	28.12	K2	K6	Earthworm
29. 1	15.12	K2	G5	Wolf	12. 2	29.12	K2	A7	Crocodile
30. 1	16.12	K2	H6	Dog	13. 2	30.12	K2	B8	Dragon

KUEI SZU YEAR

Solar date	Lunar date	Month HS/EB	Day HS/EB	Constellation	Solar date	Lunar date	Month HS/EB	Day HS/EB	Constellation
14. 2	1. 1	A3	C9	Badger	9. 4	26. 2	B4	G3	Crocodile
15. 2	2. 1	A3	D10	Hare	10. 4	27. 2	B4	H4	Dragon
16. 2	3. 1	A3	E11	Fox	11. 4	28. 2	B4	J5	Badger
17. 2	4. 1	A3	F12	Tiger	12. 4	29. 2	B4	K6	Hare
18. 2	5. 1	A3	G1	Leopard	13. 4	30. 2	B4	A7	Fox
19. 2	6. 1	A3	H2	Griffon	14. 4	1. 3	C5	B8	Tiger
20. 2	7. 1	A3	J3	Ox	15. 4	2. 3	C5	C9	Leopard
21. 2	8. 1	A3	K4	Bat	16. 4	3. 3	C5	D10	Griffon
22. 2	9. 1	A3	A5	Rat	17. 4	4. 3	C5	E11	Ox
23. 2	10. 1	A3	B6	Swallow	18. 4	5. 3	C5	F12	Bat
24. 2	11. 1	A3	C7	Pig	19. 4	6. 3	C5	G1	Rat
25. 2	12. 1	A3	D8	Porcupine	20. 4	7. 3	C5	H2	Swallow
26. 2	13. 1	A3	E9	Wolf	21. 4	8. 3	C5	J3	Pig
27. 2	14. 1	A3	F10	Dog	22. 4	9. 3	C5	K4	Porcupine
28. 2	15. 1	A3	G11	Pheasant	23. 4	10. 3	C5	A5	Wolf
1. 3	16. 1	A3	H12	Cock	24. 4	11. 3	C5	B6	Dog
2. 3	17. 1	A3	J1	Crow	25. 4	12. 3	C5	C7	Pheasant
3. 3	18. 1	A3	K2	Monkey	26. 4	13. 3	C5	D8	Cock
4. 3	19. 1	A3	A3	Gibbon	27. 4	14. 3	C5	E9	Crow
5. 3	20. 1	A3	B4	Tapir	28. 4	15. 3	C5	F10	Monkey
6. 3	21. 1	A3	C5	Sheep	29. 4	16. 3	C5	G11	Gibbon
7. 3	22. 1	A3	D6	Deer	30. 4	17. 3	C5	H12	Tapir
8. 3	23. 1	A3	E7	Horse	1. 5	18. 3	C5	J1	Sheep
9. 3	24. 1	A3	F8	Stag	2. 5	19. 3	C5	K2	Deer
10. 3	25. 1	A3	G9	Serpent	3. 5	20. 3	C5	A3	Horse
11. 3	26. 1	A3	H10	Earthworm	4. 5	21. 3	C5	B4	Stag
12. 3	27. 1	A3	J11	Crocodile	5. 5	22. 3	C5	C5	Serpent
13. 3	28. 1	A3	K12	Dragon	6. 5	23. 3	C5	D6	Earthworm
14. 3	29. 1	A3	A1	Badger	7. 5	24. 3	C5	E7	Crocodile
15. 3	1. 2	B4	B2	Hare	8. 5	25. 3	C5	F8	Dragon
16. 3	2. 2	B4	C3	Fox	9. 5	26. 3	C5	G9	Badger
17. 3	3. 2	B4	D4	Tiger	10. 5	27. 3	C5	H10	Hare
18. 3	4. 2	B4	E5	Leopard	11. 5	28. 3	C5	J11	Fox
19. 3	5. 2	B4	F6	Griffon	12. 5	29. 3	C5	K12	Tiger
20. 3	6. 2	B4	G7	Ox	13. 5	1. 4	D6	A1	Leopard
21. 3	7. 2	B4	H8	Bat	14. 5	2. 4	D6	B2	Griffon
22. 3	8. 2	B4	J9	Rat	15. 5	3. 4	D6	C3	Ox
23. 3	9. 2	B4	K10	Swallow	16. 5	4. 4	D6	D4	Bat
24. 3	10. 2	B4	A11	Pig	17. 5	5. 4	D6	E5	Rat
25. 3	11. 2	B4	B12	Porcupine	18. 5	6. 4	D6	F6	Swallow
26. 3	12. 2	B4	C1	Wolf	19. 5	7. 4	D6	G7	Pig
27. 3	13. 2	B4	D2	Dog	20. 5	8. 4	D6	H8	Porcupine
28. 3	14. 2	B4	E3	Pheasant	21. 5	9. 4	D6	J9	Wolf
29. 3	15. 2	B4	F4	Cock	22. 5	10. 4	D6	K10	Dog
30. 3	16. 2	B4	G5	Crow	23. 5	11. 4	D6	A11	Pheasant
31. 3	17. 2	B4	H6	Monkey	24. 5	12. 4	D6	B12	Cock
1. 4	18. 2	B4	J7	Gibbon	25. 5	13. 4	D6	C1	Crow
2. 4	19. 2	B4	K8	Tapir	26. 5	14. 4	D6	D2	Monkey
3. 4	20. 2	B4	A9	Sheep	27. 5	15. 4	D6	E3	Gibbon
4. 4	21. 2	B4	B10	Deer	28. 5	16. 4	D6	F4	Tapir
5. 4	22. 2	B4	C11	Horse	29. 5	17. 4	D6	G5	Sheep
6. 4	23. 2	B4	D12	Stag	30. 5	18. 4	D6	H6	Deer
7. 4	24. 2	B4	E1	Serpent	31. 5	19. 4	D6	J7	Horse
8. 4	25. 2	B4	F2	Earthworm	1. 6	20. 4	D6	K8	Stag

Solar date	Lunar date	Month HS/EB	Day HS/EB	Constellation	Solar date	Lunar date	Month HS/EB	Day HS/EB	Constellation
2. 6	21. 4	D6	A9	Serpent	14. 8	5. 7	G9	D10	Dog
3. 6	22. 4	D6	B10	Earthworm	15. 8	6. 7	G9	E11	Pheasant
4. 6	23. 4	D6	C11	Crocodile	16. 8	7. 7	G9	F12	Cock
5. 6	24. 4	D6	D12	Drgon	17. 8	8. 7	G9	G1	Crow
6. 6	25. 4	D6	E1	Badger	18. 8	9. 7	G9	H2	Monkey
7. 6	26. 4	D6	F2	Hare	19. 8	10. 7	G9	J3	Gibbon
8. 6	27. 4	D6	G3	Fox	20. 8	11. 7	G9	K4	Tapir
9. 6	28. 4	D6	H4	Tiger	21. 8	12. 7	G9	A5	Sheep
10. 6	29. 4	D6	J5	Leopard	22. 8	13. 7	G9	B6	Deer
11. 6	1. 5	E7	K6	Griffon	23. 8	14. 7	G9	C7	Horse
12. 6	2. 5	E7	A7	Ox	24. 8	15. 7	G9	D8	Stag
13. 6	3. 5	E7	B8	Bat	25. 8	16. 7	G9	E9	Serpent
14. 6	4. 5	E7	C9	Rat	26. 8	17. 7	G9	F10	Earthworm
15. 6	5. 5	E7	D10	Swallow	27. 8	18. 7	G9	G11	Crocodile
16. 6	6. 5	E7	E11	Pig	28. 8	19. 7	G9	H12	Dragon
17. 6	7. 5	E7	F12	Porcupine	29. 8	20. 7	G9	J1	Badger
18. 6	8. 5	E7	G1	Wolf	30. 8	21. 7	G9	K2	Hare
19. 6	9. 5	E7	H2	Dog	31. 8	22. 7	G9	A3	Fox
20. 6	10. 5	E7	J3	Pheasant	1. 9	23. 7	G9	B4	Tiger
21. 6	11. 5	E7	K4	Cock	2. 9	24. 7	G9	C5	Leopard
22. 6	12. 5	E7	A5	Crow	3. 9	25. 7	G9	D6	Griffon
23. 6	13. 5	E7	B6	Monkey	4. 9	26. 7	G9	E7	Ox
24. 6	14. 5	E7	C7	Gibbon	5. 9	27. 7	G9	F8	Bat
25. 6	15. 5	E7	D8	Tapir	6. 9	28. 7	G9	G9	Rat
26. 6	16. 5	E7	E9	Sheep	7. 9	29. 7	G9	H10	Swallow
27. 6	17. 5	E7	F10	Deer	8. 9	1. 8	H10	J11	Pig
28. 6	18. 5	E7	G11	Horse	9. 9	2. 8	H10	K12	Porcupine
29. 6	19. 5	E7	H12	Stag	10. 9	3. 8	H10	A1	Wolf
30. 6	20. 5	E7	J1	Serpent	11. 9	4. 8	H10	B2	Dog
1. 7	21. 5	E7	K2	Earthworm	12. 9	5. 8	H10	C3	Pheasant
2. 7	22. 5	E7	A3	Crocodile	13. 9	6. 8	H10	D4	Cock
3. 7	23. 5	E7	B4	Dragon	14. 9	7. 8	H10	E5	Crow
4. 7	24. 5	E7	C5	Badger	15. 9	8. 8	H10	F6	Monkey
5. 7	25. 5	E7	D6	Hare	16. 9	9. 8	H10	G7	Gibbon
6. 7	26. 5	E7	E7	Fox	17. 9	10. 8	H10	H8	Tapir
7. 7	27. 5	E7	F8	Tiger	18. 9	11. 8	H10	J9	Sheep
8. 7	28. 5	E7	G9	Leopard	19. 9	12. 8	H10	K10	Deer
9. 7	29. 5	E7	H10	Griffon	20. 9	13. 8	H10	A11	Horse
10. 7	30. 5	E7	J11	Ox	21. 9	14. 8	H10	B12	Stag
11. 7	1. 6	F8	K12	Bat	22. 9	15. 8	H10	C1	Serpent
12. 7	2. 6	F8	A1	Rat	23. 9	16. 8	H10	D2	Earthworm
13. 7	3. 6	F8	B2	Swallow	24. 9	17. 8	H10	E3	Crocodile
14. 7	4. 6	F8	C3	Pig	25. 9	18. 8	H10	F4	Dragon
15. 7	5. 6	F8	D4	Porcupine	26. 9	19. 8	H10	G5	Badger
16. 7	6. 6	F8	E5	Wolf	27. 9	20. 8	H10	H6	Hare
17. 7	7. 6	F8	F6	Dog	28. 9	21. 8	H10	J7	Fox
18. 7	8. 6	F8	G7	Pheasant	29. 9	22. 8	H10	K8	Tiger
19. 7	9. 6	F8	H8	Cock	30. 9	23. 8	H10	A9	Leopard
20. 7	10. 6	F8	J9	Crow	1.10	24. 8	H10	B10	Griffon
21. 7	11. 6	F8	K10	Monkey	2.10	25. 8	H10	C11	Ox
22. 7	12. 6	F8	A11	Gibbon	3.10	26. 8	H10	D12	Bat
23. 7	13. 6	F8	B12	Tapir	4.10	27. 8	H10	E1	Rat
24. 7	14. 6	F8	C1	Sheep	5.10	28. 8	H10	F2	Swallow
25. 7	15. 6	F8	D2	Deer	6.10	29. 8	H10	G3	Pig
26. 7	16. 6	F8	E3	Horse	7.10	30. 8	H10	H4	Porcupine
27. 7	17. 6	F8	F4	Stag	8.10	1. 9	J11	J5	Wolf
28. 7	18. 6	F8	G5	Serpent	9.10	2. 9	J11	K6	Dog
29. 7	19. 6	F8	H6	Earthworm	10.10	3. 9	J11	A7	Pheasant
30. 7	20. 6	F8	J7	Crocodile	11.10	4. 9	J11	B8	Cock
31. 7	21. 6	F8	K8	Dragon	12.10	5. 9	J11	C9	Crow
1. 8	22. 6	F8	A9	Badger	13.10	6. 9	J11	D10	Monkey
2. 8	23. 6	F8	B10	Hare	14.10	7. 9	J11	E11	Gibbon
3. 8	24. 6	F8	C11	Fox	15.10	8. 9	J11	F12	Tapir
4. 8	25. 6	F8	D12	Tiger	16.10	9. 9	J11	G1	Sheep
5. 8	26. 6	F8	E1	Leopard	17.10	10. 9	J11	H2	Deer
6. 8	27. 6	F8	F2	Griffon	18.10	11. 9	J11	J3	Horse
7. 8	28. 6	F8	G3	Ox	19.10	12. 9	J11	K4	Stag
8. 8	29. 6	F8	H4	Bat	20.10	13. 9	J11	A5	Serpent
9. 8	30. 6	F8	J5	Rat	21.10	14. 9	J11	B6	Earthworm
10. 8	1. 7	G9	K6	Swallow	22.10	15. 9	J11	C7	Crocodile
11. 8	2. 7	G9	A7	Pig	23.10	16. 9	J11	D8	Dragon
12. 8	3. 7	G9	B8	Porcupine	24.10	17. 9	J11	E9	Badger
13. 8	4. 7	G9	C9	Wolf	25.10	18. 9	J11	F10	Hare

Solar date	Lunar date	Month HS/EB	Day HS/EB	Constellation	Solar date	Lunar date	Month HS/EB	Day HS/EB	Constellation
26.10	19. 9	J11	G11	Fox	16.12	11.11	A1	H2	Earthworm
27.10	20. 9	J11	H12	Tiger	17.12	12.11	A1	J3	Crocodile
28.10	21. 9	J11	J1	Leopard	18.12	13.11	A1	K4	Dragon
29.10	22. 9	J11	K2	Griffon	19.12	14.11	A1	A5	Badger
30.10	23. 9	J11	A3	Ox	20.12	15.11	A1	B6	Hare
31.10	24. 9	J11	B4	Bat	21.12	16.11	A1	C7	Fox
1.11	25. 9	J11	C5	Rat	22.12	17.11	A1	D8	Tiger
2.11	26. 9	J11	D6	Swallow	23.12	18.11	A1	E9	Leopard
3.11	27. 9	J11	E7	Pig	24.12	19.11	A1	F10	Griffon
4.11	28. 9	J11	F8	Porcupine	25.12	20.11	A1	G11	Ox
5.11	29. 9	J11	G9	Wolf	26.12	21.11	A1	H12	Bat
6.11	30. 9	J11	H10	Dog	27.12	22.11	A1	J1	Rat
7.11	1.10	K12	J11	Pheasant	28.12	23.11	A1	K2	Swallow
8.11	2.10	K12	K12	Cock	29.12	24.11	A1	A3	Pig
9.11	3.10	K12	A1	Crow	30.12	25.11	A1	B4	Porcupine
10.11	4.10	K12	B2	Monkey	31.12	26.11	A1	C5	Wolf
11.11	5.10	K12	C3	Gibbon	**1954**				
12.11	6.10	K12	D4	Tapir	1. 1	27.11	A1	D6	Dog
13.11	7.10	K12	E5	Sheep	2. 1	28.11	A1	E7	Pheasant
14.11	8.10	K12	F6	Deer	3. 1	29.11	A1	F8	Cock
15.11	9.10	K12	G7	Horse	4. 1	30.11	A1	G9	Crow
16.11	10.10	K12	H8	Stag	5. 1	1.12	B2	H10	Monkey
17.11	11.10	K12	J9	Serpent	6. 1	2.12	B2	J11	Gibbon
18.11	12.10	K12	K10	Earthworm	7. 1	3.12	B2	K12	Tapir
19.11	13.10	K12	A11	Crocodile	8. 1	4.12	B2	A1	Sheep
20.11	14.10	K12	B12	Dragon	9. 1	5.12	B2	B2	Deer
21.11	15.10	K12	C1	Badger	10. 1	6.12	B2	C3	Horse
22.11	16.10	K12	D2	Hare	11. 1	7.12	B2	D4	Stag
23.11	17.10	K12	E3	Fox	12. 1	8.12	B2	E5	Serpent
24.11	18.10	K12	F4	Tiger	13. 1	9.12	B2	F6	Earthworm
25.11	19.10	K12	G5	Leopard	14. 1	10.12	B2	G7	Crocodile
26.11	20.10	K12	H6	Griffon	15. 1	11.12	B2	H8	Dragon
27.11	21.10	K12	J7	Ox	16. 1	12.12	B2	J9	Badger
28.11	22.10	K12	K8	Bat	17. 1	13.12	B2	K10	Hare
29.11	23.10	K12	A9	Rat	18. 1	14.12	B2	A11	Fox
30.11	24.10	K12	B10	Swallow	19. 1	15.12	B2	B12	Tiger
1.12	25.10	K12	C11	Pig	20. 1	16.12	B2	C1	Leopard
2.12	26.10	K12	D12	Porcupine	21. 1	17.12	B2	D2	Griffon
3.12	27.10	K12	E1	Wolf	22. 1	18.12	B2	E3	Ox
4.12	28.10	K12	F2	Dog	23. 1	19.12	B2	F4	Bat
5.12	29.10	K12	G3	Pheasant	24. 1	20.12	B2	G5	Rat
6.12	1.11	A1	H4	Cock	25. 1	21.12	B2	H6	Swallow
7.12	2.11	A1	J5	Crow	26. 1	22.12	B2	J7	Pig
8.12	3.11	A1	K6	Monkey	27. 1	23.12	B2	K8	Porcupine
9.12	4.11	A1	A7	Gibbon	28. 1	24.12	B2	A9	Wolf
10.12	5.11	A1	B8	Tapir	29. 1	25.12	B2	B10	Dog
11.12	6.11	A1	C9	Sheep	30. 1	26.12	B2	C11	Pheasant
12.12	7.11	A1	D10	Deer	31. 1	27.12	B2	D12	Cock
13.12	8.11	A1	E11	Horse	1. 2	28.12	B2	E1	Crow
14.12	9.11	A1	F12	Stag	2. 2	29.12	B2	F2	Monkey
15.12	10.11	A1	G1	Serpent					

CHIA WU YEAR

Solar date	Lunar date	Month HS/EB	Day HS/EB	Constellation	Solar date	Lunar date	Month HS/EB	Day HS/EB	Constellation
3. 2	1. 1	C3	G3	Gibbon	20. 2	18. 1	C3	D8	Bat
4. 2	2. 1	C3	H4	Tapir	21. 2	19. 1	C3	E9	Rat
5. 2	3. 1	C3	J5	Sheep	22. 2	20. 1	C3	F10	Swallow
6. 2	4. 1	C3	K6	Deer	23. 2	21. 1	C3	G11	Pig
7. 2	5. 1	C3	A7	Horse	24. 2	22. 1	C3	H12	Porcupine
8. 2	6. 1	C3	B8	Stag	25. 2	23. 1	C3	J1	Wolf
9. 2	7. 1	C3	C9	Serpent	26. 2	24. 1	C3	K2	Dog
10. 2	8. 1	C3	D10	Earthworm	27. 2	25. 1	C3	A3	Pheasant
11. 2	9. 1	C3	E11	Crocodile	28. 2	26. 1	C3	B4	Cock
12. 2	10. 1	C3	F12	Dragon	1. 3	27. 1	C3	C5	Crow
13. 2	11. 1	C3	G1	Badger	2. 3	28. 1	C3	D6	Monkey
14. 2	12. 1	C3	H2	Hare	3. 3	29. 1	C3	E7	Gibbon
15. 2	13. 1	C3	J3	Fox	4. 3	30. 1	C3	F8	Tapir
16. 2	14. 1	C3	K4	Tiger	5. 3	1. 2	D4	G9	Sheep
17. 2	15. 1	C3	A5	Leopard	6. 3	2. 2	D4	H10	Deer
18. 2	16. 1	C3	B6	Griffon	7. 3	3. 2	D4	J11	Horse
19. 2	17. 1	C3	C7	Ox	8. 3	4. 2	D4	K12	Stag

Solar date	Lunar date	Month HS/EB	Day HS/EB	Constellation
9. 3	5. 2	D4	A1	Serpent
10. 3	6. 2	D4	B2	Earthworm
11. 3	7. 2	D4	C3	Crocodile
12. 3	8. 2	D4	D4	Dragon
13. 3	9. 2	D4	E5	Badger
14. 3	10. 2	D4	F6	Hare
15. 3	11. 2	D4	G7	Fox
16. 3	12. 2	D4	H8	Tiger
17. 3	13. 2	D4	J9	Leopard
18. 3	14. 2	D4	K10	Griffon
19. 3	15. 2	D4	A11	Ox
20. 3	16. 2	D4	B12	Bat
21. 3	17. 2	D4	C1	Rat
22. 3	18. 2	D4	D2	Swallow
23. 3	19. 2	D4	E3	Pig
24. 3	20. 2	D4	F4	Porcupine
25. 3	21. 2	D4	G5	Wolf
26. 3	22. 2	D4	H6	Dog
27. 3	23. 2	D4	J7	Pheasant
28. 3	24. 2	D4	K8	Cock
29. 3	25. 2	D4	A9	Crow
30. 3	26. 2	D4	B10	Monkey
31. 3	27. 2	D4	C11	Gibbon
1. 4	28. 2	D4	D12	Tapir
2. 4	29. 2	D4	E1	Sheep
3. 4	1. 3	E5	F2	Deer
4. 4	2. 3	E5	G3	Horse
5. 4	3. 3	E5	H4	Stag
6. 4	4. 3	E5	J5	Serpent
7. 4	5. 3	E5	K6	Earthworm
8. 4	6. 3	E5	A7	Crocodile
9. 4	7. 3	E5	B8	Dragon
10. 4	8. 3	E5	C9	Badger
11. 4	9. 3	E5	D10	Hare
12. 4	10. 3	E5	E11	Fox
13. 4	11. 3	E5	F12	Tiger
14. 4	12. 3	E5	G1	Leopard
15. 4	13. 3	E5	H2	Griffon
16. 4	14. 3	E5	J3	Ox
17. 4	15. 3	E5	K4	Bat
18. 4	16. 3	E5	A5	Rat
19. 4	17. 3	E5	B6	Swallow
20. 4	18. 3	E5	C7	Pig
21. 4	19. 3	E5	D8	Porcupine
22. 4	20. 3	E5	E9	Wolf
23. 4	21. 3	E5	F10	Dog
24. 4	22. 3	E5	G11	Pheasant
25. 4	23. 3	E5	H12	Cock
26. 4	24. 3	E5	J1	Crow
27. 4	25. 3	E5	K2	Monkey
28. 4	26. 3	E5	A3	Gibbon
29. 4	27. 3	E5	B4	Tapir
30. 4	28. 3	E5	C5	Sheep
1. 5	29. 3	E5	D6	Deer
2. 5	30. 3	E5	E7	Horse
3. 5	1. 4	F6	F8	Stag
4. 5	2. 4	F6	G9	Serpent
5. 5	3. 4	F6	H10	Earthworm
6. 5	4. 4	F6	J11	Crocodile
7. 5	5. 4	F6	K12	Dragon
8. 5	6. 4	F6	A1	Badger
9. 5	7. 4	F6	B2	Hare
10. 5	8. 4	F6	C3	Fox
11. 5	9. 4	F6	D4	Tiger
12. 5	10. 4	F6	E5	Leopard
13. 5	11. 4	F6	F6	Griffon
14. 5	12. 4	F6	G7	Ox
15. 5	13. 4	F6	H8	Bat
16. 5	14. 4	F6	J9	Rat
17. 5	15. 4	F6	K10	Swallow
18. 5	16. 4	F6	A11	Pig
19. 5	17. 4	F6	B12	Porcupine
20. 5	18. 4	F6	C1	Wolf
21. 5	19. 4	F6	D2	Dog
22. 5	20. 4	F6	E3	Pheasant
23. 5	21. 4	F6	F4	Cock
24. 5	22. 4	F6	G5	Crow
25. 5	23. 4	F6	H6	Monkey
26. 5	24. 4	F6	J7	Gibbon
27. 5	25. 4	F6	K8	Tapir
28. 5	26. 4	F6	A9	Sheep
29. 5	27. 4	F6	B10	Deer
30. 5	28. 4	F6	C11	Horse
31. 5	29. 4	F6	D12	Stag
1. 6	1. 5	G7	E1	Serpent
2. 6	2. 5	G7	F2	Earthworm
3. 6	3. 5	G7	G3	Crocodile
4. 6	4. 5	G7	H4	Dragon
5. 6	5. 5	G7	J5	Badger
6. 6	6. 5	G7	K6	Hare
7. 6	7. 5	G7	A7	Fox
8. 6	8. 5	G7	B8	Tiger
9. 6	9. 5	G7	C9	Leopard
10. 6	10. 5	G7	D10	Griffon
11. 6	11. 5	G7	E11	Ox
12. 6	12. 5	G7	F12	Bat
13. 6	13. 5	G7	G1	Rat
14. 6	14. 5	G7	H2	Swallow
15. 6	15. 5	G7	J3	Pig
16. 6	16. 5	G7	K4	Porcupine
17. 6	17. 5	G7	A5	Wolf
18. 6	18. 5	G7	B6	Dog
19. 6	19. 5	G7	C7	Pheasant
20. 6	20. 5	G7	D8	Cock
21. 6	21. 5	G7	E9	Crow
22. 6	22. 5	G7	F10	Monkey
23. 6	23. 5	G7	G11	Gibbon
24. 6	24. 5	G7	H12	Tapir
25. 6	25. 5	G7	J1	Sheep
26. 6	26. 5	G7	K2	Deer
27. 6	27. 5	G7	A3	Horse
28. 6	28. 5	G7	B4	Stag
29. 6	29. 5	G7	C5	Serpent
30. 6	1. 6	H8	D6	Earthworm
1. 7	2. 6	H8	E7	Crocodile
2. 7	3. 6	H8	F8	Dragon
3. 7	4. 6	H8	G9	Badger
4. 7	5. 6	H8	H10	Hare
5. 7	6. 6	H8	J11	Fox
6. 7	7. 6	H8	K12	Tiger
7. 7	8. 6	H8	A1	Leopard
8. 7	9. 6	H8	B2	Griffon
9. 7	10. 6	H8	C3	Ox
10. 7	11. 6	H8	D4	Bat
11. 7	12. 6	H8	E5	Rat
12. 7	13. 6	H8	F6	Swallow
13. 7	14. 6	H8	G7	Pig
14. 7	15. 6	H8	H8	Porcupine
15. 7	16. 6	H8	J9	Wolf
16. 7	17. 6	H8	K10	Dog
17. 7	18. 6	H8	A11	Pheasant
18. 7	19. 6	H8	B12	Cock
19. 7	20. 6	H8	C1	Crow
20. 7	21. 6	H8	D2	Monkey
21. 7	22. 6	H8	E3	Gibbon
22. 7	23. 6	H8	F4	Tapir
23. 7	24. 6	H8	G5	Sheep
24. 7	25. 6	H8	H6	Deer
25. 7	26. 6	H8	J7	Horse
26. 7	27. 6	H8	K8	Stag
27. 7	28. 6	H8	A9	Serpent
28. 7	29. 6	H8	B10	Earthworm
29. 7	30. 6	H8	C11	Crocodile
30. 7	1. 7	J9	D12	Dragon
31. 7	2. 7	J9	E1	Badger
1. 8	3. 7	J9	F2	Hare

Solar date	Lunar date	Month HS/EB	Day HS/EB	Constellation	Solar date	Lunar date	Month HS/EB	Day HS/EB	Constellation
2. 8	4. 7	J9	G3	Fox	14.10	18. 9	A11	K4	Tapir
3. 8	5. 7	J9	H4	Tiger	15.10	19. 9	A11	A5	Sheep
4. 8	6. 7	J9	J5	Leopard	16.10	20. 9	A11	B6	Deer
5. 8	7. 7	J9	K6	Griffon	17.10	21. 9	A11	C7	Horse
6. 8	8. 7	J9	A7	Ox	18.10	22. 9	A11	D8	Stag
7. 8	9. 7	J9	B8	Bat	19.10	23. 9	A11	E9	Serpent
8. 8	10. 7	J9	C9	Rat	20.10	24. 9	A11	F10	Earthworm
9. 8	11. 7	J9	D10	Swallow	21.10	25. 9	A11	G11	Crocodile
10. 8	12. 7	J9	E11	Pig	22.10	26. 9	A11	H12	Badger
11. 8	13. 7	J9	F12	Porcupine	23.10	27. 9	A11	J1	Badger
12. 8	14. 7	J9	G1	Wolf	24.10	28. 9	A11	K2	Hare
13. 8	15. 7	J9	H2	Dog	25.10	29. 9	A11	A3	Fox
14. 8	16. 7	J9	J3	Pheasant	26.10	30. 9	A11	B4	Tiger
15. 8	17. 7	J9	K4	Cock	27.10	1.10	B12	C5	Leopard
16. 8	18. 7	J9	A5	Crow	28.10	2.10	B12	D6	Griffon
17. 8	19. 7	J9	B6	Monkey	29.10	3.10	B12	E7	Ox
18. 8	20. 7	J9	C7	Gibbon	30.10	4.10	B12	F8	Bat
19. 8	21. 7	J9	D8	Tapir	31.10	5.10	B12	G9	Rat
20. 8	22. 7	J9	E9	Sheep	1.11	6.10	B12	H10	Swallow
21. 8	23. 7	J9	F10	Deer	2.11	7.10	B12	J11	Pig
22. 8	24. 7	J9	G11	Horse	3.11	8.10	B12	K12	Porcupine
23. 8	25. 7	J9	H12	Stag	4.11	9.10	B12	A1	Wolf
24. 8	26. 7	J9	J1	Serpent	5.11	10.10	B12	B2	Dog
25. 8	27. 7	J9	K2	Earthworm	6.11	11.10	B12	C3	Pheasant
26. 8	28. 7	J9	A3	Crocodile	7.11	12.10	B12	D4	Cock
27. 8	29. 7	J9	B4	Dragon	8.11	13.10	B12	E5	Crow
28. 8	1. 8	K10	C5	Badger	9.11	14.10	B12	F6	Monkey
29. 8	2. 8	K10	D6	Hare	10.11	15.10	B12	G7	Gibbon
30. 8	3. 8	K10	E7	Fox	11.11	16.10	B12	H8	Tapir
31. 8	4. 8	K10	F8	Tiger	12.11	17.10	B12	J9	Sheep
1. 9	5. 8	K10	G9	Leopard	13.11	18.10	B12	K10	Deer
2. 9	6. 8	K10	H10	Griffon	14.11	19.10	B12	A11	Horse
3. 9	7. 8	K10	J11	Ox	15.11	20.10	B12	B12	Stag
4. 9	8. 8	K10	K12	Bat	16.11	21.10	B12	C1	Serpent
5. 9	9. 8	K10	A1	Rat	17.11	22.10	B12	D2	Earthworm
6. 9	10. 8	K10	B2	Swallow	18.11	23.10	B12	E3	Crocodile
7. 9	11. 8	K10	C3	Pig	19.11	24.10	B12	F4	Dragon
8. 9	12. 8	K10	D4	Porcupine	20.11	25.10	B12	G5	Badger
9. 9	13. 8	K10	E5	Wolf	21.11	26.10	B12	H6	Hare
10. 9	14. 8	K10	F6	Dog	22.11	27.10	B12	J7	Fox
11. 9	15. 8	K10	G7	Pheasant	23.11	28.10	B12	K8	Tiger
12. 9	16. 8	K10	H8	Cock	24.11	29.10	B12	A9	Leopard
13. 9	17. 8	K10	J9	Crow	25.11	1.11	C1	B10	Griffon
14. 9	18. 8	K10	K10	Monkey	26.11	2.11 .	C1	C11	Ox
15. 9	19. 8	K10	A11	Gibbon	27.11	3.11	C1	D12	Bat
16. 9	20. 8	K10	B12	Tapir	28.11	4.11	C1	E1	Rat
17. 9	21. 8	K10	C1	Sheep	29.11	5.11	C1	F2	Swallow
18. 9	22. 8	K10	D2	Deer	30.11	6.11	C1	G3	Pig
19. 9	23. 8	K10	E3	Horse	1.12	7.11	C1	H4	Porcupine
20. 9	24. 8	K10	F4	Stag	2.12	8.11	C1	J5	Wolf
21. 9	25. 8	K10	G5	Serpent	3.12	9.11	C1	K6	Dog
22. 9	26. 8	K10	H6	Earthworm	4.12	10.11	C1	A7	Pheasant
23. 9	27. 8	K10	J7	Crocodile	5.12	11.11	C1	B8	Cock
24. 9	28. 8	K10	K8	Dragon	6.12	12.11	C1	C9	Crow
25. 9	29. 8	K10	A9	Badger	7.12	13.11	C1	D10	Monkey
26. 9	30. 8	K10	B10	Hare	8.12	14.11	C1	E11	Gibbon
27. 9	1. 9	A11	C11	Fox	9.12	15.11	C1	F12	Tapir
28. 9	2. 9	A11	D12	Tiger	10.12	16.11	C1	G1	Sheep
29. 9	3. 9	A11	E1	Leopard	11.12	17.11	C1	H2	Deer
30. 9	4. 9	A11	F2	Griffon	12.12	18.11	C1	J3	Horse
1.10	5. 9	A11	G3	Ox	13.12	19.11	C1	K4	Stag
2.10	6. 9	A11	H4	Bat	14.12	20.11	C1	A5	Serpent
3.10	7. 9	A11	J5	Rat	15.12	21.11	C1	B6	Earthworm
4.10	8. 9	A11	K6	Swallow	16.12	22.11	C1	C7	Crocodile
5.10	9. 9	A11	A7	Pig	17.12	23.11	C1	D8	Dragon
6.10	10. 9	A11	B8	Porcupine	18.12	24.11	C1	E9	Badger
7.10	11. 9	A11	C9	Wolf	19.12	25.11	C1	F10	Hare
8.10	12. 9	A11	D10	Dog	20.12	26.11	C1	G11	Fox
9.10	13. 9	A11	E11	Pheasant	21.12	27.11	C1	H12	Tiger
10.10	14. 9	A11	F12	Cock	22.12	28.11	C1	J1	Leopard
11.10	15. 9	A11	G1	Crow	23.12	29.11	C1	K2	Griffon
12.10	16. 9	A11	H2	Monkey	24.12	30.11	C1	A3	Ox
13.10	17. 9	A11	J3	Gibbon	25.12	1. 12	D2	B4	Bat

Solar date	Lunar date	Month HS/EB	Day HS/EB	Constellation
26.12	2.12	D2	C5	Rat
27.12	3.12	D2	D6	Swallow
28.12	4.12	D2	E7	Pig
29.12	5.12	D2	F8	Porcupine
30.12	6.12	D2	G9	Wolf
31.12	7.12	D2	H10	Dog
1955				
1.1	8.12	D2	J11	Pheasant
2.1	9.12	D2	K12	Cock
3.1	10.12	D2	A1	Crow
4.1	11.12	D2	B2	Monkey
5.1	12.12	D2	C3	Gibbon
6.1	13.12	D2	D4	Tapir
7.1	14.12	D2	E5	Sheep
8.1	15.12	D2	F6	Deer
9.1	16.12	D2	G7	Horse
10.1	17.12	D2	H8	Stag
11.1	18.12	D2	J9	Serpent
12.1	19.12	D2	K10	Earthworm
13.1	20.12	D2	A11	Crocodile
14.1	21.12	D2	B12	Dragon
15.1	22.12	D2	C1	Badger
16.1	23.12	D2	D2	Hare
17.1	24.12	D2	E3	Fox
18.1	25.12	D2	F4	Tiger
19.1	26.12	D2	G5	Leopard
20.1	27.12	D2	H6	Griffon
21.1	28.12	D2	J7	Ox
22.1	29.12	D2	K8	Bat
23.1	30.12	D2	A9	Rat

YI WEI YEAR

Solar date	Lunar date	Month HS/EB	Day HS/EB	Constellation
24.1	1.1	E3	B10	Swallow
25.1	2.1	E3	C11	Pig
26.1	3.1	E3	D12	Porcupine
27.1	4.1	E3	E1	Wolf
28.1	5.1	E3	F2	Dog
29.1	6.1	E3	G3	Pheasant
30.1	7.1	E3	H4	Cock
31.1	8.1	E3	J5	Crow
1.2	9.1	E3	K6	Monkey
2.2	10.1	E3	A7	Gibbon
3.2	11.1	E3	B8	Tapir
4.2	12.1	E3	C9	Sheep
5.2	13.1	E3	D10	Deer
6.2	14.1	E3	E11	Horse
7.2	15.1	E3	F12	Stag
8.2	16.1	E3	G1	Serpent
9.2	17.1	E3	H2	Earthworm
10.2	18.1	E3	J3	Crocodile
11.2	19.1	E3	K4	Dragon
12.2	20.1	E3	A5	Badger
13.2	21.1	E3	B6	Hare
14.2	22.1	E3	C7	Fox
15.2	23.1	E3	D8	Tiger
16.2	24.1	E3	E9	Leopard
17.2	25.1	E3	F10	Griffon
18.2	26.1	E3	G11	Ox
19.2	27.1	E3	H12	Bat
20.2	28.1	E3	J1	Rat
21.2	29.1	E3	K2	Swallow
22.2	1.2	F4	A3	Pig
23.2	2.2	F4	B4	Porcupine
24.2	3.2	F4	C5	Wolf
25.2	4.2	F4	D6	Dog
26.2	5.2	F4	E7	Pheasant
27.2	6.2	F4	F8	Cock
28.2	7.2	F4	G9	Crow
1.3	8.2	F4	H10	Monkey
2.3	9.2	F4	J11	Gibbon
3.3	10.2	F4	K12	Tapir
4.3	11.2	F4	A1	Sheep
5.3	12.2	F4	B2	Deer
6.3	13.2	F4	C3	Horse
7.3	14.2	F4	D4	Stag
8.3	15.2	F4	E5	Serpent
9.3	16.2	F4	F6	Earthworm
10.3	17.2	F4	G7	Crocodile
11.3	18.2	F4	H8	Dragon
12.3	19.2	F4	H8	Badger
13.3	20.2	F4	K10	Hare
14.3	21.2	F4	A11	Fox
15.3	22.2	F4	B12	Tiger
16.3	23.2	F4	C1	Leopard
17.3	24.2	F4	D2	Griffon
18.3	25.2	F4	E3	Ox
19.3	26.2	F4	F4	Bat
20.3	27.2	F4	G5	Rat
21.3	28.2	F4	H6	Swallow
22.3	29.2	F4	J7	Pig
23.3	30.2	F4	K8	Porcupine
24.3	1.3	G5	A9	Wolf
25.3	2.3	G5	B10	Dog
26.3	3.3	G5	C11	Pheasant
27.3	4.3	G5	D12	Cock
28.3	5.3	G5	E1	Crow
29.3	6.3	G5	F2	Monkey
30.3	7.3	G5	G3	Gibbon
31.3	8.3	G5	H4	Tapir
1.4	9.3	G5	J5	Sheep
2.4	10.3	G5	K6	Deer
3.4	11.3	G5	A7	Horse
4.4	12.3	G5	B8	Stag
5.4	13.3	G5	C9	Serpent
6.4	14.3	G5	D10	Earthworm
7.4	15.3	G5	E11	Crocodile
8.4	16.3	G5	F12	Dragon
9.4	17.3	G5	G1	Badger
10.4	18.3	G5	H2	Hare
11.4	19.3	G5	J3	Fox
12.4	20.3	G5	K4	Tiger
13.4	21.3	G5	A5	Leopard
14.4	22.3	G5	B6	Griffon
15.4	23.3	G5	C7	Ox
16.4	24.3	G5	D8	Bat
17.4	25.3	G5	E9	Rat
18.4	26.3	G5	F10	Swallow
19.4	27.3	G5	G11	Pig
20.4	28.3	G5	H12	Porcupine
21.4	29.3	G5	J1	Wolf
22.4	*1.3*	*G5*	K2	Dog
23.4	*2.3*	*G5*	A3	Pheasant
24.4	*3.3*	*G5*	B4	Cock
25.4	*4.3*	*G5*	C5	Crow
26.4	*5.3*	*G5*	D6	Monkey
27.4	*6.3*	*G5*	E7	Gibbon
28.4	*7.3*	*G5*	F8	Tapir
29.4	*8.3*	*G5*	G9	Sheep
30.4	*9.3*	*G5*	H10	Deer
1.5	*10.3*	*G5*	J11	Horse
2.5	*11.3*	*G5*	K12	Stag
3.5	*12.3*	*G5*	A1	Serpent
4.5	*13.3*	*G5*	B2	Earthworm
5.5	*14.3*	*G5*	C3	Crocodile
6.5	*15.3*	*G5*	D4	Dragon
7.5	*16.3*	*G5*	E5	Badger

Solar date	Lunar date	Month HS/EB	Day HS/EB	Constellation	Solar date	Lunar date	Month HS/EB	Day HS/EB	Constellation
8. 5	17. 3	G5	F6	Hare	20. 7	2. 6	K8	J7	Gibbon
9. 5	18. 3	G5	G7	Fox	21. 7	3. 6	K8	K8	Tapir
10. 5	19. 3	G5	H8	Tiger	22. 7	4. 6	K8	A9	Sheep
11. 5	20. 3	G5	J9	Leopard	23. 7	5. 6	K8	B10	Deer
12. 5	21. 3	G5	K10	Griffon	24. 7	6. 6	K8	C11	Horse
13. 5	22. 3	G5	A11	Ox	25. 7	7. 6	K8	D12	Stag
14. 5	23. 3	G5	B12	Bat	26. 7	8. 6	K8	E1	Serpent
15. 5	24. 3	G5	C1	Rat	27. 7	9. 6	K8	F2	Earthworm
16. 5	25. 3	G5	D2	Swallow	28. 7	10. 6	K8	G3	Crocodile
17. 5	26. 3	G5	E3	Pig	29. 7	11. 6	K8	H4	Dragon
18. 5	27. 3	G5	F4	Porcupine	30. 7	12. 6	K8	J5	Badger
19. 5	28. 3	G5	G5	Wolf	31. 7	13. 6	K8	K6	Hare
20. 5	29. 3	G5	H6	Dog	1. 8	14. 6	K8	A7	Fox
21. 5	30. 3	G5	J7	Pheasant	2. 8	15. 6	K8	B8	Tiger
22. 5	1. 4	H6	K8	Cock	3. 8	16. 6	K8	C9	Leopard
23. 5	2. 4	H6	A9	Crow	4. 8	17. 6	K8	D10	Griffon
24. 5	3. 4	H6	B10	Monkey	5. 8	18. 6	K8	E11	Ox
25. 5	4. 4	H6	C11	Gibbon	6. 8	19. 6	K8	F12	Bat
26. 5	5. 4	H6	D12	Tapir	7. 8	20. 6	K8	G1	Rat
27. 5	6. 4	H6	E1	Sheep	8. 8	21. 6	K8	H2	Swallow
28. 5	7. 4	H6	F2	Deer	9. 8	22. 6	K8	J3	Pig
29. 5	8. 4	H6	G3	Horse	10. 8	23. 6	K8	K4	Porcupine
30. 5	9. 4	H6	H4	Stag	11. 8	24. 6	K8	A5	Wolf
31. 5	10. 4	H6	J5	Serpent	12. 8	25. 6	K8	B6	Dog
1. 6	11. 4	H6	K6	Earthworm	13. 8	26. 6	K8	C7	Pheasant
2. 6	12. 4	H6	A7	Crocodile	14. 8	27. 6	K8	D8	Cock
3. 6	13. 4	H6	B8	Dragon	15. 8	28. 6	K8	E9	Crow
4. 6	14. 4	H6	C9	Badger	16. 8	29. 6	K8	F10	Monkey
5. 6	15. 4	H6	D10	Hare	17. 8	30. 6	K8	G11	Gibbon
6. 6	16. 4	H6	E11	Fox	18. 8	1. 7	A9	H12	Tapir
7. 6	17. 4	H6	F12	Tiger	19. 8	2. 7	A9	J1	Sheep
8. 6	18. 4	H6	G1	Leopard	20. 8	3. 7	A9	K2	Deer
9. 6	19. 4	H6	H2	Griffon	21. 8	4. 7	A9	A3	Horse
10. 6	20. 4	H6	J3	Ox	22. 8	5. 7	A9	B4	Stag
11. 6	21. 4	H6	K4	Bat	23. 8	6. 7	A9	C5	Serpent
12. 6	22. 4	H6	A5	Rat	24. 8	7. 7	A9	D6	Earthworm
13. 6	23. 4	H6	B6	Swallow	25. 8	8. 7	A9	E7	Crocodile
14. 6	24. 4	H6	C7	Pig	26. 8	9. 7	A9	F8	Dragon
15. 6	25. 4	H6	D8	Porcupine	27. 8	10. 7	A9	G9	Badger
16. 6	26. 4	H6	E9	Wolf	28. 8	11. 7	A9	H10	Hare
17. 6	27. 4	H6	F10	Dog	29. 8	12. 7	A9	J11	Fox
18. 6	28. 4	H6	G11	Pheasant	30. 8	13. 7	A9	K12	Tiger
19. 6	29. 4	H6	H12	Cock	31. 8	14. 7	A9	A1	Leopard
20. 6	1. 5	J7	J1	Crow	1. 9	15. 7	A9	B2	Griffon
21. 6	2. 5	J7	K2	Monkey	2. 9	16. 7	A9	C3	Ox
22. 6	3. 5	J7	A3	Gibbon	3. 9	17. 7	A9	D4	Bat
23. 6	4. 5	J7	B4	Tapir	4. 9	18. 7	A9	E5	Rat
24. 6	5. 5	J7	C5	Sheep	5. 9	19. 7	A9	F6	Swallow
25. 6	6. 5	J7	D6	Deer	6. 9	20. 7	A9	G7	Pig
26. 6	7. 5	J7	E7	Horse	7. 9	21. 7	A9	H8	Porcupine
27. 6	8. 5	J7	F8	Stag	8. 9	22. 7	A9	J9	Wolf
28. 6	9. 5	J7	G9	Serpent	9. 9	23. 7	A9	K10	Dog
29. 6	10. 5	J7	H10	Earthworm	10. 9	24. 7	A9	A11	Pheasant
30. 6	11. 5	J7	J11	Crocodile	11. 9	25. 7	A9	B12	Cock
1. 7	12. 5	J7	K12	Dragon	12. 9	26. 7	A9	C1	Crow
2. 7	13. 5	J7	A1	Badger	13. 9	27. 7	A9	D2	Monkey
3. 7	14. 5	J7	B2	Hare	14. 9	28. 7	A9	E3	Gibbon
4. 7	15. 5	J7	C3	Fox	15. 9	29. 7	A9	F4	Tapir
5. 7	16. 5	J7	D4	Tiger	16. 9	1. 8	B10	G5	Sheep
6. 7	17. 5	J7	E5	Leopard	17. 9	2. 8	B10	H6	Deer
7. 7	18. 5	J7	F6	Griffon	18. 9	3. 8	B10	J7	Horse
8. 7	19. 5	J7	G7	Ox	19. 9	4. 8	B10	K8	Stag
9. 7	20. 5	J7	H8	Bat	20. 9	5. 8	B10	A9	Serpent
10. 7	21. 5	J7	J9	Rat	21. 9	6. 8	B10	B10	Earthworm
11. 7	22. 5	J7	K10	Swallow	22. 9	7. 8	B10	C11	Crocodile
12. 7	23. 5	J7	A11	Pig	23. 9	8. 8	B10	D12	Dragon
13. 7	24. 5	J7	B12	Porcupine	24. 9	9. 8	B10	E1	Badger
14. 7	25. 5	J7	C1	Wolf	25. 9	10. 8	B10	F2	Hare
15. 7	26. 5	J7	D2	Dog	26. 9	11. 8	B10	G3	Fox
16. 7	27. 5	J7	E3	Pheasant	27. 9	12. 8	B10	H4	Tiger
17. 7	28. 5	J7	F4	Cock	28. 9	13. 8	B10	J5	Leopard
18. 7	29. 5	J7	G5	Crow	29. 9	14. 8	B10	K6	Griffon
19. 7	1. 6	K8	H6	Monkey	30. 9	15. 8	B10	A7	Ox

Solar date	Lunar date	Month HS/EB	Day HS/EB	Constellation	Solar date	Lunar date	Month HS/EB	Day HS/EB	Constellation
1.10	16. 8	B10	B8	Bat	8.12	25.10	D12	K4	Tapir
2.10	17. 8	B10	C9	Rat	9.12	26.10	D12	A5	Sheep
3.10	18. 8	B10	D10	Swallow	10.12	27.10	D12	B6	Deer
4.10	19. 8	B10	E11	Pig	11.12	28.10	D12	C7	Horse
5.10	20. 8	B10	F12	Porcupine	12.12	29.10	D12	D8	Stag
6.10	21. 8	B10	G1	Wolf	13.12	30.10	D12	E9	Serpent
7.10	22. 8	B10	H2	Dog	14.12	1.11	E1	F10	Earthworm
8.10	23. 8	B10	J3	Pheasant	15.12	2.11	E1	G11	Crocodile
9.10	24. 8	B10	K4	Cock	16.12	3.11	E1	H12	Dragon
10.10	25. 8	B10	A5	Crow	17.12	4.11	E1	J1	Badger
11.10	26. 8	B10	B6	Monkey	18.12	5.11	E1	K2	Hare
12.10	27. 8	B10	C7	Gibbon	19.12	6.11	E1	A3	Fox
13.10	28. 8	B10	D8	Tapir	20.12	7.11	E1	B4	Tiger
14.10	29. 8	B10	E9	Sheep	21.12	8.11	E1	C5	Leopard
15.10	30. 8	B10	F10	Deer	22.12	9.11	E1	D6	Griffon
16.10	1. 9	C11	G11	Horse	23.12	10.11	E1	E7	Ox
17.10	2. 9	C11	H12	Stag	24.12	11.11	E1	F8	Bat
18.10	3. 9	C11	J1	Serpent	25.12	12.11	E1	G9	Rat
19.10	4. 9	C11	K2	Earthworm	26.12	13.11	E1	H10	Swallow
20.10	5. 9	C11	A3	Crocodile	27.12	14.11	E1	J11	Pig
21.10	6. 9	C11	B4	Dragon	28.12	15.11	E1	K12	Porcupine
22.10	7. 9	C11	C5	Badger	29.12	16.11	E1	A1	Wolf
23.10	8. 9	C11	D6	Hare	30.12	17.11	E1	B2	Dog
24.10	9. 9	C11	E7	Fox	31.12	18.11	E1	C3	Pheasant
25.10	10. 9	C11	F8	Tiger					
26.10	11. 9	C11	G9	Leopard	**1956**				
27.10	12. 9	C11	H10	Griffon	1. 1	19.11	E1	D4	Cock
28.10	13. 9	C11	J11	Ox	2. 1	20.11	E1	E5	Crow
29.10	14. 9	C11	K12	Bat	3. 1	21.11	E1	F6	Monkey
30.10	15. 9	C11	A1	Rat	4. 1	22.11	E1	G7	Gibbon
31.10	16. 9	C11	B2	Swallow	5. 1	23.11	E1	H8	Tapir
1.11	17. 9	C11	C3	Pig	6. 1	24.11	E1	J9	Sheep
2.11	18. 9	C11	D4	Porcupine	7. 1	25.11	E1	K10	Deer
3.11	19. 9	C11	E5	Wolf	8. 1	26.11	E1	A11	Horse
4.11	20. 9	C11	F6	Dog	9. 1	27.11	E1	B12	Stag
5.11	21. 9	C11	G7	Pheasant	10. 1	28.11	E1	C1	Serpent
6.11	22. 9	C11	H8	Cock	11. 1	29.11	E1	D2	Earthworm
7.11	23. 9	C11	J9	Crow	12. 1	30.11	E1	E3	Crocodile
8.11	24. 9	C11	K10	Monkey	13. 1	1.12	F2	F4	Dragon
9.11	25. 9	C11	A11	Gibbon	14. 1	2.12	F2	G5	Badger
10.11	26. 9	C11	B12	Tapir	15. 1	3.12	F2	H6	Hare
11.11	27. 9	C11	C1	Sheep	16. 1	4.12	F2	J7	Fox
12.11	28. 9	C11	D2	Deer	17. 1	5.12	F2	K8	Tiger
13.11	29. 9	C11	E3	Horse	18. 1	6.12	F2	A9	Leopard
14.11	1.10	D12	F4	Stag	19. 1	7.12	F2	B10	Griffon
15.11	2.10	D12	G5	Serpent	20. 1	8.12	F2	C11	Ox
16.11	3.10	D12	H6	Earthworm	21. 1	9.12	F2	D12	Bat
17.11	4.10	D12	J7	Crocodile	22. 1	10.12	F2	E1	Rat
18.11	5.10	D12	K8	Dragon	23. 1	11.12	F2	F2	Swallow
19.11	6.10	D12	A9	Badger	24. 1	12.12	F2	G3	Pig
20.11	7.10	D12	B10	Hare	25. 1	13.12	F2	H4	Porcupine
21.11	8.10	D12	C11	Fox	26. 1	14.12	F2	J5	Wolf
22.11	9.10	D12	D12	Tiger	27. 1	15.12	F2	K6	Dog
23.11	10.10	D12	E1	Leopard	28. 1	16.12	F2	A7	Pheasant
24.11	11.10	D12	F2	Griffon	29. 1	17.12	F2	B8	Cock
25.11	12.10	D12	G3	Ox	30. 1	18.12	F2	C9	Crow
26.11	13.10	D12	H4	Bat	31. 1	19.12	F2	D10	Monkey
27.11	14.10	D12	J5	Rat	1. 2	20.12	F2	E11	Gibbon
28.11	15.10	D12	K6	Swallow	2. 2	21.12	F2	F12	Tapir
29.11	16.10	D12	A7	Pig	3. 2	22.12	F2	G1	Sheep
30.11	17.10	D12	B8	Porcupine	4. 2	23.12	F2	H2	Deer
1.12	18.10	D12	C9	Wolf	5. 2	24.12	F2	J3	Horse
2.12	19.10	D12	D10	Dog	6. 2	25.12	F2	K4	Stag
3.12	20.10	D12	E11	Pheasant	7. 2	26.12	F2	A5	Serpent
4.12	21.10	D12	F12	Cock	8. 2	27.12	F2	B6	Earthworm
5.12	22.10	D12	G1	Crow	9. 2	28.12	F2	C7	Crocodile
6.12	23.10	D12	H2	Monkey	10. 2	29.12	F2	D8	Dragon
7.12	24.10	D12	J3	Gibbon	11. 2	30.12	F2	E9	Badger

PING SHEN YEAR

Solar date	Lunar date	Month HS/EB	Day HS/EB	Constellation	Solar date	Lunar date	Month HS/EB	Day HS/EB	Constellation
12. 2	1. 1	G3	F10	Hare	23. 4	13. 3	J5	G9	Crow
13. 2	2. 1	G3	G11	Fox	24. 4	14. 3	J5	H10	Monkey
14. 2	3. 1	G3	H12	Tiger	25. 4	15. 3	J5	J11	Gibbon
15. 2	4. 1	G3	J1	Leopard	26. 4	16. 3	J5	K12	Tapir
16. 2	5. 1	G3	K2	Griffon	27. 4	17. 3	J5	A1	Sheep
17. 2	6. 1	G3	A3	Ox	28. 4	18. 3	J5	B2	Deer
18. 2	7. 1	G3	B4	Bat	29. 4	19. 3	J5	C3	Horse
19. 2	8. 1	G3	C5	Rat	30. 4	20. 3	J5	D4	Stag
20. 2	9. 1	G3	D6	Swallow	1. 5	21. 3	J5	E5	Serpent
21. 2	10. 1	G3	E7	Pig	2. 5	22. 3	J5	F6	Earthworm
22. 2	11. 1	G3	F8	Porcupine	3. 5	23. 3	J5	G7	Crocodile
23. 2	12. 1	G3	G9	Wolf	4. 5	24. 3	J5	H8	Dragon
24. 2	13. 1	G3	H10	Dog	5. 5	25. 3	J5	J9	Badger
25. 2	14. 1	G3	J11	Pheasant	6. 5	26. 3	J5	K10	Hare
26. 2	15. 1	G3	K12	Cock	7. 5	27. 3	J5	A11	Fox
27. 2	16. 1	G3	A1	Crow	8. 5	28. 3	J5	B12	Tiger
28. 2	17. 1	G3	B2	Monkey	9. 5	29. 3	J5	C1	Leopard
29. 2	18. 1	G3	C3	Gibbon	10. 5	1. 4	K6	D2	Griffon
1. 3	19. 1	G3	D4	Tapir	11. 5	2. 4	K6	E3	Ox
2. 3	20. 1	G3	E5	Sheep	12. 5	3. 4	K6	F4	Bat
3. 3	21. 1	G3	F6	Deer	13. 5	4. 4	K6	G5	Rat
4. 3	22. 1	G3	G7	Horse	14. 5	5. 4	K6	H6	Swallow
5. 3	23. 1	G3	H8	Stag	15. 5	6. 4	K6	J7	Pig
6. 3	24. 1	G3	J9	Serpent	16. 5	7. 4	K6	K8	Porcupine
7. 3	25. 1	G3	K10	Earthworm	17. 5	8. 4	K6	A9	Wolf
8. 3	26. 1	G3	A11	Crocodile	18. 5	9. 4	K6	B10	Dog
9. 3	27. 1	G3	B12	Dragon	19. 5	10. 4	K6	C11	Pheasant
10. 3	28. 1	G3	C1	Badger	20. 5	11. 4	K6	D12	Cock
11. 3	29. 1	G3	D2	Hare	21. 5	12. 4	K6	E1	Crow
12. 3	1. 2	H4	E3	Fox	22. 5	13. 4	K6	F2	Monkey
13. 3	2. 2	H4	F4	Tiger	23. 5	14. 4	K6	G3	Gibbon
14. 3	3. 2	H4	G5	Leopard	24. 5	15. 4	K6	H4	Tapir
15. 3	4. 2	H4	H6	Griffon	25. 5	16. 4	K6	J5	Sheep
16. 3	5. 2	H4	J7	Ox	26. 5	17. 4	K6	K6	Deer
17. 3	6. 2	H4	K8	Bat	27. 5	18. 4	K6	A7	Horse
18. 3	7. 2	H4	A9	Rat	28. 5	19. 4	K6	B8	Stag
19. 3	8. 2	H4	B10	Swallow	29. 5	20. 4	K6	C9	Serpent
20. 3	9. 2	H4	C11	Pig	30. 5	21. 4	K6	D10	Earthworm
21. 3	10. 2	H4	D12	Porcupine	31. 5	22. 4	K6	E11	Crocodile
22. 3	11. 2	H4	E1	Wolf	1. 6	23. 4	K6	F12	Dragon
23. 3	12. 2	H4	F2	Dog	2. 6	24. 4	K6	G1	Badger
24. 3	13. 2	H4	G3	Pheasant	3. 6	25. 4	K6	H2	Hare
25. 3	14. 2	H4	H4	Cock	4. 6	26. 4	K6	J3	Fox
26. 3	15. 2	H4	J5	Crow	5. 6	27. 4	K6	K4	Tiger
27. 3	16. 2	H4	K6	Monkey	6. 6	28. 4	K6	A5	Leopard
28. 3	17. 2	H4	A7	Gibbon	7. 6	29. 4	K6	B6	Griffon
29. 3	18. 2	H4	B8	Tapir	8. 6	30. 4	K6	C7	Ox
30. 3	19. 2	H4	C9	Sheep	9. 6	1. 5	A7	D8	Bat
31. 3	20. 2	H4	D10	Deer	10. 6	2. 5	A7	E9	Rat
1. 4	21. 2	H4	E11	Horse	11. 6	3. 5	A7	F10	Swallow
2. 4	22. 2	H4	F12	Stag	12. 6	4. 5	A7	G11	Pig
3. 4	23. 2	H4	G1	Serpent	13. 6	5. 5	A7	H12	Porcupine
4. 4	24. 2	H4	H2	Earthworm	14. 6	6. 5	A7	J1	Wolf
5. 4	25. 2	H4	J3	Crocodile	15. 6	7. 5	A7	K2	Dog
6. 4	26. 2	H4	K4	Dragon	16. 6	8. 5	A7	A3	Pheasant
7. 4	27. 2	H4	A5	Badger	17. 6	9. 5	A7	B4	Cock
8. 4	28. 2	H4	B6	Hare	18. 6	10. 5	A7	C5	Crow
9. 4	29. 2	H4	C7	Fox	19. 6	11. 5	A7	D6	Monkey
10. 4	30. 2	H4	D8	Tiger	20. 6	12. 5	A7	E7	Gibbon
11. 4	1. 3	J5	E9	Leopard	21. 6	13. 5	A7	F8	Tapir
12. 4	2. 3	J5	F10	Griffon	22. 6	14. 5	A7	G9	Sheep
13. 4	3. 3	J5	G11	Ox	23. 6	15. 5	A7	H10	Deer
14. 4	4. 3	J5	H12	Bat	24. 6	16. 5	A7	J11	Horse
15. 4	5. 3	J5	J1	Rat	25. 6	17. 5	A7	K12	Stag
16. 4	6. 3	J5	K2	Swallow	26. 6	18. 5	A7	A1	Serpent
17. 4	7. 3	J5	A3	Pig	27. 6	19. 5	A7	B2	Earthworm
18. 4	8. 3	J5	B4	Porcupine	28. 6	20. 5	A7	C3	Crocodile
19. 4	9. 3	J5	C5	Wolf	29. 6	21. 5	A7	D4	Dragon
20. 4	10. 3	J5	D6	Dog	30. 6	22. 5	A7	E5	Badger
21. 4	11. 3	J5	E7	Pheasant	1. 7	23. 5	A7	F6	Hare
22. 4	12. 3	J5	F8	Cock	2. 7	24. 5	A7	G7	Fox

Solar date	Lunar date	Month HS/EB	Day HS/EB	Constellation	Solar date	Lunar date	Month HS/EB	Day HS/EB	Constellation
3. 7	25. 5	A7	H8	Tiger	14. 9	10. 8	D10	A9	Sheep
4. 7	26. 5	A7	J9	Leopard	15. 9	11. 8	D10	B10	Deer
5. 7	27. 5	A7	K10	Griffon	16. 9	12. 8	D10	C11	Horse
6. 7	28. 5	A7	A11	Ox	17. 9	13. 8	D10	D12	Stag
7. 7	29. 5	A7	B12	Bat	18. 9	14. 8	D10	E1	Serpent
8. 7	1. 6	B8	C1	Rat	19. 9	15. 8	D10	F2	Earthworm
9. 7	2. 6	B8	D2	Swallow	20. 9	16. 8	D10	G3	Crocodile
10. 7	3. 6	B8	E3	Pig	21. 9	17. 8	D10	H4	Dragon
11. 7	4. 6	B8	F4	Porcupine	22. 9	18. 8	D10	J5	Badger
12. 7	5. 6	B8	G5	Wolf	23. 9	19. 8	D10	K6	Hare
13. 7	6. 6	B8	H6	Dog	24. 9	20. 8	D10	A7	Fox
14. 7	7. 6	B8	J7	Pheasant	25. 9	21. 8	D10	B8	Tiger
15. 7	8. 6	B8	K8	Cock	26. 9	22. 8	D10	C9	Leopard
16. 7	9. 6	B8	A9	Crow	27. 9	23. 8	D10	D10	Griffon
17. 7	10. 6	B8	B10	Monkey	28. 9	24. 8	D10	E11	Ox
18. 7	11. 6	B8	C11	Gibbon	29. 9	25. 8	D10	F12	Bat
19. 7	12. 6	B8	D12	Tapir	30. 9	26. 8	D10	G1	Rat
20. 7	13. 6	B8	E1	Sheep	1.10	27. 8	D10	H2	Swallow
21. 7	14. 6	B8	F2	Deer	2.10	28. 8	D10	J3	Pig
22. 7	15. 6	B8	G3	Horse	3.10	29. 8	D10	K4	Porcupine
23. 7	16. 6	B8	H4	Stag	4.10	1. 9	E11	A5	Wolf
24. 7	17. 6	B8	J5	Serpent	5.10	2. 9	E11	B6	Dog
25. 7	18. 6	B8	K6	Earthworm	6.10	3. 9	E11	C7	Pheasant
26. 7	19. 6	B8	A7	Crocodile	7.10	4. 9	E11	D8	Cock
27. 7	20. 6	B8	B8	Dragon	8.10	5. 9	E11	E9	Crow
28. 7	21. 6	B8	C9	Badger	9.10	6. 9	E11	F10	Monkey
29. 7	22. 6	B8	D10	Hare	10.10	7. 9	E11	G11	Gibbon
30. 7	23. 6	B8	E11	Fox	11.10	8. 9	E11	H12	Tapir
31. 7	24. 6	B8	F12	Tiger	12.10	9. 9	E11	J1	Sheep
1. 8	25. 6	B8	G1	Leopard	13.10	10. 9	E11	K2	Deer
2. 8	26. 6	B8	H2	Griffon	14.10	11. 9	E11	A3	Horse
3. 8	27. 6	B8	J3	Ox	15.10	12. 9	E11	B4	Stag
4. 8	28. 6	B8	K4	Bat	16.10	13. 9	E11	C5	Serpent
5. 8	29. 6	B8	A5	Rat	17.10	14. 9	E11	D6	Earthworm
6. 8	1. 7	C9	B6	Swallow	18.10	15. 9	E11	E7	Crocodile
7. 8	2. 7	C9	C7	Pig	19.10	16. 9	E11	F8	Dragon
8. 8	3. 7	C9	D8	Porcupine	20.10	17. 9	E11	G9	Badger
9. 8	4. 7	C9	E9	Wolf	21.10	18. 9	E11	H10	Hare
10. 8	5. 7	C9	F10	Dog	22.10	19. 9	E11	J11	Fox
11. 8	6. 7	C9	G11	Pheasant	23.10	20. 9	E11	K12	Tiger
12. 8	7. 7	C9	H12	Cock	24.10	21. 9	E11	A1	Leopard
13. 8	8. 7	C9	J1	Crow	25.10	22. 9	E11	B2	Griffon
14. 8	9. 7	C9	K2	Monkey	26.10	23. 9	E11	C3	Ox
15. 8	10. 7	C9	A3	Gibbon	27.10	24. 9	E11	D4	Bat
16. 8	11. 7	C9	B4	Tapir	28.10	25. 9	E11	E5	Rat
17. 8	12. 7	C9	C5	Sheep	29.10	26. 9	E11	F6	Swallow
18. 8	13. 7	C9	D6	Deer	30.10	27. 9	E11	G7	Pig
19. 8	14. 7	C9	E7	Horse	31.10	28. 9	E11	H8	Porcupine
20. 8	15. 7	C9	F8	Stag	1.11	29. 9	E11	J9	Wolf
21. 8	16. 7	C9	G9	Serpent	2.11	30. 9	E11	K10	Dog
22. 8	17. 7	C9	H10	Earthworm	3.11	1.10	F12	A11	Pheasant
23. 8	18. 7	C9	J11	Crocodile	4.11	2.10	F12	B12	Cock
24. 8	19. 7	C9	K12	Dragon	5.11	3.10	F12	C1	Crow
25. 8	20. 7	C9	A1	Badger	6.11	4.10	F12	D2	Monkey
26. 8	21. 7	C9	B2	Hare	7.11	5.10	F12	E3	Gibbon
27. 8	22. 7	C9	C3	Fox	8.11	6.10	F12	F4	Tapir
28. 8	23. 7	C9	D4	Tiger	9.11	7.10	F12	G5	Sheep
29. 8	24. 7	C9	E5	Leopard	10.11	8.10	F12	H6	Deer
30. 8	25. 7	C9	F6	Griffon	11.11	9.10	F12	J7	Horse
31. 8	26. 7	C9	G7	Ox	12.11	10.10	F12	K8	Stag
1. 9	27. 7	C9	H8	Bat	13.11	11.10	F12	A9	Serpent
2. 9	28. 7	C9	J9	Rat	14.11	12.10	F12	B10	Earthworm
3. 9	29. 7	C9	K10	Swallow	15.11	13.10	F12	C11	Crocodile
4. 9	30. 7	C9	A11	Pig	16.11	14.10	F12	D12	Dragon
5. 9	1. 8	D10	B12	Porcupine	17.11	15.10	F12	E1	Badger
6. 9	2. 8	D10	C1	Wolf	18.11	16.10	F12	F2	Hare
7. 9	3. 8	D10	D2	Dog	19.11	17.10	F12	G3	Fox
8. 9	4. 8	D10	E3	Pheasant	20.11	18.10	F12	H4	Tiger
9. 9	5. 8	D10	F4	Cock	21.11	19.10	F12	J5	Leopard
10. 9	6. 8	D10	G5	Crow	22.11	20.10	F12	K6	Griffon
11. 9	7. 8	D10	H6	Monkey	23.11	21.10	F12	A7	Ox
12. 9	8. 8	D10	J7	Gibbon	24.11	22.10	F12	B8	Bat
13. 9	9. 8	D10	K8	Tapir	25.11	23.10	F12	C9	Rat

Solar date	Lunar date	Month HS/EB	Day HS/EB	Constellation	Solar date	Lunar date	Month HS/EB	Day HS/EB	Constellation
26.11	24.10	F12	D10	Swallow	30.12	29.11	G1	H8	Cock
27.11	25.10	F12	E11	Pig	31.12	30.11	G1	J9	Crow
28.11	26.10	F12	F12	Porcupine	**1957**				
29.11	27.10	F12	G1	Wolf	1. 1	1.12	H2	K10	Monkey
30.11	28.10	F12	H2	Dog	2. 1	2.12	H2	A11	Gibbon
1.12	29.10	F12	J3	Pheasant	3. 1	3.12	H2	B12	Tapir
2.12	1.11	G1	K4	Cock	4. 1	4.12	H2	C1	Sheep
3.12	2.11	G1	A5	Crow	5. 1	5.12	H2	D2	Deer
4.12	3.11	G1	B6	Monkey	6. 1	6.12	H2	E3	Horse
5.12	4.11	G1	C7	Gibbon	7. 1	7.12	H2	F4	Stag
6.12	5.11	G1	D8	Tapir	8. 1	8.12	H2	G5	Serpent
7.12	6.11	G1	E9	Sheep	9. 1	9.12	H2	H6	Earthworm
8.12	7.11	G1	F10	Deer	10. 1	10.12	H2	J7	Crocodile
9.12	8.11	G1	G11	Horse	11. 1	11.12	H2	K8	Dragon
10.12	9.11	G1	H12	Stag	12. 1	12.12	H2	A9	Badger
11.12	10.11	G1	J1	Serpent	13. 1	13.12	H2	B10	Hare
12.12	11.11	G1	K2	Earthworm	14. 1	14.12	H2	C11	Fox
13.12	12.11	G1	A3	Crocodile	15. 1	15.12	H2	D12	Tiger
14.12	13.11	G1	B4	Dragon	16. 1	16.12	H2	E1	Leopard
15.12	14.11	G1	C5	Badger	17. 1	17.12	H2	F2	Griffon
16.12	15.11	G1	D6	Hare	18. 1	18.12	H2	G3	Ox
17.12	16.11	G1	E7	Fox	19. 1	19.12	H2	H4	Bat
18.12	17.11	G1	F8	Tiger	20. 1	20.12	H2	J5	Rat
19.12	18.11	G1	G9	Leopard	21. 1	21.12	H2	K6	Swallow
20.12	19.11	G1	H10	Griffon	22. 1	22.12	H2	A7	Pig
21.12	20.11	G1	J11	Ox	23. 1	23.12	H2	B8	Porcupine
22.12	21.11	G1	K12	Bat	24. 1	24.12	H2	C9	Wolf
23.12	22.11	G1	A1	Rat	25. 1	25.12	H2	D10	Dog
24.12	23.11	G1	B2	Swallow	26. 1	26.12	H2	E11	Pheasant
25.12	24.11	G1	C3	Pig	27. 1	27.12	H2	F12	Cock
26.12	25.11	G1	D4	Porcupine	28. 1	28.12	H2	G1	Crow
27.12	26.11	G1	E5	Wolf	29. 1	29.12	H2	H2	Monkey
28.12	27.11	G1	F6	Dog	30. 1	30.12	H2	J3	Gibbon
29.12	28.11	G1	G7	Pheasant					

TING YU YEAR

Solar date	Lunar date	Month HS/EB	Day HS/EB	Constellation	Solar date	Lunar date	Month HS/EB	Day HS/EB	Constellation
31. 1	1. 1	J3	K4	Tapir	6. 3	5. 2	K4	D2	Earthworm
1. 2	2. 1	J3	A5	Sheep	7. 3	6. 2	K4	E3	Crocodile
2. 2	3. 1	J3	B6	Deer	8. 3	7. 2	K4	F4	Dragon
3. 2	4. 1	J3	C7	Horse	9. 3	8. 2	K4	G5	Badger
4. 2	5. 1	J3	D8	Stag	10. 3	9. 2	K4	H6	Hare
5. 2	6. 1	J3	E9	Serpent	11. 3	10. 2	K4	J7	Fox
6. 2	7. 1	J3	F10	Earthworm	12. 3	11. 2	K4	K8	Tiger
7. 2	8. 1	J3	G11	Crocodile	13. 3	12. 2	K4	A9	Leopard
8. 2	9. 1	J3	H12	Dragon	14. 3	13. 2	K4	B10	Griffon
9. 2	10. 1	J3	J1	Badger	15. 3	14. 2	K4	C11	Ox
10. 2	11. 1	J3	K2	Hare	16. 3	15. 2	K4	D12	Bat
11. 2	12. 1	J3	A3	Fox	17. 3	16. 2	K4	E1	Rat
12. 2	13. 1	J3	B4	Tiger	18. 3	17. 2	K4	F2	Swallow
13. 2	14. 1	J3	C5	Leopard	19. 3	18. 2	K4	G3	Pig
14. 2	15. 1	J3	D6	Griffon	20. 3	19. 2	K4	H4	Porcupine
15. 2	16. 1	J3	E7	Ox	21. 3	20. 2	K4	J5	Wolf
16. 2	17. 1	J3	F8	Bat	22. 3	21. 2	K4	K6	Dog
17. 2	18. 1	J3	G9	Rat	13. 3	22. 2	K4	A7	Pheasant
18. 2	19. 1	J3	H10	Swallow	24. 3	23. 2	K4	B8	Cock
19. 2	20. 1	J3	J11	Pig	25. 3	24. 2	K4	C9	Crow
20. 2	21. 1	J3	K12	Porcupine	26. 3	25. 2	K4	D10	Monkey
21. 2	22. 1	J3	A1	Wolf	27. 3	26. 2	K4	E11	Gibbon
22. 2	23. 1	J3	B2	Dog	28. 3	27. 2	K4	F12	Tapir
23. 2	24. 1	J3	C3	Pheasant	29. 3	28. 2	K4	G1	Sheep
24. 2	25. 1	J3	D4	Cock	30. 3	29. 2	K4	H2	Deer
25. 2	26. 1	J3	E5	Crow	31. 3	1. 3	A5	J3	Horse
26. 2	27. 1	J3	F6	Monkey	1. 4	2. 3	A5	K4	Stag
27. 2	28. 1	J3	G7	Gibbon	2. 4	3. 3	A5	A5	Serpent
28. 2	29. 1	J3	H8	Tapir	3. 4	4. 3	A5	B6	Earthworm
1. 3	30. 1	J3	J9	Sheep	4. 4	5. 3	A5	C7	Crocodile
2. 3	1. 2	K4	K10	Deer	5. 4	6. 3	A5	D8	Dragon
3. 3	2. 2	K4	A11	Horse	6. 4	7. 3	A5	E9	Badger
4. 3	3. 2	K4	B12	Stag	7. 4	8. 3	A5	F10	Hare
5. 3	4. 2	K4	C1	Serpent	8. 4	9. 3	A5	G11	Fox

Solar date	Lunar date	Month HS/EB	Day HS/EB	Constellation
9. 4	10. 3	A5	H12	Tiger
10. 4	11. 3	A5	J1	Leopard
11. 4	12. 3	A5	K2	Griffon
12. 4	13. 3	A5	A3	Ox
13. 4	14. 3	A5	B4	Bat
14. 4	15. 3	A5	C5	Rat
15. 4	16. 3	A5	D6	Swallow
16. 4	17. 3	A5	E7	Pig
17. 4	18. 3	A5	F8	Porcupine
18. 4	19. 3	A5	G9	Wolf
19. 4	20. 3	A5	H10	Dog
20. 4	21. 3	A5	J11	Pheasant
21. 4	22. 3	A5	K12	Cock
22. 4	23. 3	A5	A1	Crow
23. 4	24. 3	A5	B2	Monkey
24. 4	25. 3	A5	C3	Gibbon
25. 4	26. 3	A5	D4	Tapir
26. 4	27. 3	A5	E5	Sheep
27. 4	28. 3	A5	F6	Deer
28. 4	29. 3	A5	G7	Horse
29. 4	30. 3	A5	H8	Stag
30. 4	1. 4	B6	J9	Serpent
1. 5	2. 4	B6	K10	Earthworm
2. 5	3. 4	B6	A11	Crocodile
3. 5	4. 4	B6	B12	Dragon
4. 5	5. 4	B6	C1	Badger
5. 5	6. 4	B6	D2	Hare
6. 5	7. 4	B6	E3	Fox
7. 5	8. 4	B6	F4	Tiger
8. 5	9. 4	B6	G5	Leopard
9. 5	10. 4	B6	H6	Griffon
10. 5	11. 4	B6	J7	Ox
11. 5	12. 4	B6	K8	Bat
12. 5	13. 4	B6	A9	Rat
13. 5	14. 4	B6	B10	Swallow
14. 5	15. 4	B6	C11	Pig
15. 5	16. 4	B6	D12	Porcupine
16. 5	17. 4	B6	E1	Wolf
17. 5	18. 4	B6	F2	Dog
18. 5	19. 4	B6	G3	Pheasant
19. 5	20. 4	B6	H4	Cock
20. 5	21. 4	B6	J5	Crow
21. 5	22. 4	B6	K6	Monkey
22. 5	23. 4	B6	A7	Gibbon
23. 5	24. 4	B6	B8	Tapir
24. 5	25. 4	B6	C9	Sheep
25. 5	26. 4	B6	D10	Deer
26. 5	27. 4	B6	E11	Horse
27. 5	28. 4	B6	F12	Stag
28. 5	29. 4	B6	G1	Serpent
29. 5	1. 5	C7	H2	Earthworm
30. 5	2. 5	C7	J3	Crocodile
31. 5	3. 5	C7	K4	Dragon
1. 6	4. 5	C7	A5	Badger
2. 6	5. 5	C7	B6	Hare
3. 6	6. 5	C7	C7	Fox
4. 6	7. 5	C7	D8	Tiger
5. 6	8. 5	C7	E9	Leopard
6. 6	9. 5	C7	F10	Griffon
7. 6	10. 5	C7	G11	Ox
8. 6	11. 5	C7	H12	Bat
9. 6	12. 5	C7	J1	Rat
10. 6	13. 5	C7	K2	Swallow
11. 6	14. 5	C7	A3	Pig
12. 6	15. 5	C7	B4	Porcupine
13. 6	16. 5	C7	C5	Wolf
14. 6	17. 5	C7	D6	Dog
15. 6	18. 5	C7	E7	Pheasant
16. 6	19. 5	C7	F8	Cock
17. 6	20. 5	C7	G9	Crow
18. 6	21. 5	C7	H10	Monkey
19. 6	22. 5	C7	J11	Gibbon
20. 6	23. 5	C7	K12	Tapir
21. 6	24. 5	C7	A1	Sheep
22. 6	25. 5	C7	B2	Deer
23. 6	26. 5	C7	C3	Horse
24. 6	27. 5	C7	D4	Stag
25. 6	28. 5	C7	E5	Serpent
26. 6	29. 5	C7	F6	Earthworm
27. 6	30. 5	C7	G7	Crocodile
28. 6	1. 6	D8	H8	Dragon
29. 6	2. 6	D8	J9	Badger
30. 6	3. 6	D8	K10	Hare
1. 7	4. 6	D8	A11	Fox
2. 7	5. 6	D8	B12	Tiger
3. 7	6. 6	D8	C1	Leopard
4. 7	7. 6	D8	D2	Griffon
5. 7	8. 6	D8	E3	Ox
6. 7	9. 6	D8	F4	Bat
7. 7	10. 6	D8	G5	Rat
8. 7	11. 6	D8	H6	Swallow
9. 7	12. 6	D8	J7	Pig
10. 7	13. 6	D8	K8	Porcupine
11. 7	14. 6	D8	A9	Wolf
12. 7	15. 6	D8	B10	Dog
13. 7	16. 6	D8	C11	Pheasant
14. 7	17. 6	D8	D12	Cock
15. 7	18. 6	D8	E1	Crow
16. 7	19. 6	D8	F2	Monkey
17. 7	20. 6	D8	G3	Gibbon
18. 7	21. 6	D8	H4	Tapir
19. 7	22. 6	D8	J5	Sheep
20. 7	23. 6	D8	K6	Deer
21. 7	24. 6	D8	A7	Horse
22. 7	25. 6	D8	B8	Stag
23. 7	26. 6	D8	C9	Serpent
24. 7	27. 6	D8	D10	Earthworm
25. 7	28. 6	D8	E11	Crocodile
26. 7	29. 6	D8	F12	Dragon
27. 7	1. 7	E9	G1	Badger
28. 7	2. 7	E9	H2	Hare
29. 7	3. 7	E9	J3	Fox
30. 7	4. 7	E9	K4	Tiger
31. 7	5. 7	E9	A5	Leopard
1. 8	6. 7	E9	B6	Griffon
2. 8	7. 7	E9	C7	Ox
3. 8	8. 7	E9	D8	Bat
4. 8	9. 7	E9	E9	Rat
5. 8	10. 7	E9	F10	Swallow
6. 8	11. 7	E9	G11	Pig
7. 8	12. 7	E9	H12	Porcupine
8. 8	13. 7	E9	J1	Wolf
9. 8	14. 7	E9	K2	Dog
10. 8	15. 7	E9	A3	Pheasant
11. 8	16. 7	E9	B4	Cock
12. 8	17. 7	E9	C5	Crow
13. 8	18. 7	E9	D6	Monkey
14. 8	19. 7	E9	E7	Gibbon
15. 8	20. 7	E9	F8	Tapir
16. 8	21. 7	E9	G9	Sheep
17. 8	22. 7	E9	H10	Deer
18. 8	23. 7	E9	J11	Horse
19. 8	24. 7	E9	K12	Stag
20. 8	25. 7	E9	A1	Serpent
21. 8	26. 7	E9	B2	Earthworm
22. 8	27. 7	E9	C3	Crocodile
23. 8	28. 7	E9	D4	Dragon
24. 8	29. 7	E9	E5	Badger
25. 8	1. 8	F10	F6	Hare
26. 8	2. 8	F10	G7	Fox
27. 8	3. 8	F10	H8	Tiger
28. 8	4. 8	F10	J9	Leopard
29. 8	5. 8	F10	K10	Griffon
30. 8	6. 8	F10	A11	Ox
31. 8	7. 8	F10	B12	Bat
1. 9	8. 8	F10	C1	Rat

Solar date	Lunar date	Month HS/EB	Day HS/EB	Constellation	Solar date	Lunar date	Month HS/EB	Day HS/EB	Constellation
2. 9	9. 8	F10	D2	Swallow	14.11	23. 9	G11	G3	Crocodile
3. 9	10. 8	F10	E3	Pig	15.11	24. 9	G11	H4	Dragon
4. 9	11. 8	F10	F4	Porcupine	16.11	25. 9	G11	J5	Badger
5. 9	12. 8	F10	G5	Wolf	17.11	26. 9	G11	K6	Hare
6. 9	13. 8	F10	H6	Dog	18.11	27. 9	G11	A7	Fox
7. 9	14. 8	F10	J7	Pheasant	19.11	28. 9	G11	B8	Tiger
8. 9	15. 8	F10	K8	Cock	20.11	29. 9	G11	C9	Leopard
9. 9	16. 8	F10	A9	Crow	21.11	30. 9	G11	D10	Griffon
10. 9	17. 8	F10	B10	Monkey	22.11	1.10	H12	E11	Ox
11. 9	18. 8	F10	C11	Gibbon	23.11	2.10	H12	F12	Bat
12. 9	19. 8	F10	D12	Tapir	24.11	3.10	H12	G1	Rat
13. 9	20. 8	F10	E1	Sheep	25.11	4.10	H12	H2	Swallow
14. 9	21. 8	F10	F2	Deer	26.11	5.10	H12	J3	Pig
15. 9	22. 8	F10	G3	Horse	27.11	6.10	H12	K4	Porcupine
16. 9	23. 8	F10	H4	Stag	28.11	7.10	H12	A5	Wolf
17. 9	24. 8	F10	J5	Serpent	29.11	8.10	H12	B6	Dog
18. 9	25. 8	F10	K6	Earthworm	30.11	9.10	H12	C7	Pheasant
19. 9	26. 8	F10	A7	Crocodile	1.12	10.10	H12	D8	Cock
20. 9	27. 8	F10	B8	Dragon	2.12	11.10	H12	E9	Crow
21. 9	28. 8	F10	C9	Badger	3.12	12.10	H12	F10	Monkey
22. 9	29. 8	F10	D10	Hare	4.12	13.10	H12	G11	Gibbon
23. 9	30. 8	F10	E11	Fox	5.12	14.10	H12	H12	Tapir
24. 9	1. 8	F10	F12	Tiger	6.12	15.10	H12	J1	Sheep
25. 9	2. 8	F10	G1	Leopard	7.12	16.10	H12	K2	Deer
26. 9	3. 8	F10	H2	Griffon	8.12	17.10	H12	A3	Horse
27. 9	4. 8	F10	J3	Ox	9.12	18.10	H12	B4	Stag
28. 9	5. 8	F10	K4	Bat	10.12	19.10	H12	C5	Serpent
29. 9	6. 8	F10	A5	Rat	11.12	20.10	H12	D6	Earthworm
30. 9	7. 8	F10	B6	Swallow	12.12	21.10	H12	E7	Crocodile
1.10	8. 8	F10	C7	Pig	13.12	22.10	H12	F8	Dragon
2.10	9. 8	F10	D8	Porcupine	14.12	23.10	H12	G9	Badger
3.10	10. 8	F10	E9	Wolf	15.12	24.10	H12	H10	Hare
4.10	11. 8	F10	F10	Dog	16.12	25.10	H12	J11	Fox
5.10	12. 8	F10	G11	Pheasant	17.12	26.10	H12	K12	Tiger
6.10	13. 8	F10	H12	Cock	18.12	27.10	H12	A1	Leopard
7.10	14. 8	F10	J1	Crow	19.12	28.10	H12	B2	Griffon
8.10	15. 8	F10	K2	Monkey	20.12	29.10	H12	C3	Ox
9.10	16. 8	F10	A3	Gibbon	21.12	1.11	J1	D4	Bat
10.10	17. 8	F10	B4	Tapir	22.12	2.11	J1	E5	Rat
11.10	18. 8	F10	C5	Sheep	23.12	3.11	J1	F6	Swallow
12.10	19. 8	F10	D6	Deer	24.12	4.11	J1	G7	Pig
13.10	20. 8	F10	E7	Horse	25.12	5.11	J1	H8	Porcupine
14.10	21. 8	F10	F8	Stag	26.12	6.11	J1	J9	Wolf
15.10	22. 8	F10	G9	Serpent	27.12	7.11	J1	K10	Dog
16.10	23. 8	F10	H10	Earthworm	28.12	8.11	J1	A11	Pheasant
17.10	24. 8	F10	J11	Crocodile	29.12	9.11	J1	B12	Cock
18.10	25. 8	F10	K12	Dragon	30.12	10.11	J1	C1	Crow
19.10	26. 8	F10	A1	Badger	31.12	11.11	J1	D2	Monkey
20.10	27. 8	F10	B2	Hare					
21.10	28. 8	F10	C3	Fox	**1958**				
22.10	29. 8	F10	D4	Tiger	1. 1	12.11	J1	E3	Gibbon
23.10	1. 9	G11	E5	Leopard	2. 1	13.11	J1	F4	Tapir
24.10	2. 9	G11	F6	Griffon	3. 1	14.11	J1	G5	Sheep
25.10	3. 9	G11	G7	Ox	4. 1	15.11	J1	H6	Deer
26.10	4. 9	G11	H8	Bat	5. 1	16.11	J1	J7	Horse
27.10	5. 9	G11	J9	Rat	6. 1	17.11	J1	K8	Stag
28.10	6. 9	G11	K10	Swallow	7. 1	18.11	J1	A9	Serpent
29.10	7. 9	G11	A11	Pig	8. 1	19.11	J1	B10	Earthworm
30.10	8. 9	G11	B12	Porcupine	9. 1	20.11	J1	C11	Crocodile
31.10	9. 9	G11	C1	Wolf	10. 1	21.11	J1	D12	Dragon
1.11	10. 9	G11	D2	Dog	11. 1	22.11	J1	E1	Badger
2.11	11. 9	G11	E3	Pheasant	12. 1	23.11	J1	F2	Hare
3.11	12. 9	G11	F4	Cock	13. 1	24.11	J1	G3	Fox
4.11	13. 9	G11	G5	Crow	14. 1	25.11	J1	H4	Tiger
5.11	14. 9	G11	H6	Monkey	15. 1	26.11	J1	J5	Leopard
6.11	15. 9	G11	J7	Gibbon	16. 1	27.11	J1	K6	Griffon
7.11	16. 9	G11	K8	Tapir	17. 1	28.11	J1	A7	Ox
8.11	17. 9	G11	A9	Sheep	18. 1	29.11	J1	B8	Bat
9.11	18. 9	G11	B10	Deer	19. 1	30.11	J1	C9	Rat
10.11	19. 9	G11	C11	Horse	20. 1	1.12	K2	D10	Swallow
11.11	20. 9	G11	D12	Stag	21. 1	2.12	K2	E11	Pig
12.11	21. 9	G11	E1	Serpent	22. 1	3.12	K2	F12	Porcupine
13.11	22. 9	G11	F2	Earthworm	23. 1	4.12	K2	G1	Wolf

Solar date	Lunar date	Month HS/EB	Day HS/EB	Constellation	Solar date	Lunar date	Month HS/EB	Day HS/EB	Constellation
24. 1	5.12	K2	H2	Dog	6. 2	18.12	K2	A3	Crocodile
25. 1	6.12	K2	J3	Pheasant	7. 2	19.12	K2	B4	Dragon
26. 1	7.12	K2	K4	Cock	8. 2	20.12	K2	C5	Badger
27. 1	8.12	K2	A5	Crow	9. 2	21.12	K2	D6	Hare
28. 1	9.12	K2	B6	Monkey	10. 2	22.12	K2	E7	Fox
29. 1	10.12	K2	C7	Gibbon	11. 2	23.12	K2	F8	Tiger
30. 1	11.12	K2	D8	Tapir	12. 2	24.12	K2	G9	Leopard
31. 1	12.12	K2	E9	Sheep	13. 2	25.12	K2	H10	Griffon
1. 2	13.12	K2	F10	Deer	14. 2	26.12	K2	J11	Ox
2. 2	14.12	K2	G11	Horse	15. 2	27.12	K2	K12	Bat
3. 2	15.12	K2	H12	Stag	16. 2	28.12	K2	A1	Rat
4. 2	16.12	K2	J1	Serpent	17. 2	29.12	K2	B2	Swallow
5. 2	17.12	K2	K2	Earthworm					

MOU HSÜ YEAR

Solar date	Lunar date	Month HS/EB	Day HS/EB	Constellation	Solar date	Lunar date	Month HS/EB	Day HS/EB	Constellation
18. 2	1. 1	A3	C3	Pig	14. 4	26. 2	B4	H10	Swallow
19. 2	2. 1	A3	D4	Porcupine	15. 4	27. 2	B4	J11	Pig
20. 2	3. 1	A3	E5	Wolf	16. 4	28. 2	B4	K12	Porcupine
21. 2	4. 1	A3	F6	Dog	17. 4	29. 2	B4	A1	Wolf
22. 2	5. 1	A3	G7	Pheasant	18. 4	30. 2	B4	B2	Dog
23. 2	6. 1	A3	H8	Cock	19. 4	1. 3	C5	C3	Pheasant
24. 2	7. 1	A3	J9	Crow	20. 4	2. 3	C5	D4	Cock
25. 2	8. 1	A3	K10	Monkey	21. 4	3. 3	C5	E5	Crow
26. 2	9. 1	A3	A11	Gibbon	22. 4	4. 3	C5	F6	Monkey
27. 2	10. 1	A3	B12	Tapir	23. 4	5. 3	C5	G7	Gibbon
28. 2	11. 1	A3	C1	Sheep	24. 4	6. 3	C5	H8	Tapir
1. 3	12. 1	A3	D2	Deer	25. 4	7. 3	C5	J9	Sheep
2. 3	13. 1	A3	E3	Horse	26. 4	8. 3	C5	K10	Deer
3. 3	14. 1	A3	F4	Stag	27. 4	9. 3	C5	A11	Horse
4. 3	15. 1	A3	G5	Serpent	28. 4	10. 3	C5	B12	Stag
5. 3	16. 1	A3	H6	Earthworm	29. 4	11. 3	C5	C1	Serpent
6. 3	17. 1	A3	J7	Crocodile	30. 4	12. 3	C5	D2	Earthworm
7. 3	18. 1	A3	K8	Dragon	1. 5	13. 3	C5	E3	Crocodile
8. 3	19. 1	A3	A9	Badger	2. 5	14. 3	C5	F4	Dragon
9. 3	20. 1	A3	B10	Hare	3. 5	15. 3	C5	G5	Badger
10. 3	21. 1	A3	C11	Fox	4. 5	16. 3	C5	H6	Hare
11. 3	22. 1	A3	D12	Tiger	5. 5	17. 3	C5	J7	Fox
12. 3	23. 1	A3	E1	Leopard	6. 5	18. 3	C5	K8	Tiger
13. 3	24. 1	A3	F2	Griffon	7. 5	19. 3	C5	A9	Leopard
14. 3	25. 1	A3	G3	Ox	8. 5	20. 3	C5	B10	Griffon
15. 3	26. 1	A3	H4	Bat	9. 5	21. 3	C5	C11	Ox
16. 3	27. 1	A3	J5	Rat	10. 5	22. 3	C5	D12	Bat
17. 3	28. 1	A3	K6	Swallow	11. 5	23. 3	C5	E1	Rat
18. 3	29. 1	A3	A7	Pig	12. 5	24. 3	C5	F2	Swallow
19. 3	30. 1	A3	B8	Porcupine	13. 5	25. 3	C5	G3	Pig
20. 3	1. 2	B4	C9	Wolf	14. 5	26. 3	C5	H4	Porcupine
21. 3	2. 2	B4	D10	Dog	15. 5	27. 3	C5	J5	Wolf
22. 3	3. 2	B4	E11	Pheasant	16. 5	28. 3	C5	K6	Dog
23. 3	4. 2	B4	F12	Cock	17. 5	29. 3	C5	A7	Pheasant
24. 3	5. 2	B4	G1	Crow	18. 5	30. 3	C5	B8	Cock
25. 3	6. 2	B4	H2	Monkey	19. 5	1. 4	D6	C9	Crow
26. 3	7. 2	B4	J3	Gibbon	20. 5	2. 4	D6	D10	Monkey
27. 3	8. 2	B4	K4	Tapir	21. 5	3. 4	D6	E11	Gibbon
28. 3	9. 2	B4	A5	Sheep	22. 5	4. 4	D6	F12	Tapir
29. 3	10. 2	B4	B6	Deer	23. 5	5. 4	D6	G1	Sheep
30. 3	11. 2	B4	C7	Horse	24. 5	6. 4	D6	H2	Deer
31. 3	12. 2	B4	D8	Stag	25. 5	7. 4	D6	J3	Horse
1. 4	13. 2	B4	E9	Serpent	26. 5	8. 4	D6	K4	Stag
2. 4	14. 2	B4	F10	Earthworm	27. 5	9. 4	D6	A5	Serpent
3. 4	15. 2	B4	G11	Crocodile	28. 5	10. 4	D6	B6	Earthworm
4. 4	16. 2	B4	H12	Dragon	29. 5	11. 4	D6	C7	Crocodile
5. 4	17. 2	B4	J1	Badger	30. 5	12. 4	D6	D8	Dragon
6. 4	18. 2	B4	K2	Hare	31. 5	13. 4	D6	E9	Badger
7. 4	19. 2	B4	A3	Fox	1. 6	14. 4	D6	F10	Hare
8. 4	20. 2	B4	B4	Tiger	2. 6	15. 4	D6	G11	Fox
9. 4	21. 2	B4	C5	Leopard	3. 6	16. 4	D6	H12	Tiger
10. 4	22. 2	B4	D6	Griffon	4. 6	17. 4	D6	J1	Leopard
11. 4	23. 2	B4	E7	Ox	5. 6	18. 4	D6	K2	Griffon
12. 4	24. 2	B4	F8	Bat	6. 6	19. 4	D6	A3	Ox
13. 4	25. 2	B4	G9	Rat	7. 6	20. 4	D6	B4	Bat

Solar date	Lunar date	Month HS/EB	Day HS/EB	Constellation
8. 6	21. 4	D6	C5	Rat
9. 6	22. 4	D6	D6	Swallow
10. 6	23. 4	D6	E7	Pig
11. 6	24. 4	D6	F8	Porcupine
12. 6	25. 4	D6	G9	Wolf
13. 6	26. 4	D6	H10	Dog
14. 6	27. 4	D6	J11	Pheasant
15. 6	28. 4	D6	K12	Cock
16. 6	29. 4	D6	A1	Crow
17. 6	1. 5	E7	B2	Monkey
18. 6	2. 5	E7	C3	Gibbon
19. 6	3. 5	E7	D4	Tapir
20. 6	4. 5	E7	E5	Sheep
21. 6	5. 5	E7	F6	Deer
22. 6	6. 5	E7	G7	Horse
23. 6	7. 5	E7	H8	Stag
24. 6	8. 5	E7	J9	Serpent
25. 6	9. 5	E7	K10	Earthworm
26. 6	10. 5	E7	A11	Crocodile
27. 6	11. 5	E7	B12	Dragon
28. 6	12. 5	E7	C1	Badger
29. 6	13. 5	E7	D2	Hare
30. 6	14. 5	E7	E3	Fox
1. 7	15. 5	E7	F4	Tiger
2. 7	16. 5	E7	G5	Leopard
3. 7	17. 5	E7	H6	Griffon
4. 7	18. 5	E7	J7	Ox
5. 7	19. 5	E7	K8	Bat
6. 7	20. 5	E7	A9	Rat
7. 7	21. 5	E7	B10	Swallow
8. 7	22. 5	E7	C11	Pig
9. 7	23. 5	E7	D12	Porcupine
10. 7	24. 5	E7	E1	Wolf
11. 7	25. 5	E7	F2	Dog
12. 7	26. 5	E7	G3	Pheasant
13. 7	27. 5	E7	H4	Cock
14. 7	28. 5	E7	J5	Crow
15. 7	29. 5	E7	K6	Monkey
16. 7	30. 5	E7	A7	Gibbon
17. 7	1. 6	F8	B8	Tapir
18. 7	2. 6	F8	C9	Sheep
19. 7	3. 6	F8	D10	Deer
20. 7	4. 6	F8	E11	Horse
21. 7	5. 6	F8	F12	Stag
22. 7	6. 6	F8	G1	Serpent
23. 7	7. 6	F8	H2	Earthworm
24. 7	8. 6	F8	J3	Crocodile
25. 7	9. 6	F8	K4	Dragon
26. 7	10. 6	F8	A5	Badger
27. 7	11. 6	F8	B6	Hare
28. 7	12. 6	F8	C7	Fox
29. 7	13. 6	F8	D8	Tiger
30. 7	14. 6	F8	E9	Leopard
31. 7	15. 6	F8	F10	Griffon
1. 8	16. 6	F8	G11	Ox
2. 8	17. 6	F8	H12	Bat
3. 8	18. 6	F8	J1	Rat
4. 8	19. 6	F8	K2	Swallow
5. 8	20. 6	F8	A3	Pig
6. 8	21. 6	F8	B4	Porcupine
7. 8	22. 6	F8	C5	Wolf
8. 8	23. 6	F8	D6	Dog
9. 8	24. 6	F8	E7	Pheasant
10. 8	25. 6	F8	F8	Cock
11. 8	26. 6	F8	G9	Crow
12. 8	27. 6	F8	H10	Monkey
13. 8	28. 6	F8	J11	Gibbon
14. 8	29. 6	F8	K12	Tapir
15. 8	1. 7	G9	A1	Sheep
16. 8	2. 7	G9	B2	Deer
17. 8	3. 7	G9	C3	Horse
18. 8	4. 7	G9	D4	Stag
19. 8	5. 7	G9	E5	Serpent
20. 8	6. 7	G9	F6	Earthworm
21. 8	7. 7	G9	G7	Crocodile
22. 8	8. 7	G9	H8	Dragon
23. 8	9. 7	G9	J9	Badger
24. 8	10. 7	G9	K10	Hare
25. 8	11. 7	G9	A11	Fox
26. 8	12. 7	G9	B12	Tiger
27. 8	13. 7	G9	C1	Leopard
28. 8	14. 7	G9	D2	Griffon
29. 8	15. 7	G9	E3	Ox
30. 8	16. 7	G9	F4	Bat
31. 8	17. 7	G9	G5	Rat
1. 9	18. 7	G9	H6	Swallow
2. 9	19. 7	G9	J7	Pig
3. 9	20. 7	G9	K8	Porcupine
4. 9	21. 7	G9	A9	Wolf
5. 9	22. 7	G9	B10	Dog
6. 9	23. 7	G9	C11	Pheasant
7. 9	24. 7	G9	D12	Cock
8. 9	25. 7	G9	E1	Crow
9. 9	26. 7	G9	F2	Monkey
10. 9	27. 7	G9	G3	Gibbon
11. 9	28. 7	G9	H4	Tapir
12. 9	29. 7	G9	J5	Sheep
13. 9	1. 8	H10	K6	Deer
14. 9	2. 8	H10	A7	Horse
15. 9	3. 8	H10	B8	Stag
16. 9	4. 8	H10	C9	Serpent
17. 9	5. 8	H10	D10	Earthworm
18. 9	6. 8	H10	E11	Crocodile
19. 9	7. 8	H10	F12	Dragon
20. 9	8. 8	H10	G1	Badger
21. 9	9. 8	H10	H2	Hare
22. 9	10. 8	H10	J3	Fox
23. 9	11. 8	H10	K4	Tiger
24. 9	12. 8	H10	A5	Leopard
25. 9	13. 8	H10	B6	Griffon
26. 9	14. 8	H10	C7	Ox
27. 9	15. 8	H10	D8	Bat
28. 9	16. 8	H10	E9	Rat
29. 9	17. 8	H10	F10	Swallow
30. 9	18. 8	H10	G11	Pig
1.10	19. 8	H10	H12	Porcupine
2.10	20. 8	H10	J1	Wolf
3.10	21. 8	H10	K2	Dog
4.10	22. 8	H10	A3	Pheasant
5.10	23. 8	H10	B4	Cock
6.10	24. 8	H10	C5	Crow
7.10	25. 8	H10	D6	Monkey
8.10	26. 8	H10	E7	Gibbon
9.10	27. 8	H10	F8	Tapir
10.10	28. 8	H10	G9	Sheep
11.10	29. 8	H10	H10	Deer
12.10	30. 8	H10	J11	Horse
13.10	1. 9	J11	K12	Stag
14.10	2. 9	J11	A1	Serpent
15.10	3. 9	J11	B2	Earthworm
16.10	4. 9	J11	C3	Crocodile
17.10	5. 9	J11	D4	Dragon
18.10	6. 9	J11	E5	Badger
19.10	7. 9	J11	F6	Hare
20.10	8. 9	J11	G7	Fox
21.10	9. 9	J11	H8	Tiger
22.10	10. 9	J11	J9	Leopard
23.10	11. 9	J11	K10	Griffon
24.10	12. 9	J11	A11	Ox
25.10	13. 9	J11	B12	Bat
26.10	14. 9	J11	C1	Rat
27.10	15. 9	J11	D2	Swallow
28.10	16. 9	J11	E3	Pig
29.10	17. 9	J11	F4	Porcupine
30.10	18. 9	J11	G5	Wolf
31.10	19. 9	J11	H6	Dog

Solar date	Lunar date	Month HS/EB	Day HS/EB	Constellation	Solar date	Lunar date	Month HS/EB	Day HS/EB	Constellation
1.11	20. 9	J11	J7	Pheasant	22.12	12.11	A1	K10	Swallow
2.11	21. 9	J11	K8	Cock	23.12	13.11	A1	A11	Pig
3.11	22. 9	J11	A9	Crow	24.12	14.11	A1	B12	Porcupine
4.11	23. 9	J11	B10	Monkey	25.12	15.11	A1	C1	Wolf
5.11	24. 9	J11	C11	Gibbon	26.12	16.11	A1	D2	Dog
6.11	25. 9	J11	D12	Tapir	27.12	17.11	A1	E3	Pheasant
7.11	26. 9	J11	E1	Sheep	28.12	18.11	A1	F4	Cock
8.11	27. 9	J11	F2	Deer	29.12	19.11	A1	G5	Crow
9.11	28. 9	J11	G3	Horse	30.12	20.11	A1	H6	Monkey
10.11	29. 9	J11	H4	Stag	31.12	21.11	A1	J7	Gibbon
11.11	1.10	K12	J5	Serpent					
12.11	2.10	K12	K6	Earthworm	**1959**				
13.11	3.10	K12	A7	Crocodile					
14.11	4.10	K12	B8	Dragon	1. 1	22.11	A1	K8	Tapir
15.11	5.10	K12	C9	Badger	2. 1	23.11	A1	A9	Sheep
16.11	6.10	K12	D10	Hare	3. 1	24.11	A1	B10	Deer
17.11	7.10	K12	E11	Fox	4. 1	25.11	A1	C11	Horse
18.11	8.10	K12	F12	Tiger	5. 1	26.11	A1	D12	Stag
19.11	9.10	K12	G1	Leopard	6. 1	27.11	A1	E1	Serpent
20.11	10.10	K12	H2	Griffon	7. 1	28.11	A1	F2	Earthworm
21.11	11.10	K12	J3	Ox	8. 1	29.11	A1	G3	Crocodile
22.11	12.10	K12	K4	Bat	9. 1	1.12	B2	H4	Dragon
23.11	13.10	K12	A5	Rat	10. 1	2.12	B2	J5	Badger
24.11	14.10	K12	B6	Swallow	11. 1	3.12	B2	K6	Hare
25.11	15.10	K12	C7	Pig	12. 1	4.12	B2	A7	Fox
26.11	16.10	K12	D8	Porcupine	13. 1	5.12	B2	B8	Tiger
27.11	17.10	K12	E9	Wolf	14. 1	6.12	B2	C9	Leopard
28.11	18.10	K12	F10	Dog	15. 1	7.12	B2	D10	Griffon
29.11	19.10	K12	G11	Pheasant	16. 1	8.12	B2	E11	Ox
30.11	20.10	K12	H12	Cock	17. 1	9.12	B2	F12	Bat
1.12	21.10	K12	J1	Crow	18. 1	10.12	B2	G1	Rat
2.12	22.10	K12	K2	Monkey	19. 1	11.12	B2	H2	Swallow
3.12	23.10	K12	A3	Gibbon	20. 1	12.12	B2	J3	Pig
4.12	24.10	K12	B4	Tapir	21. 1	13.12	B2	K4	Porcupine
5.12	25.10	K12	C5	Sheep	22. 1	14.12	B2	A5	Wolf
6.12	26.10	K12	D6	Deer	23. 1	15.12	B2	B6	Dog
7.12	27.10	K12	E7	Horse	24. 1	16.12	B2	C7	Pheasant
8.12	28.10	K12	F8	Stag	25. 1	17.12	B2	D8	Cock
9.12	29.10	K12	G9	Serpent	26. 1	18.12	B2	E9	Crow
10.12	30.10	K12	H10	Earthworm	27. 1	19.12	B2	F10	Monkey
11.12	1.11	A1	J11	Crocodile	28. 1	20.12	B2	G11	Gibbon
12.12	2.11	A1	K12	Dragon	29. 1	21.12	B2	H12	Tapir
13.12	3.11	A1	A1	Badger	30. 1	22.12	B2	J1	Sheep
14.12	4.11	A1	B2	Hare	31. 1	23.12	B2	K2	Deer
15.12	5.11	A1	C3	Fox	1. 2	24.12	B2	A3	Horse
16.12	6.11	A1	D4	Tiger	2. 2	25.12	B2	B4	Stag
17.12	7.11	A1	E5	Leopard	3. 2	26.12	B2	C5	Serpent
18.12	8.11	A1	F6	Griffon	4. 2	27.12	B2	D6	Earthworm
19.12	9.11	A1	G7	Ox	5. 2	28.12	B2	E7	Crocodile
20.12	10.11	A1	H8	Bat	6. 2	29.12	B2	F8	Dragon
21.12	11.11	A1	J9	Rat	7. 2	30.12	B2	G9	Badger

CHI HAI YEAR

Solar date	Lunar date	Month HS/EB	Day HS/EB	Constellation	Solar date	Lunar date	Month HS/EB	Day HS/EB	Constellation
8. 2	1. 1	C3	H10	Hare	25. 2	18. 1	C3	E3	Gibbon
9. 2	2. 1	C3	J11	Fox	26. 2	19. 1	C3	F4	Tapir
10. 2	3. 1	C3	K12	Tiger	27. 2	20. 1	C3	G5	Sheep
11. 2	4. 1	C3	A1	Leopard	28. 2	21. 1	C3	H6	Deer
12. 2	5. 1	C3	B2	Griffon	1. 3	22. 1	C3	J7	Horse
13. 2	6. 1	C3	C3	Ox	2. 3	23. 1	C3	K8	Stag
14. 2	7. 1	C3	D4	Bat	3. 3	24. 1	C3	A9	Serpent
15. 2	8. 1	C3	E5	Rat	4. 3	25. 1	C3	B10	Earthworm
16. 2	9. 1	C3	F6	Swallow	5. 3	26. 1	C3	C11	Crocodile
17. 2	10. 1	C3	G7	Pig	6. 3	27. 1	C3	D12	Dragon
18. 2	11. 1	C3	H8	Porcupine	7. 3	28. 1	C3	E1	Badger
19. 2	12. 1	C3	J9	Wolf	8. 3	29. 1	C3	F2	Hare
20. 2	13. 1	C3	K10	Dog	9. 3	1. 2	D4	G3	Fox
21. 2	14. 1	C3	A11	Pheasant	10. 3	2. 2	D4	H4	Tiger
22. 2	15. 1	C3	B12	Cock	11. 3	3. 2	D4	J5	Leopard
23. 2	16. 1	C3	C1	Crow	12. 3	4. 2	D4	K6	Griffon
24. 2	17. 1	C3	D2	Monkey	13. 3	5. 2	D4	A7	Ox

Solar date	Lunar date	Month HS/EB	Day HS/EB	Constellation	Solar date	Lunar date	Month HS/EB	Day HS/EB	Constellation
14. 3	6. 2	D4	B8	Bat	26. 5	19. 4	F6	E9	Serpent
15. 3	7. 2	D4	C9	Rat	27. 5	20. 4	F6	F10	Earthworm
16. 3	8. 2	D4	D10	Swallow	28. 5	21. 4	F6	G11	Crocodile
17. 3	9. 2	D4	E11	Pig	29. 5	22. 4	F6	H12	Dragon
18. 3	10. 2	D4	F12	Porcupine	30. 5	23. 4	F6	J1	Badger
19. 3	11. 2	D4	G1	Wolf	31. 5	24. 4	F6	K2	Hare
20. 3	12. 2	D4	H4	Dog	1. 6	25. 4	F6	A3	Fox
21. 3	13. 2	D4	J3	Pheasant	2. 6	26. 4	F6	B4	Tiger
22. 3	14. 2	D4	K4	Cock	3. 6	27. 4	F6	C5	Leopard
23. 3	15. 2	D4	A5	Crow	4. 6	28. 4	F6	D6	Griffon
24. 3	16. 2	D4	B6	Monkey	5. 6	29. 4	F6	E7	Ox
25. 3	17. 2	D4	C7	Gibbon	6. 6	1. 5	G7	F8	Bat
26. 3	18. 2	D4	D8	Tapir	7. 6	2. 5	G7	G9	Rat
27. 3	19. 2	D4	E9	Sheep	8. 6	3. 5	G7	H10	Swallow
28. 3	20. 2	D4	F10	Deer	9. 6	4. 5	G7	J11	Pig
29. 3	21.1	D4	G11	Horse	10. 6	5. 5	G7	K12	Porcupine
30. 3	22. 2	D4	H12	Stag	11. 6	6. 5	G7	A1	Wolf
31. 3	23. 2	D4	J1	Serpent	12. 6	7. 5	G7	B2	Dog
1. 4	24. 2	D4	K2	Earthworm	13. 6	8. 5	G7	C3	Pheasant
2. 4	25. 2	D4	A3	Crocodile	14. 6	9. 5	G7	D4	Cock
3. 4	26. 2	D4	B4	Dragon	15. 6	10. 5	G7	E5	Crow
4. 4	27. 2	D4	C5	Badger	16. 6	11. 5	G7	F6	Monkey
5. 4	28. 2	D4	D6	Hare	17. 6	12. 5	G7	G7	Gibbon
6. 4	29. 2	D4	E7	Fox	18. 6	13. 5	G7	H8	Tapir
7. 4	30. 2	D4	F8	Tiger	19. 6	14. 5	G7	J9	Sheep
8. 4	1. 3	E5	G9	Leopard	20. 6	15. 5	G7	K10	Deer
9. 4	2. 3	E5	H10	Griffon	21. 6	16. 5	G7	A11	Horse
10. 4	3. 3	E5	J11	Ox	22. 6	17. 5	G7	B12	Stag
11. 4	4. 3	E5	K12	Bat	23. 6	18. 5	G7	C1	Serpent
12. 4	5. 3	E5	A1	Rat	24. 6	19. 5	G7	D2	Earthworm
13. 4	6. 3	E5	B2	Swallow	25. 6	20. 5	G7	E3	Crocodile
14. 4	7. 3	E5	C3	Pig	26. 6	21. 5	G7	F4	Dragon
15. 4	8. 3	E5	D4	Porcupine	27. 6	22. 5	G7	G5	Badger
16. 4	9. 3	E5	E5	Wolf	28. 6	23. 5	G7	H6	Hare
17. 4	10. 3	E5	F6	Dog	29. 6	24. 5	G7	J7	Fox
18. 4	11. 3	E5	G7	Pheasant	30. 6	25. 5	G7	K8	Tiger
19. 4	12. 3	E5	H8	Cock	1. 7	26. 5	G7	A9	Leopard
20. 4	13. 3	E5	J9	Crow	2. 7	27. 5	G7	B10	Griffon
21. 4	14. 3	E5	K10	Monkey	3. 7	28. 5	G7	C11	Ox
22. 4	15. 3	E5	A11	Gibbon	4. 7	29. 5	G7	D12	Bat
23. 4	16. 3	E5	B12	Tapir	5. 7	30. 5	G7	E1	Rat
24. 4	17. 3	E5	C1	Sheep	6. 7	1. 6	H8	F2	Swallow
25. 4	18. 3	E5	D2	Deer	7. 7	2. 6	H8	G3	Pig
26. 4	19. 3	E5	E3	Horse	8. 7	3. 6	H8	H4	Porcupine
27. 4	20. 3	E5	F4	Stag	9. 7	4. 6	H8	J5	Wolf
28. 4	21. 3	E5	G5	Serpent	10. 7	5. 6	H8	K6	Dog
29. 4	22. 3	E5	H6	Earthworm	11. 7	6. 6	H8	A7	Pheasant
30. 4	23. 3	E5	J7	Crocodile	12. 7	7. 6	H8	B8	Cock
1. 5	24. 3	E5	K8	Dragon	13. 7	8. 6	H8	C9	Crow
2. 5	25. 3	E5	A9	Badger	14. 7	9. 6	H8	D10	Monkey
3. 5	26. 3	E5	B10	Hare	15. 7	10. 6	H8	E11	Gibbon
4. 5	27. 3	E5	C11	Fox	16. 7	11. 6	H8	F12	Tapir
5. 5	28. 3	E5	D12	Tiger	17. 7	12. 6	H8	G1	Sheep
6. 5	29. 3	E5	E1	Leopard	18. 7	13. 6	H8	H2	Deer
7. 5	30. 3	E5	F2	Griffon	19. 7	14. 6	H8	J3	Horse
8. 5	1. 4	F6	G3	Ox	20. 7	15. 6	H8	K4	Stag
9. 5	2. 4	F6	H4	Bat	21. 7	16. 6	H8	A5	Serpent
10. 5	3. 4	F6	J5	Rat	22. 7	17. 6	H8	B6	Earthworm
11. 5	4. 4	F6	K6	Swallow	23. 7	18. 6	H8	C7	Crocodile
12. 5	5. 4	F6	A7	Pig	24. 7	19. 6	H8	D8	Dragon
13. 5	6. 4	F6	B8	Porcupine	25. 7	20. 6	H8	E9	Badger
14. 5	7. 4	F6	C9	Wolf	26. 7	21. 6	H8	F10	Hare
15. 5	8. 4	F6	D10	Dog	27. 7	22. 6	H8	G11	Fox
16. 5	9. 4	F6	E11	Pheasant	28. 7	23. 6	H8	H12	Tiger
17. 5	10. 4	F6	F12	Cock	29. 7	24. 6	H8	J1	Leopard
18. 5	11. 4	F6	G1	Crow	30. 7	25. 6	H8	K2	Griffon
19. 5	12. 4	F6	H2	Monkey	31. 7	26. 6	H8	A3	Ox
20. 5	13. 4	F6	J3	Gibbon	1. 8	27. 6	H8	B4	Bat
21. 5	14. 4	F6	K4	Tapir	2. 8	28. 6	H8	C5	Rat
22. 5	15. 4	F6	A5	Sheep	3. 8	29. 6	H8	D6	Swallow
23. 5	16. 4	F6	B6	Deer	4. 8	1. 7	J9	E7	Pig
24. 5	17. 4	F6	C7	Horse	5. 8	2. 7	J9	F8	Porcupine
25. 5	18. 4	F6	D8	Stag	6. 8	3. 7	J9	G9	Wolf

Solar date	Lunar date	Month HS/EB	Day HS/EB	Constellation	Solar date	Lunar date	Month HS/EB	Day HS/EB	Constellation
7. 8	4. 7	J9	H10	Dog	19.10	18. 9	A11	A11	Fox
8. 8	5. 7	J9	J11	Pheasant	20.10	19. 9	A11	B12	Tiger
9. 8	6. 7	J9	K12	Cock	21.10	20. 9	A11	C1	Leopard
10. 8	7. 7	J9	A1	Crow	22.10	21. 9	A11	D2	Griffon
11. 8	8. 7	J9	B2	Monkey	23.10	22. 9	A11	E3	Ox
12. 8	9. 7	J9	C3	Gibbon	24.10	23. 9	A11	F4	Bat
13. 8	10. 7	J9	D4	Tapir	25.10	24. 9	A11	G5	Rat
14. 8	11. 7	J9	E5	Sheep	26.10	25. 9	A11	H6	Swallow
15. 8	12. 7	J9	F6	Deer	27.10	26. 9	A11	J7	Pig
16. 8	13. 7	J9	G7	Horse	28.10	27. 9	A11	K8	Porcupine
17. 8	14. 7	J9	H8	Stag	29.10	28. 9	A11	A9	Wolf
18. 8	15. 7	J9	J9	Serpent	30.10	29. 9	A11	B10	Dog
19. 8	16. 7	J9	K10	Earthworm	31.10	30. 9	A11	C11	Pheasant
20. 8	17. 7	J9	A11	Crocodile	1.11	1.10	B12	D12	Cock
21. 8	18. 7	J9	B12	Dragon	2.11	2.10	B12	E1	Crow
22. 8	19. 7	J9	C1	Badger	3.11	3.10	B12	F2	Monkey
23. 8	20. 7	J9	D2	Hare	4.11	4.10	B12	G3	Gibbon
24. 8	21. 7	J9	E3	Fox	5.11	5.10	B12	H4	Tapir
25. 8	22. 7	J9	F4	Tiger	6.11	6.10	B12	J5	Sheep
26. 8	23. 7	J9	G4	Leopard	7.11	7.10	B12	K6	Deer
27. 8	24. 7	J9	H6	Griffon	8.11	8.10	B12	A7	Horse
28. 8	25. 7	J9	J7	Ox	9.11	9.10	B12	B8	Stag
29. 8	26. 7	J9	K8	Bat	10.11	10.10	B12	C9	Serpent
30. 8	27. 7	J9	A9	Rat	11.11	11.10	B12	D10	Earthworm
31. 8	28. 7	J9	B10	Swallow	12.11	12.10	B12	E11	Crocodile
1. 9	29. 7	J9	C11	Pig	13.11	13.10	B12	F12	Dragon
2. 9	30. 7	J9	D12	Porcupine	14.11	14.10	B12	G1	Badger
3. 9	1. 8	K10	E1	Wolf	15.11	15.10	B12	H2	Hare
4. 9	2. 8	K10	F2	Dog	16.11	16.10	B12	J3	Fox
5. 9	3. 8	K10	G3	Pheasant	17.11	17.10	B12	K4	Tiger
6. 9	4. 8	K10	H4	Cock	18.11	18.10	B12	A5	Leopard
7. 9	5. 8	K10	J5	Crow	19.11	19.10	B12	B6	Griffon
8. 9	6. 8	K10	K6	Monkey	20.11	20.10	B12	C7	Ox
9. 9	7. 8	K10	A7	Gibbon	21.11	21.10	B12	D8	Bat
10. 9	8. 8	K10	B8	Tapir	22.11	22.10	B12	E9	Rat
11. 9	9. 8	K10	C9	Sheep	23.11	23.10	B12	F10	Swallow
12. 9	10. 8	K10	D10	Deer	24.11	24.10	B12	G11	Pig
13. 9	11. 8	K10	E11	Horse	25.11	25.10	B12	H12	Porcupine
14. 9	12. 8	K10	F12	Stag	26.11	26.10	B12	J1	Wolf
15. 9	13. 8	K10	G1	Serpent	27.11	27.10	B12	K2	Dog
16. 9	14. 8	K10	H2	Earthworm	28.11	28.10	B12	A3	Pheasant
17. 9	15. 8	K10	J3	Crocodile	29.11	29.10	B12	B4	Cock
18. 9	16. 8	K10	K4	Dragon	30.11	1.11	C1	C5	Crow
19. 9	17. 8	K10	A5	Badger	1.12	2.11	C1	D6	Monkey
20. 9	18. 8	K10	B6	Hare	2.12	3.11	C1	E7	Gibbon
21. 9	19. 8	K10	C7	Fox	3.12	4.11	C1	F8	Tapir
22. 9	20. 8	K10	D8	Tiger	4.12	5.11	C1	G9	Sheep
23. 9	21. 8	K10	E9	Leopard	5.12	6.11	C1	H10	Deer
24. 9	22. 8	K10	F10	Griffon	6.12	7.11	C1	J11	Horse
25. 9	23. 8	K10	G11	Ox	7.12	8.11	C1	K12	Stag
26. 9	24. 8	K10	H12	Bat	8.12	9.11	C1	A1	Serpent
27. 9	25. 8	K10	J1	Rat	9.12	10.11	C1	B2	Earthworm
28. 9	26. 8	K10	K2	Swallow	10.12	11.11	C1	C3	Crocodile
29. 9	27. 8	K10	A3	Pig	11.12	12.11	C1	D4	Dragon
30. 9	28. 8	K10	B4	Porcupine	12.12	13.11	C1	E5	Badger
1.10	29. 8	K10	C5	Wolf	13.12	14.11	C1	F6	Hare
2.10	1. 9	A11	D6	Dog	14.12	15.11	C1	G7	Fox
3.10	2. 9	A11	E7	Pheasant	15.12	16.11	C1	H8	Tiger
4.10	3. 9	A11	F8	Cock	16.12	17.11	C1	J9	Leopard
5.10	4. 9	A11	G9	Crow	17.12	18.11	C1	K10	Griffon
6.10	5. 9	A11	H10	Monkey	18.12	19.11	C1	A11	Ox
7.10	6. 9	A11	J11	Gibbon	19.12	20.11	C1	B12	Bat
8.10	7. 9	A11	K12	Tapir	20.12	21.11	C1	C1	Rat
9.10	8. 9	A11	A1	Sheep	21.12	22.11	C1	D2	Swallow
10.10	9. 9	A11	B2	Deer	22.12	23.11	C1	E3	Pig
11.10	10. 9	A11	C3	Horse	23.12	24.11	C1	F4	Porcupine
12.10	11. 9	A11	D4	Stag	24.12	25.11	C1	G5	Wolf
13.10	12. 9	A11	E5	Serpent	25.12	26.11	C1	H6	Dog
14.10	13. 9	A11	F6	Earthworm	26.12	27.11	C1	J7	Pheasant
15.10	14. 9	A11	G7	Crocodile	27.12	28.11	C1	K8	Cock
16.10	15. 9	A11	H8	Dragon	28.12	29.11	C1	A9	Crow
17.10	16. 9	A11	J9	Badger	29.12	30.11	C1	B10	Monkey
18.10	17. 9	A11	K10	Hare	30.12	1.12	D2	C11	Gibbon

Solar date	Lunar date	Month HS/EB	Day HS/EB	Constellation	Solar date	Lunar date	Month HS/EB	Day HS/EB	Constellation
31.12	2.12	D2	D12	Tapir	13. 1	15.12	D2	G1	Leopard
1960					14. 1	16.12	D2	H2	Griffon
					15. 1	17.12	D2	J3	Ox
1. 1	3.12	D2	E1	Sheep	16. 1	18.12	D2	K4	Bat
2. 1	4.12	D2	F2	Deer	17. 1	19.12	D2	A5	Rat
3. 1	5.12	D2	G3	Horse	18. 1	20.12	D2	B6	Swallow
4. 1	6.12	D2	H4	Stag	19. 1	21.12	D2	C7	Pig
5. 1	7.12	D2	J5	Serpent	20. 1	22.12	D2	D8	Porcupine
6. 1	8.12	D2	K6	Earthworm	21. 1	23.12	D2	E9	Wolf
7. 1	9.12	D2	A7	Crocodile	22. 1	24.12	D2	F10	Dog
8. 1	10.12	D2	B8	Dragon	23. 1	25.12	D2	G11	Pheasant
9. 1	11.12	D2	C9	Badger	24. 1	26.12	D2	H12	Cock
10. 1	12.12	D2	D10	Hare	25. 1	27.12	D2	J1	Crow
11. 1	13.12	D2	E11	Fox	26. 1	28.12	D2	K2	Monkey
12. 1	14.12	D2	F12	Tiger	27. 1	29.12	D2	A3	Gibbon

KENG TZU YEAR

Solar date	Lunar date	Month HS/EB	Day HS/EB	Constellation	Solar date	Lunar date	Month HS/EB	Day HS/EB	Constellation
28. 1	1. 1	E3	B4	Tapir	21. 3	24. 2	F4	E9	Crow
29. 1	2. 1	E3	C5	Sheep	22. 3	25. 2	F4	F10	Monkey
30. 1	3. 1	E3	D6	Deer	23. 3	26. 2	F4	G11	Gibbon
31. 1	4. 1	E3	E7	Horse	24. 3	27. 2	F4	H12	Tapir
1. 2	5. 1	E3	F8	Stag	25. 3	28. 2	F4	J1	Sheep
2. 2	6. 1	E3	G9	Serpent	26. 3	29. 2	F4	K2	Deer
3. 2	7. 1	E3	H10	Earthworm	27. 3	1. 3	G5	A3	Horse
4. 2	8. 1	E3	J11	Crocodile	28. 3	2. 3	G5	B4	Stag
5. 2	9. 1	E3	K12	Dragon	29. 3	3. 3	G5	C5	Serpent
6. 2	10. 1	E3	A1	Badger	30. 3	4. 3	G5	D6	Earthworm
7. 2	11. 1	E3	B2	Hare	31. 3	5. 3	G5	E7	Crocodile
8. 2	12. 1	E3	C3	Fox	1. 4	6. 3	G5	F8	Dragon
9. 2	13. 1	E3	D4	Tiger	2. 4	7. 3	G5	G9	Badger
10. 2	14. 1	E3	E5	Leopard	3. 4	8. 3	G5	H10	Hare
11. 2	15. 1	E3	F6	Griffon	4. 4	9. 3	G5	J11	Fox
12. 2	16. 1	E3	G7	Ox	5. 4	10. 3	G5	K12	Tiger
13. 1	17. 1	E3	H8	Bat	6. 4	11. 3	G5	A1	Leopard
14. 1	18. 1	E3	J9	Rat	7. 4	12. 3	G5	B2	Griffon
15. 2	19. 1	E3	K10	Swallow	8. 4	13. 3	G5	C3	Ox
16. 2	20. 1	E3	A11	Pig	9. 4	14. 3	G5	D4	Bat
17. 2	21. 1	E3	B12	Porcupine	10. 4	15. 3	G5	E5	Rat
18. 2	22. 1	E3	C1	Wolf	11. 4	16. 3	G5	F6	Swallow
19. 2	23. 1	E3	D2	Dog	12. 4	17. 3	G5	G7	Pig
20. 2	24. 1	E3	E3	Pheasant	13. 4	18. 3	G5	H8	Porcupine
21. 2	25. 1	E3	F4	Cock	14. 4	19. 3	G5	J9	Wolf
22. 2	26. 1	E3	G5	Crow	15. 4	20. 3	G5	K10	Dog
23. 2	27. 1	E3	H6	Monkey	16. 4	21. 3	G5	A11	Pheasant
24. 2	28. 1	E3	J7	Gibbon	17. 4	22. 3	G5	B12	Cock
25. 2	29. 1	E3	K8	Tapir	18. 4	23. 3	G5	C1	Crow
26. 2	30. 1	E3	A9	Sheep	19. 4	24. 3	G5	D2	Monkey
27. 2	1. 2	F4	B10	Deer	20. 4	25. 3	G5	E3	Gibbon
28. 2	2. 2	F4	C11	Horse	21. 4	26. 3	G5	F4	Tapir
29. 2	3. 2	F4	D12	Stag	22. 4	27. 3	G5	G5	Sheep
1. 3	4. 2	F4	E1	Serpent	23. 4	28. 3	G5	H6	Deer
2. 3	5. 2	F4	F2	Earthworm	24. 4	29. 3	G5	J7	Horse
3. 3	6. 2	F4	G3	Crocodile	25. 4	30. 3	G5	K8	Stag
4. 3	7. 2	F4	H4	Dragon	26. 4	1. 4	H6	A9	Serpent
5. 3	8. 2	F4	J5	Badger	27. 4	2. 4	H6	B10	Earthworm
6. 3	9. 2	F4	K6	Hare	28. 4	3. 4	H6	C11	Crocodile
7. 3	10. 2	F4	A7	Fox	29. 4	4. 4	H6	D12	Dragon
8. 3	11. 2	F4	B8	Tiger	30. 4	5. 4	H6	E1	Badger
9. 3	12. 2	F4	C9	Leopard	1. 5	6. 4	H6	F2	Hare
10. 3	13. 2	F4	D10	Griffon	2. 5	7. 4	H6	G3	Fox
11. 3	14. 2	F4	E11	Ox	3. 5	8. 4	H6	H4	Tiger
12. 3	15. 2	F4	F12	Bat	4. 5	9. 4	H6	J5	Leopard
13. 3	16. 2	F4	G1	Rat	5. 5	10. 4	H6	K6	Griffon
14. 3	17. 2	F4	H2	Swallow	6. 5	11. 4	H6	A7	Ox
15. 3	18. 2	F4	J3	Pig	7. 5	12. 4	H6	B8	Bat
16. 3	19. 2	F4	K4	Porcupine	8. 5	13. 4	H6	C9	Rat
17. 3	20. 2	F4	A5	Wolf	9. 5	14. 4	H6	D10	Swallow
18. 3	21. 2	F4	B6	Dog	10. 5	15. 4	H6	E11	Pig
19. 3	22. 2	F4	C7	Pheasant	11. 5	16. 4	H6	F12	Porcupine
20. 3	23. 2	F4	D8	Cock	12. 5	17. 4	H6	G1	Wolf

Solar date	Lunar date	Month HS/EB	Day HS/EB	Constellation
13. 5	18. 4	H6	H2	Dog
14. 5	19. 4	H6	J3	Pheasant
15. 5	20. 4	H6	K4	Cock
16. 5	21. 4	H6	A5	Crow
17. 5	22. 4	H6	B6	Monkey
18. 5	23. 4	H6	C7	Gibbon
19. 5	24. 4	H6	D8	Tapir
20. 5	25. 4	H6	E9	Sheep
21. 5	26. 4	H6	F10	Deer
22. 5	27. 4	H6	G11	Horse
23. 5	28. 4	H6	H12	Stag
24. 5	29. 4	H6	J1	Serpent
25. 5	1. 5	J7	K2	Earthworm
26. 5	2. 5	J7	A3	Crocodile
27. 5	3. 5	J7	B4	Dragon
28. 5	4. 5	J7	C5	Badger
29. 5	5. 5	J7	D6	Hare
30. 5	6. 5	J7	E7	Fox
31. 5	7. 5	J7	F8	Tiger
1. 6	8. 5	J7	G9	Leopard
2. 6	9. 5	J7	H10	Griffon
3. 6	10. 5	J7	J11	Ox
4. 6	11. 5	J7	K12	Bat
5. 6	12. 5	J7	A1	Rat
6. 6	13. 5	J7	B2	Swallow
7. 6	14. 5	J7	C3	Pig
8. 6	15. 5	J7	D4	Porcupine
9. 6	16. 5	J7	E5	Wolf
10. 6	17. 5	J7	F6	Dog
11. 6	18. 5	J7	G7	Pheasant
12. 6	19. 5	J7	H8	Cock
13. 6	20. 5	J7	J9	Crow
14. 6	21. 5	J7	K10	Monkey
15. 6	22. 5	J7	A11	Gibbon
16. 6	23. 5	J7	B12	Tapir
17. 6	24. 5	J7	C1	Sheep
18. 6	25. 5	J7	D2	Deer
19. 6	26. 5	J7	E3	Horse
20. 6	27. 5	J7	F4	Stag
21. 6	28. 5	J7	G5	Serpent
22. 6	29. 5	J7	H6	Earthworm
23. 6	30. 5	J7	J7	Crocodile
24. 6	1. 6	K8	K8	Dragon
25. 6	2. 6	K8	A9	Badger
26. 6	3. 6	K8	B10	Hare
27. 6	4. 6	K8	C11	Fox
28. 6	5. 6	K8	D12	Tiger
29. 6	6. 6	K8	E1	Leopard
30. 6	7. 6	K8	F2	Griffon
1. 7	8. 6	K8	G3	Ox
2. 7	9. 6	K8	H4	Bat
3. 7	10. 6	K8	J5	Rat
4. 7	11. 6	K8	K6	Swallow
5. 7	12. 6	K8	A7	Pig
6. 7	13. 6	K8	B8	Porcupine
7. 7	14. 6	K8	C9	Wolf
8. 7	15. 6	K8	D10	Dog
9. 7	16. 6	K8	E11	Pheasant
10. 7	17. 6	K8	F12	Cock
11. 7	18. 6	K8	G1	Crow
12. 7	19. 6	K8	H2	Monkey
13. 7	20. 6	K8	J3	Gibbon
14. 7	21. 6	K8	K4	Tapir
15. 7	22. 6	K8	A5	Sheep
16. 7	23. 6	K8	B6	Deer
17. 7	24. 6	K8	C7	Horse
18. 7	25. 6	K8	D8	Stag
19. 7	26. 6	K8	E9	Serpent
20. 7	27. 6	K8	F10	Earthworm
21. 7	28. 6	K8	G11	Crocodile
22. 7	29. 6	K8	H12	Dragon
23. 7	30. 6	K8	J1	Badger
24. 7	1. 6	K8	K2	Hare
25. 7	2. 6	K8	A3	Fox
26. 7	3. 6	K8	B4	Tiger
27. 7	4. 6	K8	C5	Leopard
28. 7	5. 6	K8	D6	Griffon
29. 7	6. 6	K8	E7	Ox
30. 7	7. 6	K8	F8	Bat
31. 7	8. 6	K8	G9	Rat
1. 8	9. 6	K8	H10	Swallow
2. 8	10. 6	K8	J11	Pig
3. 8	11. 6	K8	K12	Porcupine
4. 8	12. 6	K8	A1	Wolf
5. 8	13. 6	K8	B2	Dog
6. 8	14. 6	K8	C3	Pheasant
7. 8	15. 6	K8	D4	Cock
8. 8	16. 6	K8	E5	Crow
9. 8	17. 6	K8	F6	Monkey
10. 8	18. 6	K8	G7	Gibbon
11. 8	19. 6	K8	H8	Tapir
12. 8	20. 6	K8	J9	Sheep
13. 8	21. 6	K8	K10	Deer
14. 8	22. 6	K8	A11	Horse
15. 8	23. 6	K8	B12	Stag
16. 8	24. 6	K8	C1	Serpent
17. 8	25. 6	K8	D2	Earthworm
18. 8	26. 6	K8	E3	Crocodile
19. 8	27. 6	K8	F4	Dragon
20. 8	28. 6	K8	G5	Badger
21. 8	29. 6	K8	H6	Hare
22. 8	1. 7	A9	J7	Fox
23. 8	2. 7	A9	K8	Tiger
24. 8	3. 7	A9	A9	Leopard
25. 8	4. 7	A9	B10	Griffon
26. 8	5. 7	A9	C11	Ox
27. 8	6. 7	A9	D12	Bat
28. 8	7. 7	A9	E1	Rat
29. 8	8. 7	A9	F2	Swallow
30. 8	9. 7	A9	G3	Pig
31. 8	10. 7	A9	H4	Porcupine
1. 9	11. 7	A9	J5	Wolf
2. 9	12. 7	A9	K6	Dog
3. 9	13. 7	A9	A7	Pheasant
4. 9	14. 7	A9	B8	Cock
5. 9	15. 7	A9	C9	Crow
6. 9	16. 7	A9	D10	Monkey
7. 9	17. 7	A9	E11	Gibbon
8. 9	18. 7	A9	F12	Tapir
9. 9	19. 7	A9	G1	Sheep
10. 9	20. 7	A9	H2	Deer
11. 9	21. 7	A9	J3	Horse
12. 9	22. 7	A9	K4	Stag
13. 9	23. 7	A9	A5	Serpent
14. 9	24. 7	A9	B6	Earthworm
15. 9	25. 7	A9	C7	Crocodile
16. 9	26. 7	A9	D8	Dragon
17. 9	27. 7	A9	E9	Badger
18. 9	28. 7	A9	F10	Hare
19. 9	29. 7	A9	G11	Fox
20. 9	30. 7	A9	H12	Tiger
21. 9	1. 8	B10	J1	Leopard
22. 9	2. 8	B10	K2	Griffon
23. 9	3. 8	B10	A3	Ox
24. 9	4. 8	B10	B4	Bat
25. 9	5. 8	B10	C5	Rat
26. 9	6. 8	B10	D6	Swallow
27. 9	7. 8	B10	E7	Pig
28. 9	8. 8	B10	F8	Porcupine
29. 9	9. 8	B10	G9	Wolf
30. 9	10. 8	B10	H10	Dog
1.10	11. 8	B10	J11	Pheasant
2.10	12. 8	B10	K12	Cock
3.10	13. 8	B10	A1	Crow
4.10	14. 8	B10	B2	Monkey
5.10	15. 8	B10	C3	Gibbon

Solar date	Lunar date	Month HS/EB	Day HS/EB	Constellation	Solar date	Lunar date	Month HS/EB	Day HS/EB	Constellation
6.10	16. 8	B10	D4	Tapir	12.12	24.10	D12	A11	Fox
7.10	17. 8	B10	E5	Sheep	13.12	25.10	D12	B12	Tiger
8.10	18. 8	B10	F6	Deer	14.12	26.10	D12	C1	Leopard
9.10	19. 8	B10	G7	Horse	15.12	27.10	D12	D2	Griffon
10.10	20. 8	B10	H8	Stag	16.12	28.10	D12	E3	Ox
11.10	21. 8	B10	J9	Serpent	17.12	29.10	D12	F4	Bat
12.10	22. 8	B10	K10	Earthworm	18.12	1.11	E1	G5	Rat
13.10	23. 8	B10	A11	Crocodile	19.12	2.11	E1	H6	Swallow
14.10	24. 8	B10	B12	Dragon	20.12	3.11	E1	J7	Pig
15.10	25. 8	B10	C1	Badger	21.12	4.11	E1	K8	Porcupine
16.10	26. 8	B10	D2	Hare	22.12	5.11	E1	A9	Wolf
17.10	27. 8	B10	E3	Fox	23.12	6.11	E1	B10	Dog
18.10	28. 8	B10	F4	Tiger	24.12	7.11	E1	C11	Pheasant
19.10	29. 8	B10	G5	Leopard	25.12	8.11	E1	D12	Cock
20.10	1. 9	C11	H6	Griffon	26.12	9.11	E1	E1	Crow
21.10	2. 9	C11	J7	Ox	27.12	10.11	E1	F2	Monkey
22.10	3. 9	C11	K8	Bat	28.12	11.11	E1	G3	Gibbon
23.10	4. 9	C11	A9	Rat	29.12	12.11	E1	H4	Tapir
24.10	5. 9	C11	B10	Swallow	30.12	13.11	E1	J5	Sheep
25.10	6. 9	C11	C11	Pig	31.12	14.11	E1	K6	Deer
26.10	7. 9	C11	D12	Porcupine					
27.10	8. 9	C11	E1	Wolf	**1961**				
28.10	9. 9	C11	F2	Dog	1. 1	15.11	E1	A7	Horse
29.10	10. 9	C11	G3	Pheasant	2. 1	16.11	E1	B8	Stag
30.10	11. 9	C11	H4	Cock	3. 1	17.11	E1	C9	Serpent
31.10	12. 9	C11	J5	Crow	4. 1	18.11	E1	D10	Earthworm
1.11	13. 9	C11	K6	Monkey	5. 1	19.11	E1	E11	Crocodile
2.11	14. 9	C11	A7	Gibbon	6. 1	20.11	E1	F12	Dragon
3.11	15. 9	C11	B8	Tapir	7. 1	21.11	E1	G1	Badger
4.11	16. 9	C11	C9	Sheep	8. 1	22.11	E1	H2	Hare
5.11	17. 9	C11	D10	Deer	9. 1	23.11	E1	J3	Fox
6.11	18. 9	C11	E11	Horse	10. 1	24.11	E1	K4	Tiger
7.11	19. 9	C11	F12	Stag	11. 1	25.11	E1	A5	Leopard
8.11	20. 9	C11	G1	Serpent	12. 1	26.11	E1	B6	Griffon
9.11	21. 9	C11	H2	Earthworm	13. 1	27.11	E1	C7	Ox
10.11	22. 9	C11	J3	Crocodile	14. 1	28.11	E1	D8	Bat
11.11	23. 9	C11	K4	Dragon	15. 1	29.11	E1	E9	Rat
12.11	24. 9	C11	A5	Badger	16. 1	30.11	E1	F10	Swallow
13.11	25. 9	C11	B6	Hare	17. 1	1.12	F2	G11	Pig
14.11	26. 9	C11	C7	Fox	18. 1	2.12	F2	H12	Porcupine
15.11	27. 9	C11	D8	Tiger	19. 1	3.12	F2	J1	Wolf
16.11	28. 9	C11	E9	Leopard	20. 1	4.12	F2	K2	Dog
17.11	29. 9	C11	F10	Griffon	21. 1	5.12	F2	A3	Pheasant
18.11	30. 9	C11	G11	Ox	22. 1	6.12	F2	B4	Cock
19.11	1.10	D12	H12	Bat	23. 1	7.12	F2	C5	Crow
20.11	2.10	D12	J1	Rat	24. 1	8.12	F2	D6	Monkey
21.11	3.10	D12	K2	Swallow	25. 1	9.12	F2	E7	Gibbon
22.11	4.10	D12	A3	Pig	26. 1	10.12	F2	F8	Tapir
23.11	5.10	D12	B4	Porcupine	27. 1	11.12	F2	G9	Sheep
24.11	6.10	D12	C5	Wolf	28. 1	12.12	F2	H10	Deer
25.11	7.10	D12	D6	Dog	29. 1	13.12	F2	J11	Horse
26.11	8.10	D12	E7	Pheasant	30. 1	14.12	F2	K12	Stag
27.11	9.10	D12	F8	Cock	31. 1	15.12	F2	A1	Serpent
28.11	10.10	D12	G9	Crow	1. 2	16.12	F2	B2	Earthworm
29.11	11.10	D12	H10	Monkey	2. 2	17.12	F2	C3	Crocodile
30.11	12.10	D12	J11	Gibbon	3. 2	18.12	F2	D4	Dragon
1.12	13.10	D12	K12	Tapir	4. 2	19.12	F2	E5	Badger
2.12	14.10	D12	A1	Sheep	5. 2	20.12	F2	F6	Hare
3.12	15.10	D12	B2	Deer	6. 2	21.12	F2	G7	Fox
4.12	16.10	D12	C3	Horse	7. 2	22.12	F2	H8	Tiger
5.12	17.10	D12	D4	Stag	8. 2	23.12	F2	J9	Leopard
6.12	18.10	D12	E5	Serpent	9. 2	24.12	F2	K10	Griffon
7.12	19.10	D12	F6	Earthworm	10. 2	25.12	F2	A11	Ox
8.12	20.10	D12	G7	Crocodile	11. 2	26.12	F2	B12	Bat
9.12	21.10	D12	H8	Dragon	12. 2	27.12	F2	C1	Rat
10.12	22.10	D12	J9	Badger	13. 2	28.12	F2	D2	Swallow
11.12	23.10	D12	K10	Hare	14. 2	29.12	F2	E3	Pig

HSIN CH'OU YEAR

Solar date	Lunar date	Month HS/EB	Day HS/EB	Constellation	Solar date	Lunar date	Month HS/EB	Day HS/EB	Constellation
15. 2	1. 1	G3	F4	Porcupine	27. 4	13. 3	J5	G3	Crocodile
16. 2	2. 1	G3	G5	Wolf	28. 4	14. 3	J5	H4	Dragon
17. 2	3. 1	G3	H6	Dog	29. 4	15. 3	J5	J5	Badger
18. 2	4. 1	G3	J7	Pheasant	30. 4	16. 3	J5	K6	Hare
19. 2	5. 1	G3	K8	Cock	1. 5	17. 3	J5	A7	Fox
20. 2	6. 1	G3	A9	Crow	2. 5	18. 3	J5	B8	Tiger
21. 2	7. 1	G3	B10	Monkey	3. 5	19. 3	J5	C9	Leopard
22. 2	8. 1	G3	C11	Gibbon	4. 5	20. 3	J5	D10	Griffon
23. 2	9. 1	G3	D12	Tapir	5. 5	21. 3	J5	E11	Ox
24. 2	10. 1	G3	E1	Sheep	6. 5	22. 3	J5	F12	Bat
25. 2	11. 1	G3	F2	Deer	7. 5	23. 3	J5	G1	Rat
26. 2	12. 1	G3	G3	Horse	8. 5	24. 3	J5	H2	Swallow
27. 2	13. 1	G3	H4	Stag	9. 5	25. 3	J5	J3	Pig
28. 2	14. 1	G3	J5	Serpent	10. 5	26. 3	J5	K4	Porcupine
1. 3	15. 1	G3	K6	Earthworm	11. 5	27. 3	J5	A5	Wolf
2. 3	16. 1	G3	A7	Crocodile	12. 5	28. 3	J5	B6	Dog
3. 3	17. 1	G3	B8	Dragon	13. 5	29. 3	J5	C7	Pheasant
4. 3	18. 1	G3	C9	Badger	14. 5	30. 3	J5	D8	Cock
5. 3	19. 1	G3	D10	Hare	15. 5	1. 4	K6	E9	Crow
6. 3	20. 1	G3	E11	Fox	16. 5	2. 4	K6	F10	Monkey
7. 3	21. 1	G3	F12	Tiger	17. 5	3. 4	K6	G11	Gibbon
8. 3	22. 1	G3	G1	Leopard	18. 5	4. 4	K6	H12	Tapir
9. 3	23. 1	G3	H2	Griffon	19. 5	5. 4	K6	J1	Sheep
10. 3	24. 1	G3	J3	Ox	20. 5	6. 4	K6	K2	Deer
11. 3	25. 1	G3	K4	Bat	21. 5	7. 4	K6	A3	Horse
12. 3	26. 1	G3	A5	Rat	22. 5	8. 4	K6	B4	Stag
13. 3	27. 1	G3	B6	Swallow	23. 5	9. 4	K6	C5	Serpent
14. 3	28. 1	G3	C7	Pig	24. 5	10. 4	K6	D6	Earthworm
15. 3	29. 1	G3	D8	Porcupine	25. 5	11. 4	K6	E7	Crocodile
16. 3	30. 1	G3	E9	Wolf	26. 5	12. 4	K6	F8	Dragon
17. 3	1. 2	H4	F10	Dog	27. 5	13. 4	K6	G9	Badger
18. 3	2. 2	H4	G11	Pheasant	28. 5	14. 4	K6	H10	Hare
19. 3	3. 2	H4	H12	Cock	29. 5	15. 4	K6	J11	Fox
20. 3	4. 2	H4	J1	Crow	30. 5	16. 4	K6	K12	Tiger
21. 3	5. 2	H4	K2	Monkey	31. 5	17. 4	K6	A1	Leopard
22. 3	6. 2	H4	A3	Gibbon	1. 6	18. 4	K6	B2	Griffon
23. 3	7. 2	H4	B4	Tapir	2. 6	19. 4	K6	C3	Ox
24. 3	8. 2	H4	C5	Sheep	3. 6	20. 4	K6	D4	Bat
25. 3	9. 2	H4	D6	Deer	4. 6	21. 4	K6	E5	Rat
26. 3	10. 2	H4	E7	Horse	5. 6	22. 4	K6	F6	Swallow
27. 3	11. 2	H4	F8	Stag	6. 6	23. 4	K6	G7	Pig
28. 3	12. 2	H4	G9	Serpent	7. 6	24. 4	K6	H8	Porcupine
29. 3	13. 2	H4	H10	Earthworm	8. 6	25. 4	K6	J9	Wolf
30. 3	14. 2	H4	J11	Crocodile	9. 6	26. 4	K6	K10	Dog
31. 3	15. 2	H4	K12	Dragon	10. 6	27. 4	K6	A11	Pheasant
1. 4	16. 2	H4	A1	Badger	11. 6	28. 4	K6	B12	Cock
2. 4	17. 2	H4	B2	Hare	12. 6	29. 4	K6	C1	Crow
3. 4	18. 2	H4	C3	Fox	13. 6	1. 5	A7	D2	Monkey
4. 4	19. 2	H4	D4	Tiger	14. 6	2. 5	A7	E3	Gibbon
5. 4	20. 2	H4	E5	Leopard	15. 6	3. 5	A7	F4	Tapir
6. 4	21. 2	H4	F6	Griffon	16. 6	4. 5	A7	G5	Sheep
7. 4	22. 2	H4	G7	Ox	17. 6	5. 5	A7	H6	Deer
8. 4	23. 2	H4	H8	Bat	18. 6	6. 5	A7	J7	Horse
9. 4	24. 2	H4	J9	Rat	19. 6	7. 5	A7	K8	Stag
10. 4	25. 2	H4	K10	Swallow	20. 6	8. 5	A7	A9	Serpent
11. 4	26. 2	H4	A11	Pig	21. 6	9. 5	A7	B10	Earthworm
12. 4	27. 2	H4	B12	Porcupine	22. 6	10. 5	A7	C11	Crocodile
13. 4	28. 2	H4	C1	Wolf	23. 6	11. 5	A7	D12	Dragon
14. 4	29. 2	H4	D2	Dog	24. 6	12. 5	A7	E1	Badger
15. 4	1. 3	J5	E3	Pheasant	25. 6	13. 5	A7	F2	Hare
16. 4	2. 3	J5	F4	Cock	26. 6	14. 5	A7	G3	Fox
17. 4	3. 3	J5	G5	Crow	27. 6	15. 5	A7	H4	Tiger
18. 4	4. 3	J5	H6	Monkey	28. 6	16. 5	A7	J5	Leopard
19. 4	5. 3	J5	J7	Gibbon	29. 6	17. 5	A7	K6	Griffon
20. 4	6. 3	J5	K8	Tapir	30. 6	18. 5	A7	A7	Ox
21. 4	7. 3	J5	A9	Sheep	1. 7	19. 5	A7	B8	Bat
22. 4	8. 3	J5	B10	Deer	2. 7	20. 5	A7	C9	Rat
23. 4	9. 3	J5	C11	Horse	3. 7	21. 5	A7	D10	Swallow
24. 4	10. 3	J5	D12	Stag	4. 7	22. 5	A7	E11	Pig
25. 4	11. 3	J5	E1	Serpent	5. 7	23. 5	A7	F12	Porcupine
26. 4	12. 3	J5	F2	Earthworm	6. 7	24. 5	A7	G1	Wolf

Solar date	Lunar date	Month HS/EB	Day HS/EB	Constellation
7.7	25.5	A7	H2	Dog
8.7	26.5	A7	J3	Pheasant
9.7	27.5	A7	K4	Cock
10.7	28.5	A7	A5	Crow
11.7	29.5	A7	B6	Monkey
12.7	30.5	A7	C7	Gibbon
13.7	1.6	B8	D8	Tapir
14.7	2.6	B8	E9	Sheep
15.7	3.6	B8	F10	Deer
16.7	4.6	B8	G11	Horse
17.7	5.6	B8	H12	Stag
18.7	6.6	B8	J1	Serpent
19.7	7.6	B8	K2	Earthworm
20.7	8.6	B8	A3	Crocodile
21.7	9.6	B8	B4	Dragon
22.7	10.6	B8	C5	Badger
23.7	11.6	B8	D6	Hare
24.7	12.6	B8	E7	Fox
25.7	13.6	B8	F8	Tiger
26.7	14.6	B8	G9	Leopard
27.7	15.6	B8	H10	Griffon
28.7	16.6	B8	J11	Ox
29.7	17.6	B8	K12	Bat
30.7	18.6	B8	A1	Rat
31.7	19.6	B8	B2	Swallow
1.8	20.6	B8	C3	Pig
2.8	21.6	B8	D4	Porcupine
3.8	22.6	B8	E5	Wolf
4.8	23.6	B8	F6	Dog
5.8	24.6	B8	G7	Pheasant
6.8	25.6	B8	H8	Cock
7.8	26.6	B8	J9	Crow
8.8	27.6	B8	K10	Monkey
9.8	28.6	B8	A11	Gibbon
10.8	29.6	B8	B12	Tapir
11.8	1.7	C9	C1	Sheep
12.8	2.7	C9	D2	Deer
13.8	3.7	C9	E3	Horse
14.8	4.7	C9	F4	Stag
15.8	5.7	C9	G5	Serpent
16.8	6.7	C9	H6	Earthworm
17.8	7.7	C9	J7	Crocodile
18.8	8.7	C9	K8	Dragon
19.8	9.7	C9	A9	Badger
20.8	10.7	C9	B10	Hare
21.8	11.7	C9	C11	Fox
22.8	12.7	C9	D12	Tiger
23.8	13.7	C9	E1	Leopard
24.8	14.7	C9	F2	Griffon
25.8	15.7	C9	G3	Ox
26.8	16.7	C9	H4	Bat
27.8	17.7	C9	J5	Rat
28.8	18.7	C9	K6	Swallow
29.8	19.7	C9	A7	Pig
30.8	20.7	C9	B8	Porcupine
31.8	21.7	C9	C9	Wolf
1.9	22.7	C9	D10	Dog
2.9	23.7	C9	E11	Pheasant
3.9	24.7	C9	F12	Cock
4.9	25.7	C9	G1	Crow
5.9	26.7	C9	H2	Monkey
6.9	27.7	C9	J3	Gibbon
7.9	28.7	C9	K4	Tapir
8.9	29.7	C9	A5	Sheep
9.9	30.7	C9	B6	Deer
10.9	1.8	D10	C7	Horse
11.9	2.8	D10	D8	Stag
12.9	3.8	D10	E9	Serpent
13.9	4.8	D10	F10	Earthworm
14.9	5.8	D10	G11	Crocodile
15.9	6.8	D10	H12	Dragon
16.9	7.8	D10	J1	Badger
17.9	8.8	D10	K2	Hare
18.9	9.8	D10	A3	Fox
19.9	10.8	D10	B4	Tiger
20.9	11.8	D10	C5	Leopard
21.9	12.8	D10	D6	Griffon
22.9	13.8	D10	E7	Ox
23.9	14.8	D10	F8	Bat
24.9	15.8	D10	G9	Rat
25.9	16.8	D10	H10	Swallow
26.9	17.8	D10	J11	Pig
27.9	18.8	D10	K12	Porcupine
28.9	19.8	D10	A1	Wolf
29.9	20.8	D10	B2	Dog
30.9	21.8	D10	C3	Pheasant
1.10	22.8	D10	D4	Cock
2.10	23.8	D10	E5	Crow
3.10	24.8	D10	F6	Monkey
4.10	25.8	D10	G7	Gibbon
5.10	26.8	D10	H8	Tapir
6.10	27.8	D10	J9	Sheep
7.10	28.8	D10	K10	Deer
8.10	29.8	D10	A11	Horse
9.10	30.8	D10	B12	Stag
10.10	1.9	E11	C1	Serpent
11.10	2.9	E11	D2	Earthworm
12.10	3.9	E11	E3	Crocodile
13.10	4.9	E11	F4	Dragon
14.10	5.9	E11	G5	Badger
15.10	6.9	E11	H6	Hare
16.10	7.9	E11	J7	Fox
17.10	8.9	E11	K8	Tiger
18.10	9.9	E11	A9	Leopard
19.10	10.9	E11	B10	Griffon
20.10	11.9	E11	C11	Ox
21.10	12.9	E11	D12	Bat
22.10	13.9	E11	E1	Rat
23.10	14.9	E11	F2	Swallow
24.10	15.9	E11	G3	Pig
25.10	16.9	E11	H4	Porcupine
26.10	17.9	E11	J5	Wolf
27.10	18.9	E11	K6	Dog
28.10	19.9	E11	A7	Pheasant
29.10	20.9	E11	B8	Cock
30.10	21.9	E11	C9	Crow
31.10	22.9	E11	D10	Monkey
1.11	23.9	E11	E11	Gibbon
2.11	24.9	E11	F12	Tapir
3.11	25.9	E11	G1	Sheep
4.11	26.9	E11	H2	Deer
5.11	27.9	E11	J3	Horse
6.11	28.9	E11	K4	Stag
7.11	29.9	E11	A5	Serpent
8.11	1.10	F12	B6	Earthworm
9.11	2.10	F12	C7	Crocodile
10.11	3.10	F12	D8	Dragon
11.11	4.10	F12	E9	Badger
12.11	5.10	F12	F10	Hare
13.11	6.10	F12	G11	Fox
14.11	7.10	F12	H12	Tiger
15.11	8.10	F12	J1	Leopard
16.11	9.10	F12	K2	Griffon
17.11	10.10	F12	A3	Ox
18.11	11.10	F12	B4	Bat
19.11	12.10	F12	C5	Rat
20.11	13.10	F12	D6	Swallow
21.11	14.10	F12	E7	Pig
22.11	15.10	F12	F8	Porcupine
23.11	16.10	F12	G9	Wolf
24.11	17.10	F12	H10	Dog
25.11	18.10	F12	J11	Pheasant
26.11	19.10	F12	K12	Cock
27.11	20.10	F12	A1	Crow
28.11	21.10	F12	B2	Monkey
29.11	22.10	F12	C3	Gibbon

Solar date	Lunar date	Month HS/EB	Day HS/EB	Constellation	Solar date	Lunar date	Month HS/EB	Day HS/EB	Constellation
30.11	23.10	F12	D4	Tapir	2.1	26.11	G1	G1	Serpent
1.12	24.10	F12	E5	Sheep	3.1	27.11	G1	H2	Earthworm
2.12	25.10	F12	F6	Deer	4.1	28.11	G1	J3	Crocodile
3.12	26.10	F12	G7	Horse	5.1	29.11	G1	K4	Dragon
4.12	27.10	F12	H8	Stag	6.1	1.12	H2	A5	Badger
5.12	28.10	F12	J9	Serpent	7.1	2.12	H2	B6	Hare
6.12	29.10	F12	K10	Earthworm	8.1	3.12	H2	C7	Fox
7.12	30.10	F12	A11	Crocodile	9.1	4.12	H2	D8	Tiger
8.12	1.11	G1	B12	Dragon	10.1	5.12	H2	E9	Leopard
9.12	2.11	G1	C1	Badger	11.1	5.12	H2	F10	Griffon
10.12	3.11	G1	D2	Hare	12.1	7.12	H2	G11	Ox
11.12	4.11	G1	E3	Fox	13.1	8.12	H2	H12	Bat
12.12	5.11	G1	F4	Tiger	14.1	9.12	H2	J1	Rat
13.12	6.11	G1	G5	Leopard	15.1	10.12	H2	K2	Swallow
14.12	7.11	G1	H6	Griffon	16.1	11.12	H2	A3	Pig
15.12	8.11	G1	J7	Ox	17.1	12.12	H2	B4	Porcupine
16.12	9.11	G1	K8	Bat	18.1	13.12	H2	C5	Wolf
17.12	10.11	G1	A9	Rat	19.1	14.12	H2	D6	Dog
18.12	11.11	G1	B10	Swallow	20.1	15.12	H2	E7	Pheasant
19.12	12.11	G1	C11	Pig	21.1	16.12	H2	F8	Cock
20.12	13.11	G1	D12	Porcupine	22.1	17.12	H2	G9	Crow
21.12	14.11	G1	E1	Wolf	23.1	18.12	H2	H10	Monkey
22.12	15.11	G1	F2	Dog	24.1	19.12	H2	J11	Gibbon
23.12	16.11	G1	G3	Pheasant	25.1	20.12	H2	K12	Tapir
24.12	17.11	G1	H4	Cock	26.1	21.12	H2	A1	Sheep
25.12	18.11	G1	J5	Crow	27.1	22.12	H2	B2	Deer
26.12	19.11	G1	K6	Monkey	28.1	23.12	H2	C3	Horse
27.12	20.11	G1	A7	Gibbon	29.1	24.12	H2	D4	Stag
28.12	21.11	G1	B8	Tapir	30.1	25.12	H2	E5	Serpent
29.12	22.11	G1	C9	Sheep	31.1	26.12	H2	F6	Earthworm
30.12	23.11	G1	D10	Deer	1.2	27.12	H2	G7	Crocodile
31.12	24.11	G1	E11	Horse	2.2	28.12	H2	H8	Dragon
1962					3.2	29.12	H2	J9	Badger
1.1	25.11	G1	F12	Stag	4.2	30.12	H2	K10	Hare

JEN YIN YEAR

Solar date	Lunar date	Month HS/EB	Day HS/EB	Constellation	Solar date	Lunar date	Month HS/EB	Day HS/EB	Constellation
5.2	1.1	J3	A11	Fox	10.3	5.2	K4	D8	Bat
6.2	2.1	J3	B12	Tiger	11.3	6.2	K4	E9	Rat
7.2	3.1	J3	C1	Leopard	12.3	7.2	K4	F10	Swallow
8.2	4.1	J3	D2	Griffon	13.3	8.2	K4	G11	Pig
9.2	5.1	J3	E3	Ox	14.3	9.2	K4	H12	Porcupine
10.2	6.1	J3	F4	Bat	15.3	10.2	K4	J1	Wolf
11.2	7.1	J3	G5	Rat	16.3	11.2	K4	K2	Dog
12.2	8.1	J3	H6	Swallow	17.3	12.2	K4	A3	Pheasant
13.2	9.1	J3	J7	Pig	18.3	13.2	K4	B4	Cock
14.2	10.1	J3	K8	Porcupine	19.3	14.2	K4	C5	Crow
15.2	11.1	J3	A9	Wolf	20.3	15.2	K4	D6	Monkey
16.2	12.1	J3	B10	Dog	21.3	16.2	K4	E7	Gibbon
17.2	13.1	J3	C11	Pheasant	22.3	17.2	K4	F8	Tapir
18.2	14.1	J3	D12	Cock	23.3	18.2	K4	G9	Sheep
19.2	15.1	J3	E1	Crow	24.3	19.2	K4	H10	Deer
20.2	16.1	J3	F2	Monkey	25.3	20.2	K4	J11	Horse
21.2	17.1	J3	G3	Gibbon	26.3	21.2	K4	K12	Stag
22.2	18.1	J3	H4	Tapir	27.3	22.2	K4	A1	Serpent
23.2	19.1	J3	J5	Sheep	28.3	23.2	K4	B2	Earthworm
24.2	20.1	J3	K6	Deer	29.3	24.2	K4	C3	Crocodile
25.2	21.1	J3	A7	Horse	30.3	25.2	K4	D4	Dragon
26.2	22.1	J3	B8	Stag	31.3	26.2	K4	E5	Badger
27.2	23.1	J3	C9	Serpent	1.4	27.2	K4	F6	Hare
28.2	24.1	J3	D10	Earthworm	2.4	28.2	K4	G7	Fox
1.3	25.1	J3	E11	Crocodile	3.4	29.2	K4	H8	Tiger
2.3	26.1	J3	F12	Dragon	4.4	30.2	K4	J9	Leopard
3.3	27.1	J3	G1	Badger	5.4	1.3	A5	K10	Griffon
4.3	28.1	J3	H2	Hare	6.4	2.3	A5	A11	Ox
5.3	29.1	J3	J3	Fox	7.4	3.3	A5	B12	Bat
6.3	1.2	K4	K4	Tiger	8.4	4.3	A5	C1	Rat
7.3	2.2	K4	A5	Leopard	9.4	5.3	A5	D2	Swallow
8.3	3.2	K4	B6	Griffon	10.4	6.3	A5	E3	Pig
9.3	4.2	K4	C7	Ox	11.4	7.3	A5	F4	Porcupine

Solar date	Lunar date	Month HS/EB	Day HS/EB	Constellation
12. 4	8. 3	A5	G5	Wolf
13. 4	9. 3	A5	H6	Dog
14. 4	10. 3	A5	J7	Pheasant
15. 4	11. 3	A5	K8	Cock
16. 4	12. 3	A5	A9	Crow
17. 4	13. 3	A5	B10	Monkey
18. 4	14. 3	A5	C11	Gibbon
19. 4	15. 3	A5	D12	Tapir
20. 4	16. 3	A5	E1	Sheep
21. 4	17. 3	A5	F2	Deer
22. 4	18. 3	A5	G3	Horse
23. 4	19. 3	A5	H4	Stag
24. 4	20. 3	A5	J5	Serpent
25. 4	21. 3	A5	K6	Earthworm
26. 4	22. 3	A5	A7	Crocodile
27. 4	23. 3	A5	B8	Dragon
28. 4	24. 3	A5	C9	Badger
29. 4	25. 3	A5	D10	Hare
30. 4	26. 3	A5	E11	Fox
1. 5	27. 3	A5	F12	Tiger
2. 5	28. 3	A5	G1	Leopard
3. 5	29. 3	A5	H2	Griffon
4. 5	1. 4	B6	J3	Ox
5. 5	2. 4	B6	K4	Bat
6. 5	3. 4	B6	A5	Rat
7. 5	4. 4	B6	B6	Swallow
8. 5	5. 4	B6	C7	Pig
9. 5	6. 4	B6	D8	Porcupine
10. 5	7. 4	B6	E9	Wolf
11. 5	8. 4	B6	F10	Dog
12. 5	9. 4	B6	G11	Pheasant
13. 5	10. 4	B6	H12	Cock
14. 5	11. 4	B6	J1	Crow
15. 5	12. 4	B6	K2	Monkey
16. 5	13. 4	B6	A3	Gibbon
17. 5	14. 4	B6	B4	Tapir
18. 5	15. 4	B6	C5	Sheep
19. 5	16. 4	B6	D6	Deer
20. 5	17. 4	B6	E7	Horse
21. 5	18. 4	B6	F8	Stag
22. 5	19. 4	B6	G9	Serpent
23. 5	20. 4	B6	H10	Earthworm
24. 5	21. 4	B6	J11	Crocodile
25. 5	22. 4	B6	K12	Dragon
26. 5	23. 4	B6	A1	Badger
27. 5	24. 4	B6	B2	Hare
28. 5	25. 4	B6	C3	Fox
29. 5	26. 4	B6	D4	Tiger
30. 5	27. 4	B6	E5	Leopard
31. 5	28. 4	B6	F6	Griffon
1. 6	29. 4	B6	G7	Ox
2. 6	1. 5	C7	H8	Bat
3. 6	2. 5	C7	J9	Rat
4. 6	3. 5	C7	K10	Swallow
5. 6	4. 5	C7	A11	Pig
6. 6	5. 5	C7	B12	Porcupine
7. 6	6. 5	C7	C1	Wolf
8. 6	7. 5	C7	D2	Dog
9. 6	8. 5	C7	E3	Pheasant
10. 6	9. 5	C7	F4	Cock
11. 6	10. 5	C7	G5	Crow
12. 6	11. 5	C7	H6	Monkey
13. 6	12. 5	C7	J7	Gibbon
14. 6	13. 5	C7	K8	Tapir
15. 6	14. 5	C7	A9	Sheep
16. 6	15. 5	C7	B10	Deer
17. 6	16. 5	C7	C11	Horse
18. 6	17. 5	C7	D12	Stag
19. 6	18. 5	C7	E1	Serpent
20. 6	19. 5	C7	F2	Earthworm
21. 6	20. 5	C7	G3	Crocodile
22. 6	21. 5	C7	H4	Dragon
23. 6	22. 5	C7	J5	Badger
24. 6	23. 5	C7	K6	Hare
25. 6	24. 5	C7	A7	Fox
26. 6	25. 5	C7	B8	Tiger
27. 6	26. 5	C7	C9	Leopard
28. 6	27. 5	C7	D10	Griffon
29. 6	28. 5	C7	E11	Ox
30. 6	29. 5	C7	F12	Bat
1. 7	30. 5	C7	G1	Rat
2. 7	1. 6	D8	H2	Swallow
3. 7	2. 6	D8	J3	Pig
4. 7	3. 6	D8	K4	Porcupine
5. 7	4. 6	D8	A5	Wolf
6. 7	5. 6	D8	B6	Dog
7. 7	6. 6	D8	C7	Pheasant
8. 7	7. 6	D8	D8	Cock
9. 7	8. 6	D8	E9	Crow
10. 7	9. 6	D8	F10	Monkey
11. 7	10. 6	D8	G11	Gibbon
12. 7	11. 6	D8	H12	Tapir
13. 7	12. 6	D8	J1	Sheep
14. 7	13. 6	D8	K2	Deer
15. 7	14. 6	D8	A3	Horse
16. 7	15. 6	D8	B4	Stag
17. 7	16. 6	D8	C5	Serpent
18. 7	17. 6	D8	D6	Earthworm
19. 7	18. 6	D8	E7	Crocodile
20. 7	19. 6	D8	F8	Dragon
21. 7	20. 6	D8	G9	Badger
22. 7	21. 6	D8	H10	Hare
23. 7	22. 6	D8	J11	Fox
24. 7	23. 6	D8	K12	Tiger
25. 7	24. 6	D8	A1	Leopard
26. 7	25. 6	D8	B2	Griffon
27. 7	26. 6	D8	C3	Ox
28. 7	27. 6	D8	D4	Bat
29. 7	28. 6	D8	E5	Rat
30. 7	29. 6	D8	F6	Swallow
31. 7	1. 7	E9	G7	Pig
1. 8	2. 7	E9	H8	Porcupine
2. 8	3. 7	E9	J9	Wolf
3. 8	4. 7	E9	K10	Dog
4. 8	5. 7	E9	A11	Pheasant
5. 8	6: 7	E9	B12	Cock
6. 8	7. 7	E9	C1	Crow
7. 8	8. 7	E9	D2	Monkey
8. 8	9. 7	E9	E3	Gibbon
9. 8	10. 7	E9	F4	Tapir
10. 8	11. 7	E9	G5	Sheep
11. 8	12. 7	E9	H6	Deer
12. 8	13. 7	E9	J7	Horse
13. 8	14. 7	E9	K8	Stag
14. 8	15. 7	E9	A9	Serpent
15. 8	16. 7	E9	B10	Earthworm
16. 8	17. 7	F9	C11	Crocodile
17. 8	18. 7	E9	D12	Dragon
18. 8	19. 7	E9	E1	Badger
19. 8	20. 7	E9	F2	Hare
20. 8	21. 7	E9	G3	Fox
21. 8	22. 7	E9	H4	Tiger
22. 8	23. 7	E9	J5	Leopard
23. 8	24. 7	E9	K6	Griffon
24. 8	25. 7	E9	A7	Ox
25. 8	26. 7	E9	B8	Bat
26. 8	27. 7	E9	C9	Rat
27. 8	28. 7	E9	D10	Swallow
28. 8	29. 7	E9	E11	Pig
29. 8	30. 7	E9	F12	Porcupine
30. 8	1. 8	F10	G1	Wolf
31. 8	2. 8	F10	H2	Dog
1. 9	3. 8	F10	J3	Pheasant
2. 9	4. 8	F10	K4	Cock
3. 9	5. 8	F10	A5	Crow
4. 9	6. 8	F10	B6	Monkey

Solar date	Lunar date	Month HS/EB	Day HS/EB	Constellation	Solar date	Lunar date	Month HS/EB	Day HS/EB	Constellation
5. 9	7. 8	F10	C7	Gibbon	16.11	20.10	H12	E7	Ox
6. 9	8. 8	F10	D8	Tapir	17.11	21.10	H12	F8	Bat
7. 9	9. 8	F10	E9	Sheep	18.11	22.10	H12	G9	Rat
8. 9	10. 8	F10	F10	Deer	19.11	23.10	H12	H10	Swallow
9. 9	11. 8	F10	G11	Horse	20.11	24.10	H12	J11	Pig
10. 9	12. 8	F10	H12	Stag	21.11	25.10	H12	K12	Porcupine
11. 9	13. 8	F10	J1	Serpent	22.11	26.10	H12	A1	Wolf
12. 9	14. 8	F10	K2	Earthworm	23.11	27.10	H12	B2	Dog
13. 9	15. 8	F10	A3	Crocodile	24.11	28.10	H12	C3	Pheasant
14. 9	16. 8	F10	B4	Dragon	25.11	29.10	H12	D4	Cock
15. 9	17. 8	F10	C5	Badger	26.11	30.10	H12	E5	Crow
16. 9	18. 8	F10	D6	Hare	27.11	1.11	J1	F6	Monkey
17. 9	19. 8	F10	E7	Fox	28.11	2.11	J1	G7	Gibbon
18. 9	20. 8	F10	F8	Tiger	29.11	3.11	J1	H8	Tapir
19. 9	21. 8	F10	G9	Leopard	30.11	4.11	J1	J9	Sheep
20. 9	22. 8	F10	H10	Griffon	1.12	5.11	J1	K10	Deer
21. 9	23. 8	F10	J11	Ox	2.12	6.11	J1	A11	Horse
22. 9	24. 8	F10	K12	Bat	3.12	7.11	J1	B12	Stag
23. 9	25. 8	F10	A1	Rat	4.12	8.11	J1	C1	Serpent
24. 9	26. 8	F10	B2	Swallow	5.12	9.11	J1	D2	Earthworm
25. 9	27. 8	F10	C3	Pig	6.12	10.11	J1	E3	Crocodile
26. 9	28. 8	F10	D4	Porcupine	7.12	11.11	J1	F4	Dragon
27. 9	29. 8	F10	E5	Wolf	8.12	12.11	J1	G5	Badger
28. 9	30. 8	F10	F6	Dog	9.12	13.11	J1	H6	Hare
29. 9	1. 9	G11	G7	Pheasant	10.12	14.11	J1	J7	Fox
30. 9	2. 9	G11	H8	Cock	11.12	15.11	J1	K8	Tiger
1.10	3. 9	G11	J9	Crow	12.12	16.11	J1	A9	Leopard
2.10	4. 9	G11	K10	Monkey	13.12	17.11	J1	B10	Griffon
3.10	5. 9	G11	A11	Gibbon	14.12	18.11	J1	C11	Ox
4.10	6. 9	G11	B12	Tapir	15.12	19.11	J1	D12	Bat
5.10	7. 9	G11	C1	Sheep	16.12	20.11	J1	E1	Rat
6.10	8. 9	G11	D2	Deer	17.12	21.11	J1	F2	Swallow
7.10	9. 9	G11	E3	Horse	18.12	22.11	J1	G3	Pig
8.10	10. 9	G11	F4	Stag	19.12	23.11	J1	H4	Porcupine
9.10	11. 9	G11	G5	Serpent	20.12	24.11	J1	J5	Wolf
10.10	12. 9	G11	H6	Earthworm	21.12	25.11	J1	K6	Dog
11.10	13. 9	G11	J7	Crocodile	22.12	26.11	J1	A7	Pheasant
12.10	14. 9	G11	K8	Dragon	23.12	27.11	J1	B8	Cock
13.10	15. 9	G11	A9	Badger	24.12	28.11	J1	C9	Crow
14.10	16. 9	G11	B10	Hare	25.12	29.11	J1	D10	Monkey
15.10	17. 9	G11	C11	Fox	26.12	30.11	J1	E11	Gibbon
16.10	18. 9	G11	D12	Tiger	27.12	1.12	K2	F12	Tapir
17.10	19. 9	G11	E1	Leopard	28.12	2.12	K2	G1	Sheep
18.10	20. 9	G11	F2	Griffon	29.12	3.12	K2	H2	Deer
19.10	21. 9	G11	G3	Ox	30.12	4.12	K2	J3	Horse
20.10	22. 9	G11	H4	Bat	31.12	5.12	K2	K4	Stag
21.10	23. 9	G11	J5	Rat					
22.10	24. 9	G11	K6	Swallow	**1963**				
23.10	25. 9	G11	A7	Pig	1. 1	6.12	K2	A5	Serpent
24.10	26. 9	G11	B8	Porcupine	2. 1	7.12	K2	B6	Earthworm
25.10	27. 9	G11	C9	Wolf	3. 1	8.12	K2	C7	Crocodile
26.10	28. 9	G11	D10	Dog	4. 1	9.12	K2	D8	Dragon
27.10	29. 9	G11	E11	Pheasant	5. 1	10.12	K2	E9	Badger
28.10	1.10	H12	F12	Cock	6. 1	11.12	K2	F10	Hare
29.10	2.10	H12	G1	Crow	7. 1	12.12	K2	G11	Fox
30.10	3.10	H12	H2	Monkey	8. 1	13.12	K2	H12	Tiger
31.10	4.10	H12	J3	Gibbon	9. 1	14.12	K2	J1	Leopard
1.11	5.10	H12	K4	Tapir	10. 1	15.12	K2	K2	Griffon
2.11	6.10	H12	A5	Sheep	11. 1	16.12	K2	A3	Ox
3.11	7.10	H12	B6	Deer	12. 1	17.12	K2	B4	Bat
4.11	8.10	H12	C7	Horse	13. 1	18.12	K2	C5	Rat
5.11	9.10	H12	D8	Stag	14. 1	19.12	K2	D6	Swallow
6.11	10.10	H12	E9	Serpent	15. 1	20.12	K2	E7	Pig
7.11	11.10	H12	F10	Earthworm	16. 1	21.12	K2	F8	Porcupine
8.11	12.10	H12	G11	Crocodile	17. 1	22.12	K2	G9	Wolf
9.11	13.10	H12	H12	Dragon	18. 1	23.12	K2	H10	Dog
10.11	14.10	H12	J1	Badger	19. 1	24.12	K2	J11	Pheasant
11.11	15.10	H12	K2	Hare	20. 1	25.12	K2	K12	Cock
12.11	16.10	H12	A3	Fox	21. 1	26.12	K2	A1	Crow
13.11	17.10	H12	B4	Tiger	22. 1	27.12	K2	B2	Monkey
14.11	18.10	H12	C5	Leopard	23. 1	28.12	K2	C3	Gibbon
15.11	19.10	H12	D6	Griffon	24. 1	29.12	K2	D4	Tapir

KUEI MAO YEAR

Solar date	Lunar date	Month HS/EB	Day HS/EB	Constellation
25. 1	1. 1	A3	E5	Sheep
26. 1	2. 1	A3	F6	Deer
27. 1	3. 1	A3	G7	Horse
28. 1	4. 1	A3	H8	Stag
29. 1	5. 1	A3	J9	Serpent
30. 1	6. 1	A3	K10	Earthworm
31. 1	7. 1	A3	A11	Crocodile
1. 2	8. 1	A3	B12	Dragon
2. 2	9. 1	A3	C1	Badger
3. 2	10. 1	A3	D2	Hare
4. 2	11. 1	A3	E3	Fox
5. 2	12. 1	A3	F4	Tiger
6. 2	13. 1	A3	G5	Leopard
7. 2	14. 1	A3	H6	Griffon
8. 2	15. 1	A3	J7	Ox
9. 2	16. 1	A3	K8	Bat
10. 2	17. 1	A3	A9	Rat
11. 2	18. 1	A3	B10	Swallow
12. 2	19. 1	A3	C1	Pig
13. 2	20. 1	A3	D12	Porcupine
14. 2	21. 1	A3	E1	Wolf
15. 2	22. 1	A3	F2	Dog
16. 2	23. 1	A3	G3	Pheasant
17. 2	24. 1	A3	H4	Cock
18. 2	25. 1	A3	J5	Crow
19. 2	26. 1	A3	K6	Monkey
20. 2	27. 1	A3	A7	Gibbon
21. 2	28. 1	A3	B8	Tapir
22. 2	29. 1	A3	C9	Sheep
23. 2	30. 1	A3	D10	Deer
24. 2	1. 2	B4	E11	Horse
25. 2	2. 2	B4	F12	Stag
26. 2	3. 2	B4	G1	Serpent
27. 2	4. 2	B4	H2	Earthworm
28. 2	5. 2	B4	J3	Crocodile
1. 3	6. 2	B4	K4	Dragon
2. 3	7. 2	B4	A5	Badger
3. 3	8. 2	B4	B6	Hare
4. 3	9. 2	B4	C7	Fox
5. 3	10. 2	B4	D8	Tiger
6. 3	11. 2	B4	E9	Leopard
7. 3	12. 2	B4	F10	Griffon
8. 3	13. 2	B4	G11	Ox
9. 3	14. 2	B4	H12	Bat
10. 3	15. 2	B4	J1	Rat
11. 3	16. 2	B4	K2	Swallow
12. 3	17. 2	B4	A3	Pig
13. 3	18. 2	B4	B4	Porcupine
14. 3	19. 2	B4	C5	Wolf
15. 3	20. 2	B4	D6	Dog
16. 3	21. 2	B4	E7	Pheasant
17. 3	22. 2	B4	F8	Cock
18. 3	23. 2	B4	G9	Crow
19. 3	24. 2	B4	H10	Monkey
20. 3	25. 2	B4	J11	Gibbon
21. 3	26. 2	B4	K12	Tapir
22. 3	27. 2	B4	A1	Sheep
23. 3	28. 2	B4	B2	Deer
24. 3	29. 2	B4	C3	Horse
25. 3	1. 3	C5	D4	Stag
26. 3	2. 3	C5	E5	Serpent
27. 3	3. 3	C5	F6	Earthworm
28. 3	4. 3	C5	G7	Crocodile
29. 3	5. 3	C5	H8	Dragon
30. 3	6. 3	C5	J9	Badger
31. 3	7. 3	C5	K10	Hare
1. 4	8. 3	C5	A11	Fox
2. 4	9. 3	C5	B12	Tiger
3. 4	10. 3	C5	C1	Leopard
4. 4	11. 3	C5	D2	Griffon
5. 4	12. 3	C5	E3	Ox
6. 4	13. 3	C5	F4	Bat
7. 4	14. 3	C5	G5	Rat
8. 4	15. 3	C5	H6	Swallow
9. 4	16. 3	C5	J7	Pig
10. 4	17. 3	C5	K8	Porcupine
11. 4	18. 3	C5	A9	Wolf
12. 4	19. 3	C5	B10	Dog
13. 4	20. 3	C5	C11	Pheasant
14. 4	21. 3	C5	D12	Cock
15. 4	22. 3	C5	E1	Crow
16. 4	23. 3	C5	F2	Monkey
17. 4	24. 3	C5	G3	Gibbon
18. 4	25. 3	C5	H4	Tapir
19. 4	26. 3	C5	J5	Sheep
20. 4	27. 3	C5	K6	Deer
21. 4	28. 3	C5	A7	Horse
22. 4	29. 3	C5	B8	Stag
23. 4	30. 3	C5	C9	Serpent
24. 4	1. 4	D6	D10	Earthworm
25. 4	2. 4	D6	E11	Crocodile
26. 4	3. 4	D6	F12	Dragon
27. 4	4. 4	D6	G1	Badger
28. 4	5. 4	D6	H2	Hare
29. 4	6. 4	D6	J3	Fox
30. 4	7. 4	D6	K4	Tiger
1. 5	8. 4	D6	A5	Leopard
2. 5	9. 4	D6	B6	Griffon
3. 5	10. 4	D6	C7	Ox
4. 5	11. 4	D6	D8	Bat
5. 5	12. 4	D6	E9	Rat
6. 5	13. 4	D6	F10	Swallow
7. 5	14. 4	D6	G11	Pig
8. 5	15. 4	D6	H12	Porcupine
9. 5	16. 4	D6	J1	Wolf
10. 5	17. 4	D6	K2	Dog
11. 5	18. 4	D6	A3	Pheasant
12. 5	19. 4	D6	B4	Cock
13. 5	20. 4	D6	C5	Crow
14. 5	21. 4	D6	D6	Monkey
15. 5	22. 4	D6	E7	Gibbon
16. 5	23. 4	D6	F8	Tapir
17. 5	24. 4	D6	G9	Sheep
18. 5	25. 4	D6	H10	Deer
19. 5	26. 4	D6	J11	Horse
20. 5	27. 4	D6	K12	Stag
21. 5	28. 4	D6	A1	Serpent
22. 5	29. 4	D6	B2	Earthworm
23. 5	*1. 4'*	*D6*	C3	Crocodile
24. 5	*2. 4'*	*D6*	D4	Dragon
25. 5	*3. 4'*	*D6*	E5	Badger
26. 5	*4. 4'*	*D6*	F6	Hare
27. 5	*5. 4'*	*D6*	G7	Fox
28. 5	*6. 4'*	*D6*	H8	Tiger
29. 5	*7. 4'*	*D6*	J9	Leopard
30. 5	*8. 4'*	*D6*	K10	Griffon
31. 5	*9. 4'*	*D6*	A11	Ox
1. 6	*10. 4'*	*D6*	B12	Bat
2. 6	*11. 4'*	*D6*	C1	Rat
3. 6	*12. 4'*	*D6*	D2	Swallow
4. 6	*13. 4'*	*D6*	E3	Pig
5. 6	*14. 4'*	*D6*	F4	Porcupine
6. 6	*15. 4'*	*D6*	G5	Wolf
7. 6	*16. 4'*	*D6*	H6	Dog
8. 6	*17. 4'*	*D6*	J7	Pheasant
9. 6	*18. 4'*	*D6*	K8	Cock
10. 6	*19. 4'*	*D6*	A9	Crow
11. 6	*20. 4'*	*D6*	B10	Monkey
12. 6	*21. 4'*	*D6*	C11	Gibbon
13. 6	*22. 4'*	*D6*	D12	Tapir
14. 6	*23. 4'*	*D6*	E1	Sheep
15. 6	*24. 4'*	*D6*	F2	Deer

Solar date	Lunar date	Month HS/EB	Day HS/EB	Constellation
16. 6	25. 4	D6	G3	Horse
17. 6	26. 4	D6	H4	Stag
18. 6	27. 4	D6	J5	Serpent
19. 6	28. 4	D6	K6	Earthworm
20. 6	29. 4	D6	A7	Crocodile
21. 6	1. 5	E7	B8	Dragon
22. 6	2. 5	E7	C9	Badger
23. 6	3. 5	E7	D10	Hare
24. 6	4. 5	E7	E11	Fox
25. 6	5. 5	E7	F12	Tiger
26. 6	6. 5	E7	G1	Leopard
27. 6	7. 5	E7	H2	Griffon
28. 6	8. 5	E7	J3	Ox
29. 6	9. 5	E7	K4	Bat
30. 6	10. 5	E7	A5	Rat
1. 7	11. 5	E7	B6	Swallow
2. 7	12. 5	E7	C7	Pig
3. 7	13. 5	E7	D8	Porcupine
4. 7	14. 5	E7	E9	Wolf
5. 7	15. 5	E7	F10	Dog
6. 7	16. 5	E7	G11	Pheasant
7. 7	17. 5	E7	H12	Cock
8. 7	18. 5	E7	J1	Crow
9. 7	19. 5	E7	K2	Monkey
10. 7	20. 5	E7	A3	Gibbon
11. 7	21. 5	E7	B4	Tapir
12. 7	22. 5	E7	C5	Sheep
13. 7	23. 5	E7	D6	Deer
14. 7	24. 5	E7	E7	Horse
15. 7	25. 5	E7	F8	Stag
16. 7	26. 5	E7	G9	Serpent
17. 7	27. 5	E7	H10	Earthworm
18. 7	28. 5	E7	J11	Crocodile
19. 7	29. 5	E7	K12	Dragon
20. 7	30. 5	E7	A1	Badger
21. 7	1. 6	F8	B2	Hare
22. 7	2. 6	F8	C3	Fox
23. 7	3. 6	F8	D4	Tiger
24. 7	4. 6	F8	E5	Leopard
25. 7	5. 6	F8	F6	Griffon
26. 7	6. 6	F8	G7	Ox
27. 7	7. 6	F8	H8	Bat
28. 7	8. 6	F8	J9	Rat
29. 7	9. 6	F8	K10	Swallow
30. 7	10. 6	F8	A11	Pig
31. 7	11. 6	F8	B12	Porcupine
1. 8	12. 6	F8	C1	Wolf
2. 8	13. 6	F8	D2	Dog
3. 8	14. 6	F8	E3	Pheasant
4. 8	15. 6	F8	F4	Cock
5. 8	16. 6	F8	G5	Crow
6. 8	17. 6	F8	H6	Monkey
7. 8	18. 6	F8	J7	Gibbon
8. 8	19. 6	F8	K8	Tapir
9. 8	20. 6	F8	A9	Sheep
10. 8	21. 6	F8	B10	Deer
11. 8	22. 6	F8	C11	Horse
12. 8	23. 6	F8	D12	Stag
13. 8	24. 6	F8	E1	Serpent
14. 8	25. 6	F8	F2	Earthworm
15. 8	26. 6	F8	G3	Crocodile
16. 8	27. 6	F8	H4	Dragon
17. 8	28. 6	F8	J5	Badger
18. 8	29. 6	F8	K6	Hare
19. 8	1. 7	G9	A7	Fox
20. 8	2. 7	G9	B8	Tiger
21. 8	3. 7	G9	C9	Leopard
22. 8	4. 7	G9	D10	Griffon
23. 8	5. 7	G9	E11	Ox
24. 8	6. 7	G9	F12	Bat
25. 8	7. 7	G9	G1	Rat
26. 8	8. 7	G9	H2	Swallow
27. 8	9. 7	G9	J3	Pig
28. 8	10. 7	G9	K4	Porcupine
29. 8	11. 7	G9	A5	Wolf
30. 8	12. 7	G9	B6	Dog
31. 8	13. 7	G9	C7	Pheasant
1. 9	14. 7	G9	D8	Cock
2. 9	15. 7	G9	E9	Crow
3. 9	16. 7	G9	F10	Monkey
4. 9	17. 7	G9	G11	Gibbon
5. 9	18. 7	G9	H12	Tapir
6. 9	19. 7	G9	J1	Sheep
7. 9	20. 7	G9	K2	Deer
8. 9	21. 7	G9	A3	Horse
9. 9	22. 7	G9	B4	Stag
10. 9	23. 7	G9	C5	Serpent
11. 9	24. 7	G9	D6	Earthworm
12. 9	25. 7	G9	E7	Crocodile
13. 9	26. 7	G9	F8	Dragon
14. 9	27. 7	G9	G9	Badger
15. 9	28. 7	G9	H10	Hare
16. 9	29. 7	G9	J11	Fox
17. 9	30. 7	G9	K12	Tiger
18. 9	1. 8	H10	A1	Leopard
19. 9	2. 8	H10	B2	Griffon
20. 9	3. 8	H10	C3	Ox
21. 9	4. 8	H10	D4	Bat
22. 9	5. 8	H10	E5	Rat
23. 9	6. 8	H10	F6	Swallow
24. 9	7. 8	H10	G7	Pig
25. 9	8. 8	H10	H8	Porcupine
26. 9	9. 8	H10	J9	Wolf
27. 9	10. 8	H10	K10	Dog
28. 9	11. 8	H10	A11	Pheasant
29. 9	12. 8	H10	B12	Cock
30. 9	13. 8	H10	C1	Crow
1.10	14. 8	H10	D2	Monkey
2.10	15. 8	H10	E3	Gibbon
3.10	16. 8	H10	F4	Tapir
4.10	17. 8	H10	G5	Sheep
5.10	18. 8	H10	H6	Deer
6.10	19. 8	H10	J7	Horse
7.10	20. 8	H10	K8	Stag
8.10	21. 8	H10	A9	Serpent
9.10	22. 8	H10	B10	Earthworm
10.10	23. 8	H10	C11	Crocodile
11.10	24. 8	H10	D12	Dragon
12.10	25. 8	H10	E1	Badger
13.10	26. 8	H10	F2	Hare
14.10	27. 8	H10	G3	Fox
15.10	28. 8	H10	H4	Tiger
16.10	29. 8	H10	J5	Leopard
17.10	1. 9	J11	K6	Griffon
18.10	2. 9	J11	A7	Ox
19.10	3. 9	J11	B8	Bat
20.20	4. 9	J11	C9	Rat
21.10	5. 9	J11	D10	Swallow
22.10	6. 9	J11	E11	Pig
23.10	7. 9	J11	F12	Porcupine
24.10	8. 9	J11	G1	Wolf
25.10	9. 9	J11	H2	Dog
26.10	10. 9	J11	J3	Pheasant
27.10	11. 9	J11	K4	Cock
28.10	12. 9	J11	A5	Crow
29.10	13. 9	J11	B6	Monkey
30.10	14. 9	J11	C7	Gibbon
31.10	15. 9	J11	D8	Tapir
1.11	16. 9	J11	E9	Sheep
2.11	17. 9	J11	F10	Deer
3.11	18. 9	J11	G11	Horse
4.11	19. 9	J11	H12	Stag
5.11	20. 9	J11	J1	Serpent
6.11	21. 9	J11	K2	Earthworm
7.11	22. 9	J11	A3	Crocodile
8.11	23. 9	J11	B4	Dragon

Solar date	Lunar date	Month HS/EB	Day HS/EB	Constellation	Solar date	Lunar date	Month HS/EB	Day HS/EB	Constellation
9.11	24. 9	J11	C5	Badger	28.12	13.11	A1	B6	Deer
10.11	25. 9	J11	D6	Hare	29.12	14.11	A1	C7	Horse
11.11	26. 9	J11	E7	Fox	30.12	15.11	A1	D8	Stag
12.11	27. 9	J11	F8	Tiger	31.12	16.11	A1	E9	Serpent
13.11	28. 9	J11	G9	Leopard	**1964**				
14.11	29. 9	J11	H10	Griffon	1. 1	17.11	A1	F10	Earthworm
15.11	30. 9	J11	J11	Ox	2. 1	18.11	A1	G11	Crocodile
16.11	1.10	K12	K12	Bat	3. 1	19.11	A1	H12	Dragon
17.11	2.10	K12	A1	Rat	4. 1	20.11	A1	J1	Badger
18.11	3.10	K12	B2	Swallow	5. 1	21.11	A1	K2	Hare
19.11	4.10	K12	C3	Pig	6. 1	22.11	A1	A3	Fox
20.11	5.10	K12	D4	Porcupine	7. 1	23.11	A1	B4	Tiger
21.11	6.10	K12	E5	Wolf	8. 1	24.11	A1	C5	Leopard
22.11	7.10	K12	F6	Dog	9. 1	25.11	A1	D6	Griffon
23.11	8.10	K12	G7	Pheasant	10. 1	26.11	A1	E7	Ox
24.11	9.10	K12	H8	Cock	11. 1	27.11	A1	F8	Bat
25.11	10.10	K12	J9	Crow	12. 1	28.11	A1	G9	Rat
26.11	11.10	K12	K10	Monkey	13. 1	29.11	A1	H10	Swallow
27.11	12.10	K12	A11	Gibbon	14. 1	30.11	A1	J11	Pig
28.11	13.10	K12	B12	Tapir	15. 1	1.12	B2	K12	Porcupine
29.11	14.10	K12	C1	Sheep	16. 1	2.12	B2	A1	Wolf
30.11	15.10	K12	D2	Deer	17. 1	3.12	B2	B2	Dog
1.12	16.10	K12	E3	Horse	18. 1	4.12	B2	C3	Pheasant
2.12	17.10	K12	F4	Stag	19. 1	5.12	B2	D4	Cock
3.12	18.10	K12	G5	Serpent	20. 1	6.12	B2	E5	Crow
4.12	19.10	K12	H6	Earthworm	21. 1	7.12	B2	F6	Monkey
5.12	20.20	K12	J7	Crocodile	22. 1	8.12	B2	G7	Gibbon
6.12	21.10	K12	K8	Dragon	23. 1	9.12	B2	H8	Tapir
7.12	22.10	K12	A9	Badger	24. 1	10.12	B2	J9	Sheep
8.12	23.10	K12	B10	Hare	25. 1	11.12	B2	K10	Deer
9.12	24.10	K12	C11	Fox	26. 1	12.12	B2	A11	Horse
10.12	25.10	K12	D12	Tiger	27. 1	13.12	B2	B12	Stag
11.12	26.10	K12	E1	Leopard	28. 1	14.12	B2	C1	Serpent
12.12	27.10	K12	F2	Griffon	29. 1	15.12	B2	D2	Earthworm
13.12	28.10	K12	G3	Ox	30. 1	16.12	B2	E3	Crocodile
14.12	29.10	K12	H4	Bat	31. 1	17.12	B2	F4	Dragon
15.12	30.10	K12	J5	Rat	1. 2	18.12	B2	G5	Badger
16.12	1.11	A1	K6	Swallow	2. 2	19.12	B2	H6	Hare
17.12	2.11	A1	A7	Pig	3. 2	20.12	B2	J7	Fox
18.12	3.11	A1	B8	Porcupine	4. 2	21.12	B2	K8	Tiger
19.12	4.11	A1	C9	Wolf	5. 2	22.12	B2	A9	Leopard
20.12	5.11	A1	D10	Dog	6. 2	23.12	B2	B10	Griffon
21.12	6.11	A1	E11	Pheasant	7. 2	24.12	B2	C11	Ox
22.12	7.11	A1	F12	Cock	8. 2	25.12	B2	D12	Bat
23.12	8.11	A1	G1	Crow	9. 2	26.12	B2	E1	Rat
24.12	9.11	A1	H2	Monkey	10. 2	27.12	B2	F2	Swallow
25.12	10.11	A1	J3	Gibbon	11. 2	28.12	B2	G3	Pig
26.12	11.11	A1	K4	Tapir	12. 2	29.12	B2	H4	Porcupine
27.12	12.11	A1	A5	Sheep					

CHIA CH'EN YEAR

Solar date	Lunar date	Month HS/EB	Day HS/EB	Constellation	Solar date	Lunar date	Month HS/EB	Day HS/EB	Constellation
13. 2	1. 1	C3	J5	Wolf	3. 3	20. 1	C3	H12	Tiger
14. 2	2. 1	C3	K6	Dog	4. 3	21. 1	C3	J1	Leopard
15. 2	3. 1	C3	A7	Pheasant	5. 3	22. 1	C3	K2	Griffon
16. 2	4. 1	C3	B8	Cock	6. 3	23. 1	C3	A3	Ox
17. 2	5. 1	C3	C9	Crow	7. 3	24. 1	C3	B4	Bat
18. 2	6. 1	C3	D10	Monkey	8. 3	25. 1	C3	C5	Rat
19. 2	7. 1	C3	E11	Gibbon	9. 3	26. 1	C3	D6	Swallow
20. 2	8. 1	C3	F12	Tapir	10. 3	27. 1	C3	E7	Pig
21. 2	9. 1	C3	G1	Sheep	11. 3	28. 1	C3	F8	Porcupine
22. 2	10. 1	C3	H2	Deer	12. 3	29. 1	C3	G9	Wolf
23. 2	11. 1	C3	J3	Horse	13. 3	30. 1	C3	H10	Dog
24. 2	12. 1	C3	K4	Stag	14. 3	1. 2	D4	J11	Pheasant
25. 2	13. 1	C3	A5	Serpent	15. 3	2. 2	D4	K12	Cock
26. 2	14. 1	C3	B6	Earthworm	16. 3	3. 2	D4	A1	Crow
27. 2	15. 1	C3	C7	Crocodile	17. 3	4. 2	D4	B2	Monkey
28. 2	16. 1	C3	D8	Dragon	18. 3	5. 2	D4	C3	Gibbon
29. 2	17. 1	C3	E9	Badger	19. 3	6. 2	D4	D4	Tapir
1. 3	18. 1	C3	F10	Hare	20. 3	7. 2	D4	E5	Sheep
2. 3	19. 1	C3	G11	Fox	21. 3	8. 2	D4	F6	Deer

Solar date	Lunar date	Month HS/EB	Day HS/EB	Constellation	Solar date	Lunar date	Month HS/EB	Day HS/EB	Constellation
22. 3	9. 2	D4	G7	Horse	3. 6	23. 4	F6	K8	Porcupine
23. 3	10. 2	D4	H8	Stag	4. 6	24. 4	F6	A9	Wolf
24. 3	11. 2	D4	J9	Serpent	5. 6	25. 4	F6	B10	Dog
25. 3	12. 2	D4	K10	Earthworm	6. 6	26. 4	F6	C11	Pheasant
26. 3	13. 2	D4	A11	Crocodile	7. 6	27. 4	F6	D12	Cock
27. 3	14. 2	D4	B12	Dragon	8. 6	28. 4	F6	E1	Crow
28. 3	15. 2	D4	C1	Badger	9. 6	29. 4	F6	F2	Monkey
29. 3	16. 2	D4	D2	Hare	10. 6	1. 5	G7	G3	Gibbon
30. 3	17. 2	D4	E3	Fox	11. 6	2. 5	G7	H4	Tapir
31. 3	18. 2	D4	F4	Tiger	12. 6	3. 5	G7	J5	Sheep
1. 4	19. 2	D4	G5	Leopard	13. 6	4. 5	G7	K6	Deer
2. 4	20. 2	D4	H6	Griffon	14. 6	5. 5	G7	A7	Horse
3. 4	21. 2	D4	J7	Ox	15. 6	6. 5	G7	B8	Stag
4. 4	22. 2	D4	K8	Bat	16. 6	7. 5	G7	C9	Serpent
5. 4	23. 2	D4	A9	Rat	17. 6	8. 5	G7	D10	Earthworm
6. 4	24. 2	D4	B10	Swallow	18. 6	9. 5	G7	E11	Crocodile
7. 4	25. 2	D4	C11	Pig	19. 6	10. 5	G7	F12	Dragon
8. 4	26. 2	D4	D12	Porcupine	20. 6	11. 5	G7	G1	Badger
9. 4	27. 2	D4	E1	Wolf	21. 6	12. 5	G7	H2	Hare
10. 4	28. 2	D4	F2	Dog	22. 6	13. 5	G7	J3	Fox
11. 4	29. 2	D4	G3	Pheasant	23. 6	14. 5	G7	K4	Tiger
12. 4	1. 3	E5	H4	Cock	24. 6	15. 5	G7	A5	Leopard
13. 4	2. 3	E5	J5	Crow	25. 6	16. 5	G7	B6	Griffon
14. 4	3. 3	E5	K6	Monkey	26. 6	17. 5	G7	C7	Ox
15. 4	4. 3	E5	A7	Gibbon	27. 6	18. 5	G7	D8	Bat
16. 4	5. 3	E5	B8	Tapir	28. 6	19. 5	G7	E9	Rat
17. 4	6. 3	E5	C9	Sheep	29. 6	20. 5	G7	F10	Swallow
18. 4	7. 3	E5	D10	Deer	30. 6	21. 5	G7	G11	Pig
19. 4	8. 3	E5	E11	Horse	1. 7	22. 5	G7	H12	Porcupine
20. 4	9. 3	E5	F12	Stag	2. 7	23. 5	G7	J1	Wolf
21. 4	10. 3	E5	G1	Serpent	3. 7	24. 5	G7	K2	Dog
22. 4	11. 3	E5	H2	Earthworm	4. 7	25. 5	G7	A3	Pheasant
23. 4	12. 3	E5	J3	Crocodile	5. 7	26. 5	G7	B4	Cock
24. 4	13. 3	E5	K4	Dragon	6. 7	27. 5	G7	C5	Crow
25. 4	14. 3	E5	A5	Badger	7. 7	28. 5	G7	D6	Monkey
26. 4	15. 3	E5	B6	Hare	8. 7	29. 5	G7	E7	Gibbon
27. 4	16. 3	E5	C7	Fox	9. 7	1. 6	H8	F8	Tapir
28. 4	17. 3	E5	D8	Tiger	10. 7	2. 6	H8	G9	Sheep
29. 4	18. 3	E5	E9	Leopard	11. 7	3. 6	H8	H10	Deer
30. 4	19. 3	E5	F10	Griffon	12. 7	4. 6	H8	J11	Horse
1. 5	20. 3	E5	G11	Ox	13. 7	5. 6	H8	K12	Stag
2. 5	21. 3	E5	H12	Bat	14. 7	6. 6	H8	A1	Serpent
3. 5	22. 3	E5	J1	Rat	15. 7	7. 6	H8	B2	Earthworm
4. 5	23. 3	E5	K2	Swallow	16. 7	8. 6	H8	C3	Crocodile
5. 5	24. 3	E5	A3	Pig	17. 7	9. 6	H8	D4	Dragon
6. 4	25. 3	E5	B4	Porcupine	18. 7	10. 6	H8	E5	Badger
7. 5	26. 3	E5	C5	Wolf	19. 7	11. 6	H8	F6	Hare
8. 5	27. 3	E5	D6	Dog	20. 7	12. 6	H8	G7	Fox
9. 5	28. 3	E5	E7	Pheasant	21. 7	13. 6	H8	H8	Tiger
10. 5	29. 3	E5	F8	Cock	22. 7	14. 6	H8	J9	Leopard
11. 5	30. 3	E5	G9	Crow	23. 7	15. 6	H8	K10	Griffon
12. 5	1. 4	F6	H10	Monkey	24. 7	16. 6	H8	A11	Ox
13. 5	2. 4	F6	J11	Gibbon	25. 7	17. 6	H8	B12	Bat
14. 5	3. 4	F6	K12	Tapir	26. 7	18. 6	H8	C1	Rat
15. 5	4. 4	F6	A1	Sheep	27. 7	19. 6	H8	D2	Swallow
16. 5	5. 4	F6	B2	Deer	28. 7	20. 6	H8	E3	Pig
17. 5	6. 4	F6	C3	Horse	29. 7	21. 6	H8	F4	Porcupine
18. 5	7. 4	F6	D4	Stag	30. 7	22. 6	H8	G5	Wolf
19. 5	8. 4	F6	E5	Serpent	31. 7	23. 6	H8	H6	Dog
20. 5	9. 4	F6	F6	Earthworm	1. 8	24. 6	H8	J7	Pheasant
21. 5	10. 4	F6	G7	Crocodile	2. 8	25. 6	H8	K8	Cock
22. 5	11. 4	F6	H8	Dragon	3. 8	26. 6	H8	A9	Crow
23. 5	12. 4	F6	J9	Badger	4. 8	27. 6	H8	B10	Monkey
24. 5	13. 4	F6	K10	Hare	5. 8	28. 6	H8	C11	Gibbon
25. 5	14. 4	F6	A11	Fox	6. 8	29. 6	H8	D12	Tapir
26. 5	15. 4	F6	B12	Tiger	7. 8	30. 6	H8	E1	Sheep
27. 5	16. 4	F6	C1	Leopard	8. 8	1. 7	J9	F2	Deer
28. 5	17. 4	F6	D2	Griffon	9. 8	2. 7	J9	G3	Horse
29. 5	18. 4	F6	E3	Ox	10. 8	3. 7	J9	H4	Stag
30. 5	19. 4	F6	F4	Bat	11. 8	4. 7	J9	J5	Serpent
31. 5	20. 4	F6	G5	Rat	12. 8	5. 7	J9	K6	Earthworm
1. 6	21. 4	F6	H6	Swallow	13. 8	6. 7	J9	A7	Crocodile
2. 6	22. 4	F6	J7	Pig	14. 8	7. 7	J9	B8	Dragon

Solar date	Lunar date	Month HS/EB	Day HS/EB	Constellation	Solar date	Lunar date	Month HS/EB	Day HS/EB	Constellation
15. 8	8. 7	J9	C9	Badger	27.10	22. 9	A11	F10	Monkey
16. 8	9. 7	J9	D10	Hare	28.10	23. 9	A11	G11	Gibbon
17. 8	10. 7	J9	E11	Fox	29.10	24. 9	A11	H12	Tapir
18. 8	11. 7	J9	F12	Tiger	30.10	25. 9	A11	J1	Sheep
19. 8	12. 7	J9	G1	Leopard	31.10	26. 9	A11	K2	Deer
20. 8	13. 7	J9	H2	Griffon	1.11	27. 9	A11	A3	Horse
21. 8	14. 7	J9	J3	Ox	2.11	28. 9	A11	B4	Stag
22. 8	15. 7	J9	K4	Bat	3.11	29. 9	A11	C5	Serpent
23. 8	16. 7	J9	A5	Rat	4.11	1.10	B12	D6	Earthworm
24. 8	17. 7	J9	B6	Swallow	5.11	2.10	B12	E7	Crocodile
25. 8	18. 7	J9	C7	Pig	6.11	3.10	B12	F8	Dragon
26. 8	19. 7	J9	D8	Porcupine	7.11	4.10	B12	G9	Badger
27. 8	20. 7	J9	E9	Wolf	8.11	5.10	B12	H10	Hare
28. 8	21. 7	J9	F10	Dog	9.11	6.10	B12	J11	Fox
29. 8	22. 7	J9	G11	Pheasant	10.11	7.10	B12	K12	Tiger
30. 8	23. 7	J9	H12	Cock	11.11	8.10	B12	A1	Leopard
31. 8	24. 7	J9	J1	Crow	12.11	9.10	B12	B2	Griffon
1. 9	25. 7	J9	K2	Monkey	13.11	10.10	B12	C3	Ox
2. 9	26. 7	J9	A3	Gibbon	14.11	11.10	B12	D4	Bat
3. 9	27. 7	J9	B4	Tapir	15.11	12.10	B12	E5	Rat
4. 9	28. 7	J9	C5	Sheep	16.11	13.10	B12	F6	Swallow
5. 9	29. 7	J9	D6	Deer	17.11	14.10	B12	G7	Pig
6. 9	1. 8	K10	E7	Horse	18.11	15.10	B12	H8	Porcupine
7. 9	2. 8	K10	F8	Stag	19.11	16.10	B12	J9	Wolf
8. 9	3. 8	K10	G9	Serpent	20.11	17.10	B12	K10	Dog
9. 9	4. 8	K10	H10	Earthworm	21.11	18.10	B12	A11	Pheasant
10. 9	5. 8	K10	J11	Crocodile	22.11	19.10	B12	B12	Cock
11. 9	6. 8	K10	K12	Dragon	23.11	20.10	B12	C1	Crow
12. 9	7. 8	K10	A1	Badger	24.11	21.10	B12	D2	Monkey
13. 9	8. 8	K10	B2	Hare	25.11	22.10	B12	E3	Gibbon
14. 9	9. 8	K10	C3	Fox	26.11	23.10	B12	F4	Tapir
15. 9	10. 8	K10	D4	Tiger	27.11	24.10	B12	G5	Sheep
16. 9	11. 8	K10	E5	Leopard	28.11	25.10	B12	H6	Deer
17. 9	12. 8	K10	F6	Griffon	29.11	26.10	B12	J7	Horse
18. 9	13. 8	K10	G7	Ox	30.11	27.10	B12	K8	Stag
19. 9	14. 8	K10	H8	Bat	1.12	28.10	B12	A9	Serpent
20. 9	15. 8	K10	J9	Rat	2.12	29.10	B12	B10	Earthworm
21. 9	16. 8	K10	K10	Swallow	3.12	30.10	B12	C11	Crocodile
22. 9	17. 8	K10	A11	Pig	4.12	1.11	C1	D12	Dragon
23. 9	18. 8	K10	B12	Porcupine	5.12	2.11	C1	E1	Badger
24. 9	19. 8	K10	C1	Wolf	6.12	3.11	C1	F2	Hare
25. 9	20. 8	K10	D2	Dog	7.12	4.11	C1	G3	Fox
26. 9	21. 8	K10	E3	Pheasant	8.12	5.11	C1	H4	Tiger
27. 9	22. 8	K10	F4	Cock	9.12	6.11	C1	J5	Leopard
28. 9	23. 8	K10	G5	Crow	10.12	7.11	C1	K6	Griffon
29. 9	24. 8	K10	H6	Monkey	11.12	8.11	C1	A7	Ox
30. 9	25. 8	K10	J7	Gibbon	12.12	9.11	C1	B8	Bat
1.10	26. 8	K10	K8	Tapir	13.12	10.11	C1	C9	Rat
2.10	27. 8	K10	A9	Sheep	14.12	11.11	C1	D10	Swallow
3.10	28. 8	K10	B10	Deer	15.12	12.11	C1	E11	Pig
4.10	29. 8	K10	C11	Horse	16.12	13.11	C1	F12	Porcupine
5.10	30. 8	K10	D12	Stag	17.12	14.11	C1	G1	Wolf
6.10	1. 9	A11	E1	Serpent	18.12	15.11	C1	H2	Dog
7.10	2. 9	A11	F2	Earthworm	19.12	16.11	C1	J3	Pheasant
8.10	3. 9	A11	G3	Crocodile	20.12	17.11	C1	K4	Cock
9.10	4. 9	A11	H4	Dragon	21.12	18.11	C1	A5	Crow
10.10	5. 9	A11	J5	Badger	22.12	19.11	C1	B6	Monkey
11.10	6. 9	A11	K6	Hare	23.12	20.11	C1	C7	Gibbon
12.10	7. 9	A11	A7	Fox	24.12	21.11	C1	D8	Tapir
13.10	8. 9	A11	B8	Tiger	25.12	22.11	C1	E9	Sheep
14.10	9. 9	A11	C9	Leopard	26.12	23.11	C1	F10	Deer
15.10	10. 9	A11	D10	Griffon	27.12	24.11	C1	G11	Horse
16.10	11. 9	A11	E11	Ox	28.12	25.11	C1	H12	Stag
17.10	12. 9	A11	F12	Bat	29.12	26.11	C1	J1	Serpent
18.10	13. 9	A11	G1	Rat	30.12	27.11	C1	K2	Earthworm
19.10	14. 9	A11	H2	Swallow	31.12	28.11	C1	A3	Crocodile
20.10	15. 9	A11	J3	Pig					
21.10	16. 9	A11	K4	Porcupine	**1965**				
22.10	17. 9	A11	A5	Wolf	1. 1	29.11	C1	B4	Dragon
23.10	18. 9	A11	B6	Dog	2. 1	30.11	C1	C5	Badger
24.10	19. 9	A11	C7	Pheasant	3. 1	1.12	D2	D6	Hare
25.10	20. 9	A11	D8	Cock	4. 1	2.12	D2	E7	Fox
26.10	21. 9	A11	E9	Crow	5. 1	3.12	D2	F8	Tiger

Solar date	Lunar date	Month HS/EB	Day HS/EB	Constellation	Solar date	Lunar date	Month HS/EB	Day HS/EB	Constellation
6. 1	4.12	D2	G9	Leopard	20. 1	18.12	D2	A11	Gibbon
7. 1	5.12	D2	H10	Griffon	21. 1	19.12	D2	B12	Tapir
8. 1	6.12	D2	J11	Ox	22. 1	20.12	D2	C1	Sheep
9. 1	7.12	D2	K12	Bat	23. 1	21.12	D2	D2	Deer
10. 1	8.12	D2	A1	Rat	24. 1	22.12	D2	E3	Horse
11. 1	9.12	D2	B2	Swallow	25. 1	23.12	D2	F4	Stag
12. 1	10.12	D2	C3	Pig	26. 1	24.12	D2	G5	Serpent
13. 1	11.12	D2	D4	Porcupine	27. 1	25.12	D2	H6	Earthworm
14. 1	12.12	D2	E5	Wolf	28. 1	26.12	D2	J7	Crocodile
15. 1	13.12	D2	F6	Dog	29. 1	27.12	D2	K8	Dragon
16. 1	14.12	D2	G7	Pheasant	30. 1	28.12	D2	A9	Badger
17. 1	15.12	D2	H8	Cock	31. 1	29.12	D2	B10	Hare
18. 1	16.12	D2	J9	Crow	1. 2	30.12	D2	C11	Fox
19. 1	17.12	D2	K10	Monkey					

YI SZU YEAR

Solar date	Lunar date	Month HS/EB	Day HS/EB	Constellation	Solar date	Lunar date	Month HS/EB	Day HS/EB	Constellation
2. 2	1. 1	E3	D12	Tiger	28. 3	26. 2	F4	H6	Hare
3. 2	2. 1	E3	E1	Leopard	29. 3	27. 2	F4	J7	Fox
4. 2	3. 1	E3	F2	Griffon	30. 3	28. 2	F4	K8	Tiger
5. 2	4. 1	E3	G3	Ox	31. 3	29. 2	F4	A9	Leopard
6. 2	5. 1	E3	H4	Bat	1. 4	30. 2	F4	B10	Griffon
7. 2	6. 1	E3	J5	Rat	2. 4	1. 3	G5	C11	Ox
8. 2	7. 1	E3	K6	Swallow	3. 4	2. 3	G5	D12	Bat
9. 2	8. 1	E3	A7	Pig	4. 4	3. 3	G5	E1	Rat
10. 2	9. 1	E3	B8	Porcupine	5. 4	4. 3	G5	F2	Swallow
11. 2	10. 1	E3	C9	Wolf	6. 4	5. 3	G5	G3	Pig
12. 2	11. 1	E3	D10	Dog	7. 4	6. 3	G5	H4	Porcupine
13. 2	12. 1	E3	E11	Pheasant	8. 4	7. 3	G5	J5	Wolf
14. 2	13. 1	E3	F12	Cock	9. 4	8. 3	G5	K6	Dog
15. 2	14. 1	E3	G1	Crow	10. 4	9. 3	G5	A7	Pheasant
16. 2	15. 1	E3	H2	Monkey	11. 4	10. 3	F5	B8	Cock
17. 2	16. 1	E3	J3	Gibbon	12. 4	11. 3	G5	C9	Crow
18. 2	17. 1	E3	K4	Tapir	13. 4	12. 3	G5	D10	Monkey
19. 2	18. 1	E3	A5	Sheep	14. 4	13. 3	G5	E11	Gibbon
20. 2	19. 1	E3	B6	Deer	15. 4	14. 3	G5	F12	Tapir
21. 2	20. 1	E3	C7	Horse	16. 4	15. 3	G5	G1	Sheep
22. 2	21. 1	E3	D8	Stag	17. 4	16. 3	G5	H2	Deer
23. 2	22. 1	E3	E9	Serpent	18. 4	17. 3	G5	J3	Horse
24. 2	23. 1	E3	F10	Earthworm	19. 4	18. 3	G5	K4	Stag
25. 2	24. 1	E3	G11	Crocodile	20. 4	19. 3	G5	A5	Serpent
26. 2	25. 1	E3	H12	Dragon	21. 4	20. 3	G5	B6	Earthworm
27. 2	26. 1	E3	J1	Badger	22. 4	21. 3	G5	C7	Crocodile
28. 2	27. 1	E3	K2	Hare	23. 4	22. 3	G5	D8	Dragon
1. 3	28. 1	E3	A3	Fox	24. 4	23. 3	G5	E9	Badger
2. 3	29. 1	E3	B4	Tiger	25. 4	24. 3	G5	F10	Hare
3. 3	1. 2	F4	C5	Leopard	26. 4	25. 3	G5	G11	Fox
4. 3	2. 2	F4	D6	Griffon	27. 4	26. 3	G5	H12	Tiger
5. 3	3. 2	F4	E7	Ox	28. 4	27. 3	G5	J1	Leopard
6. 3	4. 2	F4	F8	Bat	29. 4	28. 3	G5	K2	Griffon
7. 3	5. 2	F4	G9	Rat	30. 4	29. 3	G5	A3	Ox
8. 3	6. 2	F4	H10	Swallow	1. 5	1. 4	H6	B4	Bat
9. 3	7. 2	F4	J11	Pig	2. 5	2. 4	H6	C5	Rat
10. 3	8. 2	F4	K12	Porcupine	3. 5	3. 4	H6	D6	Swallow
11. 3	9. 2	F4	A1	Wolf	4. 5	4. 4	H6	E7	Pig
12. 3	10. 2	F4	B2	Dog	5. 5	5. 4	H6	F8	Porcupine
13. 3	11. 2	F4	C3	Pheasant	6. 5	6. 4	H6	G9	Wolf
14. 3	12. 2	F4	D4	Cock	7. 5	7. 4	H6	H10	Dog
15. 3	13. 2	F4	E5	Crow	8. 5	8. 4	H6	J11	Pheasant
16. 3	14. 2	F4	F6	Monkey	9. 5	9. 4	H6	K12	Cock
17. 3	15. 2	F4	G7	Gibbon	10. 5	10. 4	H6	A1	Crow
18. 3	16. 2	F4	H8	Tapir	11. 5	11. 4	H6	B2	Monkey
19. 3	17. 2	F4	J9	Sheep	12. 5	12. 4	H6	C3	Gibbon
20. 3	18. 2	F4	K10	Deer	13. 5	13. 4	H6	D4	Tapir
21. 3	19. 2	F4	A11	Horse	14. 5	14. 4	H6	E5	Sheep
22. 3	20. 2	F4	B12	Stag	15. 5	15. 4	H6	F6	Deer
23. 3	21. 2	F4	C1	Serpent	16. 5	16. 4	H6	G7	Horse
24. 3	22. 2	F4	D2	Earthworm	17. 5	17. 4	H6	H8	Stag
25. 3	23. 2	F4	E3	Crocodile	18. 5	18. 4	H6	J9	Serpent
26. 3	24. 2	F4	F4	Dragon	19. 5	19. 4	H6	K10	Earthworm
27. 3	25. 2	F4	G5	Badger	20. 5	20. 4	H6	A11	Crocodile

Solar date	Lunar date	Month HS/EB	Day HS/EB	Constellation	Solar date	Lunar date	Month HS/EB	Day HS/EB	Constellation
21. 5	21. 4	H6	B12	Dragon	2. 8	6. 7	A9	E1	Crow
22. 5	22. 4	H6	C1	Badger	3. 8	7. 7	A9	F2	Monkey
23. 5	23. 4	H6	D2	Hare	4. 8	8. 7	A9	G3	Gibbon
24. 5	24. 4	H6	E3	Fox	5. 8	9. 7	A9	H4	Tapir
25. 5	25. 4	H6	F4	Tiger	6. 8	10. 7	A9	J5	Sheep
26. 5	26. 4	H6	G5	Leopard	7. 8	11. 7	A9	K6	Deer
27. 5	27. 4	H6	H6	Griffon	8. 8	12. 7	A9	A7	Horse
28. 5	28. 4	H6	J7	Ox	9. 8	13. 7	A9	B8	Stag
29. 5	29. 4	H6	K8	Bat	10. 8	14. 7	A9	C9	Serpent
30. 5	30. 4	H6	A9	Rat	11. 8	15. 7	A9	D10	Earthworm
31. 5	1. 5	J7	B10	Swallow	12. 8	16. 7	A9	E11	Crocodile
1. 6	2. 5	J7	C11	Pig	13. 8	17. 7	A9	F12	Dragon
2. 6	3. 5	J7	D12	Porcupine	14. 8	18. 7	A9	G1	Badger
3. 6	4. 5	J7	E1	Wolf	15. 8	19. 7	A9	H2	Hare
4. 6	5. 5	J7	F2	Dog	16. 8	20. 7	A9	J3	Fox
5. 6	6. 5	J7	G3	Pheasant	17. 8	21. 7	A9	K4	Tiger
6. 6	7. 5	J7	H4	Cock	18. 8	22. 7	A9	A5	Leopard
7. 6	8. 5	J7	J5	Crow	19. 8	23. 7	A9	B6	Griffon
8. 6	9. 5	J7	K6	Monkey	20. 8	24. 7	A9	C7	Ox
9. 6	10. 5	J7	A7	Gibbon	21. 8	25. 7	A9	D8	Bat
10. 6	11. 5	J7	B8	Tapir	22. 8	26. 7	A9	E9	Rat
11. 6	12. 5	J7	C9	Sheep	23. 8	27. 7	A9	F10	Swallow
12. 6	13. 5	J7	D10	Deer	24. 8	28. 7	A9	G11	Pig
13. 6	14. 5	J7	E11	Horse	25. 8	29. 7	A9	H12	Porcupine
14. 6	15. 5	J7	F12	Stag	26. 8	30. 7	A9	J1	Wolf
15. 6	16. 5	J7	G1	Serpent	27. 8	1. 8	B10	K2	Dog
16. 6	17. 5	J7	H2	Earthworm	28. 8	2. 8	B10	A3	Pheasant
17. 6	18. 5	J7	J3	Crocodile	29. 8	3. 8	B10	B4	Cock
18. 6	19. 5	J7	K4	Dragon	30. 8	4. 8	B10	C5	Crow
19. 6	20. 5	J7	A5	Badger	31. 8	5. 8	B10	D6	Monkey
20. 6	21. 5	J7	B6	Hare	1. 9	6. 8	B10	E7	Gibbon
21. 6	22. 5	J7	C7	Fox	2. 9	7. 8	B10	F8	Tapir
22. 6	23. 5	J7	D8	Tiger	3. 9	8. 8	B10	G9	Sheep
23. 6	24. 5	J7	E9	Leopard	4. 9	9. 8	B10	H10	Deer
24. 6	25. 5	J7	F10	Griffon	5. 9	10. 8	B10	J11	Horse
25. 6	26. 5	J7	G11	Ox	6. 9	11. 8	B10	K12	Stag
26. 6	27. 5	J7	H12	Bat	7. 9	12. 8	B10	A1	Serpent
27. 6	28. 5	J7	J1	Rat	8. 9	13. 8	B10	B2	Earthworm
28. 6	29. 5	J7	K2	Swallow	9. 9	14. 8	B10	C3	Crocodile
29. 6	1. 6	K8	A3	Pig	10. 9	15. 8	B10	D4	Dragon
30. 6	2. 6	K8	B4	Porcupine	11. 9	16. 8	B10	E5	Badger
1. 7	3. 6	K8	C5	Wolf	12. 9	17. 8	B10	F6	Hare
2. 7	4. 6	K8	D6	Dog	13. 9	18. 8	B10	G7	Fox
3. 7	5. 6	K8	E7	Pheasant	14. 9	19. 8	B10	H8	Tiger
4. 7	6. 6	K8	F8	Cock	15. 9	20. 8	B10	J9	Leopard
5. 7	7. 6	K8	G9	Crow	16. 9	21. 8	B10	K10	Griffon
6. 7	8. 6	K8	H10	Monkey	17. 9	22. 8	B10	A11	Ox
7. 7	9. 6	K8	J11	Gibbon	18. 9	23. 8	B10	B12	Bat
8. 7	10. 6	K8	K12	Tapir	19. 9	24. 8	B10	C1	Rat
9. 7	11. 6	K8	A1	Sheep	20. 9	25. 8	B10	D2	Swallow
10. 7	12. 6	K8	B2	Deer	21. 9	26. 8	B10	E3	Pig
11. 7	13. 6	K8	C3	Horse	22. 9	27. 8	B10	F4	Porcupine
12. 7	14. 6	K8	D4	Stag	23. 9	28. 8	B10	G5	Wolf
13. 7	15. 6	K8	E5	Serpent	24. 9	29. 8	B10	H6	Dog
14. 7	16. 6	K8	F6	Earthworm	25. 9	1. 9	C11	J7	Pheasant
15. 7	17. 6	K8	G7	Crocodile	26. 9	2. 9	C11	K8	Cock
16. 7	18. 6	K8	H8	Dragon	27. 9	3. 9	C11	A9	Crow
17. 7	19. 6	K8	J9	Badger	28. 9	4. 9	C11	B10	Monkey
18. 7	20. 6	K8	K10	Hare	29. 9	5. 9	C11	C11	Gibbon
19. 7	21. 6	K8	A11	Fox	30. 9	6. 9	C11	D12	Tapir
20. 7	22. 6	K8	B12	Tiger	1. 10	7. 9	C11	E1	Sheep
21. 7	23. 6	K8	C1	Leopard	2. 10	8. 9	C11	F2	Deer
22. 7	24. 6	K8	D2	Griffon	3. 10	9. 9	C11	G3	Horse
23. 7	25. 6	K8	E3	Ox	4. 10	10. 9	C11	H4	Stag
24. 7	26. 6	K8	F4	Bat	5. 10	11. 9	C11	J5	Serpent
25. 7	27. 6	K8	G5	Rat	6. 10	12. 9	C11	K6	Earthworm
26. 7	28. 6	K8	H6	Swallow	7. 10	13. 9	C11	A7	Crocodile
27. 7	29. 6	K8	J7	Pig	8. 10	14. 9	C11	B8	Dragon
28. 7	1. 7	A9	K8	Porcupine	9. 10	15. 9	C11	C9	Badger
29. 7	2. 7	A9	A9	Wolf	10. 10	16. 9	C11	D10	Hare
30. 7	3. 7	A9	B10	Dog	11. 10	17. 9	C11	E11	Fox
31. 7	4. 7	A9	C11	Pheasant	12. 10	18. 9	C11	F12	Tiger
1. 8	5. 7	A9	D12	Cock	13. 10	19. 9	C11	G1	Leopard

Solar date	Lunar date	Month HS/EB	Day HS/EB	Constellation	Solar date	Lunar date	Month HS/EB	Day HS/EB	Constellation
14.10	20. 9	C11	H2	Griffon	4.12	12.11	E1	J5	Badger
15.10	21. 9	C11	J3	Ox	5.12	13.11	E1	K6	Hare
16. 0	22. 9	C11	K4	Bat	6.12	14.11	E1	A7	Fox
17. 0	23. 9	C11	A5	Rat	7.12	15.11	E1	B8	Tiger
18.10	24. 9	C11	B6	Swallow	8.12	16.11	E1	C9	Leopard
19.10	25. 9	C11	C7	Pig	9.12	17.11	E1	D10	Griffon
20.10	26. 9	C11	D8	Porcupine	10.12	18.11	E1	E11	Ox
21.10	27. 9	C11	E9	Wolf	11.12	19.11	E1	F12	Bat
22.10	28. 9	C11	F10	Dog	12.12	20.11	E1	G1	Rat
23.10	29. 9	C11	G11	Pheasant	13.12	21.11	E1	H2	Swallow
24.10	1.10	D12	H12	Cock	14.12	22.11	E1	J3	Pig
25.10	2.10	D12	J1	Crow	15.11	23.11	E1	K4	Porcupine
26.10	3.10	D12	K2	Monkey	16.12	24.11	E1	A5	Wolf
27.10	4.10	D12	A3	Gibbon	17.12	25.11	E1	B6	Dog
28.10	5.10	D12	B4	Tapir	18.11	26.11	E1	C7	Pheasant
29.10	6.10	D12	C5	Sheep	19.12	27.11	E1	D8	Cock
30.10	7.10	D12	D6	Deer	20.12	28.11	E1	E9	Crow
31.10	8.10	D12	E7	Horse	21.12	29.11	E1	F10	Monkey
1.11	9.10	D12	F8	Stag	22.12	30.11	E1	G11	Gibbon
2.11	10.10	D12	G9	Serpent	23.11	1.12	F2	H12	Tapir
3.11	11.10	D12	H10	Earthworm	24.12	2.12	F2	J1	Sheep
4.11	12.10	D12	J11	Crocodile	25.12	3.12	F2	K2	Deer
5.11	13.10	D12	K12	Dragon	26.12	4.12	F2	A3	Horse
6.11	14.10	D12	A1	Badger	27.12	5.12	F2	B4	Stag
7.11	15.10	D12	B2	Hare	28.12	6.12	F2	C5	Serpent
8.11	16.10	D12	C3	Fox	29.12	7.12	F2	D6	Earthworm
9.11	17.10	D12	D4	Tiger	30.12	8.12	F2	E7	Crocodile
10.11	18.10	D12	E5	Leopard	31.12	9.12	F2	F8	Dragon
11.11	19.10	D12	F6	Griffon					
12.11	20.10	D12	G7	Ox	**1966**				
13.11	21.10	D12	H8	Bat					
14.11	22.10	D12	J9	Rat	1. 1	10.12	F2	G9	Badger
15.11	23.10	D12	K10	Swallow	2. 1	11.12	F2	H10	Hare
16.11	24.10	D12	A11	Pig	3. 1	12.12	F2	J11	Fox
17.11	25.10	D12	B12	Porcupine	4. 1	13.12	F2	K12	Tiger
18.11	26.10	D12	C1	Wolf	5. 1	14.12	F2	A1	Leopard
19.11	27.10	D12	D2	Dog	6. 1	15.12	F2	B2	Griffon
20.11	28.10	D12	E3	Pheasant	7. 1	16.12	F2	C3	Ox
21.11	29.10	D12	F4	Cock	8. 1	17.12	F2	D4	Bat
22.11	30.10	D12	G5	Crow	9. 1	18.12	F2	E5	Rat
23.11	1.11	E1	H6	Monkey	10. 1	19.12	F2	F6	Swallow
24.11	2.11	E1	J7	Gibbon	11. 1	20.12	F2	G7	Pig
25.11	3.11	E1	K8	Tapir	12. 1	21.12	F2	H8	Porcupine
26.11	4.11	E1	A9	Sheep	13. 1	22.12	F2	J9	Wolf
27.11	5.11	E1	B10	Deer	14. 1	23.12	F2	K10	Dog
28.11	6.11	E1	C11	Horse	15. 1	24.12	F2	A11	Pheasant
29.11	7.11	E1	D12	Stag	16. 1	25.12	F2	B12	Cock
30.11	8.11	E1	E1	Serpent	17. 1	26.12	F2	C1	Crow
1.12	9.11	E1	F2	Earthworm	18. 1	27.12	F2	D2	Monkey
2.12	10.11	E1	G3	Crocodile	19. 1	28.12	F2	E3	Gibbon
3.12	11.11	E1	H4	Dragon	20. 1	29.12	F2	F4	Tapir

PING WU YEAR

Solar date	Lunar date	Month HS/EB	Day HS/EB	Constellation	Solar date	Lunar date	Month HS/EB	Day HS/EB	Constellation
21. 1	1. 1	G3	G5	Sheep	7. 2	18. 1	G3	D10	Swallow
22. 1	2. 1	G3	H6	Deer	8. 2	19. 1	G3	E11	Pig
23. 1	3. 1	G3	J7	Horse	9. 2	20. 1	G3	F12	Porcupine
24. 1	4. 1	G3	K8	Stag	10. 2	21. 1	G3	G1	Wolf
25. 1	5. 1	G3	A9	Serpent	11. 2	22. 1	G3	H2	Dog
26. 1	6. 1	G3	B10	Earthworm	12. 2	23. 1	G3	J3	Pheasant
27. 1	7. 1	G3	C11	Crocodile	13. 2	24. 1	G3	K4	Cock
28. 1	8. 1	G3	D12	Dragon	14. 2	25. 1	G3	A5	Crow
29. 1	9. 1	G3	E1	Badger	15. 2	26. 1	G3	B6	Monkey
30. 1	10. 1	G3	F2	Hare	16. 2	27. 1	G3	C7	Gibbon
31. 1	11. 1	G3	G3	Fox	17. 2	28. 1	G3	D8	Tapir
1. 2	12. 1	G3	H4	Tiger	18. 2	29. 1	G3	E9	Sheep
2. 2	13. 1	G3	J5	Leopard	19. 2	30. 1	G3	F10	Deer
3. 2	14. 1	G3	K6	Griffon	20. 2	1. 2	H4	G11	Horse
4. 2	15. 1	G3	A7	Ox	21. 2	2. 2	H4	H12	Stag
5. 2	16. 1	G3	B8	Bat	22. 2	3. 2	H4	J1	Serpent
6. 2	17. 1	G3	C9	Rat	23. 2	4. 2	H4	K2	Earthworm

Solar date	Lunar date	Month HS/EB	Day HS/EB	Constellation	Solar date	Lunar date	Month HS/EB	Day HS/EB	Constellation
24. 2	5. 2	H4	A3	Crocodile	8. 5	18. 3	J5	D4	Cock
25. 2	6. 2	H4	B4	Dragon	9. 5	19. 3	J5	E5	Crow
26. 2	7. 2	H4	C5	Badger	10. 5	20. 3	J5	F6	Monkey
27. 2	8. 2	H4	D6	Hare	11. 5	21. 3	J5	G7	Gibbon
28. 2	9. 2	H4	E7	Fox	12. 5	22. 3	J5	H8	Tapir
1. 3	10. 2	H4	F8	Tiger	13. 5	23. 3	J5	J9	Sheep
2. 3	11. 2	H4	G9	Leopard	14. 5	24. 3	J5	K10	Deer
3. 3	12. 2	H4	H10	Griffon	15. 5	25. 3	J5	A11	Horse
4. 3	13. 2	H4	J11	Ox	16. 5	26. 3	J5	B12	Stag
5. 3	14. 2	H4	K12	Bat	17. 5	27. 3	J5	C1	Serpent
6. 3	15. 2	H4	A1	Rat	18. 5	28. 3	J5	D2	Earthworm
7. 3	16. 2	H4	B2	Swallow	19. 5	29. 3	J5	E3	Crocodile
8. 3	17. 2	H4	C3	Pig	20. 5	1. 4	K6	F4	Dragon
9. 3	18. 2	H4	D4	Porcupine	21. 5	2. 4	K6	G5	Badger
10. 3	19. 2	H4	E5	Wolf	22. 5	3. 4	K6	H6	Hare
11. 3	20. 2	H4	F6	Dog	23. 5	4. 4	K6	J7	Fox
12. 3	21. 2	H4	G7	Pheasant	24. 5	5. 4	K6	K8	Tiger
13. 3	22. 2	H4	H8	Cock	25. 5	6. 4	K6	A9	Leopard
14. 3	23. 2	H4	J9	Crow	26. 5	7. 4	K6	B10	Griffon
15. 3	24. 2	H4	K10	Monkey	27. 5	8. 4	K6	C11	Ox
16. 3	25. 2	H4	A11	Gibbon	28. 5	9. 4	K6	D12	Bat
17. 3	26. 2	H4	B12	Tapir	29. 5	10. 4	K6	E1	Rat
18. 3	27. 2	H4	C1	Sheep	30. 5	11. 4	K6	F2	Swallow
19. 3	28. 2	H4	D2	Deer	31. 5	12. 4	K6	G3	Pig
20. 3	29. 2	H4	E3	Horse	1. 6	13. 4	K6	H4	Porcupine
21. 3	30. 2	H4	F4	Stag	2. 6	14. 4	K6	J5	Wolf
22. 3	1. 3	J5	G5	Serpent	3. 6	15. 4	K6	K6	Dog
23. 3	2. 3	J5	H6	Earthworm	4. 6	16. 4	K6	A7	Pheasant
24. 3	3. 3	J5	J7	Crocodile	5. 6	17. 4	K6	B8	Cock
25. 3	4. 3	J5	K8	Dragon	6. 6	18. 4	K6	C9	Crow
26. 3	5. 3	J5	A9	Badger	7. 6	19. 4	K6	D10	Monkey
27. 3	6. 3	J5	B10	Hare	8. 6	20. 4	K6	E11	Gibbon
28. 3	7. 3	J5	C11	Fox	9. 6	21. 4	K6	F12	Tapir
29. 3	8. 3	J5	D12	Tiger	10. 6	22. 4	K6	G1	Sheep
30. 3	9. 3	J5	E1	Leopard	11. 6	23. 4	K6	H2	Deer
31. 3	10. 3	J5	F2	Griffon	12. 6	24. 4	K6	J3	Horse
1. 4	11. 3	J5	G3	Ox	13. 6	25. 4	K6	K4	Stag
2. 4	12. 3	J5	H4	Bat	14. 6	26. 4	K6	A5	Serpent
3. 4	13. 3	J5	J5	Rat	15. 6	27. 4	K6	B6	Earthworm
4. 4	14. 3	J5	K6	Swallow	16. 6	28. 4	K6	C7	Crocodile
5. 4	15. 3	J5	A7	Pig	17. 6	29. 4	K6	D8	Dragon
6. 4	16. 3	J5	B8	Porcupine	18. 6	30. 4	K6	E9	Badger
7. 4	17. 3	J5	C9	Wolf	19. 6	1. 5	A7	F10	Hare
8. 4	18. 3	J5	D10	Dog	20. 6	2. 5	A7	G11	Fox
9. 4	19. 3	J5	E11	Pheasant	21. 6	3. 5	A7	H12	Tiger
10. 4	20. 3	J5	F12	Cock	22. 6	4. 5	A7	J1	Leopard
11. 4	21. 3	J5	G1	Crow	23. 6	5. 5	A7	K2	Griffon
12. 4	22. 3	J5	H2	Monkey	24. 6	6. 5	A7	A3	Ox
13. 4	23. 3	J5	J3	Gibbon	25. 6	7. 5	A7	B4	Bat
14. 4	24. 3	J5	K4	Tapir	26. 6	8. 5	A7	C5	Rat
15. 4	25. 3	J5	A5	Sheep	27. 6	9. 5	A7	D6	Swallow
16. 4	26. 3	J5	B6	Deer	28. 6	10. 5	A7	E7	Pig
17. 4	27. 3	J5	C7	Horse	29. 6	11. 5	A7	F8	Porcupine
18. 4	28. 3	J5	D8	Stag	30. 6	12. 5	A7	G9	Wolf
19. 4	29. 3	J5	E9	Serpent	1. 7	13. 5	A7	H10	Dog
20. 4	30. 3	J5	F10	Earthworm	2. 7	14. 5	A7	J11	Pheasant
21. 4	1. 3	J5	G11	Crocodile	3. 7	15. 5	A7	K12	Cock
22. 4	2. 3	J5	H12	Dragon	4. 7	16. 5	A7	A1	Crow
23. 4	3. 3	J5	J1	Badger	5. 7	17. 5	A7	B2	Monkey
24. 4	4. 3	J5	K2	Hare	6. 7	18. 5	A7	C3	Gibbon
25. 4	5. 3	J5	A3	Fox	7. 7	19. 5	A7	D4	Tapir
26. 4	6. 3	J5	B4	Tiger	8. 7	20. 5	A7	E5	Sheep
27. 4	7. 3	J5	C5	Leopard	9. 7	21. 5	A7	F6	Deer
28. 4	8. 3	J5	D6	Griffon	10. 7	22. 5	A7	G7	Horse
29. 4	9. 3	J5	E7	Ox	11. 7	23. 5	A7	H8	Stag
30. 4	10. 3	J5	F8	Bat	12. 7	24. 5	A7	J9	Serpent
1. 5	11. 3	J5	G9	Rat	13. 7	25. 5	A7	K10	Earthworm
2. 5	12. 3	J5	H10	Swallow	14. 7	26. 5	A7	A11	Crocodile
3. 5	13. 3	J5	J11	Pig	15. 7	27. 5	A7	B12	Dragon
4. 5	14. 3	J5	K12	Porcupine	16. 7	28. 5	A7	C1	Badger
5. 5	15. 3	J5	A1	Wolf	17. 7	29. 5	A7	D2	Hare
6. 5	16. 3	J5	B2	Dog	18. 7	1. 6	B8	E3	Fox
7. 5	17. 3	J5	C3	Pheasant	19. 7	2. 6	B8	F4	Tiger

Solar date	Lunar date	Month HS/EB	Day HS/EB	Constellation
20. 7	3. 6	B8	G5	Leopard
21. 7	4. 6	B8	H6	Griffon
22. 7	5. 6	B8	J7	Ox
23. 7	6. 6	B8	K8	Bat
24. 7	7. 6	B8	A9	Rat
25. 7	8. 6	B8	B10	Swallow
26. 7	9. 6	B8	C11	Pig
27. 7	10. 6	B8	D12	Porcupine
28. 7	11. 6	B8	E1	Wolf
29. 7	12. 6	B8	F2	Dog
30. 7	13. 6	B8	G3	Pheasant
31. 7	14. 6	B8	H4	Cock
1. 8	15. 6	B8	J5	Crow
2. 8	16. 6	B8	K6	Monkey
3. 8	17. 6	B8	A7	Gibbon
4. 8	18. 6	B8	B8	Tapir
5. 8	19. 6	B8	C9	Sheep
6. 8	20. 6	B8	D10	Deer
7. 8	21. 6	B8	E11	Horse
8. 8	22. 6	B8	F12	Stag
9. 8	23. 6	B8	G1	Serpent
10. 8	24. 6	B8	H2	Earthworm
11. 8	25. 6	B8	J3	Crocodile
12. 8	26. 6	B8	K4	Dragon
13. 8	27. 6	B8	A5	Badger
14. 8	28. 6	B8	B6	Hare
15. 8	29. 6	B8	C7	Fox
16. 8	1. 7	C9	D8	Tiger
17. 8	2. 7	C9	E9	Leopard
18. 8	3. 7	C9	F10	Griffon
19. 8	4. 7	C9	G11	Ox
20. 8	5. 7	C9	H12	Bat
21. 8	6. 7	C9	J1	Rat
22. 8	7. 7	C9	K2	Swallow
23. 8	8. 7	C9	A3	Pig
24. 8	9. 7	C9	B4	Porcupine
25. 8	10. 7	C9	C5	Wolf
26. 8	11. 7	C9	D6	Dog
27. 8	12. 7	C9	E7	Pheasant
28. 8	13. 7	C9	F8	Cock
29. 8	14. 7	C9	G9	Crow
30. 8	15. 7	C9	H10	Monkey
31. 8	16. 7	C9	J11	Gibbon
1. 9	17. 7	C9	K12	Tapir
2. 9	18. 7	C9	A1	Sheep
3. 9	19. 7	C9	B2	Deer
4. 9	20. 7	C9	C3	Horse
5. 9	21. 7	C9	D4	Stag
6. 9	22. 7	C9	E5	Serpent
7. 9	23. 7	C9	F6	Earthworm
8. 9	24. 7	C9	G7	Crocodile
9. 9	25. 7	C9	H8	Dragon
10. 9	26. 7	C9	J9	Badger
11. 9	27. 7	C9	K10	Hare
12. 9	28. 7	C9	A11	Fox
13. 9	29. 7	C9	B12	Tiger
14. 9	30. 7	C9	C1	Leopard
15. 9	1. 8	D10	D2	Griffon
16. 9	2. 8	D10	E3	Ox
17. 9	3. 8	D10	F4	Bat
18. 9	4. 8	D10	G5	Rat
19. 9	5. 8	D10	H6	Swallow
20. 9	6. 8	D10	J7	Pig
21. 9	7. 8	D10	K8	Porcupine
22. 9	8. 8	D10	A9	Wolf
23. 9	9. 8	D10	B10	Dog
24. 9	10. 8	D10	C11	Pheasant
25. 9	11. 8	D10	D12	Cock
26. 9	12. 8	D10	E1	Crow
27. 9	13. 8	D10	F2	Monkey
28. 9	14. 8	D10	G3	Gibbon
29. 9	15. 8	D10	H4	Tapir
30. 9	16. 8	D10	J5	Sheep
1.10	17. 8	D10	K6	Deer
2.10	18. 8	D10	A7	Horse
3.10	19. 8	D10	B8	Stag
4.10	20. 8	D10	C9	Serpent
5.10	21. 8	D10	D10	Earthworm
6.10	22. 8	D10	E11	Crocodile
7.10	23. 8	D10	F12	Dragon
8.10	24. 8	D10	G1	Badger
9.10	25. 8	D10	H2	Hare
10.10	26. 8	D10	J3	Fox
11.10	27. 8	D10	K4	Tiger
12.10	28. 8	D10	A5	Leopard
13.10	29. 8	D10	B6	Griffon
14.10	1. 9	E11	C7	Ox
15.10	2. 9	E11	D8	Bat
16.10	3. 9	E11	E9	Rat
17.10	4. 9	E11	F10	Swallow
18.10	5. 9	E11	G11	Pig
19.10	6. 9	E11	H12	Porcupine
20.10	7. 9	E11	J1	Wolf
21.10	8. 9	E11	K2	Dog
22.10	9. 9	E11	A3	Pheasant
23.10	10. 9	E11	B4	Cock
24.10	11. 9	E11	C5	Crow
25.10	12. 9	E11	D6	Monkey
26.10	13. 9	E11	E7	Gibbon
27.10	14. 9	E11	F8	Tapir
28.10	15. 9	E11	G9	Sheep
29.10	16. 9	E11	H10	Deer
30.10	17. 9	E11	J11	Horse
31.10	18. 9	E11	K12	Stag
1.11	19. 9	E11	A1	Serpent
2.11	20. 9	E11	B2	Earthworm
3.11	21. 9	E11	C3	Crocodile
4.11	22. 9	F11	D4	Dragon
5.11	23. 9	E11	E5	Badger
6.11	24. 9	E11	F6	Hare
7.11	25. 9	E11	G7	Fox
8.11	26. 9	E11	H8	Tiger
9.11	27. 9	E11	J9	Leopard
10.11	28. 9	E11	K10	Griffon
11.11	29. 9	E11	A11	Ox
12.11	1.10	F12	B12	Bat
13.11	2.10	F12	C1	Rat
14.11	3.10	F12	D2	Swallow
15.11	4.10	F12	E3	Pig
16.11	5.10	F12	F4	Porcupine
17.11	6.10	F12	G5	Wolf
18.11	7.10	F12	H6	Dog
19.11	8.10	F12	J7	Pheasant
20.11	9.10	F12	K8	Cock
21.11	10.10	F12	A9	Crow
22.11	11.10	F12	B10	Monkey
23.11	12.10	F12	C11	Gibbon
24.11	13.10	F12	D12	Tapir
25.11	14.10	F12	E1	Sheep
26.11	15.10	F12	F2	Deer
27.11	16.10	F12	G3	Horse
28.11	17.10	F12	H4	Stag
29.11	18.10	F12	J5	Serpent
30.11	19.10	F12	K6	Earthworm
1.12	20.10	F12	A7	Crocodile
2.12	21.10	F12	B8	Dragon
3.12	22.10	F12	C9	Badger
4.12	23.10	F12	D10	Hare
5.12	24.10	F12	E11	Fox
6.12	25.10	F12	F12	Tiger
7.12	26.10	F12	G1	Leopard
8.12	27.10	F12	H2	Griffon
9.12	28.10	F12	J3	Ox
10.12	29.10	F12	K4	Bat
11.12	30.10	F12	A5	Rat
12.12	1.11	G1	B6	Swallow

Solar date	Lunar date	Month HS/EB	Day HS/EB	Constellation	Solar date	Lunar date	Month HS/EB	Day HS/EB	Constellation
13.12	2.11	G1	C7	Pig	10. 1	30.11	G1	A11	Pig
14.12	3.11	G1	D8	Porcupine	11. 1	1.12	H2	B12	Porcupine
15.12	4.11	G1	E9	Wolf	12. 1	2.12	H2	C1	Wolf
16.12	5.11	G1	F10	Dog	13. 1	3.12	H2	D2	Dog
17.12	6.11	G1	G11	Pheasant	14. 1	4.12	H2	E3	Pheasant
18.12	7.11	G1	H12	Cock	15. 1	5.12	H2	F4	Cock
19.12	8.11	G1	J1	Crow	16. 1	6.12	H2	G5	Crow
20.12	9.11	G1	K2	Monkey	17. 1	7.12	H2	H6	Monkey
21.12	10.11	G1	A3	Gibbon	18. 1	8.12	H2	J7	Gibbon
22.12	11.11	G1	B4	Tapir	19. 1	9.12	H2	K8	Tapir
23.12	12.11	G1	C5	Sheep	20. 1	10.12	H2	A9	Sheep
24.12	13.11	G1	D6	Deer	21. 1	11.12	H2	B10	Deer
25.12	14.11	G1	E7	Horse	22. 1	12.12	H2	C11	Horse
26.12	15.11	G1	F8	Stag	23. 1	13.12	H2	D12	Stag
27.12	16.11	G1	G9	Serpent	24. 1	14.12	H2	E1	Serpent
28.12	17.11	G1	H10	Earthworm	25. 1	15.12	H2	F2	Earthworm
29.12	18.11	G1	J11	Crocodile	26. 1	16.12	H2	G3	Crocodile
30.12	19.11	G1	K12	Dragon	27. 1	17.12	H2	H4	Dragon
31.12	20.11	G1	A1	Badger	28. 1	18.12	H2	J5	Badger
1967					29. 1	19.12	H2	K6	Hare
					30. 1	20.12	H2	A7	Fox
1. 1	21.11	G1	B2	Hare	31. 1	21.12	H2	B8	Tiger
2. 1	22.11	G1	C3	Fox	1. 2	22.12	H2	C9	Leopard
3. 1	23.11	G1	D4	Tiger	2. 2	23.12	H2	D10	Griffon
4. 1	24.11	G1	E5	Leopard	3. 2	24.12	H2	E11	Ox
5. 1	25.11	G1	F6	Griffon	4. 2	25.12	H2	F12	Bat
6. 1	26.11	G1	G7	Ox	5. 2	26.12	H2	G1	Rat
7. 1	27.11	G1	H8	Bat	6. 2	27.12	H2	H2	Swallow
8. 1	28.11	G1	J9	Rat	7. 2	28.12	H2	J3	Pig
9. 1	29.11	G1	K10	Swallow	8. 2	29.12	H2	K4	Porcupine

TING WEI YEAR

Solar date	Lunar date	Month HS/EB	Day HS/EB	Constellation	Solar date	Lunar date	Month HS/EB	Day HS/EB	Constellation
9. 2	1. 1	J3	A5	Wolf	19. 3	9. 2	K4	J7	Horse
10. 2	2. 1	J3	B6	Dog	20. 3	10. 2	K4	K8	Stag
11. 2	3. 1	J3	C7	Pheasant	21. 3	11. 2	K4	A9	Serpent
12. 2	4. 1	J3	D8	Cock	22. 3	12. 2	K4	B10	Earthworm
13. 2	5. 1	J3	E9	Crow	23. 3	13. 2	K4	C11	Crocodile
14. 2	6. 1	J3	F10	Monkey	24. 3	14. 2	K4	D12	Dragon
15. 2	7. 1	J3	G11	Gibbon	25. 3	15. 2	K4	E1	Badger
16. 2	8. 1	J3	H12	Tapir	26. 3	16. 2	K4	F2	Hare
17. 2	9. 1	J3	J1	Sheep	27. 3	17. 2	K4	G3	Fox
18. 2	10. 1	J3	K2	Deer	28. 3	18. 2	K4	H4	Tiger
19. 2	11. 1	J3	A3	Horse	29. 3	19. 2	K4	J5	Leopard
20. 2	12. 1	J3	B4	Stag	30. 3	20. 2	K4	K6	Griffon
21. 2	13. 1	J3	C5	Serpent	31. 3	21. 2	K4	A7	Ox
22. 2	14. 1	J3	D6	Earthworm	1. 4	22. 2	K4	B8	Bat
23. 2	15. 1	J3	E7	Crocodile	2. 4	23. 2	K4	C9	Rat
24. 2	16. 1	J3	F8	Dragon	3. 4	24. 2	K4	D10	Swallow
25. 2	17. 1	J3	G9	Badger	4. 4	25. 2	K4	E11	Pig
26. 2	18. 1	J3	H10	Hare	5. 4	26. 2	K4	F12	Porcupine
27. 2	19. 1	J3	J11	Fox	6. 4	27. 2	K4	G1	Wolf
28. 2	20. 1	J3	K12	Tiger	7. 4	28. 2	K4	H2	Dog
1. 3	21. 1	J3	A1	Leopard	8. 4	29. 2	K4	J3	Pheasant
2. 3	22. 1	J3	B2	Griffon	9. 4	30. 2	K4	K4	Cock
3. 3	23. 1	J3	C3	Ox	10. 4	1. 3	A5	A5	Crow
4. 3	24. 1	J3	D4	Bat	11. 4	2. 3	A5	B6	Monkey
5. 3	25. 1	J3	E5	Rat	12. 4	3. 3	A5	C7	Gibbon
6. 3	26. 1	J3	F6	Swallow	13. 4	4. 3	A5	D8	Tapir
7. 3	27. 1	J3	G7	Pig	14. 4	5. 3	A5	E9	Sheep
8. 3	28. 1	J3	H8	Porcupine	15. 4	6. 3	A5	F10	Deer
9. 3	29. 1	J3	J9	Wolf	16. 4	7. 3	A5	G11	Horse
10. 3	30. 1	J3	K10	Dog	17. 4	8. 3	A5	H12	Stag
11. 3	1. 2	K4	A11	Pheasant	18. 4	9. 3	A5	J1	Serpent
12. 3	2. 2	K4	B12	Cock	19. 4	10. 3	A5	K2	Earthworm
13. 3	3. 2	K4	C1	Crow	20. 4	11. 3	A5	A3	Crocodile
14. 3	4. 2	K4	D2	Monkey	21. 4	12. 3	A5	B4	Dragon
15. 3	5. 2	K4	E3	Gibbon	22. 4	13. 3	A5	C5	Badger
16. 3	6. 2	K4	F4	Tapir	23. 4	14. 3	A5	D6	Hare
17. 3	7. 2	K4	G5	Sheep	24. 4	15. 3	A5	E7	Fox
18. 3	8. 2	K4	G6	Deer	25. 4	16. 3	A5	F8	Tiger

Solar date	Lunar date	Month HS/EB	Day HS/EB	Constellation	Solar date	Lunar date	Month HS/EB	Day HS/EB	Constellation
26. 4	17. 3	A5	G9	Leopard	8. 7	1. 6	D8	K10	Deer
27. 4	18. 3	A5	H10	Griffon	9. 7	2. 6	D8	A11	Horse
28. 4	19. 3	A5	J11	Ox	10. 7	3. 6	D8	B12	Stag
29. 4	20. 3	A5	K12	Bat	11. 7	4. 6	D8	C1	Serpent
30. 4	21. 3	A5	A1	Rat	12. 7	5. 6	D8	D2	Earthworm
1. 5	22. 3	A5	B2	Swallow	13. 7	6. 6	D8	E3	Crocodile
2. 5	23. 3	A5	C3	Pig	14. 7	7. 6	D8	F4	Dragon
3. 5	24. 3	A5	D4	Porcupine	15. 7	8. 6	D8	G5	Badger
4. 5	25. 3	A5	E5	Wolf	16. 7	9. 6	D8	H6	Hare
5. 5	26. 3	A5	F6	Dog	17. 7	10. 6	D8	J7	Fox
6. 5	27. 3	A5	G7	Pheasant	18. 7	11. 6	D8	K8	Tiger
7. 5	28. 3	A5	H8	Cock	19. 7	12. 6	D8	A9	Leopard
8. 5	29. 3	A5	J9	Crow	20. 7	13. 6	D8	B10	Griffon
9. 5	1. 4	B6	K10	Monkey	21. 7	14. 6	D8	C11	Ox
10. 5	2. 4	B6	A11	Gibbon	22. 7	15. 6	D8	D12	Bat
11. 5	3. 4	B6	B12	Tapir	23. 7	16. 6	D8	E1	Rat
12. 5	4. 4	B6	C1	Sheep	24. 7	17. 6	D8	F2	Swallow
13. 5	5. 4	B6	D2	Deer	25. 7	18. 6	D8	G3	Pig
14. 5	6. 4	B6	E3	Horse	26. 7	19. 6	D8	H4	Porcupine
15. 5	7. 4	B6	F4	Stag	27. 7	20. 6	D8	J5	Wolf
16. 5	8. 4	B6	G5	Serpent	28. 7	21. 6	D8	K6	Dog
17. 5	9. 4	B6	H6	Earthworm	29. 7	22. 6	D8	A7	Pheasant
18. 5	10. 4	B6	J7	Crocodile	30. 7	23. 6	D8	B8	Cock
19. 5	11. 4	B6	K8	Dragon	31. 7	24. 6	D8	C9	Crow
20. 5	12. 4	B6	A9	Badger	1. 8	25. 6	D8	D10	Monkey
21. 5	13. 4	B6	B10	Hare	2. 8	26. 6	D8	E11	Gibbon
22. 5	14. 4	B6	C11	Fox	3. 8	27. 6	D8	F12	Tapir
23. 5	15. 4	B6	D12	Tiger	4. 8	28. 6	D8	G1	Sheep
24. 5	16. 4	B6	F1	Leopard	5. 8	29. 6	D8	H2	Deer
25. 5	17. 4	B6	F2	Griffon	6. 8	1. 7	E9	J3	Horse
26. 5	18. 4	B6	G3	Ox	7. 8	2. 7	E9	K4	Stag
27. 5	19. 4	B6	H4	Bat	8. 8	3. 7	E9	A5	Serpent
28. 5	20. 4	B6	J5	Rat	9. 8	4. 7	E9	B6	Earthworm
29. 5	21. 4	B6	K6	Swallow	10. 8	5. 7	E9	C7	Crocodile
30. 5	22. 4	B6	A7	Pig	11. 8	6. 7	E9	D8	Dragon
31. 5	23. 4	B6	B8	Porcupine	12. 8	7. 7	E9	E9	Badger
1. 6	24. 4	B6	C9	Wolf	13. 8	8. 7	E9	F10	Hare
2. 6	25. 4	B6	D10	Dog	14. 8	9. 7	E9	G11	Fox
3. 6	26. 4	B6	E11	Pheasant	15. 8	10. 7	E9	H12	Tiger
4. 6	27. 4	B6	F12	Cock	16. 8	11. 7	E9	J1	Leopard
5. 6	28. 4	B6	G1	Crow	17. 8	12. 7	E9	K2	Griffon
6. 6	29. 4	B6	H2	Monkey	18. 8	13. 7	E9	A3	Ox
7. 6	30. 4	B6	J3	Gibbon	19. 8	14. 7	E9	B4	Bat
8. 6	1. 5	C7	K4	Tapir	20. 8	15. 7	E9	C5	Rat
9. 6	2. 5	C7	A5	Sheep	21. 8	16. 7	E9	D6	Swallow
10. 6	3. 5	C7	B6	Deer	22. 8	17. 7	E9	E7	Pig
11. 6	4. 5	C7	C7	Horse	23. 8	18. 7	E9	F8	Porcupine
12. 6	5. 5	C7	D8	Stag	24. 8	19. 7	E9	G9	Wolf
13. 6	6. 5	C7	E9	Serpent	25. 8	20. 7	E9	H10	Dog
14. 6	7. 5	C7	F10	Earthworm	26. 8	21. 7	E9	J11	Pheasant
15. 6	8. 5	C7	G11	Crocodile	27. 8	22. 7	E9	K12	Cock
16. 6	9. 5	C7	H12	Dragon	28. 8	23. 7	E9	A1	Crow
17. 6	10. 5	C7	J1	Badger	29. 8	24. 7	E9	B2	Monkey
18. 6	11. 5	C7	K2	Hare	30. 8	25. 7	E9	C3	Gibbon
19. 6	12. 5	C7	A3	Fox	31. 8	26. 7	E9	D4	Tapir
20. 6	13. 5	C7	B4	Tiger	1. 9	27. 7	E9	E5	Sheep
21. 6	14. 5	C7	C5	Leopard	2. 9	28. 7	E9	F6	Deer
22. 6	15. 5	C7	D6	Griffon	3. 9	29. 7	E9	G7	Horse
23. 6	16. 5	C7	E7	Ox	4. 9	1. 8	F10	H8	Stag
24. 6	17. 5	C7	F8	Bat	5. 9	2. 8	F10	J9	Serpent
25. 6	18. 5	C7	G9	Rat	6. 9	3. 8	F10	K10	Earthworm
26. 6	19. 5	C7	H10	Swallow	7. 9	4. 8	F10	A11	Crocodile
27. 6	20. 5	C7	J11	Pig	8. 9	5. 8	F10	B12	Dragon
28. 6	21. 5	C7	K12	Porcupine	9. 9	6. 8	F10	C1	Badger
29. 6	22. 5	C7	A1	Wolf	10. 9	7. 8	F10	D2	Hare
30. 6	23. 5	C7	B2	Dog	11. 9	8. 8	F10	E3	Fox
1. 7	24. 5	C7	C3	Pheasant	12. 9	9. 8	F10	F4	Tiger
2. 7	25. 5	C7	D4	Cock	13. 9	10. 8	F10	G5	Leopard
3. 7	26. 5	C7	E5	Crow	14. 9	11. 8	F10	H6	Griffon
4. 7	27. 5	C7	F6	Monkey	15. 9	12. 8	F10	J7	Ox
5. 7	28. 5	C7	G7	Gibbon	16. 9	13. 8	F10	K8	Bat
6. 7	29. 5	C7	H8	Tapir	18. 9	15. 8	F10	B10	Swallow
7. 7	30. 5	C7	J9	Sheep	19. 9	16. 8	F10	C11	Pig

Solar date	Lunar date	Month HS/EB	Day HS/EB	Constellation	Solar date	Lunar date	Month HS/EB	Day HS/EB	Constellation
20. 9	17. 8	F10	D12	Porcupine	26.11	25.10	H12	A7	Horse
21. 9	18. 8	F10	E1	Wolf	27.11	26.10	H12	B8	Stag
22. 9	19. 8	F10	F2	Dog	28.11	27.10	H12	C9	Serpent
23. 9	20. 8	F10	G3	Pheasant	29.11	28.10	H12	D10	Earthworm
24. 9	21. 8	F10	H4	Cock	30.11	29.10	H12	E11	Crocodile
25. 9	22. 8	F10	J5	Crow	1.12	30.10	H12	F12	Dragon
26. 9	23. 8	F10	K6	Monkey	2.12	1.11	J1	G1	Badger
27. 9	24. 8	F10	A7	Gibbon	3.12	2.11	J1	H2	Hare
28. 9	25. 8	F10	B8	Tapir	4.12	3.11	J1	J3	Fox
29. 9	26. 8	F10	C9	Sheep	5.12	4.11	J1	K4	Tiger
30. 9	27. 8	F10	D10	Deer	6.12	5.11	J1	A5	Leopard
1.10	28. 8	F10	E11	Horse	7.12	6.11	J1	B6	Griffon
2.10	29. 8	F10	F12	Stag	8.12	7.11	J1	C7	Ox
3.10	30. 8	F10	G1	Serpent	9.12	8.11	J1	D8	Bat
4.10	1. 9	G11	H2	Earthworm	10.12	9.11	J1	E9	Rat
5.10	2. 9	G11	J3	Crocodile	11.12	10.11	J1	F10	Swallow
6.10	3. 9	G11	K4	Dragon	12.12	11.11	J1	G11	Pig
7.10	4. 9	G11	A5	Badger	13.12	12.11	J1	H12	Porcupine
8.10	5. 9	G11	B6	Hare	14.12	13.11	J1	J1	Wolf
9.10	6. 9	G11	C7	Fox	15.12	14.11	J1	K2	Dog
10.10	7. 9	G11	D8	Tiger	16.12	15.11	J1	A3	Pheasant
11.10	8. 9	G11	E9	Leopard	17.12	16.11	J1	B4	Cock
12.10	9. 9	G11	F10	Griffon	18.12	17.11	J1	C5	Crow
13.10	10. 9	G11	G11	Ox	19.12	18.11	J1	D6	Monkey
14.10	11. 9	G11	H12	Bat	20.12	19.11	J1	E7	Gibbon
15.10	12. 9	G11	J1	Rat	21.12	20.11	J1	F8	Tapir
16.10	13. 9	G11	K2	Swallow	22.12	21.11	J1	G9	Sheep
17.10	14. 9	G11	A3	Pig	23.12	22.11	J1	H10	Deer
18.10	15. 9	G11	B4	Porcupine	24.12	23.11	J1	J11	Horse
19.10	16. 9	G11	C5	Wolf	25.12	24.11	J1	K12	Stag
20.10	17. 9	G11	D6	Dog	26.12	25.11	J1	A1	Serpent
21.10	18. 9	G11	E7	Pheasant	27.12	26.11	J1	B2	Earthworm
22.10	19. 9	G11	F8	Cock	28.12	27.11	J1	C3	Crocodile
23.10	20. 9	G11	G9	Crow	29.12	28.11	J1	D4	Dragon
24.10	21. 9	G11	H10	Monkey	30.12	29:11	J1	E5	Badger
25.10	22. 9	G11	J11	Gibbon	31.12	1.12	K2	F6	Hare
26.10	23. 9	G11	K12	Tapir					
27.10	24. 9	G11	A1	Sheep	**1968**				
28.10	25. 9	G11	B2	Deer	1. 1	2.12	K2	G7	Fox
29.10	26. 9	G11	C3	Horse	2. 1	3.12	K2	H8	Tiger
30.10	27. 9	G11	D4	Stag	3. 1	4.12	K2	J9	Leopard
31.10	28. 9	G11	E5	Serpent	4. 1	5.12	K2	K10	Griffon
1.11	29. 9	G11	F6	Earthworm	5. 1	6.12	K2	A11	Ox
2.11	1.10	H12	G7	Crocodile	6. 1	7.12	K2	B12	Bat
3.11	2.10	H12	H8	Dragon	7. 1	8.12	K2	C1	Rat
4.11	3.10	H12	J9	Badger	8. 1	9.12	K2	D2	Swallow
5.11	4.10	H12	K10	Hare	9. 1	10.12	K2	E3	Pig
6.11	5.10	H12	A11	Fox	10. 1	11.12	K2	F4	Porcupine
7.11	6.10	H12	B12	Tiger	11. 1	12.12	K2	G5	Wolf
8.11	7.10	H12	C1	Leopard	12. 1	13.12	K2	H6	Dog
9.11	8.10	H12	D2	Griffon	13. 1	14.12	K2	J7	Pheasant
10.11	9.10	H12	E3	Ox	14. 1	15.12	K2	K8	Cock
11.11	10.10	H12	F4	Bat	15. 1	16.12	K2	A9	Crow
12.11	11.10	H12	G5	Rat	16. 1	17.12	K2	B10	Monkey
13.11	12.10	H12	H6	Swallow	17. 1	18.12	K2	C11	Gibbon
14.11	13.10	H12	J7	Pig	18. 1	19.12	K2	D12	Tapir
15.11	14.10	H12	K8	Porcupine	19. 1	20.12	K2	E1	Sheep
16.11	15.10	H12	A9	Wolf	20. 1	21.12	K2	F2	Deer
17.11	16.10	H12	B10	Dog	21. 1	22.12	K2	G3	Horse
18.11	17.10	H12	C11	Pheasant	22. 1	23.12	K2	H4	Stag
19.11	18.10	H12	D12	Cock	23. 1	24.12	K2	J5	Serpent
20.11	19.10	H12	E1	Crow	24. 1	25.12	K2	K6	Earthworm
21.11	20.10	H12	F2	Monkey	25. 1	26.12	K2	A7	Crocodile
22.11	21.10	H12	G3	Gibbon	26. 1	27.12	K2	B8	Dragon
23.11	22.10	H12	H4	Tapir	27. 1	28.12	K2	C9	Badger
24.11	23.10	H12	J5	Sheep	28. 1	29.12	K2	D10	Hare
25.11	24.10	H12	K6	Deer	29. 1	30.12	K2	E11	Fox

MOU SHEN YEAR

Solar date	Lunar date	Month HS/EB	Day HS/EB	Constellation	Solar date	Lunar date	Month HS/EB	Day HS/EB	Constellation
30. 1	1. 1	A3	F12	Tiger	10. 4	13. 3	C5	G11	Gibbon
31. 1	2. 1	A3	G1	Leopard	11. 4	14. 3	C5	H12	Tapir
1. 2	3. 1	A3	H2	Griffon	12. 4	15. 3	C5	J1	Sheep
2. 2	4. 1	A3	J3	Ox	13. 4	16. 3	C5	K2	Deer
3. 2	5. 1	A3	K4	Bat	14. 4	17. 3	C5	A3	Horse
4. 2	6. 1	A3	A5	Rat	15. 4	18. 3	C5	B4	Stag
5. 2	7. 1	A3	B6	Swallow	16. 4	19. 3	C5	C5	Serpent
6. 2	8. 1	A3	C7	Pig	17. 4	20. 3	C5	D6	Earthworm
7. 2	9. 1	A3	D8	Porcupine	18. 4	21. 3	C5	E7	Crocodile
8. 2	10. 1	A3	E9	Wolf	19. 4	22. 3	C5	F8	Dragon
9. 2	11. 1	A3	F10	Dog	20. 4	23. 3	C5	G9	Badger
10. 2	12. 1	A3	G11	Pheasant	21. 4	24. 3	C5	H10	Hare
11. 2	13. 1	A3	H12	Cock	22. 4	25. 3	C5	J11	Fox
12. 2	14. 1	A3	J1	Crow	23. 4	26. 3	C5	K12	Tiger
13. 2	15. 1	A3	K2	Monkey	24. 4	27. 3	C5	A1	Leopard
14. 2	16. 1	A3	A3	Gibbon	25. 4	28. 3	C5	B2	Griffon
15. 2	17. 1	A3	B4	Tapir	26. 4	29. 3	C5	C3	Ox
16. 2	18. 1	A3	C5	Sheep	27. 4	1. 4	D6	D4	Bat
17. 2	19. 1	A3	D6	Deer	28. 4	2. 4	D6	E5	Rat
18. 2	20. 1	A3	E7	Horse	29. 4	3. 4	D6	F6	Swallow
19. 2	21. 1	A3	F8	Stag	30. 4	4. 4	D6	G7	Pig
20. 2	22. 1	A3	G9	Serpent	1. 5	5. 4	D6	H8	Porcupine
21. 2	23. 1	A3	H10	Earthworm	2. 5	6. 4	D6	J9	Wolf
22. 2	24. 1	A3	J11	Crocodile	3. 5	7. 4	D6	K10	Dog
23. 2	25. 1	A3	K12	Dragon	4. 5	8. 4	D6	A11	Pheasant
24. 2	26. 1	A3	A1	Badger	5. 5	9. 4	D6	B12	Cock
25. 2	27. 1	A3	B2	Hare	6. 5	10. 4	D6	C1	Crow
26. 2	28. 1	A3	C3	Fox	7. 5	11. 4	D6	D2	Monkey
27. 2	29. 1	A3	D4	Tiger	8. 5	12. 4	D6	E3	Gibbon
28. 2	1. 2	B4	E5	Leopard	9. 5	13. 4	D6	F4	Tapir
29. 2	2. 2	B4	F6	Griffon	10. 5	14. 4	D6	G5	Sheep
1. 3	3. 2	B4	G7	Ox	11. 5	15. 4	D6	H6	Deer
2. 3	4. 2	B4	H8	Bat	12. 5	16. 4	D6	J7	Horse
3. 3	5. 2	B4	J9	Rat	13. 5	17. 4	D6	K8	Stag
4. 3	6. 2	B4	K10	Swallow	14. 5	18. 4	D6	A9	Serpent
5. 3	7. 2	B4	A11	Pig	15. 5	19. 4	D6	B10	Earthworm
6. 3	8. 2	B4	B12	Porcupine	16. 5	20. 4	D6	C11	Crocodile
7. 3	9. 2	B4	C1	Wolf	17. 5	21. 4	D6	D12	Dragon
8. 3	10. 2	B4	D2	Dog	18. 5	22. 4	D6	E1	Badger
9. 3	11. 2	B4	E3	Pheasant	19. 5	23. 4	D6	F2	Hare
10. 3	12. 2	B4	F4	Cock	20. 5	24. 4	D6	G3	Fox
11. 3	13. 2	B4	G5	Crow	21. 5	25. 4	D6	H4	Tiger
12. 3	14. 2	B4	H6	Monkey	22. 5	26. 4	D6	J5	Leopard
13. 3	15. 2	B4	J7	Gibbon	23. 5	27. 4	D6	K6	Griffon
14. 3	16. 2	B4	K8	Tapir	24. 5	28. 4	D6	A7	Ox
15. 3	17. 2	B4	A9	Sheep	25. 5	29. 4	D6	B8	Bat
16. 3	18. 2	B4	B10	Deer	26. 5	30. 4	D6	C9	Rat
17. 3	19. 2	B4	C11	Horse	27. 5	1. 5	E7	D10	Swallow
18. 3	20. 2	B4	D12	Stag	28. 5	2. 5	E7	E11	Pig
19. 3	21. 2	B4	E1	Serpent	29. 5	3. 5	E7	F12	Porcupine
20. 3	22. 2	B4	F2	Earthworm	30. 5	4. 5	E7	G1	Wolf
21. 3	23. 2	B4	G3	Crocodile	31. 5	5. 5	E7	H2	Dog
22. 3	24. 2	B4	H4	Dragon	1. 6	6. 5	E7	J3	Pheasant
23. 3	25. 2	B4	J5	Badger	2. 6	7. 5	E7	K4	Cock
24. 3	26. 2	B4	K6	Hare	3. 6	8. 5	E7	A5	Crow
25. 3	27. 2	B4	A7	Fox	4. 6	9. 5	E7	B6	Monkey
26. 3	28. 2	B4	B8	Tiger	5. 6	10. 5	E7	C7	Gibbon
27. 3	29. 2	B4	C9	Leopard	6. 6	11. 5	E7	D8	Tapir
28. 3	30. 2	B4	D10	Griffon	7. 6	12. 5	E7	E9	Sheep
29. 3	1. 3	C5	E11	Ox	8. 6	13. 5	E7	F10	Deer
30. 3	2 3	C5	F12	Bat	9. 6	14. 5	E7	G11	Horse
31. 3	3. 3	C5	G1	Rat	10. 6	15. 5	E7	H12	Stag
1. 4	4. 3	C5	H2	Swallow	11. 6	16. 5	E7	J1	Serpent
2. 4	5. 3	C5	J3	Pig	12. 6	17. 5	E7	K2	Earthworm
3. 4	6. 3	C5	K4	Porcupine	13. 6	18. 5	E7	A3	Crocodile
4. 4	7. 3	C5	A5	Wolf	14. 6	19. 5	E7	B4	Dragon
5. 4	8. 3	C5	B6	Dog	15. 6	20. 5	E7	C5	Badger
6. 4	9. 3	C5	C7	Pheasant	16. 6	21. 5	E7	D6	Hare
7. 4	10. 3	C5	D8	Cock	17. 6	22. 5	E7	E7	Fox
8. 4	11. 3	C5	E9	Crow	18. 6	23. 5	E7	F8	Tiger
9. 4	12. 3	C5	F10	Monkey	19. 6	24. 5	E7	G9	Leopard

Solar date	Lunar date	Month HS/EB	Day HS/EB	Constellation
20. 6	25. 5	E7	H10	Griffon
21. 6	26. 5	E7	J11	Ox
22. 6	27. 5	E7	K12	Bat
23. 6	28. 5	E7	A1	Rat
24. 6	29. 5	E7	B2	Swallow
25. 6	30. 5	E7	C3	Pig
26. 6	1. 6	F8	D4	Porcupine
27. 6	2. 6	F8	E5	Wolf
28. 6	3. 6	F8	F6	Dog
29. 6	4. 6	F8	G7	Pheasant
30. 6	5. 6	F8	H8	Cock
1. 7	6. 6	F8	J9	Crow
2 7	7. 6	F8	K10	Monkey
3. 7	8. 6	F8	A11	Gibbon
4. 7	9. 6	F8	B12	Tapir
5. 7	10. 6	F8	C1	Sheep
6. 7	11. 6	F8	D2	Deer
7. 7	12. 6	F8	E3	Horse
8. 7	13. 6	F8	F4	Stag
9. 7	14. 6	F8	G5	Serpent
10. 7	15. 6	F8	H6	Earthworm
11. 7	16. 6	F8	J7	Crocodile
12. 7	17. 6	F8	K8	Dragon
13. 7	18. 6	F8	A9	Badger
14. 7	19. 6	F8	B10	Hare
15. 7	20. 6	F8	C11	Fox
16. 7	21. 6	F8	D12	Tiger
17. 7	22. 6	F8	E1	Leopard
18. 7	23. 6	F8	F2	Griffon
19. 7	24. 6	F8	G3	Ox
20. 7	25. 6	F8	H4	Bat
21. 7	26. 6	F8	J5	Rat
22. 7	27. 6	F8	K6	Swallow
23. 7	28. 6	F8	A7	Pig
24. 7	29. 6	F8	B8	Porcupine
25. 7	1. 7	G9	C9	Wolf
26. 7	2. 7	G9	D10	Dog
27. 7	3. 7	G9	E11	Pheasant
28. 7	4. 7	G9	F12	Cock
29. 7	5. 7	G9	G1	Crow
30. 7	6. 7	G9	H2	Monkey
31. 7	7. 7	G9	J3	Gibbon
1. 8	8. 7	G9	K4	Tapir
2. 8	9. 7	G9	A5	Sheep
3. 8	10. 7	G9	B6	Deer
4. 8	11. 7	G9	C7	Horse
5. 8	12. 7	G9	D8	Stag
6. 8	13. 7	G9	E9	Serpent
7. 8	14. 7	G9	F10	Earthworm
8. 8	15. 7	G9	G11	Crocodile
9. 8	16. 7	G9	H12	Dragon
10. 8	17. 7	G9	J1	Badger
11. 8	18. 7	G9	K2	Hare
12. 8	19. 7	G9	A3	Fox
13. 8	20. 7	G9	B4	Tiger
14. 8	21. 7	G9	C5	Leopard
15. 8	22. 7	G9	D6	Griffon
16. 8	23. 7	G9	E7	Ox
17. 8	24. 7	G9	F8	Bat
18. 8	25. 7	G9	G9	Rat
19. 8	26. 7	G9	H10	Swallow
20. 8	27. 7	G9	J11	Pig
21. 8	28. 7	G9	K12	Porcupine
22. 8	29. 7	G9	A1	Wolf
23. 8	30. 7	C9	B2	Dog
24. 8	1. 7	G9	C3	Pheasant
25. 8	2. 7	G9	D4	Cock
26. 8	3. 7	G9	E5	Crow
27. 8	4. 7	G9	F6	Monkey
28. 8	5. 7	G9	G7	Gibbon
29. 8	6. 7	G9	H8	Tapir
30. 8	7. 7	G9	J9	Sheep
31. 8	8. 7	G9	K10	Deer
1. 9	9. 7	G9	A11	Horse
2. 9	10. 7	G9	B12	Stag
3. 9	11. 7	G9	C1	Serpent
4. 9	12. 7	G9	D2	Earthworm
5. 9	13. 7	G9	E3	Crocodile
6. 9	14. 7	G9	F4	Dragon
7. 9	15. 7	G9	G5	Badger
8. 9	16. 7	G9	H6	Hare
9. 9	17. 7	G9	J7	Fox
10. 9	18. 7	G9	K8	Tiger
11. 9	19. 7	G9	A9	Leopard
12. 9	20. 7	G9	B10	Griffon
13. 9	21. 7	G9	C11	Ox
14. 9	22. 7	G9	D12	Bat
15. 9	23. 7	G9	E1	Rat
16. 9	24. 7	G9	F2	Swallow
17. 9	25. 7	G9	G3	Pig
18. 9	26. 7	G9	H4	Porcupine
19. 9	27. 7	G9	J5	Wolf
20. 9	28. 7	G9	K6	Dog
21. 9	29. 7	G9	A7	Pheasant
22. 9	1. 8	H10	B8	Cock
23. 9	2. 8	H10	C9	Crow
24. 9	3. 8	H10	D10	Monkey
25. 9	4. 8	H10	E11	Gibbon
26. 9	5. 8	H10	F12	Tapir
27. 9	6. 8	H10	G1	Sheep
28. 9	7. 8	H10	H2	Deer
29. 9	8. 8	H10	J3	Horse
30. 9	9. 8	H10	K4	Stag
1.10	10. 8	H10	A5	Serpent
2.10	11. 8	H10	B6	Earthworm
3.10	12. 8	H10	C7	Crocodile
4.10	13. 8	H10	D8	Dragon
5.10	14. 8	H10	E9	Badger
6.10	15. 8	H10	F10	Hare
7.10	16. 8	H10	G11	Fox
8.10	17. 8	H10	H12	Tiger
9.10	18. 8	H10	J1	Leopard
10.10	19. 8	H10	K2	Griffon
11.10	20. 8	H10	A3	Ox
12.10	21. 8	H10	B4	Bat
13.10	22. 8	H10	C5	Rat
14.10	23. 8	H10	D6	Swallow
15.10	24. 8	H10	E7	Pig
16.10	25. 8	H10	F8	Porcupine
17.10	26. 8	H10	G9	Wolf
18.10	27. 8	H10	H10	Dog
19.10	28. 8	H10	J11	Pheasant
20.10	29. 8	H10	K12	Cock
21.10	30. 8	H10	A1	Crow
22.10	1. 9	J11	B2	Monkey
23.10	2. 9	J11	C3	Gibbon
24.10	3. 9	J11	D4	Tapir
25.10	4. 9	J11	E5	Sheep
26.10	5. 9	J11	F6	Deer
27.10	6. 9	J11	G7	Horse
28.10	7. 9	J11	H8	Stag
29.10	8. 9	J11	J9	Serpent
30.10	9. 9	J11	K10	Earthworm
31.10	10. 9	J11	A11	Crocodile
1.11	11. 9	J11	B12	Dragon
2.11	12. 9	J11	C1	Badger
3.11	13. 9	J11	D2	Hare
4.11	14. 9	J11	E3	Fox
5.11	15. 9	J11	F4	Tiger
6.11	16. 9	J11	G5	Leopard
7.11	17. 9	J11	H6	Griffon
8.11	18. 9	J11	J7	Ox
9.11	19. 9	J11	K8	Bat
10.11	20. 9	J11	A9	Rat
11.11	21. 9	J11	B10	Swallow
12.11	22. 9	J11	C11	Pig

Solar date	Lunar date	Month HS/EB	Day HS/EB	Constellation
13.11	23. 9	J11	D12	Porcupine
14.11	24. 9	J11	E1	Wolf
15.11	25. 9	J11	F2	Dog
16.11	26. 9	J11	G3	Pheasant
17.11	27. 9	J11	H4	Cock
18.11	28. 9	J11	J5	Crow
19.11	29. 9	J11	K6	Monkey
20.11	1.10	K12	A7	Gibbon
21.11	2.10	K12	B8	Tapir
22.11	3.10	K12	C9	Sheep
23.11	4.10	K12	D10	Deer
24.11	5.10	K12	E11	Horse
25.11	6.10	K12	F12	Stag
26.11	7.10	K12	G1	Serpent
27.11	8.10	K12	H2	Earthworm
28.11	9.10	K12	J3	Crocodile
29.11	10.10	K12	K4	Dragon
30.11	11.10	K12	A5	Badger
1.12	12.10	K12	B6	Hare
2.12	13.10	K12	C7	Fox
3.12	14.10	K12	D8	Tiger
4.12	15.10	K12	E9	Leopard
5.12	16.10	K12	F10	Griffon
6.12	17.10	K12	G11	Ox
7.12	18.10	K12	H12	Bat
8.12	19.10	K12	J1	Rat
9.12	20.10	K12	K2	Swallow
10.12	21.10	K12	A3	Pig
11.12	22.10	K12	B4	Porcupine
12.12	23.10	K12	C5	Wolf
13.12	24.10	K12	D6	Dog
14.12	25.10	K12	E7	Pheasant
15.12	26.10	K12	F8	Cock
16.12	27.10	K12	G9	Crow
17.12	28.10	K12	H10	Monkey
18.12	29.10	K12	J11	Gibbon
19.12	30.10	K12	K12	Tapir
20.12	1.11	A1	A1	Sheep
21.12	2.11	A1	B2	Deer
22.12	3.11	A1	C3	Horse
23.12	4.11	A1	D4	Stag
24.12	5.11	A1	E5	Serpent
25.12	6.11	A1	F6	Earthworm
26.12	7.11	A1	G7	Crocodile
27.12	8.11	A1	H8	Dragon
28.12	9.11	A1	J9	Badger
29.12	10.11	A1	K10	Hare
30.12	11.11	A1	A11	Fox
31.12	12.11	A1	B12	Tiger

1969

Solar date	Lunar date	Month HS/EB	Day HS/EB	Constellation
1. 1	13.11	A1	C1	Leopard
2. 1	14.11	A1	D2	Griffon
3. 1	15.11	A1	E3	Ox
4. 1	16.11	A1	F4	Bat
5. 1	17.11	A1	G5	Rat
6. 1	18.11	A1	H6	Swallow
7. 1	19.11	A1	J7	Pig
8. 1	20.11	A1	K8	Porcupine
9. 1	21.11	A1	A9	Wolf
10. 1	22.11	A1	B10	Dog
11. 1	23.11	A1	C11	Pheasant
12. 1	24.11	A1	D12	Cock
13. 1	25.11	A1	E1	Crow
14. 1	26.11	A1	F2	Monkey
15. 1	27.11	A1	G3	Gibbon
16. 1	28.11	A1	H4	Tapir
17. 1	29.11	A1	J5	Sheep
18. 1	1.12	B2	K6	Deer
19. 1	2.12	B2	A7	Horse
20. 1	3.12	B2	B8	Stag
21. 1	4.12	B2	C9	Serpent
22. 1	5.12	B2	D10	Earthworm
23. 1	6.12	B2	E11	Crocodile
24. 1	7.12	B2	F12	Dragon
25. 1	8.12	B2	G1	Badger
26. 1	9.12	B2	H2	Hare
27. 1	10.12	B2	J3	Fox
28. 1	11.12	B2	K4	Tiger
29. 1	12.12	B2	A5	Leopard
30. 1	13.12	B2	B6	Griffon
31. 1	14.12	B2	C7	Ox
1. 2	15.12	B2	D8	Bat
2. 2	16.12	B2	E9	Rat
3. 2	17.12	B2	F10	Swallow
4. 2	18.12	B2	G11	Pig
5. 2	19.12	B2	H12	Porcupine
6. 2	20.12	B2	J1	Wolf
7. 2	21.12	B2	K2	Dog
8. 2	22.12	B2	A3	Pheasant
9. 2	23.12	B2	B4	Cock
10. 2	24.12	B2	C5	Crow
11. 2	25.12	B2	D6	Monkey
12. 2	26.12	B2	E7	Gibbon
13. 2	27.12	B2	F8	Tapir
14. 2	28.12	B2	G9	Sheep
15. 2	29.12	B2	H10	Deer
16. 2	30.12	B2	J11	Horse

CHI YU YEAR

Solar date	Lunar date	Month HS/EB	Day HS/EB	Constellation
17. 2	1. 1	C3	K12	Stag
18. 2	2. 1	C3	A1	Serpent
19. 2	3. 1	C3	B2	Earthworm
20. 2	4. 1	C3	C3	Crocodile
21. 2	5. 1	C3	D4	Dragon
22. 2	6. 1	C3	E5	Badger
23. 2	7. 1	C3	F6	Hare
24. 2	8. 1	C3	G7	Fox
25. 2	9. 1	C3	H8	Tiger
26. 2	10. 1	C3	J9	Leopard
27. 2	11. 1	C3	K10	Griffon
28. 2	12. 1	C3	A11	Ox
1. 3	13. 1	C3	B12	Bat
2. 3	14. 1	C3	C1	Rat
3. 3	15. 1	C3	D2	Swallow
4. 3	16. 1	C3	E3	Pig
5. 3	17. 1	C3	F4	Porcupine
6. 3	18. 1	C3	G5	Wolf
7. 3	19. 1	C3	H6	Dog
8. 3	20. 1	C3	J7	Pheasant
9. 3	21. 1	C3	K8	Cock
10. 3	22. 1	C3	A9	Crow
11. 3	23. 1	C3	B10	Monkey
12. 3	24. 1	C3	C11	Gibbon
13. 3	25. 1	C3	D12	Tapir
14. 3	26. 1	C3	E1	Sheep
15. 3	27. 1	C3	F2	Deer
16. 3	28. 1	C3	G3	Horse
17. 3	29. 1	C3	H4	Stag
18. 3	1. 2	D4	J5	Serpent
19. 3	2. 2	D4	K6	Earthworm
20. 3	3. 2	D4	A7	Crocodile
21. 3	4. 2	D4	B8	Dragon
22. 3	5. 2	D4	C9	Badger
23. 3	6. 2	D4	D10	Hare
24. 3	7. 2	D4	E11	Fox

Solar date	Lunar date	Month HS/EB	Day HS/EB	Constellation	Solar date	Lunar date	Month HS/EB	Day HS/EB	Constellation
25. 3	8. 2	D4	F12	Tiger	6. 6	22. 4	F6	J1	Sheep
26. 3	9. 2	D4	G1	Leopard	7. 6	23. 4	F6	K2	Deer
27. 3	10. 2	D4	H2	Griffon	8. 6	24. 4	F6	A3	Horse
28. 3	11. 2	D4	J3	Ox	9. 6	25. 4	F6	B4	Stag
29. 3	12. 2	D4	K4	Bat	10. 6	26. 4	F6	C5	Serpent
30. 3	13. 2	D4	A5	Rat	11. 6	27. 4	F6	D6	Earthworm
31. 3	14. 2	D4	B6	Swallow	12. 6	28. 4	F6	E7	Crocodile
1. 4	15. 2	D4	C7	Pig	13. 6	29. 4	F6	F8	Dragon
2. 4	16. 2	D4	D8	Porcupine	14. 6	30. 4	F6	G9	Badger
3. 4	17. 2	D4	E9	Wolf	15. 6	1. 5	G7	H10	Hare
4. 4	18. 2	D4	F10	Dog	16. 6	2. 5	G7	J11	Fox
5. 4	19. 2	D4	G11	Pheasant	17. 6	3. 5	G7	K12	Tiger
6. 4	20. 2	D4	H12	Cock	18. 6	4. 5	G7	A1	Leopard
7. 4	21. 2	D4	J1	Crow	19. 6	5. 5	G7	B2	Griffon
8. 4	22. 2	D4	K2	Monkey	20. 6	6. 5	G7	C3	Ox
9. 4	23. 2	D4	A3	Gibbon	21. 6	7. 5	G7	D4	Bat
10. 4	24. 2	D4	B4	Tapir	22. 6	8. 5	G7	E5	Rat
11. 4	25. 2	D4	C5	Sheep	23. 6	9. 5	G7	F6	Swallow
12. 4	26. 2	D4	D6	Deer	24. 6	10. 5	G7	G7	Pig
13. 4	27. 2	D4	E7	Horse	25. 6	11. 5	G7	H8	Porcupine
14. 4	28. 2	D4	F8	Stag	26. 6	12. 5	G7	J9	Wolf
15. 4	29. 2	D4	G9	Serpent	27. 6	13. 5	G7	K10	Dog
16. 4	30. 2	D4	H10	Earthworm	28. 6	14. 5	G7	A11	Pheasant
17. 4	1. 3	E5	J11	Crocodile	29. 6	15. 5	G7	B12	Cock
18. 4	2. 3	E5	K12	Dragon	30. 6	16. 5	G7	C1	Crow
19. 4	3. 3	E5	A1	Badger	1. 7	17. 5	G7	D2	Monkey
20. 4	4. 3	E5	B2	Hare	2. 7	18. 5	G7	E3	Gibbon
21. 4	5. 3	E5	C3	Fox	3. 7	19. 5	G7	F4	Tapir
22. 4	6. 3	E5	D4	Tiger	4. 7	20. 5	G7	G5	Sheep
23. 4	7. 3	E5	E5	Leopard	5. 7	21. 5	G7	H6	Deer
24. 4	8. 3	E5	F6	Griffon	6. 7	22. 5	G7	J7	Horse
25. 4	9. 3	E5	G7	Ox	7. 7	23. 5	G7	K8	Stag
26. 4	10. 3	E5	H8	Bat	8. 7	24. 5	G7	A9	Serpent
27. 4	11. 3	E5	J9	Rat	9. 7	25. 5	G7	B10	Earthworm
28. 4	12. 3	E5	K10	Swallow	10. 7	26. 5	G7	C11	Crocodile
29. 4	13. 3	E5	A11	Pig	11. 7	27. 5	G7	D12	Dragon
30. 4	14. 3	E5	B12	Porcupine	12. 7	28. 5	G7	E1	Badger
1. 5	15. 3	E5	C1	Wolf	13. 7	29. 5	G7	F2	Hare
2. 5	16. 3	E5	D2	Dog	14. 7	1. 6	H8	G3	Fox
3. 5	17. 3	E5	E3	Pheasant	15. 7	2. 6	H8	H4	Tiger
4. 5	18. 3	E5	F4	Cock	16. 7	3. 6	H8	J5	Leopard
5. 5	19. 3	E5	G5	Crow	17. 7	4. 6	H8	K6	Griffon
6. 5	20. 3	E5	H6	Monkey	18. 7	5. 6	H8	A7	Ox
7. 5	21. 3	E5	J7	Gibbon	19. 7	6. 6	H8	B8	Bat
8. 5	22. 3	E5	K8	Tapir	20. 7	7. 6	H8	C9	Rat
9. 5	23. 3	E5	A9	Sheep	21. 7	8. 6	H8	D10	Swallow
10. 5	24. 3	E5	B10	Deer	22. 7	9. 6	H8	E11	Pig
11. 5	25. 3	E5	C11	Horse	23. 7	10. 6	H8	F12	Porcupine
12. 5	26. 3	E5	D12	Stag	24. 7	11. 6	H8	G1	Wolf
13. 5	27. 3	E5	E1	Serpent	25. 7	12. 6	H8	H2	Dog
14. 5	28. 3	E5	F2	Earthworm	26. 7	13. 6	H8	J3	Pheasant
15. 5	29. 3	E5	G3	Crocodile	27. 7	14. 6	H8	K4	Cock
16. 5	1. 4	F6	H4	Dragon	28. 7	15. 6	H8	A5	Crow
17. 5	2. 4	F6	J5	Badger	29. 7	16. 6	H8	B6	Monkey
18. 5	3. 4	F6	K6	Hare	30. 7	17. 6	H8	C7	Gibbon
19. 5	4. 4	F6	A7	Fox	31. 7	18. 6	H8	D8	Tapir
20. 5	5. 4	F6	B8	Tiger	1. 8	19. 6	H8	E9	Sheep
21. 5	6. 4	F6	C9	Leopard	2. 8	20. 6	H8	F10	Deer
22. 5	7. 4	F6	D10	Griffon	3. 8	21. 6	H8	G11	Horse
23. 5	8. 4	F6	E11	Ox	4. 8	22. 6	H8	H12	Stag
24. 5	9. 4	F6	F12	Bat	5. 8	23. 6	H8	J1	Serpent
25. 5	10. 4	F6	G1	Rat	6. 8	24. 6	H8	K2	Earthworm
26. 5	11. 4	F6	H2	Swallow	7. 8	25. 6	H8	A3	Crocodile
27. 5	12. 4	F6	J3	Pig	8. 8	26. 6	I10	B4	Dragon
28. 5	13. 4	F6	K4	Porcupine	9. 8	27. 6	H8	C5	Badger
29. 5	14. 4	F6	A5	Wolf	10. 8	28. 6	H8	D6	Hare
30. 5	15. 4	F6	B6	Dog	11. 8	29. 6	H8	E7	Fox
31. 5	16. 4	F6	C7	Pheasant	12. 8	30. 6	H8	F8	Tiger
1. 6	17. 4	F6	D8	Cock	13. 8	1. 7	J9	G9	Leopard
2. 6	18. 4	F6	E9	Crow	14. 8	2. 7	J9	H10	Griffon
3. 6	19. 4	F6	F10	Monkey	15. 8	3. 7	J9	J11	Ox
4. 6	20. 4	F6	G11	Gibbon	16. 8	4. 7	J9	K12	Bat
5. 6	21. 4	F6	H12	Tapir	17. 8	5. 7	J9	A1	Rat

Solar date	Lunar date	Month HS/EB	Day HS/EB	Constellation
18. 8	6. 7	J9	B2	Swallow
19. 8	7. 7	J9	C3	Pig
20. 8	8. 7	J9	D4	Porcupine
21. 8	9. 7	J9	E5	Wolf
22. 8	10. 7	J9	F6	Dog
23. 8	11. 7	J9	G7	Pheasant
24. 8	12. 7	J9	H8	Cock
25. 8	13. 7	J9	J9	Crow
26. 8	14. 7	J9	K10	Monkey
27. 8	15. 7	J9	A11	Gibbon
28. 8	16. 7	J9	B12	Tapir
29. 8	17. 7	J9	C1	Sheep
30. 8	18. 7	J9	D2	Deer
31. 8	19. 7	J9	E3	Horse
1. 9	20. 7	J9	F4	Stag
2. 9	21. 7	J9	G5	Serpent
3. 9	22. 7	J9	H6	Earthworm
4. 9	23. 7	J9	J7	Crocodile
5. 9	24. 7	J9	K8	Dragon
6. 9	25. 7	J9	A9	Badger
7. 9	26. 7	J9	B10	Hare
8. 9	27. 7	J9	C11	Fox
9. 9	28. 7	J9	D12	Tiger
10. 9	29. 7	J9	E1	Leopard
11. 9	30. 7	J9	F2	Griffon
12. 9	1. 8	K10	G3	Ox
13. 9	2. 8	K10	H4	Bat
14. 9	3. 8	K10	J5	Rat
15. 9	4. 8	K10	K6	Swallow
16. 9	5. 8	K10	A7	Pig
17. 9	6. 8	K10	B8	Porcupine
18. 9	7. 8	K10	C9	Wolf
19. 9	8. 8	K10	D10	Dog
20. 9	9. 8	K10	E11	Pheasant
21. 9	10. 8	K10	F12	Cock
22. 9	11. 8	K10	G1	Crow
23. 9	12. 8	K10	H2	Monkey
24. 9	13. 8	K10	J3	Gibbon
25. 9	14. 8	K10	K4	Tapir
26. 9	15. 8	K10	A5	Sheep
27. 9	16. 8	K10	B6	Deer
28. 9	17. 8	K10	C7	Horse
29. 9	18. 8	K10	D8	Stag
30. 9	19. 8	K10	E9	Serpent
1.10	20. 8	K10	F10	Earthworm
2.10	21. 8	K10	G11	Crocodile
3.10	22. 8	K10	H12	Dragon
4.10	23. 8	K10	J1	Badger
5.10	24. 8	K10	K2	Hare
6.10	25. 8	K10	A3	Fox
7.10	26. 8	K10	B4	Tiger
8.10	27. 8	K10	C5	Leopard
9.10	28. 8	K10	D6	Griffon
10.10	29. 8	K10	E7	Ox
11.10	1. 9	A11	F8	Bat
12.10	2. 9	A11	G9	Rat
13.10	3. 9	A11	H10	Swallow
14.10	4. 9	A11	J11	Pig
15.10	5. 9	A11	K12	Porcupine
16.10	6. 9	A11	A1	Wolf
17.10	7. 9	A11	B2	Dog
18.10	8. 9	A11	C3	Pheasant
19.10	9. 9	A11	D4	Cock
20.10	10. 9	A11	E5	Crow
21.10	11. 9	A11	F6	Monkey
22.10	12. 9	A11	G7	Gibbon
23.10	13. 9	A11	H8	Tapir
24.10	14. 9	A11	J9	Sheep
25.10	15. 9	A11	K10	Deer
26.10	16. 9	A11	A11	Horse
27.10	17. 9	A11	B12	Stag
28.10	18. 9	A11	C1	Serpent
29.10	19. 9	A11	D2	Earthworm
30.10	20. 9	A11	E3	Crocodile
31.10	21. 9	A11	F4	Dragon
1.11	22. 9	A11	G5	Badger
2.11	23. 9	A11	H6	Hare
3.11	24. 9	A11	J7	Fox
4.11	25. 9	A11	K8	Tiger
5.11	26. 9	A11	A9	Leopard
6.11	27. 9	A11	B10	Griffon
7.11	28. 9	A11	C11	Ox
8.11	29. 9	A11	D12	Bat
9.11	30. 9	A11	E1	Rat
10.11	1.10	B12	F2	Swallow
11.11	2.10	B12	G3	Pig
12.11	3.10	B12	H4	Porcupine
13.11	4.10	B12	J5	Wolf
14.11	5.10	B12	K6	Dog
15.11	6.10	B12	A7	Pheasant
16.11	7.10	B12	B8	Cock
17.11	8.10	B12	C9	Crow
18.11	9.10	B12	D10	Monkey
19.11	10.10	B12	E11	Gibbon
20.11	11.10	B12	F12	Tapir
21.11	12.10	B12	G1	Sheep
22.11	13.10	B12	H2	Deer
23.11	14.10	B12	J3	Horse
24.11	15.10	B12	K4	Stag
25.11	16.10	B12	A5	Serpent
26.11	17.10	B12	B6	Earthworm
27.11	18.10	B12	C7	Crocodile
28.11	19.10	B12	D8	Dragon
29.11	20.10	B12	E9	Badger
30.11	21.10	B12	F10	Hare
1.12	22.10	B12	G11	Fox
2.12	23.10	B12	H12	Tiger
3.12	24.10	B12	J1	Leopard
4.12	25.10	B12	K2	Griffon
5.12	26.10	B12	A3	Ox
6.12	27.10	B12	B4	Bat
7.12	28.10	B12	C5	Rat
8.12	29.10	B12	D6	Swallow
9.12	1.11	C1	E7	Pig
10.12	2.11	C1	F8	Porcupine
11.12	3.11	C1	G9	Wolf
12.12	4.11	C1	H10	Dog
13.12	5.11	C1	J11	Pheasant
14.12	6.11	C1	K12	Cock
15.12	7.11	C1	A1	Crow
16.12	8.11	C1	B2	Monkey
17.12	9.11	C1	C3	Gibbon
18.12	10.11	C1	D4	Tapir
19.12	11.11	C1	E5	Sheep
20.12	12.11	C1	F6	Deer
21.12	13.11	C1	G7	Horse
22.12	14.11	C1	H8	Stag
23.12	15.11	C1	J9	Serpent
24.12	16.11	C1	K10	Earthworm
25.12	17.11	C1	A11	Crocodile
26.12	18.11	C1	B12	Dragon
27.12	19.11	C1	C1	Badger
28.12	20.11	C1	D2	Hare
29.12	21.11	C1	E3	Fox
30.12	22.11	C1	F4	Tiger
31.12	23.11	C1	G5	Leopard

1970

Solar date	Lunar date	Month HS/EB	Day HS/EB	Constellation
1. 1	24.11	C1	H6	Griffon
2. 1	25.11	C1	J7	Ox
3. 1	26.11	C1	K8	Bat
4. 1	27.11	C1	A9	Rat
5. 1	28.11	C1	B10	Swallow
6. 1	29.11	C1	C11	Pig
7. 1	30.11	C1	D12	Porcupine
8. 1	1.12	D2	E1	Wolf

Solar date	Lunar date	Month HS/EB	Day HS/EB	Constellation	Solar date	Lunar date	Month HS/EB	Day HS/EB	Constellation
9. 1	2.12	D2	F2	Dog	23. 1	16.12	D2	K4	Dragon
10. 1	3.12	D2	G3	Pheasant	24. 1	17.12	D2	A5	Badger
11. 1	4.12	D2	H4	Cock	25. 1	18.12	D2	B6	Hare
12. 1	5.12	D2	J5	Crow	26. 1	19.12	D2	C7	Fox
13. 1	6.12	D2	K6	Monkey	27. 1	20.12	D2	D8	Tiger
14. 1	7.12	D2	A7	Gibbon	28. 1	21.12	D2	E9	Leopard
15. 1	8.12	D2	B8	Tapir	29. 1	22.12	D2	F10	Griffon
16. 1	9.12	D2	C9	Sheep	30. 1	23.12	D2	G11	Ox
17. 1	10.12	D2	D10	Deer	31. 1	24.12	D2	H12	Bat
18. 1	11.12	D2	E11	Horse	1. 2	25.12	D2	J1	Rat
19. 1	12.12	D2	F12	Stag	2. 2	26.12	D2	K2	Swallow
20. 1	13.12	D2	G1	Serpent	3. 2	27.12	D2	A3	Pig
21. 1	14.12	D2	H2	Earthworm	4. 2	28.12	D2	B4	Porcupine
22. 1	15.12	D2	J3	Crocodile	5. 2	29.12	D2	C5	Wolf

KENG HSÜ YEAR

Solar date	Lunar date	Month HS/EB	Day HS/EB	Constellation	Solar date	Lunar date	Month HS/EB	Day HS/EB	Constellation
6. 2	1. 1	E3	D6	Dog	1. 4	25. 2	F4	H12	Porcupine
7. 2	2. 1	E3	E7	Pheasant	2. 4	26. 2	F4	J1	Wolf
8. 2	3. 1	E3	F8	Cock	3. 4	27. 2	F4	K2	Dog
9. 2	4. 1	E3	G9	Crow	4. 4	28. 2	F4	A3	Pheasant
10. 1	5. 1	E3	H10	Monkey	5. 4	29. 2	F4	B4	Cock
11. 2	6. 1	E3	J11	Gibbon	6. 4	1. 3	G5	C5	Crow
12. 2	7. 1	E3	K12	Tapir	7. 4	2. 3	G5	D6	Monkey
13. 2	8. 1	E3	A1	Sheep	8. 4	3. 3	G5	E7	Gibbon
14. 2	9. 1	E3	B2	Deer	9. 4	4. 3	G5	F8	Tapir
15. 2	10. 1	E3	C3	Horse	10. 4	5. 3	G5	G9	Sheep
16. 2	11. 1	E3	D4	Stag	11. 4	6. 3	G5	H10	Deer
17. 2	12. 1	E3	E5	Serpent	12. 4	7. 3	G5	J11	Horse
18. 2	13. 1	E3	F6	Earthworm	13. 4	8. 3	G5	K12	Stag
19. 2	14. 1	E3	G7	Crocodile	14. 4	9. 3	G5	A1	Serpent
20. 2	15. 1	E3	H8	Dragon	15. 4	10. 3	G5	B2	Earthworm
21. 2	16. 1	E3	J9	Badger	16. 4	11. 3	G5	C3	Crocodile
22. 2	17. 1	E3	K10	Hare	17. 4	12. 3	G5	D4	Dragon
23. 2	18. 1	E3	A11	Fox	18. 4	13. 3	G5	E5	Badger
24. 2	19. 1	E3	B12	Tiger	19. 4	14. 3	G5	F6	Hare
25. 2	20. 1	E3	C1	Leopard	20. 4	15. 3	G5	G7	Fox
26. 2	21. 1	E3	D2	Griffon	21. 4	16. 3	G5	H8	Tiger
27. 2	22. 1	E3	E3	Ox	22. 4	17. 3	G5	J9	Leopard
28. 2	23. 1	E3	F4	Bat	23. 4	18. 3	G5	K10	Griffon
1. 3	24. 1	E3	G5	Rat	24. 4	19. 3	G5	A11	Ox
2. 3	25. 1	E3	H6	Swallow	25. 4	20. 3	G5	B12	Bat
3. 3	26. 1	E3	J7	Pig	26. 4	21. 3	G5	C1	Rat
4. 3	27. 1	E3	K8	Porcupine	27. 4	22. 3	G5	D2	Swallow
5. 3	28. 1	E3	A9	Wolf	28. 4	23. 3	G5	E3	Pig
6. 3	29. 1	E3	B10	Dog	29. 4	24. 3	G5	F4	Porcupine
7. 3	30. 1	E3	C11	Pheasant	30. 4	25. 3	'G5	G5	Wolf
8. 3	1. 2	F4	D12	Cock	1. 5	26. 3	G5	H6	Dog
9. 3	2. 2	F4	E1	Crow	2. 5	27. 3	G5	J7	Pheasant
10. 3	3. 2	F4	F2	Monkey	3. 5	28. 3	G5	K8	Cock
11. 3	4. 2	F4	G3	Gibbon	4. 5	29. 3	G5	A9	Crow
12. 3	5. 2	F4	H4	Tapir	5. 5	1. 4	H6	B10	Monkey
13. 3	6. 2	F4	J5	Sheep	6. 5	2. 4	H6	C11	Gibbon
14. 3	7. 2	F4	K6	Deer	7. 5	3. 4	H6	D12	Tapir
15. 3	8. 2	F4	A7	Horse	8. 5	4. 4	H6	E1	Sheep
16. 3	9. 2	F4	B8	Stag	9. 5	5. 4	H6	F2	Deer
17. 3	10. 2	F4	C9	Serpent	10. 5	6. 4	H6	G3	Horse
18. 3	11. 2	F4	D10	Earthworm	11. 5	7. 4	H6	H4	Stag
19. 3	12. 2	F4	E11	Crocodile	12. 5	8. 4	H6	J5	Serpent
20. 3	13. 2	F4	F12	Dragon	13. 5	9. 4	H6	K6	Earthworm
21. 3	14. 2	F4	G1	Badger	14. 5	10. 4	H6	A7	Crocodile
22. 3	15. 2	F4	H2	Hare	15. 5	11. 4	H6	B8	Dragon
23. 3	16. 2	F4	J3	Fox	16. 5	12. 4	H6	C9	Badger
24. 3	17. 2	F4	K4	Tiger	17. 5	13. 4	H6	D10	Hare
25. 3	18. 2	F4	A5	Leopard	18. 5	14. 4	H6	E11	Fox
26. 3	19. 2	F4	B6	Griffon	19. 5	15. 4	H6	F12	Tiger
27. 3	20. 2	F4	C7	Ox	20. 5	16. 4	H6	G1	Leopard
28. 3	21. 2	F4	D8	Bat	21. 5	17. 4	H6	H2	Griffon
29. 3	22. 2	F4	E9	Rat	22. 5	18. 4	H6	J3	Ox
30. 3	23. 2	F4	F10	Swallow	23. 5	19. 4	H6	K4	Bat
31. 3	24. 2	F4	G11	Pig	24. 5	20. 4	H6	A5	Rat

Solar date	Lunar date	Month HS/EB	Day HS/EB	Constellation	Solar date	Lunar date	Month HS/EB	Day HS/EB	Constellation
25. 5	21. 4	H6	B6	Swallow	6. 8	5. 7	A9	E7	Crocodile
26. 5	22. 4	H6	C7	Pig	7. 8	6. 7	A9	F8	Dragon
27. 5	23. 4	H6	D8	Porcupine	8. 8	7. 7	A9	G9	Badger
28. 5	24. 4	H6	E9	Wolf	9. 8	8. 7	A9	H10	Hare
29. 5	25. 4	H6	F10	Dog	10. 8	9. 7	A9	J11	Fox
30. 5	26. 4	H6	G11	Pheasant	11. 8	10. 7	A9	K12	Tiger
31. 5	27. 4	H6	H12	Cock	12. 8	11. 7	A9	A1	Leopard
1. 6	28. 4	H6	J1	Crow	13. 8	12. 7	A9	B2	Griffon
2. 6	29. 4	H6	K2	Monkey	14. 8	13. 7	A9	C3	Ox
3. 6	30. 4	H6	A3	Gibbon	15. 8	14. 7	A9	D4	Bat
4. 6	1. 5	J7	B4	Tapir	16. 8	15. 7	A9	E5	Rat
5. 6	2. 5	J7	C5	Sheep	17. 8	16. 7	A9	F6	Swallow
6. 6	3. 5	J7	D6	Deer	18. 8	17. 7	A9	G7	Pig
7. 6	4. 5	J7	E7	Horse	19. 8	18. 7	A9	H8	Porcupine
8. 6	5. 5	J7	F8	Stag	20. 8	19. 7	A9	J9	Wolf
9. 6	6. 5	J7	G9	Serpent	21. 8	20. 7	A9	K10	Dog
10. 6	7. 5	J7	H10	Earthworm	22. 8	21. 7	A9	A11	Pheasant
11. 6	8. 5	J7	J11	Crocodile	23. 8	22. 7	A9	B12	Cock
12. 6	9. 5	J7	K12	Dragon	24. 8	23. 7	A9	C1	Crow
13. 6	10. 5	J7	A1	Badger	25. 8	24. 7	A9	D2	Monkey
14. 6	11. 5	J7	B2	Hare	26. 8	25. 7	A9	E3	Gibbon
15. 6	12. 5	J7	C3	Fox	27. 8	26. 7	A9	F4	Tapir
16. 6	13. 5	J7	D4	Tiger	28. 8	27. 7	A9	G5	Sheep
17. 6	14. 5	J7	E5	Leopard	29. 8	28. 7	A9	H6	Deer
18. 6	15. 5	J7	F6	Griffon	30. 8	29. 7	A9	J7	Horse
19. 6	16. 5	J7	G7	Ox	31. 8	30. 7	A9	K8	Stag
20. 6	17. 5	J7	H8	Bat	1. 9	1. 8	B10	A9	Serpent
21. 6	18. 5	J7	J9	Rat	2. 9	2. 8	B10	B10	Earthworm
22. 6	19. 5	J7	K10	Swallow	3. 9	3. 8	B10	C11	Crocodile
23. 6	20. 5	J7	A11	Pig	4. 9	4. 8	B10	D12	Dragon
24. 6	21. 5	J7	B12	Porcupine	5. 9	5. 8	B10	E1	Badger
25. 6	22. 5	J7	C1	Wolf	6. 9	6. 8	B10	F2	Hare
26. 6	23. 5	J7	D2	Dog	7. 9	7. 8	B10	G3	Fox
27. 6	24. 5	J7	E3	Pheasant	8. 9	8. 8	B10	H4	Tiger
28. 6	25. 5	J7	F4	Cock	9. 9	9. 8	B10	J5	Leopard
29. 6	26. 5	J7	G5	Crow	10. 9	10. 8	B10	K6	Griffon
30. 6	27. 5	J7	H6	Monkey	11. 9	11. 8	B10	A7	Ox
1. 7	28. 5	J7	J7	Gibbon	12. 9	12. 8	B10	B8	Bat
2. 7	29. 5	J7	K8	Tapir	13. 9	13. 8	B10	C9	Rat
3. 7	1. 6	K8	A9	Sheep	14. 9	14. 8	B10	D10	Swallow
4. 7	2. 6	K8	B10	Deer	15. 9	15. 8	B10	E11	Pig
5. 7	3. 6	K8	C11	Horse	16. 9	16. 8	B10	F12	Porcupine
6. 7	4. 6	K8	D12	Stag	17. 9	17. 8	B10	G1	Wolf
7. 7	5. 6	K8	E1	Serpent	18. 9	18. 8	B10	H2	Dog
8. 7	6. 6	K8	F2	Earthworm	19. 9	19. 8	B10	J3	Pheasant
9. 7	7. 6	K8	G3	Crocodile	20. 9	20. 8	B10	K4	Cock
10. 7	8. 6	K8	H4	Dragon	21. 9	21. 8	B10	A5	Crow
11. 7	9. 6	K8	J5	Badger	22. 9	22. 8	B10	B6	Monkey
12. 7	10. 6	K8	K6	Hare	23. 9	23. 8	B10	C7	Gibbon
13. 7	11. 6	K8	A7	Fox	24. 9	24. 8	B10	D8	Tapir
14. 7	12. 6	K8	B8	Tiger	25. 9	25. 8	B10	E9	Sheep
15. 7	13. 6	K8	C9	Leopard	26. 9	26. 8	B10	F10	Deer
16. 7	14. 6	K8	D10	Griffon	27. 9	27. 8	B10	G11	Horse
17. 7	15. 6	K8	E11	Ox	28. 9	28. 8	B10	H12	Stag
18. 7	16. 6	K8	F12	Bat	29. 9	29. 8	B10	J1	Serpent
19. 7	17. 6	K8	G1	Rat	30. 9	1. 9	C11	K2	Earthworm
20. 7	18. 6	K8	H2	Swallow	1.10	2. 9	C11	A3	Crocodile
21. 7	19. 6	K8	J3	Pig	2.10	3. 9	C11	B4	Dragon
22. 7	20. 6	K8	K4	Porcupine	3.10	4. 9	C11	C5	Badger
23. 7	21. 6	K8	A5	Wolf	4.10	5. 9	C11	D6	Hare
24. 7	22. 6	K8	B6	Dog	5.10	6. 9	C11	E7	Fox
25. 7	23. 6	K8	C7	Pheasant	6.10	7. 9	C11	F8	Tiger
26. 7	24. 6	K8	D8	Cock	7.10	8. 9	C11	G9	Leopard
27. 7	25. 6	K8	E9	Crow	8.10	9. 9	C11	H10	Griffon
28. 7	26. 6	K8	F10	Monkey	9.10	10. 9	C11	J11	Ox
29. 7	27. 6	K8	G11	Gibbon	10.10	11. 9	C11	K12	Bat
30. 7	28. 6	K8	H12	Tapir	11.10	12. 9	C11	A1	Rat
31. 7	29. 6	K8	J1	Sheep	12.10	13. 9	C11	B2	Swallow
1. 8	30. 6	K8	K2	Deer	13.10	14. 9	C11	C3	Pig
2. 8	1. 7	A9	A3	Horse	14.10	15. 9	C11	D4	Porcupine
3. 8	2. 7	A9	B4	Stag	15.10	16. 9	C11	E5	Wolf
4. 8	3. 7	A9	C5	Serpent	16.10	17. 9	C11	F6	Dog
5. 8	4. 7	A9	D6	Earthworm	17.10	18. 9	C11	G7	Pheasant

Solar date	Lunar date	Month HS/EB	Day HS/EB	Constellation
18.10	19. 9	C11	H8	Cock
19.10	20. 9	C11	J9	Crow
20.10	21. 9	C11	K10	Monkey
21.10	22. 9	C11	A11	Gibbon
22.10	23. 9	C11	B12	Tapir
23.10	24. 9	C11	C1	Sheep
24.10	25. 9	C11	D2	Deer
25.10	26. 9	C11	E3	Horse
26.10	27. 9	C11	F4	Stag
27.10	28. 9	C11	G5	Serpent
28.10	29. 9	C11	H6	Earthworm
29.10	30. 9	C11	J7	Crocodile
30.10	1.10	D12	K8	Dragon
31.10	2.10	D12	A9	Badger
1.11	3.10	D12	B10	Hare
2.11	4.10	D12	C11	Fox
3.11	5.10	D12	D12	Tiger
4.11	6.10	D12	E1	Leopard
5.11	7.10	D12	F2	Griffon
6.11	8.10	D12	G3	Ox
7.11	9.10	D12	H4	Bat
8.11	10.10	D12	J5	Rat
9.11	11.10	D12	K6	Swallow
10.11	12.10	D12	A7	Pig
11.11	13.10	D12	B8	Porcupine
12.11	14.10	D12	C9	Wolf
13.11	15.10	D12	D10	Dog
14.11	16.10	D12	E11	Pheasant
15.11	17.10	D12	F12	Cock
16.11	18.10	D12	G1	Crow
17.11	19.10	D12	H2	Monkey
18.11	20.10	D12	J3	Gibbon
19.11	21.10	D12	K4	Tapir
20.11	22.10	D12	A5	Sheep
21.11	23.10	D12	B6	Deer
22.11	24.10	D12	C7	Horse
23.11	25.10	D12	D8	Stag
24.11	26.10	D12	E9	Serpent
25.11	27.10	D12	F10	Earthworm
26.11	28.10	D12	G11	Crocodile
27.11	29.10	D12	H12	Dragon
28.11	30.10	D12	J1	Badger
29.11	1.11	E1	K2	Hare
30.11	2.11	E1	A3	Fox
1.12	3.11	E1	B4	Tiger
2.12	4.11	E1	C5	Leopard
3.12	5.11	E1	D6	Griffon
4.12	6.11	E1	E7	Ox
5.12	7.11	E1	F8	Bat
6.12	8.11	E1	G9	Rat
7.12	9.11	E1	H10	Swallow
8.10	10.11	E1	J11	Pig
9.12	11.11	E1	K12	Porcupine
10.12	12.11	E1	A1	Wolf
11.12	13.11	E1	B2	Dog
12.12	14.11	E1	C3	Pheasant
13.12	15.11	E1	D4	Cock
14.12	16.11	E1	E5	Crow
15.12	17.11	E1	F6	Monkey
16.12	18.11	E1	G7	Gibbon
17.12	19.11	E1	H8	Tapir
18.12	20.11	E1	J9	Sheep
19.12	21.11	E1	K10	Deer
20.12	22.11	E1	A11	Horse
21.12	23.11	E1	B12	Stag
22.12	24.11	E1	C1	Serpent
23.12	25.11	E1	D2	Earthworm
24.12	26.11	E1	E3	Crocodile
25.12	27.11	E1	F4	Dragon
26.12	28.11	E1	G5	Badger
27.12	29.11	E1	H6	Hare
28.12	1.12	F2	J7	Fox
29.12	2.12	F2	K8	Tiger
30.12	3.12	F2	A9	Leopard
31.12	4.12	F2	B10	Griffon

1971

Solar date	Lunar date	Month HS/EB	Day HS/EB	Constellation
1. 1	5.12	F2	C11	Ox
2. 1	6.12	F2	D12	Bat
3. 1	7.12	F2	E1	Rat
4. 1	8.12	F2	F2	Swallow
5. 1	9.12	F2	G3	Pig
6. 1	10.12	F2	H4	Porcupine
7. 1	11.12	F2	J5	Wolf
8. 1	12.12	F2	K6	Dog
9. 1	13.12	F2	A7	Pheasant
10. 1	14.12	F2	B8	Cock
11. 1	15.12	F2	C9	Crow
12. 1	16.12	F2	D10	Monkey
13. 1	17.12	F2	E11	Gibbon
14. 1	18.12	F2	F12	Tapir
15. 1	19.12	F2	G1	Sheep
16. 1	20.12	F2	H2	Deer
17. 1	21.12	F2	J3	Horse
18. 1	22.12	F2	K4	Stag
19. 1	23.12	F2	A5	Serpent
20. 1	24.12	F2	B6	Earthworm
21. 1	25.12	F2	C7	Crocodile
22. 1	26.12	F2	D8	Dragon
23. 1	27.12	F2	E9	Badger
24. 1	28.12	F2	F10	Hare
25. 1	29.12	F2	G11	Fox
26. 1	30.12	F2	H12	Tiger

HSIN HAI YEAR

Solar date	Lunar date	Month HS/EB	Day HS/EB	Constellation
27. 1	1. 1	G3	J1	Leopard
28. 1	2. 1	G3	K2	Griffon
29. 1	3. 1	G3	A3	Ox
30. 1	4. 1	G3	B4	Bat
31. 1	5. 1	G3	C5	Rat
1. 2	6. 1	G3	D6	Swallow
2. 2	7. 1	G3	E7	Pig
3. 2	8. 1	G3	F8	Porcupine
4. 2	9. 1	G3	G9	Wolf
5. 2	10. 1	G3	H10	Dog
6. 2	11. 1	G3	J11	Pheasant
7. 2	12. 1	G3	K12	Cock
8. 2	13. 1	G3	A1	Crow
9. 2	14. 1	G3	B2	Monkey
10. 2	15. 1	G3	C3	Gibbon
11. 2	16. 1	G3	D4	Tapir
12. 2	17. 1	G3	E5	Sheep
13. 2	18. 1	G3	F6	Deer
14. 2	19. 1	G3	G7	Horse
15. 2	20. 1	G3	H8	Stag
16. 2	21. 1	G3	J9	Serpent
17. 2	22. 1	G3	K10	Earthworm
18. 2	23. 1	G3	A11	Crocodile
19. 2	24. 1	G3	B12	Dragon
20. 2	25. 1	G3	C1	Badger
21. 2	26. 1	G3	D2	Hare
22. 2	27. 1	G3	E3	Fox
23. 2	28. 1	G3	F4	Tiger
24. 2	29. 1	G3	G5	Leopard
25. 2	1. 2	H4	H6	Griffon
26. 2	2. 2	H4	J7	Ox
27. 2	3. 2	H4	K8	Bat

Solar date	Lunar date	Month HS/EB	Day HS/EB	Constellation	Solar date	Lunar date	Month HS/EB	Day HS/EB	Constellation
28. 2	4. 2	H4	A9	Rat	12. 5	18. 4	K6	D10	Earthworm
1. 3	5. 2	H4	B10	Swallow	13. 5	19. 4	K6	E11	Crocodile
2. 3	6. 2	H4	C11	Pig	14. 5	20. 4	K6	F12	Dragon
3. 3	7. 2	H4	D12	Porcupine	15. 5	21. 4	K6	G1	Badger
4. 3	8. 2	H4	E1	Wolf	16. 5	22. 4	K6	H2	Hare
5. 3	9. 2	H4	F2	Dog	17. 5	23. 4	K6	J3	Fox
6. 3	10. 2	H4	G3	Pheasant	18. 5	24. 4	K6	K4	Tiger
7. 3	11. 2	H4	H4	Cock	19. 5	25. 4	K6	A5	Leopard
8. 3	12. 2	H4	J5	Crow	20. 5	26. 4	K6	B6	Griffon
9. 3	13. 2	H4	K6	Monkey	21. 5	27. 4	K6	C7	Ox
10. 3	14. 2	H4	A7	Gibbon	22. 5	28. 4	K6	D8	Bat
11. 3	15. 2	H4	B8	Tapir	23. 5	29. 4	K6	E9	Rat
12. 3	16. 2	H4	C9	Sheep	24. 5	1. 5	A7	F10	Swallow
13. 3	17. 2	H4	D10	Deer	25. 5	2. 5	A7	G11	Pig
14. 3	18. 2	H4	E11	Horse	26. 5	3. 5	A7	H12	Porcupine
15. 3	19. 2	H4	F12	Stag	27. 5	4. 5	A7	J1	Wolf
16. 3	20. 2	H4	G1	Serpent	28. 5	5. 5	A7	K2	Dog
17. 3	21. 2	H4	H2	Earthworm	29. 5	6. 5	A7	A3	Pheasant
18. 3	22. 2	H4	J3	Crocodile	30. 5	7. 5	A7	B4	Cock
19. 3	23. 2	H4	K4	Dragon	31. 5	8. 5	A7	C5	Crow
20. 3	24. 2	H4	A5	Badger	1. 6	9. 5	A7	D6	Monkey
21. 3	25. 2	H4	B6	Hare	2. 6	10. 5	A7	E7	Gibbon
22. 3	26. 2	H4	C7	Fox	3. 6	11. 5	A7	F8	Tapir
23. 3	27. 2	H4	D8	Tiger	4. 6	12. 5	A7	G9	Sheep
24. 3	28. 2	H4	E9	Leopard	5. 6	13. 5	A7	H10	Deer
25. 3	29. 2	H4	F10	Griffon	6. 6	14. 5	A7	J11	Horse
26. 3	30. 2	H4	G11	Ox	7. 6	15. 5	A7	K12	Stag
27. 3	1. 3	5	H12	Bat	8. 6	16. 5	A7	A1	Serpent
28. 3	2. 3	J5	J1	Rat	9. 6	17. 5	A7	B2	Earthworm
29. 3	3. 3	J5	K2	Swallow	10. 6	18. 5	A7	C3	Crocodile
30. 3	4. 3	J5	A3	Pig	11. 6	19. 5	A7	D4	Dragon
31. 3	5. 3	J5	B4	Porcupine	12. 6	20. 5	A7	E5	Badger
1. 4	6. 3	J5	C5	Wolf	13. 6	21. 5	A7	F6	Hare
2. 4	7. 3	J5	D6	Dog	14. 6	22. 5	A7	G7	Fox
3. 4	8. 3	J5	E7	Pheasant	15. 6	23. 5	A7	H8	Tiger
4. 4	9. 3	J5	F8	Cock	16. 6	24. 5	A7	J9	Leopard
5. 4	10. 3	J5	G9	Crow	17. 6	25. 5	A7	K10	Griffon
6. 4	11. 3	J5	H10	Monkey	18. 6	26. 5	A7	A11	Ox
7. 4	12. 3	J5	J11	Gibbon	19. 6	27. 5	A7	B12	Bat
8. 4	13. 3	J5	K12	Tapir	20. 6	28. 5	A7	C1	Rat
9. 4	14. 3	J5	A1	Sheep	21. 6	29. 5	A7	D2	Swallow
10. 4	15. 3	J5	B2	Deer	22. 6	30. 5	A7	E3	Pig
11. 4	16. 3	J5	C3	Horse	23. 6	1. 5	A7	F4	Porcupine
12. 4	17. 3	J5	D4	Stag	24. 6	2. 5	A7	G5	Wolf
13. 4	18. 3	J5	E5	Serpent	25. 6	3. 5	A7	H6	Dog
14. 4	19. 3	J5	F6	Earthworm	26. 6	4. 5	A7	J7	Pheasant
15. 4	20. 3	J5	G7	Crocodile	27. 6	5. 5	A7	K8	Cock
16. 4	21. 3	J5	H8	Dragon	28. 6	6. 5	A7	A9	Crow
17. 4	22. 3	J5	J9	Badger	29. 6	7. 5	A7	B10	Monkey
18. 4	23. 3	J5	K10	Hare	30. 6	8. 5	A7	C11	Gibbon
19. 4	24. 3	J5	A11	Fox	1. 7	9. 5	A7	D12	Tapir
20. 4	25. 3	J5	B12	Tiger	2. 7	10. 5	A7	E1	Sheep
21. 4	26. 3	J5	C1	Leopard	3. 7	11. 5	A7	F2	Deer
22. 4	27. 3	J5	D2	Griffon	4. 7	12. 5	A7	G3	Horse
23. 4	28. 3	J5	E3	Ox	5. 7	13. 5	A7	H4	Stag
24. 4	29. 3	J5	F4	Bat	6. 7	14. 5	A7	J5	Serpent
25. 4	1. 4	K6	G5	Rat	7. 7	15. 5	A7	K6	Earthworm
26. 4	2. 4	K6	H6	Swallow	8. 7	16. 5	A7	A7	Crocodile
27. 4	3. 4	K6	J7	Pig	9. 7	17. 5	A7	B8	Dragon
28. 4	4. 4	K6	K8	Porcupine	10. 7	18. 5	A7	C9	Badger
29. 4	5. 4	K6	A9	Wolf	11. 7	19. 5	A7	D10	Hare
30. 4	6. 4	K6	B10	Dog	12. 7	20. 5	A7	E11	Fox
1. 5	7. 4	K6	C11	Pheasant	13. 7	21. 5	A7	F12	Tiger
2. 5	8. 4	K6	D12	Cock	14. 7	22. 5	A7	G1	Leopard
3. 5	9. 4	K6	E1	Crow	15. 7	23. 5	A7	H2	Griffon
4. 5	10. 4	K6	F2	Monkey	16. 7	24. 5	A7	J3	Ox
5. 5	11. 4	K6	G3	Gibbon	17. 7	25. 5	A7	K4	Bat
6. 5	12. 4	K6	H4	Tapir	18. 7	26. 5	A7	A5	Rat
7. 5	13. 4	K6	J5	Sheep	19. 7	27. 5	A7	B6	Swallow
8. 5	14. 4	K6	K6	Deer	20. 7	28. 5	A7	C7	Pig
9. 5	15. 4	K6	A7	Horse	21. 7	29. 5	A7	D8	Porcupine
10. 5	16. 4	K6	B8	Stag	22. 7	1. 6	B8	E9	Wolf
11. 5	17. 4	K6	C9	Serpent	23. 7	2. 6	B8	F10	Dog

Solar date	Lunar date	Month HS/EB	Day HS/EB	Constellation	Solar date	Lunar date	Month HS/EB	Day HS/EB	Constellation
24. 7	3. 6	B8	G11	Pheasant	5.10	17. 8	D10	K12	Tiger
25. 7	4. 6	B8	H12	Cock	6.10	18. 8	D10	A1	Leopard
26. 7	5. 6	B8	J1	Crow	7.10	19. 8	D10	B2	Griffon
27. 7	6. 6	B8	K2	Monkey	8.10	20. 8	D10	C3	Ox
28. 7	7. 6	B8	A3	Gibbon	9.10	21. 8	D10	D4	Bat
29. 7	8. 6	B8	B4	Tapir	10.10	22. 8	D10	E5	Rat
30. 7	9. 6	B8	C5	Sheep	11.10	23. 8	D10	F6	Swallow
31. 7	10. 6	B8	D6	Deer	12.10	24. 8	D10	G7	Pig
1. 8	11. 6	B8	E7	Horse	13.10	25. 8	D10	H8	Porcupine
2. 8	12. 6	B8	F8	Stag	14.10	26. 8	D10	J9	Wolf
3. 8	13. 6	B8	G9	Serpent	15.10	27. 8	D10	K10	Dog
4. 8	14. 6	B8	H10	Earthworm	16.10	28. 8	D10	A11	Pheasant
5. 8	15. 6	B8	J11	Crocodile	17.10	29. 8	D10	B12	Cock
6. 8	16. 6	B8	K12	Dragon	18.10	30. 8	D10	C1	Crow
7. 8	17. 6	B8	A1	Badger	19.10	1. 9	E11	D2	Monkey
8. 8	18. 6	B8	B2	Hare	20.10	2. 9	E11	E3	Gibbon
9. 8	19. 6	B8	C3	Fox	21.10	3. 9	E11	F4	Tapir
10. 8	20. 6	B8	D4	Tiger	22.10	4. 9	E11	G5	Sheep
11. 8	21. 6	B8	E5	Leopard	23.10	5. 9	E11	H6	Deer
12. 8	22. 6	B8	F6	Griffon	24.10	6. 9	E11	J7	Horse
13. 8	23. 6	B8	G7	Ox	25.10	7. 9	E11	K8	Stag
14. 8	24. 6	B8	H8	Bat	26.10	8. 9	E11	A9	Serpent
15. 8	25. 6	B8	J9	Rat	27.10	9. 9	E11	B10	Earthworm
16. 8	26. 6	B8	K10	Swallow	28.10	10. 9	E11	C11	Crocodile
17. 8	27. 6	B8	A11	Pig	29.10	11. 9	E11	D12	Dragon
18. 8	28. 6	B8	B12	Porcupine	20.10	12. 9	E11	E1	Badger
19. 8	29. 6	B8	C1	Wolf	31.10	13. 9	E11	F2	Hare
20. 8	30. 6	B8	D2	Dog	1.11	14. 9	E11	G3	Fox
21. 8	1. 7	C9	E3	Pheasant	2.11	15. 9	E11	H4	Tiger
22. 8	2. 7	C9	F4	Cock	3.11	16. 9	E11	J5	Leopard
23. 8	3. 7	C9	G5	Crow	4.11	17. 9	E11	K6	Griffon
24. 8	4. 7	C9	H6	Monkey	5.11	18. 9	E11	A7	Ox
25. 8	5. 7	C9	J7	Gibbon	6.11	19. 9	E11	B8	Bat
26. 8	6. 7	C9	K8	Tapir	7.11	20. 9	E11	C9	Rat
27. 8	7. 7	C9	A9	Sheep	8.11	21. 9	E11	D10	Swallow
28. 8	8. 7	C9	B10	Deer	9.11	22. 9	E11	E11	Pig
29. 8	9. 7	C9	C11	Horse	10.11	23. 9	E11	F12	Porcupine
30. 8	10. 7	C9	D12	Stag	11.11	24. 9	E11	G1	Wolf
31. 8	11. 7	C9	E1	Serpent	12.11	25. 9	E11	H2	Dog
1. 9	12. 7	C9	F2	Earthworm	13.11	26. 9	E11	J3	Pheasant
2. 9	13. 7	C9	G3	Crocodile	14.11	27. 9	E11	K4	Cock
3. 9	14. 7	C9	H4	Dragon	15.11	28. 9	E11	A5	Crow
4. 9	15. 7	C9	J5	Badger	16.11	29. 9	E11	B6	Monkey
5. 9	16. 7	C9	K6	Hare	17.11	30. 9	E11	C7	Gibbon
6. 9	17. 7	C9	A7	Fox	18.11	1.10	F12	D8	Tapir
7. 9	18. 7	C9	B8	Tiger	19.11	2.10	F12	E9	Sheep
8. 9	19. 7	C9	C9	Leopard	20.11	3.10	F12	F10	Deer
9. 9	20. 7	C9	D10	Griffon	21.11	4.10	F12	G11	Horse
10. 9	21. 7	C9	E11	Ox	22.11	5.10	F12	H12	Stag
11. 9	22. 7	C9	F12	Bat	23.11	6.10	F12	J1	Serpent
12. 9	23. 7	C9	G1	Rat	24.11	7.10	F12	K2	Earthworm
13. 9	24. 7	C9	H2	Swallow	25.11	8.10	F12	A3	Crocodile
14. 9	25. 7	C9	J3	Pig	26.11	9.10	F12	B4	Dragon
15. 9	26. 7	C9	K4	Porcupine	27.11	10.10	F12	C5	Badger
16. 9	27. 7	C9	A5	Wolf	28.11	11.10	F12	D6	Hare
17. 9	28. 7	C9	B6	Dog	29.11	12.10	F12	E7	Fox
18. 9	29. 7	C9	C7	Pheasant	30.11	13.10	F12	F8	Tiger
19. 9	1. 8	D10	D8	Cock	1.12	14.10	F12	G9	Leopard
20. 9	2. 8	D10	E9	Crow	2.12	15.10	F12	H10	Griffon
21. 9	3. 8	D10	F10	Monkey	3.12	16.10	F12	J11	Ox
22. 9	4. 8	D10	G11	Gibbon	4.12	17.10	F12	K12	Bat
23. 9	5. 8	D10	H12	Tapir	5.12	18.10	F12	A1	Rat
24. 9	6. 8	D10	J1	Sheep	6.12	19.10	F12	B2	Swallow
25. 9	7. 8	D10	K2	Deer	7.12	20.10	F12	C3	Pig
26. 9	8. 8	D10	A3	Horse	8.12	21.10	F12	D4	Porcupine
27. 9	9. 8	D10	B4	Stag	9.12	22.10	F12	E5	Wolf
28. 9	10. 8	D10	C5	Serpent	10.12	23.10	F12	F6	Dog
29. 9	11. 8	D10	D6	Earthworm	11.12	24.10	F12	G7	Pheasant
30. 9	12. 8	D10	E7	Crocodile	12.12	25.10	F12	H8	Cock
1. 0	13. 8	D10	F8	Dragon	13.12	26.10	F12	J9	Crow
2.10	14. 8	D10	G9	Badger	14.12	27.10	F12	K10	Monkey
3.10	15. 8	D10	H10	Hare	15.12	28.10	F12	A11	Gibbon
4.10	16. 8	D10	J11	Fox	16.12	29.10	F12	B12	Tapir

Solar date	Lunar date	Month HS/EB	Day HS/EB	Constellation	Solar date	Lunar date	Month HS/EB	Day HS/EB	Constellation
17.12	30.10	F12	C1	Sheep	15. 1	29.11	G1	B6	Deer
18.12	1.11	G1	D2	Deer	16. 1	1.12	H2	C7	Horse
19.12	2.11	G1	E3	Horse	17. 1	2.12	H2	D8	Stag
20.12	3.11	G1	F4	Stag	18. 1	3.12	H2	E9	Serpent
21.12	4.11	G1	G5	Serpent	19. 1	4.12	H2	F10	Earthworm
22.12	5.11	G1	H6	Earthworm	20. 1	5.12	H2	G11	Crocodile
23.12	6.11	G1	J7	Crocodile	21. 1	6.12	H2	H12	Dragon
24.12	7.11	G1	K8	Dragon	22. 1	7.12	H2	J1	Badger
25.12	8.11	G1	A9	Badger	23. 1	8.12	H2	K2	Hare
26.12	9.11	G1	B10	Hare	24. 1	9.12	H2	A3	Fox
27.12	10.11	G1	C11	Fox	25. 1	10.12	H2	B4	Tiger
28.12	11.11	G1	D12	Tiger	26. 1	11.12	H2	C5	Leopard
29.12	12.11	G1	E1	Leopard	27. 1	12.12	H2	D6	Griffon
30.12	13.11	G1	F2	Griffon	28. 1	13.12	H2	E7	Ox
31.12	14.11	G1	G3	Ox	29. 1	14.12	H2	F8	Bat
					30. 1	15.12	H2	G9	Rat
1972					31. 1	16.12	H2	H10	Swallow
1. 1	15.11	G1	H4	Bat	1. 2	17.12	H2	J11	Pig
2. 1	16.11	G1	J5	Rat	2. 2	18.12	H2	K12	Porcupine
3. 1	17.11	G1	K6	Swallow	3. 2	19.12	H2	A1	Wolf
4. 1	18.11	G1	A7	Pig	4. 2	20.12	H2	B2	Dog
5. 1	19.11	G1	B8	Porcupine	5. 2	21.12	H2	C3	Pheasant
6. 1	20.11	G1	C9	Wolf	6. 2	22.12	H2	D4	Cock
7. 1	21.11	G1	D10	Dog	7. 2	23.12	H2	E5	Crow
8. 1	22.11	G1	E11	Pheasant	8. 2	24.12	H2	F6	Monkey
9. 1	23.11	G1	F12	Cock	9. 2	25.12	H2	G7	Gibbon
10. 1	24.11	G1	G1	Crow	10. 2	26.12	H2	H8	Tapir
11. 1	25.11	G1	H2	Monkey	11. 2	27.12	H2	J9	Sheep
12. 1	26.11	G1	J3	Gibbon	12. 2	28.12	H2	K10	Deer
13. 1	27.11	G1	K4	Tapir	13. 2	29.12	H2	A11	Horse
14. 1	28.11	G1	A5	Sheep	14. 2	30.12	H2	B12	Stag

JEN TZU YEAR

Solar date	Lunar date	Month HS/EB	Day HS/EB	Constellation	Solar date	Lunar date	Month HS/EB	Day HS/EB	Constellation
15. 2	1. 1	J3	C1	Serpent	23. 3	9. 2	K4	K2	Griffon
16. 2	2. 1	J3	D2	Earthworm	24. 3	10. 2	K4	A3	Ox
17. 2	3. 1	J3	E3	Crocodile	25. 3	11. 2	K4	B4	Bat
18. 2	4. 1	J3	F4	Dragon	26. 3	12. 2	K4	C5	Rat
19. 2	5. 1	J3	G5	Badger	27. 3	13. 2	K4	D6	Swallow
20. 2	6. 1	J3	H6	Hare	28. 3	14. 2	K4	E7	Pig
21. 2	7. 1	J3	J7	Fox	29. 3	15. 2	K4	F8	Porcupine
22. 2	8. 1	J3	K8	Tiger	30. 3	16. 2	K4	G9	Wolf
23. 2	9. 1	J3	A9	Leopard	31. 3	17. 2	K4	H10	Dog
24. 2	10. 1	J3	B10	Griffon	1. 4	18. 2	K4	J11	Pheasant
25. 2	11. 1	J3	C11	Ox	2. 4	19. 2	K4	K12	Cock
26. 2	12. 1	J3	D12	Bat	3. 4	20. 2	K4	A1	Crow
27. 2	13. 1	J3	E1	Rat	4. 4	21. 2	K4	B2	Monkey
28. 2	14. 1	J3	F2	Swallow	5. 4	22. 2	K4	C3	Gibbon
29. 2	15. 1	J3	G3	Pig	6. 4	23. 2	K4	D4	Tapir
1. 3	16. 1	J3	H4	Porcupine	7. 4	24. 2	K4	E5	Sheep
2. 3	17. 1	J3	J5	Wolf	8. 4	25. 2	K4	F6	Deer
3. 3	18. 1	J3	K6	Dog	9. 4	26. 2	K4	G7	Horse
4. 3	19. 1	J3	A7	Pheasant	10. 4	27. 2	K4	H8	Stag
5. 3	20. 1	J3	B8	Cock	11. 4	28. 2	K4	J9	Serpent
6. 3	21. 1	J3	C9	Crow	12. 4	29. 2	K4	K10	Earthworm
7. 3	22. 1	J3	D10	Monkey	13. 4	30. 2	K4	A11	Crocodile
8. 3	23. 1	J3	E11	Gibbon	14. 4	1. 3	A5	B12	Dragon
9. 3	24. 1	J3	F12	Tapir	15. 4	2. 3	A5	C1	Badger
10. 3	25. 1	J3	G1	Sheep	16. 4	3. 3	A5	D2	Hare
11. 3	26. 1	J3	H2	Deer	17. 4	4. 3	A5	E3	Fox
12. 3	27. 1	J3	J3	Horse	18. 4	5. 3	A5	F4	Tiger
13. 3	28. 1	J3	K4	Stag	19. 4	6. 3	A5	G5	Leopard
14. 3	29. 1	J3	A5	Serpent	20. 4	7. 3	A5	H6	Griffon
15. 3	1. 2	K4	B6	Earthworm	21. 4	8. 3	A5	J7	Ox
16. 3	2. 2	K4	C7	Crocodile	22. 4	9. 3	A5	K8	Bat
17. 3	3. 2	K4	D8	Dragon	23. 4	10. 3	A5	A9	Rat
18. 3	4. 2	K4	E9	Badger	24. 4	11. 3	A5	B10	Swallow
19. 3	5. 2	K4	F10	Hare	25. 4	12. 3	A5	C11	Pig
20. 3	6. 2	K4	G11	Fox	26. 4	13. 3	A5	D12	Porcupine
21. 3	7. 2	K4	H12	Tiger	27. 4	14. 3	A5	E1	Wolf
22. 3	8. 2	K4	J1	Leopard	28. 4	15. 3	A5	F2	Dog

Solar date	Lunar date	Month HS/EB	Day HS/EB	Constellation	Solar date	Lunar date	Month HS/EB	Day HS/EB	Constellation
29. 4	16. 3	A5	G3	Pheasant	11. 7	1. 6	D8	K4	Tiger
30. 4	17. 3	A5	H4	Cock	12. 7	2. 6	D8	A5	Leopard
1. 5	18. 3	A5	J5	Crow	13. 7	3. 6	D8	B6	Griffon
2. 5	19. 3	A5	K6	Monkey	14. 7	4. 6	D8	C7	Ox
3. 5	20. 3	A5	A7	Gibbon	15. 7	5. 6	D8	D8	Bat
4. 5	21. 3	A5	B8	Tapir	16. 7	6. 6	D8	E9	Rat
5. 5	22. 3	A5	C9	Sheep	17. 7	7. 6	D8	F10	Swallow
6. 5	23. 3	A5	D10	Deer	18. 7	8. 6	D8	G11	Pig
7. 5	24. 3	A5	E11	Horse	19. 7	9. 6	D8	H12	Porcupine
8. 5	25. 3	A5	F12	Stag	20. 7	10. 6	D8	J1	Wolf
9. 5	26. 3	A5	G1	Serpent	21. 7	11. 6	D8	K2	Dog
10. 5	27. 3	A5	H2	Earthworm	22. 7	12. 6	D8	A3	Pheasant
11. 5	28. 3	A5	J3	Crocodile	23. 7	13. 6	D8	B4	Cock
12. 5	29. 3	A5	K4	Dragon	24. 7	14. 6	D8	C5	Crow
13. 5	1. 4	B6	A5	Badger	25. 7	15. 6	D8	D6	Monkey
14. 5	2. 4	B6	B6	Hare	26. 7	16. 6	D8	E7	Gibbon
15. 5	3. 4	B6	C7	Fox	27. 7	17. 6	D8	F8	Tapir
16. 5	4. 4	B6	D8	Tiger	28. 7	18. 6	D8	G9	Sheep
17. 5	5. 4	B6	E9	Leopard	29. 7	19. 6	D8	H10	Deer
18. 5	6. 4	B6	F10	Griffon	30. 7	20. 6	D8	J11	Horse
19. 5	7. 4	B6	G11	Ox	31. 7	21. 6	D8	K12	Stag
20. 5	8. 4	B6	H12	Bat	1. 8	22. 6	D8	A1	Serpent
21. 5	9. 4	B6	J1	Rat	2. 8	23. 6	D8	B2	Earthworm
22. 5	10. 4	B6	K2	Swallow	3. 8	24. 6	D8	C3	Crocodile
23. 5	11. 4	B6	A3	Pig	4. 8	25. 6	D8	D4	Dragon
24. 5	12. 4	B6	B4	Porcupine	5. 8	26. 6	D8	E5	Badger
25. 5	13. 4	B6	C5	Wolf	6. 8	27. 6	D8	F6	Hare
26. 5	14. 4	B6	D6	Dog	7. 8	28. 6	D8	G7	Fox
27. 5	15. 4	B6	E7	Pheasant	8. 8	29. 6	D8	H8	Tiger
28. 5	16. 4	B6	F8	Cock	9. 8	1. 7	E9	J9	Leopard
29. 5	17. 4	B6	G9	Crow	10. 8	2. 7	E9	K10	Griffon
30. 5	18. 4	B6	H10	Monkey	11. 8	3. 7	E9	A11	Ox
31. 5	19. 4	B6	J11	Gibbon	12. 8	4. 7	E9	B12	Bat
1. 6	20. 4	B6	K12	Tapir	13. 8	5. 7	E9	C1	Rat
2. 6	21. 4	B6	A1	Sheep	14. 8	6. 7	E9	D2	Swallow
3. 6	22. 4	B6	B2	Deer	15. 8	7. 7	E9	E3	Pig
4. 6	23. 4	B6	C3	Horse	16. 8	8. 7	E9	F4	Porcupine
5. 6	24. 4	B6	D4	Stag	17. 8	9. 7	E9	G5	Wolf
6. 6	25. 4	B6	E5	Serpent	18. 8	10. 7	E9	H6	Dog
7. 6	26. 4	B6	F6	Earthworm	19. 8	11. 7	E9	J7	Pheasant
8. 6	27. 4	B6	G7	Crocodile	20. 8	12. 7	E9	K8	Cock
9. 6	28. 4	B6	H8	Dragon	21. 8	13. 7	E9	A9	Crow
10. 6	29. 4	B6	J9	Badger	22. 8	14. 7	E9	B10	Monkey
11. 6	1. 5	C7	K10	Hare	23. 8	15. 7	E9	C11	Gibbon
12. 6	2. 5	C7	A11	Fox	24. 8	16. 7	E9	D12	Tapir
13. 6	3. 5	C7	B12	Tiger	25. 8	17. 7	E9	E1	Sheep
14. 6	4. 5	C7	C1	Leopard	26. 8	18. 7	E9	F2	Deer
15. 6	5. 5	C7	D2	Griffon	27. 8	19. 7	E9	G3	Horse
16. 6	6. 5	C7	E3	Ox	28. 8	20. 7	E9	H4	Stag
17. 6	7. 5	C7	F4	Bat	29. 8	21. 7	E9	J5	Serpent
18. 6	8. 5	C7	G5	Rat	30. 8	22. 7	E9	K6	Earthworm
19. 6	9. 5	C7	H6	Swallow	31. 8	23. 7	E9	A7	Crocodile
20. 6	10. 5	C7	J7	Pig	1. 9	24. 7	E9	B8	Dragon
21. 6	11. 5	C7	K8	Porcupine	2. 9	25. 7	E9	C9	Badger
22. 6	12. 5	C7	A9	Wolf	3. 9	26. 7	E9	D10	Hare
23. 6	13. 5	C7	B10	Dog	4. 9	27. 7	E9	E11	Fox
24. 6	14. 5	C7	C11	Pheasant	5. 9	28. 7	E9	F12	Tiger
25. 6	15. 5	C7	D12	Cock	6. 9	29. 7	E9	G1	Leopard
26. 6	16. 5	C7	E1	Crow	7. 9	30. 7	E9	H2	Griffon
27. 6	17. 5	C7	F2	Monkey	8. 9	1. 8	F10	J3	Ox
28. 6	18. 5	C7	G3	Gibbon	9. 9	2. 8	F10	K4	Bat
29. 6	19. 5	C7	H4	Tapir	10. 9	3. 8	F10	A5	Rat
30. 6	20. 5	C7	J5	Sheep	11. 9	4. 8	F10	B6	Swallow
1. 7	21. 5	C7	K6	Deer	12. 9	5. 8	F10	C7	Pig
2. 7	22. 5	C7	A7	Horse	13. 9	6. 8	F10	D8	Porcupine
3. 7	23. 5	C7	B8	Stag	14. 9	7. 8	F10	E9	Wolf
4. 7	24. 5	C7	C9	Serpent	15. 9	8. 8	F10	F10	Dog
5. 7	25. 5	C7	D10	Earthworm	16. 9	9. 8	F10	G11	Pheasant
6. 7	26. 5	C7	E11	Crocodile	17. 9	10. 8	F10	H12	Cock
7. 7	27. 5	C7	F12	Dragon	18. 9	11. 8	F10	J1	Crow
8. 7	28. 5	C7	G1	Badger	19. 9	12. 8	F10	K2	Monkey
9. 7	29. 5	C7	H2	Hare	20. 9	13. 8	F10	A3	Gibbon
10. 7	30. 5	C7	J3	Fox	21. 9	14. 8	F10	B4	Tapir

Solar date	Lunar date	Month HS/EB	Day HS/EB	Constellation
22. 9	15. 8	F10	C5	Sheep
23. 9	16. 8	F10	D6	Deer
24. 9	17. 8	F10	E7	Horse
25. 9	18. 8	F10	F8	Stag
26. 9	19. 8	F10	G9	Serpent
27. 9	20. 8	F10	H10	Earthworm
28. 9	21. 8	F10	J11	Crocodile
29. 9	22. 8	F10	K12	Dragon
30. 9	23. 8	F10	A1	Badger
1.10	24. 8	F10	B2	Hare
2.10	25. 8	F10	C3	Fox
3.10	26. 8	F10	D4	Tiger
4.10	27. 8	F10	E5	Leopard
5.10	28. 8	F10	F6	Griffon
6.10	29. 8	F10	G7	Ox
7.10	1. 9	G11	H8	Bat
8.10	2. 9	G11	J9	Rat
9.10	3. 9	G11	K10	Swallow
10.10	4. 9	G11	A11	Pig
11.10	5. 9	G11	B12	Porcupine
12.10	6. 9	G11	C1	Wolf
13.10	7. 9	G11	D2	Dog
14.10	8. 9	G11	E3	Pheasant
15.10	9. 9	G11	F4	Cock
16.10	10. 9	G11	C5	Crow
17.10	11. 9	G11	H6	Monkey
18.10	12. 9	G11	J7	Gibbon
19.10	13. 9	G11	K8	Tapir
20.10	14. 9	G11	A9	Sheep
21.10	15. 9	G11	B10	Deer
22.10	16. 9	G11	C11	Horse
23.10	17. 9	G11	D12	Stag
24.10	18. 9	G11	E1	Serpent
25.10	19. 9	G11	F2	Earthworm
26.10	20. 9	G11	G3	Crocodile
27.10	21. 9	G11	H4	Dragon
28.10	22. 9	G11	J5	Badger
29.10	23. 9	G11	K6	Hare
30.10	24. 9	G11	A7	Fox
31.10	25. 9	G11	B8	Tiger
1.11	26. 9	G11	C9	Leopard
2.11	27. 9	G11	D10	Griffon
3.11	28. 9	G11	E1	Ox
4.11	29. 9	G11	F12	Bat
5.11	30. 9	G11	G1	Rat
6.11	1.10	H12	H2	Swallow
7.11	2.10	H12	J3	Pig
8.11	3.10	H12	K4	Porcupine
9.11	4.10	H12	A5	Wolf
10.11	5.10	H12	B6	Dog
11.11	6.10	H12	C7	Pheasant
12.11	7.10	H12	D8	Cock
13.11	8.10	H12	E9	Crow
14.11	9.10	H12	F10	Monkey
15.11	10.10	H12	G11	Gibbon
16.11	11.10	H12	H12	Tapir
17.11	12.10	H12	J1	Sheep
18.11	13.10	H12	K2	Deer
19.11	14.10	H12	A3	Horse
20.11	15.10	H12	B4	Stag
21.11	16.10	H12	C5	Serpent
22.11	17.10	H12	D6	Earthworm
23.11	18.10	H12	E7	Crocodile
24.11	19.10	H12	F8	Dragon
25.11	20.10	H12	G9	Badger
26.11	21.10	H12	H10	Hare
27.11	22.10	H12	J11	Fox
28.11	23.10	H12	K12	Tiger

Solar date	Lunar date	Month HS/EB	Day HS/EB	Constellation
29.11	24.10	H12	A1	Leopard
30.11	25.10	H12	B2	Griffon
1.12	26.10	H12	C3	Ox
2.12	27.10	H12	D4	Bat
3.12	28.10	H12	E5	Rat
4.12	29.10	H12	F6	Swallow
5.12	30.10	H12	G7	Pig
6.12	1.11	J1	H8	Porcupine
7.12	2.11	J1	J9	Wolf
8.12	3.11	J1	K10	Dog
9.12	4.11	J1	A11	Pheasant
10.12	5.11	J1	B12	Cock
11.12	6.11	J1	C1	Crow
12.12	7.11	J1	D2	Monkey
13.12	8.11	J1	E3	Gibbon
14.12	9.11	J1	F4	Tapir
15.12	10.11	J1	G5	Sheep
16.12	11.11	J1	H6	Deer
17.12	12.11	J1	J7	Horse
18.12	13.11	J1	K8	Stag
19.12	14.11	J1	A9	Serpent
20.12	15.11	J1	B10	Earthworm
21.12	16.11	J1	C11	Crocodile
22.12	17.11	J1	D12	Dragon
23.12	18.11	J1	E1	Badger
24.12	19.11	J1	F2	Hare
25.12	20.11	J1	G3	Fox
26.12	21.11	J1	H4	Tiger
27.12	22.11	J1	J5	Leopard
28.12	23.11	J1	K6	Griffon
29.12	24.11	J1	A7	Ox
30.12	25.11	J1	B8	Bat
31.12	26.11	J1	C9	Rat
1973				
1. 1	27.11	J1	D10	Swallow
2. 1	28.11	J1	E11	Pig
3. 1	29.11	J1	F12	Porcupine
4. 1	1.12	K2	G1	Wolf
5. 1	2.12	K2	H2	Dog
6. 1	3.12	K2	J3	Pheasant
7. 1	4.12	K2	K4	Cock
8. 1	5.12	K2	A5	Crow
9. 1	6.12	K2	B6	Monkey
10. 1	7.12	K2	C7	Gibbon
11. 1	8.12	K2	D8	Tapir
12. 1	9.12	K2	E9	Sheep
13. 1	10.12	K2	F10	Deer
14. 1	11.12	K2	G11	Horse
15. 1	12.12	K2	H12	Stag
16. 1	13.12	K2	J1	Serpent
17. 1	14.12	K2	K2	Earthworm
18. 1	15.12	K2	A3	Crocodile
19. 1	16.12	K2	B4	Dragon
20. 1	17.12	K2	C5	Badger
21. 1	18.12	K2	D6	Hare
22. 1	19.12	K2	E7	Fox
23. 1	20.12	K2	F8	Tiger
24. 1	21.12	K2	G9	Leopard
25. 1	22.12	K2	H10	Griffon
26. 1	23.12	K2	J11	Ox
27. 1	24.12	K2	K12	Bat
28. 1	25.12	K2	A1	Rat
29. 1	26.12	K2	B2	Swallow
30. 1	27.12	K2	C3	Pig
31. 1	28.12	K2	D4	Porcupine
1. 2	29.12	K2	E5	Wolf
2. 2	30.12	K2	F6	Dog

KUEI CH'OU YEAR

Solar date	Lunar date	Month HS/EB	Day HS/EB	Constellation	Solar date	Lunar date	Month HS/EB	Day HS/EB	Constellation
3. 2	1. 1	A3	G7	Pheasant	15. 4	13. 3	C5	H6	Hare
4. 2	2. 1	A3	H8	Cock	16. 4	14. 3	C5	J7	Fox
5. 2	3. 1	A3	J9	Crow	17. 4	15. 3	C5	K8	Tiger
6. 2	4. 1	A3	K10	Monkey	18. 4	16. 3	C5	A9	Leopard
7. 2	5. 1	A3	A11	Gibbon	19. 4	17. 3	C5	B10	Griffon
8. 2	6. 1	A3	B12	Tapir	20. 4	18. 3	C5	C11	Ox
9. 2	7. 1	A3	C1	Sheep	21. 4	19. 3	C5	D12	Bat
10. 2	8. 1	A3	D2	Deer	22. 4	20. 3	C5	E1	Rat
11. 2	9. 1	A3	E3	Horse	23. 4	21. 3	C5	F2	Swallow
12. 2	10. 1	A3	F4	Stag	24. 4	22. 3	C5	G3	Pig
13. 2	11. 1	A3	G5	Serpent	25. 4	23. 3	C5	H4	Porcupine
14. 2	12. 1	A3	H6	Earthworm	26. 4	24. 3	C5	J5	Wolf
15. 2	13. 1	A3	J7	Crocodile	27. 4	25. 3	C5	K6	Dog
16. 2	14. 1	A3	K8	Dragon	28. 4	26. 3	C5	A7	Pheasant
17. 2	15. 1	A3	A9	Badger	29. 4	27. 3	C5	B8	Cock
18. 2	16. 1	A3	B10	Hare	30. 4	28. 3	C5	C9	Crow
19. 2	17. 1	A3	C11	Fox	1. 5	29. 3	C5	D10	Monkey
20. 2	18. 1	A3	D12	Tiger	2. 5	30. 3	C5	E11	Gibbon
21. 2	19. 1	A3	E1	Leopard	3. 5	1. 4	D6	F12	Tapir
22. 2	20. 1	A3	F2	Griffon	4. 5	2. 4	D6	G1	Sheep
23. 2	21. 1	A3	G3	Ox	5. 5	3. 4	D6	H2	Deer
24. 2	22. 1	A3	H4	Bat	6. 5	4. 4	D6	J3	Horse
25. 2	23. 1	A3	J5	Rat	7. 5	5. 4	D6	K4	Stag
26. 2	24. 1	A3	K6	Swallow	8. 5	6. 4	D6	A5	Serpent
27. 2	25. 1	A3	A7	Pig	9. 5	7. 4	D6	B6	Earthworm
28. 2	26. 1	A3	B8	Porcupine	10. 5	8. 4	D6	C7	Crocodile
1. 3	27. 1	A3	C9	Wolf	11. 5	9. 4	D6	D8	Dragon
2. 3	28. 1	A3	D10	Dog	12. 5	10. 4	D6	E9	Badger
3. 3	29. 1	A3	E11	Pheasant	13. 5	11. 4	D6	F10	Hare
4. 3	30. 1	A3	F12	Cock	14. 5	12. 4	D6	G11	Fox
5. 3	1. 2	B4	G1	Crow	15. 5	13. 4	D6	H12	Tiger
6. 3	2. 2	B4	H2	Monkey	16. 5	14. 4	D6	J1	Leopard
7. 3	3. 2	B4	J3	Gibbon	17. 5	15. 4	D6	K2	Griffon
8. 3	4. 2	B4	K4	Tapir	18. 5	16. 4	D6	A3	Ox
9. 3	5. 2	B4	A5	Sheep	19. 5	17. 4	D6	B4	Bat
10. 3	6. 2	B4	B6	Deer	20. 5	18. 4	D6	C5	Rat
11. 3	7. 2	B4	C7	Horse	21. 5	19. 4	D6	D6	Swallow
12. 3	8. 2	B4	D8	Stag	22. 5	20. 4	D6	E7	Pig
13. 3	9. 2	B4	E9	Serpent	23. 5	21. 4	D6	F8	Porcupine
14. 3	10. 2	B4	F10	Earthworm	24. 5	22. 4	D6	G9	Wolf
15. 3	11. 2	B4	G11	Crocodile	25. 5	23. 4	D6	H10	Dog
16. 3	12. 2	B4	H12	Dragon	26. 5	24. 4	D6	J11	Pheasant
17. 3	13. 2	B4	J1	Badger	27. 5	25. 4	D6	K12	Cock
18. 3	14. 2	B4	K2	Hare	28. 5	26. 4	D6	A1	Crow
19. 3	15. 2	B4	A3	Fox	29. 5	27. 4	D6	B2	Monkey
20. 3	16. 2	B4	B4	Tiger	30. 5	28. 4	D4	C3	Gibbon
21. 3	17. 2	B4	C5	Leopard	31. 5	29. 4	D6	D4	Tapir
22. 3	18. 2	B4	D6	Griffon	1. 6	1. 5	E7	E5	Sheep
23. 3	19. 2	B4	E7	Ox	2. 6	2. 5	E7	F6	Deer
24. 3	20. 2	B4	F8	Bat	3. 6	3. 5	E7	G7	Horse
25. 3	21. 2	B4	G9	Rat	4. 6	4. 5	E7	H8	Stag
26. 3	22. 2	B4	H10	Swallow	5. 6	5. 5	E7	J9	Serpent
27. 3	23. 2	B4	J11	Pig	6. 6	6. 5	E7	K10	Earthworm
28. 3	24. 2	B4	K12	Porcupine	7. 6	7. 5	E7	A11	Crocodile
29. 3	25. 2	B4	A1	Wolf	8. 6	8. 5	E7	B12	Dragon
30. 3	26. 2	B4	B2	Dog	9. 6	9. 5	E7	C1	Badger
31. 3	27. 2	B4	C3	Pheasant	10. 6	10. 5	E7	D2	Hare
1. 4	28. 2	B4	D4	Cock	11. 6	11. 5	E7	E3	Fox
2. 4	29. 2	B4	E5	Crow	12. 6	12. 5	E7	F4	Tiger
3. 4	1. 3	C5	F6	Monkey	13. 6	13. 5	E7	G5	Leopard
4. 4	2. 3	C5	G7	Gibbon	14. 6	14. 5	E7	H6	Griffon
5. 4	3. 3	C5	H8	Tapir	15. 6	15. 5	E7	J7	Ox
6. 4	4. 3	C5	J9	Sheep	16. 6	16. 5	E7	K8	Bat
7. 4	5. 3	C5	K10	Deer	17. 6	17. 5	E7	A9	Rat
8. 4	6. 3	C5	A11	Horse	18. 6	18. 5	E7	B10	Swallow
9. 4	7. 3	C5	B12	Stag	19. 6	19. 5	E7	C11	Pig
10. 4	8. 3	C5	C1	Serpent	20. 6	20. 5	E7	D12	Porcupine
11. 4	9. 3	C5	D2	Earthworm	21. 6	21. 5	E7	E1	Wolf
12. 4	10. 3	C5	E3	Crocodile	22. 6	22. 5	E7	F2	Dog
13. 4	11. 3	C5	F4	Dragon	23. 6	23. 5	E7	G3	Pheasant
14. 4	12. 3	C5	G5	Badger	24. 6	24. 5	E7	H4	Cock

Solar date	Lunar date	Month HS/EB	Day HS/EB	Constellation	Solar date	Lunar date	Month HS/EB	Day HS/EB	Constellation
25. 6	25. 5	E7	J5	Crow	6. 9	10. 8	H10	B6	Griffon
26. 6	26. 5	E7	K6	Monkey	7. 9	11. 8	H10	C7	Ox
27. 6	27. 5	E7	A7	Gibbon	8. 9	12. 8	H10	D8	Bat
28. 6	28. 5	E7	B8	Tapir	9. 9	13. 8	H10	E9	Rat
29. 6	29. 5	E7	C9	Sheep	10. 9	14. 8	H10	F10	Swallow
30. 6	1. 6	F8	D10	Deer	11. 9	15. 8	H10	G11	Pig
1. 7	2. 6	F8	E11	Horse	12. 9	16. 8	H10	H12	Porcupine
2. 7	3. 6	F8	F12	Stag	13. 9	17. 8	H10	J1	Wolf
3. 7	4. 6	F8	G1	Serpent	14. 9	18. 8	H10	K2	Dog
4. 7	5. 6	F8	H2	Earthworm	15. 9	19. 8	H10	A3	Pheasant
5. 7	6. 6	F8	J3	Crocodile	16. 9	20. 8	H10	B4	Cock
6. 7	7. 6	F8	K4	Dragon	17. 9	21. 8	H10	C5	Crow
7. 7	8. 6	F8	A5	Badger	18. 9	22. 8	H10	D6	Monkey
8. 7	9. 6	F8	B6	Hare	19. 9	23. 8	H10	E7	Gibbon
9. 7	10. 6	F8	C7	Fox	20. 9	24. 8	H10	F8	Tapir
10. 7	11. 6	F8	D8	Tiger	21. 9	25. 8	H10	G9	Sheep
11. 7	12. 6	F8	E9	Leopard	22. 9	26. 8	H10	H10	Deer
12. 7	13. 6	F8	F10	Griffon	23. 9	27. 8	H10	J11	Horse
13. 7	14. 6	F8	G11	Ox	24. 9	28. 8	H10	K12	Stag
14. 7	15. 6	F8	H12	Bat	25. 9	29. 8	H10	A1	Serpent
15. 7	16. 6	F8	J1	Rat	26. 9	1. 9	J11	B2	Earthworm
16. 7	17. 6	F8	K2	Swallow	27. 9	2. 9	J11	C3	Crocodile
17. 7	18. 6	F8	A3	Pig	28. 9	3. 9	J11	D4	Dragon
18. 7	19. 6	F8	B4	Porcupine	29. 9	4. 9	J11	E5	Badger
19. 7	20. 6	F8	C5	Wolf	30. 9	5. 9	J11	F6	Hare
20. 7	21. 6	F8	D6	Dog	1.10	6. 9	J11	G7	Fox
21. 7	22. 6	F8	E7	Pheasant	2.10	7. 9	J11	H8	Tiger
22. 7	23. 6	F8	F8	Cock	3.10	8. 9	J11	J9	Leopard
23. 7	24. 6	F8	G9	Crow	4.10	9. 9	J11	K10	Griffon
24. 7	25. 6	F8	H10	Monkey	5.10	10. 9	J11	A11	Ox
25. 7	26. 6	F8	J11	Gibbon	6.10	11. 9	J11	B12	Bat
26. 7	27. 6	F8	K12	Tapir	7.10	12. 9	J11	C1	Rat
27. 7	28. 6	F8	A1	Sheep	8.10	13. 9	J11	D2	Swallow
28. 7	29. 6	F8	B2	Deer	9.10	14. 9	J11	E3	Pig
29. 7	30. 6	F8	C3	Horse	10.10	15. 9	J11	F4	Porcupine
30. 7	1. 7	G9	D4	Stag	11. 0	16. 9	J11	G5	Wolf
31. 7	2. 7	G9	E5	Serpent	12.10	17. 9	J11	H6	Dog
1. 8	3. 7	G9	F6	Earthworm	13.10	18. 9	J11	J7	Pheasant
2. 8	4. 7	G9	G7	Crocodile	14.10	19. 9	J11	K8	Cock
3. 8	5. 7	G9	H8	Dragon	15.10	20. 9	J11	A9	Crow
4. 8	6. 7	G9	J9	Badger	16.10	21. 9	J11	B10	Monkey
5. 8	7. 7	G9	K10	Hare	17.10	22. 9	J11	C11	Gibbon
6. 8	8. 7	G9	A11	Fox	18.10	23. 9	J11	D12	Tapir
7. 8	9. 7	G9	B12	Tiger	19.10	24. 9	J11	E1	Sheep
8. 8	10. 7	G9	C1	Leopard	20.10	25. 9	J11	F2	Deer
9. 8	11. 7	G9	D2	Griffon	21.10	26. 9	J11	G3	Horse
10. 8	12. 7	G9	E3	Ox	22.10	27. 9	J11	H4	Stag
11. 8	13. 7	G9	F4	Bat	23.10	28. 9	J11	J5	Serpent
12. 8	14. 7	G9	G5	Rat	24.10	29. 9	J11	K6	Earthworm
13. 8	15. 7	G9	H6	Swallow	25.10	30. 9	J11	A7	Crocodile
14. 8	16. 7	G9	J7	Pig	26.10	1.10	K12	B8	Dragon
15. 8	17. 7	G9	K8	Porcupine	27.10	2.10	K12	C9	Badger
16. 8	18. 7	G9	A9	Wolf	28.10	3.10	K12	D10	Hare
17. 8	19. 7	G9	B10	Dog	29.10	4.10	K12	E11	Fox
18. 8	20. 7	G9	C11	Pheasant	30.10	5.10	K12	F12	Tiger
19. 8	21. 7	G9	D12	Cock	31.10	6.10	K12	G1	Leopard
20. 8	22. 7	G9	E1	Crow	1.11	7.10	K12	H2	Griffon
21. 8	23. 7	G9	F2	Monkey	2.11	8.10	K12	J3	Ox
22. 8	24. 7	G9	G3	Gibbon	3.11	9.10	K12	K4	Bat
23. 8	25. 7	G9	H4	Tapir	4.11	10.10	K12	A5	Rat
24. 8	26. 7	G9	J5	Sheep	5.11	11.10	K12	B6	Swallow
25. 8	27. 7	G9	K6	Deer	6.11	12.10	K12	C7	Pig
26. 8	28. 7	G9	A7	Horse	7.11	13.10	K12	D8	Porcupine
27. 8	29. 7	G9	B8	Stag	8.11	14.10	K12	E9	Wolf
28. 8	1. 8	H10	C9	Serpent	9.11	15.10	K12	F10	Dog
29. 8	2. 8	H10	D10	Earthworm	10.11	16.10	K12	G11	Pheasant
30. 8	3. 8	H10	E11	Crocodile	11.11	17.10	K12	H12	Cock
31. 8	4. 8	H10	F12	Dragon	12.11	18.10	K12	J1	Crow
1. 9	5. 8	H10	G1	Badger	13.11	19.10	K12	K2	Monkey
2. 9	6. 8	H10	H2	Hare	14.11	20.10	K12	A3	Gibbon
3. 9	7. 8	H10	J3	Fox	15.11	21.10	K12	B4	Tapir
4. 9	8. 8	H10	K4	Tiger	16.11	22.10	K12	C5	Sheep
5. 9	9. 8	H10	A5	Leopard	17.11	23.10	K12	D6	Deer

Solar date	Lunar date	Month HS/EB	Day HS/EB	Constellation	Solar date	Lunar date	Month HS/EB	Day HS/EB	Constellation
18.11	24.10	K12	E7	Horse	22.12	28.11	A1	J5	Badger
19.11	25.10	K12	F8	Stag	23.12	29.11	A1	K6	Hare
20.11	26.10	K12	G9	Serpent	24.12	1.12	B2	A7	Fox
21.11	27.10	K12	H10	Earthworm	25.12	2.12	B2	B8	Tiger
22.11	28.10	K12	J11	Crocodile	26.12	3.12	B2	C9	Leopard
23.11	29.10	K12	K12	Dragon	27.12	4.12	B2	D10	Griffon
24.11	30.10	K12	A1	Badger	28.12	5.12	B2	E11	Ox
25.11	1.11	A1	B2	Hare	29.12	6.12	B2	F12	Bat
26.11	2.11	A1	C3	Fox	30.12	7.12	B2	G1	Rat
27.11	3.11	A1	D4	Tiger	31.12	8.12	B2	H2	Swallow
28.11	4.11	A1	E5	Leopard	**1974**				
29.11	5.11	A1	F6	Griffon	1. 1	9.12	B2	J3	Pig
30.11	6.11	A1	G7	Ox	2. 1	10.12	B2	K4	Porcupine
1.12	7.11	A1	H8	Bat	3. 1	11.12	B2	A5	Wolf
2.12	8.11	A1	J9	Rat	4. 1	12.12	B2	B6	Dog
3.12	9.11	A1	K10	Swallow	5. 1	13.12	B2	C7	Pheasant
4.12	10.11	A1	A11	Pig	6. 1	14.12	B2	D8	Cock
5.12	11.11	A1	B12	Porcupine	7. 1	15.12	B2	E9	Crow
6.12	12.11	A1	C1	Wolf	8. 1	16.12	B2	F10	Monkey
7.12	13.11	A1	D2	Dog	9. 1	17.12	B2	G11	Gibbon
8.12	14.11	A1	E3	Pheasant	10. 1	18.12	B2	H12	Tapir
9.12	15.11	A1	F4	Cock	11. 1	19.12	B2	J1	Sheep
10.12	16.11	A1	G5	Crow	12. 1	20.12	B2	K2	Deer
11.12	17.11	A1	H6	Monkey	13. 1	21.12	B2	A3	Horse
12.12	18.11	A1	J7	Gibbon	14. 1	22.12	B2	B4	Stag
13.12	19.11	A1	K8	Tapir	15. 1	23.12	B2	C5	Serpent
14.12	20.11	A1	A9	Sheep	16. 1	24.12	B2	D6	Earthworm
15.12	21.11	A1	B10	Deer	17. 1	25.12	B2	E7	Crocodile
16.12	22.11	A1	C11	Horse	18. 1	26.12	B2	F8	Dragon
17.12	23.11	A1	D12	Stag	19. 1	27.12	B2	G9	Badger
18.12	24.11	A1	E1	Serpent	20. 1	28.12	B2	H10	Hare
19.12	25.11	A1	F2	Earthworm	21. 1	29.12	B2	J11	Fox
20.12	26.11	A1	G3	Crocodile	22. 1	30.12	B2	K12	Tiger
21.12	27.11	A1	H4	Dragon					

CHIA YIN YEAR

Solar date	Lunar date	Month HS/EB	Day HS/EB	Constellation	Solar date	Lunar date	Month HS/EB	Day HS/EB	Constellation
23. 1	1. 1	C3	A1	Leopard	26. 2	5. 2	D4	E11	Pig
24. 1	2. 1	C3	B2	Griffon	27. 2	6. 2	D4	F12	Porcupine
25. 1	3. 1	C3	C3	Ox	28. 2	7. 2	D4	G1	Wolf
26. 1	4. 1	C3	D4	Bat	1. 3	8. 2	D4	H2	Dog
27. 1	5. 1	C3	E5	Rat	2. 3	9. 2	D4	J3	Pheasant
28. 1	6. 1	C3	F6	Swallow	3. 3	10. 2	D4	K4	Cock
29. 1	7. 1	C3	G7	Pig	4. 3	11. 2	D4	A5	Crow
30. 1	8. 1	C3	H8	Porcupine	5. 3	12. 2	D4	B6	Monkey
31. 1	9. 1	C3	J9	Wolf	6. 3	13. 2	D4	C7	Gibbon
1. 2	10. 1	C3	K10	Dog	7. 3	14. 2	D4	D8	Tapir
2. 2	11. 1	C3	A11	Pheasant	8. 3	15. 2	D4	E9	Sheep
3. 2	12. 1	C3	B12	Cock	9. 3	16. 2	D4	F10	Deer
4. 2	13. 1	C3	C1	Crow	10. 3	17. 2	D4	G11	Horse
5. 2	14. 1	C3	D2	Monkey	11. 3	18. 2	D4	H12	Stag
6. 2	15. 1	C3	E3	Gibbon	12. 3	19. 2	D4	J1	Serpent
7. 2	16. 1	C3	F4	Tapir	13. 3	20. 2	D4	K2	Earthworm
8. 2	17. 1	C3	G5	Sheep	14. 3	21. 2	D4	A3	Crocodile
9. 2	18. 1	C3	H6	Deer	15. 3	22. 2	D4	B4	Dragon
10. 2	19. 1	C3	J7	Horse	16. 3	23. 2	D4	C5	Badger
11. 2	20. 1	C3	K8	Stag	17. 3	24. 2	D4	D6	Hare
12. 2	21. 1	C3	A9	Serpent	18. 3	25. 2	D4	E7	Fox
13. 2	22. 1	C3	B10	Earthworm	19. 3	26. 2	D4	F8	Tiger
14. 2	23. 1	C3	C11	Crocodile	20. 3	27. 2	D4	G9	Leopard
15. 2	24. 1	C3	D12	Dragon	21. 3	28. 2	D4	H10	Griffon
16. 2	25. 1	C3	E1	Badger	22. 3	29. 2	D4	J11	Ox
17. 2	26. 1	C3	F2	Hare	23. 3	30. 2	D4	K12	Bat
18. 2	27. 1	C3	G3	Fox	24. 3	1. 3	E5	A1	Rat
19. 2	28. 1	C3	H4	Tiger	25. 3	2. 3	E5	B2	Swallow
20. 2	29. 1	C3	J5	Leopard	26. 3	3. 3	E5	C3	Pig
21. 2	30. 1	C3	K6	Griffon	27. 3	4. 3	E5	D4	Porcupine
22. 2	1. 2	D4	A7	Ox	28. 3	5. 3	E5	E5	Wolf
23. 2	2. 2	D4	B8	Bat	29. 3	6. 3	E5	F6	Dog
24. 2	3. 2	D4	C9	Rat	30. 3	7. 3	E5	G7	Pheasant
25. 2	4. 2	D4	D10	Swallow	31. 3	8. 3	E5	H8	Cock

Solar date	Lunar date	Month HS/EB	Day HS/EB	Constellation	Solar date	Lunar date	Month HS/EB	Day HS/EB	Constellation
1. 4	9. 3	E5	J9	Crow	13. 6	23. 4	F6	B10	Griffon
2. 4	10. 3	E5	K10	Monkey	14. 6	24. 4	F6	C11	Ox
3. 4	11. 3	E5	A11	Gibbon	15. 6	25. 4	F6	D12	Bat
4. 4	12. 3	E5	B12	Tapir	16. 6	26. 4	F6	E1	Rat
5. 4	13. 3	E5	C1	Sheep	17. 6	27. 4	F6	F2	Swallow
6. 4	14. 3	E5	D2	Deer	18. 6	28. 4	F6	G3	Pig
7. 4	15. 3	E5	E3	Horse	19. 6	29. 4	F6	H4	Porcupine
8. 4	16. 3	E5	F4	Stag	20. 6	1. 5	G7	J5	Wolf
9. 4	17. 3	E5	G5	Sterpent	21. 6	2. 5	G7	K6	Dog
10. 4	18. 3	E5	H6	Earthworm	22. 6	3. 5	G7	A7	Pheasant
11. 4	19. 3	E5	J7	Crocodile	23. 6	4. 5	G7	B8	Cock
12. 4	20. 3	E5	K8	Dragon	24. 6	5. 5	G7	C9	Crow
13. 4	21. 3	E5	A9	Badger	25. 6	6. 5	G7	D10	Monkey
14. 4	22. 3	E5	B10	Hare	26. 6	7. 5	G7	E11	Gibbon
15. 4	23. 3	E5	C11	Fox	27. 6	8. 5	G7	F12	Tapir
16. 4	24. 3	E5	D12	Tiger	28. 6	9. 5	G7	G1	Sheep
17. 4	25. 3	E5	E1	Leopard	29. 6	10. 5	G7	H2	Deer
18. 4	26. 3	E5	F2	Griffon	30. 6	11. 5	G7	J3	Horse
19. 4	27. 3	E5	G3	Ox	1. 7	12. 5	G7	K4	Stag
20. 4	28. 3	E5	H4	Bat	2. 7	13. 5	G7	A5	Serpent
21. 4	29. 3	E5	J5	Rat	3. 7	14. 5	G7	B6	Earthworm
22. 4	1. 4	F6	K6	Swallow	4. 7	15. 5	G7	C7	Crocodile
23. 4	2. 4	F6	A7	Pig	5. 7	16. 5	G7	D8	Dragon
24. 4	3. 4	F6	B8	Porcupine	6. 7	17. 5	G7	E9	Badger
25. 4	4. 4	F6	C9	Wolf	7. 7	18. 5	G7	F10	Hare
26. 4	5. 4	F6	D10	Dog	8. 7	19. 5	G7	G11	Fox
27. 4	6. 4	F6	E11	Pheasant	9. 7	20. 5	G7	H12	Tiger
28. 4	7. 4	F6	F12	Cock	10. 7	21. 5	G7	J1	Leopard
29. 4	8. 4	F6	G1	Crow	11. 7	22. 5	G7	K2	Griffon
30. 4	9. 4	F6	H2	Monkey	12. 7	23. 5	G7	A3	Ox
1. 5	10. 4	F6	J3	Gibbon	13. 7	24. 5	G7	B4	Bat
2. 5	11. 4	F6	K4	Tapir	14. 7	25. 5	G7	C5	Rat
3. 5	12. 4	F6	A5	Sheep	15. 7	26. 5	G7	D6	Swallow
4. 5	13. 4	F6	B6	Deer	16. 7	27. 5	G7	E7	Pig
5. 5	14. 4	F6	C7	Horse	17. 7	28. 5	G7	F8	Porcupine
6. 5	15. 4	F6	D8	Stag	18. 7	29. 5	G7	G9	Wolf
7. 5	16. 4	F6	E9	Serpent	19. 7	1. 6	H8	H10	Dog
8. 5	17. 4	F6	F10	Earthworm	20. 7	2. 6	H8	J11	Pheasant
9. 5	18. 4	F6	G11	Crocodile	21. 7	3. 6	H8	K12	Cock
10. 5	19. 4	F6	H12	Dragon	22. 7	4. 6	H8	A1	Crow
11. 5	20. 4	F6	J1	Badger	23. 7	5. 6	H8	B2	Monkey
12. 5	21. 4	F6	K2	Hare	24. 7	6. 6	H8	C3	Gibbon
13. 5	22. 4	F6	A3	Fox	25. 7	7. 6	H8	D4	Tapir
14. 5	23. 4	F6	B4	Tiger	26. 7	8. 6	H8	E5	Sheep
15. 5	24. 4	F6	C5	Leopard	27. 7	9. 6	H8	F6	Deer
16. 5	25. 4	F6	D6	Griffon	28. 7	10. 6	H8	F7	Horse
17. 5	26. 4	F6	E7	Ox	29. 7	11. 6	H8	H8	Stag
18. 5	27. 4	F6	F8	Bat	30. 7	12. 6	H8	J9	Serpent
19. 5	28. 4	F6	G9	Rat	31. 7	13. 6	H8	K10	Earthworm
20. 5	29. 4	F6	H10	Swallow	1. 8	14. 6	H8	A11	Crocodile
21. 5	30. 4	F6	J11	Pig	2. 8	15. 6	H8	B12	Dragon
22. 5	1. 4	F6	K12	Porcupine	3. 8	16. 6	H8	C1	Badger
23. 5	2. 4	F6	A1	Wolf	4. 8	17. 6	H8	D2	Hare
24. 5	3. 4	F6	B2	Dog	5. 8	18. 6	H8	E3	Fox
25. 5	4. 4	F6	C3	Pheasant	6. 8	19. 6	H8	F4	Tiger
26. 5	5. 4	F6	D4	Cock	7. 8	20. 6	H8	G5	Leopard
27. 5	6. 4	F6	E5	Crow	8. 8	21. 6	H8	H6	Griffon
28. 5	7. 4	F6	F6	Monkey	9. 8	22. 6	H8	J7	Ox
29. 5	8. 4	F6	G7	Gibbon	10. 8	23. 6	H8	K8	Bat
30. 5	9. 4	F6	H8	Tapir	11. 8	24. 6	H8	A9	Rat
31. 5	10. 4	F6	J9	Sheep	12. 8	25. 6	H8	B10	Swallow
1. 6	11. 4	F6	K10	Deer	13. 8	26. 6	H8	C11	Pig
2. 6	12. 4	F6	A11	Horse	14. 8	27. 6	H8	D12	Porcupine
3. 6	13. 4	F6	B12	Stag	15. 8	28. 6	H8	E1	Wolf
4. 6	14. 4	F6	C1	Serpent	16. 8	29. 6	H8	F2	Dog
5. 6	15. 4	F6	D2	Earthworm	17. 8	30. 6	H8	G3	Pheasant
6. 6	16. 4	F6	E3	Crocodile	18. 8	1. 7	J9	H4	Cock
7. 6	17. 4	F6	F4	Dragon	19. 8	2. 7	J9	J5	Crow
8. 6	18. 4	F6	G5	Badger	20. 8	3. 7	J9	K6	Monkey
9. 6	19. 4	F6	H6	Hare	21. 8	4. 7	J9	A7	Gibbon
10. 6	20. 4	F6	J7	Fox	22. 8	5. 7	J9	B8	Tapir
11. 6	21. 4	F6	K8	Tiger	23. 8	6. 7	J9	C9	Sheep
12. 6	22. 4	F6	A9	Leopard	24. 8	7. 7	J9	D10	Deer

Solar date	Lunar date	Month HS/EB	Day HS/EB	Constellation	Solar date	Lunar date	Month HS/EB	Day HS/EB	Constellation
25. 8	8. 7	J9	E11	Horse	6.11	23. 9	A11	H12	Porcupine
26. 8	9. 7	J9	F12	Stag	7.11	24. 9	A11	J1	Wolf
27. 8	10. 7	J9	G1	Serpent	8.11	25. 9	A11	K2	Dog
28. 8	11. 7	J9	H2	Earthworm	9.11	26. 9	A11	A3	Pheasant
29. 8	12. 7	J9	J3	Crocodile	10.11	27. 9	A11	B4	Cock
30. 8	13. 7	J9	K4	Dragon	11.11	28. 9	A11	C5	Crow
31. 8	14. 7	J9	A5	Badger	12.11	29. 9	A11	D6	Monkey
1. 9	15. 7	J9	B6	Hare	13.11	30. 9	A11	E7	Gibbon
2. 9	16. 7	J9	C7	Fox	14.11	1.10	B12	F8	Tapir
3. 9	17. 7	J9	D8	Tiger	15.11	2.10	B12	G9	Sheep
4. 9	18. 7	J9	E9	Leopard	16.11	3.10	B12	H10	Deer
5. 9	19. 7	J9	F10	Griffon	17.11	4.10	B12	J11	Horse
6. 9	20. 7	J9	G11	Ox	18.11	5.10	B12	K12	Stag
7. 9	21. 7	J9	H12	Bat	19.11	6.10	B12	A1	Serpent
8. 9	22. 7	J9	J1	Rat	20.11	7.10	B12	B2	Earthworm
9. 9	23. 7	J9	K2	Swallow	21.11	8.10	B12	C3	Crocodile
10. 9	24. 7	J9	A3	Pig	22.11	9.10	B12	D4	Dragon
11. 9	25. 7	J9	B4	Porcupine	23.11	10.10	B12	E5	Badger
12. 9	26. 7	J9	C5	Wolf	24.11	11.10	B12	F6	Hare
13. 9	27. 7	J9	D6	Dog	25.11	12.10	B12	G7	Fox
14. 9	28. 7	J9	E7	Pheasant	26.11	13.10	B12	H8	Tiger
15. 9	29. 7	J9	F8	Cock	27.11	14.10	B12	J9	Leopard
16. 9	1. 8	K10	G9	Crow	28.11	15.10	B12	K10	Griffon
17. 9	2. 8	K10	H10	Monkey	29.11	16.10	B12	A11	Ox
18. 9	3. 8	K10	J11	Gibbon	30.11	17.10	B12	B12	Bat
19. 9	4. 8	K10	K12	Tapir	1.12	18.10	B12	C1	Rat
20. 9	5. 8	K10	A1	Sheep	2.12	19.10	B12	D2	Swallow
21. 9	6. 8	K10	B2	Deer	3.12	20.10	B12	E3	Pig
22. 9	7. 8	K10	C3	Horse	4.12	21.10	B12	F4	Porcupine
23. 9	8. 8	K10	D4	Stag	5.12	22.10	B12	G5	Wolf
24. 9	9. 8	K10	E5	Serpent	6.12	23.10	B12	H6	Dog
25. 9	10. 8	K10	F6	Earthworm	7.12	24.10	B12	J7	Pheasant
26. 9	11. 8	K10	G7	Crocodile	8.12	25.10	B12	K8	Cock
27. 9	12. 8	K10	H8	Dragon	9.12	26.10	B12	A9	Crow
28. 9	13. 8	K10	J9	Badger	10.12	27.10	B12	B10	Monkey
29. 9	14. 8	K10	K10	Hare	11.12	28.10	B12	C11	Gibbon
30. 9	15. 8	K10	A11	Fox	12.12	29.10	B12	D12	Tapir
1.10	16. 8	K10	B12	Tiger	13.12	30.10	B12	E1	Sheep
2.10	17. 8	K10	C1	Leopard	14.12	1.11	C1	F2	Deer
3.10	18. 8	K10	D2	Griffon	15.12	2.11	C1	G3	Horse
4.10	19. 8	K10	E3	Ox	16.12	3.11	C1	H4	Stag
5.10	20. 8	K10	F4	Bat	17.12	4.11	C1	J5	Serpent
6.10	21. 8	K10	G5	Rat	18.12	5.11	C1	K6	Earthworm
7.10	22. 8	K10	H6	Swallow	19.12	6.11	C1	A7	Crocodile
8.10	23. 8	K10	J7	Pig	20.12	7.11	C1	B8	Dragon
9.10	24. 8	K10	K8	Porcupine	21.12	8.11	C1	C9	Badger
10.10	25. 8	K10	A9	Wolf	22.12	9.11	C1	D10	Hare
11.10	26. 8	K10	B10	Dog	23.12	10.11	C1	E11	Fox
12.10	27. 8	K10	C11	Pheasant	24.12	11.11	C1	F12	Tiger
13.10	28. 8	K10	D12	Cock	25.12	12.11	C1	G1	Leopard
14.10	29. 8	K10	E1	Crow	26.12	13.11	C1	H2	Griffon
15.10	1. 9	A11	F2	Monkey	27.12	14.11	C1	J3	Ox
16.10	2. 9	A11	G3	Gibbon	28.12	15.11	C1	K4	Bat
17.10	3. 9	A11	H4	Tapir	29.12	16.11	C1	A5	Rat
18.10	4. 9	A11	J5	Sheep	30.12	17.11	C1	B6	Swallow
19.10	5. 9	A11	K6	Deer	31.12	18.11	C1	C7	Pig
20.10	6. 9	A11	A7	Horse					
21.10	7. 9	A11	B8	Stag	**1975**				
22.10	8. 9	A11	C9	Serpent	1. 1	19.11	C1	D8	Porcupine
23.10	9. 9	A11	D10	Earthworm	2. 1	20.11	C1	E9	Wolf
24.10	10. 9	A11	E11	Crocodile	3. 1	21.11	C1	F10	Dog
25.10	11. 9	A11	F12	Dragon	4. 1	22.11	C1	G11	Pheasant
26.10	12. 9	A11	G1	Badger	5. 1	23.11	C1	H12	Cock
27.10	13. 9	A11	H2	Hare	6. 1	24.11	C1	J1	Crow
28.10	14. 9	A11	J3	Fox	7. 1	25.11	C1	K2	Monkey
29.10	15. 9	A11	K4	Tiger	8. 1	26.11	C1	A3	Gibbon
30.10	16. 9	A11	A5	Leopard	9. 1	27.11	C1	B4	Tapir
31.10	17. 9	A11	B6	Griffon	10. 1	28.11	C1	C5	Sheep
1.11	18. 9	A11	C7	Ox	11. 1	29.11	C1	D6	Deer
2.11	19. 9	A11	D8	Bat	12. 2	1.12	D2	E7	Horse
3.11	20. 9	A11	E9	Rat	13. 1	2.12	D2	F8	Stag
4.11	21. 9	A11	F10	Swallow	14. 1	3.12	D2	G9	Serpent
5.11	22. 9	A11	G11	Pig	15. 1	4.12	D2	H10	Earthworm

Solar date	Lunar date	Month HS/EB	Day HS/EB	Constellation
16. 1	5.12	D2	J11	Crocodile
17. 1	6.12	D2	K12	Dragon
18. 1	7.12	D2	A1	Badger
19. 1	8.12	D2	B2	Hare
20. 1	9.12	D2	C3	Fox
21. 1	10.12	D2	D4	Tiger
22. 1	11.12	D2	E5	Leopard
23. 1	12.12	D2	F6	Griffon
24. 1	13.12	D2	G7	Ox
25. 1	14.12	D2	H8	Bat
26. 1	15.12	D2	J9	Rat
27. 1	16.12	D2	K10	Swallow
28. 1	17.12	D2	A11	Pig
29. 1	18.12	D2	B12	Porcupine
30. 1	19.12	D2	C1	Wolf
31. 1	20.12	D2	D2	Dog
1. 2	21.12	D2	E3	Pheasant
2. 2	22.12	D2	F4	Cock
3. 2	23.12	D2	G5	Crow
4. 2	24.12	D2	H6	Monkey
5. 2	25.12	D2	J7	Gibbon
6. 2	26.12	D2	K8	Tapir
7. 2	27.12	D2	A9	Sheep
8. 2	28.12	D2	B10	Deer
9. 2	29.12	D2	C11	Horse
10. 2	30.12	D2	D12	Stag

YI MAO YEAR

Solar date	Lunar date	Month HS/EB	Day HS/EB	Constellation
11. 2	1. 1	E3	E1	Serpent
12. 2	2. 1	E3	F2	Earthworm
13. 2	3. 1	E3	G3	Crocodile
14. 2	4. 1	E3	H4	Dragon
15. 2	5. 1	E3	J5	Badger
16. 2	6. 1	E3	K6	Hare
17. 2	7. 1	E3	A7	Fox
18. 2	8. 1	E3	B8	Tiger
19. 2	9. 1	E3	C9	Leopard
20. 2	10. 1	E3	D10	Griffon
21. 2	11. 1	E3	E11	Ox
22. 2	12. 1	E3	F12	Bat
23. 2	13. 1	E3	G1	Rat
24. 2	14. 1	E3	H2	Swallow
25. 2	15. 1	E3	J3	Pig
26. 2	16. 1	E3	K4	Porcupine
27. 2	17. 1	E3	A5	Wolf
28. 2	18. 1	E3	B6	Dog
1. 3	19. 1	E3	C7	Pheasant
2. 3	20. 1	E3	D8	Cock
3. 3	21. 1	E3	E9	Crow
4. 3	22. 1	E3	F10	Monkey
5. 3	23. 1	E3	G11	Gibbon
6. 3	24. 1	E3	H12	Tapir
7. 3	25. 1	E3	J1	Sheep
8. 3	26. 1	E3	K2	Deer
9. 3	27. 1	E3	A3	Horse
10. 3	28. 1	E3	B4	Stag
11. 3	29. 1	E3	C5	Serpent
12. 3	30. 1	E3	D6	Earthworm
13. 3	1. 2	F4	E7	Crocodile
14. 3	2. 2	F4	F8	Dragon
15. 3	3. 2	F4	G9	Badger
16. 3	4. 2	F4	H10	Hare
17. 3	5. 2	F4	J11	Fox
18. 3	6. 2	F4	K12	Tiger
19. 3	7. 2	F4	A1	Leopard
20. 3	8. 2	F4	B2	Griffon
21. 3	9. 2	F4	C3	Ox
22. 3	10. 2	F4	D4	Bat
23. 3	11. 2	F4	E5	Rat
24. 3	12. 2	F4	F6	Swallow
25. 3	13. 2	F4	G7	Pig
26. 3	14. 2	F4	H8	Porcupine
27. 3	15. 2	F4	J9	Wolf
28. 3	16. 2	F4	K10	Dog
29. 3	17. 2	F4	A11	Pheasant
30. 3	18. 2	F4	B12	Cock
31. 3	19. 2	F4	C1	Crow
1. 4	20. 2	F4	D2	Monkey
2. 4	21. 2	F4	E3	Gibbon
3. 4	22. 2	F4	F4	Tapir
4. 4	23. 2	F4	G5	Sheep
5. 4	24. 2	F4	H6	Deer
6. 4	25. 2	F4	J7	Horse
7. 4	26. 2	F4	K8	Stag
8. 4	27. 2	F4	A9	Serpent
9. 4	28. 2	F4	B10	Earthworm
10. 4	29. 2	F4	C11	Crocodile
11. 4	30. 2	F4	D12	Dragon
12. 4	1. 3	G5	E1	Badger
13. 4	2. 3	G5	F2	Hare
14. 4	3. 3	G5	G3	Fox
15. 4	4. 3	G5	H4	Tiger
16. 4	5. 3	G5	J5	Leopard
17. 4	6. 3	G5	K6	Griffon
18. 4	7. 3	G5	A7	Ox
19. 4	8. 3	G5	B8	Bat
20. 4	9. 3	G5	C9	Rat
21. 4	10. 3	G5	D10	Swallow
22. 4	11. 3	G5	E11	Pig
23. 4	12. 3	G5	F12	Porcupine
24. 4	13. 3	G5	G1	Wolf
25. 4	14. 3	G5	H2	Dog
26. 4	15. 3	G5	J3	Pheasant
27. 4	16. 3	G5	K4	Cock
28. 4	17. 3	G5	A5	Crow
29. 4	18. 3	G5	B6	Monkey
30. 4	19. 3	G5	C7	Gibbon
1. 5	20. 3	G5	D8	Tapir
2. 5	21. 3	G5	E9	Sheep
3. 5	22. 3	G5	F10	Deer
4. 5	23. 3	G5	G11	Horse
5. 5	24. 3	G5	H12	Stag
6. 5	25. 3	G5	J1	Serpent
7. 5	26. 3	G5	K2	Earthworm
8. 5	27. 3	G5	A3	Crocodile
9. 5	28. 3	G5	B4	Dragon
10. 5	29. 3	G5	C5	Badger
11. 5	1. 4	H6	D6	Hare
12. 5	2. 4	H6	E7	Fox
13. 5	3. 4	H6	F8	Tiger
14. 5	4. 4	H6	G9	Leopard
15. 5	5. 4	H6	H10	Griffon
16. 5	6. 4	H6	J11	Ox
17. 5	7. 4	H6	K12	Bat
18. 5	8. 4	H6	A1	Rat
19. 5	9. 4	H6	B2	Swallow
20. 5	10. 4	H6	C3	Pig
21. 5	11. 4	H6	D4	Porcupine
22. 5	12. 4	H6	E5	Wolf
23. 5	13. 4	H6	F6	Dog
24. 5	14. 4	H6	G7	Pheasant
25. 5	15. 4	H6	H8	Cock
26. 5	16. 4	H6	J9	Crow
27. 5	17. 4	H6	K10	Monkey
28. 5	18. 4	H6	A11	Gibbon
29. 5	19. 4	H6	B12	Tapir
30. 5	20. 4	H6	C1	Sheep
31. 5	21. 4	H6	D2	Deer

Solar date	Lunar date	Month HS/EB	Day HS/EB	Constellation	Solar date	Lunar date	Month HS/EB	Day HS/EB	Constellation
1. 6	22. 4	H6	E3	Horse	13. 8	7. 7	A9	H4	Porcupine
2. 6	23. 4	H6	F4	Stag	14. 8	8. 7	A9	J5	Wolf
3. 6	24. 4	H6	G5	Serpent	15. 8	9. 7	A9	K6	Dog
4. 6	25. 4	H6	H6	Earthworm	16. 8	10. 7	A9	A7	Pheasant
5. 6	26. 4	H6	J7	Crocodile	17. 8	11. 7	A9	B8	Cock
6. 6	27. 4	H6	K8	Dragon	18. 8	12. 7	A9	C9	Crow
7. 6	28. 4	H6	A9	Badger	19. 8	13. 7	A9	D10	Monkey
8. 6	29. 4	H6	B10	Hare	20. 8	14. 7	A9	E11	Gibbon
9. 6	30. 4	H6	C11	Fox	21. 8	15. 7	A9	F12	Tapir
10. 6	1. 5	J7	D12	Tiger	22. 8	16. 7	A9	G1	Sheep
11. 6	2. 5	J7	E1	Leopard	23. 8	17. 7	A9	H2	Deer
12. 6	3. 5	J7	F2	Griffon	24. 8	18. 7	A9	J3	Horse
13. 6	4. 5	J7	G3	Ox	25. 8	19. 7	A9	K4	Stag
14. 6	5. 5	J7	H4	Bat	26. 8	20. 7	A9	A5	Serpent
15. 6	6. 5	J7	J5	Rat	27. 8	21. 7	A9	B6	Earthworm
16. 6	7. 5	J7	K6	Swallow	28. 8	22. 7	A9	C7	Crocodile
17. 6	8. 5	J7	A7	Pig	29. 8	23. 7	A9	D8	Dragon
18. 6	9. 5	J7	B8	Porcupine	30. 8	24. 7	A9	E9	Badger
19. 6	10. 5	J7	C9	Wolf	31. 8	25. 7	A9	F10	Hare
20. 6	11. 5	J7	D10	Dog	1. 9	26. 7	A9	G11	Fox
21. 6	12. 5	J7	E11	Pheasant	2. 9	27. 7	A9	H12	Tiger
22. 6	13. 5	J7	F12	Cock	3. 9	28. 7	A9	J1	Leopard
23. 6	14. 5	J7	G1	Crow	4. 9	29. 7	A9	K2	Griffon
24. 6	15. 5	J7	H2	Monkey	5. 9	30. 7	A9	A3	Ox
25. 6	16. 5	J7	J3	Gibbon	6. 9	1. 8	B10	B4	Bat
26. 6	17. 5	J7	K4	Tapir	7. 9	2. 8	B10	C5	Rat
27. 6	18. 5	J7	A5	Sheep	8. 9	3. 8	B10	D6	Swallow
28. 6	19. 5	J7	B6	Deer	9. 9	4. 8	B10	E7	Pig
29. 6	20. 5	J7	C7	Horse	10. 9	5. 8	B10	F8	Porcupine
30. 6	21. 5	J7	D8	Stag	11. 9	6. 8	B10	G9	Wolf
1. 7	22. 5	J7	E9	Serpent	12. 9	7. 8	B10	H10	Dog
2. 7	23. 5	J7	F10	Earthworm	13. 9	8. 8	B10	J11	Pheasant
3. 7	24. 5	J7	G11	Crocodile	14. 9	9. 8	B10	K12	Cock
4. 7	25. 5	J7	H12	Dragon	15. 9	10. 8	B10	A1	Crow
5. 7	26. 5	J7	J1	Badger	16. 9	11. 8	B10	B2	Monkey
6. 7	27. 5	J7	K2	Hare	17. 9	12. 8	B10	C3	Gibbon
7. 7	28. 5	J7	A3	Fox	18. 9	13. 8	B10	D4	Tapir
8. 7	29. 5	J7	B4	Tiger	19. 9	14. 8	B10	E5	Sheep
9. 7	1. 6	K8	C5	Leopard	20. 9	15. 8	B10	F6	Deer
10. 7	2. 6	K8	D6	Griffon	21. 9	16. 8	B10	G7	Horse
11. 7	3. 6	K8	E7	Ox	22. 9	17. 8	B10	H8	Stag
12. 7	4. 6	K8	F8	Bat	23. 9	18.18	B10	J9	Serpent
13. 7	5. 6	K8	G9	Rat	24. 9	19. 8	B10	K10	Earthworm
14. 7	6. 6	K8	H10	Swallow	25. 9	20. 8	B10	A11	Crocodile
15. 7	7. 6	K8	J11	Pig	26. 9	21. 8	B10	B12	Dragon
16. 7	8. 6	K8	K12	Porcupine	27. 9	22. 8	B10	C1	Badger
17. 7	9. 6	K8	A1	Wolf	28. 9	23. 8	B10	D2	Hare
18. 7	10. 6	K8	B2	Dog	29. 9	24. 8	B10	E3	Fox
19. 7	11. 6	K8	C3	Pheasant	30. 9	25. 8	B10	F4	Tiger
20. 7	12. 6	K8	D4	Cock	1.10	26. 8	B10	G5	Leopard
21. 7	13. 6	K8	E5	Crow	2.10	27. 8	B10	H6	Griffon
22. 7	14. 6	K8	F6	Monkey	3.10	28. 8	B10	J7	Ox
23. 7	15. 6	K8	G7	Gibbon	4.10	29. 8	B10	K8	Bat
24. 7	16. 6	K8	H8	Tapir	5.10	1. 9	C11	A9	Rat
25. 7	17. 6	K8	J9	Sheep	6.10	2. 9	C11	B10	Swallow
26. 7	18. 6	K8	K10	Deer	7.10	3. 9	C11	C11	Pig
27. 7	19. 6	K8	A11	Horse	8.10	4. 9	C11	D12	Porcupine
28. 7	20. 6	K8	B12	Stag	9.10	5. 9	C11	E1	Wolf
29. 7	21. 6	K8	C1	Serpent	10.10	6. 9	C11	F2	Dog
30. 7	22. 6	K8	D2	Earthworm	11.10	7. 9	C11	G3	Pheasant
31. 7	23. 6	K8	E3	Crocodile	12.10	8. 9	C11	H4	Cock
1. 8	24. 6	K8	F4	Dragon	13.10	9. 9	C11	J5	Crow
2. 8	25. 6	K8	G5	Badger	14.10	10. 9	C11	K6	Monkey
3. 8	26. 6	K8	H6	Hare	15.10	11. 9	C11	A7	Gibbon
4. 8	27. 6	K8	J7	Fox	16.10	12. 9	C11	B8	Tapir
5. 8	28. 6	K8	K8	Tiger	17.10	13. 9	C11	C9	Sheep
6. 8	29. 6	K8	A9	Leopard	18.10	14. 9	C11	D10	Deer
7. 8	1. 7	A9	B10	Griffon	19.10	15. 9	C11	E11	Horse
8. 8	2. 7	A9	C11	Ox	20.10	16. 9	C11	F12	Stag
9. 8	3. 7	A9	D12	Bat	21.10	17. 9	C11	G1	Serpent
10. 8	4. 7	A9	E1	Rat	22.10	18. 9	C11	H2	Earthworm
11. 8	5. 7	A9	F2	Swallow	23.10	19. 9	C11	J3	Crocodile
12. 8	6. 7	A9	G3	Pig	24.10	20. 9	C11	K4	Dragon

Solar date	Lunar date	Month HS/EB	Day HS/EB	Constellation
25.10	21. 9	C11	A5	Badger
26.10	22. 9	C11	B6	Hare
27.10	23. 9	C11	C7	Fox
28.10	24. 9	C11	D8	Tiger
29.10	25. 9	C11	E9	Leopard
30.10	26. 9	C11	F10	Griffon
31.10	27. 9	C11	G11	Ox
1.11	28. 9	C11	H12	Bat
2.11	29. 9	C11	J1	Rat
3.11	1.10	D12	K2	Swallow
4.11	2.10	D12	A3	Pig
5.11	3.10	D12	B4	Porcupine
6.11	4.10	D12	C5	Wolf
7.11	5.10	D12	D6	Dog
8.11	6.10	D12	E7	Pheasant
9.11	7.10	D12	F8	Cock
10.11	8.10	D12	G9	Crow
11.11	9.10	D12	H10	Monkey
12.11	10.10	D12	J11	Gibbon
13.11	11.10	D12	K12	Tapir
14.11	12.10	D12	A1	Sheep
15.11	13.10	D12	B2	Deer
16.11	14.10	D12	C3	Horse
17.11	15.10	D12	D4	Stag
18.11	16.10	D12	E5	Serpent
19.11	17.10	D12	F6	Earthworm
20.11	18.10	D12	G7	Crocodile
21.11	19.10	D12	H8	Dragon
22.11	20.10	D12	J9	Badger
23.11	21.10	D12	K10	Hare
24.11	22.10	D12	A11	Fox
25.11	23.10	D12	B12	Tiger
26.11	24.10	D12	C1	Leopard
27.11	25.10	D12	D2	Griffon
28.11	26.10	D12	E3	Ox
29.11	27.10	D12	F4	Bat
30.11	28.10	D12	G5	Rat
1.12	29.10	D12	H6	Swallow
2.12	20.10	D12	J7	Pig
3.12	1.11	E1	K8	Porcupine
4.12	2.11	E1	A9	Wolf
5.12	3.11	E1	B10	Dog
6.12	4.11	E1	C11	Pheasant
7.12	5.11	E1	D12	Cock
8.12	6.11	E1	E1	Crow
9.12	7.11	E1	F2	Monkey
10.12	8.11	E1	G3	Gibbon
11.12	9.11	E1	H4	Tapir
12.12	10.11	E1	J5	Sheep
13.12	11.11	E1	K6	Deer
14.12	12.11	E1	A7	Horse
15.12	13.11	E1	B8	Stag
16.12	14.11	E1	C9	Serpent
17.12	15.11	E1	D10	Earthworm
18.12	16.11	E1	E11	Crocodile
19.12	17.11	E1	F12	Dragon
20.12	18.11	E1	G1	Badger
21.12	19.11	E1	H2	Hare
22.12	20.11	E1	J3	Fox
23.12	21.11	E1	K4	Tiger
24.12	22.11	E1	A5	Leopard
25.12	23.11	E1	B6	Griffon
26.12	24.11	E1	C7	Ox
27.12	25.11	E1	D8	Bat
28.12	26.11	E1	E9	Rat
29.12	27.11	E1	F10	Swallow
30.12	28.11	E1	G11	Pig
31.12	29.11	E1	H12	Porcupine

1976

Solar date	Lunar date	Month HS/EB	Day HS/EB	Constellation
1. 1	1.12	F2	J1	Wolf
2. 1	2.12	F2	K2	Dog
3. 1	3.12	F2	A3	Pheasant
4. 1	4.12	F2	B4	Cock
5. 1	5.12	F2	C5	Crow
6. 1	6.12	F2	D6	Monkey
7. 1	7.12	F2	E7	Gibbon
8. 1	8.12	F2	F8	Tapir
9. 1	9.12	F2	G9	Sheep
10. 1	10.12	F2	H10	Deer
11. 1	11.12	F2	J11	Horse
12. 1	12.12	F2	K12	Stag
13. 1	13.12	F2	A1	Serpent
14. 1	14.12	F2	B2	Earthworm
15. 1	15.12	F2	C3	Crocodile
16. 1	16.12	F2	D4	Dragon
17. 1	17.12	F2	E5	Badger
18. 1	18.12	F2	F6	Hare
19. 1	19.12	F2	G7	Fox
20. 1	20.12	F2	H8	Tiger
21. 1	21.12	F2	J9	Leopard
22. 1	22.12	F2	K10	Griffon
23. 1	23.12	F2	A11	Ox
24. 1	24.12	F2	B12	Bat
25. 1	25.12	F2	C1	Rat
26. 1	26.12	F2	D2	Swallow
27. 1	27.12	F2	E3	Pig
28. 1	28.12	F2	F4	Porcupine
29. 1	29.12	F2	G5	Wolf
30. 1	30.12	F2	H6	Dog

PING CH'EN YEAR

Solar date	Lunar date	Month HS/EB	Day HS/EB	Constellation
31. 1	1. 1	G3	J7	Pheasant
1. 2	2. 1	G3	K8	Cock
2. 2	3. 1	G3	A9	Crow
3. 2	4. 1	G3	B10	Monkey
4. 2	5. 1	G3	C11	Gibbon
5. 2	6. 1	G3	D12	Tapir
6. 2	7. 1	G3	E1	Sheep
7. 2	8. 1	G3	F2	Deer
8. 2	9. 1	G3	G3	Horse
9. 2	10. 1	G3	H4	Stag
10. 2	11. 1	G3	J5	Serpent
11. 2	12. 1	G3	K6	Earthworm
12. 2	13. 1	G3	A7	Crocodile
13. 2	14. 1	G3	B8	Dragon
14. 2	15. 1	G3	C9	Badger
15. 2	16. 1	G3	D10	Hare
16. 2	17. 1	G3	E11	Fox
17. 2	18. 1	G3	F12	Tiger
18. 2	19. 1	G3	G1	Leopard
19. 2	20. 1	G3	H2	Griffon
20. 2	21. 1	G3	J3	Ox
21. 2	22. 1	G3	K4	Bat
22. 2	23. 1	G3	A5	Rat
23. 2	24. 1	G3	B6	Swallow
24. 2	25. 1	G3	C7	Pig
25. 2	26. 1	G3	D8	Porcupine
26. 2	27. 1	G3	E9	Wolf
27. 2	28. 1	G3	F10	Dog
28. 2	29. 1	G3	G11	Pheasant
29. 2	30. 1	G3	H12	Cock
1. 3	1. 2	H4	J1	Crow
2. 3	2. 2	H4	K2	Monkey
3. 3	3. 2	H4	A3	Gibbon
4. 3	4. 2	H4	B4	Tapir
5. 3	5. 2	H4	C5	Sheep
6. 3	6. 2	H4	D6	Deer

Solar date	Lunar date	Month HS/EB	Day HS/EB	Constellation	Solar date	Lunar date	Month HS/EB	Day HS/EB	Constellation
7. 3	7. 2	H4	E7	Horse	19. 5	21. 4	K6	H8	Porcupine
8. 3	8. 2	H4	F8	Stag	20. 5	22. 4	K6	J9	Wolf
9. 3	9. 2	H4	G9	Serpent	21. 5	23. 4	K6	K10	Dog
10. 3	10. 2	H4	H10	Earthworm	22. 5	24. 4	K6	A11	Pheasant
11. 3	11. 2	H4	J11	Crocodile	23. 5	25. 4	K6	B12	Cock
12. 3	12. 2	H4	K12	Dragon	24. 5	26. 4	K6	C1	Crow
13. 3	13. 2	H4	A1	Badger	25. 5	27. 4	K6	D2	Monkey
14. 3	14. 2	H4	B2	Hare	26. 5	28. 4	K6	E3	Gibbon
15. 3	15. 2	H4	C3	Fox	27. 5	29. 4	K6	F4	Tapir
16. 3	16. 2	H4	D4	Tiger	28. 5	30. 4	K6	G5	Sheep
17. 3	17. 2	H4	E5	Leopard	29. 5	1. 5	A7	H6	Deer
18. 3	18. 2	H4	F6	Griffon	30. 5	2. 5	A7	J7	Horse
19. 3	19. 2	H4	G7	Ox	31. 5	3. 5	A7	K8	Stag
20. 3	20. 2	H4	H8	Bat	1. 6	4. 5	A7	A9	Serpent
21. 3	21. 2	H4	J9	Rat	2. 6	5. 5	A7	B10	Earthworm
22. 3	22. 2	H4	K10	Swallow	3. 6	6. 5	A7	C11	Crocodile
23. 3	23. 2	H4	A11	Pig	4. 6	7. 5	A7	D12	Dragon
24. 3	24. 2	H4	B12	Porcupine	5. 6	8. 5	A7	E1	Badger
25. 3	25. 2	H4	C1	Wolf	6. 6	9. 5	A7	F2	Hare
26. 3	26. 2	H4	D2	Dog	7. 6	10. 5	A7	G3	Fox
27. 3	27. 2	H4	E3	Pheasant	8. 6	11. 5	A7	H4	Tiger
28. 3	28. 2	H4	F4	Cock	9. 6	12. 5	A7	J5	Leopard
29. 3	29. 2	H4	G5	Crow	10. 6	13. 5	A7	K6	Griffon
30. 3	30. 2	H4	H6	Monkey	11. 6	14. 5	A7	A7	Ox
31. 3	1. 3	J5	J7	Gibbon	12. 6	15. 5	A7	B8	Bat
1. 4	2. 3	J5	K8	Tapir	13. 6	16. 5	A7	C9	Rat
2. 4	3. 3	J5	A9	Sheep	14. 6	17. 5	A7	D10	Swallow
3. 4	4. 3	J5	B10	Deer	15. 6	18. 5	A7	E11	Pig
4. 4	5. 3	J5	C11	Horse	16. 6	19. 5	A7	F12	Porcupine
5. 4	6. 3	J5	D12	Stag	17. 6	20. 5	A7	G1	Wolf
6. 4	7. 3	J5	E1	Serpent	18. 6	21. 5	A7	H2	Dog
7. 4	8. 3	J5	F2	Earthworm	19. 6	22. 5	A7	J3	Pheasant
8. 4	9. 3	J5	G3	Crocodile	20. 6	23. 5	A7	K4	Cock
9. 4	10. 3	J5	H4	Dragon	21. 6	24. 5	A7	A5	Crow
10. 4	11. 3	J5	J5	Badger	22. 6	25. 5	A7	B6	Monkey
11. 4	12. 3	J5	K6	Hare	23. 6	26. 5	A7	C7	Gibbon
12. 4	13. 3	J5	A7	Fox	24. 6	27. 5	A7	D8	Tapir
13. 4	14. 3	J5	B8	Tiger	25. 6	28. 5	A7	E9	Sheep
14. 4	15. 3	J5	C9	Leopard	26. 6	29. 5	A7	F10	Deer
15. 4	16. 3	J5	D10	Griffon	27. 6	1. 6	B8	G11	Horse
16. 4	17. 3	J5	E11	Ox	28. 6	2. 6	B8	H12	Stag
17. 4	18. 3	J5	F12	Bat	29. 6	3. 6	B8	J1	Serpent
18. 4	19. 3	J5	G1	Rat	30. 6	4. 6	B8	K2	Earthworm
19. 4	20. 3	J5	H2	Swallow	1. 7	5. 6	B8	A3	Crocodile
20. 4	21. 3	J5	J3	Pig	2. 7	6. 6	B8	B4	Dragon
21. 4	22. 3	J5	K4	Porcupine	3. 7	7. 6	B8	C5	Badger
22. 4	23. 3	J5	A5	Wolf	4. 7	8. 6	B8	D6	Hare
23. 4	24. 3	J5	B6	Dog	5. 7	9. 6	B8	E7	Fox
24. 4	25. 3	J5	C7	Pheasant	6. 7	10. 6	B8	F8	Tiger
25. 4	26. 3	J5	D8	Cock	7. 7	11. 6	B8	G9	Leopard
26. 4	27. 3	J5	E9	Crow	8. 7	12. 6	B8	H10	Griffon
27. 4	28. 3	J5	F10	Monkey	9. 7	13. 6	B8	J11	Ox
28. 4	29. 3	J5	G11	Gibbon	10. 7	14. 6	B8	K12	Bat
29. 4	1. 4	K6	H12	Tapir	11. 7	15. 6	B8	A1	Rat
30. 4	2. 4	K6	J1	Sheep	12. 7	16. 6	B8	B2	Swallow
1. 5	3. 4	K6	K2	Deer	13. 7	17. 6	B8	C3	Pig
2. 5	4. 4	K6	A3	Horse	14. 7	18. 6	B8	D4	Porcupine
3. 5	5. 4	K6	B4	Stag	15. 7	19. 6	B8	E5	Wolf
4. 5	6. 4	K6	C5	Serpent	16. 7	20. 6	B8	F6	Dog
5. 5	7. 4	K6	D6	Earthworm	17. 7	21. 6	B8	G7	Pheasant
6. 5	8. 4	K6	E7	Crocodile	18. 7	22. 6	B8	H8	Cock
7. 5	9. 4	K6	F8	Dragon	19. 7	23. 6	B8	J9	Crow
8. 5	10. 4	K6	G9	Badger	20. 7	24. 6	B8	K10	Monkey
9. 5	11. 4	K6	H10	Hare	21. 7	25. 6	B8	A11	Gibbon
10. 5	12. 4	K6	J11	Fox	22. 7	26. 6	B8	B12	Tapir
11. 5	13. 4	K6	K12	Tiger	23. 7	27. 6	B8	C1	Sheep
12. 5	14. 4	K6	A1	Leopard	24. 7	28. 6	B8	D2	Deer
13. 5	15. 4	K6	B2	Griffon	25. 7	29. 6	B8	E3	Horse
14. 5	16. 4	K6	C3	Ox	26. 7	30. 6	B8	F4	Stag
15. 5	17. 4	K6	D4	Bat	27. 7	1. 7	C9	G5	Serpent
16. 5	18. 4	K6	E5	Rat	28. 7	2. 7	C9	H6	Earthworm
17. 5	19. 4	K6	F6	Swallow	29. 7	3. 7	C9	J7	Crocodile
18. 5	20. 4	K6	G7	Pig	30. 7	4. 7	C9	K8	Dragon

Solar date	Lunar date	Month HS/EB	Day HS/EB	Constellation
31. 7	5. 7	C9	A9	Badger
1. 8	6. 7	C9	B10	Hare
2. 8	7. 7	C9	C11	Fox
3. 8	8. 7	C9	D12	Tiger
4. 8	9. 7	C9	E1	Leopard
5. 8	10. 7	C9	F2	Griffon
6. 8	11. 7	C9	G3	Ox
7. 8	12. 7	C9	H4	Bat
8. 8	13. 7	C9	J5	Rat
9. 8	14. 7	C9	K6	Swallow
10. 8	15. 7	C9	A7	Pig
11. 8	16. 7	C9	B8	Porcupine
12. 8	17. 7	C9	C9	Wolf
13. 8	18. 7	C9	D10	Dog
14. 8	19. 7	C9	E11	Pheasant
15. 8	20. 7	C9	F12	Cock
16. 8	21. 7	C9	G1	Crow
17. 8	22. 7	C9	H2	Monkey
18. 8	23. 7	C9	J3	Gibbon
19. 8	24. 7	C9	K4	Tapir
20. 8	25. 7	C9	A5	Sheep
21. 8	26. 7	C9	B6	Deer
22. 8	27. 7	C9	C7	Horse
23. 8	28. 7	C9	D8	Stag
24. 8	29. 7	C9	E9	Serpent
25. 8	1. 8	D10	F10	Earthworm
26. 8	2. 8	D10	G11	Crocodile
27. 8	3. 8	D10	H12	Dragon
28. 8	4. 8	D10	J1	Badger
29. 8	5. 8	D10	K2	Hare
30. 8	6. 8	D10	A3	Fox
31. 8	7. 8	D10	B4	Tiger
1. 9	8. 8	D10	C5	Leopard
2. 9	9. 8	D10	D6	Griffon
3. 9	10. 8	D10	E7	Ox
4. 9	11. 8	D10	F8	Bat
5. 9	12. 8	D10	G9	Rat
6. 9	13. 8	D10	H10	Swallow
7. 9	14. 8	D10	J11	Pig
8. 9	15. 8	D10	K12	Porcupine
9. 9	16. 8	D10	A1	Wolf
10. 9	17. 8	D10	B2	Dog
11. 9	18. 8	D10	C3	Pheasant
12. 9	19. 8	D10	D4	Cock
13. 9	20. 8	D10	E5	Crow
14. 9	21. 8	D10	F6	Monkey
15. 9	22. 8	D10	G7	Gibbon
16. 9	23. 8	D10	H8	Tapir
17. 9	24. 8	D10	J9	Sheep
18. 9	25. 8	D10	K10	Deer
19. 9	26. 8	D10	A11	Horse
20. 9	27. 8	D10	B12	Stag
21. 9	28. 8	D10	C1	Serpent
22. 9	29. 8	D10	D2	Earthworm
23. 9	30. 8	D10	E3	Crocodile
24. 9	1. 8	D10	F4	Dragon
25. 9	2. 8	D10	G5	Badger
26. 9	3. 8	D10	H6	Hare
27. 9	4. 8	D10	J7	Fox
28. 9	5. 8	D10	K8	Tiger
29. 9	6. 8	D10	A9	Leopard
30. 9	7. 8	D10	B10	Griffon
1. 0	8. 8	D10	C11	Ox
2.10	9. 8	D10	D12	Bat
3.10	10. 8	D10	E1	Rat
4.10	11. 8	D10	F2	Swallow
5.10	12. 8	D10	G3	Pig
6.10	13. 8	D10	H4	Porcupine
7.10	14. 8	D10	J5	Wolf
8.10	15. 8	D10	K6	Dog
9.10	16. 8	D10	A7	Pheasant
10.10	17. 8	D10	B8	Cock
11.10	18. 8	D10	C9	Crow
12.10	19. 8	D10	D10	Monkey
13.10	20. 8	D10	E11	Gibbon
14.10	21. 8	D10	F12	Tapir
15.10	22. 8	D10	G1	Sheep
16. 0	23. 8	D10	H2	Deer
17. 0	24. 8	D10	J3	Horse
18.10	25. 8	D10	K4	Stag
19.10	26. 8	D10	A5	Serpent
20.10	27. 8	D10	B6	Earthworm
21.10	28. 8	D10	C7	Crocodile
22.10	29. 8	D10	D8	Dragon
23.10	1. 9	E11	E9	Badger
24.10	2. 9	E11	F10	Hare
25.10	3. 9	E11	G11	Fox
26.10	4. 9	E11	H12	Tiger
27.10	5. 9	E11	J1	Leopard
28.10	6. 9	E11	K2	Griffon
29.10	7. 9	E11	A3	Ox
30.10	8. 9	E11	B4	Bat
31.10	9. 9	E11	C5	Rat
1.11	10. 9	E11	D6	Swallow
2.11	11. 9	E11	E7	Pig
3.11	12. 9	E11	F8	Porcupine
4.11	13. 9	E11	G9	Wolf
5.11	14. 9	E11	H10	Dog
6.11	15. 9	E11	J11	Pheasant
7.11	16. 9	E11	K12	Cock
8.11	17. 9	E11	A1	Crow
9.11	18. 9	E11	B2	Monkey
10.11	19. 9	E11	C3	Gibbon
11.11	20. 9	E11	D4	Tapir
12.11	21. 9	E11	E5	Sheep
13.11	22. 9	E11	F6	Deer
14.11	23. 9	E11	G7	Horse
15.11	24. 9	E11	H8	Stag
16.11	25. 9	E11	J9	Serpent
17.11	26. 9	E11	K10	Earthworm
18.11	27. 9	E11	A11	Crocodile
19.11	28. 9	E11	B12	Dragon
20.11	29. 9	E11	C1	Badger
21.11	1.10	F12	D2	Hare
22.11	2.10	F12	E3	Fox
23.11	3.10	F12	F4	Tiger
24.11	4.10	F12	G5	Leopard
25.11	5.10	F12	H6	Griffon
26.11	6.10	F12	J7	Ox
27.11	7.10	F12	K8	Bat
28.11	8.10	F12	A9	Rat
29.11	9.10	F12	B10	Swallow
30.11	10.10	F12	C11	Pig
1.12	11.10	F12	D12	Porcupine
2.12	12.10	F12	E1	Wolf
3.12	13.10	F12	F2	Dog
4.12	14.10	F12	G3	Pheasant
5.12	15.10	F12	H4	Cock
6.12	16.10	F12	J5	Crow
7.12	17.10	F12	K6	Monkey
8.12	18.10	F12	A7	Gibbon
9.12	19.10	F12	B8	Tapir
10.12	20.10	F12	C9	Sheep
11.12	21.10	F12	D10	Deer
12.12	22.10	F12	E11	Horse
13.12	23.10	F12	F12	Stag
14.12	24.10	F12	G1	Serpent
15.12	25.10	F12	H2	Earthworm
16.12	26.10	F12	J3	Crocodile
17.12	27.10	F12	K4	Dragon
18.12	28.10	F12	A5	Badger
19.12	29.10	F12	B6	Hare
20.12	30.10	F12	C7	Fox
21.12	1.11	G1	D8	Tiger
22.12	2.11	G1	E9	Leopard
23.12	3.11	G1	F10	Griffon

Solar date	Lunar date	Month HS/EB	Day HS/EB	Constellation
24.12	4.11	G1	G11	Ox
25.12	5.11	G1	H12	Bat
26.12	6.11	G1	J1	Rat
27.12	7.11	G1	K2	Swallow
28.12	8.11	G1	A3	Pig
29.12	9.11	G1	B4	Porcupine
30.12	10.11	G1	C5	Wolf
31.12	11.11	G1	D6	Dog
1977				
1. 1	12.11	G1	E7	Pheasant
2. 1	13.11	G1	F8	Cock
3. 1	14.11	G1	G9	Crow
4. 1	15.11	G1	H10	Monkey
5. 1	16.11	G1	J11	Gibbon
6. 1	17.11	G1	K12	Tapir
7. 1	18.11	G1	A1	Sheep
8. 1	19.11	G1	B2	Deer
9. 1	20.11	G1	C3	Horse
10. 1	21.11	G1	D4	Stag
11. 1	22.11	G1	E5	Serpent
12. 1	23.11	G1	F6	Earthworm
13. 1	24.11	G1	G7	Crocodile
14. 1	25.11	G1	H8	Dragon
15. 1	26.11	G1	J9	Badger
16. 1	27.11	G1	K10	Hare
17. 1	28.11	G1	A11	Fox
18. 1	29.11	G1	B12	Tiger
19. 1	1.12	H2	C1	Leopard
20. 1	2.12	H2	D2	Griffon
21. 1	3.12	H2	E3	Ox
22. 1	4.12	H2	F4	Bat
23. 1	5.12	H2	G5	Rat
24. 1	6.12	H2	H6	Swallow
25. 1	7.12	H2	J7	Pig
26. 1	8.12	H2	K8	Porcupine
27. 1	9.12	H2	A9	Wolf
28. 1	10.12	H2	B10	Dog
29. 1	11.12	H2	C11	Pheasant
30. 1	12.12	H2	D12	Cock
31. 1	13.12	H2	E1	Crow
1. 2	14.12	H2	F2	Monkey
2. 2	15.12	H2	G3	Gibbon
3. 2	16.12	H2	H4	Tapir
4. 2	17.12	H2	J5	Sheep
5. 2	18.12	H2	K6	Deer
6. 2	19.12	H2	A7	Horse
7. 2	10.12	H2	B8	Stag
8. 2	21.12	H2	C9	Serpent
9. 2	22.12	H2	D10	Earthworm
10. 2	23.12	H2	E11	Crocodile
11. 2	24.12	H2	F12	Dragon
12. 2	25.12	H2	G1	Badger
13. 2	26.12	H2	H2	Hare
14. 2	27.12	H2	J3	Fox
15. 2	28.12	H2	K4	Tiger
16. 2	29.12	H2	A5	Leopard
17. 2	30.12	H2	B6	Griffon

TING SZU YEAR

Solar date	Lunar date	Month HS/EB	Day HS/EB	Constellation
18. 2	1. 1	J3	C7	Ox
19. 2	2. 1	J3	D8	Bat
20. 2	3. 1	J3	E9	Rat
21. 2	4. 1	J3	F10	Swallow
22. 2	5. 1	J3	G11	Pig
23. 2	6. 1	J3	H12	Porcupine
24. 2	7. 1	J3	J1	Wolf
25. 2	8. 1	J3	K2	Dog
26. 2	9. 1	J3	A3	Pheasant
27. 2	10. 1	J3	B4	Cock
28. 2	11. 1	J3	C5	Crow
1. 3	12. 1	J3	D6	Monkey
2. 3	13. 1	J3	E7	Gibbon
3. 3	14. 1	J3	F8	Tapir
4. 3	15. 1	J3	G9	Sheep
5. 3	16. 1	J3	H10	Deer
6. 3	17. 1	J3	J11	Horse
7. 3	18. 1	J3	K12	Stag
8. 3	19. 1	J3	A1	Serpent
9. 3	20. 1	J3	B2	Earthworm
10. 3	21. 1	J3	C3	Crocodile
11. 3	22. 1	J3	D4	Dragon
12. 3	23. 1	J3	E5	Badger
13. 3	24. 1	J3	F6	Hare
14. 3	25. 1	J3	G7	Fox
15. 3	26. 1	J3	H8	Tiger
16. 3	27. 1	J3	J9	Leopard
17. 3	28. 1	J3	K10	Griffon
18. 3	29. 1	J3	A11	Ox
19. 3	30. 1	J3	B12	Bat
20. 3	1. 2	K4	C1	Rat
21. 3	2. 2	K4	D2	Swallow
22. 3	3. 2	K4	E3	Pig
23. 3	4. 2	K4	F4	Porcupine
24. 3	5. 2	K4	G5	Wolf
25. 3	6. 2	K4	H6	Dog
26. 3	7. 2	K4	J7	Pheasant
27. 3	8. 2	K4	K8	Cock
28. 3	9. 2	K4	A9	Crow
29. 3	10. 2	K4	B10	Monkey
30. 3	11. 2	K4	C11	Gibbon
31. 3	12. 2	K4	D12	Tapir
1. 4	13. 2	K4	E1	Sheep
2. 4	14. 2	K4	F2	Deer
3. 4	15. 2	K4	G3	Horse
4. 4	16. 2	K4	H4	Stag
5. 4	17. 2	K4	J5	Serpent
6. 4	18. 2	K4	K6	Earthworm
7. 4	19. 2	K4	A7	Crocodile
8. 4	20. 2	K4	B8	Dragon
9. 4	21. 2	K4	C9	Badger
10. 4	22. 2	K4	D10	Hare
11. 4	23. 2	K4	E11	Fox
12. 4	24. 2	K4	F12	Tiger
13. 4	25. 2	K4	G1	Leopard
14. 4	26. 2	K4	H2	Griffon
15. 4	27. 2	K4	J3	Ox
16. 4	28. 2	K4	K4	Bat
17. 4	29. 2	K4	A5	Rat
18. 4	1. 3	A5	B6	Swallow
19. 4	2. 3	A5	C7	Pig
20. 4	3. 3	A5	D8	Porcupine
21. 4	4. 3	A5	E9	Wolf
22. 4	5. 3	A5	F10	Dog
23. 4	6. 3	A5	G11	Pheasant
24. 4	7. 3	A5	H12	Cock
25. 4	8. 3	A5	J1	Crow
26. 4	9. 3	A5	K2	Monkey
27. 4	10. 3	A5	A3	Gibbon
28. 4	11. 3	A5	B4	Tapir
29. 4	12. 3	A5	C5	Sheep
30. 4	13. 3	A5	D6	Deer
1. 5	14. 3	A5	E7	Horse
2. 5	15. 3	A5	F8	Stag
3. 5	16. 3	A5	G9	Serpent
4. 5	17. 3	A5	H10	Earthworm
5. 5	18. 3	A5	J11	Crocodile
6. 5	19. 3	A5	K12	Dragon

Solar date	Lunar date	Month HS/EB	Day HS/EB	Constellation	Solar date	Lunar date	Month HS/EB	Day HS/EB	Constellation
7. 5	20. 3	A5	A1	Badger	19. 7	4. 6	D8	D2	Monkey
8. 5	21. 3	A5	B2	Hare	20. 7	5. 6	D8	E3	Gibbon
9. 5	22. 3	A5	C3	Fox	21. 7	6. 6	D8	F4	Tapir
10. 5	23. 3	A5	D4	Tiger	22. 7	7. 6	D8	G5	Sheep
11. 5	24. 3	A5	E5	Leopard	23. 7	8. 6	D8	H6	Deer
12. 5	25. 3	A5	F6	Griffon	24. 7	9. 6	D8	J7	Horse
13. 5	26. 3	A5	G7	Ox	25. 7	10. 6	D8	K8	Stag
14. 5	27. 3	A5	H8	Bat	26. 7	11. 6	D8	A9	Serpent
15. 5	28. 3	A5	J9	Rat	27. 7	12. 6	D8	B10	Earthworm
16. 5	29. 3	A5	K10	Swallow	28. 7	13. 6	D8	C11	Crocodile
17. 5	30. 3	A5	A11	Pig	29. 7	14. 6	D8	D12	Dragon
18. 5	1. 4	B6	B12	Porcupine	30. 7	15. 6	D8	E1	Badger
19. 5	2. 4	B6	C1	Wolf	31. 7	16. 6	D8	F2	Hare
20. 5	3. 4	B6	D2	Dog	1. 8	17. 6	D8	G3	Fox
21. 5	4. 4	B6	E3	Pheasant	2. 8	18. 6	D8	H4	Tiger
22. 5	5. 4	B6	F4	Cock	3. 8	19. 6	D8	J5	Leopard
23. 5	6. 4	B6	G5	Crow	4. 8	20. 6	D8	K6	Griffon
24. 5	7. 4	B6	H6	Monkey	5. 8	21. 6	D8	A7	Ox
25. 5	8. 4	B6	J7	Gibbon	6. 8	22. 6	D8	B8	Bat
26. 5	9. 4	B6	K8	Tapir	7. 8	23. 6	D8	C9	Rat
27. 5	10. 4	B6	A9	Sheep	8. 8	24. 6	D8	D10	Swallow
28. 5	11. 4	B6	B10	Deer	9. 8	25. 6	D8	E11	Pig
29. 5	12. 4	B6	C11	Horse	10. 8	26. 6	D8	F12	Porcupine
30. 5	13. 4	B6	D12	Stag	11. 8	27. 6	D8	G1	Wolf
31. 5	14. 4	B6	E1	Serpent	12. 8	28. 6	D8	H2	Dog
1. 6	15. 4	B6	F2	Earthworm	13. 8	29. 6	D8	J3	Pheasant
2. 6	16. 4	B6	G3	Crocodile	14. 8	30. 6	D8	K4	Cock
3. 6	17. 4	B6	H4	Dragon	15. 8	1. 7	E9	A5	Crow
4. 6	18. 4	B6	J5	Badger	16. 8	2. 7	E9	B6	Monkey
5. 6	19. 4	B6	K6	Hare	17. 8	3. 7	E9	C7	Gibbon
6. 6	20. 4	B6	A7	Fox	18. 8	4. 7	E9	D8	Tapir
7. 6	21. 4	B6	B8	Tiger	19. 8	5. 7	E9	E9	Sheep
8. 6	22. 4	B6	C9	Leopard	20. 8	6. 7	E9	F10	Deer
9. 6	23. 4	B6	D10	Griffon	21. 8	7. 7	E9	G11	Horse
10. 6	24. 4	B6	E11	Ox	22. 8	8. 7	E9	H12	Stag
11. 6	25. 4	B6	F12	Bat	23. 8	9. 7	E9	J1	Serpent
12. 6	26. 4	B6	G1	Rat	24. 8	10. 7	E9	K2	Earthworm
13. 6	27. 4	B6	H2	Swallow	25. 8	11. 7	E9	A3	Crocodile
14. 6	28. 4	B6	J3	Pig	26. 8	12. 7	E9	B4	Dragon
15. 6	29. 4	B6	K4	Porcupine	27. 8	13. 7	E9	C5	Badger
16. 6	30. 4	B6	A5	Wolf	28. 8	14. 7	E9	D6	Hare
17. 6	1. 5	C7	B6	Dog	29. 8	15. 7	E9	E7	Fox
18. 6	2. 5	C7	C7	Pheasant	30. 8	16. 7	E9	F8	Tiger
19. 6	3. 5	C7	D8	Cock	31. 8	17. 7	E9	G9	Leopard
20. 6	4. 5	C7	E9	Crow	1. 9	18. 7	E9	H10	Griffon
21. 6	5. 5	C7	F10	Monkey	2. 9	19. 7	E9	J11	Ox
22. 6	6. 5	C7	G11	Gibbon	3. 9	20. 7	E9	K12	Bat
23. 6	7. 5	C7	H12	Tapir	4. 9	21. 7	E9	A1	Rat
24. 6	8. 5	C7	J1	Sheep	5. 9	22. 7	E9	B2	Swallow
25. 6	9. 5	C7	K2	Deer	6. 9	23. 7	E9	C3	Pig
26. 6	10. 5	C7	A3	Horse	7. 9	24. 7	E9	D4	Porcupine
27. 6	11. 5	C7	B4	Stag	8. 9	25. 7	E9	E5	Wolf
28. 6	12. 5	C7	C5	Serpent	9. 9	26. 7	E9	F6	Dog
29. 6	13. 5	C7	D6	Earthworm	10. 9	27. 7	E9	G7	Pheasant
30. 6	14. 5	C7	E7	Crocodile	11. 9	28. 7	E9	H8	Cock
1. 7	15. 5	C7	F8	Dragon	12. 9	29. 7	E9	J9	Crow
2. 7	16. 5	C7	G9	Badger	13. 9	1. 8	F10	K10	Monkey
3. 7	17. 5	C7	H10	Hare	14. 9	2. 8	F10	A11	Gibbon
4. 7	18. 5	C7	J11	Fox	15. 9	3. 8	F10	B12	Tapir
5. 7	19. 5	C7	K12	Tiger	16. 9	4. 8	F10	C1	Sheep
6. 7	20. 5	C7	A1	Leopard	17. 9	5. 8	F10	D2	Deer
7. 7	21. 5	C7	B2	Griffon	18. 9	6. 8	F10	E3	Horse
8. 7	22. 5	C7	C3	Ox	19. 9	7. 8	F10	F4	Stag
9. 7	23. 5	C7	D4	Bat	20. 9	8. 8	F10	G5	Serpent
10. 7	24. 5	C7	E5	Rat	21. 9	9. 8	F10	H6	Earthworm
11. 7	25. 5	C7	F6	Swallow	22. 9	10. 8	F10	J7	Crocodile
12. 7	26. 5	C7	G7	Pig	23. 9	11. 8	F10	K8	Dragon
13. 7	27. 5	C7	H8	Porcupine	24. 9	12. 8	F10	A9	Badger
14. 7	28. 5	C7	J9	Wolf	25. 9	13. 8	F10	B10	Hare
15. 7	29. 5	C7	K10	Dog	26. 9	14. 8	F10	C11	Fox
16. 7	1. 6	D8	A11	Pheasant	27. 9	15. 8	F10	D12	Tiger
17. 7	2. 6	D8	B12	Cock	28. 9	16. 8	F10	E1	Leopard
18. 7	3. 6	D8	C1	Crow	29. 9	17. 8	F10	F2	Griffon

Solar date	Lunar date	Month HS/EB	Day HS/EB	Constellation	Solar date	Lunar date	Month HS/EB	Day HS/EB	Constellation
30. 9	18. 8	F10	G3	Ox	6.12	26.10	H12	D10	Monkey
1.10	19. 8	F10	H4	Bat	7.12	27.10	H12	E11	Gibbon
2.10	20. 8	F10	J5	Rat	8.12	28.10	H12	F12	Tapir
3.10	21. 8	F10	K6	Swallow	9.12	29.10	H12	G1	Sheep
4.10	22. 8	F10	A7	Pig	10.12	30.10	H12	H2	Deer
5.10	23. 8	F10	B8	Porcupine	11.12	1.11	J1	J3	Horse
6.10	24. 8	F10	C9	Wolf	12.12	2.11	J1	K4	Stag
7.10	25. 8	F10	D10	Dog	13.12	3.11	J1	A5	Serpent
8.10	26. 8	F10	E11	Pheasant	14.12	4.11	J1	B6	Earthworm
9.10	27. 8	F10	F12	Cock	15.12	5.11	J1	C7	Crocodile
10.10	28. 8	F10	G1	Crow	16.12	6.11	J1	D8	Dragon
11.10	29. 8	F10	H2	Monkey	17.12	7.11	J1	E9	Badger
12.10	30. 8	F10	J3	Gibbon	18.12	8.11	J1	F10	Hare
13.10	1. 9	G11	K4	Tapir	19.12	9.11	J1	G11	Fox
14.10	2. 9	G11	A5	Sheep	20.12	10.11	J1	H12	Tiger
15.10	3. 9	G11	B6	Deer	21.12	11.11	J1	J1	Leopard
16.10	4. 9	G11	C7	Horse	22.12	12.11	J1	K2	Griffon
17.10	5. 9	G11	D8	Stag	23.12	13.11	J1	A3	Ox
19.10	6. 9	G11	E9	Serpent	24.12	14.11	J1	B4	Bat
20.10	8. 9	G11	G11	Crocodile	25.12	15.11	J1	C5	Rat
21.10	9. 9	G11	H12	Dragon	26.12	16.11	J1	D6	Swallow
22.10	10. 9	G11	J1	Badger	27.12	17.11	J1	E7	Pig
23.10	11. 9	G11	K2	Hare	28.12	18.11	J1	F8	Porcupine
24.10	12. 9	G11	A3	Fox	29.12	19.11	J1	G9	Wolf
25.10	13. 9	G11	B4	Tiger	30.12	20.11	J1	H10	Dog
26.10	14. 9	G11	C5	Leopard	31.12	21.11	J1	J11	Pheasant
27.10	15. 9	G11	D6	Griffon					
28.10	16. 9	G11	E7	Ox					
29.10	17. 9	G11	F8	Bat	**1978**				
30.10	18. 9	G11	G9	Rat	1. 1	22.11	J1	K12	Cock
31.10	19. 9	G11	H10	Swallow	2. 1	23.11	J1	A1	Crow
1.11	20. 9	G11	J11	Pig	3. 1	24.11	J1	B2	Monkey
2.11	21. 9	G11	K12	Porcupine	4. 1	25.11	J1	C3	Gibbon
3.11	22. 9	G11	A1	Wolf	5. 1	26.11	J1	D4	Tapir
4.11	23. 9	G11	B2	Dog	6. 1	27.11	J1	E5	Sheep
5.11	24. 9	G11	C3	Pheasant	7. 1	28.11	J1	F6	Deer
6.11	25. 9	G11	D4	Cock	8. 1	29.11	J1	G7	Horse
7.11	26. 9	G11	E5	Crow	9. 1	1.12	K2	H8	Stag
8.11	27. 9	G11	F6	Monkey	10. 1	2.12	K2	J9	Serpent
9.11	28. 9	G11	G7	Gibbon	11. 1	3.12	K2	K10	Earthworm
10.11	29. 9	G11	H8	Tapir	12. 1	4.12	K2	A11	Crocodile
11.11	1.10	H12	J9	Sheep	13. 1	5.12	K2	B12	Dragon
12.11	2.10	H12	K10	Deer	14. 1	6.12	K2	C1	Badger
13.11	3.10	H12	A11	Horse	15. 1	7.12	K2	D2	Hare
14.11	4.10	H12	B12	Stag	16. 1	8.12	K2	E3	Fox
15.11	5.10	H12	C1	Serpent	17. 1	9.12	K2	F4	Tiger
16.11	6.10	H12	D2	Earthworm	18. 1	10.12	K2	G5	Leopard
17.11	7.10	H12	E3	Crocodile	19. 1	11.12	K2	H6	Griffon
18.11	8.10	H12	F4	Dragon	20. 1	12.12	K2	J7	Ox
19.11	9.10	H12	G5	Badger	21. 1	13.12	K2	K8	Bat
20.11	10.10	H12	H6	Hare	22. 1	14.12	K2	A9	Rat
21.11	11.10	H12	J7	Fox	23. 1	15.12	K2	B10	Swallow
22.11	12.10	H12	K8	Tiger	24. 1	16.12	K2	C11	Pig
23.11	13.10	H12	A9	Leopard	25. 1	17.12	K2	D12	Porcupine
24.11	14.10	H12	H10	Griffon	26. 1	18.12	K2	E1	Wolf
25.11	15.10	H12	C11	Ox	27. 1	19.12	K2	F2	Dog
26.11	16.10	H12	D12	Bat	28. 1	20.12	K2	G3	Pheasant
27.11	17.10	H12	E1	Rat	29. 1	21.12	K2	H4	Cock
28.11	18.10	H12	F2	Swallow	30. 1	22.12	K2	J5	Crow
29.11	19.10	H12	G3	Pig	31. 1	23.12	K2	K6	Monkey
30.11	20.10	H12	H4	Porcupine	1. 2	24.12	K2	A7	Gibbon
1.12	21.10	H12	J5	Wolf	2. 2	25.12	K2	B8	Tapir
2.12	22.10	H12	K6	Dog	3. 2	26.12	K2	C9	Sheep
3.12	23.10	H12	A7	Pheasant	4. 2	27.12	K2	D10	Deer
4.12	24.10	H12	B8	Cock	5. 2	28.12	K2	E11	Horse
5.12	25.10	H12	C9	Crow	6. 2	29.12	K2	F12	Stag

MOU WU YEAR

Solar date	Lunar date	Month HS/EB	Day HS/EB	Constellation	Solar date	Lunar date	Month HS/EB	Day HS/EB	Constellation
7. 2	1. 1	A3	G1	Serpent	19. 4	13. 3	C5	H12	Porcupine
8. 2	2. 1	A3	H2	Earthworm	20. 4	14. 3	C5	J1	Wolf
9. 2	3. 1	A3	J3	Crocodile	21. 4	15. 3	C5	K2	Dog
10. 2	4. 1	A3	K4	Dragon	22. 4	16. 3	C5	A3	Pheasant
11. 2	5. 1	A3	A5	Badger	23. 4	17. 3	C5	B4	Cock
12. 2	6. 1	A3	B6	Hare	24. 4	18. 3	C5	C5	Crow
13. 2	7. 1	A3	C7	Fox	25. 4	19. 3	C5	D6	Monkey
14. 2	8. 1	A3	D8	Tiger	26. 4	20. 3	C5	E7	Gibbon
15. 2	9. 1	A3	E9	Leopard	27. 4	21. 3	C5	F8	Tapir
16. 2	10. 1	A3	F10	Griffon	28. 4	22. 3	C5	G9	Sheep
17. 2	11. 1	A3	G11	Ox	29. 4	23. 3	C5	H10	Deer
18. 2	12. 1	A3	H12	Bat	30. 4	24. 3	C5	J11	Horse
19. 2	13. 1	A3	J1	Rat	1. 5	25. 3	C5	K12	Stag
20. 2	14. 1	A3	K2	Swallow	2. 5	26. 3	C5	A1	Serpent
21. 2	14. 1	A3	A3	Pig	3. 5	27. 3	C5	B2	Earthworm
22. 2	16. 1	A3	B4	Porcupine	4. 5	28. 3	C5	C3	Crocodile
23. 2	17. 1	A3	C5	Wolf	5. 5	29. 3	C5	D4	Dragon
24. 2	18. 1	A3	D6	Dog	6. 5	30. 3	C5	E5	Badger
25. 2	19. 1	A3	E7	Pheasant	7. 5	1. 4	D6	F6	Hare
26. 2	20. 1	A3	F8	Cock	8. 5	2. 4	D6	G7	Fox
27. 2	21. 1	A3	G9	Crow	9. 5	3. 4	D6	H8	Tiger
28. 2	22. 1	A3	H10	Monkey	10. 5	4. 4	D6	J9	Leopard
1. 3	23. 1	A3	J11	Gibbon	11. 5	5. 4	D6	K10	Griffon
2. 3	24. 1	A3	K12	Tapir	12. 5	6. 4	D6	A11	Ox
3. 3	25. 1	A3	A1	Sheep	13. 5	7. 4	D6	B12	Bat
4. 3	26. 1	A3	B2	Deer	14. 5	8. 4	D6	C1	Rat
5. 3	27. 1	A3	C3	Horse	15. 5	9. 4	D6	D2	Swallow
6. 3	28. 1	A3	D4	Stag	16. 5	10. 4	D6	E3	Pig
7. 3	29. 1	A3	E5	Serpent	17. 5	11. 4	D6	F4	Porcupine
8. 3	30. 1	A3	F6	Earthworm	18. 5	12. 4	D6	G5	Wolf
9. 3	1. 2	B4	G7	Crocodile	19. 5	13. 4	D6	H6	Dog
10. 3	2. 2	B4	H8	Dragon	20. 5	14. 4	D6	J7	Pheasant
11. 3	3. 2	B4	J9	Badger	21. 5	15. 4	D6	K8	Cock
12. 3	4. 2	B4	K10	Hare	22. 5	16. 4	D6	A9	Crow
13. 3	5. 2	B4	A11	Fox	23. 5	17. 4	D6	B10	Monkey
14. 3	6. 2	B4	B12	Tiger	24. 5	18. 4	D6	C11	Gibbon
15. 3	7. 2	B4	C1	Leopard	25. 5	19. 4	D6	D12	Tapir
16. 3	8. 2	B4	D2	Griffon	26. 5	20. 4	D6	E1	Sheep
17. 3	9. 2	B4	E3	Ox	27. 5	21. 4	D6	F2	Deer
18. 3	10. 2	B4	F4	Bat	28. 5	22. 4	D6	G3	Horse
19. 3	11. 2	B4	G5	Rat	29. 5	23. 4	D6	H4	Stag
20. 3	12. 2	B4	H6	Swallow	30. 5	24. 4	D6	J5	Serpent
21. 3	13. 2	B4	J7	Pig	31. 5	25. 4	D6	K6	Earthworm
22. 3	14. 2	B4	K8	Porcupine	1. 6	26. 4	D6	A7	Crocodile
23. 3	15. 2	B4	A9	Wolf	2. 6	27. 4	D6	B8	Dragon
24. 3	16. 2	B4	B10	Dog	3. 6	28. 4	D6	C9	Badger
25. 3	17. 2	B4	C11	Pheasant	4. 6	29. 4	D6	D10	Hare
26. 3	18. 2	B4	D12	Cock	5. 6	30. 4	D6	E11	Fox
27. 3	19. 2	B4	E1	Crow	6. 6	1. 5	E7	F12	Tiger
28. 3	20. 2	B4	F2	Monkey	7. 6	2. 5	E7	G1	Leopard
29. 3	21. 2	B4	G3	Gibbon	8. 6	3. 5	E7	H2	Griffon
30. 3	22. 2	B4	H4	Tapir	9. 6	4. 5	E7	J3	Ox
31. 3	23. 2	B4	J5	Sheep	10. 6	5. 5	E7	K4	Bat
1. 4	24. 2	B4	K6	Deer	11. 6	6. 5	E7	A5	Rat
2. 4	25. 2	B4	A7	Horse	12. 6	7. 5	E7	B6	Swallow
3. 4	26. 2	B4	B8	Stag	13. 6	8. 5	E7	C7	Pig
4. 4	27. 2	B4	C9	Serpent	14. 6	9. 5	E7	D8	Porcupine
5. 4	28. 2	B4	D10	Earthworm	15. 6	10. 5	E7	E9	Wolf
6. 4	29. 2	B4	E11	Crocodile	16. 6	11. 5	E7	F10	Dog
7. 4	1. 3	C5	F12	Dragon	17. 6	12. 5	E7	G11	Pheasant
8. 4	2. 3	C5	G1	Badger	18. 6	13. 5	E7	H12	Cock
9. 4	3. 3	C5	H2	Hare	19. 6	14. 5	E7	J1	Crow
10. 4	4. 3	C5	J3	Fox	20. 6	15. 5	E7	K2	Monkey
11. 4	5. 3	C5	K4	Tiger	21. 6	16. 5	E7	A3	Gibbon
12. 4	6. 3	C5	A5	Leopard	22. 6	17. 5	E7	B4	Tapir
13. 4	7. 3	C5	B6	Griffon	23. 6	18. 5	E7	C5	Sheep
14. 4	8. 3	C5	C7	Ox	24. 6	19. 5	E7	D6	Deer
15. 4	9. 3	C5	D8	Bat	25. 6	20. 5	E7	E7	Horse
16. 4	10. 3	C5	E9	Rat	26. 6	21. 5	E7	F8	Stag
17. 4	11. 3	C5	F10	Swallow	27. 6	22. 5	E7	G9	Serpent
18. 4	12. 3	C5	G11	Pig	28. 6	23. 5	E7	H10	Earthworm

Solar date	Lunar date	Month HS/EB	Day HS/EB	Constellation
29. 6	24. 5	E7	J11	Crocodile
30. 6	25. 5	E7	K12	Dragon
1. 7	26. 5	E7	A1	Badger
2. 7	27. 5	E7	B2	Hare
3. 7	28. 5	E7	C3	Fox
4. 7	29. 5	E7	D4	Tiger
5. 7	1. 6	F8	E5	Leopard
6. 7	2. 6	F8	F6	Griffon
7. 7	3. 6	F8	G7	Ox
8. 7	4. 6	F8	H8	Bat
9. 7	5. 6	F8	J9	Rat
10. 7	6. 6	F8	K10	Swallow
11. 7	7. 6	F8	A11	Pig
12. 7	8. 6	F8	B12	Porcupine
13. 7	9. 6	F8	C1	Wolf
14. 7	10. 6	F8	D2	Dog
15. 7	11. 6	F8	E3	Pheasant
16. 7	12. 6	F8	F4	Cock
17. 7	13. 6	F8	G5	Crow
18. 7	14. 6	F8	H6	Monkey
19. 7	15. 6	F8	J7	Gibbon
20. 7	16. 6	F8	K8	Tapir
21. 7	17. 6	F8	A9	Sheep
22. 7	18. 6	F8	B10	Deer
23. 7	19. 6	F8	C11	Horse
24. 7	20. 6	F8	D12	Stag
25. 7	21. 6	F8	E1	Serpent
26. 7	22. 6	F8	F2	Earthworm
27. 7	23. 6	F8	G3	Crocodile
28. 7	24. 6	F8	H4	Dragon
29. 7	25. 6	F8	J5	Badger
30. 7	26. 6	F8	K6	Hare
31. 7	27. 6	F8	A7	Fox
1. 8	28. 6	F8	B8	Tiger
2. 8	29. 6	F8	C9	Leopard
3. 8	30. 6	F8	D10	Griffon
4. 8	1. 7	G9	E11	Ox
5. 8	2. 7	G9	F12	Bat
6. 8	3. 7	G9	G1	Rat
7. 8	4. 7	G9	H2	Swallow
8. 8	5. 7	G9	J3	Pig
9. 8	6. 7	G9	K4	Porcupine
10. 8	7. 7	G9	A5	Wolf
11. 8	8. 7	G9	B6	Dog
12. 8	9. 7	G9	C7	Pheasant
13. 8	10. 7	G9	D8	Cock
14. 8	11. 7	G9	E9	Crow
15. 8	12. 7	G9	F10	Monkey
16. 8	13. 7	G9	G11	Gibbon
17. 8	14. 7	G9	H12	Tapir
18. 8	15. 7	G9	J1	Sheep
19. 8	16. 7	G9	K2	Deer
20. 8	17. 7	G9	A3	Horse
21. 8	18. 7	G9	B4	Stag
22. 8	19. 7	G9	C5	Serpent
23. 8	20. 7	G9	D6	Earthworm
24. 8	21. 7	G9	E7	Crocodile
25. 8	22. 7	G9	F8	Dragon
26. 8	23. 7	G9	G9	Badger
27. 8	24. 7	G9	H10	Hare
28. 8	25. 7	G9	J11	Fox
29. 8	26. 7	G9	K12	Tiger
30. 8	27. 7	G9	A1	Leopard
31. 8	28. 7	G9	B2	Griffon
1. 9	29. 7	G8	C3	Ox
2. 9	30. 7	G9	D4	Bat
3. 9	1. 8	H10	E5	Rat
4. 9	2. 8	H10	F6	Swallow
5. 9	3. 8	H10	G7	Pig
6. 9	4. 8	H10	H8	Porcupine
7. 9	5. 8	H10	J9	Wolf
8. 9	6. 8	H10	K10	Dog
9. 9	7. 8	H10	A11	Pheasant
10. 9	8. 8	H10	B12	Cock
11. 9	9. 8	H10	C1	Crow
12. 9	10. 8	H10	D2	Monkey
13. 9	11. 8	H10	E3	Gibbon
14. 9	12. 8	H10	F4	Tapir
15. 9	13. 8	H10	G5	Sheep
16. 9	14. 8	H10	H6	Deer
17. 9	15. 8	H10	J7	Horse
18. 9	16. 8	H10	K8	Stag
19. 9	17. 8	H10	A9	Serpent
20. 9	18. 8	H10	B10	Earthworm
21. 9	19. 8	H10	C11	Crocodile
22. 9	20. 8	H10	D12	Dragon
23. 9	21. 8	H10	E1	Badger
24. 9	22. 8	H10	F2	Hare
25. 9	23. 8	H10	G3	Fox
26. 9	24. 8	H10	H4	Tiger
27. 9	25. 8	H10	J5	Leopard
28. 9	26. 8	H10	K6	Griffon
29. 9	27. 8	H10	A7	Ox
30. 9	28. 8	H10	B8	Bat
1.10	29. 8	H10	C9	Rat
2.10	1. 9	J11	D10	Swallow
3.10	2. 9	J11	E11	Pig
4.10	3. 9	J11	F12	Porcupine
5.10	4. 9	J11	G1	Wolf
6.10	5. 9	J11	H2	Dog
7.10	6. 9	J11	J3	Pheasant
8.10	7. 9	J11	K4	Cock
9.10	8. 9	J11	A5	Crow
10.10	9. 9	J11	B6	Monkey
11.10	10. 9	J11.	C7	Gibbon
12.10	11. 9	J11	D8	Tapir
13.10	12. 9	J11	E9	Sheep
14.10	13. 9	J11	F10	Deer
15.10	14. 9	J11	G11	Horse
16.10	15. 9	J11	H12	Stag
17.10	16. 9	J11	J1	Serpent
18.10	17. 9	J11	K2	Earthworm
19.10	18. 9	J11	A3	Crocodile
20.10	19. 9	J11	B4	Dragon
21.10	20. 9	J11	C5	Badger
22.10	21. 9	J11	D6	Hare
23.10	22. 9	J11	E7	Fox
24.10	23. 9	J11	F8	Tiger
25.10	24. 9	J11	G9	Leopard
26.10	25. 9	J11	H10	Griffon
27.10	26. 9	J11	J11	Ox
28.10	27. 9	J11	K12	Bat
29.10	28. 9	J11	A1	Rat
30.10	29. 9	J11	B2	Swallow
31.10	30. 9	J11	C3	Pig
1.11	1.10	K12	D4	Porcupine
2.11	2.10	K12	E5	Wolf
3.11	3.10	K12	F6	Dog
4.11	4.10	K12	G7	Pheasant
5.11	5.10	K12	H8	Cock
6.11	6.10	K12	J9	Crow
7.11	7.10	K12	K10	Monkey
8.11	8.10	K12	A11	Gibbon
9.11	9.10	K12	B12	Tapir
10.11	10.10	K12	C1	Sheep
11.11	11.10	K12	D2	Deer
12.11	12.10	K12	E3	Horse
13.11	13.10	K12	F4	Stag
14.11	14.10	K12	G5	Serpent
15.11	15.10	K12	H6	Earthworm
16.11	16.10	K12	J7	Crocodile
17.11	17.10	K12	K8	Dragon
18.11	18.10	K12	A9	Badger
19.11	19.10	K12	B10	Hare
20.11	20.10	K12	C11	Fox
21.11	21.10	K12	D12	Tiger

Solar date	Lunar date	Month HS/EB	Day HS/EB	Constellation	Solar date	Lunar date	Month HS/EB	Day HS/EB	Constellation
22.11	22.10	K12	E1	Leopard	27.12	28.11	A1	K12	Porcupine
23.11	23.10	K12	F2	Griffon	28.12	29.11	A1	A1	Wolf
24.11	24.10	K12	G3	Ox	29.12	30.11	A1	B2	Dog
25.11	25.10	K12	H4	Bat	30.12	1.12	B2	C3	Pheasant
26.11	26.10	K12	J5	Rat	31.12	2.12	B2	D4	Cock
27.11	27.10	K12	K6	Swallow					
28.11	28.10	K12	A7	Pig	**1979**				
29.11	29.10	K12	B8	Porcupine	1. 1	3.12	B2	E5	Crow
30.11	1.11	A1	C9	Wolf	2. 1	4.12	B2	F6	Monkey
1.12	2.11	A1	D10	Dog	3. 1	5.12	B2	G7	Gibbon
2.12	3.11	A1	E11	Pheasant	4. 1	6.12	B2	H8	Tapir
3.12	4.11	A1	F12	Cock	5. 1	7.12	B2	J9	Sheep
4.12	5.11	A1	G1	Crow	6. 1	8.12	B2	K10	Deer
5.12	6.11	A1	H2	Monkey	7. 1	9.12	B2	A11	Horse
6.12	7.11	A1	J3	Gibbon	8. 1	10.12	B2	B12	Stag
7.12	8.11	A1	K4	Tapir	9. 1	11.12	B2	C1	Serpent
8.12	9.11	A1	A5	Sheep	10. 1	12.12	B2	D2	Earthworm
9.12	10.11	A1	B6	Deer	11. 1	13.12	B2	E3	Crocodile
10.12	11.11	A1	C7	Horse	12. 1	14.12	B2	F4	Dragon
11.12	12.11	A1	D8	Stag	13. 1	15.12	B2	G5	Badger
12.12	13.11	A1	E9	Serpent	14. 1	16.12	B2	H6	Hare
13.12	14.11	A1	F10	Earthworm	15. 1	17.12	B2	J7	Fox
14.12	15.11	A1	G11	Crocodile	16. 1	18.12	B2	K8	Tiger
15.12	16.11	A1	H12	Dragon	17. 1	19.12	B2	A9	Leopard
16.12	17.11	A1	J1	Badger	18. 1	20.12	B2	B10	Griffon
17.12	18.11	A1	K2	Hare	19. 1	21.12	B2	C11	Ox
18.12	19.11	A1	A3	Fox	20. 1	22.12	B2	D12	Bat
19.12	20.11	A1	B4	Tiger	21. 1	23.12	B2	E1	Rat
20.12	21.11	A1	C5	Leopard	22. 1	24.12	B2	F2	Swallow
21.12	22.11	A1	D6	Griffon	23. -1	25.12	B2	G3	Pig
22.12	23.11	A1	E7	Ox	24. 1	26.12	B2	H4	Porcupine
23.12	24.11	A1	F8	Bat	25. 1	27.12	B2	J5	Wolf
24.12	25.11	A1	G9	Rat	26. 1	28.12	B2	K6	Dog
25.12	26.11	A1	H10	Swallow	27. 1	29.12	B2	A7	Pheasant
26.12	27.11	A1	J11	Pig					

CHI WEI YEAR

Solar date	Lunar date	Month HS/EB	Day HS/EB	Constellation	Solar date	Lunar date	Month HS/EB	Day HS/EB	Constellation
28. 1	1. 1	C3	B8	Cock	2. 3	4. 2	D4	E5	Sheep
29. 1	2. 1	C3	C9	Crow	3. 3	5. 2	D4	F6	Deer
30. 1	3. 1	C3	D10	Monkey	4. 3	6. 2	D4	G7	Horse
31. 1	4. 1	C3	E11	Gibbon	5. 3	7. 2	D4	H8	Stag
1. 2	5. 1	C3	F12	Tapir	6. 3	8. 2	D4	J9	Serpent
2. 2	6. 1	C3	G1	Sheep	7. 3	9. 2	D4	K10	Earthworm
3. 2	7. 1	C3	H2	Deer	8. 3	10. 2	D4	A11	Crocodile
4. 2	8. 1	C3	J3	Horse	9. 3	11. 2	D4	B12	Dragon
5. 2	9. 1	C3	K4	Stag	10. 3	12. 2	D4	C1	Badger
6. 2	10. 1	C3	A5	Serpent	11. 3	13. 2	D4	D2	Hare
7. 2	11. 1	C3	B6	Earthworm	12. 3	14. 2	D4	E3	Fox
8. 2	12. 1	C3	C7	Crocodile	13. 3	15. 2	D4	F4	Tiger
9. 2	13. 1	C3	D8	Dragon	14. 3	16. 2	D4	G5	Leopard
10. 2	14. 1	C3	E9	Badger	15. 3	17. 2	D4	H6	Griffon
11. 2	15. 1	C3	F10	Hare	16. 3	18. 2	D4	J7	Ox
12. 2	16. 1	C3	G11	Fox	17. 3	19. 2	D4	K8	Bat
13. 2	17. 1	C3	H12	Tiger	18. 3	20. 2	D4	A9	Rat
14. 2	18. 1	C3	J1	Leopard	19. 3	21. 2	D4	B10	Swallow
15. 2	19. 9	C3	K2	Griffon	20. 3	22. 2	D4	C11	Pig
16. 2	20. 1	C3	A3	Ox	21. 3	23. 2	D4	D12	Porcupine
17. 2	21. 1	C3	B4	Bat	22. 3	24. 2	D4	E1	Wolf
18. 2	22. 1	C3	C5	Rat	23. 3	25. 2	D4	F2	Dog
19. 2	23. 1	C3	D6	Swallow	24. 3	26. 2	D4	G3	Pheasant
20. 2	24. 1	C3	E7	Pig	25. 3	27. 2	D4	H4	Cock
21. 2	25. 1	C3	F8	Porcupine	26. 3	28. 2	D4	J5	Crow
22. 2	26. 1	C3	G9	Wolf	27. 3	29. 2	D4	K6	Monkey
23. 2	27. 1	C3	H10	Dog	28. 3	1. 3	E5	A7	Gibbon
24. 2	28. 1	C3	J11	Pheasant	29. 3	2. 3	E5	B8	Tapir
25. 2	29. 1	C3	K12	Cock	30. 3	3. 3	E5	C9	Sheep
26. 2	30. 1	C3	A1	Crow	31. 3	4. 3	E5	D10	Deer
27. 2	1. 2	D4	B2	Monkey	1. 4	5. 3	E5	E11	Horse
28. 2	2. 2	D4	C3	Gibbon	2. 4	6. 3	E5	F12	Stag
1. 3	3. 2	D4	D4	Tapir	3. 4	7. 3	E5	G1	Serpent

Solar date	Lunar date	Month HS/EB	Day HS/EB	Constellation	Solar date	Lunar date	Month HS/EB	Day HS/EB	Constellation
4. 4	8. 3	E5	H2	Earthworm	16. 6	22. 5	G7	A3	Pheasant
5. 4	9. 3	E5	J3	Crocodile	17. 6	23. 5	G7	B4	Cock
6. 4	10. 3	E5	K4	Dragon	18. 6	24. 5	G7	C5	Crow
7. 4	11. 3	E5	A5	Badger	19. 6	25. 5	G7	D6	Monkey
8. 4	12. 3	E5	B6	Hare	20. 6	26. 5	G7	E7	Gibbon
9. 4	13. 3	E5	C7	Fox	21. 6	27. 5	G7	F8	Tapir
10. 4	14. 3	E5	D8	Tiger	22. 6	28. 5	G7	G9	Sheep
11. 4	15. 3	E5	E9	Leopard	23. 6	29. 5	G7	H10	Deer
12. 4	16. 3	E5	F10	Griffon	24. 6	1. 6	H8	J11	Horse
13. 4	17. 3	E5	G11	Ox	25. 6	2. 6	H8	K12	Stag
14. 4	18. 3	E5	H12	Bat	26. 6	3. 6	H8	A1	Serpent
15. 4	19. 3	E5	J1	Rat	27. 6	4. 6	H8	B2	Earthworm
16. 4	20. 3	E5	K2	Swallow	28. 6	5. 6	H8	C3	Crocodile
17. 4	21. 3	E5	A3	Pig	29. 6	6. 6	H8	D4	Dragon
18. 4	22. 3	E5	B4	Porcupine	30. 6	7. 6	H8	E5	Badger
19. 4	23. 3	E5	C5	Wolf	1. 7	8. 6	H8	F6	Hare
20. 4	24. 3	E5	D6	Dog	2. 7	9. 6	H8	G7	Fox
21. 4	25. 3	E5	E7	Pheasant	3. 7	10. 6	H8	H8	Tiger
22. 4	26. 3	E5	F8	Cock	4. 7	11. 6	H8	J9	Leopard
23. 4	27. 3	E5	G9	Crow	5. 7	12. 6	H8	K10	Griffon
24. 4	28. 3	E5	H10	Monkey	6. 7	13. 6	H8	A11	Ox
25. 4	29. 3	E5	J11	Gibbon	7. 7	14. 6	H8	B12	Bat
26. 4	1. 4	F6	K12	Tapir	8. 7	15. 6	H8	C1	Rat
27. 4	2. 4	F6	A1	Sheep	9. 7	16. 6	H8	D2	Swallow
28. 4	3. 4	F6	B2	Deer	10. 7	17. 6	H8	E3	Pig
29. 4	4. 4	F6	C3	Horse	11. 7	18. 6	H8	F4	Porcupine
30. 4	5. 4	F6	D4	Stag	12. 7	19. 6	H8	G5	Wolf
1. 5	6. 4	F6	E5	Serpent	13. 7	20. 6	H8	H6	Dog
2. 5	7. 4	F6	F6	Earthworm	14. 7	21. 6	H8	J7	Pheasant
3. 5	8. 4	F6	G7	Crocodile	15. 7	22. 6	H8	K8	Cock
4. 5	9. 4	F6	H8	Dragon	16. 7	23. 6	H8	A9	Crow
5. 5	10. 4	F6	J9	Badger	17. 7	24. 6	H8	B10	Monkey
6. 5	11. 4	F6	K10	Hare	18. 7	25. 6	H8	C11	Gibbon
7. 5	12. 4	F6	A11	Fox	19. 7	26. 6	H8	D12	Tapir
8. 5	13. 4	F6	B12	Tiger	20. 7	27. 6	H8	E1	Sheep
9. 5	14. 4	F6	C1	Leopard	21. 7	28. 6	H8	F2	Deer
10. 5	15. 4	F6	D2	Griffon	22. 7	29. 6	H8	G3	Horse
11. 5	16. 4	F6	E3	Ox	23. 7	30. 6	H8	H4	Stag
12. 5	17. 4	F6	F4	Bat	24. 7	1. 6	H8	J5	Serpent
13. 5	18. 4	F6	G5	Rat	25. 7	2. 6	H8	K6	Earthworm
14. 5	19. 4	F6	H6	Swallow	26. 7	3. 6	H8	A7	Crocodile
15. 5	20. 4	F6	J7	Pig	27. 7	4. 6	H8	B8	Dragon
16. 5	21. 4	F6	K8	Porcupine	28. 7	5. 6	H8	C9	Badger
17. 5	22. 4	F6	A9	Wolf	29. 7	6. 6	H8	D10	Hare
18. 5	23. 4	F6	B10	Dog	30. 7	7. 6	H8	E11	Fox
19. 5	24. 4	F6	C11	Pheasant	31. 7	8. 6	H8	F12	Tiger
20. 5	25. 4	F6	D12	Cock	1. 8	9. 6	H8	G1	Leopard
21. 5	26. 4	F6	E1	Crow	2. 8	10. 6	H8	H2	Griffon
22. 5	27. 4	F6	F2	Monkey	3. 8	11. 6	H8	J3	Ox
23. 5	28. 4	F6	G3	Gibbon	4. 8	12. 6	H8	K4	Bat
24. 5	29. 4	F6	H4	Tapir	5. 8	13. 6	H8	A5	Rat
25. 5	30. 4	F6	J5	Sheep	6. 8	14. 6	H8	B6	Swallow
26. 5	1. 5	G7	K6	Deer	7. 8	15. 6	H8	C7	Pig
27. 5	2. 5	G7	A7	Horse	8. 8	16. 6	H8	D8	Porcupine
28. 5	3. 5	G7	B8	Stag	9. 8	17. 6	H8	E9	Wolf
29. 5	4. 5	G7	C9	Serpent	10. 8	18. 6	H8	F10	Dog
30. 5	5. 5	G7	D10	Earthworm	11. 8	19. 6	H8	G11	Pheasant
31. 5	6. 5	G7	E11	Crocodile	12. 8	20. 6	H8	H12	Cock
1. 6	7. 5	G7	F12	Dragon	13. 8	21. 6	H8	J1	Crow
2. 6	8. 5	G7	G1	Badger	14. 8	22. 6	H8	K2	Monkey
3. 6	9. 5	G7	H2	Hare	15. 8	23. 6	H8	A3	Gibbon
4. 6	10. 5	G7	J3	Fox	16. 8	24. 6	H8	B4	Tapir
5. 5	11. 5	G7	K4	Tiger	17. 8	25. 6	H8	C5	Sheep
6. 5	12. 5	G7	A5	Leopard	18. 8	26. 6	H8	D6	Deer
7. 5	13. 5	G7	B6	Griffon	19. 8	27. 6	H8	E7	Horse
8. 5	14. 5	G7	C7	Ox	20. 8	28. 6	H8	F8	Stag
9. 5	15. 5	G7	D8	Bat	21. 8	29. 6	H8	G9	Serpent
10. 5	16. 5	G7	E9	Rat	22. 8	30. 6	H8	H10	Earthworm
11. 6	17. 5	G7	F10	Swallow	23. 8	1. 7	J9	J11	Crocodile
12. 6	18. 5	G7	G11	Pig	24. 8	2. 7	J9	K12	Dragon
13. 6	19. 5	G7	H12	Porcupine	25. 8	3. 7	J9	A1	Badger
14. 6	20. 5	G7	J1	Wolf	26. 8	4. 7	J9	B2	Hare
15. 6	21. 5	G7	K2	Dog	27. 8	5. 7	J9	C3	Fox

Solar date	Lunar date	Month HS/EB	Day HS/EB	Constellation	Solar date	Lunar date	Month HS/EB	Day HS/EB	Constellation
28. 8	6. 7	J9	D4	Tiger	9.11	20. 9	A11	G5	Sheep
29. 8	7. 7	J9	E5	Leopard	10.11	21. 9	A11	H6	Deer
30. 8	8. 7	J9	F6	Griffon	11.11	22. 9	A11	J7	Horse
31. 8	9. 7	J9	G7	Ox	12.11	23. 9	A11	K8	Stag
1. 9	10. 7	J9	H8	Bat	13.11	24. 9	A11	A9	Serpent
2. 9	11. 7	J9	J9	Rat	14.11	25. 9	A11	B10	Earthworm
3. 9	12. 7	J9	K10	Swallow	15.11	26. 9	A11	C11	Crocodile
4. 9	13. 7	J9	A11	Pig	16.11	27. 9	A11	D12	Dragon
5. 9	14. 7	J9	B12	Porcupine	17.11	28. 9	A11	E1	Badger
6. 9	15. 7	J9	C1	Wolf	18.11	29. 9	A11	F2	Hare
7. 9	16. 7	J9	D2	Dog	19.11	30. 9	A11	G3	Fox
8. 9	17. 7	J9	E3	Pheasant	20.11	1.10	B12	H4	Tiger
9. 9	18. 7	J9	F4	Cock	21.11	2.10	B12	J5	Leopard
10. 9	19. 7	J9	G5	Crow	22.11	3.10	B12	K6	Griffon
11. 9	20. 7	J9	H6	Monkey	23.11	4.10	B12	A7	Ox
12. 9	21. 7	J9	J7	Gibbon	24.11	5.10	B12	B8	Bat
13. 9	22. 7	J9	K8	Tapir	25.11	6.10	B12	C9	Rat
14. 9	23. 7	J9	A9	Sheep	26.11	7.10	B12	D10	Swallow
15. 9	24. 7	J9	B10	Deer	27.11	8.10	B12	E11	Pig
16. 9	25. 7	J9	C11	Horse	28.11	9.10	B12	F12	Porcupine
17. 9	26. 7	J9	D12	Stag	29.11	10.10	B12	G1	Wolf
18. 9	27. 7	J9	E1	Serpent	30.11	11.10	B12	H2	Dog
19. 9	28. 7	J9	F2	Earthworm	1.12	12.10	B12	J3	Pheasant
20. 9	29. 7	J9	G3	Crocodile	2.12	13.10	B12	K4	Cock
21. 9	1. 8	K10	H4	Dragon	3.12	14.10	B12	A5	Crow
22. 9	2. 8	K10	J5	Badger	4.12	15.10	B12	B6	Monkey
23. 9	3. 8	K10	K6	Hare	5.12	16.10	B12	C7	Gibbon
24. 9	4. 8	K10	A7	Fox	6.12	17.10	B12	D8	Tapir
25. 9	5. 8	K10	B8	Tiger	7.12	18.10	B12	E9	Sheep
26. 9	6. 8	K10	C9	Leopard	8.12	19.10	B12	F10	Deer
27. 9	7. 8	K10	D10	Griffon	9.12	20.10	B12	G11	Horse
28. 9	8. 8	K10	E11	Ox	10.12	21.10	B12	H12	Stag
29. 9	9. 8	K10	F12	Bat	11.12	22.10	B12	J1	Serpent
30. 9	10. 8	K10	G1	Rat	12.12	23.10	B12	K2	Earthworm
1.10	11. 8	K10	H2	Swallow	13.12	24.10	B12	A3	Crocodile
2.10	12. 8	K10	J3	Pig	14.12	25.10	B12	B4	Dragon
3.10	13. 8	K10	K4	Porcupine	15.12	26.10	B12	C5	Badger
4.10	14. 8	K10	A5	Wolf	16.12	27.10	B12	D6	Hare
5.10	15. 8	K10	B6	Dog	17.12	28.10	B12	E7	Fox
6.10	16. 8	K10	C7	Pheasant	18.12	29.10	B12	F8	Tiger
7.10	17. 8	K10	D8	Cock	19.12	1.11	C1	G9	Leopard
8.10	18. 8	K10	E9	Crow	20.12	2.11	C1	H10	Griffon
9.10	19. 8	K10	F10	Monkey	21.12	3.11	C1	J11	Ox
10.10	20. 8	K10	G11	Gibbon	22.12	4.11	C1	K12	Bat
11.10	21. 8	K10	H12	Tapir	23.12	5.11	C1	A1	Rat
12.10	22. 8	K10	J1	Sheep	24.12	6.11	C1	B2	Swallow
13.10	23. 8	K10	K2	Deer	25.12	7.11	C1	C3	Pig
14.10	24. 8	K10	A3	Horse	26.12	8.11	C1	D4	Porcupine
15.10	25. 8	K10	B4	Stag	27.12	9.11	C1	E5	Wolf
16.10	26. 8	K10	C5	Serpent	28.12	10.11	C1	F6	Dog
17.10	27. 8	K10	D6	Earthworm	29.12	11.11	C1	G7	Pheasant
18.10	28. 8	K10	E7	Crocodile	30.12	12.11	C1	H8	Cock
19.10	29. 8	K10	F8	Dragon	31.12	13.11	C1	J9	Crow
20.10	30. 8	K10	G9	Badger	**1980**				
21.10	1. 9	A11	H10	Hare	1. 1	14.11	C1	K10	Monkey
22.10	2. 9	A11	J11	Fox	2. 1	15.11	C1	A11	Gibbon
23.10	3. 9	A11	K12	Tiger	3. 1	16.11	C1	B12	Tapir
24.10	4. 9	A11	A1	Leopard	4. 1	17.11	C1	C1	Sheep
25.10	5. 9	A11	B2	Griffon	5. 1	18.11	C1	D2	Deer
26.10	6. 9	A11	C3	Ox	6. 1	19.11	C1	E3	Horse
27.10	7. 9	A11	D4	Bat	7. 1	20.11	C1	F4	Stag
28.10	8. 9	A11	E5	Rat	8. 1	21.11	C1	G5	Serpent
29.10	9. 9	A11	F6	Swallow	9. 1	22.11	C1	H6	Earthworm
30.10	10. 9	A11	G7	Pig	10. 1	23.11	C1	J7	Crocodile
31.10	11. 9	A11	H8	Porcupine	11. 1	24.11	C1	K8	Dragon
1.11	12. 9	A11	J9	Wolf	12. 1	25.11	C1	A9	Badger
2.11	13. 9	A11	K10	Dog	13. 1	26.11	C1	B10	Hare
3.11	14. 9	A11	A11	Pheasant	14. 1	27.11	C1	C11	Fox
4.11	15. 9	A11	B12	Cock	15. 1	28.11	C1	D12	Tiger
5.11	16. 9	A11	C1	Crow	16. 1	29.11	C1	E1	Leopard
6.11	17. 9	A11	D2	Monkey	17. 1	30.11	C1	F2	Griffon
7.11	18. 9	A11	E3	Gibbon	18. 1	1.12	D2	G3	Ox
8.11	19. 9	A11	F4	Tapir					

Solar date	Lunar date	Month HS/EB	Day HS/EB	Constellation	Solar date	Lunar date	Month HS/EB	Day HS/EB	Constellation
19. 1	2.12	D2	H4	Bat	2. 2	16.12	D2	B6	Deer
20. 1	3.12	D2	J5	Rat	3. 2	17.12	D2	C7	Horse
21. 1	4.12	D2	K6	Swallow	4. 2	18.12	D2	D8	Stag
22. 1	5.12	D2	A7	Pig	5. 2	19.12	D2	E9	Serpent
23. 1	6.12	D2	B8	Porcupine	6. 2	20.12	D2	F10	Earthworm
24. 1	7.12	D2	C9	Wolf	7. 2	21.12	D2	G11	Crocodile
25. 1	8.12	D2	D10	Dog	8. 2	22.12	D2	H12	Dragon
26. 1	9.12	D2	E11	Pheasant	9. 2	23.12	D2	J1	Badger
27. 1	10.12	D2	F12	Cock	10. 2	24.12	D2	K2	Hare
28. 1	11.12	D2	G1	Crow	11. 2	25.12	D2	A3	Fox
29. 1	12.12	D2	H2	Monkey	12. 2	26.12	D2	B4	Tiger
30. 1	13.12	D2	J3	Gibbon	13. 2	27.12	D2	C5	Leopard
31. 1	14.12	D2	K4	Tapir	14. 2	28.12	D2	D6	Griffon
1. 2	15.12	D2	A5	Sheep	15. 2	29.12	D2	E7	Ox

KENG SHEN YEAR

Solar date	Lunar date	Month HS/EB	Day HS/EB	Constellation	Solar date	Lunar date	Month HS/EB	Day HS/EB	Constellation
16. 2	1. 1	E3	F8	Bat	10. 4	25. 2	F4	K2	Griffon
17. 2	2. 1	E3	G9	Rat	11. 4	26. 2	F4	A3	Ox
18. 2	3. 1	E3	H10	Swallow	12. 4	27. 2	F4	B4	Bat
19. 2	4. 1	E3	J11	Pig	13. 4	28. 2	F4	C5	Rat
20. 2	5. 1	E3	K12	Porcupine	14. 4	29. 2	F4	D6	Swallow
21. 2	6. 1	E3	A1	Wolf	15. 4	1. 3	G5	E7	Pig
22. 2	7. 1	E3	B2	Dog	16. 4	2. 3	G5	F8	Porcupine
23. 2	8. 1	E3	C3	Pheasant	17. 4	3. 3	G5	G9	Wolf
24. 2	9. 1	E3	D4	Cock	18. 4	4. 3	G5	H10	Dog
25. 2	10. 1	E3	E5	Crow	19. 4	5. 3	G5	J11	Pheasant
26. 2	11. 1	E3	F6	Monkey	20. 4	6. 3	G5	K12	Cock
27. 2	12. 1	E3	G7	Gibbon	21. 4	7. 3	G5	A1	Crow
28. 2	13. 1	E3	H8	Tapir	22. 4	8. 3	G5	B2	Monkey
29. 2	14. 1	E3	J9	Sheep	23. 4	9. 3	G5	C3	Gibbon
1. 3	15. 1	E3	K10	Deer	24. 4	10. 3	G5	D4	Tapir
2. 3	16. 1	E3	A11	Horse	25. 4	11. 3	G5	E5	Sheep
3. 3	17. 1	E3	B12	Stag	26. 4	12. 3	G5	F6	Deer
4. 3	18. 1	E3	C1	Serpent	27. 4	13. 3	G5	G7	Horse
5. 3	19. 1	E3	D2	Earthworm	28. 4	14. 3	G5	H8	Stag
6. 3	20. 1	E3	E3	Crocodile	29. 4	15. 3	G5	J9	Serpent
7. 3	21. 1	E3	F4	Dragon	30. 4	16. 3	G5	K10	Earthworm
8. 3	22. 1	E3	G5	Badger	1. 5	17. 3	G5	A11	Crocodile
9. 3	23. 1	E3	H6	Hare	2. 5	18. 3	G5	B12	Dragon
10. 3	24. 1	E3	J7	Fox	3. 5	19. 3	G5	C1	Badger
11. 3	25. 1	E3	K8	Tiger	4. 5	20. 3	G5	D2	Hare
12. 3	26. 1	E3	A9	Leopard	5. 5	21. 3	G5	E3	Fox
13. 3	27. 1	E3	B10	Griffon	6. 5	22. 3	G5	F4	Tiger
14. 3	28. 1	E3	C11	Ox	7. 5	23. 3	G5	G5	Leopard
15. 3	29. 1	E3	D12	Bat	8. 5	24. 3	G5	H6	Griffon
16. 3	30. 1	E3	E1	Rat	9. 5	25. 3	G5	J7	Ox
17. 3	1. 2	F4	F2	Swallow	10. 5	26. 3	G5	K8	Bat
18. 3	2. 2	F4	G3	Pig	11. 5	27. 3	G5	A9	Rat
19. 3	3. 2	F4	H4	Porcupine	12. 5	28. 3	G5	B10	Swallow
20. 3	4. 2	F4	J5	Wolf	13. 5	29. 3	G5	C11	Pig
21. 3	5. 2	F4	K6	Dog	14. 5	1. 4	H6	D12	Porcupine
22. 3	6. 2	F4	A7	Pheasant	15. 5	2. 4	H6	E1	Wolf
23. 3	7. 2	F4	B8	Cock	16. 5	3. 4	H6	F2	Dog
24. 3	8. 2	F4	C9	Crow	17. 5	4. 4	H6	G3	Pheasant
25. 3	9. 2	F4	D10	Monkey	18. 5	5. 4	H6	H4	Cock
26. 3	10. 2	F4	E11	Gibbon	19. 5	6. 4	H6	J5	Crow
27. 3	11. 2	F4	F12	Tapir	20. 5	7. 4	H6	K6	Monkey
28. 3	12. 2	F4	G1	Sheep	21. 5	8. 4	H6	A7	Gibbon
29. 3	13. 2	F4	H2	Deer	22. 5	9. 4	H6	B8	Tapir
30. 3	14. 2	F4	J3	Horse	23. 5	10. 4	H6	C9	Sheep
31. 3	15. 2	F4	K4	Stag	24. 5	11. 4	H6	D10	Deer
1. 4	16. 2	F4	A5	Serpent	25. 5	12. 4	H6	E11	Horse
2. 4	17. 2	F4	B6	Earthworm	26. 5	13. 4	H6	F12	Stag
3. 4	18. 2	F4	C7	Crocodile	27. 5	14. 4	H6	G1	Serpent
4. 4	19. 2	F4	D8	Dragon	28. 5	15. 4	H6	H2	Earthworm
5. 4	20. 2	F4	E9	Badger	29. 5	16. 4	H6	J3	Crocodile
6. 4	21. 2	F4	F10	Hare	30. 5	17. 4	H6	K4	Dragon
7. 4	22. 2	F4	G11	Fox	31. 5	18. 4	H6	A5	Badger
8. 4	23. 2	F4	H12	Tiger	1. 6	19. 4	H6	B6	Hare
9. 4	24. 2	F4	J1	Leopard	2. 6	20. 4	H6	C7	Fox

Solar date	Lunar date	Month HS/EB	Day HS/EB	Constellation	Solar date	Lunar date	Month HS/EB	Day HS/EB	Constellation
3. 6	21. 4	H6	D8	Tiger	15. 8	5. 7	A9	G9	Sheep
4. 6	22. 4	H6	E9	Leopard	16. 8	6. 7	A9	H10	Deer
5. 6	23. 4	H6	F10	Griffon	17. 8	7. 7	A9	J11	Horse
6. 6	24. 4	H6	G11	Ox	18. 8	8. 7	A9	K12	Stag
7. 6	25. 4	H6	H12	Bat	19. 8	9. 7	A9	A1	Serpent
8. 6	26. 4	H6	J1	Rat	20. 8	10. 7	A9	B2	Earthworm
9. 6	27. 4	H6	K2	Swallow	21. 8	11. 7	A9	C3	Crocodile
10. 6	28. 4	H6	A3	Pig	22. 8	12. 7	A9	D4	Dragon
11. 6	29. 4	H6	B4	Porcupine	23. 8	13. 7	A9	E5	Badger
12. 6	30. 4	H6	C5	Wolf	24. 8	14. 7	A9	F6	Hare
13. 6	1. 5	J7	D6	Dog	25. 8	15. 7	A9	G7	Fox
14. 6	2. 5	J7	E7	Pheasant	26. 8	16. 7	A9	H8	Tiger
15. 6	3. 5	J7	F8	Cock	27. 8	17. 7	A9	J9	Leopard
16. 6	4. 5	J7	G9	Crow	28. 8	18. 7	A9	K10	Griffon
17. 6	5. 5	J7	H10	Monkey	29. 8	19. 7	A9	A11	Ox
18. 6	6. 5	J7	J11	Gibbon	30. 8	20. 7	A9	B12	Bat
19. 6	7. 5	J7	K12	Tapir	31. 8	21. 7	A9	C1	Rat
20. 6	8. 5	J7	A1	Sheep	1. 9	22. 7	A9	D2	Swallow
21. 6	9. 5	J7	B2	Deer	2. 9	23. 7	A9	E3	Pig
22. 6	10. 5	J7	C3	Horse	3. 9	24. 7	A9	F4	Porcupine
23. 6	11. 5	J7	D4	Stag	4. 9	25. 7	A9	G5	Wolf
24. 6	12. 5	J7	E5	Serpent	5. 9	26. 7	A9	H6	Dog
25. 6	13. 5	J7	F6	Earthworm	6. 9	27. 7	A9	J7	Pheasant
26. 6	14. 5	J7	G7	Crocodile	7. 9	28. 7	A9	K8	Cock
27. 6	15. 5	J7	H8	Dragon	8. 9	29. 7	A9	A9	Crow
28. 6	16. 5	J7	J9	Badger	9. 9	1. 8	B10	B10	Monkey
29. 6	17. 5	J7	K10	Hare	10. 9	2. 8	B10	C11	Gibbon
30. 6	18. 5	J7	A11	Fox	11. 9	3. 8	B10	D12	Tapir
1. 7	19. 5	J7	B12	Tiger	12. 9	4. 8	B10	E1	Sheep
2. 7	20. 5	J7	C1	Leopard	13. 9	5. 8	B10	F2	Deer
3. 7	21. 5	J7	D2	Griffon	14. 9	6. 8	B10	G3	Horse
4. 7	22. 5	J7	E3	Ox	15. 9	7. 8	B10	H4	Stag
5. 7	23. 5	J7	F4	Bat	16. 9	8. 8	B10	J5	Serpent
6. 7	24. 5	J7	G5	Rat	17. 9	9. 8	B10	K6	Earthworm
7. 7	25. 5	J7	H6	Swallow	18. 9	10. 8	B10	A7	Crocodile
8. 7	26. 5	J7	J7	Pig	19. 9	11. 8	B10	B8	Dragon
9. 7	27. 5	J7	K8	Porcupine	20. 9	12. 8	B10	C9	Badger
10. 7	28. 5	J7	A9	Wolf	21. 9	13. 8	B10	D10	Hare
11. 7	29. 5	J7	B10	Dog	22. 9	14. 8	B10	E11	Fox
12. 7	1. 6	K8	C11	Pheasant	23. 9	15. 8	B10	F12	Tiger
13. 7	2. 6	K8	D12	Cock	24. 9	16. 8	B10	G1	Leopard
14. 7	3. 6	K8	E1	Crow	25. 9	17. 8	B10	H2	Griffon
15. 7	4. 6	K8	F2	Monkey	26. 9	18. 8	B10	J3	Ox
16. 7	5. 6	K8	G3	Gibbon	27. 9	19. 8	B10	K4	Bat
17. 7	6. 6	K8	H4	Tapir	28. 9	20. 8	B10	A5	Rat
18. 7	7. 6	K8	J5	Sheep	29. 9	21. 8	B10	B6	Swallow
19. 7	8. 6	K8	K6	Deer	30. 9	22. 8	B10	C7	Pig
20. 7	9. 6	K8	A7	Horse	1.10	23. 8	B10	D8	Porcupine
21. 7	10. 6	K8	B8	Stag	2.10	24. 8	B10	E9	Wolf
22. 7	11. 6	K8	C9	Serpent	3.10	25. 8	B10	F10	Dog
23. 7	12. 6	K8	D10	Earthworm	4.10	26. 8	B10	G11	Pheasant
24. 7	13. 6	K8	E11	Crocodile	5.10	27. 8	B10	H12	Cock
25. 7	14. 6	K8	F12	Dragon	6.10	28. 8	B10	J1	Crow
26. 7	15. 6	K8	G1	Badger	7.10	29. 8	B10	K2	Monkey
27. 7	16. 6	K8	H2	Hare	8.10	30. 8	B10	A3	Gibbon
28. 7	17. 6	K8	J3	Fox	9.10	1. 9	C11	B4	Tapir
29. 7	18. 6	K8	K4	Tiger	10.10	2. 9	C11	C5	Sheep
30. 7	19. 6	K8	A5	Leopard	11.10	3. 9	C11	D6	Deer
31. 7	20. 6	K8	B6	Griffon	12.10	4. 9	C11	E7	Horse
1. 8	21. 6	K8	C7	Ox	13.10	5. 9	C11	F8	Stag
2. 8	22. 6	K8	D8	Bat	14.10	6. 9	C11	G9	Serpent
3. 8	23. 6	K8	E9	Rat	15.10	7. 9	C11	H10	Earthworm
4. 8	24. 6	K8	F10	Swallow	16.10	8. 9	C11	J11	Crocodile
5. 8	25. 6	K8	G11	Pig	17.10	9. 9	C11	K12	Dragon
6. 8	26. 6	K8	H12	Porcupine	18.10	10. 9	C11	A1	Badger
7. 8	27. 6	K8	J1	Wolf	19.10	11. 9	C11	B2	Hare
8. 8	28. 6	K8	K2	Dog	20.10	12. 9	C11	C3	Fox
9. 8	29. 6	K8	A3	Pheasant	21.10	13. 9	C11	D4	Tiger
10. 8	30. 6	K8	B4	Cock	22.10	14. 9	C11	E5	Leopard
11. 8	1. 7	A9	C5	Crow	23.10	15. 9	C11	F6	Griffon
12. 8	2. 7	A9	D6	Monkey	24.10	16. 9	C11	G7	Ox
13. 8	3. 7	A9	E7	Gibbon	25.10	17. 9	C11	H8	Bat
14. 8	4. 7	A9	F8	Tapir	26.10	18. 9	C11	J9	Rat

Solar date	Lunar date	Month HS/EB	Day HS/EB	Constellation
27.10	19. 9	C11	K10	Swallow
28.10	20. 9	C11	A11	Pig
29.10	21. 9	C11	B12	Porcupine
30.10	22. 9	C11	C1	Wolf
31.10	23. 9	C11	D2	Dog
1.11	24. 9	C11	E3	Pheasant
2.11	25. 9	C11	F4	Cock
3.11	26. 9	C11	G5	Crow
4.11	27. 9	C11	H6	Monkey
5.11	28. 9	C11	J7	Gibbon
6.11	29. 9	C11	K8	Tapir
7.11	30. 9	C11	A9	Sheep
8.11	1.10	D12	B10	Deer
9.11	2.10	D12	C11	Horse
10.11	3.10	D12	D12	Stag
11.11	4.10	D12	E1	Serpent
12.11	5.10	D12	F2	Earthworm
13.11	6.10	D12	G3	Crocodile
14.11	7.10	D12	H4	Dragon
15.11	8.10	D12	J5	Badger
16.11	9.10	D12	K6	Hare
17.11	10.10	D12	A7	Fox
18.11	11.10	D12	B8	Tiger
19.11	12.10	D12	C9	Leopard
20.11	13.10	D12	D10	Griffon
21.11	14.10	D12	E11	Ox
22.11	15.10	D12	F12	Bat
23.11	16.10	D12	G1	Rat
24.11	17.10	D12	H2	Swallow
25.11	18.10	D12	J3	Pig
26.11	19.10	D12	K4	Porcupine
27.11	20.10	D12	A5	Wolf
28.11	21.10	D12	B6	Dog
29.11	22.10	D12	C7	Pheasant
30.11	23.10	D12	D8	Cock
1.12	24.10	D12	E9	Crow
2.12	25.10	D12	F10	Monkey
3.12	26.10	D12	G11	Gibbon
4.12	27.10	D12	H12	Tapir
5.12	28.10	D12	J1	Sheep
6.12	29.10	D12	K2	Deer
7.12	1.11	E1	A3	Horse
8.12	2.11	E1	B4	Stag
9.12	3.11	E1	C5	Serpent
10.12	4.11	E1	D6	Earthworm
11.12	5.11	E1	E7	Crocodile
12.12	6.11	E1	F8	Dragon
13.12	7.11	E1	G9	Badger
14.12	8.11	E1	H10	Hare
15.12	9.11	E1	J11	Fox
16.12	10.11	E1	K12	Tiger
17.12	11.11	E1	A1	Leopard
18.12	12.11	E1	B2	Griffon
19.12	13.11	E1	C3	Ox
20.12	14.11	E1	D4	Bat
21.12	15.11	E1	E5	Rat
22.12	16.11	E1	F6	Swallow
23.12	17.11	E1	G7	Pig
24.12	18.11	E1	H8	Porcupine
25.12	19.11	E1	J9	Wolf
26.12	20.11	E1	K10	Dog
27.12	21.11	E1	A11	Pheasant
28.12	22.11	E1	B12	Cock
29.12	23.11	E1	C1	Crow
30.12	24.11	E1	D2	Monkey
31.12	25.11	E1	E3	Gibbon

1981

Solar date	Lunar date	Month HS/EB	Day HS/EB	Constellation
1. 1	26.11	E1	F4	Tapir
2. 1	27.11	E1	G5	Sheep
3. 1	28.11	E1	H6	Deer
4. 1	29.11	E1	J7	Horse
5. 1	30.11	E1	K8	Stag
6. 1	1.12	F2	A9	Serpent
7. 1	2.12	F2	B10	Earthworm
8. 1	3.12	F2	C11	Crocodile
9. 1	4.12	F2	D12	Dragon
10. 1	5.12	F2	E1	Badger
11. 1	6.12	F2	F2	Hare
12. 1	7.12	F2	G3	Fox
13. 1	8.12	F2	H4	Tiger
14. 1	9.12	F2	J5	Leopard
15. 1	10.12	F2	K6	Griffon
16. 1	11.12	F2	A7	Ox
17. 1	12.12	F2	B8	Bat
18. 1	13.12	F2	C9	Rat
19. 1	14.12	F2	D10	Swallow
20. 1	15.12	F2	E11	Pig
21. 1	16.12	F2	F12	Porcupine
22. 1	17.12	F2	G1	Wolf
23. 1	18.12	F2	H2	Dog
24. 1	19.12	F2	J3	Pheasant
25. 1	20.12	F2	K4	Cock
26. 1	21.12	F2	A5	Crow
27. 1	22.12	F2	B6	Monkey
28. 1	23.12	F2	C7	Gibbon
29. 1	24.12	F2	D8	Tapir
30. 1	25.12	F2	E9	Sheep
31. 1	26.12	F2	F10	Deer
1. 2	27.12	F2	G11	Horse
2. 2	28.12	F2	H12	Stag
3. 2	29.12	F2	J1	Serpent
4. 2	30.12	F2	K2	Earthworm

HSIN YU YEAR

Solar date	Lunar date	Month HS/EB	Day HS/EB	Constellation
5. 2	1. 1	G3	A3	Crocodile
6. 2	2. 1	G3	B4	Dragon
7. 2	3. 1	G3	C5	Badger
8. 2	4. 1	G3	D6	Hare
9. 2	5. 1	G3	E7	Fox
10. 2	6. 1	G3	F8	Tiger
11. 2	7. 1	G3	G9	Leopard
12. 2	8. 1	G3	H10	Griffon
13. 2	9. 1	G3	J11	Ox
14. 2	10. 1	G3	K12	Bat
15. 2	11. 1	G3	A1	Rat
16. 2	12. 1	G3	B2	Swallow
17. 2	13. 1	G3	C3	Pig
18. 2	14. 1	G3	D4	Porcupine
19. 2	15. 1	G3	E5	Wolf
20. 2	16. 1	G3	F6	Dog
21. 2	17. 1	G3	G7	Pheasant
22. 2	18. 1	G3	H8	Cock
23. 2	19. 1	G3	J9	Crow
24. 2	20. 1	G3	K10	Monkey
25. 2	21. 1	G3	A11	Gibbon
26. 2	22. 1	G3	B12	Tapir
27. 2	23. 1	G3	C1	Sheep
28. 2	24. 1	G3	D2	Deer
1. 3	25. 1	G3	E3	Horse
2. 3	26. 1	G3	F4	Stag
3. 3	27. 1	G3	G5	Serpent
4. 3	28. 1	G3	H6	Earthworm
5. 3	29. 1	G3	J7	Crocodile
6. 3	1. 2	H4	K8	Dragon
7. 3	2. 2	H4	A9	Badger
8. 3	3. 2	H4	B10	Hare

Solar date	Lunar date	Month HS/EB	Day HS/EB	Constellation	Solar date	Lunar date	Month HS/EB	Day HS/EB	Constellation
9. 3	4. 2	H4	C11	Fox	21. 5	18. 4	K6	F12	Tapir
10. 3	5. 2	H4	D12	Tiger	22. 5	19. 4	K6	G1	Sheep
11. 3	6. 2	H4	E1	Leopard	23. 5	20. 4	K6	H2	Deer
12. 3	7. 2	H4	F2	Griffon	24. 5	21. 4	K6	J3	Horse
13. 3	8. 2	H4	G3	Ox	25. 5	22. 4	K6	K4	Stag
14. 3	9. 2	H4	H4	Bat	26. 5	23. 4	K6	A5	Serpent
15. 3	10. 2	H4	J5	Rat	27. 5	24. 4	K6	B6	Earthworm
16. 3	11. 2	H4	K6	Swallow	28. 5	25. 4	K6	C7	Crocodile
17. 3	12. 2	H4	A7	Pig	29. 5	26. 4	K6	D8	Dragon
18. 3	13. 2	H4	B8	Porcupine	30. 5	27. 4	K6	E9	Badger
19. 3	14. 2	H4	C9	Wolf	31. 5	28. 4	K6	F10	Hare
20. 3	15. 2	H4	D10	Dog	1. 6	29. 4	K6	G11	Fox
21. 3	16. 2	H4	E11	Pheasant	2. 6	1. 4	A7	H12	Tiger
22. 3	17. 2	H4	F12	Cock	3. 6	2. 4	A7	J1	Leopard
23. 3	18. 2	H4	G1	Crow	4. 6	3. 4	A7	K2	Griffon
24. 3	19. 2	H4	H2	Monkey	5. 6	4. 4	A7	A3	Ox
25. 3	20. 2	H4	J3	Gibbon	6. 6	5. 4	A7	B4	Bat
26. 3	21. 2	H4	K4	Tapir	7. 6	6. 4	A7	C5	Rat
27. 3	22. 2	H4	A5	Sheep	8. 6	7. 4	A7	D6	Swallow
28. 3	23. 2	H4	B6	Deer	9. 6	8. 4	A7	E7	Pig
29. 3	24. 2	H4	C7	Horse	10. 6	9. 4	A7	F8	Porcupine
30. 3	25. 2	H4	D8	Stag	11. 6	10. 4	A7	G9	Wolf
31. 3	26. 2	H4	E9	Serpent	12. 6	11. 4	A7	H10	Dog
1. 4	27. 2	H4	F10	Earthworm	13. 6	12. 4	A7	J11	Pheasant
2. 4	28. 2	H4	G11	Crocodile	14. 6	13. 4	A7	K12	Cock
3. 4	29. 2	H4	H12	Dragon	15. 6	14. 4	A7	A1	Crow
4. 4	30. 2	H4	J1	Badger	16. 6	15. 5	A7	B2	Monkey
5. 4	1. 3	J5	K2	Hare	17. 6	16. 5	A7	C3	Gibbon
6. 4	2. 3	J5	A3	Fox	18. 6	17. 5	A7	D4	Tapir
7. 4	3. 3	J5	B4	Tiger	19. 6	18. 5	A7	E5	Sheep
8. 4	4. 3	J5	C5	Leopard	20. 6	19. 5	A7	F6	Deer
9. 4	5. 3	J5	D6	Griffon	21. 6	20. 5	A7	G7	Horse
10. 4	6. 3	J5	E7	Ox	22. 6	21. 5	A7	H8	Stag
11. 4	7. 3	J5	F8	Bat	23. 6	22. 5	A7	J9	Serpent
12. 4	8. 3	J5	G9	Rat	24. 6	23. 5	A7	K10	Earthworm
13. 4	9. 3	J5	H10	Swallow	25. 6	24. 5	A7	A11	Crocodile
14. 4	10. 3	J5	J11	Pig	26. 6	25. 5	A7	B12	Dragon
15. 4	11. 3	J5	K12	Porcupine	27. 6	26. 5	A7	C1	Badger
16. 4	12. 3	J5	A1	Wolf	28. 6	27. 5	A7	D2	Hare
17. 4	13. 3	J5	B2	Dog	29. 6	28. 5	A7	E3	Fox
18. 4	14. 3	J5	C3	Pheasant	30. 6	29. 5	A7	F4	Tiger
19. 4	15. 3	J5	D4	Cock	1. 7	30. 5	A7	G5	Leopard
20. 4	16. 3	J5	E5	Crow	2. 7	1. 6	B8	H6	Griffon
21. 4	17. 3	J5	F6	Monkey	3. 7	2. 6	B8	J7	Ox
22. 4	18. 3	J5	G7	Gibbon	4. 7	3. 6	B8	K8	Bat
23. 4	19. 3	J5	H8	Tapir	5. 7	4. 6	B8	A9	Rat
24. 4	20. 3	J5	J9	Sheep	6. 7	5. 6	B8	B10	Swallow
25. 4	21. 3	J5	K10	Deer	7. 7	6. 6	B8	C11	Pig
26. 4	22. 3	J5	A11	Horse	8. 7	7. 6	B8	D12	Porcupine
27. 4	23. 3	J5	B12	Stag	9. 7	8. 6	B8	E1	Wolf
28. 4	24. 3	J5	C1	Serpent	10. 7	9. 6	B8	F2	Dog
29. 4	25. 3	J5	D2	Earthworm	11. 7	10. 6	B8	G3	Pheasant
30. 4	26. 3	J5	E3	Crocodile	12. 7	11. 6	B8	H4	Cock
1. 5	27. 3	J5	F4	Dragon	13. 7	12. 6	B8	J5	Crow
2. 5	28. 3	J5	G5	Badger	14. 7	13. 6	B8	K6	Monkey
3. 5	29. 3	J5	H6	Hare	15. 7	14. 6	B8	A7	Gibbon
4. 5	1. 4	K6	J7	Fox	16. 7	15. 6	B8	B8	Tapir
5. 5	2. 4	K6	K8	Tiger	17. 7	16. 6	B8	C9	Sheep
6. 5	3. 4	K6	A9	Leopard	18. 7	17. 6	B8	D10	Deer
7. 5	4. 4	K6	B10	Griffon	19. 7	18. 6	B8	E11	Horse
8. 5	5. 4	K6	C11	Ox	20. 7	19. 6	B8	F12	Stag
9. 5	6. 4	K6	D12	Bat	21. 7	20. 6	B8	G1	Serpent
10. 5	7. 4	K6	E1	Rat	22. 7	21. 6	B8	H2	Earthworm
11. 5	8. 4	K6	F2	Swallow	23. 7	22. 6	B8	J3	Crocodile
12. 5	9. 4	K6	G3	Pig	24. 7	23. 6	B8	K4	Dragon
13. 5	10. 4	K6	H4	Porcupine	25. 7	24. 6	B8	A5	Badger
14. 5	11. 4	K6	J5	Wolf	26. 7	25. 6	B8	B6	Hare
15. 5	12. 4	K6	K6	Dog	27. 7	26. 6	B8	C7	Fox
16. 5	13. 4	K6	A7	Pheasant	28. 7	27. 6	B8	D8	Tiger
17. 5	14. 4	K6	B8	Cock	29. 7	28. 6	B8	E9	Leopard
18. 5	15. 4	K6	C9	Crow	30. 7	29. 6	B8	F10	Griffon
19. 5	16. 4	K6	D10	Monkey	31. 7	1. 7	C9	G11	Ox
20. 5	17. 4	K6	E11	Gibbon	1. 8	2. 7	C9	H12	Bat

Solar date	Lunar date	Month HS/EB	Day HS/EB	Constellation	Solar date	Lunar date	Month HS/EB	Day HS/EB	Constellation
2. 8	3. 7	C9	J1	Rat	14.10	17. 9	E11	B2	Earthworm
3. 8	4. 7	C9	K2	Swallow	15.10	18. 9	E11	C3	Crocodile
4. 8	5. 7	C9	A3	Pig	16.10	19. 9	E11	D4	Dragon
5. 8	6. 7	C9	B4	Porcupine	17.10	20. 9	E11	E5	Badger
6. 8	7. 7	C9	C5	Wolf	18.10	21. 9	E11	F6	Hare
7. 8	8. 7	C9	D6	Dog	19.10	22. 9	E11	G7	Fox
8. 8	9. 7	C9	E7	Pheasant	20.10	23. 9	E11	H8	Tiger
9. 8	10. 7	C9	F8	Cock	21.10	24. 9	E11	J9	Leopard
10. 8	11. 7	C9	G9	Crow	22.10	25. 9	E11	K10	Griffon
11. 8	12. 7	C9	H10	Monkey	23.10	26. 9	E11	A11	Ox
12. 8	13. 7	C9	J11	Gibbon	24.10	27. 9	E11	B12	Bat
13. 8	14. 7	C9	K12	Tapir	25.10	28. 9	E11	C1	Rat
14. 8	15. 7	C9	A1	Sheep	26.10	29. 9	E11	D2	Swallow
15. 8	16. 7	C9	B2	Deer	27.10	30. 9	E11	E3	Pig
16. 8	17. 7	C9	C3	Horse	28.10	1.10	F12	F4	Porcupine
17. 8	18. 7	C9	D4	Stag	29.10	2.10	F12	G5	Wolf
18. 8	19. 7	C9	E5	Serpent	30.10	3.10	F12	H6	Dog
19. 8	20. 7	C9	F6	Earthworm	31.10	4.10	F12	J7	Pheasant
20. 8	21. 7	C9	G7	Crocodile	1.11	5.10	F12	K8	Cock
21. 8	22. 7	C9	H8	Dragon	2.11	6.10	F12	A9	Crow
22. 8	23. 7	C9	J9	Badger	3.11	7.10	F12	B10	Monkey
23. 8	24. 7	C9	K10	Hare	4.11	8.10	F12	C11	Gibbon
24. 8	25. 7	C9	A11	Fox	5.11	9.10	F12	D12	Tapir
25. 8	26. 7	C9	B12	Tiger	6.11	10.10	F12	E1	Sheep
26. 8	27. 7	C9	C1	Leopard	7.11	11.10	F12	F2	Deer
27. 8	28. 7	C9	D2	Griffon	8.11	12.10	F12	G3	Horse
28. 8	29. 7	C9	E3	Ox	9.11	13.10	F12	H4	Stag
29. 8	1. 8	D10	F4	Bat	10.11	14.10	F12	J5	Serpent
30. 8	2. 8	D10	G5	Rat	11.11	15.10	F12	K6	Earthworm
31. 8	3. 8	D10	H6	Swallow	12.11	16.10	F12	A7	Crocodile
1. 9	4. 8	D10	J7	Pig	13.11	17.10	F12	B8	Dragon
2. 9	5. 8	D10	K8	Porcupine	14.11	18.10	F12	C9	Badger
3. 9	6. 8	D10	A9	Wolf	15.11	19.10	F12	D10	Hare
4. 9	7. 8	D10	B10	Dog	16.11	20.10	F12	E11	Fox
5. 9	8. 8	D10	C11	Pheasant	17.11	21.10	F12	F12	Tiger
6. 9	9. 8	D10	D12	Cock	18.11	22.10	F12	G1	Leopard
7. 9	10. 8	D10	E1	Crow	19.11	23.10	F12	H2	Griffon
8. 9	11. 8	D10	F2	Monkey	20.11	24.10	F12	J3	Ox
9. 9	12. 8	D10	G3	Gibbon	21.11	25.10	F12	K4	Bat
10. 9	13. 8	D10	H4	Tapir	22.11	26.10	F12	A5	Rat
11. 9	14. 8	D10	J5	Sheep	23.11	27.10	F12	B6	Swallow
12. 9	15. 8	D10	K6	Deer	24.11	28.10	F12	C7	Pig
13. 9	16. 8	D10	A7	Horse	25.11	29.10	F12	D8	Porcupine
14. 9	17. 8	D10	B8	Stag	26.11	1.11	G1	E9	Wolf
15. 9	18. 8	D10	C9	Serpent	27.11	2.11	G1	F10	Dog
16. 9	19. 8	D10	D10	Earthworm	28.11	3.11	G1	G11	Pheasant
17. 9	20. 8	D10	E11	Crocodile	29.11	4.11	G1	H12	Cock
18. 9	21. 8	D10	F12	Dragon	30.11	5.11	G1	J1	Crow
19. 9	22. 8	D10	G1	Badger	1.12	6.11	G1	K2	Monkey
20. 9	23. 8	D10	H2	Hare	2.12	7.11	G1	A3	Gibbon
21. 9	24. 8	D10	J3	Fox	3.12	8.11	G1	B4	Tapir
22. 9	25. 8	D10	K4	Tiger	4.12	9.11	G1	C5	Sheep
23. 9	26. 8	D10	A5	Leopard	5.12	10.11	G1	D6	Deer
24. 9	27. 8	D10	B6	Griffon	6.12	11.11	G1	E7	Horse
25. 9	28. 8	D10	C7	Ox	7.12	12.11	G1	F8	Stag
26. 9	29. 8	D10	D8	Bat	8.12	13.11	G1	G9	Serpent
27. 9	30. 8	D10	E9	Rat	9.12	14.11	G1	H10	Earthworm
28. 9	1. 9	E11	F10	Swallow	10.12	15.11	G1	J11	Crocodile
29. 9	2. 9	E11	G11	Pig	11.12	16.11	G1	K12	Dragon
30. 9	3. 9	E11	H12	Porcupine	12.12	17.11	G1	A1	Badger
1.10	4. 9	E11	J1	Wolf	13.12	18.11	G1	B2	Hare
2.10	5. 9	E11	K2	Dog	14.12	19.11	G1	C3	Fox
3.10	6. 9	E11	A3	Pheasant	15.12	20.11	G1	D4	Tiger
4. 0	7. 9	E11	B4	Cock	16.12	21.11	G1	E5	Leopard
5.10	8. 9	E11	C5	Crow	17.12	22.11	G1	F6	Griffon
6.10	9. 9	E11	D6	Monkey	18.12	23.11	G1	G7	Ox
7.10	10. 9	E11	E7	Gibbon	19.12	24.11	G1	H8	Bat
8.10	11. 9	E11	F8	Tapir	20.12	25.11	G1	J9	Rat
9.10	12. 9	E11	G9	Sheep	21.12	26.11	G1	K10	Swallow
10.10	13. 9	E11	H10	Deer	22.12	27.11	G1	A11	Pig
11.10	14. 9	E11	J11	Horse	23.12	28.11	G1	B12	Porcupine
12.10	15. 9	E11	K12	Stag	24.12	29.11	G1	C1	Wolf
13.10	16. 9	E11	A1	Serpent	25.12	30.11	G1	D2	Dog

Solar date	Lunar date	Month HS/EB	Day HS/EB	Constellation
26.12	1.12	H2	E3	Pheasant
27.12	2.12	H2	F4	Cock
28.12	3.12	H2	G5	Crow
29.12	4.12	H2	H6	Monkey
30.12	5.12	H2	J7	Gibbon
31.12	6.12	H2	K8	Tapir
1982				
1. 1	7.12	H2	A9	Sheep
2. 1	8.12	H2	B10	Deer
3. 1	9.12	H2	C11	Horse
4. 1	10.12	H2	D12	Stag
5. 1	11.12	H2	E1	Serpent
6. 1	12.12	H2	F2	Earthworm
7. 1	13.12	H2	G3	Crocodile
8. 1	14.12	H2	H4	Dragon
9. 1	15.12	H2	J5	Badger
10. 1	16.12	H2	K6	Hare
11. 1	17.12	H2	A7	Fox
12. 1	18.12	H2	B8	Tiger
13. 1	19.12	H2	C9	Leopard
14. 1	20.12	H2	D10	Griffon
15. 1	21.12	H2	E11	Ox
16. 1	22.12	H2	F12	Bat
17. 1	23.12	H2	G1	Rat
18. 1	24.12	H2	H2	Swallow
19. 1	25.12	H2	J3	Pig
20. 1	26.12	H2	K4	Porcupine
21. 1	27.12	H2	A5	Wolf
22. 1	28.12	H2	B6	Dog
23. 1	29.12	H2	C7	Pheasant
24. 1	30.12	H2	D8	Cock

JEN HSÜ YEAR

Solar date	Lunar date	Month HS/EB	Day HS/EB	Constellation
25. 1	1. 1	J3	E9	Crow
26. 1	2. 1	J3	F10	Monkey
27. 1	3. 1	J3	G11	Gibbon
28. 1	4. 1	J3	H12	Tapir
29. 1	5. 1	J3	J1	Sheep
30. 1	6. 1	J3	K2	Deer
31. 1	7. 1	J3	A3	Horse
1. 2	8. 1	J3	B4	Stag
2. 2	9. 1	J3	C5	Serpent
3. 2	10. 1	J3	D6	Earthworm
4. 2	11. 1	J3	E7	Crocodile
5. 2	12. 1	J3	F8	Dragon
6. 2	13. 1	J3	G9	Badger
7. 2	14. 1	J3	H10	Hare
8. 2	15. 1	J3	J11	Fox
9. 2	16. 1	J3	K12	Tiger
10. 2	17. 1	J3	A1	Leopard
11. 2	18. 1	J3	B2	Griffon
12. 2	19. 1	J3	C3	Ox
13. 2	20. 1	J3	D4	Bat
14. 2	21. 1	J3	E5	Rat
15. 2	22. 1	J3	F6	Swallow
16. 2	23. 1	J3	G7	Pig
17. 2	24. 1	J3	H8	Porcupine
18. 2	25. 1	J3	J9	Wolf
19. 2	26. 1	J3	K10	Dog
20. 2	27. 1	J3	A11	Pheasant
21. 2	28. 1	J3	B12	Cock
22. 2	29. 1	J3	C1	Crow
23. 2	30. 1	J3	D2	Monkey
24. 2	1. 2	K4	E3	Gibbon
25. 2	2. 2	K4	F4	Tapir
26. 2	3. 2	K4	G5	Sheep
27. 2	4. 2	K4	H6	Deer
28. 2	5. 2	K4	J7	Horse
1. 3	6. 2	K4	K8	Stag
2. 3	7. 2	K4	A9	Serpent
3. 3	8. 2	K4	B10	Earthworm
4. 3	9. 2	K4	C11	Crocodile
5. 3	10. 2	K4	D12	Dragon
6. 3	11. 2	K4	E1	Badger
7. 3	12. 2	K4	F2	Hare
8. 3	13. 2	K4	G3	Fox
9. 3	14. 2	K4	H4	Tiger
10. 3	15. 2	K4	J5	Leopard
11. 3	16. 2	K4	K6	Griffon
12. 3	17. 2	K4	A7	Ox
13. 3	18. 2	K4	B8	Bat
14. 3	19. 2	K4	C9	Rat
15. 3	20. 2	K4	D10	Swallow
16. 3	21. 2	K4	E11	Pig
17. 3	22. 2	K4	F12	Porcupine
18. 3	23. 2	K4	G1	Wolf
19. 3	24. 2	K4	H4	Dog
20. 3	25. 2	K4	J3	Pheasant
21. 3	26. 2	K4	K4	Cock
22. 3	27. 2	K4	A5	Crow
23. 3	28. 2	K4	B6	Monkey
24. 3	29. 2	K4	C7	Gibbon
25. 3	1. 3	A5	D8	Tapir
26. 3	2. 3	A5	E9	Sheep
27. 3	3. 3	A5	F10	Deer
28. 3	4. 3	A5	G11	Horse
29. 3	5. 3	A5	H12	Stag
30. 3	6. 3	A5	J1	Serpent
31. 3	7. 3	A5	K2	Earthworm
1. 4	8. 3	A5	A3	Crocodile
2. 4	9. 3	A5	B4	Dragon
3. 4	10. 3	A5	C5	Badger
4. 4	11. 3	A5	D6	Hare
5. 4	12. 3	A5	E7	Fox
6. 4	13. 3	A5	F8	Tiger
7. 4	14. 3	A5	G9	Leopard
8. 4	15. 3	A5	H10	Griffon
9. 4	16. 3	A5	J11	Ox
10. 4	17. 3	A5	K12	Bat
11. 4	18. 3	A5	A1	Rat
12. 4	19. 3	A5	B2	Swallow
13. 4	20. 3	A5	C3	Pig
14. 4	21. 3	A5	D4	Porcupine
15. 4	22. 3	A5	E5	Wolf
16. 4	23. 3	A5	F6	Dog
17. 4	24. 3	A5	G7	Pheasant
18. 4	25. 3	A5	H8	Cock
19. 4	26. 3	A5	J9	Crow
20. 4	27. 3	A5	K10	Monkey
21. 4	28. 3	A5	A11	Gibbon
22. 4	29. 3	A5	B12	Tapir
23. 4	30. 3	A5	C1	Sheep
24. 4	1. 4	B6	D2	Deer
25. 4	2. 4	B6	E3	Horse
26. 4	3. 4	B6	F4	Stag
27. 4	4. 4	B6	G5	Serpent
28. 4	5. 4	B6	H6	Earthworm
29. 4	6. 4	B6	J7	Crocodile
30. 4	7. 4	B6	K8	Dragon
1. 5	8. 4	B6	A9	Badger
2. 5	9. 4	B6	B10	Hare
3. 5	10. 4	B6	C11	Fox
4. 5	11. 4	B6	D12	Tiger
5. 5	12. 4	B6	E1	Leopard
6. 5	13. 4	B6	F2	Griffon
7. 5	14. 4	B6	G3	Ox
8. 5	15. 4	B6	H4	Bat

Solar date	Lunar date	Month HS/EB	Day HS/EB	Constellation	Solar date	Lunar date	Month HS/EB	Day HS/EB	Constellation
9. 5	16. 4	B6	J5	Rat	21. 7	1. 6	D8	B6	Earthworm
10. 5	17. 4	B6	K6	Swallow	22. 7	2. 6	D8	C7	Crocodile
11. 5	18. 4	B6	A7	Pig	23. 7	3. 6	D8	D8	Dragon
12. 5	19. 4	B6	B8	Porcupine	24. 7	4. 6	D8	E9	Badger
13. 5	20. 4	B6	C9	Wolf	25. 7	5. 6	D8	F10	Hare
14. 5	21. 4	B6	D10	Dog	26. 7	6. 6	D8	G11	Fox
15. 5	22. 4	B6	E11	Pheasant	27. 7	7. 6	D8	H12	Tiger
16. 5	23. 4	B6	F12	Cock	28. 7	8. 6	D8	J1	Leopard
17. 5	24. 4	B6	G1	Crow	29. 7	9. 6	D8	K2	Griffon
18. 5	25. 4	B6	H2	Monkey	30. 7	10. 6	D8	A3	Ox
19. 5	26. 4	B6	J3	Gibbon	31. 7	11. 6	D8	B4	Bat
20. 5	27. 4	B6	K4	Tapir	1. 8	12. 6	D8	C5	Rat
21. 5	28. 4	B6	A5	Sheep	2. 8	13. 6	D8	D6	Swallow
22. 5	29. 4	B6	B6	Deer	3. 8	14. 6	D8	E7	Pig
23. 5	1. 5	B6	C7	Horse	4. 8	15. 6	D8	F8	Porcupine
24. 5	2. 4	B6	D8	Stag	5. 8	16. 6	D8	G9	Wolf
25. 5	3. 4	B6	E9	Serpent	6. 8	17. 6	D8	H10	Dog
26. 5	4. 4	B6	F10	Earthworm	7. 8	18. 6	D8	J11	Pheasant
27. 5	5. 4	B6	G11	Crocodile	8. 8	19. 6	D8	K12	Cock
28. 5	6. 4	B6	H12	Dragon	9. 8	20. 6	D8	A1	Crow
29. 5	7. 4	B6	J1	Badger	10. 8	21. 6	D8	B2	Monkey
30. 5	8. 4	B6	K2	Hare	11. 8	22. 6	D8	C3	Gibbon
31. 5	9. 4	B6	A3	Fox	12. 8	23. 6	D8	D4	Tapir
1. 6	10. 4	B6	B4	Tiger	13. 8	24. 6	D8	E5	Sheep
2. 6	11. 4	B6	C5	Leopard	14. 8	25. 6	D8	F6	Deer
3. 6	12. 4	B6	D6	Griffon	15. 8	26. 6	D8	G7	Horse
4. 6	13. 4	B6	E7	Ox	16. 8	27. 6	D8	H8	Stag
5. 6	14. 4	B6	F8	Bat	17. 8	28. 6	D8	J9	Serpent
6. 6	15. 4	B6	G9	Rat	18. 8	29. 6	D8	K10	Earthworm
7. 6	16. 4	B6	H10	Swallow	19. 8	1. 7	E9	A11	Crocodile
8. 6	17. 4	B6	J11	Pig	20. 8	2. 7	E9	B12	Dragon
9. 6	18. 4	B6	K12	Porcupine	21. 8	3. 7	E9	C1	Badger
10. 6	19. 4	B6	A1	Wolf	22. 8	4. 7	E9	D2	Hare
11. 6	20. 4	B6	B2	Dog	23. 8	5. 7	E9	E3	Fox
12. 6	21. 4	B6	C3	Pheasant	24. 8	6. 7	E9	F4	Tiger
13. 6	22. 4	B6	D4	Cock	25. 8	7. 7	E9	G4	Leopard
14. 6	23. 4	B6	E5	Crow	26. 8	8. 7	E9	H6	Griffon
15. 6	24. 4	B6	F6	Monkey	27. 8	9. 7	E9	J7	Ox
16. 6	25. 4	B6	G7	Gibbon	28. 8	10. 7	E9	K8	Bat
17. 6	26. 4	B6	H8	Tapir	29. 8	11. 7	E9	A9	Rat
18. 6	27. 4	B6	J9	Sheep	30. 8	12. 7	E9	B10	Swallow
19. 6	28. 4	B6	K10	Deer	31. 8	13. 7	E9	C11	Pig
20. 6	29. 4	B6	A11	Horse	1. 9	14. 7	E9	D12	Porcupine
21. 6	1. 5	C7	B12	Stag	2. 9	15. 7	E9	E1	Wolf
22. 6	2. 5	C7	C1	Serpent	3. 9	16. 7	E9	F2	Dog
23. 6	3. 5	C7	D2	Earthworm	4. 9	17. 7	E9	G3	Pheasant
24. 6	4. 5	C7	E3	Crocodile	5. 9	18. 7	E9	H4	Cock
25. 6	5. 5	C7	F4	Dragon	6. 9	19. 7	E9	J5	Crow
26. 6	6. 5	C7	G5	Badger	7. 9	20. 7	E9	K6	Monkey
27. 6	7. 5	C7	H6	Hare	8. 9	21. 7	E9	A7	Gibbon
28. 6	8. 5	C7	J7	Fox	9. 9	22. 7	E9	B8	Tapir
29. 6	9. 5	C7	K8	Tiger	10. 9	23. 7	E9	C9	Sheep
30. 6	10. 5	C7	A9	Leopard	11. 9	24. 7	E9	D10	Deer
1. 7	11. 5	C7	B10	Griffon	12. 9	25. 7	E9	E11	Horse
2. 7	12. 5	C7	C11	Ox	13. 9	26. 7	E9	F12	Stag
3. 7	13. 5	C7	D12	Bat	14. 9	27. 7	E9	G1	Serpent
4. 7	14. 5	C7	E1	Rat	15. 9	28. 7	E9	H2	Earthworm
5. 7	15. 5	C7	F2	Swallow	16. 9	29. 7	E9	J3	Crocodile
6. 7	16. 5	C7	G3	Pig	17. 9	1. 8	F10	K4	Dragon
7. 7	17. 5	C7	H4	Porcupine	18. 9	2. 8	F10	A5	Badger
8. 7	18. 5	C7	J5	Wolf	19. 9	3. 8	F10	B6	Hare
9. 7	19. 5	C7	K6	Dog	20. 9	4. 8	F10	C7	Fox
10. 7	20. 5	C7	A7	Pheasant	21. 9	5. 8	F10	D8	Tiger
11. 7	21. 5	C7	B8	Cock	22. 9	6. 8	F10	E9	Leopard
12. 7	22. 5	C7	C9	Crow	23. 9	7. 8	F10	F10	Griffon
13. 7	23. 5	C7	D10	Monkey	24. 9	8. 8	F10	G11	Ox
14. 7	24. 5	C7	E11	Gibbon	25. 9	9. 8	F10	H12	Bat
15. 7	25. 5	C7	F12	Tapir	26. 9	10. 8	F10	J1	Rat
16. 7	26. 5	C7	G1	Sheep	27. 9	11. 8	F10	K2	Swallow
17. 7	27. 5	C7	H2	Deer	28. 9	12. 8	F10	A3	Pig
18. 7	28. 5	C7	J3	Horse	29. 9	13. 8	F10	B4	Porcupine
19. 7	29. 5	C7	K4	Stag	30. 9	14. 8	F10	C5	Wolf
20. 7	30. 5	C7	A5	Serpent	1.10	15. 8	F10	D6	Dog

Solar date	Lunar date	Month HS/EB	Day HS/EB	Constellation	Solar date	Lunar date	Month HS/EB	Day HS/EB	Constellation
2.10	16. 8	F10	E7	Pheasant	9.12	25.10	H12	C3	Crocodile
3.10	17. 8	F10	F8	Cock	10.12	26.10	H12	D4	Dragon
4.10	18. 8	F10	G9	Crow	11.12	27.10	H12	E5	Badger
5.10	19. 8	F10	H10	Monkey	12.12	28.10	H12	F6	Hare
6.10	20. 8	F10	J11-	Gibbon	13.12	29.10	H12	G7	Fox
7.10	21. 8	F10	K12	Tapir	14.12	30.10	H12	H8	Tiger
8.10	22. 8	F10	A1	Sheep	15.12	1.11	J1	J9	Leopard
9.10	23. 8	F10	B2	Deer	16.12	2.11	J1	K10	Griffon
10.10	24. 8	F10	C3	Horse	17.12	3.11	J1	A11	Ox
11.10	25. 8	F10	D4	Stag	18.12	4.11	J1	B12	Bat
12.10	26. 8	F10	E5	Serpent	19.12	5.11	J1	C1	Rat
13.10	27. 8	F10	F6	Earthworm	20.12	6.11	J1	D2	Swallow
14.10	28. 8	F10	G7	Crocodile	21.12	7.11	J1	E3	Pig
15.10	29. 8	F10	H8	Dragon	22.12	8.11	J1	F4	Porcupine
16.10	30. 8	F10	J9	Badger	23.12	9.11	J1	G5	Wolf
17.10	1. 9	G11	K10	Hare	24.12	10.11	J1	H6	Dog
18.10	2. 9	G11	A11	Fox	25.12	11.11	J1	J7	Pheasant
19.10	3. 9	G11	B12	Tiger	26.12	12.11	J1	K8	Cock
20.10	4. 9	G11	C1	Leopard	27.12	13.11	J1	A9	Crow
21.10	5. 9	G11	D2	Griffon	28.12	14.11	J1	B10	Monkey
22.10	6. 9	G11	E3	Ox	29.12	15.11	J1	C11	Gibbon
23.10	7. 9	G11	F4	Bat	30.12	16.11	J1	D12	Tapir
24.10	8. 9	G11	G5	Rat	31.12	17.11	J1	E1	Sheep
25.10	9. 9	G11	H6	Swallow					
26.10	10. 9	G11	J7	Pig	**1983**				
27.10	11. 9	G11	K8	Porcupine	1. 1	18.11	J1	F2	Deer
28.10	12. 9	G11	A9	Wolf	2. 1	19.11	J1	G3	Horse
29.10	13. 9	G11	B10	Dog	3. 1	20.11	J1	H4	Stag
30.10	14. 9	G11	C11	Pheasant	4. 1	21.11	J1	J5	Serpent
31.10	15. 9	G11	D12	Cock	5. 1	22.11	J1	K6	Earthworm
1.11	16. 9	G11	E1	Crow	6. 1	23.11	J1	A7	Crocodile
2.11	17. 9	G11	F2	Monkey	7. 1	24.11	J1	B8	Dragon
3.11	18. 9	G11	G3	Gibbon	8. 1	25.11	J1	C9	Badger
4.11	19. 0	G11	H4	Tapir	9. 1	26.11	J1	D10	Hare
5.11	20. 9	G11	J5	Sheep	10. 1	27.11	J1	E11	Fox
6.11	21. 9	G11	K6	Deer	11. 1	28.11	J1	F12	Tiger
7.11	22. 9	G11	A7	Horse	12. 1	29.11	J1	G1	Leopard
8.11	23. 9	G11	B8	Stag	13. 1	30.11	J1	H2	Griffon
9.11	24. 9	G11	C9	Serpent	14. 1	1.12	K2	J3	Ox
10.11	25. 9	G11	D10	Earthworm	15. 1	2.12	K2	K4	Bat
11.11	26. 9	G11	E11	Crocodile	16. 1	3.12	K2	A5	Rat
12.11	27. 9	G11	F12	Dragon	17. 1	4.12	K2	B6	Swallow
13.11	28. 9	G11	G1	Badger	18. 1	5.12	K2	C7	Pig
14.11	29. 9	G11	H2	Hare	19. 1	6.12	K2	D8	Porcupine
15.11	1.10	H12	J3	Fox	20. 1	7.12	K2	E9	Wolf
16.11	2.10	H12	K4	Tiger	21. 1	8.12	K2	F10	Dog
17.11	3.10	H12	A5	Leopard	22. 1	9.12	K2	G11	Pheasant
18.11	4.10	H12	B6	Griffon	23. 1	10.12	K2	H12	Cock
19.11	5.10	H12	C7	Ox	24. 1	11.12	K2	J1	Crow
20.11	6.10	H12	D8	Bat	25. 1	12.12	K2	K2	Monkey
21.11	7.10	H12	E9	Rat	26. 1	13.12	K2	A3	Gibbon
22.11	8.10	H12	F10	Swallow	27. 1	14.12	K2	B4	Tapir
23.11	9.10	H12	G11	Pig	28. 1	15.12	K2	C5	Sheep
24.11	10.10	H12	H12	Porcupine	29. 1	16.12	K2	D6	Deer
25.11	11.10	H12	J1	Wolf	30. 1	17.12	K2	E7	Horse
26.11	12.10	H12	K2	Dog	31. 1	18.12	K2	F8	Stag
27.11	13.10	H12	A3	Pheasant	1. 2	19.12	K2	G9	Serpent
28.11	14.10	H12	B4	Cock	2. 2	20.12	K2	H10	Earthworm
29.11	15.10	H12	C5	Crow	3. 2	21.12	K2	J11	Crocodile
30.11	16.10	H12	D6	Monkey	4. 2	22.12	K2	K12	Dragon
1.12	17.10	H12	E7	Gibbon	5. 2	23.12	K2	A1	Badger
2.12	18.10	H12	F8	Tapir	6. 2	24.12	K2	B2	Hare
3.12	19.10	H12	G9	Sheep	7. 2	25.12	K2	C3	Fox
4.12	20.10	H12	H10	Deer	8. 2	26.12	K2	D4	Tiger
5.12	21.10	H12	J11	Horse	9. 2	27.12	K2	E5	Leopard
6.12	22.10	H12	K12	Stag	10. 2	28.12	K2	F6	Griffon
7.12	23.10	H12	A1	Serpent	11. 2	29.12	K2	G7	Ox
8.12	24.10	H12	B2	Earthworm	12. 2	30.12	K2	H8	Bat

KUEI HAI YEAR

Solar date	Lunar date	Month HS/EB	Day HS/EB	Constellation	Solar date	Lunar date	Month HS/EB	Day HS/EB	Constellation
13. 2	1. 1	A3	J9	Rat	25. 4	13. 3	C5	K8	Stag
14. 2	2. 1	A3	K10	Swallow	26. 4	14. 3	C5	A9	Serpent
15. 2	3. 1	A3	A11	Pig	27. 4	15. 3	C5	B10	Earthworm
16. 2	4. 1	A3	B12	Porcupine	28. 4	16. 3	C5	C11	Crocodile
17. 2	5. 1	A3	C1	Wolf	29. 4	17. 3	C5	D12	Dragon
18. 2	6. 1	A3	D2	Dog	30. 4	18. 3	C5	E1	Badger
19. 2	7. 1	A3	E3	Pheasant	1. 5	19. 3	C5	F2	Hare
20. 2	8. 1	A3	F4	Cock	2. 5	20. 3	C5	G3	Fox
21. 2	9. 1	A3	G5	Crow	3. 5	21. 3	C5	H4	Tiger
22. 2	10. 1	A3	H6	Monkey	4. 5	22. 3	C5	J5	Leopard
23. 2	11. 1	A3	J7	Gibbon	5. 5	23. 3	C5	K6	Griffon
24. 2	12. 1	A3	K8	Tapir	6. 5	24. 3	C5	A7	Ox
25. 2	13. 1	A3	A9	Sheep	7. 5	25. 3	C5	B8	Bat
26. 2	14. 1	A3	B10	Deer	8. 5	26. 3	C5	C9	Rat
27. 2	15. 1	A3	C11	Horse	9. 5	27. 3	C5	D10	Swallow
28. 2	16. 1	A3	D12	Stag	10. 5	28. 3	C5	E11	Pig
1. 3	17. 1	A3	E1	Serpent	11. 5	29. 3	C5	F12	Porcupine
2. 3	18. 1	A3	F2	Earthworm	12. 5	30. 3	C5	G1	Wolf
3. 3	19. 1	A3	G3	Crocodile	13. 5	1. 4	D6	H2	Dog
4. 3	20. 1	A3	H4	Dragon	14. 5	2. 4	D6	J3	Pheasant
5. 3	21. 1	A3	J5	Badger	15. 5	3. 4	D6	K4	Cock
6. 3	22. 1	A3	K6	Hare	16. 5	4. 4	D6	A5	Crow
7. 3	23. 1	A3	A7	Fox	17. 5	5. 4	D6	B6	Monkey
8. 3	24. 1	A3	B8	Tiger	18. 5	6. 4	D6	C7	Gibbon
9. 3	25. 1	A3	C9	Leopard	19. 5	7. 4	D6	D8	Tapir
10. 3	26. 1	A3	D10	Griffon	20. 5	8. 4	D6	E9	Sheep
11. 3	27. 1	A3	E11	Ox	21. 5	9. 4	D6	F10	Deer
12. 3	28. 1	A3	F12	Bat	22. 5	10. 4	D6	G11	Horse
13. 3	29. 1	A3	G1	Rat	23. 5	11. 4	D6	H12	Stag
14. 3	30. 1	A3	H2	Swallow	24. 5	12. 4	D6	J1	Serpent
15. 3	1. 2	B4	J3	Pig	25. 5	13. 4	D6	K2	Earthworm
16. 3	2. 2	B4	K4	Porcupine	26. 5	14. 4	D6	A3	Crocodile
17. 3	3. 2	B4	A5	Wolf	27. 5	15. 4	D6	B4	Dragon
18. 3	4. 2	B4	B6	Dog	28. 5	16. 4	D6	C5	Badger
19. 3	5. 2	B4	C7	Pheasant	29. 5	17. 4	D6	D6	Hare
20. 3	6. 2	B4	D8	Cock	30. 5	18. 4	D6	E7	Fox
21. 3	7. 2	B4	E9	Crow	31. 5	19. 4	D6	F8	Tiger
22. 3	8. 2	B4	F10	Monkey	1. 6	20. 4	D6	G9	Leopard
23. 3	9. 2	B4	G11	Gibbon	2. 6	21. 4	D6	H10	Griffon
24. 3	10. 2	B4	H12	Tapir	3. 6	22. 4	D6	J11	Ox
25. 3	11. 2	B4	J1	Sheep	4. 6	23. 4	D6	K12	Bat
26. 3	12. 2	B4	K2	Deer	5. 6	24. 4	D6	A1	Rat
27. 3	13. 2	B4	A3	Horse	6. 6	25. 4	D6	B2	Swallow
28. 3	14. 2	B4	B4	Stag	7. 6	26. 4	D6	C3	Pig
29. 3	15. 2	B4	C5	Serpent	8. 6	27. 4	D6	D4	Porcupine
30. 3	16. 2	B4	D6	Earthworm	9. 6	28. 4	D6	E5	Wolf
31. 3	17. 2	B4	E7	Crocodile	10. 6	29. 4	D6	F6	Dog
1. 4	18. 2	B4	F8	Dragon	11. 6	1. 5	E7	G7	Pheasant
2. 4	19. 2	B4	G9	Badger	12. 6	2. 5	E7	H8	Cock
3. 4	20. 2	B4	H10	Hare	13. 6	3. 5	E7	J9	Crow
4. 4	21. 2	B4	J11	Fox	14. 6	4. 5	E7	K10	Monkey
5. 4	22. 2	B4	K12	Tiger	15. 6	5. 5	E7	A11	Gibbon
6. 4	23. 2	B4	A1	Leopard	16. 6	6. 5	E7	B12	Tapir
7. 4	24. 2	B4	B2	Griffon	17. 6	7. 5	E7	C1	Sheep
8. 4	25. 2	B4	C3	Ox	18. 6	8. 5	E7	D2	Deer
9. 4	26. 2	B4	D4	Bat	19. 6	9. 5	E7	E3	Horse
10. 4	27. 2	B4	E5	Rat	20. 6	10. 5	E7	F4	Stag
11. 4	28. 2	B4	F6	Swallow	21. 6	11. 5	E7	G5	Serpent
12. 4	29. 2	B4	G7	Pig	22. 6	12. 5	E7	H6	Earthworm
13. 4	1. 3	C5	H8	Porcupine	23. 6	13. 5	E7	J7	Crocodile
14. 4	2. 3	C5	J9	Wolf	24. 6	14. 5	E7	K8	Dragon
15. 4	3. 3	C5	K10	Dog	25. 6	15. 5	E7	A9	Badger
16. 4	4. 3	C5	A11	Pheasant	26. 6	16. 5	E7	B10	Hare
17. 4	5. 3	C5	B12	Cock	27. 6	17. 5	E7	C11	Fox
18. 4	6. 3	C5	C1	Crow	28. 6	18. 5	E7	D12	Tiger
19. 4	7. 3	C5	D2	Monkey	29. 6	19. 5	E7	E1	Leopard
20. 4	8. 3	C5	E3	Gibbon	30. 6	20. 5	E7	F2	Griffon
21. 4	9. 3	C5	F4	Tapir	1. 7	21. 5	E7	G3	Ox
22. 4	10. 3	C5	G5	Sheep	2. 7	22. 5	E7	H4	Bat
23. 4	11. 3	C5	H6	Deer	3. 7	23. 5	E7	J5	Rat
24. 4	12. 3	C5	J7	Horse	4. 7	24. 5	E7	K6	Swallow

Solar date	Lunar date	Month HS/EB	Day HS/EB	Constellation	Solar date	Lunar date	Month HS/EB	Day HS/EB	Constellation
5. 7	25. 5	E7	H7	Pig	16. 9	10. 8	H10	D8	Dragon
6. 7	26. 5	E7	B8	Porcupine	17. 9	11. 8	H10	E9	Badger
7. 7	27. 5	E7	C9	Wolf	18. 9	12. 8	H10	F10	Hare
8. 7	28. 5	E7	D10	Dog	19. 9	13. 8	H10	G11	Fox
9. 7	29. 5	E7	E11	Pheasant	20. 9	14. 8	H10	H12	Tiger
10. 7	1. 6	F8	F12	Cock	21. 9	15. 8	H10	J1	Leopard
11. 7	2. 6	F8	G1	Crow	22. 9	16. 8	H10	K2	Griffon
12. 7	3. 6	F8	H2	Monkey	23. 9	17. 8	H10	A3	Ox
13. 7	4. 6	F8	J3	Gibbon	24. 9	18. 8	H10	B4	Bat
14. 7	5. 6	F8	K4	Tapir	25. 9	19. 8	H10	C5	Rat
15. 7	6. 6	F8	A5	Sheep	26. 9	20. 8	H10	D6	Swallow
16. 7	7. 6	F8	B6	Deer	27. 9	21. 8	H10	E7	Pig
17. 7	8. 6	F8	C7	Horse	28. 9	22. 8	H10	F8	Porcupine
18. 7	9. 6	F8	D8	Stag	29. 9	23. 8	H10	G9	Wolf
19. 7	10. 6	F8	E9	Serpent	30. 9	24. 8	H10	H10	Dog
20. 7	11. 6	F8	F10	Earthworm	1.10	25. 8	H10	J11	Pheasant
21. 7	12. 6	F8	G11	Crocodile	2.10	26. 8	H10	K12	Cock
22. 7	13. 6	F8	H12	Dragon	3.10	27. 8	H10	A1	Crow
23. 7	14. 6	F8	J1	Badger	4.10	28. 8	H10	B2	Monkey
24. 7	15. 6	F8	K2	Hare	5.10	29. 8	H10	C3	Gibbon
25. 7	16. 6	F8	A3	Fox	6.10	1. 9	J11	D4	Tapir
26. 7	17. 6	F8	B4	Tiger	7.10	2. 9	J11	E5	Sheep
27. 7	18. 6	F8	C5	Leopard	8.10	3. 9	J11	F6	Deer
28. 7	19. 6	F8	D6	Griffon	9.10	4. 9	J11	G7	Horse
29. 7	20. 6	F8	E7	Ox	10.10	5. 9	J11	H8	Stag
30. 7	21. 6	F8	F8	Bat	11.10	6. 9	J11	J9	Serpent
31. 7	22. 6	F8	G9	Rat	12.10	7. 9	J11	K10	Earthworm
1. 8	23. 6	F8	H10	Swallow	13.10	8. 9	J11	A11	Crocodile
2. 8	24. 6	F8	J11	Pig	14.10	9. 9	J11	B12	Dragon
3. 8	25. 6	F8	K12	Porcupine	15.10	10. 9	J11	C1	Badger
4. 8	26. 6	F8	A1	Wolf	16.10	11. 9	J11	D2	Hare
5. 8	27. 6	F8	B2	Dog	17.10	12. 9	J11	E3	Fox
6. 8	28. 6	F8	C3	Pheasant	18.10	13. 9	J11	F4	Tiger
7. 8	29. 6	F8	D4	Cock	19.10	14. 9	J11	G5	Leopard
8. 8	30. 6	F8	E5	Crow	20.10	15. 9	J11	H6	Griffon
9. 8	1. 7	G9	F6	Monkey	21.10	16. 9	J11	J7	Ox
10. 8	2. 7	G9	G7	Gibbon	22.10	17. 9	J11	K8	Bat
11. 8	3. 7	G9	H8	Tapir	23.10	18. 9	J11	A9	Rat
12. 8	4. 7	G9	J9	Sheep	24.10	19. 9	J11	B10	Swallow
13. 8	5. 7	G9	K10	Deer	25.10	20. 9	J11	C11	Pig
14. 8	6. 7	G9	A11	Horse	26.10	21. 9	J11	D12	Porcupine
15. 8	7. 7	G9	B12	Stag	27.10	22. 9	J11	E1	Wolf
16. 8	8. 7	G9	C1	Serpent	28.10	23. 9	J11	F2	Dog
17. 8	9. 7	G9	D2	Earthworm	29.10	24. 9	J11	G3	Pheasant
18. 8	10. 7	G9	E3	Crocodile	30.10	25. 9	J11	H4	Cock
19. 8	11. 7	G9	F4	Dragon	31.10	26. 9	J11	J5	Crow
20. 8	12. 7	G9	G5	Badger	1.11	27. 9	J11	K6	Monkey
21. 8	13. 7	G9	H6	Hare	2.11	28. 9	J11	A7	Gibbon
22. 8	14. 7	G9	J7	Fox	3.11	29. 9	J11	B8	Tapir
23. 8	15. 7	G9	K8	Tiger	4.11	30. 9	J11	C9	Sheep
24. 8	16. 7	G9	A9	Leopard	5.11	1.10	K12	D10	Deer
25. 8	17. 7	G9	B10	Griffon	6.11	2.10	K12	E11	Horse
26. 8	18. 7	G9	C11	Ox	7.11	3.10	K12	F12	Stag
27. 8	19. 7	G9	D12	Bat	8.11	4.10	K12	G1	Serpent
28. 8	20. 7	G9	E1	Rat	9.11	5.10	K12	H2	Earthworm
29. 8	21. 7	G9	F2	Swallow	10.11	6.10	K12	J3	Crocodile
30. 8	22. 7	G9	G3	Pig	11.11	7.10	K12	K4	Dragon
31. 8	23. 7	G9	H4	Porcupine	12.11	8.10	K12	A5	Badger
1. 9	24. 7	G9	J5	Wolf	13.11	9.10	K12	B6	Hare
2. 9	25. 7	G9	K6	Dog	14.11	10.10	K12	C7	Fox
3. 9	26. 7	G9	A7	Pheasant	15.11	11.10	K12	D8	Tiger
4. 9	27. 7	G9	B8	Cock	16.11	12.10	K12	E9	Leopard
5. 9	28. 7	G9	C9	Crow	17.11	13.10	K12	F10	Griffon
6. 9	29. 7	G9	D10	Monkey	18.11	14.10	K12	G11	Ox
7. 9	1. 8	H10	E11	Gibbon	19.11	15.10	K12	H12	Bat
8. 9	2. 8	H10	F12	Tapir	20.11	16.10	K12	J1	Rat
9. 9	3. 8	H10	G1	Sheep	21.11	17.10	K12	K2	Swallow
10. 9	4. 8	H10	H2	Deer	22.11	18.10	K12	A3	Pig
11. 9	5. 8	H10	J3	Horse	23.11	19.10	K12	B4	Porcupine
12. 9	6. 8	H10	K4	Stag	24.11	20.10	K12	C5	Wolf
13. 9	7. 8	H10	A5	Serpent	25.11	21.10	K12	D6	Dog
14. 9	8. 8	H10	B6	Earthworm	26.11	22.10	K12	E7	Pheasant
15. 9	9. 8	H10	C7	Crocodile	27.11	23.10	K12	F8	Cock

Solar date	Lunar date	Month HS/EB	Day HS/EB	Constellation	Solar date	Lunar date	Month HS/EB	Day HS/EB	Constellation
28.11	24.10	K12	G9	Crow	**1984**				
29.11	25.10	K12	H10	Monkey	1. 1	29.11	A1	A7	Horse
30.11	26.10	K12	J11	Gibbon	2. 1	30.11	A1	B8	Stag
1.12	27.10	K12	K12	Tapir	3. 1	1.12	B2	C9	Serpent
2.12	28.10	K12	A1	Sheep	4. 1	2.12	B2	D10	Earthworm
3.12	29.10	K12	B2	Deer	5. 1	3.12	B2	E11	Crocodile
4.12	1.11	A1	C3	Horse	6. 1	4.12	B2	F12	Dragon
5.12	2.11	A1	D4	Stag	7. 1	5.12	B2	G1	Badger
6.12	3.11	A1	E5	Serpent	8. 1	6.12	B2	H2	Hare
7.12	4.11	A1	F6	Earthworm	9. 1	7.12	B2	J3	Fox
8.12	5.11	A1	G7	Crocodile	10. 1	8.12	B2	K4	Tiger
9.12	6.11	A1	H8	Dragon	11. 1	9.12	B2	A5	Leopard
10.12	7.11	A1	J9	Badger	12. 2	10.12	B2	B6	Griffon
11.12	8.11	A1	K10	Hare	13. 1	11.12	B2	C7	Ox
12.12	9.11	A1	A11	Fox	14. 1	12.12	B2	D8	Bat
13.12	10.11	A1	B12	Tiger	15. 1	13.12	B2	E9	Rat
14.12	11.11	A1	C1	Leopard	16. 1	14.12	B2	F10	Swallow
15.12	12.11	A1	D2	Griffon	17. 1	15.12	B2	G11	Pig
16.12	13.11	A1	E3	Ox	18. 1	16.12	B2	H12	Porcupine
17.12	14.11	A1	F4	Bat	19. 1	17.12	B2	J1	Wolf
18.12	15.11	A1	G5	Rat	20. 1	18.12	B2	K2	Dog
19.12	16.11	A1	H6	Swallow	21. 1	19.12	B2	A3	Pheasant
20.12	17.11	A1	J7	Pig	22. 1	20.12	B2	B4	Cock
21.12	18.11	A1	K8	Porcupine	23. 1	21.12	B2	C5	Crow
22.12	19.11	A1	A9	Wolf	24. 1	22.12	B2	D6	Monkey
23.12	20.11	A1	B10	Dog	25. 1	23.12	B2	E7	Gibbon
24.12	21.11	A1	C11	Pheasant	26. 1	24.12	B2	F8	Tapir
25.12	22.11	A1	D12	Cock	27. 1	25.12	B2	G9	Sheep
26.12	23.11	A1	E1	Crow	28. 1	26.12	B2	H10	Deer
27.12	24.11	A1	F2	Monkey	29. 1	27.12	B2	J11	Horse
28.12	25.11	A1	G3	Gibbon	30. 1	28.12	B2	K12	Stag
29.12	26.11	A1	H4	Tapir	31. 1	29.12	B2	A1	Serpent
30.12	27.11	A1	J5	Sheep	1. 2	30.12	B2	B2	Earthworm
31.12	28.11	A1	K6	Deer					

CHIA TZU YEAR

Solar date	Lunar date	Month HS/EB	Day HS/EB	Constellation	Solar date	Lunar date	Month HS/EB	Day HS/EB	Constellation
2. 2	1.12	C3	C3	Crocodile	7. 3	5. 1	D4	G1	Leopard
3. 2	2.12	C3	D4	Dragon	8. 3	6. 1	D4	H2	Griffon
4. 2	3.12	C3	E5	Badger	9. 3	7. 1	D4	J3	Ox
5. 2	4.12	C3	F6	Hare	10. 3	8. 1	D4	K4	Bat
6. 2	5.12	C3	G7	Fox	11. 3	9. 1	D4	A5	Rat
7. 2	6.12	C3	H8	Tiger	12. 3	10. 1	D4	B6	Swallow
8. 2	7.12	C3	J9	Leopard	13. 3	11. 1	D4	C7	Pig
9. 2	8.12	C3	K10	Griffon	14. 3	12. 1	D4	D8	Porcupine
10. 2	9.12	C3	A11	Ox	15. 3	13. 1	D4	E9	Wolf
11. 2	10.12	C3	B12	Bat	16. 3	14. 2	D4	F10	Dog
12. 2	11.12	C3	C1	Rat	17. 3	15. 2	D4	G11	Pheasant
13. 2	12.12	C3	D2	Swallow	18. 3	16. 2	D4	H12	Cock
14. 2	13.12	C3	E3	Pig	19. 3	17. 2	D4	J1	Crow
15. 2	14. 1	C3	F4	Porcupine	20. 3	18. 2	D4	K2	Monkey
16. 2	15. 1	C3	G5	Wolf	21. 3	19. 2	D4	A3	Gibbon
17. 2	16. 1	C3	H6	Dog	22. 3	20. 2	D4	B4	Tapir
18. 2	17. 1	C3	J7	Pheasant	23. 3	21. 2	D4	C5	Sheep
19. 2	18. 1	C3	K8	Cock	24. 3	22. 2	D4	D6	Deer
20. 2	19. 1	C3	A9	Crow	25. 3	23. 2	D4	E7	Horse
21. 2	20. 1	C3	B10	Monkey	26. 3	24. 2	D4	F8	Stag
22. 2	21. 1	C3	C11	Gibbon	27. 3	25. 2	D4	G9	Serpent
23. 2	22. 1	C3	D12	Tapir	28. 3	26. 2	D4	H10	Earthworm
24. 2	23. 1	C3	E1	Sheep	29. 3	27. 2	D4	J11	Crocodile
25. 2	24. 1	C3	F2	Deer	30. 3	28. 2	D4	K12	Dragon
26. 2	25. 1	C3	G3	Horse	31. 3	29. 2	D4	A1	Badger
27. 2	26. 1	C3	H4	Stag	1. 4	1. 2	E5	B2	Hare
28. 2	27. 1	C3	J5	Serpent	2. 4	2. 2	E5	C3	Fox
29. 2	28. 1	C3	K6	Earthworm	3. 4	3. 2	E5	D4	Tiger
1. 3	29. 1	C3	A7	Crocodile	4. 4	4. 2	E5	E5	Leopard
2. 3	30. 1	C3	B8	Dragon	5. 4	5. 2	E5	F6	Griffon
3. 3	1. 1	D4	C9	Badger	6. 4	6. 2	E5	G7	Ox
4. 3	2. 1	D4	D10	Hare	7. 4	7. 2	E5	H8	Bat
5. 3	3. 1	D4	E11	Fox	8. 4	8. 2	E5	J9	Rat
6. 3	4. 1	D4	F12	Tiger	9. 4	9. 2	E5	K10	Swallow

Solar date	Lunar date	Month HS/EB	Day HS/EB	Constellation	Solar date	Lunar date	Month HS/EB	Day HS/EB	Constellation
10. 4	10. 2	E5	A11	Pig	22. 6	23. 5	G7	D12	Dragon
11. 4	11. 2	E5	B12	Porcupine	23. 6	24. 5	G7	E1	Badger
12. 4	12. 2	E5	C1	Wolf	24. 6	25. 5	G7	F2	Hare
13. 4	13. 2	E5	D2	Dog	25. 6	26. 5	G7	G3	Fox
14. 4	14. 3	E5	E3	Pheasant	26. 6	27. 5	G7	H4	Tiger
15. 4	15. 3	E5	F4	Cock	27. 6	28. 5	G7	J5	Leopard
16. 4	16. 3	E5	G5	Crow	28. 6	29. 5	G7	K6	Griffon
17. 4	17. 3	E5	H6	Monkey	29. 6	1. 6	H8	A7	Ox
18. 4	18. 3	E5	J7	Gibbon	30. 6	2. 6	H8	B8	Bat
19. 4	19. 3	E5	K8	Tapir	1. 7	3. 6	H8	C9	Rat
20. 4	20. 3	E5	A9	Sheep	2. 7	4. 6	H8	D10	Swallow
21. 4	21. 3	E5	B10	Deer	3. 7	5. 6	H8	E11	Pig
22. 4	22. 3	E5	C11	Horse	4. 7	6. 6	H8	F12	Porcupine
23. 4	23. 3	E5	D12	Stag	5. 7	7. 6	H8	G1	Wolf
24. 4	24. 3	E5	E1	Serpent	6. 7	8. 6	H8	H2	Dog
25. 4	25. 3	E5	F2	Earthworm	7. 7	9. 6	H8	J3	Pheasant
26. 4	26. 3	E5	G3	Crocodile	8. 7	10. 6	H8	K4	Cock
27. 4	27. 3	E5	H4	Dragon	9. 7	11. 6	H8	A5	Crow
28. 4	28. 3	E5	J5	Badger	10. 7	12. 6	H8	B6	Monkey
29. 4	29. 3	E5	K6	Hare	11. 7	13. 6	H8	C7	Gibbon
30. 4	30. 3	E5	A7	Fox	12. 7	14. 6	H8	D8	Tapir
1. 5	1. 4	F6	B8	Tiger	13. 7	15. 6	H8	E9	Sheep
2. 5	2. 4	F6	C9	Leopard	14. 7	16. 6	H8	F10	Deer
3. 5	3. 4	F6	D10	Griffon	15. 7	17. 6	H8	G11	Horse
4. 5	4. 4	F6	E11	Ox	16. 7	18. 6	H8	H12	Stag
5. 5	5. 4	F6	F12	Bat	17. 7	19. 6	H8	J1	Serpent
6. 5	6. 4	F6	G1	Rat	18. 7	20. 6	H8	K2	Earthworm
7. 5	7. 4	F6	H2	Swallow	19. 7	21. 6	H8	A3	Crocodile
8. 5	8. 4	F6	J3	Pig	20. 7	22. 6	H8	B4	Dragon
9. 5	9. 4	F6	K4	Porcupine	21. 7	23. 6	H8	C5	Badger
10. 5	10. 4	F6	A5	Wolf	22. 7	24. 6	H8	D6	Hare
11. 5	11. 4	F6	B6	Dog	23. 7	25. 6	H8	E7	Fox
12. 5	12. 4	F6	C7	Pheasant	24. 7	26. 6	H8	F8	Tiger
13. 5	13. 4	F6	D8	Cock	25. 7	27. 6	H8	G9	Leopard
14. 5	14. 4	F6	E9	Crow	26. 7	28. 6	H8	H10	Griffon
15. 5	15. 4	F6	F10	Monkey	27. 7	29. 6	H8	J11	Ox
16. 5	16. 4	F6	G11	Gibbon	28. 7	1. 7	J9	K12	Bat
17. 5	17. 4	F6	H12	Tapir	29. 7	2. 7	J9	A1	Rat
18. 5	18. 4	F6	J1	Sheep	30. 7	3. 7	J9	B2	Swallow
19. 5	19. 4	F6	K2	Deer	31. 7	4. 7	J9	C3	Pig
20. 5	20. 4	F6	A3	Horse	1. 8	5. 7	J9	D4	Porcupine
21. 5	21. 4	F6	B4	Stag	2. 8	6. 7	J9	E5	Wolf
22. 5	22. 4	F6	C5	Serpent	3. 8	7. 7	J9	F6	Dog
23. 5	23. 4	F6	D6	Earthworm	4. 8	8. 7	J9	G7	Pheasant
24. 5	24. 4	F6	E7	Crocodile	5. 8	9. 7	J9	H8	Cock
25. 5	25. 4	F6	F8	Dragon	6. 8	10. 7	J9	J9	Crow
26. 5	26. 4	F6	G9	Badger	7. 8	11. 7	J9	K10	Monkey
27. 5	27. 4	F6	H10	Hare	8. 8	12. 7	J9	A11	Gibbon
28. 5	28. 4	F6	J11	Fox	9. 8	13. 7	J9	B12	Tapir
29. 5	29. 4	F6	K12	Tiger	10. 8	14. 7	J9	C1	Sheep
30. 5	30. 4	F6	A1	Leopard	11. 8	15. 7	J9	D2	Deer
31. 5	1. 5	G7	B2	Griffon	12. 8	16. 7	J9	E3	Horse
1. 6	2. 5	G7	C3	Ox	13. 8	17. 7	J9	F4	Stag
2. 6	3. 5	G7	D4	Bat	14. 8	18. 7	J9	G5	Serpent
3. 6	4. 5	G7	E5	Rat	15. 8	19. 7	J9	H6	Earthworm
4. 6	5. 5	G7	F6	Swallow	16. 8	20. 7	J9	J7	Crocodile
5. 6	6. 5	G7	G7	Pig	17. 8	21. 7	J9	K8	Dragon
6. 6	7. 5	G7	H8	Porcupine	18. 8	22. 7	J9	A9	Badger
7. 6	8. 5	G7	J9	Wolf	19. 8	23. 7	J9	B10	Hare
8. 6	9. 5	G7	K10	Dog	20. 8	24. 7	J9	C11	Fox
9. 6	10. 5	G7	A11	Pheasant	21. 8	25. 7	J9	D12	Tiger
10. 6	11. 5	G7	B12	Cock	22. 8	26. 7	J9	E1	Leopard
11. 6	12. 5	G7	C1	Crow	23. 8	27. 7	J9	F2	Griffon
12. 6	13. 5	G7	D2	Monkey	24. 8	28. 7	J9	G3	Ox
13. 6	14. 5	G7	E3	Gibbon	25. 8	29. 7	J9	H4	Bat
14. 6	15. 5	G7	F4	Tapir	26. 8	30. 7	J9	J5	Rat
15. 6	16. 5	G7	G5	Sheep	27. 8	1. 8	K10	K6	Swallow
16. 6	17. 5	G7	H6	Deer	28. 8	2. 8	K10	A7	Pig
17. 6	18. 5	G7	J7	Horse	29. 8	3. 8	K10	B8	Porcupine
18. 6	19. 5	G7	K8	Stag	30. 8	4. 8	K10	C9	Wolf
19. 6	20. 5	G7	A9	Serpent	31. 8	5. 8	K10	D10	Dog
20. 6	21. 5	G7	B10	Earthworm	1. 9	6. 8	K10	E11	Pheasant
21. 6	22. 5	G7	C11	Crocodile	2. 9	7. 8	K10	F12	Cock

Solar date	Lunar date	Month HS/EB	Day HS/EB	Constellation	Solar date	Lunar date	Month HS/EB	Day HS/EB	Constellation
3. 9	8. 8	K10	G1	Crow	15.11	23.10	B12	K2	Griffon
4. 9	9. 8	K10	H2	Monkey	16.11	24.10	B12	A3	Ox
5. 9	10. 8	K10	J3	Gibbon	17.11	25.10	B12	B4	Bat
6. 9	11. 8	K10	K4	Tapir	18.11	26.10	B12	C5	Rat
7. 9	12. 8	K10	A5	Sheep	19.11	27.10	B12	D6	Swallow
8. 9	13. 8	K10	B6	Deer	20.11	28.10	B12	E7	Pig
9. 9	14. 8	K10	C7	Horse	21.11	29.10	B12	F8	Porcupine
10. 9	15. 8	K10	D8	Stag	22.11	30.10	B12	G9	Wolf
11. 9	16. 8	K10	E9	Serpent	23.11	1.10	B12	H10	Dog
12. 9	17. 8	K10	F10	Earthworm	24.11	2.10	B12	J11	Pheasant
13. 9	18. 8	K10	G11	Crocodile	25.11	3.10	B12	K12	Cock
14. 9	19. 8	K10	H12	Dragon	26.11	4.10	B12	A1	Crow
15. 9	20. 8	K10	J1	Badger	27.11	5.10	B12	B2	Monkey
16. 9	21. 8	K10	K2	Hare	28.11	6.10	B12	C3	Gibbon
17. 9	22. 8	K10	A3	Fox	29.11	7.10	B12	D4	Tapir
18. 9	23. 8	K10	B4	Tiger	30.11	8.10	B12	E5	Sheep
19. 9	24. 8	K10	C5	Leopard	1.12	9.10	B12	F6	Deer
20. 9	25. 8	K10	D6	Griffon	2.12	10.10	B12	G7	Horse
21. 9	26. 8	K10	E7	Ox	3.12	11.10	B12	H8	Stag
22. 9	27. 8	K10	F8	Bat	4.12	12.10	B12	J9	Serpent
23. 9	28. 8	K10	G9	Rat	5.12	13.10	B12	K10	Earthworm
24. 9	29. 8	K10	H10	Swallow	6.12	14.10	B12	A11	Crocodile
25. 9	1. 9	A11	J11	Pig	7.12	15.10	B12	B12	Dragon
26. 9	2. 9	A11	K12	Porcupine	8.12	16.10	B12	C1	Badger
27. 9	3. 9	A11	A1	Wolf	9.12	17.10	B12	D2	Hare
28. 9	4. 9	A11	B2	Dog	10.12	18.10	B12	E3	Fox
29. 9	5. 9	A11	C3	Pheasant	11.12	19.10	B12	F4	Tiger
30. 9	6. 9	A11	D4	Cock	12.12	20.10	B12	G5	Leopard
1.10	7. 9	A11	E5	Crow	13.12	21.10	B12	H6	Griffon
2.10	8. 9	A11	F6	Monkey	14.12	22.10	B12	J7	Ox
3.10	9. 9	A11	G7	Gibbon	15.12	23.10	B12	K8	Bat
4.10	10. 9	A11	H8	Tapir	16.12	24.10	B12	A9	Rat
5.10	11. 9	A11	J9	Sheep	17.12	25.10	B12	B10	Swallow
6.10	12. 9	A11	K10	Deer	18.12	26.10	B12	C11	Pig
7.10	13. 9	A11	A11	Horse	19.12	27.10	B12	D12	Porcupine
8.10	14. 9	A11	B12	Stag	20.12	28.10	B12	E1	Wolf
9.10	15. 9	A11	C1	Serpent	21.12	29.10	B12	F2	Dog
10.10	16. 9	A11	D2	Earthworm	22.12	1.11	C1	G3	Pheasant
11.10	17. 9	A11	E3	Crocodile	23.12	2.11	C1	H4	Cock
12.10	18. 9	A11	F4	Dragon	24.12	3.11	C1	J5	Crow
13.10	19. 9	A11	G5	Badger	25.12	4.11	C1	K6	Monkey
14.10	20. 9	A11	H6	Hare	26.12	5.11	C1	A7	Gibbon
15.10	21. 9	A11	J7	Fox	27.12	6.11	C1	B8	Tapir
16.10	22. 9	A11	K8	Tiger	28.12	7.11	C1	C9	Sheep
17.10	23. 9	A11	A9	Leopard	29.12	8.11	C1	D10	Deer
18.10	24. 9	A11	B10	Griffon	30.12	9.11	C1	E11	Horse
19.10	25. 9	A11	C11	Ox	31.12	10.11	C1	F12	Stag
20.10	26. 9	A11	D12	Bat					
21.10	27. 9	A11	E1	Rat	**1985**				
22.10	28. 9	A11	F2	Swallow	1. 1	11.11	C1	G1	Serpent
23.10	29. 9	A11	G3	Pig	2. 1	12.11	C1	H2	Earthworm
24.10	1.10	B12	H4	Porcupine	3. 1	13.11	C1	J3	Crocodile
25.10	2.10	B12	J5	Wolf	4. 1	14.11	C1	K4	Dragon
26.10	3.10	B12	K6	Dog	5. 1	15.11	C1	A5	Badger
27.10	4.10	B12	A7	Pheasant	6. 1	16.11	C1	B6	Hare
28.10	5.10	B12	B8	Cock	7. 1	17.11	C1	C7	Fox
29.10	6.10	B12	C9	Crow	8. 1	18.11	C1	D8	Tiger
30.10	7.10	B12	D10	Monkey	9. 1	19.11	C1	E9	Leopard
31.10	8.10	B12	E11	Gibbon	10. 1	20.11	C1	F10	Griffon
1.11	9.10	B12	F12	Tapir	11. 1	21.11	C1	G11	Ox
2.11	10.10	B12	G1	Sheep	12. 1	22.11	C1	H12	Bat
3.11	11.10	B12	H2	Deer	13. 1	23.11	C1	J1	Rat
4.11	12.10	B12	J3	Horse	14. 1	24.11	C1	K2	Swallow
5.11	13.10	B12	K4	Stag	15. 1	25.11	C1	A3	Pig
6.11	14.10	B12	A5	Serpent	16. 1	26.11	C1	B4	Porcupine
7.11	15.10	B12	B6	Earthworm	17. 1	27.11	C1	C5	Wolf
8.11	16.10	B12	C7	Crocodile	18. 1	28.11	C1	D6	Dog
9.11	17.10	B12	D8	Dragon	19. 1	29.11	C1	E7	Pheasant
10.11	18.10	B12	E9	Badger	20. 1	30.11	C1	F8	Cock
11.11	19.10	B12	F10	Hare	21. 1	1.12	D2	G9	Crow
12.11	20.10	B12	G11	Fox	22. 1	2.12	D2	H10	Monkey
13.11	21.10	B12	H12	Tiger	23. 1	3.12	D2	J11	Gibbon
14.11	22.10	B12	J1	Leopard	24. 1	4.12	D2	K12	Tapir

Solar date	Lunar date	Month HS/EB	Day HS/EB	Constellation	Solar date	Lunar date	Month HS/EB	Day HS/EB	Constellation
25. 1	5.12	D2	A1	Sheep	7. 2	18.12	D2	D2	Griffon
26. 1	6.12	D2	B2	Deer	8. 2	19.12	D2	E3	Ox
27. 1	7.12	D2	C3	Horse	9. 2	20.12	D2	F4	Bat
28. 1	8.12	D2	D4	Stag	10. 2	21.12	D2	G5	Rat
29. 1	9.12	D2	E5	Serpent	11. 2	22.12	D2	H6	Swallow
30. 1	10.12	D2	F6	Earthworm	12. 2	23.12	D2	J7	Pig
31. 1	11.12	D2	G7	Crocodile	13. 2	24.12	D2	K8	Porcupine
1. 2	12.12	D2	H8	Dragon	14. 2	25.12	D2	A9	Wolf
2. 2	13.12	D2	J9	Badger	15. 2	26.12	D2	B10	Dog
3. 2	14.12	D2	K10	Hare	16. 2	27.12	D2	C11	Pheasant
4. 2	15.12	D2	A11	Fox	17. 2	28.12	D2	D12	Cock
5. 2	16.12	D2	B12	Tiger	18. 2	29.12	D2	E1	Crow
6. 2	17.12	D2	C1	Leopard	19. 2	30.12	D2	F2	Monkey

YI CH'OU YEAR

Solar date	Lunar date	Month HS/EB	Day HS/EB	Constellation	Solar date	Lunar date	Month HS/EB	Day HS/EB	Constellation
20. 2	1. 1	E3	G3	Gibbon	16. 4	27. 2	F4	B10	Monkey
21. 2	2. 1	E3	H4	Tapir	17. 4	28. 2	F4	C11	Gibbon
22. 2	3. 1	E3	J5	Sheep	18. 4	29. 2	F4	D12	Tapir
23. 2	4. 1	E3	K6	Deer	19. 4	30. 2	F4	E1	Sheep
24. 2	5. 1	E3	A7	Horse	20. 4	1. 3	G5	F2	Deer
25. 2	6. 1	E3	B8	Stag	21. 4	2. 3	G5	G3	Horse
26. 2	7. 1	E3	C9	Serpent	22. 4	3. 3	G5	H4	Stag
27. 2	8. 1	E3	D10	Earthworm	23. 4	4. 3	G5	J5	Serpent
28. 2	9. 1	E3	E11	Crocodile	24. 4	5. 3	G5	K6	Earthworm
1. 3	10. 1	E3	F12	Dragon	25. 4	6. 3	G5	A7	Crocodile
2. 3	11. 1	E3	G1	Badger	26. 4	7. 3	G5	B8	Dragon
3. 3	12. 1	E3	H2	Hare	27. 4	8. 3	G5	C9	Badger
4. 3	13. 1	E3	J3	Fox	28. 4	9. 3	G5	D10	Hare
5. 3	14. 1	E3	K4	Tiger	29. 4	10. 3	G5	E11	Fox
6. 3	15. 1	E3	A5	Leopard	30. 4	11. 3	G5	F12	Tiger
7. 3	16. 1	E3	B6	Griffon	1. 5	12. 3	G5	G1	Leopard
8. 3	17. 1	E3	C7	Ox	2. 5	13. 3	G5	H2	Griffon
9. 3	18. 1	E3	D8	Bat	3. 5	14. 3	G5	J3	Ox
10. 3	19. 1	E3	E9	Rat	4. 5	15. 3	G5	K4	Bat
11. 3	20. 1	E3	F10	Swallow	5. 5	16. 3	G5	A5	Rat
12. 3	21. 1	E3	G11	Pig	6. 5	17. 3	G5	B6	Swallow
13. 3	22. 1	E3	H12	Porcupine	7. 5	18. 3	G5	C7	Pig
14. 3	23. 1	E3	J1	Wolf	8. 5	19. 3	G5	D8	Porcupine
15. 3	24. 1	E3	K2	Dog	9. 5	20. 3	G5	E9	Wolf
16. 3	25. 1	E3	A3	Pheasant	10. 5	21. 3	G5	F10	Dog
17. 3	26. 1	E3	B4	Cock	11. 5	22. 3	G5	G11	Pheasant
18. 3	27. 1	E3	C5	Crow	12. 5	23. 3	G5	H12	Cock
19. 3	28. 1	E3	D6	Monkey	13. 5	24. 3	G5	J1	Crow
20. 3	29. 1	E3	E7	Gibbon	14. 5	25. 3	G5	K2	Monkey
21. 3	1. 2	F4	F8	Tapir	15. 5	26. 3	G5	A3	Gibbon
22. 3	2. 2	F4	G9	Sheep	16. 5	27. 3	G5	B4	Tapir
23. 3	3. 2	F4	H10	Deer	17. 5	28. 3	G5	C5	Sheep
24. 3	4. 2	F4	J11	Horse	18. 5	29. 3	G5	D6	Deer
25. 3	5. 2	F4	K12	Stag	19. 5	30. 3	G5	E7	Horse
26. 3	6. 2	F4	A1	Serpent	20. 5	1. 4	H6	F8	Stag
27. 3	7. 2	F4	B2	Earthworm	21. 5	2. 4	H6	G9	Serpent
28. 3	8. 2	F4	C3	Crocodile	22. 5	3. 4	H6	H10	Earthworm
29. 3	9. 2	F4	D4	Dragon	23. 5	4. 4	H6	J11	Crocodile
30. 3	10. 2	F4	E5	Badger	24. 5	5. 4	H6	K12	Dragon
31. 3	11. 2	F4	F6	Hare	25. 5	6. 4	H6	A1	Badger
1. 4	12. 2	F4	G7	Fox	26. 5	7. 4	H6	B2	Hare
2. 4	13. 2	F4	H8	Tiger	27. 5	8. 4	H6	C3	Fox
3. 4	14. 2	F4	J9	Leopard	28. 5	9. 4	H6	D4	Tiger
4. 4	15. 2	F4	K10	Griffon	29. 5	10. 4	H6	E5	Leopard
5. 4	16. 2	F4	A11	Ox	30. 5	11. 4	H6	F6	Griffon
6. 4	17. 2	F4	B12	Bat	31. 5	12. 4	H6	G7	Ox
7. 4	18. 2	F4	C1	Rat	1. 6	13. 4	H6	H8	Bat
8. 4	19. 2	F4	D2	Swallow	2. 6	14. 4	H6	J9	Rat
9. 4	20. 2	F4	E3	Pig	3. 6	15. 4	H6	K10	Swallow
10. 4	21. 2	F4	F4	Porcupine	4. 6	16. 4	H6	A11	Pig
11. 4	22. 2	F4	G5	Wolf	5. 6	17. 4	H6	B12	Porcupine
12. 4	23. 2	F4	H6	Dog	6. 6	18. 4	H6	C1	Wolf
13. 4	24. 2	F4	J7	Pheasant	7. 6	19. 4	H6	D2	Dog
14. 4	25. 2	F4	K8	Cock	8. 6	20. 4	H6	E3	Pheasant
15. 4	26. 2	F4	A9	Crow	9. 6	21. 4	H6	F4	Cock

Solar date	Lunar date	Month HS/EB	Day HS/EB	Constellation	Solar date	Lunar date	Month HS/EB	Day HS/EB	Constellation
10. 6	22. 4	H6	G5	Crow	22. 8	7. 7	A9	K6	Griffon
11. 6	23. 4	H6	H6	Monkey	23. 8	8. 7	A9	A7	Ox
12. 6	24. 4	H6	J7	Gibbon	24. 8	9. 7	A9	B8	Bat
13. 6	25. 4	H6	K8	Tapir	25. 8	10. 7	A9	C9	Rat
14. 6	26. 4	H6	A9	Sheep	26. 8	11. 7	A9	D10	Swallow
15. 6	27. 4	H6	B10	Deer	27. 8	12. 7	A9	E11	Pig
16. 6	28. 4	H6	C11	Horse	28. 8	13. 7	A9	F12	Porcupine
17. 6	29. 4	H6	D12	Stag	29. 8	14. 7	A9	G1	Wolf
18. 6	1. 5	J7	E1	Serpent	30. 8	15. 7	A9	H2	Dog
19. 6	2. 5	J7	F2	Earthworm	31. 8	16. 7	A9	J3	Pheasant
20. 6	3. 5	J7	G3	Crocodile	1. 9	17. 7	A9	K4	Cock
21. 6	4. 5	J7	H4	Dragon	2. 9	18. 7	A9	A5	Crow
22. 6	5. 5	J7	J5	Badger	3. 9	19. 7	A9	B6	Monkey
23. 6	6. 5	J7	K6	Hare	4. 9	20. 7	A9	C7	Gibbon
24. 6	7. 5	J7	A7	Fox	5. 9	21. 7	A9	D8	Tapir
25. 6	8. 5	J7	B8	Tiger	6. 9	22. 7	A9	E9	Sheep
26. 6	9. 5	J7	C9	Leopard	7. 9	23. 7	A9	F10	Deer
27. 6	10. 5	J7	D10	Griffon	8. 9	24. 7	A9	G11	Horse
28. 6	11. 5	J7	E11	Ox	9. 9	25. 7	A9	H12	Stag
29. 6	12. 5	J7	F12	Bat	10. 9	26. 7	A9	J1	Serpent
30. 6	13. 5	J7	G1	Rat	11. 9	27. 7	A9	K2	Earthworm
1. 7	14. 5	J7	H2	Swallow	12. 9	28. 7	A9	A3	Crocodile
2. 7	15. 5	J7	J3	Pig	13. 9	29. 7	A9	B4	Dragon
3. 7	16. 5	J7	K4	Porcupine	14. 9	30. 7	A9	C5	Badger
4. 7	17. 5	J7	A5	Wolf	15. 9	1. 8	B10	D6	Hare
5. 7	18. 5	J7	B6	Dog	16. 9	2. 8	B10	E7	Fox
6. 7	19. 5	J7	C7	Pheasant	17. 9	3. 8	B10	F8	Tiger
7. 7	20. 5	J7	D8	Cock	18. 9	4. 8	B10	G9	Leopard
8. 7	21. 5	J7	E9	Crow	19. 9	5. 8	B10	H10	Griffon
9. 7	22. 5	J7	F10	Monkey	20. 9	6. 8	B10	J11	Ox
10. 7	23. 5	J7	G11	Gibbon	21. 9	7. 8	B10	K12	Bat
11. 7	24. 5	J7	H12	Tapir	22. 9	8. 8	B10	A1	Rat
12. 7	25. 5	J7	J1	Sheep	23. 9	9. 8	B10	B2	Swallow
13. 7	26. 5	J7	K2	Deer	24. 9	10. 8	B10	C3	Pig
14. 7	27. 5	J7	A3	Horse	25. 9	11. 8	B10	D4	Porcupine
15. 7	28. 5	J7	B4	Stag	26. 9	12. 8	B10	E5	Wolf
16. 7	29. 5	J7	C5	Serpent	27. 9	13. 8	B10	F6	Dog
17. 7	30. 5	J7	D6	Earthworm	28. 9	14. 8	B10	G7	Pheasant
18. 7	1. 6	K8	E7	Crocodile	29. 9	15. 8	B10	H8	Cock
19. 7	2. 6	K8	F8	Dragon	30. 9	16. 8	B10	J9	Crow
20. 7	3. 6	K8	G9	Badger	1.10	17. 8	B10	K10	Monkey
21. 7	4. 6	K8	H10	Hare	2.10	18. 8	B10	A11	Gibbon
22. 7	5. 6	K8	J11	Fox	3.10	19. 8	B10	B12	Tapir
23. 7	6. 6	K8	K12	Tiger	4.10	20. 8	B10	C1	Sheep
24. 7	7. 6	K8	A1	Leopard	5.10	21. 8	B10	D2	Deer
25. 7	8. 6	K8	B2	Griffon	6.10	22. 8	B10	E3	Horse
26. 7	9. 6	K8	C3	Ox	7.10	23. 8	B10	F4	Stag
27. 7	10. 6	K8	D4	Bat	8.10	24. 8	B10	G5	Serpent
28. 7	11. 6	K8	E5	Rat	9.10	25. 8	B10	H6	Earthworm
29. 7	12. 6	K8	F6	Swallow	10.10	26. 8	B10	J7	Crocodile
30. 7	13. 6	K8	G7	Pig	11.10	27. 8	B10	K8	Dragon
31. 7	14. 6	K8	H8	Porcupine	12.10	28. 8	B10	A9	Badger
1. 8	15. 6	K8	J9	Wolf	13.10	29. 8	B10	B10	Hare
2. 8	16. 6	K8	K10	Dog	14.10	1. 9	C11	C11	Fox
3. 8	17. 6	K8	A11	Pheasant	15.10	2. 9	C11	D12	Tiger
4. 8	18. 6	K8	B12	Cock	16.10	3. 9	C11	E1	Leopard
5. 8	19. 6	K8	C1	Crow	17.10	4. 9	C11	F2	Griffon
6. 8	20. 6	K8	D2	Monkey	18.10	5. 9	C11	G3	Ox
7. 8	21. 6	K8	E3	Gibbon	19.10	6. 9	C11	H4	Bat
8. 8	22. 6	K8	F4	Tapir	20.10	7. 9	C11	J5	Rat
9. 8	23. 6	K8	G5	Sheep	21.10	8. 9	C11	K6	Swallow
10. 8	24. 6	K8	H6	Deer	22.10	9. 9	C11	A7	Pig
11. 8	25. 6	K8	J7	Horse	23.10	10. 9	C11	B8	Porcupine
12. 8	26. 6	K8	K8	Stag	24.10	11. 9	C11	C9	Wolf
13. 8	27. 6	K8	A9	Serpent	25.10	12. 9	C11	D10	Dog
14. 8	28. 6	K8	B10	Earthworm	26.10	13. 9	C11	E11	Pheasant
15. 8	29. 6	K8	C11	Crocodile	27.10	14. 9	C11	F12	Cock
16. 8	1. 7	A9	D12	Dragon	28.10	15. 9	C11	G1	Crow
17. 8	2. 7	A9	E1	Badger	29.10	16. 9	C11	H2	Monkey
18. 8	3. 7	A9	F2	Hare	30.10	17. 9	C11	J3	Gibbon
19. 8	4. 7	A9	G3	Fox	31.10	18. 9	C11	K4	Tapir
20. 8	5. 7	A9	H4	Tiger	1.11	19. 9	C11	A5	Sheep
21. 8	6. 7	A9	J5	Leopard	2.11	20. 9	C11	B6	Deer

Solar date	Lunar date	Month HS/EB	Day HS/EB	Constellation		Solar date	Lunar date	Month HS/EB	Day HS/EB	Constellation
3.11	21. 9	C11	C7	Horse		23.12	12.11	E1	C9	Crow
4.11	22. 9	C11	D8	Stag		24.12	13.11	E1	D10	Monkey
5.11	23. 9	C11	E9	Serpent		25.12	14.11	E1	E11	Gibbon
6.11	24. 9	C11	F10	Earthworm		26.12	15.11	E1	F12	Tapir
7.11	25. 9	C11	G11	Crocodile		27.12	16.11	E1	G1	Sheep
8.11	26. 9	C11	H12	Dragon		28.12	17.11	E1	H2	Deer
9.11	27. 9	C11	J1	Badger		29.12	18.11	E1	J3	Horse
10.11	28. 9	C11	K2	Hare		30.12	19.11	E1	K4	Stag
11.11	29. 9	C11	A3	Fox		31.12	20.11	E1	A5	Serpent
12.11	1.10	D12	B4	Tiger						
13.11	2.10	D12	C5	Leopard		**1986**				
14.11	3.10	D12	D6	Griffon		1. 1	21.11	E1	B6	Earthworm
15.11	4.10	D12	E7	Ox		2. 1	22.11	E1	C7	Crocodile
16.11	5.10	D12	F8	Bat		3. 1	23.11	E1	D8	Dragon
17.11	6.10	D12	G9	Rat		4. 1	24.11	E1	E9	Badger
18.11	7.10	D12	H10	Swallow		5. 1	25.11	E1	F10	Hare
19.11	8.10	D12	J11	Pig		6. 1	26.11	E1	G11	Fox
20.11	9.10	D12	K12	Porcupine		7. 1	27.11	E1	H12	Tiger
21.11	10.10	D12	A1	Wolf		8. 1	28.11	E1	J1	Leopard
22.11	11.10	D12	B2	Dog		9. 1	29.11	E1	K2	Griffon
23.11	12.10	D12	C3	Pheasant		10. 1	1.12	F2	A3	Ox
24.11	13.10	D12	D4	Cock		11. 1	2.12	F2	B4	Bat
25.11	14.10	D12	E5	Crow		12. 1	3.12	F2	C5	Rat
26.11	15.10	D12	F6	Monkey		13. 1	4.12	F2	D6	Swallow
27.11	16.10	D12	G7	Gibbon		14. 1	5.12	F2	E7	Pig
28.11	17.10	D12	H8	Tapir		15. 1	6.12	F2	F8	Porcupine
29.11	18.10	D12	J9	Sheep		16. 1	7.12	F2	G9	Wolf
30.11	19.10	D12	K10	Deer		17. 1	8.12	F2	H10	Dog
1.12	20.10	D12	A11	Horse		18. 1	9.12	F2	J11	Pheasant
2.12	21.10	D12	B12	Stag		19. 1	10.12	F2	K12	Cock
3.12	22.10	D12	C1	Serpent		20. 1	11.12	F2	A1	Crow
4.12	23.10	D12	D2	Earthworm		21. 1	12.12	F2	B2	Monkey
5.12	24.10	D12	E3	Crocodile		22. 1	13.12	F2	C3	Gibbon
6.12	25.10	D12	F4	Dragon		23. 1	14.12	F2	D4	Tapir
7.12	26.10	D12	G5	Badger		24. 1	15.12	F2	E5	Sheep
8.12	27.10	D12	H6	Hare		25. 1	16.12	F2	F6	Deer
9.12	28.10	D12	J7	Fox		26. 1	17.12	F2	G7	Horse
10.12	29.10	D12	K8	Tiger		27. 1	18.12	F2	H8	Stag
11.12	30.10	D12	A9	Leopard		28. 1	19.12	F2	J9	Serpent
12.12	1.11	E1	B10	Griffon		29. 1	20.12	F2	K10	Earthworm
13.12	2.11	E1	C11	Ox		30. 1	21.12	F2	A11	Crocodile
14.12	3.11	E1	D12	Bat		31. 1	22.12	F2	B12	Dragon
15.12	4.11	E1	E1	Rat		1. 2	23.12	F2	C1	Badger
16.12	5.11	E1	F2	Swallow		2. 2	24.12	F2	D2	Hare
17.12	6.11	E1	G3	Pig		3. 2	25.12	F2	E3	Fox
18.12	7.11	E1	H4	Porcupine		4. 2	26.12	F2	F4	Tiger
19.12	8.11	E1	J5	Wolf		5. 2	27.12	F2	G5	Leopard
20.12	9.11	E1	K6	Dog		6. 2	28.12	F2	H6	Griffon
21.12	10.11	E1	A7	Pheasant		7. 2	29.12	F2	J7	Ox
22.12	11.11	E1	B8	Cock		8. 2	30.12	F2	K8	Bat

PING YIN YEAR

Solar date	Lunar date	Month HS/EB	Day HS/EB	Constellation		Solar date	Lunar date	Month HS/EB	Day HS/EB	Constellation
9. 2	1. 1	G3	A9	Rat		26. 2	18. 1	G3	H2	Earthworm
10. 2	2. 1	G3	B10	Swallow		27. 2	19. 1	G3	J3	Crocodile
11. 2	3. 1	G3	C1	Pig		28. 2	20. 1	G3	K4	Dragon
12. 2	4. 1	G3	D12	Porcupine		1. 3	21. 1	G3	A5	Badger
13. 2	5. 1	G3	E1	Wolf		2. 3	22. 1	G3	B6	Hare
14. 2	6. 1	G3	F2	Dog		3. 3	23. 1	G3	C7	Fox
15. 2	7. 1	G3	G3	Pheasant		4. 3	24. 1	G3	D8	Tiger
16. 2	8. 1	G3	H4	Cock		5. 3	25. 1	G3	E9	Leopard
17. 2	9. 1	G3	J5	Crow		6. 3	26. 1	G3	F10	Griffon
18. 2	10. 1	G3	K6	Monkey		7. 3	27. 1	G3	G11	Ox
19. 2	11. 1	G3	A7	Gibbon		8. 3	28. 1	G3	H12	Bat
20. 2	12. 1	G3	B8	Tapir		9. 3	29. 1	G3	J1	Rat
21. 2	13. 1	G3	C9	Sheep		10. 3	1. 2	H4	K2	Swallow
22. 2	14. 1	G3	D10	Deer		11. 3	2. 2	H4	A3	Pig
23. 2	15. 1	G3	E11	Horse		12. 3	3. 2	H4	B4	Porcupine
24. 2	16. 1	G3	F12	Stag		13. 3	4. 2	H4	C5	Wolf
25. 2	17. 1	G3	G1	Serpent		14. 3	5. 2	H4	D6	Dog

Solar date	Lunar date	Month HS/EB	Day HS/EB	Constellation	Solar date	Lunar date	Month HS/EB	Day HS/EB	Constellation
15. 3	6. 2	H4	E7	Pheasant	27. 5	19. 4	K6	H8	Tiger
16. 3	7. 2	H4	F8	Cock	28. 5	20. 4	K6	J9	Leopard
17. 3	8. 2	H4	G9	Crow	29. 5	21. 4	K6	K10	Griffon
18. 3	9. 2	H4	H10	Monkey	30. 5	22. 4	K6	A11	Ox
19. 3	10. 2	H4	J11	Gibbon	31. 5	23. 4	K6	B12	Bat
20. 3	11. 2	H4	K12	Tapir	1. 6	24. 4	K6	C1	Rat
21. 3	12. 2	H4	A1	Sheep	2. 6	25. 4	K6	D2	Swallow
22. 3	13. 2	H4	B2	Deer	3. 6	26. 4	K6	E3	Pig
23. 3	14. 2	H4	C3	Horse	4. 6	27. 4	K6	F4	Porcupine
24. 3	15. 2	H4	D4	Stag	5. 6	28. 4	K6	G5	Wolf
25. 3	16. 2	H4	E5	Serpent	6. 6	29. 4	K6	H6	Dog
26. 3	17. 2	H4	F6	Earthworm	7. 6	1. 5	A7	J7	Pheasant
27. 3	18. 2	H4	G7	Crocodile	8. 6	2. 5	A7	K8	Cock
28. 3	19. 2	H4	H8	Dragon	9. 6	3. 5	A7	A9	Crow
29. 3	20. 2	H4	J9	Badger	10. 6	4. 5	A7	B10	Monkey
30. 3	21. 2	H4	K10	Hare	11. 6	5. 5	A7	C11	Gibbon
31. 3	22. 2	H4	A11	Fox	12. 6	6. 5	A7	D12	Tapir
1. 4	23. 2	H4	B12	Tiger	13. 6	7. 5	A7	E1	Sheep
2. 4	24. 2	H4	C1	Leopard	14. 6	8. 5	A7	F2	Deer
3. 4	25. 2	H4	D2	Griffon	15. 6	9. .5	A7	G3	Horse
4. 4	26. 2	H4	E3	Ox	16. 6	10. 5	A7	H4	Stag
5. 4	27. 2	H4	F4	Bat	17. 6	11. 5	A7	J5	Serpent
6. 4	28. 2	H4	G5	Rat	18. 6	12. 5	A7	K6	Earthworm
7. 4	29. 2	H4	H6	Swallow	19. 6	13. 5	A7	A7	Crocodile
8. 4	30. 2	H4	J7	Pig	20. 6	14. 5	A7	B8	Dragon
9. 4	1. 3	J5	K8	Porcupine	21. 6	15. 5	A7	C9	Badger
10. 4	2. 3	J5	A9	Wolf	22. 6	16. 5	A7	D10	Hare
11. 4	3. 3	J5	B10	Dog	23. 6	17. 5	A7	E11	Fox
12. 4	4. 3	J5	C11	Pheasant	24. 6	18. 5	A7	F12	Tiger
13. 4	5. 3	J5	D12	Cock	25. 6	19. 5	A7	G1	Leopard
14. 4	6. 3	J5	E1	Crow	26. 6	20. 5	A7	H2	Griffon
15. 4	7. 3	J5	F2	Monkey	27. 6	21. 5	A7	J3	Ox
16. 4	8. 3	J5	G3	Gibbon	28. 6	22. 5	A7	K4	Bat
17. 4	9. 3	J5	H4	Tapir	29. 6	23. 5	A7	A5	Rat
18. 4	10. 3	J5	J5	Sheep	30. 6	24. .5	A7	B6	Swallow
19. 4	11. 3	J5	K6	Deer	1. 7	25. 5	A7	C7	Pig
20. 4	12. 3	J5	A7	Horse	2. 7	26. 5	A7	D8	Porcupine
21. 4	13. 3	J5	B8	Stag	3. 7	27. 5	A7	E9	Wolf
22. 4	14. 3	J5	C9	Serpent	4. 7	28. 5	A7	F10	Dog
23. 4	15. 3	J5	D10	Earthworm	5. 7	29. 5	A7	G11	Pheasant
24. 4	16. 3	J5	E11	Crocodile	6. 7	30. 5	A7	H12	Cock
25. 4	17. 3	J5	F12	Dragon	7. 7	1. 6	B8	J1	Crow
26. 4	18. 3	J5	G1	Badger	8. 7	2. 6	B8	K2	Monkey
27. 4	19. 3	J5	H2	Hare	9. 7	3. 6	B8	A3	Gibbon
28. 4	20. 3	J5	J3	Fox	10. 7	4. 6	B8	B4	Tapir
29. 4	21. 3	J5	K4	Tiger	11. 7	5. 6	B8	C5	Sheep
30. 4	22. 3	J5	A5	Leopard	12. 7	6. 6	B8	D6	Deer
1. 5	23. 3	J5	B6	Griffon	13. 7	7. 6	B8	E7	Horse
2. 5	24. 3	J5	C7	Ox	14. 7	8. 6	B8	F8	Stag
3. 5	25. 3	J5	D8	Bat	15. 7	9. 6	B8	G9	Serpent
4. 5	26. 3	J5	E9	Rat	16. 7	10. 6	B8	H10	Earthworm
5. 5	27. 3	J5	F10	Swallow	17. 7	11. 6	B8	J11	Crocodile
6. 5	28. 3	J5	G11	Pig	18. 7	12. 6	B8	K12	Dragon
7. 5	29. 3	J5	H12	Porcupine	19. 7	13. 6	B8	A1	Badger
8. 5	30. 3	J5	J1	Wolf	20. 7	14. 6	B8	B2	Hare
9. 5	1. 4	K6	K2	Dog	21. 7	15. 6	B8	C3	Fox
10. 5	2. 4	K6	A3	Pheasant	22. 7	16. 6	B8	D4	Tiger
11. 5	3. 4	K6	B4	Cock	23. 7	17. 6	B8	E5	Leopard
12. 5	4. 4	K6	C5	Crow	24. 7	18. 6	B8	F6	Griffon
13. 5	5. 4	K6	D6	Monkey	25. 7	19. 6	B8	G7	Ox
14. 5	6. 4	K6	E7	Gibbon	26. 7	20. 6	B8	H8	Bat
15. 5	7. 4	K6	F8	Tapir	27. 7	21. 6	B8	J9	Rat
16. 5	8. 4	K6	G9	Sheep	28. 7	22. 6	B8	K10	Swallow
17. 5	9. 4	K6	H10	Deer	29. 7	23. 6	B8	A11	Pig
18. 5	10. 4	K6	J11	Horse	30. 7	24. 6	B8	B12	Porcupine
19. 5	11. 4	K6	K12	Stag	31. 7	25. 6	B8	C1	Wolf
20. 5	12. 4	K6	A1	Serpent	1. 8	26. 6	B8	D2	Dog
21. 5	13. 4	K6	B2	Earthworm	2. 8	27. 6	B8	E3	Pheasant
22. 5	14. 4	K6	C3	Crocodile	3. 8	28. 6	B8	F4	Cock
23. 5	15. 4	K6	D4	Dragon	4. 8	29. 6	B8	G5	Crow
24. 5	16. 4	K6	E5	Badger	5. 8	30. 6	B8	H6	Monkey
25. 5	17. 4	K6	F6	Hare	6. 8	1. 7	C9	J7	Gibbon
26. 5	18. 4	K6	G7	Fox	7. 8	2. 7	C9	K8	Tapir

Solar date	Lunar date	Month HS/EB	Day HS/EB	Constellation	Solar date	Lunar date	Month HS/EB	Day HS/EB	Constellation
8. 8	3. 7	C9	A9	Sheep	20.10	17. 9	E11	D10	Swallow
9. 8	4. 7	C9	B10	Deer	21.10	18. 9	E11	E11	Pig
10. 8	5. 7	C9	C11	Horse	22.10	19. 9	E11	F12	Porcupine
11. 8	6. 7	C9	D12	Stag	23.10	20. 9	E11	G1	Wolf
12. 8	7. 7	C9	E1	Serpent	24.10	21. 9	E11	H2	Dog
13. 8	8. 7	C9	F2	Earthworm	25.10	22. 9	E11	J3	Pheasant
14. 8	9. 7	C9	G3	Crocodile	26.10	23. 9	E11	K4	Cock
15. 8	10. 7	C9	H4	Dragon	27.10	24. 9	E11	A5	Crow
16. 8	11. 7	C9	J5	Badger	28.10	25. 9	E11	B6	Monkey
17. 8	12. 7	C9	K6	Hare	29.10	26. 9	E11	C7	Gibbon
18. 8	13. 7	C9	A7	Fox	30.10	27. 9	E11	D8	Tapir
19. 8	14. 7	C9	B8	Tiger	31.10	28. 9	E11	E9	Sheep
20. 8	15. 7	C9	C9	Leopard	1.11	29. 9	E11	F10	Deer
21. 8	16. 7	C9	D10	Griffon	2.11	1.10	F12	G11	Horse
22. 8	17. 7	C9	E11	Ox	3.11	2.10	F12	H12	Stag
23. 8	18. 7	C9	F12	Bat	4.11	3.10	F12	J1	Serpent
24. 8	19. 7	C9	G1	Rat	5.11	4.10	F12	K2	Earthworm
25. 8	20. 7	C9	H2	Swallow	6.11	5.10	F12	A3	Crocodile
26. 8	21. 7	C9	J3	Pig	7.11	6.10	F12	B4	Dragon
27. 8	22. 7	C9	K4	Porcupine	8.11	7.10	F12	C5	Badger
28. 8	23. 7	C9	A5	Wolf	9.11	8.10	F12	D6	Hare
29. 8	24. 7	C9	B6	Dog	10.11	9.10	F12	E7	Fox
30. 8	25. 7	C9	C7	Pheasant	11.11	10.10	F12	F8	Tiger
31. 8	26. 7	C9	D8	Cock	12.11	11.10	F12	G9	Leopard
1. 9	27. 7	C9	E9	Crow	13.11	12.10	F12	H10	Griffon
2. 9	28. 7	C9	F10	Monkey	14.11	13.10	F12	J11	Ox
3. 9	29. 7	C9	G11	Gibbon	15.11	14.10	F12	K12	Bat
4. 9	1. 8	D10	H12	Tapir	16.11	15.10	F12	A1	Rat
5. 9	2. 8	D10	J1	Sheep	17.11	16.10	F12	B2	Swallow
6. 9	3. 8	D10	K2	Deer	18.11	17.10	F12	C3	Pig
7. 9	4. 8	D10	A3	Horse	19.11	18.10	F12	D4	Porcupine
8. 9	5. 8	D10	B4	Stag	20.11	19.10	F12	E5	Wolf
9. 9	6. 8	D10	C5	Serpent	21.11	20.10	F12	F6	Dog
10. 9	7. 8	D10	D6	Earthworm	22.11	21.10	F12	G7	Pheasant
11. 9	8. 8	D10	E7	Crocodile	23.11	22.10	F12	H8	Cock
12. 9	9. 8	D10	F8	Dragon	24.11	23.10	F12	J9	Crow
13. 9	10. 8	D10	G9	Badger	25.11	24.10	F12	K10	Monkey
14. 9	11. 8	D10	H10	Hare	26.11	25.10	F12	A11	Gibbon
15. 9	12. 8	D10	J11	Fox	27.11	26.10	F12	B12	Tapir
16. 9	13. 8	D10	K12	Tiger	28.11	27.10	F12	C1	Sheep
17. 9	14. 8	D10	A1	Leopard	29.11	28.10	F12	D2	Deer
18. 9	15. 8	D10	B2	Griffon	30.11	29.10	F12	E3	Horse
19. 9	16. 8	D10	C3	Ox	1.12	30.10	F12	F4	Stag
20. 9	17. 8	D10	D4	Bat	2.12	1.11	G1	G5	Serpent
21. 9	18. 8	D10	E5	Rat	3.12	2.11	G1	H6	Earthworm
22. 9	19. 8	D10	F6	Swallow	4.12	3.11	G1	J7	Crocodile
23. 9	20. 8	D10	G7	Pig	5.12	4.11	G1	K8	Dragon
24. 9	21. 8	D10	H8	Porcupine	6.12	5.11	G1	A9	Badger
25. 9	22. 8	D10	J9	Wolf	7.12	6.11	G1	B10	Hare
26. 9	23. 8	D10	K10	Dog	8.12	7.11	G1	C11	Fox
27. 9	24. 8	D10	A11	Pheasant	9.12	8.11	G1	D12	Tiger
28. 9	25. 8	D10	B12	Cock	10.12	9.11	G1	E1	Leopard
29. 9	26. 8	D10	C1	Crow	11.12	10.11	G1	F2	Griffon
30. 9	27. 8	D10	D2	Monkey	12.12	11.11	G1	G3	Ox
1.10	28. 8	D10	E3	Gibbon	13.12	12.11	G1	H4	Bat
2.10	29. 8	D10	F4	Tapir	14.12	13.11	G1	J5	Rat
3.10	30. 8	D10	G5	Sheep	15.12	14.11	G1	K6	Swallow
4.10	1. 9	E11	H6	Deer	16.12	15.11	G1	A7	Pig
5.10	2. 9	E11	J7	Horse	17.12	16.11	G1	B8	Porcupine
6.10	3. 9	E11	K8	Stag	18.12	17.11	G1	C9	Wolf
7.10	4. 9	E11	A9	Serpent	19.12	18.11	G1	D10	Dog
8.10	5. 9	E11	B10	Earthworm	20.12	19.11	G1	E11	Pheasant
9.10	6. 9	E11	C11	Crocodile	21.12	20.11	G1	F12	Cock
10.10	7. 9	E11	D12	Dragon	22.12	21.11	G1	G1	Crow
11.10	8. 9	E11	E1	Badger	23.12	22.11	G1	H2	Monkey
12.10	9. 9	E11	F2	Hare	24.12	23.11	G1	J3	Gibbon
13.10	10. 9	E11	G3	Fox	25.12	24.11	G1	K4	Tapir
14.10	11. 9	E11	H4	Tiger	26.12	25.11	G1	A5	Sheep
15.10	12. 9	E11	J5	Leopard	27.12	26.11	G1	B6	Deer
16.10	13. 9	E11	K6	Griffon	28.12	27.11	G1	C7	Horse
17.10	14. 9	E11	A7	Ox	29.12	28.11	G1	D8	Stag
18.10	15. 9	E11	B8	Bat	30.12	29.11	G1	E9	Serpent
19.10	16. 9	E11	C9	Rat	31.12	1.12	H2	F10	Earthworm

Solar date	Lunar date	Month HS/EB	Day HS/EB	Constellation	Solar date	Lunar date	Month HS/EB	Day HS/EB	Constellation
1987					14. 1	15.12	H2	K12	Porcupine
					15. 1	16.12	H2	A1	Wolf
1. 1	2.12	H2	G11	Crocodile	16. 1	17.12	H2	B2	Dog
2. 1	3.12	H2	H12	Dragon	17. 1	18.12	H2	C3	Pheasant
3. 1	4.12	H2	J1	Badger	18. 1	19.12	H2	D4	Cock
4. 1	5.12	H2	K2	Hare	19. 1	20.12	H2	E5	Crow
5. 1	6.12	H2	A3	Fox	20. 1	21.12	H2	F6	Monkey
6. 1	7.12	H2	B4	Tiger	21. 1	22.12	H2	G7	Gibbon
7. 1	8.12	H2	C5	Leopard	22. 1	23.12	H2	H8	Tapir
8. 1	9.12	H2	D6	Griffon	23. 1	24.12	H2	J9	Sheep
9. 1	10.12	H2	E7	Ox	24. 1	25.12	H2	K10	Deer
10. 1	11.12	H2	F8	Bat	25. 1	26.12	H2	A11	Horse
11. 1	12.12	H2	G9	Rat	26. 1	27.12	H2	B12	Stag
12. 1	13.12	H2	H10	Swallow	27. 1	28.12	H2	C1	Serpent
13. 1	14.12	H2	J11	Pig	28. 1	29.12	H2	D2	Earthworm

TING MAO YEAR

Solar date	Lunar date	Month HS/EB	Day HS/EB	Constellation	Solar date	Lunar date	Month HS/EB	Day HS/EB	Constellation
29. 1	1. 1	J3	E3	Crocodile	23. 3	24. 2	K4	H8	Stag
30. 1	2. 1	J3	F4	Dragon	24. 3	25. 2	K4	J9	Serpent
31. 1	3. 1	J3	G5	Badger	25. 3	26. 2	K4	K10	Earthworm
1. 2	4. 1	J3	H6	Hare	26. 3	27. 2	K4	A11	Crocodile
2. 2	5. 1	J3	J7	Fox	27. 3	28. 2	K4	B12	Dragon
3. 2	6. 1	J3	K8	Tiger	28. 3	29. 2	K4	C1	Badger
4. 2	7. 1	J3	A9	Leopard	29. 3	1. 3	A5	D2	Hare
5. 2	8. 1	J3	B10	Griffon	30. 3	2. 3	A5	E3	Fox
6. 2	9. 1	J3	C11	Ox	31. 3	3. 3	A5	F4	Tiger
7. 2	10. 1	J3	D12	Bat	1. 4	4. 3	A5	G5	Leopard
8. 2	11. 1	J3	E1	Rat	2. 4	5. 3	A5	H6	Griffon
9. 2	12. 1	J3	F2	Swallow	3. 4	6. 3	A5	J7	Ox
10. 2	13. 1	J3	G3	Pig	4. 4	7. 3	A5	K8	Bat
11. 2	14. 1	J3	H4	Porcupine	5. 4	8. 3	A5	A9	Rat
12. 2	15. 1	J3	J5	Wolf	6. 4	9. 3	A5	B10	Swallow
13. 2	16. 1	J3	K6	Dog	7. 4	10. 3	A5	C11	Pig
14. 2	17. 1	J3	A7	Pheasant	8. 4	11. 3	A5	D12	Porcupine
15. 2	18. 1	J3	B8	Cock	9. 4	12. 3	A5	E1	Wolf
16. 2	19. 1	J3	C9	Crow	10. 4	13. 3	A5	F2	Dog
17. 2	20. 1	J3	D10	Monkey	11. 4	14. 3	A5	G3	Pheasant
18. 2	21. 1	J3	E11	Gibbon	12. 4	15. 3	A5	H4	Cock
19. 2	22. 1	J3	F12	Tapir	13. 4	16. 3	A5	J5	Crow
20. 2	23. 1	J3	G1	Sheep	14. 4	17. 3	A5	K6	Monkey
21. 2	24. 1	J3	H2	Deer	15. 4	18. 3	A5	A7	Gibbon
22. 2	25. 1	J3	J3	Horse	16. 4	19. 3	A5	B8	Tapir
23. 2	26. 1	J3	K4	Stag	17. 4	20. 3	A5	C9	Sheep
24. 2	27. 1	J3	A5	Serpent	18. 4	21. 3	A5	D10	Deer
25. 2	28. 1	J3	B6	Earthworm	19. 4	22. 3	A5	E11	Horse
26. 2	29. 1	J3	C7	Crocodile	20. 4	23. 3	A5	F12	Stag
27. 2	30. 1	J3	D8	Dragon	21. 4	24. 3	A5	G1	Serpent
28. 2	1. 2	K4	E9	Badger	22. 4	25. 3	A5	H2	Earthworm
1. 3	2. 2	K4	F10	Hare	23. 4	26. 3	A5	J3	Crocodile
2. 3	3. 2	K4	G11	Fox	24. 4	27. 3	A5	K4	Dragon
3. 3	4. 2	K4	H12	Tiger	25. 4	28. 3	A5	A5	Badger
4. 3	5. 2	K4	J1	Leopard	26. 4	29. 3	A5	B6	Hare
5. 3	6. 2	K4	K2	Griffon	27. 4	30. 3	A5	C7	Fox
6. 3	7. 2	K4	A3	Ox	28. 4	1. 4	B6	D8	Tiger
7. 3	8. 2	K4	B4	Bat	29. 4	2. 4	B6	E9	Leopard
8. 3	9. 2	K4	C5	Rat	30. 4	3. 4	B6	F10	Griffon
9. 3	10. 2	K4	D6	Swallow	1. 5	4. 4	B6	G11	Ox
10. 3	11. 2	K4	E7	Pig	2. 5	5. 4	B6	H12	Bat
11. 3	12. 2	K4	F8	Porcupine	3. 5	6. 4	B6	J1	Rat
12. 3	13. 2	K4	G9	Wolf	4. 5	7. 4	B6	K2	Swallow
13. 3	14. 2	K4	H10	Dog	5. 5	8. 4	B6	A3	Pig
14. 3	15. 2	K4	J11	Pheasant	6. 5	9. 4	B6	B4	Porcupine
15. 3	16. 2	K4	K12	Cock	7. 5	10. 4	B6	C5	Wolf
16. 3	17. 2	K4	A1	Crow	8. 5	11. 4	B6	D6	Dog
17. 3	18. 2	K4	B2	Monkey	9. 5	12. 4	B6	E7	Pheasant
18. 3	19. 2	K4	C3	Gibbon	10. 5	13. 4	B6	F8	Cock
19. 3	20. 2	K4	D4	Tapir	11. 5	14. 4	B6	G9	Crow
20. 3	21. 2	K4	E5	Sheep	12. 5	15. 4	B6	H10	Monkey
21. 3	22. 2	K4	F6	Deer	13. 5	16. 4	B6	J11	Gibbon
22. 3	23. 2	K4	G7	Horse	14. 5	17. 4	B6	K12	Tapir

Solar date	Lunar date	Month HS/EB	Day HS/EB	Constellation	Solar date	Lunar date	Month HS/EB	Day HS/EB	Constellation
15. 5	18. 4	B6	A1	Sheep	27. 7	2. 6	D8	D2	Swallow
16. 5	19. 4	B6	B2	Deer	28. 7	3. 6	D8	E3	Pig
17. 5	20. 4	B6	C3	Horse	29. 7	4. 6	D8	F4	Porcupine
18. 5	21. 4	B6	D4	Stag	30. 7	5. 6	D8	G5	Wolf
19. 5	22. 4	B6	E5	Serpent	31. 7	6. 6	D8	H6	Dog
20. 5	23. 4	B6	F6	Earthworm	1. 8	7. 6	D8	J7	Pheasant
21. 5	24. 4	B6	G7	Crocodile	2. 8	8. 6	D8	K8	Cock
22. 5	25. 4	B6	H8	Dragon	3. 8	9. 6	D8	A9	Crow
23. 5	26. 4	B6	J9	Badger	4. 8	10. 6	D8	B10	Monkey
24. 5	27. 4	B6	K10	Hare	5. 8	11. 6	D8	C11	Gibbon
25. 5	28. 4	B6	A11	Fox	6. 8	12. 6	D8	D12	Tapir
26. 5	29. 4	B6	B12	Tiger	7. 8	13. 6	D8	E1	Sheep
27. 5	1. 5	C7	C1	Leopard	8. 8	14. 6	D8	F2	Deer
28. 5	2. 5	C7	D2	Griffon	9. 8	15. 6	D8	G3	Horse
29. 5	3. 5	C7	E3	Ox	10. 8	16. 6	D8	H4	Stag
30. 5	4. 5	C7	F4	Bat	11. 8	17. 6	D8	J5	Serpent
31. 5	5. 5	C7	G5	Rat	12. 8	18. 6	D8	K6	Earthworm
1. 6	6. 5	C7	H6	Swallow	13. 8	19. 6	D8	A7	Crocodile
2. 6	7. 5	C7	J7	Pig	14. 8	20. 6	D8	B8	Dragon
3. 6	8. 5	C7	K8	Porcupine	15. 8	21. 6	D8	C9	Badger
4. 6	9. 5	C7	A9	Wolf	16. 8	22. 6	D8	D10	Hare
5. 6	10. 5	C7	B10	Dog	17. 8	23. 6	D8	E11	Fox
6. 6	11. 5	C7	C11	Pheasant	18. 8	24. 6	D8	F12	Tiger
7. 6	12. 5	C7	D12	Cock	19. 8	25. 6	D8	G1	Leopard
8. 6	13. 5	C7	E1	Crow	20. 8	26. 6	D8	H2	Griffon
9. 6	14. 5	C7	F2	Monkey	21. 8	27. 6	D8	J3	Ox
10. 6	15. 5	C7	G3	Gibbon	22. 8	28. 6	D8	K4	Bat
11. 6	16. 5	C7	H4	Tapir	23. 8	29. 6	D8	A5	Rat
12. 6	17. 5	C7	J5	Sheep	24. 8	1. 7	E9	B6	Swallow
13. 6	18. 5	C7	K6	Deer	25. 8	2. 7	E9	C7	Pig
14. 6	19. 5	C7	A7	Horse	26. 8	3. 7	E9	D8	Porcupine
15. 6	20. 5	C7	B8	Stag	27. 8	4. 7	E9	E9	Wolf
16. 6	21. 5	C7	C9	Serpent	28. 8	5. 7	E9	F10	Dog
17. 6	22. 5	C7	D10	Earthworm	29. 8	6. 7	E9	G11	Pheasant
18. 6	23. 5	C7	E11	Crocodile	30. 8	7. 7	E9	H12	Cock
19. 6	24. 5	C7	F12	Dragon	31. 8	8. 7	E9	J1	Crow
20. 6	25. 5	C7	G1	Badger	1. 9	9. 7	E9	K2	Monkey
21. 6	26. 5	C7	H2	Hare	2. 9	10. 7	E9	A3	Gibbon
22. 6	27. 5	C7	J3	Fox	3. 9	11. 7	E9	B4	Tapir
23. 6	28. 5	C7	K4	Tiger	4. 9	12. 7	E9	C5	Sheep
24. 6	29. 5	C7	A5	Leopard	5. 9	13. 7	E9	D6	Deer
25. 6	30. 5	C7	B6	Griffon	6. 9	14. 7	E9	E7	Horse
26. 6	1. 6	D8	C7	Ox	7. 9	15. 7	E9	F8	Stag
27. 6	2. 6	D8	D8	Bat	8. 9	16. 7	E9	G9	Serpent
28. 6	3. 6	D8	E9	Rat	9. 9	17. 7	E9	H10	Earthworm
29. 6	4. 6	D8	F10	Swallow	10. 9	18. 7	E9	J11	Crocodile
30. 6	5. 6	D8	G11	Pig	11. 9	19. 7	E9	K12	Dragon
1. 7	6. 6	D8	H12	Porcupine	12. 9	20. 7	E9	A1	Badger
2. 7	7. 6	D8	J1	Wolf	13. 9	21. 7	E9	B2	Hare
3. 7	8. 6	D8	K2	Dog	14. 9	22. 7	E9	C3	Fox
4. 7	9. 6	D8	A3	Pheasant	15. 9	23. 7	E9	D4	Tiger
5. 7	10. 6	D8	B4	Cock	16. 9	24. 7	E9	E5	Leopard
6. 7	11. 6	D8	C5	Crow	17. 9	25. 7	E9	F6	Griffon
7. 7	12. 6	D8	D6	Monkey	18. 9	26. 7	E9	G7	Ox
8. 7	13. 6	D8	E7	Gibbon	19. 9	27. 7	E9	H8	Bat
9. 7	14. 6	D8	F8	Tapir	20. 9	28. 7	E9	J9	Rat
10. 7	15. 6	D8	G9	Sheep	21. 9	29. 7	E9	K10	Swallow
11. 7	16. 6	D8	H10	Deer	22. 9	30. 7	E9	A11	Pig
12. 7	17. 6	D8	J11	Horse	23. 9	1. 8	F10	B12	Porcupine
13. 7	18. 6	D8	K12	Stag	24. 9	2. 8	F10	C1	Wolf
14. 7	19. 6	D8	A1	Serpent	25. 9	3. 8	F10	D2	Dog
15. 7	20. 6	D8	B2	Earthworm	26. 9	4. 8	F10	E3	Pheasant
16. 7	21. 6	D8	C3	Crocodile	27. 9	5. 8	F10	F4	Cock
17. 7	22. 6	D8	D4	Dragon	28. 9	6. 8	F10	G5	Crow
18. 7	23. 6	D8	E5	Badger	29. 9	7. 8	F10	H6	Monkey
19. 7	24. 6	D8	F6	Hare	30. 9	8. 8	F10	J7	Gibbon
20. 7	25. 6	D8	G7	Fox	1.10	9. 8	F10	K8	Tapir
21. 7	26. 6	D8	H8	Tiger	2.10	10. 8	F10	A9	Sheep
22. 7	27. 6	D8	J9	Leopard	3.10	11. 8	F10	B10	Deer
23. 7	28. 6	D8	K10	Griffon	4.10	12. 8	F10	C11	Horse
24. 7	29. 6	D8	A11	Ox	5.10	13. 8	F10	D12	Stag
25. 7	30. 6	D8	B12	Bat	6.10	14. 8	F10	E1	Serpent
26. 7	1. 6	D8	C1	Rat	7.10	15. 8	F10	F2	Earthworm

Solar date	Lunar date	Month HS/EB	Day HS/EB	Constellation	Solar date	Lunar date	Month HS/EB	Day HS/EB	Constellation
8.10	16. 8	F10	G3	Crocodile	14.12	24.10	H12	D10	Swallow
9.10	17. 8	F10	H4	Dragon	15.12	25.10	H12	E11	Pig
10.10	18. 8	F10	J5	Badger	16.12	26.10	H12	F12	Porcupine
11.10	19. 8	F10	K6	Hare	17.12	27.10	H12	G1	Wolf
12.10	20. 8	F10	A7	Fox	18.12	28.10	H12	H2	Dog
13.10	21. 8	F10	B8	Tiger	19.12	29.10	H12	J3	Pheasant
14.10	22. 8	F10	C9	Leopard	20.12	30.10	H12	K4	Cock
15.10	23. 8	F10	D10	Griffon	21.12	1.11	J1	A5	Crow
16.10	24. 8	F10	E11	Ox	22.12	2.11	J1	B6	Monkey
17.10	25. 8	F10	F12	Bat	23.12	3.11	J1	C7	Gibbon
18.10	26. 8	F10	G1	Rat	24.12	4.11	J1	D8	Tapir
19.10	27. 8	F10	H2	Swallow	25.12	5.11	J1	E9	Sheep
20.10	28. 8	F10	J3	Pig	26.12	6.11	J1	F10	Deer
21.10	29. 8	F10	K4	Porcupine	27.12	7.11	J1	G11	Horse
22.10	30. 8	F10	A5	Wolf	28.12	8.11	J1	H12	Stag
23.10	1. 9	G11	B6	Dog	29.12	9.11	J1	J1	Serpent
24.10	2. 9	G11	C7	Pheasant	30.12	10.11	J1	K2	Earthworm
25.10	3. 9	G11	D8	Cock	31.12	11.11	J1	A3	Crocodile
26.10	4. 9	G11	E9	Crow					
27.10	5. 9	G11	F10	Monkey	**1988**				
28.10	6. 9	G11	G11	Gibbon	1. 1	12.11	J1	B4	Dragon
29.10	7. 9	G11	H12	Tapir	2. 1	13.11	J1	C5	Badger
30.10	8. 9	G11	J1	Sheep	3. 1	14.11	J1	D6	Hare
31.10	9. 9	G11	K2	Deer	4. 1	15.11	J1	E7	Fox
1.11	10. 9	G11	A3	Horse	5. 1	16.11	J1	F8	Tiger
2.11	11. 9	G11	B4	Stag	6. 1	17.11	J1	G9	Leopard
3.11	12. 9	G11	C5	Serpent	7. 1	18.11	J1	H10	Griffon
4.11	13. 9	G11	D6	Earthworm	8. 1	19.11	J1	J11	Ox
5.11	14. 9	G11	E7	Crocodile	9. 1	20.11	J1	K12	Bat
6.11	15. 9	G11	F8	Dragon	10. 1	21.11	J1	A1	Rat
7.11	16. 9	G11	G9	Badger	11. 1	22.11	J1	B2	Swallow
8.11	17. 9	G11	H10	Hare	12. 1	23.11	J1	C3	Pig
9.11	18. 9	G11	J11	Fox	13. 1	24.11	J1	D4	Porcupine
10.11	19. 9	G11	K12	Tiger	14. 1	25.11	J1	E5	Wolf
11.11	20. 9	G11	A1	Leopard	15. 1	26.11	J1	F6	Dog
12.11	21. 9	G11	B2	Griffon	16. 1	27.11	J1	G7	Pheasant
13.11	22. 9	G11	C3	Ox	17. 1	28.11	J1	H8	Cock
14.11	23. 9	G11	D4	Bat	18. 1	29.11	J1	J9	Crow
15.11	24. 9	G11	E5	Rat	19. 1	1.12	K2	K10	Monkey
16.11	25. 9	G11	F6	Swallow	20. 1	2.12	K2	A11	Gibbon
17.11	26. 9	G11	G7	Pig	21. 1	3.12	K2	B12	Tapir
18.11	27. 9	G11	H8	Porcupine	22. 1	4.12	K2	C1	Sheep
19.11	28. 9	G11	J9	Wolf	23. 1	5.12	K2	D2	Deer
20.11	29. 9	G11	K10	Dog	24. 1	6.12	K2	E3	Horse
21.11	1.10	H12	A11	Pheasant	25. 1	7.12	K2	F4	Stag
22.11	2.10	H12	B12	Cock	26. 1	8.12	K2	G5	Serpent
23.11	3.10	H12	C1	Crow	27. 1	9.12	K2	H6	Earthworm
24.11	4.10	H12	D2	Monkey	28. 1	10.12	K2	J7	Crocodile
25.11	5.10	H12	E3	Gibbon	29. 1	11.12	K2	K8	Dragon
26.11	6.10	H12	F4	Tapir	30. 1	12.12	K2	A9	Badger
27.11	7.10	H12	G5	Sheep	31. 1	13.12	K2	B10	Hare
28.11	8.10	H12	H6	Deer	1. 2	14.12	K2	C11	Fox
29.11	9.10	H12	J7	Horse	2. 2	15.12	K2	D12	Tiger
30.11	10.10	H12	K8	Stag	3. 2	16.12	K2	E.1	Leopard
1.12	11.10	H12	A9	Serpent	4. 2	17.12	K2	F2	Griffon
2.12	12.10	H12	B10	Earthworm	5. 2	18.12	K2	G3	Ox
3.12	13.10	H12	C11	Crocodile	6. 2	19.12	K2	H4	Bat
4.12	14.10	H12	D12	Dragon	7. 2	20.12	K2	J5	Rat
5.12	15.10	H12	E1	Badger	8. 2	21.12	K2	K6	Swallow
6.12	16.10	H12	F2	Hare	9. 2	22.12	K2	A7	Pig
7.12	17.10	H12	G3	Fox	10. 2	23.12	K2	B8	Porcupine
8.12	18.10	H12	H4	Tiger	11. 2	24.12	K2	C9	Wolf
9.12	19.10	H12	J5	Leopard	12. 2	25.12	K2	D10	Dog
10.12	20.10	H12	K6	Griffon	13. 2	26.12	K2	E11	Pheasant
11.12	21.10	H12	A7	Ox	14. 2	27.12	K2	F12	Cock
12.12	22.10	H12	B8	Bat	15. 2	28.12	K2	G1	Crow
13.12	23.10	H12	C9	Rat	16. 2	29.12	K2	H2	Monkey

MOU CH'EN YEAR

Solar date	Lunar date	Month HS/EB	Day HS/EB	Constellation	Solar date	Lunar date	Month HS/EB	Day HS/EB	Constellation
17. 2	1. 1	A3	J3	Gibbon	28. 4	13. 3	C5	K2	Griffon
18. 2	2. 1	A3	K4	Tapir	29. 4	14. 3	C5	A3	Ox
19. 2	3. 1	A3	A5	Sheep	30. 4	15. 3	C5	B4	Bat
20. 2	4. 1	A3	B6	Deer	1. 5	16. 3	C5	C5	Rat
21. 2	5. 1	A3	C7	Horse	2. 5	17. 3	C5	D6	Swallow
22. 2	6. 1	A3	D8	Stag	3. 5	18. 3	C5	E7	Pig
23. 2	7. 1	A3	E9	Serpent	4. 5	19. 3	C5	F8	Porcupine
24. 2	8. 1	A3	F10	Earthworm	5. 5	20. 3	C5	G9	Wolf
25. 2	9. 1	A3	G11	Crocodile	6. 5	21. 3	C5	H10	Dog
26. 2	10. 1	A3	H12	Dragon	7. 5	22. 3	C5	J11	Pheasant
27. 2	11. 1	A3	J1	Badger	8. 5	23. 3	C5	K12	Cock
28. 2	12. 1	A3	K2	Hare	9. 5	24. 3	C5	A1	Crow
29. 2	13. 1	A3	A3	Fox	10. 5	25. 3	C5	B2	Monkey
1. 3	14. 1	A3	B4	Tiger	11. 5	26. 3	C5	C3	Gibbon
2. 3	15. 1	A3	C5	Leopard	12. 5	27. 3	C5	D4	Tapir
3. 3	16. 1	A3	D6	Griffon	13. 5	28. 3	C5	E5	Sheep
4. 3	17. 1	A3	E7	Ox	14. 5	29. 3	C5	F6	Deer
5. 3	18. 1	A3	F8	Bat	15. 5	30. 3	C5	G7	Horse
6. 3	19. 1	A3	G9	Rat	16. 5	1. 4	D6	H8	Stag
7. 3	20. 1	A3	H10	Swallow	17. 5	2. 4	D6	J9	Serpent
8. 3	21. 1	A3	J11	Pig	18. 5	3. 4	D6	K10	Earthworm
9. 3	22. 1	A3	K12	Porcupine	19. 5	4. 4	D6	A11	Crocodile
10. 3	23. 1	A3	A1	Wolf	20. 5	5. 4	D6	B12	Dragon
11. 3	24. 1	A3	B2	Dog	21. 5	6. 4	D6	C1	Badger
12. 3	25. 1	A3	C3	Pheasant	22. 5	7. 4	D6	D2	Hare
13. 3	26. 1	A3	D4	Cock	23. 5	8. 4	D6	E3	Fox
14. 3	27. 1	A3	E5	Crow	24. 5	9. 4	D6	F4	Tiger
15. 3	28. 1	A3	F6	Monkey	25. 5	10. 4	D6	G5	Leopard
16. 3	29. 1	A3	G7	Gibbon	26. 5	11. 4	D6	H6	Griffon
17. 3	30. 1	A3	H8	Tapir	27. 5	12. 4	D6	J7	Ox
18. 3	1. 2	B4	J9	Sheep	28. 5	13. 4	D6	K8	Bat
19. 3	2. 2	B4	K10	Deer	29. 5	14. 4	D6	A9	Rat
20. 3	3. 2	B4	A11	Horse	30. 5	15. 4	D6	B10	Swallow
21. 3	4. 2	B4	B12	Stag	31. 5	16. 4	D6	C11	Pig
22. 3	5. 2	B4	C1	Serpent	1. 6	17. 4	D6	D12	Porcupine
23. 3	6. 2	B4	D2	Earthworm	2. 6	18. 4	D6	E1	Wolf
24. 3	7. 2	B4	E3	Crocodile	3. 6	19. 4	D6	F2	Dog
25. 3	8. 2	B4	F4	Dragon	4. 6	20. 4	D6	G3	Pheasant
26. 3	9. 2	B4	G5	Badger	5. 6	21. 4	D6	H4	Cock
27. 3	10. 2	B4	H6	Hare	6. 6	22. 4	D6	J5	Crow
28. 3	11. 2	B4	J7	Fox	7. 6	23. 4	D6	K6	Monkey
29. 3	12. 2	B4	K8	Tiger	8. 6	24. 4	D6	A7	Gibbon
30. 3	13. 2	B4	A9	Leopard	9. 6	25. 4	D6	B8	Tapir
31. 3	14. 2	B4	B10	Griffon	10. 6	26. 4	D6	C9	Sheep
1. 4	15. 2	B4	C11	Ox	11. 6	27. 4	D6	D10	Deer
2. 4	16. 2	B4	D12	Bat	12. 6	28. 4	D6	E11	Horse
3. 4	17. 2	B4	E1	Rat	13. 6	29. 4	D6	F12	Stag
4. 4	18. 2	B4	F2	Swallow	14. 6	1. 5	E7	G1	Serpent
5. 4	19. 2	B4	G3	Pig	15. 6	2. 5	E7	H2	Earthworm
6. 4	20. 2	B4	H4	Porcupine	16. 6	3. 5	E7	J3	Crocodile
7. 4	21. 2	B4	J5	Wolf	17. 6	4. 5	E7	K4	Dragon
8. 4	22. 2	B4	K6	Dog	18. 6	5. 5	E7	A5	Badger
9. 4	23. 2	B4	A7	Pheasant	19. 6	6. 5	E7	B6	Hare
10. 4	24. 2	B4	B8	Cock	20. 6	7. 5	E7	C7	Fox
11. 4	25. 2	B4	C9	Crow	21. 6	8. 5	E7	D8	Tiger
12. 4	26. 2	B4	D10	Monkey	22. 6	9. 5	E7	E9	Leopard
13. 4	27. 2	B4	E11	Gibbon	23. 6	10. 5	E7	F10	Griffon
14. 4	28. 2	B4	F12	Tapir	24. 6	11. 5	E7	G11	Ox
15. 4	29. 2	B4	G1	Sheep	25. 6	12. 5	E7	H12	Bat
16. 4	1. 3	C5	H2	Deer	26. 6	13. 5	E7	J1	Rat
17. 4	2. 3	C5	J3	Horse	27. 6	14. 5	E7	K2	Swallow
18. 4	3. 3	C5	K4	Stag	28. 6	15. 5	E7	A3	Pig
19. 4	4. 3	C5	A5	Serpent	29. 6	16. 5	E7	B4	Porcupine
20. 4	5. 3	C5	B6	Earthworm	30. 6	17. 5	E7	C5	Wolf
21. 4	6. 3	C5	C7	Crocodile	1. 7	18. 5	E7	D6	Dog
22. 4	7. 3	C5	D8	Dragon	2. 7	19. 5	E7	E7	Pheasant
23. 4	8. 3	C5	E9	Badger	3. 7	20. 5	E7	F8	Cock
24. 4	9. 3	C5	F10	Hare	4. 7	21. 5	E7	G9	Crow
25. 4	10. 3	C5	G11	Fox	5. 7	22. 5	E7	H10	Monkey
26. 4	11. 3	C5	H12	Tiger	6. 7	23. 5	E7	J11	Gibbon
27. 4	12. 3	C5	J1	Leopard	7. 7	24. 5	E7	K12	Tapir

Solar date	Lunar date	Month HS/EB	Day HS/EB	Constellation	Solar date	Lunar date	Month HS/EB	Day HS/EB	Constellation
8. 7	25. 5	E7	A1	Sheep	19. 9	9. 8	H10	D2	Swallow
9. 7	26. 5	E7	B2	Deer	20. 9	10. 8	H10	E3	Pig
10. 7	27. 5	E7	C3	Horse	21. 9	11. 8	H10	F4	Porcupine
11. 7	28. 5	E7	D4	Stag	22. 9	12. 8	H10	G5	Wolf
12. 7	29. 5	E7	E5	Serpent	23. 9	13. 8	H10	H6	Dog
13. 7	30. 5	E7	F6	Earthworm	24. 9	14. 8	H10	J7	Pheasant
14. 7	1. 6	F8	G7	Crocodile	25. 9	15. 8	H10	K8	Cock
15. 7	2. 6	F8	H8	Dragon	26. 9	16. 8	H10	A9	Crow
16. 7	3. 6	F8	J9	Badger	27. 9	17. 8	H10	B10	Monkey
17. 7	4. 6	F8	K10	Hare	28. 9	18.18	H10	C11	Gibbon
18. 7	5. 6	F8	A11	Fox	29. 9	19. 8	H10	D12	Tapir
19. 7	6. 6	F8	B12	Tiger	30. 9	20. 8	H10	E1	Sheep
20. 7	7. 6	F8	C1	Leopard	1.10	21. 8	H10	F2	Deer
21. 7	8. 6	F8	D2	Griffon	2.10	22. 8	H10	G3	Horse
22. 7	9. 6	F8	E3	Ox	3.10	23. 8	H10	H4	Stag
23. 7	10. 6	F8	F4	Bat	4.10	24. 8	H10	J5	Serpent
24. 7	11. 6	F8	G5	Rat	5.10	25. 8	H10	K6	Earthworm
25. 7	12. 6	F8	H6	Swallow	6.10	26. 8	H10	A7	Crocodile
26. 7	13. 6	F8	J7	Pig	7.10	27. 8	H10	B8	Dragon
27. 7	14. 6	F8	K8	Porcupine	8.10	28. 8	H10	C9	Badger
28. 7	15. 6	F8	A9	Wolf	9.10	29. 8	H10	D10	Hare
29. 7	16. 6	F8	B10	Dog	10.10	30. 8	H10	E11	Fox
30. 7	17. 6	F8	C11	Pheasant	11.10	1. 9	J11	F12	Tiger
31. 7	18. 6	F8	D12	Cock	12.10	2. 9	J11	G1	Leopard
1. 8	19. 6	F8	E1	Crow	13.10	3. 9	J11	H2	Griffon
2. 8	20. 6	F8	F2	Monkey	14.10	4. 9	J11	J3	Ox
3. 8	21. 6	F8	G3	Gibbon	15.10	5. 9	J11	K4	Bat
4. 8	22. 6	F8	H4	Tapir	16.10	6. 9	J11	A5	Rat
5. 8	23. 6	F8	J5	Sheep	17.10	7. 9	J11	B6	Swallow
6. 8	24. 6	F8	K6	Deer	18.10	8. 9	J11	C7	Pig
7. 8	25. 6	F8	A7	Horse	19.10	9. 9	J11	D8	Porcupine
8. 8	26. 6	F8	B8	Stag	20.10	10. 9	J11	E9	Wolf
9. 8	27. 6	F8	C9	Serpent	21.10	11. 9	J11	F10	Dog
10. 8	28. 6	F8	D10	Earthworm	22.10	12. 9	J11	G11	Pheasant
11. 8	29. 6	F8	E11	Crocodile	23.10	13. 9	J11	H12	Cock
12. 8	1. 7	G9	F12	Dragon	24.10	14. 9	J11	J1	Crow
13. 8	2. 7	G9	G1	Badger	25.10	15. 9	J11	K2	Monkey
14. 8	3. 7	G9	H2	Hare	26.10	16. 9	J11	A3	Gibbon
15. 8	4. 7	G9	J3	Fox	27.10	17. 9	J11	B4	Tapir
16. 8	5. 7	G9	K4	Tiger	28.10	18. 9	J11	C5	Sheep
17. 8	6. 7	G9	A5	Leopard	29.10	19. 9	J11	D6	Deer
18. 8	7. 7	G9	B6	Griffon	30.10	20. 9	J11	E7	Horse
19. 8	8. 7	G9	C7	Ox	31.10	21. 9	J11	F8	Stag
20. 8	9. 7	G9	D8	Bat	1.11	22. 9	J11	G9	Serpent
21. 8	10. 7	G9	E9	Rat	2.11	23. 9	J11	H10	Earthworm
22. 8	11. 7	G9	F10	Swallow	3.11	24. 9	J11	J11	Crocodile
23. 8	12. 7	G9	G11	Pig	4.11	25. 9	J11	K12	Dragon
24. 8	13. 7	G9	H12	Porcupine	5.11	26. 9	J11	A1	Badger
25. 8	14. 7	G9	J1	Wolf	6.11	27. 9	J11	B2	Hare
26. 8	15. 7	G9	K2	Dog	7.11	28. 9	J11	C3	Fox
27. 8	16. 7	G9	A3	Pheasant	8.11	29. 9	J11	D4	Tiger
28. 8	17. 7	G9	B4	Cock	9.11	1.10	K12	E5	Leopard
29. 8	18. 7	G9	C5	Crow	10.11	2.10	K12	F6	Griffon
30. 8	19. 7	G9	D6	Monkey	11.11	3.10	K12	G7	Ox
31. 8	20. 7	G9	E7	Gibbon	12.11	4.10	K12	H8	Bat
1. 9	21. 7	G9	F8	Tapir	13.11	5.10	K12	J9	Rat
2. 9	22. 7	G9	G9	Sheep	14.11	6.10	K12	K10	Swallow
3. 9	23. 7	G9	H10	Deer	15.11	7.10	K12	A11	Pig
4. 9	24. 7	G9	J11	Horse	16.11	8.10	K12	B12	Porcupine
5. 9	25. 7	G9	K12	Stag	17.11	9.10	K12	C1	Wolf
6. 9	26. 7	G9	A1	Serpent	18.11	10.10	K12	D2	Dog
7. 9	27. 7	G9	B2	Earthworm	19.11	11.10	K12	E3	Pheasant
8. 9	28. 7	G9	C3	Crocodile	20.11	12.10	K12	F4	Cock
9. 9	29. 7	G9	D4	Dragon	21.11	13.10	K12	G5	Crow
10. 9	30. 7	G9	E5	Badger	22.11	14.10	K12	H6	Monkey
11. 9	1. 8	H10	F6	Hare	23.11	15.10	K12	J7	Gibbon
12. 9	2. 8	H10	G7	Fox	24.11	16.10	K12	K8	Tapir
13. 9	3. 8	H10	H8	Tiger	25.11	17.10	K12	A9	Sheep
14. 9	4. 8	H10	J9	Leopard	26.11	18.10	K12	B10	Deer
15. 9	5. 8	H10	K10	Griffon	27.11	19.10	K12	C11	Horse
16. 9	6. 8	H10	A11	Ox	28.11	20.10	K12	D12	Stag
17. 9	7. 8	H10	B12	Bat	29.11	21.10	K12	E1	Serpent
18. 9	8. 8	H10	C1	Rat	30.11	22.10	K12	F2	Earthworm

Solar date	Lunar date	Month HS/EB	Day HS/EB	Constellation
1.12	23.10	K12	G3	Crocodile
2.12	24.10	K12	H4	Dragon
3.12	25.10	K12	J5	Badger
4.12	26.10	K12	K6	Hare
5.12	27.10	K12	A7	Fox
6.12	28.10	K12	B8	Tiger
7.12	29.10	K12	C9	Leopard
8.12	30.10	K12	D10	Griffon
9.12	1.11	A1	E11	Ox
10.12	2.11	A1	F12	Bat
11.12	3.11	A1	G1	Rat
12.12	4.11	A1	H2	Swallow
13.12	5.11	A1	J3	Pig
14.12	6.11	A1	K4	Porcupine
15.12	7.11	A1	A5	Wolf
16.12	8.11	A1	B6	Dog
17.12	9.11	A1	C7	Pheasant
18.12	10.11	A1	D8	Cock
19.12	11.11	A1	E9	Crow
20.12	12.11	A1	F10	Monkey
21.12	13.11	A1	G11	Gibbon
22.12	14.11	A1	H12	Tapir
23.12	15.11	A1	J1	Sheep
24.12	16.11	A1	K2	Deer
25.12	17.11	A1	A3	Horse
26.12	18.11	A1	B4	Stag
27.12	19.11	A1	C5	Serpent
28.12	20.11	A1	D6	Earthworm
29.12	21.11	A1	E7	Crocodile
30.12	22.11	A1	F8	Dragon
31.12	23.11	A1	G9	Badger
1989				
1. 1	24.11	A1	H10	Hare
2. 1	25.11	A1	J11	Fox
3. 1	26.11	A1	K12	Tiger
4. 1	27.11	A1	A1	Leopard
5. 1	28.11	A1	B2	Griffon
6. 1	29.11	A1	C3	Ox
7. 1	30.11	A1	D4	Bat
8. 1	1.12	B2	E5	Rat
9. 1	2.12	B2	F6	Swallow
10. 1	3.12	B2	G7	Pig
11. 1	4.12	B2	H8	Porcupine
12. 1	5.12	B2	J9	Wolf
13. 1	6.12	B2	K10	Dog
14. 1	7.12	B2	A11	Pheasant
15. 1	8.12	B2	B12	Cock
16. 1	9.12	B2	C1	Crow
18. 1	10.12	B2	D2	Monkey
18. 1	11.12	B2	E3	Gibbon
19. 1	12.12	B2	F4	Tapir
20. 1	13.12	B2	G5	Sheep
21. 1	14.12	B2	H6	Deer
22. 1	15.12	B2	J7	Horse
23. 1	16.12	B2	K8	Stag
24. 1	17.12	B2	A9	Serpent
25. 1	18.12	B2	B10	Earthworm
26. 1	19.12	B2	C11	Crocodile
27. 1	20.12	B2	D12	Dragon
28. 1	21.12	B2	E1	Badger
29. 1	22.12	B2	F2	Hare
30. 1	23.12	B2	G3	Fox
31. 1	24.12	B2	H4	Tiger
1. 2	25.12	B2	J5	Leopard
2. 2	26.12	B2	K6	Griffon
3. 2	27.12	B2	A7	Ox
4. 2	28.12	B2	B8	Bat
5. 2	29.12	B2	C9	Rat

CHI SZU YEAR

Solar date	Lunar date	Month HS/EB	Day HS/EB	Constellation
6. 2	1. 1	C3	D10	Swallow
7. 2	2. 1	C3	E11	Pig
8. 2	3. 1	C3	F12	Porcupine
9. 2	4. 1	C3	G1	Wolf
10. 2	5. 1	C3	H2	Dog
11. 2	6. 1	C3	J3	Pheasant
12. 2	7. 1	C3	K4	Cock
13. 2	8. 1	C3	A5	Crow
14. 2	9. 1	C3	B6	Monkey
15. 2	10. 1	C3	C7	Gibbon
16. 2	11. 1	C3	D8	Tapir
17. 2	12. 1	C3	E9	Sheep
18. 2	13. 1	C3	F10	Deer
19. 2	14. 1	C3	G11	Horse
20. 2	15. 1	C3	H12	Stag
21. 2	16. 1	C3	J1	Serpent
22. 2	17. 1	C3	K2	Earthworm
23. 2	18. 1	C3	A3	Crocodile
24. 2	19. 1	C3	B4	Dragon
25. 2	20. 1	C3	C5	Badger
26. 2	21. 1	C3	D6	Hare
27. 2	22. 1	C3	E7	Fox
28. 2	23. 1	C3	F8	Tiger
1. 3	24. 1	C3	G9	Leopard
2. 3	25. 1	C3	H10	Griffon
3. 3	26. 1	C3	J11	Ox
4. 3	27. 1	C3	K12	Bat
5. 3	28. 1	C3	A1	Rat
6. 3	29. 1	C3	B2	Swallow
7. 3	30. 1	C3	C3	Pig
8. 3	1. 2	D4	D4	Porcupine
9. 3	2. 2	D4	E5	Wolf
10. 3	3. 2	D4	F6	Dog
11. 3	4. 2	D4	G7	Pheasant
12. 3	5. 2	D4	H8	Cock
13. 3	6. 2	D4	J9	Crow
14. 3	7. 2	D4	K10	Monkey
15. 3	8. 2	D4	A11	Gibbon
16. 3	9. 2	D4	B12	Tapir
17. 3	10. 2	D4	C1	Sheep
18. 3	11. 2	D4	D2	Deer
19. 3	12. 2	D4	E3	Horse
20. 3	13. 2	D4	F4	Stag
21. 3	14. 2	D4	G5	Serpent
22. 3	15. 2	D4	H6	Earthworm
23. 3	16. 2	D4	J7	Crocodile
24. 3	17. 2	D4	K8	Dragon
25. 3	18. 2	D4	A9	Badger
26. 3	19. 2	D4	B10	Hare
27. 3	20. 2	D4	C11	Fox
28. 3	21. 2	D4	D12	Tiger
29. 3	22. 2	D4	E1	Leopard
30. 3	23. 2	D4	F2	Griffon
31. 3	24. 2	D4	G3	Ox
1. 4	25. 2	D4	H4	Bat
2. 4	26. 2	D4	J5	Rat
3. 4	27. 2	D4	K6	Swallow
4. 4	28. 2	D4	A7	Pig
5. 4	29. 2	D4	B8	Porcupine
6. 4	1. 3	E5	C9	Wolf
7. 4	2. 3	E5	D10	Dog
8. 4	3. 3	E5	E11	Pheasant
9. 4	4. 3	E5	F12	Cock
10. 4	5. 3	E5	G1	Crow
11. 4	6. 3	E5	H2	Monkey
12. 4	7. 3	E5	J3	Gibbon

Solar date	Lunar date	Month HS/EB	Day HS/EB	Constellation
13. 4	8. 3	E5	K4	Tapir
14. 4	9. 3	E5	A5	Sheep
15. 4	10. 3	E5	B6	Deer
16. 4	11. 3	E5	C7	Horse
17. 4	12. 3	E5	D8	Stag
18. 4	13. 3	E5	E9	Serpent
19. 4	14. 3	E5	F10	Earthworm
20. 4	15. 3	E5	G11	Crocodile
21. 4	16. 3	E5	H12	Dragon
22. 4	17. 3	E5	J1	Badger
23. 4	18. 3	E5	K2	Hare
24. 4	19. 3	E5	A3	Fox
25. 4	20. 3	E5	B4	Tiger
26. 4	21. 3	E5	C5	Leopard
27. 4	22. 3	E5	D6	Griffon
28. 4	23. 3	E5	E7	Ox
29. 4	24. 3	E5	F8	Bat
30. 4	25. 3	E5	G9	Rat
1. 5	26. 3	E5	H10	Swallow
2. 5	27. 3	E5	J11	Pig
3. 5	28. 3	E5	K12	Porcupine
4. 5	29. 3	E5	A1	Wolf
5. 5	1. 4	F6	B2	Dog
6. 5	2. 4	F6	C3	Pheasant
7. 5	3. 4	F6	D4	Cock
8. 5	4. 4	F6	E5	Crow
9. 5	5. 4	F6	F6	Monkey
10. 5	6. 4	F6	G7	Gibbon
11. 5	7. 4	F6	H8	Tapir
12. 5	8. 4	F6	J9	Sheep
13. 5	9. 4	F6	K10	Deer
14. 5	10. 4	F6	A11	Horse
15. 5	11. 4	F6	B12	Stag
16. 5	12. 4	F6	C1	Serpent
17. 5	13. 4	F6	D2	Earthworm
18. 5	14. 4	F6	E3	Crocodile
19. 5	15. 4	F6	F4	Dragon
20. 5	16. 4	F6	G5	Badger
21. 5	17. 4	F6	H6	Hare
22. 5	18. 4	F6	J7	Fox
23. 5	19. 4	F6	K8	Tiger
24. 5	20. 4	F6	A9	Leopard
25. 5	21. 4	F6	B10	Griffon
26. 5	22. 4	F6	C11	Ox
27. 5	23. 4	F6	D12	Bat
28. 5	24. 4	F6	E1	Rat
29. 5	25. 4	F6	F2	Swallow
30. 5	26. 4	F6	G3	Pig
31. 5	27. 4	F6	H4	Porcupine
1. 6	28. 4	F6	J5	Wolf
2. 6	29. 4	F6	K6	Dog
3. 6	30. 4	F6	A7	Pheasant
4. 6	1. 5	G7	B8	Cock
5. 6	2. 5	G7	C9	Crow
6. 6	3. 5	G7	D10	Monkey
7. 6	4. 5	G7	E11	Gibbon
8. 6	5. 5	G7	F12	Tapir
9. 6	6. 5	G7	G1	Sheep
10. 6	7. 5	G7	H2	Deer
11. 6	8. 5	G7	J3	Horse
12. 6	9. 5	G7	K4	Stag
13. 6	10. 5	G7	A5	Serpent
14. 6	11. 5	G7	B6	Earthworm
15. 6	12. 5	G7	C7	Crocodile
16. 6	13. 5	G7	D8	Dragon
17. 6	14. 5	G7	E9	Badger
18. 6	15. 5	G7	F10	Hare
19. 6	16. 5	G7	G11	Fox
20. 6	17. 5	G7	H12	Tiger
21. 6	18. 5	G7	J1	Leopard
22. 6	19. 5	G7	K2	Griffon
23. 6	20. 5	G7	A3	Ox
24. 6	21. 5	G7	B4	Bat
25. 6	22. 5	G7	C5	Rat
26. 6	23. 5	G7	D6	Swallow
27. 6	24. 5	G7	E7	Pig
28. 6	25. 5	G7	F8	Porcupine
29. 6	26. 5	G7	G9	Wolf
30. 6	27. 5	G7	H10	Dog
1. 7	28. 5	G7	J11	Pheasant
2. 7	29. 5	G7	K12	Cock
3. 7	1. 6	H8	A1	Crow
4. 7	2. 6	H8	B2	Monkey
5. 7	3. 6	H8	C3	Gibbon
6. 7	4. 6	H8	D4	Tapir
7. 7	5. 6	H8	E5	Sheep
8. 7	6. 6	H8	F6	Deer
9. 7	7. 6	H8	G7	Horse
10. 7	8. 6	H8	H8	Stag
11. 7	9. 6	H8	J9	Serpent
12. 7	10. 6	H8	K10	Earthworm
13. 7	11. 6	H8	A11	Crocodile
14. 7	12. 6	H8	B12	Dragon
15. 7	13. 6	H8	C1	Badger
16. 7	14. 6	H8	D2	Hare
17. 7	15. 6	H8	E3	Fox
18. 7	16. 6	H8	F4	Tiger
19. 7	17. 6	H8	G5	Leopard
20. 7	18. 6	H8	H6	Griffon
21. 7	19. 6	H8	J7	Ox
22. 7	20. 6	H8	K8	Bat
23. 7	21. 6	H8	A9	Rat
24. 7	22. 6	H8	B10	Swallow
25. 7	23. 6	H8	C11	Pig
26. 7	24. 6	H8	D12	Porcupine
27. 7	25. 6	H8	E1	Wolf
28. 7	26. 6	H8	F2	Dog
29. 7	27. 6	H8	G3	Pheasant
30. 7	28. 6	H8	H4	Cock
31. 7	29. 6	H8	J5	Crow
1. 8	1. 7	J9	K6	Monkey
2. 8	2. 7	J9	A7	Gibbon
3. 8	3. 7	J9	B8	Tapir
4. 8	4. 7	J9	C9	Sheep
5. 8	5. 7	J9	D10	Deer
6. 8	6. 7	J9	E11	Horse
7. 8	7. 7	J9	F12	Stag
8. 8	8. 7	J9	G1	Serpent
9. 8	9. 7	J9	H2	Earthworm
10. 8	10. 7	J9	J3	Crocodile
11. 8	11. 7	J9	K4	Dragon
12. 8	12. 7	J9	A5	Badger
13. 8	13. 7	J9	B6	Hare
14. 8	14. 7	J9	C7	Fox
15. 8	15. 7	J9	D8	Tiger
16. 8	16. 7	J9	E9	Leopard
17. 8	17. 7	J9	F10	Griffon
18. 8	18. 7	J9	G11	Ox
19. 8	19. 7	J9	H12	Bat
20. 8	20. 7	J9	J1	Rat
21. 8	21. 7	J9	K2	Swallow
22. 8	22. 7	J9	A3	Pig
23. 8	23. 7	J9	B4	Porcupine
24. 8	24. 7	J9	C5	Wolf
25. 8	25. 7	J9	D6	Dog
26. 8	26. 7	J9	E7	Pheasant
27. 8	27. 7	J9	F8	Cock
28. 8	28. 7	J9	G9	Crow
29. 8	29. 7	J9	H10	Monkey
30. 8	30. 7	J9	J11	Gibbon
31. 8	1. 8	K10	K12	Tapir
1. 9	2. 8	K10	A1	Sheep
2. 9	3. 8	K10	B2	Deer
3. 9	4. 8	K10	C3	Horse
4. 9	5. 8	K10	D4	Stag
5. 9	6. 8	K10	E5	Serpent

Solar date	Lunar date	Month HS/EB	Day HS/EB	Constellation	Solar date	Lunar date	Month HS/EB	Day HS/EB	Constellation
6. 9	7. 8	K10	F6	Earthworm	18.11	21.10	B12	J7	Pheasant
7. 9	8. 8	K10	G7	Crocodile	19.11	22.10	B12	K8	Cock
8. 9	9. 8	K10	H8	Dragon	20.11	23.10	B12	A9	Crow
9. 9	10. 8	K10	J9	Badger	21.11	24.10	B12	B10	Monkey
10. 9	11. 8	K10	K10	Hare	22.11	25.10	B12	C11	Gibbon
11. 9	12. 8	K10	A11	Fox	23.11	26.10	B12	D12	Tapir
12. 9	13. 8	K10	B12	Tiger	24.11	27.10	B12	E1	Sheep
13. 9	14. 8	K10	C1	Leopard	25.11	28.10	B12	F2	Deer
14. 9	15. 8	K10	D2	Griffon	26.11	29.10	B12	G3	Horse
15. 9	16. 8	K10	E3	Ox	27.11	30.10	B12	H4	Stag
16. 9	17. 8	K10	F4	Bat	28.11	1.11	C1	J5	Serpent
17. 9	18. 8	K10	G5	Rat	29.11	2.11	C1	K6	Earthworm
18. 9	19. 8	K10	H6	Swallow	30.11	3.11	C1	A7	Crocodile
19. 9	20. 8	K10	J7	Pig	1.12	4.11	C1	B8	Dragon
20. 9	21. 8	K10	K8	Porcupine	2.12	5.11	C1	C9	Badger
21. 9	22. 8	K10	A9	Wolf	3.12	6.11	C1	D10	Hare
22. 9	23. 8	K10	B10	Dog	4.12	7.11	C1	E11	Fox
23. 9	24. 8	K10	C11	Pheasant	5.12	8.11	C1	F12	Tiger
24. 9	25. 8	K10	D12	Cock	6.12	9.11	C1	G1	Leopard
25. 9	26. 8	K10	E1	Crow	7.12	10.11	C1	H2	Griffon
26. 9	27. 8	K10	F2	Monkey	8.12	11.11	C1	J3	Ox
27. 9	28. 8	K10	G3	Gibbon	9.12	12.11	C1	K4	Bat
28. 9	29. 8	K10	H4	Tapir	10.12	13.11	C1	A5	Rat
29. 9	30. 8	K10	J5	Sheep	11.12	14.11	C1	B6	Swallow
30. 9	1. 9	A11	K6	Deer	12.12	15.11	C1	C7	Pig
1.10	2. 9	A11	A7	Horse	13.12	16.11	C1	D8	Porcupine
2.10	3. 9	A11	B8	Stag	14.12	17.11	C1	E9	Wolf
3.10	4. 9	A11	C9	Serpent	15.12	18.11	C1	F10	Dog
4.10	5. 9	A11	D10	Earthworm	16.12	19.11	C1	G11	Pheasant
5.10	6. 9	A11	E11	Crocodile	17.12	20.11	C1	H12	Cock
6.10	7. 9	A11	F12	Dragon	18.12	21.11	C1	J1	Crow
7.10	8. 9	A11	G1	Badger	19.12	22.11	C1	K2	Monkey
8.10	9. 9	A11	H2	Hare	20.12	23.11	C1	A3	Gibbon
9.10	10. 9	A11	J3	Fox	21.12	24.11	C1	B4	Tapir
10.10	11. 9	A11	K4	Tiger	22.12	25.11	C1	C5	Sheep
11.10	12. 9	A11	A5	Leopard	23.12	26.11	C1	D6	Deer
12.10	13. 9	A11	B6	Griffon	24.12	27.11	C1	E7	Horse
13.10	14. 9	A11	C7	Ox	25.12	28.11	C1	F8	Stag
14.10	15. 9	A11	D8	Bat	26.12	29.11	C1	G9	Serpent
15.10	16. 9	A11	E9	Rat	27.12	30.11	C1	H10	Earthworm
16.10	17. 9	A11	F10	Swallow	28.12	1.12	D2	J11	Crocodile
17.10	18. 9	A11	G11	Pig	29.12	2.12	D2	K12	Dragon
18.10	19. 9	A11	H12	Porcupine	30.12	3.12	D2	A1	Badger
19.10	20. 9	A11	J1	Wolf	31.12	4.12	D2	B2	Hare
20.10	21. 9	A11	K2	Dog					
21.10	22. 9	A11	A3	Pheasant	**1990**				
22.10	23. 9	A11	B4	Cock	1. 1	5.12	D2	C3	Fox
23.10	24. 9	A11	C5	Crow	2. 1	6.12	D2	D4	Tiger
24.10	25. 9	A11	D6	Monkey	3. 1	7.12	D2	E5	Leopard
25.10	26. 9	A11	E7	Gibbon	4. 1	8.12	D2	F6	Griffon
26.10	27. 9	A11	F8	Tapir	5. 1	9.12	D2	G7	Ox
27.10	28. 9	A11	G9	Sheep	6. 1	10.12	D2	H8	Bat
28.10	29. 9	A11	H10	Deer	7. 1	11.12	D2	J9	Rat
29.10	1.10	B12	J11	Horse	8. 1	12.12	D2	K10	Swallow
30.10	2.10	B12	K12	Stag	9. 1	13.12	D2	A11	Pig
31.10	3.10	B12	A1	Serpent	10. 1	14.12	D2	B12	Porcupine
1.11	4.10	B12	B2	Earthworm	11. 1	15.12	D2	C1	Wolf
2.11	5.10	B12	C3	Crocodile	12. 1	16.12	D2	D2	Dog
3.11	6.10	B12	D4	Dragon	13. 1	17.12	D2	E3	Pheasant
4.11	7.10	B12	E5	Badger	14. 1	18.12	D2	F4	Cock
5.11	8.10	B12	F6	Hare	15. 1	19.12	D2	G5	Crow
6.11	9.10	B12	G7	Fox	16. 1	20.12	D2	H6	Monkey
7.11	10.10	B12	H8	Tiger	17. 1	21.12	D2	J7	Gibbon
8.11	11.10	B12	J9	Leopard	18. 1	22.12	D2	K8	Tapir
9.11	12.10	B12	K10	Griffon	19. 1	23.12	D2	A9	Sheep
10.11	13.10	B12	A11	Ox	20. 1	24.12	D2	B10	Deer
11.11	14.10	B12	B12	Bat	21. 1	25.12	D2	C11	Horse
12.11	15.10	B12	C1	Rat	22. 1	26.12	D2	D12	Stag
13.11	16.10	B12	D2	Swallow	23. 1	27.12	D2	E1	Serpent
14.11	17.10	B12	E3	Pig	24. 1	28.12	D2	F2	Earthworm
15.11	18.10	B12	F4	Porcupine	25. 1	29.12	D2	G3	Crocodile
16.11	19.10	B12	G5	Wolf	26. 1	30.12	D2	H4	Dragon
17.11	20.10	B12	H6	Dog					

KENG WU YEAR

Solar date	Lunar date	Month HS/EB	Day HS/EB	Constellation	Solar date	Lunar date	Month HS/EB	Day HS/EB	Constellation
27. 1	1. 1	E3	J5	Badger	8. 4	13. 3	G5	K4	Cock
28. 1	2. 1	E3	K6	Hare	9. 4	14. 3	G5	A5	Crow
29. 1	3. 1	E3	A7	Fox	10. 4	15. 3	G5	B6	Monkey
30. 1	4. 1	E3	B8	Tiger	11. 4	16. 3	G5	C7	Gibbon
31. 1	5. 1	E3	C9	Leopard	12. 4	17. 3	G5	D8	Tapir
1. 2	6. 1	E3	D10	Griffon	13. 4	18. 3	G5	E9	Sheep
2. 2	7. 1	E3	D11	Ox	14. 4	19. 3	G5	F10	Deer
3. 2	8. 1	E3	F12	Bat	15. 4	20. 3	G5	G11	Horse
4. 2	9. 1	E3	G1	Rat	16. 4	21. 3	G5	H12	Stag
5. 2	10. 1	E3	H2	Swallow	17. 4	22. 3	G5	J1	Serpent
6. 2	11. 1	E3	J3	Pig	18. 4	23. 3	G5	K2	Earthworm
7. 2	12. 1	E3	K4	Porcupine	19. 4	24. 3	G5	A3	Crocodile
8. 2	13. 1	E3	A5	Wolf	20. 4	25. 3	G5	B4	Dragon
9. 2	14. 1	E3	B6	Dog	21. 4	26. 3	G5	C5	Badger
10. 2	15. 1	E3	C7	Pheasant	22. 4	27. 3	G5	D6	Hare
11. 2	16. 1	E3	D8	Cock	23. 4	28. 3	G5	E7	Fox
12. 2	17. 1	E3	E9	Crow	24. 4	29. 3	G5	F8	Tiger
13. 2	18. 1	E3	F10	Monkey	25. 4	1. 4	H6	G9	Leopard
14. 2	19. 1	E3	G11	Gibbon	26. 4	2. 4	H6	H10	Griffon
15. 2	20. 1	E3	H12	Tapir	27. 4	3. 4	H6	J11	Ox
16. 2	21. 1	E3	J1	Sheep	28. 4	4. 4	H6	K12	Bat
17. 2	22. 1	E3	K2	Deer	29. 4	5. 4	H6	A1	Rat
18. 2	23. 1	E3	A3	Horse	30. 4	6. 4	H6	B2	Swallow
19. 2	24. 1	E3	B4	Stag	1. 5	7. 4	H6	C3	Pig
20. 2	25. 1	E3	C5	Serpent	2. 5	8. 4	H6	D4	Porcupine
21. 2	26. 1	E3	D6	Earthworm	3. 5	9. 4	H6	E5	Wolf
22. 2	27. 1	E3	E7	Crocodile	4. 5	10. 4	H6	F6	Dog
23. 2	28. 1	E3	F8	Dragon	5. 5	11. 4	H6	G7	Pheasant
24. 2	29. 1	E3	G9	Badger	6. 5	12. 4	H6	H8	Cock
25. 2	1. 2	F4	H10	Hare	7. 5	13. 4	H6	J9	Crow
26. 2	2. 2	F4	J11	Fox	8. 5	14. 4	H6	K10	Monkey
27. 2	3. 2	F4	K12	Tiger	9. 5	15. 4	H6	A11	Gibbon
28. 2	4. 2	F4	A1	Leopard	10. 5	16. 4	H6	B12	Tapir
1. 3	5. 2	F4	B2	Griffon	11. 5	17. 4	H6	C1	Sheep
2. 3	6. 2	F4	C3	Ox	12. 5	18. 4	H6	D2	Deer
3. 3	7. 2	F4	D4	Bat	13. 5	19. 4	H6	E3	Horse
4. 3	8. 2	F4	E5	Rat	14. 5	20. 4	H6	F4	Stag
5. 3	9. 2	F4	F6	Swallow	15. 5	21. 4	H6	G5	Serpent
6. 3	10. 2	F4	G7	Pig	16. 5	22. 4	H6	H6	Earthworm
7. 3	11. 2	F4	H8	Porcupine	17. 5	23. 4	H6	J7	Crocodile
8. 3	12. 2	F4	J9	Wolf	18. 5	24. 4	H6	K8	Dragon
9. 3	13. 2	F4	K10	Dog	19. 5	25. 4	H6	A9	Badger
10. 3	14. 2	F4	A11	Pheasant	20. 5	26. 4	H6	B10	Hare
11. 3	15. 2	F4	B12	Cock	21. 5	27. 4	H6	C11	Fox
12. 3	16. 2	F4	C1	Crow	22. 5	28. 4	H6	D12	Tiger
13. 3	17. 2	F4	D2	Monkey	23. 5	29. 4	H6	E1	Leopard
14. 3	18. 2	F4	E3	Gibbon	24. 5	1. 5	J7	F2	Griffon
15. 3	19. 2	F4	F4	Tapir	25. 5	2. 5	J7	G3	Ox
16. 3	20. 2	F4	G5	Sheep	26. 5	3. 5	J7	H4	Bat
17. 3	21. 2	F4	H6	Deer	27. 5	4. 5	J7	J5	Rat
18. 3	22. 2	F4	J7	Horse	28. 5	5. 5	J7	K6	Swallow
19. 3	23. 2	F4	K8	Stag	29. 5	6. 5	J7	A7	Pig
20. 3	24. 2	F4	A9	Serpent	30. 5	7. 5	J7	B8	Porcupine
21. 3	25. 2	F4	B10	Earthworm	31. 5	8. 5	J7	C9	Wolf
22. 3	26. 2	F4	C11	Crocodile	1. 6	9. 5	J7	D10	Dog
23. 3	27. 2	F4	D12	Dragon	2. 6	10. 5	J7	E11	Pheasant
24. 3	28. 2	F4	E1	Badger	3. 6	11. 5	J7	F12	Cock
25. 3	29. 2	F4	F2	Hare	4. 6	12. 5	J7	G1	Crow
26. 3	30. 2	F4	G3	Fox	5. 6	13. 5	J7	H2	Monkey
27. 3	1. 3	G5	H4	Tiger	6. 6	14. 5	J7	J3	Gibbon
28. 3	2. 3	G5	J5	Leopard	7. 6	15. 5	J7	K4	Tapir
29. 3	3. 3	G5	K6	Griffon	8. 6	16. 5	J7	A5	Sheep
30. 3	4. 3	G5	A7	Ox	9. 6	17. 5	J7	B6	Deer
31. 3	5. 3	G5	B8	Bat	10. 6	18. 5	J7	C7	Horse
1. 4	6. 3	G5	C9	Rat	11. 6	19. 5	J7	D8	Stag
2. 4	7. 3	G5	D10	Swallow	12. 16	20. 5	J7	E9	Serpent
3. 4	8. 3	G5	E11	Pig	13. 6	21. 5	J7	F10	Earthworm
4. 4	9. 3	G5	F12	Porcupine	14. 6	22. 5	J7	G11	Crocodile
5. 4	10. 3	G5	G1	Wolf	15. 6	23. 5	J7	H12	Dragon
6. 4	11. 3	G5	H2	Dog	16. 6	24. 5	J7	J1	Badger
7. 4	12. 3	G5	J3	Pheasant	17. 6	25. 5	J7	K2	Hare

Solar date	Lunar date	Month HS/EB	Day HS/EB	Constellation	Solar date	Lunar date	Month HS/EB	Day HS/EB	Constellation
18. 6	26. 5	J7	A3	Fox	30. 8	11. 7	A9	D4	Tapir
19. 6	27. 5	J7	B4	Tiger	31. 8	12. 7	A9	E5	Sheep
20. 6	28. 5	J7	C5	Leopard	1. 9	13. 7	A9	F6	Deer
21. 6	29. 5	J7	D6	Griffon	2. 9	14. 7	A9	G7	Horse
22. 6	30. 5	J7	E7	Ox	3. 9	15. 7	A9	H8	Stag
23. 6	1. 5	J7	F8	Bat	4. 9	16. 7	A9	J9	Serpent
24. 6	2. 5	J7	G9	Rat	5. 9	17. 7	A9	K10	Earthworm
25. 6	3. 5	J7	H10	Swallow	6. 9	18. 7	A9	A11	Crocodile
26. 6	4. 5	J7	J11	Pig	7. 9	19. 7	A9	B12	Dragon
27. 6	5. 5	J7	K12	Porcupine	8. 9	20. 7	A9	C1	Badger
28. 6	6. 5	J7	A1	Wolf	9. 9	21. 7	A9	D2	Hare
29. 6	7. 5	J7	B2	Dog	10. 9	22. 7	A9	E3	Fox
30. 6	8. 5	J7	C3	Pheasant	11. 9	23. 7	A9	F4	Tiger
1. 7	9. 5	J7	D4	Cock	12. 9	24. 7	A9	G5	Leopard
2. 7	10. 5	J7	E5	Crow	13. 9	25. 7	A9	H6	Griffon
3. 7	11. 5	J7	F6	Monkey	14. 9	26. 7	A9	J7	Ox
4. 7	12. 5	J7	G7	Gibbon	15. 9	27. 7	A9	K8	Bat
5. 7	13. 5	J7	H8	Tapir	16. 9	28. 7	A9	A9	Rat
6. 7	14. 5	J7	J9	Sheep	17. 9	29. 7	A9	B10	Swallow
7. 7	15. 5	J7	K10	Deer	18. 9	30. 7	A9	C11	Pig
8. 7	16. 5	J7	A11	Horse	19. 9	1. 8	B10	D12	Porcupine
9. 7	17. 5	J7	B12	Stag	20. 9	2. 8	B10	E1	Wolf
10. 7	18. 5	J7	C1	Serpent	21. 9	3. 8	B10	F2	Dog
11. 7	19. 5	J7	D2	Earthworm	22. 9	4. 8	B10	G3	Pheasant
12. 7	20. 5	J7	E3	Crocodile	23. 9	5. 8	B10	H4	Cock
13. 7	21. 5	J7	F4	Dragon	24. 9	6. 8	B10	J5	Crow
14. 7	22. 5	J7	G5	Badger	25. 9	7. 8	B10	K6	Monkey
15. 7	23. 5	J7	H6	Hare	26. 9	8. 8	B10	A7	Gibbon
16. 7	24. 5	J7	J7	Fox	27. 9	9. 8	B10	B8	Tapir
17. 7	25. 5	J7	K8	Tiger	28. 9	10. 8	B10	C9	Sheep
18. 7	26. 5	J7	A9	Leopard	29. 9	11. 8	B10	D10	Deer
19. 7	27. 5	J7	B10	Griffon	30. 9	12. 8	B10	E11	Horse
20. 7	28. 5	J7	C11	Ox	1.10	13. 8	B10	F12	Stag
21. 7	29. 5	J7	D12	Bat	2.10	14. 8	B10	G1	Serpent
22. 7	1. 6	K8	E1	Rat	3.10	15. 8	B10	H2	Earthworm
23. 7	2. 6	K8	F2	Swallow	4.10	16. 8	B10	J3	Crocodile
24. 7	3. 6	K8	G3	Pig	5.10	17. 8	B10	K4	Dragon
25. 7	4. 6	K8	H4	Porcupine	6.10	18. 8	B10	A5	Badger
26. 7	5. 6	K8	J5	Wolf	7.10	19. 8	B10	B6	Hare
27. 7	6. 6	K8	K6	Dog	8.10	20. 8	B10	C7	Fox
28. 7	7. 6	K8	A7	Pheasant	9.10	21. 8	B10	D8	Tiger
29. 7	8. 6	K8	B8	Cock	10.10	22. 8	B10	E9	Leopard
30. 7	9. 6	K8	C9	Crow	11.10	23. 8	B10	F10	Griffon
31. 7	10. 6	K8	D10	Monkey	12.10	24. 8	B10	G11	Ox
1. 8	11. 6	K8	E11	Gibbon	13.10	25. 8	B10	H12	Bat
2. 8	12. 6	K8	F12	Tapir	14.10	26. 8	B10	J1	Rat
3. 8	13. 6	K8	G1	Sheep	15.10	27. 8	B10	K2	Swallow
4. 8	14. 6	K8	H2	Deer	16.10	28. 8	B10	A3	Pig
5. 8	15. 6	K8	J3	Horse	17.10	29. 8	B10	B4	Porcupine
6. 8	16. 6	K8	K4	Stag	18.10	1. 9	C11	C5	Wolf
7. 8	17. 6	K8	A5	Serpent	19.10	2. 9	C11	D6	Dog
8. 8	18. 6	K8	B6	Earthworm	20.10	3. 9	C11	E7	Pheasant
9. 8	19. 6	K8	C7	Crocodile	21.10	4. 9	C11	F8	Cock
10. 8	20. 6	K8	D8	Dragon	22.10	5. 9	C11	G9	Crow
11. 8	21. 6	K8	E9	Badger	23.10	6. 9	C11	H10	Monkey
12. 8	22. 6	K8	F10	Hare	24.10	7. 9	C11	J11	Gibbon
13. 8	23. 6	K8	G11	Fox	25.10	8. 9	C11	K12	Tapir
14. 8	24. 6	K8	H12	Tiger	26.10	9. 9	C11	A1	Sheep
15. 8	25. 6	K8	J1	Leopard	27.10	10. 9	C11	B2	Deer
16. 8	26. 6	K8	K2	Griffon	28.10	11. 9	C11	C3	Horse
17. 8	27. 6	K8	A3	Ox	29.10	12. 9	C11	D4	Stag
18. 8	28. 6	K8	B4	Bat	30.10	13. 9	C11	E5	Serpent
19. 8	29. 6	K8	C5	Rat	31.10	14. 9	C11	F6	Earthworm
20. 8	1. 7	A9	D6	Swallow	1.11	15. 9	C11	G7	Crocodile
21. 8	2. 7	A9	E7	Pig	2.11	16. 9	C11	H8	Dragon
22. 8	3. 7	A9	F8	Porcupine	3.11	17. 9	C11	J9	Badger
23. 8	4. 7	A9	G9	Wolf	4.11	18. 9	C11	K10	Hare
24. 8	5. 7	A9	H10	Dog	5.11	19. 9	C11	A11	Fox
25. 8	6. 7	A9	J11	Pheasant	6.11	20. 9	C11	B12	Tiger
26. 8	7. 7	A9	K12	Cock	7.11	21. 9	C11	C1	Leopard
27. 8	8. 7	A9	A1	Crow	8.11	22. 9	C11	D2	Griffon
28. 8	9. 7	A9	B2	Monkey	9.11	23. 9	C11	E3	Ox
29. 8	10. 7	A9	C3	Gibbon	10.11	24. 9	C11	F4	Bat

Solar date	Lunar date	Month HS/EB	Day HS/EB	Constellation	Solar date	Lunar date	Month HS/EB	Day HS/EB	Constellation
11.11	25. 9	C11	G5	Rat	30.12	14.11	E1	F6	Hare
12.11	26. 9	C11	H6	Swallow	31.12	15.11	E1	G7	Fox
13.11	27. 9	C11	J7	Pig	**1991**				
14.11	28. 9	C11	K8	Porcupine					
15.11	29. 9	C11	A9	Wolf	1. 1	16.11	E1	H8	Tiger
16.11	30. 9	C11	B10	Dog	2. 1	17.11	E1	J9	Leopard
17.11	1.10	D12	C11	Pheasant	3. 1	18.11	E1	K10	Griffon
18.11	2.10	D12	D12	Cock	4. 1	19.11	E1	A11	Ox
19.11	3.10	D12	E1	Crow	5. 1	20.11	E1	B12	Bat
20.11	4.10	D12	F2	Monkey	6. 1	21.11	E1	C1	Rat
21.11	5.10	D12	G3	Gibbon	7. 1	22.11	E1	D2	Swallow
22.11	6.10	D12	H4	Tapir	8. 1	23.11	E1	E3	Pig
23.11	7.10	D12	J5	Sheep	9. 1	24.11	E1	F4	Porcupine
24.11	8.10	D12	K6	Deer	10. 1	25.11	E1	G5	Wolf
25.11	9.10	D12	A7	Horse	11. 1	26.11	E1	H6	Dog
26.11	10.10	D12	B8	Stag	12. 1	27.11	E1	J7	Pheasant
27.11	11.10	D12	C9	Serpent	13. 1	28.11	E1	K8	Cock
28.11	12.10	D12	D10	Earthworm	14. 1	29.11	E1	A9	Crow
29.11	13.10	D12	E11	Crocodile	15. 1	30.11	E1	B10	Monkey
30.11	14.10	D12	F12	Dragon	16. 1	1.12	F2	C11	Gibbon
1.12	15.10	D12	G1	Badger	17. 1	2.12	F2	D12	Tapir
2.12	16.10	D12	H2	Hare	18. 1	3.12	F2	E1	Sheep
3.12	17.10	D12	J3	Fox	19. 1	4.12	F2	F2	Deer
4.12	18.10	D12	K4	Tiger	20. 1	5.12	F2	G3	Horse
5.12	19.10	D12	A5	Leopard	21. 1	6.12	F2	H4	Stag
6.12	20.10	D12	B6	Griffon	22. 1	7.12	F2	J5	Serpent
7.12	21.10	D12	C7	Ox	23. 1	8.12	F2	K6	Earthworm
8.12	22.10	D12	D8	Bat	24. 1	9.12	F2	A7	Crocodile
9.12	23.10	D12	E9	Rat	25. 1	10.12	F2	B8	Dragon
10.12	24.10	D12	F10	Swallow	26. 1	11.12	F2	C9	Badger
11.12	25.10	D12	G11	Pig	27. 1	12.12	F2	D10	Hare
12.12	26.10	D12	H12	Porcupine	28. 1	13.12	F2	E11	Fox
13.12	27.10	D12	J1	Wolf	29. 1	14.12	F2	F12	Tiger
14.12	28.10	D12	K2	Dog	30. 1	15.12	F2	G1	Leopard
15.12	29.10	D12	A3	Pheasant	31. 1	16.12	F2	H2	Griffon
16.12	30.10	D12	B4	Cock	1. 2	17.12	F2	J3	Ox
17.12	1.11	E1	C5	Crow	2. 2	18.12	F2	K4	Bat
18.12	2.11	E1	D6	Monkey	3. 2	19.12	F2	A5	Rat
19.12	3.11	E1	E7	Gibbon	4. 2	20.12	F2	B6	Swallow
20.12	4.11	E1	F8	Tapir	5. 2	21.12	F2	C7	Pig
21.12	5.11	E1	G9	Sheep	6. 2	22.12	F2	D8	Porcupine
22.12	6.11	E1	H10	Deer	7. 2	23.12	F2	E9	Wolf
23.12	7.11	E1	J11	Horse	8. 2	24.12	F2	F10	Dog
24.12	8.11	E1	K12	Stag	9. 2	25.12	F2	G11	Pheasant
25.12	9.11	E1	A1	Serpent	10. 2	26.12	F2	H12	Cock
26.12	10.11	E1	B2	Earthworm	11. 2	27.12	F2	J1	Crow
27.12	11.11	E1	C3	Crocodile	12. 2	28.12	F2	K2	Monkey
28.12	12.11	E1	D4	Dragon	13. 2	29.12	F2	A3	Gibbon
29.12	13.11	E1	E5	Badger	14. 2	30.12	F2	B4	Tapir

HSIN WEI YEAR

Solar date	Lunar date	Month HS/EB	Day HS/EB	Constellation	Solar date	Lunar date	Month HS/EB	Day HS/EB	Constellation
15. 2	1. 1	G3	C5	Sheep	6. 3	20. 1	G3	B12	Porcupine
16. 2	2. 1	G3	D6	Deer	7. 3	21. 1	G3	C1	Wolf
17. 2	3. 1	G3	E7	Horse	8. 3	22. 1	G3	D2	Dog
18. 2	4. 1	G3	F8	Stag	9. 3	23. 1	G3	E3	Pheasant
19. 2	5. 1	G3	G9	Serpent	10. 3	24. 1	G3	F4	Cock
20. 2	6. 1	G3	H10	Earthworm	11. 3	25. 1	G3	G5	Crow
21. 2	7. 1	G3	J11	Crocodile	12. 3	26. 1	G3	H6	Monkey
22. 2	8. 1	G3	K12	Dragon	13. 3	27. 1	G3	J7	Gibbon
23. 2	9. 1	G3	A1	Badger	14. 3	28. 1	G3	K8	Tapir
24. 2	10. 1	G3	B2	Hare	15. 3	29. 1	G3	A9	Sheep
25. 2	11. 1	G3	C3	Fox	16. 3	1. 2	H4	B10	Deer
26. 2	12. 1	G3	D4	Tiger	17. 3	2. 2	H4	C11	Horse
27. 2	13. 1	G3	E5	Leopard	18. 3	3. 2	H4	D12	Stag
28. 2	14. 1	G3	F6	Griffon	19. 3	4. 2	H4	E1	Serpent
1. 3	15. 1	G3	G7	Ox	20. 3	5. 2	H4	F2	Earthworm
2. 3	16. 1	G3	H8	Bat	21. 3	6. 2	H4	G3	Crocodile
3. 3	17. 1	G3	J9	Rat	22. 3	7. 2	H4	H4	Dragon
4. 3	18. 1	G3	K10	Swallow	23. 3	8. 2	H4	J5	Badger
5. 3	19. 1	G3	A11	Pig	24. 3	9. 2	H4	K6	Hare

Solar date	Lunar date	Month HS/EB	Day HS/EB	Constellation
25. 3	10. 2	H4	A7	Fox
26. 3	11. 2	H4	B8	Tiger
27. 3	12. 2	H4	C9	Leopard
28. 3	13. 2	H4	D10	Griffon
29. 3	14. 2	H4	E11	Ox
30. 3	15. 2	H4	F12	Bat
31. 3	16. 2	H4	G1	Rat
1. 4	17. 2	H4	H2	Swallow
2. 4	18. 2	H4	J3	Pig
3. 4	19. 2	H4	K4	Porcupine
4. 4	20. 2	H4	A5	Wolf
5. 4	21. 2	H4	B6	Dog
6. 4	22. 2	H4	C7	Pheasant
7. 4	23. 2	H4	D8	Cock
8. 4	24. 2	H4	E9	Crow
9. 4	25. 2	H4	F10	Monkey
10. 4	26. 2	H4	G11	Gibbon
11. 4	27. 2	H4	H12	Tapir
12. 4	28. 2	H4	J1	Sheep
13. 4	29. 2	H4	K2	Deer
14. 4	30. 2	H4	A3	Horse
15. 4	1. 3	J5	B4	Stag
16. 4	2. 3	J5	C5	Serpent
17. 4	3. 3	J5	D6	Earthworm
18. 4	4. 3	J5	E7	Crocodile
19. 4	5. 3	J5	F8	Dragon
20. 4	6. 3	J5	G9	Badger
21. 4	7. 3	J5	H10	Hare
22. 4	8. 3	J5	J11	Fox
23. 4	9. 3	J5	K12	Tiger
24. 4	10. 3	J5	A1	Leopard
25. 4	11. 3	J5	B2	Griffon
26. 4	12. 3	J5	C3	Ox
27. 4	13. 3	J5	D4	Bat
28. 4	14. 3	J5	E5	Rat
29. 4	15. 3	J5	F6	Swallow
30. 4	16. 3	J5	G7	Pig
1. 5	17. 3	J5	H8	Porcupine
2. 5	18. 3	J5	J9	Wolf
3. 5	19. 3	J5	K10	Dog
4. 5	20. 3	J5	A11	Pheasant
5. 5	21. 3	J5	B12	Cock
6. 5	22. 3	J5	C1	Crow
7. 5	23. 3	J5	D2	Monkey
8. 5	24. 3	J5	E3	Gibbon
9. 5	25. 3	J5	F4	Tapir
10. 5	26. 3	J5	G5	Sheep
11. 5	27. 3	J5	H6	Deer
12. 5	28. 3	J5	J7	Horse
13. 5	29. 3	J5	K8	Stag
14. 5	1. 4	K6	A9	Serpent
15. 5	2. 4	K6	B10	Earthworm
16. 5	3. 4	K6	C11	Crocodile
17. 5	4. 4	K6	D12	Dragon
18. 5	5. 4	K6	E1	Badger
19. 5	6. 4	K6	F2	Hare
20. 5	7. 4	K6	G3	Fox
21. 5	8. 4	K6	H4	Tiger
22. 5	9. 4	K6	J5	Leopard
23. 5	10. 4	K6	K6	Griffon
24. 5	11. 4	K6	A7	Ox
25. 5	12. 4	K6	B8	Bat
26. 5	13. 4	K6	C9	Rat
27. 5	14. 4	K6	D10	Swallow
28. 5	15. 4	K6	E11	Pig
29. 5	16. 4	K6	F12	Porcupine
30. 5	17. 4	K6	G1	Wolf
31. 5	18. 4	K6	H2	Dog
1. 6	19. 4	K6	J3	Pheasant
2. 6	20. 4	K6	K4	Cock
3. 6	21. 4	K6	A5	Crow
4. 6	22. 4	K6	B6	Monkey
5. 6	23. 4	K6	C7	Gibbon
6. 6	24. 4	K6	D8	Tapir
7. 6	25. 4	K6	E9	Sheep
8. 6	26. 4	K6	F10	Deer
9. 6	27. 4	K6	G11	Horse
10. 6	28. 4	K6	H12	Stag
11. 6	29. 4	K6	J1	Serpent
12. 6	1. 5	A7	K2	Earthworm
13. 6	2. 5	A7	A3	Crocodile
14. 6	3. 5	A7	B4	Dragon
15. 6	4. 5	A7	C5	Badger
16. 6	5. 5	A7	D6	Hare
17. 6	6. 5	A7	E7	Fox
18. 6	7. 5	A7	F8	Tiger
19. 6	8. 5	A7	G9	Leopard
20. 6	9. 5	A7	H10	Griffon
21. 6	10. 5	A7	J11	Ox
22. 6	11. 5	A7	K12	Bat
23. 6	12. 5	A7	A1	Rat
24. 6	13. 5	A7	B2	Swallow
25. 6	14. 5	A7	C3	Pig
26. 6	15. 5	A7	D4	Porcupine
27. 6	16. 5	A7	E5	Wolf
28. 6	17. 5	A7	F6	Dog
29. 6	18. 5	A7	G7	Pheasant
30. 6	19. 5	A7	H8	Cock
1. 7	20. 5	A7	J9	Crow
2. 7	21. 5	A7	K10	Monkey
3. 7	22. 5	A7	A11	Gibbon
4. 7	23. 5	A7	B12	Tapir
5. 7	24. 5	A7	C1	Sheep
6. 7	25. 5	A7	D2	Deer
7. 7	26. 5	A7	E3	Horse
8. 7	27. 5	A7	F4	Stag
9. 7	28. 5	A7	G5	Serpent
10. 7	29. 5	A7	H6	Earthworm
11. 7	30. 5	A7	J7	Crocodile
12. 7	1. 6	B8	K8	Dragon
13. 7	2. 6	B8	A9	Badger
14. 7	3. 6	B8	B10	Hare
15. 7	4. 6	B8	C11	Fox
16. 7	5. 6	B8	D12	Tiger
17. 7	6. 6	B8	E1	Leopard
18. 7	7. 6	B8	F2	Griffon
19. 7	8. 6	B8	G3	Ox
20. 7	9. 6	B8	H4	Bat
21. 7	10. 6	B8	J5	Rat
22. 7	11. 6	B8	K6	Swallow
23. 7	12. 6	B8	A7	Pig
24. 7	13. 6	B8	B8	Porcupine
25. 7	14. 6	B8	C9	Wolf
26. 7	15. 6	B8	D10	Dog
27. 7	16. 6	B8	E11	Pheasant
28. 7	17. 6	B8	F12	Cock
29. 7	18. 6	B8	G1	Crow
30. 7	19. 6	B8	H2	Monkey
31. 7	20. 6	B8	J3	Gibbon
1. 8	21. 6	B8	K4	Tapir
2. 8	22. 6	B8	A5	Sheep
3. 8	23. 6	B8	B6	Deer
4. 8	24. 6	B8	C7	Horse
5. 8	25. 6	B8	D8	Stag
6. 8	26. 6	B8	E9	Serpent
7. 8	27. 6	B8	F10	Earthworm
8. 8	28. 6	B8	G11	Crocodile
9. 8	29. 6	B8	H12	Dragon
10. 8	1. 7	C9	J1	Badger
11. 8	2. 7	C9	K2	Hare
12. 8	3. 7	C9	A3	Fox
13. 8	4. 7	C9	B4	Tiger
14. 8	5. 7	C9	C5	Leopard
15. 8	6. 7	C9	D6	Griffon
16. 8	7. 7	C9	E7	Ox
17. 8	8. 7	C9	F8	Bat

Solar date	Lunar date	Month HS/EB	Day HS/EB	Constellation
18. 8	9. 7	C9	G9	Rat
19. 8	10. 7	C9	H10	Swallow
20. 8	11. 7	C9	J11	Pig
21. 8	12. 7	C9	K12	Porcupine
22. 8	13. 7	C9	A1	Wolf
23. 8	14. 7	C9	B2	Dog
24. 8	15. 7	C9	C3	Pheasant
25. 8	16. 7	C9	D4	Cock
26. 8	17. 7	C9	E5	Crow
27. 8	18. 7	C9	F6	Monkey
28. 8	19. 7	C9	G7	Gibbon
29. 8	20. 7	C9	H8	Tapir
30. 8	21. 7	C9	J9	Sheep
31. 8	22. 7	C9	K10	Deer
1. 9	23. 7	C9	A11	Horse
2. 9	24. 7	C9	B12	Stag
3. 9	25. 7	C9	C1	Serpent
4. 9	26. 7	C9	D2	Earthworm
5. 9	27. 7	C9	E3	Crocodile
6. 9	28. 7	C9	F4	Dragon
7. 9	29. 7	C9	G5	Badger
8. 9	1. 8	D10	H6	Hare
9. 9	2. 8	D10	J7	Fox
10. 9	3. 8	D10	K8	Tiger
11. 9	4. 8	D10	A9	Leopard
12. 9	5. 8	D10	B10	Griffon
13. 9	6. 8	D10	C11	Ox
14. 9	7. 8	D10	D12	Bat
15. 9	8. 8	D10	E1	Rat
16. 9	9. 8	D10	F2	Swallow
17. 9	10. 8	D10	G3	Pig
18. 9	11. 8	D10	H4	Porcupine
19. 9	12. 8	D10	J5	Wolf
20. 9	13. 8	D10	K6	Dog
21. 9	14. 8	D10	A7	Pheasant
22. 9	15. 8	D10	B8	Cock
23. 9	16. 8	D10	C9	Crow
24. 9	17. 8	D10	D10	Monkey
25. 9	18. 8	D10	E11	Gibbon
26. 9	19. 8	D10	F12	Tapir
27. 9	20. 8	D10	G1	Sheep
28. 9	21. 8	D10	H2	Deer
29. 9	22. 8	D10	J3	Horse
30. 9	23. 8	D10	K4	Stag
1.10	24. 8	D10	A5	Serpent
2.10	25. 8	D10	B6	Earthworm
3.10	26. 8	D10	C7	Crocodile
4.10	27. 8	D10	D8	Dragon
5.10	28. 8	D10	E9	Badger
6.10	29. 8	D10	F10	Hare
7.10	30. 8	D10	G11	Fox
8.10	1. 9	E11	H12	Tiger
9.10	2. 9	E11	J1	Leopard
10.10	3. 9	E11	K2	Griffon
11.10	4. 9	E11	A3	Ox
12.10	5. 9	E11	B4	Bat
13.10	6. 9	E11	C5	Rat
14.10	7. 9	E11	D6	Swallow
15.10	8. 9	E11	E7	Pig
16.10	9. 9	E11	F8	Porcupine
17.10	10. 9	E11	G9	Wolf
18.10	11. 9	E11	H10	Dog
19.10	12. 9	E11	J11	Pheasant
20.10	13. 9	E11	K12	Cock
21.10	14. 9	E11	A1	Crow
22.10	15. 9	E11	B2	Monkey
23.10	16. 9	E11	C3	Gibbon
24.10	17. 9	E11	D4	Tapir
25.10	18. 9	E11	E5	Sheep
26.10	19. 9	E11	F6	Deer
27.10	20. 9	E11	G7	Horse
28.10	21. 9	E11	H8	Stag
29.10	22. 9	E11	J9	Serpent
30.10	23. 9	E11	K10	Earthworm
31.10	24. 9	E11	A11	Crocodile
1.11	25. 9	E11	B12	Dragon
2.11	26. 9	E11	C1	Badger
3.11	27. 9	E11	D2	Hare
4.11	28. 9	E11	E3	Fox
5.11	29. 9	E11	F4	Tiger
6.11	1.10	F12	G5	Leopard
7.11	2.10	F12	H6	Griffon
8.11	3.10	F12	J7	Ox
9.11	4.10	F12	K8	Bat
10.11	5.10	F12	A9	Rat
11.11	6.10	F12	B10	Swallow
12.11	7.10	F12	C11	Pig
13.11	8.10	F12	D12	Porcupine
14.11	9.10	F12	E1	Wolf
15.11	10.10	F12	F2	Dog
16.11	11.10	F12	G3	Pheasant
17.11	12.10	F12	H4	Cock
18.11	13.10	F12	J5	Crow
19.11	14.10	F12	K6	Monkey
20.11	15.10	F12	A7	Gibbon
21.11	16.10	F12	B8	Tapir
22.11	17.10	F12	C9	Sheep
23.11	18.10	F12	D10	Deer
24.11	19.10	F12	E11	Horse
25.11	20.10	F12	F12	Stag
26.11	21.10	F12	G1	Serpent
27.11	22.10	F12	H2	Earthworm
28.11	23.10	F12	J3	Crocodile
29.11	24.10	F12	K4	Dragon
30.11	25.10	F12	A5	Badger
1.12	26.10	F12	B6	Hare
2.12	27.10	F12	C7	Fox
3.12	28.10	F12	D8	Tiger
4.12	29.10	F12	E9	Leopard
5.12	30.10	F12	F10	Griffon
6.12	1.11	G1	G11	Ox
7.12	2.11	G1	H12	Bat
8.12	3.11	G1	J1	Rat
9.12	4.11	G1	K2	Swallow
10.12	5.11	G1	A3	Pig
11.12	6.11	G1	B4	Porcupine
12.12	7.11	G1	C5	Wolf
13.12	8.11	G1	D6	Dog
14.12	9.11	G1	E7	Pheasant
15.12	10.11	G1	F8	Cock
16.12	11.11	G1	G9	Crow
17.12	12.11	G1	H10	Monkey
18.12	13.11	G1	J11	Gibbon
19.12	14.11	G1	K12	Tapir
20.12	15.11	G1	A1	Sheep
21.12	16.11	G1	B2	Deer
22.12	17.11	G1	C3	Horse
23.12	18.11	G1	D4	Stag
24.12	19.11	G1	E5	Serpent
25.12	20.11	G1	F6	Earthworm
26.12	21.11	G1	G7	Crocodile
27.12	22.11	G1	H8	Dragon
28.12	23.11	G1	J9	Badger
29.12	24.11	G1	K10	Hare
30.12	25.11	G1	A11	Fox
31.12	26.11	G1	B12	Tiger
1992				
1. 1	27.11	G1	C1	Leopard
2. 1	28.11	G1	D2	Griffon
3. 1	29.11	G1	E3	Ox
4. 1	30.11	G1	F4	Bat
5. 1	1.12	H2	G5	Rat
6. 1	2.12	H2	H6	Swallow
7. 1	3.12	H2	J7	Pig
8. 1	4.12	H2	K8	Porcupine

Solar date	Lunar date	Month HS/EB	Day HS/EB	Constellation
9. 1	5.11	H2	A9	Wolf
10. 1	6.11	H2	B10	Dog
11. 1	7.11	H2	C11	Pheasant
12. 1	8.11	H2	D12	Cock
13. 1	9.11	H2	E1	Crow
14. 1	10.11	H2	F2	Monkey
15. 1	11.11	H2	G3	Gibbon
16. 1	12.11	H2	H4	Tapir
17. 1	13.11	H2	J5	Sheep
18. 1	14.12	H2	K6	Deer
19. 1	15.12	H2	A7	Horse
20. 1	16.12	H2	B8	Stag
21. 1	17.12	H2	C9	Serpent
22. 1	18.12	H2	D10	Earthworm
23. 1	19.12	H2	E11	Crocodile
24. 1	20.12	H2	F12	Dragon
25. 1	21.12	H2	G1	Badger
26. 1	22.12	H2	H2	Hare
27. 1	23.12	H2	J3	Fox
28. 1	24.12	H2	K4	Tiger
29. 1	25.12	H2	A5	Leopard
30. 1	26.12	H2	B6	Griffon
31. 1	27.12	H2	C7	Ox
1. 2	28.12	H2	D8	Bat
2. 2	29.12	H2	E9	Rat
3. 2	30.12	H2	F10	Swallow

JEN SHEN YEAR

Solar date	Lunar date	Month HS/EB	Day HS/EB	Constellation
4. 2	1. 1	J3	G11	Pig
5. 2	2. 1	J3	H12	Porcupine
6. 2	3. 1	J3	J1	Wolf
7. 2	4. 1	J3	K2	Dog
8. 2	5. 1	J3	A3	Pheasant
9. 2	6. 1	J3	B4	Cock
10. 2	7. 1	J3	C5	Crow
11. 2	8. 1	J3	D6	Monkey
12. 2	9. 1	J3	E7	Gibbon
13. 2	10. 1	J3	F8	Tapir
14. 2	11. 1	J3	G9	Sheep
15. 2	12. 1	J3	H10	Deer
16. 2	13. 1	J3	J11	Horse
17. 2	14. 1	J3	K12	Stag
18. 2	15. 1	J3	A1	Serpent
19. 2	16. 1	J3	B2	Earthworm
20. 2	17. 1	J3	C3	Crocodile
21. 2	18. 1	J3	D4	Dragon
22. 2	19. 1	J3	E5	Badger
23. 2	20. 1	J3	F6	Hare
24. 2	21. 1	J3	G7	Fox
25. 2	22. 1	J3	H8	Tiger
26. 2	23. 1	J3	J9	Leopard
27. 2	24. 1	J3	K10	Griffon
28. 2	25. 1	J3	A11	Ox
29. 2	26. 1	J3	B12	Bat
1. 3	27. 1	J3	C1	Rat
2. 3	28. 1	J3	D2	Swallow
3. 3	29. 1	J3	E3	Pig
4. 3	1. 2	K4	F4	Porcupine
5. 3	2. 2	K4	G5	Wolf
6. 3	3. 2	K4	H6	Dog
7. 3	4. 2	K4	J7	Pheasant
8. 3	5. 2	K4	K8	Cock
9. 3	6. 2	K4	A9	Crow
10. 3	7. 2	K4	B10	Monkey
11. 3	8. 2	K4	C11	Gibbon
12. 3	9. 2	K4	D12	Tapir
13. 3	10. 2	K4	E1	Sheep
14. 3	11. 2	K4	F2	Deer
15. 3	12. 2	K4	G3	Horse
16. 3	13. 2	K4	H4	Stag
17. 3	14. 2	K4	J5	Serpent
18. 3	15. 2	K4	K6	Earthworm
19. 3	16. 2	K4	A7	Crocodile
20. 3	17. 2	K4	B8	Dragon
21. 3	18. 2	K4	C9	Badger
22. 3	19. 2	K4	D10	Hare
23. 3	20. 2	K4	E11	Fox
24. 3	21. 2	K4	F12	Tiger
25. 3	22. 2	K4	G1	Leopard
26. 3	23. 2	K4	H2	Griffon
27. 3	24. 2	K4	J3	Ox
28. 3	25. 2	K4	K4	Bat
29. 3	26. 2	K4	A5	Rat
30. 3	27. 2	K4	B6	Swallow
31. 3	28. 2	K4	C7	Pig
1. 4	29. 2	K4	D8	Porcupine
2. 4	30. 2	K4	E9	Wolf
3. 2	1. 3	A5	F10	Dog
4. 4	2. 3	A5	G11	Pheasant
5. 4	3. 3	A5	H12	Cock
6. 4	4. 3	A5	J1	Crow
7. 4	5. 3	A5	K2	Monkey
8. 4	6. 3	A5	A3	Gibbon
9. 4	7. 3	A5	B4	Tapir
10. 4	8. 3	A5	C5	Sheep
11. 4	9. 3	A5	D6	Deer
12. 4	10. 3	A5	E7	Horse
13. 4	11. 3	A5	F8	Stag
14. 4	12. 3	A5	G9	Serpent
15. 4	13. 3	A5	H10	Earthworm
16. 4	14. 3	A5	J11	Crocodile
17. 4	15. 3	A5	K12	Dragon
18. 4	16. 3	A5	A1	Badger
19. 4	17. 3	A5	B2	Hare
20. 4	18. 3	A5	C3	Fox
21. 4	19. 3	A5	D4	Tiger
22. 4	20. 3	A5	E5	Leopard
23. 4	21. 3	A5	F6	Griffon
24. 4	22. 3	A5	G7	Ox
25. 4	23. 3	A5	H8	Bat
26. 4	24. 3	A5	J9	Rat
27. 4	25. 3	A5	K10	Swallow
28. 4	26. 3	A5	A11	Pig
29. 4	27. 3	A5	B12	Porcupine
30. 4	28. 3	A5	C1	Wolf
1. 5	29. 3	A5	D2	Dog
2. 5	30. 3	A5	E3	Pheasant
3. 5	1. 4	B6	F4	Cock
4. 5	2. 4	B6	G5	Crow
5. 5	3. 4	B6	H6	Monkey
6. 5	4. 4	B6	J7	Gibbon
7. 5	5. 4	B6	K8	Tapir
8. 5	6. 4	B6	A9	Sheep
9. 5	7. 4	B6	B10	Deer
10. 5	8. 4	B6	C11	Horse
11. 5	9. 4	B6	D12	Stag
12. 5	10. 4	B6	E1	Serpent
13. 5	11. 4	B6	F2	Earthworm
14. 5	12. 4	B6	G3	Crocodile
15. 5	13. 4	B6	H4	Dragon
16. 5	14. 4	B6	J5	Badger
17. 5	15. 4	B6	K6	Hare
18. 5	16. 4	B6	A7	Fox
19. 5	17. 4	B6	B8	Tiger
20. 5	18. 4	B6	C9	Leopard
21. 5	19. 4	B6	D10	Griffon
22. 5	20. 4	B6	E11	Ox
23. 5	21. 4	B6	F12	Bat

Solar date	Lunar date	Month HS/EB	Day HS/EB	Constellation	Solar date	Lunar date	Month HS/EB	Day HS/EB	Constellation
24. 5	22. 4	B6	G1	Rat	5. 8	7. 7	E9	K2	Earthworm
25. 5	23. 4	B6	H2	Swallow	6. 8	8. 7	E9	A3	Crocodile
26. 5	24. 4	B6	J3	Pig	7. 8	9. 7	E9	B4	Dragon
27. 5	25. 4	B6	K4	Porcupine	8. 8	10. 7	E9	C5	Badger
28. 5	26. 4	B6	A5	Wolf	9. 8	11. 7	E9	D6	Hare
29. 5	27. 4	B6	B6	Dog	10. 8	12. 7	E9	E7	Fox
30. 5	28. 4	B6	C7	Pheasant	11. 8	13. 7	E9	F8	Tiger
31. 5	29. 4	B6	D8	Cock	12. 8	14. 7	E9	G9	Leopard
1. 6	1. 5	C7	E9	Crow	13. 8	15. 7	E9	H10	Griffon
2. 6	2. 5	C7	F10	Monkey	14. 8	16. 7	E9	J11	Ox
3. 6	3. 5	C7	G11	Gibbon	15. 8	17. 7	E9	K12	Bat
4. 6	4. 5	C7	H12	Tapir	16. 8	18. 7	E9	A1	Rat
5. 6	5. 5	C7	J1	Sheep	17. 8	19. 7	E9	B2	Swallow
6. 6	6. 5	C7	K2	Deer	18. 8	20. 7	E9	C3	Pig
7. 6	7. 5	C7	A3	Horse	19. 8	21. 7	E9	D4	Porcupine
8. 6	8. 5	C7	B4	Stage	20. 8	22. 7	E9	E5	Wolf
9. 6	9. 5	C7	C5	Serpent	21. 8	23. 7	E9	F6	Dog
10. 6	10. 5	C7	D6	Earthworm	22. 8	24. 7	E9	G7	Pheasant
11. 6	11. 5	C7	E7	Crocodile	23. 8	25. 7	E9	H8	Cock
12. 6	12. 5	C7	F8	Dragon	24. 8	26. 7	E9	J9	Crow
13. 6	13. 5	C7	G9	Badger	25. 8	27. 7	E9	K10	Monkey
14. 6	14. 5	C7	H10	Hare	26. 8	28. 7	E9	A11	Gibbon
15. 6	15. 5	C7	J11	Fox	27. 8	29. 7	E9	B12	Tapir
16. 6	16. 5	C7	K12	Tiger	28. 8	1. 8	F10	C1	Sheep
17. 6	17. 5	C7	A1	Leopard	29. 8	2. 8	F10	D2	Deer
18. 6	18. 5	C7	B2	Griffon	30. 8	3. 8	F10	E3	Horse
19. 6	19. 5	C7	C3	Ox	31. 8	4. 8	F10	F4	Stag
20. 6	20. 5	C7	D4	Bat	1. 9	5. 8	F10	G5	Serpent
21. 6	21. 5	C7	E5	Rat	2. 9	6. 8	F10	H6	Earthworm
22. 6	22. 5	C7	F6	Swallow	3. 9	7. 8	F10	J7	Crocodile
23. 6	23. 5	C7	G7	Pig	4. 9	8. 8	F10	K8	Dragon
24. 6	24. 5	C7	H8	Porcupine	5. 9	9. 8	F10	A9	Badger
25. 6	25. 5	C7	J9	Wolf	6. 9	10. 8	F10	B10	Hare
26. 6	26. 5	C7	K10	Dog	7. 9	11. 8	F10	C11	Fox
27. 6	27. 5	C7	A11	Pheasant	8. 9	12. 8	F10	D12	Tiger
28. 6	28. 5	C7	B12	Cock	9. 9	13. 8	F10	E1	Leopard
29. 6	29. 5	C7	C1	Crow	10. 9	14. 8	F10	F2	Griffon
30. 6	1. 6	D8	D2	Monkey	11. 9	15. 8	F10	G3	Ox
1. 7	2. 6	D8	E3	Gibbon	12. 9	16. 8	F10	H4	Bat
2. 7	3. 6	D8	F4	Tapir	13. 9	17. 8	F10	J5	Rat
3. 7	4. 6	D8	G5	Sheep	14. 9	18. 8	F10	K6	Swallow
4. 7	5. 6	D8	H6	Deer	15. 9	19. 8	F10	A7	Pig
5. 7	6. 6	D8	J7	Horse	16. 9	20. 8	F10	B8	Porcupine
6. 7	7. 6	D8	K8	Stag	17. 9	21. 8	F10	C9	Wolf
7. 7	8. 6	D8	A9	Serpent	18. 9	22. 8	F10	D10	Dog
8. 7	9. 6	D8	B10	Earthworm	19. 9	23. 8	F10	E11	Pheasant
9. 7	10. 6	D8	C11	Crocodile	20. 9	24. 8	F10	F12	Cock
10. 7	11. 6	D8	D12	Dragon	21. 9	25. 8	F10	G1	Crow
11. 7	12. 6	D8	E1	Badger	22. 9	26. 8	F10	H2	Monkey
12. 7	13. 6	D8	F2	Hare	23. 9	27. 8	F10	J3	Gibbon
13. 7	14. 6	D8	G3	Fox	24. 9	28. 8	F10	K4	Tapir
14. 7	15. 6	D8	H4	Tiger	25. 9	29. 8	F10	A5	Sheep
15. 7	16. 6	D8	J5	Leopard	26. 9	1. 9	G11	B6	Deer
16. 7	17. 6	D8	K6	Griffon	27. 9	2. 9	G11	C7	Horse
17. 7	18. 6	D8	A7	Ox	28. 9	3. 9	G11	D8	Stag
18. 7	19. 6	D8	B8	Bat	29. 9	4. 9	G11	E9	Serpent
19. 7	20. 6	D8	C9	Rat	30. 9	5. 9	G11	F10	Earthworm
20. 7	21. 6	D8	D10	Swallow	1.10	6. 9	G11	G11	Crocodile
21. 7	22. 6	D8	E11	Pig	2.10	7. 9	G11	H12	Dragon
22. 7	23. 6	D8	F12	Porcupine	3.10	8. 9	G11	J1	Badger
23. 7	24. 6	D8	G1	Wolf	4.10	9. 9	G11	K2	Hare
24. 7	25. 6	D8	H2	Dog	5.10	10. 9	G11	A3	Fox
25. 7	26. 6	D8	J3	Pheasant	6.10	11. 9	G11	B4	Tiger
26. 7	27. 6	D8	K4	Cock	7.10	12. 9	G11	C5	Leopard
27. 7	28. 6	D8	A5	Crow	8.10	13. 9	G11	D6	Griffon
28. 7	29. 6	D8	B6	Monkey	9.10	14. 9	G11	E7	Ox
29. 7	30. 6	D8	C7	Gibbon	10.10	15. 9	G11	F8	Bat
30. 7	1. 7	E9	D8	Tapir	11.10	16. 9	G11	G9	Rat
31. 7	2. 7	E9	E9	Sheep	12.10	17. 9	G11	H10	Swallow
1. 8	3. 7	E9	F10	Deer	13.10	18. 9	G11	J11	Pig
2. 8	4. 7	E9	G11	Horse	14.10	19. 9	G11	K12	Porcupine
3. 8	5. 7	E9	H12	Stag	15.10	20. 9	G11	A1	Wolf
4. 8	6. 7	E9	J1	Serpent	16.10	21. 9	G11	B2	Dog

Solar date	Lunar date	Month HS/EB	Day HS/EB	Constellation
17.10	22. 9	G11	C3	Pheasant
18.10	23. 9	G11	D4	Cock
19.10	24. 9	G11	E5	Crow
20.10	25. 9	G11	F6	Monkey
21.10	26. 9	G11	G7	Gibbon
22.10	27. 9	G11	H8	Tapir
23.10	28. 9	G11	J9	Sheep
24.10	29. 9	G11	K10	Deer
25.10	30. 9	G11	A11	Horse
26.10	1.10	H12	B12	Stag
27.10	2.10	H12	C1	Serpent
28.10	3.10	H12	D2	Earthworm
29.10	4.10	H12	E3	Crocodile
30.10	5.10	H12	F4	Dragon
31.10	6.10	H12	G5	Badger
1.11	7.10	H12	H6	Hare
2.11	8.10	H12	J7	Fox
3.11	9.10	H12	K8	Tiger
4.11	10.10	H12	A9	Leopard
5.11	11.10	H12	B10	Griffon
6.11	12.10	H12	C11	Ox
7.11	13.10	H12	D12	Bat
8.11	14.10	H12	E1	Rat
9.11	15.10	H12	F2	Swallow
10.11	16.10	H12	G3	Pig
11.11	17.10	H12	H4	Porcupine
12.11	18.10	H12	J5	Wolf
13.11	19.10	H12	K6	Dog
14.11	20.10	H12	A7	Pheasant
15.11	21.10	H12	B8	Cock
16.11	22.10	H12	C9	Crow
17.11	23.10	H12	D10	Monkey
18.11	24.10	H12	E11	Gibbon
19.11	25.10	H12	F12	Tapir
20.11	26.10	H12	G1	Sheep
21.11	27.10	H12	H2	Deer
22.11	28.10	H12	J3	Horse
23.11	29.10	H12	K4	Stag
24.11	1.11	J1	A5	Serpent
25.11	2.11	J1	B6	Earthworm
26.11	3.11	J1	C7	Crocodile
27.11	4.11	J1	D8	Dragon
28.11	5.11	J1	E9	Badger
29.11	6.11	J1	F10	Hare
30.11	7.11	J1	G11	Fox
1.12	8.11	J1	H12	Tiger
2.12	9.11	J1	J1	Leopard
3.12	10.11	J1	K2	Griffon
4.12	11.11	J1	A3	Ox
5.12	12.11	J1	B4	Bat
6.12	13.11	J1	C5	Rat
7.12	14.11	J1	D6	Swallow
8.12	15.11	J1	E7	Pig
9.12	16.11	J1	F8	Porcupine
10.12	17.11	J1	G9	Wolf
11.12	18.11	J1	H10	Dog
12.12	19.11	J1	J11	Pheasant
13.12	20.11	J1	K12	Cock
14.12	21.11	J1	A1	Crow
15.12	22.11	J1	B2	Monkey
16.12	23.11	J1	C3	Gibbon
17.12	24.11	J1	D4	Tapir
18.12	25.11	J1	E5	Sheep
19.12	26.11	J1	F6	Deer
20.12	27.11	J1	G7	Horse
21.12	28.11	J1	H8	Stag
22.12	29.11	J1	J9	Serpent
23.12	30.11	J1	K10	Earthworm
24.12	1.12	K2	A1	Crocodile
25.12	2.12	K2	B12	Dragon
26.12	3.12	K2	C1	Badger
27.12	4.12	K2	D2	Hare
28.12	5.12	K2	E3	Fox
29.12	6.12	K2	F4	Tiger
30.12	7.12	K2	G5	Leopard
31.12	8.12	K2	H6	Griffon

1993

Solar date	Lunar date	Month HS/EB	Day HS/EB	Constellation
1. 1	9.12	K2	J7	Ox
2. 1	10.12	K2	K8	Bat
3. 1	11.12	K2	A9	Rat
4. 1	12.12	K2	B10	Swallow
5. 1	13.12	K2	C11	Pig
6. 1	14.12	K2	D12	Porcupine
7. 1	15.12	K2	E1	Wolf
8. 1	16.12	K2	F2	Dog
9. 1	17.12	K2	G3	Pheasant
10. 1	18.12	K2	H4	Cock
11. 1	19.12	K2	J5	Crow
12. 1	20.12	K2	K6	Monkey
13. 1	21.12	K2	A7	Gibbon
14. 1	22.12	K2	B8	Tapir
15. 1	23.12	K2	C9	Sheep
16. 1	24.12	K2	D10	Deer
17. 1	25.12	K2	E11	Horse
18. 1	26.12	K2	F12	Stag
19. 1	27.12	K2	G1	Serpent
20. 1	28.12	K2	H2	Earthworm
21. 1	29.12	K2	J3	Crocodile
22. 1	30.12	K2	K4	Dragon

KUEI YU YEAR

Solar date	Lunar date	Month HS/EB	Day HS/EB	Constellation
23. 1	1. 1	A3	A5	Badger
24. 1	2. 1	A3	B6	Hare
25. 1	3. 1	A3	C7	Fox
26. 1	4. 1	A3	D8	Tiger
27. 1	5. 1	A3	E9	Leopard
28. 1	6. 1	A3	F10	Griffon
29. 1	7. 1	A3	G11	Ox
30. 1	8. 1	A3	H12	Bat
31. 1	9. 1	A3	J1	Rat
1. 2	10. 1	A3	K2	Swallow
2. 2	11. 1	A3	A3	Pig
3. 2	12. 1	A3	B4	Porcupine
4. 2	13. 1	A3	C5	Wolf
5. 2	14. 1	A3	D6	Dog
6. 2	15. 1	A3	E7	Pheasant
7. 2	16. 1	A3	F8	Cock
8. 2	17. 1	A3	G9	Crow
9. 2	18. 1	A3	H10	Monkey
10. 2	19. 1	A3	J11	Gibbon
11. 2	20. 1	A3	K12	Tapir
12. 2	21. 1	A3	A1	Sheep
13. 2	22. 1	A3	B2	Deer
14. 2	23. 1	A3	C3	Horse
15. 2	24. 1	A3	D4	Stag
16. 2	25. 1	A3	E5	Serpent
17. 2	26. 1	A3	F6	Earthworm
18. 2	27. 1	A3	G7	Crocodile
19. 2	28. 1	A3	H8	Dragon
20. 2	29. 1	A3	J9	Badger
21. 2	1. 2	B4	K10	Hare
22. 2	2. 2	B4	A11	Fox
23. 2	3. 2	B4	B12	Tiger
24. 2	4. 2	B4	C1	Leopard
25. 2	5. 2	B4	D2	Griffon
26. 2	6. 2	B4	E3	Ox
27. 2	7. 2	B4	F4	Bat

Solar date	Lunar date	Month HS/EB	Day HS/EB	Constellation	Solar date	Lunar date	Month HS/EB	Day HS/EB	Constellation
28. 2	8. 2	B4	G5	Rat	12. 5	*21. 3*	*C5*	K6	Earthworm
1. 3	9. 2	B4	H6	Swallow	13. 5	*22. 3*	*C5*	A7	Crocodile
2. 3	10. 2	B4	J7	Pig	14. 5	*23. 3*	*C5*	B8	Dragon
3. 3	11. 2	B4	K8	Porcupine	15. 5	*24. 3*	*C5*	C9	Badger
4. 3	12. 2	B4	A9	Wolf	16. 5	*25. 3*	*C5*	D10	Hare
5. 3	13. 2	B4	B10	Dog	17. 5	*26. 3*	*C5*	E11	Fox
6. 3	14. 2	B4	C11	Pheasant	18. 5	*27. 3*	*C5*	F12	Tiger
7. 3	15. 2	B4	D12	Cock	19. 5	*28. 3*	*C5*	G1	Leopard
8. 3	16. 2	B4	E1	Crow	20. 5	*29. 3*	*C5*	H2	Griffon
9. 3	17. 2	B4	F2	Monkey	21. 5	1. 4	D6	J3	Ox
10. 3	18. 2	B4	G3	Gibbon	22. 5	2. 4	D6	K4	Bat
11. 3	19. 2	B4	H4	Tapir	23. 5	3. 4	D6	A5	Rat
12. 3	20. 2	B4	J5	Sheep	24. 5	4. 4	D6	B6	Swallow
13. 3	21. 2	B4	K6	Deer	25. 5	5. 4	D6	C7	Pig
14. 3	22. 2	B4	A7	Horse	26. 5	6. 4	D6	D8	Porcupine
15. 3	23. 2	B4	B8	Stag	27. 5	7. 4	D6	E9	Wolf
16. 3	24. 2	B4	C9	Serpent	28. 5	8. 4	D6	F10	Dog
17. 3	25. 2	B4	D10	Earthworm	29. 5	9. 4	D6	G11	Pheasant
18. 3	26. 2	B4	E11	Crocodile	30. 5	10. 4	D6	H12	Cock
19. 3	27. 2	B4	F12	Dragon	31. 5	11. 4	D6	J1	Crow
20. 3	28. 2	B4	G1	Badger	1. 6	12. 4	D6	K2	Monkey
21. 3	29. 2	B4	H2	Hare	2. 6	13. 4	D6	A3	Gibbon
22. 3	30. 2	B4	J3	Fox	3. 6	14. 4	D6	B4	Tapir
23. 3	1. 3	C5	K4	Tiger	4. 6	15. 4	D6	C5	Sheep
24. 3	2. 3	C5	A5	Leopard	5. 6	16. 4	D6	D6	Deer
25. 3	3. 3	C5	B6	Griffon	6. 6	17. 4	D6	E7	Horse
26. 3	4. 3	C5	C7	Ox	7. 6	18. 4	D6	F8	Stag
27. 3	5. 3	C5	D8	Bat	8. 6	19. 4	D6	G9	Serpent
28. 3	6. 3	C5	E9	Rat	9. 6	20. 4	D6	H10	Earthworm
29. 3	7. 3	C5	F10	Swallow	10. 6	21. 4	D6	J11	Crocodile
30. 3	8. 3	C5	G11	Pig	11. 6	22. 4	D6	K12	Dragon
31. 3	9. 3	C5	H12	Porcupine	12. 6	23. 4	D6	A1	Badger
1. 4	10. 3	C5	J1	Wolf	13. 6	24. 4	D6	B2	Hare
2. 4	11. 3	C5	K2	Dog	14. 6	25. 4	D6	C3	Fox
3. 4	12. 3	C5	A3	Pheasant	15. 6	26. 4	D6	D4	Tiger
4. 4	13. 3	C5	B4	Cock	16. 6	27. 4	D6	E5	Leopard
5. 4	14. 3	C5	C5	Crow	17. 6	28. 4	D6	F6	Griffon
6. 4	15. 3	C5	D6	Monkey	18. 6	29. 4	D6	G7	Ox
7. 4	16. 3	C5	E7	Gibbon	19. 6	30. 4	D6	H8	Bat
8. 4	17. 3	C5	F8	Tapir	20. 6	1. 5	E7	J9	Rat
9. 4	18. 3	C5	G9	Sheep	21. 6	2. 5	E7	K10	Swallow
10. 4	19. 3	C5	H10	Deer	22. 6	3. 5	E7	A11	Pig
11. 4	20. 3	C5	J11	Horse	23. 6	4. 5	E7	B12	Porcupine
12. 4	21. 3	C5	K12	Stag	24. 6	5. 5	E7	C1	Wolf
13. 4	22. 3	C5	A1	Serpent	25. 6	6. 5	E7	D2	Dog
14. 4	23. 3	C5	B2	Earthworm	26. 6	7. 5	E7	E3	Pheasant
15. 4	24. 3	C5	C3	Crocodile	27. 6	8. 5	E7	F4	Cock
16. 4	25. 3	C5	D4	Dragon	28. 6	9. 5	E7	G5	Crow
17. 4	26. 3	C5	E5	Badger	29. 6	10. 5	E7	H6	Monkey
18. 4	27. 3	C5	F6	Hare	30. 6	11. 5	E7	J7	Gibbon
19. 4	28. 3	C5	G7	Fox	1. 7	12. 5	E7	K8	Tapir
20. 4	29. 3	C5	H8	Tiger	2. 7	13. 5	E7	A9	Sheep
21. 4	30. 3	C5	J9	Leopard	3. 7	14. 5	E7	B10	Deer
22. 4	*1. 3*	*C5*	K10	Griffon	4. 7	15. 5	E7	C11	Horse
23. 4	*2. 3*	*C5*	A11	Ox	5. 7	16. 5	E7	D12	Stag
24. 4	*3. 3*	*C5*	B12	Bat	6. 7	17. 5	E7	E1	Serpent
25. 4	*4. 3*	*C5*	C1	Rat	7. 7	18. 5	E7	F2	Earthworm
26. 4	*5. 3*	*C5*	D2	Swallow	8. 7	19. 5	E7	G3	Crocodile
27. 4	*6. 3*	*C5*	E3	Pig	9. 7	20. 5	E7	H4	Dragon
28. 4	*7. 3*	*C5*	F4	Porcupine	10. 7	21. 5	E7	J5	Badger
29. 4	*8. 3*	*C5*	G5	Wolf	11. 7	22. 5	E7	K6	Hare
30. 4	*9. 3*	*C5*	H6	Dog	12. 7	23. 5	E7	A7	Fox
1. 5	*10. 3*	*C5*	J7	Pheasant	13. 7	24. 5	E7	B8	Tiger
2. 5	*11. 3*	*C5*	K8	Cock	14. 7	25. 5	E7	C9	Leopard
3. 5	*12. 3*	*C5*	A9	Crow	15. 7	26. 5	E7	D10	Griffon
4. 5	*13. 3*	*C5*	B10	Monkey	16. 7	27. 5	E7	E11	Ox
5. 5	*14. 3*	*C5*	C11	Gibbon	17. 7	28. 5	E7	F12	Bat
6. 5	*15. 3*	*C5*	D12	Tapir	18. 7	29. 5	E7	G1	Rat
7. 5	*16. 3*	*C5*	E1	Sheep	19. 7	1. 6	F8	H2	Swallow
8. 5	*17. 3*	*C5*	F2	Deer	20. 7	2. 6	F8	J3	Pig
9. 5	*18. 3*	*C5*	G3	Horse	21. 7	3. 6	F8	K4	Porcupine
10. 5	*19. 3*	*C5*	H4	Stag	22. 7	4. 6	F8	A5	Wolf
11. 5	*20. 3*	*C5*	J5	Serpent	23. 7	5. 6	F8	B6	Dog

Solar date	Lunar date	Month HS/EB	Day HS/EB	Constellation	Solar date	Lunar date	Month HS/EB	Day HS/EB	Constellation
24. 7	6. 6	F8	C7	Pheasant	5.10	20. 8	H10	F8	Tiger
25. 7	7. 6	F8	D8	Cock	6.10	21. 8	H10	G9	Leopard
26. 7	8. 6	F8	E9	Crow	7.10	22. 8	H10	H10	Griffon
27. 7	9. 6	F8	F10	Monkey	8.10	23. 8	H10	J11	Ox
28. 7	10. 6	F8	G11	Gibbon	9.10	24. 8	H10	K12	Bat
29. 7	11. 6	F8	H12	Tapir	10.10	25. 8	H10	A1	Rat
30. 7	12. 6	F8	J1	Sheep	11.10	26. 8	H10	B2	Swallow
31. 7	13. 6	F8	K2	Deer	12.10	27. 8	H10	C3	Pig
1. 8	14. 6	F8	A3	Horse	13.10	28. 8	H10	D4	Porcupine
2. 8	15. 6	F8	B4	Stag	14.10	29. 8	H10	E5	Wolf
3. 8	16. 6	F8	C5	Serpent	15.10	1. 9	J11	F6	Dog
4. 8	17. 6	F8	D6	Earthworm	16.10	2. 9	J11	G7	Pheasant
5. 8	18. 6	F8	E7	Crocodile	17.10	3. 9	J11	H8	Cock
6. 8	19. 6	F8	F8	Dragon	18.10	4. 9	J11	J9	Crow
7. 8	20. 6	F8	G9	Badger	19.10	5. 9	J11	K10	Monkey
8. 8	21. 6	F8	H10	Hare	20.10	6. 9	J11	A11	Gibbon
9. 8	22. 6	F8	J11	Fox	21.10	7. 9	J11	B12	Tapir
10. 8	23. 6	F8	K12	Tiger	22.10	8. 9	J11	C1	Sheep
11. 8	24. 6	F8	A1	Leopard	23.10	9. 9	J11	D2	Deer
12. 8	25. 6	F8	B2	Griffon	24.10	10. 9	J11	E3	Horse
13. 8	26. 6	F8	C3	Ox	25.10	11. 9	J11	F4	Stag
14. 8	27. 6	F8	D4	Bat	26.10	12. 9	J11	G5	Serpent
15. 8	28. 6	F8	E5	Rat	27.10	13. 9	J11	H6	Earthworm
16. 8	29. 6	F8	F6	Swallow	28.10	14. 9	J11	J7	Crocodile
17. 8	30. 6	F8	G7	Pig	29.10	15. 9	J11	K8	Dragon
18. 8	1. 7	G9	H8	Porcupine	30.10	16. 9	J11	A9	Badger
19. 8	2. 7	G9	J9	Wolf	31.10	17. 9	J11	B10	Hare
20. 8	3. 7	G9	K10	Dog	1.11	18. 9	J11	C11	Fox
21. 8	4. 7	G9	A11	Pheasant	2.11	19. 9	J11	D12	Tiger
22. 8	5. 7	G9	B12	Cock	3.11	20. 9	J11	E1	Leopard
23. 8	6. 7	G9	C1	Crow	4.11	21. 9	J11	F2	Griffon
24. 8	7. 7	G9	D2	Monkey	5.11	22. 9	J11	G3	Ox
25. 8	8. 7	G9	E3	Gibbon	6.11	23. 9	J11	H4	Bat
26. 8	9. 7	G9	F4	Tapir	7.11	24. 9	J11	J5	Rat
27. 8	10. 7	G9	G5	Sheep	8.11	25. 9	J11	K6	Swallow
28. 8	11. 7	G9	H6	Deer	9.11	26. 9	J11	A7	Pig
29. 8	12. 7	G9	J7	Horse	10.11	27. 9	J11	B8	Porcupine
30. 8	13. 7	G9	K8	Stag	11.11	28. 9	J11	C9	Wolf
31. 8	14. 7	G9	A9	Serpent	12.11	29. 9	J11	D10	Dog
1. 9	15. 7	G9	B10	Earthworm	13.11	30. 9	J11	E11	Pheasant
2. 9	16. 7	G9	C11	Crocodile	14.11	1.10	K12	F12	Cock
3. 9	17. 7	G9	D12	Dragon	15.11	2.10	K12	G1	Crow
4. 9	18. 7	G9	E1	Badger	16.11	3.10	K12	H2	Monkey
5. 9	19. 7	G9	F2	Hare	17.11	4.10	K12	J3	Gibbon
6. 9	20. 7	G9	G3	Fox	18.11	5.10	K12	K4	Tapir
7. 9	21. 7	G9	H4	Tiger	19.11	6.10	K12	A5	Sheep
8. 9	22. 7	G9	J5	Leopard	20.11	7.10	K12	B6	Deer
9. 9	23. 7	G9	K6	Griffon	21.11	8.10	K12	C7	Horse
10. 9	24. 7	G9	A7	Ox	22.11	9.10	K12	D8	Stag
11. 9	25. 7	G9	B8	Bat	23.11	10.10	K12	E9	Serpent
12. 9	26. 7	G9	C9	Rat	24.11	11.10	K12	F10	Earthworm
13. 9	27. 7	G9	D10	Swallow	25.11	12.10	K12	G11	Crocodile
14. 9	28. 7	G9	E11	Pig	26.11	13.10	K12	H12	Dragon
15. 9	29. 7	G9	F12	Porcupine	27.11	14.10	K12	J1	Badger
16. 9	1. 8	H10	G1	Wolf	28.11	15.10	K12	K2	Hare
17. 9	2. 8	H10	H2	Dog	29.11	16.10	K12	A3	Fox
18. 9	3. 8	H10	J3	Pheasant	30.11	17.10	K12	B4	Tiger
19. 9	4. 8	H10	K4	Cock	1.12	18.10	K12	C5	Leopard
20. 9	5. 8	H10	A5	Crow	2.12	19.10	K12	D6	Griffon
21. 9	6. 8	H10	B6	Monkey	3.12	20.10	K12	E7	Ox
22. 9	7. 8	H10	C7	Gibbon	4.12	21.10	K12	F8	Bat
23. 9	8. 8	H10	D8	Tapir	5.12	22.10	K12	G9	Rat
24. 9	9. 8	H10	E9	Sheep	6.12	23.10	K12	H10	Swallow
25. 9	10. 8	H10	F10	Deer	7.12	24.10	K12	J11	Pig
26. 9	11. 8	H10	G11	Horse	8.12	25.10	K12	K12	Porcupine
27. 9	12. 8	H10	H12	Stag	9.12	26.10	K12	A1	Wolf
28. 9	13. 8	H10	J1	Serpent	10.12	27.10	K12	B2	Dog
29. 9	14. 8	H10	K2	Earthworm	11.12	28.10	K12	C3	Pheasant
30. 9	15. 8	H10	A3	Crocodile	12.12	29.10	K12	D4	Cock
1.10	16. 8	H10	B4	Dragon	13.12	1.11	A1	E5	Crow
2.10	17. 8	H10	C5	Badger	14.12	2.11	A1	F6	Monkey
3.10	18. 8	H10	D6	Hare	15.12	3.11	A1	G7	Gibbon
4.10	19. 8	H10	E7	Fox	16.12	4.11	A1	H8	Tapir

Solar date	Lunar date	Month HS/EB	Day HS/EB	Constellation	Solar date	Lunar date	Month HS/EB	Day HS/EB	Constellation
17.12	5.11	A1	J9	Sheep	12. 1	1.12	B2	E11	Gibbon
18.12	6.11	A1	K10	Deer	13. 1	2.12	B2	F12	Tapir
19.12	7.11	A1	A11	Horse	14. 1	3.12	B2	G1	Sheep
20.12	8.11	A1	B12	Stag	15. 1	4.12	B2	H2	Deer
21.12	9.11	A1	C1	Serpent	16. 1	5.12	B2	J3	Horse
22.12	10.11	A1	D2	Earthworm	17. 1	6.12	B2	K4	Stag
23.12	11.11	A1	E3	Crocodile	18. 1	7.12	B2	A5	Serpent
24.12	12.11	A1	F4	Dragon	19. 1	8.12	B2	B6	Earthworm
25.12	13.11	A1	G5	Badger	20. 1	9.12	B2	C7	Crocodile
26.12	14.11	A1	H6	Hare	21. 1	10.12	B2	D8	Dragon
27.12	15.11	A1	J7	Fox	22. 1	11.12	B2	E9	Badger
28.12	16.11	A1	K8	Tiger	23. 1	12.12	B2	F10	Hare
29.12	17.11	A1	A9	Leopard	24. 1	13.12	B2	G11	Fox
30.12	18.11	A1	B10	Griffon	25. 1	14.12	B2	H12	Tiger
31.12	19.11	A1	C11	Ox	26. 1	15.12	B2	J1	Leopard
					27. 1	16.12	B2	K2	Griffon
1994					28. 1	17.12	B2	A3	Ox
					29. 1	18.12	B2	B4	Bat
1. 1	20.11	A1	D12	Bat	30. 1	19.12	B2	C5	Rat
2. 1	21.11	A1	E1	Rat	31. 1	20.12	B2	D6	Swallow
3. 1	22.11	A1	F2	Swallow	1. 2	21.12	B2	E7	Pig
4. 1	23.11	A1	G3	Pig	2. 2	22.12	B2	F8	Porcupine
5. 1	24.11	A1	H4	Porcupine	3. 2	23.12	B2	G9	Wolf
6. 1	25.11	A1	J5	Wolf	4. 2	24.12	B2	H10	Dog
7. 1	26.11	A1	K6	Dog	5. 2	25.12	B2	J11	Pheasant
8. 1	27.11	A1	A7	Pheasant	6. 2	26.12	B2	K12	Cock
9. 1	28.11	A1	B8	Cock	7. 2	27.12	B2	A1	Crow
10. 1	29.11	A1	C9	Crow	8. 2	28.12	B2	B2	Monkey
11. 1	30.11	A1	D10	Monkey	9. 2	29.12	B2	C3	Gibbon

CHIA HSÜ YEAR

Solar date	Lunar date	Month HS/EB	Day HS/EB	Constellation	Solar date	Lunar date	Month HS/EB	Day HS/EB	Constellation
10. 2	1. 1	C3	D4	Tapir	21. 3	10. 2	D4	C7	Fox
11. 2	2. 1	C3	E5	Sheep	22. 3	11. 2	D4	D8	Tiger
12. 2	3. 1	C3	F6	Deer	23. 3	12. 2	D4	E9	Leopard
13. 2	4. 1	C3	G7	Horse	24. 3	13. 2	D4	F10	Griffon
14. 2	5. 1	C3	H8	Stag	25. 3	14. 2	D4	G11	Ox
15. 2	6. 1	C3	J9	Serpent	26. 3	15. 2	D4	H12	Bat
16. 2	7. 1	C3	K10	Earthworm	27. 3	16. 2	D4	J1	Rat
17. 2	8. 1	C3	A11	Crocodile	28. 3	17. 2	D4	K2	Swallow
18. 2	9. 1	C3	B12	Dragon	29. 3	18. 2	D4	A3	Pig
19. 2	10. 1	C3	C1	Badger	30. 3	19. 2	D4	B4	Porcupine
20. 2	11. 1	C3	D2	Hare	31. 3	20. 2	D4	C5	Wolf
21. 2	12. 1	C3	E3	Fox	1. 4	21. 2	D4	D6	Dog
22. 2	13. 1	C3	F4	Tiger	2. 4	22. 2	D4	E7	Pheasant
23. 2	14. 1	C3	G5	Leopard	3. 4	23. 2	D4	F8	Cock
24. 2	15. 1	C3	H6	Griffon	4. 4	24. 2	D4	G9	Crow
25. 2	16. 1	C3	J7	Ox	5. 4	25. 2	D4	H10	Monkey
26. 2	17. 1	C3	K8	Bat	6. 4	26. 2	D4	J11	Gibbon
27. 2	18. 1	C3	A9	Rat	7. 4	27. 2	D4	K12	Tapir
28. 2	19. 1	C3	B10	Swallow	8. 4	28. 2	D4	A1	Sheep
1. 3	20. 1	C3	C11	Pig	9. 4	29. 2	D4	B2	Deer
2. 3	21. 1	C3	D12	Porcupine	10. 4	30. 2	D4	C3	Horse
3. 3	22. 1	C3	E1	Wolf	11. 4	1. 3	E5	D4	Stag
4. 3	23. 1	C3	F2	Dog	12. 4	2. 3	E5	E5	Serpent
5. 3	24. 1	C3	G3	Pheasant	13. 4	3. 3	E5	F6	Earthworm
6. 3	25. 1	C3	H4	Cock	14. 4	4. 3	E5	G7	Crocodile
7. 3	26. 1	C3	J5	Crow	15. 4	5. 3	E5	H8	Dragon
8. 3	27. 1	C3	K6	Monkey	16. 4	6. 3	E5	J9	Badger
9. 3	28. 1	C3	A7	Gibbon	17. 4	7. 3	E5	K10	Hare
10. 3	29. 1	C3	B8	Tapir	18. 4	8. 3	E5	A11	Fox
11. 3	30. 1	C3	C9	Sheep	19. 4	9. 3	E5	B12	Tiger
12. 3	1. 2	D4	D10	Deer	20. 4	10. 3	E5	C1	Leopard
13. 3	2. 2	D4	E11	Horse	21. 4	11. 3	E5	D2	Griffon
14. 3	3. 2	D4	F12	Stag	22. 4	12. 3	E5	E3	Ox
15. 3	4. 2	D4	G1	Serpent	23. 4	13. 3	E5	F4	Bat
16. 3	5. 2	D4	H2	Earthworm	24. 4	14. 3	E5	G5	Rat
17. 3	6. 2	D4	J3	Crocodile	25. 4	15. 3	E5	H6	Swallow
18. 3	7. 2	D4	K4	Dragon	26. 4	16. 3	E5	J7	Pig
19. 3	8. 2	D4	A5	Badger	27. 4	17. 3	E5	K8	Porcupine
20. 3	9. 2	D4	B6	Hare	28. 4	18. 3	E5	A9	Wolf

Solar date	Lunar date	Month HS/EB	Day HS/EB	Constellation	Solar date	Lunar date	Month HS/EB	Day HS/EB	Constellation
29. 4	19. 3	E5	B10	Dog	11. 7	3. 6	H8	E11	Fox
30. 4	20. 3	E5	C11	Pheasant	12. 7	4. 6	H8	F12	Tiger
1. 5	21. 3	E5	D12	Cock	13. 7	5. 6	H8	G1	Leopard
2. 5	22. 3	E5	E1	Crow	14. 7	6. 6	H8	H2	Griffon
3. 5	23. 3	E5	F2	Monkey	15. 7	7. 6	H8	J3	Ox
4. 5	24. 3	E5	G3	Gibbon	16. 7	8. 6	H8	K4	Bat
5. 5	25. 3	E5	H4	Tapir	17. 7	9. 6	H8	A5	Rat
6. 5	26. 3	E5	J5	Sheep	18. 7	10. 6	H8	B6	Swallow
7. 5	27. 3	E5	K6	Deer	19. 7	11. 6	H8	C7	Pig
8. 5	28. 3	E5	A7	Horse	20. 7	12. 6	H8	D8	Porcupine
9. 5	29. 3	E5	B8	Stag	21. 7	13. 6	H8	E9	Wolf
10. 5	30. 3	E5	C9	Serpent	22. 7	14. 6	H8	F10	Dog
11. 5	1. 4	F6	D10	Earthworm	23. 7	15. 6	H8	G11	Pheasant
12. 5	2. 4	F6	E11	Crocodile	24. 7	16. 6	H8	H12	Cock
13. 5	3. 4	F6	F12	Dragon	25. 7	17. 6	H8	J1	Crow
14. 5	4. 4	F6	G1	Badger	26. 7	18. 6	H8	K2	Monkey
15. 5	5. 4	F6	H2	Hare	27. 7	19. 6	H8	A3	Gibbon
16. 5	6. 4	F6	J3	Fox	28. 7	20. 6	H8	B4	Tapir
17. 5	7. 4	F6	K4	Tiger	29. 7	21. 6	H8	C5	Sheep
18. 5	8. 4	F6	A5	Leopard	30. 7	22. 6	H8	D6	Deer
19. 5	9. 4	F6	B6	Griffon	31. 7	23. 6	H8	E7	Horse
20. 5	10. 4	F6	C7	Ox	1. 8	24. 6	H8	F8	Stag
21. 5	11. 4	F6	D8	Bat	2. 8	25. 6	H8	G9	Serpent
22. 5	12. 4	F6	E9	Rat	3. 8	26. 6	H8	H10	Earthworm
23. 5	13. 4	F6	F10	Swallow	4. 8	27. 6	H8	J11	Crocodile
24. 5	14. 4	F6	G11	Pig	5. 8	28. 6	H8	K12	Dragon
25. 5	15. 4	F6	H12	Porcupine	6. 8	29. 6	H8	A1	Badger
26. 5	16. 4	F6	J1	Wolf	7. 8	1. 7	J9	B2	Hare
27. 5	17. 4	F6	K2	Dog	8. 8	2. 7	J9	C3	Fox
28. 5	18. 4	F6	A3	Pheasant	9. 8	3. 7	J9	D4	Tiger
29. 5	19. 4	F6	B4	Cock	10. 8	4. 7	J9	E5	Leopard
30. 5	20. 4	F6	C5	Crow	11. 8	5. 7	J9	F6	Griffon
31. 5	21. 4	F6	D6	Monkey	12. 8	6. 7	J9	G7	Ox
1. 6	22. 4	F6	E7	Gibbon	13. 8	7. 7	J9	H8	Bat
2. 6	23. 4	F6	F8	Tapir	14. 8	8. 7	J9	J9	Rat
3. 6	24. 4	F6	G9	Sheep	15. 8	9. 7	J9	K10	Swallow
4. 6	25. 4	F6	H10	Deer	16. 8	10. 7	J9	A11	Pig
5. 6	26. 4	F6	J11	Horse	17. 8	11. 7	J9	B12	Porcupine
6. 6	27. 4	F6	K12	Stag	18. 8	12. 7	J9	C1	Wolf
7. 6	28. 4	F6	A1	Serpent	19. 8	13. 7	J9	D2	Dog
8. 6	29. 4	F6	B2	Earthworm	20. 8	14. 7	J9	E3	Pheasant
9. 6	1. 5	G7	C3	Crocodile	21. 8	15. 7	J9	F4	Cock
10. 6	2. 5	G7	D4	Dragon	22. 8	16. 7	J9	G5	Crow
11. 6	3. 5	G7	E5	Badger	23. 8	17. 7	J9	H6	Monkey
12. 6	4. 5	G7	F6	Hare	24. 8	18. 7	J9	J7	Gibbon
13. 6	5. 5	G7	G7	Fox	25. 8	19. 7	J9	K8	Tapir
14. 6	6. 5	G7	H8	Tiger	26. 8	20. 7	J9	A9	Sheep
15. 6	7. 5	G7	J9	Leopard	27. 8	21. 7	J9	B10	Deer
16. 6	8. 5	G7	K10	Griffon	28. 8	22. 7	J9	C11	Horse
17. 6	9. 5	G7	A11	Ox	29. 8	23. 7	J9	D12	Stag
18. 6	10. 5	G7	B12	Bat	30. 8	24. 7	J9	E1	Serpent
19. 6	11. 5	G7	C1	Rat	31. 8	25. 7	J9	F2	Earthworm
20. 6	12. 5	G7	D2	Swallow	1. 9	26. 7	J9	G3	Crocodile
21. 6	13. 5	G7	E3	Pig	2. 9	27. 7	J9	H4	Dragon
22. 6	14. 5	G7	F4	Porcupine	3. 9	28. 7	J9	J5	Badger
23. 6	15. 5	G7	G5	Wolf	4. 9	29. 7	J9	K6	Hare
24. 6	16. 5	G7	H6	Dog	5. 9	30. 7	J9	A7	Fox
25. 6	17. 5	G7	J7	Pheasant	6. 9	1. 8	K10	B8	Tiger
26. 6	18. 5	G7	K8	Cock	7. 9	2. 8	K10	C9	Leopard
27. 6	19. 5	G7	A9	Crow	8. 9	3. 8	K10	D10	Griffon
28. 6	20. 5	G7	B10	Monkey	9. 9	4. 8	K10	E11	Ox
29. 6	21. 5	G7	C11	Gibbon	10. 9	5. 8	K10	F12	Bat
30. 6	22. 5	G7	D12	Tapir	11. 9	6. 8	K10	G1	Rat
1. 7	23. 5	G7	E1	Sheep	12. 9	7. 8	K10	H2	Swallow
2. 7	24. 5	G7	F2	Deer	13. 9	8. 8	K10	J3	Pig
3. 7	25. 5	G7	G3	Horse	14. 9	9. 8	K10	K4	Porcupine
4. 7	26. 5	G7	H4	Stag	15. 9	10. 8	K10	A5	Wolf
5. 7	27. 5	G7	J5	Serpent	16. 9	11. 8	K10	B6	Dog
6. 7	28. 5	G7	K6	Earthworm	17. 9	12. 8	K10	C7	Pheasant
7. 7	29. 5	G7	A7	Crocodile	18. 9	13. 8	K10	D8	Cock
8. 7	30. 5	G7	B8	Dragon	19. 9	14. 8	K10	E9	Crow
9. 7	1. 6	H8	C9	Badger	20. 9	15. 8	K10	F10	Monkey
10. 7	2. 6	H8	D10	Hare	21. 9	16. 8	K10	G11	Gibbon

Solar date	Lunar date	Month HS/EB	Day HS/EB	Constellation	Solar date	Lunar date	Month HS/EB	Day HS/EB	Constellation
22. 9	17. 8	K10	H12	Tapir	28.11	26.10	B12	E7	Fox
23. 9	18. 8	K10	J1	Sheep	29.11	27.10	B12	F8	Tiger
24. 9	19. 8	K10	K2	Deer	30.11	28.10	B12	G9	Leopard
25. 9	20. 8	K10	A3	Horse	1.12	29.10	B12	H10	Griffon
26. 9	21. 8	K10	B4	Stag	2.12	30.10	B12	J11	Ox
27. 9	22. 8	K10	C5	Serpent	3.12	1.11	C1	K12	Bat
28. 9	23. 8	K10	D6	Earthworm	4.12	2.11	C1	A1	Rat
29. 9	24. 8	K10	E7	Crocodile	5.12	3.11	C1	B2	Swallow
30. 9	25. 8	K10	F8	Dragon	6.12	4.11	C1	C3	Pig
1.10	26. 8	K10	G9	Badger	7.12	5.11	C1	D4	Porcupine
2.10	27. 8	K10	H10	Hare	8.12	6.11	C1	E5	Wolf
3.10	28. 8	K10	J11	Fox	9.12	7.11	C1	F6	Dog
4.10	29. 8	K10	K12	Tiger	10.12	8.11	C1	G7	Pheasant
5.10	1. 9	A11	A1	Leopard	11.12	9.11	C1	H8	Cock
6.10	2. 9	A11	B2	Griffon	12.12	10.11	C1	J9	Crow
7.10	3. 9	A11	C3	Ox	13.12	11.11	C1	K10	Monkey
8.10	4. 9	A11	D4	Bat	14.12	12.11	C1	A11	Gibbon
9.10	5. 9	A11	E5	Rat	15.12	13.11	C1	B12	Tapir
10.10	6. 9	A11	F6	Swallow	16.12	14.11	C1	C1	Sheep
11.10	7. 9	A11	G7	Pig	17.12	15.11	C1	D2	Deer
12.10	8. 9	A11	H8	Porcupine	18.12	16.11	C1	E3	Horse
13.10	9. 9	A11	J9	Wolf	19.12	17.11	C1	F4	Stag
14.10	10. 9	A11	K10	Dog	20.12	18.11	C1	G5	Serpent
15.10	11. 9	A11	A11	Pheasant	21.12	19.11	C1	H6	Earthworm
16.10	12. 9	A11	B12	Cock	22.12	20.11	C1	J7	Crocodile
17.10	13. 9	A11	C1	Crow	23.12	21.11	C1	K8	Dragon
18.10	14. 9	A11	D2	Monkey	24.12	22.11	C1	A9	Badger
19.10	15. 9	A11	E3	Gibbon	25.12	23.11	C1	B10	Hare
20.10	16. 9	A11	F4	Tapir	26.12	24.11	C1	C11	Fox
21.10	17. 9	A11	G5	Sheep	27.12	25.11	C1	D12	Tiger
22.10	18. 9	A11	H6	Deer	28.12	26.11	C1	E1	Leopard
23.10	19. 9	A11	J7	Horse	29.12	27.11	C1	F2	Griffon
24.10	20. 9	A11	K8	Stag	30.12	28.11	C1	G3	Ox
25.10	21. 9	A11	A9	Serpent	31.12	29.11	C1	H4	Bat
26.10	22. 9	A11	B10	Earthworm					
27.10	23. 9	A11	C11	Crocodile					
28.10	24. 9	A11	D12	Dragon	**1995**				
29.10	25. 9	A11	E1	Badger	1. 1	1.12	D2	J5	Rat
30.10	26. 9	A11	F2	Hare	2. 1	2.12	D2	K6	Swallow
31.10	27. 9	A11	G3	Fox	3. 1	3.12	D2	A7	Pig
1.11	28. 9	A11	H4	Tiger	4. 1	4.12	D2	B8	Porcupine
2.11	29. 9	A11	J5	Leopard	5. 1	5.12	D2	C9	Wolf
3.11	1.10	B12	K6	Griffon	6. 1	6.12	D2	D10	Dog
4.11	2.10	B12	A7	Ox	7. 1	7.12	D2	E11	Pheasant
5.11	3.10	B12	B8	Bat	8. 1	8.12	D2	F12	Cock
6.11	4.10	B12	C9	Rat	9. 1	9.12	D2	G1	Crow
7.11	5.10	B12	D10	Swallow	10. 1	10.12	D2	H2	Monkey
8.11	6.10	B12	E11	Pig	11. 1	11.12	D2	J3	Gibbon
9.11	7.10	B12	F12	Porcupine	12. 1	12.12	D2	K4	Tapir
10.11	8.10	B12	G1	Wolf	13. 1	13.12	D2	A5	Sheep
11.11	9.10	B12	H2	Dog	14. 1	14.12	D2	B6	Deer
12.11	10.10	B12	J3	Pheasant	15. 1	15.12	D2	C7	Horse
13.11	11.10	B12	K4	Cock	16. 1	16.12	D2	D8	Stag
14.11	12.10	B12	A5	Crow	17. 1	17.12	D2	E9	Serpent
15.11	13.10	B12	B6	Monkey	18. 1	18.12	D2	F10	Earthworm
16.11	14.10	B12	C7	Gibbon	19. 1	19.12	D2	G11	Crocodile
17.11	15.10	B12	D8	Tapir	20. 1	20.12	D2	H12	Dragon
18.11	16.10	B12	E9	Sheep	21. 1	21.12	D2	J1	Badger
19.11	17.10	B12	F10	Deer	22. 1	22.12	D2	K2	Hare
20.11	18.10	B12	G11	Horse	23. 1	23.12	D2	A3	Fox
21.11	19.10	B12	H12	Stag	24. 1	24.12	D2	B4	Tiger
22.11	20.10	B12	J1	Serpent	25. 1	25.12	D2	C5	Leopard
23.11	21.10	B12	K2	Earthworm	26. 1	26.12	D2	D6	Griffon
24.11	22.10	B12	A3	Crocodile	27. 1	27.12	D2	E7	Ox
25.11	23.10	B12	B4	Dragon	28. 1	28.12	D2	F8	Bat
26.11	24.10	B12	C5	Badger	29. 1	29.12	D2	G9	Rat
27.11	25.10	B12	D6	Hare	30. 1	30.12	D2	H10	Swallow

YI HAI YEAR

Solar date	Lunar date	Month HS/EB	Day HS/EB	Constellation	Solar date	Lunar date	Month HS/EB	Day HS/EB	Constellation
31. 1	1. 1	E3	J11	Pig	12. 4	13. 3	G5	K10	Earthworm
1. 2	2. 1	E3	K12	Porcupine	13. 4	14. 3	G5	A11	Crocodile
2. 2	3. 1	E3	A1	Wolf	14. 4	15. 3	G5	B12	Dragon
3. 2	4. 1	E3	B2	Dog	15. 4	16. 3	G5	C1	Badger
4. 2	5. 1	E3	C3	Pheasant	16. 4	17. 3	G5	D2	Hare
5. 2	6. 1	E3	D4	Cock	17. 4	18. 3	G5	E3	Fox
6. 2	7. 1	E3	E5	Crow	18. 4	19. 3	G5	F4	Tiger
7. 2	8. 1	E3	F6	Monkey	19. 4	20. 3	G5	G5	Leopard
8. 2	9. 1	E3	G7	Gibbon	20. 4	21. 3	G5	H6	Griffon
9. 2	10. 1	E3	H8	Tapir	21. 4	22. 3	G5	J7	Ox
10. 2	11. 1	E3	J9	Sheep	22. 4	23. 3	G5	K8	Bat
11. 2	12. 1	E3	K10	Deer	23. 4	24. 3	G5	A9	Rat
12. 2	13. 1	E3	A11	Horse	24. 4	25. 3	G5	B10	Swallow
13. 2	14. 1	E3	B12	Stag	25. 4	26. 3	G5	C11	Pig
14. 2	15. 1	E3	C1	Serpent	26. 4	27. 3	G5	D12	Porcupine
15. 2	16. 1	E3	D2	Earthworm	27. 4	28. 3	G5	E1	Wolf
16. 2	17. 1	E3	E3	Crocodile	28. 4	29. 3	G5	F2	Dog
17. 2	18. 1	E3	F4	Dragon	29. 4	30. 3	G5	G3	Pheasant
18. 2	19. 1	E3	G5	Badger	30. 4	1. 4	H6	H4	Cock
19. 2	20. 1	E3	H6	Hare	1. 5	2. 4	H6	J5	Crow
20. 2	21. 1	E3	J7	Fox	2. 5	3. 4	H6	K6	Monkey
21. 2	22. 1	E3	K8	Tiger	3. 5	4. 4	H6	A7	Gibbon
22. 2	23. 1	E3	A9	Leopard	4. 5	5. 4	H6	B8	Tapir
23. 2	24. 1	E3	B10	Griffon	5. 5	6. 4	H6	C9	Sheep
24. 2	25. 1	E3	C11	Ox	6. 5	7. 4	H6	D10	Deer
25. 2	26. 1	E3	D12	Bat	7. 5	8. 4	H6	E11	Horse
26. 2	27. 1	E3	E1	Rat	8. 5	9. 4	H6	F12	Stag
27. 2	28. 1	E3	F2	Swallow	9. 5	10. 4	H6	G1	Serpent
28. 2	29. 1	E3	G3	Pig	10. 5	11. 4	H6	H2	Earthworm
1. 3	1. 2	F4	H4	Porcupine	11. 5	12. 4	H6	J3	Crocodile
2. 3	2. 2	F4	J5	Wolf	12. 5	13. 4	H6	K4	Dragon
3. 3	3. 2	F4	K6	Dog	13. 5	14. 4	H6	A5	Badger
4. 3	4. 2	F4	A7	Pheasant	14. 5	15. 4	H6	B6	Hare
5. 3	5. 2	F4	B8	Cock	15. 5	16. 4	H6	C7	Fox
6. 3	6. 2	F4	C9	Crow	16. 5	17. 4	H6	D8	Tiger
7. 3	7. 2	F4	D10	Monkey	17. 5	18. 4	H6	E9	Leopard
8. 3	8. 2	F4	E11	Gibbon	18. 5	19. 4	H6	F10	Griffon
9. 3	9. 2	F4	F12	Tapir	19. 5	20. 4	H6	G11	Ox
10. 3	10. 2	F4	G1	Sheep	20. 5	21. 4	H6	H12	Bat
11. 3	11. 2	F4	H2	Deer	21. 5	22. 4	H6	J1	Rat
12. 3	12. 2	F4	J3	Horse	22. 5	23. 4	H6	K2	Swallow
13. 3	13. 2	F4	K4	Stag	23. 5	24. 4	H6	A3	Pig
14. 3	14. 2	F4	A5	Serpent	24. 5	25. 4	H6	B4	Porcupine
15. 3	15. 2	F4	B6	Earthworm	25. 5	26. 4	H6	C5	Wolf
16. 3	16. 2	F4	C7	Crocodile	26. 5	27. 4	H6	D6	Dog
17. 3	17. 2	F4	D8	Dragon	27. 5	28. 4	H6	E7	Pheasant
18. 3	18. 2	F4	E9	Badger	28. 5	29. 4	H6	F8	Cock
19. 3	19. 2	F4	F10	Hare	29. 5	1. 5	J7	G9	Cock
20. 3	20. 2	F4	G11	Fox	30. 5	2. 5	J7	H10	Monkey
21. 3	21. 2	F4	H12	Tiger	31. 5	3. 5	J7	J11	Gibbon
22. 3	22. 2	F4	J1	Leopard	1. 6	4. 5	J7	K12	Tapir
23. 3	23. 2	F4	K2	Griffon	2. 6	5. 5	J7	A1	Sheep
24. 3	24. 2	F4	A3	Ox	3. 6	6. 5	J7	B2	Deer
25. 3	25. 2	F4	B4	Bat	4. 6	7. 5	J7	C3	Horse
26. 3	26. 2	F4	C5	Rat	5. 6	8. 5	J7	D4	Stag
27. 3	27. 2	F4	D6	Swallow	6. 6	9. 5	J7	E5	Serpent
28. 3	29. 2	F4	E7	Pig	7. 6	10. 5	J7	F6	Earthworm
29. 3	29. 2	F4	F8	Porcupine	8. 6	11. 5	J7	G7	Crocodile
30. 3	30. 2	F4	G9	Wolf	9. 6	12. 5	J7	H8	Dragon
31. 3	1. 3	G5	H10	Dog	10. 6	13. 5	J7	J9	Badger
1. 4	2. 3	G5	J11	Pheasant	11. 6	14. 5	J7	K10	Hare
2. 4	3. 3	G5	K12	Cock	12. 6	15. 5	J7	A11	Fox
3. 4	4. 3	G5	A1	Crow	13. 6	16. 5	J7	B12	Tiger
4. 4	5. 3	G5	B2	Monkey	14. 6	17. 5	J7	C1	Leopard
5. 4	6. 3	G5	C3	Gibbon	15. 6	18. 5	J7	D2	Griffon
6. 4	7. 3	G5	D4	Tapir	16. 6	19. 5	J7	E3	Ox
7. 4	8. 3	G5	E5	Sheep	17. 6	20. 5	J7	F4	Bat
8. 4	9. 3	G5	F6	Deer	18. 6	21. 5	J7	G5	Rat
9. 4	10. 3	G5	G7	Horse	19. 6	22. 5	J7	H6	Swallow
10. 4	11. 3	G5	H8	Stag	20. 6	23. 5	J7	J7	Pig
11. 4	12. 3	G5	J9	Serpent	21. 6	24. 5	J7	K8	Porcupine

Solar date	Lunar date	Month HS/EB	Day HS/EB	Constellation	Solar date	Lunar date	Month HS/EB	Day HS/EB	Constellation
22. 6	25. 5	J7	A9	Wolf	3. 9	9. 8	B10	D10	Hare
23. 6	26. 5	J7	B10	Dog	4. 9	10. 8	B10	E11	Fox
24. 6	27. 5	J7	C11	Pheasant	5. 9	11. 8	B10	F12	Tiger
25. 6	28. 5	J7	D12	Cock	6. 9	12. 8	B10	G1	Leopard
26. 6	29. 5	J7	E1	Crow	7. 9	13. 8	B10	H2	Griffon
27. 6	30. 5	J7	F2	Monkey	8. 9	14. 8	B10	J3	Ox
28. 6	1. 6	K8	G3	Gibbon	9. 9	15. 8	B10	K4	Bat
29. 6	2. 6	K8	H4	Tapir	10. 9	16. 8	B10	A5	Rat
30. 6	3. 6	K8	J5	Sheep	11. 9	17. 8	B10	B6	Swallow
1. 7	4. 6	K8	K6	Deer	12. 9	18. 8	B10	C7	Pig
2. 7	5. 6	K8	A7	Horse	13. 9	19. 8	B10	D8	Porcupine
3. 7	6. 6	K8	B8	Stag	14. 9	20. 8	B10	E9	Wolf
4. 7	7. 6	K8	C9	Serpent	15. 9	21. 8	B10	F10	Dog
5. 7	8. 6	K8	D10	Earthworm	16. 9	22. 8	B10	G11	Pheasant
6. 7	9. 6	K8	E11	Crocodile	17. 9	23. 8	B10	H12	Cock
7. 7	10. 6	K8	F12	Dragon	18. 9	24. 8	B10	J1	Crow
8. 7	11. 6	K8	G1	Badger	19. 9	25. 8	B10	K2	Monkey
9. 7	12. 6	K8	H2	Hare	20. 9	26. 8	B10	A3	Gibbon
10. 7	13. 6	K8	J3	Fox	21. 9	27. 8	B10	B4	Tapir
11. 7	14. 6	K8	K4	Tiger	22. 9	28. 8	B10	C5	Sheep
12. 7	15. 6	K8	A5	Leopard	23. 9	29. 8	B10	D6	Deer
13. 7	16. 6	K8	B6	Griffon	24. 9	30. 8	B10	E7	Horse
14. 7	17. 6	K8	C7	Ox	25. 9	1. 8	B10	F8	Stag
15. 7	18. 6	K8	D8	Bat	26. 9	2. 8	B10	G9	Serpent
16. 7	19. 6	K8	E9	Rat	27. 9	3. 8	B10	H10	Earthworm
17. 7	20. 6	K8	E10	Swallow	28. 9	4. 8	B10	J11	Crocodile
18. 7	21. 6	K8	G11	Pig	29. 9	5. 8	B10	K12	Dragon
19. 7	22. 6	K8	H12	Porcupine	30. 9	6. 8	B10	A1	Badger
20. 7	23. 6	K8	J1	Wolf	1.10	7. 8	B10	B2	Hare
21. 7	24. 6	K8	K2	Dog	2.10	8. 8	B10	C3	Fox
22. 7	25. 6	K8	A3	Pheasant	3.10	9. 8	B10	D4	Tiger
23. 7	26. 6	K8	B4	Cock	4.10	10. 9	B10	E5	Leopard
24. 7	27. 6	K8	C5	Crow	5.10	11. 8	B10	F6	Griffon
25. 7	28. 6	K8	D6	Monkey	6.10	12. 8	B10	G7	Ox
26. 7	29. 6	K8	E7	Gibbon	7.10	13. 8	B10	H8	Bat
27. 7	1. 7	A9	F8	Tapir	8.10	14. 8	B10	J9	Rat
28. 7	2. 7	A9	G9	Sheep	9.10	15. 8	B10	K10	Swallow
29. 7	3. 7	A9	H10	Deer	10.10	16. 8	B10	A11	Pig
30. 7	4. 7	A9	J11	Horse	11.10	17. 8	B10	B12	Porcupine
31. 7	5. 7	A9	K12	Stag	12.10	18. 8	B10	C1	Wolf
1. 8	6. 7	A9	A1	Serpent	13.10	19. 8	B10	D2	Dog
2. 8	7. 7	A9	B2	Earthworm	14.10	20. 8	B10	E3	Pheasant
3. 8	8. 7	A9	C3	Crocodile	15.10	21. 8	B10	F4	Cock
4. 8	9. 7	A9	D4	Dragon	16.10	22. 8	B10	G5	Crow
5. 8	10. 7	A9	E5	Badger	17.10	23. 8	B10	H6	Monkey
6. 8	11. 7	A9	F6	Hare	18.10	24. 8	B10	J7	Gibbon
7. 8	12. 7	A9	G7	Fox	19.10	25. 8	B10	K8	Tapir
8. 8	13. 7	A9	H8	Tiger	20.10	26. 8	B10	A9	Sheep
9. 8	14. 7	A9	J9	Leopard	21.10	27. 8	B10	B10	Deer
10. 8	15. 7	A9	K10	Griffon	22.10	28. 8	B10	C11	Horse
11. 8	16. 7	A9	A11	Ox	23.10	29. 8	B10	D12	Stag
12. 8	17. 7	A9	B12	Bat	24.10	1. 9	C11	E1	Serpent
13. 8	18. 7	A9	C1	Rat	25.10	2. 9	C11	F2	Earthworm
14. 8	19. 7	A9	D2	Swallow	26.10	3. 9	C11	G3	Crocodile
15. 8	20. 7	A9	E3	Pig	27.10	4. 9	C1	H4	Dragon
16. 8	21. 7	A9	F4	Porcupine	28.10	5. 9	C11	J5	Badger
17. 8	22. 7	A9	G5	Wolf	29.10	6. 9	C11	K6	Hare
18. 8	23. 7	A9	H6	Dog	30.10	7. 9	C11	A7	Fox
19. 8	24. 7	A9	J7	Pheasant	31.10	8. 9	C11	B8	Tiger
20. 8	25. 7	A9	K8	Cock	1.11	9. 9	C11	C9	Leopard
21. 8	26. 7	A9	A9	Crow	2.11	10. 9	C11	D10	Griffon
22. 8	27. 7	A9	B10	Monkey	3.11	11. 9	C11	E11	Ox
23. 8	28. 7	A9	C11	Gibbon	4.11	12. 9	C11	F12	Bat
24. 8	29. 7	A9	D12	Tapir	5.11	13. 9	C11	G1	Rat
25. 8	30. 7	A9	E1	Sheep	6.11	14. 9	C11	H2	Swallow
26. 8	1. 8	B10	F2	Deer	7.11	15. 9	C11	J3	Pig
27. 8	2. 8	B10	G3	Horse	8.11	16. 9	C11	K4	Porcupine
28. 8	3. 8	B10	H4	Stag	9.11	17. 9	C11	A5	Wolf
29. 8	4. 8	B10	J5	Serpent	10.11	18. 9	C11	B6	Dog
30. 8	5. 8	B10	K6	Earthworm	11.11	19. 9	C11	C7	Pheasant
31. 8	6. 8	B10	A7	Crocodile	12.11	20. 9	C11	D8	Cock
1. 9	7. 8	B10	B8	Dragon	13.11	21. 9	C11	E9	Crow
2. 9	8. 8	B10	C9	Badger	14.11	22. 9	C11	F10	Monkey

Solar date	Lunar date	Month HS/EB	Day HS/EB	Constellation
15.11	23. 9	C11	G11	Gibbon
16.11	24. 9	C11	H12	Tapir
17.11	25. 9	C11	J1	Sheep
18.11	26. 9	C11	K2	Deer
19.11	27. 9	C11	A3	Horse
20.11	28. 9	C11	B4	Stag
21.11	29. 9	C11	C5	Serpent
22.11	1.10	D12	D6	Earthworm
23.11	2.10	D12	E7	Crocodile
24.11	3.10	D12	F8	Dragon
25.11	4.10	D12	G9	Badger
26.11	5.10	D12	H10	Hare
27.11	6.10	D12	J11	Fox
28.11	7.10	D12	K12	Tiger
29.11	8.10	D12	A1	Leopard
30.11	9.10	D12	B2	Griffon
1.12	10.10	D12	C3	Ox
2.12	11.10	D12	D4	Bat
3.12	12.10	D12	E5	Rat
4.12	13.10	D12	F6	Swallow
5.12	14.10	D12	G7	Pig
6.12	15.10	D12	H8	Porcupine
7.12	16.10	D12	J9	Wolf
8.12	17.10	D12	K10	Dog
9.12	18.10	D12	A11	Pheasant
10.12	19.10	D12	B12	Cock
11.12	20.10	D12	C1	Crow
12.12	21.10	D12	D2	Monkey
13.12	22.10	D12	E3	Gibbon
14.12	23.10	D12	F4	Tapir
15.12	24.10	D12	G5	Sheep
16.12	25.10	D12	H6	Deer
17.12	26.10	D12	J7	Horse
18.12	27.10	D12	K8	Stag
19.12	28.10	D12	A9	Serpent
20.12	29.10	D12	B10	Earthworm
21.12	30.10	D12	C11	Crocodile
22.12	1.11	E1	D12	Dragon
23.12	2.11	E1	E1	Badger
24.12	3.11	E1	F2	Hare
25.12	4.11	E1	G3	Fox
26.12	5.11	E1	H4	Tiger
27.12	6.11	E1	J5	Leopard
28.12	7.11	E1	K6	Griffon
29.12	8.11	E1	A7	Ox
30.12	9.11	E1	B8	Bat
31.12	10.11	E1	C9	Rat
1996				
1. 1	11.11	E1	D10	Swallow
2. 1	12.11	E1	E11	Pig
3. 1	13.11	E1	F12	Porcupine
4. 1	14.11	E1	G1	Wolf
5. 1	15.11	E1	H2	Dog
6. 1	16.11	E1	J3	Pheasant
7. 1	17.11	E1	K4	Cock
8. 1	18.11	E1	A5	Crow
9. 1	19.11	E1	B6	Monkey
10. 1	20.11	E1	C7	Gibbon
11. 1	21.11	E1	D8	Tapir
12. 1	22.11	E1	E9	Sheep
13. 1	23.11	E1	F10	Deer
14. 1	24.11	E1	G11	Horse
15. 1	25.11	E1	H12	Stag
16. 1	26.11	E1	J1	Serpent
17. 1	27.11	E1	K2	Earthworm
18. 1	28.11	E1	A3	Crocodile
19. 1	29.11	E1	B4	Dragon
20. 1	1.12	F2	C5	Badger
21. 1	2.12	F2	D6	Hare
22. 1	3.12	F2	E7	Fox
23. 1	4.12	F2	F8	Tiger
24. 1	5.12	F2	G9	Leopard
25. 1	6.12	F2	H10	Griffon
26. 1	7.12	F2	J11	Ox
27. 1	8.12	F2	K12	Bat
28. 1	9.12	F2	A1	Rat
29. 1	10.12	F2	B2	Swallow
30. 1	11.12	F2	C3	Pig
31. 1	12.12	F2	D4	Porcupine
1. 2	13.12	F2	E5	Wolf
2. 2	14.12	F2	F6	Dog
3. 2	25.12	F2	G7	Pheasant
4. 2	16.12	f2	H8	Cock
5. 2	17.12	F2	J9	Crow
6. 2	18.12	F2	K10	Monkey
7. 2	19.12	F2	A11	Gibbon
8. 2	20.12	F2	B12	Tapir
9. 2	21.12	F2	C1	Sheep
10. 2	22.12	F2	D2	Deer
11. 2	23.12	F2	E3	Horse
12. 2	24.12	F2	F4	Stag
13. 2	25.12	F2	G5	Serpent
14. 2	26.12	F2	H6	Earthworm
15. 2	27.12	F2	J7	Crocodile
16. 2	28.12	F2	K8	Dragon
17. 2	29.12	F2	A9	Badger
18. 2	30.12	F2	B10	Hare

PING TZU YEAR

Solar date	Lunar date	Month HS/EB	Day HS/EB	Constellation
19. 2	1. 1	G3	C11	Fox
20. 2	2. 1	G3	D12	Tiger
21. 2	3. 1	G3	E1	Leopard
22. 2	4. 1	G3	F2	Griffon
23. 2	5. 1	G3	G3	Ox
24. 2	6. 1	G3	H4	Bat
25. 2	7. 1	G3	J5	Rat
26. 2	8. 1	G3	K6	Swallow
27. 2	9. 1	G3	A7	Pig
28. 2	10. 1	G3	B8	Porcupine
29. 2	11. 1	G3	C9	Wolf
1. 3	12. 1	G3	D10	Dog
2. 3	13. 1	G3	E11	Pheasant
3. 3	14. 1	G3	F12	Cock
4. 3	15. 1	G3	G1	Crow
5. 3	16. 1	G3	H2	Monkey
6. 3	17. 1	G3	J3	Gibbon
7. 3	18. 1	G3	K4	Tapir
8. 3	19. 1	G3	A5	Sheep
9. 3	20. 1	G3	B6	Deer
10. 3	21. 1	G3	C7	Horse
11. 3	22. 1	G3	D8	Stag
12. 3	23. 1	G3	E9	Serpent
13. 3	24. 1	G3	F10	Earthworm
14. 3	25. 1	G3	G11	Crocodile
15. 3	26. 1	G3	H12	Dragon
16. 3	27. 1	G3	J1	Badger
17. 3	28. 1	G3	K2	Hare
18. 3	29. 1	G3	A3	Fox
19. 3	1. 2	H4	B4	Tiger
20. 3	2. 2	H4	C5	Leopard
21. 3	3. 2	H4	D6	Griffon
22. 3	4. 2	H4	E7	Ox
23. 3	5. 2	H4	F8	Bat
24. 3	6. 2	H4	G9	Rat
25. 3	7. 2	H4	H10	Swallow

Solar date	Lunar date	Month HS/EB	Day HS/EB	Constellation	Solar date	Lunar date	Month HS/EB	Day HS/EB	Constellation
26. 3	8. 2	H4	J11	Pig	7. 6	22. 4	K6	B12	Dragon
27. 3	9. 2	H4	K12	Porcupine	8. 6	23. 4	K6	C1	Badger
28. 3	10. 2	H4	A1	Wolf	9. 6	24. 4	K6	D2	Hare
29. 3	11. 2	H4	B2	Dog	10. 6	25. 4	K6	E3	Fox
30. 3	12. 2	H4	C3	Pheasant	11. 6	26. 4	K6	F4	Tiger
31. 3	13. 2	H4	D4	Cock	12. 6	27. 4	K6	G5	Leopard
1. 4	14. 2	H4	E5	Crow	13. 6	28. 4	K6	H6	Griffon
2. 4	15. 2	H4	F6	Monkey	14. 6	29. 4	K6	J7	Ox
3. 4	16. 2	H4	G7	Gibbon	15. 6	30. 4	K6	K8	Bat
4. 4	17. 2	H4	H8	Tapir	16. 6	1. 5	A7	A9	Rat
5. 2	18. 2	H4	J9	Sheep	17. 6	2. 5	A7	B10	Swallow
6. 4	19. 2	H4	K10	Deer	18. 6	3. 5	A7	C11	Pig
7. 4	21. 2	H4	A11	Horse	19. 6	4. 5	A7	D12	Porcupine
8. 4	21. 2	H4	B12	Stag	20. 6	5. 5	A7	E1	Wolf
9. 4	22. 2	H4	C1	Serpent	21. 6	6. 5	A7	F2	Dog
10. 4	23. 2	H4	D2	Earthworm	22. 6	7. 5	A7	G3	Pheasant
11. 4	24. 2	H4	E3	Crocodile	23. 6	8. 5	A7	H4	Cock
12. 4	25. 2	H4	F4	Dragon	24. 6	9. 5	A7	J5	Crow
13. 4	26. 2	H4	G5	Badger	25. 6	10. 5	A7	K6	Monkey
14. 4	27. 2	H4	H6	Hare	26. 6	11. 5	A7	A7	Gibbon
15. 4	28. 2	H4	J7	Fox	27. 6	12. 5	A7	B8	Tapir
16. 4	29. 2	H4	K8	Tiger	28. 6	13. 5	A7	C9	Sheep
17. 4	30. 2	H4	A9	Leopard	29. 6	14. 5	A7	D10	Deer
18. 4	1. 3	J5	B10	Griffon	30. 6	15. 5	A7	E11	Horse
19. 4	2. 3	J5	C11	Ox	1. 7	16; 5	A7	F12	Stag
20. 4	3. 3	J5	D12	Bat	2. 7	17. 5	A7	G1	Serpent
21. 4	4. 3	J5	E1	Rat	3. 7	18. 5	A7	H2	Earthworm
22. 4	5. 3	J5	F2	Swallow	4. 7	19. 5	A7	J3	Crocodile
23. 4	6. 3	J5	G3	Pig	5. 7	20. 5	A7	K4	Dragon
24. 4	7. 3	J5	H4	Porcupine	6. 7	21. 5	A7	A5	Badger
25. 4	8. 3	J5	J5	Wolf	7. 7	22. 5	A7	B6	Hare
26. 4	9. 3	J5	K6	Dog	8. 7	23. 5	A7	C7	Fox
27. 4	10. 3	J5	A7	Pheasant	9. 7	24. 5	A7	D8	Tiger
28. 4	11. 3	J5	B8	Cock	10. 7	25. 5	A7	E9	Leopard
29. 4	12. 3	J5	C9	Crow	11. 7	26. 5	A7	F10	Griffon
30. 4	13. 3	J5	D10	Monkey	12. 7	27. 5	A7	G11	Ox
1. 5	14. 3	J5	E11	Gibbon	13. 7	28. 5	A7	H12	Bat
2. 5	15. 3	J5	F12	Tapir	14. 7	29. 5	A7	J1	Rat
3. 5	16. 3	J5	G1	Sheep	15. 7	30. 5	A7	K2	Swallow
4. 5	17. 3	J5	H2	Deer	16. 7	1. 6	B8	A3	Pig
5. 5	18. 3	J5	J3	Horse	17. 7	2. 6	B8	B4	Porcupine
6. 5	19. 3	J5	K4	Stag	18. 7	3. 6	B8	C5	Wolf
7. 5	20. 3	J5	A5	Serpent	19. 7	4. 6	B8	D6	Dog
8. 5	21. 3	J5	B6	Earthworm	20. 7	5. 6	B8	E7	Pheasant
9. 5	22. 3	J5	C7	Crocodile	21. 7	6. 6	B8	F8	Cock
10. 5	23. 3	J5	D8	Dragon	22. 7	7. 6	B8	G9	Crow
11. 5	24. 3	J5	E9	Badger	23. 7	8. 6	B8	H10	Monkey
12. 5	25. 3	J5	F10	Hare	24. 7	9. 6	B8	J11	Gibbon
13. 5	26. 3	J5	G11	Fox	25. 7	10. 6	B8	K12	Tapir
14. 5	27. 3	J5	H12	Tiger	26. 7	11. 6	B8	A1	Sheep
15. 5	28. 3	J5	J1	Leopard	27. 7	12. 6	B8	B2	Deer
16. 5	29. 3	J5	K2	Griffon	28. 7	13. 6	B8	C3	Horse
17. 5	1. 4	K6	A3	Ox	29. 7	14. 6	B8	D4	Stag
18. 5	2. 4	K6	B4	Bat	30. 7	15. 6	B8	E5	Serpent
19. 5	3. 4	K6	C5	Rat	31. 7	16. 6	B8	F6	Earthworm
20. 5	4. 4	K6	D6	Swallow	1. 8	17. 6	B8	G7	Crocodile
21. 5	5. 4	K6	E7	Pig	2. 8	18. 6	B8	H8	Dragon
22. 5	6. 4	K6	F8	Porcupine	3. 8	19. 6	B8	J9	Badger
23. 5	7. 4	K6	G9	Wolf	4. 8	20. 6	B8	K10	Hare
24. 5	8. 4	K6	H10	Dog	5. 8	21. 6	B8	A11	Fox
25. 5	9. 4	K6	J11	Pheasant	6. 8	22. 6	B8	B12	Tiger
26. 5	10. 4	K6	K12	Cock	7. 8	23. 6	B8	C1	Leopard
27. 5	11. 4	K6	A1	Crow	8. 8	24. 6	B8	D2	Griffon
28. 5	12. 4	K6	B2	Monkey	9. 8	25. 6	B8	E3	Ox
29. 5	13. 4	K6	C3	Gibbon	10. 8	26. 6	B8	F4	Bat
30. 5	14. 4	K6	D4	Tapir	11. 8	27. 6	B8	G5	Rat
31. 5	15. 4	K6	E5	Sheep	12. 8	28. 6	B8	H6	Swallow
1. 6	16. 4	K6	F6	Deer	13. 8	29. 6	B8	J7	Pig
2. 6	17. 4	K6	G7	Horse	14. 8	1. 7	C9	K8	Porcupine
3. 6	18. 4	K6	H8	Stag	15. 8	2. 7	C9	A9	Wolf
4. 6	19. 4	K6	J9	Serpent	16. 8	3. 7	C9	B10	Dog
5. 6	20. 4	K6	K10	Earthworm	17. 8	4. 7	C9	C11	Pheasant
6. 6	21. 4	K6	A11	Crocodile	18. 8	5. 7	C9	D12	Cock

Solar date	Lunar date	Month HS/EB	Day HS/EB	Constellation	Solar date	Lunar date	Month HS/EB	Day HS/EB	Constellation
19. 8	6. 7	C9	E1	Crow	31.10	20. 9	E11	H2	Griffon
20. 8	7. 7	C9	F2	Monkey	1.11	21. 9	E11	J3	Ox
21. 8	8. 7	C9	G3	Gibbon	2.11	22. 9	E11	K4	Bat
22. 8	9. 7	C9	H4	Tapir	3.11	23. 9	E11	A5	Rat
23. 8	10. 7	C9	J5	Sheep	4.11	24. 9	E11	B6	Swallow
24. 8	11. 7	C9	K6	Deer	5.11	25. 9	E11	C7	Pig
25. 8	12. 7	C9	A7	Horse	6.11	26. 9	E11	D8	Porcupine
26. 8	13. 7	C9	B8	Stag	7.11	27. 9	E11	E9	Wolf
27. 8	14. 7	C9	C9	Serpent	8.11	28. 9	E11	F10	Dog
28. 8	15. 7	C9	D10	Earthworm	9.11	29. 9	E11	G11	Pheasant
29. 8	16. 7	C9	E11	Crocodile	10.11	30. 9	E11	H12	Cock
30. 8	17. 7	C9	F12	Dragon	11.11	1.10	F12	J1	Crow
31. 8	18. 7	C9	G1	Badger	12.11	2.10	F12	K2	Monkey
1. 9	19. 7	C9	H2	Hare	13.11	3.10	F12	A3	Gibbon
2. 9	20. 7	C9	J3	Fox	14.11	4.10	F12	B4	Tapir
3. 9	21. 7	C9	K4	Tiger	15.11	5.10	F12	C5	Sheep
4. 9	22. 7	C9	A5	Leopard	16.11	6.10	F12	D6	Deer
5. 9	23. 7	C9	B6	Griffon	17.11	7.10	F12	E7	Horse
6. 9	24. 7	C9	C7	Ox	18.11	8.10	F12	F8	Stag
7. 9	25. 7	C9	D8	Bat	19.11	9.10	F12	G9	Serpent
8. 9	26. 7	C9	E9	Rat	20.11	10.10	F12	H10	Earthworm
9. 9	27. 7	C9	F10	Swallow	21.11	11.10	F12	J11	Crocodile
10. 9	28. 7	C9	G11	Pig	22.11	12.10	F12	K12	Dragon
11. 9	29. 7	C9	H12	Porcupine	23.11	13.10	F12	A1	Badger
12. 9	30. 7	C9	J1	Wolf	24.11	14.10	F12	B2	Hare
13. 9	1. 8	D10	K2	Dog	25.11	15.10	F12	C3	Fox
14. 9	2. 8	D10	A3	Pheasant	26.11	16.10	F12	D4	Tiger
15. 9	3. 8	D10	B4	Cock	27.11	17.10	F12	E5	Leopard
16. 9	4. 8	D10	C5	Crow	28.11	18.10	F12	F6	Griffon
17. 9	5. 8	D10	D6	Monkey	29.11	19.10	F12	G7	Ox
18. 9	6. 8	D10	E7	Gibbon	30.11	20.10	F12	H8	Bat
19. 9	7. 8	D10	F8	Tapir	1.12	21.10	F12	J9	Rat
20. 9	8. 8	D10	G9	Sheep	2.12	22.10	F12	K10	Swallow
21. 9	9. 8	D10	H10	Deer	3.12	23.10	F12	A11	Pig
22. 9	10. 8	D10	J11	Horse	4.12	24.10	F12	B12	Porcupine
23. 9	11. 8	D10	K12	Stag	5.12	25.10	F12	C1	Wolf
24. 9	12. 8	D10	A1	Serpent	6.12	26.10	F12	D2	Dog
25. 9	13. 8	D10	B2	Earthworm	7.12	27.10	F12	E3	Pheasant
26. 9	14. 8	D10	C3	Crocodile	8.12	28.10	F12	F4	Cock
27. 9	15. 8	D10	D4	Dragon	9.12	29.10	F12	G5	Crow
28. 9	16. 8	D10	E5	Badger	10.12	30.10	F12	H6	Monkey
29. 9	17. 8	D10	F6	Hare	11.12	1.11	G1	J7	Gibbon
30. 9	18. 8	D10	G7	Fox	12.12	2.11	G1	K8	Tapir
1.10	19. 8	D10	H8	Tiger	13.12	3.11	G1	A9	Sheep
2.10	20. 8	D10	J9	Leopard	14.12	4.11	G1	B10	Deer
3.10	21. 8	D10	K10	Griffon	15.12	5.11	G1	C11	Horse
4.10	22. 8	D10	A11	Ox	16.12	6.11	G1	D12	Stag
5.10	23. 8	D10	B12	Bat	17.12	7.11	G1	E1	Serpent
6.10	24. 8	D10	C1	Rat	18.12	8.11	G1	F2	Earthworm
7.10	25. 8	D10	D2	Swallow	19.12	9.11	G1	G3	Crocodile
8.10	26. 8	D10	E3	Pig	20.12	10.11	G1	H4	Dragon
9.10	27. 8	D10	F4	Porcupine	21.12	11.11	G1	J5	Badger
10.10	28. 8	D10	G5	Wolf	22.12	12.11	G1	K6	Hare
11. 0	29. 8	D10	H6	Dog	23.12	13.11	G1	A7	Fox
12.10	1. 9	E11	J7	Pheasant	24.12	14.11	G1	B8	Tiger
13.10	2. 9	E11	K8	Cock	25.12	15.11	G1	C9	Leopard
14.10	3. 9	E11	A9	Crow	26.12	16.11	G1	D10	Griffon
15.10	4. 9	E11	B10	Monkey	27.12	17.11	G1	E11	Ox
16.10	5. 9	E11	C11	Gibbon	28.12	18.11	G1	F12	Bat
17.10	6. 9	E11	D12	Tapir	29.12	19.11	G1	G1	Rat
18.10	7. 9	E11	E1	Sheep	30.12	20.11	G1	H2	Swallow
19.10	8. 9	E11	F2	Deer	31.12	21.11	G1	J3	Pig
20.10	9. 9	E11	G3	Horse					
21.10	10. 9	E11	H4	Stag	**1997**				
22.10	11. 9	E11	J5	Serpent	1. 1	22.11	G1	K4	Porcupine
23.10	12. 9	E11	K6	Earthworm	2. 1	23.11	G1	A5	Wolf
24.10	13. 9	E11	A7	Crocodile	3. 1	24.11	G1	B6	Dog
25.10	14. 9	E11	B8	Dragon	4. 1	25.11	G1	C7	Pheasant
26.10	15. 9	E11	C9	Badger	5. 1	26.11	G1	D8	Cock
27.10	16. 9	E11	D10	Hare	6. 1	27.11	G1	E9	Crow
28.10	17. 9	E11	E11	Fox	7. 1	28.11	G1	F10	Monkey
29.10	18. 9	E11	F12	Tiger	8. 1	29.11	G1	G11	Gibbon
30.10	19. 9	E11	G1	Leopard	9. 1	1.12	H2	H12	Tapir

Solar date	Lunar date	Month HS/EB	Day HS/EB	Constellation	Solar date	Lunar date	Month HS/EB	Day HS/EB	Constellation
10. 1	2.12	H2	J1	Sheep	24. 1	16.12	H2	C3	Ox
11. 1	3.12	H2	K2	Deer	25. 1	17.12	H2	D4	Bat
12. 1	4.12	H2	A3	Horse	26. 1	18.12	H2	E5	Rat
13. 1	5.12	H2	B4	Stag	27. 1	19.12	H2	F6	Swallow
14. 1	6.12	H2	C5	Serpent	28. 1	10.12	H2	G7	Pig
15. 1	7.12	H2	D6	Earthworm	29. 1	21.12	H2	H8	Porcupine
16. 1	8.12	H2	E7	Crocodile	30. 1	22.12	H2	J9	Wolf
17. 1	9.12	H2	F8	Dragon	31. 1	23.12	H2	K10	Dog
18. 1	10.12	H2	G9	Badger	1. 2	24.12	H2	A11	Pheasant
19. 1	11.12	H2	H10	Hare	2. 2	25.12	H2	B12	Cock
20. 1	12.12	H2	J11	Fox	3. 2	26.12	H2	C1	Crow
21. 1	13.12	H2	K12	Tiger	4. 2	27.12	H2	D2	Monkey
22. 1	14.12	H2	A1	Leopard	5. 2	28.12	H2	E3	Gibbon
23. 1	15.12	H2	B2	Griffon	6. 2	29.12	H2	F4	Tapir

TING CH'OU YEAR

Solar date	Lunar date	Month HS/EB	Day HS/EB	Constellation	Solar date	Lunar date	Month HS/EB	Day HS/EB	Constellation
7. 2	1. 1	J3	G5	Sheep	2. 4	25. 2	K4	A11	Gibbon
8. 2	2. 1	J3	H6	Deer	3. 4	26. 2	K4	B12	Tapir
9. 2	3. 1	J3	J7	Horse	4. 4	27. 2	K4	C1	Sheep
10. 2	4. 1	J3	K8	Stag	5. 4	28. 2	K4	D2	Deer
11. 2	5. 1	J3	A9	Serpent	6. 4	29. 2	K4	E3	Horse
12. 2	6. 1	J3	B10	Earthworm	7. 4	1. 3	A5	F4	Stag
13. 2	7. 1	J3	C11	Crocodile	8. 4	2. 3	A5	G5	Serpent
14. 2	8. 1	J3	D12	Dragon	9. 4	3. 3	A5	H6	Earthworm
15. 2	9. 1	J3	E1	Badger	10. 4	4. 3	A5	J7	Crocodile
16. 2	10. 1	J3	F2	Hare	11. 4	5. 3	A5	K8	Dragon
17. 2	11. 1	J3	G3	Fox	12. 4	6. 3	A5	A9	Badger
18. 2	12. 1	J3	H4	Tiger	13. 4	7. 3	A5	B10	Hare
19. 2	13. 1	J3	J5	Leopard	14. 4	8. 3	A5	C11	Fox
20. 2	14. 1	J3	K6	Griffon	15. 4	9. 3	A5	D12	Tiger
21. 2	15. 1	J3	A7	Ox	16. 4	10. 3	A5	E1	Leopard
22. 2	16. 1	J3	B8	Bat	17. 4	11. 3	A5	F2	Griffon
23. 2	17. 1	J3	C9	Rat	18. 4	12. 3	A5	G3	Ox
24. 2	18. 1	J3	D10	Swallow	19. 4	13. 3	A5	H4	Bat
25. 2	19. 1	J3	E11	Pig	20. 4	14. 3	A5	J5	Rat
26. 2	20. 1	J3	F12	Porcupine	21. 4	15. 3	A5	K6	Swallow
27. 2	21. 1	J3	G1	Wolf	22. 4	16. 3	A5	A7	Pig
28. 2	22. 1	J3	H2	Dog	23. 4	17. 3	A5	B8	Porcupine
1. 3	23. 1	J3	J3	Pheasant	24. 4	18. 3	A5	C9	Wolf
2. 3	24. 1	J3	K4	Cock	25. 4	19. 3	A5	D10	Dog
3. 3	25. 1	J3	A5	Crow	26. 4	20. 3	A5	E11	Pheasant
4. 3	26. 1	J3	B6	Monkey	27. 4	21. 3	A5	F12	Cock
5. 3	27. 1	J3	C7	Gibbon	28. 4	22. 3	A5	G1	Crow
6. 3	28. 1	J3	D8	Tapir	29. 4	23. 3	A5	H2	Monkey
7. 3	29. 1	J3	E9	Sheep	30. 4	24. 3	A5	J3	Gibbon
8. 3	30. 1	J3	F10	Deer	1. 5	25. 3	A5	K4	Tapir
9. 3	1. 2	K4	G11	Horse	2. 5	26. 3	A5	A5	Sheep
10. 3	2. 2	K4	H12	Stag	3. 5	27. 3	A5	B6	Deer
11. 3	3. 2	K4	J1	Serpent	4. 5	28. 3	A5	C7	Horse
12. 3	4. 2	K4	K2	Earthworm	5. 5	29. 3	A5	D8	Stag
13. 3	5. 2	K4	A3	Crocodile	6. 5	30. 3	A5	E9	Serpent
14. 3	6. 2	K4	B4	Dragon	7. 5	1. 4	B6	F10	Earthworm
15. 3	7. 2	K4	C5	Badger	8. 5	2. 4	B6	G11	Crocodile
16. 3	8. 2	K4	D6	Hare	9. 5	3. 4	B6	H12	Dragon
17. 3	9. 2	K4	E7	Fox	10. 5	4. 4	B6	J1	Badger
18. 3	10. 2	K4	F8	Tiger	11. 5	5. 4	B6	K2	Hare
19. 3	11. 2	K4	G9	Leopard	12. 5	6. 4	B6	A3	Fox
20. 3	12. 2	K4	H10	Griffon	13. 5	7. 4	B6	B4	Tiger
21. 3	13. 2	K4	J11	Ox	14. 5	8. 4	B6	C5	Leopard
22. 3	14. 2	K4	K12	Bat	15. 5	9. 4	B6	D6	Griffon
23. 3	15. 2	K4	A1	Rat	16. 5	10. 4	B6	E7	Ox
24. 3	16. 2	K4	B2	Swallow	17. 5	11. 4	B6	F8	Bat
25. 3	17. 2	K4	C3	Pig	18. 5	12. 4	B6	G9	Rat
26. 3	18. 2	K4	D4	Porcupine	19. 5	13. 4	B6	H10	Swallow
27. 3	19. 2	K4	E5	Wolf	20. 5	14. 4	B6	J11	Pig
28. 3	20. 2	K4	F6	Dog	21. 5	15. 4	B6	K12	Porcupine
29. 3	21. 2	K4	G7	Pheasant	22. 5	16. 4	B6	A1	Wolf
30. 3	22. 2	K4	H8	Cock	23. 5	17. 4	B6	B2	Dog
31. 3	23. 2	K4	J9	Crow	24. 5	18. 4	B6	C3	Pheasant
1. 4	24. 2	K4	K10	Monkey	25. 5	19. 4	B6	D4	Cock

Solar date	Lunar date	Month HS/EB	Day HS/EB	Constellation	Solar date	Lunar date	Month HS/EB	Day HS/EB	Constellation
26. 5	20. 4	B6	E5	Crow	7. 8	5. 7	E9	H6	Griffon
27. 5	21. 4	B6	F6	Monkey	8. 8	6. 7	E9	J7	Ox
28. 5	22. 4	B6	G7	Gibbon	9. 8	7. 7	E9	K8	Bat
29. 5	23. 4	B6	H8	Tapir	10. 8	8. 7	E9	A9	Rat
30. 5	24. 4	B6	J9	Sheep	11. 8	9. 7	E9	B10	Swallow
31. 5	25. 4	B6	K10	Deer	12. 8	10. 7	E9	C11	Pig
1. 6	26. 4	B6	A11	Horse	13. 8	11. 7	E9	D12	Porcupine
2. 6	27. 4	B6	B12	Stag	14. 8	12. 7	E9	E1	Wolf
3. 6	28. 4	B6	C1	Serpent	15. 8	13. 7	E9	F2	Dog
4. 6	29. 4	B6	D2	Earthworm	16. 8	14. 7	E9	G3	Pheasant
5. 6	1. 5	C7	E3	Crocodile	17. 8	15. 7	E9	H4	Cock
6. 6	2. 5	C7	F4	Dragon	18. 8	16. 7	E9	J5	Crow
7. 6	3. 5	C7	G5	Badger	19. 8	17. 7	E9	K6	Monkey
8. 6	4. 5	C7	H6	Hare	20. 8	18. 7	E9	A7	Gibbon
9. 6	5. 5	C7	J7	Fox	21. 8	19. 7	E9	B8	Tapir
10. 6	6. 5	C7	K8	Tiger	22. 8	20. 7	E9	C9	Sheep
11. 6	7. 5	C7	A9	Leopard	23. 8	21. 7	E9	D10	Deer
12. 6	8. 5	C7	B10	Griffon	24. 8	22. 7	E9	E11	Horse
13. 6	9. 5	C7	C11	Ox	25. 8	23. 7	E9	F12	Stag
14. 6	10. 5	C7	D12	Bat	26. 8	24. 7	E9	G1	Serpent
15. 6	11. 5	C7	E1	Rat	27. 8	25. 7	E9	H2	Earthworm
16. 6	12. 5	C7	F2	Swallow	28. 8	26. 7	E9	J3	Crocodile
17. 6	13. 5	C7	G3	Pig	29. 8	27. 7	E9	K4	Dragon
18. 6	14. 5	C7	H4	Porcupine	30. 8	28. 7	E9	A5	Badger
19. 6	15. 5	C7	J5	Wolf	31. 8	29. 7	E9	B6	Hare
20. 6	16. 5	C7	K6	Dog	1. 9	30. 7	E9	C7	Fox
21. 6	17. 5	C7	A7	Pheasant	2. 9	1. 8	F10	D8	Tiger
22. 6	18. 5	C7	B8	Cock	3. 9	2. 8	F10	E9	Leopard
23. 6	19. 5	C7	C9	Crow	4. 9	3. 8	F10	F10	Griffon
24. 6	20. 5	C7	D10	Monkey	5. 9	4. 8	F10	G11	Ox
25. 6	21. 5	C7	E11	Gibbon	6. 9	5. 8	F10	H12	Bat
26. 6	22. 5	C7	F12	Tapir	7. 9	6. 8	F10	J1	Rat
27. 6	23. 5	C7	G1	Sheep	8. 9	7. 8	F10	K2	Swallow
28. 6	24. 5	C7	H2	Deer	9. 9	8. 8	F10	A3	Pig
29. 6	25. 5	C7	J3	Horse	10. 9	9. 8	F10	B4	Porcupine
30. 6	26. 5	C7	K4	Stag	11. 9	10. 8	F10	C5	Wolf
1. 7	27. 5	C7	A5	Serpent	12. 9	11. 8	F10	D6	Dog
2. 7	28. 5	C7	B6	Earthworm	13. 9	12. 8	F10	E7	Pheasant
3. 7	29. 5	C7	C7	Crocodile	14. 9	13. 8	F10	F8	Cock
4. 7	30. 5	C7	D8	Dragon	15. 9	14. 8	F10	G9	Crow
5. 7	1. 6	D8	E9	Badger	16. 9	15. 8	F10	H10	Monkey
6. 7	2. 6	D8	F10	Hare	17. 9	16. 8	F10	J11	Gibbon
7. 7	3. 6	D8	G11	Fox	18. 9	17. 8	F10	K12	Tapir
8. 7	4. 6	D8	H12	Tiger	19. 9	18. 8	F10	A1	Sheep
9. 7	5. 6	D8	J1	Leopard	20. 9	19. 8	F10	B2	Deer
10. 7	6. 6	D8	K2	Griffon	21. 9	20. 8	F10	C3	Horse
11. 7	7. 6	D8	A3	Ox	22. 9	21. 8	F10	D4	Stag
12. 7	8. 6	D8	B4	Bat	23. 9	22. 8	F10	E5	Serpent
13. 7	9. 6	D8	C5	Rat	24. 9	23. 8	F10	F6	Earthworm
14. 7	10. 6	D8	D6	Swallow	25. 9	24. 8	F10	G7	Crocodile
15. 7	11. 6	D8	E7	Pig	26. 9	25. 8	F10	H8	Dragon
16. 7	12. 6	D8	F8	Porcupine	27. 9	26. 8	F10	J9	Badger
17. 7	13. 6	D8	G9	Wolf	28. 9	27. 8	F10	K10	Hare
18. 7	14. 6	D8	H10	Dog	29. 9	28. 8	F10	A11	Fox
19. 7	15. 6	D8	J11	Pheasant	30. 9	29. 8	F10	B12	Tiger
20. 7	16. 6	D8	K12	Cock	1.10	30. 8	F10	C1	Leopard
21. 7	17. 6	D8	A1	Crow	2.10	1. 9	G11	D2	Griffon
22. 7	18. 6	D8	B2	Monkey	3.10	2. 9	G11	E3	Ox
23. 7	19. 6	D8	C3	Gibbon	4.10	3. 9	G11	F4	Bat
24. 7	20. 6	D8	D4	Tapir	5.10	4. 9	G11	G5	Rat
25. 7	21. 6	D8	E5	Sheep	6.10	5. 9	G11	H6	Swallow
26. 7	22. 6	D8	F6	Deer	7.10	6. 9	G11	J7	Pig
27. 7	23. 6	D8	G7	Horse	8.10	7. 9	G11	K8	Porcupine
28. 7	24. 6	D8	H8	Stag	9.10	8. 9	G11	A9	Wolf
29. 7	25. 6	D8	J9	Serpent	10.10	9. 9	G11	B10	Dog
30. 7	26. 6	D8	K10	Earthworm	11.10	10. 9	G11	C11	Pheasant
31. 7	27. 6	D8	A11	Crocodile	12.10	11. 9	G11	D12	Cock
1. 8	28. 6	D8	B12	Dragon	13.10	12. 9	G11	E1	Crow
2. 8	29. 6	D8	C1	Badger	14.10	13. 9	G11	F2	Monkey
3. 8	1. 7	E9	D2	Hare	15.10	14. 9	G11	G3	Gibbon
4. 8	2. 7	E9	E3	Fox	16.10	15. 9	G11	H4	Tapir
5. 8	3. 7	E9	F4	Tiger	17.10	16. 9	G11	J5	Sheep
6. 8	4. 7	E9	G5	Leopard	18.10	17. 9	G11	K6	Deer

Solar date	Lunar date	Month HS/EB	Day HS/EB	Constellation
19.10	18. 9	G11	A7	Horse
20.10	19. 9	G11	B8	Stag
21.10	20. 9	G11	C9	Serpent
22.10	21. 9	G11	D10	Earthworm
23.10	22. 9	G11	E11	Crocodile
24.10	23. 9	G11	F12	Dragon
25.10	24. 9	G11	G1	Badger
26.10	25. 9	G11	H2	Hare
27.10	26. 9	G11	J3	Fox
28.10	27. 9	G11	K4	Tiger
29.10	28. 9	G11	A5	Leopard
30.10	29. 9	G11	B6	Griffon
31.10	1.10	H12	C7	Ox
1.11	2.10	H12	D8	Bat
2.11	3.10	H12	E9	Rat
3.11	4.10	H12	F10	Swallow
4.11	5.10	H12	G11	Pig
5.11	6.10	H12	H12	Porcupine
6.11	7.10	H12	J1	Wolf
7.11	8.10	H12	K2	Dog
8.11	9.10	H12	A3	Pheasant
9.11	10.10	H12	B4	Cock
10.11	11.10	H12	C5	Crow
11.11	12.10	H12	D6	Monkey
12.11	13.10	H12	E7	Gibbon
13.11	14.10	H12	F8	Tapir
14.11	15.10	H12	G9	Sheep
15.11	16.10	H12	H10	Deer
16.11	17.10	H12	J11	Horse
17.11	18.10	H12	K12	Stag
18.11	19.10	H12	A1	Serpent
19.11	20.10	H12	B2	Earthworm
20.11	21.10	H12	C3	Crocodile
21.11	22.10	H12	D4	Dragon
22.11	23.10	H12	E5	Badger
23.11	24.10	H12	F6	Hare
24.11	25.10	H12	G7	Fox
25.11	26.10	H12	H8	Tiger
26.11	27.10	H12	J9	Leopard
27.11	28.10	H12	K10	Griffon
28.11	29.10	H12	A11	Ox
29.11	30.10	H12	B12	Bat
30.11	1.11	J1	C1	Rat
1.12	2.11	J1	D2	Swallow
2.12	3.11	J1	E3	Pig
3.12	4.11	J1	F4	Porcupine
4.12	5.11	J1	G5	Wolf
5.12	6.11	J1	H6	Dog
6.12	7.11	J1	J7	Pheasant
7.12	8.11	J1	K8	Cock
8.12	9.11	J1	A9	Crow
9.12	10.11	J1	B10	Monkey
10.12	11.11	J1	C11	Gibbon
11.12	12.11	J1	D12	Tapir
12.12	13.11	J1	E1	Sheep
13.12	14.11	J1	F2	Deer
14.12	15.11	J1	G3	Horse
15.12	16.11	J1	H4	Stag
16.12	17.11	J1	J5	Serpent
17.12	18.11	J1	K6	Earthworm
18.12	19.11	J1	A7	Crocodile
19.12	20.11	J1	B8	Dragon
20.12	21.11	J1	C9	Badger
21.12	22.11	J1	D10	Hare
22.12	23.11	J1	E11	Fox
23.12	24.11	J1	F12	Tiger
24.12	25.11	J1	G1	Leopard
25.12	26.11	J1	H2	Griffon
26.12	27.11	J1	J3	Ox
27.12	28.11	J1	K4	Bat
28.12	29.11	J1	A5	Rat
29.12	30.11	J1	B6	Swallow
30.12	1.12	K2	C7	Pig
31.12	2.12	K2	D8	Porcupine

1998

Solar date	Lunar date	Month HS/EB	Day HS/EB	Constellation
1. 1	3.12	K2	E9	Wolf
2. 1	4.12	K2	F10	Dog
3. 1	5.12	K2	G11	Pheasant
4. 1	6.12	K2	H12	Cock
5. 1	7.12	K2	J1	Crow
6. 1	8.12	K2	K2	Monkey
7. 1	9.12	K2	A3	Gibbon
8. 1	10.12	K2	B4	Tapir
9. 1	11.12	K2	C5	Sheep
10. 1	12.12	K2	D6	Deer
11. 1	13.12	K2	E7	Horse
12. 1	14.12	K2	F8	Stag
13. 1	15.12	K2	G9	Serpent
14. 1	16.12	K2	H10	Earthworm
15. 1	17.12	K2	J11	Crocodile
16. 1	18.12	K2	K12	Dragon
17. 1	19.12	K2	A1	Badger
18. 1	20.12	K2	B2	Hare
19. 1	21.12	K2	C3	Fox
20. 1	22.12	K2	D4	Tiger
21. 1	23.12	K2	E5	Leopard
22. 1	24.12	K2	F6	Griffon
23. 1	25.12	K2	G7	Ox
24. 1	26.12	K2	H8	Bat
25. 1	27.12	K2	J9	Rat
26. 1	28.12	K2	K10	Swallow
27. 1	29.12	K2	A11	Pig

MOU YIN YEAR

Solar date	Lunar date	Month HS/EB	Day HS/EB	Constellation
28. 1	1. 1	A3	B12	Porcupine
29. 1	2. 1	A3	C1	Wolf
30. 1	3. 1	A3	D2	Dog
31. 1	4. 1	A3	E3	Pheasant
1. 2	5. 1	A3	F4	Cock
2. 2	6. 1	A3	G5	Crow
3. 2	7. 1	A3	H6	Monkey
4. 2	8. 1	A3	J7	Gibbon
5. 2	9. 1	A3	K8	Tapir
6. 2	10. 1	A3	A9	Sheep
7. 2	11. 1	A3	B10	Deer
8. 2	12. 1	A3	C11	Horse
9. 2	13. 1	A3	D12	Stag
10. 2	14. 1	A3	E1	Serpent
11. 2	15. 1	A3	F2	Earthworm
12. 2	16. 1	A3	G3	Crocodile
13. 2	17. 1	A3	H4	Dragon
14. 2	18. 1	A3	J5	Badger
15. 2	19. 1	A3	K6	Hare
16. 2	20. 1	A3	A7	Fox
17. 2	21. 1	A3	B8	Tiger
18. 2	22. 1	A3	C9	Leopard
19. 2	23. 1	A3	D10	Griffon
20. 2	24. 1	A3	E11	Ox
21. 2	25. 1	A3	F12	Bat
22. 2	26. 1	A3	G1	Rat
23. 2	27. 1	A3	H2	Swallow
24. 2	28. 1	A3	J3	Pig
25. 2	29. 1	A3	K4	Porcupine
26. 2	30. 1	A3	A5	Wolf
27. 2	1. 2	B4	B6	Dog
28. 2	2. 2	B4	C7	Pheasant

Solar date	Lunar date	Month HS/EB	Day HS/EB	Constellation	Solar date	Lunar date	Month HS/EB	Day HS/EB	Constellation
1. 3	3. 2	B4	D8	Cock	13. 5	18. 4	D6	G9	Leopard
2. 3	4. 2	B4	E9	Crow	14. 5	19. 4	D6	H10	Griffon
3. 3	5. 2	B4	F10	Monkey	15. 5	20. 4	D6	J11	Ox
4. 3	6. 2	B4	G11	Gibbon	16. 5	21. 4	D6	K12	Bat
5. 3	7. 2	B4	H12	Tapir	17. 5	22. 4	D6	A1	Rat
6. 3	8. 2	B4	J1	Sheep	18. 5	23. 4	D6	B2	Swallow
7. 3	9. 2	B4	K2	Deer	19. 5	24. 4	D6	C3	Pig
8. 3	10. 2	B4	A3	Horse	20. 5	25. 4	D6	D4	Porcupine
9. 3	11. 2	B4	B4	Stag	21. 5	26. 4	D6	E5	Wolf
10. 3	12. 2	B4	C5	Serpent	22. 5	27. 4	D6	F6	Dog
11. 3	13. 2	B4	D6	Earthworm	23. 5	28. 4	D6	G7	Pheasant
12. 3	14. 2	B4	E7	Crocodile	24. 5	29. 4	D6	H8	Cock
13. 3	15. 2	B4	F8	Dragon	25. 5	30. 4	D6	J9	Crow
14. 3	16. 2	B4	G9	Badger	26. 5	1. 5	E7	K10	Monkey
15. 3	17. 2	B4	H10	Hare	27. 5	2. 5	E7	A11	Gibbon
16. 3	18. 2	B4	J11	Fox	28. 5	3. 5	E7	B12	Tapir
17. 3	19. 2	B4	K12	Tiger	29. 5	4. 5	E7	C1	Sheep
18. 3	20. 2	B4	A1	Leopard	30. 5	5. 5	E7	D2	Deer
19. 3	21. 2	R4	B2	Griffon	31. 5	6. 5	E7	E3	Horse
20. 3	22. 2	B4	C3	Ox	1. 6	7. 5	E7	F4	Stag
21. 3	23. 2	B4	D4	Bat	2. 6	8. 5	E7	G5	Serpent
22. 3	24. 2	B4	E5	Rat	3. 6	9. 5	E7	H6	Earthworm
23. 3	25. 2	B4	F6	Swallow	4. 6	10. 5	E7	J7	Crocodile
24. 3	26. 2	B4	G7	Pig	5. 6	11. 5	E7	K8	Dragon
25. 3	27. 2	B4	H8	Porcupine	6. 6	12. 5	E7	A9	Badger
26. 3	28. 2	B4	J9	Wolf	7. 6	13. 5	E7	B10	Hare
27. 3	29. 2	B4	K10	Dog	8. 6	14. 5	E7	C11	Fox
28. 3	1. 3	C5	A11	Pheasant	9. 6	15. 5	E7	D12	Tiger
29. 3	2. 3	C5	B12	Cock	10. 6	16. 5	E7	E1	Leopard
30. 3	3. 3	C5	C1	Crow	11. 6	17. 5	E7	F2	Griffon
31. 3	4. 3	C5	D2	Monkey	12. 6	18. 5	E7	G3	Ox
1. 4	5. 3	C5	E3	Gibbon	13. 6	19. 5	E7	H4	Bat
2. 4	6. 3	C5	F4	Tapir	14. 6	20. 5	E7	J5	Rat
3. 4	7. 3	C5	G5	Sheep	15. 6	21. 5	E7	K6	Swallow
4. 4	8. 3	C5	H6	Deer	16. 6	22. 5	E7	A7	Pig
5. 4	9. 3	C5	J7	Horse	17. 6	23. 5	E7	B8	Porcupine
6. 4	10. 3	C5	K8	Stag	18. 6	24. 5	E7	C9	Wolf
7. 4	11. 3	C5	A9	Serpent	19. 6	25. 5	E7	D10	Dog
8. 4	12. 3	C5	B10	Earthworm	20. 6	26. 5	E7	E11	Pheasant
9. 4	13. 3	C5	C11	Crocodile	21. 6	27. 5	E7	F12	Cock
10. 4	14. 3	C5	D12	Dragon	22. 6	28. 5	E7	G1	Crow
11. 4	15. 3	C5	E1	Badger	23. 6	29. 5	E7	H2	Monkey
12. 4	16. 3	C5	F2	Hare	24. 6	1. 5	E7	J3	Gibbon
13. 4	17. 3	C5	G3	Fox	25. 6	2. 5	E7	K4	Tapir
14. 4	18. 3	C5	H4	Tiger	26. 6	3. 5	E7	A5	Sheep
15. 4	19. 3	C5	J5	Leopard	27. 6	4. 5	E7	B6	Deer
16. 4	20. 3	C5	K6	Griffon	28. 6	5. 5	E7	C7	Horse
17. 4	21. 3	C5	A7	Ox	29. 6	6. 5	E7	D8	Stag
18. 4	22. 3	C5	B8	Bat	30. 6	7. 5	E7	E9	Serpent
19. 4	23. 3	C5	C9	Rat	1. 7	8. 5	E7	F10	Earthworm
20. 4	24. 3	C5	D10	Swallow	2. 7	9. 5	E7	G11	Crocodile
21. 4	25. 3	C5	E11	Pig	3. 7	10. 5	E7	H12	Dragon
22. 4	26. 3	C5	F12	Porcupine	4. 7	11. 5	E7	J1	Badger
23. 4	27. 3	C5	G1	Wolf	5. 7	12. 5	E7	K2	Hare
24. 4	28. 3	C5	H2	Dog	6. 7	13. 5	E7	A3	Fox
25. 4	29. 3	C5	J3	Pheasant	7. 7	14. 5	E7	B4	Tiger
26. 4	1. 4	D6	K4	Cock	8. 7	15. 5	E7	C5	Leopard
27. 4	2. 4	D6	A5	Crow	9. 7	16. 5	E7	D6	Griffon
28. 4	3. 4	D6	B6	Monkey	10. 7	17. 5	E7	E7	Ox
29. 4	4. 4	D6	C7	Gibbon	11. 7	18. 5	E7	F8	Bat
30. 4	5. 4	D6	D8	Tapir	12. 7	19. 5	E7	G9	Rat
1. 5	6. 4	D6	E9	Sheep	13. 7	20. 5	E7	H10	Swallow
2. 5	7. 4	D6	F10	Deer	14. 7	21. 5	E7	J11	Pig
3. 5	8. 4	D6	G11	Horse	15. 7	22. 5	E7	K12	Porcupine
4. 5	9. 4	D6	H12	Stag	16. 7	23. 5	E7	A1	Wolf
5. 5	10. 4	D6	J1	Serpent	17. 7	24. 5	E7	B2	Dog
6. 5	11. 4	D6	K2	Earthworm	18. 7	25. 5	E7	C3	Pheasant
7. 5	12. 4	D6	A3	Crocodile	19. 7	26. 5	E7	D4	Cock
8. 5	13. 4	D6	B4	Dragon	20. 7	27. 5	E7	E5	Crow
9. 5	14. 4	D6	C5	Badger	21. 7	28. 5	E7	F6	Monkey
10. 5	15. 4	D6	D6	Hare	22. 7	29. 5	E7	G7	Gibbon
11. 5	16. 4	D6	E7	Fox	23. 7	1. 6	F8	H8	Tapir
12. 5	17. 4	D6	F8	Tiger	24. 7	2. 6	F8	J9	Sheep

Solar date	Lunar date	Month HS/EB	Day HS/EB	Constellation	Solar date	Lunar date	Month HS/EB	Day HS/EB	Constellation
25. 7	3. 6	F8	K10	Deer	6.10	16. 8	H10	C11	Pig
26. 7	4. 6	F8	A11	Horse	7.10	17. 8	H10	D12	Porcupine
27. 7	5. 6	F8	B12	STag	8.10	18. 8	H10	E1	Wolf
28. 7	6. 6	F8	C1	Serpent	9.10	19. 8	H10	F2	Dog
29. 7	7. 6	F8	D2	Earthworm	10.10	20. 8	H10	G3	Pheasant
30. 7	8. 6	F8	E3	Crocodile	11.10	21. 8	H10	H4	Cock
31. 7	9. 6	F8	F4	Dragon	12.10	22. 8	H10	J5	Crow
1. 8	10. 6	F8	G5	Badger	13.10	23. 8	H10	K6	Monkey
2. 8	11. 6	F8	H6	Hare	14.10	24. 8	H10	A7	Gibbon
3. 8	12. 6	F8	J7	Fox	15.10	25. 8	H10	B8	Tapir
4. 8	13. 6	F8	K8	Tiger	16.10	26. 8	H10	C9	Sheep
5. 8	14. 6	F8	A9	Leopard	17.10	27. 8	H10	D10	Deer
6. 8	15. 6	F8	B10	Griffon	18.10	28. 8	H10	E11	Horse
7. 8	16. 6	F8	C11	Ox	19.10	29. 8	H10	F12	Stag
8. 8	17. 6	F8	D12	Bat	20.10	1. 9	J11	G1	Serpent
9. 8	18. 6	F8	E1	Rat	21.10	2. 9	J11	H2	Earthworm
10. 8	19. 6	F8	F2	Swallow	22.10	3. 9	J11	J3	Crocodile
11. 8	20. 6	F8	G3	Pig	23.10	4. 9	J11	K4	Dragon
12. 8	21. 6	F8	H4	Porcupine	24.10	5. 9	J11	A5	Badger
13. 8	22. 6	F8	J5	Wolf	25.10	6. 9	J11	B6	Hare
14. 8	23. 6	F8	K6	Dog	26.10	7. 9	J11	C7	Fox
15. 8	24. 6	F8	A7	Pheasant	27.10	8. 9	J11	D8	Tiger
16. 8	25. 6	F8	B8	Cock	28.10	9. 9	J11	E9	Leopard
17. 8	26. 6	F8	C9	Crow	29.10	10. 9	J11	F10	Griffon
18. 8	27. 6	F8	D10	Monkey	30.10	11. 9	J11	G11	Ox
19. 8	28. 6	F8	E11	Gibbon	31.10	12. 9	J11	H12	Bat
20. 8	29. 6	F8	F12	Tapir	1.11	13. 9	J11	J1	Rat
21. 8	30. 6	F8	G1	Sheep	2.11	14. 9	J11	K2	Swallow
22. 8	1. 7	G9	H2	Deer	3.11	15. 9	J11	A3	Pig
23. 8	2. 7	G9	J3	Horse	4.11	16. 9	J11	B4	Porcupine
24. 8	3. 7	G9	K4	Stag	5.11	17. 9	J11	C5	Wolf
25. 8	4. 7	G9	A5	Serpent	6.11	18. 9	J11	D6	Dog
26. 8	5. 7	G9	B6	Earthworm	7.11	19. 9	J11	E7	Pheasant
27. 8	6. 7	G9	C7	Crocodile	8.11	20. 9	J11	F8	Cock
28. 8	7. 7	G9	D8	Dragon	9.11	21. 9	J11	G9	Crow
29. 8	8. 7	G9	E9	Badger	10.11	22. 9	J11	H10	Monkey
30. 8	9. 7	G9	F10	Hare	11.11	23. 9	J11	J11	Gibbon
31. 8	10. 7	G9	G11	Fox	12.11	24. 9	J11	K12	Tapir
1. 9	11. 7	G9	H12	Tiger	13.11	25. 9	J11	A1	Sheep
2. 9	12. 7	G9	J1	Leopard	14.11	26. 9	J11	B2	Deer
3. 9	13. 7	G9	K2	Griffon	15.11	27. 9	J11	C3	Horse
4. 9	14. 7	G9	A3	Ox	16.11	28. 9	J11	D4	Stag
5. 9	15. 7	G9	B4	Bat	17.11	29. 9	J11	E5	Serpent
6. 9	16. 7	G9	C5	Rat	18.11	30. 9	J11	F6	Earthworm
7. 9	17. 7	G0	D6	Swallow	19.11	1.10	K12	G7	Crocodile
8. 9	18. 7	G9	E7	Pig	20.11	2.10	K12	H8	Dragon
9. 9	19. 7	G9	F8	Porcupine	21.11	3.10	K12	J9	Badger
10. 9	20. 7	G9	G9	Wolf	22.11	4.10	K12	K10	Hare
11. 9	21. 7	G9	H10	Dog	23.11	5.10	K12	A11	Fox
12. 9	22. 7	G9	J11	Pheasant	24.11	6.10	K12	B12	Tiger
13. 9	23. 7	G9	K12	Cock	25.11	7.10	K12	C1	Leopard
14. 9	24. 7	G9	A1	Crow	26.11	8.10	K12	D2	Griffon
15. 9	25. 7	G9	B2	Monkey	27.11	9.10	K12	E3	Ox
16. 9	26. 7	G9	C3	Gibbon	28.11	10.10	K12	F4	Bat
17. 9	27. 7	G9	D4	Tapir	29.11	11.10	K12	G5	Rat
18. 9	28. 7	G9	E5	Sheep	20.11	12.10	K12	H6	Swallow
19. 9	29. 7	G9	F6	Deer	1.12	13.10	K12	J7	Pig
20. 9	30. 7	G9	G7	Horse	2.12	14.10	K12	K8	Porcupine
21. 9	1. 8	H10	H8	Stag	3.12	15.10	K12	A9	Wolf
22. 9	2. 8	H10	J9	Serpent	4.12	16.10	K12	B10	Dog
23. 9	3. 8	H10	K10	Earthworm	5.12	17.10	K12	C11	Pheasant
24. 9	4. 8	H10	A11	Crocodile	6.12	18.10	K12	D12	Cock
25. 9	5. 8	H10	B12	Dragon	7.12	19.10	K12	E1	Crow
26. 9	6. 8	H10	C1	Badger	8.12	20.10	K12	F2	Monkey
27. 9	7. 8	H10	D2	Hare	9.12	21.10	K12	G3	Gibbon
28. 9	8. 8	H10	E3	Fox	10.12	22.10	K12	H4	Tapir
29. 9	9. 8	H10	F4	Tiger	11.12	23.10	K12	J5	Sheep
30. 9	10. 8	H10	G5	Leopard	12.12	24.10	K12	K6	Deer
1.10	11. 8	H10	H6	Griffon	13.12	25.10	K12	A7	Horse
2.10	12. 8	H10	J7	Ox	14.12	26.10	K12	B8	Stag
3.10	13. 8	H10	K8	Bat	15.12	27.10	K12	C9	Serpent
4.10	14. 8	H10	A9	Rat	16.12	28.10	K12	D10	Earthworm
5.10	15. 8	H10	B10	Swallow	17.12	29.10	K12	E11	Crocodile

Solar date	Lunar date	Month HS/EB	Day HS/EB	Constellation	Solar date	Lunar date	Month HS/EB	Day HS/EB	Constellation
18.12	30.10	K12	F12	Dragon	16. 1	29.11	A1	E5	Badger
19.12	1.11	A1	G1	Badger	17. 1	1.12	B2	F6	Hare
20.12	2.11	A1	H2	Hare	18. 1	2.12	B2	G7	Fox
21.12	3.11	A1	J3	Fox	19. 1	3.12	B2	H8	Tiger
22.12	4.11	A1	K4	Tiger	20. 1	4.12	B2	J9	Leopard
23.12	5.11	A1	A5	Leopard	21. 1	5.12	B2	K10	Griffon
24.12	6.11	A1	B6	Griffon	22. 1	6.12	B2	A11	Ox
25.12	7.11	A1	C7	Ox	23. 1	7.12	B2	B12	Bat
26.12	8.11	A1	D8	Bat	24. 1	8.12	B2	C1	Rat
27.12	9.11	A1	E9	Rat	25. 1	9.12	B2	D2	Swallow
28.12	10.11	A1	F10	Swallow	26. 1	10.12	B2	E3	Pig
29.12	11.11	A1	G11	Pig	27. 1	11.12	B2	F4	Porcupine
30.12	12.11	A1	H12	Porcupine	28. 1	12.12	B2	G5	Wolf
31.12	13.11	A1	J1	Wolf	29. 1	13.12	B2	H6	Dog
1999					30. 1	14.12	B2	J7	Pheasant
1. 1	14.11	A1	K2	Dog	31. 1	15.12	B2	K8	Cock
2. 1	15.11	A1	A3	Pheasant	1. 2	16.12	B2	A9	Crow
3. 1	16.11	A1	B4	Cock	2. 2	17.12	B2	B10	Monkey
4. 1	17.11	A1	C5	Crow	3. 2	18.12	B2	C11	Gibbon
5. 1	18.11	A1	D6	Monkey	4. 2	19.12	B2	D12	Tapir
6. 1	19.11	A1	E7	Gibbon	5. 2	20.12	B2	E1	Sheep
7. 1	20.11	A1	F8	Tapir	6. 2	21.12	B2	F2	Deer
8. 1	21.11	A1	G9	Sheep	7. 2	22.12	B2	G3	Horse
9. 1	22.11	A1	H10	Deer	8. 2	23.12	B2	H4	Stag
10. 1	23.11	A1	J11	Horse	9. 2	24.12	B2	J5	Serpent
11. 1	24.11	A1	K12	Stag	10. 2	25.12	B2	K6	Earthworm
12. 1	25.11	A1	A1	Serpent	11. 2	26.12	B2	A7	Crocodile
13. 1	26.11	A1	B2	Earthworm	12. 2	27.12	B2	B8	Dragon
14. 1	27.11	A1	C3	Crocodile	13. 2	28.12	B2	C9	Badger
15. 1	28.11	A1	D4	Dragon	14. 2	29.12	B2	D10	Hare
					15. 2	30.12	B2	E11	Fox

CHI MAO YEAR

Solar date	Lunar date	Month HS/EB	Day HS/EB	Constellation	Solar date	Lunar date	Month HS/EB	Day HS/EB	Constellation
16. 2	1. 1	C3	F12	Tiger	25. 3	8. 2	D4	C1	Wolf
17. 2	2. 1	C3	G1	Leopard	26. 3	9. 2	D4	D2	Dog
18. 2	3. 1	C3	H2	Griffon	27. 3	10. 2	D4	E3	Pheasant
19. 2	4. 1	C3	J3	Ox	28. 3	11. 2	D4	F4	Cock
20. 2	5. 1	C3	K4	Bat	29. 3	12. 2	D4	G5	Crow
21. 2	6. 1	C3	A5	Rat	30. 3	13. 2	D4	H6	Monkey
22. 2	7. 1	C3	B6	Swallow	31. 3	14. 2	D4	J7	Gibbon
23. 2	8. 1	C3	C7	Pig	1. 4	15. 2	D4	K8	Tapir
24. 2	9. 1	C3	D8	Porcupine	2. 4	16. 2	D4	A9	Sheep
25. 2	10. 1	C3	E9	Wolf	3. 4	17. 2	D4	B10	Deer
26. 2	11. 1	C3	F10	Dog	4. 4	18. 2	D4	C11	Horse
27. 2	12. 1	C3	G11	Pheasant	5. 4	19. 2	D4	D12	Stag
28. 2	13. 1	C3	H12	Cock	6. 4	20. 2	D4	E1	Serpent
1. 3	14. 1	C3	J1	Crow	7. 4	21. 2	D4	F2	Earthworm
2. 3	15. 1	C3	K2	Monkey	8. 4	22. 2	D4	G3	Crocodile
3. 3	16. 1	C3	A3	Gibbon	9. 4	23. 2	D4	H4	Dragon
4. 3	17. 1	C3	B4	Tapir	10. 4	24. 2	D4	J5	Badger
5. 3	18. 1	C3	C5	Sheep	11. 4	25. 2	D4	K6	Hare
6. 3	19. 1	C3	D6	Deer	12. 4	26. 2	D4	A7	Fox
7. 3	20. 1	C3	E7	Horse	13. 4	27. 2	D4	B8	Tiger
8. 3	21. 1	C3	F8	Stag	14. 4	28. 2	D4	C9	Leopard
9. 3	22. 1	C3	G9	Serpent	15. 4	29. 2	D4	D10	Griffon
10. 3	23. 1	C3	H10	Earthworm	16. 4	1. 3	E5	E11	Ox
11. 3	24. 1	C3	J11	Crocodile	17. 4	2. 3	E5	F12	Bat
12. 3	25. 1	C3	K12	Dragon	18. 4	3. 3	E5	G1	Rat
13. 3	26. 1	C3	A1	Badger	19. 4	4. 3	E5	H2	Swallow
14. 3	27. 1	C3	B2	Hare	20. 4	5. 3	E5	J3	Pig
15. 3	28. 1	C3	C3	Fox	21. 4	6. 3	E5	K4	Porcupine
16. 3	29. 1	C3	D4	Tiger	22. 4	7. 3	E5	A5	Wolf
17. 3	30. 1	C3	E5	Leopard	23. 4	8. 3	E5	B6	Dog
18. 3	1. 2	D4	F6	Griffon	24. 4	9. 3	E5	C7	Pheasant
19. 3	2. 2	D4	G7	Ox	25. 4	10. 3	E5	D8	Cock
20. 3	3. 2	D4	H8	Bat	26. 4	11. 3	E5	E9	Crow
21. 3	4. 2	D4	J9	Rat	27. 4	12. 3	E5	F10	Monkey
22. 3	5. 2	D4	K10	Swallow	28. 4	13. 3	E5	G11	Gibbon
23. 3	6. 2	D4	A11	Pig	29. 4	14. 3	E5	H12	Tapir
24. 3	7. 2	D4	B12	Porcupine	30. 4	15. 3	E5	J1	Sheep

Solar date	Lunar date	Month HS/EB	Day HS/EB	Constellation	Solar date	Lunar date	Month HS/EB	Day HS/EB	Constellation
1. 5	16. 3	E5	K2	Deer	13. 7	1. 6	H8	C3	Pig
2. 5	17. 3	E5	A3	Horse	14. 7	2. 6	H8	D4	Porcupine
3. 5	18. 3	E5	B4	Stag	15. 7	3. 6	H8	E5	Wolf
4. 5	19. 3	E5	C5	Serpent	16. 7	4. 6	H8	F6	Dog
5. 5	20. 3	E5	D6	Earthworm	17. 7	5. 6	H8	G7	Pheasant
6. 5	21. 3	E5	E7	Crocodile	18. 7	6. 6	H8	H8	Cock
7. 5	22. 3	E5	F8	Dragon	19. 7	7. 6	H8	J9	Crow
8. 5	23. 3	E5	G9	Badger	20. 7	8. 6	H8	K10	Monkey
9. 5	24. 3	E5	H10	Hare	21. 7	9. 6	H8	A11	Gibbon
10. 5	25. 3	E5	J11	Fox	22. 7	10. 6	H8	B12	Tapir
11. 5	26. 3	E5	K12	Tiger	23. 7	11. 6	H8	C1	Sheep
12. 5	27. 3	E5	A1	Leopard	24. 7	12. 6	H8	D2	Deer
13. 5	28. 3	E5	B2	Griffon	25. 7	13. 6	H8	E3	Horse
14. 5	29. 3	E5	C3	Ox	26. 7	14. 6	H8	F4	Stag
15. 5	1. 4	F6	D4	Bat	27. 7	15. 6	H8	G5	Serpent
16. 5	2. 4	F6	E5	Rat	28. 7	16. 6	H8	H6	Earthworm
17. 5	3. 4	F6	F6	Swallow	29. 7	17. 6	H8	J7	Crocodile
18. 5	4. 4	F6	G7	Pig	30. 7	18. 6	H8	K8	Dragon
19. 5	5. 4	F6	H8	Porcupine	31. 7	19. 6	H8	A9	Badger
20. 5	6. 4	F6	J9	Wolf	1. 8	20. 6	H8	B10	Hare
21. 5	7. 4	F6	K10	Dog	2. 8	21. 6	H8	C11	Fox
22. 5	8. 4	F6	A11	Pheasant	3. 8	22. 6	H8	D12	Tiger
23. 5	9. 4	F6	B12	Cock	4. 8	23. 6	H8	E1	Leopard
24. 5	10. 4	F6	C1	Crow	5. 8	24. 6	H8	F2	Griffon
25. 5	11. 4	F6	D2	Monkey	6. 8	25. 6	H8	G3	Ox
26. 5	12. 4	F6	E3	Gibbon	7. 8	26. 6	H8	H4	Bat
27. 5	13. 4	F6	F4	Tapir	8. 8	27. 6	H8	J5	Rat
28. 5	14. 4	F6	G5	Sheep	9. 8	28. 6	H8	K6	Swallow
29. 5	15. 4	F6	H6	Deer	10. 8	29. 6	H8	A7	Pig
30. 5	16. 4	F6	J7	Horse	11. 8	1. 7	J9	B8	Porcupine
31. 5	17. 4	F6	K8	Stag	12. 8	2. 7	J9	C9	Wolf
1. 6	18. 4	F6	A9	Serpent	13. 8	3. 7	J9	D10	Dog
2. 6	19. 4	F6	B10	Earthworm	14. 8	4. 7	J9	E11	Pheasant
3. 6	20. 4	F6	C11	Crocodile	15. 8	5. 7	J9	F12	Cock
4. 6	21. 4	F6	D12	Dragon	16. 8	6. 7	J9	G1	Crow
5. 6	22. 4	F6	E1	Badger	17. 8	7. 7	J9	H2	Monkey
6. 6	23. 4	F6	F2	Hare	18. 8	8. 7	J9	J3	Gibbon
7. 6	24. 4	F6	G3	Fox	19. 8	9. 7	J9	K4	Tapir
8. 6	25. 4	F6	H4	Tiger	20. 8	10. 7	J9	A5	Sheep
9. 6	26. 4	F6	J5	Leopard	21. 8	11. 7	J9	B6	Deer
10. 6	27. 4	F6	K6	Griffon	22. 8	12. 7	J9	C7	Horse
11. 6	28. 4	F6	A7	Ox	23. 8	13. 7	J9	D8	Stag
12. 6	29. 4	F6	B8	Bat	24. 8	14. 7	J9	E9	Serpent
13. 6	30. 4	F6	C9	Rat	25. 8	15. 7	J9	F10	Earthworm
14. 6	1. 5	G7	D10	Swallow	26. 8	16. 7	J9	G11	Crocodile
15. 6	2. 5	G7	E11	Pig	27. 8	17. 7	J9	H12	Dragon
16. 6	3. 5	G7	F12	Porcupine	28. 8	18. 7	J9	J1	Badger
17. 6	4. 5	G7	G1	Wolf	29. 8	19. 7	J9	K2	Hare
18. 6	5. 5	G7	H2	Dog	30. 8	20. 7	J9	A3	Fox
19. 6	6. 5	G7	J3	Pheasant	31. 8	21. 7	J9	B4	Tiger
20. 6	7. 5	G7	K4	Cock	1. 9	22. 7	J9	C5	Leopard
21. 6	8. 5	G7	A5	Crow	2. 9	23. 7	J9	D6	Griffon
22. 6	9. 5	G7	B6	Monkey	3. 9	24. 7	J9	E7	Ox
23. 6	10. 5	G7	C7	Gibbon	4. 9	25. 7	J9	F8	Bat
24. 6	11. 5	G7	D8	Tapir	5. 9	26. 7	J9	G9	Rat
25. 6	12. 5	G7	E9	Sheep	6. 9	27. 7	J9	H10	Swallow
26. 6	13. 5	G7	F10	Deer	7. 9	28. 7	J9	J11	Pig
27. 6	14. 5	G7	G11	Horse	8. 9	29. 7	J9	K12	Porcupine
28. 6	15. 5	G7	H12	Stag	9. 9	30. 7	J9	A1	Wolf
29. 6	16. 5	G7	J1	Serpent	10. 9	1. 8	K10	B2	Dog
30. 6	17. 5	G7	K2	Earthworm	11. 9	2. 8	K10	C3	Pheasant
1. 7	18. 5	G7	A3	Crocodile	12. 9	3. 8	K10	D4	Cock
2. 7	19. 5	G7	B4	Dragon	13. 9	4. 8	K10	E5	Crow
3. 7	20. 5	G7	C5	Badger	14. 9	5. 8	K10	F6	Monkey
4. 7	21. 5	G7	D6	Hare	15. 9	6. 8	K10	G7	Gibbon
5. 7	22. 5	G7	E7	Fox	16. 9	7. 8	K10	H8	Tapir
6. 7	23. 5	G7	F8	Tiger	17. 9	8. 8	K10	J9	Sheep
7. 7	24. 5	G7	G9	Leopard	18. 9	9. 8	K10	K10	Deer
8. 7	25. 5	G7	H10	Griffon	19. 9	10. 8	K10	A11	Horse
9. 7	26. 5	G7	J11	Ox	20. 9	11. 8	K10	B12	Stag
10. 7	27. 5	G7	K12	Bat	21. 9	12. 8	K10	C1	Serpent
11. 7	28. 5	G7	A1	Rat	22. 9	13. 8	K10	D2	Earthworm
12. 7	29. 5	G7	B2	Swallow	23. 9	14. 8	K10	E3	Crocodile

Solar date	Lunar date	Month HS/EB	Day HS/EB	Constellation	Solar date	Lunar date	Month HS/EB	Day HS/EB	Constellation
24. 9	15. 8	K10	F4	Dragon	1.12	24.10	B12	D12	Porcupine
25. 9	16. 8	K10	G5	Badger	2.12	25.10	B12	E1	Wolf
26. 9	17. 8	K10	H6	Hare	3.12	26.10	B12	F2	Dog
27. 9	18. 8	K10	J7	Fox	4.12	27.10	B12	G3	Pheasant
28. 9	19. 8	K10	K8	Tiger	5.12	28.10	B12	H4	Cock
29. 9	20. 8	K10	A9	Leopard	6.12	29.10	B12	J5	Crow
30. 9	21. 8	K10	B10	Griffon	7.12	30.10	B12	K6	Monkey
1.10	22. 8	K10	C11	Ox	8.12	1.11	C1	A7	Gibbon
2.10	23. 8	K10	D12	Bat	9.12	2.11	C1	B8	Tapir
3.10	24. 8	K10	E1	Rat	10.12	3.11	C1	C9	Sheep
4.10	25. 8	K10	F2	Swallow	11.12	4.11	C1	D10	Deer
5.10	26. 8	K10	G3	Pig	12.12	5.11	C1	E11	Horse
6.10	27. 8	K10	H4	Porcupine	13.12	6.11	C1	F12	Stag
7.10	28. 8	K10	J5	Wolf	14.12	7.11	C1	G1	Serpent
8.10	29. 8	K10	K6	Dog	15.12	8.11	C1	H2	Earthworm
9.10	1. 9	A11	A7	Pheasant	16.12	9.11	C1	J3	Crocodile
10.10	2. 9	A11	B8	Cock	17.12	10.11	C1	K4	Dragon
11.10	3. 9	A11	C9	Crow	18.12	11.11	C1	A5	Badger
12.10	4. 9	A11	D10	Monkey	19.12	12.11	C1	B6	Hare
13.10	5. 9	A11	E11	Gibbon	20.12	13.11	C1	C7	Fox
14.10	6. 9	A11	F12	Tapir	21.12	14.11	C1	D8	Tiger
15.10	7. 9	A11	G1	Sheep	22.12	15.11	C1	E9	Leopard
16.10	8. 9	A11	H2	Deer	23.12	16.11	C1	F10	Griffon
17.10	9. 9	A11	J3	Horse	24.12	17.11	C1	G11	Ox
18.10	10. 9	A11	K4	Stag	25.12	18.11	C1	H12	Bat
19.10	11. 9	A11	A5	Serpent	26.12	19.11	C1	J1	Rat
20.10	12. 9	A11	B6	Earthworm	27.12	20.11	C1	K2	Swallow
21.10	13. 9	A11	C7	Crocodile	28.12	21.11	C1	A3	Pig
22.10	14. 9	A11	D8	Dragon	29.12	22.11	C1	B4	Porcupine
23.10	15. 9	A11	E9	Badger	30.12	23.11	C1	C5	Wolf
24.10	16. 9	A11	F10	Hare	31.12	24.11	C1	D6	Dog
25.10	17. 9	A11	G11	Fox					
26.10	18. 9	A11	H12	Tiger	**2000**				
27.10	19. 9	A11	J1	Leopard	1. 1	25.11	C1	E7	Pheasant
28.10	20. 9	A11	K2	Griffon	2. 1	26.11	C1	F8	Cock
29.10	21. 9	A11	A3	Ox	3. 1	27.11	C1	G9	Crow
30.10	22. 9	A11	B4	Bat	4. 1	28.11	C1	H10	Monkey
31.10	23. 9	A11	C5	Rat	5. 1	29.11	C1	J11	Gibbon
1.11	24. 9	A11	D6	Swallow	6. 1	30.11	C1	K12	Tapir
2.11	25. 9	A11	E7	Pig	7. 1	1.12	D2	A1	Sheep
3.11	26. 9	A11	F8	Porcupine	8. 1	2.12	D2	B2	Deer
4.11	27. 9	A11	G9	Wolf	9. 1	3.12	D2	C3	Horse
5.11	28. 9	A11	H10	Dog	10. 1	4.12	D2	D4	Stag
6.11	29. 9	A11	J11	Pheasant	11. 1	5.12	D2	E5	Serpent
7.11	30. 9	A11	K12	Cock	12. 1	6.12	D2	F6	Earthworm
8.11	1.10	B12	A1	Crow	13. 1	7.12	D2	G7	Crocodile
9.11	2.10	B12	B2	Monkey	14. 1	8.12	D2	H8	Dragon
10.11	3.10	B12	C3	Gibbon	15. 1	9.12	D2	J9	Badger
11.11	4.10	B12	D4	Tapir	16. 1	10.12	D2	K10	Hare
12.11	5.10	B12	E5	Sheep	17. 1	11.12	D2	A11	Fox
13.11	6.10	B12	F6	Deer	18. 1	12.12	D2	B12	Tiger
14.11	7.10	B12	G7	Horse	19. 1	13.12	D2	C1	Leopard
15.11	8.10	B12	H8	Stag	20. 1	14.12	D2	D2	Griffon
16.11	9.10	B12	J9	Serpent	21. 1	15.12	D2	E3	Ox
17.11	10.10	B12	K10	Earthworm	22. 1	16.12	D2	F4	Bat
18.11	11.10	B12	A11	Crocodile	23. 1	17.12	D2	G5	Rat
19.11	12.10	B12	B12	Dragon	24. 1	18.12	D2	H6	Swallow
20.11	13.10	B12	C1	Badger	25. 1	19.12	D2	J7	Pig
21.11	14.10	B12	D2	Hare	26. 1	20.12	D2	K8	Porcupine
22.11	15.10	B12	E3	Fox	27. 1	21.12	D2	A9	Wolf
23.11	16.10	B12	F4	Tiger	28. 1	22.12	D2	B10	Dog
24.11	17.10	B12	G5	Leopard	29. 1	23.12	D2	C11	Pheasant
25.11	18.10	B12	H6	Griffon	30. 1	24.12	D2	D12	Cock
26.11	19.10	B12	J7	Ox	31. 1	25.12	D2	E1	Crow
27.11	20.10	B12	K8	Bat	1. 2	26.12	D2	F2	Monkey
28.11	21.10	B12	A9	Rat	2. 2	27.12	D2	G3	Gibbon
29.11	22.10	B12	B10	Swallow	3. 2	28.12	D2	H4	Tapir
30.11	23.10	B12	C11	Pig	4. 2	29.12	D2	J5	Sheep

KENG CH'EN YEAR

Solar date	Lunar date	Month HS/EB	Day HS/EB	Constellation
5. 2	1. 1	E3	K6	Deer
6. 2	2. 1	E3	A7	Horse
7. 2	3. 1	E3	B8	Stag
8. 2	4. 1	E3	C9	Serpent
9. 2	5. 1	E3	D10	Earthworm
10. 2	6. 1	E3	E11	Crocodile
11. 2	7. 1	E3	F12	Dragon
12. 2	8. 1	E3	G1	Badger
13. 2	9. 1	E3	H2	Hare
14. 2	10. 1	E3	J3	Fox
15. 2	11. 1	E3	K4	Tiger
16. 2	12. 1	E3	A5	Leopard
17. 2	13. 1	E3	B6	Griffon
18. 2	14. 1	E3	C7	Ox
19. 2	15. 1	E3	D8	Bat
20. 2	16. 1	E3	E9	Rat
21. 2	17. 1	E3	F10	Swallow
22. 2	18. 1	E3	G11	Pig
23. 2	19. 1	E3	H12	Porcupine
24. 2	20. 1	E3	J1	Wolf
25. 2	21. 1	E3	K2	Dog
26. 2	22. 1	E3	A3	Pheasant
27. 2	23. 1	E3	B4	Cock
28. 2	24. 1	E3	C5	Crow
29. 2	25. 1	E3	D6	Monkey
1. 3	26. 1	E3	E7	Gibbon
2. 3	27. 1	E3	F8	Tapir
3. 3	28. 1	E3	G9	Sheep
4. 3	29. 1	E3	H10	Deer
5. 3	30. 1	E3	J11	Horse
6. 3	1. 2	F4	K12	Stag
7. 3	2. 2	F4	A1	Serpent
8. 3	3. 2	F4	B2	Earthworm
9. 3	4. 2	F4	C3	Crocodile
10. 3	5. 2	F4	D4	Dragon
11. 3	6. 2	F4	E5	Badger
12. 3	7. 2	F4	F6	Hare
13. 3	8. 2	F4	G7	Fox
14. 3	9. 2	F4	H8	Tiger
15. 3	10. 2	F4	J9	Leopard
16. 3	11. 2	F4	K10	Griffon
17. 3	12. 2	F4	A11	Ox
18. 3	13. 2	F4	B12	Bat
19. 3	14. 2	F4	C1	Rat
20. 3	15. 2	F4	D2	Swallow
21. 3	16. 2	F4	E3	Pig
22. 3	17. 2	F4	F4	Porcupine
23. 3	18. 2	F4	G5	Wolf
24. 3	19. 2	F4	H6	Dog
25. 3	20. 2	F4	J7	Pheasant
26. 3	21. 2	F4	K8	Cock
27. 3	22. 2	F4	A9	Crow
28. 3	23. 2	F4	B10	Monkey
29. 3	24. 2	F4	C11	Gibbon
30. 3	25. 2	F4	D12	Tapir
31. 3	26. 2	F4	E1	Sheep
1. 4	27. 2	F4	F2	Deer
2. 4	28. 2	F4	G3	Horse
3. 4	29. 2	F4	H4	Stag
4. 4	30. 2	F4	J5	Serpent
5. 4	1. 3	G5	K6	Earthworm
6. 4	2. 3	G5	A7	Crocodile
7. 4	3. 3	G5	B8	Dragon
8. 4	4. 3	G5	C9	Badger
9. 4	5. 3	G5	D10	Hare
10. 4	6. 3	G5	E11	Fox
11. 4	7. 3	G5	F12	Tiger
12. 4	8. 3	G5	G1	Leopard
13. 4	9. 3	G5	H2	Griffon
14. 4	10. 3	G5	J3	Ox
15. 4	11. 3	G5	K4	Bat
16. 4	12. 3	G5	A5	Rat
17. 4	13. 3	G5	B6	Swallow
18. 4	14. 3	G5	C7	Pig
19. 4	15. 3	G5	D8	Porcupine
20. 4	16. 3	G5	E9	Wolf
21. 4	17. 3	G5	F10	Dog
22. 4	18. 3	G5	G11	Pheasant
23. 4	19. 3	G5	H12	Cock
24. 4	20. 3	G5	J1	Crow
25. 4	21. 3	G5	K2	Monkey
26. 4	22. 3	G5	A3	Gibbon
27. 4	23. 3	G5	B4	Tapir
28. 4	24. 3	G5	C5	Sheep
29. 4	25. 3	G5	D6	Deer
30. 4	26. 3	G5	E7	Horse
1. 5	27. 3	G5	F8	Stag
2. 5	28. 3	G5	G9	Serpent
3. 5	29. 3	G5	H10	Earthworm
4. 5	1. 4	H6	J11	Crocodile
5. 5	2. 4	H6	K12	Dragon
6. 5	3. 4	H6	A1	Badger
7. 5	4. 4	H6	B2	Hare
8. 5	5. 4	H6	C3	Fox
9. 5	6. 4	H6	D4	Tiger
10. 5	7. 4	H6	E5	Leopard
11. 5	8. 4	H6	F6	Griffon
12. 5	9. 4	H6	G7	Ox
13. 5	10. 4	H6	H8	Bat
14. 5	11. 4	H6	J9	Rat
15. 5	12. 4	H6	K10	Swallow
16. 5	13. 4	H6	A11	Pig
17. 5	14. 4	H6	B12	Porcupine
18. 5	15. 4	H6	C1	Wolf
19. 5	16. 4	H6	D2	Dog
20. 5	17. 4	H6	E3	Pheasant
21. 5	18. 4	H6	F4	Cock
22. 5	19. 4	H6	G5	Crow
23. 5	20. 4	H6	H6	Monkey
24. 5	21. 4	H6	J7	Gibbon
25. 5	22. 4	H6	K8	Tapir
26. 5	23. 4	H6	A9	Sheep
27. 5	24. 4	H6	B10	Deer
28. 5	25. 4	H6	C11	Horse
29. 5	26. 4	H6	D12	Stag
30. 5	27. 4	H6	E1	Serpent
31. 5	28. 4	H6	F2	Earthworm
1. 6	29. 4	H6	G3	Crocodile
2. 6	1. 5	J7	H4	Dragon
3. 6	2. 5	J7	J5	Badger
4. 6	3. 5	J7	K6	Hare
5. 6	4. 5	J7	A7	Fox
6. 6	5. 5	J7	B8	Tiger
7. 6	6. 5	J7	C9	Leopard
8. 6	7. 5	J7	D10	Griffon
9. 6	8. 5	J7	E11	Ox
10. 6	9. 5	J7	F12	Bat
11. 6	10. 5	J7	G1	Rat
12. 6	11. 5	J7	H2	Swallow
13. 6	12. 5	J7	J3	Pig
14. 6	13. 5	J7	K4	Porcupine
15. 6	14. 5	J7	A5	Wolf
16. 6	15. 5	J7	B6	Dog
17. 6	16. 5	J7	C7	Pheasant
18. 6	17. 5	J7	D8	Cock
19. 6	18. 5	J7	E9	Crow
20. 6	19. 5	J7	F10	Monkey
21. 6	20. 5	J7	G11	Gibbon
22. 6	21. 5	J7	H12	Tapir
23. 6	22. 5	J7	J1	Sheep
24. 6	23. 5	J7	K2	Deer
25. 6	24. 5	J7	A3	Horse

Solar date	Lunar date	Month HS/EB	Day HS/EB	Constellation	Solar date	Lunar date	Month HS/EB	Day HS/EB	Constellation
26. 6	25. 5	J7	B4	Stag	7. 9	10. 8	B10	E5	Wolf
27. 6	26. 5	J7	C5	Serpent	8. 9	11. 8	B10	F6	Dog
28. 6	27. 5	J7	D6	Earthworm	9. 9	12. 8	B10	G7	Pheasant
29. 6	28. 5	J7	E7	Crocodile	10. 9	13. 8	B10	H8	Cock
30. 6	29. 5	J7	F8	Dragon	11. 9	14. 8	B10	J9	Crow
1. 7	30. 5	J7	G9	Badger	12. 9	15. 8	B10	K10	Monkey
2. 7	1. 6	K8	H10	Hare	13. 9	16. 8	B10	A11	Gibbon
3. 7	2. 6	K8	J11	Fox	14. 9	17. 8	B10	B12	Tapir
4. 7	3. 6	K8	K12	Tiger	15. 9	18. 8	B10	C1	Sheep
5. 7	4. 6	K8	A1	Leopard	16. 9	19. 8	B10	D2	Deer
6. 7	5. 6	K8	B2	Griffon	17. 9	20. 8	B10	E3	Horse
7. 7	6. 6	K8	C3	Ox	18. 9	21. 8	B10	F4	Stag
8. 7	7. 6	K8	D4	Bat	19. 9	22. 8	B10	G5	Serpent
9. 7	8. 6	K8	E5	Rat	20. 9	23. 8	B10	H6	Earthworm
10. 7	9. 6	K8	F6	Swallow	21. 9	24. 8	B10	J7	Crocodile
11. 7	10. 6	K8	G7	Pig	22. 9	25. 8	B10	K8	Dragon
12. 7	11. 6	K8	H8	Porcupine	23. 9	26. 8	B10	A9	Badger
13. 7	12. 6	K8	J9	Wolf	24. 9	27. 8	B10	B10	Hare
14. 7	13. 6	K8	K10	Dog	25. 9	28. 8	B10	C11	Fox
15. 7	14. 6	K8	A11	Pheasant	26. 9	29. 8	B10	D12	Tiger
16. 7	15. 6	K8	B12	Cock	27. 9	30. 8	B10	E1	Leopard
17. 7	16. 6	K8	C1	Crow	28. 9	1. 9	C11	F2	Griffon
18. 7	17. 6	K8	D2	Monkey	29. 9	2. 9	C11	G3	Ox
19. 7	18. 6	K8	E3	Gibbon	30. 9	3. 9	C11	H4	Bat
20. 7	19. 6	K8	F4	Tapir	1.10	4. 9	C11	J5	Rat
21. 7	20. 6	K8	G5	Sheep	2.10	5. 9	C11	K6	Swallow
22. 7	21. 6	K8	H6	Deer	3.10	6. 9	C11	A7	Pig
23. 7	22. 6	K8	J7	Horse	4.10	7. 9	C11	B8	Porcupine
24. 7	23. 6	K8	K8	Stag	5.10	8. 9	C11	C9	Wolf
25. 7	24. 6	K8	A9	Serpent	6.10	9. 9	C11	D10	Dog
26. 7	25. 6	K8	B10	Earthworm	7.10	10. 9	C11	E11	Pheasant
27. 7	26. 6	K8	C11	Crocodile	8.10	11. 9	C11	F12	Cock
28. 7	27. 6	K8	D12	Dragon	9.10	12. 9	C11	G1	Crow
29. 7	28. 6	K8	E1	Badger	10.10	13. 9	C11	H2	Monkey
30. 7	29. 6	K8	F2	Hare	11.10	14. 9	C11	J3	Gibbon
31. 7	1. 7	A9	G3	Fox	12.10	15. 9	C11	K4	Tapir
1. 8	2. 7	A9	H4	Tiger	13.10	16. 9	C11	A5	Sheep
2. 8	3. 7	A9	J5	Leopard	14.10	17. 9	C11	B6	Deer
3. 8	4. 7	A9	K6	Griffon	15.10	18. 9	C11	C7	Horse
4. 8	5. 7	A9	A7	Ox	16.10	19. 9	C11	D8	Stag
5. 8	6. 7	A9	B8	Bat	17.10	20. 9	C11	E9	Serpent
6. 8	7. 7	A9	C9	Rat	18.10	21. 9	C11	F10	Earthworm
7. 8	8. 7	A9	D10	Swallow	19.10	22. 9	C11	G11	Crocodile
8. 8	9. 7	A9	E11	Pig	20.10	23. 9	C11	H12	Dragon
9. 8	10. 7	A9	F12	Porcupine	21.10	24. 9	C11	J1	Badger
10. 8	11. 7	A9	G1	Wolf	22.10	25. 9	C11	K2	Hare
11. 8	12. 7	A9	H2	Dog	23.10	26. 9	C11	A3	Fox
12. 8	13. 7	A9	J3	Pheasant	24.10	27. 9	C11	B4	Tiger
13. 8	14. 7	A9	K4	Cock	25.10	28. 9	C11	C5	Leopard
14. 8	15. 7	A9	A5	Crow	26.10	29. 9	C11	D6	Griffon
15. 8	16. 7	A9	B6	Monkey	27.10	1.10	D12	E7	Ox
16. 8	17. 7	A9	C7	Gibbon	28.10	2.10	D12	F8	Bat
17. 8	18. 7	A9	D8	Tapir	29.10	3.10	D12	G9	Rat
18. 8	19. 7	A9	E9	Sheep	30.10	4.10	D12	H10	Swallow
19. 8	20. 7	A9	F10	Deer	31.10	5.10	D12	J11	Pig
20. 8	21. 7	A9	G11	Horse	1.11	6.10	D12	K12	Porcupine
21. 8	22. 7	A9	H12	Stag	2.11	7.10	D12	A1	Wolf
22. 8	23. 7	A9	J1	Serpent	3.11	8.10	D12	B2	Dog
23. 8	24. 7	A9	K2	Earthworm	4.11	9.10	D12	C3	Pheasant
24. 8	25. 7	A9	A3	Crocodile	5.11	10.10	D12	D4	Cock
25. 8	26. 7	A9	B4	Dragon	6.11	11.10	D12	E5	Crow
26. 8	27. 7	A9	C5	Badger	7.11	12.10	D12	F6	Monkey
27. 8	28. 7	A9	D6	Hare	8.11	13.10	D12	G7	Gibbon
28. 8	29. 7	A9	E7	Fox	9.11	14.10	D12	H8	Tapir
29. 8	1. 8	B10	F8	Tiger	10.11	15.10	D12	J9	Sheep
30. 8	2. 8	B10	G9	Leopard	11.11	16.10	D12	K10	Deer
31. 8	3. 8	B10	H10	Griffon	12.11	17.10	D12	A11	Horse
1. 9	4. 8	B10	J11	Ox	13.11	18.10	D12	B12	Stag
2. 9	5. 8	B10	K12	Bat	14.11	19.10	D12	C1	Serpent
3. 9	6. 8	B10	A1	Rat	15.11	20.10	D12	D2	Earthworm
4. 9	7. 8	B10	B2	Swallow	16.11	21.10	D12	E3	Crocodile
5. 9	8. 8	B10	C3	Pig	17.11	22.10	D12	F4	Dragon
6. 9	9. 8	B10	D4	Porcupine	18.11	23.10	D12	G5	Badger

Solar date	Lunar date	Month HS/EB	Day HS/EB	Constellation	Solar date	Lunar date	Month HS/EB	Day HS/EB	Constellation
19.11	24.10	D12	H6	Hare	23.12	28.11	E1	B4	Bat
20.11	25.10	D12	J7	Fox	24.12	29.11	E1	C5	Rat
21.11	26.10	D12	K8	Tiger	25.12	30.11	E1	D6	Swallow
22.11	27.10	D12	A9	Leopard	26.12	1.12	F2	E7	Pig
23.11	28.10	D12	B10	Griffon	27.12	2.12	F2	F8	Porcupine
24.11	29.10	D12	C11	Ox	28.12	3.12	F2	G9	Wolf
25.11	30.10	D12	D12	Bat	29.12	4.12	F2	H10	Dog
26.11	1.11	E1	E1	Rat	30.12	5.12	F2	J11	Pheasant
27.11	2.11	E1	F2	Swallow	31.12	6.12	F2	K12	Cock
28.11	3.11	E1	G3	Pig					
29.11	4.11	E1	H4	Porcupine	**2001**				
30.11	5.11	E1	J5	Wolf	1. 1	7.12	F2	A1	Crow
1.12	6.11	E1	K6	Dog	2. 1	8.12	F2	B2	Monkey
2.12	7.11	E1	A7	Pheasant	3. 1	9.12	F2	C3	Gibbon
3.12	8.11	E1	B8	Cock	4. 1	10.12	F2	D4	Tapir
4.12	9.11	E1	C9	Crow	5. 1	11.12	F2	E5	Sheep
5.12	10.11	E1	D10	Monkey	6. 1	12.12	F2	F6	Deer
6.12	11.11	E1	E11	Gibbon	7. 1	13.12	F2	G7	Horse
7.12	12.11	E1	F12	Tapir	8. 1	14.12	F2	H8	Stag
8.12	13.11	E1	G1	Sheep	9. 1	15.12	F2	J9	Serpent
9.12	14.11	E1	H2	Deer	10. 1	16.12	F2	K10	Earthworm
10.12	15.11	E1	J3	Horse	11. 1	17.12	F2	A11	Crocodile
11.12	16.11	E1	K4	Stag	12. 1	18.12	F2	B12	Dragon
12.12	17.11	E1	A5	Serpent	13. 1	19.12	F2	C1	Badger
13.12	18.11	E1	B6	Earthworm	14. 1	20.12	F2	D2	Hare
14.12	19.11	E1	C7	Crocodile	15. 1	21.12	F2	E3	Fox
15.12	20.11	E1	D8	Dragon	16. 1	22.12	F2	F4	Tiger
16.12	21.11	E1	E9	Badger	17. 1	23.12	F2	G5	Leopard
17.12	22.11	E1	F10	Hare	18. 1	24.12	F2	H6	Griffon
18.12	23.11	E1	G11	Fox	19. 1	25.12	F2	J7	Ox
19.12	24.11	E1	H12	Tiger	20. 1	26.12	F2	K8	Bat
20.12	25.11	E1	J1	Leopard	21. 1	27.12	F2	A9	Rat
21.12	26.11	E1	K2	Griffon	22. 1	28.12	F2	B10	Swallow
22.12	27.11	E1	A3	Ox	23. 1	29.12	F2	C11	Pig